W9-CDF-745

Summary of Contents

SIMPLY
JAVASCRIPT

BY **KEVIN YANK**
& CAMERON ADAMS

Simply JavaScript

by Kevin Yank and Cameron Adams

Copyright © 2007 SitePoint Pty. Ltd.

Managing Editor: Simon Mackie

Technical Editor: Kevin Yank

Technical Director: Kevin Yank

Printing History:

   First Edition: June 2007

Editor: Georgina Laidlaw

Index Editor: Max McMaster

Cover Design: Alex Walker

Latest Update: September 2007

Notice of Rights

Notice of Liability

Trademark Notice

Published by SitePoint Pty. Ltd.

424 Smith Street Collingwood
VIC Australia 3066
Web: www.sitepoint.com
Email: business@sitepoint.com

ISBN 978-0-9802858-0-2
Printed and bound in Canada

About Kevin Yank

As Technical Director for SitePoint, Kevin Yank keeps abreast of all that is new and exciting in web technology. Best known for his book, *Build Your Own Database Driven Website Using PHP & MySQL*,[1] now in its third edition, Kevin also writes the *SitePoint Tech Times*,[2] a free, biweekly email newsletter that goes out to over 150,000 subscribers worldwide.

When he isn't speaking at a conference or visiting friends and family in Canada, Kevin lives in Melbourne, Australia, and enjoys performing improvised comedy theater with Impro Melbourne,[3] and flying light aircraft. His personal blog is *Yes, I'm Canadian*.[4]

About Cameron Adams

Cameron Adams melds a background in Computer Science with almost a decade's experience in graphic design, resulting in a unique approach to interface design. He uses these skills to play with the intersection between design and code, always striving to create interesting and innovative sites and applications.

Having worked with large corporations, government departments, nonprofit organizations, and tiny startups, he's starting to get the gist of this Internet thing. In addition to the projects that pay his electricity bills, Cameron muses about web design on his well-respected weblog—*The Man in Blue*[5]—and has written several books on topics ranging from JavaScript to CSS and design.

Sometimes he's in Melbourne, other times he likes to fly around the world to talk about design and programming with other friendly geeks. If you ever see him standing at a bar, buy him a Baileys and say "hi."

About SitePoint

SitePoint specializes in publishing fun, practical, and easy-to-understand content for web professionals. Visit http://www.sitepoint.com/ to access our books, newsletters, articles, and community forums.

---

[1] http://www.sitepoint.com/books/phpmysql1/
[2] http://www.sitepoint.com/newsletter/
[3] http://www.impromelbourne.com.au/
[4] http://yesimcanadian.com/
[5] http://themaninblue.com/

To Jessica,
my partner in crime,
the lemon to my lime.

—Kevin

Without you, Lisa, this book would
never have been written. I can
only hope to return the same
amount of love and support that
you have given me.

—Cameron

Table of Contents

Chapter 5   Animation

Preface

On the surface, JavaScript is a simple programming language that lets you make changes to your web pages on the fly, while they're being displayed in a web browser. How hard could that be to learn, right? It sounds like something you could knock over in an afternoon.

But JavaScript is bigger on the inside than it seems from the outside. If you were a *Dr. Who* fan, you might call it the TARDIS of programming languages. If you're *not* a *Dr. Who* fan, roll your eyes with me as the fanboys (and girls) geek out.

Everyone back with me? Put your Daleks away, Jimmy.

As I was saying, JavaScript *sounds* like it should be simple. Nevertheless, throughout its ten year history (so far), the best ways of doing things with JavaScript have seemed to change with the seasons. And advice on how to write good JavaScript can be found everywhere: "Do it this way—it'll run faster!" "Use this code—it'll run on more browsers!" "Stay away from that feature—it causes memory leaks!"

Too many other JavaScript books—some of them from very respected names in the industry—will teach you a handful of simple solutions to simple problems and then call it a day, leaving you with just enough rope with which to hang yourself when you actually try to solve a real-world problem on your own. And when in desperation you go looking on the Web for an example that does what you need it to, you'll likely be unable to make sense of the JavaScript code you find, because the book you bought didn't cover many of the truly useful features of the language, such as object literals, event listeners, or closures.

This book aims to be different. From the very first page, we'll show you the *right* way to use JavaScript. By working through fully fleshed-out examples that are ready to be plugged right into a professionally-designed web site, you'll gain the confidence not only to write JavaScript code of your own, but to understand code that was written by others, and even to spot harmful, old-fashioned code that's more trouble than it's worth!

Throughout this book, we've tried to go the extra mile by giving you more than just the basics. In particular, we've covered some of the new JavaScript-powered development techniques—like Ajax—that are changing the face of the Web. We've also included sections that explore the new crop of JavaScript libraries like jQuery, Prototype, Yahoo! UI, and Dojo, making this the only beginner's JavaScript book to cover these powerful time-savers.

… all of which made this book a lot harder to write, but that's why they pay us the big bucks.

Who Should Read this Book?

Whether you've never seen a line of JavaScript code in your life, or you've seen one too many lines that doesn't do what you expect, this book will show you how to make JavaScript work for you.

We assume going in that you've got a good handle on web design with HyperText Markup Language (HTML) and Cascading Style Sheets (CSS). You needn't be an expert in these languages, but as we'll see, JavaScript is just another piece in the puzzle. The better you understand basic web design techniques, the more you can enhance them with JavaScript.

If you need a refresher, we highly recommend *Build Your Own Web Site The Right Way Using HTML & CSS*[1] (Melbourne: SitePoint, 2006).

What's Covered in this Book?

Chapter 1: The Three Layers of the Web
A big part of learning JavaScript is learning when it's the right tool for the job, and when ordinary HTML and CSS can offer a better solution. Before we dive into learning JavaScript, we'll take a little time to review how to build web sites with HTML and CSS, and see just how JavaScript fits into the picture.

Chapter 2: Programming with JavaScript
JavaScript is a programming language. To work with it, then, you must get your head around the way computer programs work—which to some extent means learning to think like a computer. The simple concepts introduced in this

---

[1] http://www.sitepoint.com/books/html1/

chapter—statements, variables, expressions, loops, functions, and objects—are the building blocks for every JavaScript program you'll ever write.

Chapter 3: Document Access

While certain people enjoy writing JavaScript code for its own sake, you wouldn't want to run into them in a dark alley at night. As a well-adjusted web developer, you'll probably want to use JavaScript to make changes to the contents of your web pages using the Document Object Model (DOM). Lucky for you, we wrote a whole chapter to show you how!

Chapter 4: Events

By far the most *event*ful portion of this book (ha ha ha … I slay me), this chapter shows you how to write JavaScript programs that will respond to the actions of your users as they interact with a web page. As you'll see, this can be done in a number of ways, for which varying degrees of support are provided by current browsers.

Chapter 5: Animation

Okay, okay. We can talk all day about the subtle usability enhancements that JavaScript makes possible, but we know you won't be satisfied until you can make things swoosh around the page. In this chapter, you'll get all the swooshing you can handle.

Chapter 6: Form Enhancements

I know what you're thinking: forms are boring. Nobody leaps out of bed in the morning, cracks their knuckles, and shouts, "Today, I'm going to fill in some *forms*!" Well, once you trick out your forms with the enhancements in this chapter, they just might. Oh, and just to spice up this chapter a bit more, we'll show you how to make an element on your page draggable.

Chapter 7: Errors and Debugging

When things go wrong in other programming languages, your computer will usually throw a steady stream of error messages at you until you fix the problem. With JavaScript, however, your computer just folds its arms and gives you a look that seems to say, "You were expecting, maybe, something to happen?" No, English is not your computer's first language. What did you expect? It was made in Taiwan. In this chapter, we'll show you how to fix scripts that don't behave the way they should.

Chapter 8: Ajax

You might have heard about this thing called Ajax that makes web pages look like desktop applications, and shaky business ventures look like solid investments. We put it into this book for both those reasons.

Chapter 9: Looking Forward

JavaScript doesn't just *have* a future; JavaScript *is* the future! Okay, you might think that's taking it a bit far, but when you read this chapter and see the many amazing things that JavaScript makes possible, you might reconsider.

Appendix A: The Core JavaScript Library

As we progress through the book, we'll write code to solve many common problems. Rather than making you rewrite that code every time you need it, we've collected it all into a JavaScript library that you can reuse in your own projects to save yourself a *ton* of typing. This appendix will provide a summary and breakdown of all the code that's collected in this library, with instructions on how to use it.

The Book's Web Site

Located at http://www.sitepoint.com/books/javascript1/, the web site that supports this book will give you access to the following facilities.

The Code Archive

As you progress through this book, you'll note file names above many of the code listings. These refer to files in the code archive, a downloadable ZIP file that contains all of the finished examples presented in this book. Simply click the **Code Archive** link on the book's web site to download it.

Updates and Errata

No book is error-free, and attentive readers will no doubt spot at least one or two mistakes in this one. The Corrections and Typos page on the book's web site[2] will provide the latest information about known typographical and code errors, and will offer necessary updates for new releases of browsers and related standards.

---

[2] http://www.sitepoint.com/books/javascript1/errata.php

The SitePoint Forums

If you'd like to communicate with other web developers about this book, you should join SitePoint's online community.[3] The JavaScript forum,[4] in particular, offers an abundance of information above and beyond the solutions in this book, and a lot of fun and experienced JavaScript developers hang out there. It's a good way to learn new tricks, get questions answered in a hurry, and just have a good time.

The SitePoint Newsletters

In addition to books like this one, SitePoint publishes free email newsletters including *The SitePoint Tribune*, *The SitePoint Tech Times*, and *The SitePoint Design View*. Reading them will keep you up to date on the latest news, product releases, trends, tips, and techniques for all aspects of web development. If nothing else, you'll get useful CSS articles and tips, but if you're interested in learning other technologies, you'll find them especially valuable. Sign up to one or more SitePoint newsletters at http://www.sitepoint.com/newsletter/.

Your Feedback

If you can't find an answer through the forums, or if you wish to contact us for any other reason, the best place to write is books@sitepoint.com. We have an email support system set up to track your inquiries, and friendly support staff members who can answer your questions. Suggestions for improvements as well as notices of any mistakes you may find are especially welcome.

Acknowledgments

Kevin Yank

I'd like to thank Mark Harbottle and Luke Cuthbertson, SitePoint's Co-founder and General Manager, who sat me down late in 2006 and—for the second time in my career—convinced me that stepping away from SitePoint's day-to-day operations to write a book wouldn't be the worst career move ever. I also owe a beverage to

---

[3] http://www.sitepoint.com/forums/
[4] http://www.sitepoint.com/launch/jsforum/

Simon Mackie, whose idea it was in the first place. Let's hope someone buys it, guys!

To Jessica, for the many evenings that I stayed at the office to write long past the hour I said I'd be home, and for the boundless support and patience with which she greeted my eventual arrival, I owe something big and chocolaty.

And to the more than 150,000 readers of the *SitePoint Tech Times* newsletter,[5] with whom I shared many of the ideas that made their way into this book, and who provided valuable and challenging feedback in return, my gratitude.

Cameron Adams

The knowledge I've accrued on JavaScript has been drawn from so many sources that it would be impossible to name them all. Anything that I can pass on is only due to the contributions of hundreds—if not thousands—of charitable individuals who use their valuable time to lay out their knowledge for the advantage of others. If you're ever in a position to add to those voices, try your hardest to do so. Still, I'd like to put out an old school shout-out to the *Webmonkey* team, in particular Thau and Taylor, who inspired me in the beginning. I'd also like to thank my coding colleagues, who are always available for a quick question or an extended discussion whenever I'm stuck: Derek Featherstone, Dustin Diaz, Jonathan Snook, Jeremy Keith, Peter-Paul Koch, and Dan Webb.

---

[5] http://www.sitepoint.com/newsletter/

Conventions Used in this Book

You'll notice that we've used certain typographic and layout styles throughout this book to signify different types of information. Look out for the following items.

Code Samples

Any code will be displayed using a fixed-width font like so:

```
<h1>A perfect summer's day</h1>
<p>It was a lovely day for a walk in the park. The birds
were singing and the kids were all back at school.</p>
```

If the code may be found in the book's code archive, the name of the file will appear at the top of the program listing, like this:

```
                                                      example.css
.footer {
  background-color: #CCC;
  border-top: 1px solid #333;
}
```

If only part of the file is displayed, this is indicated by the word *excerpt*:

```
                                              example.css (excerpt)
  border-top: 1px solid #333;
```

Tips, Notes, and Warnings

 Hey, You!

Tips will give you helpful little pointers.

 Ahem, Excuse Me ...

Notes are useful asides that are related—but not critical—to the topic at hand. Think of them as extra tidbits of information.

 Make Sure you Always ...

... pay attention to these important points.

 Watch Out!

Warnings will highlight any gotchas that are likely to trip you up along the way.

The Three Layers of the Web

Once upon a time, there was ... 'A king!' my little readers will say right away. No, children, you are wrong. Once upon a time there was a piece of wood...
—The Adventures of Pinocchio

You can do a lot without JavaScript. Using Hypertext Markup Language (HTML),[1] you can produce complex documents that intricately describe the content of a page—and that content's meaning—to the minutest detail. Using Cascading Style Sheets (CSS), you can present that content in myriad ways, with variations as subtle as a single color, as striking as replacing text with an image.

No matter how you dress it up, though, HTML and CSS can only achieve the static beauty of the department store mannequin—or at best, an animatronic monstrosity that wobbles precariously when something moves nearby. With JavaScript, you can bring that awkward puppet to life, lifting you as its creator from humble shop clerk to web design mastery!

---

[1] Throughout this book, we'll refer to HTML and XHTML as just HTML. Which *you* choose is up to you, and doesn't have much to do with JavaScript. In case it matters to you, the HTML code we'll present in this book will be valid XHTML 1.0 Strict.

But whether your new creation has the graceful stride of a runway model, or the shuffling gait of Dr. Frankenstein's monster, depends as much on the quality of its HTML and CSS origins as it does on the JavaScript code that brought it to life.

Before we learn to work miracles, therefore, let's take a little time to review how to build web sites that look good both inside *and* out, and see how JavaScript fits into the picture.

Keep 'em Separated

Not so long ago, professional web designers would gleefully pile HTML, CSS, and JavaScript code into a single file, name it **index.html**,[2] and call it a web page. You can still do this today, but be prepared for your peers to call it something rather less polite.

Somewhere along the way, web designers realized that the code they write when putting together a web page does three fundamental things:

---

[2] Or **default.htm**, if they had been brainwashed by Microsoft.

- It describes the *content* of the page.
- It specifies the *presentation* of that content.
- It controls the *behavior* of that content.

They also realized that keeping these three types of code separate, as depicted in Figure 1.1, made their jobs easier, and helped them to make web pages that work better under adverse conditions, such as when users have JavaScript disabled in their browsers.

Computer geeks have known about this for years, and have even given this principle a geeky name: the **separation of concerns**.

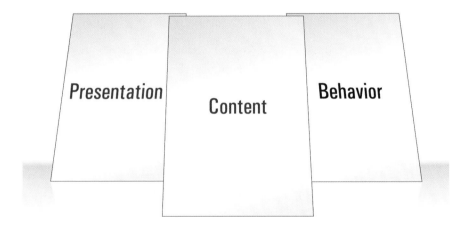

Figure 1.1. Separation of concerns

Now, realizing this is one thing, but actually *doing* it is another—especially if you're not a computer geek. I *am* a computer geek, and I'm tempted to do the wrong thing all the time.

I'll be happily editing the HTML code that describes a web page's content, when suddenly I'll find myself thinking how nice that text would look if it were in a slightly different shade of gray, if it were nudged a little to the left, and if it had that hee-larious photocopy of my face I made at the last SitePoint office party in the background. Prone to distraction as I am, I want to make those changes right away.

Now which is easier: opening up a separate CSS file to modify the page's style sheet, or just typing those style properties into the HTML code I'm already editing?

Like behaving yourself at work functions, keeping the types of code you write separate from one another takes discipline. But once you understand the benefits, you too will be able to summon the willpower it takes to stay on the straight and narrow.

Three Layers

Keeping different kinds of code as separate as possible is a good idea in any kind of programming. It makes it easier to reuse portions of that code in future projects, it reduces the amount of duplicate code you end up writing, and it makes it easier to find and fix problems months and years later.

When it comes to the Web, there's one more reason to keep your code separate: it lets you cater for the many different ways in which people access web pages.

Depending on your audience, the majority of your visitors may use well-appointed desktop browsers with cutting-edge CSS and JavaScript support, but many might be subject to corporate IT policies that force them to use older browsers, or to browse with certain features (like JavaScript) disabled.

Visually impaired users often browse using screen reader or screen magnifier software, and for these users your slick visual design can be more of a hindrance than a help.

Some users won't even *visit* your site, preferring to read content feeds in RSS or similar formats if you offer them. When it comes time to build these feeds, you'll want to be able to send your HTML content to these users without any JavaScript or CSS junk.

The key to accommodating the broadest possible range of visitors to your site is to think of the Web in terms of **three layers**, which conveniently correspond to the three kinds of code I mentioned earlier. These layers are illustrated in Figure 1.2.

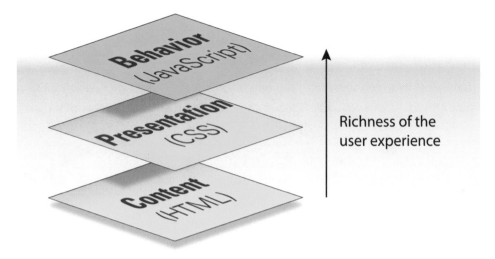

Figure 1.2. The three layers of the Web

When building a site, we work through these layers from the bottom up:

1. We start by producing the **content** in HTML format. This is the base layer, which any visitor using any kind of browser should be able to view.

2. With that done, we can focus on making the site look better, by adding a layer of **presentation** information using CSS. The site will now look good to users able to display CSS styles.

3. Lastly, we can use JavaScript to introduce an added layer of interactivity and dynamic **behavior**, which will make the site easier to use in browsers equipped with JavaScript.

If we keep the HTML, CSS, and JavaScript code separate, we'll find it much easier to make sure that the content layer remains readable in browsing environments where the presentation and/or behavior layers are unable to operate. This "start at the bottom" approach to web design is known in the trade as **progressive enhancement**.

Let's look at each of these layers in isolation to see how we can best maintain this separation of code.

HTML for Content

Everything that's needed to read and understand the content of a web page belongs in the HTML code for that page—nothing more, nothing less. It's that simple. Web designers get into trouble when they forget the K.I.S.S. principle,[3] and cram non-content information into their HTML code, or alternatively move some of the page's content into the CSS or JavaScript code for the page.

A common example of non-content information that's crammed into pages is **presentational HTML**—HTML code that describes how the content should *look* when it's displayed in the browser. This can include old-fashioned HTML tags like <b>, <i>, <u>, <tt>, and <font>:

```
<p>Whatever you do, <a href="666.html"><font color="red">don't
  click this link</font></a>!</p>
```

It can take the form of inline CSS applied with the style attribute:

```
<p>Whatever you do, <a href="666.html" style="color: red;">don't
  click this link</a>!</p>
```

It can also include the secret shame of many well-intentioned web designers—CSS styles applied with presentational class names:

```
<p>Whatever you do, <a href="666.html" class="red">don't click
  this link</a>!</p>
```

 Presentational Class Names?

If that last example looks okay to you, you're not alone, but it's definitely bad mojo. If you later decide you want that link to be yellow, you're either stuck updating both the class name and the CSS styles that apply to it, or living with the embarrassment of a class named "red" that is actually styled yellow. *That'll* turn your face yellow—er, red!

---

[3] Keep It Simple, Stupid.

Rather than embedding presentation information in your HTML code, you should focus on the *reason* for the action—for example, you want a link to be displayed in a different color. Is the link especially important? Consider surrounding it with a tag that describes the emphasis you want to give it:

```
<p>Whatever you do, <em><a href="evil.html">don't click this
  link</a></em>!</p>
```

Is the link a warning? HTML doesn't have a tag to describe a warning, but you could choose a CSS class name that conveys this information:

```
<p>Whatever you do, <a href="evil.html" class="warning">don't
  click this link</a>!</p>
```

You can take this approach too far, of course. Some designers mistake tags like <h1> as presentational, and attempt to remove this presentational code from their HTML:

```
<p class="heading">A heading with an identity crisis</p>
```

Really, the presentational information that you should keep out of your document is the font, size, and color in which a heading is to be displayed. The fact that a piece of text *is* a heading is part of the content, and as such should be reflected in the HTML code. So this code is perfectly fine:

```
<h1>A heading at peace with itself</h1>
```

In short, your HTML should do everything it can to convey the meaning, or **semantics** of the content in the page, while steering clear of describing how it should look. Web standards geeks call HTML code that does this **semantic markup**.

Writing semantic markup allows your HTML files to stand on their own as meaningful documents. People who, for whatever reason, cannot read these documents by viewing them in a typical desktop web browser will be better able to make sense of them this way. Visually impaired users, for example, will be able to use assistive software like screen readers to listen to the page as it's read aloud, and the more clearly your HTML code describes the content's meaning, the more sense tools like these will be able to make of it.

Best of all, however, semantic markup lets you apply new styles (presentation) and interactive features (behavior) without having to make many (or, in some cases, any!) changes to your HTML code.

CSS for Presentation

Obviously, if the content of a page should be entirely contained within its HTML code, its style—or presentation—should be fully described in the CSS code that's applied to the page.

With all the work you've done to keep your HTML free of presentational code and rich with semantics, it would be a shame to mess up that file by filling it with snippets of CSS.

As you probably know, CSS styles can be applied to your pages in three ways:

inline styles

```
<a href="evil.html" style="color: red;">
```

Inline styles are tempting for the reasons I explained earlier: you can apply styles to your content as you create it, without having to switch gears and edit a separate style sheet. But as we saw in the previous section, you'll want to avoid inline styles like the plague if you want to keep your HTML code meaningful to those who cannot see the styles.

embedded styles

```
<style type="text/css">
  .warning {
    color: red;
  }
</style>
⋮
<a href="evil.html" class="warning">
```

Embedded styles keep your markup clean, but tie your styles to a single document. In most cases, you'll want to share your styles across multiple pages on your site, so it's best to steer clear of this approach as well.

external styles

```
<link rel="stylesheet" href="styles.css" />
  ⋮
<a href="evil.html" class="warning">
```

```
                                                    styles.css

.warning {
  color: red;
}
```

External styles are really the way to go, because they let you share your styles between multiple documents, they reduce the amount of code browsers need to download, and they also let you modify the look of your site without having to get your hands dirty editing HTML.

But you knew all that, right? This is a JavaScript book, after all, so let's talk about the JavaScript that goes into your pages.

JavaScript for Behavior

As with CSS, you can add JavaScript to your web pages in a number of ways:

■ You can embed JavaScript code directly in your HTML content:

```
<a href="evil.html" onclick="JavaScript code here">
```

■ You can include JavaScript code at the top of your HTML document in a `<script>` tag:

```
<script type="text/javascript"><!--//--><![CDATA[//><!--
  JavaScript code here
//--><!]]></script>
  ⋮
<a href="evil.html" class="warning">
```

CDATA?

If you're wondering what all that gobbledygook is following the `<script>` tag and preceding the `</script>` tag, that's what it takes to legitimately embed JavaScript in an XHTML document without confusing web browsers that don't understand XHTML (like Internet Explorer).

If you write your page with HTML instead of XHTML, you can get away with this much simpler syntax:

```
<script type="text/javascript">
  JavaScript code here
</script>
```

You can put your JavaScript code in a separate file, then link to that file from as many HTML documents as you like:

```
<script type="text/javascript" src="script.js"></script>
⋮
<a href="evil.html" class="warning">
```

script.js *(excerpt)*

```
JavaScript code here
```

Guess which method you should use.

Writing JavaScript that enhances usability without cluttering up the HTML document(s) it is applied to, without locking out users that have JavaScript disabled in their browsers, and without interfering with *other* JavaScript code that might be applied to the same page, is called **unobtrusive scripting**.

Unfortunately, while many professional web developers have clued in to the benefits of keeping their CSS code in separate files, there is still a lot of JavaScript code mixed into HTML out there. By showing you the *right* way to use JavaScript in this book, we hope to help change that.

The Right Way

So, how much does all this stuff really matter? After all, people have been building web sites with HTML, CSS, and JavaScript mixed together for years, and for the majority of people browsing the Web, those sites have worked.

Well, as you come to learn JavaScript, it's arguably more important to get it right than ever before. JavaScript is by far the most powerful of the three languages that you'll use to design web sites, and as such it gives you unprecedented freedom to completely mess things up.

As an example, if you really, really like JavaScript, you could go so far as to put everything—content, presentation, and behavior—into your JavaScript code. I've actually seen this done, and it's not pretty—especially when a browser with Java-Script disabled comes along.

Even more telling is the fact that JavaScript is the only one of these three languages that has the ability to hang the browser, making it unresponsive to the user.[4]

Therefore, through the rest of this book, we'll do our darnedest to show you the right way to use JavaScript, not just because it keeps your code tidy, but because it helps to keep the Web working the way it's meant to—by making content accessible to as many people as possible, no matter which web browser they choose to use.

JavaScript Libraries

As I mentioned, one of the benefits of keeping different kinds of code separate is that it makes it easier to take code that you've written for one site and reuse it on another. Certain JavaScript maniacs (to be referred to from this point on as "people") have taken the time to assemble vast **libraries** of useful, unobtrusive JavaScript code that you can download and use on your own web sites for free.

Throughout this book, we'll build each of the examples from scratch—all of the JavaScript code you need can be found right here in these pages. Since there isn't always time to do this in the real world, however, and because libraries are quickly

---

[4] We'll show you an example of this in Chapter 7.

becoming an important part of the JavaScript landscape, we'll also look at how the popular JavaScript libraries do things whenever the opportunity presents itself.

Here are the libraries that we'll use in this book:

Prototype	http://www.prototypejs.org/
script.aculo.us	http://script.aculo.us/
Yahoo! User Interface Library (YUI)	http://developer.yahoo.com/yui/
Dojo	http://dojotoolkit.org/
jQuery	http://jquery.com/
MooTools	http://mootools.net/

 Not All Libraries are Created Equal

Watch out for sites offering snippets of JavaScript code for you to copy and paste into your web pages to achieve a particular effect. There is a lot of free code out there, but not all of it is good.

In general, the good libraries come in the form of JavaScript (**.js**) files that you can link into your pages unobtrusively, instead of pasting JavaScript directly into your HTML code.

If you don't feel confident to judge whether a particular JavaScript library is good or bad, ask for some advice in the SitePoint Forums,[5] or just stick with the libraries mentioned in this book—they're all very good.

Let's Get Started!

Enough preaching—you picked up this book to learn JavaScript, right? (If you didn't, I'm afraid you're in for a bit of a disappointment.) Clean HTML and CSS are nice and all, but it's time to take the plunge into the third layer of the Web: behavior.

Turn the page, and get ready to start using some cool (and unobtrusive) JavaScript.

---

[5] http://www.sitepoint.com/forums/

2

Programming with JavaScript

Programming is all about speaking the language of computers. If you're a robot, this should be pretty easy for you, but if you're unlucky enough to be a human, it might take a bit of adjustment.

If you want to learn how to program, there are really two things you have to get your head around. First, you have to think about reducing one big problem into small, digestible chunks that are just right for a computer to crunch. Second, you have to know how to translate those chunks into a language that the computer understands.

I find that the second part—the **syntax**—gradually becomes second nature (much like when you learn a *real* second language), and experienced programmers have very little trouble switching between different languages (like JavaScript, PHP, Ruby, or Algol 60). Most of the thought in programming is focused on the first part—thinking about how you can break down a problem so that the computer can solve it.

By the time you've finished this book, you'll understand most of the syntax that JavaScript has to offer, but you'll continue learning new ways to solve programming problems for as long as you continue to program. We'll tell you how to solve quite a few problems in this book, but there are always different ways to achieve a given task, and there will always be new problems to solve, so don't think that your learning will stop on the last page of this book.

Running a JavaScript Program

Before you even start writing your first JavaScript program, you'll have to know how to run it.

Every JavaScript program designed to run in a browser has to be attached to a document. Most of the time this will be an HTML or XHTML document, but exciting new uses for JavaScript emerge every day, and in the future you might find yourself using JavaScript on XML, SVG, or something else that we haven't even thought of yet. We're just going to worry about HTML in this book, because that's what 99% of people use JavaScript with.

To include some JavaScript on an HTML page, we have to include a `<script>` tag inside the `head` of the document. A script doesn't necessarily have to be JavaScript, so we need to tell the browser what type of script we're including by adding a `type` attribute with a value of `text/javascript`:

```
<!DOCTYPE HTML PUBLIC "-//W3C//DTD HTML 4.01//EN"
    "http://www.w3.org/TR/html4/strict.dtd">
<html lang="en-US">
  <head>
    <title>The Running Man</title>
    <meta http-equiv="Content-Type"
        content="text/html; charset=utf-8">

    <script type="text/javascript">
    </script>

  </head>
</html>
```

You can put as much JavaScript code as you want inside that `<script>` tag—the browser will execute it as soon as it has been downloaded:

```
<!DOCTYPE HTML PUBLIC "-//W3C//DTD HTML 4.01//EN"
    "http://www.w3.org/TR/html4/strict.dtd">
<html lang="en-US">
  <head>
    <title>The Running Man</title>
    <meta http-equiv="Content-Type"
        content="text/html; charset=utf-8">

    <script type="text/javascript">
      alert("Arnie says hi!");
    </script>

  </head>
</html>
```

XHTML and Embedded JavaScript don't Mix

For this one example, we've switched from an XHTML DOCTYPE to an HTML DOCTYPE. As mentioned in Chapter 1, embedding JavaScript in XHTML requires gobbledygook that few mortals can remember:

```
<script type="text/javascript"><!--//--><![CDATA[//><!--
    alert("Arnie says hi!");
//--><!]]></script>
```

For many, this is reason enough to avoid embedded JavaScript.

Even though it's nice and easy to just type some JavaScript straight into your HTML code, it's preferable to include your JavaScript in an external file. This approach provides several advantages:

- It maintains the separation between content and behavior (HTML and JavaScript).
- It makes it easier to maintain your web pages.
- It allows you to easily reuse the same JavaScript programs on different pages of your site.

To reference an external JavaScript file, you need to use the src attribute on the `<script>` tag:

```
<!DOCTYPE html PUBLIC "-//W3C//DTD XHTML 1.0 Strict//EN"
    "http://www.w3.org/TR/xhtml1/DTD/xhtml1-strict.dtd">
<html xmlns="http://www.w3.org/1999/xhtml" lang="en-US">
  <head>
    <title>The Running Man</title>
    <meta http-equiv="Content-Type"
        content="text/html; charset=utf-8" />

    <script type="text/javascript" src="example.js"></script>

  </head>
</html>
```

Any JavaScript that you might have included between your `<script>` and `</script>` tags can now be put into that external file and the browser will download the file and run the code.

The file can be called whatever you want, but the common practice is to include a **.js** extension at the end of it.

If you'd like to try out the little program above, create a new HTML document (or open the closest one to hand) and insert the `<script>` tag inside the `head`. Once you've done that, put this snippet into a file called **example.js** in the same directory or folder:

```
alert("Arnie says hi!");
```

Now, open the HTML file in your browser, and see what happens! As you read through the rest of this chapter, you can replace the contents of **example.js** with each of the simple programs that I'll show you, and try them for yourself!

 Absolute URLs Work Too

As with the `src` attribute of an image, you can reference a file anywhere on your server, or anyone else's server:

```
<script type="text/javascript"
    src="http://www.example.com/script.js"></script>
```

It's possible to include as many external scripts on your page as you want:

```
<script type="text/javascript" src="library.js"></script>
<script type="text/javascript" src="more.js"></script>
<script type="text/javascript" src="example.js"></script>
```

This capability is what makes JavaScript libraries, where you include a standard library file on your page alongside other code that uses the contents of that library, possible.

Every time you load a page with JavaScript on it, the browser will interpret all of the included JavaScript code and figure out what to do with it. If you've loaded a page into your browser, and then you make some changes to that page's JavaScript (either on the page itself or in an external file), you'll need to refresh the page before those changes will be picked up by the browser.

Statements: Bite-sized Chunks for your Browser

So now you know how to tell the browser that it needs to run some JavaScript, but you don't know any JavaScript for it to run. We'd better fix that!

Earlier, we were talking about reducing a problem into steps that a computer can understand. Each small step you take in a program is called a **statement**, and it tells the browser to perform an action. By building up a series of these actions, we create a **program**. Statements are to programs as sentences are to books.

In JavaScript each statement has to be separated by a new line or a semicolon. So, two statements could be written like this:

```
Statement one
Statement 2.0
```

Or they could be written like this:

```
Statement one;Statement 2.0;
```

It is generally considered best practice, however, to do both—separate statements by a semicolon *and* a new line:

```
Statement one;
Statement 2.0;
```

This way, each of your statements will be easy to read, and you'll have removed the potential for any ambiguity that might occur if two statements accidentally run together.

There's a whole bunch of different tasks you can achieve inside each statement; the first one that we'll look at shortly is creating variables.

Comments: Bite-sized Chunks Just for You

If you follow the advice in this book and keep your JavaScript code simple and well structured, you should be able to get the gist of how it works just by looking at it. Every once in a while, however, you'll find yourself crafting a particularly tricky segment of code, or some esoteric browser compatibility issue will force you to insert a statement that might seem like nonsense if you had to come back and work on the program later. In situations like these, you may want to insert a comment.

A **comment** is a note in your code that browsers will ignore completely. Unlike the rest of the code you write, comments are there to be read by *you* (or other programmers who might later need to work on your code). In general, they explain the surrounding code, making it easier to update the program in future.

JavaScript supports two types of comments. The first is a single-line comment, which begins with two slashes (//) and runs to the end of the line:

```
Statement one; // I'm especially proud of this one
Statement 2.0;
```

As soon as the browser sees two slashes, it closes its eyes and sings a little song to itself until it reaches the end of the line, after which it continues to read the program as usual.

If you need to write a more sizable comment, you can use a multi-line comment, starting with /* and ending with */:

```
/* This is my first JavaScript program. Please forgive any
   mistakes you might find here.
   If you have any suggestions, write to n00b@example.com. */
Statement one; // I'm especially proud of this one
Statement 2.0;
```

You'll notice a distinct lack of comments in the code presented in this book. The main reason for this is that all of the code is explained in the surrounding text, so why not save a few trees? In real-world programs, you should always include a comment if you suspect that you might not understand a piece of code when you return to work on it later.

Variables: Storing Data for your Program

It's possible to write a program that defines the value of every single piece of data it uses, but that's like driving a ski lift—you don't really get to choose where you're going. If you want your program to be able to take user input, and adapt to different pages and situations, you have to have some way of working with values that you don't know in advance.

As with most programming concepts, it's very useful at this point to think of your computer as a BGC (Big, Giant Calculator). You know where you are with a calculator, so it makes programming a bit easier to understand.

Now, we could write a program for a calculator that said:

```
4 + 2
```

But every time we run that program, we're going to get exactly the same answer. There's no way that we can substitute the values in the equation for something else—values from another calculation, data from a file, or even user input.

If we want the program to be a bit more flexible, we need to abstract some of its components. Take a look at the equation above and ask yourself, "What does it really do?"

It adds two numbers.

If we're getting those numbers when we *run* the program, we don't know what they'll be when we *write* the program, so we need some way of referring to them without using actual numbers. How about we give them names? Say … "x" and "y."

Using those names, we could rewrite the program as:

```
x + y
```

Then, when we get our data values from some faraway place, we just need to make sure it's called x and y. Once we've done that, we've got **variables**.

Variables allow us to give a piece of data a name, then reference that data by its name further along in our program. This way, we can reuse a piece of data without having to remember what its actual value was; all we have to do is remember a variable name.

In JavaScript, we create a variable by using the keyword var and specifying the name we want to use:

```
var chameleon;
```

This is called **declaring** a variable.

Having been declared, `chameleon` is ready to have some data assigned to it. We can do this using the **assignment operator** (=), placing the variable name on the left and the data on the right:

```
var chameleon;
chameleon = "blue";
```

This whole process can be shortened by declaring and assigning the variable in one go:

```
var chameleon = "blue";
```

In practice, this is what most JavaScript programmers do—declare a variable whenever that variable is first assigned some data.

If you've never referenced a particular variable name before, you can actually assign that variable without declaring it using var:

```
chameleon = "blue";
```

The JavaScript interpreter will detect that this variable hasn't been declared before, and will automatically declare it when you try to assign a value to it. At first glance, this statement seems to do exactly the same thing as using the var keyword; however, the variable that it declares is actually quite different, as we'll see later in this chapter when we discuss functions and scoping. For now, take it from me—it's always safest to use var.

The var keyword has to be used only when you first declare a variable. If you want to change the value of the variable later, you do so without var:

```
var chameleon = "blue";
⋮
chameleon = "red";
```

You can use the value of a variable just by calling its name. Any occurrence of the variable name will automatically be replaced with its value when the program is run:

```
var chameleon = "blue";
alert(chameleon);
```

The second statement in this program tells your browser to display an alert box with the supplied value, which in this case will be the value of the variable chameleon, as shown in Figure 2.1.

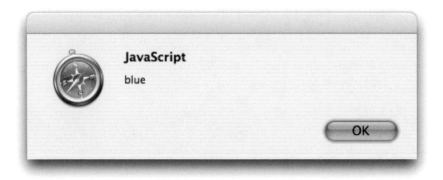

Figure 2.1. JavaScript replacing the variable name with its value

Your variable names can comprise almost any combination of letters and numbers, though no spaces are allowed. Most punctuation and symbols have special meaning inside JavaScript, so the dollar sign ($) and the underscore (_) are the only non-alphanumeric characters allowed in variable names. Variable names are also case-sensitive, so the names chameleon, Chameleon, and CHAMELEON refer to unique variables that could exist simultaneously.

Given those rules, these are all acceptable variable declarations:

```
var chameleon = "blue";
var Chameleon = "red";
var CHAMELEON = "green";
var yellow_chameleon = "yellow";
var orangeChameleon = "orange";
var chameleon$ = "greedy";
```

It's standard practice to create variable names in lowercase letters, unless you're concatenating more than one word. And as I mentioned, variable names can't have spaces in them, so if you want a variable name to include more than one word, you can separate each word with an underscore (multi_word_variable) or capitalize the first letter of each word except for the first (multiWordVariable)—an approach called **camel casing**, because the name has humps like a camel (if you squint your eyes and tilt your head slightly … kind of).

The approach you use to name variables really comes down to personal preference, and which name style you find more readable. I use camel casing because some long-forgotten lecturer beat it into me with a big plank.

Variable Types: Different Types for Different Data

A lot of programming languages feature **strictly typed** variables. With these, you have to tell the program what type of data the variable is going to hold when it's declared, and you can't change a variable's type once it has been created.

JavaScript, however, is **loosely typed**—the language doesn't care *what* your variables hold. A variable could start off holding a number, then change to holding a character, a word, or anything else you want it to hold.

Even though you don't have to declare the data type up front, it's still vital to know what types of data a variable can store, so that you can use and manipulate them properly inside your own programs. In JavaScript, you can work with numbers, strings, Booleans, arrays and objects. We'll take a look at the first four of these types now, but you'll have to wait till the end of the chapter to read about objects, because they're a bit trickier.

Numbers

Eventually, everything inside a computer is broken down into numbers (see the Big Giant Calculator theory we explored earlier). Numbers in JavaScript come in two flavors: whole numbers and decimals. The technical term for a whole number is an **integer** or **int**. A decimal is called a **floating point number**, or **float**. These terms are used in most programming languages, including JavaScript.

To create a variable with numerical data, you just assign a number to a variable name:

```
var whole = 3;
var decimal = 3.14159265;
```

Floating point numbers can have a practically unlimited number of decimal places:

```
var shortDecimal = 3.1;
var longDecimal = 3.14159265358979323846264338327950288419716939937;
```

And both floats and integers can have negative values if you place a minus sign (-) in front of them:

```
var negativeInt = -3;
var negativeFloat = -3.14159265;
```

Mathematical Operations

Numbers can be combined with all of the mathematical operations you'd expect: addition (+), subtraction (-), multiplication (*), and division (/). They're written in fairly natural notation:

```
var addition = 4 + 6;
var subtraction = 6 − 4;
var multiplication = 5 * 9;
var division = 100 / 10;
var longEquation = 4 + 6 + 5 * 9 − 100 / 10;
```

The symbols that invoke these operations in JavaScript—+, -, *, and /—are called **operators**, and as we'll see through the rest of this chapter, JavaScript has a lot of them!

In a compound equation like the one assigned to longEquation, each of the operations is subject to standard mathematical precedence (that is, multiplication and division operations are calculated first, from left to right, after which the addition and subtraction operations are calculated from left to right).

If you want to override the standard precedence of these operations, you can use brackets, just like you learned in school. Any operations that occur inside brackets will be calculated before any multiplication or division is done:

```
var unbracketed = 4 + 6 * 5;
var bracketed = (4 + 6) * 5;
```

Here, the value of unbracketed will be 34, because 6 * 5 is calculated first. The value of bracketed will be 50, because (4 + 6) is calculated first.

You can freely combine integers and floats in your calculations, but the result will always be a float:

```
var whole = 3;
var decimal = 3.14159265;
var decimal2 = decimal - whole;
var decimal3 = whole * decimal;
```

`decimal2` now equals `0.14159265` and `decimal3` equals `9.42477795`.

If you divide two integers and the result is not a whole number, it will automatically become a float:

```
var decimal = 5 / 4;
```

The value of `decimal` will be `1.25`.

Calculations can also involve any combination of numbers or numerical variables:

```
var dozen = 12;
var halfDozen = dozen / 2;
var fullDozen = halfDozen + halfDozen;
```

A handy feature of JavaScript is the fact that you can refer to the current value of a variable in describing a new value to be assigned to it. This capability lets you do things like increase a variable's value by one:

```
var age = 26;
age = age + 1;
```

In the second of these statements, the `age` reference on the right uses the value of `age` *before* the calculation; the result of the calculation is then assigned to `age`, which ends up being 27. This means you can keep calculating new values for the same variable without having to create temporary variables to store the results of those calculations.

The program above can actually be shortened using the handy += operator, which tells your program to add and assign in one fell swoop:

```
var age = 26;
age += 1;
```

Now, age will again equal 27.

It turns out that adding 1 to a variable is something that happens quite frequently in programming (you'll see why when we get to loops later in this chapter), and there's an even shorter shortcut for adding 1 to a variable:

```
var age = 26;
age++;
```

By adding the special ++ operator to the end of age, we tell the program to increment the value of age by 1 and assign the result of this operation as the new value. After those calculations, age again equals 27.

Before or After?

As an alternative to placing the increment operator at the end of a variable name, you can also place it at the beginning:

```
var age = 26;
++age;
```

This achieves exactly the same end result, with one subtle difference in the processing: the value of age is incremented *before* the variable's value is read. This has no effect in the code above, because we're not using the variable's value there, but consider this code:

```
var age = 26;
var ageCopy = age++;
```

Here, ageCopy will equal 26. Now consider this:

```
var age = 26;
var ageCopy = ++age;
```

In this code, ageCopy will equal 27.

Due to the possible confusion arising from this situation, the tasks of incrementing a variable and reading its value are not often completed in a single step. It's safer to increment and assign variables separately.

As well as these special incrementing operators, JavaScript also has the corresponding decrementing operators, `-=` and `--`:

```
var age = 26;
age -= 8;
```

Now `age` will be 18, but let's imagine we just wanted to decrease it by one:

```
var age = 26;
age--;
```

`age` will now be 25.

You can also perform quick assignment multiplication and division using `*=` and `/=`, but these operators are far less common.

Strings

A string is a series of characters of any length, from zero to infinity (or as many as you can type in your lifetime; ready … set … go!). Those characters could be letters, numbers, symbols, punctuation marks, or spaces—basically anything you can find on your keyboard.

To specify a string, we surround a series of characters with quote marks. These can either be single or double straight quote marks,[1] just as long as the opening quote mark matches the closing quote mark:

```
var single = 'Just single quotes';
var double = "Just double quotes";
var crazyNumbers = "18 crazy numb3r5";
var crazyPunctuation = '~cr@zy_punctu&t!on';
```

The quote marks don't appear in the value of the string, they just mark its boundaries. You can prove this to yourself by putting the following code into a test JavaScript file:

---

[1] Some text editors will let you insert curly quotes around a string, "like this." JavaScript will not recognize strings surrounded by curly quotes; it only recognizes straight quotes, "like this."

```
var single = 'Just single quotes';
alert(single);
```

When you load the HTML page that this file's attached to, you'll see the alert shown in Figure 2.2.

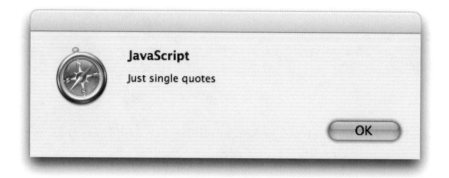

Figure 2.2. The string's value displaying without the quotes used to create the string

It's okay to include a single quote inside a double-quoted string, or a double quote inside a single-quoted string, but if you want to include a quote mark inside a string that's quoted with the same mark, you must precede the internal quote marks with a backslash (\). This is called **escaping** the quote marks:

```
var singleEscape = 'He said \'RUN\' ever so softly.';
var doubleEscape = "She said \"hide\" in a loud voice.";
```

Don't worry—those backslashes disappear when the string is actually used. Let's put this code into a test JavaScript file:

```
var doubleEscape = "She said \"hide\" in a loud voice.";
alert(doubleEscape);
```

When you load the HTML page the file's attached to, you'll see the alert box shown in Figure 2.3.

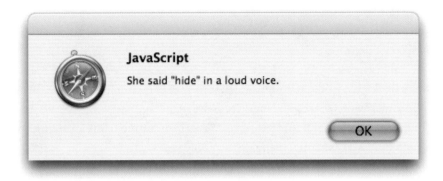

Figure 2.3. The string's value displaying without the backslashes used to escape quote marks in the string

It doesn't matter whether you use single or double quotes for your strings—it's just a matter of personal preference. I tend to use double quotes, but if I'm creating a string with a lot of double quotes in it (such as HTML code), I'll switch to using single quotes around that string, just so I don't have to escape all the double quotes it contains.

String Operations

We can't perform as many operations on strings as we can on numbers, but a couple of very useful operators are available to us.

If you'd like to add two strings together, or **concatenate** them, you use the same + operator that you use for numbers:

```
var complete = "com" + "plete";
```

The value of `complete` will now be `"complete"`.

Again, you can use a combination of strings and string variables with the + operator:

```
var name = "Slim Shady";
var sentence = "My name is " + name;
```

The value of `sentence` will be `"My name is Slim Shady"`.

You can use the += operator with strings, but not the ++ operator—it doesn't make sense to increment strings. So the previous set of statements could be rewritten as:

```
var name = "Slim Shady";
var sentence = "My name is ";
sentence += name;
```

There's one last trick to concatenating strings: you can concatenate numbers and strings, but the result will always end up being a string. If you try to add a number to a string, JavaScript will automatically convert the number into a string, then concatenate the two resulting strings:

```
var sentence = "You are " + 1337
```

`sentence` now contains `"You are 1337"`. Use this trick when you want to output sentences for your h4x0r friends.

Booleans

Boolean values are fairly simple, really—they can be either `true` or `false`. It's probably easiest to think of a Boolean value as a switch that can either be on or off. They're used mainly when we're making decisions, as we'll see in a few pages time.

In order to assign a Boolean value to a variable, you simply specify which state you want it to be in. `true` and `false` are keywords in JavaScript, so you don't need to put any quote marks around them:

```
var lying = true;
var truthful = false;
```

If you were to surround the keywords in quote marks, they'd just be normal strings, not Boolean values.

Arrays

Numbers, strings and Booleans are good ways to store individual pieces of data, but what happens when you have a group of data values that you want to work with, like a list of names or a series of numbers? You could create a whole bunch of variables, but they still wouldn't be grouped together, and you'd have a hard time keeping track of them all.

Arrays solve this problem by providing you with an ordered structure for storing a group of values. You can think of an array as being like a rack in which each slot is able to hold a distinct value.

In order to create an array, we use the special array markers, which are the opening and closing square brackets:

```
var rack = [];
```

The variable `rack` is now an array, but there's nothing stored in it.

Each "slot" in an array is actually called an **element**, and in order to put some data into an element you have to correctly reference which element you want to put it in. This reference is called an **index**, which is a number that represents an element's position in an array. The first element in an array has an index of 0, which can be a little confusing at first, but it's just a programming quirk you have to get used to. The second element has an index of 1, the third: 2, and so on.

To reference a particular element, we use the variable name, followed by an opening square bracket, then the index and a closing square bracket, like this:

```
var rack = [];
rack[0] = "First";
rack[1] = "Second";
```

With that data in the array, you could imagine it looking like Figure 2.4.

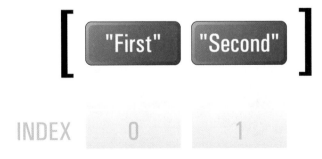

Figure 2.4. An array storing data sequentially, with an index for each element, starting at 0

When we want to retrieve a particular element, we use the array-index notation just like a normal variable name. So, if we had an array like the one above, we could create an alert box displaying the value of the second element like this:

```
alert(rack[1]);
```

The resulting alert is shown in Figure 2.5.

Figure 2.5. An alert box displaying a value retrieved from an array

It's possible to populate an array when it's declared. We simply insert values, separated with commas, between the square brackets:

```
var rack = ["First", "Second", "Third", "Fourth"];
```

That statement says that we should create an array—rack—that has four elements with the values specified here. The first value will have an index of 0, the second value an index of 1, and so on. The array that's created will look like Figure 2.6.

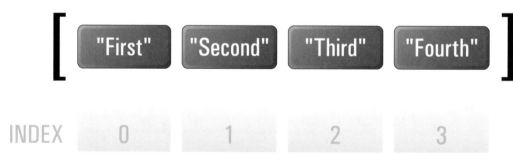

Figure 2.6. The resulting array

Arrays can contain any data type—not just strings—so you could have an array of numbers:

```
var numberArray = [1, 2, 3, 5, 8, 13, 21, 34];
```

You might have an array of strings:

```
var stringArray = ["Veni", "Vidi", "Vici"];
```

A mixed array, containing multiple data types, would look like this:

```
var mixedArray = [235, "Parramatta", "Road"];
```

Here's an array of arrays:

```
var subArray1 = ["Paris", "Lyon", "Nice"];
var subArray2 = ["Amsterdam", "Eindhoven", "Utrecht"];
var subArray3 = ["Madrid", "Barcelona", "Seville"];

var superArray = [subArray1, subArray2, subArray3];
```

That last example is what we call a **multi-dimensional array**—it's a two-dimensional array, to be precise—and it's useful if you want to create a group of groups. In order to retrieve a value from one of the sub-arrays, you have to reference two indices, like so:

```
var city = superArray[0][2];
```

If we translate that statement, starting from the right side, it says:

[2] Get the third element …

[0] of the first array …

superArray in superArray …

var city = and save that value in a new variable, city.

It's possible to have arrays of arrays of arrays, and arrays of arrays of arrays of arrays, but as you can probably tell from these descriptions, such arrangements quickly become unmanageable, so two-dimensional arrays are normally as far as you ever need to go.

The last thing to understand about arrays is the fact that a very useful property is attached to them: `length`. Sometimes, you'll be dealing with an unknown array—an array you've obtained from somewhere else—and you won't know how many elements it contains. In order to avoid referencing an element that doesn't exist, you can check the array's `length` to see how many items it actually contains. We perform this check by adding `.length` to the end of the array name:

```
var shortArray = ["First", "Second", "Third"];
var total = shortArray.length;
```

The value of `total` will now be 3 because there are three items in the array `shortArray`.

It's important to note that you can't use `array.length` to get the index of the last item in the array. Because the first item's index is 0, the last item's index is actually `array.length - 1`:

```
var lastItem = shortArray[shortArray.length - 1];
```

This situation might seem a bit annoying, until you realize that this makes it easy to add an element to the end of the array:

```
shortArray[shortArray.length] = "Fourth";
```

Associative Arrays

Normal arrays are great for holding big buckets of data, but they can sometimes make it difficult to find the exact piece of data you're looking for.

Associative arrays provide a way around this problem—they let you specify key-value pairs. In most respects an associative array is just like an ordinary array, except that instead of the indices being numbers, they're strings, which can be a lot easier to remember and reference:

```
var postcodes = [];
postcodes["Armadale"] = 3143;
postcodes["North Melbourne"] = 3051;
postcodes["Camperdown"] = 2050;
postcodes["Annandale"] = 2038;
```

Now that we've created our associative array, it's not hard to get the postcode for Annandale. All we have to do is specify the right key, and the value will appear:

```
alert(postcodes["Annandale"]);
```

The resulting alert is shown in Figure 2.7.

Figure 2.7. Finding a postcode using an associative array

Although the keys for an associative array have to be strings, the values can be of any data type, including other arrays or associative arrays.

Conditions and Loops: Controlling Program Flow

So far, we've seen statements that allow you to set and retrieve variables inside your program. For a program to be really useful, however, it has to be able to make decisions based on the values of those variables.

The way we make those decisions is through the use of special structures called conditions and loops, which help to control which parts of your program will run under particular conditions, and how many times those parts will be run.

Conditions: Making Decisions

If you think of your program as being like a road map, and the browser as a car navigating those roads, you'll realize that the browser has to be able to take different paths depending on where the user wants to go. Although a program might seem like a linear path—one statement following another—**conditional statements** act like intersections, allowing you to change directions on the basis of a given condition.

`if` Statements

The most common conditional statement is an `if` statement. An `if` statement checks a condition, and if that condition is met, allows the program to execute some code. If the condition isn't met, the code is skipped.

The flow of a program through an `if` statement can be visualized as in Figure 2.8.

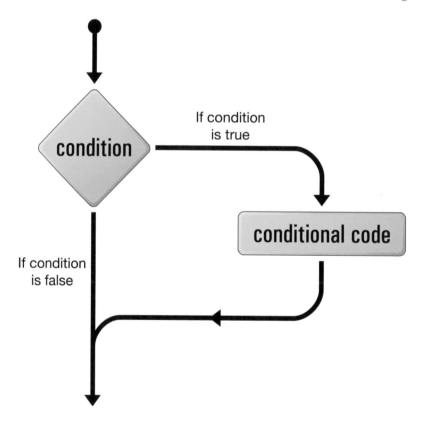

Figure 2.8. The logical flow of an `if` statement

Written as code, `if` statements take this form:

```
if (condition)
{
  conditional code;
}
```

Instead of a semicolon, an `if` statement ends with the conditional code between curly braces (`{…}`).[2] It's considered best practice to put each of these braces on its own line, to make it as easy as possible to spot where blocks of code begin and end.

Indenting Code

It's standard practice to indent the code that's inside curly braces.

On each indented line, a standard number of spaces or tab characters should appear before the first character of the statement. This helps to improve the readability of your code and makes it easier to follow the flow of your programs.

We use two spaces as the standard indentation in this book, but you can use four spaces, one tab—whatever looks best to you. Just be consistent. Every time you nest curly braces (for instance, in another `if` statement inside a block of conditional code), you should increase the indentation for the nested lines by one standard indent.

The condition has to be contained within round brackets (also called parentheses) and will be evaluated as a Boolean, with `true` meaning the code between the curly braces will be executed and `false` indicating it will be skipped. However, the condition doesn't have to be an explicit Boolean value—it can be any **expression** that evaluates to a value that's able to be used as a Boolean.

Expressions

An expression is a combination of values, variable references, operators, and function calls that, when evaluated, produce another value. Wherever a JavaScript value (like a number or a string) is expected, you can use an expression instead.

---

[2] If the conditional code consists of just one statement, you can choose to omit the curly braces. I find it clearer to always include the braces, which is what we'll do in this book.

Here's a simple expression:

```
4 + 6
```

When evaluated, it produces a value (10). We can write a statement that uses this expression like so:

```
var effect = 4 + 6;
```

We now have in our program a variable called `effect`, with a value of 10.

With conditional statements, the most useful types of expressions are those that use **comparison operators** to test a condition and return a Boolean value indicating its outcome.

You might remember comparison operators such as **greater than** (>) and **less than** (<) from some of your old mathematics classes, but there are also **equality** (==) and **inequality** (!=) operators, and various combinations of these. Basically, each comparison operator compares what's on the left of the operator with what's on the right, then evaluates to `true` or `false`. You can then use that result in a conditional statement like this:

```
var age = 27;

if (age > 20)
{
   alert("Drink to get drunk");
}
```

The greater than and less than operators are really only useful with numbers, because it feels a bit too Zen to ask "is one string greater than another?"

However, the equality operator (==) is useful with both strings and numbers:

```
var age = 27;

if (age == 50){
   alert("Half century");
}
```

```
var name = "Maximus";

if (name == "Maximus")
{
  alert("Good afternoon, General.");
}
```

In the first condition, age is 27 and we're testing whether it is equal to 50; obviously, this condition will evaluate to false, so the conditional code will not be run.

In the second condition, name is "Maximus" and we're testing whether it is equal to "Maximus". This condition will evaluate to true and the conditional code will be executed.

== versus =

Be careful to use two equals signs rather than one when you intend to check for equality. If you use only one, you'll be assigning the value on the right to the variable on the left, rather than comparing them, so you'll end up losing your original value rather than checking it!

We can reverse the equality test by using the inequality operator (!=):

```
var name = "Decimus";

if (name != "Maximus")
{
  alert("You are not allowed in.");
}
```

Now, because name is "Decimus" and we're testing whether it *isn't* equal to "Maximus" that condition will evaluate to true and the conditional code will be run.

Table 2.1 lists the most commonly used comparison operators, and the results they'll return with different values:

Table 2.1. Commonly Used Comparison Operators

Operator	Example	Result
>	A > B	true if A is greater than B
>=	A >= B	true if A is greater than or equal to B
<	A < B	true if A is less than B
<=	A <= B	true if A is less than or equal to B
==	A == B	true if A equals B
!=	A != B	true if A does not equal B
!	!A	true if A's Boolean value is false

Multiple Conditions

Instead of using just one test as a condition, you can create a whole chain of them using the logical operators AND (&&) and OR (||).[3]

Both of these operators may be used to combine conditional tests. The AND operator specifies that *both* tests must evaluate to true in order for the whole expression to evaluate to true. The OR operator specifies that only one of the tests has to evaluate to true in order for the whole expression to evaluate to true.

Take a look at this conditional statement:

```
var age = 27;

if (age > 17 && age < 21)
{
  alert("Old enough to vote, too young to drink");
}
```

Here, age is greater than 17 but it's not less than 21, so, since one of the tests evaluated to false, the entire condition evaluates to false. This is a good way to check if a number falls within a specific range.

On the other hand, the OR operator is good for checking whether a variable matches one of a few values:

---

[3] That's two vertical bars, not lowercase Ls or number 1s.

```
var sport = "Skydiving";

if (sport == "Bungee jumping" || sport == "Cliff diving" ||
    sport == "Skydiving")
{
  alert("You're extreme!");
}
```

Although the first two tests in this expression evaluate to `false`, `sport` matches the last test in the OR expression, so the whole condition will evaluate to `true`.

if-else Statements

An `if` statement allows you to execute some code when a condition is met, but doesn't offer any alternative code for cases when the condition *isn't* met. That's the purpose of the `else` statement.

In an `if-else` statement, you begin just as you would for an `if` statement, but immediately after the closing brace of the `if`, you include an `else`, which specifies code to be executed when the condition of the `if` statement fails:

```
if (condition)
{
  conditional code;
}
else
{
  alternative conditional code;
}
```

The flow of this construct can be visualized as shown in Figure 2.9.

To provide some alternative code, all you have to do is append an `else` statement to the end of the `if`:

```
var name = "Marcus";

if (name == "Maximus")
{
  alert("Good afternoon, General.");
}
```

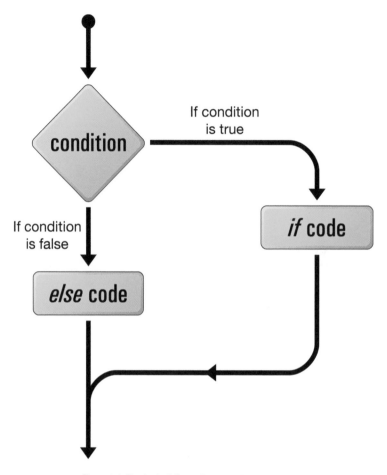

Figure 2.9. The logical flow of an `if-else` statement

```
else
{
  alert("You are not allowed in.");
}
```

This approach saves you from creating a separate `if` statement with a negative formulation of the original condition.

`else-if` Statements

Technically speaking, `else-if` isn't a separate type of statement from `if-else`, but you should be aware of it, because it can be quite useful.

If you want to provide some alternative code for cases in which an `if` statement fails, but you want to further assess the data in order to decide what course of action to take, an `else-if` statement is what you need. Instead of just typing `else`, type `else if`, followed by the extra condition you want to test:

```
var name = "Marcus";

if (name == "Maximus")
{
  alert("Good afternoon, General.");
}
else if (name == "Marcus")
{
  alert("Good afternoon, Emperor.");
}
else
{
  alert("You are not allowed in.");
}
```

You can chain together as many `else-if` statements as you want, and at the end, you can include a normal `else` statement for use when everything fails (though it's not necessary).

Loops: Minimizing Repetition

Computers are meant to make life easier, right? Well, where are those darn robot servants, huh?

Luckily, computers have a few capabilities that will save you thinking and typing time when you're programming. The most effective of these are **loops**, which automate repetitive tasks like modifying each element in an array.

There are a couple of different loop statements but they essentially do the same thing: repeat a set of actions for as long as a specified condition is `true`.

`while` Loops

`while` is the simplest of the loops. All it needs is a condition, and some conditional code:

```
while (condition)
{
  conditional code;
}
```

When the program first encounters the `while` loop, it checks the condition. If the condition evaluates to `true`, the conditional code will be executed. When the program reaches the end of the conditional code, it goes back up to the condition, checks it, and if it evaluates to `true`, the conditional code will be executed ... and so on, as Figure 2.10 shows.

A `while` loop only finishes when its condition evaluates to `false`. This means it's important to have something inside the conditional code that will affect the condition, eventually making it evaluate to `false`. Otherwise, your program will never escape the `while` loop, and will repeat the conditional code forever, causing the browser to become unresponsive.[4]

Loops are extremely handy when they're used in conjunction with arrays, because they allow you to step sequentially through the array and perform the same operation on each element.

To step through an array with a `while` loop, you need an incrementing counter that starts at 0 and increases by one each time the loop executes. This incrementer will keep track of the index of the element that we're currently working with. When we reach the end of the array, we need to make it stop—that's where we use the array's `length` property.

In this example, we'll multiply each element of the `numbers` array by two:

```
var numbers = [1, 2, 3, 4, 5];
var incrementer = 0;
while (incrementer < numbers.length)
{
  numbers[incrementer] *= 2;
  incrementer++;
}
```

---

[4] In Firefox, the browser will eventually display a message to the user complaining that your script is taking a long time to execute. Oh, the shame!

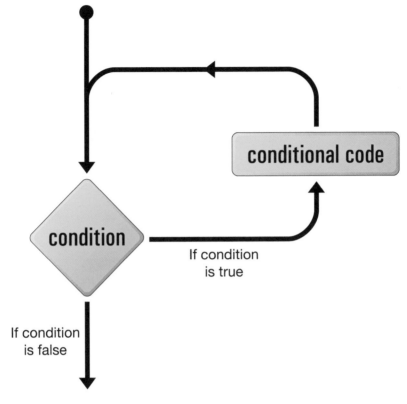

Figure 2.10. The logical flow of a `while` loop

The conditional code inside that `while` loop uses `incrementer` as the index for the array. Starting at `0`, this variable will reference the first element, but because we increase it by one for each execution of the loop, it will step through all of the elements in turn. Once `incrementer` has the same value as `numbers.length`, the condition will fail and the program will exit the `while` loop, having doubled all the elements in the array.

 `i` is for `incrementer`

The variable name `incrementer` is frequently shortened to `i`, which is a commonly used name for a variable that increments inside a loop. This variable is often called a **counter variable**, because it counts how many times the loop has been executed.

do-while Loops

A do-while loop behaves almost identically to a while loop, with one key difference: the conditional code is placed before the condition, so the conditional code is always executed at least once, even if the condition is immediately false.

The conditional code is placed inside the curly braces of the do; the while statement contains the condition right after that:

```
do
{
  conditional code;
}
while (condition);
```

The flow of the program can be described as in Figure 2.11.

do-while loops aren't used very much. In fact, I don't think I've used one in ten years of programming.[5] Your friends and family will be impressed if you know about them, though.

for Loops

for loops are my favorite kind of loops—they're so succinct!

They're a lot like while loops, but they offer a couple of handy shortcuts for statements that we commonly use with loops. Consider this while loop:

```
var numbers = [1, 2, 3, 4, 5];
var i = 0;
while (i < numbers.length)
{
  numbers[i] *= 2;
  i++;
}
```

With a for loop, you can reduce the code above to:

---

[5] The co-author wishes it noted that he uses them all the time ... possibly just because he likes to show off.

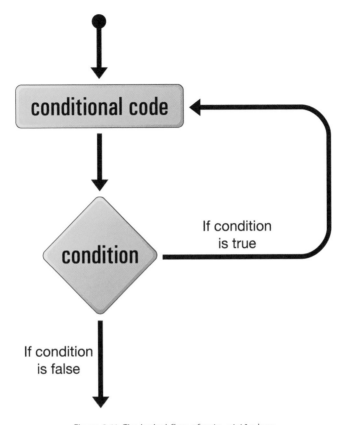

Figure 2.11. The logical flow of a do-while loop

```
var numbers = [1, 2, 3, 4, 5];

for (var i = 0; i < numbers.length; i++)
{
  numbers[i] *= 2;
}
```

A for loop shortens two aspects of the while loop: the declaration of a counter variable, and the incrementing of that variable.

If you look inside the round brackets immediately after the for keyword, you'll see three different statements separated by semicolons. The first statement is the declaration. It allows us to declare a counter variable—in this case i—and set its initial value.

The second statement is the condition that controls the loop. Just like the condition in a `while` loop, this condition must evaluate to `true` in order for the conditional code to be executed. It's evaluated as soon as the program reaches the `for` loop (but after the counter has been declared), so if it evaluates to `false` immediately, the conditional code will never be executed.

The third statement is an action that will be executed every time the program reaches the end of the conditional code. It is normally used to increment (or decrement) the counter, but you could theoretically put anything in there.

A `for` loop can be thought to exhibit a flow similar to that shown in Figure 2.12.

Functions: Writing Code for Later

So far, all the JavaScript code we've seen (and you've perhaps tried out) executes as soon as the page loads in your browser. It runs from top to bottom and then stops, never to run again (at least, until the page is reloaded).

Quite often, we'll want to execute different parts of our program at different times, or re-run the same code quite a few times. In order to do this, you have to put your code into **functions**.

Functions are like little packages of JavaScript code waiting to be called into action. You've seen one function already in this chapter—the `alert` function we used to pop up an alert box in the browser. `alert` is a function that's native to all browsers—that means it comes built-in with the browser's JavaScript interpreter—but it's possible to create your own functions, which you can call whenever you want.

A function can essentially be seen as a wrapper for a block of code. All you need to do is name that block, and you'll be able to call it from other areas of your program, whenever you like.

You can define your own functions using the `function` keyword. This tells the program that you're defining a new function, and that the code contained between the curly braces that follow should be executed whenever that function is called:

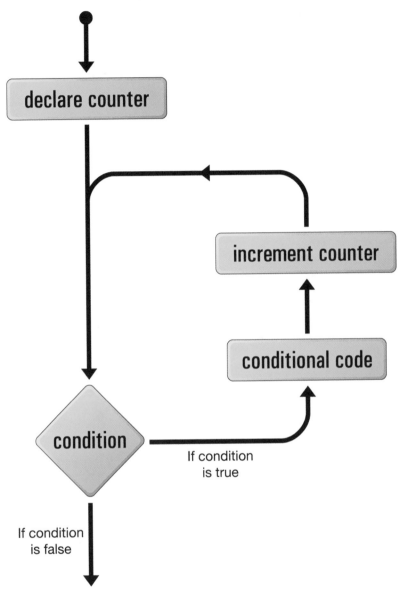

Figure 2.12. The logical flow of a for loop

```
function warning()
{
  alert("This is your final warning");
}
```

The name that follows the `function` keyword is the name that you want to give your function (function names have the same restrictions as variable names). This is the name you'll call whenever you want your program to run the code inside the function. The name must be followed by round brackets—they're empty in this instance, but as you'll see in the next section, this will not always be the case.

In the example above, we created a new function called `warning`, so whenever we make a call to this function, the statements inside the function will be executed, causing an alert box to appear, displaying the text, "This is your final warning."

As in the function declaration above, round brackets must appear immediately after the function name in a function call:

```
warning();
```

These brackets serve two purposes: they tell the program that you want to execute the function, and they contain the data—also known as **arguments**—that you want to pass to the function.[6] Not every function has to have arguments passed to it, but you always have to use the brackets in a function call.

Arguments: Passing Data to a Function

If you look at the ways we used the `alert` function on previous pages, you'll notice that we always inserted a string between the brackets of the function call:

```
alert("Insert and play");
```

The string `"Insert and play"` is actually an argument that we're passing to the `alert` function; the `alert` is designed to take that argument and display it in the browser's alert box.

Functions can be designed to take as many arguments as you want, and those arguments don't have to be strings—they can be any sort of data that you can create in JavaScript.

---

[6] Some people like to call these "parameters." Some people also like to eat sheep's brains.

When you define your function, you can provide names for the arguments that are to be passed to it. These are included in the round brackets immediately after the function name, with a comma separating arguments in cases where there's more than one:

```
function sandwich(bread, meat)
{
  alert(bread + meat + bread);
}
```

Once an argument name has been defined in the function declaration, that argument becomes a variable that's available every time the function is run, allowing you to use the data passed to the function *inside* the function itself.

As you can see in the sandwich function above, two arguments are defined: bread and meat. These two arguments are used in a call to alert and produce a little nonsensical message to the user.

Let's call the function sandwich with the arguments "Rye" and "Pastrami":

```
sandwich("Rye", "Pastrami");
```

When the code for sandwich is executed, those arguments become available as the variables bread and meat, respectively. So, as Figure 2.13 indicates, the user would end up with a pastrami on rye.

Figure 2.13. Using a function argument as a variable

The arguments Array

In addition to being available in their assigned argument names, the values that are passed to a function are also made available inside an automatically generated array variable named `arguments`.

Even if you don't declare any argument names in your function declaration, you can actually pass one or more arguments when you call the function. These arguments will still be available in the `arguments` array. This can be useful for writing functions that will accept any number of arguments.

Imagine we called a function with these arguments:

```
debate("affirmative", "negative");
```

We could access those arguments via the `arguments` array inside the function, like this:

```
function debate()
{
  var affirmative = arguments[0];
  var negative = arguments[1];
}
```

Return Statements: Outputting Data from a Function

Thus far, the outcome of most of our functions has been to display an alert box to the user with a message in it. But most of the time, you'll want your functions to be silent, simply passing data to other parts of your program.

A function may **return** data to the statement that called it. The neat thing about that is that you can assign a function call as the value of a variable, and that variable's value will become whatever was returned by the function.

To get a function to return a value, we use the `return` keyword, followed by the value we want it to return:

```
function sandwich(bread, meat)
{
  var assembled = bread + meat + bread;

  return assembled;
}
```

Then, the function's all ready to be used in an expression:

```
var lunch = sandwich("Rye", "Pastrami");
```

The lunch variable now contains the string "RyePastramiRye".

If you want to get *really* tricky, you'll be pleased to hear that the return value can even be an expression:

```
function sandwich(bread, meat)
{
  return bread + meat + bread;
}
```

The expression will be evaluated and the result will be returned, producing the same effect as the previous version of the code.

A return statement is always the final act of a function; nothing else is processed after a function has returned. Consider this code:

```
function prematureReturner()
{
  return "Too quick";

  alert("Was it good for you?");
}
```

The alert function wouldn't be called, because the return statement would always "cut off" execution of the function. This ability to "cut off" execution of a function with a return statement can be handy when used in conjunction with a conditional statement, where you only want the rest of the function to be executed if a certain condition is met.

Scope: Keeping your Variables Separate

Right back at the start of this chapter I mentioned that you should avoid using variables without first declaring them using the var keyword. This will help you prevent variable clashes in your functions.

Most of the variables we saw in this chapter weren't declared inside a function, and therefore reside in what's known as global scope. Variables declared in **global scope** may be accessed from any other JavaScript code running in the current web page. This mightn't sound too bad, and it often won't be a problem … until you start using common variable names inside your functions.

Take a look at this program:

```
function countWiis()
{
  stock = 5;
  sales = 3;

  return stock - sales;
}

stock = 0;
wiis = countWiis();
```

What will be the value of stock after this code has run?

You'd probably expect it still to be 0, which is what we set it to be before calling countWiis. However, countWiis *also* uses a variable called stock. But because the function doesn't use var to declare this variable, JavaScript will go looking *outside* the function—in the global scope—to see whether or not that variable already exists. Indeed it does, so JavaScript will assign the value 5 to that global variable.

What we really intended was for countWiis to use its own *separate* stock variable. To achieve this, we need to declare that variable with **local scope**. A variable with local scope exists only within the confines of the function in which it was created. It also takes precedence over variables with global scope—if a local variable and a global variable both have the same name, a function will always use the local variable, leaving the global variable untouched.

How do you declare a local variable? Put `var` in front of it.

Let's reformulate our code with all our variables correctly declared:

```javascript
function countWiis()
{
  var stock = 5;
  var sales = 3;

  return stock - sales;
}

var stock = 0;
var wiis = countWiis();
```

The `stock` variable declared *outside* the `countWiis` function will remain untouched by the `stock` variable declared *inside* `countWiis`—our function can live in peace and harmony with the rest of the universe!

The lesson here is that unless you intend a variable to be shared throughout your program, always declare it with `var`.[7]

Objects

Now that we've looked at variables and functions, we can finally take a look at **objects**.

Objects are really just amorphous programming blobs. They're an amalgam of all the other data types, existing mainly to make life easier for programmers. Still, their vagueness of character doesn't mean they're not useful.

Objects exist as a way of organizing variables and functions into logical groups. If your program deals with bunnies and robots, it'll make sense to have all the functions and variables that relate to robots in one area, and all the functions and variables

---

[7] Strictly speaking, variables created outside of functions will always be in the global scope, whether they are declared with `var` or created simply by assigning a value to an undeclared variable name. Nevertheless, declaring all your variables with `var` is a good habit to get into, and is considered best practice.

that relate to bunnies in another area. Objects do this by grouping together sets of **properties** and **methods**.

Properties are *variables* that are only accessible via their object, and methods are *functions* that are only accessible via their object. By requiring all access to properties and methods to go through the objects that contain them, JavaScript objects make it much easier to manage your programs.

We've actually played with objects already—when you create a new array, you're creating a new instance of the built-in `Array` object. The `length` of an array is actually a property of that object, and arrays also have methods like `push` and `splice`, which we'll use later in this book.

An array is a native object, because it's built in to the JavaScript language, but it's easy to create your own objects using the `Object` constructor:

```
var Robot = new Object();
```

 Naming Conventions

Variable names start with a lowercase letter, while object names start with an uppercase letter. That's just the way it is. After decades of finely honed programming practice, this convention helps everyone distinguish between the two.

Once you've instantiated your new object, you're then free to add properties and methods to it, to modify the values of existing properties, and to call the object's methods. The properties and methods of an object are both accessed using the dot (.) syntax:

```
Robot.metal = "Titanium";
Robot.killAllHumans = function()
{
  alert("Exterminate!");
};

Robot.killAllHumans();
```

The first line of this code adds to our empty `Robot` object a `metal` property, assigning it a value of `"Titanium"`. Note that we don't need to use the `var` keyword when we're declaring properties, since properties are always in **object scope**—they must be accessed via the object that contains them.

The statement that begins on the second line adds a `killAllHumans` method to our `Robot` object. Note that this is a little different from the syntax that we used previously to declare a standalone function; here, our method declaration takes the form of an assignment statement (note the assignment operator, =, and the semicolon at the end of the code block).

 ## Alternative Syntax for Standalone Functions

As it turns out, you can also use this syntax to declare standalone functions if you want to. Never let it be said that JavaScript doesn't give you options! Before, we used this function declaration:

```
function sandwich(bread, meat)
{
  alert(bread + meat + bread);
}
```

JavaScript lets you write this in the form of a variable assignment, if you prefer:

```
var sandwich = function(bread, meat)
{
  alert(bread + meat + bread);
};
```

As you might expect, there is a very subtle difference between the effects of these two code styles: a function declared with the former syntax can be used by any code in the file, even if it comes before the function declaration. A function declared with the latter syntax can only be used by code that executes after the assignment statement that declares the function. If your code is well organized, however, this difference won't matter.

Finally, the last line of our program calls the `Robot` object's `killAllHumans` method.

As with a lot of JavaScript, we can shortcut this whole sequence using the object literal syntax:

```
var Robot =
{
  metal: "Titanium",
  killAllHumans: function()
  {
    alert("Exterminate!");
  }
};
```

Rather than first creating an empty object and then populating it with properties and methods using a series of assignment statements, **object literal syntax** lets you create the object and its contents with a single statement.

In object literal syntax, we represent a new object with curly braces; inside those braces, we list the properties and methods of the object, separated by commas. For each property and method, we assign a value using a colon (:) instead of the assignment operator.

Object literal syntax can be a little difficult to read once you've been using the standard assignment syntax for a while, but it *is* slightly more succinct.

We're going to use this object literal syntax throughout this book to create neatly self-contained packages of functionality that you can easily transport from page to page.

Unobtrusive Scripting in the Real World

After reading Chapter 1, you no doubt have it fairly clear in your head that HTML is for content and JavaScript is for behavior, and never the twain shall meet. However, it's not quite that simple in the real world.

If you have a close look at the way JavaScript is downloaded alongside the HTML page that links to it, you should notice that sometimes—in fact *most* of the time—the JavaScript will download before all of the HTML has downloaded. This presents us with a slight problem.

Browsers execute JavaScript files as soon as the *JavaScript file* is downloaded—not the HTML file. So chances are that the JavaScript will be executed before all of the HTML has been downloaded. If your JavaScript executes and is trying to enhance the HTML content with behavior before it's ready, you're probably going to start seeing JavaScript errors about HTML elements not being where they're supposed to be.

One way around this problem is to wait until all of the HTML is ready before you run any JavaScript that modifies or uses the HTML. Luckily, JavaScript has a way of detecting when the web page is ready to do this. Unluckily, the code involved is rather complicated.

To get you up to speed quickly, I've created a special library object, Core. This object includes a method called start that monitors the status of the page, and lets your JavaScript objects know when it's safe to start playing around with the HTML. It does this by calling your object's init method. All you have to do is let the function know which objects require this notification, and make sure each of those objects has an init method that will start working with the web page when it's called.

So, if you had a Robot object that wanted to find all the robots on your page, you'd write the following code:

```
var Robot =
{
  init: function()
  {
    Your HTML modifying code;
  }
};

Core.start(Robot);
```

By registering Robot with Core.start on the final line, you can rest assured that Robot.init will be run only when it's safe to do so.

Core.start uses some JavaScript voodoo that we'll learn about in later chapters, but if you want to know all the details now, flick to Appendix A.

Summary

If you've never programmed before, stepping into JavaScript can be a little daunting, so don't think you have to understand it straight away. Take the time to read through this chapter's explanations again, and maybe try out some of the examples—I find I learn best by practical experience and experimentation.

Once you've got a firm understanding of the concepts behind programming and the basics of JavaScript, continue on to the next chapter, where we'll learn how to work with the contents of web pages and create some real-world programs.

Chapter 3

Document Access

Without a document, JavaScript would have no way to make its presence felt. It's HTML that creates the tangible interface through which JavaScript can reach its users.

This relationship makes it vital that JavaScript be able to access, create, and manipulate every part of the document. To this end, the W3C created the Document Object Model—a system through which scripts can influence the document. This system not only allows JavaScript to make changes to the structure of the document, but enables it to access a document's styles and change the way it looks.

If you want to take control of your interfaces, you'll first have to master the DOM.

The Document Object Model: Mapping your HTML

When an HTML document is downloaded to your browser, that browser has to do the job of turning what is essentially one long string of characters into a web page. To do this, the browser decides which parts are paragraphs, which parts are headings, which parts are text, and so on. In order to save poor JavaScript programmers from having to do the exact same work, the browser stores its interpretation of the HTML code as a structure of JavaScript objects, called the **Document Object Model**, or **DOM**.

Within this model, each element in the HTML document becomes an object, as do all the attributes and text. JavaScript can access each of these objects independently, using built-in functions that make it easy to find and change what we want on the fly.

As a result of the way in which HTML is written—as a hierarchy of nested elements marked with start and end tags—the DOM creates a different object for each element, but links each element object to its enclosing (or parent) element. This creates an explicit parent-child relationship between elements, and lends the visualization of the DOM most readily to a tree structure.

Take, for example, this HTML:

```
<!DOCTYPE html PUBLIC "-//W3C//DTD XHTML 1.0 Strict//EN"
    "http://www.w3.org/TR/xhtml1/DTD/xhtml1-strict.dtd">
<html xmlns="http://www.w3.org/1999/xhtml" lang="en-US">
  <head>
    <title>DOMinating JavaScript</title>
    <meta http-equiv="Content-Type"
        content="text/html; charset=utf-8" />
  </head>
  <body>
    <h1>
      DOMinating JavaScript
    </h1>
    <p>
      If you need some help with your JavaScript, you might like
      to read articles from <a href="http://www.danwebb.net/"
          rel="external">Dan Webb</a>,
      <a href="http://www.quirksmode.org/" rel="external">PPK</a>
      and <a href="http://adactio.com/" rel="external">Jeremy
      Keith</a>.
    </p>
  </body>
</html>
```

These elements, as mapped out in the DOM, can most easily be thought of as shown in Figure 3.1.

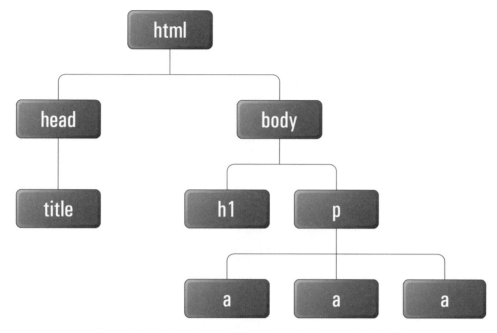

Figure 3.1. Each element on an HTML page linking to its parent in the DOM

To create the DOM for a document, each element in the HTML is represented by what's known as a **node**. A node's position in the DOM tree is determined by its parent and child nodes.

An element node is distinguished by its element name (head, body, h1, etc.), but this doesn't have to be unique. Unless you supply some identifying characteristic—like an id attribute—one paragraph node will appear much the same as another.

Technically, there's a special node that's always contained in a document, no matter what that document's content is. It always sits right at the top of the tree and it's called the **document node**. With that in mind, Figure 3.2 would be a more accurate representation of the DOM.

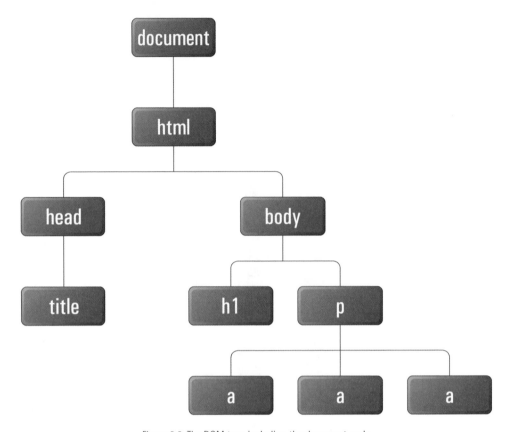

Figure 3.2. The DOM tree, including the document node

Element nodes (that is, nodes that represent HTML elements) are one type of node, and they define most of the structure of the DOM, but the actual *content* of a document is contained in two other types of nodes: text nodes and attribute nodes.

Text Nodes

In HTML code, anything that's not contained between angled brackets will be interpreted as a **text node** in the DOM. Structurally, text nodes are treated almost exactly like element nodes: they sit in the same tree structure and can be reached just like element nodes; however, they cannot have children.

If we reconsider the HTML example we saw earlier, and include the text nodes in our visualization of the DOM, it becomes a lot bigger, as Figure 3.3 illustrates.

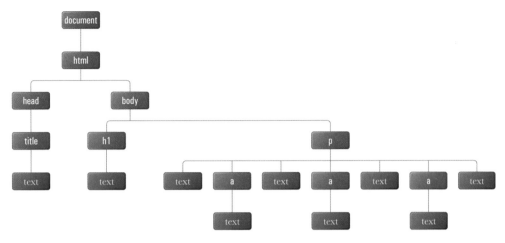

Figure 3.3. The complete DOM tree, including text nodes

Although those text nodes all look fairly similar, each node has its own value, which stores the actual text that the node represents. So the value of the text node inside the `title` element in this example would be "DOMinating JavaScript."

Whitespace May Produce Text Nodes

As well as visible characters, text nodes contain invisible characters such as new lines and tabs. If you indent your code to make it more readable (as we do in this book), each of the lines and tabs that you use to separate any tags or text will be included in a text node.

This means you may end up with text nodes in between adjacent elements, or with extra white space at the beginning or end of a text node. Browsers handle these **whitespace nodes** differently, and this variability in DOM parsing is the reason why you have to be very careful when relying upon the number or order of nodes in the DOM.

Attribute Nodes

With tags and text covered by element and text nodes, the only pieces of information that remain to be accounted for in the DOM are attributes. At first glance, attributes would appear to be part of an element—and they are, in a way—but they still occupy their own type of nodes, handily called **attribute nodes**.

Any of the three anchor elements in the example DOM we saw earlier could be visualized as shown in Figure 3.4 with the element's attribute nodes.

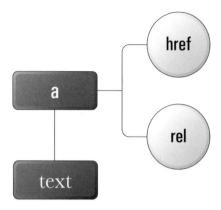

Figure 3.4. The `href` and `rel` attributes represented as attribute nodes in the DOM

Attribute nodes are always attached to an element node, but they don't fit into the structure of the DOM like element and text nodes do—they're not counted as children of the element they're attached to. Because of this, we use different functions to work with attribute nodes—we'll discuss those functions later in the chapter.

As you can see from the diagrams presented here, the DOM quickly becomes complex—even with a simple document—so you'll need some powerful ways to identify and manipulate the parts you want. That's what we'll be looking at next.

Accessing the Nodes you Want

Now that we know how the DOM is structured, we've got a good idea of the sorts of things we'll want to access. Each node—be it an element, text, or attribute node—contains information that we can use to identify it, but it's a delicate matter to sort through all of the nodes in a document to find those we want.

In many ways, manipulating an element via the DOM is a lot like applying element styles via CSS. Both tasks take this general pattern:

1.   Specify the element or group of elements that you want to affect.

2.   Specify the effect you want to have on them.

Although the ways in which we manipulate elements vary greatly between the two technologies, the processes we use to find the elements we want to work on are strikingly similar.

Finding an Element by ID

The most direct path to an element is via its `id` attribute. `id` is an optional HTML attribute that can be added to any element on the page, but each ID you use has to be unique within that document:

```
<p id="uniqueElement">
  ⋮
</p>
```

If you set out to find an element by ID, you'll need to make one big assumption: that the element you want has an ID. Sometimes, this assumption will mean that you need to massage your HTML code ahead of time, to make sure that the required element has an ID; at other times, that ID will naturally appear in the HTML (as part of the document's semantic structure). But once an element does have an ID, it becomes particularly easy for JavaScript to find.

If you wanted to reference a particular element by ID in CSS, you'd use an ID selector beginning with #:

```
#uniqueElement ❶
{
  color: blue; ❷
}
```

Roughly translated, that CSS says:

❶   Find the element with the ID `uniqueElement`.

❷   Make its color blue.

CSS is quite a succinct language. JavaScript is not. So, to reference an element by ID in JavaScript, we use the `getElementById` method, which is available only from the `document` node. It takes a string as an argument, then finds the element that has that string as its ID. I like to think of `getElementById` as a sniper that can pick out one element at a time—highly targeted. For instance, imagine that our document included this HTML:

```
<h1>
  Sniper (1993)
</h1>
<p>
  In this cinema masterpiece,
  <a id="berenger" href="/name/nm0000297/">Tom Berenger</a> plays
  a US soldier working in the Panamanian jungle.
</p>
```

We can obtain a reference to the HTML element with the ID berenger, irrespective of what type of element it is:

```
var target = document.getElementById("berenger");
```

The variable target will now reference the DOM node for the anchor element around Tom Berenger's name. But let's suppose that the ID was moved onto another element:

```
<h1 id="berenger">
  Sniper (1993)
</h1>
<p>
  In this cinema masterpiece,
  <a href="/name/nm0000297/">Tom Berenger</a> plays a US soldier
  working in the Panamanian jungle.
</p>
```

Now, if we execute the same JavaScript code, our target would reference the h1 element.

Once you have a reference to an element node, you can use lots of native methods and properties on it to gain information about the element, or modify its contents. You'll explore a lot of these methods and properties as you progress through this book.

If you'd like to try to get some information about the element we just found, you can access one or more of the element node's native properties. One such property is nodeName, which tells you the exact tag name of the node you're referencing. To display the tag name of the element captured by getElementById, you could run this code:

```
var target = document.getElementById("berenger");
alert(target.nodeName);
```

An alert dialog will pop up displaying the tag name, as shown in Figure 3.5.

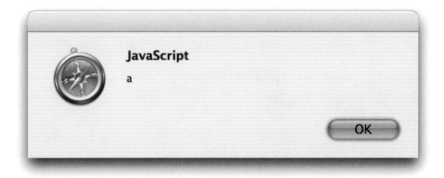

Figure 3.5. Displaying an element's tag name using the nodeName property

If an element with the particular ID you're looking for doesn't exist, getElementById won't return a reference to a node—instead, it will return the value null. null is a special value that usually indicates some type of error. Essentially, it indicates the absence of an object when one might normally be expected.

If you're not sure that your document will contain an element with the particular ID you're looking for, it's safest to check that getElementById actually returns a node object, because performing most operations on a null value will cause your program to report an error and stop running. You can perform this check easily using a conditional statement that verifies that the reference returned from getElementById isn't null:

```
var target = document.getElementById("berenger");

if (target != null)
{
  alert(target.nodeName);
}
```

Finding Elements by Tag Name

Using IDs to locate elements is excellent if you want to modify one element at a time, but if you want to find a group of elements, getElementsByTagName is the method for you.

Its equivalent in CSS would be the element type selector:

```
li
{
  color: blue;
}
```

Unlike getElementById, getElementsByTagName can be executed as a method of any element node, but it's most commonly called on the document node.

Take a look at this document:

```
<!DOCTYPE html PUBLIC "-//W3C//DTD XHTML 1.0 Strict//EN"
    "http://www.w3.org/TR/xhtml1/DTD/xhtml1-strict.dtd">
<html xmlns="http://www.w3.org/1999/xhtml" lang="en-US">
  <head>
    <title>Tag Name Locator</title>
    <meta http-equiv="Content-Type"
        content="text/html; charset=utf-8" />
  </head>
  <body>
    <p>
      There are 3 different types of element in this body:
    </p>
    <ul>
      <li>
        paragraph
      </li>
      <li>
        unordered list
      </li>
      <li>
        list item
      </li>
```

```
    </ul>
  </body>
</html>
```

We can retrieve all these list item elements using one line of JavaScript:

```
var listItems = document.getElementsByTagName("li");
```

By executing that code, you're telling your program to search through all of the descendants of the document node, get all the nodes with a tag name of "li", and assign that group to the listItems variable.

listItems ends up containing a collection of nodes called a **node list**. A node list is a JavaScript object that contains a list of node objects in source order. In the example we just saw, all the nodes in the node list have a tag name of "li".

Node lists behave a lot like arrays, which we saw in Chapter 2, although they lack some of the useful methods that arrays provide. In general, however, you can treat them the same way. Since getElementsByTagName always returns a node list in source order, we know that the second node in the list will actually be the second node in the HTML source, so to reference it you would use the index 1 (remember, the first index in an array is 0):

```
var listItems = document.getElementsByTagName("li");
var secondItem = listItems[1];
```

secondItem would now be a reference to the list item containing the text "unordered list."

Node lists also have a length property, so you can retrieve the number of nodes in a collection by referencing its length:

```
var listItems = document.getElementsByTagName("li");
var numItems = listItems.length;
```

Given that the document contained three list items, numItems will be 3.

The fact that a node list is referenced similarly to an array means that it's easy to use a loop to perform the same task on each of the nodes in the list. If we wanted to check that getElementsByTagName only returned elements with the same tag name, we could output the tag name of each of the nodes using a for loop:

```
var listItems = document.getElementsByTagName("li");

for (var i = 0; i < listItems.length; i++)
{
  alert(listItems[i].nodeName);
}
```

Unlike getElementById, getElementsByTagName will return a node list even if no elements matched the supplied tag name. The length of this node list will be 0. This means it's safe to use statements that check the length of the node list, as in the loop above, but it's *not* safe to directly reference an index in the list without first checking the length to make sure that the index will be valid. Looping through the node list using its length property as part of the loop condition is usually the best way to do this.

Restricting Tag Name Selection

At the start of this section, I mentioned that getElementsByTagName can be executed from any element node, not just the document node. Calling this method from an element node allows you to restrict the area of the DOM from which you want to select nodes.

For instance, imagine that your document included multiple unordered lists, like this:

```
<!DOCTYPE html PUBLIC "-//W3C//DTD XHTML 1.0 Strict//EN"
    "http://www.w3.org/TR/xhtml1/DTD/xhtml1-strict.dtd">
<html xmlns="http://www.w3.org/1999/xhtml" lang="en-US">
  <head>
    <title>Tag Name Locator</title>
    <meta http-equiv="Content-Type"
        content="text/html; charset=utf-8" />
  </head>
  <body>
    <p>
```

```
      There are 3 different types of element in this body:
    </p>
    <ul>
      <li>
        paragraph
      </li>
      <li>
        unordered list
      </li>
      <li>
        list item
      </li>
    </ul>
    <p>
      There are 2 children of html:
    </p>
    <ul>
      <li>
        head
      </li>
      <li>
        body
      </li>
    </ul>
  </body>
</html>
```

Now, you might want to get the list items from the second list only—not the first. If you were to call document.getElementsByTagName("li"), you'd end up with a collection that contained all five list items in the document, which, obviously, is not what you want. But if you get a reference to the second list and use *that* reference to call the method, it's possible to get the list items from that list alone:

```
var lists = document.getElementsByTagName("ul");
var secondList = lists[1];
var secondListItems = secondList.getElementsByTagName("li");
```

secondListItems now contains just the two list items from the second list.

Here, we've used two getElementsByTagName calls to get the elements we wanted, but there is an alternative. We could use a getElementById call to get the required reference to the second list (if the second list had an ID) before we called `getElementsByTagName`, to get the list items it contains. Combining multiple DOM method calls is something you should get a feel for fairly quickly. The best approach will often depend upon the structure of the HTML you're dealing with.

Finding Elements by Class Name

It's quite often very handy to find elements based on a class rather than a tag name. Although we're stuck with the same 91 HTML elements wherever we go, we can readily customize our classes to create easily referenced groups of elements that suit our purposes.

Compared to searching by tag name, using a class as a selector can be a more granular way to find elements (as it lets you get a subset of a particular tag name group) as well as a broader way to find elements (as it lets you select a group of elements that have a range of tag names).

Unfortunately, no built-in DOM function lets you get elements by class, so I think it's time we created our first real function! Once that's done, we can add the function to our custom JavaScript library and call it whenever we want to get all elements with a particular class.

Starting your First Function

When you're writing a function or a program, your first step should be to define clearly in plain English what you want it to do. If you're tackling a relatively simple problem, you might be able to translate that description straight into JavaScript, but usually you'll need to break the task down into simple steps.

The full description of what we want to do here could be something like, "find all elements with a particular class in the document."

That sounds deceptively simple; let's break it down into more logical steps:

1. Look at each element in the document.

2. For each element, perform a check that compares its class against the one we're looking for.

3. If the classes match, add the element to our group of elements.

A couple of things should jump out at you immediately from those steps. Firstly, whenever you see the phrase "for each," chances are that you're going to need a loop. Secondly, whenever there's a condition such as "if it matches," you're going to need a conditional statement. Lastly, when we talk about a "group," that usually means an array or node list.

With those predictions in mind, let's turn these three steps into code.

Looking at All the Elements

First of all, we'll need to get all the elements in the document. We do this using `getElementsByTagName`, but we're not going to look for a particular tag; instead, we're going to pass this method the special value `"*"`, which tells it to return all elements.

Unfortunately, Internet Explorer 5.x doesn't understand that special value, so we have to write some additional code in order to support that browser. In Internet Explorer 5.x, Microsoft created a special object that contains all the elements in the document, and called it `document.all`. `document.all` is basically a node list containing all the elements, so it's synonymous with calling `document.getElementsByTagName("*")`.

Most other browsers don't have the `document.all` object, but those that do implement it just like Internet Explorer, so our code can simply test to see whether `document.all` exists. If it does, we use the Internet Explorer 5.x way of getting all the elements. If it doesn't, we use the normal approach:

```
var elementArray = [];

if (typeof document.all != "undefined")
{
  elementArray = document.all;
}
else
{
  elementArray = document.getElementsByTagName("*");
}
```

The conditional statement above uses the `typeof` operator to check for the existence of `document.all`. `typeof` checks the data type of the value that follows it, and produces a string that describes the value's type (for instance, `"number"`, `"string"`, `"object"`, etc.). Even if the value is `null`, it will still return a type (`"object"`), but if you supply `typeof` with a variable or property name that hasn't been assigned any value whatsoever, it will return the string `"undefined"`. This technique, called **object detection**, is the safest way of testing whether an object—such as `document.all`—exists. If `typeof` returns `"undefined"`, we know that the browser doesn't implement that feature.

Whichever part of the conditional statement the browser decides to execute, we end up correctly assigning to `elementArray` a node list of every element in the document.

Checking the Class of Each Element

Now that we have a collection of elements to look at, we can check the class of each:

```
var pattern = new RegExp("(^| )" + theClass + "( |$)");

for (var i = 0; i < elementArray.length; i++)
{
  if (pattern.test(elementArray[i].className))
  {
    ⋮
  }
}
```

The value that we assign to the variable `pattern` on the first line will probably look rather alien to you. In fact, this is a **regular expression**, which we'll explore more fully in Chapter 6. For now, what you need to know is that regular expressions help us search strings for a particular pattern. In this case, our regular expression uses the variable `theClass` as the class we want to match against; `theClass` will be passed into our function as an argument.

Once we've set up our regular expression with that class name, we use a `for` loop to step through each of the elements in `elementArray`.

Every time we move through the `for` loop, we use the `pattern` regular expression, testing the current element's `class` attribute against it. We do this by passing the element's `className` property—a string value—to the regular expression's `test` method. Every element node has a `className` property, which corresponds directly to that element's `class` attribute in the HTML.

When `pattern.test` is run, it checks the string argument that's passed to it against the regular expression. If the string matches the regular expression (that is, it contains the specified class name), it will return `true`; if the string doesn't match the regular expression, it will return `false`. In this way, we can use a regular expression test as the condition for an `if` statement. In this example, we use the conditional statement to tell us if the current element has a class that matches the one we're looking for.

But why can't we just perform a direct string comparison on the class, like this?

```
if (elementArray[i].className == theClass) // this won't work
```

The thing about dealing with an element's `className` property is that it can actually contain multiple classes, separated by spaces, like this:

```
<div class="article summary clicked">
```

For this reason, simply checking whether the `class` attribute's value equals the class that we're interested in is not always sufficient. When checking to see whether `class` contains a particular class, we need to use a more advanced method of searching within the attribute value, which is why we used a regular expression.

Adding Matching Elements to our Group of Elements

Once we've decided that an element matches the criteria we've set, we need to add it to our group of elements. But where's our group? Earlier, I said that a node list is a lot like an array. We can't actually create our own node lists—the closest thing we can create is an array.

Outside the `for` loop, we create the array that's going to hold the group of elements, then add each matched element to the array as we find it:

```
var matchedArray = [];
var pattern = new RegExp("(^| )" + theClass + "( |$)");

for (var i = 0; i < elementArray.length; i++)
```

```
{
  if (pattern.test(elementArray[i].className))
  {
    matchedArray[matchedArray.length] = elementArray[i];
  }
}
```

Within the `if` statement we wrote in the previous step, we add any newly matched elements to the end of `matchedArray`, using its current `length` as the index of the new element (remember that the `length` of an array will always be one more than the index of the last element).

Once the `for` loop has finished executing, all of the elements in the document that have the required class will be referenced inside `matchedArray`. We're almost done!

Putting it All Together

The guts of our function are now pretty much written. All we have to do it paste them together and put them inside a function:

core.js *(excerpt)*

```
Core.getElementsByClass = function(theClass)
{
  var elementArray = [];

  if (typeof document.all != "undefined")
  {
    elementArray = document.all;
  }
  else
  {
    elementArray = document.getElementsByTagName("*");
  }

  var matchedArray = [];
  var pattern = new RegExp("(^| )" + theClass + "( |$)");

  for (var i = 0; i < elementArray.length; i++)
  {
    if (pattern.test(elementArray[i].className))
    {
```

```
      matchedArray[matchedArray.length] = elementArray[i];
    }
  }

  return matchedArray;
};
```

We've called our new function `Core.getElementsByClass`, and our function definition contains one argument—`theClass`—which is the class we use to construct our regular expression. As well as placing the code inside a function block, we include a `return` statement that passes `matchedArray` back to the statement that called `Core.getElementsByClass`.

Now that it's part of our `Core` library, we can use this function to find a group of elements by class from anywhere in our JavaScript code:

```
var elementArray = Core.getElementsByClass("dataTable");
```

Navigating the DOM Tree

The methods for finding DOM elements that I've described so far have been fairly targeted—we're jumping straight to a particular node in the tree without worrying about the connections in between.

This works fine when there's some distinguishing feature about the element in question that allows us to identify it: an ID, a tag name, or a class. But what if you want to get an element on the basis of its relationship with the nodes that surround it? For instance, if we have a list item node and want to retrieve its parent `ul`, how do we do that? For that matter, how do we get the next item in the list?

For each node in the tree, the DOM specifies a number of properties, and it's these properties that allow us to move around the tree one step at a time. Where `document.getElementById` and its ilk are like direct map references ("go to S37° 47.75', E144° 59.01'"), these DOM properties are like giving directions: "turn left onto the Bayshore Freeway and a right onto Amphitheater Parkway." Some people call this process **walking the DOM**.

Finding a Parent

Every element node—except for the document node—has a parent. Consequently, each element node has a property called parentNode. When we use this property, we receive a reference to the target element's parent.

Consider this HTML:

```
<p>
  <a id="oliver" href="/oliver/">Oliver Twist</a>
</p>
```

Once we have a reference to the anchor element, we can get a reference to its parent paragraph using parentNode like so:

```
var oliver = document.getElementById("oliver");
var paragraph = oliver.parentNode;
```

Finding Children

The parent-child relationship isn't just one way. You can find all of the children of an element using the childNodes property.

An element can only have one parent, but it can have many children, so childNodes is actually a node list that contains all of the element's children, in source order.

Take, for instance, a list like this:

```
<ul id="baldwins">
  <li>
    Alec
  </li>
  <li>
    Daniel
  </li>
  <li>
    William
  </li>
  <li>
```

```
    Stephen
  </li>
</ul>
```

The unordered list node will have four child nodes,[1] each of which matches a list item. To get the third list item (the one containing "William") in the list above, we'd get the third element in the `childNodes` list:

```
var baldwins = document.getElementById("baldwins");
var william = baldwins.childNodes[2];
```

Two shortcut properties are available to help us get the first child or last child of an element: the `firstChild` and `lastChild` properties, respectively.

To get the "Alec" list item, we could just use:

```
var alec = baldwins.firstChild;
```

And to get the "Stephen" list item, we can use:

```
var stephen = baldwins.lastChild;
```

I don't think `firstChild` is all that much easier than typing `childNodes[0]`, but `lastChild` is definitely shorter than `childNodes[childNodes.length − 1]`, so it's a shortcut that I use regularly.

Finding Siblings

As well as moving up and down the DOM tree, we can move from side to side by getting the next or previous node on the same level. The properties we use to do so are `nextSibling` and `previousSibling`.

If we continued on from the example we saw a moment ago, we could get to the "Stephen" list item from "William" using `nextSibling`:

```
var stephen = william.nextSibling;
```

---

[1] As noted at the start of this chapter, the number of nodes may vary depending on whether the browser in question counts the whitespace between each of the list items.

We could get to the "Daniel" list item using `previousSibling`:

```
var daniel = william.previousSibling;
```

If we're at the last node on a level, and try to get the `nextSibling`, the property will be `null`. Similarly, if we're at the first node on a level and try to get `previousSibling`, that property will also be `null`. You should check to make sure you have a valid node reference whenever you use either of these properties.

Figure 3.6 provides a clear visualization of where each of these DOM-walking properties will get you to from a given node in the DOM tree.

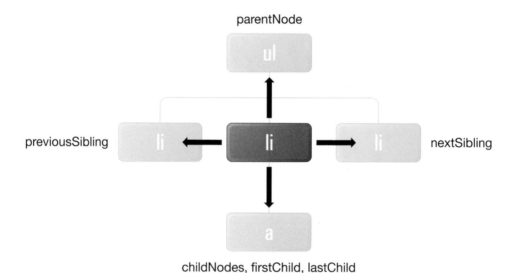

Figure 3.6. Moving around the DOM tree using the element node's DOM properties

Interacting with Attributes

As I mentioned when we discussed the structure of the DOM, attributes are localized to the elements they're associated with—they don't have much relevance in the larger scheme of things. Therefore, we don't have DOM functions that will let you find a particular attribute node, or all attributes with a certain value.

Attributes are more focused on reading and modifying the data related to an element. As such, the DOM only offers two methods related to attributes, and both of them can only be used once you have an element reference.

Getting an Attribute

With a reference to an element already in hand, you can get the value of one of its attributes by calling the method `getAttribute` with the attribute name as an argument.

Let's get the `href` attribute value for this link:

```
<a id="koko" href="http://www.koko.org/">Let's all hug Koko</a>
```

We need to create a reference to the anchor element, then use `getAttribute` to retrieve the value:

```
var koko = document.getElementById("koko");
var kokoHref = koko.getAttribute("href");
```

The value of `kokoHref` will now be `"http://www.koko.org/"`.

This approach works for any of the attributes that have been set for an element:

```
var koko = document.getElementById("koko");
var kokoId = koko.getAttribute("id");
```

The value of `kokoId` will now be `"koko"`.

At least, that's how it's *supposed* to work, according to the W3C. But in reality, `getAttribute` is beset by problems in quite a few of the major browsers.[2] Firefox returns `null` for unset values when it's supposed to return a string, as does Opera 9. Internet Explorer returns a string for most unset attributes, but returns `null` for non-string attributes like `onclick`. When it does return a value, Internet Explorer subtly alters a number of the attribute values it returns, making them different from those returned by other browsers. For example, it converts `href` attribute values to absolute URLs.

---

[2] `getAttribute` is a bit of a mess across all browsers, but most noticeably in Internet Explorer. For a complete rundown of what's going on, visit http://tobielangel.com/2007/1/11/attribute-nightmare-in-ie.

With all of these problems currently in play, at the moment it's safer to use the old-style method of getting attributes, which we can do by accessing each attribute as a dot property of an element.

In using this approach to get the href on our anchor, we'd rewrite the code as follows:

```
var koko = document.getElementById("koko");
var kokoHref = koko.href;
```

In most cases, fetching an attribute value is just a matter of appending the attribute name to the end of the element, but in a couple of cases the attribute name is a reserved word in JavaScript. This is why we use *element*.className for the class attribute, and why, if you ever need to get the for attribute, you'll need to use *element*.htmlFor.

Setting an Attribute

As well as being readable, all HTML attributes are writable via the DOM.

To write an attribute value, we use the setAttribute method on an element, specifying both the attribute name we want to set and the value we want to set it to:

```
var koko = document.getElementById("koko");
koko.setAttribute("href", "/koko/");
```

When we run those lines of code, the href for Koko's link will change from http://www.koko.org/ to /koko/.

Thankfully, there are no issues with setAttribute across browsers, so we can safely use it anywhere.

setAttribute can be used not only to change preexisting attributes, but also to add new attributes. So if we wanted to add a title that described the link in more detail, we could use setAttribute to specify the value of the new title attribute, which would be added to the anchor element:

```
var koko = document.getElementById("koko");
koko.setAttribute("title", "Web site of the Gorilla Foundation");
```

If you were to take the browser's internal representation of the document following this DOM change and convert it to HTML, here's what you'd get:

```
<a id="koko" href="http://www.koko.org/"
    title="Web site of the Gorilla Foundation">Let's all hug
  Koko</a>
```

Changing Styles

Almost every aspect of your web page is accessible via the DOM, including the way it looks.

Each element node has a property called `style`. `style` is a deceptively expansive object that lets you change every aspect of an element's appearance, from the color of its text, to its line height, to the type of border that's drawn around it. For every CSS property that's applicable to an element, `style` has an equivalent property that allows us to change that property's value.

To change the text color of an element, we'd use `style.color`:

```
var scarlet = document.getElementById("scarlet");
scarlet.style.color = "#FF0000";
```

To change its background color, we'd use `style.backgroundColor`:

```
var indigo = document.getElementById("indigo");
indigo.style.backgroundColor = "#000066";
```

We don't have enough space here to list every property you could change, but there's a good rule of thumb: if you wish to access a particular CSS property, simply append it as a property of the `style` object. Any properties that include hyphens (like `text-indent`) should be converted to camel case (`textIndent`). If you leave the hyphen in there, JavaScript will try to subtract one word from the other, which makes about as much sense as that sentence!

Any changes to the `style` object will take immediate effect on the display of the page. Using `style`, it's possible to change a page like Figure 3.7 into a page like Figure 3.8 using just three lines of code.

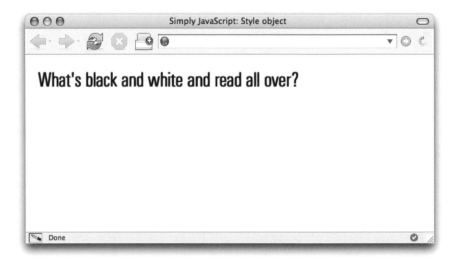

Figure 3.7. A standard page

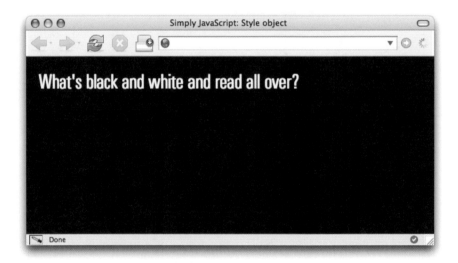

Figure 3.8. The same page, altered using `style`

Here's the code that makes all the difference:

style_object.js *(excerpt)*

```
var body = document.getElementsByTagName("body")[0];
body.style.backgroundColor = "#000000";
body.style.color = "#FFFFFF";
```

The `color` CSS property is inherited by child elements, so changing `style.color` on the `body` element will also affect every element inside the `body` to which a specific color is not assigned.

The `style` object directly accesses the HTML `style` attribute, so the JavaScript code we just saw is literally equivalent to this HTML:

```
<body style="background-color: #000000; color: #FFFFFF;">
```

As it *is* the inline style of an element, if you make a change to an element's `style` property, and that change conflicts with any of the rules in your CSS files, the `style` property will take precedence (except, of course, for properties marked `!important`).

Changing Styles with Class

In the world of CSS, it's considered bad practice to use inline styles to style an element's appearance. Equally, in JavaScript it's considered bad practice to use the `style` property as a means of styling an element's appearance.

As we discussed in Chapter 1, you want to keep the layers separated, so HTML shouldn't include style information, and JavaScript shouldn't include style information.

The best way to change an element's appearance with JavaScript is to change its class. This approach has several advantages:

- We don't mix behavior with style.
- We don't have to hunt through a JavaScript file to change styles.
- Style changes can be made by those who make the styles, not the JavaScript programmers.
- It's more succinct to write styles in CSS.

Most of the time, changes to an element's appearance can be defined as distinct changes to its state, as described in its `class`. It's these state changes that you should be controlling through JavaScript, not specific properties of its appearance.

The only situation in which it's okay to use the `style` property arises when you need to calculate a CSS value on the fly. This often occurs when you're moving objects around the screen (for instance, to follow the cursor), or when you animate a particular property, such as in the "yellow fade" technique (which changes an element's background-color by increments).

Comparing Classes

When we're checking to see whether className contains a particular class, we need to use a special search, like the one we used to write Core.getElementsByClass earlier in this chapter. In fact, we can use that same regular expression to create a function that will tell us whether or not an element has a particular class attached to it:

core.js *(excerpt)*

```
Core.hasClass = function(target, theClass)
{
  var pattern = new RegExp("(^| )" + theClass + "( |$)");

  if (pattern.test(target.className))
  {
    return true;
  }

  return false;
};
```

Core.hasClass takes two arguments: an element and a class. The class is used inside the regular expression and compared with the className of the element. If the pattern.test method returns true, it means that the element *does* have the specified class, and we can return true from the function. If pattern.test returns false, Core.hasClass returns false by default.

Now, we can very easily use this function inside a conditional statement to execute some code when an element has (or doesn't have) a matching class:

```
var scarlet = document.getElementById("scarlet");

if (Core.hasClass(scarlet, "clicked"))
{
  ⋮
}
```

Adding a Class

When we're *adding* a class, we have to take the same amount of care as we did when comparing it. The main thing we have to be careful about here is to not overwrite an element's existing classes. Also, to make it easy to remove a class, we shouldn't add a class to an element that already has that class. To make sure we don't, we'll use `Core.hasClass` inside `Core.addClass`:

core.js *(excerpt)*

```
Core.addClass = function(target, theClass)
{
  if (!Core.hasClass(target, theClass))
  {
    if (target.className == "")
    {
      target.className = theClass;
    }
    else
    {
      target.className += " " + theClass;
    }
  }
};
```

The first conditional statement inside `Core.addClass` uses `Core.hasClass` to check whether or not the `target` element already has the class we're trying to add. If it does, there's no need to add the class again.

If the `target` *doesn't* have the class, we have to check whether that element has *any* classes at all. If it has none (that is, the `className` is an empty string), it's safe to assign `theClass` directly to `target.className`. But if the element has some preexisting classes, we have to follow the syntax for multiple classes, whereby each class is separated by a space. Thus, we add a space to the end of `className`, followed by `theClass`. Then we're done.

Now that `Core.addClass` performs all these checks for us, it's easy to use it whenever we want to add a new class to an element:

class.js (excerpt)

```
var body = document.getElementsByTagName("body")[0];
Core.addClass(body, "unreadable");
```

Then, we specify some CSS rules for that class in our CSS file:

class.css

```
.unreadable
{
  background-image: url(polka_dots.gif);
  background-repeat: 15px 15px;
  color: #FFFFFF;
}
```

The visuals for our page will swap from those shown in Figure 3.9 to those depicted in Figure 3.10.

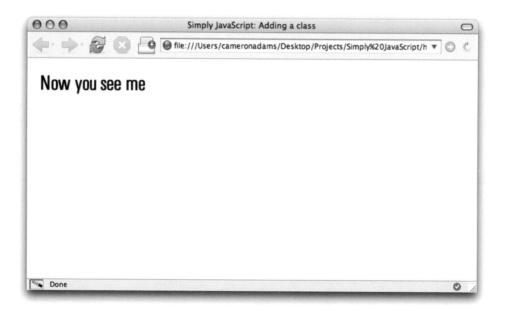

Figure 3.9. The page before we start work

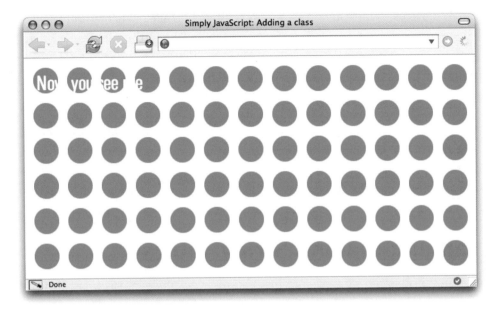

Figure 3.10. The display after we change the class of the body element

Removing a Class

When we want to remove a class from an element, we use that same regular expression (it's a pretty handy one, huh?), but with a slightly different twist:

```
                                                    core.js (excerpt)

Core.removeClass = function(target, theClass)
{
  var pattern = new RegExp("(^| )" + theClass + "( |$)");

  target.className = target.className.replace(pattern, "$1");
  target.className = target.className.replace(/ $/, "");
};
```

In `Core.removeClass`, instead of using the regular expression to check whether or not the target element has the class, we assume that it does have the class, and instead use the regular expression to replace the class with an empty string, effectively removing it from `className`.

To do this, we use a built-in string method called `replace`. This method takes a regular expression and a replacement string, then replaces the occurrences that match the regular expression with the replacement string. In this case, we're using an empty string as the replacement, so any matches will be erased. If the class exists inside `className`, it will disappear.

The second call to `replace` just tidies up `className`, removing any extraneous spaces that might be hanging around after the class was removed (some browsers will choke if any spaces are present at the start of `className`). Since we assign both these operations back to `className`, the `target` element's class will be updated with the changes straight away, and we can return from the function without fuss.

Example: Making Stripy Tables

Earlier in this chapter, we made our first real *function*, `Core.getElementsByClass`, but now I think you're ready to make your first real *program*, and a useful one it is too!

In my days as an HTML jockey, there was one task I dreaded more than any other, and that was making stripy tables. On static pages, you had to hand code tables so that every odd row had a special class like `alt`, but I just knew that as soon as I finished classing 45 different rows my manager was going to come along and tell me he wanted to add one more row right at the top. Every odd row would become even and every even row would become odd. Then I'd have to remove 45 classes and add them to 45 other rows. Argh!

Of course, that was before I knew about JavaScript. With JavaScript and the magic of the `for` loop, you can include one JavaScript file in your page, sit back, and change tables to your heart's delight. Obviously we're going to be using JavaScript to add a class to every second row in this example. But it might help to break down the desired outcome into a series of simple steps again.

In order to achieve stripy tables, we'll want to:

1. Find all tables with a class of `dataTable` in the document.

2. For each table, get the table rows.

3. For every second row, add the class `alt`.

By now, glancing at that list should cause a few key ideas to spring to mind. On the programming structure side of the equation, you should be thinking about loops, and plenty of them. But on the DOM side you should be thinking about `getElementsByTagName`, `className`, and maybe even our own custom function, `Core.getElementsByClass`. If you found yourself muttering any of those names under your breath while you read through the steps in that list, give yourself a pat on the back.

Finding All Tables with Class `dataTable`

This first step's pretty simple, since we did most of the related work mid-chapter. We don't want to apply striping to every table in the document (just in case someone's been naughty and used one for layout), so we'll apply it only to the tables marked with a class of `dataTable`. To do this, all we have to do is dust off `Core.getElementsByClass`—it will be able to go and find all the `dataTable` elements:

stripy_tables.js (excerpt)

```
var tables = Core.getElementsByClass("dataTable");
```

Done. You can't beat your own custom library!

 Remember to Load your Library

Remember to add a `<script>` tag to your HTML document to load the Core library of functions (**core.js**) before the `<script>` tag that runs your program, as shown in the code below. Otherwise, your program won't be able to find `Core.getElementsByClass`, and your browser will report a JavaScript error.

stripy_tables.html (excerpt)

```
<script type="text/javascript" src="core.js"></script>
<script type="text/javascript" src="stripy_tables.js">
</script>
```

Getting the Table Rows for Each Table

There's that phrase "for each" again. Inside the variable `tables` we have the collection of tables waiting to be striped—we just need to iterate through each of them using a `for` loop.

Every time we move through the `for` loop, we'll want to get the rows for that particular table. This sounds okay, but it's not that simple. Let's look at the markup for a nicely semantic and accessible table:

stripy_tables.html *(excerpt)*

```
<table class="dataTable">
  <thead>
    <tr>
      <th scope="col">
        Web Luminary
      </th>
      <th scope="col">
        Height
      </th>
      <th scope="col">
        Hobbies
      </th>
      <th scope="col">
        Digs microformats?
      </th>
    </tr>
  </thead>
  <tbody>
    <tr>
      <td>
        John Allsopp
      </td>
      <td class="number">
        6'1"
      </td>
      <td>
        Surf lifesaving, skateboarding, b-boying
      </td>
      <td class="yesno">
        <img src="tick.gif" alt="Yes" />
      </td>
```

```
    </tr>
     ⋮
  </tbody>
</table>
```

There's one row in there that we don't want to be susceptible to striping—the row inside the thead.

To avoid affecting this row through our row striping shenanigans, we need to get only the rows that are inside a tbody. This means we must add a step to our code—we need to get all of the tbody elements in the table (HTML allows more than one to exist), then get all the rows inside each tbody. This process will actually require *two* for loops—one to step through each of the table elements in the document, and another *inside* that to step through each of the tbody elements—but that's fine; it just means more work for the computer. Since the variable name i is used for the counter in the outer for loop, we'll name the counter variable in our inner for loop j:

stripy_tables.js (excerpt)

```
for (var i = 0; i < tables.length; i++)
{
  var tbodys = tables[i].getElementsByTagName("tbody");

  for (var j = 0; j < tbodys.length; j++)
  {
    var rows = tbodys[j].getElementsByTagName("tr");
     ⋮
  }
}
```

The results for both uses of getElementsByTagName in the code above will be limited to the current table, because we're using it as a method of a particular element, not the entire document. The variable rows now contains a collection of all the tr elements that exist inside a tbody element of the current table.

Adding the Class `alt` to Every Second Row

"For every" is equivalent to "for each" here, so we know that we're going to use yet another `for` loop. It will be a slightly different `for` loop though, because we only want to modify every second row.

To do this, we'll start the counter on the *second* index of the collection and increment it by two, not one:

```
                                                    stripy_tables.js (excerpt)

for (var i = 0; i < tables.length; i++)
{
  var tbodys = tables[i].getElementsByTagName("tbody");

  for (var j = 0; j < tbodys.length; j++)
  {
    var rows = tbodys[j].getElementsByTagName("tr");

    for (var k = 1; k < rows.length; k += 2)
    {
      Core.addClass(rows[k], "alt");
    }
  }
}
```

We're already using the variables i and j as the counters for the outer `for` loops, and we don't want to overwrite their values, so we create a new counter variable called k. k starts at 1 (the second index), and for every execution of this inner loop we increase its value by 2.

The conditional code for this inner loop is just one line that uses our pre-rolled `Core.addClass` function to add the class `alt` to the current row. Once the inner `for` loop finishes, every second row will be marked with this class, and once the outer `for` loops finish, every data table will be stripy.

Putting it All Together

The main code for our function is now complete; we just have to wrap it inside a self-contained object:

```
                                              stripy_tables.js (excerpt)

var StripyTables =
{
  init: function()
  {
    var tables = Core.getElementsByClass("dataTable");

    for (var i = 0; i < tables.length; i++)
    {
      var tbodys = tables[i].getElementsByTagName("tbody");

      for (var j = 0; j < tbodys.length; j++)
      {
        var rows = tbodys[j].getElementsByTagName("tr");

        for (var k = 1; k < rows.length; k += 2)
        {
          Core.addClass(rows[k], "alt");
        }
      }
    }
  }
};
```

Kick-start it when the page loads, using Core.start:

```
                                              stripy_tables.js (excerpt)

Core.start(StripyTables);
```

Now, whenever you include this script file (and the Core library) on your page, StripyTables will go into action to automatically stripe all your tables:

```
                                              stripy_tables.html (excerpt)

<!DOCTYPE html PUBLIC "-//W3C//DTD XHTML 1.0 Strict//EN"
    "http://www.w3.org/TR/xhtml1/DTD/xhtml1-strict.dtd">
<html xmlns="http://www.w3.org/1999/xhtml" lang="en-US">
  <head>
    <title>Stripy Tables</title>
    <meta http-equiv="Content-Type"
```

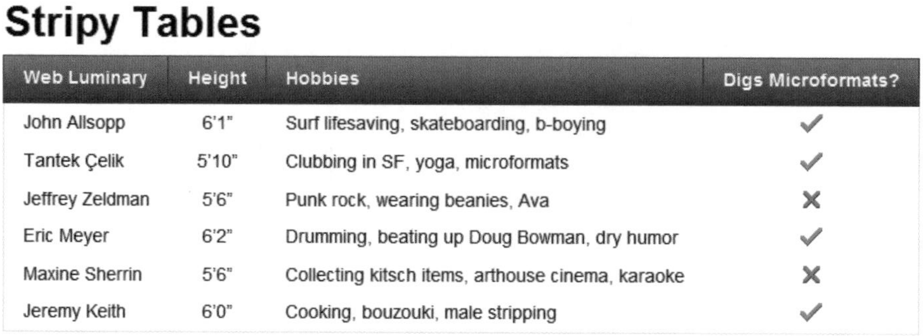

Stripy Tables

Web Luminary	Height	Hobbies	Digs Microformats?
John Allsopp	6'1"	Surf lifesaving, skateboarding, b-boying	✓
Tantek Çelik	5'10"	Clubbing in SF, yoga, microformats	✓
Jeffrey Zeldman	5'6"	Punk rock, wearing beanies, Ava	✗
Eric Meyer	6'2"	Drumming, beating up Doug Bowman, dry humor	✓
Maxine Sherrin	5'6"	Collecting kitsch items, arthouse cinema, karaoke	✗
Jeremy Keith	6'0"	Cooking, bouzouki, male stripping	✓

Figure 3.11. Hard-to-scan table content without stripes

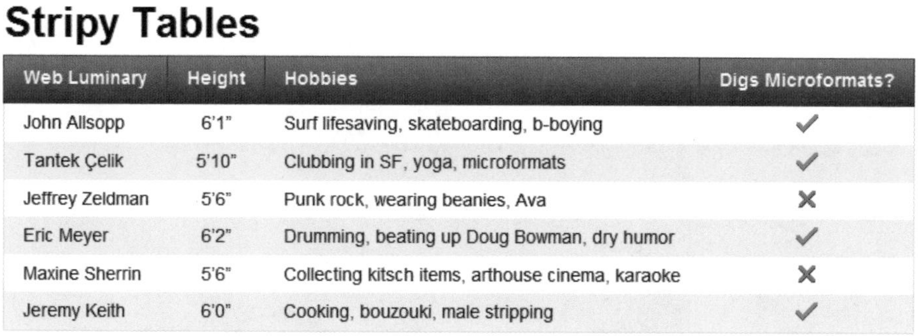

Stripy Tables

Web Luminary	Height	Hobbies	Digs Microformats?
John Allsopp	6'1"	Surf lifesaving, skateboarding, b-boying	✓
Tantek Çelik	5'10"	Clubbing in SF, yoga, microformats	✓
Jeffrey Zeldman	5'6"	Punk rock, wearing beanies, Ava	✗
Eric Meyer	6'2"	Drumming, beating up Doug Bowman, dry humor	✓
Maxine Sherrin	5'6"	Collecting kitsch items, arthouse cinema, karaoke	✗
Jeremy Keith	6'0"	Cooking, bouzouki, male stripping	✓

Figure 3.12. Using a script to produce stripy tables and improve the usability of the document

```
      content="text/html; charset=utf-8" />
<link rel="stylesheet" type="text/css"
    href="stripy_tables.css" />
<script type="text/javascript" src="core.js"></script>
<script type="text/javascript"
    src="stripy_tables.js"></script>
```

You can style the `alt` class however you want with a simple CSS rule:

stripy_tables.css (excerpt)

```
tr.alt
{
  background-color: #EEEEEE;
}
```

You can turn a plain, hard-to-follow table like the one in Figure 3.11 into something that's much more usable—like that pictured in Figure 3.12—with very little effort.

This type of script is a great example of progressive enhancement. Users who browse with JavaScript disabled will still be able to access the table perfectly well; however, the script provides a nice improvement for those who can run it.

Exploring Libraries

Most of the available JavaScript libraries have little helper functions that can help you expand the functionality of the DOM. These range from neat little shortcuts to entirely different ways of finding and manipulating elements.

Prototype

Prototype was one of the first libraries to swap the painful-to-type `document.getElementById` for the ultra-compact $.

The $ function in Prototype not only acts as a direct substitute for `document.getElementById`, it also expands upon it. You can get a reference to a single element by ID, so this normal code:

```
var money = document.getElementById("money");
```

would become:

```
var money = $("money");
```

But you don't have stop at getting just one element; you can specify a whole list of element IDs that you want, and $ will return them all as part of an array. So this normal code:

```
var elementArray = [];
elementArray[0] = document.getElementById("kroner");
elementArray[1] = document.getElementById("dollar");
elementArray[2] = document.getElementById("yen");
```

becomes considerably shorter:

```
var elementArray = $("kroner", "dollar", "yen");
```

Earlier in this chapter we created our own library function to get elements by class. Prototype has a similar function, which is slightly more powerful. It creates an extension to the document node, called `getElementsByClassName`. Like our function `Core.getElementsByClass`, this method allows us to retrieve an array of elements that have a particular class:

```
var tables = document.getElementsByClassName("dataTable");
```

It also takes an optional second argument, which allows us to specify a parent element under which to search. Only elements that are descendants of the specified element, and have a particular class, will be included in the array:

```
var tables =
    document.getElementsByClassName("dataTable", $("content"));
```

The variable `tables` will now be an array containing elements that are descendants of the element with ID `content`, and that have a class of `dataTable`.

Prototype also replicates all of the class functions that we created for our own library. These functions take exactly the same arguments that ours did, but the functions themselves are methods of Prototype's `Element` object. So Prototype offers `Element.hasClassName`, `Element.addClassName`, and `Element.removeClassName`:

```
var body = document.getElementsByTagName("body")[0];
Element.addClassName(body, "unreadable");

if (Element.hasClassName(body, "unreadable"))
{
  Element.removeClassName(body, "unreadable");
}
```

jQuery

jQuery was one of the first libraries to support an entirely different way of finding elements with JavaScript: it allows us to find groups of elements using CSS selectors.

The main function in jQuery is also called $, but because it uses CSS selectors, this function is much more powerful than Prototype's version, and manages to roll a number of Prototype's functions into one.[3]

If you wanted to use jQuery to get an element by ID, you'd type the following:

```
var money = $("#money");
```

# indicates an ID selector in CSS, so $("#money") is the equivalent of typing document.getElementById("money").

To get a group of elements by tag name, you'd pass $ a CSS element type selector:

```
var paragraphs = $("p");
```

And to get a group of elements by class, you'd use a class selector:

```
var tables = $(".dataTable");
```

And, as with CSS, you can combine all these simple selector types in, say, a descendant selector:

```
var tables = $("#content table.dataTable");
```

tables is now an array of table elements that are descendants of the element with ID content, and that have a class of dataTable.

The CSS rule parsing in jQuery is really quite spectacular, and it supports the majority of selectors from CSS1, CSS2, and CSS3, as well as XPath.[4] This makes it possible for us to use selectors like this:

```
var complex = $("form > fieldset:only-child input[@type=radio]");
```

---

[3] In fact, based on the popularity of this feature in jQuery, Prototype went on to include similar functionality in a function named $$.

[4] XPath is a zany language for selecting nodes from XML documents (including XHTML documents). While XPath is extremely powerful, the process of learning it is likely to give you a facial tick.

Once you break it down, that query finds all radio button `input` elements inside `fieldsets` that are direct children of form elements, but only where the `fieldset` is the only child of the form. Phew!

Dojo

Dojo follows the previous two libraries closely in how they deal with the DOM.

It has its own shortcut to `document.getElementById`, but it doesn't expand upon the DOM's native functionality:

```
var money = Dojo.byId("money");
```

It also has its own `getElementsByClass` function inside the `html` module:

```
var tables = dojo.html.getElementsByClass("dataTable");
```

This function allows you to get elements by class under a particular parent:

```
var tables = Dojo.html.getElementsByClass("dataTable",
    dojo.byId("content"));
```

For completeness, it has the usual class handling functions, which take the same form as our own `Core` functions:

```
var body = document.getElementsByTagName("body")[0];
Dojo.html.addClass(body, "unreadable");

if (Dojo.html.hasClass(body, "unreadable"))
{
  Dojo.html.removeClass(body, "unreadable");
}
```

Summary

An understanding of the DOM is central to using JavaScript, which is why the use of JavaScript on the Web is sometimes referred to as "DOM scripting."

As you delve further into this book, and we begin to look at more complex interfaces, our manipulation of the DOM will also become more complex, so your familiarity with the basics presented in this chapter is vital.

In the next chapter, we take a look at events, which allow your JavaScript programs to respond to users' interactions with your web pages. Dynamic interfaces, here we come!

Events

When we started out in Chapter 2, every script that we looked at would be loaded by the browser and executed right away. Since then, we've learned how to wait until the HTML document has finished loading before unleashing the awesome power of JavaScript. In every case, however, the script will work its magic (for instance, making the rows of your tables stripy), then fizzle out, leaving behind an enhanced—but still very static—page.

You don't need to suffer with scripts that peak too quickly! With the simple techniques we'll explore in this chapter, you'll learn to take control, write scripts that last longer, and become a superstar … well, in your favorite JavaScript chat room, anyway.

Don't get me wrong—scripts that enhance web pages the instant they're loaded (let's call them "quickies") have their place, but there are limits to how much they can improve the user experience of a site. JavaScript *really* gets interesting when you start to write scripts that are triggered by **events** that occur during the user's interaction with the page, like clicking a hyperlink, scrolling the browser's viewport, or typing a value into a form field.

An Eventful History

Thanks to the wide adoption of the Document Object Model (DOM) standard, accessing HTML elements in your JavaScript code works very similarly in every browser. If only the same could be said for every aspect of JavaScript! As it happens, running JavaScript code in response to an event stands out as one of the few remaining features that are implemented in wildly varying ways in current browsers.

The news isn't all bad. There is a certain amount of common ground. For as long as they've supported JavaScript, browsers have had a simple model for dealing with events—using event handlers—and all current browsers provide compatible support for these handlers, despite the fact that a complete standard was never written for them.[1] As we'll see, these techniques come with limitations that you'll want to avoid when you can, but they offer a good fallback option.

DOM Level 0

The first version of the W3C DOM specification was called Document Object Model Level 1. Since event handlers (along with a number of other nonstandard JavaScript features) predate this specification, developers like to call them Document Object Model Level 0.

Stepping into the 21st century, the World Wide Web Consortium (W3C) has developed the DOM Level 2 Events standard,[2] which provides a more powerful means of dealing with events, called event listeners. Almost all browsers now support this standard, the notable exception being Internet Explorer up to and including IE 7.0. Internet Explorer has its own way of doing things, and though its approach is almost as powerful, it's also sufficiently different to force us to write extra code to cater for this popular browser.

It's interesting to note that Microsoft participated in the development of the DOM Level 2 Events specification within the W3C, but when it came time to release IE 5.5, Microsoft chose not to support the specification in that browser. In the two

---

[1] The HTML 4 specification briefly discusses them under the heading Intrinsic Events [http://www.w3.org/TR/html4/interact/scripts.html#h-18.2.3].

[2] http://www.w3.org/TR/DOM-Level-2-Events/

major releases of Internet Explorer since then (IE 6.0 and 7.0), there has been no sign of Microsoft adding support for this standard.

Thankfully, we don't have to wait for Microsoft. The benefits of using event listeners, be they the W3C standard version or Internet Explorer's peculiar alternative, are so great that legions of dedicated geeks have investigated the incompatibilities and come up with reasonable solutions. With a little work, we can build these solutions into our `Core` library so that we can use event listeners freely, without encountering browser compatibility issues.

Event Handlers

The simplest way to run JavaScript code in response to an event is to use an **event handler**. Event handlers have been around for as long as browsers have supported JavaScript, and predate the DOM standard. An event handler is a JavaScript function that's "plugged into" a node in the DOM so that it's called automatically when a particular event occurs in relation to that element. Figure 4.1 illustrates this concept.

Figure 4.1. Plugging in a single event handler function to respond to a particular event

Let's start with an obvious example—the user clicking on a link like this:

linkhandler.html *(excerpt)*

```
<p>The first captain of the USS Enterprise NCC-1701 was
  <a id="wikipedia" href="http://en.wikipedia.org/…">Christopher
  Pike</a>.</p>
```

When a user clicks on a link like this one, the browser generates a `click` event. By default, the browser will respond to that `click` event by navigating to the URL specified by the link. But before this happens, we can plug in our own event handler to respond to the event.

Let's say you want to display an alert to notify users that they're leaving your site. An event handler is just a JavaScript function, so we can write a function to present the alert. As usual, we don't want to interfere with other scripts, so we'll wrap this function in an object with a unique name:

linkhandler.js *(excerpt)*

```
var WikipediaLink =
{
  clickHandler: function()
  {
    alert("Don't believe everything you read on Wikipedia!");
  }
};
```

Setting up a function as an event handler is easy. All you need is a reference to the DOM element for which you want to handle events. Then, you set the element's on*event* property, where *event* is the type of event you want to handle:

```
element.onevent = eventHandler;
```

To handle `click` events for the `wikipedia` link above with our `clickHandler` function (which is a method of our `WikipediaLink` object), we write this code:

linkhandler.js *(excerpt)*

```
var link = document.getElementById("wikipedia");
link.onclick = WikipediaLink.clickHandler;
```

But there's a catch: we can't assign an event handler to our element until the element has loaded. Thankfully, we already know how to write code that's executed only after the entire document is loaded:

```
                                                          linkhandler.js

var WikipediaLink =
{
  init: function()
  {
    var link = document.getElementById("wikipedia");
    link.onclick = WikipediaLink.clickHandler;
  },

  clickHandler: function()
  {
    alert("Don't believe everything you read on Wikipedia!");
  }
};

Core.start(WikipediaLink);
```

The code for this example is deceptively simple. As Figure 4.2 reveals, our code is actually executed in three stages:

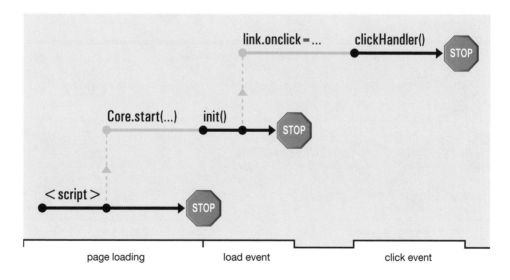

Figure 4.2. The three stages of script execution

1. The browser encounters the `<script>` tag in the HTML document's header and loads the JavaScript file. Our code declares the `WikipediaLink` object, then

calls `Core.start` to request that the object's `init` method be called when the whole document has loaded.

2. The page finishes loading, and the `WikipediaLink` object's `init` method is called. This method finds the `wikipedia` link and sets up the `clickHandler` method as its `click` event handler.

3. The user clicks the link, which generates a `click` event. The browser calls `clickHandler`, the link's `click` event handler, which displays the alert shown in Figure 4.3.

Figure 4.3. The event handler in action

Once the user clicks the **OK** button to dismiss the alert, the browser follows the link as normal.

Event Handlers as HTML Attributes

If you go looking, you'll find that a lot of sites set up JavaScript event handlers using HTML attributes, like this:

```
<a href="…" onclick="JavaScript code here">…</a>
```

As I mentioned in Chapter 1, this is the JavaScript equivalent of assigning CSS properties to your elements using the HTML `style` attribute. It's messy, it violates the principle of keeping code for dynamic behavior separate from your document content, and it's *so* 1998.

Default Actions

As we've just seen, event handlers let you respond to user actions by running any JavaScript code you like. But often, the browser still gets the last word. Take the example we just saw: no matter how creative and amazing the code in our event handler, when it's done, the browser will take over and follow the link as normal. I don't know about you, but I call that being a slave to the Man, and I won't take it.

Browsers take all sorts of actions like this:

- They follow links that users click.
- They submit forms when users click a **Submit** button, or hit **Enter**.
- They move keyboard focus around the page when the user hits **Tab**.

These are called **default actions**—things the browser *normally* does in response to events. In most cases you'll want the browser to do these things, but sometimes you'll want to prevent them from occurring.

The easiest way to stop the browser from performing a default action in response to an event is to create for that event an event handler that returns `false`. For example, we can modify the link `click` event handler we created above to ask the user for confirmation before the link is followed:

clickprompt.js *(excerpt)*

```
clickHandler: function()
{
  if (!confirm("Are you sure you want to leave this site?"))
  {
    return false;
  }
}
```

The `confirm` function used in this code is built into the browser, just like `alert`. And it displays a message to the user just like `alert` does, except that it offers the user two buttons to click: **OK** and **Cancel**. If the user clicks **OK**, the function returns `true`. If the user clicks **Cancel**, the function returns `false`. We then use the `!` operator introduced in Table 2.1 to reverse that value so that the body of the `if` statement is executed when the user clicks **Cancel**.

As shown in Figure 4.4, this new code prompts the user with the message "Are you sure you want to leave this site?" and causes our `clickHandler` method to return `false` if the user clicks **Cancel**. This, in turn, prevents the browser from performing the default action for the `click` event, so the browser does not follow the link.

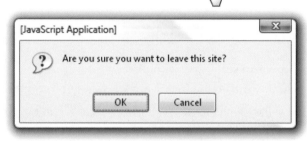

Figure 4.4. The user choosing whether or not to take the default action

 Cutting Down on Code

If you're feeling especially zen, you might have spotted the fact that `confirm` returns `false` when we want `clickHandler` to return `false`. Since these values match, you can simplify the code of `clickHandler` if you want to:

```
clickHandler: function()
{
  return confirm(
      "Are you sure you want to leave this site?");
}
```

This version of the code simply returns whatever `confirm` returns, which turns out to be exactly what we want.

The `this` Keyword

So far, we've created one event handler that handles one particular event occurring on one particular HTML element—pretty pathetic, if you ask me. The real fun is in writing an event handler that can handle events for *many* HTML elements!

Now, while assigning an event handler to many different elements is relatively straightforward, making it do something *sensible* for each element can be tricky, and that's where the `this` keyword comes into play.

A popular request from web development clients is for links to external sites to open in a new browser window or tab. However you feel about this in principle, the way a link opens is considered a part of the *behavior* of the page, and thus should be controlled by your JavaScript code (if at all).[3]

To open a URL in a new window or tab, simply use JavaScript's built-in `open` function:[4]

```
open(URL);
```

Writing a `click` event handler that opens a particular URL in a new window is therefore trivial:

```
clickHandler: function()
{
  open("http://en.wikipedia.org/wiki/Christopher_Pike");
  return false;
}
```

But how do we do this for *every* external link in the page? We definitely don't want to write a separate `click` handler for every external link.

The solution is to write a single handler that can retrieve the URL of the link that has just been clicked, using the `this` keyword:

---

[3] In past versions of the HTML standard, you could set the `target` attribute of a link to control how it would open. This attribute was deprecated in HTML 4 in favor of JavaScript alternatives.

[4] You'll see this referred to as `window.open` in many other books and online tutorials, because technically, all built-in functions are actually methods of the global `window` object. But you don't see them talking about `window.alert`, do you?

```
                                                    newwindow.js (excerpt)

clickHandler: function()
{
  open(this.href);
  return false;
}
```

this is a special JavaScript keyword that behaves like a variable, except that you can't assign it a value—its value is the object upon which the currently-executing function was invoked as a method. In other words, if you call *object*.*method*(), then within the code of *method*, the this keyword will refer to *object*. When the code currently being executed is not within a function, or when the function was not called as a method of an object, then this points to the global object that contains all global variables and functions.

Since the browser calls an event handler as a method of the element on which the event occurred, you can use this within an event handler to get a reference to that element. In the above code, we use this to get a reference to the link that the user has clicked, then use its href property to obtain the URL to which the link points.

By using this to retrieve from the element itself the information we need in order to respond to an event, we have created an event handler that can be assigned to all of the external links on the page. We just need to identify them with a class in our HTML code, and use that in our script's init method:

```
                                                              newwindow.js

var ExternalLinks =
{
  init: function()
  {
    var extLinks = Core.getElementsByClass("external");

    for (var i = 0; i < extLinks.length; i++)
    {
      extLinks[i].onclick = ExternalLinks.clickHandler;
    }
  },
```

```
  clickHandler: function()
  {
    open(this.href);
    return false;
  }
};

Core.start(ExternalLinks);
```

The Problem with Event Handlers

Many JavaScript developers like event handlers because they're simple to use, and they work in all browsers. Unfortunately, they come with one big, honking limitation: *you can only assign one event handler to a given event on a given HTML element.*

In simple terms, you can't easily make more than one thing happen when an event occurs. Consider this code:

```
element.onclick = script1.clickHandler;
element.onclick = script2.clickHandler;
```

Only the `clickHandler` in *script2* will be executed when a click occurs on *element*, because assigning the second event handler replaces the first.

You might wonder if we really *need* to assign more than one event handler. After all, how often are you going to want more than one script to respond to the `click` event of a link? And as long as we were just talking about `click` events, you'd be right to wonder.

But there are all sorts of events that you can respond to, and for some of them it would be extremely useful to have multiple handlers. As we'll see in Chapter 6, for example, a form's `submit` event often requires multiple scripts to check that the various form fields have been filled out correctly.

The commonly used workaround to this problem is to assign as the event handler a function that calls multiple event handling functions:

```
element.onclick = function()
{
  script1.clickHandler();
  script2.clickHandler();
}
```

But all sorts of things are wrong with this approach:

- `this` will no longer point to the *element* within the `clickHandler` methods.

- If either `clickHandler` method returns `false`, it will not cancel the default action for the event.

- Instead of assigning event handlers neatly inside a script's `init` method, you have to perform these assignments in a separate script, since you have to reference both *script1* and *script2*.

There are solutions to all of these problems, of course, but they involve complicated and twisty code[5] that you really shouldn't have to deal with to accomplish something as basic as responding to events.

In addition to the simple event handlers we've just looked at, most browsers today have built-in support for a more advanced way of handling events: event listeners, which do not suffer from the one-handler-only restriction.

Event Listeners

The good news is that **event listeners** are just like event handlers, except that you can assign as many event listeners as you like to a particular event on a particular element, and there is a W3C specification that explains how they should work.[6]

The bad news is that Internet Explorer has its own completely different, and somewhat buggy version of event listeners that you also need to support if you want your scripts to work in that browser. Oh, and sometimes Safari likes to do things slightly differently, too.

---

[5] http://dean.edwards.name/weblog/2005/10/add-event/
[6] http://www.w3.org/TR/DOM-Level-2-Events/

Like an event handler, an event listener is just a JavaScript function that is "plugged into" a DOM node. Where you could only plug in one event handler at a time, however, you can plug multiple listeners in, as Figure 4.5 illustrates.

Figure 4.5. Plugging in only one handler, but many listeners

The code that sets up an event listener is quite different from that used to set up an event handler, but it's still fairly easy:

```
element.addEventListener("event", eventListener, false);
```

In browsers that support W3C-standard event listeners, the `addEventListener` method is available on every object that supports events. This method takes three arguments: the name of the event to which you want to assign the listener (e.g. `"click"`), the listener function itself, and a Boolean value that you'll usually want to set to `false` (more on this last argument in the section called "Event Propagation").

To set up an event listener in Internet Explorer, however, you need to use a method called `attachEvent`. This method works a lot like `addEventListener`, but it takes slightly different arguments:

```
element.attachEvent("onevent", eventListener);
```

Spot the differences? The first argument—the name of the event you're interested in—must be prefixed with `on` (for example, `"onclick"`), and there is no mysterious third argument.

Any script that uses event listeners will need to use addEventListener for all browsers that support it, and attachEvent for Internet Explorer browsers that don't. Ensuring that your script uses the right method is a simple matter of using an if-else statement that checks if the addEventListener or attachEvent methods exist in the current browser:

```
if (typeof element.addEventListener != "undefined")
{
  element.addEventListener("event", eventListener, false);
}
else if (typeof element.attachEvent != "undefined")
{
  element.attachEvent("onevent", eventListener);
}
```

This is another example of the object detection technique that we first saw at work in Chapter 3.

Let's employ this technique to display an alert in response to the click event of a particular link, as we did using event handlers earlier in this chapter:

linklistener.js (excerpt)

```
var WikipediaLink =
{
  init: function()
  {
    var link = document.getElementById("wikipedia");

    if (typeof link.addEventListener != "undefined")
    {
      link.addEventListener(
          "click", WikipediaLink.clickListener, false);
    }
    else if (typeof link.attachEvent != "undefined")
    {
      link.attachEvent("onclick", WikipediaLink.clickListener);
    }
  },

  clickListener: function()
  {
```

```
    alert("Don't believe everything you read on Wikipedia!");
  }
};

Core.start(WikipediaLink);
```

It's not as simple as setting up an event handler, of course, but this code isn't too complex, and it allows for another script to add its own `click` event listener to the link without dislodging the one we've set up here.

Although you'll usually just add event listeners to your DOM nodes and forget about them, you can "unplug" an event listener from a DOM node if you need to. In the W3C's standard event listener model, we use the `removeEventListener` method to achieve this, whereas in Internet Explorer, we use `detachEvent`. In either case, we pass the method the same arguments we passed when adding the listener:

```
if (typeof element.removeEventListener != "undefined")
{
  element.removeEventListener("event", eventListener, false);
}
else if (typeof element.detachEvent != "undefined")
{
  element.detachEvent("onevent", eventListener);
}
```

Default Actions

You'll remember that you can simply return `false` from an event handler in order to prevent the browser from carrying out the default action for an event, such as following a clicked hyperlink. Event listeners let you do this too, but in a slightly different way.

In the W3C standard event listener model, the browser will always pass an **event object** to the event listener function. The event object's properties contain information about the event (for instance, the position of the cursor when the event occurred), while its methods let us control how the event is processed by the browser.

In order to prevent the browser from performing the default action for an event, we simply call the event object's `preventDefault` method:

```
clickListener: function(event)
{
  if (!confirm("Are you sure you want to leave this site?"))
  {
    event.preventDefault();
  }
}
```

If multiple listeners are associated with an event, any one of those listeners calling preventDefault is enough to stop the default action from occurring.

Internet Explorer's event model is, of course, similar but different. In Internet Explorer, the event object isn't passed to the event listener as an argument; it's available as a global variable named event. Also, the event object doesn't have a preventDefault method; instead, it has a property named returnValue that we can set to false in order to prevent the default action from taking place:

```
clickListener: function()
{
  if (!confirm("Are you sure you want to leave this site?"))
  {
    event.returnValue = false;
  }
}
```

Again, using the technique of object detection to figure out which event model the current browser supports, we can write an event listener that's able to cancel the default action in either event model:

```
                                          clickpromptlistener.js (excerpt)
clickListener: function(event)
{
  if (typeof event == "undefined")
  {
    event = window.event;
  }

  if (!confirm("Are you sure you want to leave this site?"))
  {
    if (typeof event.preventDefault != "undefined")
```

```
    {
      event.preventDefault();
    }
    else
    {
      event.returnValue = false;
    }
  }
}
```

At the start of this listener, we check if we've actually been passed an event object as an argument according to the W3C event model. If we haven't, we set our `event` variable to `window.event`, which is Internet Explorer's global event object. We refer to it as `window.event` instead of just `event` because our function already has its own variable named `event`.

Then, when it comes time to cancel the default action, we check to see whether or not the event object has a `preventDefault` method. If it does, we call it. If it doesn't, we set the object's `returnValue` property to `false` instead. Either way, the default action is prevented.

 Preventing Default Actions in Safari 2.0.3 and Earlier

Although it did an admirable job of supporting the rest of the DOM 2 Events standard, prior to version 2.0.4 the Safari browser could not stop a default action from occurring in an event listener. The `preventDefault` method was there; it just didn't do anything.

As I write this, a lot of Mac users are still using Safari 1.2, which is affected by this issue. If you need to support Safari version 2.0.3 or earlier, the only way to cancel a default action is to use an old-style event handler. If you're lucky enough to be working on a script that will *always* cancel the default event, you can use an event listener in combination with an event handler that simply returns `false`:

```
element.onevent = function()
{
  return false;
}
```

Event Propagation

Obviously, if you stick a `click` event listener on a hyperlink, then click on that link, the listener will be executed. But if, instead, you assign the `click` listener to the paragraph containing the link, or even the document node at the top of the DOM tree, clicking the link will still trigger the listener. That's because events don't just affect the target element that generated the event—they travel through the tree structure of the DOM. This is known as **event propagation**, and I should warn you: it's not sexy or exciting.

The W3C event model is very specific about how event propagation works. As illustrated in Figure 4.6, an event propagates in three phases:

1. In the **capture phase**, the event travels down through the DOM tree, visiting each of the target element's ancestors on its way to the target element. For example, if the user clicked a hyperlink, that `click` event would pass through the document node, the `html` element, the `body` element, and the paragraph containing the link.

    At each stop along the way, the browser checks for **capturing event listeners** for that type of event, and runs them.

    What's that? You don't know what a capturing event listener is? Remember when I mentioned the third argument of the `addEventListener` method and I told you that you'd usually want to set it to `false`? Well, if you set it to `true`, you'll create a capturing event listener.

    You'll also recall that Internet Explorer's `attachEvent` method doesn't support a third argument. That's because Internet Explorer's event model doesn't have a capture phase. Consequently, most developers avoid using capturing event listeners.

2. In the **target phase**, the browser looks for event listeners that have been assigned to the target of the event, and runs them. The target is the DOM node on which the event is focused. For example, if the user clicks a hyperlink, the target node is the hyperlink.[7]

---

[7] This is the case except in Safari, where the target is actually the text node *inside* the hyperlink. The W3C events specification is ambiguous about which behavior is correct, but in practice it doesn't make

3. In the **bubbling phase**, the event travels back up the DOM tree, again visiting the element's ancestors one by one until it reaches the document node. At each stop along the way, the browser checks for event listeners that are *not* capturing event listeners, and runs them.

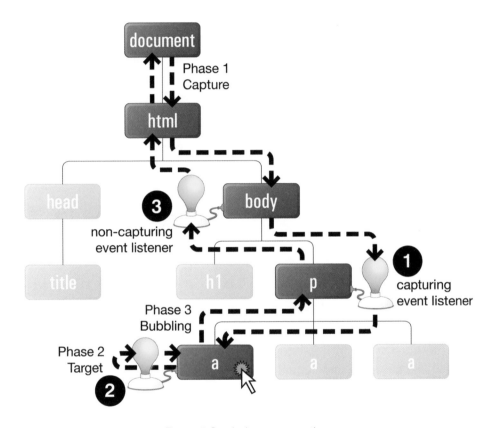

Figure 4.6. Standard event propagation

Not All Events Bubble

All events go through the capture and target phases, but certain events skip the bubbling phase. Specifically, `focus` and `blur` events, which occur when keyboard focus is given to and removed from an element, respectively, do not bubble. In most cases, this isn't a detail you need to lose much sleep over, but as we'll see

a big difference, since an event listener that's assigned to the hyperlink itself will still be triggered in the bubbling phase.

in the section called "Example: Accordion" later in this chapter, it'll make your life more difficult every once in a while.

So why am I boring you with all these details on event propagation? After all, you can assign an event listener to an element on which you expect an event to occur, and your listener will run when that event occurs. Does it have to be any more complicated than that? In most cases, no—it doesn't. But sometimes you want to get a little more creative, and creativity inevitably breeds complexity. Stay with me, here.

Let's say you were an especially helpful sort of person—I'm talking about the kind of helpful that most people find annoying. You might want to display a "helpful" message if a user were to accidentally click on a part of your page that wasn't a hyperlink:

strayclickcatcher.js (excerpt)

```
strayClickListener: function(event)
{
  alert("Did you mean to click a link? " +
      "It's that blue, underlined text.");
},
```

In order to catch clicks anywhere in the document, you can just assign this as a `click` listener for the document node. The listener will be triggered in the bubbling phase of every `click` event, no matter where in the document the target element is located.

But how do you keep the message from appearing when the user *does* click a link? What you need to do is prevent *those* `click` events from bubbling up to trigger your event listener. To do this, you need to set up another event listener that stops the propagation of those events.

To stop the propagation of an event in the W3C event model, you call the `stopPropagation` method of the event object that's passed to your event listener. In Internet Explorer's event model there's no such method; instead, you need to set the `cancelBubble` property of the event object to `true`. Here's what the resulting listener looks like:

```
                                            strayclickcatcher.js (excerpt)
linkClickListener: function(event)
{
  if (typeof event == "undefined")
  {
    event = window.event;
  }

  if (typeof event.stopPropagation != "undefined")
  {
    event.stopPropagation();
  }
  else
  {
    event.cancelBubble = true;
  }
}
```

Just assign this second listener function to every link in your document, and it will stop the propagation of `click` events when they reach a link. This prevents those clicks from bubbling up to the document element to trigger the first event listener.

Figure 4.7 shows what happens when you click on a part of the document that doesn't link to anything. If you click on a link, however, the browser will follow it without complaint.

Figure 4.7. A stray click producing a helpful/annoying message

Here's the complete, and very helpful/annoying script:

```javascript
var StrayClickCatcher =
{
  init: function()
  {
    var links = document.getElementsByTagName("a");

    if (typeof document.addEventListener != "undefined")
    {
      document.addEventListener("click",
          StrayClickCatcher.strayClickListener, false);
      for (var i = 0; i < links.length; i++)
      {
        links[i].addEventListener("click",
            StrayClickCatcher.linkClickListener, false);
      }
    }
    else if (typeof document.attachEvent != "undefined")
    {
      document.attachEvent("onclick",
          StrayClickCatcher.strayClickListener);
      for (var i = 0; i < links.length; i++)
      {
        links[i].attachEvent("onclick",
            StrayClickCatcher.linkClickListener);
      }
    }
  },

  strayClickListener: function(event)
  {
    alert("Did you mean to click a link? " +
        "It's that blue, underlined text.");
  },

  linkClickListener: function(event)
  {
    if (typeof event == "undefined")
    {
      event = window.event;
    }

    if (typeof event.stopPropagation != "undefined")
```

```
  {
    event.stopPropagation();
  }
  else
  {
    event.cancelBubble = true;
  }
 }
};

Core.start(StrayClickCatcher);
```

The this Keyword

Earlier in this chapter, we grappled with the problem of how to write a single event handler that could be applied to many different elements. We learned that we could use this to reference the element to which the handler was assigned, and retrieve from it information that we could use to control how the handler would respond. It would be nice if we could do the same with our event listeners … so, can we?

Keep in mind that the value of this within a JavaScript function is determined by the way in which a function is called. If it's called as a method of an object, this refers to that object. If it's called as a standalone function, this refers to the global object that contains all global variables and functions. The question is, how are event listeners called by the browser?

Surprisingly, the W3C event model standard has nothing to say on the subject, so it's left up to each browser to decide which object this refers to when it's used within an event listener. Thankfully, every browser that supports the W3C event model calls an event listener as a method of the element to which it was assigned, so this refers to that element, just like it does in an event handler.

Less surprisingly, Internet Explorer went a different way with its event listeners: Internet Explorer event listeners are called as standalone functions, so this points to the relatively useless global object.

So far, we've been able to deal with every incompatibility between the two event listener models by using simple object detection to run the code required by each browser. When it comes to solving the issue with `this`, however, things aren't so simple. In case you're curious, here's the solution:

```
if (typeof element.addEventListener != "undefined")
{
  element.addEventListener("event", eventListener, false);
}
else if (typeof element.attachEvent != "undefined")
{
  var thisListener = function()
  {
    var event = window.event;
    if (Function.prototype.call)
    {
      eventListener.call(element, event);
    }
    else
    {
      target._currentListener = eventListener;
      target._currentListener(event);
      target._currentListener = null;
    }
  };
  element.attachEvent("onevent", thisListener);
}
```

Now, leaving aside for the moment the details of how this code works, can you imagine having to type out that entire monstrosity every time you want to set up an event listener? I don't mind telling you that I wouldn't be sitting here writing this book if that's how JavaScript made us do things.

There's a way to make life easier for yourself, and I'll show it to you in the section called "Putting it All Together."

The Internet Explorer Memory Leak

When it comes to making your life difficult, Internet Explorer has one more trick up its sleeve. If the disaster surrounding the `this` keyword wasn't enough to make you want to give up on Internet Explorer's event model, this will.

In Internet Explorer, if you set up for an element an event listener that contains a reference to that element (or indeed, any other node in the DOM), the memory occupied by that listener and the associated DOM nodes will not be released when the user navigates to another page. I'll grant you that this is pretty technical stuff, but what it comes down to is that certain types of event listeners can cause Internet Explorer to leak memory, thereby causing users' computers to slow down until those users are forced to restart their browsers.

The solution to this issue is to set up a special event listener for the `unload` event of the global `window` object, which represents the browser window containing the page. When the user navigates to another page, the `unload` event will occur and the special event listener will be triggered. Within this event listener, you can take the opportunity to remove all of the event listeners that you set up in your document, thereby preventing them from causing memory leaks.

While this solution is quite elegant, the JavaScript code to make it happen is not. For the moment, I'll spare you the details, because as we'll see in the next section, you shouldn't have to worry about them.

Putting it All Together

Have you been keeping track of all the cross-browser compatibility issues that we need to deal with when using event listeners? That's okay—I have:

- Internet Explorer uses `attachEvent`/`detachEvent` to add and remove event listeners, instead of `addEventListener`/`removeEventListener`.

- Internet Explorer uses an `"onevent"` naming style for its events, instead of just `"event"`.

- Internet Explorer uses a global `event` variable instead of passing the event object to the listener as an argument.

- To prevent a default action from taking place, Internet Explorer requires you to set the event object's `returnValue` property, instead of calling its `preventDefault` method.

- Internet Explorer doesn't support the capture phase of event propagation.

- To stop an event from propagating, Internet Explorer requires you to set the event object's `cancelBubble` property, instead of calling its `stopPropagation` method.

■ Internet Explorer calls event listeners as standalone functions, rather than as methods, requiring the developer to jump through hoops to get a reference to the target element, instead of just using `this`.

■ When using event listeners in a certain way, Internet Explorer leaks memory unless you go to great lengths to clean up all of your event listeners.

… and that's without even getting into the differences when it comes to retrieving the details of keyboard and mouse events.[8]

These problems have led some developers to throw in the towel and just use event handlers. In fact, some experts have gone so far as to write their own event listener systems using event handlers as a foundation.[9] While there is certainly a case to be made for such an approach, I believe in embracing the support for event listeners that's built into most browsers, and saving the complex code for the browser that really needs it—Internet Explorer.

To that end, the **core.js** library that you'll find in the code archive for this book includes four methods that enable you to use event listeners without worrying about any of the issues I listed above. Here's how they work:

Core.addEventListener

This method sets up an event listener function for a particular event type on a particular element. It works just like the standard `addEventListener` method, except that we pass the element as the first argument of the method. It doesn't support the creation of capturing event listeners, and therefore doesn't take a final Boolean argument:

```
Core.addEventListener(element, "event", eventListener);
```

In Internet Explorer, this method sets up the event listener so that the event object is passed to the listener function as an argument (just as it is in the standard event model), and so that the listener is called as a method of the element to which it is assigned (so that we can use `this` to refer to that element).

---

[8] For complete coverage of these headaches, and some of the solutions that are available, pick up a copy of *The JavaScript Anthology* (Melbourne: SitePoint, 2006).
[9] http://dean.edwards.name/weblog/2005/10/add-event/

It also takes care of automatically cleaning up the listener when the document is unloaded, so that it does not cause memory leaks in Internet Explorer.

Core.removeEventListener

This method removes an event listener that was previously added to an element. It works just like the standard `removeEventListener` method, except that we pass the element as the first argument of the method, and like `Core.addEventListener`, it takes no final Boolean argument:

```
Core.removeEventListener(element, "event", eventListener);
```

Core.preventDefault

This method prevents the default action associated with an event from occurring. It works just like the standard `preventDefault` method, except that we pass the event object as an argument of the method:

```
Core.preventDefault(event);
```

Core.stopPropagation

This method stops the event from propagating further, and potentially triggering event listeners assigned to ancestors of the element to which the current event listener is assigned:

```
Core.stopPropagation(event);
```

And just like that, all your event listener compatibility headaches vanish! Through the rest of this book, whenever we deal with event listeners, we'll use these methods.

In fact, if you've been following along up until this point, you'll already have used one of these methods without knowing it! The `Core.start` method that we used to start running a script only once the document had finished loading relies on `Core.addEventListener`. Take a look for yourself:

```
                                                          core.js (excerpt)
Core.start = function(runnable)
{
  Core.addEventListener(window, "load", runnable.init);
};
```

As you can see, `Core.start` simply sets up the `init` method of the script you pass it as an event listener for the `load` event of the `window` object, which represents the browser window that contains the current page.

Now, you might be feeling a little uneasy about trusting those four methods to handle all of your event listening tasks without having seen how they work. If you aren't, you should be! As you can imagine, a lot of developers have put their minds to solving these problems, and the solutions they've produced have not always been particularly good. How do you know that this solution is the one you should be using?

Before drinking the Kool-Aid,[10] you should take a look at Appendix A, in which the inner workings of the four methods are described in detail. Some of the code involved is rather advanced, and uses features of JavaScript that we won't talk about until later in this book—if at all. But if nothing else, the discussion there should let you rest assured that we've done our homework.

Now that we have these shiny, new event listener methods in hand, let's use them for something more exciting than displaying an alert box when the user clicks on the page.

Example: Rich Tooltips

In some browsers, when the user mouses over, or gives keyboard focus to a link (for instance, when **Tab**bing to it), a tooltip will appear, displaying the value of the link's `title` attribute. In many browsers, however, this attribute is never displayed to the user, or is limited to a brief, one-line description. In any case, plain-text

---

[10] The closest that many geeks will come to making a pop culture reference, "drinking the Kool-Aid" refers to the all-too-common practice of enthusiastically embracing a library or other programming aid without understanding how it works (or doesn't work, as the case may be).

tooltips look fairly boring, and tend to be overlooked by users even when they *are* displayed. But, as shown in Figure 4.8, we can use JavaScript—with a healthy dose of event listeners—to produce our own, more eye-catching tooltips.

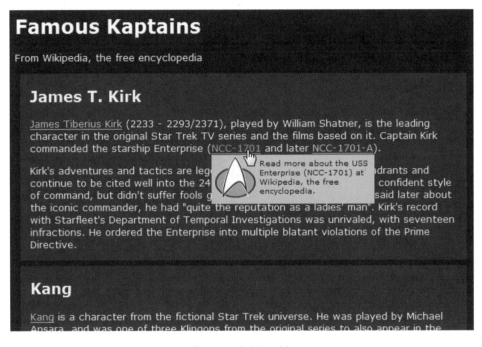

Figure 4.8. A rich tooltip

The Static Page

Let's start by looking at the HTML code for this example. We want the browser's standard tooltips to display if the user has JavaScript disabled for some reason, so we'll code our hyperlinks with the tooltip text in the `title` attribute as usual:

tooltips.html *(excerpt)*

```
<p><a class="federation" title="Read more …" href="…">James
   Tiberius Kirk</a> (2233 - 2293/2371), played by William Shatner,
   is the leading character in the original Star Trek TV series and
   the films based on it. Captain Kirk commanded the starship
   Enterprise (<a class="federation" title="Read more …"
      href="…">NCC-1701</a> and later <a class="federation"
   title="Read more …" href="…">NCC-1701-A</a>).</p>
```

Making Things Happen

With a finely-crafted static page all ready to go, we can look at setting up some event listeners to make the changes we want to occur in response to user events.

For each link that has a `title` attribute, we want to show a rich tooltip in two situations: when the cursor hovers over the link (a `mouseover` event), or the link receives keyboard focus (a `focus` event). When the mouse is moved away (a `mouseout` event), or keyboard focus is removed (a `blur` event), we want to hide that tooltip. You should be getting fairly good at belting out the `init` method for a script like this:

tooltips.js *(excerpt)*

```javascript
var Tooltips =
{
  init: function()
  {
    var links = document.getElementsByTagName("a");

    for (var i = 0; i < links.length; i++)
    {
      var title = links[i].getAttribute("title");

      if (title && title.length > 0)
      {
        Core.addEventListener(links[i], "mouseover",
            Tooltips.showTipListener);
        Core.addEventListener(links[i], "focus",
            Tooltips.showTipListener);
        Core.addEventListener(links[i], "mouseout",
            Tooltips.hideTipListener);
        Core.addEventListener(links[i], "blur",
            Tooltips.hideTipListener);
      }
    }
  },
```

As you can see, this code uses `getElementsByTagName` to obtain a list of all the a elements in the page, and get the value of the `title` attribute for each one. If the `title` attribute exists, and has a value longer than zero characters (if (title &&

`title.length > 0)`, we set up event listeners for the four different events that we're interested in.

Although we've registered four event listeners on each of our links, you can see that there are actually only two event listener methods: `showTipListener`, which will display a tooltip in response to either a `mouseover` or `focus` event, and `hideTipListener`, which hides the tooltip in response to a `mouseout` or a `blur`.

Now, we could write the code that actually shows and hides tooltips directly inside these two methods, but I prefer to implement the "actions" in my scripts in separate methods, so that the code that controls *what* happens in response to an event is separate from the code that controls *how* it happens. Our event listener methods, therefore, tend to be relatively simple:

tooltips.js *(excerpt)*

```
showTipListener: function(event)
{
  Tooltips.showTip(this);
  Core.preventDefault(event);
},

hideTipListener: function(event)
{
  Tooltips.hideTip(this);
}
```

`showTipListener` calls `showTip`, the method that will actually display the tooltip, passing it a reference to the hyperlink that has been moused-over, or given keyboard focus. It then calls `preventDefault` to keep the browser from displaying a tooltip of its own in response to the event.

`hideTipListener` is even simpler: it just calls `hideTip`, which will do the work of hiding the tooltip.

The Workhorse Methods

We've put it off as long as we can, but the time has come to write the code that will actually create our rich tooltips.

Until this point, every script we've written has either displayed a message box of some sort, or modified the style of an existing element in the page. To actually display something *new*, however—to dynamically add content to the page on the fly—is a very different trick.

There are two ways to modify the HTML content of a page using JavaScript:

- via the DOM API
- through the nonstandard `innerHTML` property

In this book, we'll only use the first option. As we learned in Chapter 3, the DOM API is a W3C standard that is likely to be supported in all web browsers for the foreseeable future, and its document modification features are up to almost any task. The `innerHTML` property, by contrast, is not described in any standard, and indeed browsers like Firefox have on occasion struggled to implement it consistently in combination with new standards like XHTML. That said, there is an argument to be made for `innerHTML`, and if you're curious you can read more about this alternative in The `innerHTML` Option, at the end of this section.

In Chapter 3, we concentrated on how to access and modify existing elements in an HTML document, but the DOM also lets us create and add new content to the page. Web developers who secretly wish they had the biceps of bricklayers call this **DOM building**.

To display a tooltip on the page, we'll add a `span` element that contains the text of the tooltip just inside the relevant link. Here's what the markup would look like if the tooltip were coded right into the document:

```
<a href="…">Link text<span class="tooltip">Tooltip text</span></a>
```

To create this element via the DOM, we'll use the `createElement` method of the document node:

tooltips.js (excerpt)

```
var tip = document.createElement("span");
```

Once we've created the `span`, we can set its `class` attribute:

```
tip.className = "tooltip";
```

Next, we need to put the tooltip text inside the `span`. In the DOM, this will be a text node, which we can create with the `document` node's `createTextNode` method. We need to pass this method the text that we want the node to contain; we can grab it using the link's `title` property:

```
var tipText = document.createTextNode(link.title);
```

To put our new text node inside our new `span`, we need to use the `span`'s `appendChild` method:

```
tip.appendChild(tipText);
```

Every element in the DOM tree supports the `appendChild` method, which you can use to add any node as the last child of the element upon which you are calling the method. It's the DOM builder's best friend! To show you what I mean, we'll use it again—to add the tooltip to the document as a child of the link:

```
link.appendChild(tip);
```

That's our DOM building done, and with just a few finishing touches, we have our `showTip` method:

```
showTip: function(link)
{
  Tooltips.hideTip(link);
```

```
  var tip = document.createElement("span");
  tip.className = "tooltip";
  var tipText = document.createTextNode(link.title);
  tip.appendChild(tipText);
  link.appendChild(tip);

  link._tooltip = tip;
  link.title = "";

  // Fix for Safari2/Opera9 repaint issue
  document.documentElement.style.position = "relative";
},
```

Before building a new tooltip, this method calls `hideTip` to make sure that any existing tooltip has been removed, so that we don't end up with two (which might happen if the user hovered the cursor over a link that already had keyboard focus).

Once the new tooltip has been built and inserted, this method stores a reference to the tooltip as a property of the link named `_tooltip`.[11] This will make it easier for `hideTip` to remove the tooltip later, using only the reference to the link that it gets as an argument. Finally, the method sets the link's `title` property to an empty string, so the document doesn't contain the tooltip text twice. Cleanliness is next to godliness, they say!

Finally, both Safari 2 and Opera 9 have difficulty with some dynamically-inserted content like our tooltip, and won't refresh the page display fully. We can force these browsers to fully refresh the page display by changing the value of the CSS `position` property on the `html` element (`document.documentElement`).

That takes care of the creation and inserting of new DOM nodes, but to hide the tooltip you need to be able to *remove* content from the page. Predictably, the DOM provides a method to do this: `removeChild`. To see how it works, take a look at the code for `hideTip`:

---

[11] The underscore (_) at the start of this property name indicates that it's a "private" property—a property that isn't meant to be used by other scripts. It doesn't actually *prevent* other scripts from accessing it, but it's a clear indication to other developers that it's not a standard DOM property, which will make them think twice about using it.

tooltips.js *(excerpt)*

```
hideTip: function(link)
{
  if (link._tooltip)
  {
    link.title = link._tooltip.childNodes[0].nodeValue;
    link.removeChild(link._tooltip);
    link._tooltip = null;

    // Fix for Safari2/Opera9 repaint issue
    document.documentElement.style.position = "static";
  }
},
```

Before removing the tooltip, this method needs to check if there is actually a tooltip to remove. Since we stored a reference to the currently displayed tooltip in the link's _tooltip property, we just have to check if the property has a value.

With the certain knowledge that a tooltip is currently displayed, we need to retrieve from it the tooltip text and store it in the link's title property. You can get the text stored in a text node using its nodeValue property, and since the text node is the first child node of the tooltip element, we can access this as link._tooltip.child-Nodes[0].nodeValue. It's a little long-winded, but it works.

With the tooltip text safely tucked away, we can remove the tooltip using removeChild. Since the tooltip is a child of the link, we call removeChild on the link, and pass it a reference to the node that we want to remove from the document—the tooltip.

And last of all, to indicate that there is no longer a tooltip displayed for this link, we set its _tooltip property to null.

As with showTip, we need to cap this method off with the fix for the repainting bugs in Safari 2 and Opera 9. Since we set position to relative when showing the tooltip, we can just set it back to static when hiding the tooltip to force another repaint.

The `innerHTML` Option

Although it's not a part of any W3C standard, every major browser supports an `innerHTML` property on every DOM element node. The value of this property is the HTML code of the content that it currently contains, and by changing that value, you can change the content of that element.

The biggest advantage offered by `innerHTML` is performance. If you're creating or modifying complex document structures, it can be a lot quicker for the browser to make document modifications in bulk using `innerHTML` than by stepping through a series of separate DOM modifications. In some cases, very complex JavaScript applications *must* use `innerHTML` to achieve reasonable performance.

Additionally, many developers quickly tire of writing the verbose JavaScript code that DOM manipulation requires, and the "one stop shop" that `innerHTML` offers is a tempting alternative. As a result, most of the major JavaScript libraries contain utilities for making DOM manipulation more convenient, and a number of mini-libraries like Dan Webb's DOM Builder have even sprung up to tackle this issue specifically.[12]

The Dynamic Styles

Having written all the JavaScript code required to add and remove tooltips on cue, all that's left for us to do is to write the CSS code that will make these ordinary `spans` really grab users' attention.

To begin with, we need to make sure our tooltips sit on top of the surrounding document content. Since our tooltips are generated inside hyperlinks, we can apply the necessary styles to our links. First, we set the positioning mode of all links to `relative`:

tooltips.css *(excerpt)*

```
a:link, a:visited {
  position: relative;
}
```

---

[12] http://www.webstandards.org/2006/04/13/dom-builder/

This alone does nothing to the appearance of our links, but it does enable us to modify the z-index property of these links when we need to—specifically, when the link is hovered or has keyboard focus:

tooltips.css *(excerpt)*

```
a:hover, a:focus, a:active {
  ⋮
  z-index: 1;
}
```

That takes care of displaying the tooltips on top of the surrounding elements. Now let's look at the tooltips themselves:

tooltips.css *(excerpt)*

```
/* Tooltips (dynamic styles) */

.tooltip {
  display: block;
  font-size: smaller;
  left: 0;
  padding: 5px;
  position: absolute;
  text-decoration: none;
  top: 1.7em;
  width: 15em;
}
```

Here's a breakdown of the various property declarations in this rule:

`text-decoration: none;`	removes the underline from the text that is inherited from the link in some browsers
`display: block;` `width: 15em;`	displays the tooltip as a block 15 ems wide

`position: absolute;`
`top: 1.7em;`
`left: 0;`
	positions the box just below the link, in alignment with its left edge

```
font-size: smaller;        tweaks the appearance of the tooltip to more clearly
padding: 5px;              set it apart from the main document content
```

Those declarations look after the basic appearance of a tooltip. We can now play with details like text color, background, and border to get the effect we want. In this example, I've put together a couple of different tooltip styles, based on the class of the link to which the tooltip refers:

tooltips.css *(excerpt)*

```css
.federation .tooltip {
  background: #C0C0FF url(starfleet.png) top left no-repeat;
  color: #2E2E33;
  min-height: 54px;
  padding-left: 64px;
}

.klingon .tooltip {
  background: #BF0000 url(klingonempire.png) top left no-repeat;
  color: #FFF;
  min-height: 54px;
  padding-left: 64px;
}
```

Putting it All Together

That's all you need to produce great looking tooltips! Here's the complete JavaScript code for easy reference:

tooltips.js

```javascript
var Tooltips =
{
  init: function()
  {
    var links = document.getElementsByTagName("a");

    for (var i = 0; i < links.length; i++)
    {
      var title = links[i].getAttribute("title");

      if (title && title.length > 0)
```

```
      {
        Core.addEventListener(
            links[i], "mouseover", Tooltips.showTipListener);
        Core.addEventListener(
            links[i], "focus", Tooltips.showTipListener);
        Core.addEventListener(
            links[i], "mouseout", Tooltips.hideTipListener);
        Core.addEventListener(
            links[i], "blur", Tooltips.hideTipListener);
      }
    }
},

showTip: function(link)
{
  Tooltips.hideTip(link);

  var tip = document.createElement("span");
  tip.className = "tooltip";
  var tipText = document.createTextNode(link.title);
  tip.appendChild(tipText);
  link.appendChild(tip);

  link._tooltip = tip;
  link.title = "";

  // Fix for Safari2/Opera9 repaint issue
  document.documentElement.style.position = "relative";
},

hideTip: function(link)
{
  if (link._tooltip)
  {
    link.title = link._tooltip.childNodes[0].nodeValue;
    link.removeChild(link._tooltip);
    link._tooltip = null;

  // Fix for Safari2/Opera9 repaint issue
  document.documentElement.style.position = "static";
  }
},

showTipListener: function(event)
```

```
{
  Tooltips.showTip(this);
  Core.preventDefault(event);
},

hideTipListener: function(event)
{
  Tooltips.hideTip(this);
}
};

Core.start(Tooltips);
```

Example: Accordion

As shown in Figure 4.9, an accordion control collapses content to save space on the page, allowing the user to expand one "fold" of content at a time to read it.

This sort of interface enhancement is a great example of how JavaScript can improve the user experience on a page that works just fine without it. Making such enhancements work smoothly not just for mouse users, but for visitors who navigate using the keyboard (not to mention users of assistive technologies like screen readers), requires careful thought, and extensive use of event listeners.

The Static Page

As usual, we'll start by creating a static page with clean HTML and CSS code before we add any JavaScript. The accordion is essentially a collapsible list, so we'll use a ul element of class accordion to represent it:

accordion.html (excerpt)

```
<ul class="accordion">
  <li id="archer">
    <h2><a href="#archer">Jonathan Archer</a></h2>
    <p>Vessel registry: NX-01</p>
    <p>Assumed command: 2151</p>
    <div class="links">
      <h3>Profiles</h3>
      <ul>
```

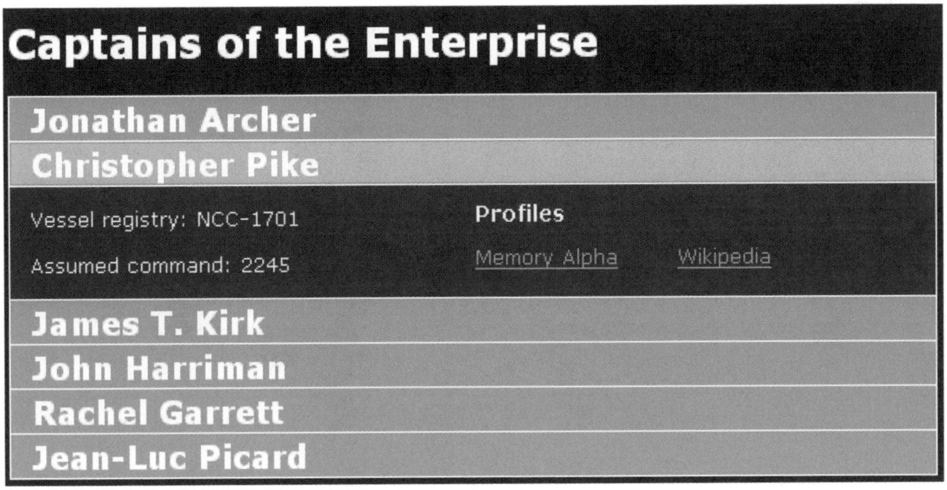

Figure 4.9. An accordion control

```
      <li><a href="…">Memory Alpha</a></li>
      <li><a href="…">Wikipedia</a></li>
    </ul>
  </div>
</li>
<li id="pike">
  ⋮
</li>
  ⋮
</ul>
```

Note that we've applied an ID to each list item, and linked to that ID from the heading just inside the item. Although we're focused on creating a sensible HTML document at this stage, you can also look for opportunities to add meaningful structure that will help you to script the dynamic behaviour you want.

In this case, we can predict that we'll want users to be able to click on a heading in order to expand the corresponding fold of the accordion. Although we could implement this functionality by adding a `click` event listener directly to the heading, using a link makes it easier to support keyboard users. Links can be tabbed to and "clicked" using the browser's built-in keyboard support, whereas extra JavaScript code would be necessary to make a clickable heading accessible from the keyboard.

The next step is to write the CSS code that will style the static version of the page, so that it looks nice even in browsers where JavaScript is not available. Since this isn't a CSS book, I'll spare you the code and just show you the result in Figure 4.10. You can always check out the code in the code archive if you're curious.

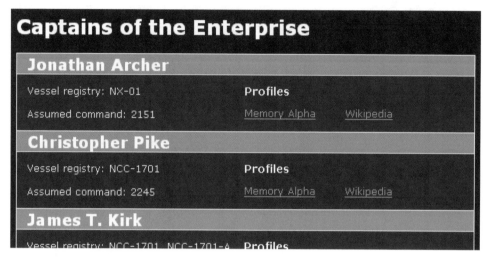

Figure 4.10. The styled page as it will appear without JavaScript

The Workhorse Methods

With a perfectly good page in hand, we can now write a script to enhance it. We'll start with our usual script skeleton:

```
                                                      accordion.js (excerpt)
var Accordion =
{
  init: function()
  {
    ⋮
  },
  ⋮
};


Core.start(Accordion);
```

This script will be concerned primarily with expanding and collapsing the folds of our accordion list, so let's begin by writing the methods that will accomplish this task.

As we learned in Chapter 3, the best approach for modifying the appearance of elements on the fly is to assign CSS classes to them, and then define the actual appearance of each of those classes in our style sheet. So let's assign the expanded and collapsed folds the class names expanded and collapsed, respectively. With this decision made, writing a method that collapses a given fold couldn't be simpler:

accordion.js (excerpt)

```
collapse: function(fold)
{
  Core.removeClass(fold, "expanded");
  Core.addClass(fold, "collapsed");
},
```

Now feel free to go a different way on this point, but personally, I want to allow only one fold of the accordion to be expanded at a time. Expanding a fold, therefore, should also collapse all the other folds on the page. Because collapsing all the folds on the page is a useful thing to be able to do in any case, we'll write a separate method to accomplish this:

accordion.js (excerpt)

```
collapseAll: function(accordion)
{
  var folds = accordion.childNodes;
  for (var i = 0; i < folds.length; i++)
  {
    if (folds[i].nodeType == 1)
    {
      Accordion.collapse(folds[i]);
    }
  }
},
```

This method takes as an argument a reference to the accordion element you want to collapse completely, so logically the very first thing we want to do is get a list of the children of that element—the li elements of the list that represent the folds of the accordion.

This code uses a new trick in the DOM access department: the if statement that checks the nodeType property of each of those list items. We need to do this because there's no guarantee that all the child nodes of the list will be element nodes (that is, list items). Depending on the browser in which our accordion is being used,[13] the whitespace between the list items in our code may be represented as text nodes, which will be listed as children of the ul element as well. The nodeType property of a node tells you whether you're dealing with an element node, a text node, or an attribute node. Since we're only interested in elements (the list items in the list), we check for a nodeType value of 1.

Other than this new trick, the method is fairly straightforward. It gets a list of all the folds in the accordion, then calls Accordion.collapse to collapse each one.

We now have what we need to write our expand method:

accordion.js *(excerpt)*

```
expand: function(fold)
{
  Accordion.collapseAll(fold.parentNode);
  Core.removeClass(fold, "collapsed");
  Core.addClass(fold, "expanded");
},
```

The Dynamic Styles

Now that we have the methods responsible for changing the appearance of our accordion, let's switch gears and write the CSS code that will control exactly what those appearance changes are.

---

[13] Safari is particularly prone to interpreting whitespace as a text node when you least expect it.

The appearance changes that we need for an accordion are really simple. With the exception of the heading of each fold, which should always remain visible, we need to hide the contents of a collapsed fold (an `li` element of class `collapsed`).

Now, we could naively achieve this by setting the `display` property to `none` or `block` where appropriate:

```
ul.accordion li.collapsed * {
  display: none;
}

ul.accordion li.collapsed h2, ul.accordion li.expanded h2,
ul.accordion li.collapsed h2 a:link,
ul.accordion li.collapsed h2 a:visited,
ul.accordion li.expanded h2 a:link,
ul.accordion li.expanded h2 a:visited {
  display: block;
}
```

… but doing it this way would effectively prevent users of screen readers from accessing the contents of our accordion. Screen readers don't read content that's hidden with `display: none`, even when it is later revealed. If there's another way to show and hide content dynamically in your JavaScript projects, you should use it.

In this case, there is definitely another way to hide the contents of the accordion. It's a technique called **offleft positioning**, which is just a fancy way of saying "hide stuff by positioning it off the left-hand side of the page:"

accordion.css *(excerpt)*

```
/* Accordion styles (dynamic) */

ul.accordion li.collapsed * {
  position: absolute;
  left: -10000px;
}

ul.accordion li.collapsed h2, ul.accordion li.expanded h2,
ul.accordion li.collapsed h2 a:link,
ul.accordion li.collapsed h2 a:visited,
ul.accordion li.expanded h2 a:link,
```

```
ul.accordion li.expanded h2 a:visited {
  position: static;
}
```

Offleft positioning is a great boon to screen reader users, because the screen reader software will read the hidden content just as if it were visible on the page.

The inconvenient side-effect of this approach is that the content also remains a part of the page for keyboard users, who will be forced to **Tab** through any links or form elements within that hidden content, even though the content isn't visible to them. In this particular example, however, we can make that work to our advantage, so offleft positioning is the best choice.

The work we've done so far takes care of the essentials, but for a little added spice, we can change the background color of the header of a fold that is either expanded, has the cursor over it, or has keyboard focus:

accordion.css (excerpt)

```
ul.accordion li.collapsed h2 a:hover,
ul.accordion li.collapsed h2 a:focus,
ul.accordion li.collapsed h2 a:active,
ul.accordion li.expanded h2 a:link,
ul.accordion li.expanded h2 a:visited {
  background-color: #F0A000;
}
```

Putting it All Together

Back in the world of JavaScript, we can now write the code that makes things happen, setting up the event listeners that will respond to user actions. Since we want to set up our event listeners as soon as the document has finished loading, we turn our attention to our script's init method.

Let's break down the tasks we want to achieve in this method:

1. Find the accordion list(s) in the page.

2. For each accordion, collapse each of the folds it contains.

3. When the user clicks on the link in the title of an accordion fold, expand it, or collapse it if it's already expanded.

That's not a bad start, so let's convert these plans into JavaScript code. If you're feeling confident, try doing this yourself before looking at the following code—you can implement each of those steps using only the techniques and features of JavaScript that we have already seen in this book:

accordion.js (excerpt)

```
init: function()
{
  var accordions = Core.getElementsByClass("accordion");

  for (var i = 0; i < accordions.length; i++)
  {
    var folds = accordions[i].childNodes;
    for (var j = 0; j < folds.length; j++)
    {
      if (folds[j].nodeType == 1)
      {
        Accordion.collapse(folds[j]);
        var foldLinks = folds[j].getElementsByTagName("a");
        var foldTitleLink = foldLinks[0];
        Core.addEventListener(foldTitleLink, "click",
            Accordion.clickListener);
```

This code gets a list of all elements with a class of `accordion` and uses a `for` loop to process them one at a time. For each accordion list, it retrieves the list of its child nodes (its folds) and again uses a `for` loop to step through them one at time.

After confirming that each node in the list is in fact an element node, it calls the `collapse` method to collapse the fold.

It then obtains a reference to the first link in the fold (which will be the one inside the fold's title), and adds to it an event listener that will respond to the user clicking on it. Here's that event listener:

```
clickListener: function(event)
{
  var fold = this.parentNode.parentNode;
  if (Core.hasClass(fold, "collapsed"))
  {
    Accordion.expand(fold);
  }
  else
  {
    Accordion.collapse(fold);
  }
  Core.preventDefault(event);
},
```

Again, things here are relatively straightforward. The listener obtains a reference to the fold, which is the parent node of the parent node of the link that has just been clicked. It then checks the fold's current CSS class to determine if the fold is collapsed or not. If it's collapsed, the code expands it. If it's expanded, the code collapses it.

The listener ends with a call to `Core.preventDefault`, which keeps the browser from attempting to follow the link. Although it wouldn't be disastrous if the browser *did* follow the link (after all, it just links to the fold itself), this could cause the page to scroll to the fold, when what we're after is a slick, seamless effect.

With the code we've seen so far, the accordion will work exactly the way we want it to for mouse and screen reader users, but we still have to solve the problem that offleft positioning causes for keyboard users. Remember, even though the contents of collapsed folds are hidden off the left of the screen, keyboard users will still find themselves **Tab**bing through the contents of those folds.

On the surface, this seems like a no-win situation, but let's try a strategy in use at most major software companies: what if we think of this as feature and not a bug?

If we can't keep keyboard users from **Tab**bing into hidden folds, why not make something *useful* happen when they do? Specifically, we can expand a fold when the user **Tab**s into it!

In an ideal world, an easy way to do this would be to add a `focus` event listener to each fold and catch the `focus` events as they bubbled up from the specific element within the fold that has received focus, but as we learned earlier in this chapter, `focus` events do not bubble.[14]

Instead, we need to attach a `focus` event listener to every element within our accordion that we expect might receive keyboard focus. For this example, we'll limit ourselves to hyperlinks, but if you were to add form elements to an accordion, you'd want to set them up with this listener as well:[15]

accordion.js (excerpt)

```
init: function()
{
  var accordions = Core.getElementsByClass("accordion");

  for (var i = 0; i < accordions.length; i++)
  {
    var folds = accordions[i].childNodes;
    for (var j = 0; j < folds.length; j++)
    {
      if (folds[j].nodeType == 1)
      {
        Accordion.collapse(folds[j]);
        var foldLinks = folds[j].getElementsByTagName("a");
        var foldTitleLink = foldLinks[0];
        Core.addEventListener(foldTitleLink, "click",
            Accordion.clickListener);

        for (var k = 1; k < foldLinks.length; k++)
        {
          Core.addEventListener(foldLinks[k], "focus",
              Accordion.focusListener);
        }
      }
    }
  }
}
```

[14] If you want to get picky, they do bubble in Mozilla browsers like Firefox, but this behavior is in direct violation of the W3C standard for events, so I wouldn't be surprised to see it changed in future versions of these browsers.

[15] If you wanted to be especially thorough, you could add this listener to *every* element within your accordion, but the sheer number of listeners this might entail could put a real drag on the browser's performance, so I recommend the lighter—if riskier—approach we've used here.

Here's the focus event listener:

accordion.js (excerpt)

```javascript
focusListener: function(event)
{
  var element = this;
  while (element.parentNode)
  {
    if (element.parentNode.className == "accordion")
    {
      Accordion.expand(element);
      return;
    }
    element = element.parentNode;
  }
}
```

This code showcases a common way of using the parentNode property to reach up through the DOM tree. Since all we know is that this is an element somewhere inside a fold of an accordion, you need to use a while loop to climb up through parent nodes of parent nodes until you find an element whose parent node has a class of accordion. That tells you that you've found the fold element, which you can promptly expand in the usual way.

As a finishing touch to our menu, let's add a bonus feature that takes advantage of the fact that, in the HTML code of the page, each of our folds has a unique ID:

accordion.html (excerpt)

```html
<ul class="accordion">
  <li id="archer">
    ⋮
  </li>
  <li id="pike">
    ⋮
  </li>
  ⋮
</ul>
```

If a link on another page points to a specific fold of our accordion (e.g. `<a href="accordion.html#pike">`), it would be nice to automatically expand that fold when the page is loaded. All this effect takes is a brief addition to our `init` method:

```
init: function()
{
  var accordions = Core.getElementsByClass("accordion");

  for (var i = 0; i < accordions.length; i++)
  {
    ⋮

    if (location.hash.length > 1)
    {
      var activeFold = document.getElementById(
          location.hash.substring(1));
      if (activeFold && activeFold.parentNode == accordions[i])
      {
        Accordion.expand(activeFold);
      }
    }
  }
},
```

The global `location` variable is an object that contains information about the URL of the current page. Its `hash` property contains the fragment identifier portion of that URL (e.g. `"#pike"`), which we can use to identify and expand the requested fold.

First, we obtain a reference to the element with the specified ID. Since the ID we're after is the fragment identifier minus the leading # character, we can use the `substring` method that's built into every JavaScript string value to fetch a portion of the fragment identifier, starting at the second character (`location.hash.substring(1)`):

```
var activeFold = document.getElementById(
      location.hash.substring(1));
```

Before expanding the element, we need to check if that ID actually corresponds to an element in the page, and if the parent of that element is the accordion that we're currently setting up:

accordion.js *(excerpt)*

```
if (activeFold && activeFold.parentNode == accordions[i])
{
  Accordion.expand(activeFold);
}
```

And there you have it: a robust and accessible accordion control that you can easily plug into any web page you like. Load it up in your favorite browser and take it for a spin. Be sure to try using the keyboard to **Tab** through the accordion and its contents to see how a little extra code can go a long way toward making your site work well for a wider audience.

Here's the complete JavaScript code:

accordion.js

```
var Accordion =
{
  init: function()
  {
    var accordions = Core.getElementsByClass("accordion");

    for (var i = 0; i < accordions.length; i++)
    {
      var folds = accordions[i].childNodes;
      for (var j = 0; j < folds.length; j++)
      {
        if (folds[j].nodeType == 1)
        {
          Accordion.collapse(folds[j]);
          var foldLinks = folds[j].getElementsByTagName("a");
          var foldTitleLink = foldLinks[0];
          Core.addEventListener(
              foldTitleLink, "click", Accordion.clickListener);

          for (var k = 1; k < foldLinks.length; k++)
          {
```

```
            Core.addEventListener(
                foldLinks[k], "focus", Accordion.focusListener);
          }
        }
      }

      if (location.hash.length > 1)
      {
        var activeFold = document.getElementById(
            location.hash.substring(1));
        if (activeFold && activeFold.parentNode == accordions[i])
        {
          Accordion.expand(activeFold);
        }
      }
    }
},

collapse: function(fold)
{
  Core.removeClass(fold, "expanded");
  Core.addClass(fold, "collapsed");
},

collapseAll: function(accordion)
{
  var folds = accordion.childNodes;
  for (var i = 0; i < folds.length; i++)
  {
    if (folds[i].nodeType == 1)
    {
      Accordion.collapse(folds[i]);
    }
  }
},

expand: function(fold)
{
  Accordion.collapseAll(fold.parentNode);
  Core.removeClass(fold, "collapsed");
  Core.addClass(fold, "expanded");
},

clickListener: function(event)
```

```
  {
    var fold = this.parentNode.parentNode;
    if (Core.hasClass(fold, "collapsed"))
    {
      Accordion.expand(fold);
    }
    else
    {
      Accordion.collapse(fold);
    }
    Core.preventDefault(event);
  },

  focusListener: function(event)
  {
    var element = this;
    while (element.parentNode)
    {
      if (element.parentNode.className == "accordion")
      {
        Accordion.expand(element);
        return;
      }
      element = element.parentNode;
    }
  }
};

Core.start(Accordion);
```

Exploring Libraries

Most JavaScript libraries contain solutions to the browser compatibility issues surrounding event listeners that we tackled in this chapter. Although we believe the Core library that we have developed for this book to be well worth using, depending on your preferences, you may find these alternatives slightly more convenient, efficient, or confusing.

The Prototype library, for example, offers cross-browser alternatives for the standard addEventListener and removeEventListener methods, called Event.observe and Event.stopObserving, respectively:

```
Event.observe(element, "event", eventListener);
```

```
Event.stopObserving(element, "event", eventListener);
```

These methods work much like our own `Core.addEventListener` and `Core.removeEventListener` methods, in that they transparently call the correct methods to add and remove event listeners in the current browser, and ensure that the necessary cleanup is done to avoid listener-related memory leaks in Internet Explorer.

These methods leave a couple of issues unresolved, however—the inconsistency surrounding the value of `this` within the listener function, for example. Instead of automatically ensuring that `this` refers to the element to which the event listener was applied, Prototype lets you specify exactly which object you'd like `this` to refer to by adding a `bindAsEventListener` method to every function.

Therefore, the correct way to set up an event listener in Prototype is as follows:

```
Event.observe(element, "event",
    eventListener.bindAsEventListener(element));
```

I've assumed here that we want `this` to refer to the element to which the listener was added, but we can pass any object we like as an argument to `bindAsEventListener`, and it will be used as the value of `this` when the event listener function is called.

Calling `bindAsEventListener` also resolves the remaining cross-browser compatibility issues, for example, ensuring that the event object is passed to the listener function as an argument, even in Internet Explorer.

Unfortunately, this approach complicates the process of *removing* an event listener slightly. As we need to pass the same arguments to `Event.stopObserving` in order for it to work, we need to store the result of calling `bindAsEventListener`:

```
var myEventListener = eventListener.bindAsEventListener(element);
Event.observe(element, "event", myEventListener);
⋮
Event.stopObserving(element, "event", myEventListener);
```

If Prototype makes registering event listeners a little complicated, it simplifies the control of event propagation and default actions. Instead of separate `preventDefault` and `stopPropagation` methods, Prototype gives you a single method that does both:

```
Event.stop(event);
```

At the opposite end of the spectrum in terms of complexity is the jQuery library, which makes the code for managing event listeners extremely simple. It has extremely easy-to-use `bind` and `unbind` methods that take care of all the cross-browser compatibility headaches associated with adding and removing event listeners:

```
$("#id").bind("event", eventListener);
```

```
$("#id").unbind("event", eventListener);
```

jQuery also provides for each event type a convenient method that lets us set up an event listener for that event with even less code than the above. For example, the `click` method lets us set up a `click` event listener:

```
$("#id").click(clickListener);
```

Note that we can call any of these methods on a jQuery node list in order to add the listener to every node in the list. For example, we can add a `click` listener to every link in the document with just one statement:

```
$("a[href]").click(clickListener);
```

Nestled halfway between Prototype and jQuery in terms of complexity is the Yahoo! UI Library, which works almost exactly like our own `Core.addEventListener` and `Core.removeEventListener` methods.

Summary

You've taken a huge step in this chapter! Instead of just running JavaScript code as the page is loaded, painting a pretty picture for the user to gaze at in vague disappointment, you can now attach your code to events, following the user's lead like a practiced dance partner, adjusting and responding to his or her every whim.

But in some ways, this can still be quite limiting. After all, just because the user stops dancing doesn't mean your code should have to!

In Chapter 5, we'll finally set JavaScript free! We'll explore the secrets of animation, and learn how to produce effects that take place over a period of time, independent of the user's interaction with the page. We'll also learn how this freedom can be used to further improve the examples we created in this chapter.

Animation

Are you ready for your journey into the ... *fourth dimension!?* (Cue spooky theramin music.)

Animation is all about time—stopping time, starting time, and bending time to produce the effect you want: movement. You don't actually have to learn much new JavaScript in order to create web page animation—just two little functions. One and a half, really. What are they? You'll have to read on to find out!

But first, let's take a look at exactly what animation is, and how we can best go about producing it on a computer screen.

The Principles of Animation

If, like me, you're a connoisseur of Saturday morning cartoons, you'll probably be familiar with the basic principles of animation. As illustrated in Figure 5.1, what we see on the TV screen isn't actually Astroboy jetting around, but a series of images played rapidly, with minute changes between each one, producing the illusion that Astroboy can move.

Standard TV displays between 25 and 30 pictures (or **frames**) per second, but we don't perceive each picture individually—we see them as one continuous, moving image. Animation differs from live TV only in the way it is produced. The actual display techniques are identical—a series of rapidly displayed images that fools our brains into seeing continuous movement.

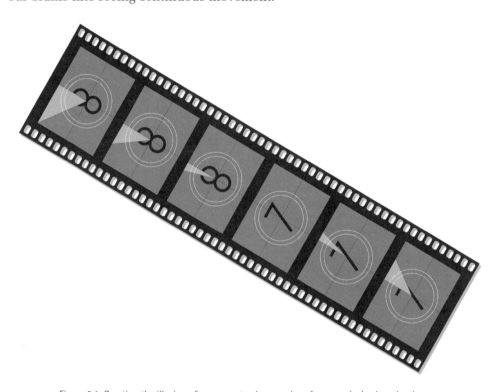

Figure 5.1. Creating the illusion of movement using a series of progressively changing images

Adding animation to your interfaces is no different from animating something for TV, although it may seem somewhat less artistic. If you want a drop-down menu to actually drop *down*, you start it closed, end it open, and include a whole bunch of intermediate steps that make it look like it moved.

The faster you want to move it, the fewer steps you put in between the starting and finishing frames. As it is, a drop-down menu without animation is akin to teleport-ation—the menu moves directly from point A to point B, without any steps in between. If you add just one step, it's not quite teleportation, but it's still faster than you can blink. Add ten steps and the menu begins to look like it's moving smoothly. Add 50 and it's probably behaving a bit too much like a tortoise. It's really up to you to find the optimal intervals that give you that nice, pleasing feeling of the menu opening.

Controlling Time with JavaScript

The most intuitive way of thinking about animations is as slices of time. We're capturing and displaying discrete moments in time so that they look like one continuous experience. But, given the way we handle animation in JavaScript, it's probably more accurate to think of ourselves as inserting the *pauses*—putting gaps *between* the slices, as is illustrated in Figure 5.2.

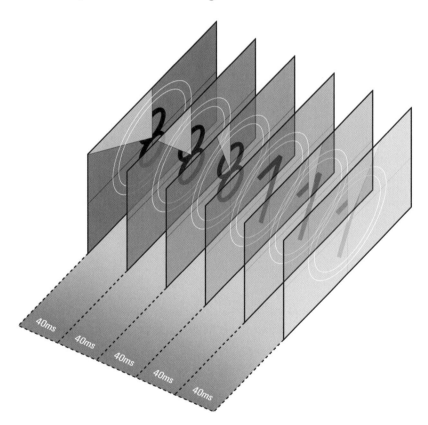

Figure 5.2. An animation running at 25 frames per second, in which the gap between each "slice" of time is 40 milliseconds

In normal program flow a browser will execute JavaScript as quickly as it can, pumping instructions to the CPU whenever they can be processed. This means that your entire, 5,000-line program could execute faster than you can take a breath. That's great if you're performing long calculations, but it's useless if you're creating animation. Watching *Snow White and the Seven Dwarfs* in 7.3 seconds might be efficient, but it doesn't do much for the storyline.

To create smooth, believable animation we need to be able to control when each frame is displayed. In traditional animation, the **frame rate** (that is, the number of images displayed per second) is fixed. Decisions about how you slice the intervals, where you slice them, and what you slice, are all up to you, but they're displayed at the same, measured pace all the time.

In JavaScript, you can create the same slices and control the same aspects, but you're also given control of the pauses—how long it takes for one image to be displayed after another. You can vary the pauses however you like, slowing time down, speeding it up, or stopping it entirely (though most of the time you'll want to keep it steady). We control time in JavaScript using `setTimeout`.

Instead of allowing your program to execute each statement as quickly as it can, `setTimeout` tells your program to wait awhile—to take a breather. The function takes two arguments: the statement you want it to run next, and the time that the program should wait before executing that statement (in milliseconds).

In order to stop the statement inside the `setTimeout` call from being evaluated immediately, we must make it into a string. So if we wanted to display an alert after one second, the `setTimeout` call would look like this:

```
setTimeout("alert('Was it worth the wait?')", 1000);
```

From the moment this statement is executed, our program will wait 1000 milliseconds (one second) before it executes the code inside the string, and produces the popup shown in Figure 5.3.

Technically speaking, what happens when `setTimeout` is called is that the browser adds the statement to a "to-do list" of sorts, while the rest of your program continues to run without pausing. Once it finishes what it's currently doing (for instance, executing an event listener), the browser consults its to-do list and executes any tasks it finds scheduled there.

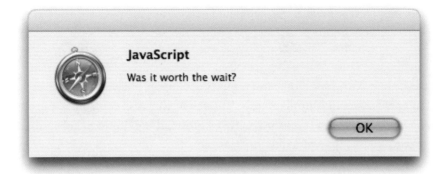

Figure 5.3. Using `setTimeout` to execute code after a specified number of milliseconds have elapsed

Usually, when you call a function from inside another function, the execution of the outer function halts until the inner function has finished executing. So a function like the one shown here actually executes as depicted in Figure 5.4:

```
function fabric()
{
  ⋮
  alert("Stop that man!");
  ⋮
}
```

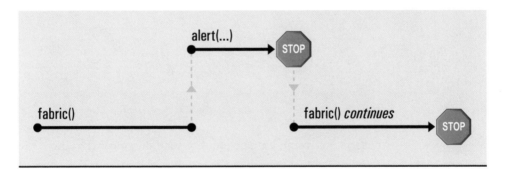

Figure 5.4. Calling a function inside another function

But what happens if you have a `setTimeout` call in the middle of your code?

```
function fabric()
{
  ⋮
```

```
  setTimeout("alert('Was it worth the wait?');", 1000);
  ⋮
}
```

In this case, the execution of the statement passed to `setTimeout` is deferred, while the rest of `fabric` executes immediately. The scheduled task waits until the specified time has elapsed, *and* the browser has finished what it's doing, before executing. Figure 5.5 illustrates this concept.

Strictly speaking, the delay that you specify when calling `setTimeout` will be the *minimum* amount of time that must elapse before the scheduled task will occur. If the browser is still tied up doing other things when that time arrives, your task will be put off until all others have been completed, as Figure 5.6 indicates.[1]

Using Variables with `setTimeout`

Statements passed to `setTimeout` are run in global scope. We talked about scope in Chapter 2, so if you'd like to refresh your memory, flick back to that chapter. The effect that scope has here is that the code run by `setTimeout` will not have access to any variables that are local to the function from which `setTimeout` was called.

Take a look at this example:

```
function periscope()
{
  var message = "Prepare to surface!";

  setTimeout("alert(message);", 2000);
}
```

Here, the variable `message` is local to `periscope`, but the code passed to the `setTimeout` will be run with global scope, entirely separately from `periscope`. Therefore, it won't have access to `message` when it runs, and we'll receive the error shown in Figure 5.7.

---

[1] If you specify a delay of zero milliseconds when you call `setTimeout`, the browser will execute the task as soon as it's finished what it's currently doing.

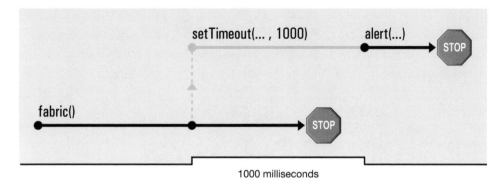

Figure 5.5. Calling `setTimeout` schedules a task to be run after a delay

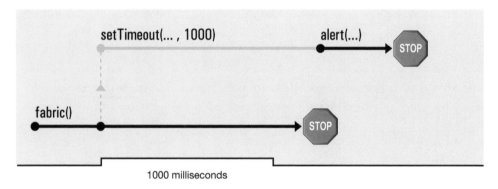

Figure 5.6. `setTimeout` waits until JavaScript is free before running the newly specified task

Figure 5.7. The error that occurs when we try to use a locally scoped variable as part of `setTimeout` code

There are three ways around this problem.

The first is to make `message` a global variable. This isn't that great an idea, because it's not good practice to have variables floating around, cluttering up the global namespace, and causing possible clashes with other scripts. But if we *were* to go down this path, we could just leave the `var` keyword off our variable declaration:

```
function periscope()
{
  message = "Prepare to surface!";

  setTimeout("alert(message)", 2000);
}
```

`message` would be a global variable that's accessible from any function, including the code passed to `setTimeout`.

The second option is available when the variable we're using is a string. In this case, we can encode the value of the variable directly into the `setTimeout` code simply by concatenating the variable into the string:

```
function periscope()
{
  message = "Prepare to surface!";

  setTimeout("alert('" + message + "')", 2000);
}
```

Since we want the string to be interpreted as a string—not a variable name—we have to include single quote marks inside the `setTimeout` code string, and in between those marks, insert the value of the variable. Though the above code is equivalent to the code below, we have the advantage of being able to use dynamically assigned text with the variable:

```
setTimeout("alert('Prepare to surface!')", 2000);
```

 Troublesome Quotes

Of course, if the variable's string value happens to contain one or more single quotes, this approach will fall to pieces unless you go to the trouble of escaping

> each of the single quotes with a backslash. And while that is certainly possible, the code involved isn't much fun.

The final option, and the one that's used more regularly in complex scripts, is to use a **closure**. A closure is a tricky JavaScript concept that allows any function that's defined inside another function to access the outer function's local variables, regardless of when it's run. Put another way, functions have access to the context in which they're defined, even if that context is a function that's no longer executing. So, even though the outer function may have finished executing minutes ago, functions that were declared while it was executing will still be able to access its local variables.

How does this help us given the fact that `setTimeout` takes a string as its first argument? Well, it can also take a function:

```
function periscope()
{
  var message = "Prepare to surface!";

  var theFunction = function()
  {
    alert(message);
  };

  setTimeout(theFunction, 2000);
}
```

Or, more briefly:

```
function periscope()
{
  var message = "Prepare to surface!";

  setTimeout(function(){alert(message);}, 2000);
}
```

When you pass a function to `setTimeout`, `setTimeout` doesn't execute it then and there; it executes the function after the specified delay. Since that function was declared within `periscope`, the function creates a closure, giving it access to `periscope`'s local variables (in this case, `message`).

Even though `periscope` will have finished executing when the inner function is run in two seconds' time, `message` will still be available, and the call to `alert` will bring up the right message.

The concept of closures is difficult to get your head around, so for the moment, you can be satisfied if you've just got a general feel for them.

Stopping the Timer

When `setTimeout` is executed, it creates a timer that "counts down" to the moment when the specified code should be executed. The `setTimeout` function returns the ID of this timer so that you can access it later in your script. So far, we've been calling `setTimeout` without bothering about its return value, but if you ever want to intervene in a timer's countdown, you have to pay attention to this value.

To stop a timer before its countdown has finished, we need to capture the timer's ID inside a variable and pass it to a function called `clearTimeout`. `clearTimeout` will immediately cancel the countdown of the associated timer, and the scheduled task will never occur:

```
var timer = setTimeout("alert('This will never appear')", 3000);
clearTimeout(timer);
```

The alert in the code above will never be displayed, because we stop the `setTimeout` call immediately using `clearTimeout`.

Let's consider something that's a little more useful. Suppose we create a page that displays two buttons:

clear_timeout.html (excerpt)

```
<button id="start">Start</button>
<button id="stop">Stop</button>
```

We can add some behavior to those buttons with a short program:

```
                                                          clear_timeout.js
var ClearTimer =
{
  init: function()
  {
    var start = document.getElementById("start");
    Core.addEventListener(start, "click", ClearTimer.clickStart);

    var stop = document.getElementById("stop");
    Core.addEventListener(stop, "click", ClearTimer.clickStop);
  },
  clickStart: function()
  {
    ClearTimer.timer = setTimeout("alert('Launched')", 2000);
  },
  clickStop: function()
  {
    if (ClearTimer.timer)
    {
      clearTimeout(ClearTimer.timer);
    }

    alert("Aborted");
  }
};

Core.start(ClearTimer);
```

This program begins by running `ClearTimer.init` via `Core.start`, which initializes the page by adding a `click` event listener to each of the buttons. When the **Start** button is clicked, `ClearTimer.clickStart` will be called, and when the **Stop** button is clicked, `ClearTimer.clickStop` will be called.

`ClearTimer.clickStart` uses `setTimeout` to schedule an alert, but we store the ID to that scheduled alert inside the variable `ClearTimer.timer`. Whenever `ClearTimer.clickStop` is pressed we pass `ClearTimer.timer` to `clearTimeout`, and the timer will be stopped.

So, once you click **Start** you will have two seconds to click **Stop**; otherwise, the alert dialog will appear, displaying the message "Launched." This simple example provides a good illustration of what's involved in controlling timers via user interaction; we'll look at how it can be used in a more complex interface later in this chapter.

Creating a Repeating Timer

There's another timing function that's very similar to `setTimeout`, but which allows you to schedule a repeating piece of code. This function is called `setInterval`.

`setInterval` takes exactly the same arguments as `setTimeout`, and when it's executed, it waits in exactly the same way. But the fun doesn't stop once the scheduled code has finished executing—`setInterval` schedules the code again, and again, and again, and again, until you tell it to stop. If you tell it to wait 1,000 milliseconds, `setInterval` will schedule the code to run once every 1,000 milliseconds.

Each interval is scheduled as a separate task, so if a particular occurrence of the scheduled code takes longer to run than the interval time, the next occurrence will execute immediately after it finishes, as the browser scrambles to catch up.

At the start of this chapter I mentioned that there were really one and a half functions that could be used to control time in JavaScript. That's because `setInterval` isn't used very often.

As `setInterval` relentlessly schedules tasks at the specified interval no matter how long those tasks actually take, long-running tasks can generate an undesirable backlog that causes fast-running tasks to run instantly, with no pause between them. In an animation, this can be disastrous, as the pause between each frame is crucial to generating that illusion of motion.

When it comes to animation, it's usually best to rely on chained `setTimeout` calls, including at the end of your scheduled code a `setTimeout` call to that same piece of code. This approach ensures that you only have one task scheduled at any one time, and that the crucial pauses between frames are maintained throughout the animation. You'll see examples of this technique in each of the animation programs we write in this chapter.

Stopping `setInterval`

Just like `setTimeout`, `setInterval` returns a timer ID. To stop `setInterval` from executing any more scheduled code, we pass this ID to `clearInterval`:

```
var timer = setInterval("alert('Do this over and over!')", 3000);
clearInterval(timer);
```

Done! No more timer.

Revisiting Rich Tooltips

It's probably easiest to get a feel for working with `setTimeout` if we start simply—using it to put in a short delay on an action. I'll demonstrate this by modifying the Rich Tooltips script from Chapter 4, so that the tooltips behave more like regular tooltips and appear after the user has hovered the mouse over the element for a moment. We won't need to change much of the program—just the two event listeners that handle the `mouseover`/`focus` and `mouseout`/`blur` events.

Let's think about how the delay should work. We want the tooltip to pop up about 500 milliseconds after the `mouseover` or `focus` event occurs. In our original script, the event listener `showTipListener` immediately made a call to `Tooltips.showTip`. But in the delayed script, we want to move that call into a `setTimeout`:

tooltips_delay.js *(excerpt)*

```
showTipListener: function(event)
{
  var link = this;
  this._timer = setTimeout(function()
      {
        Tooltips.showTip(link);
      }, 500);
  Core.preventDefault(event);
},
```

In order to pass `showTip` a reference to the link in question, we need to store that reference in a local variable called `link`. We can then make use of a closure by passing `setTimeout` a newly created function. That new function will have access to showTipListener's local variables, and when it's run, it will be able to pass the link to showTip.

The other point to note about this setTimeout call is that we assign the ID it returns to a custom property of the anchor element, called _timer. We store this value so that if a user mouses off the anchor before the tooltip has appeared, we can stop the showTip call from going ahead. To cancel the method call, we update hideTipListener with a clearTimeout call:

tooltip_delay.js *(excerpt)*

```
hideTipListener: function(event)
{
  clearTimeout(this._timer);
  Tooltips.hideTip(this);
}
```

The ID of the setTimeout call is passed to clearTimeout every time that hideTipListener is executed, and this will prevent premature "tooltipification."

And that's it: our Rich Tooltips script has now been modified into a moderately less annoying Rich *Delayed* Tooltips script.

Old-school Animation in a New-school Style

To demonstrate how to create a multi-stepped animation sequence in JavaScript we're going to do something novel, though you probably wouldn't implement it on a real web page. We're going to re-create a film reel in HTML.

First of all, we need a strip of film—or a graphic that looks almost like a real piece of film. As you can see in Figure 5.8, our reel contains a series of progressively changing images that are joined together in one long strip.

If you had a real reel, you'd pass it through a projector, and the frames would be projected individually onto the screen, one after the other. For this virtual film reel, our projector will be an empty `div`:

---

robot_animation.html *(excerpt)*

```
<div id="robot"></div>
```

The `div` will be styled to the exact dimensions of a frame (150x150px), so that we can show exactly one frame inside it:

---

robot_animation.css *(excerpt)*

```
#robot {
  width: 150px;
  height: 150px;
```

If we use the strip of robots as a background image, we can change the `background-position` CSS property to move the image around and display different parts of the strip:

---

robot_animation.css *(excerpt)*

```
#robot {
  width: 150px;
  height: 150px;
  background-image:
    url(../images/robot_strip.gif);
  background-repeat: no-repeat;
  background-position: 0 0;
}
```

Figure 5.8. The "reel" we'll use to create animation

Getting the idea now? You can think of the `div` as a little window inside which we're moving the strip around, as Figure 5.9 illustrates.

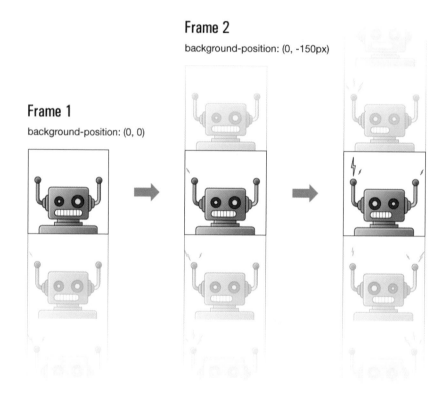

Figure 5.9. Changing the position of the background image to specify which frame is in view

So, we know how to make any one frame appear inside the `div` window, but the page is still static—there's no animation. That's what that ol' JavaScript magic is for!

In order to create a fluid animation, we're going to need to change the `background-position` at a regular interval, flicking through the frames so that they look like one fluid, moving image. With all the talk of `setTimeout` in this chapter, you could probably take a guess that the function is the key to it all. And you'd be wrong. Sorry, *right*:

```
var Robot =
{
  init: function()
  {
    Robot.div = document.getElementById("robot"); ❶
    Robot.frameHeight = 150;
    Robot.frames = 10;
    Robot.offsetY = 0; ❷

    Robot.animate(); ❸
  },
  animate: function() ❹
  {
    Robot.offsetY -= Robot.frameHeight; ❺

    if (Robot.offsetY <= -Robot.frameHeight * Robot.frames) ❻
    {
      Robot.offsetY = 0;
    }

    Robot.div.style.backgroundPosition =
        "0 " + Robot.offsetY + "px"; ❼

    setTimeout(Robot.animate, 75); ❽
  }
};

Core.start(Robot);
```

The `Robot` object contains two methods. `Robot.init` is included mainly to declare some variables and kick-start the animation. I include the variables here, rather than in `Robot.animate`, because `Robot.animate` will be called a lot, and it's more efficient to declare the variables just once than to have them declared for each frame of our animation.

Here are the highlights of this script:

1 The initialized variables include a reference to the `div` element we're modifying, as well as two constant properties— `frameHeight` and `frames`—which tell the program that each frame is 150 pixels high, and that there are ten frames in total. These values will remain fixed throughout an animation, but by declaring them up front, you'll find it easier to modify the frame dimensions and the number of frames later if you need to. If you create your own animation, you should modify these variables according to your needs.

2 The other variable, `Robot.offsetY`, is the only variable we'll be updating dynamically. It's set to `0` initially, but it's used to record the current vertical position of the animation image, just so we know which frame we're up to.

3 After the `init` method does its thing, we step into our first iteration of `Robot.animate`.

4 If you look to the end of the function, you'll see that the function calls itself with a `setTimeout` delay. This lets you know that we're setting up a timed, repeating task.

5 The first statement in the function reduces `Robot.offsetY` by the height of one frame. What we're calculating here is the vertical `background-position` required to view the next frame. However, our animation graphic isn't infinitely long; if we just kept reducing the value of `Robot.offsetY`, we'd eventually run out of frames and end up with an empty box. To avoid this, we need to return to the beginning of the strip at the right moment.

6 Next up is an `if` statement that checks whether the new `Robot.offsetY` value is outside the range of our animation strip. If it is, we set it back to `0`.

7 With our new offset value in hand, we're ready to update the position of the image. To do so, we modify the `div`'s `style.backgroundPosition` property, using `Robot.offsetY` for the vertical coordinate and `0` for the horizontal coordinate (because we don't need to move the image horizontally at all).

Units Required

Remember to include units at the end of all non-zero CSS values, otherwise your changes will be ignored. We're using pixels in this case, so we add `px` to the end of the value.

8 Changing the style of the `div` commits the new frame to the browser for the user to see. Once that's done, we have to schedule the next change using `setTimeout`. The wait until the next frame change is 75 milliseconds, which will produce a frame rate of approximately 13 frames per second. You might want to tweak this rate depending on how fast or smooth you want your animation to be. The most pleasing results are often reached by trial and error.

Once the program has made a few passes through `Robot.animate`, you have yourself an animation. Since there's nothing in our code to stop the repeated calls to that method, the animation will keep going forever. If you wanted to, you could provide start and stop buttons as we did previously in this chapter to allow users to stop and restart the animation. Alternatively, you could limit the number of cycles that the animation goes through by including a counter variable that's incremented each time `Robot.offsetY` returns to 0.

Path-based Motion

The JavaScript techniques we used to animate our digital film reel can be applied whenever you want to make a series of progressive changes to the display over time. All you have to do is replace `background-position` with the attribute you want to modify: color, width, height, position, opacity—anything you can think of.

In our next example, we're going to look at moving an HTML element along a linear path. So, instead of changing the `background-position` of the target element, we change its actual position.

In cases where you want to move an element, you usually know where it is now (that is, its starting location), and where you want it to be (its end location), as Figure 5.10 shows.

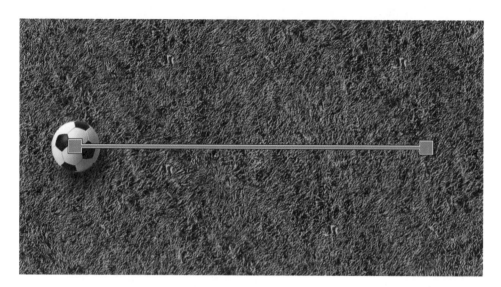

Figure 5.10. Visualizing a path from the object's starting location to the point where you want it to end up

Once you've defined the two end points of the path, it's the job of the animation program to figure out all the steps that must occur to let the animated element move smoothly from point A to point B, as shown in Figure 5.11.

Figure 5.11. Calculating the steps required to move an element from point A to point B

Given that the movement is going to be automated by an animation function, all we really have to identify at the moment is:

- the element we want to move
- where we want to move it to
- how long we want it to take to reach its destination

We'll use the soccer ball and grassy background as the basis for a working example. The HTML for this document is fairly simple:

path-based_motion.html (excerpt)

```
<div id="grass">
  <div id="soccerBall"></div>
</div>
```

There are a number of ways we could position the soccer ball, but for this example I've chosen to use absolute positioning:

path-based_motion.css (excerpt)

```
#soccerBall {
  background-image: url(soccer_ball.png);
  background-repeat: no-repeat;
  height: 125px;
  left: 0;
  margin-top: 25px;
  position: absolute;
  top: 75px;
  width: 125px;
}
```

 Positioning and Animation

If you're going to animate an element's movement, the element will need to be positioned relatively or absolutely; otherwise, changing its `left` and `top` properties won't have any effect.

The JavaScript we used to animate our previous film reel example makes a fairly good template for any animation, so we'll use its structure to help us define the movement we need in this new animation. Inside `init`, we declare some of the variables we'll need, then start the actual animation:

```
                                                    path-based_motion.js (excerpt)
var SoccerBall =
{
  init: function()
  {
    SoccerBall.frameRate = 25; ❶
    SoccerBall.duration = 2;
    SoccerBall.div = document.getElementById("soccerBall"); ❷
    SoccerBall.targetX = 600; ❸
    SoccerBall.originX = parseInt(
        Core.getComputedStyle(SoccerBall.div, "left"), 10); ❹
    SoccerBall.increment =
        (SoccerBall.targetX - SoccerBall.originX) /
        (SoccerBall.duration * SoccerBall.frameRate); ❺
    SoccerBall.x = SoccerBall.originX; ❻

    SoccerBall.animate(); ❼
  },
    ⋮
};
```

❶ The first two variables control the speed of the animation.
`SoccerBall.frameRate` specifies the number of frames per second at which
we want the animation to move. This property is used when we set the delay
time for the `setTimeout` call, and determines the "smoothness" of the soccer
ball's movement. `SoccerBall.duration` determines how long the animation
should take to complete (in seconds) and affects the speed with which the ball
appears to move.

❷ `SoccerBall.div` is self-explanatory.

❸ `SoccerBall.targetX` specifies the location to which we're moving the soccer
ball. Once it reaches this point, the animation should stop.

❹ In order to support an arbitrary starting position for the soccer ball,
`SoccerBall.originX` is actually calculated from the browser's computed style
for the `div`.

The **computed style** of an element is its style information *after* all CSS rules and
inline styles have been applied to it. So, if an element's `left` position has been

specified inside an external style sheet, obtaining the element's computed style will let you access that property value.

Unfortunately, there are differences between the way that Internet Explorer implements computed style and the way that other browsers implement it. Internet Explorer exposes a `currentStyle` property on every element. This properties has exactly the same properties as `style`, so you could ascertain an element's computed `left` position using `element.currentStyle.left`. Other browsers require you to retrieve a computed style object using the method `document.defaultView.getComputedStyle`. This method takes two arguments—the first is the element you require the styles for; the second must always be `null`—then returns a style object that has the same structure as Internet Explorer's `currentStyle` property.

To get around these browser differences, we'll create a new Core library function that will allow us to get a particular computed style property from an element:

core.js *(excerpt)*

```
Core.getComputedStyle = function(element, styleProperty)
{
  var computedStyle = null;

  if (typeof element.currentStyle != "undefined")
  {
    computedStyle = element.currentStyle;
  }
  else
  {
    computedStyle =
        document.defaultView.getComputedStyle(element, null);
  }

  return computedStyle[styleProperty];
};
```

`Core.getComputedStyle` does a little object detection to check which way we should retrieve the computed style, then passes back the value for the appropriate property. Using method, we can get the correct starting point for `SoccerBall.originX` without requiring a hard-coded value in our script.

Let's return to our `init` method above:

⑤   With `SoccerBall.originX` and `SoccerBall.targetX` in hand, we can calculate
the increment by which we'll need to move the soccer ball in each frame so
that it ends up at the target location within the duration specified for the animation. This is a simple matter of finding the distance to be traveled
(`SoccerBall.targetX − SoccerBall.originX`) and dividing it by the total
number of frames in the animation (`SoccerBall.duration *`
`SoccerBall.frameRate`). Calculating this figure during initialization—rather
than inside the actual animating function—reduces the number of calculations
that we'll have to complete for each step of the animation.

⑥   The last variable we declare is `SoccerBall.x`. It acts similarly to `Robot.offsetY`,
keeping track of the horizontal position of the element. It would be possible
to keep track of the soccer ball's position using its actual `style.left` value,
however, that value has to be an integer, whereas `SoccerBall.x` can be a
floating point number. This approach produces more accurate calculations and
smoother animation.

⑦   After `SoccerBall.init` has finished declaring all the object properties, we
start the animation by calling `SoccerBall.animate`.

Here's the code for this method:

path-based_motion.js *(excerpt)*

```
animate: function()
{
  SoccerBall.x += SoccerBall.increment;

  if ((SoccerBall.targetX > SoccerBall.originX &&
      SoccerBall.x > SoccerBall.targetX) ||
      (SoccerBall.targetX <= SoccerBall.originX &&
      SoccerBall.x <= SoccerBall.targetX))
  {
    SoccerBall.x = SoccerBall.targetX;
  }
  else
  {
    setTimeout(SoccerBall.animate, 1000 / SoccerBall.frameRate)
  }
```

```
    SoccerBall.div.style.left = Math.round(SoccerBall.x) + "px";
}
```

The similarities between this `animate` method and `Robot.animate`, which we saw in the previous example, are striking. The process for both is basically:

1. Calculate the new position.

2. Check whether the new position exceeds the limit.

3. Apply the new position to the element.

4. Repeat the process with a delay.

In this case, we're calculating a new position by adding to the current position one "slice" of the total distance to be traveled:

path-based_motion.js (excerpt)

```
SoccerBall.x += SoccerBall.increment;
```

Then, we check whether that new position goes beyond the end point of the animation:

path-based_motion.js (excerpt)

```
if ((SoccerBall.targetX > SoccerBall.originX &&
    SoccerBall.x >= SoccerBall.targetX) ||
    (SoccerBall.targetX < SoccerBall.originX &&
    SoccerBall.x <= SoccerBall.targetX))
```

That condition looks a little daunting, but we can break it down into smaller chunks. There are actually two possible states represented here, separated by an OR operator.

The first of these states (`SoccerBall.targetX > SoccerBall.originX &&` `SoccerBall.x >= SoccerBall.targetX`) checks whether `SoccerBall.targetX` is greater than `SoccerBall.originX`. If it is, we know that the soccer ball is moving to the right. If that's the case, the soccer ball will be beyond the end point if `SoccerBall.x` is greater than `SoccerBall.targetX`.

In the second state (`SoccerBall.targetX < SoccerBall.originX && SoccerBall.x <= SoccerBall.targetX`), if `SoccerBall.targetX` is *less than* `SoccerBall.originX`, the soccer ball will be moving to the *left*, and it will be beyond the end point if `SoccerBall.x` is *less than* `SoccerBall.targetX`. By including these two separate states inside the condition, we allow the soccer ball to move in any direction without having to modify the code.

If the newly calculated position for the soccer ball exceeds the end point, we automatically set the new position to be the end point:

path-based_motion.js (excerpt)

```
if ((SoccerBall.targetX > SoccerBall.originX &&
    SoccerBall.x >= SoccerBall.targetX) ||
    (SoccerBall.targetX < SoccerBall.originX &&
    SoccerBall.x <= SoccerBall.targetX))
{
  SoccerBall.x = SoccerBall.targetX;
}
```

Otherwise, the soccer ball needs to keep moving, so we schedule another animation frame:

path-based_motion.js (excerpt)

```
else
{
  setTimeout(SoccerBall.animate, 1000 / SoccerBall.frameRate)
}
```

Notice that the delay for the `setTimeout` is specified as 1000 milliseconds (one second) divided by the specified frame rate. This calculation transforms the frame rate into the millisecond format that's required for the delay.

The last thing we need to do for each frame is apply the newly calculated position to the `style.left` property of the soccer ball. This step causes the browser to display the update:

path-based_motion.js (excerpt)

```
SoccerBall.div.style.left = Math.round(SoccerBall.x) + "px";
```

That statement converts `SoccerBall.x` to an integer using `Math.round`, which rounds any number up or down to the nearest integer. We need to do this because `SoccerBall.x` might be a floating point number, and CSS pixel values can't be decimals.

The last two statements (the `setTimeout` and the `style` change) would normally be written in the reverse of the order shown here, but the `setTimeout` is placed inside the `else` statement for code efficiency. If we were to place it after the `style` assignment, `setTimeout` would require an additional conditional check. By doing it this way, we can avoid adversely affecting the performance of our script.

Once we assemble both the `init` and `animate` functions inside the one object, which we initialize using `Core.start`, we have our finished program. We're all set to roll that soccer ball over a lush, green field:

path-based_motion.js

```
var SoccerBall =
{
  init: function()
  {
    SoccerBall.frameRate = 25;
    SoccerBall.duration = 2;
    SoccerBall.div = document.getElementById("soccerBall");
    SoccerBall.targetX = 600;
    SoccerBall.originX = parseInt(
        Core.getComputedStyle(SoccerBall.div, "left"), 10);
    SoccerBall.increment =
        (SoccerBall.targetX - SoccerBall.originX) /
        (SoccerBall.duration * SoccerBall.frameRate);
    SoccerBall.x = SoccerBall.originX;
```

```
      SoccerBall.animate();
    },

  animate: function()
  {
    SoccerBall.x += SoccerBall.increment;

    if ((SoccerBall.targetX > SoccerBall.originX &&
        SoccerBall.x >= SoccerBall.targetX) ||
        (SoccerBall.targetX < SoccerBall.originX &&
        SoccerBall.x <= SoccerBall.targetX))
    {
      SoccerBall.x = SoccerBall.targetX;
    }
    else
    {
      setTimeout(SoccerBall.animate, 1000 / SoccerBall.frameRate)
    }

    SoccerBall.div.style.left = Math.round(SoccerBall.x) + "px";
  }
};

Core.start(SoccerBall);
```

Animating in Two Dimensions

The example above only animated the soccer ball horizontally, but it's quite easy
to modify our program to deal with vertical movement as well:

path-based_motion2.js

```
var SoccerBall =
{
  init: function()
  {
    SoccerBall.frameRate = 25;
    SoccerBall.duration = 2;
    SoccerBall.div = document.getElementById("soccerBall");
    SoccerBall.targetX = 600;
    SoccerBall.targetY = 150;
    SoccerBall.originX = parseInt(
```

```
            Core.getComputedStyle(SoccerBall.div, "left"), 10);
        SoccerBall.originY = parseInt(
            Core.getComputedStyle(SoccerBall.div, "top"), 10);
        SoccerBall.incrementX =
            (SoccerBall.targetX - SoccerBall.originX) /
            (SoccerBall.duration * SoccerBall.frameRate);
        SoccerBall.incrementY =
            (SoccerBall.targetY - SoccerBall.originY) /
            (SoccerBall.duration * SoccerBall.frameRate);
        SoccerBall.x = SoccerBall.originX;
        SoccerBall.y = SoccerBall.originY;

        SoccerBall.animate();
    },
    animate: function()
    {
        SoccerBall.x += SoccerBall.incrementX;
        SoccerBall.y += SoccerBall.incrementY;

        if ((SoccerBall.targetX > SoccerBall.originX &&
            SoccerBall.x >= SoccerBall.targetX) ||
            (SoccerBall.targetX < SoccerBall.originX &&
            SoccerBall.x <= SoccerBall.targetX))
        {
            SoccerBall.x = SoccerBall.targetX;
            SoccerBall.y = SoccerBall.targetY;
        }
        else
        {
            setTimeout(SoccerBall.animate, 1000 / SoccerBall.frameRate)
        }

        SoccerBall.div.style.left = Math.round(SoccerBall.x) + "px";
        SoccerBall.div.style.top = Math.round(SoccerBall.y) + "px";
    }
};

Core.start(SoccerBall);
```

For every instance in which we performed a calculation with the *x* coordinate, we add an equivalent statement for the *y* coordinate. So, `SoccerBall.init` ends up with a vertical end-point in `SoccerBall.targetY`, a vertical origin in

`SoccerBall.originY`, and a vertical position tracker in `SoccerBall.y`. These variables are used by `SoccerBall.animate` to increment the vertical position and write it to the `style.top` property.

The only other change we need to make is a small tweak to the starting position of the ball:

path-based_motion2.css *(excerpt)*

```
#soccerBall {
  ⋮
  top: 0;
  ⋮
}
```

Once that's done, we've got a ball that moves in both dimensions, as Figure 5.12 illustrates.

Figure 5.12. Adding vertical movement to the animation

Creating Realistic Movement

The animation that we've created so far treats the movement of the soccer ball homogeneously—each frame moves the ball by the same amount, and the ball stops without any deceleration. But this isn't how objects move in the real world: they speed up, they slow down, they bounce. It's possible for us to mimic this type of behavior by using different algorithms to calculate the movement of our soccer ball.

If we wanted to get our soccer ball to slow to a halt, there are just a few minor tweaks we'd have to make to our program:

path-based_motion3.js

```
var SoccerBall =
{
  init: function()
  {
    SoccerBall.frameRate = 25;
    SoccerBall.deceleration = 10;
    SoccerBall.div = document.getElementById("soccerBall");
    SoccerBall.targetX = 600;
    SoccerBall.targetY = 150;
    SoccerBall.originX = parseInt(
        Core.getComputedStyle(SoccerBall.div, "left"), 10);
    SoccerBall.originY = parseInt(
        Core.getComputedStyle(SoccerBall.div, "top"), 10);
    SoccerBall.x = SoccerBall.originX;
    SoccerBall.y = SoccerBall.originY;

    SoccerBall.animate();
  },

  animate: function()
  {
    SoccerBall.x += (SoccerBall.targetX - SoccerBall.x) /
        SoccerBall.deceleration;
    SoccerBall.y += (SoccerBall.targetY - SoccerBall.y) /
        SoccerBall.deceleration;

    if ((SoccerBall.targetX > SoccerBall.originX &&
        Math.round(SoccerBall.x) >= SoccerBall.targetX) ||
        (SoccerBall.targetX < SoccerBall.originX &&
        Math.round(SoccerBall.x) <= SoccerBall.targetX))
    {
      SoccerBall.x = SoccerBall.targetX;
      SoccerBall.y = SoccerBall.targetY;
    }
    else
    {
```

```
      setTimeout(SoccerBall.animate, 1000 / SoccerBall.frameRate)
    }

    SoccerBall.div.style.left = Math.round(SoccerBall.x) + "px";
    SoccerBall.div.style.top = Math.round(SoccerBall.y) + "px";
  }
};

Core.start(SoccerBall);
```

In this code, we've replaced `SoccerBall.duration` with
`SoccerBall.deceleration`—a deceleration factor that's applied to our new position
calculation inside `animate`. This time, instead of dividing the total distance into
neat little increments, the position calculator takes the distance *remaining* to the
end-point, and divides it by the deceleration factor. In this way, the steps start out
being big, but as the ball moves closer to its goal, the steps become smaller and
smaller. The ball travels a smaller distance between frames, creating the sense that
it's slowing down, or decelerating.

One pitfall that you need to watch out for when you're using an equation like this
is that, if left to its own devices, `SoccerBall.x` will never reach the end point. The
animation function will continually divide the remaining distance into smaller and
smaller steps, producing an infinite loop. To counteract this (and stop the animation
from going forever), we round `SoccerBall.x` to the nearest integer, using `Math.round`,
before checking whether it has reached the end point. As soon as `SoccerBall.x` is
within 0.5 pixels of the end point—which is close enough for the ball to reach its
goal when its position is expressed in pixels—the rounding will cause the animation
to end.

Using this deceleration algorithm, the movement of the ball looks more like that
depicted in Figure 5.13.

Figure 5.13. Modeling realistic deceleration by changing the algorithm that moves the soccer ball

If you want the ball to move more slowly—gliding more smoothly to its final position—increase the deceleration factor. If you want the ball to reach its destination more quickly—coming to a more sudden stop—decrease the deceleration factor. Setting the factor to 1 causes the ball to jump directly to its destination.

Faster!

If you wanted to accelerate the soccer ball—make it start off slow and get faster—then you'd have to reverse the algorithm we used for deceleration:

```
                                              path-based_motion4.js (excerpt)

var SoccerBall =
{
  init: function()
  {

    SoccerBall.frameRate = 25;
    SoccerBall.acceleration = 2;
    SoccerBall.threshold = 0.5;
    SoccerBall.div = document.getElementById("soccerBall");
    SoccerBall.targetX = 600;
    SoccerBall.targetY = 150;
    SoccerBall.originX = parseInt(
        Core.getComputedStyle(SoccerBall.div, "left"));
```

```
    SoccerBall.originY = parseInt(
        Core.getComputedStyle(SoccerBall.div, "top"));

    if (SoccerBall.targetX < SoccerBall.originX)
    {
      SoccerBall.x = SoccerBall.originX - SoccerBall.threshold;
    }
    else
    {
      SoccerBall.x = SoccerBall.originX + SoccerBall.threshold;
    }

    SoccerBall.distanceY = SoccerBall.targetY - SoccerBall.originY;

    SoccerBall.animate();
  },

  animate: function()
  {
    SoccerBall.x += (SoccerBall.x - SoccerBall.originX) /
        SoccerBall.acceleration;
    var movementRatio = (SoccerBall.x - SoccerBall.originX) /
        (SoccerBall.targetX - SoccerBall.originX);
    var y = SoccerBall.originY + SoccerBall.distanceY *
        movementRatio;

    if ((SoccerBall.targetX > SoccerBall.originX &&
        SoccerBall.x >= SoccerBall.targetX) ||
        (SoccerBall.targetX < SoccerBall.originX &&
        SoccerBall.x <= SoccerBall.targetX))
    {
      SoccerBall.x = SoccerBall.targetX;
      y = SoccerBall.targetY;
    }
    else
    {
      setTimeout(SoccerBall.animate, 1000 / SoccerBall.frameRate)
    }

    SoccerBall.div.style.left = Math.round(SoccerBall.x) + "px";
    SoccerBall.div.style.top = Math.round(y) + "px";
  }
```

```
};

Core.start(SoccerBall);
```

Here, the `SoccerBall.deceleration` variable has been replaced by `SoccerBall.acceleration`, and the value has been lowered to give us a quicker start. The algorithm that calculates the increments now uses the distance to the start point to determine them, so as the ball gets further from the start point the increments get bigger, making the ball move faster.

As this algorithm uses `SoccerBall.x` − `SoccerBall.originX` as the basis for its calculations, we need `SoccerBall.x` to initially be offset slightly from `SoccerBall.originX`, otherwise the ball would never move. `SoccerBall.x` must be offset in the direction of the destination point, so during initialization we check the direction in which the destination lies from the origin, and add or subtract a small value—`SoccerBall.threshold`—as appropriate. For a more accurate model, you could reduce `SoccerBall.threshold` below `0.5`, but you won't see much difference.

The other difference between this algorithm and the decelerating one is the way in which the vertical positions are calculated. Since we use a fixed value for acceleration, if it was calculated separately, the acceleration in either dimension would be the same—the y position would increase in speed at the same rate as the x position. If your y destination coordinate is closer than your x destination coordinate, the soccer ball would reach its final y position faster than it reached its final x position, producing some strange (non-linear) movement.

In order to prevent this eventuality, we calculate the y position of the soccer ball based on the value of its x position. After the new x position has been calculated, the ratio between the distance traveled and the total distance is calculated and placed in the variable `movementRatio`. This figure is multiplied by the total vertical distance between the origin and the target, and gives us an accurate y position for the soccer ball, producing movement in a straight line.

As the y position is calculated in terms of the x position, we no longer need `SoccerBall.y`, so this property has been removed from the object. Instead, we just calculate a normal *y* variable inside the `animate` function. As a quick reference for the vertical distance, `SoccerBall.distanceY` is calculated upon initialization.

Moving Ahead

You can give countless different types of movements to an object. Deceleration and acceleration are just two of the more simple options; there's also bouncing, circular movements, elastic movements—the list goes on. If you'd like to learn the mathematics behind other types of object movement, I highly recommend visiting Robert Penner's site.[2] He created the movement calculations for the Flash environment, so I'm pretty sure he knows his stuff.

Revisiting the Accordion Control

Well, you learned to make an accordion control in Chapter 4, and I'm sure you were clicking around it, collapsing and expanding the different sections, but thinking, "This isn't quite there; it needs some more … snap!" Well, it's now time to make it snap, move, and jiggle. Because we're going to add some animation to that accordion. After all, what's an accordion without moving parts, and a little monkey in a fez?

This upgrade will take a little more effort than the modifications we made to our Rich Tooltips script, but the effect is well worth it—we'll wind up with an animated accordion that gives the user a much better sense of what's going on, and looks very, *very* slick.

Making the Accordion Look Like it's Animated

Before we dive into the updated code, let's take a look at *how* we're going to animate the accordion. To produce the effect of the content items collapsing and expanding, we have to modify the height of an element that contains all of that content. In this case, the list items in the menu are the most likely candidates.

Normally, if no height is specified for a block-level element, it will expand to show all of the content that it contains. But if you *do* specify a height for a block-level element, it will always appear at that specified height, and any content that doesn't fit inside the container will spill out, or **overflow**, as shown in Figure 5.14.

---

[2] http://www.robertpenner.com/easing/

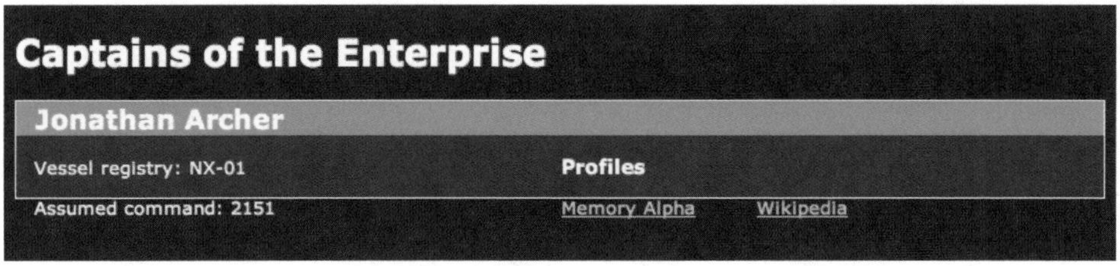

Figure 5.14. Content overflowing the bounds of a block-level element for which height is specified

Now, we don't want the content to overflow when we're animating our accordion; we want the parent element to hide any content that would ordinarily overflow. The way to do this is to adjust the CSS on the parent container, and specify the property `overflow: hidden`. When this is done, and a height (or a width) is specified, any overflowing content will be hidden from view, as illustrated in Figure 5.15.

Figure 5.15. Specifying `overflow: hidden` on the block-level element causing content that doesn't fit inside it to be hidden

Once we've made sure that the overflowing content is being hidden correctly, we can start to animate the container. To do this, we'll gradually change its height to make it look like it's expanding or collapsing.

Changing the Code

Now that you've got the general idea of how we're going to animate our accordion, our first stop is the initialization method:

accordion_animated.js *(excerpt)*

```
init: function()
{
  Accordion.frameRate = 25;
  Accordion.duration = 0.5;
```

```
var accordions = Core.getElementsByClass("accordion");

for (var i = 0; i < accordions.length; i++)
{
  var folds = accordions[i].childNodes;
  for (var j = 0; j < folds.length; j++)
  {
    if (folds[j].nodeType == 1)
    {
      var accordionContent = document.createElement("div"); ❶
      accordionContent.className = "accordionContent";

      for (var k = 0; k < folds[j].childNodes.length; k++) ❷
      {
        if (folds[j].childNodes[k].nodeName.toLowerCase() !=
            "h2") ❸
        {
          accordionContent.appendChild(folds[j].childNodes[k]); ❹
          k--; ❺
        }
      }

      folds[j].appendChild(accordionContent); ❻
      folds[j]._accordionContent = accordionContent; ❼

      Accordion.collapse(folds[j]);
      var foldLinks = folds[j].getElementsByTagName("a");
      var foldTitleLink = foldLinks[0];
      Core.addEventListener(foldTitleLink, "click",
          Accordion.clickListener);

      for (var k = 1; k < foldLinks.length; k++)
      {
        Core.addEventListener(foldLinks[k], "focus",
            Accordion.focusListener);
      }
    }
  }

  if (location.hash.length > 1)
  {
    var activeFold =
        document.getElementById(location.hash.substring(1));
    if (activeFold && activeFold.parentNode == accordions[i])
```

```
      {
        Accordion.expand(activeFold);
      }
    }
  }
}
```

In this code, we've added two familiar animation constants, as well as a whole new block of code that modifies the HTML of the menu. Why?

One point you should note about using the `overflow: hidden` CSS property is that it can produce some weird visual effects in Internet Explorer 6. Given the way we've set up the accordion headings, if we applied `overflow: hidden` to those list items, they'd look completely warped in IE. To circumvent this pitfall, we separate the heading (the part that the user clicks on) from the rest of the content in a given fold of the accordion by putting that content inside its own `div` element. It's also a lot easier to deal with the animation if we can collapse the container to zero height, rather than having to worry about leaving enough height for the heading.

But that's no reason to go in and modify your HTML by hand! We can easily make these changes with JavaScript, as the code above shows:

❶ Inside `init`, we create a new `div` and assign it a `class` of `accordionContent`.

❷ Next, we have to move the current contents of the list item into this new container. We do so using a `for` loop that iterates through each of the list item's `childNodes`.

❸ We don't want to move the `h2` into that new container, because that's the clickable part of the accordion, so we do a check for that, skip it, and include everything else.

❹ You can move an element from one parent to another simply by appending the element to the new parent. The DOM will automatically complete the process of removing and adding the element in the position you're identified.

❺ One trick with that `for` loop is that it decrements the counter every time a child element is moved. The reason for this is that the counter automatically *incre-*

ments every time the loop executes, but if we remove an element from
`childNodes`, its next sibling moves down to take its index, so if we actually
incremented the index, we'd start to skip elements. Decrementing cancels out
this effect.

6 Once all the existing content has been moved into the new container, we're
able to append that container into the list item, completing our modification
of the DOM. Now our list item contains only two elements—the title and the
content—and no one's the wiser!

7 Finally, as a shortcut for later, we store a reference to the `accordionContent`
element as a property of the list item: `_accordionContent`.

Another advantage of adding the `accordionContent` `div` is that it simplifies the
CSS. For example, the CSS code that hides the contents of collapsed folds can be
distilled down to this:

accordion_animated.css (excerpt)

```css
.accordionContent {
  overflow: hidden;
  ⋮
}

li.collapsed .accordionContent {
  position: absolute;
  left: -9999px;
}

/* Fixes Safari bug that prevents expanded content from displaying.
   See http://betech.virginia.edu/bugs/safari-stickyposition.html */
li.collapsed .accordionContent p {
  position: relative;
}
```

Thanks to this code, `overflow: hidden` will always be specified on elements with
the `class` `accordionContent`, enabling us to animate them properly.

In the original script, our expand function changed some classes to make the selected accordion item pop open, but in *animating* the accordion, we need to use expand to do a little setup first:

```
                                              accordion_animated.js (excerpt)
expand: function(fold)
{
  var content = fold._accordionContent; ❶

  Accordion.collapseAll(fold.parentNode);
  if (!Core.hasClass(fold, "expanded")) ❷
  {
    content.style.height = "0"; ❸
    content._height = 0; ❹
    Core.removeClass(fold, "collapsed");
    Core.addClass(fold, "expanded");
    content._increment = content.scrollHeight /
        (Accordion.frameRate * Accordion.duration); ❺
    Accordion.expandAnimate(content); ❻
  }
},
```

❶   The content variable is just a shortcut to the fold._accordionContent property we created earlier—it saves plenty of typing. The collapseAll method is then called to reset the accordion menu items, and we can focus our attention on the currently selected content.

❷   Although previously it didn't matter if expand was called on an already-expanded fold (for example, in response to the keyboard focus moving from link to link within an expanded fold), we've changed this method so that it kicks off an animation. As such, we need this if statement to avoid animating already-expanded folds.

❸   Before we change its classes to make it visible, we set content's style.height to 0. This step ensures that when the class change switches the content from collapsed to expanded, it will remain invisible, because it will have no height.

❹   To keep track of the actual calculated height of the content, we create the variable _height as a property of content. As in the previous animation examples, this property allows us to keep an accurate calculation of the accordion's movement. Once the height has been reset, we can remove the "collapsed" class and add the "expanded" class.

⑤ We're almost ready to perform the animation, but before we do that, we need to check the height to which we're going to expand the accordion item. As we'll be increasing the height of the item from zero, we have to know when all the content is displayed, so we can work out when to stop. The `scrollHeight` property lets us do this—it calculates the height of the content irrespective of whether we cut it off with an explicit height and `overflow: hidden`.

We can save a bit of repetitive calculation within the animating function by calculating in advance the movement increment that we'll apply in each step of the animation. This is determined by dividing the total height of the content (`content.scrollHeight`) by the total number of frames (`Accordion.frameRate * Accordion.duration`). The result of this calculation is assigned to the `_increment` property of `content`.

⑥ After all that setup, we can call `expandAnimate`, our new method that's designed to animate the expansion of an accordion item.

Let's take a look at that animation method:

accordion_animated.js (excerpt)

```
expandAnimate: function(content)
{
  var newHeight = content._height + content._increment; ❶

  if (newHeight > content.scrollHeight) ❷
  {
    newHeight = content.scrollHeight; ❸
  }
  else
  {
    content._timer = setTimeout(function() ❹
        {
          Accordion.expandAnimate(content);
        }, 1000 / Accordion.frameRate);
  }
```

```
    content._height = newHeight; ❺
    content.style.height = Math.round(newHeight) + "px";
    content.scrollTop = 0; ❻
},
```

❶ expandAnimate starts off by calculating the new height of the content:
    content._height + content._increment.

❷ This newHeight variable is used inside a conditional test to detect whether the
    animation should finish.

❸ If newHeight is larger than content.scrollHeight, we change newHeight to
    equal the height of the content, and we don't schedule any more animation
    cycles.

❹ But if newHeight is less than the content's height, we schedule another
    setTimeout call to the same function. This step produces the iterative animation
    we're looking for. The setTimeout ID is assigned to the _timer property of the
    content element, so that if another accordion item is clicked mid-animation,
    we can stop the expansion animation from continuing.

❺ After we've figured out what the new height of the content should be, we use
    that new height to update the element's _height property, then change its ap-
    pearance using a rounded value for style.height. One frame of the animation
    is now complete.

❻ In certain browsers, if keyboard focus moves to a hyperlink inside a collapsed
    fold of the accordion, the browser will make a misguided attempt to scroll that
    collapsed content in order to make the link visible. If left this way, the content,
    once expanded, will not display properly. Thankfully, the fix is easy—after
    each frame of the animation, we reset the content's scrollTop property to
    zero, which resets its vertical scrolling position.

With those two methods, you can see how animation works—the event listener is
fired only once, and sets up the initial values for the animation. Then the iterative
function is called via setTimeout to produce the visual changes needed to get to
the final state.

Collapsing an item works in much the same fashion:

accordion_animated.js *(excerpt)*

```
collapse: function(fold)
{
  var content = fold._accordionContent;
  content._height = parseInt(content.style.height, 10);
  content._increment = content._height /
      (Accordion.frameRate * Accordion.duration);

  if (Core.hasClass(fold, "expanded"))
  {
    clearTimeout(fold._accordionContent._timer);
    Accordion.collapseAnimate(fold._accordionContent);
  }
  else
  {
    Core.addClass(fold, "collapsed");
  }
},
```

For the `collapse` method, we have to move the class changes into the animation method because we need the item to remain expanded until the animation has finished (otherwise it will disappear immediately, before the animation has had a chance to take place). To kick off the animation, we check whether the current item has the class `expanded`, and if it does, we send the browser off to execute `collapseAnimate`, but not before we cancel any expansion animation that's currently taking place. If we didn't cancel the expansion first, the collapsing animation might coincide with an expansion animation that was already in progress, in which case we'd end up with a stuck accordion (never a pretty sight—or sound).

If an element doesn't have the `expanded` class on it when a collapse is initiated, we simply add the `collapsed` class and forego the animation. This takes care of the circumstance in which the page first loads and we need to hide all the menu items.

collapseAnimate is a lot like expandAnimate, but in reverse:

accordion_animated.js (excerpt)

```
collapseAnimate: function(content)
{
  var newHeight = content._height - content._increment; ❶

  if (newHeight < 0)
  {
    newHeight = 0;
    Core.removeClass(content.parentNode, "expanded"); ❷
    Core.addClass(content.parentNode, "collapsed");
  }
  else
  {
    content._timer = setTimeout(function()
        {
            Accordion.collapseAnimate(content);
        }, 1000 / Accordion.frameRate);
  }

  content._height = newHeight;
  content.style.height = Math.round(newHeight) + "px";
}
```

❶ We're aiming to get the height of the content element to 0, so instead of adding the increment, we subtract it.

❷ The if-else statement that's used when we reach our target height is slightly different than the one we saw above, because we have to change the classes on the current item. Otherwise, it's identical to expandAnimate.

With animation occurring in both directions, we now have a fully functioning animated accordion. Of course, you'll get the best view of its effect if you check out the demo in the example files, but Figure 5.16 shows what happens when you click to open a new accordion item.

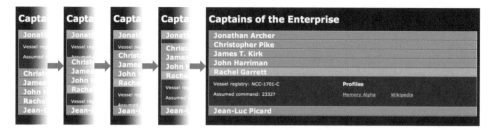

Figure 5.16. The progression of our animated accordion as one item collapses and another expands

Exploring Libraries

Quite a few of the main JavaScript libraries don't tackle animation; instead, they focus on core tasks like DOM manipulation and styling. However, around these have sprung up a number of little libraries devoted to animation tasks, and they do the job quite well.

The animation libraries are a lot more generalized than the scripts we've written here, so it's possible to use them to apply a range of effects to almost any element, depending on how adventurous you're feeling.

script.aculo.us

script.aculo.us is probably the most well-known effects library available. It's actually an add-on to Prototype, which it uses for its DOM access and architecture capabilities, so if you want to run script.aculo.us, you'll also need to include Prototype.

script.aculo.us comes with a host of effects that have become popular in the so-called Web 2.0 age: fading, highlighting, shrinking, and many other transitions. It has also more recently included larger pieces of functionality such as drag-and-drop and slider widgets. Here, we'll focus on the effects.

All of the effects in script.aculo.us are available through the **Effect** object, which will be available in your programs if you include the **scriptaculous.js** file on your page.

Let's imagine that we have a paragraph of text that we want to highlight:

scriptaculous_highlight.html (excerpt)

```
<p id="introduction">
  Industrial Light &amp; Magic (ILM) is a motion picture visual
  effects company, founded in May 1975 by George Lucas and owned
  by Lucasfilm Ltd. Lucas created the company when he discovered
  that the special effects department at Twentieth Century Fox was
  shut down after he was given the green light for his production
  of Star Wars.
</p>
```

We can do so by passing the ID string to `Effect.Highlight`:

```
new Effect.Highlight("introduction");
```

As soon as you make this call, the effect will be applied to the element, as shown in Figure 5.17.

Figure 5.17. Creating a yellow fade effect with script.aculo.us

`Effect.Highlight` also allows you to pass it a DOM node reference, so you could apply the effect to the paragraph like this:

```
new Effect.Highlight(document.getElementsByTagName("p")[0]);
```

Most of the effects in script.aculo.us have optional parameters that allow you to customize various aspects of the effect. These parameters are specified as properties inside an object literal, which itself is passed as an argument to the effect.

For instance, by default, `Effect.Highlight` fades the background from yellow to white, but it's possible to specify the start color and the end color, so we could make a particularly lurid fade from red to blue like this:

```
new Effect.Highlight("introduction",
    {startcolor: "#FF0000", endcolor: "#0000FF"});
```

These optional parameters will differ from effect to effect, so you'll have to read through the script.aculo.us documentation if you wish to customize a particular effect.

Most of the effects have a duration parameter, which lets you specify how quickly you want the effect to occur. This parameter is specified in seconds, so if you wanted a two-second, lurid red-blue fade, you'd include all these parameters:

scriptaculous_highlight.js *(excerpt)*

```
new Effect.Highlight("introduction",
    {startcolor: "#FF0000", endcolor: "#0000FF",
    duration: 2});
```

script.aculo.us also has a nice little event model that allows you to trigger functions while effects are happening, or after they have finished. These events are again specified as parameters in the object literal, and take a function name as a value. That function will be called when the event is fired:

```
function effectFinished()
{
  alert("The introduction has been effected");
}

new Effect.Highlight("introduction",
    {afterFinish: effectFinished});
```

That code pops up an alert dialog once the fade has finished, to tell us it's done.

script.aculo.us is certainly a powerful and flexible effects library. Its popularity has largely been fueled by its ease of integration and execution. In case these benefits weren't already apparent, I'll leave you with this nugget: using script.aculo.us, we could have animated our soccer ball with just one line of code:

```
new Effect.MoveBy("soccerBall", 150, 600);
```

But that wouldn't have been half as much fun, would it?

Summary

HTML was designed to be a static medium, but using JavaScript, we can bring it to life.

There's no doubt that animation can add a lot of polish to an interface—it doesn't have to be mere eye candy! Animation provides real benefits in guiding users around and providing them with visual cues as to functionality and state. I'm sure quite a few useful ideas have sprung into your mind while you've been reading. This chapter has given you a taste of what you can do with time-based processing, but there's so much more to explore once you've learned the basics.

Next up, we'll delve deeper into a subject that's central to the development of web applications: forms.

Chapter **6**

Form Enhancements

HTML hasn't changed much in the past ten years. Since browsers implemented the changes in HTML 4 around 1997, the collection of tags and attributes that we use on the web has essentially stayed the same. Thanks to ongoing improvements to CSS support in browsers, we have been able to create richer, more intricate designs with that limited markup. Like the designer fashions that are paraded down the runway each season, the styles are always fresh and new, even if the models underneath look eerily alike.

But there is one aspect of web design for which CSS can't hide the stagnation of HTML: forms. No matter how we dress them up, HTML has for the past decade supported only this limited set of form controls:

- text input fields
- checkboxes
- radio buttons
- drop-down menus and lists
- multi-line text areas
- buttons

Since this selection is so limited, forms were one of the first parts of HTML to receive the attention of developers experimenting with JavaScript enhancements.

In this chapter, we'll build a number of useful, reusable form enhancements of our own. This will give you an opportunity to apply many of the skills you've gathered in the book so far, and to learn a new trick or two.

HTML DOM Extensions

Form controls aren't your everyday HTML elements. They offer built-in behavior and interactivity far beyond that which can be described with events like `click`, `mouseover`, `mouseout`, `focus`, and `blur`, and properties like `id`, and `className`.

Consequently, in addition to the standard DOM properties, methods, and events that we've already played with in this book, form-related elements support a bunch of extra properties and methods that are defined in a separate section of the DOM standard.[1] The most useful of these properties and methods are listed in Table 6.2 and Table 6.1, respectively. Form controls also support a handful of extra events, which are listed in Table 6.3.

Table 6.1. Additional DOM Methods for HTML Form Controls

Method	Element(s)	Description
blur	input select textarea	removes keyboard focus from this form control
click	input	simulates a mouse click on this control
focus	input select textarea	gives keyboard focus to this form control
reset	form	restores all of this form's controls to their default values
select	input textarea	selects the text contents of this control
submit	form	submits the form without triggering a `submit` event

---

[1] http://www.w3.org/TR/DOM-Level-2-HTML/

In the next two examples, we'll play with some—but not all—of these form-specific DOM features. Once you've got a feel for the extra functionality that JavaScript can provide, come back to these tables and think about *other* ways you can use these tools to enhance your forms.

Table 6.2. Additional DOM Properties for HTML Form Controls

Property	Element(s)	Description
elements	form	a node list containing all of the form controls in the form
checked	input	for inputs of type checkbox and radio, this property's value is true if the control is selected
disabled	button input optgroup option select textarea	when true, the control is unavailable to the user
form	button input option select textarea	a reference to the form element that contains this control
index	option	the index of this option within the select element that contains it (0 for the first)
options	select	a node list containing all of the option elements in this menu
selected	option	true if this option is currently selected, false if not
selectedIndex	select	the index of the currently-selected option in the list (0 for the first)
value	button input option select textarea	the current value of this control, as it would be submitted to the server

Table 6.3. Additional DOM Events for HTML Form Controls

Event	Element(s)	Triggered when...
change	input select textarea	the control has lost focus after its value has been changed
select	input textarea	the user has selected some text in the field
submit	form	the user has requested that the form be submitted

Example: Dependent Fields

You don't always need your users to fill in every field in a form. Sometimes, the value a user enters into *one* form field renders *another* field irrelevant. Instead of relying on the user to figure out which fields are relevant, why not use the `disabled` property mentioned in Table 6.2 to disable the fields that the user can safely ignore?

In Figure 6.1, the checkbox following the second radio button is only relevant if that radio button is selected. We can use JavaScript to disable it in all other cases.

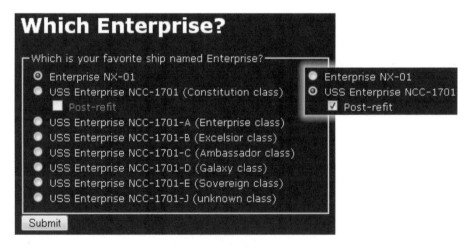

Figure 6.1. The checkbox is relevant only if the user selects the second radio button

The best way to implement dependent fields will depend (so to speak) on the specific logic of your form, but for the purposes of this example we can take an approach that's general enough to make the script useful in many situations. To this end, we'll make the following assumptions:

- Each form will have only one level of dependency (a dependent field cannot be dependent on another dependent field).

- Dependent fields can only be `input` elements of `type text`, `password`, `checkbox`, or `radio`.

- Dependent fields can only depend on `input` elements of these types.

- Dependent fields will immediately follow the fields on which they depend in the document.

- Dependent fields will be contained within `label` elements.

Here's how we'll mark up a form field (in this case, a radio button), and another field (a checkbox) that's dependent on it:

dependentfields.html *(excerpt)*

```
<div>
  <label for="ncc1701">
    <input type="radio" name="whichenterprise"
        value="ncc1701" id="ncc1701" />
    USS Enterprise NCC-1701 (Constitution class)
  </label>
  <label for="ncc1701refit" class="secondary">
    <input type="checkbox" class="dependent"
        name="ncc1701refit" id="ncc1701refit"
        value="ncc1701refit" />
    Post-refit
  </label>
</div>
```

Note that the checkbox has a `class` of `dependent`—that's how we indicate that the checkbox is dependent on the field that precedes it. If the radio button had more than one dependent field, each one would have a `class` of `dependent`.

When this markup is given to a browser in which JavaScript is disabled, the form's dependent fields will simply remain enabled at all times.

We'll put our script in an object called `DependentFields`:

```
                                        dependentfields.js (excerpt)
var DependentFields =
{
  init: function()
  {
    ⋮
  },
  ⋮
};

Core.init(DependentFields);
```

Let's start our script by writing the workhorse functions, which will actually enable and disable form fields as needed:

```
                                        dependentfields.js (excerpt)
disable: function(field)
{
  field.disabled = true;
  Core.addClass(field, "disabled");
  Core.addClass(field.parentNode, "disabled");
},

enable: function(field)
{
  field.disabled = false;
  Core.removeClass(field, "disabled");
  Core.removeClass(field.parentNode, "disabled");
},
```

That's simple enough, right? Both functions start by setting the field's `disabled` property. The first function then applies the `disabled` class on both the field itself and the element that contains it (the field's `label`); the second function removes this class from the field and its containing element. We'll use the `disabled` class to style disabled fields (and their labels):

```
                                        dependentfields.css (excerpt)
label.disabled {
  color: #A0A0A0;
}
```

If you prefer, you can actually use a technique like offleft positioning (which I described in Chapter 4) to hide disabled fields entirely!

Now, we can approach the code in a number of ways that will actually call the `disable` and `enable` methods we've just seen. The most obvious approach would be to add event listeners to each `input` element that had one or more dependent fields, and have those listeners enable or disable the relevant dependent fields.

Having attempted this, I can tell you now that this approach, though obvious, is problematic. For example, a radio button won't always produce a useful event when it's deselected. Sometimes, the only hint that JavaScript gets that a radio button has been deselected is a `click` event from the radio button next to it.

Another option is to add a couple of event listeners to each form on the page. These event listeners will watch for `click` and `change` events bubbling up from *any* of the fields in the form, and update the state of all the dependent fields in that form after every such event:

```
                                         dependentfields.js (excerpt)
init: function()
{
  var forms = document.getElementsByTagName("form");

  for (var i = 0; i < forms.length; i++)
  {
    Core.addEventListener(
        forms[i], "change", DependentFields.changeListener);
    Core.addEventListener(
        forms[i], "click", DependentFields.clickListener);
```

To make the jobs of these listeners easier (after all, they'll be running quite often), the `init` method will also scan each form to build a list of the dependent fields it contains, and to store for each one a reference to the field upon which it depends:

dependentfields.js *(excerpt)*

```
var fields = forms[i].getElementsByTagName("input"); ❶
var lastIndependentField = null;
forms[i]._dependents = []; ❷
for (var j = 0; j < fields.length; j++)
{
  if (!Core.hasClass(fields[j], "dependent")) ❸
  {
    lastIndependentField = fields[j]; ❹
  }
  else
  {
    if (lastIndependentField) ❺
    {
      forms[i]._dependents[forms[i]._dependents.length] =
          fields[j]; ❻
      fields[j]._master = lastIndependentField; ❼
    }
  }
}
```

This code may seem a little convoluted at first glance, so let me break it down for you:

❶ We get a list of all the `input` elements in the form.

❷ We create for the form a custom property named `_dependents`, in which we'll store a list of all the dependent fields in the form. To start with, however, we initialize it with an empty array.

❸ For each field in the form, we perform a check to see if it's a dependent field or not.

❹ If it's an independent field, we store a reference to it in a variable called `lastIndependentField`.

⑤ If it's a dependent field, we double-check that we've already got a reference to the field on which it will depend.

⑥ We then add to the form's _dependents array a reference to this dependent field.

⑦ Finally, we store in a custom property named _master a reference to the field upon which the dependent field depends.

What this code gives us is a list of all the dependent fields in each form (*form._dependents*), as well as a link from each dependent field to the field upon which it depends (*dependentField._master*).

The last thing our init method will do for each form is set the initial states of all the dependent fields. Since this is a fairly complex process, we'll write a separate method, called updateDependents, to achieve it:

dependentfields.js *(excerpt)*

```
    DependentFields.updateDependents(forms[i]);
  }
},
```

Both of our event listeners will kick off the same process of updating the dependent field states, so both listeners will call this same method:

dependentfields.js *(excerpt)*

```
changeListener: function(event)
{
  DependentFields.updateDependents(this);
},

clickListener: function(event)
{
  DependentFields.updateDependents(this);
}
```

All that's left is to write that all-important `updateDependents` method, which will either enable or disable each dependent field in a form on the basis of the state of the field on which it depends:

dependentfields.js *(excerpt)*

```
updateDependents: function(form)
{
  var dependents = form._dependents; ❶
  if (!dependents)
  {
    return;
  }

  for (var i = 0; i < dependents.length; i++) ❷
  {
    var disabled = true; ❸
    var master = dependents[i]._master; ❹

    if (master.type == "text" || master.type == "password") ❺
    {
      if (master.value.length > 0)
      {
        disabled = false;
      }
    }
    else if (master.type == "checkbox" ||
        master.type == "radio") ❻
    {
      if (master.checked)
      {
        disabled = false;
      }
    }

    if (disabled) ❼
    {
      DependentFields.disable(dependents[i]);
    }
    else
    {
      DependentFields.enable(dependents[i]);
```

```
      }
   }
},
```

Again, let's take this one step at a time:

1 We start by fetching the list of the form's dependent fields that was compiled by the `init` method.

2 We loop through this list, one dependent field at a time.

3 For each field, we start by assuming it will be disabled, then set out to determine whether that assumption is wrong.

4 To find out, we need to look at the field upon which this field depends—information that we can obtain from the `_master` property that we created in the `init` method.

5 If the master field is a `text` or `password` field, we check the `length` of its `value` property. If it's greater than zero, this dependent field should not be disabled.

6 If the master field is of `type` `checkbox` or `radio`, we look to see if it's `checked`. If it is, this dependent field should not be disabled.

7 Now that we know for sure whether this dependent field should or should not be disabled, we can call the `disable` or `enable` methods as required to set the appropriate state.

And there you have it! Our script has used a number of the HTML DOM extensions:

- We set up an event listener for the `change` event generated by some form controls.

- We used the `disabled` property, which is supported by all form controls, to disable dependent fields when appropriate.

- We used the `type`, `checked`, and `value` properties of various form controls to determine whether a field had been filled in, and thus whether we should enable its dependent fields.

Although our example only contains one dependent field, you can reuse this script on any page with any number of dependent fields, as long as the assumptions we stated at the start of this section are met. Here's the complete JavaScript code:

```javascript
var DependentFields =
{
  init: function()
  {
    var forms = document.getElementsByTagName("form");

    for (var i = 0; i < forms.length; i++)
    {
      Core.addEventListener(forms[i], "change",
          DependentFields.changeListener);
      Core.addEventListener(forms[i], "click",
          DependentFields.clickListener);

      var fields = forms[i].getElementsByTagName("input");
      var lastIndependentField = null;
      forms[i]._dependents = [];
      for (var j = 0; j < fields.length; j++)
      {
        if (!Core.hasClass(fields[j], "dependent"))
        {
          lastIndependentField = fields[j];
        }
        else
        {
          if (lastIndependentField)
          {
            forms[i]._dependents[
                forms[i]._dependents.length] = fields[j];
            fields[j]._master = lastIndependentField;
          }
        }
      }
      DependentFields.updateDependents(forms[i]);
    }
  },

  disable: function(field)
  {
```

```javascript
    field.disabled = true;
    Core.addClass(field, "disabled");
    Core.addClass(field.parentNode, "disabled");
  },

  enable: function(field)
  {
    field.disabled = false;
    Core.removeClass(field, "disabled");
    Core.removeClass(field.parentNode, "disabled");
  },

  updateDependents: function(form)
  {
    var dependents = form._dependents;
    if (!dependents)
    {
      return;
    }

    for (var i = 0; i < dependents.length; i++)
    {
      var disabled = true;
      var master = dependents[i]._master;

      if (master.type == "text" || master.type == "password")
      {
        if (master.value.length > 0)
        {
          disabled = false;
        }
      }
      else if (master.type == "checkbox" ||
          master.type == "radio")
      {
        if (master.checked)
        {
          disabled = false;
        }
      }

      if (disabled)
      {
        DependentFields.disable(dependents[i]);
```

```
      }
      else
      {
        DependentFields.enable(dependents[i]);
      }
    }
  },

  changeListener: function(event)
  {
    DependentFields.updateDependents(this);
  },

  clickListener: function(event)
  {
    DependentFields.updateDependents(this);
  }
};

Core.start(DependentFields);
```

Example: Cascading Menus

Another situation in which it can be useful to tie multiple form fields together with JavaScript arises when you have a complex `select` menu like that shown in Figure 6.2.

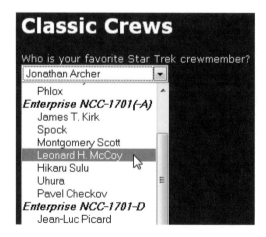

Figure 6.2. A two-level menu made up of `optgroups` and `options`

Here we have a `select` containing a number of `optgroup` elements, each of which contains a number of `option` elements. In effect, we have two levels of menus here—the user must first find the right option group, then select the desired option. Why not make it easier on the user by splitting this into two menus, as shown in Figure 6.3?

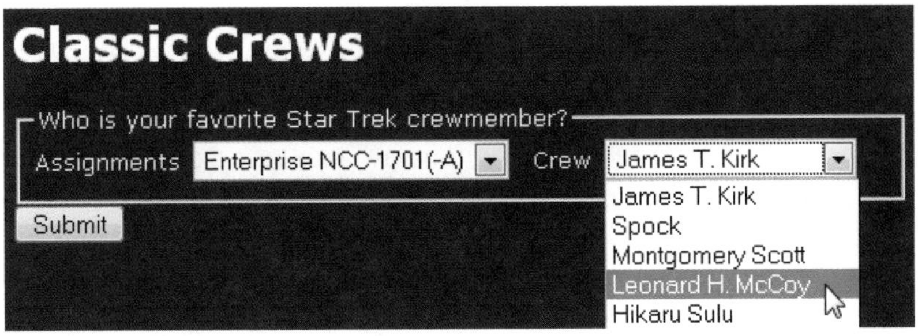

Figure 6.3. Splitting the single menu into a pair of cascading menus to improve usability

When the user selects an option from the first menu, our JavaScript code will swing into action, updating the list of options in the second menu. This saves users from having to scroll through menu choices that aren't in the group they're interested in.

Of course, our form must still work when JavaScript is disabled, so we'll write the HTML code for our form using the single `select`, then split it into the two menus during the initialization of our script. To make our script reusable, however, we need to make sure that the single menu contains all the information that's needed to produce the two cascaded menus:

cascadingmenu.html *(excerpt)*

```html
<label for="crewselect">
  Who is your favorite Star Trek crewmember?
</label>
<select id="crewselect" name="crewselect"
    class="cascading" title="Assignments">
  <optgroup title="Crew" label="Enterprise NX-01">
    <option value="1">Jonathan Archer</option>
    <option value="2">T'Pol</option>
    <option value="3">Charles Tucker III</option>
    <option value="4">Malcolm Reed</option>
    <option value="5">Hoshi Sato</option>
    <option value="6">Travis Mayweather</option>
```

```
      <option value="7">Phlox</option>
   </optgroup>
   <optgroup title="Crew" label="Enterprise NCC-1701(-A)">
      ⋮
   </optgroup>
   ⋮
</select>
```

Notice in particular the `title` attributes that are highlighted in bold. The title describes the items that are listed in each element—the `select` contains a list of assignments, and each `optgroup` contains a crew listing. As you can see in Figure 6.3, these attribute values will become the `labels` for the menus that our script will create.

This transformation from one menu into two will form the bulk of the work that the `init` method of our script will complete. As Figure 6.4 shows, we're making a fairly drastic change to the document's structure.

We can break the process into a number of steps to make it more manageable:

1. Find within the page every `select` with a `class` of `cascading`.

2. For each one, convert the single `select`'s `label` into a `fieldset` that surrounds the `select`, with the former `label`'s content contained in the `fieldset`'s `legend`.

3. Create a new "master" `select` before the existing `select`. Give it the same `title` as the existing `select`, but new `name` and `id` attributes. Fill it with `options` based on the `optgroups` of the existing `select`, then change the existing `select`'s `title` to match the `optgroups`' `titles` before removing all the contents of the existing `select`.

4. Just before each of the two `selects` that now exist, create a `label` containing the text from the `select`'s `title` attribute.

5. Fill the now-empty second `select` with the `options` that correspond to the currently-selected `option` in the new master `select`. Repeat this process whenever the selection in the master `select` changes.

We can use this breakdown as a blueprint for our script's `init` method:

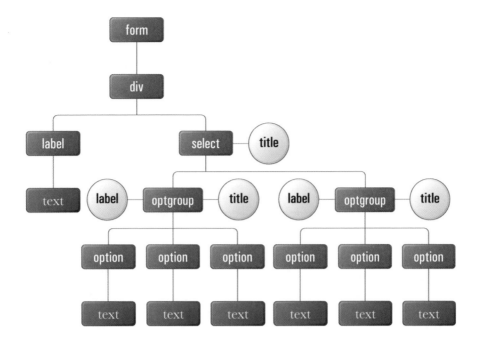

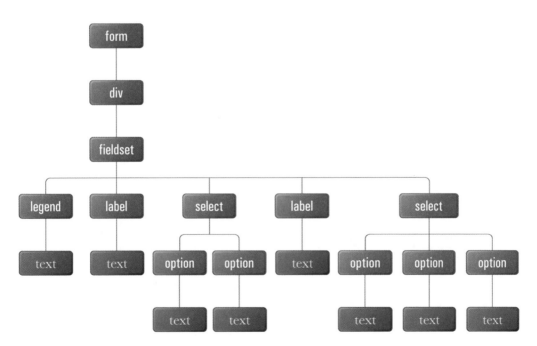

Figure 6.4. Before and after: the required alterations to the DOM structure

```
var CascadingMenu =
{
  init: function()
  {
    var menus = Core.getElementsByClass("cascading");

    for (var i = 0; i < menus.length; i++)
    {
      CascadingMenu.convertLabelToFieldset(menus[i]);
      var masterMenu = CascadingMenu.extractMasterMenu(menus[i]);
      CascadingMenu.createLabelFromTitle(masterMenu);
      CascadingMenu.createLabelFromTitle(menus[i]);

      CascadingMenu.updateSlaveMenu(masterMenu);
      Core.addEventListener(
          masterMenu, "change", CascadingMenu.changeListener);
    }
  },
    ⋮
};

Core.start(CascadingMenu);
```

The rest of the work simply consists of implementing the methods in this code: convertLabelToFieldset, extractMasterMenu, createLabelFromTitle, updateSlaveMenu, and changeListener. No sweat, right?

Let's start with an easy one: convertLabelToFieldset needs to find the label for the select element that it's given, and convert it into a fieldset and legend that will surround the select:

```
convertLabelToFieldset: function(menu)
{
  var menuId = menu.id;
  var labels = document.getElementsByTagName("label");

  for (var i = 0; i < labels.length; i++) ❶
  {
```

```
    if (labels[i].getAttribute("for") == menuId) ❷
    {
      var label = labels[i];
      label.parentNode.removeChild(label); ❸

      var legend = document.createElement("legend"); ❹
      while (label.hasChildNodes()) ❺
      {
        legend.appendChild(label.firstChild);
      }

      var fieldset = document.createElement("fieldset"); ❻
      fieldset.appendChild(legend);

      menu.parentNode.replaceChild(fieldset, menu); ❼
      fieldset.appendChild(menu);

      return; ❽
    }
  }
},
```

This method demonstrates the process of transplanting DOM nodes from one element to another with a `while` loop and the `hasChildNodes` method. It also shows how to replace one element with another, using the `replaceChild` method. Both these processes are new to us, so let's break the code down:

❶   In order to find the `label` that belongs to this field, we fetch a list of all the `label` elements in the document and loop through them with a `for` loop as usual.

❷   For each `label`, we compare the `for` attribute to the ID of the specified `select` menu. When we find a match, we'll have found the `label` that we need to convert to a `fieldset` and `legend`.

❸   We start by removing the `label` from its parent node, effectively removing it from the document. This also removes it from the node set `labels`, which is why we first created the variable `label` to store a reference to the element.

④ Next, we'll create the `legend` element, into which we need to move all the child nodes of the `label`.

⑤ Moving DOM nodes from one element to another is surprisingly easy. Simply create a `while` loop that uses the `hasChildNodes` method to check if the source element has any more child nodes, and as long as it does, keeps appending the first of its child nodes to the target element. Since a node can only exist in one location at a time, adding it to the target element automatically removes it from the source element.

⑥ We can now create the `fieldset` element, and add to it the `legend` that we've just created

⑦ Replacing the `select` menu with the newly created `fieldset` is easy, thanks to the `replaceChild` method, which will insert the `fieldset` in place of the `select` in the `select`'s parent node. Once that's done, we can insert the `select` into the `fieldset`.

⑧ Since we've found and dealt with the `label` we were looking for, we can `return` from the `convertLabelToFieldset` method immediately, rather than letting the `for` loop continue searching through the document.

Next up is the `extractMasterMenu` method, which will create and return a new `select` menu that contains as `options` the `optgroups` from the original menu:

cascadingmenu.js (excerpt)

```
extractMasterMenu: function(menu)
{
  var masterMenu = document.createElement("select"); ❶
  masterMenu.id = menu.id + "master";
  masterMenu.setAttribute("name", masterMenu.id);
  masterMenu.setAttribute("title", menu.getAttribute("title"));
  masterMenu._slave = menu; ❷

  while (menu.hasChildNodes()) ❸
  {
    var optgroup = menu.firstChild;
    if (optgroup.nodeType == 1) ❹
    {
      var masterOption = document.createElement("option"); ❺
```

```
    masterOption.appendChild(document.createTextNode(
        optgroup.getAttribute("label")));
    masterMenu.appendChild(masterOption);

    var slaveOptions = []; ⑥
    while (optgroup.hasChildNodes())
    {
      var option = optgroup.firstChild;
      slaveOptions[slaveOptions.length] = option;
      optgroup.removeChild(option);
    }
    masterOption._slaveOptions = slaveOptions;

    menu.setAttribute("title",
        optgroup.getAttribute("title")); ⑦
  }
  menu.removeChild(optgroup); ⑧
}

menu.parentNode.insertBefore(masterMenu, menu); ⑨

return masterMenu; ⑩
},
```

It's a doozy, but there's almost nothing in there that you haven't seen before. Nevertheless, let me break down the major steps of this method:

❶ We start by creating a new `select` element for the new menu. We set its `id` property and `name` attribute to match the ID of the existing `select`, but we append the word "master" to it. We grab the `title` directly from the existing `select`.

❷ Since we'll need to update the contents of the existing "slave" menu every time the user makes a selection from the new master menu, we store a reference to the slave in a custom property of the master, called `_slave`.

❸ Now we need to create in the master menu an `option` for each `optgroup` in the slave menu. As we did in the `convertLabelToFieldset` method, we'll use a `while` loop with the `hasChildNodes` method, grabbing the first `optgroup` from the slave menu, then removing it from that menu in preparation for the next time we cycle through the loop.

④ Since the menu's child nodes may include whitespace text nodes, we need to check the `nodeType` of each child to make sure we're dealing with one of the `optgroup` elements.

⑤ For each `optgroup` in the slave menu, we'll create an `option` that we'll insert into the master menu. The text for each `option` will be taken from the `label` attribute of the corresponding `optgroup`.

⑥ So that we can fill the slave menu with the `options` that correspond to the selection in the master menu, we'll bundle up the relevant `option` elements into an array, which we'll store in a custom `_slaveOptions` property of the `option` element within the master menu.

⑦ As we process each `optgroup`, we grab its `title` attribute and set the `title` of the slave menu to that value. We assume here that each `optgroup` has the same `title`, so the fact that the final `title` of the slave menu will be taken from the last `optgroup` that's processed isn't a problem.

⑧ Finally, we remove the `optgroup` from the slave menu in preparation for the next cycle of the `while` loop.

⑨ Now that we've filled the master menu with its `options`, we can insert it into the document, right before the existing menu, using the `insertBefore` method—yet another useful DOM method that we haven't seen before. Like `appendChild`, it adds the first node passed to it as a child of the element upon which it is called. Unlike `appendChild`, however, it doesn't place this child at the end of the element; it places it *before* the second node that's passed to it.

⑩ At last, we `return` a reference to the new master menu so that `init` can perform additional setup tasks on the menu.

Compared to the last method, `createLabelFromTitle` is dead simple:

cascadingmenu.js *(excerpt)*

```
createLabelFromTitle: function(menu)
{
  var title = menu.getAttribute("title");
  menu.setAttribute("title", "");

  var label = document.createElement("label");
  label.setAttribute("for", menu.id);
  label.appendChild(document.createTextNode(title));

  menu.parentNode.insertBefore(label, menu);
},
```

This method takes the `title` from the `select` element it was given, builds for the `select` a `label` element that contains that text, then inserts it into the document before the `select`. There's nothing to it!

`updateSlaveMenu`, which fills the slave menu with the `options` corresponding to the current master menu selection is almost as straightforward:

cascadingmenu.js *(excerpt)*

```
updateSlaveMenu: function(masterMenu)
{
  var selectedOption =
      masterMenu.options[masterMenu.selectedIndex]; ❶

  while (masterMenu._slave.hasChildNodes()) ❷
  {
    masterMenu._slave.removeChild(masterMenu._slave.firstChild);
  }

  for (var i = 0; i < selectedOption._slaveOptions.length; i++) ❸
  {
    masterMenu._slave.appendChild(
        selectedOption._slaveOptions[i]);
  }
  masterMenu._slave.selectedIndex = 0; ❹
},
```

This method does what you'd expect:

1 It finds the selected `option` in the master menu using its `selectedIndex` property.

2 Using a `while` loop with `hasChildNodes`, it empties the slave menu, which it finds using the custom `_slave` property that we created for the master menu in `extractMasterMenu`.

3 It inserts into the slave menu the array of `options` that corresponds to the selected `option` in the master menu. Again, this task is made simple by the custom `_slaveOptions` property that we set up in `extractMasterMenu`.

4 Finally, it sets the slave menu's `selectedIndex` property to 0, which selects the first `option` in the list.

As usual, since we're doing all the work in our workhorse methods, our event listener is as simple as they come:

cascadingmenu.js *(excerpt)*

```
changeListener: function(event)
{
  CascadingMenu.updateSlaveMenu(this);
}
```

That does it! Fire the example up in your browser and take it for a spin. Also, be sure to try disabling JavaScript to check that the single menu works just fine in that environment. Here's the completed script:

cascadingmenu.js

```
var CascadingMenu =
{
  init: function()
  {
    var menus = Core.getElementsByClass("cascading");

    for (var i = 0; i < menus.length; i++)
    {
      CascadingMenu.convertLabelToFieldset(menus[i]);
      var masterMenu = CascadingMenu.extractMasterMenu(menus[i]);
      CascadingMenu.createLabelFromTitle(masterMenu);
```

```
      CascadingMenu.createLabelFromTitle(menus[i]);

      CascadingMenu.updateSlaveMenu(masterMenu);
      Core.addEventListener(
          masterMenu, "change", CascadingMenu.changeListener);
    }
  },

  convertLabelToFieldset: function(menu)
  {
    var menuId = menu.id;
    var labels = document.getElementsByTagName("label");

    for (var i = 0; i < labels.length; i++)
    {
      if (labels[i].getAttribute("for") == menuId)
      {
        var label = labels[i];
        label.parentNode.removeChild(label);

        var legend = document.createElement("legend");
        while (label.hasChildNodes())
        {
          legend.appendChild(label.firstChild);
        }

        var fieldset = document.createElement("fieldset");
        fieldset.appendChild(legend);

        menu.parentNode.replaceChild(fieldset, menu);
        fieldset.appendChild(menu);

        return;
      }
    }
  },

  extractMasterMenu: function(menu)
  {
    var masterMenu = document.createElement("select");
    masterMenu.id = menu.id + "master";
    masterMenu.setAttribute("name", masterMenu.id);
    masterMenu.setAttribute(
        "title", menu.getAttribute("title"));
```

```
    masterMenu._slave = menu;

  while (menu.hasChildNodes())
  {
    var optgroup = menu.firstChild;
    if (optgroup.nodeType == 1)
    {
      var masterOption = document.createElement("option");
      masterOption.appendChild(document.createTextNode(
          optgroup.getAttribute("label")));
      masterMenu.appendChild(masterOption);

      var slaveOptions = [];
      while (optgroup.hasChildNodes())
      {
        var option = optgroup.firstChild;
        slaveOptions[slaveOptions.length] = option;
        optgroup.removeChild(option);
      }
      masterOption._slaveOptions = slaveOptions;

      menu.setAttribute("title",
          optgroup.getAttribute("title"));
    }
    menu.removeChild(optgroup);
  }

  menu.parentNode.insertBefore(masterMenu, menu);

  return masterMenu;
},

createLabelFromTitle: function(menu)
{
  var title = menu.getAttribute("title");
  menu.setAttribute("title", "");

  var label = document.createElement("label");
  label.setAttribute("for", menu.id);
  label.appendChild(document.createTextNode(title));

  menu.parentNode.insertBefore(label, menu);
},
```

```
updateSlaveMenu: function(masterMenu)
{
  var selectedOption =
      masterMenu.options[masterMenu.selectedIndex];

  while (masterMenu._slave.hasChildNodes())
  {
    masterMenu._slave.removeChild(masterMenu._slave.firstChild);
  }

  for (var i = 0; i < selectedOption._slaveOptions.length; i++)
  {
    masterMenu._slave.appendChild(
        selectedOption._slaveOptions[i]);
  }
  masterMenu._slave.selectedIndex = 0;
},

changeListener: function(event)
{
  CascadingMenu.updateSlaveMenu(this);
}
};

Core.start(CascadingMenu);
```

Form Validation

Usability tweaks like those we've seen so far in this chapter are all well and good, but by far the most common use of JavaScript when dealing with forms is client-side validation.

Now let me make one thing clear: every web site that accepts user input of any kind needs a program on the receiving end—the server side—to make sure that input is provided in the expected format, and is safe to use. That's **server-side validation**, and it's an absolute must, no matter what you do with JavaScript in the browser.

Client-side validation, on the other hand, is merely an early warning system. It does the same job as server-side validation—and does it much faster—but you can't rely on it to work every time.

Client-side validation takes place in the browser, before the user input is submitted for processing. The advantage here is that the user doesn't have to wait for the request to be transferred to the server, for validation to occur there, and for the response to come back in the form of a new page. With JavaScript, you can tell the user more or less instantly if there is something wrong with the values that are about to be submitted.

Of course, the user can always disable JavaScript to circumvent your client-side validation, so it's important that you also have server-side validation in place to intercept any invalid submissions.

Intercepting Form Submissions

The key to client-side validation is the `submit` event that I mentioned in Table 6.3. Whenever the user attempts to submit a form (whether by clicking a submit button or just by hitting **Enter** in a text field), a `submit` event is triggered on the corresponding `form` element. The default action for that event is to submit the form, but as we learned in Chapter 4, you can use JavaScript to cancel the default action for an event if you want to.

The basic technique for client-side validation, then, is to set up either an event handler or an event listener for the form's `submit` event, and cancel the default action if the form's contents are not acceptable. Here's roughly what this process looks like, using an event handler:

```
form.onsubmit = function()
{
  if (form input is not valid)
  {
    notify the user
    return false;
  }
};
```

Here's how it looks if you're using an event listener:

```
Core.addEventListener(form, "submit", function(event)
{
  if (form input is not valid)
```

```
  {
    notify the user
    Core.preventDefault(event);
  }
});
```

As usual, I recommend that you stick with using an event listener so that you can enjoy the benefits I described in Chapter 4, but remember that Safari versions 2.0.3 and earlier do not support the cancelling of default actions from event listeners. If you need to support client-side validation in those older Safari versions, look in the code archive for the JavaScript files whose names end in **-dom0.js**. These use event handlers instead of event listeners for each of the examples that follow.

As a trivial example, we could verify that the user had filled in a value for a particular text field:

requiredfield.js *(excerpt)*

```
var RequiredField =
{
  init: function()
  {
    var requiredField = document.getElementById("requiredfield");
    var theForm = requiredField.form; ❶

    Core.addEventListener(
        theForm, "submit", RequiredField.submitListener);
  },

  submitListener: function(event)
  {
    var requiredField = document.getElementById("requiredfield");

    if (requiredField.value == "") ❷
    {
      requiredField.focus(); ❸
      alert("Please fill in a value for this required field."); ❹
      Core.preventDefault(event); ❺
    }
  }
```

```
};

Core.start(RequiredField);
```

Most of this code should come pretty naturally to you by now, but here's a run-down of the highlights:

1 Because the `submit` event's target is the `form` element, not any single form control, we need to use the required field's `form` property to obtain a reference to the form that contains it before we can register our event listener.

2 We can check the value of a text field with its `value` property.

3 Once we've identified a problem with a field, we call its `focus` method to give it keyboard focus and help the user find and correct the mistake.

4 We display a helpful message to let the user know what he or she did wrong, as shown in Figure 6.5.

5 We prevent the form from submitting by cancelling the `submit` event's default action.

Figure 6.5. A helpful error message

Of course, sometimes it's not enough for a field just to be filled in; sometimes, the value has to conform to a particular format. That's where regular expressions come in handy.

Regular Expressions

We use **regular expressions** to search for and replace patterns of text. They're available in many different programming languages and environments, and are especially prevalent in web development languages like JavaScript.

The popularity of regular expressions has everything to do with how useful they are, and absolutely nothing to do with how easy they are to use—they're not easy at all. In fact, to most people who encounter them for the first time, regular expressions look like something that might eventuate if you fell asleep with your face on the keyboard.

Here, for example, is a relatively simple (yes, really!) regular expression that will match any string that might be a valid email address:

```
^[\w\.\-]+@([\w\-]+\.)+[a-zA-Z]+$
```

Scary, huh? By the end of this section, you'll actually be able to make sense of that.

To create a regular expression in JavaScript, use forward slashes (/) around the expression as you would use single or double quotes around a string:

```
var regex = /pattern/;
```

 Escape the Forward Slash!

To include a forward slash as part of a regular expression, you must escape it with a preceding backslash (\/); otherwise, it will be interpreted as marking the end of the pattern.

Alternatively, if you need to build a regular expression dynamically (say, using the value of a variable), you can use this alternative syntax to create the regular expression from a string:

```
var regex = new RegExp("pat" + variable + "tern");
```

Essentially, a regular expression represents a pattern specified with ordinary and special characters. For instance, if you wanted a pattern that matched the string "JavaScript," your regular expression pattern could be:

```
JavaScript
```

However, by including special characters, your pattern could also be:

```
^Java.*
```

The caret (^), the dot (.), and the asterisk (*) are all special characters that have a specific meaning inside a regular expression. Specifically, the caret means "the start of the string," the dot means "any character," and the asterisk means "zero or more of the preceding character."

Therefore, the pattern ^Java.* matches not only the string "JavaScript," but "Javascript," "JavaHouse," "Java, the most populous island in the world," and any other string beginning with "Java."

Here are some of the most commonly used regular expression special characters (try not to lose too much sleep attempting to memorize these):

. (dot)

This is the wildcard character. It matches any single character except line break characters (\r and \n).

* (asterisk)

An asterisk requires that the preceding character appear zero or more times.

When matching, the asterisk will be **greedy**, including as many characters as possible. For example, for the string "a word here, a word there," the pattern "a.*word" will match "a word here, a word." In order to make a minimal match (just "a word"), use the question mark character (explained below).

+ (plus)

This character requires that the preceding character appears one or more times. When matching, the plus will be greedy (just like the asterisk, described above) unless you use the question mark character (explained below).

? (question mark)

This character makes the preceding character optional.

If placed after a plus or an asterisk, it instead dictates that the match for this preceding symbol will be a **minimal match**, including as few characters as possible.

^ (caret)

The caret matches the start of the string. This does not include any characters—it considers merely the position itself.

$ (dollar)

A dollar character matches the end of the string. This does not include any characters—it considers merely the position itself.

| (pipe)

The pipe causes the regular expression to match either the pattern on the left of the pipe, or the pattern on the right.

(...) (round brackets)

Round brackets define a group of characters that must occur together, to which you can then apply a modifier like *, +, or ? by placing it after the closing bracket.

You can also refer to a bracketed portion of a regular expression later to obtain the *portion* of the string that it matched.

[...] (square brackets)

Square brackets define a **character class**. A character class matches *one* character out of those listed within the square brackets.

A character class can include an explicit list of characters (for instance, [aqz], which is the same as (a|q|z)), or a range of characters (such as [a-z], which is the same as (a|b|c|...|z)).

A character class can also be defined so that it matches one character that's *not* listed in the brackets. To do this, simply insert a caret (^) after the opening square bracket (so [^a] will match any single character except "a").

If you want to use one of these special characters as a literal character to be matched by the regular expression pattern, escape it by placing a backslash (\) before it (for example, 1\+1=2 will match "1+1=2").

There are also a number of so-called **escape sequences** that will match a character that either is not easily typed, or is a certain type of character:

\n   This sequence matches a newline character.

\r   This matches a carriage return character.

\t   This matches a tab character.

\s   This sequence matches any whitespace character; it's the same as [\n\r\t].

\S   This matches any non-whitespace character, and is the same as [^ \n\r\t].

\d   This matches any digit; it's the same as [0-9].

\D   This sequence matches anything but a digit, and is the same as [^0-9].

\w   This matches any "word" character. It's the same as [a-zA-Z0-9_].

\W   This sequence matches any "non-word" character, and is the same as [^a-zA-Z0-9_].

\b   This code is a little special because it doesn't actually match a character. Instead, it matches a word boundary—the start or end of a word.

\B   Like \b, this doesn't actually match a character. Rather, it matches a position in the string that is *not* a word boundary.

\\   Matches an actual backslash character. So if you want to match the string "\n" exactly, your regular expression would be \\n, not \n (which matches a newline character). Similarly, if you wanted to match the string "\\" exactly, your regular expression would be \\\\.

We now have everything we need to be able to understand the email address regular expression I showed you at the start of this section:

```
^[\w\.\-]+@([\w\-]+\.)+[a-zA-Z]+$
```

^   We start by matching the beginning of the string, to make sure that nothing appears before the email address.

`[\w\.\-]+`   The name portion of the email address is made up of one or more (+) characters that are either "word" characters, dots, or hyphens (`[\w\.\-]`).

@   The name is followed by the @ character.

`([\w\-]+\.)+` Then we have one or more (+) subdomains (such as "sitepoint."), each of which is one or more "word" characters or hyphens (`[\w\-]+`) followed by a dot (`\.`).

`[a-zA-Z]+`   Next, there's the top-level domain (for example, "com"), which is simply one or more letters (`[a-zA-Z]+`).

$ Finally, we match the end of the string, to make sure that nothing appears after the email address.

Got all that? If you're feeling anything like I was when I first learned regular expressions, you're probably a little nervous. Okay, you can follow along with a breakdown of a regular expression that someone else wrote for you, but can you really come up with this gobbledygook yourself? Don't sweat it: in the following example, we'll look at a bunch more regular expressions, and before you know it you'll be writing expressions of your own with confidence.

But hang on a minute … I've told you all about the syntax of regular expressions, but we still need to see how to actually use them in JavaScript! In fact, there are a number of different ways to do this, but the simplest—and the one we'll be using the most in this book—is the `test` method that's supported by all regular expressions:

```
regex.test(string)
```

The `test` method will return true if the regular expression it's called on matches the string that you pass to it as an argument.

For a simple example of this method in action, we can return to the `hasClass` method that we created back in Chapter 3:

core.js *(excerpt)*

```
Core.hasClass = function(target, theClass)
{
  var pattern = new RegExp("(^| )" + theClass + "( |$)"); ❶

  if (pattern.test(target.className)) ❷
  {
    return true;
  }

  return false;
};
```

This method determines if a particular class appears in the `class` attribute of a given HTML element. Remember that this attribute is a space-delimited list of classes (for example, `classa classb classc`).

❶ First, this method builds a regular expression containing the class name that we're searching for, of the form `(^| )theClass( |$)`. This expression should be fairly easy for you to decipher by now: it starts by matching either the start of the string or a space (`(^| )`), then the class name, and finally, either a space or the end of the string (`( |$)`).

❷ Next, the method tests if the value of the element's `class` attribute (`target.className`) matches the pattern. If it does, the method returns `true`. Otherwise, it returns `false`.

Not too bad, eh? Let's dive into a bigger example and see how we go. In the meantime, if you want a more extensive listing of regular expression syntax, visit regularexpressions.info,[2] and for more information on regular expressions in JavaScript, see my article *Regular Expressions in JavaScript* on SitePoint.[3]

Example: Reusable Validation Script

Before we got distracted by the bewildering glory of regular expressions, I seem to remember this chapter being about forms. How about we try to combine the two by using regular expressions to validate forms?

Regular expressions are great for validating forms, because we can express quite a complex set of requirements for a field in just a single regular expression. For example, we can test if a field has been filled in with a very simple expression:

```
.
```

That right, it's just a dot (.). Since this will match any character, the only string that won't match this is the empty string (" ").

Of course, a user could just type a space character into the field and satisfy this pattern, so how about we require at least one non-whitespace character in the field? Again, this is an easy expression to write:

```
\S
```

Let's make things a little more complicated. How about a field that requires a positive whole number, and nothing else?

```
^\d*[1-9]\d*$
```

This pattern checks that the string contains at least one digit between 1 and 9 (that is, not 0), which can be preceded and/or followed by any number of digits (including 0). The start-string (^) and end-string ($) characters ensure there is nothing else in the string.

---

[2] http://www.regularexpressions.info/
[3] http://www.sitepoint.com/article/expressions-javascript/

If we were happy to allow zero as a value, we could simplify the pattern to this:

```
^\d+$
```

Want to allow negative numbers too? Easy! Just add an optional minus sign:

```
^-?\d+$
```

How about decimal numbers like 12.345? Easy enough:

```
^-?\d+(\.\d+)?$
```

This pattern allows for an optional decimal point (\.) followed by one or more digits.

Let's get a little trickier and check for a valid phone number. Phone number formats vary from country to country, but in general they consist of an optional country code (+1 for North America, or +61 for Australia), an optional area code that may or may not be enclosed in parentheses, then one or more groups of numbers. Each of these elements may be separated by spaces, dashes, or nothing at all.

Here's the expression we'll need:

```
^(\+\d+)?( |\-)?(\(?\d+\))?( |\-)?(\d+( |\-)?)*\d+$
```

If you can get that expression straight in your head, you can safely claim to have mastered the basics of regular expressions. Good luck! For an added challenge, try adapting the pattern to allow phone numbers that are spelled out in letters, such as "1-800-YOU-RULE."

To build a reusable form validation script, we can bundle all of the regular expressions we've seen so far into a JavaScript object:

formvalidation.js (excerpt)

```
var FormValidation =
{
  ⋮
  rules:
  {
```

```
    required: /./,
    requiredNotWhitespace: /\S/,
    positiveInteger: /^\d*[1-9]\d*$/,
    positiveOrZeroInteger: /^\d+$/,
    integer: /^-?\d+$/,
    decimal: /^-?\d+(\.\d+)?$/,
    email: /^[\w\.\-]+@([\w\-]+\.)+[a-zA-Z]+$/,
    telephone:
        /^(\+\d+)?( |\-)?(\((?\d+\))?)?( |\-)?(\d+( |\-)?)*\d+$/
},
```

For each pattern, we can also store an error message for display when the pattern
is not satisfied:

formvalidation.js *(excerpt)*

```
errors:
{
  required: "Please fill in this required field.",
  requiredNotWhitespace: "Please fill in this required field.",
  positiveInteger:
      "This field may only contain a positive whole number.",
  positiveOrZeroInteger: "This field may only contain a " +
      "non-negative whole number.",
  integer: "This field may only contain a whole number.",
  decimal: "This field may only contain a number.",
  email: "Please enter a valid email address into this field.",
  telephone:
      "Please enter a valid telephone number into this field."
},
```

We can then mark the fields in our form with the labels we defined in the code
above. For example, a required field would have its `class` set to `required`:

formvalidation.html *(excerpt)*

```
<input type="text" class="required" id="username" name="username"
    />
```

Similarly, here's a field that must contain a valid email address:

formvalidation.html (excerpt)

```html
<input type="text" class="email" id="email" name="email" />
```

All that's left is to write the JavaScript required to test the fields of a form with the specified regular expressions before allowing submission to proceed.

The `init` method is simple enough. All we need to do is add a `submit` event listener to every form on the page:

formvalidation.js (excerpt)

```js
init: function()
{
  var forms = document.getElementsByTagName("form");

  for (var i = 0; i < forms.length; i++)
  {
    Core.addEventListener(
        forms[i], "submit", FormValidation.submitListener);
  }
},
```

In fact, the only tricky part of this script is in that `submit` event listener:

formvalidation.js (excerpt)

```js
submitListener: function(event)
{
  var fields = this.elements; ❶

  for (var i = 0; i < fields.length; i++)
  {
    var className = fields[i].className; ❷
    var classRegExp = /(^| )(\S+)( |$)/g; ❸
    var classResult;

    while (classResult = classRegExp.exec(className)) ❹
    {
```

```
      var oneClass = classResult[2]; ❺
      var rule = FormValidation.rules[oneClass]; ❻
      if (typeof rule != "undefined") ❼
      {
        if (!rule.test(fields[i].value)) ❽
        {
          fields[i].focus(); ❾
          alert(FormValidation.errors[oneClass]); ❿
          Core.preventDefault(event); ⓫
          return; ⓬
        }
      }
    }
  }
}
```

Thanks to the power of regular expressions, that's all the code we need to write in order to validate a form—any form—with the regular expressions that we declared earlier. Thanks to the *complexity* of regular expressions, this code is particularly difficult to understand at a glance. Let me walk you through it:

❶ First, we obtain a list of all the fields in the form, using the elements property of the form element described in Table 6.2. We can then loop through the list with a for loop.

❷ For each field, we obtain the class attribute value, which we'll use to ascertain which of the regular expressions we'll test its value against. But remember that the class attribute can contain a list of *multiple* class names, so we need to do some work to break this value up into individual class names, and check them one at a time.

❸ This regular expression will find one particular class name in a space-delimited list such as the class attribute value. It looks for the start of the string or a space, followed by one or more non-whitespace characters, and then a space or the end of the string. But, since we want to find not just *one* class name, but *all* of the class names in the attribute value, we need to apply the **global modifier** to this expression. See the g following the closing forward slash that marks the end of the regular expression? That's the global modifier, and it sets the regular expression up so that we can use it to find *all* the matches in a given string, not just the first one.

4 Most of the time, the `test` method is all that's needed to use a regular expression. But when you're working with the global modifier, you're better off using a more advanced method: `exec`. This method works just like `test`, except that it returns information about the portion of the string that it matched. When `exec` is applied to a regular expression that includes the global modifier, and it finds a match, it returns an array, which we store in the `classResult` variable.

5 The first element of that array (with array index 0) contains the portion of the string that was matched by the entire regular expression; in this case, the portion of the string may contain spaces before or after the class name, so it's no good to us. The second element in the array (array index 1) contains the portion of the string that was matched by the first parenthesized portion of the regular expression (in this case, the space before the class name, if any). The third element in the array (array index 2) contains the portion of the string matched by the second parenthesized portion of the expression, which in this case is the actual class name—exactly what we're after!

When called repeatedly, the `exec` method will search for successive matches in the string, which is the reason why we can use it in a `while` loop in this way. During the first cycle of the loop, `classResult[2]` will contain the first class name in the `class` attribute; the second time through, `classResult[2]` will contain the second class name, and so on, until all the class names in the attribute have been found. At this point, `exec` will return `null` and the `while` loop will end.

6 Now that we have an individual class name, we can check if we have a regular expression for validating fields with that class.

Remember that we've stored all of our validation expressions as properties of the `FormValidation.rules` object. Usually, you access the property of an object using a dot and the property name (for example, `FormValidation.rules.required`), but we can't do that if the name of the property is stored as a string in a variable, as it is now. If we typed `FieldValidation.rules.oneClass`, JavaScript would actually look for a property named `oneClass`, rather than using the name stored in the `oneClass` variable.

The trick to accessing a property using a property name that's stored in a variable is to treat the object like an array, and use the property name as the array index. So we can fetch the regular expression for a particular class using `FormValidation.rules[oneClass]`. This doesn't exactly make sense, but it's just one of those odd things about JavaScript that you learn from experience.

7 Because we may or may not have a regular expression that corresponds to a given class name, we need to check that we actually got a value back for the `rule` variable.

8 Finally, we can use the `test` method to check if our regular expression matches the value that the user has supplied for the field.

9 If it doesn't match, then the value is not valid, so we assign keyboard focus to the field so that the user can correct it.

10 We then display the error message corresponding to the class name, again using the trick of treating the `FormValidation.errors` object like an array.

11 Because the field's value is invalid, we cancel the default action for the `submit` event, so that the form isn't submitted.

12 And finally, we `return` immediately, so that the user is only notified of one error per submission attempt. If we left this step out, the user would be notified of each and every invalid field in the form one after another, which I think would be a little harsh if, for example, the user had simply submitted the form by accident before filling it in.

And there you have it—a reusable form validation script in just 66 lines of code. Try it out on the simple example page we've included in the code archive, then take it for a spin on some forms of your own! Finally, try adding some more regular expressions (and the corresponding error messages) of your own devising to make this library even *more* useful!

Annoyed by Alerts?

If, like many people, you find alert boxes annoying, you might like to have your validation errors displayed within the page, next to the form fields themselves, instead of in popup message boxes. This technique is demonstrated in the SitePoint book *The JavaScript Anthology* (Melbourne: SitePoint, 2006).

Custom Form Controls

Linking multiple fields together and performing client-side validation are both useful ways to enhance the rather limited form controls that are currently available in HTML, but to truly rise above the limitations of those controls, you need to create entirely new controls of your own!

Creating fully realized user interface elements using only the capabilities of HTML, CSS, and JavaScript is a tall order. The built-in form controls have a lot of subtle features that are difficult, if not impossible to achieve using JavaScript. Consider the right-click menu—not to mention all the keyboard shortcuts—that even a basic text field supports!

However, by setting realistic goals, and by taking advantage of the existing form controls where appropriate, you can produce some truly useful user interface elements. Let's look at one, shall we?

Example: Slider

A slider control can give your users a very intuitive way to select a value over a given range. The control immediately gives the user a sense of the position of the current value within the available range of values, and also allows the user to manipulate that value easily, and see the changes in real time.

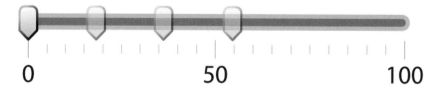

Figure 6.6. A typical slider control

A plain text field can store the same values as a slider, so in order to keep the page accessible to users who browse with JavaScript disabled, we will convert any text input field that has a class of slider into a slider control:

```
slider.html (excerpt)

<label for="percent">Percentage
  <input id="percent" name="percent" type="text" value="0"
     class="slider from0 to100 scale4" />
</label>
```

Notice the other classes that have been applied to this field: from0, to100, and scale4. These classes control various aspects of the slider control that will be created from this text field:

from0   The minimum value that you will be able to select using the slider will be 0.

to100   The maximum value that you will be able to select using the slider will be 100.

scale4 For every change of 1 in the value of the field, the slider will move four pixels.

Together, these classes describe a slider that's 400 pixels wide, and allows you to select values ranging from 0 to 100.

Before we tackle the script that will make the control work, let's figure out the HTML document structures and CSS styles that will get the browser to display the control.

We'll start by creating an image for the "track" of the slider—the labelled horizontal bar that represents the range of values from which the user can choose. To match the values specified in the code, the slider's track should be exactly 400 pixels long, but the image's actual width and height are up to you. For example, the image may be wider than 400 pixels if you want to add decorative elements to either end of the track. Figure 6.7 shows the background image I created, which is 430 pixels wide and 72 pixels high.

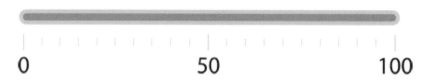

Figure 6.7. The image for the slider track

We also need a separate image for the draggable portion of the slider control—the "thumb." The one I've created is 20 pixels wide and 35 pixels high, and is shown in Figure 6.8.

Figure 6.8. The image for the slider thumb

Now, keeping in mind that we want to keep the text field visible and usable for both keyboard and screen reader users, what do we need in terms of additional DOM structure and CSS styles to produce this control? Well, I'm thinking something like this would work well:

```
<label for="percent">Percentage
  <span class="sliderControl">
    <span class="sliderTrack"></span>
    <span class="sliderThumb"></span>
    <input id="percent" name="percent" type="text"
        value="0" class="slider from0 to100 scale4" />
  </span>
<label>
```

Remember: this isn't code you'll actually add to your HTML—we'll use JavaScript to generate these new elements.

I've used spans because they're legal wherever an input is allowed in HTML. The sliderControl span provides a container for us to position the different elements of the slider control, the track span is what we'll use to display the track image, and the thumb span will display the thumb image for us. I've also put the existing input inside the sliderControl span because that gives us the freedom to position the field in relation to the elements of the slider control.

Here's the CSS that will style all this:

```
span.sliderControl {  ❶
  display: block;
  height: 79px;
  position: relative;
}

span.sliderTrack {  ❷
  background: url(slider_scale.jpg);
  display: block;
  height: 72px;
  left: 0;
  position: absolute;
  top: 7px;
  width: 430px;
}

span.sliderControl span.sliderThumb {  ❸
  background-image: url(slider_thumb.gif);
  cursor: w-resize;
  height: 35px;
  position: absolute;
  top: 0;
  width: 20px;
}

span.sliderControl input.slider {  ❹
  margin-left: 430px;
}
```

This isn't a book on CSS layout, but let me quickly sum up what each of these rules does:

❶ The span that contains all the elements that make up the slider will be displayed as a block, with a height sufficient to accommodate the slider control (specifically, the track background image, and any space you want to allow around it). Setting position: relative lets you position all the elements it contains relative to its top-left corner.

❷ The sliderTrack span is really just a canvas on which to display the slider track as a background image. It's displayed as a block of the required dimensions, and is positioned so that when the thumb is positioned at the left edge of the sliderControl container, it appears at the left end of the track.

❸ The sliderThumb span is similarly set up to adopt the exact dimensions needed to display the thumb image as its background. Notice, however, that it doesn't have a value set for its left property, because its horizontal position will be controlled dynamically by our JavaScript code. It does, however, display the horizontal-resize cursor to assist the user in discovering how to use the control.

❹ This final rule positions the text input field within the sliderControl container. In this case, I've given it sufficient left margin to place it just to the right of the slider control.

I've highlighted in bold the values in this code that are likely to change if you create a slider of your own with different dimensions and images.

Okay, the groundwork is done—let's get scripting! As usual, we start with an init method that searches the document for the elements that we want to enhance—in this case, elements of class slider:

slider.js (excerpt)

```
var Slider =
{
  init: function()
  {
    var sliderFields = Core.getElementsByClass("slider");

    for (var i = 0; i < sliderFields.length; i++)
    {
```

The first thing we need to do to each of these elements is extract the "from," "to," and "scale" values from its class attribute. This is, of course, a job for regular expressions:

slider.js (excerpt)

```
      var fromMatch = /(^| )from(\d+)( |$)/.exec(
          sliderFields[i].className);
      var from = parseInt(fromMatch[2], 10);
```

```
var toMatch = /(^| )to(\d+)( |$)/.exec(
    sliderFields[i].className);
var to = parseInt(toMatch[2], 10);

var scaleMatch = /(^| )scale(\d+)( |$)/.exec(
    sliderFields[i].className);
var scale = parseInt(scaleMatch[2], 10);
```

Because we're extracting values using regular expressions, we're using the more advanced `exec` method that we learned about in the section called "Example: Reusable Validation Script". In each regular expression, the number that we're interested in extracting is in the second parenthesized section of the expression, which we can grab out of the third element of the array returned by `exec`.

Now, regular expressions deal with strings, and what we actually need are numbers, so we need to convert each string value to a JavaScript number. JavaScript has a built-in function called `parseInt` that does exactly that; we've used it in the code. `parseInt` looks at the start of a string (the first argument), and returns any number it finds there. The second argument specifies the base of the number. Since we usually deal with decimal numbers, which are base 10, you can make a habit of always passing 10 as this function's second argument.

Now it's time to begin creating the DOM structure we looked at earlier. You should be very used to this sort of thing by now:

slider.js (excerpt)

```
var slider = document.createElement("span");
slider.id = sliderFields[i].id + "slider";
slider.className = "sliderControl";

var track = document.createElement("span");
track.id = sliderFields[i].id + "track";
track.className = "sliderTrack";

var thumb = document.createElement("span");
thumb.id = sliderFields[i].id + "thumb";
thumb.className = "sliderThumb";
```

To each of the three span elements that we create, we assign both an ID and a class to facilitate styling. The class lets you apply general style properties shared by all sliders on the page, while the ID lets you apply properties specific to an individual slider control.

Since the user will actually interact with the slider thumb (by dragging it), we'll take the opportunity to store all of the values that our event listeners will need in custom properties of the thumb element:

slider.js *(excerpt)*

```
thumb._input = sliderFields[i];
thumb._from = from;
thumb._to = to;
thumb._scale = scale;
```

The user may still choose to enter values directly into the text field, however, and since we'll need to update the position of the thumb in response to such changes, we'll store a reference to the thumb in the text field element:

slider.js *(excerpt)*

```
sliderFields[i]._thumb = thumb;
```

With all the elements created, we can now add them to the document to produce the required structure:

slider.js *(excerpt)*

```
slider.appendChild(track);
slider.appendChild(thumb);
sliderFields[i].parentNode.replaceChild(
    slider, sliderFields[i]);
slider.appendChild(sliderFields[i]);
```

The final step in building the slider is to position the thumb so that it corresponds to the current value of the text field:

slider.js *(excerpt)*

```
    var value = parseInt(sliderFields[i].value, 10);
    thumb.style.left = ((value - from) * scale) + "px";
```

The first line above obtains a number based on the string value of the text field. The second line calculates the difference between that value and the minimum value of the slider, multiplies that difference by the scale of the slider, then positions the thumb that number of pixels from the left-hand side of the slider.

That's our slider created. Now all we need are the event listeners to make it go:

slider.js *(excerpt)*

```
    Core.addEventListener(sliderFields[i], "change",
        Slider.changeListener);
    Core.addEventListener(thumb, "mousedown",
        Slider.mousedownListener);
  }
},
```

When the user changes the value of the text field, our change event listener will update the slider accordingly. Conversely, when the user clicks on the slider thumb, our mousedown event listener will handle the dragging operation, and will update the text field's value.

Let's start with the change event listener, as we've dealt with this type of event before:

slider.js *(excerpt)*

```
changeListener: function(event)
{
  var thumb = this._thumb; ❶
  var value = parseInt(this.value, 10);

  if (value < thumb._from) ❷
  {
    value = thumb._from;
  }
```

```
  else if (value > thumb._to)
  {
    value = thumb._to;
  }

  thumb.style.left =
      ((value - thumb._from) * thumb._scale) + "px"; ❸
  this.value = value; ❹
},
```

While the code here is relatively straightforward, let me explain exactly what it's doing:

❶ Since we're responding to an event targeted on the text field, we can obtain a reference to the slider thumb using the custom _thumb property that we created in init.

❷ We check the value that was entered by the user against the limits that have been specified for the slider. If the value is too big, we reduce it to the maximum allowed value. If it's too small, we increase it to the minimum allowed value.

❸ Once we've settled on an acceptable value, we move the thumb to the corresponding position.

❹ Finally, we take the value that we settled on and write it back into the form field, so that any adjustment that occurred due to the limits of the slider are reflected in the field's value.

And now for the part you've been waiting for: the code that makes the slider thumb draggable. Every drag operation involves three kinds of events:

1. A mousedown event indicates that the user has pushed down a mouse button while the cursor was positioned over the draggable element.

2. A series of mousemove events is generated as the user moves the cursor around the page.

3. A mouseup event signals that the user has released the mouse button, completing the drag operation.

We've already registered a mousedown event listener on the slider thumb in init, so let's take a look at it:

```
                                                                slider.js (excerpt)

mousedownListener: function(event)
{
  this._valueorigin =
      parseInt(this.style.left, 10) / this._scale - this._from; ❶
  this._dragorigin = event.clientX; ❷
  document._currentThumb = this; ❸

  Core.addEventListener(
      document, "mousemove", Slider.mousemoveListener); ❹
  Core.addEventListener(
      document, "mouseup", Slider.mouseupListener); ❺
  Core.preventDefault(event); ❻
},
```

This listener is responsible for kicking off the drag operation:

❶ We begin by recording a number of values that will be needed throughout the drag operation, the first of which is the value indicated by the slider when the drag began. In subsequent steps, we'll track how far the mouse has moved from its starting position, and use that figure to determine how much the slider's value should change from this starting value.

❷ Obviously, then, we also need to record the mouse pointer's starting position. The clientX property of the event object for any event gives you the horizontal position of the pointer within the browser window when that event occurred.

❸ As we'll see in a moment, we'll also need a convenient way to access the thumb throughout the drag operation, so we'll store in a custom property of the document object a reference to that element.

❹ Now that a drag operation has begun, we need to respond to every mousemove event in the document—whether the cursor remains positioned over the thumb element or not. We therefore add a mousemove event listener to the document node. This listener will catch events that bubble up from any element in the document.

⑤　Similarly, we need to know when the user releases the mouse button, no matter where the cursor is located when that happens, so we add a `mouseup` event listener to the `document` object.

Because these two event listeners are registered on the document and not the thumb, they won't be able to access the thumb element using `this`. That's why we recorded the reference to the thumb element in the document we just created.

⑥　Finally, we prevent the browser from taking any default action—such as beginning a text selection—in response to the mouse button being pressed.

As the user drags the cursor around the page with the mouse button held down, we'll respond to every `mousemove` event by dynamically updating the position of the thumb and the value in the text field:

slider.js (excerpt)

```
mousemoveListener: function(event)
{
  var thumb = document._currentThumb; ❶
  var value = thumb._valueorigin +
      (event.clientX - thumb._dragorigin) / thumb._scale; ❷

  if (value < thumb._from) ❸
  {
    value = thumb._from;
  }
  else if (value > thumb._to)
  {
    value = thumb._to;
  }

  thumb.style.left =
      ((value - thumb._from) * thumb._scale) + "px"; ❹
  thumb._input.value = value; ❺

  Core.preventDefault(event); ❻
},
```

This listener works a lot like changeListener, which we saw earlier, except that instead of fetching the updated value from a form field, it needs to calculate that value on the basis of the mouse pointer's position in relation to its starting location, and the original value when the drag operation began:

1 We're responding to a mousemove event that has bubbled up to the document node, but all the information we need is locked away in the thumb element. Thankfully, we stored a reference to that element in the custom _currentThumb property of the document object.

2 Here, we calculate the slider value corresponding to the current mouse position. We start with the value of the slider before the drag started (thumb._valueorigin), then add to it the difference between the current mouse position (event.clientX) and the starting mouse position (thumb._dragorigin) divided by the scale of the slider (thumb._scale).

3 As with changeListener, we limit the value that we just calculated so that it falls within the range allowed by the slider.

4 To produce the illusion that the user is actually dragging the slider thumb, we adjust its position based on the value that we have just calculated. Again, this code works just like the corresponding code in changeListener.

5 We also update the value of the text field on the fly.

6 Finally, we prevent the browser from doing anything it might normally do in response to the movement of the mouse.

As the French might say, *le tour est joué!*—we've pulled it off! The user can now click and drag the slider, and see the field's value update in real time. All that's left is to complete the drag operation when the user releases the mouse button:

slider.js *(excerpt)*

```
mouseupListener: function(event)
{
  document._currentThumb = null;
  Core.removeEventListener(document, "mousemove",
      Slider.mousemoveListener);
```

```
    Core.removeEventListener(document, "mouseup",
        Slider.mouseupListener);
}
```

This code is pretty self-explanatory. It removes the reference to the thumb that we stored in the document object, and it removes the mousemove and mouseup listeners, leaving the mousedown listener in place to start the next drag.

As you can probably tell, creating draggable elements on the Web is a bit of a black art, and things get even more complicated when you want to allow the user to *drop* the draggable element on one or more target elements.[4]

For now, however, we've managed to make dragging an element seem natural with an intricate mesh of listeners that finely control how the browser responds to the relevant mouse events. This demonstrates just how much you can achieve with JavaScript if you're willing to take matters into your own hands. Figure 6.9 shows what the finished slider control should look like.

Figure 6.9. The finished slider control

Here's the complete JavaScript code for the slider control. Considering what it can add to the usability of a form, I'd say it's refreshingly brief!

---

[4] This is covered at great length in the SitePoint book *The JavaScript Anthology* (Melbourne: SitePoint, 2006).

```
var Slider =
{
  init: function()
  {
    var sliderFields = Core.getElementsByClass("slider");

    for (var i = 0; i < sliderFields.length; i++)
    {
      var fromMatch = /(^| )from(\d+)( |$)/.exec(
          sliderFields[i].className);
      var from = parseInt(fromMatch[2], 10);

      var toMatch = /(^| )to(\d+)( |$)/.exec(
          sliderFields[i].className);
      var to = parseInt(toMatch[2], 10);

      var scaleMatch = /(^| )scale(\d+)( |$)/.exec(
          sliderFields[i].className);
      var scale = parseInt(scaleMatch[2], 10);

      var slider = document.createElement("span");
      slider.id = sliderFields[i].id + "slider";
      slider.className = "sliderControl";

      var track = document.createElement("span");
      track.id = sliderFields[i].id + "track";
      track.className = "sliderTrack";

      var thumb = document.createElement("span");
      thumb.id = sliderFields[i].id + "thumb";
      thumb.className = "sliderThumb";
      thumb._input = sliderFields[i];
      thumb._from = from;
      thumb._to = to;
      thumb._scale = scale;

      sliderFields[i]._thumb = thumb;

      slider.appendChild(track);
      slider.appendChild(thumb);
      sliderFields[i].parentNode.replaceChild(
          slider, sliderFields[i]);
```

```
    slider.appendChild(sliderFields[i]);

    var value = parseInt(sliderFields[i].value, 10);
    thumb.style.left = ((value - from) * scale) + "px";

    Core.addEventListener(
        sliderFields[i], "change", Slider.changeListener);
    Core.addEventListener(
        thumb, "mousedown", Slider.mousedownListener);
  }
},

changeListener: function(event)
{
  var thumb = this._thumb;
  var value = parseInt(this.value, 10);

  if (value < thumb._from)
  {
    value = thumb._from;
  }
  else if (value > thumb._to)
  {
    value = thumb._to;
  }

  thumb.style.left =
      ((value - thumb._from) * thumb._scale) + "px";
  this.value = value;
},

mousedownListener: function(event)
{
  this._valueorigin =
      parseInt(this.style.left, 10) / this._scale - this._from;
  this._dragorigin = event.clientX;
  document._currentThumb = this;

  Core.addEventListener(
      document, "mousemove", Slider.mousemoveListener);
  Core.addEventListener(
      document, "mouseup", Slider.mouseupListener);
  Core.preventDefault(event);
},
```

```
  mousemoveListener: function(event)
  {
    var thumb = document._currentThumb;
    var value = thumb._valueorigin +
        (event.clientX - thumb._dragorigin) / thumb._scale;

    if (value < thumb._from)
    {
      value = thumb._from;
    }
    else if (value > thumb._to)
    {
      value = thumb._to;
    }

    thumb.style.left =
        ((value - thumb._from) * thumb._scale) + "px";
    thumb._input.value = value;

    Core.preventDefault(event);
  },

  mouseupListener: function(event)
  {
    document._currentThumb = null;
    Core.removeEventListener(
        document, "mousemove", Slider.mousemoveListener);
    Core.removeEventListener(
        document, "mouseup", Slider.mouseupListener);
  }
};

Core.start(Slider);
```

Exploring Libraries

A little surprisingly, none of the major JavaScript libraries currently does the kinds
of simple form enhancements that we looked at earlier in this chapter—dependent
fields, cascading menus, and so on. However, many of these libraries *do* have features
that can make building these sorts of enhancements yourself a little easier.

That said, the two other types of form enhancements that we've looked at in this chapter—client-side validation and custom controls—are well served by one library or another.

Form Validation

One of the Dojo library's main strengths is its library of widgets, many of which are enhanced versions of the basic HTML form controls. Some of these widgets provide built-in validation features. For example, with Dojo loaded, you can create a text field that only accepts whole numbers (integers) like this:

```
<input type="text" name="name" class="dojo-IntegerTextbox" />
```

This code invokes Dojo's `IntegerTextbox` widget, which automatically displays an error message when the user types anything that isn't a whole number into the field.

As of this writing, however, Dojo's validation widgets aren't well documented, and the requirement that all the fields of a form are valid before the user is allowed to submit the form still necessitates your writing some JavaScript code of your own. In short, figuring out just how to use Dojo to automate your form validation can take a lot longer than writing your own validation library, as we did in this chapter.

That said, if you're willing to look beyond the major JavaScript libraries, you'll find a couple of well-developed mini-libraries that do client-side validation very well indeed.

wForms is an actively-developed library that works very much like the reusable form validation script that we developed in this chapter.[5] Like our library, it applies reusable validation rules to your form fields based on the `class` attribute. Here's a list of the class names that it recognizes, and the corresponding checks that it carries out:

required
: The field cannot be left empty. By setting this class name on an element that contains a number of form fields, you can require the user to fill in *at least one* of those fields.

---

[5] http://www.formassembly.com/wForms/

`validate-alpha`	This class allows only alphabetic characters in the value of the field.
`validate-alphanum`	This class allows only numbers and alphabetic characters.
`validate-date`	This class allows a date to be entered in any format that's recognized by the browser.
`validate-email`	This class allows an email address, or several email addresses separated by commas, spaces, or semicolons.
`validate-integer`	This class allows only a whole number.
`validate-float`	This class allows only decimal numbers.
`validate-custom` *`/regex/`*	This class allows any value that matches the specified regular expression.
`allrequired`	By setting this class name on an element that contains a number of form fields, you can require that *all* of the fields be filled in.

Forms also offers extensive control over the error messages that are displayed when validation fails. Error messages can appear in an alert box, within the page, or both. This library is full of all sorts of other useful features, including support for dependent fields that's similar to what we developed at the start of this chapter. wForms calls them "conditional sections."

Another library that's worth checking out is Really Easy Field Validation, which was developed by a fellow named Andrew Tetlaw. It works very much like wForms, except that it's based on the Prototype JavaScript library (so you need to load Protoype, and then this library, on your page). You can read all about—and download—Really Easy Field Validation at the developer's web site.[6]

---

[6] http://tetlaw.id.au/view/javascript/really-easy-field-validation

Custom Controls

As I mentioned earlier, one of the main areas of focus for the Dojo library has been the creation of rich widgets to supplement the user interface elements that plain HTML has to offer. Among these is an extensive collection of Form Widgets that work in the same way as the slider control that we developed in this chapter, providing a rich, JavaScript-powered user interface that sits atop a standard HTML form field.

Here's a quick list of some of Dojo's Form Widgets:

Button   an advanced version of the HTML `button` element

Checkbox   like a standard HTML checkbox, but uses customizable images for the checkbox

ColorPalette   displays a grid of color swatches from which the user can choose

ComboBox   like a standard text field, but pops up a list of suggested values in response to user input

DatePicker   displays an interactive calendar for selecting a date

TimePicker   displays a rich interface for selecting a time of day

Editor2 (RichText) a WYSIWYG HTML editor that lets the user input and format rich text that's submitted as HTML

HslColorPicker   displays a rich interface for selecting a color value

Select   an advanced version of the HTML `select` element

Slider   a graphical slider control, much like the one we built in this chapter

Spinner   an input field that lets you select a number by clicking up and down arrows to adjust the value

Again, as of this writing, Dojo's widgets are sparsely documented, so trying to use them without advanced JavaScript experience can be frustrating.

The Yahoo! UI Library (YUI) offers a less extensive collection of controls,[7] but those that it does provide are richly documented with plenty of beginner-friendly examples. Here's a list of the form-related YUI Controls as of this writing:

AutoComplete   a text field that can pop up a list of suggested values in response to user input

Calendar   a rich interface for selecting a date

Slider   a graphical slider control, much like the one we built in this chapter

By all means, take some time to play with these widget libraries, and pay special attention to how well (or how badly, as is more often the case) they handle issues like keyboard navigation, screen reader accessibility, and semantically meaningful HTML code. While it can be tempting to trust these widget libraries implicitly, I believe you'll find there is definitely still a lot of value in the do-it-yourself option.

Whatever you decide, it's important to go in with your eyes open, and by understanding—at least in principle—how to build custom form controls yourself, you'll be better equipped to evaluate prepackaged options like these.

Summary

Back when JavaScript support was first added to web browsers, practically the only thing anyone could think to use it for was to enhance HTML forms. The tasks we've seen in this chapter—interlinking form fields, performing client-side validation of form submissions, and creating new types of form controls—are the things JavaScript does best, if only because it has been doing them for such a long time.

Although these form enhancements may not be as shiny and new as some of the other examples in this book, the techniques we've used to implement them—progressive enhancement, DOM manipulation, and unobtrusive scripting—certainly are. If the JavaScript pioneers that first set out to enhance HTML forms had had these techniques at their disposal, the JavaScript-enhanced forms that appear all over the Web today would work a lot better than they do.

---

[7] http://developer.yahoo.com/yui/#elements

Errors and Debugging

A truth that many JavaScript books won't tell you is that JavaScript is a tough language to get right the first time.

By now you should have a fairly solid feel for JavaScript as a language, and how to use things like event listeners and the DOM API to enrich the web sites you build. But if you've actually tried to write an original script of your own, chances are that you came away feeling humbled, and maybe even a little angry.

That frustration's probably due, in part at least, to the fact that JavaScript, like all languages that run in the browser, is designed to fail silently by default. When things go wrong in the code you write, there's no point in shouting about it to your hapless visitors, so browsers just quietly set aside broken scripts and ignore them. The instructions in this chapter will show you how to get the browser to speak up, so you can find out about JavaScript errors as they happen.

However, even once you can *see* the error messages, you'll likely find that most JavaScript errors aren't all that helpful—especially if you're new to the language. Most of them are written in "programmer-ese," or complain about a perfectly good part of the code when the problem is actually elsewhere. So we'll spend some time in this chapter deciphering the most common error messages you're likely to encounter, and what they really mean.

With those tools tucked in your belt, you should be able track down problems that the browser can detect for you. But you might still have occasion to wonder why on earth your carefully scripted code (which is perfectly fine, as far as the browser is concerned) is behaving the way it is. With the right tools, you can track a problem in your code to its source, even stepping through your JavaScript code a line at a time if necessary.

Nothing Happened!

It isn't very encouraging to spend two hours piecing together the ultimate script full of whizz-bang effects only to fire up your browser and have nothing happen; but when you're first writing a new script, that's usually your first hint that something has gone wrong—nothing happens.

The good news is that, if you've done your job right, the fact that the JavaScript fails silently means that your plain HTML/CSS can work on its own, and a user need never know that your code isn't working right. See? The browser's just looking after your reputation! This isn't much help when you're trying to find out *why* the script isn't working, though.

When you're working on your JavaScript code, then, you should configure your browser of choice to let you know about JavaScript errors when they happen. Depending on which browser you're dealing with (and of course, you will eventually need to test as many as possible), the procedure is different.

Firefox has a very nice error console that you can access by selecting **Tools** > **Error Console**. This opens the window shown in Figure 7.1. The console displays not only JavaScript errors, but errors in your CSS code, and even so-called **chrome errors** generated internally by the browser (usually after you've installed a buggy browser extension).

Figure 7.1. The Firefox Error Console

As you can see, the Firefox error console displays more than just errors:

Errors   problems with your code that prevented the browser from continuing
to run the script

Warnings   problems with your code that the browser was able to work around,
but which may indicate that the script isn't doing what you expect it
to

Messages   notes from your code that tell you what it's doing, usually only used
as a debugging tool by browser extension developers—you won't see
many of these

For each entry in the console, the specific file and line number that generated the notification will be displayed. Depending on the nature of the entry, the error console may even show you the line in question, with a little arrow pointing to the exact code that generated the entry.

When you're trying to track down a problem in your code, you'll usually start by opening the error console and clicking the **Clear** button to empty out the backlog of entries that may be displayed. Then you can reload the page in your main browser window and note the notifications that appear in the error console. If there are a lot of notifications, you might start by clicking the **Errors** button to see only the most severe errors, and concentrate on fixing them first, before returning to the **All** view to fix the less serious issues.

Opera's error console, shown in Figure 7.2, works very much like Firefox's. You can get to it by clicking **Tools** > **Advanced** > **Error Console**.

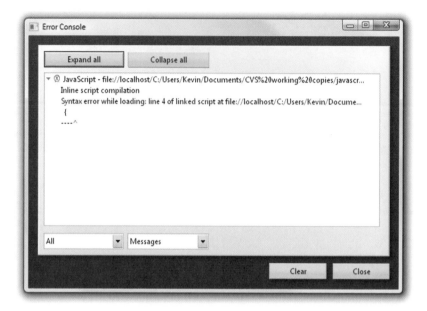

Figure 7.2. The Opera Error Console

The two drop-down menus at the bottom of this window are the key to seeing just the notifications that interest you. The first controls the source of the notifications that will be displayed, and you can choose **JavaScript** from this menu if you want to filter out things like HTML and CSS errors while working on a script. The second drop-down works much like the notification filtering buttons in Firefox's error console, enabling you to set the severity of the entries that are displayed in the console. The default selection, **Messages**, will allow messages, warnings, and errors to be displayed.

Useful error messages are harder to find in Internet Explorer. To see them, you need to open the Internet Options window (**Tools** > **Internet Options**), then, on the **Advanced** tab, look for the **Display a notification about every script error** option, under **Browsing**. Make sure it's checked, as shown in Figure 7.3.

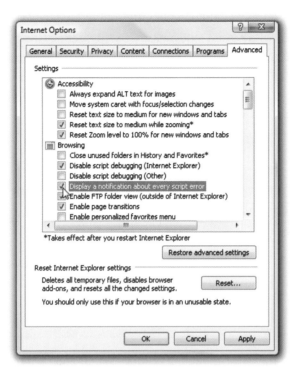

Figure 7.3. Enabling JavaScript errors in Internet Explorer

Once this option is set, you'll be notified the moment a JavaScript error has occurred, with a remarkably unhelpful message box similar to that shown in Figure 7.4.

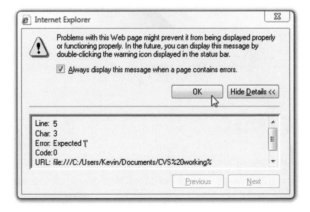

Figure 7.4. A JavaScript error notification in Internet Explorer

The only part of this window that you should really pay attention to is the line that begins with **Error:**. All the other information in this dialog (including the line and character numbers) is usually wrong. Heck, as of Internet Explorer 7, even the message at the top of this window was wrong! If you uncheck the **Always display this message when a page contains errors** checkbox, the warning icon in the status bar that it mentions will not actually be displayed.

As you can see, finding and fixing JavaScript errors in Internet Explorer is not easy. There are tools that can make it a little easier,[1] but because most JavaScript problems will affect *all* browsers, you're usually better off doing your JavaScript development in a different browser, and using Internet Explorer's JavaScript error reporting as a last resort for problems specific to that browser.

To access Safari's error console, you need to enable a hidden feature of that browser. Open a Terminal window and type:

```
defaults write com.apple.Safari IncludeDebugMenu 1
```

Press **Enter**, then quit the Terminal application. When you next launch Safari, you'll see a new **Debug** menu next to the **Help** menu. Make sure the **Log JavaScript Exceptions** option is checked in the menu, as shown in Figure 7.5, then click **Show JavaScript Console** to bring up the error console shown in Figure 7.6.

You'll note that, of the four browsers we've discussed in this section, Safari provides the tersest and least helpful error messages. It generally gets the file name and line number right, at least.

Now that you can *see* JavaScript error messages, you need to learn how to interpret them.

Common Errors

Every browser has its own particular dialect for JavaScript error messages. Almost invariably, Firefox produces the most sensible and helpful messages of current browsers, so your best bet when faced with a confusing message is to open your page in Firefox to see what its error console says.

---

[1] http://blogs.msdn.com/ie/archive/2004/10/26/247912.aspx

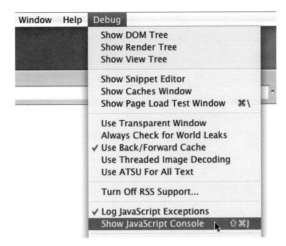

Figure 7.5. Safari's hidden **Debug** menu

Figure 7.6. Safari's Error Console

Three kinds of errors can occur in JavaScript:

- syntax errors
- runtime errors
- logic errors

Only the first two produce error messages.

Syntax Errors

A **syntax error** is caused when your code violates the fundamental rules (or syntax) of the JavaScript language. It's the browser's way of saying, "Whatchoo talkin' 'bout,

Willis?"[2] Of the errors that the browser will tell you about, syntax errors are the easiest to fix, but the hardest to spot in your code.

Here's a simple script that contains a number of syntax errors:

```
                                                          syntax.js
1  // This script contains four syntax errors
2  var MyScript = {
3    init: function
4    {
5      MyScript.doSomething();
6    }
7    doSomething: function()
8    {
9      alert("Hold onto your "hat"!");
10     \\ something happens
11   }
12 };
13
14 Core.start(MyScript);
```

If you load a page that links to this script (like **syntax.html** in the code archive) in Firefox, the error console will display the error message shown in Figure 7.7.

Figure 7.7. The first syntax error

---

[2] http://www.imdb.com/title/tt0077003/quotes

Because the browser gives up on trying to make sense of your script when it runs into a syntax error, you'll only ever be notified about the first syntax error in a given script. As you can see, the error message in this case is "missing (before formal parameters," and the browser ran into this error when it hit the opening brace ({) on line four of **syntax.js**.

Looking back at the script, it may not be immediately obvious to you what the problem is. The brace is certainly in the right place, and is required to mark the start of the `init` method's body, so why is the browser complaining about it? And what are "formal parameters" anyway?

The real problem here occurs on the previous line: the parentheses that must follow the `function` keyword were left out! These parentheses enclose the list of arguments for the function (also known as **formal parameters**), and are required. Here's what the corrected code looks like:

```
3    init: function()
4    {
5      MyScript.doSomething();
```

It turns out that most syntax errors occur when the browser was expecting one thing, but ran into something else instead. In this case, it was expecting an opening parenthesis ((), and encountered an opening brace ({) instead. That's why the error message points to the innocent-looking brace.

Usually, the error message will tell you what the browser expected to find instead (in this case, it complains about the "missing ("), but if the message doesn't make sense to you, a good tactic is to look at what immediately precedes the place in your code where the error occurred, and try to identify what you might've left out.

If you fix this error and reload the page, you'll have an excellent opportunity to try out this technique when you see the error message shown in Figure 7.8.

Can you find the problem? Again, the browser is complaining about a missing character—in this case a closing brace (})—but if you look at the line before the error, there's a closing brace there already!

Figure 7.8. Another syntax error

```
                                                           syntax.js (excerpt)

6    }
7    doSomething: function()
```

Why is the browser complaining about a missing closing brace? Well, because it thinks you need *another* closing brace. Now why would it think something like that?

The error message says "missing } after property list" because what we're doing at this point in our code is building an object (MyScript) by providing a list of its properties and methods. At the end of that list, we'd normally end the object declaration with a closing brace, but judging by the error message, JavaScript thinks we meant the object to end right here, on line seven.

Looking at the code in this light, you can probably spot what's wrong: because the first method (init) isn't followed by a comma (,), the browser doesn't know that we want to declare a second, and falsely assumes that this is the end of the object declaration. To fix this error, we must add the missing comma:

```
6    },
7    doSomething: function()
```

This case highlights the fact that error messages are often just the browser's best guess at what you meant to say with your code. In an ideal world, the message would have said something like "missing } after property list, *unless you're declaring another property, in which case you're missing a comma,*" but unfortunately browsers just aren't that smart (yet). It's up to you to notice when an error message is based on a false assumption on the browser's part, and act accordingly.

If you fix this error and reload the page, you'll see another example error, as depicted in Figure 7.9. This is an easy one, so see if you can figure it out before reading on.

Figure 7.9. Yet another syntax error

From the error message, when the browser reached the "h" in "hat," it actually expected a closing parenthesis ()), because it thought it had reached the end of the argument list for the `alert` function call. Why would it think that in the middle of an argument?

Again, look at the code that immediately precedes the error for an explanation. Just before the "h" is a double quote ("), which the browser interprets as the end of the string `"Hold onto your "`—the first argument in your `alert` function call. After this argument, it expects either a comma (,) followed by the next argument, or a closing parenthesis to complete the list of arguments. The error message assumes you meant to choose the latter option.

Of course, in this case, you meant neither—you don't actually want that double quote to signal the end of the first argument! To fix this, escape the double quotes in the string with backslashes:

```
9       alert("Hold onto your \"hat\"!");
```

Figure 7.10 shows the final error that the browser will trip over in this script.

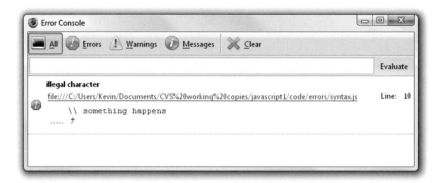

Figure 7.10. Guess what! (Yes—it's another syntax error)

Okay, I threw you a bone with this one. Just to show you that it *does* happen now and then, this error message says exactly what it means. The backslash at the start of the line is termed an **illegal character**, which is a fancy way of saying "Get a grip—you're not even *allowed* to type a backslash here!"

The problem, of course, is that comments must be preceded by a double slash, not a double backslash:

```
10      // something happens
```

As you can see, once you've figured out where you went wrong, syntax errors are easy to fix, but the error messages that the browser displays can often be misleading. Usually it comes down to a forgotten character or two, or accidentally using one type of bracket when you meant to use another.

The good news is that the more JavaScript you write, the more familiar you'll become with the nitty-gritty details of the language, and the fewer syntax errors you'll be likely to run into.

Runtime Errors

Runtime errors occur when a perfectly valid piece of JavaScript code tries to do something that it's not allowed to do, or that is flat out impossible. These errors are so named because they occur while the script is actually running. Unlike syntax error messages, the messages produced by runtime errors tend to be right on the money. The trick is figuring out why the error occurred.

This script contains a number of runtime errors:

```
                                                                    runtime.js
 1 // This script contains three runtime errors
 2 var MyScript = {
 3   init: function()
 4   {
 5     var example = document.getElementsById("example");
 6
 7     for (var i = 0; i < example.length; i++)
 8     {
 9       Core.addEventListener(example[i], "click", doSomething);
10     }
11
12     var links = documents.getElementsByTagName("a");
13     var firstLink = links[0];
14
15     if (firstLink && firstLink.className == "")
16     {
17       alert("The first link has no class assigned to it!");
18     }
19   },
20   doSomething: function(event)
21   {
22     alert("Hold onto your \"hat\"!");
23   }
24 };
25
26 Core.start(MyScript);
```

Once again, fire up Firefox and load the corresponding HTML file (**runtime.html**) to see the first error produced by this script—it's shown in Figure 7.11.

As you can see, runtime errors look just like syntax errors, except that the error console doesn't show the line of code that caused a runtime error.

An "is not a function" error usually indicates that you've misspelled the name of the function or method that you're trying to call, or that the function or method that you're trying to call simply doesn't exist.

Figure 7.11. A runtime error … how novel!

As a newcomer to JavaScript, you'll probably see this message a lot—especially if you aren't used to the case-sensitive nature of JavaScript. Attempting to call `Alert` instead of `alert`, for example, will produce this error message. But it can happen in more subtle cases too, like calling a string method like `toLowerCase` on a text node (which isn't a string), rather than the `nodeValue` of the text node (which is).

In this example, the cause is far simpler: the developer has tried to call a method called `getElementsById` when there is no such method. The method the developer was probably thinking of is `getElementById` (without the "s"). Since you can only have one element with a given ID in a document, it wouldn't make sense for there to be a method called `getElementsById`.

The fix in this case is trivial:

```
5      var example = document.getElementById("example");
```

But it turns out that fixing this problem actually causes another runtime error, shown in Figure 7.12.

A "has no properties" error means that you're trying to treat something that isn't an object as if it were an object, by trying to access a property or method on something that has neither.

The most common cause of this error is a method that normally returns an object (like `getElementById`) returning `null`, JavaScript's special "no object" value. If your code assumes that an object would be returned and treats the returned value as such, you'll end up with an error like this.

Figure 7.12. A runtime error that's slightly less clear

In this case, the error is being caused by the following line of code:

```
runtime.js (excerpt)

7    for (var i = 0; i < example.length; i++)
```

If you check **runtime.html**, you'll see that there isn't actually an element with ID `example`, so the `getElementById` call we just fixed above returns `null`, and when this `for` loop tries to read the `length` property of that `null` value, it produces the error message we're looking at now.

Apparently, whoever wrote this script assumed that the fictitious `getElementsById` method would return an empty array if it didn't find any elements with the specified ID. Since `getElementById` returns either a single element node or `null`, we need to replace the `for` loop with an `if` statement:

```
 3    init: function()
 4    {
 5      var example = document.getElementsById("example");
 6
 7      if (example)
 8      {
 9        Core.addEventListener(example, "click", doSomething);
10      }
```

With that fixed, Figure 7.13 shows the last runtime error in this script.

Figure 7.13. A runtime error that's easy to fix

An "is not defined" error is about as easy an error to fix as there is. Like the "is not a function" error we saw earlier, it usually results from a simple typing mistake, but rather than a misspelled function or method name, "is not defined" indicates you've tried to use a variable or property that doesn't exist.

In this case, the error is really straightforward:

runtime.js *(excerpt)*

```
12    var links = documents.getElementsByTagName("a");
```

As you can see, the developer has simply misspelled `document` as `documents`.

Fix this error, and the script will successfully display the alert message, "The first link has no class assigned to it!"

Logic Errors

Logic errors aren't so much errors as they are bugs in your script. The code runs fine as it was written—it just doesn't behave the way you expected it to when you wrote it. These kinds of errors can be devilishly difficult to find because as far as the browser's concerned the script is working just fine, so you never see an error message.

Since every logic error is different, each one presents a new challenge. Just in case you're not entirely clear what a logic error *is*, here's a script with a few logic errors in it:

logic.js

```
1  // This script contains three logic errors
2  var MyScript = {
3    init: function()
4    {
5      var links = document.getElementsByTagName("a");
6      var exampleLinks = [];
7      for (var i = 0; i < links.length; i++)
8      {
9        if (links[i].className = "Example")
10       {
11         Core.addEventListener(
12             links[i], "click", MyScript.doSomething);
13         exampleLinks[exampleLinks.length] = links[i];
14         i--;
15       }
16     }
17   },
18   doSomething: function(event)
19   {
20     alert("Hold onto your \"hat\"!");
21   }
22 };
23
24 Core.start(MyScript);
```

This script is *supposed* to find and build an array that contains all links in the document that have a `class` attribute of `example`, and assign to each one the `doSomething` method as a `click` event listener.

Due to what could be described as a perfect storm of logic errors, this script actually attempts to *set* the `class` attribute of *every* link in the document to `Example`, but only gets as far as setting the first one in the document before going into an infinite loop that hangs the browser. Nice, huh?

If it's any consolation, you'd have to be pretty unlucky to innocently produce a script with so serious a combination of logic errors as this. However, taken in isolation, each of the logic errors in this script is a reasonably common bug of the type you may run into when writing your own scripts.

The most serious problem in the script is the infinite loop, which is just about as bad a problem as you'll ever create with a logic error. Older browsers would become completely unresponsive, and would have to be forcibly terminated by the user in the event of an infinite loop. These days, browsers will detect when a script has been running for a long time, and will display a message like the one shown in Figure 7.14, which offers to stop the script and return control to the user.

Figure 7.14. The prompt an infinite loop will produce (eventually)

Let's start by fixing this problem. Here's the code responsible for the infinite loop:

```
                                                            logic.js (excerpt)
12        exampleLinks[exampleLinks.length] = links[i];
13        i--;
```

When the script has discovered a link that it wants to add to the exampleLinks array, it does so with the first of these two statements. Unfortunately, the developer seems to have suffered a brain fart, and assumed that adding a reference to the link to the end of the exampleLinks array would remove it from the node list stored in links. In an effort to compensate for this imagined loss of an item from links, the developer has decremented the counter variable with the second statement (i--;).

In fact, the link remains in the links node list, and all the decrementing i achieves is to cause the for loop to process the same link over and over again—our infinite loop.

We can avoid the infinite loop simply by removing the second statement:

```
7     for (var i = 0; i != links.length; i++)
8     {
9       if (links[i].className = "Example")
```

```
10        {
11          Core.addEventListener(
12              links[i], "click", MyScript.doSomething);
13          exampleLinks[exampleLinks.length] = links[i];
14        }
15    }
```

Run this corrected code, and the next thing you'll discover is that the `click` event listener is assigned to *every* link in the document. Behind the scenes, the `exampleLinks` array is also filled with all the links in the page. What's causing this issue?

The source of this bug is an extremely common mistake made by JavaScript beginners, who will often confuse the assignment operator (=) with the equality operator (==). See it now?

logic.js *(excerpt)*

```
9        if (links[i].className = "Example")
```

The condition in this `if` statement is supposed to be checking if the `className` property has a value *equal* to `"Example"`, but the developer has mistakenly used the assignment operator (=) here, causing this code to *set* the value of `className` to `"Example"`. An assignment statement used as a condition like this evaluates to the assigned value (`"Example"`), and since any non-empty string is considered "true," the `if` statement will execute for every link it processes. The solution, of course, is to use the correct operator:

```
9        if (links[i].className == "Example")
```

Run this modified code, however, and you'll suddenly find that the event listener isn't assigned to *any* of the links in the page—not even the first one in this paragraph:

logic.html *(excerpt)*

```
    <p>This is an <a href="http://www.example.com/"
        class="example">example</a>, but this
    <a href="http://www.sitepoint.com/">is not</a>.</p>
```

This one's pretty obvious. The `if` statement is looking for a `className` of `"Example"` (capital "E"), but the `class` attribute of the link is `example` (lowercase "e"). Class names are case-sensitive, so we need to make sure the script matches the actual `class` value in the document:

```
9        if (links[i].className == "example")
```

Now be honest: how many of those errors could you have spotted without my help, based only on the behavior of the browser? And if you thought spotting logic errors in someone *else's* code was difficult, just wait till you're sitting in front of your *own* code armed only with the absolute conviction that your code is perfect in every way!

In the absence of error messages, you need a specialized tool to help you track down logic errors like the ones we've just seen.

Debugging with Firebug

In the past, the most common approach to resolving logic errors in JavaScript code was liberal use of the `alert` function. If you're expecting a `for` loop to run five times, you can stick an `alert` on the first line inside the loop and see if the browser displays five alert boxes when you load the page. If it does, you move the `alert` call somewhere else, to test another theory about why your script might be misbehaving.

Sound tedious? It is.

At the time of writing, a much more powerful (not to mention sane) approach is to use a JavaScript debugger, and by far the best debugger around is Firebug. Firebug is a free extension for Firefox that adds to the browser a panel containing a rich set of tools for diagnosing problems with your HTML, CSS, and JavaScript. You can download and install it from the Firebug web site,[3] shown in Figure 7.15.

---

[3] http://www.getfirebug.com/

Figure 7.15. Getting Firebug

Let me show you how to use Firebug to track down the infinite loop that we fixed in the previous section:

1. Open the page in your browser, and wait for the "Unresponsive Script" warning. Click **Stop script**.

2. Hit **F12**, or click the new Firebug status icon at the bottom of the browser window to open the Firebug panel, shown in Figure 7.16, at the bottom of your browser.

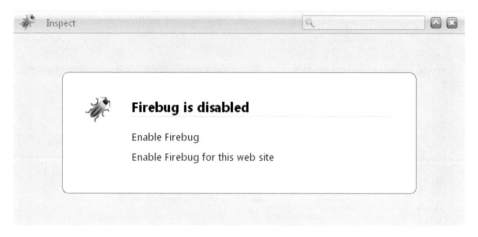

Figure 7.16. The Firebug panel

3. Since Firebug slows your browser's performance, it's disabled by default. Click either of the **Enable Firebug** links to enable Firebug. The first thing you'll see is the **Console** tab pictured in Figure 7.17.

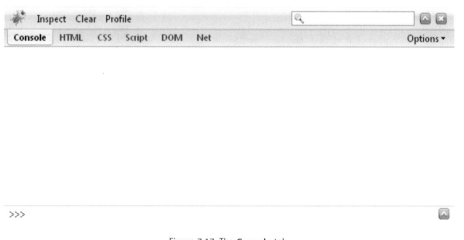

Figure 7.17. The **Console** tab

Like Firefox's error console, Firebug's **Console** tab will display JavaScript and CSS errors. It will also display useful information about Ajax requests, which you'll learn about in the next chapter, if you select **Show XMLHttpRequests** on the **Options** menu. You can type any JavaScript statement or expression into the command line at the bottom of the tab, and Firebug will execute it in the currently displayed page and display the result in the console.

4. To fix the infinite loop in this page, however, we need something more powerful than the **Console** tab. Click the **Script** tab to see Firebug's JavaScript debugger, which is depicted in Figure 7.18.

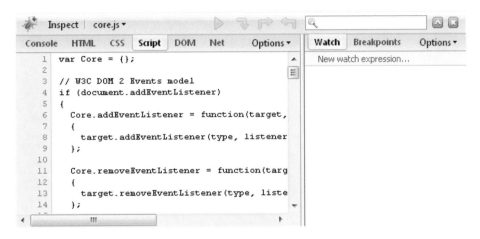

Figure 7.18. The **Script** tab

5. The debugger lets you pause the execution of your scripts and step through them one line at a time, observing the values of variables and the structure of the DOM as you go. Since the problem is likely to be in the **logic.js** file, start by selecting it from the drop-down menu at the top of the Firebug tab, as shown in Figure 7.19.

6. Firebug now displays the code of the **logic.js** file. We can tell by the way the browser is hanging that we're dealing with an infinite loop, and the only loop in the code is the `for` loop on line 7, so click in the gutter next to that line number, as shown in Figure 7.20. This sets a **breakpoint**, represented by a red circle, which tells the debugger to pause the execution of your script when it reaches that line.

7. With your breakpoint in place, reload the page. As Figure 7.21 indicates, a yellow arrow will appear on top of the breakpoint to indicate that execution of the script has been paused at that line. The **Watch** tab in the debugger's right-

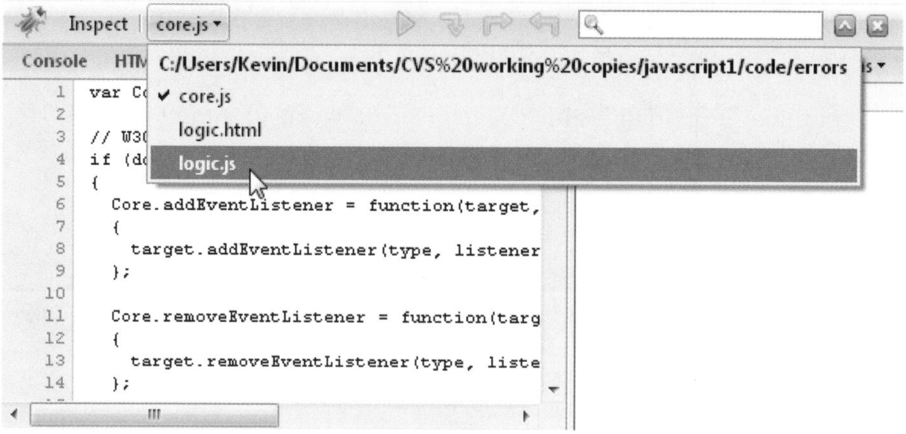

Figure 7.19. Selecting the file to debug

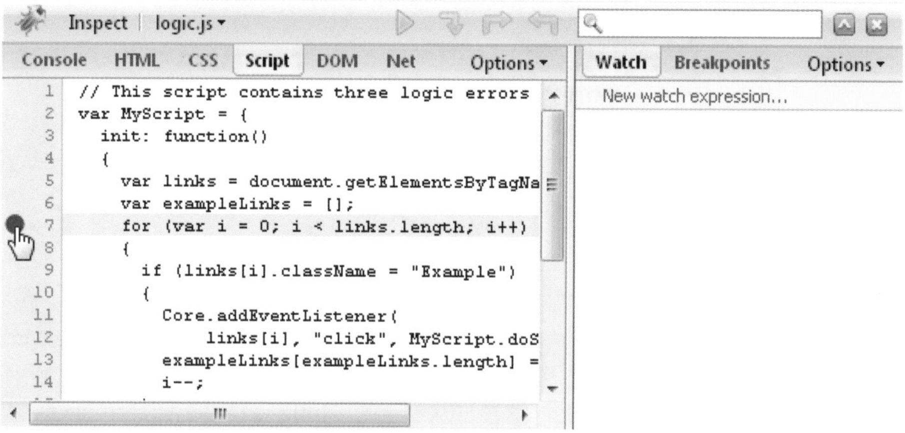

Figure 7.20. Setting a breakpoint

hand pane will also show the local variables that exist on that line, and their current values.

While the debugger is paused, you can click one of the four buttons at the top of the Firebug panel to control the execution of your script. The blue arrow resumes normal execution of the script, which will continue until it reaches the next breakpoint, if any. The three gold arrows let you step through your script one statement at a time. The first, **Step Over**, simply executes the current statement and pauses execution again on the next line of the current code listing. The second, **Step Into** works just like **Step Over**, except when the current state-

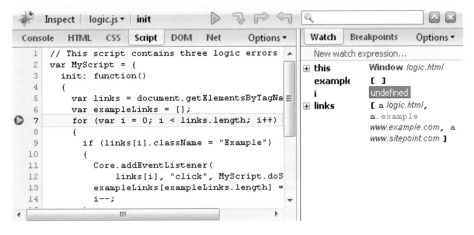

Figure 7.21. Pausing execution

ment contains a function or method call. In such cases, the debugger will step *into* the call, pausing execution on the first line inside the function/method. The third arrow, **Step Out**, allows the script to finish executing the current function, and pauses execution on the next line of the code that called it.

8. Click **Step Over** once to move to the first line inside the `for` loop.

9. Now, it would be nice to know about the current link being processed by the `for` loop, `links[i]`. You can eyeball it by looking at the value of `i` in the **Watch** pane, then expanding the `links` variable in that pane to find the corresponding element of the array. Alternatively, you can click the area labeled **New watch expression...**, type **links[i]**, and press **Enter** to add the expression to the list of local variables in the **Watch** pane, as shown in Figure 7.22.

So we can tell that the first time through the loop, `links[i]` is pointing to the hyperlink to `logic.html`.

10. Click the yellow arrow in the gutter to set another breakpoint, this time on line 9.

11. Click the blue arrow to resume execution of the script. The `for` loop finishes its first iteration and starts its second. Execution pauses at the new breakpoint on line 9. Already, as shown in Figure 7.23, you can spot a number of clues about what's going wrong:

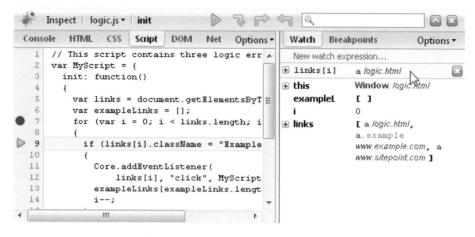

Figure 7.22. Adding a custom watch expression

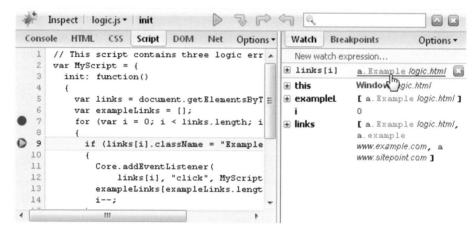

Figure 7.23. Examining the clues

- i still has a value of 0, even though we're in the second iteration of the loop.

- links[i] still refers to the link to logic.html, except that it now has a class of Example.

- The links node list still contains all three of the links in our document.

At this point, a perceptive developer would be looking very hard at that if statement and the i--; inside it. If you needed more to go on, you could step through the body of the for loop line by line to see exactly what's going on.

Firebug has *tons* of other cool stuff in it. Spend some time reading the Firebug web site to learn about the other features that it offers to aid you in your quest for the answer to the eternal question, "Why is the browser *doing* that?" And if you like what you see, think about donating a few bucks to the development of this incredible tool—I have.

Summary

That's it! You can go out and brag to your friends that you know JavaScript now. From here on in, we'll look at extra browser features and other software that can make JavaScript do more.

In the next chapter, we'll delve into the mysteries of Ajax, whose sheer buzzword power may well be the reason you *bought* this book. If so, you'll be pleased to know that the long wait is over. Turn the page, and bask in the buzz.

Ajax

It's probably not an understatement to say that Ajax has revitalized the Web. It's certainly one of the reasons for a resurgent interest in JavaScript and it might even be the reason that you're reading this book.

Irrespective of the hyperbole surrounding Ajax, the technology has dramatically affected the way in which people can interact with a web page. The ability to update individual parts of a page with information from a remote server mightn't sound like a revolutionary change, but it has facilitated a seamless type of interaction that has been missing from HTML documents since their inception.

This ability to create a fluidly updating web page has captured the imaginations of developers and interaction designers alike; they've flocked to Ajax in droves, using it to create the next generation of web applications, as well as annoy the heck out of the average user. As with any new technology, there's a temptation to overuse Ajax; but when it's used sensibly, it can definitely create more helpful, more responsive, and more enjoyable interfaces for users to explore.

Although quite a few of the JavaScript libraries out there will offer you a complete "Ajax experience" in a box, there is really no substitute for the freedom that comes with knowing how it works from the ground up. So let's dive in!

XMLHttpRequest: Chewing Bite-sized Chunks of Content

The main concept of Ajax is that you're instructing the browser to fetch small pieces of content instead of big ones; instead of a page you might request a single paragraph.

Although cross-browser Ajax-type functionality was hacked together previously with `iframes`, the current Ajax movement was sparked when `XMLHttpRequest` became available in more than just Internet Explorer.

`XMLHttpRequest` is a browser feature that allows JavaScript to make a call to a server without going through the normal browser page-request mechanism. This means that JavaScript can make additional server requests behind the scenes while a page is being viewed. In effect, this allows us to pull down extra data from the server, then manipulate the page using the DOM—replacing sections, adding sections, or deleting sections depending on the data we receive. The distinction between normal and Ajax requests is illustrated in Figure 8.1.

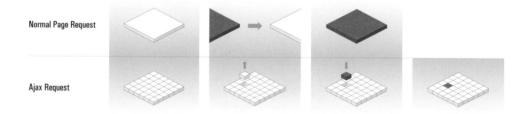

Figure 8.1. Comparing a normal page request (replacing the whole page) with an Ajax request (replacing part of the page)

Communications with the server that don't use the page-request mechanism are called **asynchronous requests**, because they can be made without interrupting the user's page interaction. A normal page request is synchronous, in that the browser waits for a response from the server before any more interaction is allowed.

`XMLHttpRequest` is really the only aspect of Ajax that's truly new. Every other part of an Ajax interaction—the event listener that triggers it, the DOM manipulation that updates the page, and so on—has been covered in previous chapters of this book already. So, once you know how to make an asynchronous request, you're ready to go.

Creating an `XMLHttpRequest` Object

Internet Explorer 5 and 6 were the first browsers to implement `XMLHttpRequest`, and they did so using an ActiveX object:[1]

```
var requester = new ActiveXObject("Microsoft.XMLHTTP");
```

Every other browser that supports `XMLHttpRequest` (including Internet Explorer 7) does so without using ActiveX. A request object for these browsers looks like this:

```
var requester = new XMLHttpRequest();
```

 ActiveX is Unreliable

The way that `XMLHttpRequest` is implemented in Internet Explorer 6 and earlier means that if a user has disabled *trusted* ActiveX controls, `XMLHttpRequest` will be unavailable to you even if JavaScript is enabled. Many people disable *untrusted* ActiveX controls, but disabling trusted ActiveX controls is less common.

We can easily reconcile the differences between the two methods of object creation using a `try-catch` statement, which will automatically detect the correct way to create an `XMLHttpRequest` object:

try-catch_test.js *(excerpt)*

```
try
{
    var requester = new XMLHttpRequest(); ❶
}
```

---

[1] An ActiveX object is Microsoft's term for a reusable software component that provides encapsulated, reusable functionality. In Internet Explorer, such objects normally give client-side scripting access to operating system facilities like the file system, or in the case of `XMLHttpRequest`, the network layer.

```
catch (error) ❷
{
  try
  {
    var requester = new ActiveXObject("Microsoft.XMLHTTP"); ❸
  }
  catch (error)
  {
    var requester = null;
  }
}
```

A `try` statement allows you to try out a block of code, but if anything inside that block causes an error, the program won't stop execution entirely; instead, it moves onto the `catch` statement and runs the code inside that. As you can see in Figure 8.2, the whole structure is like an `if-else` statement, except the branch taken is conditional on any errors occurring.

We need to use a `try-catch` statement to create ActiveX objects because an object detection test will indicate that ActiveX controls are still available even if a user has disabled them (though your script will throw an error when you actually try to create an ActiveX object).

The Damage Done

If an error occurs inside a `try` statement, the program will not revert to the state it had before the `try` statement was executed—instead, it will switch immediately to the `catch` statement. Thus, any variables that were created *before* the error occurred will still exist. However, if an error occurs while a variable is being assigned, that variable will not be created at all.

Here's what happens in the code above:

❶ We try to create an `XMLHttpRequest` object using the cross-browser method. If our attempt is successful, the variable `requester` will be a new `XMLHttpRequest` object. But if `XMLHttpRequest` is unavailable, the code will cause an error. We can try out a different method inside the `catch` statement.

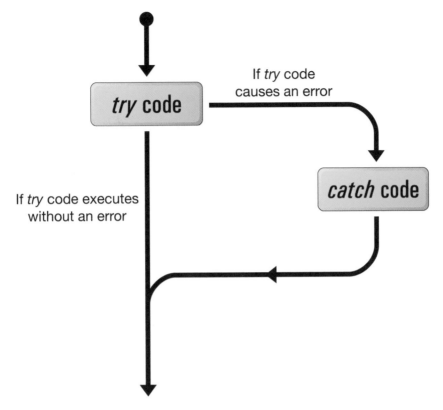

Figure 8.2. The logical structure or a `try-catch` statement

② `catch` statements "catch" the exception that caused the `try` statement to fail. This exception is identified by the variable name that appears in brackets after `catch`, and it's mandatory to give that exception a name (even if we're not going to use it). You can give the exception any name you like, but I think `error` is nicely descriptive.

③ Inside the `catch`, we try to create an `XMLHttpRequest` object via ActiveX. If that attempt is successful, `requester` will be a valid `XMLHttpRequest` object, but if we still can't create the object, the second `catch` statement sets `requester` to `null`. This makes it easy to test whether the current user agent supports `XMLHttpRequest`, and to fork to some non-Ajax fallback code (such as that which submits a form normally):

```
if (requester == null)
{
  code for non-Ajax clients
}
else
{
  code for Ajax-enabled clients
}
```

Thankfully, the significant differences between browser implementations of XMLHttpRequest end with its creation. All of the basic data communication methods can be called using the same syntax, irrespective of the browser in which they're running.

Calling a Server

Once we've created an XMLHttpRequest object, we must call two separate methods—open and send—in order to get it to retrieve data from a server.

open initializes the connection and takes two required arguments, with several optionals. The first argument is the type of HTTP request you want to send (GET, POST, DELETE, etc.); the second is the location from which you want to request data. For instance, if we wanted to use a GET request to access **feed.xml** in the root directory of a web site, we'd initialize the XMLHttpRequest object like this:

```
requester.open("GET", "/feed.xml", true);
```

The URL can be either relative or absolute, but due to cross-domain security concerns the target must reside on the same domain as the page that's requesting it.

 HTTP Only

Quite a few browsers will only allow XMLHttpRequest calls via http:// and https:// URLs, so if you're viewing your site locally via a URL beginning with file://, your XMLHttpRequest call may not be allowed.

The third argument of open is a Boolean that specifies whether the request is made asynchronously (true) or synchronously (false). A synchronous request will freeze the browser until the request has completed, disallowing user interaction in the interim. An asynchronous request occurs in the application's background, allowing other scripts to run and the user to access the browser at the same time. I recommend you use asynchronous requests; otherwise, you run the risk of users' browsers locking up while they wait for a request that has gone awry. open also has optional fourth and fifth arguments that specify the user's name and password for authentication purposes when a password-protected URL is requested.

Once open has been used to initialize a connection, the send method activates that connection and makes the request. send takes one argument that allows you to send encoded data along with a POST request, in the same format as a form submission:

```
requester.setRequestHeader("Content-Type",
    "application/x-www-form-urlencoded");
requester.open("POST", "/query.php", true);
requester.send("name=Clark&email=superman@justiceleague.xmp");
```

 Content-Type Required

Opera requires you to set the Content-Type header of a POST request using the setRequestHeader method. Other browsers don't require it, but it's the safest approach to take to allow for all browsers.

To simulate a form submission using a GET request, you need to hard-code the names and values into the open URL, then execute send with a null value:

```
requester.open("GET",
    "query.php?name=Clark&email=superman@justiceleague.xmp", true);
requester.send(null);
```

Internet Explorer doesn't require you to pass any value to send, but Mozilla browsers will return an error if no value is passed; that's why null is included in the above code.

Once you've called send, XMLHttpRequest will contact the server and retrieve the data that you requested. In the case of an asynchronous request, the function that created the connection will likely finish executing while the retrieval takes place.

In terms of program flow, making an `XMLHttpRequest` call is a lot like `setTimeout`, which you'll remember from Chapter 5.

We use an event handler to notify us that the server has returned a response. In this particular case, we'll need to handle changes in the value of the `XMLHttpRequest` object's `readyState` property, which specifies the status of the object's connection, and can take any of these values:

0   uninitialized

1   loading

2   loaded

3   interactive

4   complete

We can monitor changes in the `readyState` property by handling `readystatechange` events, which are triggered each time the property's value changes:

```
requester.onreadystatechange = readystatechangeHandler;

function readystatechangeHandler()
{
  code to handle changes in XMLHttpRequest readystate
}
```

`readyState` increments from 0 to 4, and the `readystatechange` event is triggered for each increment. However, we only really want to know when the connection has completed (that is, `readyState` equals 4), so our handling function needs to check for this value.

Upon the connection's completion, we also have to check whether the `XMLHttpRequest` object successfully retrieved the data, or was given an HTTP error code such as 404 (page not found). You can determine this from the request object's `status` property, which contains an integer value. A value of 200 is a fulfilled request; you should check for it—along with 304 (not modified)—as these values indicate successfully retrieved data. However, `status` can take as a value *any* of the HTTP codes that servers are able to return, so you may want to write some conditions that will handle some other codes. In general, however, you'll need to specify a course of action for your program to take if the request is not successful:

```
requester.onreadystatechange = readystatechangeHandler;

function readystatechangeHandler()
{
  if (requester.readyState == 4)
  {
    if (requester.status == 200 || requester.status == 304)
    {
      code to handle successful request
    }
    else
    {
      code to handle failed request
    }
  }
}
```

Instead of assigning a function that's defined elsewhere as the readystatechange event handler, you can declare a new, anonymous (unnamed) function inline:

```
requester.onreadystatechange = function()
{
  if (requester.readyState == 4)
  {
    if (requester.status == 200 || requester.status == 304)
    {
      code to handle successful request
    }
    else
    {
      code to handle failed request
    }
  }
}
```

The advantage of specifying the readystatechange callback function inline like this is that the requester object will be available inside that function via a closure. If the readystatechange handler function is declared separately, you'll need to jump through hoops to obtain a reference to the `requester` object inside the handling function.

XMLHttpRequest is Non-recyclable

Even though an `XMLHttpRequest` object allows you to call the `open` method multiple times, each object can effectively only be used for one call, as the `readystatechange` event refuses to fire again once `readyState` changes to 4 (in Mozilla browsers). Therefore, you will have to create a new `XMLHttpRequest` object every time you want to retrieve new data from the server.

Dealing with Data

If you've made a successful request, the next logical step is to read the server's response. Two properties of the `XMLHttpRequest` object can be used for this purpose:

responseXML   This property stores a DOM tree representing the retrieved data, but only if the server indicated a `content-type` of `text/xml` for the response. This DOM tree can be explored and modified using the standard JavaScript DOM access methods and properties we explored in Chapter 3, such as `getElementsByTagName`, `childNodes`, and `parentNode`.

responseText   This property stores the response data as a single string. If the `content-type` of the data supplied by the server was `text/plain` or `text/html`, this is the only property that will contain data. In the case of a `text/xml` response, this property will also contain the XML code as a text string, providing an alternative to `responseXML`.

In simple cases, plain text works perfectly well as a means of transmitting and handling the response, so the `XMLHttpRequest` object doesn't exactly live up to its name. When we're dealing with more complex data structures, however, XML can provide a convenient way to express those structures:

```
<?xml version="1.0" ?>
<user>
  <name>Doctor Who</name>
```

```
  <email>thedoctor@tardis.biz</email>
</user>
<user>
  <name>The Master</name>
  <email>themaster@gallifrey.org</email>
</user>
```

responseXML allows us to access different parts of the data using all the DOM features with which we're familiar from our dealings with HTML documents. Remember that data contained between tags is considered to be a text node inside the element in question. With that in mind, extracting a single value from a responseXML structure is reasonably easy:

```
var nameNode =
    requester.responseXML.getElementsByTagName("name")[0];
var nameTextNode = nameNode.childNodes[0];
var name = nameTextNode.nodeValue;
```

The name variable will now take as its value the first user's name: "Doctor Who".

Whitespace Generates Text Nodes

As in HTML documents, be aware that whitespace between tags in XML will often be interpreted as a text node. If in doubt, remember that you can check if a given node is an element by looking at its nodeType property, as described in Chapter 4.

We can use the data contained in the XML to modify or create new HTML content, updating the interface on the fly in the manner that has become synonymous with Ajax.

The main downside of using XML with JavaScript is that a fair amount of work can be involved in parsing XML structures and accessing the information we want. However, an alternative way to use the XMLHttpRequest object is to remove this data processing layer and allow the server to return HTML code, all ready to insert into your page. This approach is taken by libraries such as Prototype, in which HTML is delivered with a MIME type of text/html and the value of responseText is automatically inserted into the document using innerHTML, overwriting the contents of an existing element.

As with any use of `innerHTML`, this technique suffers from the disadvantages we discussed in Chapter 4, but it can certainly be a viable option if your circumstances require it.

A Word on Screen Readers

Until now, we've always taken time to make sure our JavaScript enhancements do not prevent users of assistive technologies—like screen readers—from using our sites. Unfortunately, when you add Ajax to the equation, this goal becomes extremely difficult, if not impossible to achieve for screen reader users in particular.

Most, if not all of the current screen readers are unable to handle in a sensible (let alone useful) way the on-the-fly page updates that typify Ajax development. Screen readers either will not pick up those changes at all, or they'll pick them up at the most untimely of moments.

In some very specific cases, developers have begun to produce experimental solutions that start to address these issues, but we're a long way from having reliable, best-practice techniques in hand. The prevailing wisdom suggests that any real solution will have to be developed at least in part by the screen reader vendors themselves.

This leaves web developers like you and me with a tough decision: do we abandon Ajax and the amazing usability enhancements that it makes possible, or do we shut out screen reader users and take full advantage of Ajax? Of course, if you can justify asking screen reader users to disable JavaScript when visiting your site, you can offer these users the same fallback experience as other non-JavaScript users, which can work just fine. But you'll need to make sure these users can find out enough about your site to decide if it's worth disabling JavaScript to proceed. And consider making it even easier—a link that said "Disable user interface features on this site that are not compatible with screen readers," for example, would not be out of the question.

Putting Ajax into Action

Now you know the basics of Ajax—how to create and use an `XMLHttpRequest` object. But it's probably easier to understand how Ajax fits into a JavaScript program if you try out a simple example.

In this example, we'll retrieve information that's relevant to the selections users make from the widget shown in Figure 8.3. This tool allows users to choose any of three cities; each selection will update the widget's display with the weather for that location.

Figure 8.3. In our weather widget, the user is asked to select a particular city

The HTML for the widget looks like this:

```
                                                weather_widget.html (excerpt)
<div id="weatherWidget">
  <h2>Weather</h2>
  <p>Please select a city:</p>
  <ul>
    <li>
      <a href="/weather/london/">London</a>
    </li>
    <li>
      <a href="/weather/new_york/">New York</a>
    </li>
    <li>
      <a href="/weather/melbourne/">Melbourne</a>
    </li>
  </ul>
</div>
```

We'll override those anchors with our Ajax code, but it's important to note that the href attribute of each anchor points to a valid location. This means that users who have JavaScript or XMLHttpRequest turned off will still be able to get the information; they just won't be gobsmacked by our cool use of Ajax to retrieve it.

When creating Ajax functionality, you can generally follow this pattern:

1. Initialize event listeners.

2. Handle event triggers.

3. Create an XMLHttpRequest connection.

4. Parse data.

5. Modify the page.

To handle the behavior of this weather widget, we'll create a WeatherWidget object. Its initialization function will start by adding event listeners to those anchor tags, which will capture any clicks that the user makes:

weather_widget.js *(excerpt)*

```
var WeatherWidget =
{
  init: function()
  {
    var weatherWidget = document.getElementById("weatherWidget");
    var anchors = weatherWidget.getElementsByTagName("a");

    for (var i = 0; i < anchors.length; i++)
    {
      Core.addEventListener(anchors[i], "click",
          WeatherWidget.clickListener);
    }
  },
  ⋮
};
```

Each of those anchors now has a click event listener, but what happens when the event is fired? Let's fill out the listener method, clickListener:

```
clickListener: function(event)
{
  try
  {
    var requester = new XMLHttpRequest(); ❶
  }
  catch (error)
  {
    try
    {
      var requester = new ActiveXObject("Microsoft.XMLHTTP");
    }
    catch (error)
    {
      var requester = null;
    }
  }

  if (requester != null) ❷
  {
    var widgetLink = this;
    widgetLink._timer = setTimeout(function() ❸
      {
        requester.abort();

        WeatherWidget.writeError(
          "The server timed out while making your request.");
      }, 10000);

    var city = this.firstChild.nodeValue; ❹

    requester.open("GET", "ajax_weather.php?city=" +
      encodeURIComponent(city), true); ❺
    requester.onreadystatechange = function() ❻
    {
      if (requester.readyState == 4)
      {
        clearTimeout(widgetLink._timer);

        if (requester.status == 200 || requester.status == 304)
        {
          WeatherWidget.writeUpdate(requester.responseXML);
        }
        else
```

```
        {
          WeatherWidget.writeError(
              "The server was unable to be contacted.");
        }
      }
    };
    requester.send(null); ❼

    Core.preventDefault(event); ❽
  }
}
```

❶   The start of this function is occupied by the standard XMLHttpRequest creation
    code that we looked at earlier in this chapter.

❷   Once that has been executed, the real logic of clickListener is contained inside
    the conditional statement if (requester != null). By using this condition,
    we ensure that the Ajax code is only executed if the XMLHttpRequest object is
    available. Otherwise, the event handling function will exit normally, allowing
    the browser to navigate to the href location, just as it would if JavaScript wasn't
    enabled. This approach provides an accessible alternative for users without
    Ajax capability.

❸   This is a real-world Ajax application that's subject to the unreliability of net-
    work traffic, so before the actual Ajax call is made, it's a good idea to place a
    time limit on the transaction to ensure that the user won't be sitting around
    waiting forever if the server fails to respond. To establish this limit, we assign
    a setTimeout call as a custom property of the link that was clicked
    (widgetLink), with a ten-second delay. If the Ajax request takes longer than
    ten seconds, the function supplied to setTimeout will be called, canceling the
    request via the abort method, and supplying the user with a sensible error
    message. Just like the readystatechange listener, the timeout function is spe-
    cified inline, so requester will be available via a closure. We'll have to remem-
    ber to stop this timeout later, if and when the Ajax request is actually completed.

❹   In the first line of code after the timeout function, we determine which city
    was selected. To do so, we get the value of the text from the anchor that was
    clicked. We assume that the link contains a text node—so that will be the first
    child node of the anchor—and the city name itself will be the nodeValue of

that text node. We can pass this value to our server-side script in order to access the weather data for that particular city.

5 Once the requested city has been identified, we begin our Ajax connection. For this example we're using a GET request, and the server-side script we're trying to access is at `ajax_weather.php`. Since we're using GET, the request variables have to be encoded directly into the URL. To do so, we append a question mark (?) to the script location, followed by the variables specified as *name=value* pairs. If you want to pass multiple variables (we don't in this case), each pair must be separated by an ampersand (&).

In this example, we're passing the city as a request variable called `city`; its value is the city name we extracted from the link. The actual value is generated by the built-in `escapeURIComponent` function, which will encode values so that they don't cause errors when being used as part of a URL. You should encode any string values that you attach to a URL this way.

6 Once the `requester` object has been initialized with `requester.open`, we set up our `readystatechange` event handler as an anonymous inline function. The code inside this handler is almost identical to the template that we outlined earlier in this chapter, except that we have filled in the actions that are to be taken for successful and unsuccessful requests. You should also note that once a response has been received from the server, a `clearTimeout` call is executed to cancel the `setTimeout` call we made earlier. This ensures that the user won't receive an error message about the server timing out when it hasn't actually done so.

7 Directly after the `onreadystatechange` function declaration, we fire off the requester's `send` method. The Ajax call is now in action.

8 We don't want any clicks on our Ajax links to take the user to a new page (that would defeat the links' purposes!), so the last line of `clickListener` stops the browser from performing the link's default action.

What actually occurs on the server after we make our Ajax request isn't the concern of our JavaScript. In our code, we've referred to a PHP script that will return information on the basis of the value of the city we passed it, but we could equally refer to a JSP script, a Ruby on Rails action, or a .NET controller. Whatever technology is used, we simply need it to return some correctly formatted XML.

If a successful request occurred, we call our `writeUpdate` method, and pass it the `responseXML` data returned by the server. If there was an *unsuccessful* request, we call `writeError` and give it a suitable error message.

When `writeUpdate` is called, we know that we've got some XML data waiting to be parsed and added to our HTML. In order to use it, we need to extract particular data points from the XML, then insert them into appropriate elements in our page.

When you're liaising with a custom server-side script, you'll have to agree on a format for the XML, so that the server-side script can write it correctly and the JavaScript can read it correctly. For this example, we're going to assume that the XML has a form like this:

melbourne.xml

```xml
<?xml version="1.0" ?>
<city>
  <name>Melbourne</name>
  <temperature>18</temperature>
  <description>Fine, partly cloudy</description>
  <description_class>partlyCloudy</description_class>
</city>
```

Knowing this structure makes it easy for us to write `writeUpdate` to extract the pertinent data:

weather_widget.js *(excerpt)*

```javascript
writeUpdate: function(responseXML)
{
  var nameNode = responseXML.getElementsByTagName("name")[0]; ❶
  var nameTextNode = nameNode.firstChild;
  var name = nameTextNode.nodeValue;

  var temperatureNode =
      responseXML.getElementsByTagName("temperature")[0];
  var temperatureTextNode = temperatureNode.firstChild;
  var temperature = temperatureTextNode.nodeValue;
```

```
var descriptionNode =
    responseXML.getElementsByTagName("description")[0];
var descriptionTextNode = descriptionNode.firstChild;
var description = descriptionTextNode.nodeValue;

var descriptionClassNode =
    responseXML.getElementsByTagName("description_class")[0];
var descriptionClassTextNode = descriptionClassNode.firstChild;
var descriptionClass = descriptionClassTextNode.nodeValue;

var weatherWidget = document.getElementById("weatherWidget"); ❷
while (weatherWidget.hasChildNodes())
{
  weatherWidget.removeChild(weatherWidget.firstChild);
}

var h2 = document.createElement("h2"); ❸
h2.appendChild(document.createTextNode(name + " Weather"));
weatherWidget.appendChild(h2);

var div = document.createElement("div");
div.setAttribute("id", "forecast");
div.className = descriptionClass;
weatherWidget.appendChild(div);

var paragraph = document.createElement("p");
paragraph.setAttribute("id", "temperature");
paragraph.appendChild(
    document.createTextNode(temperature + "\u00B0C")); ❹
div.appendChild(paragraph);

var paragraph2 = document.createElement("p");
paragraph2.appendChild(document.createTextNode(description));
div.appendChild(paragraph2);
}
```

❶ The first four paragraphs of code inside writeUpdate parse the XML to get a particular tag value. As you can see, parsing XML can be quite tedious, but because we know the syntax of the data, we can go directly to the elements we need and extract their values fairly easily.

② Right after we've finished parsing the data, we get a reference to the widget container and clean out its contents by removing all of its child nodes. This gives us an empty element into which we can insert our new data.

③ Using this clean slate, we can go about creating the new HTML elements that are going to represent the weather report. We'll use the data from the XML to create the relevant content.

④ If you have a sharp eye, you'll have noticed the peculiar text that we specified for the contents of `paragraph`. What the heck does `"\u00B0C"` mean, anyway?

In fact, that will be displayed as °C (as in "It's a lovely 20°C outside"). The code `\u00B0` is a JavaScript character code for Unicode character number 00B0, which is the degree symbol (°).

In an HTML document, you could just type the ° character verbatim, assuming you're hip to the whole Unicode thing and your HTML is written in UTF-8, or you could use the HTML character entity `&deg;`. JavaScript strings, on the other hand, only support Latin-1 (ISO-8859-1) characters in older browsers, and they don't support HTML character entities at all.

So whenever you need to include in a JavaScript string a character that you can't easily type on an English keyboard (which means it may not be within the Latin-1 character set), your best bet is to look up its Unicode character number (using a tool like Character Map, which is built into Windows, or Mac OS X's Character Palette) and replace it with a `\uXXXX` code.

After we finish manipulating the DOM, the HTML of the weather widget will look roughly like this:

```html
<div id="weatherWidget">
  <h1>
    Melbourne Weather
  </h1>
  <div id="forecast" class="partlyCloudy">
    <p id="temperature">
      18°C
    </p>
    <p>
      Fine, partly cloudy
```

```
      </p>
    </div>
  </div>
```

The `class` on the `forecast` element enables us to style the weather forecast with a little icon, producing an updated widget that looks like Figure 8.4.

Figure 8.4. The weather widget with its updated content

Our little Ajax program is almost finished. All that's left is to handle the error that will be returned if our server doesn't return proper data:

weather_widget.js (excerpt)

```
  writeError: function(errorMsg)
  {
    alert(errorMsg);
  }
};
```

That one's really simple: the error message supplied to `writeError` is popped up in an alert box, letting the user know that something went wrong.

With the methods written, all we have to do is throw them together into one object, and initialize it with `Core.start`:

weather_widget.js

```javascript
var WeatherWidget =
{
  init: function()
  {
    var weatherWidget = document.getElementById("weatherWidget");
    var anchors = weatherWidget.getElementsByTagName("a");

    for (var i = 0; i < anchors.length; i++)
    {
      Core.addEventListener(anchors[i], "click",
          WeatherWidget.clickListener);
    }
  },
  clickListener: function(event)
  {
    try
    {
      var requester = new XMLHttpRequest();
    }
    catch (error)
    {
      try
      {
        var requester = new ActiveXObject("Microsoft.XMLHTTP");
      }
      catch (error)
      {
        var requester = null;
      }
    }

    if (requester != null)
    {
      var widgetLink = this;
      widgetLink._timer = setTimeout(function()
          {
            requester.abort();

            WeatherWidget.writeError(
                "The server timed out while making your request.");
          }, 10000);
```

```
    var city = this.firstChild.nodeValue;

    requester.open("GET", "ajax_weather.php?city=" +
        encodeURIComponent(city), true);
    requester.onreadystatechange = function()
    {
      if (requester.readyState == 4)
      {
        clearTimeout(widgetLink._timer);

        if (requester.status == 200 || requester.status == 304)
        {
          WeatherWidget.writeUpdate(requester.responseXML);
        }
        else
        {
          WeatherWidget.writeError(
              "The server was unable to be contacted.");
        }
      }
    };
    requester.send(null);

    Core.preventDefault(event);
  }
},
writeUpdate: function(responseXML)
{
  var nameNode = responseXML.getElementsByTagName("name")[0];
  var nameTextNode = nameNode.firstChild;
  var name = nameTextNode.nodeValue;

  var temperatureNode =
      responseXML.getElementsByTagName("temperature")[0];
  var temperatureTextNode = temperatureNode.firstChild;
  var temperature = temperatureTextNode.nodeValue;

  var descriptionNode =
      responseXML.getElementsByTagName("description")[0];
  var descriptionTextNode = descriptionNode.firstChild;
  var description = descriptionTextNode.nodeValue;

  var descriptionClassNode =
      responseXML.getElementsByTagName("description_class")[0];
```

```
    var descriptionClassTextNode = descriptionClassNode.firstChild;
    var descriptionClass = descriptionClassTextNode.nodeValue;

    var weatherWidget = document.getElementById("weatherWidget");
    while (weatherWidget.hasChildNodes())
    {
      weatherWidget.removeChild(weatherWidget.firstChild);
    }

    var h2 = document.createElement("h2");
    h2.appendChild(document.createTextNode(name + " Weather"));
    weatherWidget.appendChild(h2);

    var div = document.createElement("div");
    div.setAttribute("id", "forecast");
    div.className = descriptionClass;
    weatherWidget.appendChild(div);

    var paragraph = document.createElement("p");
    paragraph.setAttribute("id", "temperature");
    paragraph.appendChild(
        document.createTextNode(temperature + "\u00B0C"));
    div.appendChild(paragraph);

    var paragraph2 = document.createElement("p");
    paragraph2.appendChild(document.createTextNode(description));
    div.appendChild(paragraph2);
  },
  writeError: function(errorMsg)
  {
    alert(errorMsg);
  }
};

Core.start(WeatherWidget);
```

And there you have it: a little Ajax weather widget that you could pop into the
sidebar of one of your sites to let users instantly check the weather without leaving
your page. Ajax offers endless possibilities; all you have to do is remember the
pattern I described at the start of this example, and you'll have even the most complex interactions within your reach.

Seamless Form Submission with Ajax

As we saw in Chapter 6, forms are integral to the user experience provided by most web sites. One of the things Ajax allows us to do is to streamline the form submission process by transmitting the contents of a form to the server without having to load an entirely new page into the browser.

It's fairly simple to extend the Ajax code that we used in the previous example so that it can submit a form. Consider the contact form pictured in Figure 8.5, which uses this code:

contact_form.html *(excerpt)*

```html
<form id="contactForm" action="form_mailer.php" method="POST">
  <fieldset>
    <legend>
      Contact Form
    </legend>
    <label for="contactName">
      Name
    </label>
    <input id="contactName" name="contactName" type="text" />
    <label for="contactEmail">
      Email Address
    </label>
    <input id="contactEmail" name="contactEmail" type="text" />
    <label for="contactType">
      Message Type
    </label>
    <select id="contactType" name="contactType">
      <option value="1">Enquiry</option>
      <option value="2">Spam</option>
      <option value="3">Wedding proposal</option>
    </select>
    <label for="contactMessage">
      Message
    </label>
    <textarea id="contactMessage" name="contactMessage"></textarea>
    <input id="contactNewsletter" name="contactNewsletter"
        type="checkbox" value="1" />
    <label for="contactNewsletter">
      I'd like to receive your hourly newsletter
    </label>
```

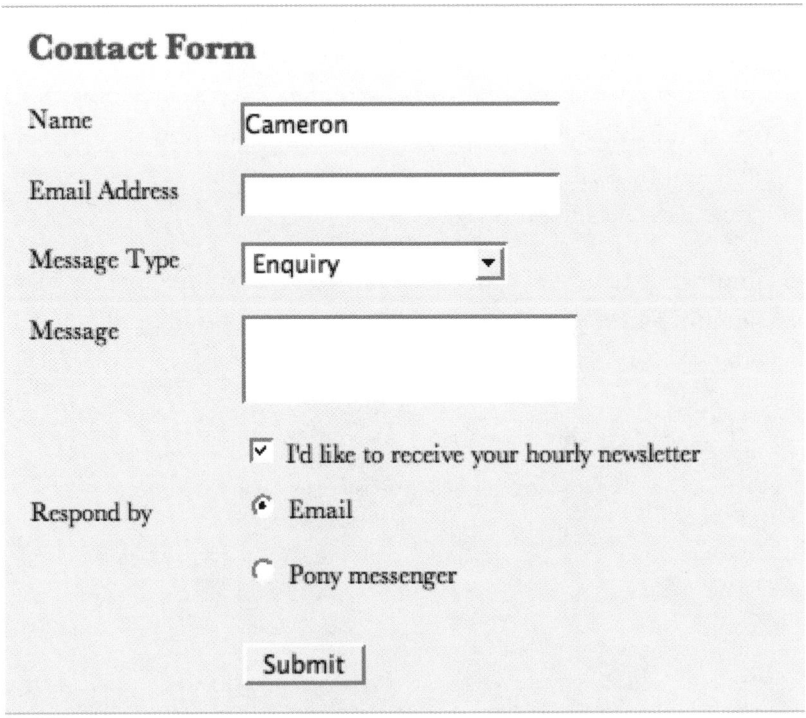

Contact Form

Name	Cameron
Email Address	
Message Type	Enquiry ▼
Message	

☑ I'd like to receive your hourly newsletter

Respond by　　⦿ Email

　　　　　　　○ Pony messenger

　　　　　　Submit

Figure 8.5. The example form to which we'll apply Ajax submission techniques

```
  <fieldset>
    <legend>
      Reply by
    </legend>
    <input id="contactMethodA" name="contactMethod" type="radio"
        value="1" />
    <label for="contactMethodA">
      Email
    </label>
    <input id="contactMethodB" name="contactMethod" type="radio"
        value="2" />
    <label for="contactMethodB">
      Pony messenger
    </label>
  </fieldset>
  <input type="hidden" name="id" value="SS56789" />
  <input type="submit" value="submit" />
  </fieldset>
</form>
```

In order to submit the form's contents using Ajax, we need to do a couple of things:

1. Override the default form submission behavior.

2. Get the form data.

3. Submit the form data to the server.

4. Check for the success or failure of submission.

We'll create this functionality inside an object called `ContactForm`. The only thing we need to do when we initialize the object is to override the form's default submission action. This can easily be done by intercepting the form's `submit` event with an event listener:

```
                                                     contact_form.js (excerpt)
var ContactForm =
{
  init: function()
  {
    var contactForm = document.getElementById("contactForm");
    Core.addEventListener(contactForm, "submit",
        ContactForm.submitListener);
  },
```

 Ajax and Form Validation

> Adding multiple event listeners to a given element for a given event can be risky business, because you have no control over the order in which they will be invoked. Thus, it isn't safe to assign an Ajax form submitter and a client-side form validator separately. If you do so, the submitter may be executed before the validator, and you might end up sending invalid data to the server. Link your validator and your submitter together to ensure that validation takes place before the form is submitted.

Now, before the form is submitted, the `submitListener` method will be run. It's inside this function that we collect the form data, send off an Ajax request, and cancel the normal form submission:

```
submitListener: function(event)
{
  var form = this;

  try
  {
    var requester = new XMLHttpRequest();
  }
  catch (error)
  {
    try
    {
      var requester = new ActiveXObject("Microsoft.XMLHTTP");
    }
    catch (error)
    {
      var requester = null;
    }
  }

  if (requester != null)
  {
    form._timer = setTimeout(function()
        {
          requester.abort();

          ContactForm.writeError(
              "The server timed out while making your request.");
        }, 10000);

    var parameters = "submitby=ajax"; ❶
    var formElements = []; ❷

    var textareas = form.getElementsByTagName("textarea");

    for (var i = 0; i < textareas.length; i++)
    {
      formElements[formElements.length] = textareas[i]; ❸
    }

    var selects = form.getElementsByTagName("select");
```

```
for (var i = 0; i < selects.length; i++)
{
  formElements[formElements.length] = selects[i];
}

var inputs = form.getElementsByTagName("input");

for (var i = 0; i < inputs.length; i++)
{
  var inputType = inputs[i].getAttribute("type");

  if (inputType == null || inputType == "text" ||
      inputType == "hidden" ||
      (typeof inputs[i].checked != "undefined" &&
      inputs[i].checked == true)) ❹
  {
    formElements[formElements.length] = inputs[i];
  }
}

for (var i = 0; i < formElements.length; i++) ❺
{
  var elementName = formElements[i].getAttribute("name");

  if (elementName != null && elementName != "") ❻
  {
    parameters += "&" + elementName + "=" +
        encodeURIComponent(formElements[i].value); ❼
  }
}

requester.setRequestHeader("Content-Type",
    "application/x-www-form-urlencoded"); ❽
requester.open("POST", form.getAttribute("action"), true); ❾
requester.onreadystatechange = function()
{
  clearTimeout(form._timer);

  if (requester.readyState == 4)
  {
    if (requester.status == 200 || requester.status == 304)
    {
      ContactForm.writeSuccess(form); ❿
    }
```

```
      else
      {
        ContactForm.writeError(
            "The server was unable to be contacted.");  ⑪
      }
    }
  };
  requester.send(parameters);  ⑫

  Core.preventDefault(event);  ⑬
  }
},
```

① One of the most important parts of the `submitForm` method is the variable `parameters`. This variable is used to store the **serialized** contents of the form—all of the field names and values combined into one long string that's suitable for sending in a POST request. We start this string off with the value `"submitby=ajax"`, which effectively adds to the form a variable named `submitby` with a value of `ajax`. The server can use this variable to identify form submissions that are transmitted via Ajax—as opposed to a standard form submission—and respond differently to them (for example, by sending the response in XML format rather than as a full HTML page).

② A form can contain a number of different elements, and we have to deal with all of them in order to produce a properly serialized version of the form's contents. There are three essential element types—`input`, `select`, and `textarea`—but `input` elements can have different types with different behaviors, so we have to cater for those as well. In order to minimize code repetition, we use the DOM to get node lists of each of the three element types, then we combine them into one big array—`formElements`—through which we can iterate in one fell swoop.

③ All of the `textareas` and `selects` can be added to `formElements` straight away, because those elements are always of the same type.

④ When it comes to `input` elements, we have to distinguish between text `inputs`, hidden `inputs`, checkboxes, and radio buttons. Text `inputs` and hidden `inputs` can always be submitted with the form, because they don't have an on/off toggle. However, we need to test whether checkboxes and radio buttons are `checked` or not before we add them to the list of submitted elements. We don't want to submit a value for a checkbox that wasn't checked, or for the wrong radio button in a group.

Inside the `for` loop that iterates over the `inputs` node list, we use a combination of each `input`'s `type` and its `checked` property to determine whether it should be added to `formElements`. The `if` statement uses a number of OR conditions to perform this check, and the logic reads like this:

1.   IF the `type` of the `input` is `null` (it will be a text `input` by default)

2.   OR the `type` of the input is `text`

3.   OR the `type` of the input is `hidden`

4.   OR the `input`'s `checked` property exists AND it is `true`

5.   THEN add the `input` to `formElements`

The fourth point above catches both checkboxes *and* radio buttons. Any checkbox that's checked should have its value submitted, and only one radio button in a radio button group will ever have `checked` set to `true`, so it's safe to submit that one as well.

❺ Once all the valid elements have been added to `formElements`, we have to write out their name/value pairs in a serialized fashion. This process is identical for all form element types, which is why we can minimize code repetition by building the `formElements` array in advance.

❻ As we add each form element to the serialized string, we have to check whether a `name` is assigned to it.

❼ If it *does* have a name, we'll want to send its value to the server, so we take the `name`, followed by `"="`, followed by the `value`, and add the whole thing to the end of `parameters`. Each of the name/value pairs in `parameters` is separated by an ampersand (`"&"`).

You'll notice that, again, we encode the names and values of our form elements using `encodeURIComponent`, to make sure that the request data remains valid no matter which special characters the user types into the form.

We're now ready to submit our serialized form data string to the server. The `XMLHttpRequest` code should be pretty familiar to you by now:

8 Remember that we have to set the `content-type` in the header of a POST request so that the request will work in Opera.

9 This time, when we `open` our `XMLHttpRequest` object, we'll use the `"POST"` method. The URL for the server request is pulled directly from the `action` of the form itself, which increases the reusability of this script.

10 In the `readystatechange` handler, all we're doing is waiting for a success code from the server. We don't actually care what data it gives us, so long as we know that it received the contact information. Once we've received that confirmation (in the form of a successful status code), we can execute `ContactForm.writeSuccess`, which will let the user know that the action was successful:

contact_form.js (excerpt)

```
writeSuccess: function(form)
{
  var newP = document.createElement("p");
  newP.setAttribute("id", "success");
  newP.appendChild(document.createTextNode(
      "Your message was submitted successfully."));
  form.parentNode.replaceChild(newP, form);
},
```

For this example, the success handler replaces the contact form with a paragraph that reads "Your message was submitted successfully," as shown in Figure 8.6.

11 Similarly, if the server does not successfully receive the contact information, `ContactForm.writeError` can handle the error in any manner it chooses—with a simple alert telling the user to try again, an error message, or even by shaking the browser window violently from side to side—whatever suits your applica-

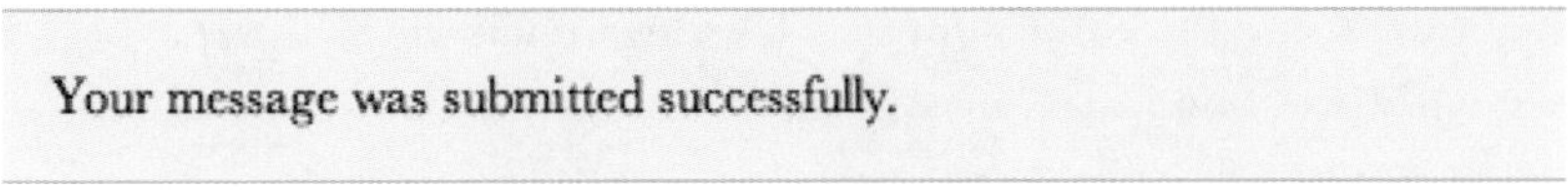

> Your message was submitted successfully.

Figure 8.6. The message that appears when the form has been submitted successfully

tion best. For reasons of simplicity, and because it's highly visible to the user, this example uses an alert box:

```
contact_form.js (excerpt)

writeError: function(errorMsg)
{
  alert(errorMsg);
}
```

⑫ With that last method in place, the readystatechange handler is ready to do its work, and submitListener is free to fire off the Ajax request. Since this is a POST request, we pass parameters to the send method, rather than including them in the URL itself (as we would for a GET request).

⑬ The very last command in submitListener is a Core.preventDefault call, which stops the browser from submitting the form (as we just did it ourselves via Ajax). And that's why we call this program "seamless form submission."

We've generalized the code that handles form elements, which means that it's really easy to take this code and use it in other applications you might work on. Just modify the init method to reference the correct form, and away you go!

Exploring Libraries

Obviously, in this age of buzzwords, every JavaScript library must support Ajax in its own special way. As a result, almost every library out there has its own abstraction of the XMLHttpRequest object, which saves you from writing your own try-catch statements, supplying request variables in the right way depending on the type of request, and wiring up functions to handle different success and error conditions. Some of them even have handy shortcuts for common Ajax interactions, which can save you from writing code.

For each of the Prototype, Dojo, jQuery, YUI, and MooTools libraries, we'll translate this low-level Ajax code into the equivalent library syntax:

```
try
{
  var requester = new XMLHttpRequest();
}
catch (error)
{
  try
  {
    var requester = new ActiveXObject("Microsoft.XMLHTTP");
  }
  catch (error)
  {
    var requester = null;
  }
}

requester.open("GET", "library.php?dewey=005", true);
requester.onreadystatechange = readystatchangeHandler;
requester.send(null);

function readystatchangeHandler()
{
  if (requester.readyState == 4)
  {
    if (requester.status == 200 || requester.status == 304)
    {
      writeUpdate(requester);
    }
  }
}

function writeUpdate(requestObject)
{
  document.getElementById("container").childNodes[0].nodeValue =
      requestObject.reponseText;
}
```

That code steps through a fairly standard Ajax program:

1. Create a new XMLHttpRequest object.

2. Set up a GET connection to a server-side script.

3. Attach a request variable to the server call.

4. Send the data to the server.

5. Monitor the request for completion.

6. Insert the returned data into an HTML element (by setting the nodeValue of the text node it contains).

This program's standard functionality should give you a fair indication of the way that each library handles Ajax connections and interactions.

Prototype

Prototype's approach to handling Ajax calls basically represents the archetype for other libraries. It gives you access to an Ajax object, which offers a couple of methods with which to make requests.

We start a basic Ajax request by calling new Ajax.Request and passing it a number of parameters in the form of an object literal. When you specify an onComplete function, it will automatically be called once the server call has successfully completed:

```
var requester = new Ajax.Request("library.php",
    {
       method: "get",
       parameters: "dewey=005",
       onComplete: writeUpdate;
    });

function writeUpdate(requestObject)
{
  document.getElementById("container").childNodes[0].nodeValue =
      requestObject.reponseText;
}
```

That code can be further shortened by replacing Ajax.Request with Ajax.Updater. The second method assumes that you will place the contents of responseText directly inside an HTML element (the most common Ajax operation), and allows you to specify the ID of that element. Thus, it circumvents the need for you to create your own callback function:

```
var requester = new Ajax.Updater("container", "library.php",
    {
      method: "get",
      parameters: "dewey=005",
    });
```

That's very succinct!

Dojo

To use Dojo's Ajax handler, we just call `dojo.io.bind` with an object literal that contains the appropriate parameters:

```
dojo.io.bind(
    {
      url: "library.php?dewey=005",
      load: writeUpdate,
      mimetype: "text/plain"
    });

function writeUpdate(type, data, event)
{
  document.getElementById("container").childNodes[0].nodeValue =
      data;
}
```

There are a couple of tricks with the Dojo Ajax implementation. Specifying `mimetype` inside the object literal determines what type of data Dojo will pass to your `load` function when the request is completed (text or XML). The `load` function receives three arguments:

type   a superfluous variable that always has a value of `"load"`

data   the only variable you'll actually use, as it contains the data from the server's response

event contains a reference to the low-level transport object that was used to perform the server communication (For the moment, it will inevitably be the XMLHttpRequest object.)

jQuery

As with everything in jQuery, Ajax functionality is available as part of the $ object. $.ajax lets you specify an all-too-familiar object literal with the particular configuration you require for the call:

```
$.ajax(
    {
        type: "GET",
        url: "library.php",
        data: "dewey=005",
        success: writeUpdate
    });

function writeUpdate(data)
{
  document.getElementById("container").childNodes[0].nodeValue =
      data;
}
```

Again, with jQuery, as with Dojo, either responseXML or responseText will be passed directly to the success function—the property that's passed will depend upon the MIME type of the data returned from the server.

YUI

In true Yahoo! UI style, the name that Yahoo! has given to its Ajax object (which it calls a Connection Manager) is rather verbose, but in most other respects it's similar to what we've seen so far:

```
var handlers = {
  success: writeUpdate
}

YAHOO.util.Connect.asyncRequest(
    "GET",
    "library.php",
```

```
    handlers,
    "dewey=005"
);

function writeUpdate(requestObject)
{
  document.getElementById("container").childNodes[0].nodeValue =
      requestObject.reponseText;
}
```

The handlers variable allows you to specify both the handler function for a successful Ajax request, and the function to be called when an error occurs. These functions are passed a full XMLHttpRequest object, rather than just the data.

MooTools

MooTools based its Ajax handler on the one that comes with Prototype, so both handlers have similar syntax. MooTools' handler even has the shortcut for placing the returned data directly into an element without specifying a callback function:

```
var requester = new Ajax("library.php?dewey=005",
    {
      method: "get",
      onComplete: writeUpdate;
    });

requester.request();

function writeUpdate(requestObject)
{
  document.getElementById("container").childNodes[0].nodeValue =
      requestObject.reponseText;
}
```

The one difference between these two libraries is that the MooTools object doesn't automatically send the request once it has been initialized; you have to call request when you want to send it.

If you wish to use the element insertion shortcut, the code looks like this:

```
var requester = new Ajax("library.php?dewey=005",
    {
      method: "get",
      update: "container";
    });

requester.request();
```

The update property takes the ID of the element whose contents you wish to update.

Summary

Ajax is definitely here to stay, and as users and developers become accustomed to its behavior, the number of ways in which it will be used to enhance web interfaces will only increase.

As you've seen in this chapter, the actual communication mechanism of Ajax is relatively straightforward. The pattern of *initialize-retrieve-modify* draws heavily on all the techniques that you've picked up as you've worked your way through the preceding seven chapters, so Ajax is the perfect finishing point for all the practical work in this book. But read on to find out where the future of JavaScript might lead you...

9

Looking Forward

When you first picked up this book, you were undoubtedly aware of JavaScript's meteoric rise in (or return to) popularity over the past couple of years. Interest in JavaScript—and its usage on the Web—is now at its highest point ever, and it's only going to keep rising.

However, for all its popularity, JavaScript is still very immature—a truth that applies to many aspects of the Web. New things are being learned about JavaScript each day, and new ideas are springing up from every corner of the globe. JavaScript is a language that's yet to reach its full potential.

It wasn't so long ago that developers could forget about being unobtrusive! *Everything* was obtrusive: we used inline event handlers in our HTML, content was being inserted with `document.write`, and we had to provide a different version of our code for every browser. How quickly we've moved on, created new rules, and almost invented a new language. The JavaScript you've learned in this book looks very different from the JavaScript that was written only a few years ago.

Some people might see this immaturity as a bad thing, but I embrace it. Why? Because it's exciting. JavaScript is on the edge. With JavaScript, you can do things that people have never done before. There are countless new ideas to be explored, and new pages to be forged.

Hopefully, all the reading you've done so far has made you as excited as I am, and you've got a million and one ideas buzzing around inside your head. You should be thinking of all the ways you can use JavaScript on your pages to create a usable and fun experience for your users.

But if, by some strange eventuality, your JavaScript juices aren't quite flowing yet, this peek at the future is sure to get them going like the Niagara.

Bringing Richness to the Web

Maybe you thought Flash brought richness to the Web. It certainly did its bit, changing the Internet from a static, page-based paradigm to a morphing, transitioning, all-singing, all-dancing "experience." But it tends to throw out the benefits of HTML, while introducing some of its own disadvantages.

JavaScript—with HTML as its foundation—manages to strike a happy medium between the interactivity of Flash and the accessibility of HTML, especially if you follow the tenets of progressive enhancement that we've been advocating in this book. If you think of JavaScript as an add-on to HTML, it makes the transition from a page-based development model to a more interactive model much less turbulent.

Although a lot of the recent focus of interaction design has been placed on Ajax, it's not the only way in which you can create a more usable interface. Sometimes, you just need to think about how you can represent your interface in a different manner.

Easy Exploration

Take, for example, the Travelocity site.[1] Its creators recognize that when you're looking for accommodation, there are normally one or two variables that you want to use to narrow down your options. To let you get feedback quickly on the effect that your choices have made, they implemented the variables as JavaScript sliders,

---

[1] http://www.travelocity.com/

as shown in Figure 9.1. These sliders allow you very easily to specify your accepted range for the variables, and immediately see how many hotels meet your criteria.

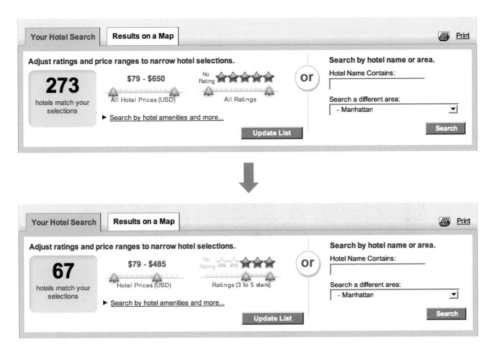

Figure 9.1. The JavaScript sliders on Travelocity providing immediate feedback

If you wanted to implement this sort of feature using nothing but server-side calculation, obtaining the correct data would take an impractical number of form submissions. The site's users would probably either give up before discovering exactly what they wanted, or settle for accommodation that wasn't really what they wanted.

By having this easy-to-use interface element, the site actually encourages users to explore all of the options, making them much happier throughout the experience, and giving them a greater chance of finding ideal accommodation matches.

Easy Visualization

Among all of the Ajax voodoo used on Flickr,[2] one of my favorite pieces of functionality is the inline editing capability shown in Figure 9.2. This type of interaction tool serves two purposes. Firstly, the use of an Ajax call to update information

---

[2] http://www.flickr.com/

means that users' changes are applied to pages very quickly. Helping this impression of speed, only small amounts of data are being sent (which is important on Flickr's sometimes slow-loading pages), and the Gallery view makes it easy to make bulk changes to multiple photos.

Figure 9.2. Inline editing areas eliminating full page loads on Flickr

The other great thing about inline editing is that you can be browsing your photo gallery pages, spot something that you want to change (like the typo in Figure 9.3), and change it right there and then. You get to see the data exactly as it appears to users, rather than in a form that's not at all connected with the way the data will be finally presented. Thus the usual disconnect between administration and presentation vanishes.

Figure 9.3. Editing data inline, just as it appears on your pages

Unique Interaction

You can perform a million and one usability tweaks with JavaScript, but they still essentially function like static HTML—with a bit less waiting. By far the most forward-thinking—and, let's face it, *sexier*—examples are those that use the interactive capabilities of JavaScript to create something that's not possible using traditional client-server techniques.

One of my favorite examples of this is Meebo, which is shown in Figure 9.4.[3] It (and its web-based IM brethren) take the originally desktop-based instant messaging applications and move them onto a freely available web-based platform, thereby multiplying their usefulness by a factor of approximately 15.[4]

With IM available through your browser, maintaining contact with your friends becomes as easy as blinking. Having an entirely browser-based chat client means

---

[3] http://www.meebo.com/

[4] Note: author's personal estimation only. Real results may differ from those shown on the pack. —Ed.

you don't have to install any software (an impossibility on many corporate systems), and you can switch workstations and still use the service—without having to transfer your IM account details. These services are also pretty good at beating firewalls that are set up to block IM ports. (I'm not sure whether this is counted as a good thing for employers, though!) Without JavaScript, this type of complex interface would be impossible—it would simply take too long using a normal page request architecture.

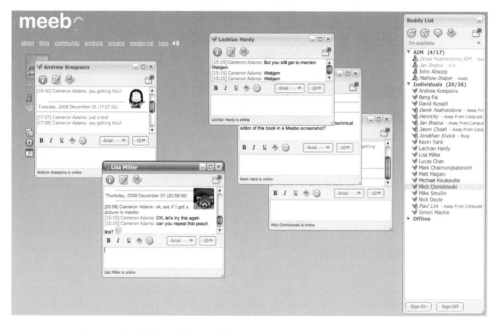

Figure 9.4. Meebo's JavaScript- and Ajax-based, in-browser instant messaging client

If you want to take a bigger step into the future, it's possible to combine JavaScript with emerging vector-rendering standards that allow you to create you own *really* customized interfaces. Brand new at the time this book was written was the Yahoo! Pipes service shown in Figure 9.5.[5] It uses the `canvas` element (which is available in quite a few browsers) to create a unique interface that's best suited to its own particular functionality: wiring together an unlimited number of data modules.

---

[5] http://www.pipes.yahoo.com

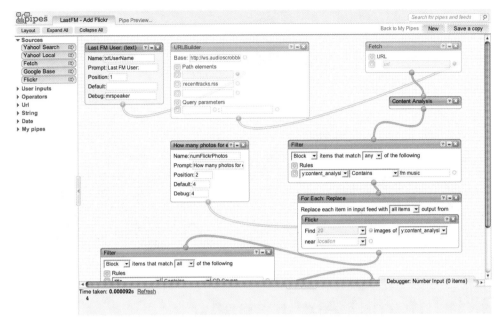

Figure 9.5. Yahoo! Pipes's intuitive and unique interface

`canvas` and its cousin SVG give designers the ability to create lightweight, highly adaptable vector graphics for use in web interfaces. Combined with the interactivity of JavaScript, these technologies are finally giving web applications the power that their desktop cousins have enjoyed for so many years, thereby removing one of the biggest barriers to the proliferation of a totally web-based application system.

And of course it's not all business suits and briefcases on the side of JavaScript; there's the potential to let your mind wander and produce some frivolous but fun entertainment of the kind for which Flash has earned a reputation—my Bunny Hunt game is a case in point.[6] The sky's the limit!

---

[6] http://www.themaninblue.com/experiment/BunnyHunt/

Figure 9.6. Bunny Hunt, a game whose style you'd normally associate with Flash

Rich Internet Applications

As you might have noticed as you read the previous section, the introduction of JavaScript and other new technologies is promoting a shift in the Web's focus. Previously, web sites were largely restricted to storing information, and offered very little interactivity, apart from the ubiquitous form fields.

As JavaScript makes more and more desktop-style interactions possible, we're beginning to see the Web transformed into an extension of the desktop. And eventually, who knows? We may lose the desktop altogether.

These next-generation web applications are distinguished from their static ancestors by the name **Rich Internet Applications** (RIAs). The important distinction here is made by the term *rich*, which refers to the styles of interaction that are available through these applications: expanding/collapsing, seamlessly updating, auto-completion, drag-and-drop, customized gestures—the list goes on.

In RIAs, most user interface actions are driven from the client side, which makes them much more responsive and flexible, because no time-consuming communication has to be performed with the server to complete these types of operations. Examples of RIAs include most of Google's recent applications[7] (Maps, Mail, Calen-

---

[7] http://www.google.com/intl/en/options/

dar—shown in Figure 9.7—and Docs & Spreadsheets), Meebo,[8] Netvibes,[9] and Zimbra.[10]

Many of these applications focus on taking functionality that currently exists on your desktop and moving it onto the Web, literally making your data available to you wherever you may be in the world. But as RIA development matures, we'll begin to see more applications that have no desktop counterpart—and never will—such as Yahoo! Pipes.

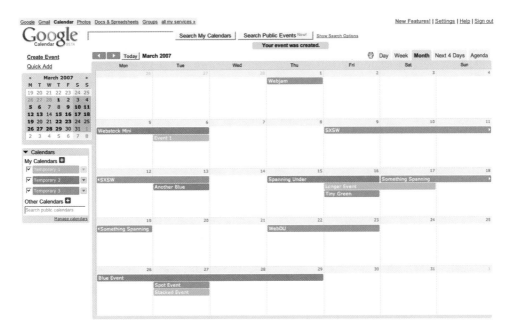

Figure 9.7. The Google Calendar interface

The main problem with RIAs is that they're extremely complex to develop—probably even more complex than their desktop equivalents. This complexity is the result of three factors, which have a lot to do with the nature of the Web itself:

▨ The interface is subject to display in a browser, which entails all the browser quirks and incompatibilities that are normally associated with web development.

---

[8] http://www.meebo.com/
[9] http://www.netvibes.com/
[10] http://www.zimbra.com/

- The behaviors required to perform much of the interaction don't natively exist on the Web or in a browser; they have to be created from the ground up using JavaScript. So if you want drag-and-drop capabilities, you'll have to include a script that creates this functionality.

- The Web was designed to be stateless, yet this clashes with the way a lot of applications are designed to work. Applications often rely upon a certain sequence of events occurring in a given order, but this order can't be guaranteed on the Web—a place where users can jump in or out at any point they choose, and can modify data without the server knowing.

One fundamental issue underlies all of these problems: the Web wasn't designed to support applications.

This fact is highlighted by the way that current accessibility technology handles RIAs: badly. Since assistive technology has been designed to work with a page-based model, the new micro-updates that lie at the heart of an RIA throw tools like screen readers into confusion—they don't know when the page has been updated, and even if they did, they wouldn't know how best to alert a user to those updates.

The blame can't be laid solely on the screen reader manufacturers, though. The structure that they're trying to translate has some inherent accessibility flaws when it comes to describing applications—flaws that can't just be patched. The thing is, browsers that render HTML have become so ubiquitous that it makes sense to create applications that take advantage of them. We just have to hack our way around all the challenges somehow. At least, that's one point of view. The other is to remodel or even recreate HTML with more application-oriented functionality.

canvas is one of the first steps in this direction. Introduced by the Web Hypertext Application Technology Working Group (WhatWG)—a community organized towards the development of a more coherent web application standard—canvas is just a small part of a greater plan that aims to create a developer-friendly, user-advantage-ous system of application delivery. However, its full potential is yet to be realized, and even after all the standards have been locked in, the standard's roll-out to a majority of browsers will take time.

For the moment, it looks like we're stuck using the sometimes clunky, always complex combination of HTML, CSS, and JavaScript for web application development. It's with this fact in mind that quite a few people are trying to find the most viable way of easing the pressure.

If JavaScript follows the path of most other programming languages—which, judging from the rise in libraries, it most likely will—it seems inevitable that popular application functionality will become invested in a few frameworks that will help ease the burden of the first two points outlined above. It remains to be seen whether or not the third problem can be solved.

Widgets

A number of common themes run through the design of a lot of applications. On the desktop, these functional commonalities include tasks like file handling and window control, and tools such as dialog boxes, toolbars, and menus. You can use a range of these standard components to build desktop applications, so you don't have to reinvent the wheel every time you create a new application. By using these components, you take advantage of established conventions that aid usability—users already know what a menu looks like, how a dialog box works, and what they should do with a button.

Parallels are starting to be drawn in application design on the Web. A few interactions are now becoming sufficiently common to warrant the creation of reusable components, or **widgets**, that, when dropped into a page, *just work*. Whereas previously these widgets might have been offered piecemeal across a dozen sites spread over the Web, now they're beginning to be aggregated in large libraries, to become what you might call **component frameworks**.

These frameworks don't provide just a bit of abstracting code that addresses specific browser differences; they offer an entirely new mode of development. Instead of writing all the HTML, all the styles, and all the JavaScript for a particular piece of functionality, you can just include a widget—maybe just one line of code—and your application will automatically boast the functionality that you once had to write hundreds of lines of code to achieve.

Frameworks don't just make coding easier, however; they also have an effect upon the language itself. If you start substituting one line of Dojo for a hundred lines of JavaScript, are you writing JavaScript, or are you writing Dojo?

JavaScript Off the Web

As the popularity of web development techniques continues to surge, JavaScript has become quite a powerful force in software development. The separation of structure, style, and behavior that is so strictly expressed in web standards is actually an ideal platform for the development of applications and widgets both on the Web, and off it.

With the introduction of Dashboard Widgets, a sampling of which is shown in Figure 9.8, Apple's Mac OS X brought the combination of HTML, CSS, and JavaScript onto the desktop, making it a much easier proposition for people to create their own native applications. The masses of people who had cut their development teeth on the pages of the Web were now able to port those skills directly to the desktop. And the growth in the number of widgets has revealed the ease with which this skills transfer can be achieved.

Figure 9.8. Creating mini-applications using HTML, CSS, and JavaScript with MacOS X widgets

Alongside MacOS X, Yahoo! released its own desktop widget tool; they've just been joined by the latest incarnation of Windows—Vista—which supports similar items, called "gadgets."

Aside from widgets, it's possible to create entire applications using JavaScript. One of the browsers with the fastest growing market share—Firefox—was built entirely with JavaScript; an application development language called XUL was used to provide the user interface elements. Again, the separation of structure, style, and behavior here allows the application to easily be skinned via CSS, and invites the addition of new functionality—contained in Firefox extensions—via JavaScript.

Exploring Libraries

The number of JavaScript libraries available on the Web is gradually being whittled down predominantly on the basis of how much they're used, but their endurance is also affected by factors such as functionality, ease of integration, and available documentation.

To my mind, a library can go in two directions—small and light, or big and heavy. There are some advantages to keeping a library small—especially on the Web, where download time is still an issue, along with client-side processing power and code complexity. Libraries such as jQuery[11] and moo.fx[12] fill that niche neatly, providing an efficient pocket knife of JavaScript functions that will help you get the job done.

At the other end of the scale, the big libraries are becoming even bigger. More and more functionality is being absorbed into their bellies, in an effort to encompass any and all types of interaction that can be imagined to take place in a browser. These libraries are becoming less like libraries from which you can pick and choose the elements you want, and more like frameworks, where the library becomes the language, and your programs become distilled into minimalistic lines of API code.

The various styles of these large frameworks differ. Some try to maintain the separation of layers that has characterized web development for some time, while others attempt to abstract the web layer entirely, by creating a translation between server-side logic and browser implementation. To cover the specifics of each of these

---

[11] http://jquery.com/
[12] http://moofx.mad4milk.net/

frameworks would take many more pages than we have available, but I'll try to give you a tiny taste of how they function here.

Dojo

We've taken a decent look at Dojo throughout this book, but only as a library, not a framework.[13] Dojo offers more than just helper functions to shortcut common scripting actions—it actually provides an entire system for developing interfaces using common widgets.

The widgets currently available in Dojo number well over a hundred and include such items as accordion menus, combo boxes, date pickers, fish-eye lists, progress bars, sliders, and tree menus. The framework also has its own layout system, which allows you to create panes with related dimensions (such as equal heights) and adjustable dimensions—something that's quite common in desktop application design.

We can implement widgets in Dojo in two ways: structurally and programmatically. If you use the structural method, you must modify the HTML structure of your page in order to include the Dojo widgets you want to use. To achieve this, you tack non-standard attributes onto particular HTML elements—a big no-no if web standards are an important consideration to you.

The programmatic creation of Dojo widgets is most useful when you want to create new interface elements on the fly, or you don't want to dirty your HTML with attributes that aren't meant to be there. You create the new widget inside your JavaScript, then include it on the page via the DOM.

Following the tenets of progressive enhancement, a lot of Dojo widgets try to use HTML elements that provide the same functionality, then transform them into more complex objects. For example, a `select` box can be turned into a combo box (a box that allows you to type and receive suggestions) with the addition of some extra attributes:

```
<select dojoType="ComboBox" dataUrl="example.php" name="state">
</select>
```

---

[13] http://dojotoolkit.org/

Next, include that element on an HTML page along with the Dojo library and
ComboBox module:

```
<!DOCTYPE html PUBLIC "-//W3C//DTD XHTML 1.0 Strict//EN"
    "http://www.w3.org/TR/xhtml1/DTD/xhtml1-strict.dtd">
<html xmlns="http://www.w3.org/1999/xhtml" lang="en-US">
  <head>
    <title>ComboBox</title>
    <meta http-equiv="Content-Type"
        content="text/html; charset=utf-8" />
    <script type="text/javascript" src="dojo.js"></script>
    <script type="text/javascript">
      dojo.require("dojo.widget.ComboBox");
    </script>
    ⋮
```

The result is a custom form element that provides users with suggestions as they
type, like the one shown in Figure 9.9.

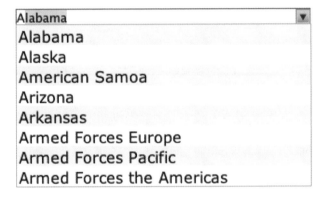

Figure 9.9. Using the Dojo ComboBox widget to transform a select element into a field that auto-completes as users type

When the page is parsed by Dojo, the dojoType attribute is used to determine which
elements are to be transformed into widgets. Then, the Dojo engine will go about
changing the page to include the specified widgets.

If you wanted to include the ComboBox programmatically, you could write a script
that creates a ComboBox widget, then adds it to the page:

```
var comboBox = dojo.widget.createWidget("ComboBox",
    {
        dataUrl: "../../tests/widget/comboBoxData.js"
    });
document.getElementsByTagName("body")[0].appendChild(
    comboBox.domNode);
```

New widgets are created using the `dojo.widget.createWidget` method, which takes the name of the widget, followed by a set of options expressed as an object literal. In this case, the only option we're supplying to the `ComboBox` widget is the `dataUrl` location.

Once that widget has been created, we'll have a reference to the widget as a JavaScript object, but in order to include it on the page, we'll have to use its `domNode` property, which acts as the HTML interface for the actual object. And once that's done, we'll have a working `ComboBox` widget in our interface.

In the example above, the `ComboBox` is actually Ajax-driven—it will use the URL specified by the `dataUrl` property to retrieve listings that match what the user types. However, this explanation highlights a flaw in the way that this widget uses progressive enhancement.

When using a `select` box, users without JavaScript would expect to click on the box, and receive a number of `options` from which they can choose. The only way that this can be done is if all the `options` are included in the HTML. One of the aims of the `ComboBox` is to *reduce* the amount of data transferred between client and server by only retrieving the data that matches what the user is typing. However, leaving the `select` box empty initially renders it useless to users who don't have JavaScript enabled. This is not progressive enhancement. Then again, if we included all the `options` for the `select` box in the HTML, we'd be removing one of the main advantages of the `ComboBox`.

Maybe a `ComboBox` could be thought of more like a plain text field (although Dojo's `ComboBox` widget doesn't work with text fields, so this is a purely academic argument). Non-JavaScript users would be able to type whatever value they wanted into the field, but they wouldn't get a list of possible values.

These questions highlight some of the problems that are being caused by Rich Internet Applications. JavaScript and HTML give us a great deal of flexibility to create whatever we want, but sometimes that flexibility comes at the cost of accessibility. Is there a better answer? Only time will tell.

Google Web Toolkit

The Google Web Toolkit (GWT) uses Java as the basis for its engine.[14] You never have to write JavaScript, HTML, or CSS if you don't want to. Using GWT's API, you can create entire applications in Java. The GWT compiler translates all of the Java into browser code (HTML, CSS, and JavaScript) for inclusion in your web site.

This style of framework makes web application development similar to traditional application development—all the code is written by the developer, then compiled for execution. In GWT's case, compilation includes the creation of HTML and JavaScript files that will help run your application in a browser.

This framework is radically different from anything we've looked at in this book, but as an example, this Java class is used to create a page with a button that launches an alert box saying, "Hello, JavaScript:"

```
public class Hello implements EntryPoint {

  public void onModuleLoad() {
    Button b = new Button("Click me", new ClickListener() {
      public void onClick(Widget sender) {
        Window.alert("Hello, JavaScript");
      }
    });

    RootPanel.get().add(b);
  }

}
```

As well as being a very quick way for Java developers to create web applications, GWT is also extremely inaccessible. No static HTML is provided as the structure for the application, and every interface element is created via JavaScript. Therefore,

---

[14] http://code.google.com/webtoolkit/

there is essentially no document for the browser to fall back on if JavaScript is not available. The unlucky user gets zip, nada, nothing. If this isn't a worry for you, you might want to give GWT a try. But, personally, it scares the pants off me.

Summary

The future is bright for JavaScript. Its dominance as the client-side language of choice on the Web has been unchallenged for well over ten years, and as long as HTML (or something like it) exists, JavaScript will be there to partner it.

Yet the question remains, what will the future hold for JavaScript? It's flexible enough to adapt to a range of environments—as we've discussed in this chapter—and its ultimate form will largely be dependent upon which technology makes its ascendance. But no matter which one rises to the top of the heap, I'm pretty certain that JavaScript will be there right alongside it, making it do all the *really* cool stuff.

Appendix A: The Core JavaScript Library

Most of the examples in this book have relied on a small library of useful methods contained in a file named **core.js**. This library enabled us to set aside the messy details of some of the common tasks you need to perform in most scripts, and focus on the more unique aspects of each example.

In some cases, this library's methods were a little too complicated to explain in detail at the moment we first needed them. This appendix, therefore, contains a complete description of the Core library, and how each of its methods works.

The Object

Like most of the scripts in this book, the Core library encloses all of its functions within a JavaScript object, making them methods of that object. In the past, we have always enclosed functions within a JavaScript object using an object literal:

```
var Core = {
  method1: function(…)
  {
     ⋮
  },
  method2: function(…)
  {
     ⋮
  },
   ⋮
};
```

While the Core library has the same basic structure as the code shown above, the code that we've used to define the object and its methods uses different syntax:

```
var Core = {};

MyObject.method1 = function(…)
{
   ⋮
};
MyObject.method2 = function(…)
```

```
{
    ⋮
};
```

The object that's produced here is identical to the first; the syntax is just a little more verbose.

The reason we use this alternative style for the Core library is that it gives us the freedom to define different versions of each method based on the browser in which the script is running—essential for compatibility mine-fields like event listeners:

core.js (excerpt)

```
var Core = {};

// W3C DOM 2 Events model
if (document.addEventListener)
{
  Core.addEventListener = function(target, type, listener)
  {
    ⋮ W3C DOM 2 Events implementation
  };
  ⋮
}
// Internet Explorer Events model
else if (document.attachEvent)
{
  Core.addEventListener = function(target, type, listener)
  {
    ⋮ Internet Explorer Events implementation
  };
  ⋮
}
```

Event Listener Methods

As we saw in Chapter 4, there are two very different models for implementing event listeners in current browsers: the Internet Explorer Events model, supported by IE browsers up to and including version 7, and the W3C DOM 2 Events model, supported by every other browser out there. The Core library bridges the gap by providing a set of methods that will work in both of these models:

Core.addEventListener(*target*, *type*, *listener*)

For the object *target* (usually a DOM element node), this method assigns the function/method *listener* as an event listener for events of type *type*. For example:

```
Core.addEventListener(theLink, "click", Obj.clickListener);
```

Core.removeEventListener(*target*, *type*, *listener*)

For the object *target* (usually a DOM element node), this method removes the function/method *listener*, previously added as an event listener for events of type *type*. Here's an example:

```
Core.removeEventListener(theLink, "click", Obj.clickListener);
```

Core.preventDefault(*event*)

This method prevents the browser from performing the default action associated with the event represented by *event*, an event object passed as an argument to an event listener.

Core.stopPropagation(*event*)

This method prevents event listeners attached to elements higher up in the DOM tree from being triggered in response to the event represented by *event*, an event object passed as an argument to an event listener.

Thanks to the code structure discussed in the previous section, we are able to implement these event listener methods separately for each of the two event models.

The W3C DOM 2 versions of the event listeners are trivial wrappers around the standard methods:

core.js (excerpt)

```
// W3C DOM 2 Events model
if (document.addEventListener)
{
  Core.addEventListener = function(target, type, listener)
  {
```

```
    target.addEventListener(type, listener, false);
  };

  Core.removeEventListener = function(target, type, listener)
  {
    target.removeEventListener(type, listener, false);
  };

  Core.preventDefault = function(event)
  {
    event.preventDefault();
  };

  Core.stopPropagation = function(event)
  {
    event.stopPropagation();
  };
}
```

The Internet Explorer versions are much more complicated, so we'll look at them one at a time. Fundamentally, however, these functions make the following enhancements to Internet Explorer's built-in event listener functionality:

◼ Prevent the same function/method from being assigned as a listener for the same event on the same element more than once.

◼ Pass Internet Explorer's global event object as an argument to the event listener.

◼ Call event listeners in such a way that, within the listener, this represents the object to which the listener was assigned.

◼ Clean up all registered event listeners when the document is unloaded, so as to prevent memory leaks in Internet Explorer.

The code for these functions is based upon a script presented in the book *JavaScript: The Definitive Guide, 5th Edition.*[1]

addEventListener is the most complex of the methods, so let's take it one step at a time:

---

[1] David Flanagan, *JavaScript: The Definitive Guide, 5th Edition* (Sebastopol: O'Reilly, 2006).

core.js *(excerpt)*

```
Core.addEventListener = function(target, type, listener)
{
  // prevent adding the same listener twice, since DOM 2 Events
  // ignores duplicates like this
  if (Core._findListener(target, type, listener) != -1) return;
```

We start by checking if the specified combination of target object, event type, and listener function has already been registered in this document. To do this, we use a private method named _findListener, the implementation of which we'll look at shortly. If the listener has already been registered, we simply do nothing, and return from this method immediately.

Now, we can't go using the listener function that was passed to addEventListener as is. If we did, Internet Explorer wouldn't pass it the event object as an argument, and this would refer to the global context within the function, rather than referring to target. To resolve these issues, we can wrap the supplied listener inside a function that makes the necessary changes:

core.js *(excerpt)*

```
  // listener2 calls listener as a method of target in one of
  // two ways, depending on what this version of IE supports,
  // and passes it the global event object as an argument
  var listener2 = function()
  {
    var event = window.event; ❶

    if (Function.prototype.call)
    {
      listener.call(target, event); ❷
    }
    else
    {
      target._currentListener = listener; ❸
      target._currentListener(event);
      target._currentListener = null;
    }
  };
```

❶ As you can see, `listener2` is a function that starts by retrieving the global event object. It then calls `listener` in such a way as to make `target` the value of `this`, and passes the event object to it as an argument. This is done in one of two ways, depending on the version of Internet Explorer that's running the script.

❷ In Internet Explorer 5.5 or later, all functions support a method named `call`, which allows the function to be called as if it were a method of a specified object. If this function is available (which we can test by checking for the presence of `Function.prototype.call`), we can use it to call `listener` as a method of `target`, and with `event` as an argument.

❸ In previous versions of Internet Explorer, the `call` method is not available, so instead we store `listener` in a temporary property of `target` named `_currentListener`, which enables us to call `listener` as a method of `target`. Again, we pass `event` as an argument. Once that's done, we set `_currentListener` to `null`.

Now that we've got our pimped-out `listener2`, we can use Internet Explorer's `attachEvent` method to register it as an event listener:

core.js *(excerpt)*

```
// add listener2 using IE's attachEvent method
target.attachEvent("on" + type, listener2);
```

Next, we need to do a little bookkeeping to ensure that the `_findListener` method we called at the top of `addEventListener` can tell that this listener has been registered. We'll create an object that contains all the pertinent information about the listener that we have just added:

core.js *(excerpt)*

```
// create an object describing this listener so we can clean
// it up later
var listenerRecord =
{
  target: target,
  type: type,
```

```
    listener: listener,
    listener2: listener2
};
```

For _findListener to do its job, we could just add this object to an array stored as a property of target. But as long as we're keeping records of our event listeners, let's set things up so that it's easy to clean up *all* the listeners in the document when the page is unloaded. To this end, we'll store our listenerRecord in an object that's shared by *all* the listeners in the document:

core.js (excerpt)

```
// get a reference to the window object containing target
var targetDocument = target.document || target; ❶
var targetWindow = targetDocument.parentWindow;

// create a unique ID for this listener
var listenerId = "l" + Core._listenerCounter++; ❷

// store a record of this listener in the window object
if (!targetWindow._allListeners)
  targetWindow._allListeners = {}; ❸
targetWindow._allListeners[listenerId] = listenerRecord; ❹
```

❶ Since we want to have one object containing all the listeners in the window, we need to get a reference to that window. To do that reliably, we need to start by getting a reference to the current document.

Now, target may be either an element in the document or the document itself, so if target.document exists we'll use that as our document; otherwise, we can just assume that target is the document, and use that. We can then get a reference to the window using the document's parentWindow property.

❷ Since our listener records will be stored in an object, not an array, we need a unique property name for each listener record. This unique listener ID will be the letter "l" followed by a counter that is incremented each time we register a new listener. This counter's initial value is declared after all the other event listener methods in this script:

```
                                                   core.js (excerpt)

  Core._listenerCounter = 0;
```

❸ The object that will contain records of all the listeners in this window will be stored in a property of the window, named _allListeners. If the property doesn't yet exist, we create it here as an empty object.

❹ Lastly, we store our listener record in the _allListeners object. As we learned in Chapter 6, when we have a property name stored in a variable, we need to use array-like syntax to access it, even though we're dealing with an object.

Since all our listeners are stored in a single object, it will be really easy to clean them up when the document is unloaded. However, it might take a long time for our _findListener method to determine if a particular listener had been assigned to a particular event on a particular element—the method will need to search through this potentially massive object. To make this search more efficient, we'll store the unique ID of the listener in an array attached to target:

```
                                                   core.js (excerpt)

  // store this listener's ID in target
  if (!target._listeners) target._listeners = [];
  target._listeners[target._listeners.length] = listenerId;
```

Lastly, we need to make sure that our script is notified when the document is unloaded, so that we can clean up all the listeners:

```
                                                   core.js (excerpt)

  // set up Core._removeAllListeners to clean up all listeners
  // on unload
  if (!targetWindow._unloadListenerAdded)
  {
    targetWindow._unloadListenerAdded = true;
    targetWindow.attachEvent(
        "onunload", Core._removeAllListeners);
  }
};
```

And that's `addEventListener` taken care of! We'll get to the method that actually removes all the listeners, `_removeAllListeners`, in a moment.

Thanks to a lot of the bookkeeping we did in `addEventListener`, `removeEventListener` is relatively straightforward:

core.js *(excerpt)*

```
Core.removeEventListener = function(target, type, listener)
{
  // find out if the listener was actually added to target
  var listenerIndex =
      Core._findListener(target, type, listener); ❶
  if (listenerIndex == -1) return;

  // get a reference to the window object containing target
  var targetDocument = target.document || target; ❷
  var targetWindow = targetDocument.parentWindow;

  // obtain the record of the listener from the window object
  var listenerId = target._listeners[listenerIndex]; ❸
  var listenerRecord = targetWindow._allListeners[listenerId];

  // remove the listener, and remove its ID from target
  target.detachEvent("on" + type, listenerRecord.listener2); ❹
  target._listeners.splice(listenerIndex, 1); ❺

  // remove the record of the listener from the window object
  delete targetWindow._allListeners[listenerId]; ❻
};
```

❶ Our first task is to find out if the specified combination of `target`, `type`, and `listener` actually corresponds to a registered event listener. We can use the same `_findListener` method that we used at the top of `addEventListener` to do this. This method returns the index of the listener in `target`'s `_listeners` array, or `-1` if no such listener has been registered.

❷ Having confirmed that the specified listener was registered, we need to get at the "listener record" object that we stored in the global `_allListeners` object for that listener. As in `addEventListener`, we start by getting a reference to the window.

❸ We get the unique ID of the listener out of target's _listeners array (using the listenerIndex that we got from _findListener), then use it to access the listener record in _allListeners.

❹ With the listener record in hand, we can use Internet Explorer's detachEvent method to unregister the listener. Remember that, since we enhanced listener by wrapping it in a new function, the listener that we need to pass to detachEvent is the listener2 property of the listenerRecord, not listener itself.

❺ With the listener unregistered, we now need to remove our own records of its existence. First, we remove the relevant item from target's _listeners array. To do so, we use a method that's supported by all JavaScript arrays: splice. We pass to this method the index of the first element that we want to remove from the array, and the number of elements to remove (in this case, 1).

❻ Finally, we remove the property from the global _allListeners object that contains the listener record. To do so, we make use of the rarely seen JavaScript delete statement, which deletes properties from objects.

Did you get all that? Don't worry too much if you're not able to follow all the code that goes into addEventListener and removeEventListener—it's fairly advanced, and when it comes right down to it, you really shouldn't have to understand JavaScript of this level of complexity to do something as simple as adding and removing event listeners. That's why we decided to hide this code at the back of this book, and why we badmouth the Internet Explorer Events model whenever we have the chance.

By comparison, the Internet Explorer versions of preventDefault and stopPropagation are simple:

core.js *(excerpt)*

```
Core.preventDefault = function(event)
{
  event.returnValue = false;
};

Core.stopPropagation = function(event)
```

```
{
  event.cancelBubble = true;
};
```

In order to prevent the default action associated with an event in IE, we simply set the event object's `returnValue` property to `false`. Similarly, in order to stop the propagation of an event in IE, we set its `cancelBubble` property to `true`. And that's all these methods need to do.

That takes care of the Internet Explorer versions of our four methods, but we still need to look at the two helper methods that they rely on—`_findListener` and `_removeAllListeners`:

core.js *(excerpt)*

```
Core._findListener = function(target, type, listener)
{
  // get the array of listener IDs added to target
  var listeners = target._listeners;
  if (!listeners) return -1;

  // get a reference to the window object containing target
  var targetDocument = target.document || target;
  var targetWindow = targetDocument.parentWindow;

  // searching backward (to speed up onunload processing),
  // find the listener
  for (var i = listeners.length - 1; i >= 0; i--)
  {
    // get the listener's ID from target
    var listenerId = listeners[i];

    // get the record of the listener from the window object
    var listenerRecord = targetWindow._allListeners[listenerId];

    // compare type and listener with the retrieved record
    if (listenerRecord.type == type &&
        listenerRecord.listener == listener)
    {
      return i;
    }
```

```
    }
    return -1;
  };
```

_findListener looks through the specified target's _listeners array, retrieving for of the each listener IDs it contains the corresponding listener record from the global _allListeners object. If it finds a listener record that matches the target, type, and listener specified, it returns the index of that listener's ID in target's _listeners array. If it doesn't find a matching record, it returns -1.

core.js *(excerpt)*

```
Core._removeAllListeners = function()
{
  var targetWindow = this;

  for (id in targetWindow._allListeners)
  {
    var listenerRecord = targetWindow._allListeners[id];
    listenerRecord.target.detachEvent(
        "on" + listenerRecord.type, listenerRecord.listener2);
    delete targetWindow._allListeners[id];
  }
};
```

_removeAllListeners does something we haven't actually had to do anywhere else in this book—step through the properties of an object one at a time. Specifically, it steps through the listener records stored as properties in the _allListeners object. To step through the properties of an object, we use a for-in loop of this form:

```
for (propertyName in object)
{
  : access each property as object[propertyName]
}
```

Aside from that extra spoonful of syntactic sugar, _removeAllListeners is self-explanatory. Within the for-in loop, this method retrieves each of the listener record objects, uses Internet Explorer's detachEvent method to remove the corresponding listener, and then deletes the property from _allListeners.

Script Bootstrapping

From almost the very first script we saw in this book, we've used the Core library's `start` method to run a script's `init` method as soon as the document has finished loading.

Core.start(*runnable*)

> This method runs the `init` method of the given script object (*runnable*) as soon as the document has finished loading.

As we've seen many times in this book, here's how we use `Core.start` to initialize an object once the page has loaded:

```
var MyScript =
{
  init: function()
  {
    ⋮
  },
  ⋮
};

Core.start(MyScript);
```

As we saw in Chapter 4, this method simply calls the `addEventListener` method to register the script's `init` method as a `load` event listener for the window:

core.js (excerpt)

```
Core.start = function(runnable)
{
  Core.addEventListener(window, "load", runnable.init);
};
```

This is a nice, simple approach to starting up a script (a process known as **bootstrapping**), but it has one important drawback: the `load` event that it depends on is not triggered until the page *and all linked resources* (such as images) have loaded. The practical consequence of this is that the page will sit there in its static form, with no added JavaScript functionality, while all the images load up. Finally, once all the static content is in play, your JavaScript will be triggered and the dynamic functionality will snap into existence. If the user started to read the page while the images were loaded, this sudden (and potentially dramatic) change can be disorienting—and annoying.

Ideally, JavaScript code should start running the moment the element(s) of the document that it requires have been loaded, and are available for scripting. Exactly how element availability can be detected, and just what JavaScript is allowed to do at the various stages of the page loading process, is another swirling morass of vague standards and cross-browser incompatibility.

In the absence of clear standards for early bootstrapping, we have elected to stick with the standard, reliable load event throughout this book.

That said, there *is* an approach that works reliably in Firefox and Opera (version 9 or later) browsers: the DOMContentLoaded event. This is a nonstandard event that these browsers generate as soon as the HTML content of the document has finished loading (that is, before the images and other external resources). If this event were supported by all browsers, we could re-implement the Core library's start method as follows:

```
Core.start = function(runnable)
{
  Core.addEventListener(document, "DOMContentLoaded",
      runnable.init);
};
```

Normally, we'd shy away from a nonstandard solution like this, but the benefit to the user is so significant that it's worth taking some time to think about how this solution could be made to work cross-browser.

It would be nice to detect if the browser supported the DOMContentLoaded event, and have the start method use it if it's available, but fall back on the load event if it's not. Unfortunately, there is no reliable and future-proof way to detect events like this.

Instead, what we can do is register the listener for *both* events, and do a little extra work to make sure that browsers that *do* support DOMContentLoaded don't end up calling the script's init method twice:

```
Core.start = function(runnable)
{
  var initOnce = function()
  {
    if (arguments.callee.done) return;
    arguments.callee.done = true;
    runnable.init();
  };

  Core.addEventListener(document, "DOMContentLoaded", initOnce);
  Core.addEventListener(window, "load", initOnce);
};
```

This version of the method starts by creating a new function called initOnce. The first time this function is called, it will call the init method of the given script. If it's called again, however, it will do nothing. How does this work? The function sets a property named done on itself (a function's code can access the function itself as arguments.callee) the first time it's called, and checks for that property to stop execution and immediately return to the code that called the method on subsequent calls.

We can now register this initOnce function as a listener for both the document's DOMContentLoaded event, and the window's load event. In Firefox and Opera, initOnce will be called for both events, but will only run the script's init method on the first event. Other browsers will only call initOnce once—when the load event occurs.

Despite its nonstandard status, this approach is reliable enough to be recommended for production use. In the spirit of progressive enhancement, it starts with an approach that works just fine in standards-compliant browsers (the load event), then adds to it an enhancement (the DOMContentLoaded event) that will improve the user experience where it is supported. If you'd like your scripts to start up sooner in Firefox and Opera browsers, feel free to replace the Core library's start method with the final version above.

Can anything be done for other browsers—like, say, Internet Explorer? Well, some high-flying members of the JavaScript community have met with some success by toying with IE's support for the defer attribute of the <script> tag. Others have tried things like repeatedly checking for the presence of a required DOM element (an approach known as **polling**) and launching the script as soon as it appears. A number of the major JavaScript libraries, such as jQuery, MooTools, and the Yahoo! UI Library, have even adopted different combinations of these solutions.

The short answer, however, is that—especially since the release of Internet Explorer 7, which apparently introduces some new bugs related to these solutions—there is no single solution that is 100% reliable. For this reason, we recommend sticking with the simple approach given above.

If you're interested in the full story on the JavaScript community's attempts to solve the early bootstrapping problem, the most complete and up-to-date article on the subject at the time of this writing is Peter Michaux's *The window.onload problem (still)*.[2]

CSS Class Management Methods

The next four methods in the Core library have to do with manipulating the CSS classes that are applied to elements in your HTML documents:

`Core.addClass(target, theClass)`

This method adds to the `className` property of *target* the specified CSS class (*theClass*), without removing any classes that may already have been applied to *target*.

`Core.getElementsByClass(theClass)`

This method returns an array of all elements in the document that have the specified CSS class (*theClass*) applied to them.

`Core.hasClass(target, theClass)`

This method returns `true` if *target* has the specified CSS class (*theClass*) applied to it, and `false` if not.

`Core.removeClass(target, theClass)`

This method removes from the `className` property of *target* the specified CSS class (*theClass*), without removing any of the other classes that may also have been applied to *target*.

---

[2] http://peter.michaux.ca/article/553

These methods are fully described in Chapter 3. For completeness, you can find the code for these methods reproduced along with the rest of the library in the section called "The Complete Library" below.

Retrieving Computed Styles

The final method in our core library is getComputedStyle:

Core.getComputedStyle(*element*, *styleProperty*)
This method retrieves the effective value of the CSS property indicated by *styleProperty* once all the various sources of CSS styles (linked style sheets, embedded styles, inline styles, and dynamically-applied styles) have all been applied to *element*.

This method is fully described in Chapter 5; however, the complete code for this method is also reproduced along with the rest of the library in the following section.

The Complete Library

Here it is—the complete code for the Core JavaScript library.

```
                                                                core.js
var Core = {};

// W3C DOM 2 Events model
if (document.addEventListener)
{
  Core.addEventListener = function(target, type, listener)
  {
    target.addEventListener(type, listener, false);
  };

  Core.removeEventListener = function(target, type, listener)
  {
    target.removeEventListener(type, listener, false);
  };

  Core.preventDefault = function(event)
  {
    event.preventDefault();
```

```
  };

  Core.stopPropagation = function(event)
  {
    event.stopPropagation();
  };
}
// Internet Explorer Events model
else if (document.attachEvent)
{
  Core.addEventListener = function(target, type, listener)
  {
    // prevent adding the same listener twice, since DOM 2
    // Events ignores duplicates like this
    if (Core._findListener(target, type, listener) != -1)
      return;

    // listener2 calls listener as a method of target in one of
    // two ways, depending on what this version of IE supports,
    // and passes it the global event object as an argument
    var listener2 = function()
    {
      var event = window.event;

      if (Function.prototype.call)
      {
        listener.call(target, event);
      }
      else
      {
        target._currentListener = listener;
        target._currentListener(event)
        target._currentListener = null;
      }
    };

    // add listener2 using IE's attachEvent method
    target.attachEvent("on" + type, listener2);

    // create an object describing this listener so we can
    // clean it up later
    var listenerRecord =
    {
      target: target,
```

```
    type: type,
    listener: listener,
    listener2: listener2
  };

  // get a reference to the window object containing target
  var targetDocument = target.document || target;
  var targetWindow = targetDocument.parentWindow;

  // create a unique ID for this listener
  var listenerId = "l" + Core._listenerCounter++;

  // store a record of this listener in the window object
  if (!targetWindow._allListeners)
    targetWindow._allListeners = {};
  targetWindow._allListeners[listenerId] = listenerRecord;

  // store this listener's ID in target
  if (!target._listeners) target._listeners = [];
  target._listeners[target._listeners.length] = listenerId;

  // set up Core._removeAllListeners to clean up all
  // listeners on unload
  if (!targetWindow._unloadListenerAdded)
  {
    targetWindow._unloadListenerAdded = true;
    targetWindow.attachEvent(
        "onunload", Core._removeAllListeners);
  }
};

Core.removeEventListener = function(target, type, listener)
{
  // find out if the listener was actually added to target
  var listenerIndex = Core._findListener(
      target, type, listener);
  if (listenerIndex == -1) return;

  // get a reference to the window object containing target
  var targetDocument = target.document || target;
  var targetWindow = targetDocument.parentWindow;

  // obtain the record of the listener from the window object
  var listenerId = target._listeners[listenerIndex];
```

```
    var listenerRecord =
        targetWindow._allListeners[listenerId];

  // remove the listener, and remove its ID from target
  target.detachEvent("on" + type, listenerRecord.listener2);
  target._listeners.splice(listenerIndex, 1);

  // remove the record of the listener from the window object
  delete targetWindow._allListeners[listenerId];
};

Core.preventDefault = function(event)
{
  event.returnValue = false;
};

Core.stopPropagation = function(event)
{
  event.cancelBubble = true;
};

Core._findListener = function(target, type, listener)
{
  // get the array of listener IDs added to target
  var listeners = target._listeners;
  if (!listeners) return -1;

  // get a reference to the window object containing target
  var targetDocument = target.document || target;
  var targetWindow = targetDocument.parentWindow;

  // searching backward (to speed up onunload processing),
  // find the listener
  for (var i = listeners.length - 1; i >= 0; i--)
  {
    // get the listener's ID from target
    var listenerId = listeners[i];

    // get the record of the listener from the window object
    var listenerRecord =
        targetWindow._allListeners[listenerId];

    // compare type and listener with the retrieved record
    if (listenerRecord.type == type &&
```

```
        listenerRecord.listener == listener)
      {
        return i;
      }
    }
    return -1;
  };

  Core._removeAllListeners = function()
  {
    var targetWindow = this;

    for (id in targetWindow._allListeners)
    {
      var listenerRecord = targetWindow._allListeners[id];
      listenerRecord.target.detachEvent(
          "on" + listenerRecord.type, listenerRecord.listener2);
      delete targetWindow._allListeners[id];
    }
  };

  Core._listenerCounter = 0;
}

Core.addClass = function(target, theClass)
{
  if (!Core.hasClass(target, theClass))
  {
    if (target.className == "")
    {
      target.className = theClass;
    }
    else
    {
      target.className += " " + theClass;
    }
  }
};

Core.getElementsByClass = function(theClass)
{
  var elementArray = [];

  if (typeof document.all != "undefined")
```

```
  {
    elementArray = document.all;
  }
  else
  {
    elementArray = document.getElementsByTagName("*");
  }

  var matchedArray = [];
  var pattern = new RegExp("(^| )" + theClass + "( |$)");

  for (var i = 0; i < elementArray.length; i++)
  {
    if (pattern.test(elementArray[i].className))
    {
      matchedArray[matchedArray.length] = elementArray[i];
    }
  }

  return matchedArray;
};

Core.hasClass = function(target, theClass)
{
  var pattern = new RegExp("(^| )" + theClass + "( |$)");

  if (pattern.test(target.className))
  {
    return true;
  }

  return false;
};

Core.removeClass = function(target, theClass)
{
  var pattern = new RegExp("(^| )" + theClass + "( |$)");

  target.className = target.className.replace(pattern, "$1");
  target.className = target.className.replace(/ $/, "");
};

Core.getComputedStyle = function(element, styleProperty)
{
```

```
  var computedStyle = null;

  if (typeof element.currentStyle != "undefined")
  {
    computedStyle = element.currentStyle;
  }
  else
  {
    computedStyle =
        document.defaultView.getComputedStyle(element, null);
  }

  return computedStyle[styleProperty];
};

Core.start = function(runnable)
{
  Core.addEventListener(window, "load", runnable.init);
};
```

Index

THE
JAVASCRIPT
ANTHOLOGY
101 ESSENTIAL TIPS, TRICKS & HACKS

BY JAMES EDWARDS
& CAMERON ADAMS

THE MOST COMPLETE QUESTION AND ANSWER BOOK ON JAVASCRIPT

THE ART & SCIENCE OF CSS

BY **CAMERON ADAMS**
JINA BOLTON
DAVID JOHNSON
STEVE SMITH
JONATHAN SNOOK

INSPIRATIONAL STANDARDS-BASED WEB DESIGN

THE PRINCIPLES OF
BEAUTIFUL
WEB DESIGN

BY JASON BEAIRD

DESIGN BEAUTIFUL WEB SITES USING THIS SIMPLE STEP-BY-STEP GUIDE

FOR
STUDENTS

Over the past four years we have spent time in classrooms across Canada, speaking to students just like you.

We've asked what you want to see in a textbook, how you learn, how many hours a week you spend online, and what you find most valuable when preparing for a test. Based on your feedback, we've developed a new hybrid learning solution—**MGMT**. Your textbook, the Chapter Review cards, and our online resources present a new, exciting, and fresh approach to learning. Check out the website at **www.icanmgmt.com** for an unrivalled set of learning tools.

- Interactive e-book
- Audio summaries
- Cases and Exercises
- Flashcards
- Games
- Videos
- Glossary
- Interactive quizzing
- PowerPoint slides
- **And more!**

Purestock/Getty Images

NELSON / E D U C A T I O N

MGMT, Canadian Edition

by Chuck Williams, Terri Champion, and Ike Hall

**Vice President,
Editorial Director:**
Evelyn Veitch

**Editor-in-Chief:
Higher Education:**
Anne Williams

Acquisitions Editor:
Amie Plourde

Marketing Manager:
Kathaleen McCormick

Developmental Editor:
Jenny O'Reilly

**Photo Researcher and
Permissions Coordinator:**
Julie Pratt

**Senior Content
Production Manager:**
Natalia Denesiuk Harris

Production Service:
MPS Limited, a Macmillan
Company

Copy Editor:
Matthew Kudelka

Proofreader:
Dianne Fowlie

Indexer:
Edwin Durbin

Manufacturing Manager:
Joanne McNeil

Design Director:
Ken Phipps

Managing Designer:
Franca Amore

Interior Design:
Ke Design

Cover Design:
Martyn Schmoll

Cover Image:
John Giustina/Iconica/Getty Images

Compositor:
MPS Limited, a Macmillan Company

Printer:
RR Donnelley

**Library and Archives Canada
Cataloguing in Publication Data**

Williams, Chuck, 1959–

   MGMT / Chuck Williams,
Terri Champion, Ike Hall. —
Canadian ed.

Includes bibliographical references
and index.
ISBN 978-0-17-650235-5

   1. Management—Textbooks.
I. Champion, Terri, 1965– II. Hall, Ike
III. Title.

HD31.W51675 2011   658
C2010-908088-2

ISBN-13: 978-0-17-650235-5
ISBN-10: 0-17-650235-1

Brief Contents

Part 1
Introduction to Management

Part 2
Planning

Part 3
Organizing

Part 4
Leading

Part 5
Controlling

Contents

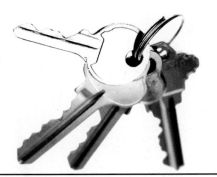

Part 2
Planning 84

Part 3
Organizing 166

Chapter 11
Managing Human Resource Systems 208

Chapter 12
Managing Individuals and a Diverse Workforce 234

Part 4
Leading 254

Chapter 13
Motivation 254

Chapter 14
Leadership 274

Part 5
Controlling 316

MANAGEMENT

What Is Management?

Management issues are fundamental to any organization: How do we plan to get things done, organize the company to be efficient and effective, lead and motivate employees, and put controls in place to make sure our plans are followed and our goals are met? Good management is basic to starting a business, growing a business, and maintaining a business once it has achieved some measure of success.

To understand how important *good* management is, think about mistakes like these: Mistake #1. A high-level bank manager reduces a marketing manager to tears by angrily criticizing her in front of others for a mistake that wasn't hers.[1] Mistake #2. Guidant Corporation, which makes cardiovascular medical products, waited for three years, forty-five device failures, and two patient deaths before recalling 50,000 defective heart defibrillators, 77 percent of which were already implanted in patients.[2]

Ah, bad managers and bad management. Is it any wonder that Canadian companies pay management consultants nearly $10 billion a year for advice on basic management issues such as how to lead people effectively, organize the company efficiently, and manage large-scale projects and processes?[3] This textbook will help you understand some of the basic issues that management consultants help companies resolve. (And it won't cost you billions of dollars.)

Learning Outcomes

1 describe what management is.

2 explain the four functions of management.

3 describe different kinds of managers.

4 explain the major roles and subroles that managers perform in their jobs.

5 explain what companies look for in managers.

6 discuss the top mistakes that managers make in their jobs.

7 describe the transition that employees go through when they are promoted to management.

8 explain how and why companies can create competitive advantage through people.

After reading the next two sections, you should be able to

1 describe what management is.

2 explain the four functions of management.

NAM Y HUH/ASSOCIATED PRESS

1 Management Is...

Many of today's managers got their start working on the factory floor, clearing dishes off tables, helping customers fit a suit, or wiping up a spill in aisle 3. Similarly, lots of you will start at the bottom and work your way up. There's no better way to get to know your competition, your customers, and your business. But whether you begin your career at the entry level or as a supervisor, your job is not to do the work but to help others do theirs. **Management** is getting work done through others. Pat Carrigan, a former elementary school principal who became a manager at a General Motors' car parts plant, says,

"I've never made a part in my life, and I don't really have any plans to make one. That's not my job. My job is to create an environment where people who do make them can make them right, can make them right the first time, can make them at a competitive cost, and can do so with some sense of responsibility and pride in what they're doing. I don't have to know how to make a part to do any of those things."[4]

Pat Carrigan's description of managerial responsibilities suggests that managers also have to be concerned with efficiency and effectiveness in the

Management getting work done through others

work process. **Efficiency** is getting work done with a minimum of effort, expense, or waste. For example, how does the Shouldice Hospital in Toronto perform more than 7,500 hernia surgeries a year on patients from all over the world even while employing only 10 full-time surgeons? The Shouldice Hernia Centre has been in operation since 1945 and is a testament to the principles of efficiency and productivity, hallmarks of Frederick Taylor's Theory of Scientific Management. The hospital is equipped with 5 operating theatres, 89 hospital beds, and a staff of 107, all focused on providing an extremely specialized, high-quality and high-volume service. A well-organized admissions screening and scheduling system allows for efficient management of demand and capacity, and the delivery system allows for maximum patient involvement to ensure efficiency and low cost. The facility is designed to encourage exercise and rapid recovery—there are no TVs or telephones in patient rooms, but there *are* 23 acres of gardens for patients to stroll in. The centre's results are impressive—at Shouldice, the chance of complication is 0.5 percent, and the average chance of recurrence after hernia repair is less than 1 percent. Compare this to the average in North America for recurrence after hernia repair, which is 10 percent. In addition, recovery times and costs are lower compared to other hospitals and clinics.[5]

You'll learn more about the principles of scientific management and other management theories in Chapter 2 on the history of management.

Efficiency alone is not enough to ensure success. Managers must also strive for **effectiveness,** which means accomplishing tasks that help fulfill organizational objectives such as customer service and satisfaction. Wal-Mart's new computerized scheduling system is an example of efficiency and effectiveness. It typically takes a manager a full day to schedule the weekly shifts for a single store. But the computerized scheduling system calculates the schedules for Wal-Mart's 1.3 million workers in one day. The system also measures trends in store sales and customer traffic so it can have more employees on the job whenever its stores are busy. Tests in 39 stores indicated that 70 percent of customers reported improved checkout times and service using this scheduling system.[6]

2 Management Functions

Henri Fayol, who was a managing director (CEO) of a large steel company in the early 1900s, was one of the founders of the field of management. You'll learn more about Fayol and management's other key contributors when you read about the history of management in Chapter 2. Based on his 20 years of experience as a CEO, Fayol argued that "the success of an enterprise generally depends much more on the administrative ability of its leaders than on their technical ability."[7] Take, as an example, Jim Balsillie and Mike Lazaridis, co-CEOs of Research in Motion Inc. Both men have expertise in engineering and computer technology; however, RIM succeeds because of their capabilities as managers, not solely because of their technical abilities.

Managers need to perform five managerial functions in order to succeed, according to Fayol: planning, organizing, coordinating, commanding, and controlling.[8] Most management textbooks today have updated this list by dropping the coordinating function and referring to Fayol's commanding function as "leading." Fayol's management functions are thus known today in this updated form as planning, organizing, leading, and controlling. Studies indicate that managers who perform these management functions well are more successful, gaining promotions for themselves and profits for their companies. One study shows that the more time CEOs spend planning, the more profitable their companies are.[9] A 25-year study at AT&T found that employees with better planning and decision-making skills were more likely to be promoted into management jobs, to be successful as managers, and to be promoted into upper levels of management.[10] The evidence is clear. Managers serve their companies well when they plan, organize, lead, and control. (That's why this book is organized around the functions of management outlined in Exhibit 1.1.)

Now let's take a closer look at each of the management functions: 2.1 planning, 2.2 organizing, 2.3 leading, and 2.4 controlling.

2.1 Planning

Planning involves determining organizational goals and a means for achieving them. As you'll learn in Chapter 5, planning is one of the best ways to

Efficiency getting work done with a minimum of effort, expense, or waste

Effectiveness accomplishing tasks that help fulfill organizational objectives

Planning (management functions) determining organizational goals and a means for achieving them

Exhibit 1.1

The Four Functions of Management

Planning | Organizing
Leading | Controlling

© iStockphoto.com/blackred

improve performance. It encourages people to work harder, to work hard for extended periods, to engage in behaviours directly related to accomplishing goals, and to think of better ways to do their jobs. But most important, companies that plan have larger profits and faster growth than companies that don't plan.

For example, the question "What business are we in?" is at the heart of strategic planning, which you'll learn about in Chapter 6. If you can answer the question "What business are you in?" in two sentences or less, chances are you have a very clear plan for your business. Christine Day, CEO of Vancouver-based athletic apparel company lululemon athletica, inc., knows precisely what business her company is in: 'creating components for people to live a longer, healthier, more fun life.'[11] Same for Google. Even though the company makes money selling search-based Internet advertising, Google says that it is not in the advertising business but in the business of organizing the world's information.[12] Not only can you search Google for websites, images, books and scholarly articles, and shopping opportunities, but you can also organize your personal life using Google's calendar, e-mail, photo, and document sharing, and feed reader applications. Even Google's $1.65 billion purchase of YouTube adheres to the business Google is in by helping users access and organize video content.

You'll learn more about planning in Chapter 5 on planning and decision making, Chapter 6 on organizational strategy, Chapter 7 on innovation and change, and Chapter 8 on global management.

2.2 Organizing

Organizing is deciding where decisions will be made, who will do what jobs and tasks, and who will work

for whom in the company. Imagine the massive effort that faced the Vancouver Organizing Committee for the 2010 Olympic and Paralympic Winter Games (VANOC). The International Olympic Committee announced on July 2, 2003, that VANOC would be tasked with the enormous challenge of organizing this worldwide event, which would attract over 6,850 athletes and officials from over 80 countries, 10,000 media representatives, and 2.3 million visitors to the City of Vancouver over 17 days of competition. Organizing efforts encompassed new sports facilities and venues, major transportation infrastructure projects, housing accommodations (including the Olympic Athletes Village), event ticket sales, the planning of the opening and closing ceremonies, medal presentations, retail merchandise sales, security measures, and the coordination of an army of over 50,000 workers and volunteers. To make the Vancouver 2010 Winter Olympics a reality, VANOC administered a budget of $580 million for capital infrastructure from the federal and provincial governments and a further $1.76 billion operating budget funded by television revenues, ticket sales, corporate sponsorships, and private contributions. Construction cost overruns and a global economic downturn presented a major challenge to VANOC's operating budget and was cause for concern. However, there was also plenty of good news: event ticket sales were oversubscribed, the sports venues were completed ahead of schedule, and major transportation projects—including rapid transit service between downtown Vancouver and the airport—were fully operational three months earlier than anticipated. There is no doubt that it took an incredible amount of organizational effort to host an international event of this calibre. With the world watching, VANOC put on an event that made Canadians proud.[13]

You'll learn more about organizing in Chapter 9 on designing organizations, Chapter 10 on managing teams, Chapter 11 on managing human resources, and Chapter 12 on managing individuals and a diverse work force.

2.3 Leading

Our third management function, **leading,** involves inspiring and motivating workers to work hard to achieve organizational

Organizing deciding where decisions will be made, who will do what jobs and tasks, and who will work for whom

Leading inspiring and motivating workers to work hard to achieve organizational goals

Rick Madonik/GetStock.com

running clinics and weekly runs for everyone from beginners to avid runners and marathoners; and promote a lifestyle of wellness and community. Much of Running Room's success in achieving this vision can be attributed to Stanton himself, who spends about 300 days a year on the road, visiting Running Room stores and participating in numerous charity runs and marathons across North America, allowing him to stay up to date on the needs of his consumers and staff. Examples of his approachable and accessible leadership style are found throughout the company: his e-mail address is posted on the company website; he acts as the voice of the company's voicemail receptionist; and he utilizes a company-wide computer network that allows store employees to stay connected with one another and head office. The results speak for themselves: the Running Room boasts an employee turnover rate that is half the industry average. It was voted one of Canada's Best Managed Companies in 2007 and continues to expand in Canada and in the United States.[14]

You'll learn more about leading in Chapter 13 on motivation, Chapter 14 on leadership, and Chapter 15 on managing communication.

2.4 Controlling

The last function of management, **controlling,** is monitoring progress toward goal achievement and taking corrective action when progress isn't being made. The basic control process involves setting standards to achieve goals, comparing actual performance to those standards, and then making changes to return performance to those standards.

Needing to cut costs (the standard) to restore profitability (the goal), Continental Airlines started giving passengers small cups of their soft drinks instead of an entire can (one corrective action among many). Company spokesperson Rahsaan Johnson defended the move, saying, "Flight attendants have been telling us that the trash bags they carry were so heavy because of all the [wasted] liquid. We were pouring almost half away."[15] Although Continental will still give entire soft drink cans to customers who request them, serving smaller drinks saves the company $100,000 a year in costs.

You'll learn more about the control function in Chapter 16 on control, Chapter 17 on managing information, and Chapter 18 on managing service and manufacturing operations.

goals. John Stanton, founder and president of the Edmonton-based Running Room chain of retail stores, which cater to running and fitness enthusiasts alike, knows how important leadership is to building a successful company. Since opening his first store in 1984, Stanton's company has grown into North America's largest specialty running and walking retailer of sporting goods, apparel, and footwear, with stores from coast to coast. He credits much of his success to his original vision for the company, which hasn't changed much over the years—locate stores near parks, trails, and post-run meeting places like cafés; provide specialized knowledge and technical expertise on shoe selection as well as health and nutrition; offer

Controlling monitoring progress toward goal achievement and taking corrective action when needed

What Do Managers Do?

Not all managerial jobs are the same. The demands and requirements placed on the CEO of Sony are significantly different from those placed on the manager of your local Wendy's restaurant.

 After reading the next two sections, you should be able to

3 describe different kinds of managers.

4 explain the major roles and subroles that managers perform in their jobs.

3 Kinds of Managers

As shown in Exhibit 1.2, there are four kinds of managers, each with different jobs and responsibilities: 3.1 top managers, 3.2 middle managers, 3.3 first-line managers, and 3.4 team leaders.

3.1 Top Managers

Top managers hold positions like chief executive officer (CEO), chief operating officer (COO), chief financial officer (CFO), and chief information officer (CIO), and are responsible for the overall direction of the organization. Top managers have the following responsibilities.[16] First, they are responsible for creating a context for change. In many large corporations it is not uncommon for a CEO to be fired because he or she failed to move fast enough to effect significant change. In fact, the most critical time for a CEO is the first 100 days. This indicates that more and more organizations today are expecting to see results quickly and that they use the first few months of a top manager's tenure as a means of determining whether that person will succeed.[17] In both Europe and the United States, 35 percent of all CEOs are eventually fired because of their failure to successfully change their companies.[18] Creating a context for change includes forming a long-range vision or mission for the company.

Once that vision or mission is set, the second responsibility of top managers is to develop employees'

commitment to and ownership of the company's performance. That is, top managers are responsible for creating employee buy-in. Third, top managers must create a positive organizational culture through language and action. Top managers impart company values, strategies, and lessons through what they do and say to others both inside and outside the company. Above all, no matter what they communicate, it's critical for CEOs to send and reinforce clear, consistent messages.[19] A former *Fortune* 500 CEO said, "I tried to [use] exactly the same words every time so that I didn't produce a lot of, 'Last time you said this, this time you said that.' You've got to say the same thing over and over and over."[20]

Finally, top managers are responsible for monitoring their business environments. This means that top managers must closely monitor customers' needs, competitors' moves, and long-term business, economic, and social trends. You'll read more about business environments in Chapter 3.

3.2 Middle Managers

Middle managers hold positions like plant manager, regional manager, or divisional manager. They are responsible for setting objectives consistent with top management's goals and for planning and implementing subunit strategies for achieving those objectives.[21] One specific middle management responsibility is to plan and allocate resources to meet objectives.

A second major responsibility is to coordinate and link groups, departments, and divisions within a company. In February 2008, a tornado destroyed a Caterpillar plant in Oxford, Mississippi, the only plant in the company that produced a particular coupling required for many of Caterpillar's machines. The disaster threatened a worldwide production shutdown. Greg Folley, a middle manager in charge of the parts division that included the plant, gave workers two weeks to restore production to pre-tornado levels. He said, "I was betting on people to get it done." He contacted new vendors, sent engineers from other Caterpillar locations to Mississippi to check for quality, and set up distribution operations in another facility. Meanwhile, Kevin Kempa, the plant manager in Oxford, moved some employees to another plant,

Top managers executives responsible for the overall direction of the organization

Middle managers managers responsible for setting objectives consistent with top management's goals and for planning and implementing subunit strategies for achieving these objectives

Exhibit 1.2

What the Four Kinds of Managers Do

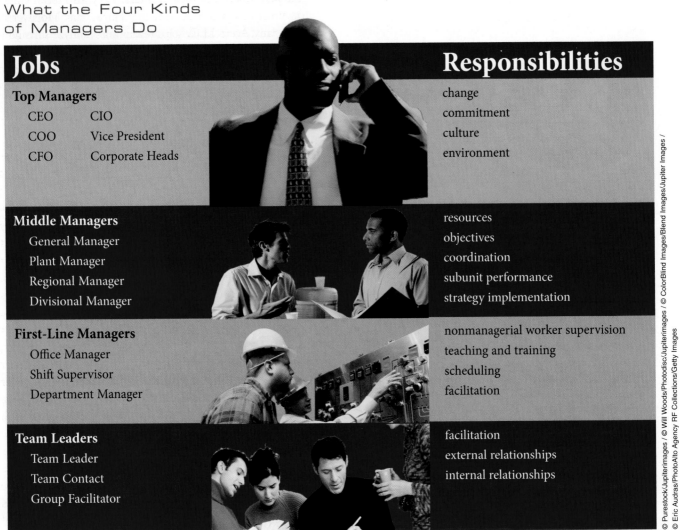

Jobs	Responsibilities
Top Managers CEO CIO COO Vice President CFO Corporate Heads	change commitment culture environment
Middle Managers General Manager Plant Manager Regional Manager Divisional Manager	resources objectives coordination subunit performance strategy implementation
First-Line Managers Office Manager Shift Supervisor Department Manager	nonmanagerial worker supervision teaching and training scheduling facilitation
Team Leaders Team Leader Team Contact Group Facilitator	facilitation external relationships internal relationships

delivered new training to employees during the production hiatus, and oversaw reconstruction of the plant. The day before the two-week deadline, the Oxford plant was up and running and produced 8,000 parts.[22]

A third responsibility of middle management is to monitor and manage the performance of the subunits and individual managers who report to them. Canada's upscale menswear retail chain, Harry Rosen Inc., invested in a customized software system to help sales associates better manage customer relationships by enabling employees to view customer preferences and buying history as well as to help develop marketing campaigns targeted to individual customer preferences. The system also provides management with important real-time information and sales reports, which are used to evaluate storewide and individual sales associate performance. In this way, management is able to assess how stores and associates are performing in terms of key performance indicators and ensures that the Harry Rosen quality and brand image is maintained.[23]

Finally, middle managers are also responsible for implementing the changes or strategies generated by top managers. Wal-Mart's strategy reflects its mission, "Saving people money so they can live better." When Wal-Mart began selling groceries in its new 200,000-square-foot supercentres, it made purchasing manager Brian Wilson responsible for buying perishable goods more cheaply than Wal-Mart's competitors. When small produce suppliers had trouble meeting Wal-Mart's needs, Wilson worked closely with them and connected them to RetailLink, Wal-Mart's computer network, "which allows our suppliers immediate

Courtesy, Whirlpool Corporation

Feats of Daring Duet

Trusting that his 61,000 employees could dramatically increase product innovation at Whirlpool appliances, CEO David Whitman told them to come up with new ideas, tell their bosses about their ideas, and, if their bosses wouldn't listen, bring their new product ideas directly to him. Employees flocked to an in-house website featuring a course on innovation and a list of all the new suggestions and ideas, racking up 300,000 "hits" on the site each month. Today, revenue from innovative products has quadrupled. And instead of cutting prices to maintain sales, Whirlpool's prices are now rising 5 percent per year because customers are willing to pay more for its innovative products, such as the Duet washer and dryer.[24]

Source: M. Arndt, "Creativity Overflowing," *Business Week*, 8 May 2006, 50.

access to all information needed to help run the business." Over time, these steps helped the produce suppliers reduce costs and deliver the enormous quantities of fresh fruits and vegetables that Wal-Mart's Supercenters need.[24] They also helped Wal-Mart become the world's largest grocer.[25]

3.3 First-Line Managers

First-line managers hold positions like office manager, shift supervisor, or department manager. The primary responsibility of first-line managers is to manage the performance of the entry-level employees who are directly responsible for producing a company's goods and services. First-line managers are the only managers who don't supervise other managers. The responsibilities of first-line managers include monitoring, teaching, and short-term planning.

First-line managers encourage, monitor, and reward the performance of their workers. They also teach entry-level employees how to do their jobs. Damian Mogavero's company, Avero LLC, helps restaurants analyze sales data for each member of a restaurant's wait staff. Restaurant managers who use these data, says Mogavero, will often take their top-selling server to lunch each week as a reward. The best managers, however, will also take their poorest-selling servers out to lunch to talk about what they can do to improve their performance.[26]

First-line managers also make detailed schedules and operating plans based on middle management's intermediate-range plans. By contrast to the long-term plans of top managers (three to five years out) and the intermediate plans of middle managers (6 to 18 months out), first-line managers engage in plans and actions that typically produce results within two weeks.[27] Consider the typical convenience store manager (e.g., 7-Eleven), who starts the day by driving past competitors' stores to inspect their gasoline prices and then checks the outside of his or her store for anything that might need maintenance, such as burned-out lights or signs, or restocking, like windshield washer fluid and paper towels. Then comes an inside check, where the manager determines what needs to be done for that day. (Are there enough coffee and donuts for breakfast or enough sandwiches for lunch?) Once the day is planned, the manager turns to weekend orders. After accounting for the weather (hot or cold) and the sales trends at the same time last year, the manager makes sure the store will have enough beer, soft drinks, and Sunday papers on hand. Finally, the manager looks 7 to 10 days ahead for hiring needs. Because of strict hiring procedures (basic math tests, drug tests, and background checks), it can take that long to hire new employees. Said one convenience store manager, "I have to continually interview, even if I am fully staffed."[28]

3.4 Team Leaders

The fourth kind of manager is a team leader. This relatively new kind of management job developed as companies shifted to self-managing teams which, by definition, have no formal supervisor. In traditional management hierarchies, first-line managers are responsible for the performance of nonmanagerial employees and have the authority to hire and fire workers, make job

First-line managers managers who train and supervise the performance of nonmanagerial employees who are directly responsible for producing the company's products or services

Getting produce to market efficiently and cheaply requires skilled execution of the four management functions.

© PhotoLink/Photodisc/Jupiterimages

assignments, and control resources. In this new structure, the teams themselves perform nearly all of the functions performed by first-line managers under traditional hierarchies.[29]

Team leaders thus have a different set of responsibilities than traditional first-line managers.[30] **Team leaders** are primarily responsible for facilitating team activities toward accomplishing a goal. This doesn't mean team leaders are responsible for team performance. They aren't. The team is. Team leaders help their team members plan and schedule work, learn to solve problems, and work effectively with one another. Management consultant Franklin Jonath says, "The idea is for the team leader to be at the service of the group. It should be clear that the team members own the outcome. The leader is there to bring intellectual, emotional, and spiritual resources to the team. Through his or her actions, the leader should

> **Team leaders** managers responsible for facilitating team activities toward accomplishing a goal

be able to show the others how to think about the work that they're doing in the context of their lives."[31]

Relationships among team members and between different teams are crucial to good team performance and must be well-managed by team leaders. Getting along with others is much more important in team structures because team members can't get work done without the help of other teammates. Team leaders are responsible for fostering good relationships and addressing problematic ones within their teams.

Team leaders are also responsible for managing external relationships. Team leaders act as the bridge or liaison between their teams and other teams, departments, and divisions in a company. For example, if a member of Team A complains about the quality of Team B's work, Team A's leader needs to initiate a meeting with Team B's leader. Together, these team leaders are responsible for getting members of both teams to work together to solve the problem. If it's done right, the problem is solved without involving company management or blaming members of the other team.[32]

Team leaders who fail to understand how their roles are different from those of traditional managers often struggle in their jobs. A team leader at Texas Instruments reacted with skepticism to his initial experience with teams: "I didn't buy into teams, partly because there was no clear plan on what I was supposed to do. . . . I never let the operators [team members] do any scheduling or any ordering of parts because that was mine. I figured as long as I had that, I had a job." After shifting jobs, however, he learned the difference in approach in a setting where members of the team took turns at the leadership role. He eventually became a consultant to help team leaders develop their skills and solve problems.[33]

You will learn more about teams in Chapter 10.

4 Managerial Roles

Although all four types of managers engage in planning, organizing, leading, and controlling, if you were to follow them around during a typical day on the job, you would probably not use these terms to describe what they actually do. Rather, what you'd see are the various roles managers play. Henry Mintzberg studied several CEOs over the course of a week, analyzing their mail, their conversations, and their actions. He concluded that managers fulfill three major roles while performing their jobs:[34]

- interpersonal roles
- informational roles
- decisional roles

In other words, managers talk to people, gather and give information, and make decisions. Furthermore, as shown in Exhibit 1.3, these three major roles can be subdivided into 10 subroles. *Let's examine each major role—**4.1 interpersonal**, **4.2 informational**, and **4.3 decisional roles**—and their 10 subroles.*

4.1 Interpersonal Roles

More than anything else, management jobs are people-intensive. Estimates vary with the level of management, but most managers spend between two-thirds and four-fifths of their time in face-to-face communication with others.[35] If you're a loner, or if you consider dealing with people a pain, then you may not be cut out for management work. In fulfilling the interpersonal role of management, managers perform three subroles: figurehead, leader, and liaison.

In the **figurehead role,** managers perform ceremonial duties like greeting company visitors, speaking at the opening of a new facility, or representing the company at

Exhibit 1.3
Mintzberg's Managerial Roles

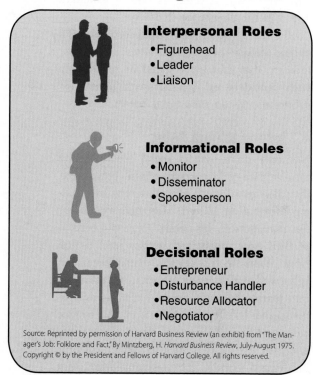

Interpersonal Roles
- Figurehead
- Leader
- Liaison

Informational Roles
- Monitor
- Disseminator
- Spokesperson

Decisional Roles
- Entrepreneur
- Disturbance Handler
- Resource Allocator
- Negotiator

a community luncheon to support local charities. In the **leader role,** managers motivate and encourage workers to accomplish organizational objectives. Vancouver-based Mountain Equipment Co-op (MEC) is an outdoor recreation retail chain known for its unique retail format. Customers are offered a lifetime membership and a share of the company for a one-time payment of five dollars. Their unique approach fits well with the culture set by MEC's leaders, who make corporate social responsibility—in particular, ethical sourcing and sustainability—a top priority, and who focus strongly on employee motivation. MEC provides employees with onsite yoga classes, shower facilities for bicycle commuters, outdoor patio areas with lounge chairs and barbeques, a climbing wall, and a sign-out system where employees can borrow outdoor equipment. Employees can listen to music at work, bring pets to work when needed, participate in after-work bike rides and company running teams, and receive tuition subsidies for courses taken at outside institutions that support

Figurehead role the interpersonal role managers play when they perform ceremonial duties

Leader role the interpersonal role managers play when they motivate and encourage workers to accomplish organizational objectives

ongoing career development. The company's culture and its leadership approach explain why MEC was selected as one of Canada's Top 100 Employers for 2010.[36]

In the **liaison role,** managers deal with people outside their units. Studies consistently indicate that managers spend as much time with outsiders as they do with their own subordinates and their own bosses.[37]

4.2 Informational Roles

Not only do managers spend most of their time in face-to-face contact with others, but they also spend much of it obtaining and sharing information. Indeed, Mintzberg found that the managers in his study spent 40 percent of their time giving and getting information from others. In this regard, management can be viewed as processing information, gathering information by scanning the business environment and listening to others in face-to-face conversations, processing that information, and then sharing that information with people inside and outside the company. Mintzberg described three informational subroles: monitor, disseminator, and spokesperson.

In the **monitor role,** managers scan their environment for information, actively contact others for information, and, because of their personal contacts, receive a great deal of unsolicited information. Besides

Liaison role the interpersonal role managers play when they deal with people outside their units

Monitor role the informational role managers play when they scan their environment for information

Disseminator role the informational role managers play when they share information with others in their departments or companies

receiving firsthand information, managers monitor their environment by reading local newspapers and national papers like the *Globe and Mail* to keep track of customers, competitors, and technological changes that may affect their businesses. Now, managers can also take advantage of electronic monitoring and distribution services that track the news wires for stories related to their businesses.

Because of their numerous personal contacts and their access to subordinates, managers are often hubs for the distribution of critical information. In the **disseminator role,** managers share the information they have collected with their subordinates and others in the company. There will never be a complete substitute for face-to-face dissemination of information. Yet technology is changing how information is shared and collected. Although the primary methods of communication in large companies are e-mail and voicemail, managers are also

© Image Source/Jupiterimages

using company intranets, online video, blogs, podcasts, and wikis to communicate internally with employees. Managers are also beginning to realize the value of social networking technologies like Facebook and Twitter to disseminate information internally. Vancouver-based lululemon athletica uses Twitter, Facebook, blogging, and Flickr to help maintain open lines of communication with employees in their 100-plus stores across North America and Australia. Carolyn Coles, lululemon's online community manager, explains that social networking "helps to keep everyone connected at every level and empowered, and really elevates internal conversation."[38]

In contrast to the disseminator role, in which managers distribute information to employees inside the company, in the **spokesperson role,** managers share information with people outside their departments and companies. One of the most common ways CEOs serve as spokespeople for their companies is at annual meetings with company shareholders or the board of directors. CEOs also serve as spokespeople to the media when their companies are involved in major news stories. When Toshiba pulled the plug on its effort to position its HD-DVD technology as the dominant format for new high-definition players, ceding the market to Sony's Blu-ray, it was the company CEO Atsutoshi Nishida who explained this move to the public. Because Japanese companies value pride and tend to choose less high-profile strategies for backing out of a business deal, it was surprising that Nishida acted as the spokesperson in this situation. But Nishida emphasized, "We were in this to win," and explained Toshiba's decision to change its strategy and invest energy in alternative avenues of growth.[39]

4.3 Decisional Roles

Mintzberg found that obtaining and sharing information is not an end in itself. Obtaining and sharing information with people inside and outside the company is useful to managers because it helps them make good decisions. According to Mintzberg, managers engage in four decisional subroles: entrepreneur, disturbance handler, resource allocator, and negotiator.

In the **entrepreneur role,** managers adapt themselves, their subordinates, and their units to change. Ontario's Lakeport Brewing Corp. was struggling to survive in the extremely competitive beer industry when Teresa Cascioli was brought in as manager to try and salvage a company that was in deep financial trouble. Cascioli's strategy of expanding the product line, redesigning the packaging and labels, switching to a can format, and—more important—reducing the price of a case of beer to $24 or a buck a beer (the lowest legal price in Ontario), was considered by many in the industry to be brash and full of risk, considering that Lakeport had been started as a premium brewery. But her gamble paid off—the company's market share began to rise as a result of her innovative discount strategy, and eventually the brewery became the fourth-largest in the province and the sixth-largest in Canada.[40]

In the **disturbance handler role,** managers respond to pressures and problems so severe that they demand immediate attention and action. Managers often play the role of disturbance handler when the board of a failing company hires a new CEO to turn the company around. After Ford Motor Company's market share shrank from 25 to 16 percent and the company lost $7 billion in nine months, Alan Mulally came from Boeing to become Ford's new CEO. Mulally quickly arranged $23.5 billion in financing to cover the losses and introduced a plan to cut costs by reducing the number of cars Ford produces, standardizing the use of shared parts across Ford vehicles, and laying off half of Ford's 82,000 factory workers.[41]

Spokesperson role the informational role managers play when they share information with people outside their departments or companies

Entrepreneur role the decisional role managers play when they adapt themselves, their subordinates, and their units to change

Disturbance handler role the decisional role managers play when they respond to severe problems that demand immediate action

In the **resource allocator role,** managers decide who will get what resources and how much of each resource they will get. Hoping to revive sales of its luxury cars, top managers at General Motors acted as resource allocators by redirecting long-term investment of $4 billion to the company's Cadillac brand. Put in perspective, that means that executives invested nearly 10 percent of GM's total capital budget in a division that accounts for only 4 percent of GM sales.[42]

In the **negotiator role,** managers negotiate schedules, projects, goals, outcomes, resources, and employee raises. When Sprint bought Nextel (another cell phone company), the U.S. Federal Communications Commission required it to buy new radios for police and firefighters because its cell phone tower transmissions were interfering with emergency service communications in hundreds of locations. Sprint Nextel, which will spend over $3 billion to fix the problem, has been negotiating with law enforcement agencies in Maryland and Washington to replace 35,000 radios. It took Sprint a year to negotiate a $609,000 deal with the city of Fairfax, Virginia, just to develop plans to replace its radios, and the company continues to negotiate with the FCC for extended deadlines to complete the transition.[43] Negotiating, as you can see from Sprint's dilemma, is a key to success and a basic part of managerial work.

Resource allocator role the decisional role managers play when they decide who gets what resources

Negotiator role the decisional role managers play when they negotiate schedules, projects, goals, outcomes, resources, and employee raises

What Does It Take to Be a Manager?

I didn't have the slightest idea what my job was. I walked in giggling and laughing because I had been promoted and had no idea what principles or style to be guided by. After the first day, I felt like I had run into a brick wall. (Sales Representative #1)

Suddenly, I found myself saying, boy, I can't be responsible for getting all that revenue. I don't have the time. Suddenly you've got to go from [taking care of] yourself and say now I'm the manager, and what does a manager do? It takes a while thinking about it for it to really hit you . . . a manager gets things done through other people. That's a very, very hard transition to make. (Sales Representative #2)[44]

The statements above come from two star sales representatives, who, on the basis of their superior performance, were promoted to the position of sales manager. As their comments indicate, at first they did not feel confident about their ability to do their jobs as managers. Like most new managers, these sales managers suddenly realized that the knowledge, skills, and abilities that led to success early in their careers (and were probably responsible for their promotion into the ranks of management) would not necessarily help them succeed as managers. As sales representatives, they were responsible for managing only their own performance. But as sales managers, they were now directly responsible for supervising all of the sales representatives in their sales territories. Furthermore, they were now directly accountable for whether those sales representatives achieved their sales goals.

If performance in nonmanagerial jobs doesn't necessarily prepare you for a managerial job, then what does it take to be a manager?

After reading the next three sections, you should be able to

5 explain what companies look for in managers.

6 discuss the top mistakes that managers make in their jobs.

7 describe the transition that employees go through when they are promoted to management.

5 What Companies Look for in Managers

When companies look for employees who would be good managers, they look for individuals who have technical skills, human skills, conceptual skills, and the motivation to manage.[45] Exhibit 1.4 shows the relative importance of these four skills to the jobs of team leaders, first-line managers, middle managers, and top managers.

Technical skills are the specialized procedures, techniques, and knowledge required to get the job done. For the sales managers described above, technical skills are the ability to find new sales prospects, develop accurate sales pitches based on customer needs, and close the sale. For a nurse supervisor, technical skills include being able to insert an IV or operate a crash cart if a patient goes into cardiac arrest.

Technical skills are most important for team leaders and lower-level managers because they supervise the workers who produce products or serve customers. Team leaders and first-line managers need technical knowledge and skills to train new employees and help employees solve problems. Technical knowledge and skills are also needed to troubleshoot problems that employees can't handle. Technical skills become less important as managers rise through the managerial ranks, but they are still important.

Human skills can be summarized as the ability to work well with others. Managers with people skills work effectively within groups, encourage others to express their thoughts and feelings, are sensitive to others' needs and viewpoints, and are good listeners and communicators. Human skills are equally important at all levels of management, from first-line supervisors to CEOs. However, because lower-level managers spend much of their time solving technical problems, upper-level managers may actually spend more time dealing directly with people. On average, first-line managers spend 57 percent of their time with people, but that percentage increases to 63 percent for middle managers and 78 percent for top managers.[46]

Conceptual skills include the ability to see the organization as a whole, to understand how the different parts of the company affect one another, and to recognize how the company fits into or is affected by elements of its external environment such as the local community, social and economic forces, customers, and the competition. Good managers have

Exhibit 1.4

Management Skills

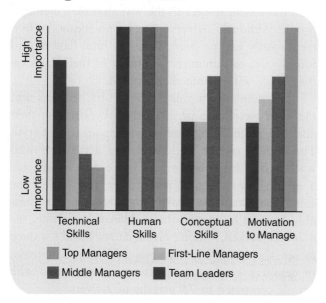

- Top Managers
- Middle Managers
- First-Line Managers
- Team Leaders

Technical skills the specialized procedures, techniques, and knowledge required to get the job done

Human skills the ability to work well with others

Conceptual skills the ability to see the organization as a whole, understand how the different parts affect each other, and recognize how the company fits into or is affected by its environment

Top Ten Mistakes Managers Make

1. **Insensitive to others:** abrasive, intimidating, bullying style
2. **Cold, aloof, arrogant**
3. **Betrays trust**
4. **Overly ambitious:** thinking of next job, playing politics
5. **Specific performance problems with the business**
6. **Overmanaging:** unable to delegate or build a team
7. **Unable to staff effectively**
8. **Unable to think strategically**
9. **Unable to adapt to boss with different style**
10. **Overdependent on advocate or mentor**

Source: M. W. McCall, Jr. and M. M. Lombardo, "What Makes a Top Executive?," *Psychology Today*, February 1983, 26–31.

to be able to recognize, understand, and reconcile multiple complex problems and perspectives. In other words, managers have to be smart! In fact, intelligence makes so much difference for managerial performance that managers with above-average intelligence typically outperform managers of average intelligence by approximately 48 percent.[47] Clearly, companies need to be careful to promote smart workers into management. Conceptual skills increase in importance as managers rise through the management hierarchy.

Good management involves much more than intelligence, however. For example, making the department genius a manager can be disastrous if that genius lacks technical skills, human skills, or one other factor known as the motivation to manage. **Motivation to manage** is an assessment of how motivated employees are to interact with superiors, participate in competitive situations, behave assertively toward others, tell others what to do, reward good behaviour and punish poor behaviour, perform actions that are highly visible to others, and handle and organize administrative tasks. Managers typically have a stronger motivation to manage than their subordinates, and managers at higher levels usually have a stronger motivation to manage than managers at lower levels. Furthermore, managers with a stronger motivation to manage are promoted faster, are rated as better managers by their employees, and earn more money than managers with a weak motivation to manage.[48]

Motivation to manage an assessment of how enthusiastic employees are about managing the work of others

6 Mistakes Managers Make

Another way to understand what it takes to be a manager is to look at the mistakes managers make. In other words, we can learn just as much from what managers shouldn't do as from what they should do.

Several studies of U.S. and British managers have compared "arrivers," or managers who made it all the way to the top of their companies, with "derailers," or managers who were successful early in their careers but were knocked off the fast track by the time they reached the middle to upper levels of management.[49] The researchers found that there were only a few differences between arrivers and derailers. For the most part, both groups were talented and both groups had weaknesses. But what distinguished derailers from arrivers was that derailers possessed two or more fatal flaws with respect to the way that they managed people. Although arrivers were by no means perfect, they usually had no more than one fatal flaw or had found ways to minimize the effects of their flaws on the people with whom they worked.

The number one mistake made by derailers was that they were insensitive to others by virtue of their abrasive, intimidating, and bullying management style. The authors of one study described a manager who walked into his subordinate's office and interrupted a meeting by saying, "I need to see you." When the subordinate tried to explain that he was not available because he was in the middle of a meeting, the manager barked, "I don't give a damn. I said I wanted to see you now."[50] Not surprisingly, only 25 percent of derailers were rated by others as being good with people compared to 75 percent of arrivers.

Konstantin Sutyagin/Shutterstock

The second mistake was that derailers were often cold, aloof, or arrogant. Although this sounds like insensitivity to others, it has more to do with derailed managers being so smart, so expert in their areas of knowledge, that they treated others with contempt because they weren't experts, too. For example, a large telecommunications company called in an industrial psychologist to counsel its vice president of human resources because she had been blamed for ruffling too many feathers at the company.[51] Interviews with the vice president's coworkers and subordinates revealed that they thought she was brilliant. Unfortunately, these smarts were accompanied by a cold, aloof, and arrogant management style. The people she worked with complained that she does "too much too fast," treats coworkers with "disdain," "impairs teamwork," "doesn't always show her warm side," and has "burned too many bridges."

The third mistake made by derailers involved betraying a trust. Betraying a trust doesn't mean being dishonest. Instead, it means making others look bad by not doing what you said you would do when you said you would do it. That mistake, in itself, is not fatal because managers and their workers aren't machines. Tasks go undone in every company every single business day. There's always too much to do and not enough time, people, money, or resources to do it. The fatal betrayal of trust is failing to inform others when things will not be done on time. This failure to admit mistakes, quickly inform others of the mistakes, take responsibility for the mistakes, and then fix them without blaming others distinguished the behaviour of derailers from that of arrivers.

The fourth mistake was being overly political and ambitious. Managers who always have their eye on their next job rarely establish more than superficial relationships with peers and coworkers. In their haste to gain credit for successes that would be noticed by upper management, they make the fatal mistake of treating people as though they don't matter. An employee with an overly ambitious boss described him this way: "He gave me a new definition of shared risk: If something I did was successful, he took the credit. If it wasn't, I got the blame."[52]

The fatal mistakes of being unable to delegate, build a team, and staff effectively indicate that many derailed managers were unable to make the most basic transition to managerial work: to quit being hands-on doers and start getting work done through others. Two things go wrong when managers make these mistakes. First, when managers meddle in decisions that their subordinates should be making—when they can't stop being doers—they alienate the people who work for them. According to Richard Kilburg of Johns Hopkins University, when managers interfere with workers' decisions, "You . . . have a tendency to lose your most creative people. They're able to say, 'Screw this. I'm not staying here.'"[53] Second, because they are trying to do their subordinates' jobs in addition to their own, managers who fail to delegate will not have enough time to do anything well.

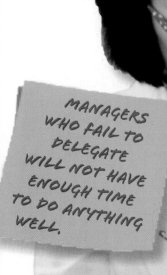

MANAGERS WHO FAIL TO DELEGATE WILL NOT HAVE ENOUGH TIME TO DO ANYTHING WELL.

Exhibit 1.5

Stages in the Transition to Management

MANAGERS' INITIAL EXPECTATIONS			AFTER SIX MONTHS AS A MANAGER			AFTER A YEAR AS A MANAGER					
JAN	FEB	MAR	APR	MAY	JUN	JUL	AUG	SEP	OCT	NOV	DEC

MANAGERS' INITIAL EXPECTATIONS	AFTER SIX MONTHS AS A MANAGER	AFTER A YEAR AS A MANAGER
⊙ Be the boss	⊙ Initial expectations were wrong	⊙ No longer "doer"
⊙ Formal authority	⊙ Fast pace	⊙ Communication, listening, & positive reinforcement
⊙ Manage tasks	⊙ Heavy workload	⊙ Learning to adapt to and control stress
⊙ Job is not managing people	⊙ Job is to be problem solver and troubleshooter for subordinates	⊙ Job is people development

Source: L.A. Hill, *Becoming a Manager: Mastery of a New Identity* (Boston: Harvard Business School Press, 1992).

7 The Transition to Management: The First Year

In her book *Becoming a Manager: Mastery of a New Identity*, Harvard Business School professor Linda Hill followed the development of 19 people in their first year as managers. Her study found that becoming a manager produced a profound psychological transition that changed the way these managers viewed themselves and others. As shown in Exhibit 1.5, the evolution of the managers' thoughts, expectations, and realities over the course of their first year in management reveals the magnitude of the changes they experienced.

Initially, the managers in Hill's study believed that their job was to exercise formal authority and to manage tasks—basically being the boss, telling others what to do, making decisions, and getting things done. In fact, most of the new managers were attracted to management positions because they wanted to be in charge. Surprisingly, the new managers did not believe that their job was to manage people. The only aspects of people management mentioned by the new managers were hiring and firing.

After six months, most of the new managers had concluded that their initial expectations about managerial work were wrong. Management wasn't just about being the boss, making decisions, and telling others what to do. The first surprise

Top managers spend an average of 9 minutes on a given task before having to switch to another.

was the fast pace and heavy workload involved. Said one manager, "This job is much harder than you think. It is 40 to 50 percent more work than being a producer! Who would have ever guessed?" The pace of managerial work was startling, too. Another manager said, "You have eight or nine people looking for your time . . . coming into and out of your office all day long." A somewhat frustrated manager declared that management was "a job that never ended . . . a job you couldn't get your hands around."

Informal descriptions like this are consistent with studies indicating that the average first-line manager spends no more than two minutes on a task before being interrupted by a request from a subordinate, a phone call, or an e-mail. The pace is somewhat less hurried for top managers, who spend an average of approximately nine minutes on a task before having to switch to another. In practice, this means that supervisors may perform 30 different tasks per hour, while top managers perform seven different tasks per hour, with each task typically different from the one that preceded it. A manager described this frenetic level of activity by saying, "The only time you are in control is when you shut your door, and then I feel I am not doing the job I'm supposed to be doing, which is being with the people."

The other major surprise after six months on the job was that the managers' expectations about what they should do as managers were very different from their subordinates' expectations. Initially, the managers defined their jobs as helping their subordinates perform their jobs well. For the managers, who still defined themselves as doers rather than managers, assisting their subordinates meant going out on sales calls or handling customer complaints. But when the managers "assisted" in this way, their subordinates were resentful and viewed their help as interference. The subordinates wanted their managers to help them by solving problems that they couldn't solve. Once the managers realized this distinction, they embraced their role as problem solver and troubleshooter. They could then help without interfering with their subordinates' jobs.

After a year on the job, most of the managers thought of themselves as managers and no longer as doers. In making the transition, they finally realized that people management was the most important part of their job. One manager summarized the lesson that had taken him a year to learn by saying, "As many demands as managers have on their time, I think their primary responsibility is people development. Not production, but people development." Another indication of how much their views had changed was that most of the managers now regretted the rather heavy-handed approach they had used in their early attempts to manage their subordinates. "I wasn't good at managing . . . , so I was bossy like a first-grade teacher." "Now I see that I started out as a drill sergeant. I was inflexible, just a lot of how-to's." By the end of the year, most of the managers had abandoned

© Anthony Marsland/Riser/Getty Images

their authoritarian approach for one based on communication, listening, and positive reinforcement.

Finally, after beginning their year as managers in frustration, the managers came to feel comfortable with their subordinates, with the demands of their jobs, and with their emerging managerial styles. While being managers had made them acutely aware of their limitations and their need to develop as people, it also provided them with an unexpected reward of coaching and developing the people who worked for them. One manager said, "I realize now that when I accepted the position of branch manager that it is truly an exciting vocation. It is truly awesome, even at this level; it can be terribly challenging and terribly exciting."

Why Management Matters

If you walk down the aisle of the business section in your local bookstore, you'll find hundreds of books that explain precisely what companies need to do to be successful. Unfortunately, the best-selling business books tend to be faddish, changing dramatically every few years. One thing that hasn't changed, though, is the importance of good people and good management: companies can't succeed for long without them.

After reading this section, you should be able to

8 explain how and why companies can create competitive advantage through people.

8 Competitive Advantage through People

In his books *Competitive Advantage Through People* and *The Human Equation: Building Profits by Putting People First,* Stanford University business professor Jeffrey Pfeffer contends that what separates top-performing companies from their competitors is the way they treat their workforces—in other words, their management style.[54]

Pfeffer found that managers in top-performing companies used ideas like employment security, selective hiring, self-managed teams and decentralization, high pay contingent on company performance, extensive training, reduced status distinctions (between managers and employees), and extensive sharing of financial information to achieve financial performance that, on average, was 40 percent higher than that of other companies. These ideas, which are explained in detail in Exhibit 1.6, help organizations develop workforces that are smarter, better trained, more motivated, and more committed than their competitors' workforces. And—as indicated by the phenomenal growth and return on investment earned by these companies—smarter, better trained, and more committed workforces provide superior products and service to customers. Such customers keep buying and, by telling others about their positive experiences, bring in new customers.

According to Pfeffer, companies that invest in their people will also create long-lasting competitive advantages that are difficult for other companies to duplicate. The importance of employee management is particularly critical during tough economic times, when morale and employee engagement often experience a downturn. This in turn is often reflected in the bottom line. The president of HiringSmart Canada believes that "engagement is the single most reliable indicator of business performance. The more engaged a group of people is, the more emotional skin they have in the game [and] the more committed they are to generating results." High levels of employee engagement can be a valuable competitive advantage to management, which is why management must identify and recruit high-potential employees and utilize best-management practices in order to hold on to them.[55]

In terms of sales revenues and profits, a study of nearly 1,000 U.S. firms found that companies using *just some* of the ideas shown in Exhibit 1.6 had $27,044 more sales per employee and

Exhibit 1.6

Competitive Advantage through People: Management Practices

1. **Employment Security**—Employment security is the ultimate form of commitment companies can make to their workers. Employees can innovate and increase company productivity without fearing the loss of their jobs.

2. **Selective Hiring**—If employees are the basis for a company's competitive advantage, and those employees have employment security, then the company needs to aggressively recruit and selectively screen applicants in order to hire the most talented employees available.

3. **Self-Managed Teams and Decentralization**—Self-managed teams are responsible for their own hiring, purchasing, job assignments, and production. Self-managed teams can often produce enormous increases in productivity through increased employee commitment and creativity. Decentralization allows employees who are closest to (and most knowledgeable about) problems, production, and customers to make timely decisions. Decentralization increases employee satisfaction and commitment.

4. **High Wages Contingent on Organizational Performance**—High wages are needed to attract and retain talented workers and to indicate that the organization values its workers. Employees, like company founders, shareholders, and managers, need to share in the financial rewards when the company is successful. Why? Because employees who have a financial stake in their companies are more likely to take a long-run view of the business and think like business owners.

5. **Training and Skill Development**—Like a high-tech company that spends millions of dollars to upgrade computers or research and development labs, a company whose competitive advantage is based on its people must invest in the training and skill development of its people.

6. **Reduction of Status Differences**—A company should treat everyone, no matter what the job, as equals. There are no reserved parking spaces. Everyone eats in the same cafeteria and has similar benefits. The result: improved communication as employees focus on problems and solutions rather than on how they are less valued than managers.

7. **Sharing Information**—If employees are to make decisions that are good for the long-run health and success of the company, they need to be given information about costs, finances, productivity, development times, and strategies that was previously known only by company managers.

Source: J. Pfeffer, *The Human Equation: Building Profits by Putting People First* (Boston: Harvard Business School Press, 1996).

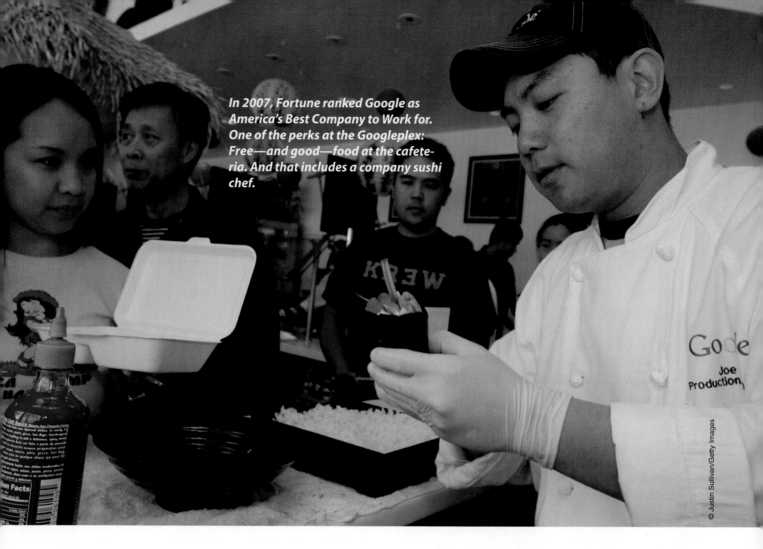

In 2007, Fortune ranked Google as America's Best Company to Work for. One of the perks at the Googleplex: Free—and good—food at the cafeteria. And that includes a company sushi chef.

© Justin Sullivan/Getty Images

$3,814 more profit per employee than companies that didn't.[56] For a 100-person company, these differences amount to $2.7 million more in sales and nearly $400,000 more in annual profit! For a 1,000-person company, the difference grows to $27 million more in sales and $4 million more in annual profit!

To determine how investing in people affects stock market performance, researchers matched companies on *Fortune* magazine's list of "100 Best Companies to Work for in America" with companies that were similar in industry, size, and—this is key—operating performance. Both sets of companies were equally good performers; the key difference was how well they treated their employees. For both sets of companies, the researchers found that employee attitudes such as job satisfaction changed little from year to year. The people who worked for the "100 Best" companies were consistently much more satisfied with their jobs and employers year after year than were employees in the matched companies. More important, those stable differences in employee attitudes were strongly related to differences in stock market performance. Over a three-year period, an investment in the "100 Best" companies would have resulted in an 82 percent cumulative stock return compared to just 37 percent for the matched companies.[57] This difference is remarkable given that both sets of companies were equally good performers at the beginning of the period.

Finally, research also indicates that managers have an important effect on customer satisfaction. Many people find this surprising. They don't understand how managers, who are largely responsible for what goes on inside the company, can affect what goes on outside the company. They wonder how managers, who often interact with customers under negative conditions (when customers are angry or dissatisfied), can actually improve customer satisfaction. It turns out that managers influence customer satisfaction through employee satisfaction. When employees are satisfied with their jobs, their bosses, and the companies they work for, they provide much better service to customers.[58] In turn, customers are more satisfied, too.

You will learn more about the service-profit chain in Chapter 18 on managing service and manufacturing operations.

Visit **icanmgmt.com** to find the resources you need today!

Located at the back of the textbook are rip-out Chapter Review cards. Make sure you also go online to check out other tools that MGMT offers to help you successfully pass your course.

- Interactive Quizzes
- Key Terms Flashcards
- Audio Chapter Summaries
- PowerPoint Slides

- Interactive Games
- Crossword Puzzles
- "Reel to Reel" and "Biz Flix" videos
- Cases and Exercises

HISTORY OF MANAGEMENT

In the Beginning

Each day, managers are asked to solve challenging problems and are given only a limited amount of time, people, or resources. Yet it's still their responsibility to get things done on time and within budget. Tell today's managers to "reward workers for improved production or performance," "set specific goals to increase motivation," or "innovate to create and sustain a competitive advantage," and they'll respond, "Duh! Who doesn't know that?" A mere 125 years ago, however, business ideas and practices were so different that today's widely accepted management ideas would have been as self-evident as space travel, cell phones, and the Internet. In fact, management jobs and management careers did not exist 125 years ago, so management was not yet a field of study. If there were no managers 125 years ago, but you can't walk down the hall today without bumping into one, where did management come from?

After reading the next section, you should be able to

1   explain the origins of management.

1 The Origins of Management

Although we can find the seeds of many of today's management ideas throughout history, not until the last two centuries did systematic changes in the nature of work and organizations create a compelling need for managers.

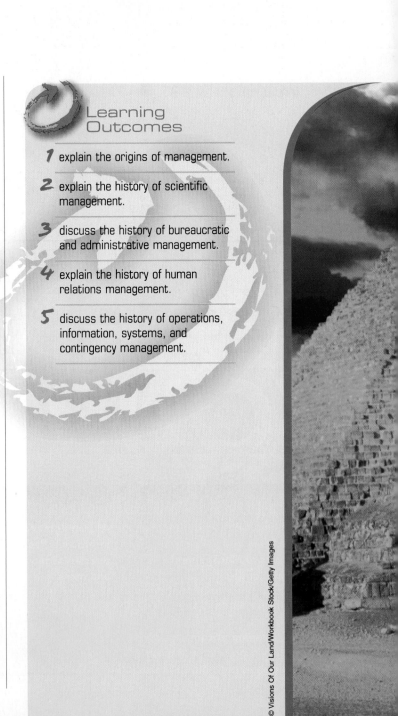

Learning Outcomes

1 explain the origins of management.

2 explain the history of scientific management.

3 discuss the history of bureaucratic and administrative management.

4 explain the history of human relations management.

5 discuss the history of operations, information, systems, and contingency management.

© Visions Of Our Land/Workbook Stock/Getty Images

*Let's begin our discussion of the origins of management by learning about **1.1 management ideas and practice throughout history** and **1.2 why we need managers today**.*

1.1 Management Ideas and Practice Throughout History

Examples of management thought and practice can be found throughout history.[1] For example, the Egyptians recognized the need for planning, organizing, and controlling; for submitting written requests; and for consulting staff for advice before making decisions. The practical problems they encountered while building the Great Pyramids no doubt led to the development of these management ideas. The enormity of the task they faced is evident in the pyramid of King Khufu, which contains 2.3 million blocks of stone. Each block had to be quarried, cut to precise size and shape, cured (hardened in the sun), transported by boat for two to three days, moved onto the construction site, numbered to identify where it would be placed, and then shaped and smoothed so that it would fit perfectly into place. It took 20,000 workers 23 years to complete this pyramid; more than 8,000 were needed just to quarry the stones and transport them.[2]

1.2 Why We Need Managers Today

Working from 8 A.M. to 5 P.M., coffee breaks, lunch hours, crushing rush hour traffic, and punching a time

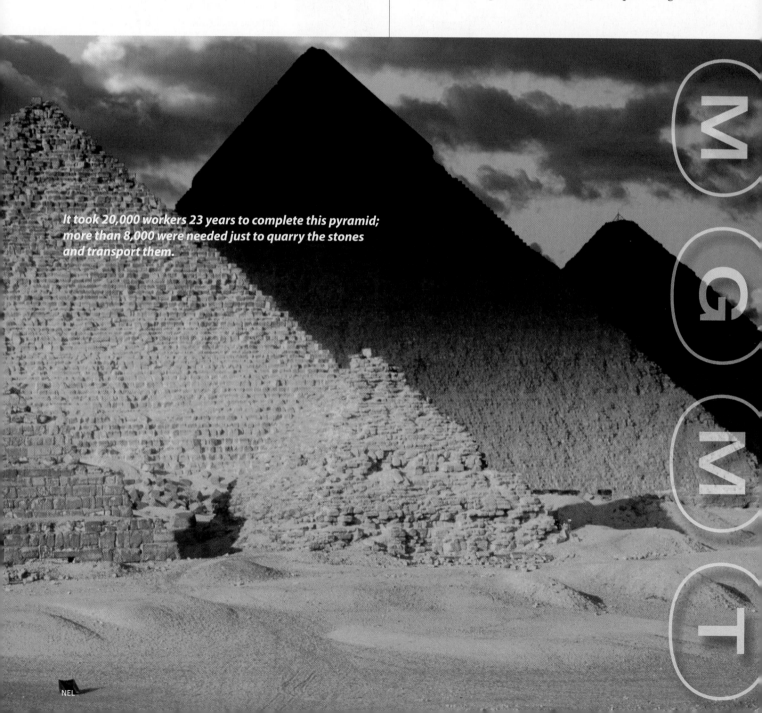

It took 20,000 workers 23 years to complete this pyramid; more than 8,000 were needed just to quarry the stones and transport them.

Company, where the assembly line was developed, the time required to assemble a car dropped from 12.5 man hours to just 93 minutes.[5]

Second, instead of being performed in fields, homes, or small shops, jobs occurred in large, formal organizations where hundreds, if not thousands, of people worked under one roof.[6] In 1913, Henry Ford employed 12,000 employees in his Highland Park, Michigan, factory alone. With individual factories employing so many workers under one roof, companies now had a strong need for disciplinary rules to impose order and structure. For the first time, they needed managers who knew how to organize large groups, work with employees, and make good decisions.

clock are things we associate with today's working world. But for most of history, people didn't commute to work. Work usually occurred in homes or on farms. Even most of those who didn't earn their living from agriculture didn't commute to work. Blacksmiths, furniture makers, leather-goods makers, and other skilled tradesmen or craftsmen, who formed trade guilds (the historical predecessors of labour unions) in England as early as 1093, typically worked out of shops in or next to their homes.[3] Likewise, until the late 1800s, cottage workers worked with one another out of small homes that were often built in a semicircle. A family in each cottage would complete a different production step, and work passed from one cottage to the next until production was complete. With small, self-organized work groups, no commute, no bosses, and no common building, there wasn't a strong need for management.

During the Industrial Revolution (1750–1900), however, jobs and organizations changed dramatically.[4] First, the availability of power (steam engines and later electricity) enabled low-paid, unskilled labourers running machines to replace high-paid, skilled artisans who made entire goods by themselves by hand. This new mass production system was based on a division of labour: each worker, interacting with machines, performed separate, highly specialized tasks that were but a small part of all the steps required to make manufactured goods. While workers focused on their singular tasks, managers were needed to coordinate the different parts of the production system and optimize its overall performance. Productivity skyrocketed at companies that understood this. At Ford Motor

The Evolution of Management

Before 1880, business educators taught only basic bookkeeping and secretarial skills, and no one published books or articles about management.[7] Today, you can turn to dozens of academic journals, hundreds of business school and practitioner journals, and thousands of books and articles if you have a question about management. In the next four sections, you will learn about other important contributors to the field of management and how their ideas shaped our current understanding of management theory and practice.

After reading the next four sections, which review the different schools of management thought, you should be able to

2   explain the history of scientific management.

3   discuss the history of bureaucratic and administrative management.

4   explain the history of human relations management.

5   discuss the history of operations, information, systems, and contingency management.

© Douglas Miller/Hulton Archive/Getty Images

2 Scientific Management

Bosses, who were hired by the company owner or founder, used to make decisions by the seat of their pants—haphazardly, without any systematic study, thought, or collection of information. Little thought was given to worker motivation as the boss dictated how fast or how hard the worker toiled. With no incentives for bosses and workers to cooperate, both groups played the system by trying to take advantage of each other. Moreover, each worker did the same job in his or her own way with different methods and different tools. In short, there were no procedures to standardize operations, no standards by which to judge whether performance was good or bad, and no follow-up to determine if productivity or quality actually improved when changes were made.[8]

This all changed with the advent of **scientific management,** which involved thorough study and testing of different work methods to identify the best, most efficient ways to complete a job.

*Let's find out more about scientific management by learning about **2.1 Frederick W. Taylor, the father of scientific management; 2.2 Frank and Lillian Gilbreth and motion studies;** and **2.3 Henry Gantt and his Gantt charts.***

2.1 Father of Scientific Management: Frederick W. Taylor

Frederick W. Taylor (1856–1915), the father of scientific management, began his career as a worker at Midvale Steel Company. He was

Scientific management
thoroughly studying and testing different work methods to identify the best, most efficient way to complete a job

> There were **no procedures** to standardize operations, **no standards** by which to judge whether performance was good or bad, and **no follow-up** to determine if productivity or quality actually improved when changes were made.

later promoted to patternmaker, supervisor, and then chief engineer.

At Midvale, Taylor was deeply affected by his three-year struggle to get the men who worked for him to do, as he called it, "a fair day's work." Taylor explained that as soon as he became the boss, "the men who were working under me . . . knew that I was onto the whole game of **soldiering,** or deliberately restricting output [to one-third of what they were capable of producing]."[9]

Initially, Taylor tried everything he could think of to improve output. By doing the job himself, he showed workers that it was possible to produce more output. He hired new workers and trained them himself, hoping they would produce more. But "very heavy social pressure" from the other workers kept them from doing so. Pushed by Taylor, the workers began breaking their machines so they couldn't produce. Taylor responded by fining them every time they broke a machine and for any violation of the rules, no matter how small, such as being late to work. Tensions became so severe that some of the workers threatened to shoot him.

The remedy that Taylor eventually developed was scientific management. The goal of scientific management was to use systematic study to find the optimal means of doing each task.

Soldiering when workers deliberately slow their pace or restrict their work outputs

To do that, managers had to follow the four principles shown in Exhibit 2.1. First, they had to "develop a science" for each element of work. That meant they had to study it. Analyze it. Determine the optimal means to do the work. For example, one of Taylor's controversial proposals at the time was to give rest breaks to factory workers doing physical labour. We take breaks for granted today, but factory workers in Taylor's day were expected to work without stopping.[10] Through systematic experiments, he showed that frequent rest breaks greatly increased daily output.

Second, managers had to scientifically select, train, teach, and develop workers to help them reach their full potential. Before Taylor, supervisors often hired on the basis of favouritism and nepotism. Who you knew was often more important than what you could do. By contrast, Taylor instructed supervisors to hire "first class" workers on the basis of their aptitude to do a job well. For similar reasons, he also recommended that companies train and develop their workers—a rare practice at the time.

The third principle instructed managers to cooperate with employees to ensure that the scientific principles were actually implemented. As Taylor knew from personal experience, workers and management more often than not viewed each other as enemies. Taylor said, "The majority of these men believe that the fundamental interests of employees and employers are necessarily antagonistic. Scientific management, on the contrary, is founded on the firm conviction that the true interests

Exhibit 2.1

Taylor's Four Principles of Scientific Management

First:	Develop a science for each element of a man's work, which replaces the old rule-of-thumb method.
Second:	Scientifically select and then train, teach, and develop the workman, whereas in the past he chose his own work and trained himself as best he could.
Third:	Heartily cooperate with the men so as to ensure all of the work being done is in accordance with the principles of the science that has been developed.
Fourth:	There is an almost equal division of the work and the responsibility between the management and the workmen. The management take over all the work for which they are better fitted than the workmen, while in the past almost all of the work and the greater part of the responsibility were thrown upon the men.

Source: F. W. Taylor, *The Principles of Scientific Management* (New York: Harper, 1911).

Want Fries with That?

Don't think scientific management has much to do with today's work life? Think again: about the last time you were at the store and the clerk said, "Have a nice day." Service providers—particularly at restaurants—use scripts to ensure that employees are following the "one best way" of interacting with the customers. McDonald's uses a speech-only script (workers must say, "May I help you, ma'am?" instead of "Can I help someone?"). At Olive Garden, workers must greet the table within thirty seconds of arrival; take the drink order within three minutes; suggest five items while taking the order; and check back with the table three minutes after the food arrives.

Source: A. Scharf, "Scripted Talk: From 'Welcome to McDonald's' to 'Paper or Plastic?' Employers Control the Speech of Service Workers," *Dollars & Sense*, September–October 2003, 35; C. McCann, "Have a Nice Day and an Icy Stare," *Marketing Week*, 2 September 2004, 27.

of the two are one and the same. Prosperity for the employer cannot exist through a long term of years unless it is accompanied by prosperity for the employee. Moreover, it is possible to give the workman what he most wants—high wages—and the employer what he wants—a low labour cost—for his manufactures."[11]

The fourth principle of scientific management was to divide the work and the responsibility equally between management and workers. Prior to Taylor, workers alone were held responsible for productivity and performance. But, said Taylor, "Almost every act of the workman should be preceded by one or more preparatory acts of the management which enable him to do his work better and quicker than he otherwise could."[12]

Above all, Taylor felt these principles could be used to determine a "fair day's work," that is, what an average worker could produce at a reasonable pace, day in and day out. Once that was determined, it was management's responsibility to pay workers fairly for that fair day's work. In essence, Taylor was trying to align management and employees so that what was good for employees was also good for management. In this way, he felt, workers and managers could avoid the conflicts he had experienced at Midvale Steel. And one of the best ways, according to Taylor, to align management and employees was to use incentives to motivate workers. In particular, Taylor believed in piece-rate incentives in which work pay was directly tied to how much workers produced.

Although Taylor remains a controversial figure among some academics, his key ideas have stood the test of time.[13]

2.2 Motion Studies: Frank and Lillian Gilbreth

The husband and wife team Frank and Lillian Gilbreth are best known for their use of motion studies to simplify work.

Frank Gilbreth (1868–1924) began his career as an apprentice bricklayer. While learning the trade, he noticed the bricklayers using three different sets of motions—one to teach others how to lay bricks, a second to work at a slow pace, and a third to work at a fast pace.[14] Wondering which was best, he studied the various approaches and began eliminating unnecessary motions. For example, by designing a stand that could be raised to waist height, he eliminated the need to bend over to pick up each brick. By having lower-paid workers place all the bricks with their most attractive side up, bricklayers didn't waste time turning a brick over to find it. By mixing a more consistent mortar, bricklayers no longer had to tap each brick numerous times to put it in the right position. Together, Gilbreth's improvements raised productivity from 120 to 350 bricks per hour and from 1,000 bricks to 2,700 bricks per day.

As a result of his experience with bricklaying, Gilbreth and his wife Lillian developed a long-term interest in using motion study to simplify work, improve productivity, and reduce the level of effort required to safely perform a job. **Motion study** broke each task or job into separate motions and then eliminated those that were unnecessary or repetitive. Because many motions were completed very

> **Motion study** breaking each task or job into its separate motions and then eliminating those that are unnecessary or repetitive

quickly, the Gilbreths used motion-picture films, a relatively new technology at the time, to analyze jobs. Most film cameras, however, were hand-cranked and thus variable in their film speed, so Frank Gilbreth invented the micro chronometer, a large clock that could record time to 1/2000th of a second. By placing the micro chronometer next to the worker in the camera's field of vision, the Gilbreths could use film to detect and precisely time even the slightest, fastest movements. Motion study typically yielded production increases of 25 to 300 percent.

Frederick W. Taylor also strove to simplify work, but he did so by managing time rather than motion.[15] Taylor developed time study to put an end to soldiering and to determine what could be considered a fair day's work. **Time study** worked by timing how long it took a "first-class man" to complete each part of his job. A standard time was established after allowing for rest periods, and a worker's pay would increase or decrease depending on whether the worker exceeded or fell below that standard.

Lillian Gilbreth (1878–1972) was an important contributor to management as well. When Frank died in 1924, she continued the work of their management consulting company (which they had shared for over a dozen years) on her own. Lillian was particularly concerned with the human side of work and was one of the first contributors to industrial psychology. She established ways to improve office communication, incentive programs, job satisfaction, and management training. Her work also convinced the government to enact laws regarding workplace safety, ergonomics, and child labour.

Time study timing how long it takes good workers to complete each part of their jobs

Gantt chart a graphic chart that shows which tasks must be completed at which times in order to complete a project or task

2.3 Charts: Henry Gantt

Henry Gantt (1861–1919) was first a protégé and then an associate of Frederick Taylor. Gantt is best known for the Gantt chart, but he also made significant contributions to management with respect to the training and development of workers. As shown in Exhibit 2.2, a **Gantt chart** visually indicates what tasks must be completed at which times in order to complete a project. It accomplishes this task by showing time in various units on the *x*-axis and tasks on the *y*-axis. For example, Exhibit 2.2 shows that the following tasks must be completed by the following dates: in order to start construction on a new company headquarters by the week of November 18, the architectural firm must be selected by October 7, the architectural planning done by November 4, permits obtained from the city by November 11, site preparation finished by November 18, and loans and financing finalized by November 18. Though simple and straightforward, Gantt charts were revolutionary in the era of seat-of-the-pants management because of the detailed planning information they provided to managers. The use of Gantt charts is so widespread today that nearly all project management software and computer spreadsheets have the capability to create charts that track and visually display the progress being made on a project.

Finally, Gantt, along with Taylor, was one of the first to strongly recommend that companies train and develop their workers.[16] In his work with companies, he found that workers achieved their best performance levels if they were trained first. At the time, however, supervisors were reluctant to teach workers what they knew for fear they could lose their jobs to more knowledgeable workers. Gantt overcame the supervisors' resistance by rewarding them with bonuses for properly training all of their workers. Gantt's approach to training was straightforward: "(1) a scientific investigation in detail of each piece of work, and the determination of the best method

Exhibit 2.2

Gantt Chart for Starting Construction on a New Headquarters

Tasks	Current Week				▼					
Weeks	23 Sep to 30 Sep	30 Sep to 7 Oct	7 Oct to 14 Oct	14 Oct to 21 Oct	21 Oct to 28 Oct	28 Oct to 4 Nov	4 Nov to 11 Nov	11 Nov to 18 Nov	18 Nov to 25 Nov
Interview and select architectural firm	Architect by October 7								
Hold weekly planning meetings with architects				Weekly planning with architects by November 4					
Obtain permits and approval from city						Permits & approval by November 11			
Begin preparing site for construction							Site preparation done by November 18		
Finalize loans and financing								Financing finalized by November 18	
Begin construction									Start building

Tasks									
Weeks	23 Sep to 30 Sep	30 Sep to 7 Oct	7 Oct to 14 Oct	14 Oct to 21 Oct	21 Oct to 28 Oct	28 Oct to 4 Nov	4 Nov to 11 Nov	11 Nov to 18 Nov	18 Nov to 25 Nov
Current Week				▲					

and the shortest time in which the work can be done. (2) A teacher capable of teaching the best method and the shortest time. (3) Reward for both teacher and pupil when the latter is successful."[17]

3 Bureaucratic and Administrative Management

The field of scientific management focused on improving the efficiency of manufacturing facilities and their workers. At about the same time, equally important ideas about bureaucratic and administrative management were developing in Europe. German sociologist Max Weber presented a new way to run entire organizations in *The Theory of Economic and Social Organization* in 1922. Henri Fayol, an experienced French CEO, published his ideas about how and what managers should do in their jobs in *General and Industrial Management* in 1916.

Let's find out more about Weber's and Fayol's contributions to management by learning about 3.1 bureaucratic management and 3.2 administrative management.

3.1 Bureaucratic Management: Max Weber

Today, when we hear the term *bureaucracy,* we think of inefficiency and red tape, incompetence and ineffectiveness, and rigid administrators blindly enforcing nonsensical rules. When German sociologist Max Weber (1864–1920) first proposed the idea of bureaucratic organizations, however, these problems were associated with monarchies and patriarchies rather than bureaucracies. In monarchies, where kings, queens, sultans, and emperors ruled, and patriarchies, where a council of elders, wise men, or male heads of extended families ruled, the top leaders typically achieved their positions by virtue of birthright. Likewise, promotion to prominent positions of authority was based on who you knew (politics), who you were (heredity), or traditions.

> An organization's rules and procedures should apply to **all** members regardless of their position or status.

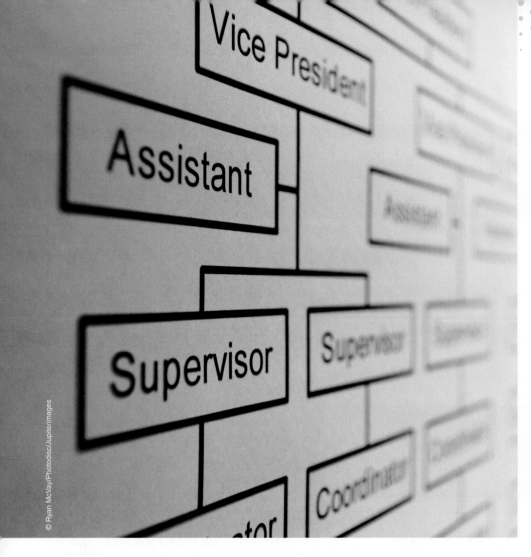

© Ryan McVay/Photodisc/Jupiterimages

It was against this historical background that Weber proposed the then new idea of bureaucracy. According to Weber, **bureaucracy** is "the exercise of control on the basis of knowledge."[18] Rather than ruling by virtue of favouritism or personal or family connections, people in a bureaucracy would lead by virtue of their rational-legal authority—in other words, their knowledge, expertise, or experience. Furthermore, the aim of bureaucracy is not to protect authority but to achieve an organization's goals in the most efficient way possible.

Exhibit 2.3 shows the seven elements that, according to Weber, characterize bureaucracies. First, instead of hiring people because of their family or political connections or personal loyalty, they should be hired because their technical training or education qualifies them to do the job well. Second, along the same lines, promotion within the company should no longer be based on who you knew or who you were (heredity), but on your experience or achievements. And to further limit the influence of personal connections in the promotion process, *managers* rather than organizational owners should

Bureaucracy the exercise of control on the basis of knowledge, expertise, or experience

decide who gets promoted. Third, each position or job should be viewed as part of a chain of command that clarifies who reports to whom throughout the organization. Those higher in the chain of command have the right, if they so choose, to give commands, take action, and make decisions concerning activities occurring anywhere below them in the chain. Fourth, to increase efficiency and effectiveness, tasks and responsibilities should be separated and assigned to those best qualified to complete them. Fifth, an organization's rules and procedures should apply to all members regardless of their position or status. Sixth, to ensure consistency and fairness over time and across different leaders, all rules, procedures, and decisions should be recorded in writing. Finally, to reduce favouritism, "professional" managers rather than company owners should manage or supervise the organization.

When viewed in historical context, Weber's ideas about bureaucracy represent a tremendous improvement. Fairness supplanted favouritism, the goal of efficiency replaced the goal of personal gain, and logical rules and procedures took the place of traditions or arbitrary decision making.

Today, however, after more than a century of experience, we recognize that bureaucracy has limitations as well. In bureaucracies, managers are supposed to influence employee behaviour by fairly rewarding or punishing employees for compliance or noncompliance with organizational policies, rules, and procedures. In reality, however, most employees would argue that bureaucratic managers emphasize punishment for noncompliance much more than reward for compliance. Ironically, bureaucratic management was created to prevent just this type of managerial behaviour.

3.2 Administrative Management: Henri Fayol

Though his work was not translated and widely recognized until 1949, Frenchman Henri Fayol (1841–1925)

Exhibit 2.3

Elements of Bureaucratic Organizations

Qualification-based hiring:	Employees are hired on the basis of their technical training or educational background.
Merit-based promotion:	Promotion is based on experience or achievement. Managers, not organizational owners, decide who is promoted.
Chain of command:	Each job occurs within a hierarchy, the chain of command, in which each position reports and is accountable to a higher position. A grievance procedure and a right to appeal protect people in lower positions.
Division of labor:	Tasks, responsibilities, and authority are clearly divided and defined.
Impartial application of rules and procedures:	Rules and procedures apply to all members of the organization and will be applied in an impartial manner, regardless of one's position or status
Recorded in writing:	All administrative decisions, acts, rules, or procedure will be recorded in writing.
Managers separate from owners:	The owners of an organization should not manage or supervise the organization.

Source: M. Weber, *The Theory of Economic and Social Organization*, trans. A. Henderson & T. Parsons (New York: The Free Press, 1947), 329–334.

was as important a contributor to the field of management as Frederick Taylor. Whereas Taylor's ideas changed companies from the shop floor up, Fayol's ideas, which were shaped by his experience as a managing director (CEO), generally changed companies from the board of directors down. Fayol is best known for developing five functions of managers and fourteen principles of management.

The most formative events in Fayol's business career came during his 20-plus years as the managing director (CEO) of a steel company that owned several coal and iron ore mines and employed 10,000 to 13,000 workers. Fayol was initially hired by the board of directors to shut the "hopeless" steel company down. But, after "four months of reflection and study," he presented the board with a plan, backed by detailed facts and figures, to save the company. With little to lose, the board agreed. Fayol then began the process of turning the company around by obtaining supplies of key resources such as coal and iron ore;

using research to develop new steel alloy products; carefully selecting key subordinates in research, purchasing, manufacturing, and sales and then delegating responsibility to them; and cutting costs by moving the company to a better location closer to key markets. Looking back 10 years later, Fayol attributed his and the company's success to changes in management practices.

Based on his experience as a CEO, Fayol argued that "the success of an enterprise generally depends much more on the administrative ability of its leaders than on their technical ability."[19] And, as you learned in Chapter 1, managers need to perform five managerial functions if they are to be successful: planning, organizing, coordinating, commanding, and controlling.[20] Because most management textbooks have dropped the coordinating function and now refer to Fayol's commanding function as "leading," these functions are widely known as planning (determining organizational goals and a means for achieving

Exhibit 2.4

Fayol's Fourteen Principles of Management

1. **Division of work**
   Increase production by dividing work so that each worker completes smaller tasks or job elements.

2. **Authority and responsibility**
   A manager's authority, which is the "right to give orders," should be commensurate with the manager's responsibility. However, organizations should enact controls to prevent managers from abusing their authority.

3. **Discipline**
   Clearly defined rules and procedures are needed at all organizational levels to ensure order and proper behaviour.

4. **Unity of command**
   To avoid confusion and conflict, each employee should report to and receive orders from just one boss.

5. **Unity of direction**
   One person and one plan should be used in deciding the activities to be used to accomplish each organizational objective.

6. **Subordination of individual interests to the general interest**
   Employees must put the organization's interests and goals before their own.

7. **Remuneration**
   Compensation should be fair and satisfactory to both the employees and the organization; that is, don't overpay or underpay employees.

8. **Centralization**
   Avoid too much centralization or decentralization. Strike a balance depending on the circumstances and employees involved.

9. **Scalar chain**
   From the top to the bottom of an organization, each position is part of a vertical chain of authority in which each worker reports to just one boss. For the sake of simplicity, communication outside normal work groups or departments should follow the vertical chain of authority.

10. **Order**
    To avoid conflicts and confusion, order can be obtained by having a place for everyone and having everyone in his or her place; in other words, there should be no overlapping responsibilities.

11. **Equity**
    Kind, fair, and just treatment for all will develop devotion and loyalty. This does not exclude discipline, if warranted, and consideration of the broader general interest of the organization.

12. **Stability of tenure of personnel**
    Low turnover, meaning a stable work force with high tenure, benefits an organization by improving performance, lowering costs, and giving employees, especially managers, time to learn their jobs.

13. **Initiative**
    Because it is a "great source of strength for business," managers should encourage the development of initiative, or the ability to develop and implement a plan, in others.

14. ***Esprit de corps***
    Develop a strong sense of morale and unity among workers that encourages coordination of efforts.

Sources: H. Fayol, *General and Industrial Management* (London: Pittman & Sons, 1949); M. Fells, "Fayol Stands the Test of Time," *Journal of Management History* 6 (2000): 345–360; C. Rodrigues, "Fayol's 14 Principles of Management Then and Now: A Framework for Managing Today's Organizations Effectively" *Management Decision* 39 (2001): 880–889.

them), organizing (deciding where decisions will be made, who will do what jobs and tasks, and who will work for whom), leading (inspiring and motivating workers to work hard to achieve organizational goals), and controlling (monitoring progress toward goal achievement and taking corrective action when needed). In addition, according to Fayol, effective management is based on the 14 principles in Exhibit 2.4.

4 Human Relations Management

As we have seen, scientific management focuses on improving efficiency; bureaucratic management focuses on using knowledge, fairness, and logical rules and procedures; and administrative management focuses on how and what managers should do in their jobs. The human

© Dmitriy Shironosov/Shutterstock

relations approach to management focuses on people. This approach to management sees people not as just extensions of machines but as valuable organizational resources in their own right. Human relations management holds that people's needs are important and understands that their efforts, motivation, and performance are affected by the work they do and their relationships with their bosses, coworkers, and work groups. In other words, efficiency alone is not enough. Organizational success also depends on treating workers well.

*Let's find out more about human relations management by learning about **4.1 Mary Parker Follett's theories of constructive conflict; 4.2 Elton Mayo's Hawthorne Studies; and 4.3 Chester Barnard's theories of cooperation and acceptance of authority.***

4.1 Constructive Conflict : Mary Parker Follett

Mary Parker Follett (1868–1933) was a social worker who, after 25 years of working with schools and non-profit organizations, began lecturing and writing about management and working extensively as a consultant for business and government. Many of today's "new" management ideas can be traced clearly to her work.

Follett is known for developing ideas regarding constructive conflict, also called cognitive conflict, which is discussed in Chapter 5 on decision making and Chapter 10 on teams. Unlike most people, then

and now, who view conflict as bad, Follett believed that conflict could be beneficial. She said that conflict is "the appearance of difference, difference of opinions, of interests. For that is what conflict means—difference." She went on to say, "As conflict—difference—is here in this world, as we cannot avoid it, we should, I think, use it to work for us. Instead of condemning it, we should set it to work for us. Thus we shall not be afraid of conflict, but shall recognize that there is a destructive way of dealing with such moments and a constructive way."[21]

Follett believed that the best way to deal with conflict was not domination, where one side wins and the other loses, nor compromise, where each side gives up some of what they want, but integration. Rather than one side dominating the other or both sides compromising, the point of **integrative conflict resolution** is to have both parties indicate their preferences and then work together to find an alternative that meets the needs of both. According to Follett, "Integration involves invention, and the clever thing is to recognize this, and not to let one's thinking stay within the boundaries of two alternatives which are mutually exclusive."

> **Integrative conflict resolution** an approach to dealing with conflict in which both parties deal with the conflict by indicating their preferences and then working together to find an alternative that meets the needs of both

Follet also believed that authority flows from job knowledge and experience rather than position. Leadership involves setting the tone for the team rather than being aggressive and dominating, which may be harmful. Control, by contrast, should be based on facts, information, and coordination. In the end, Follett's contributions added significantly to our understanding of the human, social, and psychological sides of management. Peter Parker, the former chairman of the London School of Economics, said about Follett: "People often puzzle about who is the father of management. I don't know who the father was, but I have no doubt about who was the mother."[22]

4.2 Hawthorne Studies: Elton Mayo

Australian-born Elton Mayo (1880–1948) is best known for his role in the famous Hawthorne Studies at the Western Electric Company in Chicago between 1924 and 1932. Although Mayo didn't join the studies until 1928, he played a significant role thereafter, writing about the results in his book, *The Human Problems of an Industrial Civilization*.[23] The first stage of the Hawthorne Studies investigated the effects of lighting levels and incentives on employee productivity in the Relay Test Assembly Room, where workers took approximately a minute to put "together a coil, armature, contact springs, and insulators in a fixture and secure the parts by means of four machine screws."[24]

Multiple spindle drill presses. Western Electric Company photograph album, ca. 1925. Baker Library Historical Collections. Harvard Business School (olvwork278788).

Two groups of six experienced female workers, five to do the work and one to supply needed parts, were separated from the main part of the factory by a 10-foot partition and placed at a standard work bench with the necessary parts and tools. Over the next five years, the experimenters introduced various levels and combinations of lighting, financial incentives, and rest pauses (work breaks) to study the effect on productivity. Curiously, however, production levels increased whether the experimenters increased or decreased the lighting, paid workers based on individual production or group production, or increased or decreased the number and length of rest pauses. The question was: Why?

Mayo and his colleagues eventually concluded that two things accounted for the results. First, substantially more attention was paid to these workers than to workers in the rest of the plant. Mayo wrote, "Before every change of program [in the study], the group is consulted. Their comments are listened to and discussed; sometimes their objections are allowed to negate a suggestion. The group unquestionably develops a sense of participation in the critical determinations and becomes something of a social unit."[25]

For years, the Hawthorne Effect has been *incorrectly* defined as increasing productivity by paying more attention to workers.[26] But it is not simply about attention from management. This effect cannot be understood without giving equal importance to the "social units," which became intensively cohesive groups. Mayo said, "What actually happened was that six individuals became a team and the team gave itself wholeheartedly and spontaneously to cooperation in the experiment. The consequence was that they felt themselves to be participating freely and without afterthought, and were happy in the knowledge that they were working without coercion from above or limits from below."[27]

Tough Jobs

During the early twentieth century, labour unrest, dissatisfaction, and protests (some of them violent) were widespread in North America, Europe, and Asia. In 1919 alone, for example, more than four million American workers went on strike. Working conditions contributed to the unrest. Millions of workers in large factories toiled at boring, repetitive, unsafe jobs for low pay. Employee turnover was high and absenteeism was rampant. With employee turnover approaching 380 percent in his automobile factories, Henry Ford had to double the daily wage of his manufacturing workers from $2.50, the going wage at the time, to $5.00 to keep enough workers at their jobs. It's not surprising that Mayo's ideas became popular during this period.

© Bettmann/CORBIS

For the first time, human factors related to work were found to be more important than the physical conditions or design of the work. Together, the increased attention from management and the development of a cohesive work group led to significantly higher levels of job satisfaction and productivity. In short, the Hawthorne studies found that workers' feelings and attitudes affected their work.

The next stage of the Hawthorne Studies was conducted in the Bank Wiring Room, where "the group consisted of nine wiremen, three solderers, and two inspectors. Each of these groups performed a specific task and collaborated with the other two in completion of each unit of equipment. The task consisted of setting up the banks of terminals side-by-side on frames, wiring the corresponding terminals from bank to bank, soldering the connections, and inspecting with a test set for short circuits or breaks in the wire. One solderman serviced the work of the three wiremen."[28] While productivity increased in the Relay Test Assembly Room no matter what the researchers did, productivity dropped in the Bank Wiring Room. Again, the question was: Why?

Mayo and his colleagues found that different group dynamics were responsible. The workers in the Bank Wiring Room had been an existing work group for some time and had already developed strong negative norms that governed their behaviour. For instance, despite a group financial incentive for production, the group members decided that they would wire only 6,000 to 6,600 connections a day (depending on the kind of equipment they were wiring), well below the production goal of 7,300 connections that management had set for them. Individual workers who worked at a faster pace were socially ostracized from the group, or "binged" (hit on the arm), until they slowed their work pace. The group's behaviour was reminiscent of the soldiering that Frederick Taylor had observed.

In the end, the Hawthorne Studies demonstrated that the workplace was more complex than previously thought, that workers were not just extensions of machines, and that financial incentives weren't necessarily the most important motivator for workers. Thanks to Mayo and

Organization a system of consciously coordinated activities or forces created by two or more people

the Hawthorne Studies, managers better understood the effect that group social interactions, employee satisfaction, and attitudes had on individual and group performance.

4.3 Cooperation and Acceptance of Authority: Chester Barnard

Like Henri Fayol, Chester Barnard (1886–1961) had experience as a top executive that shaped his views of management. Barnard began his career as an engineer and went on to become president of a telephone company. Barnard's ideas, published in his classic book, *The Functions of the Executive,* influenced companies from the board of directors down. He is best known for his ideas about cooperation and the acceptance of authority.

Barnard proposed a comprehensive theory of cooperation in formal organizations. In fact, he defines an **organization** as a "system of consciously coordinated activities or forces of two or more persons." In other words, organization occurs whenever two people work together for some purpose, whether it be classmates working together to complete a class project, Habitat for Humanity volunteers donating their time to build a house, or managers working with subordinates to reduce costs, improve quality, or increase sales. Why did Barnard place so much emphasis on cooperation? Because cooperation is *not* the normal state of affairs: "Failure to cooperate, failure of cooperation, failure of organization, disorganization, disintegration, destruction of organization—and reorganization—are characteristic facts of human history."[29]

According to Barnard, the extent to which people willingly cooperate in an organization depends on how workers perceive executive authority and whether they're willing to accept it. Many managerial requests or directives have a *zone of indifference* in which acceptance of managerial authority is automatic. For example, if your boss asks you for a copy of the monthly inventory report, and compiling and writing that report is part of your job, you think nothing of the request and automatically send it. In general, people will be indifferent to managerial directives or orders if they (1) are understood, (2) are consistent with the purpose of the organization, (3) are compatible with the people's personal interests, and (4) can actually be carried out by those

people. Acceptance of managerial authority (i.e., cooperation) is not automatic, however. Ask people to do things contrary to the organization's purpose or to their own benefit and they'll put up a fight. While many people assume that managers have the authority to do whatever they want, Barnard, referring to the "fiction of superior authority," believed that workers ultimately grant managers their authority.

5 Operations, Information, Systems, and Contingency Management

In this last section, we review four other significant historical approaches to management that have influenced how today's managers produce goods and services on a daily basis, gather and manage the information they need to understand their businesses and make good decisions, understand how the different parts of the

company work together as a whole, and recognize when and where particular management practices are likely to work.

*To better understand these ideas, let's learn about **5.1 operations management; 5.2 information management; 5.3 systems management;** and **5.4 contingency management.***

5.1 Operations Management

In Chapter 18, you will learn about *operations management*, which involves managing the daily production of goods and services. In general, operations management uses a quantitative or mathematical approach to find ways to increase productivity, improve quality, and manage or reduce costly inventories. The most commonly used operations management tools and methods are quality control, forecasting techniques, capacity planning, productivity measurement and improvement, linear programming, scheduling systems, inventory systems, work measurement techniques (similar to the Gilbreths' motion studies), project management (similar to Gantt's charts), and cost-benefit analysis.[30]

Today, with these tools and techniques, we take it for granted that manufactured goods will be made with standardized, interchangeable parts; that the design of those parts will be based on specific, detailed plans; and that manufacturing companies will aggressively manage inventories to keep costs low and increase productivity. These key elements of operations management have some rather strange origins: guns, geometry, and fire.

Since the 1500s, skilled craftsmen had made the lock, stock, and barrel of a gun by hand. After each part was made, a skilled gun finisher assembled the parts into a complete gun. But the gun finisher did not simply screw the different parts of a gun together, as is done today. Instead, each handmade part required extensive finishing and adjusting so that it would fit together with the other handmade gun parts. Hand fitting was necessary because, even when made by the same skilled craftsman, no two parts were alike. Today, we would say that these parts were low quality because they varied so much from part to part.

All this changed in 1791 when the U.S. government, worried about a possible war with France, ordered 40,000 muskets from private gun contractors. Because each handmade musket was unique, a replacement part had to be handcrafted if a part broke. One contractor, Eli Whitney (who is better known for his invention of the cotton gin), determined that if gun parts were made accurately enough, guns could be made with standardized, interchangeable parts. So he designed machine tools that allowed unskilled workers to make each gun part the same as the next. In 1801, he demonstrated the superiority of interchangeable parts to President-elect Thomas Jefferson by quickly and easily assembling complete muskets from randomly picked piles of musket parts. Today, most products are manufactured using standardized, interchangeable parts.

Once standardized, interchangeable parts became the norm and could be made from design drawings alone, manufacturers ran into a costly problem that they had never faced before: too much inventory. *Inventory* is the amount and number of raw materials, parts, and finished products that a company has in its

The cash register, invented in 1879, kept sales clerks honest by recording all sales transactions on a roll of paper securely locked inside the machine. But managers soon realized that its most important contribution was better management and control of their business. For example, department stores could track performance and sales by installing separate cash registers in the food, clothing, and hardware departments.

Cash Management

© Comstock Images/Jupiterimages

possession. A solution to this problem was found in 1905 when the Oldsmobile Motor Works in Detroit burned down. Management rented a new production facility to get production up and running as quickly as possible after the fire. But because the new facility was much smaller, there was no room to store large stockpiles of inventory. Therefore, the company made do with what it called "hand-to-mouth inventories," in which each production station had only enough parts on hand to do a short production run. Since all of its parts suppliers were close by, Oldsmobile could place orders in the morning and receive them in the afternoon (even without telephones), just like today's computerized, just-in-time inventory systems. So, contrary to common belief, just-in-time inventory systems were not invented by Japanese manufacturers. Instead, they were invented out of necessity a century ago because of a fire.

5.2 Information Management

For most of recorded history, information has been costly, difficult to obtain, and slow to spread compared to modern standards. Documents were written by hand. Books and manuscripts were extremely labour-intensive and therefore expensive. Although letters and other such documents were relatively easy to produce, transporting the information in them relied on horses, foot travellers, and ships.

Consequently, throughout history, organizations have pushed for and quickly adopted new information technologies that reduce the cost or increase the speed with which they can acquire, retrieve, or communicate information. The first technologies to truly revolutionize the business use of information were paper and the printing press. In the 14th century, water-powered machines were created to pulverize rags into pulp to make paper. Paper prices quickly dropped by 400 percent. Less than a half-century later, Johannes Gutenberg invented the printing press, which reduced the cost and time needed to copy written information by 99.8 percent. In 15th-century Florence, Italy, a scribe would charge one florin (an Italian unit of money) to hand-copy one document page. By contrast, a printer would set up and print 1,025 copies of the same document for just three florins.

What Gutenberg's printing press did for publishing, the manual typewriter did for daily communication. Before 1850, most business correspondence was written by hand and copied using the letter press. With the ink still wet, the letter would be placed into a tissue paper book. A hand press would then be used to squeeze the book and copy the still-wet ink onto the tissue paper. By the 1870s, manual typewriters made it cheaper, easier, and faster to produce and copy business correspondence. Of course, in the 1980s, slightly more than a century later, typewriters were replaced by personal computers and word processing software for identical reasons.

Finally, businesses have always looked for information technologies that would speed access to timely information. The Medici family, which opened banks throughout Europe in the early 1400s, used posting messengers to keep in contact with their more than 40 branch managers. The post messengers, who predated the U.S. Postal Service Pony Express by 400 years, could travel 90 miles per day, twice what average riders could cover, because the Medicis were willing to pay for the expense of providing them with fresh horses. The need for timely information also led companies to quickly adopt the telegraph in the 1860s, the telephone in the 1880s, and, of course, Internet technologies in the last decade.

5.3 Systems Management

Today's companies are much larger and more complex. They most likely manufacture, service, *and* finance what they sell. They also operate in complex, fast-changing, competitive, global environments that can quickly turn competitive advantages into competitive disadvantages.

How can managers make sense of this complexity both within and outside their organizations? One way to deal with organizational and environmental complexity is to take a systems view of organizations.[31] A **system** is a set of interrelated elements or parts that function as a whole. Rather than viewing one part of an organization as separate from the other parts, a systems approach encourages managers to complicate their thinking by looking for connections between the different parts of the organization. Indeed, one of the more important ideas in the systems approach to management is that organizational systems are composed of parts or **subsystems,** which are simply smaller systems within larger systems. Subsystems and their connections matter in systems theory because of the possibility for managers to create synergy. **Synergy** occurs when two or more subsystems working together can produce more than they can working apart. In other words, synergy occurs when $1 + 1 = 3$.

Exhibit 2.5 illustrates how the elements of systems management work together. Whereas **closed systems** can function without interacting with their environments, nearly all organizations should be viewed as **open systems** that interact with their environments and depend on them for survival. Therefore, rather than viewing what goes on within the organization as separate from what goes on outside it, the systems approach encourages managers to look for connections between the different parts of the organization and the different parts of its environment.

A systems view of organizations offers several advantages. First, it forces managers to view their organizations as part of and subject to the competitive, economic, social, technological, and legal/regulatory forces in their environments.[32] Second, it also forces managers to be aware of how the environment affects specific parts of the organization. Third, because of the complexity and difficulty of trying to achieve synergies between different parts of the organization, the systems view encourages managers to focus on better communication and cooperation within the organization. Finally, survival also depends on

System a set of interrelated elements or parts that function as a whole

Subsystems smaller systems that operate within the context of a larger system

Synergy when two or more subsystems working together can produce more than they can working apart

Closed systems systems that can sustain themselves without interacting with their environments

Open systems systems that can sustain themselves only by interacting with their environments, on which they depend for their survival

Exhibit 2.5

The Organization as an Open System

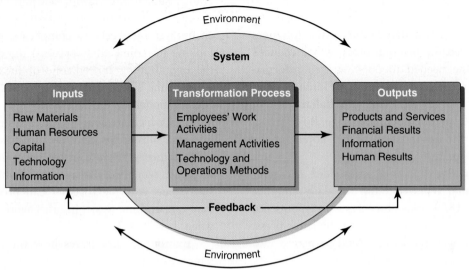

Source: Robbins, Coulter & Langton, *Fundamentals of Management*, Sixth Canadian Edition, Toronto: Pearson (2011) p. 29. Reprinted with permission by Pearson Education Canada Inc.

making sure that the organization continues to satisfy critical environmental stakeholders such as shareholders, employees, customers, suppliers, governments, and local communities.

5.4 Contingency Management

Earlier you learned that the goal of scientific management was to use systematic study to find the one best way of doing each task and then use that one best way everywhere. The problem, as you may have gathered from reading about the various approaches to management, is that no one in management seems to agree on what that one best way is. In fact, there isn't *one* best way. More than a century of management research has shown that there are clear boundaries or limitations to most management theories and practices. None is universal. Though any theory or practice may work much of the time, none works all the time. How, then, is a manager to decide what theory to use? Well, it depends on the situation. The **contingency approach** to management clearly states that there are no universal management theories and that the most effective management theory or idea depends on the kinds of problems or situations that managers or organizations are facing at a particular time.[33]

One of the practical implications of the contingency approach is that management is much harder than it looks. In fact, because of the clarity and obviousness of management theories (OK, most of them), students and workers often wrongly assume that a company's problems would be quickly and easily solved if management would take just a few simple steps. If this were true, few companies would have problems.

A second implication of the contingency approach is that managers need to look for key contingencies that differentiate today's situation or problems from yesterday's situation or problems. Moreover, it means that managers need to spend more time analyzing problems, situations, and employees before taking action to fix them. Finally, it means that as you read this text and learn about management ideas and practices, you need to pay particular attention to qualifying phrases such as "usually," "in these situations," "for this to work," and "under these circumstances." Doing so will help you identify the key contingencies that will help you become a better manager.

Contingency approach holds that there are no universal management theories and that the most effective management theory or idea depends on the kinds of problems or situations that managers are facing at a particular time and place

Visit **icanmgmt.com** to find the resources you need today!

Located at the back of the textbook are rip-out Chapter Review cards. Make sure you also go online to check out other tools that MGMT offers to help you successfully pass your course.

- Interactive Quizzes
- Key Terms Flashcards
- Audio Chapter Summaries
- PowerPoint Slides
- Interactive Games
- Crossword Puzzles
- "Reel to Reel" and "Biz Flix" videos
- Cases and Exercises

ORGANIZATIONAL ENVIRONMENTS AND CULTURES

This chapter examines the internal and external forces that affect business. First we'll examine the two types of external organizational environments: the general environment that affects all organizations and the specific environment unique to each company. Then we'll learn how managers make sense of their changing general and specific environments. The chapter finishes with a discussion of internal organizational environments by focusing on organizational culture. But first, let's see how the changes in external organizational environments affect the decisions and performance of a company.

Sony is one of the world's top electronics companies because of its ability to innovate, from the first commercially successful transistor radio to the Walkman, the first portable music player. The company has recently experienced a downturn, however, due to elements in its external environment, including heavy price competition in consumer electronics and the development of innovative products such as the Apple iPod and digital video recorders. Executives at Sony have responded by generating a shift in the company's internal culture. Engineers from what were once separate divisions of the company are now sharing ideas and working together to develop new products that respond to consumer demand. In particular, customers want their various electronic devices to connect easily to one another and to the Internet. Sony has also released the Bravia LCD television, a no-frills response to the demand for lower-priced products.[1]

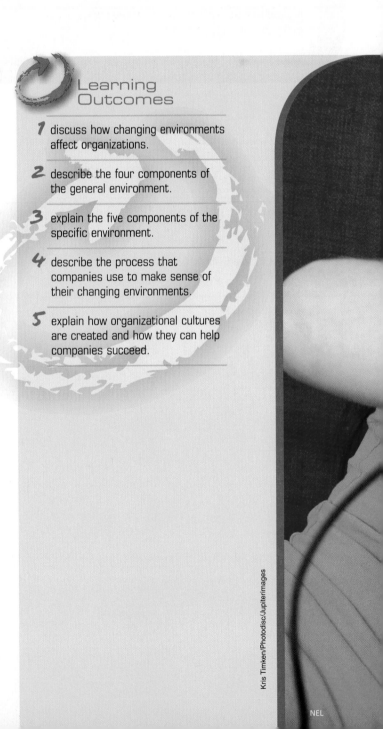

Learning Outcomes

1 discuss how changing environments affect organizations.

2 describe the four components of the general environment.

3 explain the five components of the specific environment.

4 describe the process that companies use to make sense of their changing environments.

5 explain how organizational cultures are created and how they can help companies succeed.

Kris Timken/Photodisc/Jupiterimages

External Environments

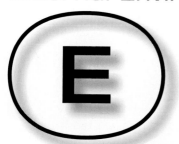

External environments are the forces and events outside a company that have the potential to influence or affect it.

After reading the next four sections, you should be able to

1 discuss how changing environments affect organizations.

2 describe the four components of the general environment.

3 explain the five components of the specific environment.

4 describe the process that companies use to make sense of their changing environments.

1 Changing Environments

Let's examine the three basic characteristics of changing external environments: 1.1 environmental change, 1.2 environmental complexity, and 1.3 resource scarcity,

External environments all events outside a company that have the potential to influence or affect it

*and **1.4** the uncertainty that environmental change, complexity, and resource scarcity can create for organizational managers.*

1.1 Environmental Change

Environmental change is the rate at which a company's general and specific environments change. In **stable environments**, the rate of environmental change is slow. For instance, apart from the fact that ovens are more efficient, bread is baked, wrapped, and delivered fresh to stores each day much as it was decades ago. Although some new breads have become popular, the white and wheat breads that customers bought 20 years ago are still today's best sellers.

While baking companies have stable environments, EA Sports, whose best-selling products are sports games like FIFA soccer and NHL hockey, competes in one of the most dynamic external environments: video games. In **dynamic environments**, the rate of environmental change is fast. EA Sports' business environment is dynamic primarily because gaming technology changes so quickly. The company's first product was designed for the Atari 800, which was soon replaced by the more powerful Commodore 64, the Commodore Amiga, the 8-bit Nintendo, the 16-bit Sega Genesis, the 32-bit and 64-bit Segas, Nintendos, Sony PlayStations, desktop computers, and now the Sony PlayStation3, Nintendo's Gamecube and Wii, and Microsoft's Xbox 360. With development costs exceeding $10 million per game and marketing costs running as high as $15 million for some games, if EA Sports guesses wrong and develops games that prove to be unpopular or quickly become obsolete, it could join the dozens of game companies that have already closed their doors.[2]

Although you might think that a company's external environment would be *either* stable *or* dynamic, research suggests that companies often experience both. According to **punctuated equilibrium theory,** companies go through long, simple periods of stability (equilibrium) during which incremental changes occur, followed by short, complex periods of dynamic, fundamental change (revolutionary periods), finishing with a return to stability (new equilibrium).[3]

One example of punctuated equilibrium is the Canadian airline industry. Twice in the past 30 years, the Canadian airline industry has experienced revolutionary periods. The first occurred with the advent of airline deregulation, which began in 1978 in response to U.S. deregulation. Prior to deregulation, the industry was dominated by the "friendly duopoly" of CP Air and Air Canada, which shared over 95 percent of the market; however, the federal government controlled where airlines could fly, when they could fly, the prices they could charge, and the number of flights they could have on a particular route. Although full deregulation was not seen in Canada until 1988, airlines had more choices to make. Many competitors—such as Wardair, which was primarily a charter airline, and Pacific Western Airlines, a regional carrier—expanded, and new air carriers were started. Competition among the airlines was fierce, and Pacific Western purchased several smaller airlines, including Wardair. In 1987 it purchased the much larger CP Air to form Canadian Airlines. Canadian Airlines was a truly national carrier; although somewhat smaller than Air Canada, it was in a position to compete with Air Canada on an even basis. After substantially increased competition, two companies again dominated the skies, Canadian Airlines and Air Canada, and a period of relative stability developed. The dominance of these two carriers was first seriously challenged in 1996 with the emergence of WestJet Airlines, which started as a Western-based airline. Canadian, too, was a Western-based airline. Competition once again increased, and a faltering Canadian Airlines was purchased by Air Canada in 2000, leaving only two national carriers, Air Canada and WestJet. Several smaller carriers tried to

Ilja Mašík/Dreamstime.com

Environmental change the rate at which a company's general and specific environments change

Stable environment an environment in which the rate of change is slow

Dynamic environment an environment in which the rate of change is fast

Punctuated equilibrium theory a theory according to which companies go through long, simple periods of stability (equilibrium), followed by short periods of dynamic, fundamental change (revolution), and ending with a return to stability (new equilibrium)

take advantage of the failure of Canadian Airlines; some of these have since gone bankrupt. Now Air Canada and WestJet dominate the Canadian skies, and no serious challengers are on the horizon. These two periods of stability followed by revolution and regained stability illustrate punctuated equilibrium theory well.[4]

1.2 Environmental Complexity

Environmental complexity refers to the number and intensity of external factors in the environment that affect organizations. **Simple environments** have few environmental factors, whereas **complex environments** have many environmental factors. The dairy industry is an excellent example of a relatively simple external environment. Even accounting for decades-old advances in processing and automatic milking machines, milk is produced the same way today as it was 100 years ago. And while food manufacturers introduce dozens of new dairy-based products each year, Canadian milk production has grown only 3.5 percent per year over the last decade. In short, producing milk is a highly competitive but simple business that has experienced few changes.[5]

At the other end of the spectrum, few industries find themselves in more complex environments today than the recording industry. The music industry was fairly simple during its first century: Make recordings on records, 8-track tapes, cassette tapes, or compact discs. Then sell those recordings to retailers, who, in turn, would sell them to consumers.

But things got much more complex after Napster created a peer-to-peer network that allowed users to easily (and usually illegally) share digital files with one another. Within a year, 30 percent of all PCs were running Napster, and the recording industry blamed illegal file sharing for sharp declines in CD sales. In an effort to create a legal downloading mechanism that would support the rights of the recording industry, Apple Computer developed iTunes.com, where individual songs could be legally purchased and downloaded for 99 cents per song. Apple followed this up with the October 2001 release of its iPod, which uses an internal hard drive to store and play thousands of songs. More than 10 billion songs have been downloaded from iTunes since the inception of the iTunes/iPod model, clearly changing the way the recording industry distributes and profits from music.[6]

1.3 Resource Scarcity

The third characteristic of external environments is resource scarcity. **Resource scarcity** is the abundance or shortage of critical organizational resources in an organization's external environment. For example, when flat-screen LCD (liquid crystal display) televisions entered the North American market, prices were six times higher per inch than for regular TVs, two times higher than for rear-projection TVs, and 25 percent higher than for plasma TVs, partly because there weren't enough LCD screen factories to meet demand. LCD factories were a scarce resource in this industry; because they were expensive to build ($2 to $4 billion each) and the manufacturing process was complex and difficult to manage. As a result of these resource shortages, consumer electronics companies found themselves susceptible to price volatility and subsequently charged higher prices to consumers. Since then, the demand for LCD television has continued to grow, helped along by the growing popularity of digital and high-definition television and (most recently) 3D television. This has prompted companies to expand production at existing factories and build new ones. As resources became less scarce,

> **Environmental complexity** the number of external factors in the environment that affect organizations
>
> **Simple environment** an environment with few environmental factors
>
> **Complex environment** an environment with many environmental factors
>
> **Resource scarcity** the abundance or shortage of critical organizational resources in an organization's external environment

Exhibit 3.1

Environmental Change, Environmental Complexity, and Resource Scarcity

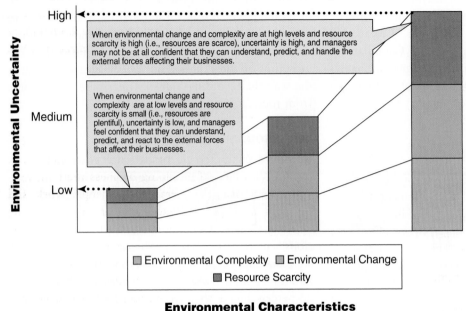

When environmental change and complexity are at high levels and resource scarcity is high (i.e., resources are scarce), uncertainty is high, and managers may not be at all confident that they can understand, predict, and handle the external forces affecting their businesses.

When environmental change and complexity are at low levels and resource scarcity is small (i.e., resources are plentiful), uncertainty is low, and managers feel confident that they can understand, predict, and react to the external forces that affect their businesses.

☐ Environmental Complexity   ☐ Environmental Change
☐ Resource Scarcity

Environmental Characteristics

competition intensified, which led to the entry of discount LCD makers, which drove down consumer prices. In this industry, resource scarcity undoubtedly plays an important role in the changing external environment.[7]

1.4 Uncertainty

As Exhibit 3.1 shows, environmental change, environmental complexity, and resource scarcity affect environmental **uncertainty,** which is how well managers can understand or predict the external changes and trends affecting their businesses. Starting at the left side of the figure, environmental uncertainty is lowest when environmental change and environmental complexity are at low levels and resource scarcity is small (i.e., resources are plentiful). In these environments, managers feel confident that they can understand, predict, and react to the external forces that affect their businesses. By contrast, the right side of the figure shows that environmental uncertainty is highest

Uncertainty extent to which managers can understand or predict which environmental changes and trends will affect their businesses

General environment the economic, technological, sociocultural, and political trends that indirectly affect all organizations

when environmental change and complexity are extensive and resource scarcity is a problem. In these environments, managers may not be confident that they can understand, predict, and handle the external forces affecting their businesses.

2 General Environment

As Exhibit 3.2 shows, two kinds of external environments influence organizations: the general environment and the specific environment. The **general environment** consists of the economy and the technological, sociocultural, and political/legal trends that indirectly affect *all* organizations. Changes in any sector of the general environment eventually affect most organizations. For example, when the Federal

Exhibit 3.2

General and Specific Environments

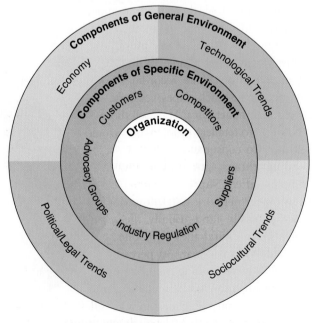

Source: From WILLIAMS/KONDRA/VIBERT. *Management*, 2E. © 2008 Nelson Education Ltd. Reproduced by permission. www.cengage.com/permissions

The Economic Ripple Effect

A sudden change in a country's economy can send a ripple effect through the entire country or even the world. Difficulties in the U.S. housing market began in 2008 when a large number of Americans, many of whom had poor credit histories, took advantage of low interest rates and forgiving credit standards in the form of subprime mortgages. As home prices fell and interest rates began to rise, many of these borrowers found themselves unable to meet their mortgage payments; the result was a record number of loan defaults and foreclosures, which forced a number of financial institutions into bankruptcy. As a result, consumer confidence began to slide, stock prices fell, and the credit market stalled. This led to reduced retail spending, especially in big-ticket purchases such as automobiles, an industry that relies on a stable credit market. The faltering of the U.S. economy ignited a global financial crisis that had an impact on other industrialized countries, including Canada. The economic challenges facing the United States, Canada's largest trading partner, led to a decrease in Canadian exports and resulting slowdowns in the manufacturing sector. Managers and business analysts keeping a close eye on these economic developments have been buoyed by early indications that Canada is expected to weather the global recession better than most other countries.

Source: P. Bergevin, "The Global Financial Crisis and Its Impact on Canada," Library of Parliament, December 2008; J. Lorio, "October Auto Sales Screech to a Halt," *Automobile*; R. Ray, "Canada to Feel Impact from Slowing U.S. Growth, Economists Say Good News Is the Worst Is Already Behind Us," *Investment Executive*, February 2008; http://www.conferenceboard.ca/HCP/Details/Economy/forecast-2010.aspx [accessed 6 May 2010].

Feng Yu/Shutterstock

includes customers, competitors, suppliers, industry regulation, and advocacy groups.

Let's take a closer look at the four components of the general environment: 2.1 the economy, and 2.2 the technological, 2.3 sociocultural, and 2.4 political/legal trends that indirectly affect all organizations.

2.1 Economy

The current state of a country's economy affects virtually every organization doing business there. In general, more people work and wages increase in a growing economy, so consumers have relatively more money to spend. More products are bought and sold in a growing economy than in a static or shrinking economy. Though an individual firm's sales will not necessarily increase, a growing economy does provide an environment favourable to business growth. In a shrinking economy, on the other hand, consumers have less money to spend and relatively fewer products are bought and sold. A shrinking economy thus makes growth for individual businesses more difficult. Because the economy influences basic business decisions such as whether to hire more employees, expand production, or take out loans to purchase equipment, managers scan their economic environments for signs of significant change.

Some managers try to predict future economic activity by keeping track of business confidence. **Business confidence indices** show how confident actual managers are about future business growth. The Conference Board of Canada surveys more than 1,500 business executives in Canada each quarter to compile the Index of Business Confidence (IBC), a measure of the business community's perceptions of the current economic situation and an indication of future plans relating to business growth. The same board surveys Canadian consumers to gauge

Reserve lowers its prime lending rate, most businesses benefit because banks and credit card companies often lower the interest rates they charge for loans. Consumers can then borrow money more cheaply to buy homes, cars, refrigerators, and plasma or LCD large-screen TVs. By contrast, each organization also has a **specific environment** that is unique to that firm's industry and that directly affects the way it conducts day-to-day business. For example, when the cost of coffee beans increased dramatically, Starbucks increased its prices, as did Kraft Foods, the maker of Maxwell House coffee.[8] But only coffee-related businesses were affected. The specific environment, which will be discussed in detail in Section 3 of this chapter,

Specific environment the customers, competitors, suppliers, industry regulations, and advocacy groups that are unique to an industry and directly affect how a company does business

Business confidence indices indices that show managers' level of confidence about future business growth

consumer confidence by asking how they feel about the economy and their employment situation and whether they plan to purchase any big-ticket items. In addition, the Small Business Research Board surveys Canadian small business owners for their opinions on significant business issues and topics in order to gain valuable insight into the small business environment in Canada.[9] Managers often prefer business confidence indices to economic statistics because they know that other managers make business decisions that are in line with their expectations concerning the economy's future. So if business confidence indices are dropping, a manager might decide against hiring new employees, increasing production, or taking out additional loans to expand the business.

2.2 Technological Component

Technology is an umbrella term for the knowledge, tools, and techniques used to transform inputs (raw materials, information, and so on) into outputs (products and services). For example, the inputs of authors, editors, and artists (knowledge and skills) and the use of equipment such as computers and printing presses (technology) transformed paper, ink, and glue (raw material) into this book (the finished product). In the case of a service company such as an airline, the technology consists of equipment, including airplanes, repair tools, and computers, as well as the knowledge of mechanics, ticketers, and flight crews. The output is the service of transporting people from one place to another.

Changes in technology can help companies provide better products or produce their products more efficiently. For example, advances in surgical techniques and imaging equipment have made open-heart surgery much faster and safer in recent years. While technological changes can benefit a business, they can also threaten it. Companies must embrace new technology and find effective ways to use it to improve their products and services or decrease costs. If they don't, they will lose out to those companies that do.

2.3 Sociocultural Component

The sociocultural component of the general environment refers to the demographic characteristics, general behaviour, attitudes, and beliefs of people in a particular society. Sociocultural changes and trends influence organizations in two important ways.

Technology the knowledge, tools, and techniques used to transform input into output

Exhibit 3.3

Demographics: Percentage of Married Women (with Children) Who Work

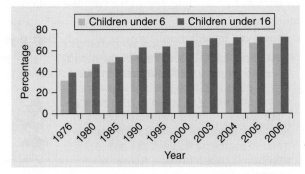

Source: Statistics Canada, Labour Force Survey, *Women in Canada: Work Chapter Updates 2006*, Catalogue no. 89F0133XIE, available at: http://www.statcan.gc.ca/pub/89f0133x/89f0133x2006000-eng.pdf [accessed 5 May 2010].

First, changes in demographic characteristics, such as the number of people with particular skills or the growth/decline in particular population segments and cultural norms, such as gender roles, affect how companies staff their businesses. Married women with children are much more likely to work today than they were four decades ago, as illustrated in Exhibit 3.3. In 1976, only 31.4 percent of women with children under six years old and 39.1 percent of women with children between the ages of six and sixteen worked. By 2006, those percentages had risen to 66.4 percent and 72.9 percent, respectively.

Second, sociocultural changes in behaviour, attitudes, and beliefs also affect the demand for a business's products and services. With traffic congestion creating longer commutes and both parents working longer hours, employees today are much more likely to value products and services that allow them to recapture free time with their families. Balancing work and home life is a major concern for many Canadians and is a factor in determining commitment to an employer. Edmonton-based VIP Concierge & Errand was launched to meet the needs of busy working Canadians who want to spend more time with family and leisure activities and less time running errands. Services provided include these: shopping (personal and grocery), meal delivery, pet sitting and dog walking, travel planning, car cleaning, and a wait service for cable, phone, or other home services. A recent study found that employees with greater work–life support are more balanced and committed to their employers and more likely to achieve greater work outcomes.[10]

2.4 Political/Legal Component

The political/legal component of the general environment includes the legislation, regulations, and court decisions that govern and regulate business behaviour. New laws and regulations continue to impose additional responsibilities on companies. For example, in Canada, the Personal Information Protection and Electronic Documents Act (PIPEDA) came into full effect in 2004. It applies to all personal information collected, used, or disclosed by private-sector organizations in the course of commercial activities. This federal legislation was introduced in response to growing consumer concerns about privacy and the handling of personal information in the digital age. Canadian businesses are now required to put systems in place to ensure that personal information such as names, addresses, phone numbers, and e-mails is not disclosed and is protected from theft. Also in 2004, Bill C-45, an amendment to the Canadian Criminal Code, was passed, establishing rules

Failure to do so may put you and your company at risk of sizable penalties, fines, or legal charges.

3 Specific Environment

As you just learned, changes in any sector of the general environment (economic, technological, socio-cultural, and political/legal) eventually affect most organizations. Each organization also has a specific environment that is unique to that firm's industry and that directly affects the way it conducts day-to-day business. For instance, if your customers decide to use another product, your main competitor cuts prices 10 percent, your best supplier can't deliver raw materials, federal regulators mandate reductions in pollutants in your industry, or environmental groups accuse your company of selling unsafe products, the impact from the specific environment on your business is immediate.

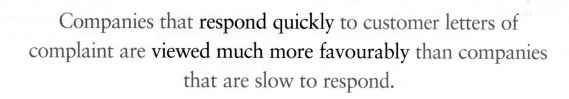

Companies that **respond quickly** to customer letters of complaint are **viewed much more favourably** than companies that are slow to respond.

for criminal liability for organizations' actions in terms of workplace health and safety, including penalties for violations resulting in injury or death.

Canada's Employment Standards Code includes a number of options allowing employees time to deal with family demands, including maternity, parental, family, and compassionate care leave. By combining maternity with parental leave, some mothers are able to stay home with their child for a full year without risk of losing their job.

Even though legal systems differ between Canada to the United States, there is sometimes a trickle-down effect whereby a law introduced in the U.S. may result in similar legislation being passed in Canada. Most recently, an increasing number of climate change lawsuits levelled against U.S. oil companies, auto makers, and electrical utilities has signalled to many Canadian companies and legal advisers that it would be wise to prepare for similar developments in Canada.[11] From a managerial perspective, the best medicine against legal risk is prevention. As a manager, it is your responsibility to educate yourself about the laws, regulations, and potential lawsuits that could affect your business.

*Let's examine how the **3.1 customer, 3.2 competitor, 3.3 supplier, 3.4 industry regulation,** and **3.5 advocacy group** components of the specific environment affect businesses.*

3.1 Customer Component

Customers purchase products and services. Companies cannot exist without customer support. Monitoring customers' changing wants and needs is therefore critical to business success. There are two basic strategies for monitoring customers: reactive and proactive.

Reactive customer monitoring involves identifying and addressing customer trends and problems after they occur. One reactive strategy is to listen closely to customer complaints and respond to customer concerns. Companies that respond quickly to customer letters of complaint are viewed much more favourably than companies that are slow to respond or never respond.[12] In particular, studies have shown that when a company's follow-up letter thanks the customer for writing, offers a sincere, specific response to the complaint (not a form letter, but an explanation of how the problem will be handled), and contains

© Bruno Vincent/Getty Images

a small gift, coupons, or a refund to make up for the problem, customers are much more likely to purchase products or services again from that company.[13]

Proactive monitoring of customers, on the other hand, means identifying and addressing customer needs, trends, and issues before they occur. An example of proactive monitoring is the fast-food industry's use of multibranding, in which two or more food chains share space under the same roof. Multibranding brings in more customers by giving them more choice. Customer research suggested that people dining together might like to eat at different places at the same time. Priszm Income Fund, Canada's largest independent restaurant operator, continues to expand through multibranding with its KFC, Taco Bell, and Pizza Hut franchises, offering customers greater selection. Prizm benefits from shared construction and operating costs—and even better, higher sales volumes relative to traditional single-brand restaurants.[14]

3.2 Competitor Component

Competitors are companies in the same industry that sell similar products or services to customers. General Motors, Ford, Toyota, Honda, Nissan, Hyundai, Kia, and DaimlerChrysler all compete for automobile customers. CBC, CTV, and CanWest Global (along with hundreds of regional cable channels) compete for TV viewers' attention. Often the difference between business success and failure comes down to whether your company is doing a better job of satisfying customer wants and needs than the competition. Consequently, companies need to keep close track of what their competitors are doing. To do this, managers perform a **competitive analysis**, which involves deciding who your competitors are, anticipating competitors' moves, and determining competitors' strengths and weaknesses.

Surprisingly, managers often do a poor job of identifying potential competitors because they tend to focus on only two or three well-known competitors with similar goals and resources.[15] Hoover, Dirt Devil, and, more recently, Oreck compete fiercely in the market for vacuum cleaners. Because these companies produced relatively similar vacuum cleaners, they paid attention to one another and competed mostly on price. When Dyson entered the market with its radically different vacuum that developed and maintained significantly more suction power, the company garnered 20 percent market share within its first twelve months on the shelves.[16] Only then did Hoover and Dirt Devil design their own bagless vacuums.

Another mistake managers may make when analyzing the competition is to underestimate potential competitors' capabilities. When this happens, managers don't take the steps they should to continue to improve their products or services. The result can be significant decreases in both market share and profits. For nearly a decade, traditional phone companies ignored the threat to their business from Voice over Internet Protocol (VoIP)—that is, the technology for making telephone calls over the Internet at a fraction of the cost. Phone companies in Canada were used to limited competition owing to the high costs associated with establishing traditional telecommunications networks. However, with VoIP technology, telecommunications providers, cable providers, and Internet service providers (ISPs) can now all offer similar services. Many companies are now entering the Canadian market hoping to capitalize on this growing market opportunity, especially in the business sector, and in doing so have heightened competition. How much of a threat is phone Internet service? Statistics Canada reports that "between December 2006 and December 2007, the proportion of households that reported using cable or VoIP telephone services rose from 10.7% to 14.9%," with Quebec and Alberta reporting the highest household penetration.[17] According to Joe Parent, VP of Vonage Canada, "if you look at reports from analysts, they're predicting that well over 10 million Canadians will have adopted this type of phone service over the next two to three years."[18]

Competitors companies in the same industry that sell similar products or services to customers

Competitive analysis a process for monitoring the competition that involves identifying competition, anticipating their moves, and determining their strengths and weaknesses

3.3 Supplier Component

Suppliers are companies that provide material, human, financial, and informational resources to other companies. A key factor influencing the impact and quality of the relationship between companies and their suppliers is how dependent they are on each other.[19] **Supplier dependence** is the degree to which a company relies on that supplier because of the importance of the supplier's product to the company and the difficulty of finding other sources for that product. Supplier dependence is very strong in the diamond business, given that De Beers Consolidated Mines provides 66 percent of the wholesale diamonds in the world and controls the supply, price, and quality of the best diamonds on the market. The company's 125 customers, or "sightholders," as they're known in the industry, are summoned to De Beers's London office 10 times a year and given a shoebox of diamonds that they are required to buy. If they refuse, they lose the opportunity to purchase any more diamonds.[20]

Buyer dependence is the degree to which a supplier relies on a buyer because of the importance of that buyer to the supplier's sales and the difficulty of finding other buyers for its products. For example, Superior Industries, which makes car wheels, gets 85 percent of its $840 million in annual sales from Ford and General Motors. When the two auto makers demanded that Superior match the low prices that Chinese wheel suppliers were offering, it had little choice. Superior's president, Steve Borick, says the ultimatum was presented very simply: "They said, 'This is the price we are getting [from Chinese suppliers], for this product. You either match that, or we'll take our business to them.'" He adds, "It's that black and white. Close the [cost] gap [of 20 to 40 percent] no matter how" you do it.[21]

As the De Beers and Superior Industries examples show, a high degree of buyer or seller dependence can lead to **opportunistic behaviour,** in which one party benefits at the expense of the other. Suppliers are beginning to hit back at auto makers that expect them to supply parts at prices that are attractive for the auto maker and crippling for the supplier, pushing many of them to bankruptcy or out of business as a result. When Michael Lord, the CEO of Bluewater Plastics, refused to sell parts at a too-low price, the purchasing manager of a Detroit auto maker told him, "Obviously, you don't want to be strategic with us." Lord, however, was unfazed and confident that the purchasing manager would call back. "I know we aren't the only ones pushing back—the supplier world is changing."[22] Though opportunistic behaviour between buyers and suppliers will never be completely eliminated, many companies believe that both buyers and suppliers can benefit by improving the buyer–supplier relationship.[23]

In contrast to opportunistic behaviour, **relationship behaviour** focuses on establishing a mutually beneficial, long-term relationship between buyers and suppliers.[24] Toyota is well known for developing positive long-term relationships with its key suppliers.

> ### Talk Any Time Anywhere . . . and Virtually Any Way
>
> The nature of telecommunications changed in 2003 with the release of Skype. With only a broadband connection, a headset, and Skype software, you could talk to anyone anywhere in the world over the Internet . . . for free. Skype has continued to push the envelope by enabling users to do video and conference calls and to connect with landlines at a lower cost than standard phone service. You can now get Skype on mobile devices and use it 24/7 from your cordless phone. Being low-cost, versatile, mobile, and integrated with traditional systems, Skype gives competitors a run for their money.

Mario Tama/Getty Images

Take a deep breath

Suppliers companies that provide material, human, financial, and informational resources to other companies

Supplier dependence the degree to which a company relies on a supplier because of the importance of the supplier's product to the company and the difficulty of finding other sources that product

Buyer dependence the degree to which a supplier relies on a buyer because of the importance of that buyer to the supplier and the difficulty of finding other buyers for its products

Opportunistic behaviour a transaction in which one party in the relationship benefits at the expense of the other

Relationship behaviour mutually beneficial, long-term exchanges between buyers and suppliers

Donald Esmond, who runs Toyota's U.S. division, says of suppliers, "I think what they appreciate ... is we don't go in and say, 'Reduce the costs by 6 percent; if you don't, somebody else is going to get the business.' We go in and say we want to come in and help you [figure out] where you can save costs so we can reduce our overall price. So it's a different approach."[25]

3.4 Industry Regulation Component

Whereas the political/legal component of the general environment affects all businesses, the **industry regulation** component consists of regulations and rules that govern the practices and procedures of specific industries, businesses, and professions. Regulatory agencies affect businesses by creating and enforcing rules and regulations to protect consumers, workers, or society as a whole. For example, the responsibility for toy safety is shared among governments, the toy industry, and safety associations as well as consumers. The Canadian Toy Association's mission is to work at a national and international level to protect and improve industry practices through various committees such as the Safety and Government Relations Committee, which helps develop toy safety standards. All toys sold in Canada must meet safety requirements defined in the Hazardous Products Act and the Hazardous

Products (Toys) Regulations. The toy industry recognizes that liaison between the various stakeholders is needed especially in terms of packaging, labelling, advertising, and the environment.[26]

3.5 Advocacy Groups

Advocacy groups are groups of concerned citizens who band together to try to influence the business practices of specific industries, businesses, and professions. The members of a group generally share the same point of view on a particular issue. For example, environmental advocacy groups might try to get manufacturers to reduce smokestack pollution emissions. Unlike the industry regulation component of the specific environment, advocacy groups cannot force organizations to change their practices. Nevertheless, they can use a number of techniques to try to influence companies, including public communications, media advocacy, Web pages, blogs, and product boycotts.

The **public communications** approach relies on voluntary participation by the news media and the advertising industry to send out an advocacy group's message. Media advocacy is much more aggressive than the public communications approach. A **media advocacy** approach typically involves framing the group's concerns as public issues (affecting everyone); exposing questionable, exploitative, or unethical practices; and forcing media coverage by buying media time or creating controversy that is likely to receive extensive news coverage.

For example, the Liquor Control Board of Ontario's (LCBO) $1.6 million "Deflate the Elephant"

Industry regulation regulations and rules that govern the business practices and procedures of specific industries, businesses, and professions

Advocacy groups groups of concerned citizens who band together to try to influence the business practices of specific industries, businesses, and professions

Public communications an advocacy group tactic that relies on voluntary participation by the news media and the advertising industry to get the advocacy group's message out

Media advocacy an advocacy group tactic that involves framing issues as public issues; exposing questionable, exploitative, or unethical practices; and forcing media coverage by buying media time or creating controversy that is likely to receive extensive news coverage

Bunny Butchers

PETA (People for the Ethical Treatment of Animals), which has offices in the United States, England, Italy, and Germany, uses controversial publicity stunts and advertisements to try to change the behaviour of large organizations, fashion designers, medical researchers, and anyone else it believes is hurting or mistreating animals. In one of its latest protests, PETA released a series of attention-getting advertisements featuring nude celebrities who would "rather go naked than wear fur" and "rather bare skin than wear skin". Although a number of designers have pledged to go animal-free, PETA is active against those that have not, engaging in activities such as smearing the windows of Jean-Paul Gaultier's Paris boutique with red "blood."

FEDERAL REGULATORY AGENCIES AND RESPONSIBILITES

Environmental Assessment Agency
Reduces and controls pollution through research, monitoring, standard setting, and enforcement activities
www.ceaa-acee.gc.ca

Candian Human Rights Commission
Promotes fair hiring and promotion practices   www.chrc-ccdp.ca

Canadian Radio-Television and Telecommunications Commission (CRTC)
Regulates communications by radio, television, wire, satellite, and cable   www.crtc.gc.ca

Bank of Canada
As the nation's central bank, controls interest rates and money supply, and monitors the Canadian banking system to produce a growing economy with stable prices   www.bank-banque-canada.ca

Competition Tribunal
Restricts unfair methods of business competition and misleading advertising   www.ct-tc.gc.ca

Health Canada
Protects nation's health by making sure food, drugs, and cosmetics are safe   www.hc-sc.gc.ca

Canadian Industrial Relations Board
Monitors union elections and stops companies from engaging in unfair labour practices   www.cirb-ccri.gc.ca

Canadian Centre for Occupational Health and Safety
Saves lives, prevent injuries, and protects the health of workers   www.ccohs.ca

Source: From WILLIAMS/KONDRA/VIBERT. *Management*, 2E. © 2008 Nelson Education Ltd. Reproduced by permission. www.cengage.com/permissions

campaign aimed at helping people open what is often an uncomfortable conversation (the elephant in the room) to prevent their friends or guests from drinking and driving. This campaign featured television commercials, online and print ads, and a special website; its purpose was to engage those people who are in a position to intervene when family or friends are at risk of getting behind the wheel when they have had too much to drink.[27]

A **product boycott** is a tactic in which an advocacy group actively tries to persuade consumers not to purchase a company's product or service. One example of this is the Rainforest Action Network (RAN), whose members have chained themselves to woodpiles at select Home Depot stores to get the company to stop selling old-growth lumber.

RAN has also partnered with Greenpeace Canada as part of a Canadian/U.S. coalition aimed at promoting a boycott of products from Canada's boreal forest, one of the last intact forests in North America, which starts in Alaska and extends all the way to the Atlantic. In question are the logging practices used by the forest companies that supply many large U.S. corporations with boreal wood. The coalition has sent correspondence to 500 major corporations, urging them to stop buying from logging companies that haven't shifted to sustainable logging and to strongly reconsider decreasing the number of flyers, catalogues, and magazines being produced.[28]

4 Making Sense of Changing Environments

In Chapter 1, you learned that managers are responsible for making sense of their business environments. As our discussions of the general and specific environments have indicated, however, making sense of business environments is not an easy task. Because external environments can be dynamic, confusing, and complex, managers use a three-step process to make sense of the changes in their external environments:

Product boycott an advocacy group tactic that involves protesting a company's actions by convincing consumers not to purchase its product or service

Chapter 3: Organizational Environments and Cultures

4.1 environmental scanning, 4.2 interpreting environmental factors, and 4.3 acting on threats and opportunities

4.1 Environmental Scanning

Environmental scanning involves searching the environment for important events or issues that might affect an organization. Managers scan the environment to stay up to date on important factors in their industry. For example, with one out of every four new car buyers purchasing highly profitable sports utility vehicles (SUVs), auto executives hadn't paid much attention to environmental groups' complaints about SUVs' extremely poor gas mileage. Now, however, market research is showing that current SUV owners are unhappy with their vehicles' poor gas mileage. In addition, the rapid rise in retail gas prices and increasingly strong disapproval of SUVs by younger car buyers have resulted in large unsold inventories of SUVs.[29]

Managers also scan their environments to reduce uncertainty. Faced with the responsibility of developing the marketing campaigns that sell their companies' most important products, the chief marketing officers (CMOs) of the world's best organizations willingly pay $50,000 a year to join the "Marketing 50," an exclusive group of CMOs who meet several times a year to

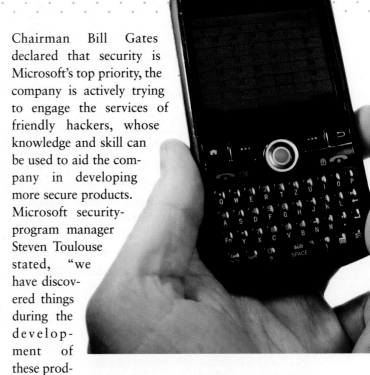

Chairman Bill Gates declared that security is Microsoft's top priority, the company is actively trying to engage the services of friendly hackers, whose knowledge and skill can be used to aid the company in developing more secure products. Microsoft security-program manager Steven Toulouse stated, "we have discovered things during the development of these products that we might not have discovered otherwise."[32]

Finally, environmental scanning is important because it contributes to organizational performance. Environmental scanning helps managers detect environmental changes and problems before they become organizational crises.[33] Furthermore, companies whose

dwphotos/Shutterstock

> Managers pay **close attention** to **trends** and **events** that are directly related to their company's **ability to compete.**

exchange ideas and pick one another's brains. Michael Linton, Best Buy's CMO, believes the "Marketing 50" is fantastic for finding out what other companies and CMOs are doing, thereby reducing uncertainty. He says, "It's impossible for any one company to know about every new tool, so hearing what is working for others helps."[30]

Organizational strategies also affect environmental scanning. In other words, managers pay close attention to trends and events that are directly related to their company's ability to compete in the marketplace.[31] Microsoft used to take software hackers to court to prosecute them for the damage caused by their efforts. However, since

Environmental scanning searching the environment for important events or issues that might affect an organization

CEOs do more environmental scanning have higher profits.[34] CEOs in better performing firms scan their firm's environments more frequently and scan more key factors in their environments in more depth and detail than do CEOs in poorer performing firms.[35]

4.2 Interpreting Environmental Factors

After scanning, managers determine what environmental events and issues mean to the organization. Typically, managers view environmental events and issues as either threats or opportunities. When managers interpret environmental events as threats, they take steps to protect the company from further harm. For example, now that Internet phone service (VoIP) has emerged as a threat, traditional phone companies have responded by announcing billion-dollar

Exhibit 3.4
Cognitive Maps

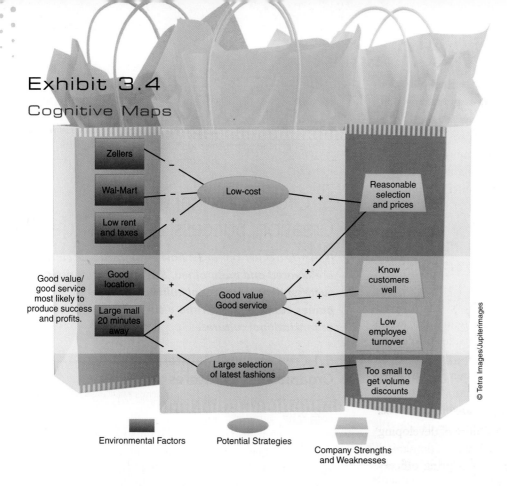

Environmental Factors | Potential Strategies | Company Strengths and Weaknesses

© Tetra Images/Jupiterimages

devices in the belief that there is better value for the money in a smartphone because of its multifunctionality.[37]

4.3 Acting on Threats and Opportunities

After scanning for information on environmental events and issues and interpreting them as threats or opportunities, managers have to decide how to respond to these environmental factors. Deciding what to do under conditions of uncertainty is always difficult. Managers can never be completely confident that they have all the information they need or that they correctly understand the information they have.

Because it is impossible to comprehend all the factors and changes, managers often rely on simplified models of external environments called cognitive maps. **Cognitive maps** summarize the perceived relationships between environmental factors and possible organizational actions. For example, the cognitive map shown in Exhibit 3.4 represents a small clothing store owner's interpretation of her business environment. The map shows three kinds of variables. The first set of variables, shown as blue rectangles, are environmental factors, such as a Wal-Mart or a large mall 20 minutes away. The second set of variables, shown in green ovals, are potential actions that the store owner might take, such as a low-cost strategy; a good-value, good-service strategy; or a large selection of the latest fashions strategy. The third set of variables, shown as gold trapezoids, are company strengths such as low employee turnover and weaknesses such as small size.

The plus and minus signs on the map indicate whether the manager believes there is a positive or negative relationship between variables. For example, the manager believes that a low-cost strategy won't work because Wal-Mart and Zellers are nearby. Offering a large selection

> **Cognitive maps**
> graphic depictions of how managers believe environmental factors relate to possible organizational actions

plans to expand their fibre-optic networks so that they can offer phone (using VoIP), Internet service, and TV packages just like those the cable and satellite companies offer.[36]

By contrast, when managers interpret environmental events as opportunities, they consider strategic alternatives for taking advantage of those events to improve company performance. The global market for high-end "smartphones"—full-featured mobile phones that also function as handheld personal computers—continues to grow and is expected to account for 23 percent of all new handsets sold by 2013. Apple developed the iPhone to meet consumer demand for multimedia devices that combined consumer electronics, telecommunications, and computer needs, thus allowing users to e-mail, take pictures, surf the Web, update and browse social networking sites, use Bluetooth devices and faster WiFi networks, and (of course) download and play iTunes music. The popularity of the iPhone (as of April 2010, 50 million had been sold) fuelled the introduction of more new phones on the market, along with specialized applications that can be tailored to an individual user's needs. Even though smartphones cost more and were introduced during a recession, consumers have embraced these new

of the latest fashions would not work either—not with the small size of the store and that large nearby mall. However, the manager believes that a good-value, good-service strategy would lead to success and profits because of the store's low employee turnover, good knowledge of customers, reasonable selection of clothes at reasonable prices, and good location.

Internal Environments

We have been looking at trends and events outside of companies that have the potential to affect them. By contrast, the **internal environment** consists of the trends and events *within* an organization that affect the management, employees, and organizational culture. Internal environments are important because they affect what people think, feel, and do at work. The internal environment at SAS, the leading provider of statistical software, is unlike that of most software companies. Instead of expecting employees to work 12- to 14-hour days, SAS has a seven-hour workday and closes its offices at 6 P.M. every evening. Employees receive unlimited sick days each year. To encourage employees to spend time with their families, there's an on-site day-care facility, and the company cafeteria has plenty of high chairs and baby seats. Given SAS's internal environment, it shouldn't surprise you to learn that almost no one quits. In a typical software company, 25 percent of the workforce quits each year to take another job. At SAS, only 4 percent leave.[38]

The key component in internal environments is **organizational culture,** which is the set of key values, beliefs, and attitudes shared by members of the organization.

Internal environment the events and trends inside an organization that affect management, employees, and organizational culture

Organizational culture the values, beliefs, and attitudes shared by members of the organization

Organizational stories stories told by members to make sense of events and changes in an organization and to emphasize culturally consistent assumptions, decisions, and actions

After reading the next section, you should be able to

5 explain how organizational cultures are created and how they can help companies succeed.

5 Organizational Cultures: Creation, Success, and Change

*Let's take a closer look at **5.1 how organizational cultures are created and maintained, 5.2 the characteristics of successful organizational cultures,** and **5.3 how companies can accomplish the difficult task of changing organizational cultures.***

5.1 Creation and Maintenance of Organizational Cultures

A primary source of organizational culture is the company founder. Founders like Bill Gates (Microsoft) create organizations in their own image and imprint them with their beliefs, attitudes, and values. Microsoft employees share founder Bill Gates's determination to stay ahead of software competitors. Says a Microsoft vice president, "No matter how good your product, you are only 18 months away from failure."[39] Though company founders are instrumental in the creation of organizational cultures, eventually founders retire, die, or choose to leave their companies. When the founders are gone, how are their values, attitudes, and beliefs sustained in the organizational culture? Answer: stories and heroes.

Members tell **organizational stories** to make sense of events and changes in an organization and to emphasize culturally consistent assumptions, decisions, and actions.[40] At Wal-Mart, stories abound about founder Sam Walton's thriftiness as he strove to make Wal-Mart the low-cost retailer that it is today. Gary Reinboth, one of Wal-Mart's first store managers, tells the following story:

In those days, we would go on buying trips with Sam, and we'd all stay, as much as we could, in one room or two. I remember one time in Chicago when we stayed eight of us to a room. And the room wasn't very big to begin with. You might say we were on a pretty restricted budget.[41]

Sam Walton's thriftiness permeates Wal-Mart to this day. Everyone, including top executives and the CEO, flies coach rather than business or first class. When employees travel on business, it's still the norm to share rooms (though two to a room, not eight!) at relatively inexpensive motels. Likewise, Wal-Mart will reimburse only up to $15 per meal on business travel, which is half to one-third the reimbursement rate at similar-sized companies. (Remember, Wal-Mart is one of the largest companies in the world.)

A second way in which organizational culture is sustained is by recognizing and celebrating heroes. By definition, **organizational heroes** are people admired for their qualities and achievements within the organization. Clive Beddoe, founding shareholder, past president, and now chairman of the board of WestJet, earned his reputation for being a hands-on leader partly owing to his practice of spending time at

Exhibit 3.5

Keys to Successful Organizational Culture

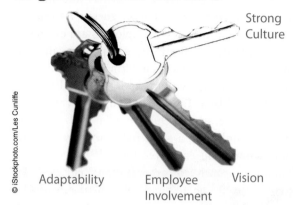

Strong Culture

Adaptability   Employee Involvement   Vision

© iStockphoto.com/Les Cunliffe

> If you want employees to be **productive**, you have to create a nurturing environment and let them be **creative**.

airports across the country during the busy Christmas travel season, doing whatever was needed to help out, checking and loading bags, and even changing an airplane tire on one occasion. Besides not shying away from the front lines, Beddoe was known to celebrate the company's success randomly with employees, once renting out a sports bar in Calgary to throw a staff party for 700 employees *just because*—no official reason or milestone was being celebrated. The company continues to grow and prosper in a difficult industry and recently earned the title of Canada's Most Admired Corporate Culture for the third year in a row.[42]

5.2 Successful Organizational Cultures

Preliminary research shows that organizational culture is related to business success. As shown in Exhibit 3.5, cultures based on adaptability, involvement, a clear vision, and consistency can help companies achieve higher sales growth, return on assets, profits, quality, and employee satisfaction.[43]

Adaptability is the ability to notice and respond to changes in the organization's environment. Cultures need to reinforce important values and behaviours, but a culture becomes dysfunctional if it prevents change.

In cultures that promote higher levels of *employee involvement* in decision making, employees feel a greater sense of ownership and responsibility. Employee involvement has been part of the WestJet corporate culture since the Calgary-based airline was founded in

1996. Employees are empowered to rely on their own integrity and decision making to solve WestJet guest problems personally. They can issue flight credits to customers when situations arise such as overbookings or late plane arrivals; they can even order in refreshments for tired passengers who are stranded at the airport. In addition, the Employee Share Purchase Plan means that employees are also "owners" and are integral to the company's success. Recently, the employee-owners were asked to weigh in and provide their opinions during meetings with WestJet executives to discuss possible strategies to help guide the company in the future, in light of the economic challenges facing the airline industry. Company founder Clive Beddoe sums up the role of employees: "If there is one defining lesson to be drawn from WestJet, it's this: Put your employees first."[44]

Company vision is the business's purpose or reason for existing. In organizational cultures with a clear company vision, the organization's strategic purpose and direction are apparent to everyone in the company. At the Four Seasons luxury hotel chain, "treating all others as we would wish to be treated" is the company's Golden Rule. It was established by the company's founder, Isadore Sharp, and is the guiding principle that applies to all interactions

Organizational heroes people celebrated for their qualities and achievements within an organization

Company vision a business's purpose or reason for existing

with guests, business partners, and employees. Besides the Golden Rule, the company's goals, beliefs, and principles are formally communicated to help guide employees in their day-to-day activities and interactions with one another and with guests. As part of annual performance reviews, employees are evaluated on how well they embody the company's values as well as on their achievements in terms of development, mentorship, and interactions with people. President and COO Kathleen Taylor sums up the company's vision when she says: "Our founder had a theory that you couldn't have a guest focus in a luxury hotel business without an employee focus."[45]

Finally, in **consistent organizational cultures**, the company actively defines and teaches organizational values, beliefs, and attitudes. Consistent organizational cultures are also called *strong cultures* because the core beliefs are widely shared and strongly held. Everyone who has ever worked at McDonald's has been taught its four core values: quality, service, cleanliness, and value. Studies show that companies with consistent or strong corporate cultures will generally outperform those with inconsistent or weak cultures.[46] Why? The reason is that when core beliefs are widely shared and strongly held, it is easy for everyone to figure out what to do and what *not* to do in their efforts to achieve organizational goals.

Having a consistent or strong organizational culture doesn't guarantee good company performance. When core beliefs are widely shared and strongly held, it is very difficult to bring about needed change. Consequently, companies with strong cultures tend to perform poorly when they need to adapt to dramatic changes in their external environments. Their consistency sometimes prevents them from adapting to those changes.[47] Indeed, McDonald's saw its sales and profits decline over the last decade as customer eating patterns began to change. To turn around performance, McDonald's developed hospitality and multilingual computer training programs and expanded its menu to include more healthful and snack-oriented selections. Over 5,000 McDonald's restaurants were remodelled in a three-year period and now feature warmer lighting, upbeat music, flat screen TVs, and WiFi networks. And the company's promotional message "I'm lovin' it" went from being derided by advertising executives to one of the most recognizable jingles in any market. Only a few

Consistent organizational culture when a company actively defines and teaches organizational values, beliefs, and attitudes

years into the plan, McDonald's achieved 32 consecutive months of positive sales (its longest streak in 25 years), reached record annual revenues of more than $20 billion, and tripled the cash dividend paid to shareholders.[48]

5.3 Changing Organizational Cultures

As shown in Exhibit 3.6, organizational cultures exist on three levels.[49] On the first, or surface, level are the elements of an organization's culture that can be seen and observed, such as symbolic artifacts (e.g., dress codes and office layouts) and workers' and managers' behaviours. Next, just below the surface, are the values and beliefs expressed by people in the company. You can't see these values and beliefs, but they become clear if you listen carefully to what people say and to how decisions are made or explained. Finally, unconsciously held assumptions and beliefs about the company are buried deep below the surface. These are the unwritten views and rules that are so strongly held and so widely shared that they are rarely discussed or even thought about unless someone attempts to change them or unknowingly violates them. Changing such assumptions and beliefs can be very difficult. Instead, managers should focus on the parts of the organizational culture they can control. These include observable surface-level items, such as workers' behaviours and symbolic artifacts, and expressed values and beliefs, which can be influenced through employee selection.

Marc Tellier, president and CEO of Yellow Pages Group, has witnessed his share of changes at the Quebec-based publishing company, which is famous for its telephone directories. In 2002, a major ownership change occurred when the company became independent. The resulting reorganization saw the exit of many senior managers at a time when competition in the industry was beginning to heat up and when the need to adapt to new technologies was apparent. According to Tellier, these changes created an opportunity for the company to change its corporate attitude from one of entitlement to one that would promote excellence.

Yellow Pages managers adopted a back-to-basics approach, examining the type of corporate culture they wanted and then giving thought to what values and behaviours were needed to achieve that vision. The desire for a customer-focused and performance-based culture emerged. With that, six values or "ground rules" were developed to help guide employee behaviour: customer focus, compete to win, teamwork,

Exhibit 3.6

Three Levels of Organizational Culture

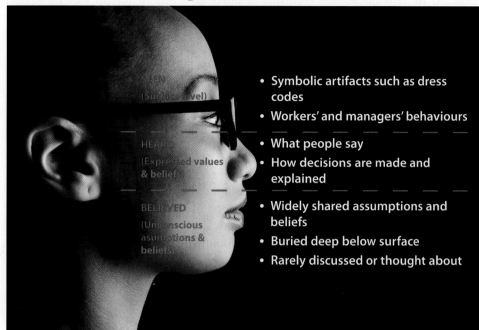

SEEN
(Surface level)

HEARD
(Expressed values & beliefs)

BELIEVED
(Unconscious assumptions & beliefs)

- Symbolic artifacts such as dress codes
- Workers' and managers' behaviours

- What people say
- How decisions are made and explained

- Widely shared assumptions and beliefs
- Buried deep below surface
- Rarely discussed or thought about

©Thinkstock/Jupiterimages

passion, respect, and open communication.[50] In order to communicate the new values and ultimately achieve the desired corporate philosophy, management used traditional communication channels with a twist, printing the six values on employee security passes and running town hall–style meetings to spread the vision of the "new" Yellow Pages.[51] In addition, the company refocused its selection process for new hires, looking for individuals with values and beliefs consistent with the company's desired culture.

To facilitate the new organizational direction in a tangible way, the company brought its Montreal and Laval offices together in a new centralized head office location complete with on-site fitness facility (with free memberships, organized walking groups, and instructor-led fitness classes); a healthy eating cafeteria; self-serve kitchen areas on every floor; outdoor eating areas to take advantage of the beautiful view of the St. Lawrence River; transit subsidies for employees; and a car pool sign-up system. Employees can listen to music while working and can participate in the many employee sports teams and social events organized throughout the year. As well, skills development is encouraged through tuition subsidies for courses or professional accreditations, in-house and online training programs, and a formal mentoring program.[52] Besides the visible transformation, changes to management and

employee behaviours have been made to facilitate the new corporate culture. For example, employee opinions were solicited in the development of the company's six ground rules; some internal processes were redesigned to encourage greater individual accountability; senior management spent a day a week working alongside the sales force; and focus groups were established to provide feedback on the new head office location.[53]

The experience at Yellow Pages demonstrates that although it is a daunting task, changes to corporate culture can be accomplished. As Josée Dykun, VP of Human Resources, explains, "strong corporate culture translates into alignment, performance and then financial results."[54] According to the *2008 Corporate Culture Study*, 82 percent of Canadian senior executives believe there is a direct correlation between corporate culture and financial performance; in fact, 20 percent claim that it's the number-one driver of success. The top 10 companies on Canada's 10 Most Admired Corporate Cultures list boasted a three-year average revenue growth 63 percent higher than that of the 60 largest public companies in Canada. A strong corporate culture is associated with more productive employees, greater customer satisfaction, better innovation, stronger confidence to develop new strategies, and improved hiring and employee retention; these factors combine to impact company performance.[55] See Exhibit 3.7 for a list of the 10 most admired Canadian corporate cultures.

It's obvious that many organizations believe that developing and maintaining the right corporate culture is integral to success. Yet according to a 2006 study, 65 percent of executives surveyed say they do not regularly measure their organization's corporate culture. Starbucks Canada is an exception is this regard. Starbucks management asks its employees to complete a Partner View Survey (Starbucks employees are considered "partners") every 18 months; the purpose is to measure the corporate culture. Participants

Exhibit 3.7

Canada's 10 Most Admired Corporate Cultures (2008)

1.	Boston Pizza International Inc. (Richmond, BC)
2.	Four Seasons Hotels and Resorts (Toronto, ON)
3.	Intuit Canada (Edmonton, AB)
4.	McDonald's Restaurants of Canada Ltd. (Toronto, ON)
5.	Purolator Courier Ltd. (Mississauga, ON)
6.	RBC (Toronto, ON)
7.	Shoppers Drug Mart (Toronto, ON)
8.	Tim Hortons (Oakville, ON)
9.	WestJet (Calgary, AB)
10.	Yellow Pages Group (Montreal, QC)

Source: Waterstone Human Capital Ltd.

are asked questions relating to job satisfaction and commitment to the company to help gauge how the company is doing in terms of one of its key values, which is, creating a great work environment for all partners. Although the survey is voluntary, by encouraging partners to complete the survey online at their individual store (on company time), and using the feedback to implement company-wide changes and initiatives, the company has achieved a greater than 90 percent participation rate. Survey results are compared to Starbucks operations in other countries and to the entire Starbucks organization; they are also tracked over time to see whether improvements are being made. According to Starbucks Canada President Colin Moore, "the Partner View Survey is a quantitative way for us to continue to ensure we're doing things that are consistent with our guiding principles and what we say we're going to do." Graham Lowe, founding partner of the Great Place to Work Institute Canada, in Kelowna, B.C., believes that "it's only now being recognized that an organization's culture can be a strategic advantage."[56]

Visit **icanmgmt.com** to find the resources you need today!

Located at the back of the textbook are rip-out Chapter Review cards. Make sure you also go online to check out other tools that MGMT offers to help you successfully pass your course.

- Interactive Quizzes
- Key Terms Flashcards
- Audio Chapter Summaries
- PowerPoint Slides

- Interactive Games
- Crossword Puzzles
- "Reel to Reel" and "Biz Flix" videos
- Cases and Exercises

© Andrew Rich/Getty Images

LOG IN!

MGMT was designed for students just like you—busy people who want choices, flexibility, and multiple learning options.

MGMT delivers concise, electronic resources such as discipline-specific activities, flashcards, test yourself questions, crossword puzzles and more!

At **icanmgmt.com**, you'll find electronic resources such as **printable interactive flashcards, downloadable study aids, games, quizzes, and videos** to test your knowledge of key concepts. These resources will help supplement your understanding of core **Principles of Management** concepts in a format that fits your busy lifestyle.

"I really like how you use students' opinions on how to study and made a website that encompasses everything we find useful. Seeing this website makes me excited to study!"

—Abby Boston, Fanshawe College

Visit **icanmgmt.com** to find the resources you need today!

ETHICS AND SOCIAL RESPONSIBILITY

Today, it's not enough for companies to make a profit. We also expect managers to make a profit by doing the right things. Unfortunately, no matter what managers decide to do, someone or some group will be unhappy with the outcome. Managers don't have the luxury of choosing theoretically optimal, win-win solutions that are obviously desirable to everyone involved. In practice, solutions to ethical and social responsibility problems aren't optimal. Often, managers must be satisfied with a solution that just makes do or does the least harm. Rights and wrongs are rarely crystal-clear to managers charged with doing the right thing. The business world is much messier than that.

What Is Ethical and Unethical Workplace Behaviour?

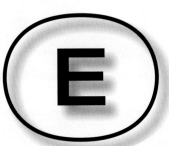

Ethics is the set of moral principles or values that defines right and wrong for a person or group. Unfortunately, numerous studies have consistently produced distressing results about the state of ethics in today's business world. In a recent survey on workplace integrity, 74 percent of employees reported having observed misconduct in the workplace during the previous 12 months, with half of employees reporting that

Ethics the set of moral principles or values that defines right and wrong for a person or group

Learning Outcomes

1 identify common kinds of workplace deviance.

2 describe ethics guidelines and legislation in North America.

3 describe what influences ethical decision making.

4 explain what practical steps managers can take to improve ethical decision making.

5 explain to whom organizations are socially responsible.

6 explain for what organizations are socially responsible.

7 explain how organizations can choose to respond to societal demands for social responsibility.

8 explain whether social responsibility hurts or helps an organization's economic performance.

© iStockphoto.com/Joselito Briones

what had been observed would lead to "a significant loss of public trust if discovered."[1] The increased use of technology in the workplace presents new challenges in terms of ethical behaviour. A 2009 Ethics and Workplace Survey explored the implications of online social networks and found that 74 percent of employees surveyed believed that it was possible to damage a company's reputation through social media; however, 53 percent believed that their social networking pages were none of their employers' business.[2] Another survey of white-collar workers found that 45 percent of workers had engaged in unethical behaviour related to technology over a 12-month period. The most reported actions included these: sabotage of a coworker or employer's systems or data; accessing private computer files without permission; listening to private cell phone conversations; and visiting pornographic websites using office equipment. Of concern is that two-thirds of employees felt that traditional standards of right and wrong were no longer relevant in the work environment due to the introduction of new technologies.[3]

A 2006 study contains more positive news, pointing to the fact that ethics is a growing concern among employees. Indeed, 94 percent of respondents said it was either critical or important that the company they work for be ethical; and 82 percent of a group of employees surveyed said "they would work

for less to be at a company that had ethical business practices, and more than a third left a job because they disagreed with the actions of fellow employees or managers."[4]

According to Dwight Reighard, the chief people officer at HomeBanc Mortgage Corp. in Atlanta, "people want to work for leaders they trust."[5] In short, much needs to be done to make workplaces more ethical, but—and this is very important—most managers and employees want this to happen.

 After reading the next two sections, you should be able to

1 identify common kinds of workplace deviance.

2 describe ethics guidelines and legislation in North America.

1 Workplace Deviance

Ethical behaviour follows accepted principles of right and wrong. Depending on which study you look at, however, one-third to three-quarters of all employees admit that they have stolen from their employers, committed computer fraud, embezzled funds, vandalized company property, sabotaged company projects, faked injuries to receive workers' compensation benefits or insurance, or been "sick" from work when they weren't really sick. Experts estimate that unethical behaviours like these, which researchers call *workplace deviance*, may cost companies nearly $1 trillion a year, or roughly 7 percent of their revenues.[6]

Workplace deviance is unethical behaviour that violates organizational norms about right and wrong. As Exhibit 4.1 shows, workplace deviance can be categorized by how deviant the behaviour is, from minor to serious, and by the target of the deviant behaviour, either the organization or particular people in the workplace.[7]

Company-related deviance can affect both tangible and intangible assets. One kind of workplace deviance, called **production deviance,** hurts the

Ethical behaviour
behaviour that conforms to a society's accepted principles of right and wrong

Workplace deviance
unethical behaviour that violates organizational norms about right and wrong

Production deviance
unethical behaviour that hurts the quality and quantity of work produced

Property deviance
unethical behaviour aimed at the organization's property or products

Employee shrinkage
employee theft of company merchandise

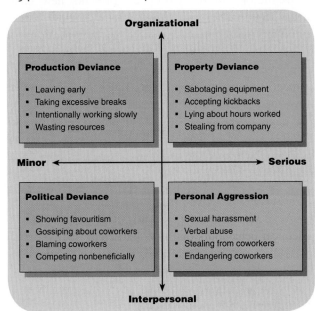

Exhibit 4.1

Types of Workplace Deviance

Source: S. L. Robinson & R. J. Bennett, "A Typology of Deviant Workplace Behaviors," (Figure), *Academy Management Journal*, 1995, Vol 38.

quality and quantity of work produced. Examples include leaving early, taking excessively long work breaks, intentionally working more slowly, or wasting resources. **Property deviance** is unethical behaviour aimed at company property or products. Examples include sabotaging, stealing, or damaging equipment or products and overcharging for services and then pocketing the difference. Fifty-eight percent of office workers acknowledge taking company property for personal use, according to a survey conducted for Lawyers.com.[8] Property deviance also includes the sabotage of company property, such as using "software bombs" to destroy company programs and data.[9]

The theft of company merchandise by employees, called **employee shrinkage,** is another common form of property deviance. Retail shrinkage costs Canadian retailers over $3.6 billion annually, which represents about 1.49 percent of sales.[10] According to the Retail Council of Canada (RCC), small and independent retailers are exposed to greater risk and lose an average of $1,005 per month from theft.[11] A 2008 RCC survey reports that 33 percent of merchandise stolen is by employees and that the average loss per incident is $370.[12] Retail employees use a variety of methods to commit crimes against their employers—leaving the store with merchandise; stashing unloaded merchandise in dumpsters and then returning after their shift to retrieve it (referred to as "dumpster diving"); acting as "sweethearts" for friends and family by discounting purchases; not charging for items at the checkout counter; allowing refunds with no receipts; or passing on credit card numbers to process gift cards.[13]

Whereas production and property deviance harm companies, political deviance and personal aggression are unethical behaviours that hurt particular people within companies. **Political deviance** is using one's influence to harm others in the company. Examples include making decisions based on favouritism rather than performance, spreading rumours about coworkers, or blaming others for mistakes they didn't make. **Personal aggression** is hostile or aggressive behaviour toward others. Examples include sexual harassment, verbal abuse, stealing from coworkers, or personally threatening coworkers. One of the fastest-growing kinds of personal aggression is workplace violence. According to Statistics Canada's 2004 General Social Survey, almost one in five violent incidents in Canada occurs in the workplace of the victim and 71 percent of all incidents of workplace violence are physical assaults.[14]

Political deviance
using one's influence to harm others in the company

Personal aggression
hostile or aggressive behaviour toward others

Life Imitates . . . Tony Soprano

If you think workplace violence is really only an issue for jobs like police officer, taxi driver, and convenient store clerk, consider this: Chris Albrecht resigned his position as the head of HBO after being arrested for assault in Las Vegas. He had previously been involved with a female subordinate, who received a settlement of $400,000 from Time Warner (HBO's parent company) for allegedly kicking and shoving her. Albrecht was a key figure in developing the popular programs *Sex and the City* and *The Sopranos*.

Source: B. Steinberg, "Incidents Bring Down HBO Chief," *The Wall Street Journal*, 10 May 2007, B1, B2.

Anthony Neste/Time & Life Pictures/Getty Images

Exhibit 4.2

International Code of Ethics for Canadian Business Principles

A. Concerning community participation and environmental protection, we will:

- strive within our sphere of influence to ensure a fair share of benefits to stakeholders impacted by our activities;
- ensure meaningful and transparent consultation with all stakeholders and attempt to integrate our corporate activities with local communities as good corporate citizens;
- ensure our activities are consistent with sound environmental management and conservation practices; and
- provide meaningful opportunities for technology cooperation, training and capacity building within the host nation.

B. Concerning human rights, we will:

- support and respect the protection of international human rights within our sphere of influence; and
- not be complicit in human rights abuses.

C. Concerning business conduct, we will:

- not make illegal and improper payments and bribes and will refrain from participating in any corrupt business practices;
- comply with all applicable laws and conduct business activities with integrity; and
- ensure contractors', suppliers' and agents' activities are consistent with these principles.

D. Concerning employee rights and health and safety, we will:

- ensure health and safety of workers is protected;
- strive for social justice and respect freedom of association and expression in the workplace; and
- ensure consistency with other universally accepted labour standards related to exploitation of child labour, forced labour and non-discrimination in employment.

Source: W. Cragg and K. McKague, *"Compendium of Ethics Codes and Instruments of Corporate Responsibility"*. Toronto: Schulich School of Business York University, 2005.

2 Ethics Guidelines and Legislation in North America

At present there is no national ethics legislation in Canada. However, in 1997 an International Code of Ethics was released by a group of Canadian companies to provide a general guideline for acceptable standards of conduct when doing business at home and in other countries. As illustrated in Exhibit 4.2, this voluntary code covers issues relating to community participation, environmental protection, human rights, business conduct, and employee rights. The code is intended to establish Canadian businesses as respected members of the global business community and is supported by the Department of Foreign Affairs and International Trade.[15]

In the United States, the establishment of the U.S. Sentencing Commission Guidelines for Organizations in 1991 signalled a change in the legal approach to handling unethical activities in business. Until that time, a company that was unaware of an employee's unethical activities could not be held responsible; however, since the new guidelines were established, companies can be prosecuted and punished *even if management doesn't* *know about the unethical behaviour*. Penalties can be substantial, with maximum fines approaching $300 million.[16] A 2004 amendment outlines much stricter ethics training requirements and emphasizes creating company cultures that value legal and ethical behaviour.[17]

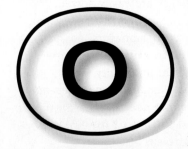

Feng Yu/Shutterstock

How Do You Make Ethical Decisions?

On a cold morning in the midst of a winter storm, schools were closed, and most people had decided to stay home from work. Nevertheless, Richard Addessi had already showered, shaved, and dressed for the office. He kissed his wife Joan goodbye, but before he could get to his car, he fell dead on the garage floor of a sudden heart attack. Addessi was four months short of his 30-year anniversary with the company. Having begun work at IBM at the age of 18, he was just 48 years old.[18]

You're the vice president in charge of benefits at IBM. Given that he was only four months short of full retirement, do you award full retirement benefits to Richard Addessi's wife and daughters? If the answer is yes, they will receive his full retirement benefits of $1,800 a month and free lifetime medical coverage. If you say no, his widow and two daughters will receive only $340 a month. They will also have to pay $473 a month just to continue their current medical coverage. As the VP in charge of benefits at IBM, what would be the ethical thing for you to do?

After reading the next two sections, you should be able to

3 describe what influences ethical decision making.

4 explain what practical steps managers can take to improve ethical decision making.

3 Influences on Ethical Decision Making

Although some ethical issues are easily solved, many do not have clearly right or wrong answers. Although the answers are rarely clear, managers do need to have a clear sense of *how* to arrive at an answer in order to manage this ethical ambiguity well.

The ethical answers that managers choose depend on **3.1 the ethical intensity of the decision, 3.2 the moral development of the manager,** *and* **3.3 the ethical principles used to solve the problem.**

3.1 Ethical Intensity of the Decision

Managers don't treat all ethical decisions the same. The manager who has to decide whether to deny or extend full benefits to Joan Addessi and her family is going to treat that decision much more seriously than the decision of how to deal with an assistant who has been taking computer paper home for personal use. These decisions differ in their **ethical intensity,** or the degree of concern people have about an ethical issue. When addressing an issue of high ethical intensity, managers are more aware of the impact their decision will have on others. They are more likely to view the decision as an ethical or moral decision rather than as an economic decision. They are also more likely to worry about doing the right thing.

Six factors must be taken into account when determining the ethical intensity of an action, as shown in Exhibit 4.3. **Magnitude of consequences** is the total harm or benefit derived from an ethical decision. The more people who are harmed or the greater the harm to those

> **Ethical intensity** the degree of concern people have about an ethical issue
>
> **Magnitude of consequences** the total harm or benefit derived from an ethical decision

Exhibit 4.3

Six Factors that Contribute to Ethical Intensity

Magnitude of consequences
Social consensus
Probability of effect
Temporal immediacy
Proximity of effect
Concentration of effect

Source: T. M. Jones, "Ethical Decision Making by Individuals in Organizations: An Issue-Contingent Model," *Academy of Management Review* 16 (1991): 366–395.

people, the larger the consequences. **Social consensus** is agreement on whether behaviour is bad or good. **Probability of effect** is the chance that something will happen and then result in harm to others. If we combine these factors, we can see the effect they can have on ethical intensity. For example, if there is *clear agreement* (social consensus) that a managerial decision or action is *certain* (probability of effect) to have *large negative consequences* (magnitude of consequences) in some way, then people will be highly concerned about that managerial decision or action, and ethical intensity will be high. Although Adessi's family will be profoundly affected by the decision, they are one family, and the magnitude of consequences and possibility of effect beyond them would be quite low if IBM decided to deny the benefits.

Temporal immediacy is the time between an act and the consequences the act produces. Temporal immediacy is stronger if a manager has to lay off workers next week as opposed to three months from now. **Proximity of effect** is the social, psychological, cultural, or physical distance of a decision maker from those affected by his or her decisions. Thus, proximity of effect is greater for the manager who works with employees who are to be laid off than it is for a manager who works where no layoffs will occur. If the person responsible for the decision were Adessi's direct supervisor, who had known him and his family through his tenure at the company, the ethical intensity would be higher than it would be for an executive who had never met him. Finally, whereas the magnitude of consequences is the total effect across all people, **concentration of effect** is how much an act affects the average person. Temporarily laying off 100 employees for 10 months without pay is a greater concentration of effect than temporarily laying off 1,000 employees for one month.

Which of these six factors has the most impact on ethical intensity? Studies indicate that managers are much more likely to view decisions as ethical when the magnitude of consequences (total harm) is high and there is a social consensus (agreement) that a behaviour or action is bad.[19]

3.2 Moral Development

A friend of yours has given you the latest version of Microsoft Office. She stuffed the software disks in your backpack with a note saying that you should install it on your computer and get it back to her in a couple of days. You're tempted. No one would find out. Even if someone does, Microsoft probably isn't going to come after you. Microsoft goes after the big fish—companies that illegally copy and distribute software to their workers. What would you do?[20]

In part, according to psychologist Lawrence Kohlberg, your decision will be based on your level of moral development. Kohlberg identified three phases of moral development with two stages in each phase (see Exhibit 4.4).[21] At the **preconventional level of moral development**, people decide based on selfish reasons. For example, if you are in Stage 1, the punishment and obedience stage, your primary concern will be to avoid trouble for yourself. So you won't copy the software

Social consensus agreement on whether behaviour is bad or good

Probability of effect the chance that something will happen and then harm others

Temporal immediacy the time between an act and the consequences the act produces

Proximity of effect the social, psychological, cultural, or physical distance between a decision maker and those affected by his or her decisions

Concentration of effect the total harm or benefit that an act produces on the average person

Preconventional level of moral development the first level of moral development in which people make decisions based on selfish reasons

Exhibit 4.4

Kohlberg's Stages of Moral Development

Stage 1	Stage 2	Stage 3	Stage 4	Stage 5	Stage 6
Punishment and Obedience	Instrumental Exchange	Good Boy, Nice Girl	Law and Order	Social Contract	Universal Principle
Preconventional		Conventional		Postconventional	
Self-Interest		Societal Expectations		Internalized Principles	

Source: W. Davidson III and D. Worrell, "Influencing Managers to Change Unpopular Corporate Behaviour through Boycotts and Divestitures," *Business & Society* 34 (1995): 171–196.

because you are afraid of being caught and punished. Yet in Stage 2, the instrumental exchange stage, you worry less about punishment and more about doing things that directly advance your wants and needs. So you copy the software.

People at the **conventional level of moral development** make decisions that conform to societal expectations. In other words, they look to others for guidance on ethical issues. In Stage 3, the "good boy, nice girl" stage, you normally do what the other "good boys" and "nice girls" are doing. If everyone else is illegally copying software, you will, too. But if they aren't, you won't either. In the law and order stage, Stage 4, you again look for external guidance, but do whatever the *law* permits, so you won't copy the software.

People at the **postconventional level of moral development** use internalized ethical principles to solve ethical dilemmas. In Stage 5, the social contract stage, you will refuse to copy the software because, as a whole, society is better off when the rights of others—in this case, the rights of software authors and manufacturers—are not violated. In Stage 6, the universal principle stage, you might or might not copy the software, depending on your principles of right and wrong. Moreover, you will stick to your principles even if your decision conflicts with the law

(Stage 4) or what others believe is best for society (Stage 5). For example, those with socialist or communist beliefs might choose to copy the software because they believe goods and services should be owned by society rather than by individuals and corporations.

Kohlberg believed that people would progress sequentially from earlier to later stages as they became more educated and mature. But only 20 percent of adults ever reach the postconventional stage of moral development where internal principles guide their decisions. Most adults are in the conventional stage of moral development and look to others for guidance on ethical issues. This means that most people in the workplace look to and need leadership when it comes to ethical decision making.[22]

3.3 Principles of Ethical Decision Making

Beyond an issue's ethical intensity and a manager's level of moral maturity, the particular ethical principles that managers use will also affect how they solve ethical dilemmas. Unfortunately, there is no one ideal principle to use when making ethical business decisions. According to professor LaRue Hosmer, a number of different ethical principles can be used to make business decisions: long-term self-interest, personal virtue, religious injunctions, government requirements, utilitarian benefits, individual rights, and distributive justice.[23] All of these ethical principles encourage managers and employees to take others' interests into account when making ethical decisions. At the same time, however, these principles can lead to very different ethical actions, as we can see by using these principles to decide whether to award full benefits to Joan Addessi and her children.

According to the **principle of long-term self-interest,** you should never take any action that is not in your or your organization's long-term self-interest. Although this sounds as if the principle promotes selfishness, it doesn't. What we do to maximize our long-term interests (save more, spend

Conventional level of moral development the second level of moral development in which people make decisions that conform to societal expectations

Postconventional level of moral development the third level of moral development in which people make decisions based on internalized principles

Principle of long-term self-interest an ethical principle that holds that you should never take any action that is not in your or your organization's long-term self-interest

Drugs and Scientific Credibility

Merck, one of the largest U.S. pharmaceutical companies, has come under fire from members of the medical community. The *Journal of the American Medical Association* accused the company of paying academic authors to publish ghostwritten stories about its now-withdrawn painkiller, Vioxx, and selectively reporting information about how the drug may have been linked with the deaths of Alzheimer's patients. Academic studies offer valuable information about drugs but can also be a powerful marketing tool. Ethical standards in carrying out and publishing drug studies are critical in maintaining scientific credibility. Merck defended its procedures as normative, but its questionable actions put the company's virtue at risk and could undermine its long-term credibility. Using a defensive strategy, Merck has now promised to cease the practice of ghostwriting.

Source: R. Winslow and A. Johnson, "Merck's Publishing Ethics Are Questioned by Studies," The Wall Street Journal 16 April 2008 B4, J. Goldstein, "In Latest Vioxx Settlement, Merck Swears Off Ghostwriting," The Wall Street Journal 20 May, 2008.

Principle of personal virtue an ethical principle that holds that you should never do anything that is not honest, open, and truthful and that you would not be glad to see reported in the newspapers or on TV

Principle of religious injunctions an ethical principle that holds that you should never take any action that is not kind and that does not build a sense of community

Principle of government requirements an ethical principle that holds that you should never take any action that violates the law, for the law represents the minimal moral standard

Principle of utilitarian benefits an ethical principle that holds that you should never take any action that does not result in greater good for society

Principle of individual rights an ethical principle that holds that you should never take any action that infringes on others' agreed-upon rights

---

less, exercise every day, watch what we eat) is often very different from what we do to maximize short-term interests (max out our credit cards, be couch potatoes, eat whatever we want). At any given time, IBM has nearly 1,000 employees who are just months away from retirement. Because of the costs involved, it serves IBM's long-term interest to pay full benefits only after employees have put in their 30 years.

The **principle of personal virtue** holds that you should never do anything that is not honest, open, and truthful and that you would not be glad to see reported in the newspapers or on TV. Using the principle of personal virtue, IBM should quietly award Joan Addessi her husband's full benefits, avoiding the potential for negative media coverage.

The **principle of religious injunctions** holds that you should never take an action that is unkind or that harms a sense of community, such as the positive feelings that come from working together to accomplish a commonly accepted goal. Using this principle, IBM would be concerned foremost with compassion and kindness and award full benefits to Joan Addessi.

According to the **principle of government requirements,** the law represents the minimal moral standards of society, so you should never take any action that violates the law. Using this principle, IBM would deny full benefits to Joan Addessi because her husband did not work for the company for 30 years.

The **principle of utilitarian benefits** states that you should never take an action that does not result in greater good for society. In short, you should do whatever creates the greatest good for the greatest number. At first, this principle seems to suggest that IBM should award full benefits to Joan Addessi. If IBM did this with any regularity, however, the costs would be enormous, profits would shrink, and IBM would have to cut its stock dividend, harming countless shareholders, many of whom rely on IBM dividends for retirement income. In this case, the principle does not lead to a clear choice.

The **principle of individual rights** holds that you should never take an action that infringes on others' agreed-upon rights. Using this principle, IBM would deny Joan Addessi full benefits. If it carefully followed the rules specified in its pension plan and granted Mrs. Addessi due process, meaning the right to appeal the decision, then IBM would not be violating her rights. In fact, it could be argued that providing full benefits to Mrs. Addessi would violate the rights of employees who had to wait 30 years to receive full benefits.

Finally, under the **principle of distributive justice,** you should never take any action that harms the least fortunate among us in some way. This principle is designed to protect the poor, the uneducated, and the unemployed. Although Joan Addessi could probably find a job, it's unlikely that she could easily find one that would support her and her daughters in the manner to which they were accustomed after 20 years as a stay-at-home mom. Using the principle of distributive justice, IBM would award her full benefits.

As mentioned at the beginning of this chapter, one of the practical aspects of ethical decisions is that no matter *what* you decide, someone or some group will be unhappy. This corollary is also true: No matter *how* you decide, someone or some group will be unhappy. Some will argue that you should have used a different principle or weighed concerns differently. Consequently, although all of these ethical principles encourages managers to balance others' needs against their own, they can also lead to very different ethical actions. So even when managers strive to be ethical, there are often no clear answers when it comes to doing the right thing.

So, what did IBM decide to do? Since Richard Addessi had not completed 30 full years with the company, IBM officials felt they had no choice but to give Joan Addessi and her two daughters the smaller, partial retirement benefits. Do you think IBM's decision was ethical? It's likely many of you don't. You may wonder how the company could be so heartless as to deny Richard Addessi's family the full benefits to which you believe they were entitled. Yet others might argue that IBM did the ethical thing by strictly following the rules laid out in its pension benefit plan. Indeed, an IBM spokesperson stated that making exceptions would violate the federal Employee Retirement Income Security Act of 1974. After all, being fair means applying the rules to everyone.

4 Practical Steps to Ethical Decision Making

*Managers can encourage more ethical decision making in their organizations by **4.1 carefully selecting and hiring ethical employees, 4.2 establishing a specific code of ethics, 4.3 training employees to make ethical decisions, and 4.4 creating an ethical climate.***

4.1 Selecting and Hiring Ethical Employees

As an employer, you can increase your chances of hiring an honest person by giving job applicants integrity tests.

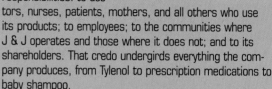

Corporate Responsibility

Johnson & Johnson knows the value of a strong code of ethics. The company has a credo that outlines four main responsibilities: to doctors, nurses, patients, mothers, and all others who use its products; to employees; to the communities where J & J operates and those where it does not; and to its shareholders. That credo undergirds everything the company produces, from Tylenol to prescription medications to baby shampoo.

Source: "Our Credo," Johnson & Johnson, available online at http://www.jnj.com/connect/about-jnj/jnj-credo, [accessed 13 November 2008].

© Susan Trigg/iStockphoto.com

Overt integrity tests estimate job applicants' honesty by directly asking them what they think or feel about theft or about punishment of unethical behaviours.[24] For example, an employer might ask an applicant, "Don't most people steal from their companies?" Surprisingly, unethical people will usually answer "yes" to such questions, because they believe that the world is basically dishonest and that dishonest behaviour is normal.[25]

Personality-based integrity tests indirectly estimate job applicants' honesty by measuring psychological traits such as dependability and conscientiousness. For example, prison inmates serving time for white-collar crimes (counterfeiting, embezzlement, and fraud) scored much lower than a comparison group of middle-level managers on scales measuring reliability, dependability, honesty, conscientiousness, and abiding by rules.[26] These results show that companies can selectively hire and promote people who will be more ethical.[27]

4.2 Codes of Ethics

Today, almost all large corporations have similar ethics codes in place. Still, two things must happen if

Principle of distributive justice an ethical principle that holds that you should never take any action that harms the least fortunate among us: the poor, the uneducated, the unemployed

Overt integrity test a written test that estimates job applicants' honesty by directly asking them what they think or feel about theft or about punishment of unethical behaviours

Personality-based integrity test a written test that indirectly estimates job applicants' honesty by measuring psychological traits, such as dependability and conscientiousness

those codes are to encourage ethical decision making and behaviour.[28] First, a company must communicate its code inside and outside the company. Johnson & Johnson's credo is an example of a well-communicated code of ethics. With the click of a computer mouse, anyone inside or outside the company can obtain detailed information about the company's specific ethical business practices.

Second, in addition to having an ethics code with general guidelines like "do unto others as you would have others do unto you," management must also develop practical ethical standards and procedures specific to the company's line of business. Canadian Tire established a set of ethical standards known as its Code of Business Conduct to help direct the actions of employees and individuals who act on behalf of the company. For example, a Canadian Tire employee who is unsure whether to accept an invitation to a business function can refer to the code and find that the expected procedure is to seek approval prior to accepting any invitation and to consider whether the event is relevant to his or her role in the company, whether the event is a networking opportunity, and whether acceptance would reduce his or her ability to be objective in making decisions regarding this business partner. The code is available on the company's website, so it is easily accessible to employees, suppliers, and customers alike. Complaints or concerns regarding potential violations of the code can be submitted to the company using the Business Conduct Hotline, or they can be reported through the company's website as part of the company's Business Conduct Compliance Program.[29]

4.3 Ethics Training

The first objective of ethics training is to develop employees' awareness of ethics.[30] This means helping employees recognize which issues are ethical issues and then avoid rationalizing unethical behaviour by thinking, "This isn't really illegal or immoral" or "No one will ever find out." To ensure that employees of the Royal Bank of Canada understand the company's code of conduct, at least once every two years, employees participate in a Web-based ethics training program that incorporates role plays as well as a testing feature designed to evaluate awareness of company principles and how an employee would respond to an ethical dilemma.[31] Several companies have even created board games to improve awareness of ethical issues.[32] Defence contractor Martin's ethics training program is aimed at creating "A Culture of Trust." Employees form small groups and engage in role playing and dialogue with one another about real-life scenarios such as managing relationships with coworkers, ethical use of company credit cards while on business travel, and managing conflicts of interest. The groups then come up with outcomes to the scenarios. Because it is collective, this program not only conveys information about ethical behaviour but also builds accountability and a sense of "we're all in this together."[33]

The second objective for ethics training programs is to achieve credibility with employees. Some companies have hurt the credibility of their ethics programs by having outside instructors and consultants conduct the classes.[34] Employees often complain that outside instructors and consultants are teaching theory that has nothing to do with their jobs and the practical dilemmas they actually face on a daily basis. Boeing has established a number of ways to educate employees about and help them manage ethical issues right in-house. These include a handbook which outlines how to make ethical decisions and presents information in response to FAQs as well as ethics advisors who serve as mentors. Answers to "What do I do if...?" questions are easily accessible in the handbook and through the company's Ethics Line, which is available to employees throughout the company as well as concerned stakeholders.[35] Ethics training becomes even more credible when top managers teach the initial ethics classes to their subordinates who in turn teach their subordinates.[36] Unfortunately, though, 25 percent of large companies don't require top managers to attend, much less teach, ethics training.[37]

The third objective of ethics training is to teach employees a practical model of ethical decision making. A basic model should help them think about the consequences their choices will have on others and consider how they will choose between different solutions. Exhibit 4.5 presents a basic model of ethical decision making.

4.4 Ethical Climate

Organizational culture is key to fostering ethical decision making. Management consultant Andrea Plotnick observes about an ethics code: "You want it to be about embedding the right behaviours and the right decision-making process within everybody in the organization, so that it becomes part of the culture. That is how you will have success."[38] The 2009 National Business Ethics Survey found that 62 percent of American employees perceived their culture as very or somewhat ethically strong; however,

Exhibit 4.5

A Basic Model of Ethical Decision Making

1. **Identify the problem.** What makes it an ethical problem? Think in terms of rights, obligations, fairness, relationships, and integrity. How would you define the problem if you stood on the other side of the fence?

2. **Identify the constituents.** Who has been hurt? Who could be hurt? Who could be helped? Are they willing players, or are they victims? Can you negotiate with them?

3. **Diagnose the situation.** How did it happen in the first place? What could have prevented it? Is it going to get worse or better? Can the damage now be undone?

4. **Analyze your options.** Imagine the range of possibilities. Limit yourself to the two or three most manageable. What are the likely outcomes of each? What are the likely costs? Look to the company mission statement or code of ethics for guidance.

5. **Make your choice.** What is your intention in making this decision? How does it compare with the probable results? Can you discuss the problem with the affected parties before you act? Could you disclose without qualm your decision to your boss, the CEO, the board of directors, your family, or society as a whole?

6. **Act.** Do what you have to do. Don't be afraid to admit errors. Be as bold in confronting a problem as you were in causing it.

Source: L. A. Berger, "Train All Employees to Solve Ethical Dilemmas," *Best's Review—Life-Health Insurance Edition* 95 (1995): 70–80.

---

49 percent of employees had witnessed misconduct on the job (a decrease from 56 percent in 2007). The strength of ethical culture in the workplace increased from 53 percent in 2007 to 62 percent in 2009. The Ethics Resource Center (ERC) suggests that these positive trends are likely part of an "ethics bubble" resulting from the downturn in the economy. During tough economic times, a company's future stability may be in jeopardy and management may emphasize the importance of high standards; as a result, employees may be less inclined to participate in unethical behaviours. The ERC cautions that when the economic business environment improves, misconduct may rise unless a strong ethical culture is in place.[39] Management sets the tone. We learned in Chapter 3 that leadership is an important factor in creating an organizational culture. In study after study, when researchers ask, "What is the most important influence on your ethical behaviour at work?" the answer comes back, "My manager." The first step in establishing an ethical climate is for managers, especially top managers, to act ethically themselves.

A second step in establishing an ethical climate is for top management to be active in and committed to the company ethics program.[40] Business writer Dayton Fandray says, "You can have ethics offices and officers and training programs and reporting systems, but if the CEO doesn't seem to care, it's all just a sham. It's not surprising to find that the companies that really do care about ethics make a point of including senior management in all of their ethics and compliance programs."[41]

A third step is to put in place a reporting system that encourages managers and employees to report potential ethics violations. **Whistle-blowing**, that is, reporting others' ethics violations, is a difficult step for most people to take. Potential whistle-blowers often feel that their reporting won't make

> **Whistle-blowing**
> reporting others' ethics violations to management or legal authorities

AMAZINGLY, THOUGH, **NOT ALL COMPANIES** FIRE ETHICS VIOLATORS.

Whistle-Blowing

In Canada, several high-profile cases of whistle-blowing by federal and provincial employees signalled a need for whistle-blowing legislation dealing specifically with public service employees. Former Olympic athlete Myriam Bedard claimed that she had been fired from her marketing job at VIA Rail after questioning invoices from advertising agencies—invoices indicating that public funds intended for government advertising in Quebec had been misused. This cracked open what would later be referred to as the Sponsorship Scandal. In 2004, Dr. Shiv Chopra and two other scientists were fired from their jobs at Health Canada after criticizing the department's drug approval processes and expressing concern over public health and safety in relation to the bovine growth hormone used in meat and milk production. As a result, Ontario's Public Service Act of 1993 was passed; later, in 2005, the Public Servants Disclosure Protection Act signalled "the federal government's broader commitment to ensure transparency, accountability, financial responsibility and ethical conduct in the public sector."

Sources: Whistleblower legislation Bill C-25, Disclosure Protection. CBC News Online, 28 April 2004. Accessed from: http://www.cbc.c*Globe and Mail*, 29 September 2006; D. Johansen and S. Spano, Bill C-11 The Public Servants Disclosure Protection Act 18 October 2004, Revised 2 November 2005. Law and Government Division, Library of Parliament. Accessed from: http://www2.parl.gc.ca/Sites/LOP/LegislativeSummaries/Bills_ls.asp?Parl=38&Ses=1&1s=C11.

an impact and fear that they, and not the ethics violators, will be punished. According to the 2009 National Business Ethics Survey, whistle-blowing is on the rise: 63 percent of employees surveyed said they had reported workplace misconduct when they observed it, compared to 58 percent in 2007.[42] However, 15 percent of employees who reported misconduct perceived that they were retaliated against as a result—an increase from 12 percent in 2007.[43] According to the survey, retaliation mainly involved interpersonal responses from coworkers, rather than a direct impact on their job (see Exhibit 4.6).

Exhibit 4.6

Forms of Retaliation Experienced as a Result of Reported Misconduct (2009)

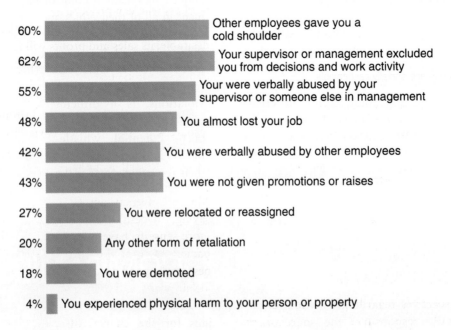

Percentage	Form of Retaliation
60%	Other employees gave you a cold shoulder
62%	Your supervisor or management excluded you from decisions and work activity
55%	Your were verbally abused by your supervisor or someone else in management
48%	You almost lost your job
42%	You were verbally abused by other employees
43%	You were not given promotions or raises
27%	You were relocated or reassigned
20%	Any other form of retaliation
18%	You were demoted
4%	You experienced physical harm to your person or property

Source: "2009 National Business Ethics Survey." Ethics Resource Center, available online at http://www.ethics.org/nbes/files/nbes-final.pdf.

The factor that does the most to discourage whistle-blowers from reporting problems, however, is lack of company action on their complaints.[44] Thus, the final step in developing an ethical climate is for management to fairly and consistently punish those who violate the company's code of ethics. Amazingly, though, not all companies fire ethics violators. In fact, 8 percent of surveyed companies admit that they would promote top performers even if they had violated ethical standards.[45]

What Is Social Responsibility?

Social responsibility is a business's obligation to pursue policies, make decisions, and take actions that benefit society.[46] Unfortunately, because there are strong disagreements over to whom and for what in society organizations are responsible, it can be difficult for managers to know what is or will be perceived as socially responsible corporate behaviour. In a recent McKinsey & Co. study of 1,144 top global executives, 79 percent predicted that at least some responsibility for dealing with future social and political issues would fall on corporations, but only 3 percent said they do a good job of dealing with these issues.[47]

After reading the next four sections, you should be able to explain

5   to whom organizations are socially responsible.

6   for what organizations are socially responsible.

7   how organizations can choose to respond to societal demands for social responsibility.

8   whether social responsibility hurts or helps an organization's economic performance.

5 To Whom Are Organizations Socially Responsible?

There are two perspectives regarding to whom organizations are socially responsible: the shareholder model and the stakeholder model. According to the late Nobel Prize–winning economist Milton Friedman, the only social responsibility that organizations have is to satisfy their owners, that is, company shareholders. This view—called the **shareholder model**—holds that the only social responsibility that businesses have is to maximize profits. By maximizing profit, the firm maximizes shareholder wealth and satisfaction. More specifically, as profits rise, the company shares owned by shareholders generally increase in value.

Friedman argued that it is socially irresponsible for companies to divert time, money, and attention from maximizing profits to social causes and charitable organizations. The first problem, he believed, is that organizations cannot act effectively as moral agents for all company shareholders. Although shareholders are likely to agree on investment issues concerning a company, it's highly unlikely that they have common views on what social causes a company should or should not support. Rather than act as moral agents, Friedman argued, companies should maximize profits for shareholders. Shareholders can then use their time and increased wealth to contribute to the social causes, charities, or institutions they want rather than those that companies want.

The second major problem, Friedman said, is that the time, money, and attention diverted to social causes undermine market efficiency.[48] In competitive markets, companies compete for raw materials, talented workers, customers, and investment funds. A company that spends money on social causes will have less money to purchase quality materials or to hire talented workers who can produce a valuable product at a good price. If customers find the company's product less desirable, its sales and profits will fall. If profits fall, the company's stock price will decline, and the company will have difficulty attracting investment funds that could be used to fund long-term growth. In the end, Friedman argues, diverting the firm's money, time, and resources to social causes hurts customers, suppliers, employees, and shareholders. Russell Roberts, an economist at George Mason University, agrees, saying, "Doesn't it make more sense to have companies do what they do best, make good products at fair prices, and then let consumers use the savings for the charity of their choice?"[49]

Social responsibility a business's obligation to pursue policies, make decisions, and take actions that benefit society

Shareholder model a view of social responsibility that holds that an organization's overriding goal should be to maximize profit for the benefit of shareholders

By contrast, under the **stakeholder model,** management's most important responsibility is not just maximizing profits, but the firm's long-term survival, which is achieved by satisfying not just shareholders, but the interests of multiple corporate stakeholders.[50] **Stakeholders** are persons or groups who are interested in and affected by the organization's actions.[51] They are called stakeholders because they have a stake in what those actions are. Consequently, stakeholder groups may try to influence the firm to act in their own interests. Exhibit 4.7 shows the various stakeholder groups that the organization must satisfy to ensure its long-term survival.

Being responsible to multiple stakeholders raises two basic questions. First, how does a company identify its stakeholders? Second, how does a company balance the needs of different stakeholders? Distinguishing between primary and secondary stakeholders can help answer these questions.[52]

Some stakeholders are more important to the firm's survival than others. **Primary stakeholders** are groups on which the organization depends for its long-term survival. They include shareholders, employees, customers, suppliers, governments, and local communities. When managers are struggling to balance the needs of different stakeholders, the stakeholder model suggests that the needs of primary stakeholders take precedence over the needs of secondary stakeholders. But among primary stakeholders, are some more important than others? In practice, yes, as CEOs typically give somewhat higher priority to shareholders, employees, and customers than to suppliers, governments, and local communities.[53] Addressing the concerns of primary stakeholders is important because if a stakeholder group becomes dissatisfied and terminates its relationship with the company, the company could be seriously harmed or go out of business.

Secondary stakeholders, such as the media and special interest groups, can influence or be influenced by the company. Unlike the

Exhibit 4.7

Stakeholder Model of Corporate Social Responsibility

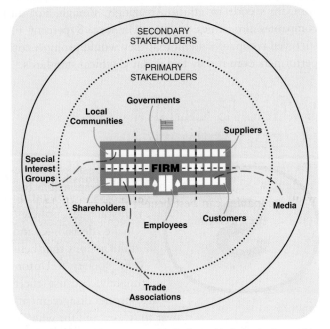

Source: T. Donaldson and L.E. Preston, "The Stakeholder Theory of the Corporation; Concepts, Evidence and Implications," *Academy of Management Review* 20 (1995): 65-91.

primary stakeholders, however, they do not engage in regular transactions with the company and are not critical to its long-term survival. Nevertheless, secondary stakeholders are still important because they can affect public perceptions and opinions about socially responsible behaviour. In 2008, for example, after five years of battling with People for the Ethical Treatment of Animals (PETA), KFC Canada signed an agreement promising to buy from suppliers who use "animal-welfare friendly" practices and announced it would begin to offer vegan options in its restaurants. The agreement effectively ended the boycott imposed by PETA on the Canadian division of KFC, although the campaign against KFC continued in the United States and worldwide. PETA's "Kentucky Fried Cruelty" campaign gained international exposure and included more than 12,000 protests at KFC restaurants as well as outside the homes of KFC executives.[54]

So, to whom are organizations socially responsible? Many commentators, especially economists and financial analysts, continue to argue that organizations are responsible only to shareholders. Increasingly, however, top managers have come to believe

Stakeholder model a theory of corporate responsibility that holds that management's most important responsibility, long-term survival, is achieved by satisfying the interests of multiple corporate stakeholders

Stakeholders persons or groups with a "stake" or legitimate interest in a company's actions

Primary stakeholder any group on which an organization relies for its long-term survival

Secondary stakeholder any group that can influence or be influenced by a company and can affect public perceptions about its socially responsible behaviour

that they and their companies must be socially responsible to their stakeholders. Today, surveys show that as many as 80 percent of top-level managers believe that it is unethical to focus just on shareholders. Although there is not complete agreement, a majority of opinion makers would argue that companies must be socially responsible to their stakeholders.

6 For What Are Organizations Socially Responsible?

If organizations are to be socially responsible to stakeholders, what are they to be socially responsible for? Well, companies can best benefit their stakeholders by fulfilling their economic, legal, ethical, and discretionary responsibilities. Economic and legal responsibilities play a larger part in a company's social responsibility than do ethical and discretionary responsibilities. However, the relative importance of these various responsibilities depends on society's expectations of corporate social responsibility at a particular point in time.[55] A century ago, society expected businesses to meet their economic and legal responsibilities and little else. Today, when society judges whether businesses are socially responsible, ethical and discretionary responsibilities are considerably more important than they used to be.

Historically, **economic responsibility,** making a profit by producing a product or service valued by society, has been a business's most basic social responsibility. Organizations that don't meet their financial and economic expectations come under tremendous pressure. For example, company boards are very, very quick these days to fire CEOs. CEOs are three times more likely to be fired today than two decades ago. Typically, all it takes is two or three bad quarters in a row. William Rollnick, who became acting chairman of Mattel after the company fired its previous CEO, says, "There's zero forgiveness. You screw up and you're dead."[56] Indeed, in both Europe and the United States, nearly one-third of all CEOs are fired because of their inability to successfully change their companies.[57]

Legal responsibility is a company's social responsibility to obey society's laws and regulations as it tries to meet its economic responsibilities. For example, various municipalities across Ontario have adopted anti-drive-through ordinances in response to environmental concerns over emissions generated by vehicles using drive-throughs. These bans pose a challenge for businesses with drive-throughs. One of these is TDL, the parent company of Tim Hortons, which responded by commissioning a study that

Economic responsibility the expectation that a company will make a profit by producing a valued product or service

Legal responsibility a company's social responsibility to obey society's laws and regulations

To Give or Not to Give?

Following the devastating earthquake in Haiti in 2010, many Canadian companies and organizations were quick to donate supplies, services, and funds to help with what was a staggering loss to a country ill-equipped to deal with such a monumental natural disaster. However, a recent poll of Canadian executives by Compas Inc. suggests that there are varying views regarding what a company's role should be in terms of charitable donations. Of those polled, 45 percent expressed their belief that charitable donations should be at the discretion of the individual shareholder. "Public corporations should leave it to the shareholders to give to charities," one CEO argued. Also, 35 percent of those polled believed that corporations should indeed support charitable causes. "Being a good corporate citizen means assisting those less fortunate—as long as it is done in the context of the entities' aims, objectives, and employees' desires," said another executive. When selecting a charity to support, executives valued efficiency and honesty, wanting to be assured that the donation would actually reach the intended recipients. In addition, local charities that benefit the surrounding community were preferred over those that were geographically far away. When asked whether they were in favour of encouraging employees to contribute to charities, the executives were split: 45 percent were in favour, 34% opposed.

Source: J. Nelson, "A Corporate Responsibility," *Canadian Business*, 1 March 2010, page 19.

Steve Russell/GetStock.com

Shane Link/iStockphoto.com

concluded that drive-throughs actually generate fewer vehicle emissions than parking lots. Tim Hortons cannot afford to walk away from this legal issue, considering that drive-throughs make up 50 percent of the company's revenue. TDL has succeeded in fighting restrictions in several Ontario cities; in Kingston, Ontario, however, the city planning committee prohibited the building of any new drive-throughs in the city's historic downtown core.[58]

Ethical responsibility is a company's social responsibility not to violate accepted principles of right and wrong when conducting its business. For example, most people believe that KFC was wrong to run ads implying that its fried chicken was good for you and could help you lose weight. In one ad, one friend said to another, "Is that you? Man you look fantastic! What the heck you been doin'?" With his mouth full, the friend says, "Eatin' chicken." A voice-over then says, "So if you're watching carbs and going high protein, go KFC!" Two of KFC's fried chicken breasts, however, contain 780 calories and 38 grams of fat. Michael Jacobsen, executive director of the Center for Science in the Public Interest, says "These ads take the truth, dip it in batter and deep-fry it. Colonel Sanders himself would have a hard time swallowing this ad campaign."[59] After running the ads for a brief time, KFC quietly pulled them.

Discretionary responsibilities pertain to the social roles that businesses play in society beyond their economic, legal, and ethical responsibilities. Discretionary responsibilities are voluntary and can be undertaken by large, multinational corporations as well as by small businesses. For example, MasterCard and its cardholders have teamed up with Canadian organizations such as the Juvenile Diabetes Research Foundation, the Ontario Soccer Association, and Scouts Canada, to support research, minor soccer, and the scouting movement respectively. Every time someone uses a MasterCard to make a purchase, MasterCard donates a small portion of that purchase to its designated partners.[60] At the opposite end of the spectrum, Bargains Group, a small, Toronto-based company that sources discounted clothing for resale to retailers, uses industry contacts and suppliers to donate sleeping bags and survival kits for street people, toys for the Salvation Army, and emergency supplies for victims of natural disasters.[61] Discretionary responsibilities such as these are voluntary. Companies are not considered unethical if they don't perform them. Today, however, corporate stakeholders expect companies to do much more than in the past to meet their discretionary responsibilities.

7 Responses to Demands for Social Responsibility

Social responsiveness refers to a company's strategy for responding to stakeholders' economic, legal, ethical, or discretionary expectations concerning social responsibility. A social responsibility problem exists whenever company actions do not meet stakeholder expectations. One model of social responsiveness identifies four strategies for responding to social responsibility problems: reactive, defensive, accommodative, and proactive. These strategies differ in the extent to which the company is willing to act to meet or exceed society's expectations.

A company using a **reactive strategy** will do less than society expects. It may deny responsibility for a problem or fight any suggestions that the company should solve a problem. By contrast, a company using a **defensive strategy** would admit responsibility for a problem but would do the least required to meet societal expectations. Second Chance Body Armor

---

Ethical responsibility a company's social responsibility not to violate accepted principles of right and wrong when conducting its business

Discretionary responsibility the expectation that a company will voluntarily serve a social role beyond its economic, legal, and ethical responsibilities

Social responsiveness refers to a company's strategy for responding to stakeholders' economic, legal, ethical, or discretionary expectations concerning social responsibility

Reactive strategy a social responsiveness strategy in which a company does less than society expects

Defensive strategy a social responsiveness strategy in which a company admits responsibility for a problem but does the least required to meet societal expectations

makes bulletproof vests for police officers. According to company founder Richard Davis, tests indicated that the protective material in its vests deteriorated quickly under high temperatures and humidity, conditions under which they're typically used. As a result, Davis concluded that even vests that were only two years old were potentially unsafe. Nevertheless, he couldn't convince the company's executive committee to recall the vests (an accommodative strategy). Davis says he told the committee that it had three choices: recall the vests and stop selling them, do nothing and wait "until a customer is injured or killed," or wait until the problem becomes public and "be forced to make excuses as to why we didn't recognize and correct the problem."[62] After two vests were pierced by bullets, killing one police officer and wounding another, Second Chance announced that it would fix or replace 130,000 potentially defective vests. Although the company finally admitted responsibility for the problem, management decided to do only the minimum of what society expects (fix a defective product). Second Chance, therefore, used a defensive strategy.

A company using an **accommodative strategy** will accept responsibility for a problem and take a progressive approach by doing all that could be expected to solve the problem. For example, after a recall of millions of toys by Mattel Inc. in 2007, the Walt Disney Company announced it was going to begin independently testing toys featuring its characters. Disney hired companies to make random purchases of Disney-branded toys at retailers across the country to test for safety issues relating to small parts and the use of potentially hazardous lead paint. Disney also started requiring licensees to submit their own test results, and it increased staffing in its Product Integrity Office.[63]

Finally, a company using a **proactive strategy** will anticipate responsibility for a problem before it occurs, do more than expected to address the problem, and lead the industry in its approach. Honda Motors announced that it would include side-curtain air bags (that drop from the roof and protect passengers' heads) and front-side air bags (that come out of the door to protect against side-impact collisions) as standard equipment on all of its cars. Although more expensive car brands, such as Lexus and Volvo, already included these safety features, Honda was the first to make them standard on all models. Exhibit 4.8 summarizes the discussion of social responsiveness.

© dpa/Landov

Exhibit 4.8

Social Responsiveness

Reactive	Defensive	Accommodative	Proactive
Fight all the way	Do only what is required	Be progressive	Lead the industry
Withdrawal	Public Relations Approach	Legal Approach	Bargaining	Problem Solving

DO NOTHING ←————————————————————→ DO MUCH

Source: A. B. Carroll, "A Three-Dimensional Conceptual Model of Corporate Performance," *Academy of Management Review*, 1979, Vol 4 497–505.

8 Social Responsibility and Economic Performance

One question that managers often ask is, "Does it pay to be socially responsible?" This particular topic has garnered a lot of attention in recent years as researchers from around the world study the relationship between corporate social responsibility (CSR) and economic performance. A report presented at the World Economic Forum suggests that indeed there is a positive relationship— a study of the 100 most sustainable public corporations showed they outperformed the Morgan Stanley Capital International index by 7.1 percent during a five-year period and by an

Accommodative strategy a social responsiveness strategy in which a company accepts responsibility for a problem and does all that society expects to solve that problem

Proactive strategy a social responsiveness strategy in which a company anticipates responsibility for a problem before it occurs and does more than society expects to address the problem

impressive 23 percent during 2005. Canadian companies on that list included Royal Bank of Canada, TransAlta, Enbridge, Sun Life Financial, and Alcan.[64] Canadians support socially responsible investments to the tune of over $54 billion, or 3.5 percent of the total Canadian mutual fund market. From 2006 to 2008, assets invested in socially responsible investments experienced a 21 percent increase.[65] Furthermore, the JANTZI index, which contains a portfolio of 60 CSR firms, consistently outperforms the Canadian stock market.[66] At the same time, critics have plenty of facts to indicate that social responsibility hurts economic performance. A U.S. study of 42 socially responsible mutual funds found that the CSR firms underperformed the Standard and Poor's 500 (an index of 500 stocks representative of the entire economy) by 8 percent.[67]

When it comes to social responsibility and economic performance, the reality is that being socially responsible can sometimes cost a company significantly. Boston-based Timberland closes the entire company for one day each year so that all of its 5,400 workers can spend the day working on charitable projects sponsored by the company. This commitment to giving back doesn't come cheap—closing down for one day costs Timberland $2 million.[68]

Nonetheless, sometimes it does pay to be socially responsible. Terracycle, a multinational company that produces organic fertilizer, has demonstrated its commitment to CSR since the company's inception. "In its early cash-strapped days, Terracycle realized it could package liquid fertilizer in used plastic pop bottles. It was a perfect solution—zero costs for inputs and good for the environment, too."[69] Socially responsible energy policy may be good for the environment *and* good for business.

A 2009 experiment concluded that consumers are willing to pay more for what they know to be ethically produced goods and that they will "punish" a company that produces unethically produced goods by either not purchasing their products or by doing so only at a substantial discount.[70] Nonetheless, although socially responsible behaviour may be the right thing to do, it does not guarantee profitability. Socially responsible companies experience the same ups and downs in economic performance that traditional businesses do. In the end, if company management chooses a proactivex or accommodative strategy toward social responsibility (rather than a defensive or reactive strategy), it should do so because it wants to benefit society and its corporate stakeholders, not because it expects a better financial return.

Givaga/Shutterstock

Visit **icanmgmt.com** to find the resources you need today!

Located at the back of the textbook are rip-out Chapter Review cards. Make sure you also go online to check out other tools that MGMT offers to help you successfully pass your course.

- Interactive Quizzes
- Key Terms Flashcards
- Audio Chapter Summaries
- PowerPoint Slides
- Interactive Games
- Crossword Puzzles
- "Reel to Reel" and "Biz Flix" videos
- Cases and Exercises

86% of Canadian students surveyed find PowerPoint notes a valuable way to help them study.

GET ONLINE

The easy-to-navigate website for **MGMT** offers guidance on key topics in **Principles of Management** in a variety of engaging formats. You have the opportunity to refine and check your understanding via interactive quizzes and flashcards. Videos and audio summaries provide inspiration for your own further exploration. And, in order to make **MGMT** an even better learning tool, we invite you to speak up about your experience with **MGMT** by completing a survey form and sending us your comments.

Get online and discover the following resources:
- Printable and Interactive PowerPoints
- Flashcards
- Interactive Quizzing
- Crossword Puzzles

"I think this book is awesome for students of all ages. It is a much simpler way to study."

—Yasmine Al-Hashimi, Fanshawe College

Visit **icanmgmt.com** to find the resources you need today!

PLANNING AND DECISION MAKING

Even inexperienced managers know that planning and decision making are central parts of their jobs. Figure out what the problem is. Generate potential solutions or plans. Pick the best one. Make it work. Experienced managers, however, know how hard it really is to make good plans and decisions. One seasoned manager says: "I think the biggest surprises are the problems. Maybe I had never seen it before. Maybe I was protected by my management when I was in sales. Maybe I had delusions of grandeur, I don't know. I just know how disillusioning and frustrating it is to be hit with problems and conflicts all day and not be able to solve them very cleanly."[1]

Planning

Planning is choosing a goal and developing a method or strategy to achieve that goal. In the face of tougher regulations and an industry-wide reputation for purveying junk food, General Mills sought to have 20 percent of its products meet nutrition standards. To accomplish this goal, the company had to shift its strategy from products that would be popular in the short-term to those that would meet more long-range goals. Managers had to adapt old products and develop new ones that were higher in whole grains and lower in sugar and salt and that would encourage people to eat their vegetables. Setting clear standards for nutritional value and tying annual executive bonuses to achievement of these goals helped General Mills meet

Planning choosing a goal and developing a strategy to achieve that goal

Learning Outcomes

1 discuss the benefits and pitfalls of planning.

2 describe how to make a plan that works.

3 discuss how companies can use plans at all management levels, from top to bottom.

4 explain the steps and limits to rational decision making.

5 explain how group decisions and group decision-making techniques can improve decision making.

© matka_Wariatka/Shutterstock

its goal by 2006. At the end of fiscal year 2008, the company was already well on its way to the next goal: 40 percent of products meeting nutrition standards by 2010. And this with $12.4 billion in annual sales.[2]

After reading the next three sections, you should be able to

1   discuss the benefits and pitfalls of planning.

2   describe how to make a plan that works.

3   discuss how companies can use plans at all management levels, from top to bottom.

1 Benefits and Pitfalls of Planning

Are you one of those naturally organized people who always make a daily to-do list and never miss a deadline? Or are you one of those flexible, creative, go-with-the-flow people who dislike planning because it restricts their freedom? Some people are natural planners. They love it and can see only its benefits. Others dislike planning and can see only its disadvantages. It turns out that *both* views have real value.

*Planning has advantages and disadvantages. Let's learn about **1.1 the benefits** and **1.2 the pitfalls of planning**.*

1.1 Benefits of Planning

Planning offers four important benefits: intensified effort, persistence, direction, and creation of task strategies.[3] First, managers and employees put forth greater effort when following a plan. Take two workers. Instruct one to "do your best" to increase production. Instruct the other to achieve a 2 percent increase in production each month. Research shows that the one with the specific plan will work harder.[4]

Second, planning leads to persistence, that is, working hard for long periods. In fact, planning encourages persistence even when there may be little chance of short-term success.[5] Canadian golfer Mike Weir knows how important hard work and persistence are to achieving success. He has eight PGA tour victories under his belt, including a Masters championship in 2003, and has recently been inducted into the Canadian Golf Hall of Fame. His success in golf has a lot to do with his dedication and his long hours of practice. He started his regimen when he was young and has continued it into adulthood. As a child, Mike would spend entire summer days playing at the neighbourhood golf course. He would also hit balls into a driving net his parents set up in their garage. He would even practise at the local beach, hitting golf balls over frozen Lake Huron. "I was out there all the time," he says, "that's where I wanted to be."[6]

The third benefit of planning is direction. Plans encourage managers and employees to direct their persistent efforts *toward* activities that help accomplish their goals and *away* from activities that don't.[7] The fourth benefit of planning is that it encourages the development of task strategies. In other words, planning not only encourages people to work hard for extended periods and to engage in behaviours directly related to goal accomplishment, but also encourages them to think of better ways to do their jobs. Finally, perhaps the most compelling benefit of planning is that it has been proven to work for both companies and individuals. On average, companies with plans have larger profits and grow much faster than companies that don't.[8] The same holds true for individual managers and employees: There is no better way to improve the performance of the people who work in a company than to have them set goals and develop strategies for achieving those goals.

1.2 Planning Pitfalls

Despite the significant benefits associated with planning, it is not a cure-all. Plans won't fix all organizational problems. In fact, many management authors and consultants believe that planning can harm companies in several ways.[9]

The first pitfall of planning is that it can impede change and prevent or slow needed adaptation. Sometimes companies become so committed to achieving the goals set forth in their plans or following the strategies and tactics spelled out in them that they fail to notice when their plans aren't working or their goals need to change. When it comes to environmentally sound cars, General Motors may have missed the boat because of its "culture wedded to big cars and horsepower." GM developed experimental technology for an electric car in 2003, but dropped the project,

> **DESPITE THE SIGNIFICANT BENEFITS ASSOCIATED WITH PLANNING, PLANNING IS NOT A CURE-ALL.**

Planning . . .

Working for you by:
- intensifying effort
- increasing persistence
- providing direction
- creating task strategies

Working against you by:
- impeding change
- creating a false sense of certainty
- allowing planners to plan things they don't understand how to accomplish

© Mikhail Solovev/iStockphoto.com

electing to continue with its strategy of selling SUVs and fighting government fuel restrictions. Meanwhile, oil prices rose drastically, restrictions were tightened, and Toyota developed its popular Prius. Although Toyota formed its "green group" in the mid-1990s, GM only established its group dedicated to developing hybrids and electrics in 2006. They have brought the electric car idea back, but slow adaptation to new circumstances has them racing to develop the technology they need to keep the company afloat and competitive.[10]

The second pitfall is that planning can create a false sense of certainty. Planners sometimes feel that they know exactly what the future holds for their competitors, their suppliers, and their companies. However, all plans are based on assumptions. "The price of gasoline will increase by 4 percent per year." "Exports will continue to rise." For plans to work, the assumptions on which they are based must hold true. If the assumptions turn out to be false, then the plans based on them are likely to fail.

The third potential pitfall of planning is the detachment of planners. In theory, strategic planners and top-level managers are supposed to focus on the big picture and not concern themselves with the details of implementation (that is, carrying out the plan). According to management professor Henry Mintzberg, detachment leads planners to plan for things they don't understand.[11] Plans are meant to be guidelines for action, not abstract theories. Consequently, planners need to be familiar with the daily details of their businesses if they are to produce plans that can work.

2 How to Make a Plan That Works

Planning is a double-edged sword. If done right, planning brings about tremendous increases in individual and organizational performance. If planning is done wrong, however, it can have just the opposite effect and harm individual and organizational performance.

*In this section, you will learn how to make a plan that works. As depicted in Exhibit 5.1, planning consists of **2.1 setting goals, 2.2 developing commitment to the goals, 2.3 developing effective action plans, 2.4 tracking progress toward goal achievement,** and **2.5 maintaining flexibility in planning.***

Exhibit 5.1
How to Make a Plan That Works

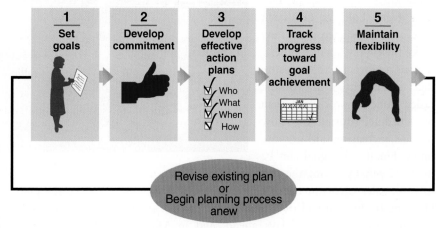

2.1 Setting Goals

The first step in planning is to set goals. To direct behaviour and increase effort, goals need to be specific and challenging.[12] For example, deciding to "increase sales this year" won't direct and energize workers as much as deciding to "increase North American sales by 4 percent in the next six months." Specific, challenging goals provide a target for which to aim and a standard against which to measure success.

One way of writing effective goals for yourself, your job, or your company is to use the S.M.A.R.T. guidelines. **S.M.A.R.T. goals** are **S**pecific, **M**easurable, **A**ttainable, **R**ealistic, and **T**imely.[13] Let's see how a heating, ventilation, and air-conditioning (HVAC) company might use S.M.A.R.T. goals in its business.

The HVAC business is cyclical. It's extremely busy at the beginning of summer when homeowners find that their air-conditioning isn't working, and at the beginning of winter, when furnaces and heat pumps need repair. During these times, most HVAC companies have more business than they can handle, while at other times of year their business can be very slow. So a *Specific* goal would be to increase sales by 50 percent during the fall and spring when business is slower. This goal could be *Measured* by keeping track of the number of annual maintenance contracts sold to customers. This goal of increasing sales during the off-seasons is *Attainable* because maintenance contracts typically include spring tune-ups (air-conditioning systems) and fall tune-ups (furnace or heating systems). Moreover, a 50 percent increase in sales during the slow seasons appears to

> **S.M.A.R.T. goals** goals that are specific, measurable, attainable, realistic, and timely

be *Realistic*. Because customers want their furnaces and air conditioners to work the first time it gets cold (or hot) each year, a well-designed pitch may make them very open to buying service contracts that ensure their equipment is in working order. Tune-up work can then be scheduled during the slow seasons, increasing sales at those times. Finally, this goal can be made *Timely* by asking the staff

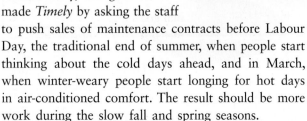

to push sales of maintenance contracts before Labour Day, the traditional end of summer, when people start thinking about the cold days ahead, and in March, when winter-weary people start longing for hot days in air-conditioned comfort. The result should be more work during the slow fall and spring seasons.

2.2 Developing Commitment to Goals

Just because a company sets a goal doesn't mean that people will try to accomplish it. If workers don't care about a goal, that goal won't encourage them to work harder or smarter. Thus, the second step in planning is to develop commitment to goals.[14]

Goal commitment is the determination to achieve a goal. Commitment to achieve a goal is not automatic. Managers and workers must choose to commit themselves to a goal. Facing a company-wide slowdown in revenue, the management at 1-800-GOT-JUNK, North America's largest junk removal franchise network, came up with a new business strategy for combating the recession, one that would allow the company to grow and become more sustainable in the future. The "100-Day Plan" was introduced with the clear expectation that the new strategy would be executed throughout the organization in 100 days. Brian Scudamore, founder and CEO of the company, explains that "having everyone moving with the same purpose in the same direction, we figured, would allow us to gain maximum momentum." "With only 100 days to execute," he added, "we had to be driving hard every single day."[15] Put another way, goal commitment is about really wanting to achieve a goal.

So how can managers bring about goal commitment? The most popular approach is to set goals collectively, as a team. At 1-800-GOT-JUNK, each franchisee was asked to set a revenue goal for the 100 Day Plan and to sign a commitment to that goal. Goals are more likely to be realistic and attainable when individuals participate in setting them. Another technique for gaining commitment to a goal is to make that goal public, as was the case at 1-800-GOT-JUNK. It held a company-wide conference call and Web presentation to introduce the plan, following that up with regular 100 Day Updates and a 100 Day Plan blog. Support from top management was also important and included providing funds, speaking publicly about the plan, and participating in the plan itself. At 1-800-GOT-JUNK, frequent communication from top management ensured that the plan was being adopted throughout the organization.[16]

2.3 Developing Effective Action Plans

The third step in planning is to develop effective action plans. An **action plan** lists the specific steps (how), people (who), resources (what), and time period (when) for accomplishing a goal. Unlike most CEOs, Randy Papadellis has a unique goal that requires an extraordinary action plan. As the CEO of Ocean Spray, Papadellis has to buy all of the cranberries that his farmers produce (Ocean Spray is a farmer cooperative). His goal must be to buy the crop at the highest possible price. So he needs to figure out an action plan for how to sell the entire crop of high-cost berries. He says, "Imagine if Pepsi had to maximize the aluminum it used, and at the highest price it could afford!" Under Papadellis's direction, Ocean Spray began looking for alternative uses for cranberries beyond the traditional

Ocean Spray has been able to increase the price it pays its farmers over 100 percent in the past 3 years.

Goal commitment the determination to achieve a goal

Action plan the specific steps, people, and resources needed to accomplish a goal

Exhibit 5.2

Effects of Goal Setting, Training, and Feedback on Safe Behaviour in a Bread Factory

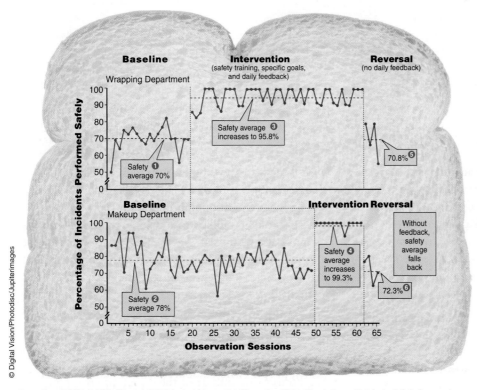

Source: Komaki, J., Barwick K. D., & Scott, L. R., "A Behavioural Approach to Occupational Safety: Pinpointing and Reinforcing Safe Performance in a Food Manufacturing Plant." *Journal of Applied Psychology* 63, (1978).

juice and canned products, uses that would involve new methods, people, and resources. The company invented dried-fruit Craisins by reinfusing juice into husks that used to be thrown away. Craisins have grown into a $100 million product line. Ocean Spray also developed a set of light drinks that had just 40 calories, as well as mock berries that could be infused with other flavours (blueberry, strawberry, etc.) and used in muffins and cereals. And it was the first company to introduce juice

boxes. Because of these effective actions, Ocean Spray has been able to increase the price it pays its farmers over 100 percent in the past three years.[17]

2.4 Tracking Progress

The fourth step in planning is to track progress toward goal achievement. There are two accepted methods of tracking progress. The first is to set proximal goals and distal goals. **Proximal goals** are short-term goals or subgoals, whereas **distal goals** are long-term or primary goals.[18] The idea behind setting proximal goals is that achieving them may be more motivating and rewarding than waiting to reach far-off distal goals. Proximal goals are less intimidating and more attainable than distal goals, which often feel like biting off more than you can chew. Proximal goals enable you to achieve a distal goal one little piece at a time.

The second method of tracking progress is to gather and provide performance feedback. Regular, frequent performance feedback allows workers and managers to track their progress toward goal achievement and make adjustments in effort, direction, and strategies.[19] Proper action on performance feedback can keep you from failing to adapt, one of the pitfalls of planning. Exhibit 5.2 shows the impact of feedback on safety behaviour at a large bakery company. During the baseline period, workers in the wrapping department, who measure and mix ingredients, roll the bread dough, and put it into baking pans, performed their jobs safely about 70 percent of the time (see dialogue box 1 in Exhibit 5.2). The baseline safety record for workers in the makeup department, who bag and seal baked bread and assemble, pack, and tape cardboard cartons for shipping, was somewhat better at 78 percent (see dialogue box 2). The company gave workers 30 minutes of safety training, set a goal of 90 percent safe behaviour, and then provided daily feedback (such as a chart similar to Exhibit 5.2). Performance

Proximal goals short-term goals or subgoals

Distal goals long-term or primary goals

Chapter 5: Planning and Decision Making

improved dramatically. During the intervention period, safely-performed behaviours rose to an average of 95.8 percent for wrapping workers (see dialogue box 3) and 99.3 percent for workers in the makeup department (see dialogue box 4), and never fell below 83 percent. In this instance, the combination of training, a challenging goal, and feedback led to a dramatic increase in performance.

The importance of feedback can be seen in the reversal stage, when the company quit posting daily feedback on safe behaviour. Without daily feedback, the percentage of safely-performed behaviour returned to baseline levels, 70.8 percent for the wrapping department (see dialogue box 5) and 72.3 percent for the makeup department (see dialogue box 6). For planning to be effective, workers need both a specific, challenging goal and regular feedback to track their progress. Indeed, further research indicates that the effectiveness of goal setting can be doubled by the addition of feedback.[20]

2.5 Maintaining Flexibility

Because action plans are sometimes poorly conceived and goals sometimes turn out not to be achievable, the last step in developing an effective plan is to maintain flexibility. One method of maintaining flexibility while planning is to adopt an options-based approach.[21] The goal of **options-based planning** is to keep options open by making small, simultaneous investments in many alternative plans. Then, when one or a few of these plans emerge as likely winners, you invest even more in these plans while discontinuing or reducing investment in the others. In part, options-based planning is the opposite of traditional planning. Whereas the purpose of an action plan is to commit people and resources to a particular course of action, the purpose of options-based planning is to leave those commitments open

Options-based planning maintaining flexibility by making small, simultaneous investments in many alternative plans

Slack resources a cushion of extra resources that can be used with options-based planning to adapt to unanticipated change, problems, or opportunities

Strategic plans overall company plans that clarify how the company will serve customers and position itself against competitors over the next two to five years

Vision statement a statement of a company's purpose and the ultimate destination it hopes to reach, acting as a guide to individuals in an organization.

Exhibit 5.3

Planning from Top to Bottom

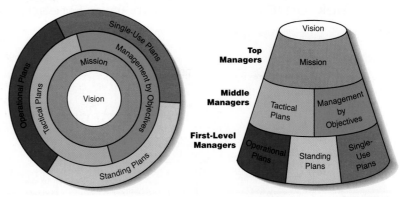

by maintaining **slack resources,** that is, a cushion of resources such as extra time, people, money, or production capacity, that can be used to address and adapt to unanticipated changes, problems, or opportunities.[22] Holding options open gives you choices. And choices, combined with slack resources, give you flexibility.

3 Planning from Top to Bottom

Planning works best when the goals and action plans at the bottom and middle of the organization support the goals and action plans at the top of the organization. In other words, planning works best when everybody pulls in the same direction. Exhibit 5.3 illustrates this planning continuity, beginning at the top with a clear definition of the company vision and ending at the bottom with the execution of operational plans.

Let's see how **3.1 top managers create the organizational vision and mission, 3.2 middle managers develop tactical plans and use management by objectives to motivate employee efforts toward the overall vision and mission, and 3.3 first-level managers use operational, single-use, and standing plans to implement the tactical plans.**

3.1 Starting at the Top

Top management is responsible for developing long-term **strategic plans** that make clear how the company will serve customers and position itself against competitors in the next two to five years. Strategic planning begins with the creation of an organizational vision or mission.

A **vision statement** is a statement of a company's purpose and the ultimate destination it hopes to reach. It serves as a guide to individuals in an organization. A vision statement should be brief—no more than two sentences—and should also be enduring, inspirational,

Dreams on the Back of a Napkin

Company mission statements are often a source of frustration for members of a committee charged with writing one. Employees often read a cliché mission statement like "We continually revolutionize business data to allow us to quickly integrate unique solutions to stay competitive in tomorrow's world" with glazed eyes. Such documents often get shoved in a drawer and make little impact on how people work. The process of plugging nouns and verbs into a formula, combined with a desire for it to be all-encompassing, can make a mission statement uninspiring and meaningless. According to Carmine Gallo, what makes a real difference in the work of an organization is not a bulky mission statement, but a concise and inspiring vision that can fit on the back of a napkin. It'll stick. It'll inspire members of the organization to be creative, and it'll motivate them to invest their energies into a shared dream.

Source: Gallo, C., "The Napkin Test; Why it's time to replace your company's bulky mission statement with a vision concise enough to fit on the back of a napkin." *BusinessWeek Online*, 10 December 2007, available online at http://www.business-week.com/smallbiz/content/dec2007/sb2007127_010305.htm?chan=search [accessed 28 July 2008].

© iStockphoto.com/Chad McDermott

clear, and consistent with widely shared company beliefs and values. An example: "To be the No. 1 executive recruiter in B.C." Another, in this case Google's: "To organize the world's information and make it universally accessible and useful."[23]

An organization's mission, which should flow from its vision, is about how the organization plans to get there—in other words, how it plans to achieve its vision. To define the mission, a formal **mission statement** can be developed to provide a broad statement of an organization's purpose that distinguishes it from others of a similar type.[24] A mission statement can be an effective way to inspire employees and create shared values. For example, here is the mission statement for Starbucks: "To inspire and nurture the human spirit—one person, one cup and one neighbourhood at a time." That statement guides everyone in the organization and provides a focal point for the delivery of the company's products to its customers around the world. Even though regional differences are integrated into the company's strategy across the globe, the vision is the same whether Starbucks is selling its Assam black tea latte in Tokyo, its lemon poppy muffin in Moscow, or its iced caffe latte in Edmonton. The Starbucks vision is clear, inspirational, and consistent with the company's values and principles, which are meant to guide the organization on a day-to-day basis.[25] Other examples of organizational visions include these: yoga-inspired athletic apparel company lululemon's "creating components for people to live a longer, healthier, more fun life," and the Royal Canadian Legion's "to serve veterans and their dependants, promote remembrance and act in the service of Canada and its communities."[26]

3.2 Bending in the Middle

Middle management is responsible for developing and carrying out tactical plans to accomplish the organization's mission. **Tactical plans** specify how a company will use resources, budgets, and people to accomplish specific goals within its mission. Whereas strategic plans and objectives are used to focus company efforts over the next two to five years, tactical plans and objectives are used to direct behaviour, efforts, and attention over the next six months to two years. For example, two weeks before the official launch of Magnotta Wines, the company learned that the Liquor Control Board of Ontario (LCBO), the only retail distribution outlet for wine in Ontario, did not have any shelf space available for the fledgling winery. To continue with the company's mission, the company put an emergency plan in place that included selling its wines on-site at its winery for $3.95 a bottle—a considerably lower price than comparable wines sold at the LCBO. The company's tactical plans succeeded, garnering the winery valuable media and consumer attention—key elements needed to succeed in this competitive industry. As a result, Magnotta Wines was able to grow and expand its market, eventually establishing distributorships across Canada and international exports to the United States, Taiwan, and China. It is now Ontario's third largest winery in volume sales.[27]

Management by objectives is a management

Mission statement a broad statement of an organization's purpose that distinguishes the organization from others of a similar type.

Tactical plans plans created and implemented by middle managers that specify how the company will use resources, budgets, and people over the next six months to two years to accomplish specific goals within its mission

technique often used to develop and carry out tactical plans. **Management by objectives,** or MBO, is a four-step process in which managers and their employees (1) discuss possible goals; (2) collectively select goals that are challenging, attainable, and consistent with the company's overall goals; (3) jointly develop tactical plans that lead to the accomplishment of tactical goals and objectives; and (4) meet regularly to review progress toward accomplishment of those goals.

3.3 Finishing at the Bottom

Lower-level managers are responsible for developing and carrying out **operational plans,** which are the day-to-day plans for producing or delivering the organization's products and services. Operational plans direct the behaviour, efforts, and priorities of operative employees for periods ranging from 30 days to six months. There are three kinds of operational plans: single-use plans, standing plans, and budgets.

Single-use plans deal with unique, one-time-only events. For example, when the new owners of Alberta-based Blue Falls Manufacturing, a maker of portable hot tubs and spas, took over the company they quickly found out that there was no inventory control system to identify component parts needed to service older hot tub models that had been sold to customers and dealers. There were over 1,100 components that didn't have part numbers, and searching for parts became a frustrating exercise; it sometimes took hours to find which part was needed for a particular model. So the company came up with a plan for an inventory system that would allow it to catalogue each piece of equipment for almost every model built since the company began in the late 1980s. Although time consuming, this plan allowed it to continue servicing its network of existing customers and dealers; it also established a process by which subsequent hot tub models and components could be tracked.[28]

Unlike single-use plans that are created, carried out, and then never used again, **standing plans** can be used repeatedly to handle frequently recurring events. If you encounter a problem that you've seen before, someone in your company has probably written a standing plan that explains how to address it. Using this plan rather than reinventing the wheel will save you time. There are three kinds of standing plans: policies, procedures, and rules and regulations.

Policies indicate the general course of action that company managers should take in response to a particular event or situation. A well-written policy will also specify why the policy exists and what outcome the policy is intended to produce. Concerns surrounding the amount of time employees spend surfing the Internet while at work, as well as fears about computer virus attacks, have prompted many organizations to develop policies for managing Internet use. A 2007 study reports that in Canada, 61 percent of companies monitor the Web surfing of their employees; that 34 percent of the companies surveyed have corporate policies to define acceptable Web browsing; and that 18 percent have guidelines in place, as well as software that effectively blocks access to non-work-related websites and to sites with inappropriate content.[29] A 2000 Angus Reid poll found that Canadian workers spend an average of eight hours a day online at work, and of that, at least two hours is spent on non-work-related matters.[30] Chaparral Energy, an oil and gas company, switched to software that blocks access to religious, political, and sexually oriented websites and saw its employee Web surfing times drop to less than 15 minutes a day compared to an hour a day.[31]

Procedures are more specific than policies because they indicate the series of steps that should be taken in response to a particular event. A manufacturer's procedure for handling defective products might include the following steps. Step 1: Rejected material is locked in a secure area with "reject" documentation attached. Step 2: Material Review Board (MRB) identifies the defect and how far outside the standard the rejected products are. Step 3: MRB determines the disposition of the defective product as either scrap or as rework. Step 4: Scrap is either discarded or recycled, and rework is sent back through the production line to be fixed. Step 5: If delays in delivery will result, MRB member notifies customer.[32]

Rules and regulations are even more specific than procedures because they specify what must or must not

Management by objectives (MBO) a four-step process in which managers and employees discuss and select goals, develop tactical plans, and meet regularly to review progress toward goal accomplishment

Operational plans day-to-day plans, developed and implemented by lower-level managers, for producing or delivering the organization's products and services over a 30-day to six-month period

Single-use plans plans that cover unique, one-time-only events

Standing plans plans used repeatedly to handle frequently recurring events

Policy a standing plan that indicates the general course of action that should be taken in response to a particular event or situation

Procedure a standing plan that indicates the specific steps that should be taken in response to a particular event

Rules and regulations standing plans that describe how a particular action should be performed or what must happen or not happen in response to a particular event

happen. They describe precisely how a particular action should be performed. For instance, many companies have rules and regulations forbidding managers from writing job reference letters for employees who have worked at their firms because a negative reference may prompt a former employee to sue for defamation of character.[33]

After single-use plans and standing plans, budgets are the third kind of operational plan. **Budgeting** is quantitative planning because it forces managers to decide how to allocate available money to best accomplish company goals. According to Jan King, author of *Business Plans to Game Plans,* "Money sends a clear message about your priorities. Budgets act as a language for communicating your goals to others."

What Is Rational Decision Making?

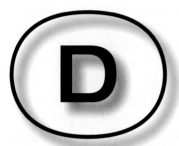

Decision making is the process of choosing a solution from available alternatives.[34] **Rational decision making** is a systematic process in which managers define problems, evaluate alternatives, and choose optimal solutions that provide maximum benefits to their organizations.

After reading the next two sections, you should be able to

4 explain the steps and limits to rational decision making.

5 explain how group decisions and group decision-making techniques can improve decision making.

Steps of the Rational Decision-Making Process

1. Define the Problem
2. Identify Decision Criteria
3. Weight the Criteria
4. Generate Alternative Courses of Action
5. Evaluate Each Alternative
6. Compute the Optimal Decision

4 Steps and Limits to Rational Decision Making

There are six steps in the rational decision-making process: 4.1 define the problem, 4.2 identify decision criteria, 4.3 weight the criteria, 4.4 generate alternative courses of action, 4.5 evaluate each alternative, and 4.6 compute the optimal decision. Then we'll consider 4.7 limits to rational decision making.

4.1 Define the Problem

The first step in decision making is to identify and define the problem. A **problem** exists when there is a gap between a desired state (what is wanted) and an existing state (the situation you are actually facing). Women want to look good and feel comfortable in clothes that fit properly, but sizes are not universal. There are no industry standards, which means it's hard for a woman to know her size as she could in the past. Today's sizes vary from brand to brand and don't take into account body type. As a result, women either leave the store without purchasing anything because they can't find a perfect fit, or purchase an imperfectly fitting garment, discard it after a couple of wears, and decide not to buy the brand again. Either way, garment companies lose customers.

The presence of a gap between an existing state and a desired state is no guarantee that managers will make decisions to solve

Photo credit: © Brian Hagiwara/Brand X Pictures/Jupiterimages

Budgeting quantitative planning through which managers decide how to allocate available money to best accomplish company goals

Decision making the process of choosing a solution from available alternatives

Rational decision making a systematic process of defining problems, evaluating alternatives, and choosing optimal solutions

Problem a gap between a desired state and an existing state

problems. Two things must occur for this to happen.[35] First, managers have to be aware of the gap. But that isn't enough. Managers also have to be motivated to reduce the gap. In other words, managers have to know there is a problem and *want* to solve it. Finally, it's not enough to be aware of a problem and be motivated to solve it. Managers must also have the knowledge, skills, abilities, and resources to fix the problem. Cricket Lee has tried to solve the sizing problem in the women's clothing industry by developing Fitlogic, a simple sizing standard that takes account of body type and is not intimidating for larger women. Although she lacked name recognition, she recruited help in licensing her system to Jones Apparel for one line of pants sold on a home shopping network. She has so far met with limited success in selling Fitlogic, but has influenced the industry as more companies start accounting for body shape, as Banana Republic does by assigning different names to pants with different fit.[36]

4.2 Identify Decision Criteria

Decision criteria are the standards used to guide judgments and decisions. Typically, the more criteria a potential solution meets, the better that solution will be.

Imagine that your boss asks for a recommendation on outfitting the sales force, many of whom travel regularly, with new computers. What general factors would be important when purchasing these computers? Reliability, price, warranty, on-site service, and compatibility with existing software, printers, and computers would all be important, but you must also consider the technical details. With technology changing so quickly, you'll probably want to buy laptops with as much capability and flexibility as you can afford. What are your options? Well, laptops come in four distinct model types. There are budget models that are good for routine office work but are usually saddled with a slower processor; workhorse models that are not lightweight, but have everything included; slim models for traveling but that usually require an external drive to read/write to a DVD/CD; and tablet models that include extra features like handwriting-recognition software.[37] But what will the sales force really need? Will they need to burn CDs and DVDs or just read them? How much

Decision criteria the standards used to guide judgments and decisions

Absolute comparisons a process in which each criterion is compared to a standard or ranked on its own merits

memory will the users need? How many files and programs will they need to store on their hard drives? Answering questions like these will help you identify the criteria that will guide the purchase of the new equipment.

4.3 Weight the Criteria

After identifying decision criteria, the next step is deciding which criteria are more or less important. Although there are numerous mathematical models for weighting decision criteria, all require the decision maker to provide an initial ranking of the criteria. Some use **absolute comparisons,** in which each criterion is compared to a standard or ranked on its own merits. Someone who would like to purchase a new car might consider the following criteria: predicted reliability, previous owners' satisfaction, predicted depreciation (the price you could expect if you sold the car), ability to avoid an accident, fuel economy, crash protection, acceleration, ride, and front seat comfort.

Different individuals will rank these criteria differently, depending on what they value or require in a car. Exhibit 5.4 shows the absolute weights that someone buying a car might use. Because these weights are absolute, each criterion is judged on its own importance, using a five-point scale, with "5" representing "critically important" and "1" representing "completely unimportant." In this instance, predicted reliability,

Exhibit 5.4

Absolute Weighting of Decision Criteria for a Car Purchase

5 critically important				
4 important				
3 somewhat important				
2 not very important				
1 completely unimportant				

	1	2	3	4	5
1. Predicted reliability	1	2	3	4	(5)
2. Owner satisfaction	1	(2)	3	4	5
3. Predicted depreciation	(1)	2	3	4	5
4. Avoiding accidents	1	2	3	(4)	5
5. Fuel economy	1	2	3	4	(5)
6. Crash protection	1	2	3	(4)	5
7. Acceleration	(1)	2	3	4	5
8. Ride	1	2	(3)	4	5
9. Front seat comfort	1	2	3	4	(5)

Exhibit 5.5

Relative Comparison of Home Characteristics

Home Characteristics	L	PS	IP	RR	QS	NBH
Daily commute (L)		+1	−1	−1	−1	0
Proximity to schools (PS)	−1		−1	−1	−1	−1
Inground pool (IP)	+1	+1		0	0	+1
Recreation room (RR)	+1	+1	0		0	0
Quiet street (QS)	+1	+1	0	0		0
Newly built house (NBH)	0	+1	−1	0	0	
Total weight	+2	+5	−3	−2	−2	0

fuel economy, and front seat comfort were rated most important, and acceleration and predicted depreciation were rated least important.

Another method uses **relative comparisons,** in which each criterion is compared directly to every other criterion.[38] Exhibit 5.5 shows six criteria that someone might use when buying a house. Moving across the first row, we see that the time of the daily commute has been rated more important (+1) than proximity to schools; less important (−1) than having an inground pool, recreation room, or a quiet street, and just as important as the house being brand new (0). Total weights, which are obtained by summing the scores in each column, indicate that the daily commute and proximity to schools are the most important factors to this home buyer, whereas an inground pool, recreation room, and a quiet street are the least important.

4.4 Generate Alternative Courses of Action

After identifying and weighting the criteria that will guide the decision-making process, the next step is to identify possible courses of action that could solve the problem. The idea is to generate as many alternatives as possible. Let's assume that you're trying to select a city in Europe to be the location of a major office. After meeting with your staff, you generate a list of possible alternatives: Amsterdam, the Netherlands; Barcelona or Madrid, Spain; Berlin or Frankfurt, Germany; Brussels, Belgium; London, England; Milan, Italy; Paris, France; and Zurich, Switzerland.

4.5 Evaluate Each Alternative

The next step is to systematically evaluate each alternative against each criterion. Because of the amount of information that must be collected, this step can take

much longer and be much more expensive than other steps in the decision-making process. When selecting a European city for your office, you could contact economic development offices in each city, systematically interview businesspeople or executives who operate there, retrieve and use published government data on each location, or rely on published studies such as Cushman & Wakefield's *European Cities Monitor,* which conducts an annual survey of more than 500 senior European executives who rate 33 European cities on 12 business-related criteria.[39]

No matter how you gather the information, the key is to use that information to systematically evaluate each alternative against each criterion once you have it. Exhibit 5.6 on the next page shows how each of the 10 cities on your staff's list fared on each of the 12 criteria (higher scores are better), from qualified staff to freedom from pollution. Although London is the easiest place to get to and from work, it is also one of the most polluted cities on the list. Although telecommunications in Barcelona might not be optimal, that city offers your employees the highest quality of life. Paris offers excellent access to markets and clients, but if your staff is multilingual, Amsterdam may be a better choice.

4.6 Compute the Optimal Decision

The final step in the decision-making process is to compute the optimal decision by determining the optimal value of each alternative. This is done by multiplying the rating for each criterion (Step 4.5) by the weight for that criterion (Step 4.3), and then summing those scores

Relative comparisons
a process in which each criterion is compared directly to every other

Exhibit 5.6

Criteria Ratings Used to Determine the Best Locations for a New Office

	Qualified Staff	Access to Markets	Communications	Intercity Transport	Staff Cost	Languages	Government Climate	Office Value	Office Availability	Intracity Transport	Quality of Life	Pollution	Ranking
Weights	62%	58%	55%	52%	36%	29%	27%	26%	26%	24%	21%	16%	
Amsterdam	0.38	0.60	0.34	0.71	0.25	1.05	0.37	0.42	0.28	0.50	0.43	0.49	5
Barcelona	0.29	0.26	0.17	0.28	0.54	0.26	0.47	0.50	0.38	0.48	1.16	0.43	4
Berlin	0.41	0.30	0.56	0.24	0.30	0.39	0.36	0.63	0.75	0.64	0.36	0.24	8
Brussels	0.32	0.43	0.30	0.45	0.15	0.95	0.36	0.33	0.36	0.30	0.32	0.26	6
Frankfurt	0.54	0.65	0.61	1.04	0.18	0.51	0.16	0.26	0.38	0.32	0.12	0.17	3
London	1.44	1.41	1.39	1.75	0.13	1.41	0.60	0.28	0.57	1.20	0.40	0.08	1
Madrid	0.24	0.31	0.25	0.41	0.49	0.21	0.38	0.43	0.44	0.40	0.62	0.14	7
Milan	0.31	0.33	0.14	0.22	0.26	0.25	0.13	0.20	0.17	0.19	0.28	0.06	10
Paris	0.78	1.02	0.84	1.30	0.19	0.50	0.27	0.32	0.41	0.96	0.59	0.13	2
Zurich	0.27	0.19	0.22	0.24	0.04	0.50	0.42	0.10	0.18	0.37	0.48	0.72	13

Source: "European Cities Monitor 2007," Cushman & Wakefield, available at http://www.berlin-partner.de/fileadmin/chefredaktion/documents/pdf_Presse/European_Investment_Monitor_2007.pdf, accessed 2 October 2008.

for each alternative course of action that you generated (Step 4.4). The 500 executives participating in Cushman & Wakefield's survey of the best European cities for business rated the 12 decision criteria in terms of importance, as shown in the first line of Exhibit 5.6. Access to quality staff was deemed most important. Freedom from pollution, on the other hand, while a concern, was not high on the list of priorities. To calculate the optimal value for Paris, its score in each category is multiplied by the weight for each category (.78 x .62 in the qualified staff category, for example). Then all of these scores are added together to produce the optimal value, as follows:

$$(.78 \times .62) + (1.02 \times .58) + (.84 \times .55) +$$
$$(1.30 \times .52) + (.19 \times .36) + (.5 \times .29) +$$
$$(.27 \times .27) + (.32 \times .26) + (.41 \times .26) +$$
$$(.96 \times .24) + (.59 \times .21) + (.13 \times .16) = 3.06$$

Since London has a weighted average of 4.6 compared to 3.06 for Paris and 2.14 for Frankfurt, London clearly ranks as the best location for your company's new European office because of its large number of qualified staff; easy access to markets; outstanding ease of travel to, from, and within the city; excellent telecommunications; and top-notch business climate.

4.7 Limits to Rational Decision Making

In general, managers who diligently complete all six steps of the rational decision-making model will make better decisions than those who don't. So, when they can, managers should try to follow the steps in the rational decision-making model, especially for big decisions with long-range consequences.

And the winner is . . . London. When all the weights are calculated and compared, London is the best city in Europe for business.

To make perfect rational decisions, managers would have to operate in a perfect world with no real-world constraints. Of course, it never actually works like that in the real world. Managers face time and money constraints. They often don't have time to make extensive lists of decision criteria. And they often don't have the resources to test all possible solutions against all possible criteria.

In theory, fully rational decision makers **maximize** decisions by choosing the optimal solution. In practice, however, limited resources along with attention, memory, and expertise problems make it nearly impossible for managers to maximize decisions. Consequently, most managers don't maximize—they satisfice. Whereas maximizing is choosing the best alternative, **satisficing** is choosing a "good enough" alternative. In reality, however, the manager's limited time, money, and expertise mean that only a few alternatives will be assessed against a few decision criteria. In practice, the manager will visit two or three computer or electronic stores, read a few recent computer reviews, and get bids from Dell, Lenovo, Gateway, and Hewlett-Packard. The decision will be complete when the manager finds a good enough laptop computer that meets a few decision criteria.

Reasons Groups Are Better at Defining Problems and Generating Possible Solutions

1. Group members usually possess different knowledge, skills, abilities, and experiences, so groups are able to view problems from multiple perspectives. Being able to view problems from different perspectives, in turn, can help groups perform better on complex tasks and make better decisions than individuals.

2. Groups can find and access much more information than can individuals alone.

3. The increased knowledge and information available to groups make it easier for them to generate more alternative solutions. Studies show that generating lots of alternative solutions is critical to improving the quality of decisions.

4. If groups are involved in the decision-making process, group members will be more committed to making chosen solutions work.

Source: L. Pelled, K. Eisenhardt, and K. Xin, "Exploring the Black Box: An Analysis of Work Group Diversity, Conflict, and Performance," *Administrative Science Quarterly* 44, no. 1 (1 March 1999): 1.

5 Using Groups to Improve Decision Making

According to Blanchard's annual survey on corporate issues, 84 percent of companies use teams to handle special projects (i.e., to make decisions).[40] Why so many? When done properly, group decision making can lead to much better decisions than those typically made by individuals. In fact, numerous studies show that groups consistently outperform individuals on complex tasks.

*Let's explore the **5.1 advantages and pitfalls of group decision making** and the following group decision-making methods—**5.2 structured conflict, 5.3 the nominal group technique, 5.4 the Delphi technique.***

5.1 Advantages and Pitfalls of Group Decision Making

Groups can do a much better job than individuals in two important steps of the decision-making process: defining the problem and generating alternative solutions.

Still, group decision making is subject to some pitfalls that can quickly erase these gains. One possible pitfall is groupthink. **Groupthink** occurs in highly cohesive groups when group members feel intense pressure to agree with one another so that the group

can approve a proposed solution.[41] Because groupthink leads to consideration of a limited number of solutions and restricts discussion of any considered solutions, it usually results in poor decisions. Groupthink is most likely to occur under the following conditions:

- The group is insulated from others with different perspectives.
- The group leader begins by expressing a strong preference for a particular decision.
- The group has no established procedure for systematically defining problems and exploring alternatives.
- Group members have similar backgrounds and experiences.[42]

Groupthink is thought to have contributed to the explosion of the space shuttle *Columbia* in February 2003. Foam used to insulate the shuttle frequently causes damage to the wing during a shuttle's launch. When *Columbia* re-entered the atmosphere, wing damage allowed superhot gas to enter the wing, which caused the shuttle to explode. Previous shuttle missions made the possibility of this problem

Maximizing choosing the best alternative

Satisficing choosing a "good enough" alternative

Groupthink a barrier to good decision making caused by pressure within a group for members to agree with one another

Chapter 5: Planning and Decision Making

known, and damage on this particular mission was suspected. However, NASA's culture does not allow individuals to be wrong, and its dependence on public and political support for its existence can influence decisions in favour of keeping missions on schedule even when delay would allow such problems to be investigated. Managers were reluctant to be the first to point out the problem, and requests for satellite images of the damage to *Columbia* during flight were ignored. The result? Loss of lives and a negative reputation for NASA, consequences worse than those that would have resulted from a delay to investigate the problems.[43]

A second potential problem with group decision making is that it takes considerable time. Reconciling schedules so that group members can meet takes time. Furthermore, it's a rare group that consistently holds productive task-oriented meetings to work through the decision process effectively. Some of the most common complaints

the meeting should (5) discourage office politics and rely on data, and above all, they should (6) stick to the clock. Mayer's guidelines help meetings stay focused and productive.[44]

Strong-willed group members can constitute a third possible pitfall to group decision making. Such an individual, whether the boss or a vocal group member, dominates group discussion and puts limits on how the problem is defined and what the solutions can be. Another potential problem is the group members may not feel accountable for the decisions made and actions taken by the group unless they are personally responsible for some aspect of carrying out those decisions.

Although these pitfalls can lead to poor decision making, this doesn't mean that managers should avoid using groups to make decisions.

Photos.com

WHEN DONE PROPERLY, GROUP DECISION MAKING CAN LEAD TO MUCH BETTER DECISIONS.

about meetings (and thus decision making) are that the meeting's purpose is unclear, participants are unprepared, critical people are absent or late, conversation doesn't stay focused on the problem, and no one follows up on the decisions that were made. Google's vice president of search products and user experience, Marissa Mayer, holds over 70 meetings a week and is the last executive to hear a pitch before it is made to the cofounders. To keep meetings on track, Mayer has set down six guidelines. Meetings must (1) have a firm agenda and (2) an assigned note taker. Meetings must occur (3) during established office hours, and (4) preferably in short, ten-minute micro-meetings. Those running

C-type conflict (cognitive conflict) disagreement that focuses on problem- and issue-related differences of opinion

When facilitated well, group decision making can lead to much better decisions. The pitfalls of group decision making are not inevitable. Managers can overcome most of them by using the various techniques described next.

5.2 Structured Conflict

Most people view conflict negatively. Yet the right kind of conflict can lead to much better group decision making. **C-type conflict,** or "cognitive conflict," focuses on problem- and issue-related differences of opinion.[45] In c-type conflict, group members disagree because their different experiences and expertise lead them to view the problem and its potential solutions differently. C-type conflict is also characterized by a willingness to examine, compare, and reconcile those differences to produce the best possible solution. Alteon WebSystems, now a division of Nortel Networks, makes critical use of c-type conflict. Top manager Dominic Orr described Alteon's c-type conflict this way:

> *After an idea is presented, we open the floor to objective, and often withering, critiques. And if the idea collapses under scrutiny, we move on to another: no hard feelings. We're judging the idea, not the person. At the same time, we don't really try to regulate emotions. Passionate conflict means that we're getting somewhere, not that the discussion is out of control. But one person does act as referee— by asking basic questions like "Is this good for the customer?" or "Does it keep our time-to-market advantage intact?" By focusing relentlessly on the facts, we're able to see the strengths and weaknesses of an idea clearly and quickly.*[46]

By contrast, **a-type conflict,** meaning "affective conflict," refers to the emotional reactions that can occur when disagreements become personal rather than professional. A-type conflict often results in hostility, anger, resentment, distrust, cynicism, and apathy. Unlike c-type conflict, a-type conflict undermines team effectiveness by preventing teams from engaging in the activities characteristic of c-type conflict that are critical to team effectiveness. Examples of a-type conflict statements are "your idea," "our idea," "my department," "you don't know what you are talking about," or "you don't understand our situation." Rather than focusing on issues and ideas, these statements focus on individuals.[47]

The **devil's advocacy** approach can be used to create c-type conflict by assigning an individual or a subgroup the role of critic. The following five steps establish a devil's advocacy program:

1. Generate a potential solution.
2. Assign a devil's advocate to criticize and question the solution.
3. Present the critique of the potential solution to key decision makers.
4. Gather additional relevant information.
5. Decide whether to use, change, or not use the originally proposed solution.[48]

When properly used, the devil's advocacy approach introduces c-type conflict into the decision-making process. Contrary to the common belief that conflict is bad, studies show that structured conflict leads to less a-type conflict, improved decision quality, and greater acceptance of decisions once they have been made.[49]

5.3 Nominal Group Technique

Nominal means "in name only." Accordingly, the **nominal group technique** received its name because it begins with a quiet time in which group members independently write down as many problem definitions and alternative solutions as possible. In other words, the nominal group technique begins by having group members act as individuals. After the quiet time the group leader asks each group member to share one idea at a time with the group. As they are read aloud, ideas are posted on flipcharts or wallboards for all to see. This step continues until all ideas have been shared. In the next step, the group discusses the advantages and disadvantages of the ideas. The nominal group technique closes with a second quiet time in which group members independently rank the ideas presented. Group members then read their rankings aloud, and the idea with the highest average rank is selected.[50]

The nominal group technique improves group decision making by decreasing a-type conflict. But it also restricts c-type conflict. Consequently, the nominal group technique typically produces poorer decisions than does the

A-type conflict (affective conflict) disagreement that focuses on individual or personal issues

Devil's advocacy a decision-making method in which an individual or a subgroup is assigned the role of a critic

Nominal group technique a decision-making method that begins and ends by having group members quietly write down and evaluate ideas to be shared with the group

devil's advocacy approach. Nonetheless, more than 80 studies have found that nominal groups produce better ideas than those produced by traditional groups.[51]

5.4 Delphi Technique

In the **Delphi technique,** the members of a panel of experts respond to questions and to each other until reaching agreement on an issue. The first step is to assemble a panel of experts. Unlike other approaches to group decision making, however, it isn't necessary to bring the panel members together in one place. Because the Delphi technique does not require the experts to leave their offices or disrupt their schedules, they are more likely to participate.

The second step is to create a questionnaire consisting of a series of open-ended questions for the experts. In the third step, the panel members' written responses are analyzed, summarized, and fed back to the panel for reactions until the members reach agreement. Asking the members why they agree or disagree is important because it helps uncover their unstated assumptions and beliefs. Again, this process of summarizing panel feedback and obtaining reactions to that feedback continues until the panel members reach agreement.

5.5 Electronic Brainstorming

Brainstorming, in which group members build on others' ideas, is a technique for generating a large number of alternative solutions. Brainstorming has four rules:

1. The more ideas, the better.

2. All ideas are acceptable, no matter how wild or crazy they might seem.

3. Other group members' ideas should be used to come up with even more ideas.

4. Criticism or evaluation of ideas is not allowed.

In terms of decision making, brainstorming can generate a large number of ideas and possible solutions, although there are some disadvantages associated with this process. Fortunately, technology has been able to address some of these challenges with the advent of electronic meeting system (EMS) software and **electronic brainstorming,** where team members use computers to communicate possible solutions. These systems have helped remove some of the drawbacks of traditional face-to-face brainstorming, which can inhibit effective group decision making.

For example, the first disadvantage that electronic brainstorming overcomes is **production blocking,** which occurs when you have an idea but have to wait to share it because someone else is already presenting an idea to the group. During this short delay, you may forget your idea or decide that it really wasn't worth sharing. Production blocking doesn't happen with electronic brainstorming. All group members are seated at computers, so everyone can type in ideas whenever they occur. There's no waiting your turn to be heard by the group.

The second disadvantage that electronic brainstorming overcomes is **evaluation apprehension,** that is, being afraid of what others will think of your ideas. With electronic brainstorming, all ideas are anonymous. When you type in an idea and hit the Enter key to share it with the group, group members see only the idea. Furthermore, many brainstorming software programs also protect anonymity by displaying ideas in random order. So, if you laugh maniacally when you type "Cut top management's pay by 50 percent!" and then hit the Enter key, it won't show up immediately on everyone's screen. This makes it doubly difficult to determine who is responsible for which comments.

In the typical layout for electronic brainstorming, all participants sit in front of computers around a U-shaped table. This configuration allows them to see their computer screens, the other participants, a large main screen, and a meeting leader or facilitator. Step 1 in electronic brainstorming is to anonymously generate as many ideas as possible. Groups commonly generate 100 ideas in a half-hour period. Step 2 is to edit the generated ideas, categorize them, and eliminate redundancies. Step 3 involves ranking the categorized ideas in terms of quality. Step 4, the last step, has three parts: generate a series of action steps, decide the best order for accomplishing these steps,

Delphi technique a decision-making method in which members of a panel of experts respond to questions and to one another until reaching agreement on an issue

Brainstorming a decision-making method in which group members build on one anothers' ideas to generate as many alternative solutions as possible

Electronic brainstorming a decision-making method in which group members use computers to build on one anothers' ideas and generate many alternative solutions

Production blocking a disadvantage of face-to-face brainstorming in which a group member must wait to share an idea because another member is presenting an idea

Evaluation apprehension fear of what others will think of your ideas

and identify who is responsible for each step. All four steps are accomplished with computers and electronic brainstorming software.[52]

Studies show that electronic brainstorming is much more productive than face-to-face brainstorming. Four-person electronic brainstorming groups produce 25 to 50 percent more ideas than four-person regular brainstorming groups, and 12-person electronic brainstorming groups produce 200 percent more ideas than regular groups of the same size! In fact, because production blocking (i.e., waiting your turn) is not a problem for electronic brainstorming, the number and quality of ideas generally increase with group size.[53]

Even though it works much better than traditional brainstorming, electronic brainstorming has disadvantages, too. An obvious problem is the expense of computers, networks, software, and other equipment. As these costs continue to drop, however, electronic brainstorming will become a viable option for more groups.

Another problem is that the anonymity of ideas may bother people who are used to having their ideas accepted by virtue of their position (i.e., the boss). On the other hand, one CEO said, "Because the process is anonymous, the sky's the limit in terms of what you can say, and as a result it is more thought-provoking. As a CEO, you'll probably discover things you might not want to hear but need to be aware of."[54]

A third disadvantage is that outgoing individuals who are more comfortable expressing themselves verbally may find it difficult to express themselves in writing. Finally, the most obvious problem is that participants have to be able to type. Those who can't type, or who type slowly, may be easily frustrated and find themselves at a disadvantage to experienced typists.

Avoiding Blamestorming and Coblabberation

Without serious planning and adherence to brainstorming guidelines and procedures, brainstorming can quickly degenerate into blamestorming (where zero progress is made) or coblabberation (settling for an unimaginative solution just to get the session over with). Indeed, Professor Paul Paulus of the University of Texas at Arlington conducted a study comparing the number and quality of ideas of four people brainstorming versus four individuals working alone. Results: the brainstormers were only half as effective as the solo thinkers. Professor David Perkins of Harvard is not surprised. He prefers having people write down their ideas then bring them in. That way, you get diversity without all the politicking.

Source: Sandberg, J., "Brainstorming Works Best If People Scramble for Ideas on Their Own," *Wall Street Journal*, 13 June 2006, B1.

© iStockphoto.com

Visit **icanmgmt.com** to find the resources you need today!

Located at the back of the textbook are rip-out Chapter Review cards. Make sure you also go online to check out other tools that MGMT offers to help you successfully pass your course.

- Interactive Quizzes
- Key Terms Flashcards
- Audio Chapter Summaries
- PowerPoint Slides

- Interactive Games
- Crossword Puzzles
- "Reel to Reel" and "Biz Flix" videos
- Cases and Exercises

87% Percent of Canadian students surveyed would use the Chapter Review cards to study for a test or prepare for class.

TEST COMING UP? NOW WHAT?

With **MGMT** you have a multitude of study aids at your fingertips. After reading the chapters, check out these ideas for further help:

Chapter Review cards include learning outcomes, definitions, and visual summaries for each chapter.

Printable flashcards give you three additional ways to check your comprehension of key **Principles of Management** concepts.

Other great ways to help you study include **interactive games, audio summaries, quizzes,** and **flashcards**.

"I like the flashcards, the videos, and the quizzes. Great format! I love the cards in the back of the book!"

—Asha Thtodort, Algonquin College

Visit **icanmgmt.com** to find the resources you need today!

ORGANIZATIONAL STRATEGY

Basics of Organizational Strategy

Less than a decade ago, Apple Computer was not in the music business. And then it released the iPod, which quickly set the standard for all other digital music devices. Designed around a 1.8-inch-diameter hard drive, the iPod boasted low battery consumption and enough storage to hold literally thousands of songs in an easy-to-use product smaller than a deck of cards. Because Apple used existing technology to make the iPod, Sony, Samsung, Dell, Creative, and Microsoft moved quickly to produce their own MP3 players.

As the market matured, competitors tried to steal—or at least minimize—Apple's competitive advantage by adding unique features to their MP3 players. Sony entered the market, and so did SanDisk, Microsoft, and a host of other large players. Yet it was Apple's continual progress that made the iPod emerge on top—but for how long? Apple dominates the recording industry, yet it is a computer company—its release of the iPad in 2010 continues to cause quite a stir in the computer industry. Canada's Research in Motion (RIM) did not exist until fairly recently, yet its BlackBerry took the cellular phone industry by storm. Apple has also had a huge impact on the cellular phone industry with its G4 entry, yet it is a computer company—or is it? Google is a computer company, yet it has entered the cellular phone industry with its Android phone, with Microsoft and Motorola fast on its heels. How does a company decide which industries to enter, in which markets, and with which products?[1]

Learning Outcomes

1 specify the components of sustainable competitive advantage and explain why it is important.

2 describe the steps involved in the strategy-making process.

3 explain the different kinds of corporate-level strategies.

4 describe the different kinds of industry-level strategies.

5 explain the components and kinds of firm-level strategies.

How can a company like Apple, or Microsoft, or Google, or RIM, which dominates a particular industry, maintain its competitive advantage as strong, well-financed competitors enter the market? What steps can companies take to better manage their strategy-making process? How does strategy relate to sustainable competitive advantage?

After reading the next two sections, you should be able to

1 specify the components of sustainable competitive advantage and explain why it is important.

2 describe the steps involved in the strategy-making process.

1 Sustainable Competitive Advantage

Resources are the assets, capabilities, processes, employee time, information, and knowledge that an organization controls. Firms use their resources to improve organizational effectiveness and efficiency. Resources are critical to organizational strategy because they can help companies create and sustain an advantage over competitors.[2]

> **Resources** the assets, capabilities, processes, information, and knowledge that an organization uses to improve its effectiveness and efficiency, create and sustain competitive advantage, and fulfill a need or solve a problem

New Technology, Whole New Business

Apple developed its iPod out of existing technology. But CJ-Global Logistics Service, a Korean third-party logistics company, created new technology to solve old problems and, in the process, created a whole new business. Getting products to consumers efficiently involves managing not just boxes, but a lot of information as well. Invoices must be tracked. Boxes must be stored and inventory managed. Customers need to know when to expect delivery. CJ-GLS used a number of innovative methods to do this, including Internet-based delivery routing, sending delivery schedules to customers' PDAs, and tracking shipments with GPS. One of the most inefficient parts of the old process was managing inventory with bar codes. CJ-GLS replaced bar codes with an attachable chip containing inventory, storage, and delivery data that can be managed remotely through radio frequency identification (RFID). This approach to inventory yields no scanning errors and takes less time to manage. Plus, the chips have the capacity to store more information than a bar code and can easily be updated. RFID didn't just strengthen CJ-GLS's competitive advantage; it turned out to be a whole new way to manage logistics information.

Source: C. Kim, K. Yang, & J. Kim, "A Strategy for Third-Party Logistics Systems: A Case Analysis Using the Blue Ocean Strategy," Omega 36 (August 2008) 522–534.

© Ryan McVay/Photodisc/Jupiterimages

Organizations can achieve a **competitive advantage** by using their resources to provide greater value for customers than competitors can. For example, the iPod's competitive advantage came from its simple, attractive design relative to its price. But Apple's most important advantage was being the first company to make it easy to use MP3 players to legally buy and download music from iTunes.com. (Prior to the iTunes store at iTunes.com, the only means of acquiring digital music was illegal file swapping.) Apple negotiated agreements with nearly all of the major record labels to sell their music, and iTunes.com quickly became the premier platform for music downloading. The easy-to-understand site came with free downloadable software that customers could use to organize and manage their digital music libraries.[3]

The goal of most organizational strategies is to create and then sustain a competitive advantage. A competitive advantage becomes a **sustainable competitive advantage** when other companies cannot duplicate the value a firm is providing to customers. Sustainable competitive advantage is *not* the same as a long-lasting competitive advantage, though companies obviously want a competitive advantage to last a long time. Instead, a competitive advantage is *sustained* if competitors have tried unsuccessfully to duplicate the advantage and have, for the moment, stopped trying to duplicate it. It's the corporate equivalent of your competitors saying, "We give up. You win. We can't do what you do, and we're not even going to try to do it any more." Four conditions must be met if a firm's resources are to be used to achieve a sustainable competitive advantage. The resources must be valuable, rare, imperfectly imitable, *and* nonsubstitutable.

Valuable resources allow companies to improve their efficiency and effectiveness. Unfortunately, changes in customer demand and preferences, competitors' actions, and technology can make once-valuable resources much less valuable. Throughout the 1980s, Sony controlled the portable music market with its Sony Walkman, which has sold over 230 million units worldwide since its introduction in 1979. Sony leveraged the capabilities of its engineers and inventors (more resources) to make incremental changes to the Walkman that were unmatched by the competition—until the MP3 player came along. With the introduction

Competitive advantage providing greater value for customers than competitors can

Sustainable competitive advantage a competitive advantage that other companies have tried unsuccessfully to duplicate and have, for the moment, stopped trying to duplicate

Valuable resource a resource that allows companies to improve efficiency and effectiveness

> To achieve a **sustainable** competitive **advantage**, the resources must be valuable, rare, imperfectly imitable, *and* nonsubstitutable.

of Apple's iPod to the market, Sony's previous valuable technology lost nearly all its value. Sony finally changed the Walkman to a portable digital device and created its own online music store (Connect), which does not yet match iTunes' simplicity of song selection.[4]

For sustained competitive advantage, valuable resources must also be rare resources. Think about it: How can a company sustain a competitive advantage if all of its competitors have similar resources and capabilities? Consequently, **rare resources,** resources that are not controlled or possessed by many competing firms, are necessary to sustain a competitive advantage. When Apple introduced the iPod, no other portable music players on the market used existing hard drive technology in their design. The iPod gained an immediate advantage over competitors because it was able to satisfy the desire of consumers to carry large numbers of songs in a portable device, something the newer MP3 systems and older individual CD players could not do. The technology that powered the iPod, however, was readily available, so competitors were able to quickly imitate iPod's basic storage capacity. As competitors began introducing iPod look-alikes, Apple released a model with double the storage and replaced the original mechanical wheel with a solid-state touch wheel. Once again, Apple used its design talents (resources) to gain an advantage over the competition.

As this shows, valuable and rare resources can create temporary competitive advantage. For sustained competitive advantage, however, other firms must be unable to imitate or find substitutes for those valuable, rare resources. **Imperfectly imitable resources** are those resources that are impossible or extremely costly or difficult to duplicate. For example, despite numerous attempts by competitors to imitate it, iTunes has retained its competitive lock on the music download business. Because it capitalized on Apple's reputation for developing customer-friendly software, the library of music, movies, and podcasts on iTunes is still two to three times larger than those of other music download sites. Because the company has developed a closed system for its iTunes and iPod, iPod owners can only download music from Apple's iTunes store. But consumers don't seem to mind. Kelly Moore, a sales representative for a Texas software company, takes her pink iPod everywhere she goes and keeps it synchronized with her iPad. She says, "Once I find something I like, I don't switch brands."[5] She's not alone: people with iPads, iPods, and iPhones have used iTunes to download over a billion songs. No other competitor comes close to those numbers.

Valuable, rare, imperfectly imitable resources can produce sustainable competitive advantage only if they are also **nonsubstitutable resources,** meaning that no other resources can replace them and produce similar value or competitive advantage. The industry has produced equivalent substitutes for iTunes, but competitors have had to experiment with different business models in order to get customers to accept them. Napster founders Shawn Fanning and Wayne Rosso created a subscription-based service called Mashboxx that charged $15 a month for unlimited downloads, and Zune Marketplace established a similar system with over 3 million songs, although no video.[6] In addition to straight subscription models, some companies are experimenting with price. Where iTunes charges 99 cents per song, period, Amazon's online store will allow the record companies to charge different amounts for different songs based upon popularity. At Amie Street, a newly posted track can be downloaded for free, but as the number of downloads increases, so does the song's price, until it reaches the maximum of 98 cents.[7] In response to competitors' experimentation, Apple has stated that its one-flat-price model has been both effective and lucrative and that it has no plans to change. It will take years to find out whether competing music download sites will be an effective substitute to iTunes.[8]

In summary, Apple has reaped the rewards of a first mover advantage from its interdependent iPod and iTunes. The company's history of developing customer-friendly software, the innovative capabilities of the iPod, the simple 99-cent-pay-as-you-go sales model of iTunes, and the unmatched list of music and movies available for download provide customers with a service that

Rare resources
resources that are not controlled or possessed by many competing firms

Imperfectly imitable resources resources that are impossible or extremely costly or difficult for other firms to duplicate

Nonsubstitutable resource a resource that produces value or competitive advantage and has no equivalent substitutes or replacements

has been valuable, rare, relatively non-substitutable, and, in the past, imperfectly imitable. Past success is, however, no guarantee of future success: Apple needs to continually change and develop its offerings or risk being unseated by a more nimble competitor whose products are more relevant and have higher perceived value to consumers.

2 Strategy-Making Process

*In order to produce sustainable competitive advantage, a company must have a strategy.[9] Exhibit 6.1 displays the three steps of the strategy-making process: **2.1 assess the need for strategic change, 2.2 conduct a situational analysis,** and then **2.3 choose strategic alternatives.** Let's examine each of these steps in more detail.*

2.1 Assessing the Need for Strategic Change

The external business environment is much more turbulent than it used to be. With customers' needs constantly growing and changing, and with competitors working harder, faster, and smarter to meet those needs, the first step to creating a strategy is determining the need for strategic change. In other words, the company should determine whether it needs to change its strategy to sustain a competitive advantage.[10]

Determining the need for strategic change might seem easy to do, but it's really not. There's a great deal of uncertainty in strategic business environments. Furthermore, top-level managers are often slow to recognize the need for strategic change, especially at successful companies that have created and sustained competitive advantages. Because they are acutely aware of the strategies that made their companies successful, they continue to rely on those strategies even as the competition changes. In other words, success often leads to **competitive inertia**—a reluctance to change strategies or competitive practices that have been successful in the past.

Besides being aware of the dangers of competitive

Competitive inertia a reluctance to change strategies or competitive practices that have been successful in the past

Strategic dissonance a discrepancy between a company's intended strategy and the strategic actions managers take when implementing that strategy

Situational (SWOT) analysis an assessment of the strengths and weaknesses in an organization's internal environment and the opportunities and threats in its external environment

Distinctive competence what a company can make, do, or perform better than its competitors

inertia, what can managers do to improve the speed and accuracy with which they determine the need for strategic change? One method is to actively look for signs of strategic dissonance. **Strategic dissonance** is a discrepancy between a company's intended strategy and the strategic actions managers take when actually implementing that strategy.[11]

For example, when prominant Canadian businessman Edgar Bronfman, Jr., bought the struggling Warner Music Group, his strategy was to cut costs and change a company culture where excessive spending—not uncommon in the entertainment industry—was the norm. Accordingly, he laid off 1,200 employees to save $250 million and cut remaining salaries by as much as 50 percent. A few weeks later, however, he contradicted his new cost-cutting strategy. First, he signed off on a $13,000 bill to charter a private jet to fly top company managers and the agents of the company's best-selling artists to the Grammy awards in Los Angeles. Then, despite his insistence that music industry professionals shouldn't be paid more than their counterparts in other industries, Bronfman quietly restored the salary cuts he had made after top executives complained.[12]

Finally, while strategic dissonance can indicate that managers are not doing what they should to carry out company strategy, it can also mean that the intended strategy is out of date and needs to be changed.

2.2 Situational Analysis

A situational analysis can also help managers determine the need for strategic change. A **situational analysis,** also called a **SWOT analysis** for *strengths, weaknesses, opportunities,* and *threats,* is an assessment of the strengths and weaknesses in an organization's internal environment and the opportunities and threats in its external environment.[13] Ideally, as shown in Step 2 of Exhibit 6.1 (p. 109), a SWOT analysis helps a company determine how to increase internal strengths and minimize internal weaknesses while maximizing external opportunities and minimizing external threats.

An analysis of an organization's internal environment—that is, a company's strengths and weaknesses—often begins with an assessment of its distinctive competencies and core capabilities. A **distinctive competence** is something that a company can make, do, or perform better than its competitors. For example, *Consumer Reports* magazine consistently ranks Toyota cars number one in quality and reliability.[14] Similarly, *PC Magazine* readers ranked Apple's desktop and laptop computers best in terms of service and reliability.[15]

Whereas distinctive competencies are tangible—for example, a product or service is faster, cheaper, or better—the core capabilities that produce distinctive competencies are not. **Core capabilities** are the less visible, internal decision-making routines, problem-solving processes, and organizational cultures that determine how efficiently inputs can be turned into outputs.[16] Distinctive competencies cannot be sustained for long without superior core capabilities. Offering Asian food products is a distinctive competence at T & T Supermarkets. At these stores, one can find every kind of Asian food imaginable. Most of the products sold are exotic and unique. T & T Supermarkets' goal is to enrich the lifestyle of Asian families in Canada by offering them choice food and household items in a comfortable shopping environment. They also hope to introduce the colourful Asian food culture to Canada's multicultural society. "Freshness" is their most important operating value, which is practised along with "customer satisfaction" to enhance their one-stop shopping convenience and personable service standards. This is an example of a focused differentiated approach (see Section 6.4.2). Loblaw's purchased the T & T chain in 2009 to enhance Weston's corporate strategy (see Section 6.3).[17]

After examining internal strengths and weaknesses, the second part of a situational analysis is to look outside the company and assess the opportunities and threats in the external environment. In Chapter 3, you learned that *environmental scanning* involves searching the environment for important events or issues that might affect the organization such as pricing trends or new products and technology. In a situational analysis, however, managers use environmental scanning to identify specific opportunities and threats that can either improve or

Exhibit 6.1

Three Steps of the Strategy-Making Process

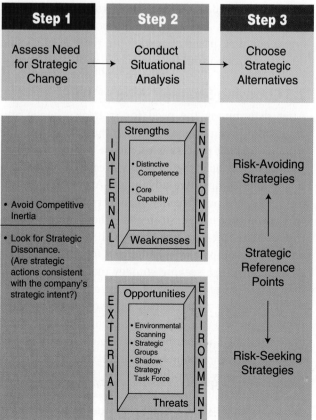

Step 1	Step 2	Step 3
Assess Need for Strategic Change	Conduct Situational Analysis	Choose Strategic Alternatives

Step 1:
- Avoid Competitive Inertia
- Look for Strategic Dissonance. (Are strategic actions consistent with the company's strategic intent?)

Step 2 — INTERNAL ENVIRONMENT:
Strengths
- Distinctive Competence
- Core Capability
Weaknesses

EXTERNAL ENVIRONMENT:
Opportunities
- Environmental Scanning
- Strategic Groups
- Shadow-Strategy Task Force
Threats

Step 3:
Risk-Avoiding Strategies
↑
Strategic Reference Points
↓
Risk-Seeking Strategies

Core capabilities the internal decision-making routines, problem-solving processes, and organizational cultures that determine how efficiently inputs can be turned into outputs

harm the company's ability to sustain its competitive advantage. One can do this by identifying strategic groups and forming shadow-strategy task forces.

A **strategic group** is a group of other companies within an industry that top managers choose and follow closely in order to compare, evaluate, and benchmark their company's strategic threats and opportunities.[18] (*Benchmarking* involves identifying outstanding practices, processes, and standards at other companies and adapting them to your own company.) Typically, managers include a company as part of their strategic group if they compete directly with it for customers or if it uses strategies similar to theirs. It's likely that the managers at Home Depot, a large Canadian home improvement and hardware retailer, assess strategic threats and opportunities by comparing their company to a strategic group consisting of the other home improvement and hardware retailers as illustrated in Exhibit 6.2.

In fact, when scanning the environment for strategic threats and opportunities, managers tend to categorize the different companies in their industries as core or secondary firms.[19] **Core firms** are the central companies in a strategic group. Home Depot operates 180 stores covering all 10 provinces of Canada. The company has more than 35,000 employees in Canada and annual revenue of over $8 billion. By comparison, Rona has 680 stores in 10 provinces and has 27,000 employees in Canada. Clearly, Rona is the closest competitor to Home Depot and would probably be classified as the core firm in Home Depot's strategic group. Lowe's is a recent entry into the Canadian market, and currently has only 16 stores (mostly in Ontario). It stocks 40,000 products in each store and has a total annual revenue of more than $2 billion. Lowe's is in Home Depot's strategic group and must be a competitor that they keep an eye on.[20]

Secondary firms are firms that use strategies related to but somewhat different from those of core firms. TIM-BR MART has more stores than Home Depot: 700 in Canada. But

Exhibit 6.2

Core and Secondary Firms in the Home Improvement Industry

Canac - Marquis - Grenier (limited to Quebec)

Home Depot
Lowe's
RONA

franchise stores

© iStockphoto.com/Tom McNemar / © C. Borland/PhotoLink/Photodisc/Jupiterimages

TIM-BR MART's franchise structure and small, individualized stores keep it from being a core firm in Home Depot's strategic group.[21] Likewise, Home Depot's management probably doesn't concern itself much with Canac-Marquis-Grenier, which has only two dozen stores in Quebec.[22] Managers need to be aware of the potential threats and opportunities posed by secondary firms, but they usually spend more time assessing the threats and opportunities associated with core firms.

2.3 Choosing Strategic Alternatives

After determining the need for strategic change and conducting a situational analysis, the last step in the strategy-making process is to choose strategic alternatives that will help the company create or maintain a sustainable competitive advantage. According to strategic reference point theory, managers choose between two basic alternative strategies. They can choose a conservative *risk-avoiding strategy* that aims to protect an existing competitive advantage. Or they can choose an aggressive *risk-seeking strategy* that aims to extend or create a sustainable competitive advantage.

The choice to seek risk or avoid risk typically depends on whether top management views the company as falling above or below strategic reference points. **Strategic reference points** are the targets that managers use to measure whether their firm has developed the core competencies that it needs to achieve a sustainable competitive advantage. If a hotel chain decides to compete

Exhibit 6.3

Strategic Reference Points

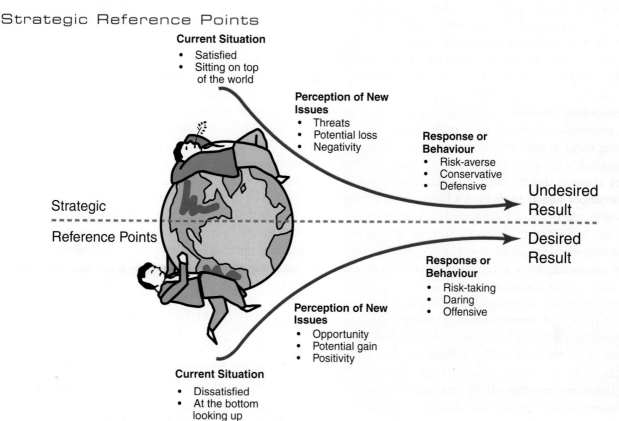

Current Situation
- Satisfied
- Sitting on top of the world

Perception of New Issues
- Threats
- Potential loss
- Negativity

Response or Behaviour
- Risk-averse
- Conservative
- Defensive

Undesired Result

Strategic

Reference Points

Desired Result

Response or Behaviour
- Risk-taking
- Daring
- Offensive

Perception of New Issues
- Opportunity
- Potential gain
- Positivity

Current Situation
- Dissatisfied
- At the bottom looking up

Source: A. Fiegenbaum, S. Hart, & D. Schendel, "Strategic Reference Point Theory," *Strategic Management Journal* 17 (1996): 219–235.

by providing superior quality and service, then top management will track the success of this strategy through customer surveys or published hotel ratings such as those provided by the prestigious *vacationcanada.com*. By contrast, if a hotel chain decides to compete on price, it will regularly conduct market surveys to check the prices of other hotels. The competitors' prices are the hotel managers' strategic reference points against which to compare their own pricing strategy. If competitors can consistently underprice them, then the managers need to determine whether their staff and resources have the core competencies to compete on price.

As shown in Exhibit 6.3, when a company is performing above or better than its strategic reference points, top management will typically be satisfied with the company's strategy. Ironically, this satisfaction tends to make top management conservative and risk-averse. Since the company already has a sustainable competitive advantage, the worst thing that could happen would be to lose it, so new issues or changes in the company's external environments are viewed as threats. By contrast, when a company is performing below or worse than its strategic reference points, top

management will typically be dissatisfied with the company's strategy. In this instance, managers are much more likely to choose a daring, risk-taking strategy. If the current strategy is producing substandard results, the company has nothing to lose by switching to risky new strategies in the hopes that it can create a sustainable competitive advantage. Managers of companies in this situation view new issues or changes in external environments as opportunities for potential gain.

Strategic reference point theory is not deterministic, however. Managers are not predestined to choose risk-averse or risk-seeking strategies for their companies depending solely on their current situation. Indeed, one of the most important elements of the theory is that managers can influence the strategies chosen by their company by *actively changing and adjusting* the strategic reference points they use to judge strategic performance. If a company has become complacent after consistently surpassing its strategic reference points, then top management can change from a risk-averse to a risk-taking orientation by raising the standards of performance (i.e., strategic reference points). This is just what happened at Menards.

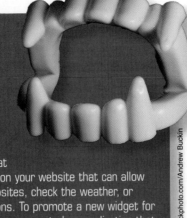

Werewolves or Widgets?

New opportunities make you re-evaluate your strategy, but change is not always good. ChipIn makes widgets, small programs that place an interactive icon on your website that can allow you to shop at other websites, check the weather, or conduct online transactions. To promote a new widget for Facebook pages, the company created an application that allows users to become a werewolf or a vampire and "bite" or "infect" other users. The application became one of the top 100 most downloaded widgets on Facebook, and other companies began to show interest in ChipIn's werewolves and vampires as tools for advertising their own products (which meant cash for ChipIn). The popularity of werewolves and vampires presented ChipIn with a potential strategy shift: Should the company start making Facebook applications? Carnet Williams remembered the Internet bubble days and decided to stick with what his company knew best: he sold off the werewolves and vampires in the interest of long-term growth.

Source: A. Salkever, "To Embrace or Flee Facebook?," *Inc.* (January 2008) 56–58.

Canadian Tire is one of Canada's 35 largest publicly traded companies. It operates an interrelated network of businesses engaged in retailing (hard goods, apparel, petroleum) and services (financial, automotive). Well known for its Canadian Tire money, the company has over 475 stores. Each Canadian Tire store is operated by a franchisee. The buildings and lands are owned or leased by the company; everything inside the building, from fixtures to merchandise, is owned by the franchisee. Canadian Tire Corporation has tried twice to expand into the U.S. market. In the 1980s it acquired the White Auto Store chain, concentrated in Texas; that attempt cost Canadian Tire $200 million to wind up its operations. In 1991 it made a second attempt by acquiring the Auto Source chain, with grand plans for 100 to 120 outlets in the U.S. Midwest. It later sold the Auto Source chain. That attempt cost it a reported $80.6 million. Both attempts were examples of a firm using an offensive-minded strategy that ultimately failed.[23] A daring strategy like this is emblematic of a red ocean (see box on page 119).

Corporate-level strategy the overall organizational strategy that addresses the question "What business or businesses are we in or should we be in?"

Canadian Tire has since stayed with a risk-averse strategy, protecting its existing stores, and has experienced a period of significant growth and success. Since 1994 it has transformed its store network in three major waves. In its last five-year strategic plan it attained top-quartile total returns to shareholders among all publicly traded North American retailers, with a total return of 286 percent.[24]

So even when (perhaps *especially* when) companies have achieved a sustainable competitive advantage, top managers must adjust or change strategic reference points to challenge themselves and their employees to develop new core competencies for the future. In the long run, effective organizations will frequently revise their strategic reference points to better focus managers' attention on the new challenges and opportunities that occur in their ever-changing business environments.

Corporate-, Industry-, and Firm-Level Strategies

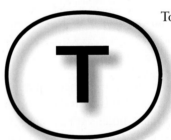

To formulate effective strategies, companies must be able to answer these three basic questions:

- What business are we in?
- How should we compete in this industry?
- Who are our competitors, and how should we respond to them?

These simple but powerful questions are at the heart of corporate-, industry-, and firm-level strategies.

After reading the next three sections, you should be able to

3   explain the different kinds of corporate-level strategies.

4   describe the different kinds of industry-level strategies.

5   explain the components and kinds of firm-level strategies.

3 Corporate-Level Strategies

Corporate-level strategy is the overall organizational strategy that addresses the question "What business or businesses are we in or should we be in?"

*There are two major approaches to corporate-level strategy that companies use to decide which businesses they should be in: **3.1 portfolio strategy** and **3.2 grand strategies**.*

3.1 Portfolio Strategy

One of the standard strategies for stock market investors is **diversification,** or owning stocks in a variety of companies in different industries. The purpose of this strategy is to reduce risk in the overall stock portfolio (the entire collection of stocks). The basic idea is simple. If you invest in 10 companies in 10 different industries, you won't lose your entire investment if one company performs poorly. Furthermore, because they're in different industries, one company's losses are likely to be offset by another company's gains. Portfolio strategy is based on these same ideas. We'll start by taking a look at the theory and ideas behind portfolio strategy and then proceed with a critical review that suggests that some of the key ideas behind portfolio strategy are *not* supported.

Portfolio strategy is a corporate-level strategy that minimizes risk by diversifying investment among various businesses or product lines.[25] Just as a diversification strategy guides an investor who invests in a variety of stocks, portfolio strategy guides the strategic decisions of corporations that compete in a variety of businesses. For example, portfolio strategy could be used to guide the strategy of a company like 3M, with many locations in Canada, which makes 55,000 products for seven different business sectors: consumers and offices (Post-its, Scotch tape, etc.); display and graphics (for computers, cell phones, PDAs, TVs); electronics and communications (flexible circuits used in printers and electronic displays); health care (medical, surgical, dental, and personal care products); industrial (tapes, adhesives, supply chain software); safety, security, and protection services (glass safety, fire protection, respiratory products); and transportation (products and components for the manufacture, repair, and maintenance of autos, aircraft, boats, and other vehicles).[26] Furthermore, just as investors consider the mix of stocks in their stock portfolio when deciding which stocks to buy or sell, managers following portfolio strategy try to acquire companies that fit well with the rest of their corporate portfolio and sell those that don't. Portfolio strategy provides the following guidelines to help companies make these difficult decisions.

First, according to portfolio strategy, the more businesses in which a corporation competes, the smaller its overall chances of failing. Think of a corporation as a stool and its businesses as the legs of the stool. The more legs or businesses added to the stool, the less likely it is to tip over. Using this analogy, portfolio strategy reduces 3M's risk of failing because the corporation's survival depends on essentially seven different business sectors. Managers employing portfolio strategy can either develop new businesses internally or look for potential new **acquisitions,** that is, other companies to buy.

Second, beyond adding new businesses to the corporate portfolio, portfolio strategy predicts that companies can reduce risk even more through **unrelated diversification**—creating or acquiring companies in completely unrelated businesses (more on the accuracy of this prediction later). According to portfolio strategy, when businesses are unrelated, losses in one business or industry should have minimal effect on the performance of other companies in the corporate portfolio. One of the best examples of unrelated diversification is Samsung of Korea. Samsung has businesses in electronics, machinery and heavy industries, chemicals, financial services, and other areas ranging from automobiles to hotels and entertainment.[27] Because most internally grown businesses tend to be related to existing products or services, portfolio strategy

---

Corporate-Level Strategies

PORTFOLIO STRATEGY	GRAND STRATEGIES
• Acquisitions, unrelated diversification, related diversification, single businesses • Boston Consulting Group matrix • Stars • Question marks • Cash cows • Dogs	• Growth • Stability • Retrenchment/recovery

---

Diversification a strategy for reducing risk by owning a variety of items (stocks or, in the case of a corporation, types of businesses) so that the failure of one stock or one business does not doom the entire portfolio

Portfolio strategy a corporate-level strategy that minimizes risk by diversifying investment among various businesses or product lines

Acquisition the purchase of a company by another company

Unrelated diversification creating or acquiring companies in completely unrelated businesses

suggests that acquiring new businesses is the preferred method of unrelated diversification.

Third, investing the profits and cash flows from mature, slow-growth businesses into newer, faster-growing businesses can reduce long-term risk. The best-known portfolio strategy for guiding investment in a corporation's businesses is the Boston Consulting Group (BCG) matrix. The **BCG matrix** is a portfolio strategy that managers use to categorize their corporation's businesses by growth rate and relative market share, helping them decide how to invest corporate funds. BCG, which began as a consulting business in 1963, also introduced the now-ubiquitous concept of the experience curve (costs go down as experience increases) in 1968, followed by the growth share matrix, shown in Exhibit 6.4.

The BGC matrix separates businesses into four categories based on how fast the market is growing (high-growth or low-growth) and the size of the business's share of that market (small or large). **Stars** are companies that have a large share of a fast-growing market. To take advantage of a star's fast-growing market and its strength in that market (large share), the corporation must invest substantially in it. The investment is usually worthwhile, however, because many stars produce sizable future profits.

Exhibit 6.4

Boston Consulting Group Matrix

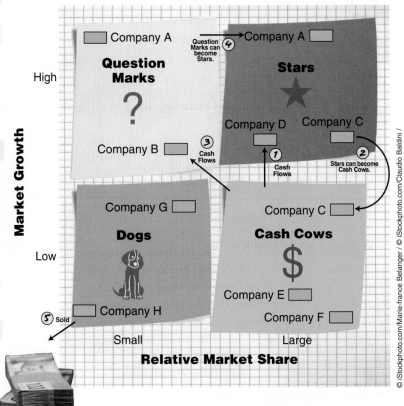

BCG matrix a portfolio strategy, developed by the Boston Consulting Group, that categorizes a corporation's businesses by growth rate and relative market share and helps managers decide how to invest corporate funds

Star a company with a large share of a fast-growing market

Question mark a company with a small share of a fast-growing market

Cash cow a company with a large share of a slow-growing market

Dog a company with a small share of a slow-growing market

Question marks are companies that have a small share of a fast-growing market. If the corporation invests in these companies, they may eventually become stars, but their relative weakness in the market (small share) makes investing in question marks more risky than investing in stars. **Cash cows** are companies that have a large share of a slow-growing market. Companies in this situation are often highly profitable, hence the name "cash cow." Finally, **dogs** are companies that have a small share of a slow-growing market. As the name suggests, having

a small share of a slow-growth market is often not profitable.

Since the idea is to redirect investment from slow-growing to fast-growing companies, the BCG matrix starts by recommending that the substantial cash flows from cash cows should be reinvested in stars while the cash lasts (see arrow 1 in Exhibit 6.4) to help them grow even faster and obtain even more market share. Using this strategy, current profits help produce future profits. As their market growth slows over time, some stars may turn into cash cows (see arrow 2).

Cash flows should also be directed to some question marks (see arrow 3). Though riskier than stars, question marks have great potential because of their fast-growing market. Managers must decide which question marks are most likely to turn into stars (and therefore warrant further investment) and which ones are too risky and should be sold. Over time, it is hoped that some question marks will become stars as their small markets become large ones (see arrow 4). Finally, because dogs lose money, the corporation should "find them new owners" or "take them to the pound." In other words, dogs should either be sold to other companies or be closed down and liquidated for their assets (see arrow 5).

Although the BCG matrix and other forms of portfolio strategy are relatively popular among managers, portfolio strategy has some drawbacks. The most significant: Contrary to the predictions of portfolio strategy, evidence suggests that acquiring unrelated businesses is *not* useful. As shown in Exhibit 6.5, there is a U-shaped relationship between diversification and risk. The left side of the curve shows that single businesses with no diversification are extremely risky (if the single business fails, the entire business fails). So, in part, the portfolio strategy of diversifying is correct—competing in a variety of different businesses can lower risk. However, portfolio strategy is partly wrong, too—the right side of the curve shows that conglomerates composed of completely unrelated businesses are even riskier than single, undiversified businesses.

A second set of problems with portfolio strategy has to do with the dysfunctional consequences that occur when companies are categorized as stars, cash cows, question marks, or dogs. The BCG matrix often yields incorrect judgments about a company's potential. This is because it relies on past performance (i.e., previous market share and previous market growth), which is a notoriously poor predictor of future company performance.

Furthermore, using the BCG matrix can also weaken the strongest performer in the corporate portfolio, the cash cow. As funds are redirected from cash cows to stars, corporate managers essentially take away the resources needed to take advantage of the cash cow's new business opportunities. As a result, the cash cow becomes less aggressive in seeking new business or in defending its present business. Finally, labelling a top performer as a cash cow can harm

© AP Images

Exhibit 6.5

U-Shaped Relationship Between Diversification and Risk

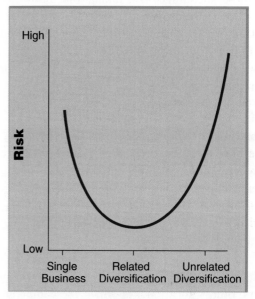

Source: Republished with permission of Academy of Management, P.O. Box 3020, Briar Cliff Manor, NY, 10510–8020. M. Lubatkin & P. J. Lane, "Psst . . . The Merger Mavens Still Have It Wrong!" *Academy of Management Executive* 10 (1996): 21–39.

employee morale. Cash cow employees realize that they have inferior status and that they are now working to fund the growth of stars and question marks instead of working for themselves.

So, what kind of portfolio strategy does the best job of helping managers decide which companies to buy or sell? The U-shaped curve in Exhibit 6.5 indicates that the best approach is probably **related diversification,** in which the different business units share similar products, manufacturing, marketing, technology, or cultures. The key to related diversification is to acquire or create new companies with core capabilities that complement the core capabilities of businesses already in the corporate portfolio. Hormel Foods is an example of related diversification in the food business. The company both manufactures and markets a variety of foods from deli meats to salsa to the infamous SPAM®.

We began this section with the example of 3M and its 55,000 products sold in over seven different business sectors. While seemingly different, most of 3M's product divisions are based in some fashion on its distinctive competencies in adhesives and tape (e.g., wet or dry sandpaper, Post-it notes, Scotchgard fabric

Related diversification creating or acquiring companies that share similar products, manufacturing, marketing, technology, or cultures

protector, transdermal skin patches, reflective material used in traffic signs, etc.). Furthermore, all of 3M's divisions share its strong corporate culture that promotes and encourages risk taking and innovation. In sum, in contrast to a single, undiversified business or unrelated diversification, related diversification reduces risk because the different businesses can work as a team, relying on one another for needed experience, expertise, and support.

3.2 Grand Strategies

A **grand strategy** is a broad strategic plan used to help an organization achieve its strategic goals.[28] Grand strategies guide the strategic alternatives that managers of individual businesses or subunits may use in deciding what businesses they should be in. There are three kinds of grand strategies: growth, stability, and retrenchment/recovery.

The purpose of a **growth strategy** is to increase profits, revenues, market share, or the number of places (stores, offices, locations) in which the company does business. Companies can grow in several ways. They can grow externally by merging with or acquiring other companies in the same or different businesses.

Another way to grow is internally, directly expanding the company's existing business or creating and growing new businesses. Staples sells office supplies in retail stores, online, and through catalogues to individuals as well as small and large businesses. The company wants to strengthen its ability to deliver supplies directly to consumers. In order to accomplish this, the company seeks to grow externally by acquiring other companies that specialize in delivery.[29]

The purpose of a **stability strategy** is to continue doing what the company has been doing, just do it better. Companies following a stability strategy try to improve the way in which they sell the same products or services to the same customers. For example, Subaru has been making four-wheel-drive station wagons for 30 years. Over the last decade, it strengthened this focus by manufacturing only all-wheel-drive vehicles, like the Subaru Legacy and Outback (both come in four-door sedans or two-door coupes), which are popular in snowy and mountainous regions.[30] Companies often choose a stability strategy when their external environment doesn't change much or after they have struggled with periods of explosive growth.

The purpose of a **retrenchment strategy** is to turn around very poor company performance by shrinking the size or scope of the business or, if a company is in multiple businesses, by closing or shutting down different lines of the business. The first step of a typical retrenchment strategy might include making significant cost reductions; laying off employees; closing poorly performing stores, offices, or manufacturing plants; or closing or selling entire lines of products or services.[31] Between the fourth quarter of 2006 and the first quarter of 2008, Sears, the parent company that purchased Eaton's in Canada, saw its earnings drop from $800 million to a loss of $50 million. One approach was to keep sales growing at a modest level but do so without heavy discounts or expenditures of cash. Other strategies involved restructuring the company by closing stores.[32]

After cutting costs and reducing a business's size or scope, the second step in a retrenchment strategy is recovery. **Recovery** consists of the strategic actions that a company takes to return to a growth strategy. This two-step process of cutting and recovery is analogous to pruning roses. Prior to each growing season, roses should be cut back to two-thirds their normal size. Pruning doesn't damage the roses; it makes them stronger and more likely to produce beautiful, fragrant flowers. The retrenchment-and-recovery process is similar. Cost reductions, layoffs, and plant closings are sometimes necessary to restore companies to good health. Like pruning, those cuts are intended to allow companies to eventually return to growth strategies (i.e., recovery). When company performance drops significantly, a strategy of retrenchment and recovery may help the company return to a successful growth strategy. Daimler experienced just this after it split from Chrysler. The company's ability to focus on its strengths in the luxury car industry (Daimler makes Mercedes-Benz) took it from a loss of 12 million euros to a profit of 1.69 billion.[33]

Grand strategy a broad corporate-level strategic plan used to achieve strategic goals and guide the strategic alternatives that managers of individual businesses or subunits may use

Growth strategy a strategy that focuses on increasing profits, revenues, market share, or the number of places in which the company does business

Stability strategy a strategy that focuses on improving the way in which the company sells the same products or services to the same customers

Retrenchment strategy a strategy that focuses on turning around very poor company performance by shrinking the size or scope of the business

Recovery the strategic actions taken after retrenchment to return to a growth strategy

4 Industry-Level Strategies

Industry-level strategy addresses the question "How should we compete in this industry?"

Let's find out more about industry-level strategies by discussing **4.1 the five industry forces that determine overall levels of competition in an industry** *and* **4.2 the positioning strategies** *and* **4.3 adaptive strategies that companies can use to achieve sustained competitive advantage and above-average profits.**

4.1 Five Industry Forces

According to Harvard professor Michael Porter, five industry forces determine an industry's overall attractiveness and potential for long-term profitability. These include the character of the rivalry, the threat of new entrants, the threat of substitute products or services, the bargaining power of suppliers, and the bargaining power of buyers and are illustrated in Exhibit 6.6. The stronger these forces, the less attractive the industry becomes to corporate investors because it is more difficult for companies to be profitable. Let's examine how these industry forces are bringing changes to several kinds of industries.

Character of the rivalry is a measure of the intensity of competitive behaviour between companies in an industry. Is the competition among firms aggressive and cutthroat, or do competitors focus more on serving customers than on attacking one another? Both industry attractiveness and profitability decrease when rivalry is cutthroat.

The **threat of new entrants** is a measure of the degree to which barriers to entry make it easy or difficult for new companies to get started in an industry. If new companies can easily enter the industry, then competition will increase and prices and profits will fall. On the other hand, if there are sufficient barriers to entry, such as large capital requirements to buy expensive equipment or plant facilities or the need for specialized knowledge, then competition will be weaker and prices and profits will generally be higher. For instance, high costs and intense competition make it very difficult to enter the video game business. With today's average video game taking 12 to 36 months to create, $5 million to $10 million to develop, and teams of high-paid creative workers to develop realistic graphics, captivating story lines, and innovative game capabilities, the barriers to entry for this business are obviously extremely high.

The **threat of substitute products or services** is a measure of the ease with which customers can find substitutes for an industry's products or

Exhibit 6.6

Porter's Five Industry Forces

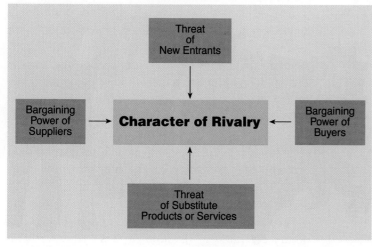

Industry-level strategy a corporate strategy that addresses the question "How should we compete in this industry?"

Character of the rivalry a measure of the intensity of competitive behaviour between companies in an industry

Threat of new entrants a measure of the degree to which barriers to entry make it easy or difficult for new companies to get started in an industry

Threat of substitute products or services a measure of the ease with which customers can find substitutes for an industry's products or services

services. If customers can easily find substitute products or services, the competition will be greater and profits will be lower. If there are few or no substitutes, competition will be weaker, and profits will be higher. Generic medicines are some of the best-known examples of substitute products. Under Canadian patent law, a company that develops a drug has exclusive rights to produce and market that drug for 17 years. Prices and profits are generally high during this period if the drug sells well. After 17 years, however, the patent will expire, and any pharmaceutical company can manufacture and sell the same drug. When this happens, drug prices drop substantially, and the company that developed the drug typically sees its revenues drop sharply.

Bargaining power of suppliers is a measure of the influence that suppliers of parts, materials, and services to firms in an industry have on the prices of these inputs. When companies can buy parts, materials, and services from numerous suppliers, the companies will be able to bargain with the suppliers to keep prices low. Today, there are so many suppliers of inexpensive, standardized parts, computer chips, and video screens that dozens of new companies are beginning to manufacture flat-screen TVs. In other words, the weak bargaining power of suppliers has made it easier for new firms to enter the HDTV business. On the other hand, if there are few suppliers, or if a company is dependent on a supplier with specialized skills and knowledge, then the suppliers will have the bargaining power to dictate price levels.

Bargaining power of buyers is a measure of the influence that customers have on the firm's prices. If a company sells a popular product or service to multiple buyers, then the company has more power to set prices. By contrast, if a company is dependent on just a few high-volume buyers, those buyers will typically have enough bargaining power to dictate prices. Wal-Mart is the largest single buyer in the history of retailing. The company buys 30 percent of all toothpaste, shampoo, and paper towels made by retail suppliers; 15 to 20 percent of all CDs, videos, and DVDs; 15 percent of all magazines; 14 percent of all groceries; and 20 percent of all toys. And, of course, Wal-Mart uses its purchasing power as a buyer to push down prices.[34]

4.2 Positioning Strategies

After analyzing industry forces, the next step in industry-level strategy is to protect your company from the negative effects of industry-wide competition and to create a sustainable competitive advantage. According to Michael Porter, there are three positioning strategies: cost leadership, differentiation, and focus.

Cost leadership means producing a product or service of acceptable quality at consistently lower production costs than competitors so that the firm can offer the product or service at the lowest price in the industry. Cost leadership protects companies from industry forces by deterring new entrants, who will have to match low costs and prices. Cost leadership also forces down the prices of substitute products and services, attracts bargain-seeking buyers, and increases bargaining power with suppliers, who have to keep their prices low if they want to do business with the cost leader.[35]

Differentiation means making your product or service sufficiently different from competitors' offerings such that customers are willing to pay a premium price for the extra value

Bargaining power of suppliers a measure of the influence that suppliers of parts, materials, and services to firms in an industry have on the prices of these inputs

Bargaining power of buyers a measure of the influence that customers have on a firm's prices

Cost leadership the positioning strategy of producing a product or service of acceptable quality at consistently lower production costs than competitors can, so that the firm can offer the product or service at the lowest price in the industry

Differentiation the positioning strategy of providing a product or service that is sufficiently different from competitors' offerings that customers are willing to pay a premium price for it

Differentiation is what makes Whirlpool's $2,300 washer-dryer combination a hot product.

ADAPTIVE

Fashion for the Rest of Us

Demand for products is changing strategies in the fashion world. Runway shows traditionally occur twice each year, exhibiting clothes for the next season six months out. But broader interest in Fashion Week among "real consumers" is creating demand for cheaper merchandise much sooner. This may change how the fashion industry works. Natalie Massenet, founder of the ready-to-wear website Net-a-Porter.com suggests an adaptive strategy: four shows each year plus faster designing and manufacture.

Source: C. Binkley, R. Dodes, & R. Smith, "Notes From Fashion Week: Styles That Are Really Ready-to-Wear; New Economic Realities," *The Wall Street Journal* (7 February 2008) D10.

or performance that it provides. Differentiation protects companies from industry forces by reducing the threat of substitute products. It also protects companies by making it easier to retain customers and more difficult for new entrants trying to attract new customers. For example, why would anyone pay $2,300 for Whirlpool's Duet, a deluxe washer-dryer combination, when they could purchase a regular washer-dryer combination for $700 or less? The answer is that the Duet washer does huge loads, almost twice what normal washers hold, with less than half the water—just 16 gallons compared to 40 for conventional washers. So it's incredibly efficient in terms of water and energy and saves consumers time because they can wash and dry twice as many clothes at the same time.[36]

With a **focus strategy,** a company uses either cost leadership or differentiation to produce a specialized product or service for a limited, specially targeted group of customers in a particular geographic region or market segment. Focus strategies typically work in market niches that competitors have overlooked or have difficulty serving. The Containerstore.com sells products in Canada to reorganize and rebuild your closets, sort out your kitchen drawers and cabinets, or add shelves, hooks, and storage anywhere in your home, office, or dorm room. But, unlike Wal-Mart or Canadian Tire, that's all it does.

4.3 Adaptive Strategies

Adaptive strategies are another set of industry-level strategies. Whereas the aim of positioning strategies is to minimize the effects of industry competition and build a sustainable competitive advantage, the purpose of adaptive strategies is to choose an industry-level strategy that is best suited to changes in the organization's external environment. There are four kinds of adaptive strategies: defending, prospecting, analyzing, and reacting.[37]

Defenders seek moderate, steady growth by offering a limited range of products and services to a well-defined set of customers. In other words, defenders aggressively "defend" their current strategic position by doing the best job they can to hold on to customers in a particular market segment.

Prospectors seek fast growth by searching for new market opportunities, encouraging risk taking, and being the first to bring innovative new products to market. Prospectors are analogous to gold miners who "prospect" for gold nuggets (i.e., new products) in hopes that the nuggets will lead them to a rich deposit of gold (i.e., fast growth).

Analyzers blend the defending and prospecting

Focus strategy the positioning strategy of using cost leadership or differentiation to produce a specialized product or service for a limited, specially targeted group of customers in a particular geographic region or market segment

Defenders those who adopt an adaptive strategy aimed at defending strategic positions by seeking moderate, steady growth and by offering a limited range of high-quality products and services to a well-defined set of customers

Prospectors those who adopt an adaptive strategy that seeks fast growth by searching for new market opportunities, encouraging risk taking, and being the first to bring innovative new products to market

Analyzers those who adopt an adaptive strategy that seeks to minimize risk and maximize profits by following or imitating the proven successes of prospectors

© Dennis Hallinan/Hulton Archive/Getty Images

strategies. Analyzers seek moderate, steady growth *and* limited opportunities for fast growth. Analyzers are rarely first to market with new products or services. Instead, they try to simultaneously minimize risk and maximize profits by following or imitating the proven successes of prospectors. Tempur-Pedic, which is sold by Sleep Country Canada, is the fastest-growing bed company in part because it replaced bed springs with visco foam. Traditional bed makers Sealy and Simmons (also major brands carried by Sleep Country Canada) sat back, analyzed, and came up with their own answers to visco foam. Simmons came out with its own visco bed, while Sealy moved to natural latex, which has many of the same qualities but which Sealy claims to be better. Analyzing the market after Tempur-Pedic's

release of visco helped Sealy and Simmons determine their strategies.[38]

Finally, unlike defenders, prospectors, or analyzers, **reactors** do not follow a consistent strategy. Rather than anticipating and preparing for external opportunities and threats, reactors tend to react to changes in their external environment after they occur. Not surprisingly, reactors tend to be poorer performers than defenders, prospectors, or analyzers. A reactor approach is inherently unstable, and firms that fall into this mode of operation must change their approach or face almost certain failure.

5 Firm-Level Strategies

Microsoft brings out its Xbox 360 video-game console; Sony counters with its PlayStation 3. Telus drops prices and increases monthly cell phone minutes; Bell Mobility strikes back with better reception and even lower prices and more minutes. Attack and respond, respond and attack. **Firm-level strategy** addresses the question "How should we compete against a particular firm?"

Let's find out more about the firm-level strategies (i.e., direct competition between companies) by reading about 5.1 the basics of direct competition, and 5.2 the strategic moves involved in direct competition between companies.

5.1 Direct Competition

Although Porter's five industry forces indicate the overall level of competition in an industry, most companies do not compete directly with all the firms in their industry. For example, McDonald's and Red Lobster are both in the restaurant business, but no one would characterize them as competitors. McDonald's offers low-cost, convenient fast food in a seat-yourself restaurant, while Red Lobster offers mid-priced, sit-down seafood dinners complete with servers and a bar.

Instead of competing with an industry, most firms compete directly with just a few companies within it. **Direct competition** is the rivalry between two companies offering similar products and services that acknowledge each other as rivals and take offensive and defensive positions as they act and react to each other's strategic actions.[39] Two factors determine the extent to which firms will be in direct competition with each other: market commonality and resource similarity. **Market commonality** is the degree to which two companies have overlapping products, services, or customers in multiple markets. The more markets in

Reactors those who take an adaptive strategy of not following a consistent strategy, but instead reacting to changes in the external environment after they occur

Firm-level strategy a corporate strategy that addresses the question "How should we compete against a particular firm?"

Direct competition the rivalry between two companies that offer similar products and services, acknowledge each other as rivals, and react to each other's strategic actions

Market commonality the degree to which two companies have overlapping products, services, or customers in multiple markets

which there is product, service, or customer overlap, the more intense the direct competition between the two companies. **Resource similarity** is the extent to which a competitor has similar amounts and kinds of resources, that is, similar assets, capabilities, processes, information, and knowledge used to create and sustain an advantage over competitors. From a competitive standpoint, resource similarity means that your direct competitors can probably match the strategic actions that your company takes.

Exhibit 6.7 shows how market commonality and resource similarity interact to determine when and where companies are in direct competition.[40] The overlapping area in each quadrant (between the triangle and the rectangle, or between the differently coloured rectangles) depicts market commonality. The larger the overlap, the greater the market commonality. Shapes depict resource similarity, with rectangles representing one set of competitive resources and triangles representing another.

Quadrant I shows two companies in direct competition because they have similar resources at their disposal and a high degree of market commonality. These companies try to sell similar products and services to similar customers. McDonald's and Burger King would clearly fit here as direct competitors.

In Quadrant II, the overlapping parts of the triangle and rectangle show two companies going after similar customers with some similar products or services, but doing so with different competitive resources. McDonald's and Wendy's restaurants would fit here. Wendy's is after the same lunchtime and dinner crowds that McDonald's is. Nevertheless, with its more expensive hamburgers, fries, shakes, and salads, Wendy's is less of a direct competitor to McDonald's than Burger King is. For example, Wendy's Garden Sensation salads (using fancy lettuce varieties, grape tomatoes, and mandarin oranges) bring in customers who would have eaten at more expensive casual dining restaurants like Applebee's.[41] A representative from Wendy's says, "We believe you win customers by consistently offering a better product at a strong, everyday value."[42]

In Quadrant III, the very small overlap shows two companies with different competitive resources and little market commonality. McDonald's and Denny's, with restaurants in most major Canadian cities, fit here. Although both are in the fast-food business, there's almost no overlap in terms of products and customers.

> Instead of "competing" with the **industry**, most firms compete directly with **just a few companies**.

Furthermore, Denny's customers aren't likely to eat at McDonald's. In fact, Denny's is not really competing with other fast-food restaurants, but with eating at home. Denney's sells full omelettes, pork chops, steaks, and full-fare dinners.[43]

Finally, in Quadrant IV, the small overlap between the two rectangles shows that McDonald's and Subway compete with similar resources but with little market commonality. In terms of resources, McDonald's sales are much larger, but Subway, with its 29,590 stores worldwide, much faster growth, and plans to have 30,000 stores worldwide by 2010, has nearly approached McDonald's.[44] Though Subway and McDonald's compete, they aren't direct competitors in terms of market commonality in the way that McDonald's and Burger King are, because Subway, unlike McDonald's, sells itself as a provider of healthy fast food. Thus, the overlap is much smaller in Quadrant IV than in Quadrant I.

Resource similarity
the extent to which a competitor has similar amounts and kinds of resources

Exhibit 6.7
A Framework of Direct Competition

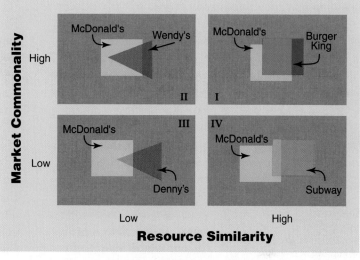

Source: Reprinted with permission of Academy of Management, P O Box 3020, Briar Cliff Manor, NY, 10510-8020. M. Chen, "Competitor Analysis and InterFirm Rivalry: Toward a Theoretical Integration," *Academy of Management Review* 21 (1996): 100-134.) 21–39.

Dukin' Donuts

Canadian icon Tim Hortons has 2,711 donut stores in Canada; 76 percent market share in coffee and baked goods; and an entry in the Canadian Oxford dictionary for one of the chain's shorthand orders, a "double-double" (coffee with two creams and two sugars). Such entrenched success should indicate that Tim Hortons would follow a risk-avoiding strategy. In seven years, however, the company will have built as many stores as Canada can support, so Tim Hortons entered the U.S. market in New England, home turf for Dunkin' Donuts and thousands of other small independents. Boston has five times the national average of donut shops per capita at one shop per 5,143 residents. Providence has one shop per 4,226 people. Implementing such a risky strategy has been brutal. At a recent annual shareholder meeting, Hortons CEO Paul House told investors, "We got our a** kicked in New England," but the company is still committed to a "good old street fight." One of the partners in the original Tim Hortons was optimistic: "America is a big country"; but in November of 2010, Tim Hortons closed all 36 money-losing restaurants.

Sources: D. Belkin, "A Canadian Icon Turns Its Glaze Southward," Wall Street Journal, 14 May 2007, B1. ; "Tim Hortons to Close 36 Restaurants in New England," November 11, 2010, http://abcnews.go.com/Business/wireStory?id=12119540.

© iStockphoto.com/Yong Hian Lim

5.2 Strategic Moves of Direct Competition

While corporate-level strategies help managers decide what business to be in and industry-level strategies help them determine how to compete within an industry, firm-level strategies help managers determine when, where, and what strategic actions should be taken against a direct competitor. Firms in direct competition can make two basic strategic moves: attacks and responses. These moves occur all the time in virtually every industry, but they are most noticeable in industries where multiple large competitors are pursuing customers in the same market space.

An **attack** is a competitive move designed to reduce a rival's market share or profits. Hoping to increase its market share at Burger King's expense, McDonald's began a brutal price war by putting eight items on a new $1 value menu, including two sandwiches, the Big N' Tasty quarter-pounder and the McChicken sandwich, that usually sold for $1.99.[45] Sales of those sandwiches doubled within weeks.

A **response** is a countermove, prompted by a rival's attack, that is designed to defend or improve a company's market share or profit.

Attack a competitive move designed to reduce a rival's market share or profits

Response a competitive countermove, prompted by a rival's attack, to defend or improve a company's market share or profit

There are two kinds of responses.[46] The first is to match or mirror your competitor's move. This is what Burger King did to McDonald's by selling 11 menu items at 99 cents each, including its popular double cheeseburgers. The second kind of response, however, is to respond along a different dimension from your competitor's move or attack. For example, instead of cutting prices, Burger King could have introduced a new menu item to attract customers away from McDonald's.

Market commonality and resource similarity determine the likelihood of an attack or response, that is, whether a company is likely to attack a direct competitor or to strike back with a strong response when attacked. When market commonality is strong and companies have overlapping products, services, or customers in multiple markets, there is less motivation to attack and more motivation to respond to an attack. The reason for this is straightforward: when firms are direct competitors in a large number of markets, they have a great deal at stake. So when McDonald's launched an aggressive price war with its value menu, Burger King had no choice but to respond by cutting its own prices.

Whereas market commonality affects the likelihood of an attack or a response to an attack, resource similarity largely affects response capability, that is, how quickly and forcefully a company can respond to an attack. When resource similarity is strong, the responding firm will generally be able to match the strategic moves of the attacking firm. Consequently, a firm is less likely to attack firms with similar levels of resources because it is unlikely to gain any sustained advantage when the responding firms strike back. On the other hand, if one firm is substantially stronger than another (i.e., low resource similarity), then a competitive attack is more likely to produce sustained competitive advantage. With over 30,000 stores to Burger King's 11,000 stores and much greater financial resources, McDonald's hoped its price war would inflict serious financial damage on Burger King while suffering minimal financial damage itself. This strategy worked to some extent. Although Burger King already sold 11 menu items for 99 cents, it wasn't willing or able to cut the price of its best-selling Whopper sandwiches to 99 cents (from $1.99). Basically admitting that it couldn't afford to match McDonald's price cuts on more expensive sandwiches, a Burger King spokesperson insisted, "McDonald's can't sell those sandwiches at $1 without losing money. It isn't sustainable." Thanks to its much larger financial resources, McDonald's had the funds to outlast Burger King in the price war. As often happens, though, the price war ended up hurting both companies' profits.[47] McDonald's ended the price war when it became clear that lower prices didn't draw more customers to its restaurants.

In general, the more moves (i.e., attacks) a company initiates against direct competitors and the greater a company's tendency to respond when attacked, the better its performance. More specifically, attackers and early responders (companies that are quick to launch a retaliatory attack) tend to gain market share and profits at the expense of late responders. This is not to suggest that a "full-attack" strategy always works best. In fact, attacks can provoke harsh retaliatory responses. Consequently, when deciding when, where, and what strategic actions to take against a direct competitor, managers should always consider the possibility of retaliation.

Red Ocean, Blue Ocean

Using the ocean as a metaphor, Professors Renée Mauborgne and W. Chan Kim describe highly competitive markets as shark-infested waters. The water is red with blood from continual attacks and responses, and any gains made by one company are incremental at best and bound to be ceded in the next shark fight. Canadian Tire's forays into the United States are an example of a red ocean. As outlined later, Canada's Cirque du Soleil is an example of a blue ocean.

The only hope for survival is to pursue innovations that take you out of the red ocean and into the deep blue ocean, where there are no competitors. If it sounds hard, it is; but it's not impossible. Canada's own Cirque du Soleil created a whole new category of entertainment; Gmail lets you store unlimited email for free; and Nintendo's Wii has redefined videogaming with simple games that combine elements of virtual reality. Read more in *Blue Ocean Strategy* (Harvard University Press, 2005).

© iStockphoto.com / © Ethan Miller/Reuters/Landov

Visit **icanmgmt.com** to find the resources you need today!

Located at the back of the textbook are rip-out Chapter Review cards. Make sure you also go online to check out other tools that MGMT offers to help you successfully pass your course.

- Interactive Quizzes
- Key Terms Flashcards
- Audio Chapter Summaries
- PowerPoint Slides

- Interactive Games
- Crossword Puzzles
- "Reel to Reel" and "Biz Flix" videos
- Cases and Exercises

INNOVATION AND CHANGE

Organizational Innovation

Sometimes the solution to a problem causes another problem. Jernhusen AB, a Swedish property administration firm, is building a new office and retail building near Stockholm's Central Station. How should they heat it? Problem number two: How should they get rid of excess heat in the train station, generated by the 250,000 people who pass through it every day? As Karl Sundholm, representative of Jernhusen, puts it, "All people produce heat, and that heat is in fact fairly difficult to get rid of. Instead of opening windows and letting all that heat go to waste we want to harness it through the ventilation system." The innovative solution to both problems? Convert the heat in the station to hot water and pump it through the heating system of the new building using pipes that connect the building to the station. Sundholm estimates the system will cost about 300,000 kronor (32,000 Euros; Cdn $52,000) to install, and it is likely to reduce energy consumption by 15 percent. Per Berggren, Jernhusen's managing director notes, "It's more like thinking out of the box, being environmentally smart."[1]

Organizational innovation is the successful implementation of creative ideas in an organization.[2] **Creativity,** which is a form of organizational innovation, is the production of novel and useful ideas.[3] In the

Organizational innovation the successful implementation of creative ideas in organizations

Creativity the production of novel and useful ideas

Learning Outcomes

1 explain why innovation matters to companies.

2 discuss the different methods that managers can use to effectively manage innovation in their organizations.

3 discuss why not changing can lead to organizational decline.

4 discuss the different methods that managers can use to better manage change as it occurs.

first part of this chapter, you will learn why innovation matters and how to manage innovation to create and sustain a competitive advantage. In the second part, you will learn about **organizational change,** which is a difference in the form, quality, or condition of an organization over time.[4] You will also learn about the risk of not changing and the ways in which companies can manage change. But first, let's deal with organizational innovations like using body heat to warm buildings.[5]

After reading the next two sections on organizational innovation, you should be able to

1 explain why innovation matters to companies.

2 discuss the different methods that managers can use to effectively manage innovation in their organizations.

1 Why Innovation Matters

We can only guess what changes technological innovations will bring in the next 20 years. It is likely that many of us will carry very powerful telecomputers in our pockets. But will our printer send a message to the supplier when it's out of ink? Will the Internet make movie theatres and televisions obsolete? Will we edit

> **Organizational change** a difference in the form, quality, or condition of an organization over time

our own news?[6] Who knows? The only thing we do know for sure about the next 20 years is that innovation will continue to change our lives.

Let's begin our discussion of innovation by learning about: **1.1 technology cycles** and **1.2 innovation streams**.

1.1 Technology Cycles

In Chapter 3, you learned that *technology* consists of the knowledge, tools, and techniques used to transform inputs (raw materials, information, etc.) into outputs (products and services). A **technology cycle** begins with the birth of a new technology and ends when that technology reaches its limits and dies as it is replaced by a newer, substantially better technology.[7] For example, technology cycles occurred when air-conditioning supplanted fans, when Henry Ford's Model T replaced horse-drawn carriages, and when planes replaced trains as a means of cross-country travel.

From Gutenberg's invention of the printing press in the 1400s to the rapid advance of the Internet, studies of hundreds of technological innovations have shown that nearly all technology cycles follow the typical **S-curve pattern of innovation** shown in Exhibit 7.1.[8] Early in a technology cycle, there is still much to learn, so progress is slow, as depicted by point A on the S-curve. The flat slope indicates that increased effort (i.e., money, research and development) brings only small improvements in technological performance. Fortunately, as the new technology matures, researchers figure out how to get better performance from it. This is represented by point B of the S-curve in Exhibit 7.1. The steeper slope indicates that small amounts of effort will result in significant increases in performance. At point C, the flat slope again indicates that further efforts to develop this particular technology will result in only small increases in performance. More important,

Exhibit 7.1

S-Curves and Technological Innovation

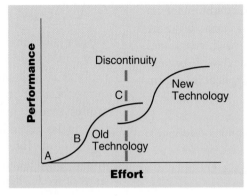

Source: R. N. Foster, *Innovation: The Attacker's Advantage* (New York: Summitt, 1986).

however, point C indicates that the performance limits of that particular technology are being reached. In other words, additional significant improvements in performance are highly unlikely.

Intel's technology cycles have followed this pattern. Intel spends billions to develop new computer chips and to build new production facilities to produce them. Intel has found that the technology cycle for its integrated circuits is about three years. In each three-year cycle, Intel spends billions to introduce a new chip, improves the chip by making it a little bit faster each year, and then replaces that chip at the end of the cycle with a brand new, different chip that is substantially faster than the old chip. At first, though (point A), the billions Intel spends typically produce only small improvements in performance. But after six months to a year with a new chip design, Intel's engineering and production people typically figure out how to make the new chips much faster than they were initially (point B). Yet despite impressive gains in performance, Intel is unable to make a particular computer chip run any faster because the chip reaches its design limits.

After a technology has reached its limits at the top of the S-curve, significant improvements in performance usually come from radical new designs or new performance-enhancing materials (point C). In Exhibit 7.1, that new technology is represented by the second S-curve.

Joseph Balgazette designed the first interceptor sewers to carry London's sewage down the banks of the Thames to be dumped into the estuary.

© Otto Herschan/Hulton Archive/Getty Images

The changeover or discontinuity between the old and new technologies is represented by the dotted line. At first, the old and new technologies will likely coexist. Eventually, however, the new technology will replace the old technology. When that happens, the old technology cycle will be complete, and a new one will have started. The changeover between Intel's newer and older computer chip designs typically takes about one year. Over time, improving existing technology (tweaking the performance of the current technology cycle), combined with replacing old technology with new technology cycles (i.e., new, faster computer chip designs replacing older ones), has increased the speed of Intel's computer processors by a factor of 70 in just 19 years.

Though the evolution of Intel's Pentium chips has been used to illustrate S-curves and technology cycles, it's important to note that technology cycles and technological innovation don't necessarily involve faster computer chips or cleaner-burning automobile engines. Remember, *technology* is simply the knowledge, tools, and techniques used to transform inputs into outputs. So a technology cycle occurs whenever there are major advances or changes in the *knowledge, tools,* and *techniques* of a field or discipline, whatever they may be. For example, one of the most important technology cycles in the history of civilization occurred in 1859, when 1,300 miles of central sewer line were constructed throughout London to carry human waste to the sea more than 11 miles away. This sewer system replaced the practice of dumping raw sewage into streets where it drained into public wells that supplied drinking water. Preventing waste runoff from contaminating water supplies stopped the spread of cholera that had killed millions of people for centuries in cities throughout

© iStockphoto.com/Murat Baysan

Patent #4,131,919

the world.[9] Indeed, the water you drink today is safe thanks to this technological breakthrough. So, when you think about technology cycles, don't automatically think "high technology." Instead, broaden your perspective by considering advances or changes in any kind of knowledge, tools, and techniques.

1.2 Innovation Streams

In Chapter 6, you learned that organizations can create *competitive advantage* for themselves if they have a *distinctive competence* that allows them to make, do, or perform something better than their competitors. A competitive advantage becomes sustainable if other companies cannot duplicate the benefits obtained from that distinctive competence. Technological innovation can enable competitors to duplicate the benefits obtained from a company's distinctive advantage. It can also quickly turn a company's competitive advantage into a competitive disadvantage. For more than 110 years, Eastman Kodak was the dominant producer of photographic film worldwide. That is, until Kodak invented the digital camera (patent 4,131,919). But Kodak itself was unprepared for the rapid acceptance of its new technology, and its managers watched film quickly become obsolete for the majority of camera users. Technological innovation turned Kodak's competitive advantage into a competitive disadvantage.[10]

As the Kodak example shows, companies that want to sustain a competitive advantage must understand and protect themselves from the strategic threats of innovation. Over the long run, the best way for a company to do that is to create a stream of its own innovative ideas and products year after year.

Consequently, we define **innovation streams** as patterns of innovation over time that can create sustainable competitive advantage.[11] Exhibit 7.2 on the next page shows a typical innovation consisting of a series of technology cycles. Recall that a technology cycle begins with a new technology and ends when that technology is replaced by a newer, substantially better technology. The innovation stream in Exhibit 7.2 shows three such technology cycles.

An innovation stream begins with a **technological discontinuity,** in which a scientific advance or a unique combination of existing technologies creates a significant breakthrough in performance or function. Technological discontinuities are followed by a **discontinuous change,** which is characterized by technological substitution and design competition. **Technological substitution** occurs when customers then purchase new technologies to replace older technologies.

Discontinuous change is also characterized by **design competition,** in which the old technology and several different new technologies compete to establish a new technological standard or dominant design. For example, Toshiba and Sony competed for dominance in a new standard format for home video, Toshiba with its HD DVD technology and Sony with Blu-ray. Because of large investments in old technology, and because the new and old technologies are often incompatible with each other, companies and consumers are reluctant to switch to a different technology during a design competition. Toshiba lost the design competition because Warner Bros., which had been using both technologies, decided to go exclusively with Blu-ray. Retailers followed suit, announcing intentions to focus on Blu-ray equipment

Innovation streams patterns of innovation over time that can create sustainable competitive advantage

Technological discontinuity a scientific advance or a unique combination of existing technologies creates a significant breakthrough in performance or function

Discontinuous change the phase of a technology cycle characterized by technological substitution and design competition

Technological substitution the purchase of new technologies to replace older ones

Design competition competition between old and new technologies to establish a new technological standard or dominant design

Dominant design a new technological design or process that becomes the accepted market standard

Exhibit 7.2

Innovation Streams: Technology Cycles over Time

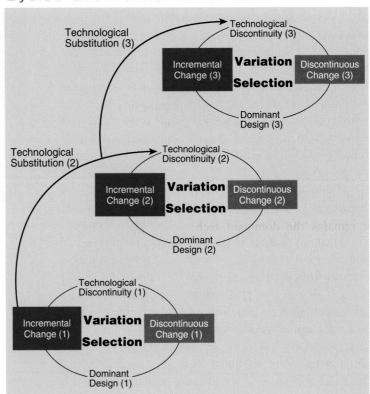

"Technology Cycles, Innovation Streams and Ambidextrous Organizations," in MANAGING STRATEGIC INNOVATION AND CHANGE edited by M.L. Tushman & P.C. Anderson & C. O'Reilly: Redrawn figure 1.2 (p. 8) © 1997 by Oxford University Press, Inc. By Permission of Oxford University Press, Inc.

and videos. Some "early adopters" of HD DVD will continue to use the technology for their collections, but most people will eventually use Blu-ray because it will dominate the market.[12] In addition, during design competition, the older technology usually improves significantly in response to the competitive threat from the new technologies; this response also slows the changeover from older to newer technologies.

Discontinuous change is followed by the emergence of a **dominant design,** which becomes the new accepted market standard for technology.[13] Dominant designs emerge in several ways. The best technology doesn't always become the dominant design because a number of other factors come into play. One is critical mass, meaning that a particular technology can become the dominant design simply because most people use it. As of April 2008, Blu-ray held 64 percent of the market share while HD DVD had only 36 percent. Toshiba dropped HD DVD in part because, with a critical mass of Blu-ray adopters, Blu-ray had become the dominant design.

A design can also become dominant if it solves a practical problem. For example, the QWERTY keyboard (named for the top left line of letters) became the dominant design for typewriters because it slowed typists who caused mechanical typewriter keys to jam because they typed too fast. Though computers can easily be switched to the DVORAK keyboard layout, which doubles typing speed and cuts typing errors by half, QWERTY lives on as the standard keyboard. In this instance, the QWERTY keyboard solved a problem that, with computers, is no longer relevant. Yet it remains the dominant technology because most people learned to type that way and continue to use it.

Dominant designs can also emerge through independent standards bodies. The International Telecommunications Union (**http://www.itu.ch**) is the leading United Nations agency that establishes standards for the communications industry. The ITU was founded in Paris in 1865 because European countries all had different telegraph systems that could not communicate with one another. After three months of negotiations, 20 countries signed the International Telegraph Convention, which standardized equipment and instructions, enabling telegraph messages to flow seamlessly from country to country. Today, as in 1865, various standards are proposed, discussed, negotiated, and changed until agreement is reached on a final set of standards that communication industries (i.e., Internet, telephone, satellites, radio, etc.) will follow worldwide.

Canada and the United States have the weakest standards with respect to automobile fuel consumption; however, they also have the toughest emission requirements. Auto makers are pursuing alternative fuel technologies such as ethanol and diesel in an effort to increase fuel economy and meet these legal standards. Although research into alternative fuel technologies tends to be adopted in a climate of high oil prices and abandoned when they fall, it is not impossible to envision a future in which gasoline-burning engines are no longer the dominant technology on the road.[14]

Protecting Innovation

One of the risks in coming up with great new ideas is that someone might steal them. Published work, such as books and magazine articles, are protected by copyrights, while designs for new devices such as the iPhone are protected by patents. Research In Motion® (RIM®), the Canadian designer and manufacturer of the BlackBerry® smartphone, is headquartered in Waterloo, Ontario. Its legal department deals with patents, trademarks(™), industrial designs, integrated circuit topography, and copyrights©. It has paid more than $600 million in settlements to fight off various companies, including Prism Technologies LLC and NTP. Patent battles are very difficult, and expensive, to defend. The Government of Canada does not help on behalf of companies such as RIM. The present lawsuit with Prism Technologies dates back to 2001 and is only just coming to an end (for now) in late 2010. "It is a rather unusual situation that they are refusing to accept a check for $450 million when the validity of their IPR [intellectual property rights] is at issue," surmised RIM chairman Jim Balsillie. RIM has maintained that U.S. patent law should not have jurisdiction in the case because its BlackBerry relay server, which handles its e-mails, is in Waterloo, but various courts do not accept RIM's argument. The international law that deals with all of these issues is very complex.

Sources: "RIM settles BlackBerry patent dispute with Prism (Update 2)," *Bloomberg Businessweek*, May 18, 2010, online at http://www.businessweek.com/news/2010-05-18/rim-settles-blackberry-patent-dispute-with-prism-update2-.html; "RIM shares jump on settlement of BlackBerry patent lawsuit," CBC News, March 16, 2005, online at http://www.cbc.ca/money/story/2005/03/16/rimsettle-050316.html; Tom Krazit, "Patent Office weakens NTP's BlackBerry patent case: Seven of eight patents thrown out in initial assessment," *Techworld*, 24 June 2005, online at http://news.techworld.com/mobile-wireless/3913/patent-office-weakens-ntps-blackberry-patent-case/. [accessed June 7, 2010].

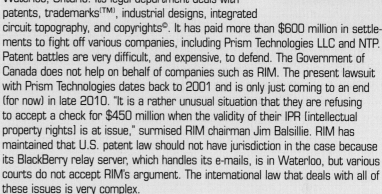

Associated Press/PR NEWSWIRE

© iStockphoto.com/MidwestWilderness

No matter how it happens, the emergence of a dominant design is a key event in an innovation stream. First, the emergence of a dominant design indicates that there are winners and losers. Technological innovation both enhances and destroys competence. Companies that bet on the now-dominant design usually prosper. In contrast, when companies bet on the wrong design or the old technology, they may experience **technological lockout,** which occurs when a new dominant design (i.e., a significantly better technology) prevents a company

Technological lockout
when a new dominant design (i.e., a significantly better technology) prevents a company from competitively selling its products or makes it difficult to do so

from competitively selling its products or makes it difficult to do so.[15] Toshiba has now stopped producing HD DVD players. It will continue to make spare parts for existing machines and may apply the technology to downloading videos online. But it will shift its business strategy to other sectors, such as flash drives, which are replacing hard drives in computers.[16] In fact, more companies are likely to go out of business in a time of discontinuous change and changing standards than in an economic recession or slowdown.

Second, the emergence of a dominant design signals a shift from design experimentation and competition to **incremental change,** a phase in which companies innovate by lowering the cost and improving the functioning and performance of the dominant design. For example, manufacturing efficiencies enable Intel to cut the cost of its chips by one-half to two-thirds during a technology cycle, while doubling or tripling their speed. This focus on improving the dominant design continues until the next technological discontinuity occurs.

2 Managing Innovation

One consequence of technology cycles and innovation streams is that managers must be equally good at managing innovation in two very different circumstances. First, during discontinuous change, companies must find a way to anticipate and survive the technological changes that can suddenly transform industry leaders into losers and industry unknowns into powerhouses. Companies that can't manage innovation following technological discontinuities risk quick organizational decline and dissolution. Second, after a new dominant design emerges following discontinuous change, companies must manage the very different process

of incremental improvement and innovation. Companies that can't manage incremental innovation slowly deteriorate as they fall farther behind industry leaders.

Unfortunately, what works well when managing innovation during discontinuous change doesn't work well when managing innovation during periods of incremental change (and vice versa). Consequently, to successfully manage innovation streams, companies need to be good at three things: **2.1 managing sources of innovation, 2.2 managing innovation during discontinuous change,** and **2.3 managing innovation during incremental change.**

2.1 Managing Sources of Innovation

Innovation comes from great ideas. So a starting point for managing innovation is to manage the sources of innovation, that is, where new ideas come from. One place that new ideas originate is brilliant inventors. But only a few companies have the likes of an Edison, Marconi, or Canada's Alexander Graham Bell working for them. Given that great thinkers and inventors are in short supply, what might companies do to ensure a steady flow of good ideas?

Well, when we say that innovation begins with great ideas, we're really saying that innovation begins with creativity. As we defined it at the beginning of this chapter, creativity is the production of novel and useful ideas.[17] Although companies can't command employees to be creative ("You *will* be more creative!"), they can jump-start innovation by building **creative work environments** in which workers perceive that creative thoughts and ideas are welcomed and valued. As Exhibit 7.3 shows, creative work environments have six components that encourage creativity: challenging work, organizational encouragement,

Incremental change the phase of a technology cycle in which companies innovate by lowering costs and improving the functioning and performance of the dominant technological design

Creative work environments workplace cultures in which workers perceive that new ideas are welcomed, valued, and encouraged

Exhibit 7.3
Components of Creative Work Environments

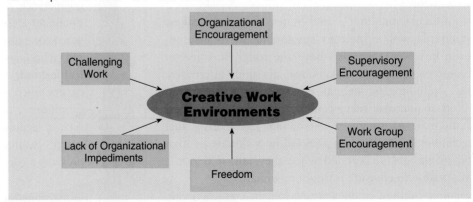

Source: T. M. Amabile, R. Conti, H. Coon, J. Lazenby, and M. Herron, "Assessing the Work Environment for Creativity," *Academy of Management Journal* 39 (1996): 1154–1184.

supervisory encouragement, work group encouragement, freedom, and a lack of organizational impediments.[18]

Work is *challenging* when it requires effort, demands attention and focus, and is perceived as important to others in the organization. According to researcher Mihaly Csikszentmihalyi (pronounced ME-high-ee CHICK-sent-me-high-ee), challenging work promotes creativity because it creates a rewarding psychological experience known as "flow." **Flow** is a psychological state of effortlessness in which you become completely absorbed in what you're doing and time seems to fly.[19] A key part of creating flow experiences, and thus creative work environments, is to achieve a balance between skills and task challenge. When workers can do more than is required of them, they become bored, and when their skills aren't sufficient to accomplish a task, they become anxious. When skills and task challenge are balanced, however, flow and creativity can occur.

A creative work environment requires three kinds of encouragement: organizational, supervisory, and work group encouragement. *Organizational encouragement* of creativity occurs when management encourages risk taking and new ideas, supports and fairly evaluates new ideas, rewards and recognizes creativity, and encourages the sharing of new ideas throughout different parts of the company. Many companies keep technology on a tight leash. But Douglas Merrill, chief information officer at Google, allows employees to use whatever hardware, operating systems, and software helps them be creative and get the job done efficiently, whether Google or another company designed them.[20] *Supervisory encouragement* of creativity occurs when supervisors provide clear goals, encourage open interaction with subordinates, and actively support development teams' work and ideas. *Work group encouragement* occurs when group members have diverse experience, education, and backgrounds and the group fosters mutual openness to ideas; positive, constructive challenge to ideas; and shared commitment to ideas.

An example of organizational and supervisory encouragement can be found at Adobe, which builds software for business and publishing. Every quarter, Adobe hosts the Idea Champion Showcase, a Canadian Idol-style "ideathon" in which six presenters get ten minutes each to pitch a new business idea involving product concept, packaging, technology, whatever.

Top executives are not invited to the showcase because their tendency to be cautious makes them want to "hurl rocks" at nascent ideas before they have a chance to develop. Rick Bess is an idea mentor at Adobe. He developed the showcase after an internal study showed that too many roadblocks were being thrown in front of new ideas, keeping them from penetrating the organizational hierarchy.[21]

Freedom means having autonomy over one's day-to-day work and a sense of ownership and control over one's ideas. Numerous studies have indicated that creative ideas thrive under conditions of freedom. At Royal Philips Electronics (Philips), all groups within the company have been given complete freedom to rethink every product with the goal of making it simpler for the end user to install and use.[22]

To foster creativity, companies may also have to *remove impediments* to creativity from their work environments. Internal conflict and power struggles, rigid management structures, and a conservative bias toward the status quo can all discourage creativity. They create the perception that others in the organization will decide which ideas are acceptable and deserve support.

2.2 Experiential Approach: Managing Innovation during Discontinuous Change

A study of 72 product-development projects (i.e., innovation) in 36 computer companies across Canada, Europe, and Asia sheds light on how to manage innovation. Companies that succeeded in periods of discontinuous change (characterized by technological substitution and design competition, as described earlier) typically followed an experiential approach to innovation.[23] The **experiential approach to innovation** assumes that innovation is occurring within a highly uncertain environment and that the key to fast product innovation is to use intuition, flexible options, and hands-on experience to reduce uncertainty and accelerate learning and understanding. The experiential approach to innovation has five aspects: design

Flow a psychological state of effortlessness, in which you become completely absorbed in what you're doing and time seems to pass quickly

Experiential approach to innovation an approach to innovation that assumes a highly uncertain environment and uses intuition, flexible options, and hands-on experience to reduce uncertainty and accelerate learning and understanding

iterations, testing, milestones, multifunctional teams, and powerful leaders.[24]

An "iteration" is a repetition. So a **design iteration** is a cycle of repetition in which a company tests a prototype of a new product or service, improves on the design, and then builds and tests the improved product or service prototype. A **product prototype** is a full-scale working model that is being tested for design, function, and reliability. **Testing** is a systematic comparison of different product designs or design iterations. Companies that want to create a new dominant design following a technological discontinuity quickly build, test, improve, and retest a series of different product prototypes. Rickster Powell has jumped from an airplane 20,000 times in order to test parachute designs. He and a partner strap cameras to their bodies to film the chute's deployment, which enables the manufacturers to look for problems. Only 9 out of 50 designs he's tested have actually been produced. Needless to say, he always wears a spare chute.[25]

By trying a number of very different designs or making successive improvements and changes in the same design, frequent design iterations reduce uncertainty and improve understanding. Simply put, the more prototypes you build, the more likely you are to learn what works and what doesn't. Also, when designers and engineers build a number of prototypes, they are less likely to fall in love with a particular prototype. Instead, they'll be more concerned with improving the product or technology as much as they can. Testing speeds up and improves the innovation process, too. When two very different design prototypes are tested against each other or the new design iteration is tested against the previous iteration, product design strengths and weaknesses quickly become apparent. Likewise, testing uncovers errors early in the design process when they are easiest to correct. Finally, testing accelerates learning and understanding by forcing engineers and product designers to examine hard data about product performance. When there's hard evidence that prototypes are testing well, the confidence of the design team grows. Also, personal conflict between design team members is less likely when testing focuses on hard measurements and facts rather than personal hunches and preferences.

Milestones are formal project review points used to assess progress and performance. For example, a company that has put itself on a 12-month schedule to complete a project might schedule milestones at the 3-month, 6-month, and 9-month points on the schedule. By making people regularly assess what they're doing, how well they're performing, and whether they need to take corrective action, milestones provide structure to the general chaos that follows technological discontinuities. Milestones also shorten the innovation process by creating a sense of urgency that keeps everyone on task.

Multifunctional teams are work teams composed of people from different departments. Multifunctional teams accelerate learning and understanding by mixing and integrating technical, marketing, and manufacturing activities. By involving all key departments in development from the start, multifunctional teams

Design iteration a cycle of repetition in which a company tests a prototype of a new product or service, improves on that design, and then builds and tests the improved prototype

Product prototype a full-scale, working model that is being tested for design, function, and reliability

Testing the systematic comparison of different product designs or design iterations

Milestones formal project review points used to assess progress and performance

Multifunctional teams work teams composed of people from different departments speed innovation through early identification of new ideas or problems that would typically not have been generated or addressed until much later.

Powerful leaders provide the vision, discipline, and motivation to keep the innovation process focused, on time, and on target. Powerful leaders are able to get resources when they are needed, are typically more experienced, have high status in the company, and are held directly responsible for the product's success or failure. On average, powerful leaders can get innovation-related projects done nine months faster than leaders with little power or influence. One such powerful leader was Phil Martens, the former head of Ford's product development. With a year to go before introduction and Ford's hybrid Escape months behind schedule, he told the team, "We are going to deliver on time.... Anything you need you'll get."[26] Despite daily inquiries "from above," he promised no interruptions or interference from anyone—even top management. And, when the team members needed something, they got it without waiting.

2.3 Compression Approach: Managing Innovation during Incremental Change

Whereas the experiential approach is used to manage innovation in highly uncertain environments during periods of discontinuous change, the compression approach is used to manage innovation in more certain environments during periods of incremental change. Whereas the goals of the experiential approach are significant improvements in performance and the establishment of a *new* dominant design, the goals of the compression approach are lower costs and incremental improvements in the performance and function of the *existing* dominant design.

The general strategies in each approach are different, too. With the experiential approach, the general strategy is to build something new, different, and substantially better. Because there's so much uncertainty—no one knows which technology will become the market leader—companies adopt a winner-take-all approach by trying to create the market-leading, dominant design. With the compression approach, the general strategy is to compress the time and steps needed to bring about small, consistent improvements in performance and functionality. Because a dominant technology design already exists, the general strategy is to continue improving the existing technology as rapidly as possible.

In short, a **compression approach to innovation** assumes that innovation is a predictable process, that

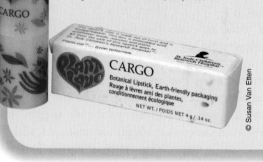

Extreme Makeover

Standing in front of her mirror, Hana Zalal, the president of Cargo Cosmetics, was holding a tube of lipstick and wondering how to redesign it. Then came a packaging epiphany: make it completely biodegradable. An alumna of the University of Toronto's civil engineering program, she went to the university for help. Professor Mohini Sain took up the project and worked with Cargo and a local injection-molding company for two years to figure out how to form corn into a lipstick tube at a "fast and cheap commercial rate." They succeeded. Not only does the new PlantLove lipstick tube decompose in 47 days with composting, the box it comes in is embedded with wildflower seeds and can be planted instead of discarded. And as you would expect, the lipstick itself is environmentally friendly and uses no mineral or petroleum oils or derivatives.

Source: S. Bhattacharya, "Cosmetics Company Cargo Takes Green and Floral Path," *Toronto Star*, 16 January 2007; "Lipstick Maker Goes Green with Biodegradable Tube," *CBC Canada*, 20 April 2007.

incremental innovation can be planned using a series of steps, and that compressing the time it takes to complete those steps can speed up innovation. The compression approach to innovation has five aspects: planning, supplier involvement, shortening the time of individual steps, overlapping steps, and multifunctional teams.[27]

In Chapter 5, *planning* was defined as choosing a goal and a method or strategy to achieve that goal. When *planning for incremental innovation*, the goal is to squeeze or compress development time as much as possible, and the general strategy is to create a series of planned steps to accomplish that goal. Planning for incremental innovation helps avoid unnecessary steps and enables developers to sequence steps in the right order to avoid wasted time and delays between steps. Planning also reduces misunderstandings and improves coordination.

Compression approach to innovation an approach to innovation that assumes that incremental innovation can be planned using a series of steps and that compressing those steps can speed innovation

Most planning for incremental innovation is based on the idea of generational change. **Generational change** occurs when incremental improvements are made to a dominant technological design such that the improved version of the technology is fully backward compatible with the older version.[28] Software is backward compatible if a new version of the software will work with files created by older versions. Likewise, one of the important features of gaming machines, like the Xbox 360 and the Nintendo Wii, is their ability to play games purchased for earlier machines. In fact, the latest Game Boy can play games originally purchased more than 20 years ago.

Because the compression approach assumes that innovation can follow a series of preplanned steps, one of the ways to shorten development time is *supplier involvement.* Delegating some of the preplanned steps in the innovation process to outside suppliers reduces the amount of work that internal development teams must do. Plus, suppliers provide an alternative source of ideas and expertise that can lead to better designs. Rowmark, an international firms, produces thin plastic sheets that can be engraved or shaped by a thermoforming process. In an effort to improve the performance of their product, lower the cost of raw materials, and avoid disruptions in supply, it recruits the companies that supply its resin and additives to participate in the product design and manufacturing processes. Suppliers have knowledge that can help Rowmark put out a better product at lower cost. Loyalty and flexibility is important, as is cultural fit between the supplier and the manufacturer, because

Generational change
change based on incremental improvements to a dominant technological design such that the improved technology is fully backward compatible with the older technology

they are effectively becoming a single team. Eric Hausserman, Rowmark's vice president for manufacturing and technology, points out, "We see our suppliers as partners in every sense of the term."[29] In general, the earlier suppliers are involved, the quicker they catch and prevent future problems, such as unrealistic designs or mismatched product specifications.

Another way to shorten development time is simply to *shorten the time of individual steps* in the innovation process. A common way to do that is through computer-aided design (CAD). CAD speeds up the design process by allowing designers and engineers to make and test design changes using computer models rather than physically testing expensive prototypes. CAD also speeds innovation by making it easy to see how design changes affect engineering, purchasing, and production.

In a sequential design process, each step must be completed before the next step begins. But sometimes multiple development steps can be performed at the same time. *Overlapping steps* shorten the development process by reducing delays or waiting time between steps. Warner Bros. is using overlapping steps to reduce the time it takes to make the entire series of seven *Harry Potter* films—one for each of the seven books in J.K. Rowling's series. Because the actors were aging and would soon resemble adults more than high school students, Warner Bros. used new directors and new production teams for each of the movies in the *Harry Potter* series so that it could begin shooting the next film while the previous one was in post production and the one prior to that was in the theatres.[30]

Beating a Sluggish Economy

Starbucks, the ubiquitous coffee shop that popularized gourmet coffee, posted its first ever loss in July 2008. What's got them down? Overexpansion, increase in the price of commodities, competition from companies like McDonald's, which are making improved (and less expensive) coffee, and an overall slower economy. CEO Howard Schultz aimed to give the company a jolt in early 2008 by introducing the new Pike Place roast, among other tactics. But even a venti strategy couldn't wake up the company, which announced plans to close 680 stores in 2008, on top of the 300 stores closed worldwide in 2008 (including 61 in Australia). But you still probably won't have to walk far to get your next caffeine fix.

Sources: L. Gunnison, "Black and Brew," Portfolio.com; J. Riley, "Starbucks Closures—Global Economy or Other Factors to Blame?" *Tutor2u*; Starbucks (2008). Starbucks Newsroom 31 July 2008.

© D. Hurst/Getstock.com

Organizational Change

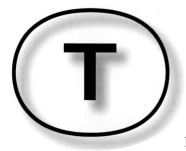

The idea was simple. Build a series of electronics superstores and watch the customers and profits pour in. For a while, it seemed to work. Radio Shack created Incredible Universe and it grew to $72.5 million in less than four years as the company expanded to 17 stores, including several in Canada, each of which stocked an average of 85,000 products in a 185,000-square-foot building. That was more than four times the size of the now bankrupt Circuit City stores, a rival at the time. At the time, the largest big-box store in Canada was an Incredible Universe. Yet because of the size, inventory, and extras, the breakeven point for each store was $70 million in sales per year. So despite rapid growth, the company was losing money at record rates. Managers were unable to change the store concept quickly enough to reverse the situation, so the parent company, Radio Shack, closed Incredible Universe just four years after its founding. Businesses operate in a constantly changing environment. Recognizing and adapting to internal and external changes can mean the difference between continued success and going out of business. Companies that fail to change run the risk of organizational decline.[31]

 After reading the next two sections on organizational change, you should be able to

3 discuss why not changing can lead to organizational decline.

4 discuss the different methods that managers can use to better manage change as it occurs.

3 Organizational Decline: The Risk of Not Changing

Businesses operate in a constantly changing environment. Recognizing and adapting to internal and external changes can mean the difference between continued success and going out of business. Companies that fail to change run the risk of organizational decline.[32]

Organizational decline occurs when companies don't anticipate, recognize, neutralize, or adapt to the internal or external pressures that threaten their survival.[33] In other words, decline occurs when organizations don't recognize the need for change. General Motors' loss of market share and eventual bankruptcy in late 2009, in the automobile industry is an example of organizational decline. There are five stages of organizational decline: blinded, inaction, faulty action, crisis, and dissolution.[34]

In the *blinded stage*, decline begins because key managers fail to recognize the internal or external changes that will harm their organization. This "blindness" may be due to a simple lack of awareness about changes or an inability to understand their significance. It may also come from the overconfidence that can develop when a company has been successful.

In the *inaction stage*, as organizational performance problems become more visible, management may recognize the need to change but still take no action. The managers may be waiting to see if the problems will correct themselves. Or, they may find it difficult to change the practices and policies that previously led to success. Possibly, too, they wrongly assume that they can easily correct the problems, so they don't feel the situation is urgent.

In the *faulty action stage*, faced with rising costs and decreasing profits and market share, management will announce "belt tightening" plans designed to cut costs, increase efficiency, and restore profits. In other words, rather than recognizing the need for fundamental changes, managers assume that if they just run a tighter ship, company performance will return to previous levels.

In the *crisis stage*, bankruptcy or dissolution (i.e., breaking up the company and selling its parts) is likely to occur unless the company completely reorganizes the way it does business. At this point, however, companies typically lack the resources to fully change how they run their businesses. Cutbacks and layoffs will have reduced the level of talent among employees. Furthermore, talented managers who were savvy enough to see the crisis coming will have found jobs with other companies, often with competitors.

In the *dissolution stage*, after failing to make the changes needed to sustain the organization, the company is dissolved through bankruptcy proceedings or by selling assets in order to pay suppliers,

> **Organizational decline** a large decrease in organizational performance that occurs when companies don't anticipate, recognize, neutralize, or adapt to the internal or external pressures that threaten their survival

banks, and creditors. At this point, a new CEO may be brought in to oversee the closing of stores, offices, and manufacturing facilities, the final layoff of managers and employees, and the sale of assets.

Because decline is reversible at each of the first four stages, not all companies in decline reach final dissolution. GM aggressively cut costs, stabilized its shrinking market share, and used innovative production techniques in an effort to reverse a decline that resulted in bankruptcy.

4 Managing Change

According to social psychologist Kurt Lewin, change is a function of the forces that promote change and the opposing forces that slow or resist change.[35] **Change forces** lead to differences in the form, quality, or condition of an organization over time.

By contrast, **resistance forces** support the status quo, that is, the existing conditions in organizations. Change is difficult under any circumstances. In a study of heart bypass patients, doctors told participants straight-forwardly to change their eating and health habits or they would die. Unbelievably, a full 90 percent of participants did *not* change their habits at all![36] This fierce resistance to change also applies to organizations.

Resistance to change is caused by self-interest, misunderstanding and distrust, and a general intolerance for change.[37] People resist change out of *self-interest* because they fear that change will cost or deprive them of something they value. For example, resistance might stem from a fear that the changes will result in a loss of pay, power, responsibility, or even perhaps one's job. People also resist change because of *misunderstanding and distrust*; they don't understand the change or the reasons for it, or they distrust the people—typically management—behind the

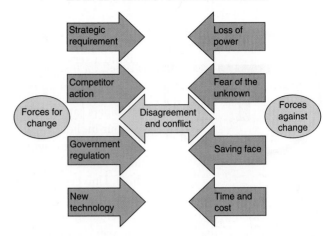

EXAMPLE of LEWIN'S FORCE FIELD ANALYSIS

Forces for change: Strategic requirement, Competitor action, Government regulation, New technology

Disagreement and conflict

Forces against change: Loss of power, Fear of the unknown, Saving face, Time and cost

Source: Adapted from Lewin.

change. Resistance isn't always visible at first, however. Some of the strongest resisters may initially support the changes in public, nodding and smiling their agreement, but then ignore the changes in private and do their jobs as they always have. Management consultant Michael Hammer calls this deadly form of resistance the "Kiss of Yes."[38]

Resistance may also come from a generally low tolerance for change. Some people are simply less capable of handling change than others. People with a *low tolerance for change* feel threatened by the uncertainty associated with change and worry that they won't be able to learn the new skills and behaviours needed to successfully negotiate change in their companies.

Because resistance to change is inevitable, successful change efforts require careful management. In this section you will learn about **4.1 managing resistance to change, 4.2 what not to do when leading organizational change,** and **4.3 different change tools and techniques.**

4.1 Managing Resistance to Change

According to Kurt Lewin, managing organizational change is a basic process of unfreezing, change intervention, and refreezing. **Unfreezing** is getting the people affected by change to believe that change is needed. During the **change intervention** itself, workers and managers change their behaviour and work practices. **Refreezing** is supporting and reinforcing the new changes so that they stick.

Resistance to change is an example of frozen behaviour. Given the choice between changing and not changing, most people would rather not change. Because resistance to change is natural and inevitable, managers need to unfreeze resistance to change to

Change forces forces that produce differences in the form, quality, or condition of an organization over time

Resistance forces forces that support the existing state of conditions in organizations

Resistance to change opposition to change resulting from self-interest, misunderstanding and distrust, and a general intolerance for change

Unfreezing getting the people affected by change to believe that change is needed

Change intervention the process used to get workers and managers to change their behaviour and work practices

Refreezing supporting and reinforcing new changes so that they stick

create successful change programs. The following methods can be used to manage resistance to change: education and communication, participation, negotiation, top management support, and coercion.[39]

When resistance to change is based on insufficient, incorrect, or misleading information, managers should *educate* employees about the need for change and *communicate* change-related information to them. Managers must also supply the information and funding or other support employees need to make changes. For example, resistance to change can be particularly strong when one company buys another company.

Another way to reduce resistance to change is to have those affected by the change *participate in planning and implementing the change process.* Employees who participate have a better understanding of the change and the need for it. Furthermore, employee concerns about change can be addressed as they occur if employees participate in the planning and implementation process. The original Swiffer duster was developed by a Japanese company; P&G then teamed up with it to take the product global.[40] Innovation on a global scale is sometimes required. Tim Penner, CEO of P&G Canada, has indicated that P&G will become an innovator online and that he will be assigning as much as 20 percent of the advertising budget to digital media. Canada has often served as a testing ground for new products that P&G has eventually rolled out elsewhere in the world. Penner led the launch of Swiffer WetJet in Canada a year before its American rollout.[41] P&G Canada tries to blend the best R&D practices in the world with an understanding of local Canadian markets. "We truly think globally and act locally," states Penner. In doing so, P&G hopes to become the fastest growing consumer products company in Canada. It plans to achieve that leadership position "through innovation in everything we do," from innovative marketing programs that foster meaningful relationships with consumers, to productive partnerships with retailers and leading workplace practices for employees.[42]

Employees are also less likely to resist change if they are allowed to discuss and agree on who will do what after change occurs. Resistance to change also decreases when change efforts receive *significant managerial support.* Managers must do more than talk about the importance of change, though. They must provide the training, resources, and autonomy needed to make change happen. For example, with a distinguished 70-year history of hand-drawing Hollywood's most successful animated films (*Snow White,*

GOOD TIP!

What to Do When Employees Resist Change

UNFREEZING

- **Share reasons** Share the reasons for change with employees.
- **Empathize** Be empathetic to the difficulties that change will create for managers and employees.
- **Communicate** Communicate the details simply, clearly, extensively, verbally, and in writing.

CHANGE

- **Explain** Explain the benefits, "what's in it for them."
- **Champion** Identify a highly respected manager to manage the change effort.
- **Create opportunities for feedback** Allow the people who will be affected by change to express their needs and offer their input.
- **Time it right** Don't begin change at a bad time, for example, during the busiest part of the year or month.
- **Offer security** If possible, maintain employees' job security to minimize fear of change.
- **Educate** Offer training to ensure that employees are both confident and competent to handle new requirements.
- **Don't rush** Change at a manageable pace.

Source: G. J. Iskat and J. Liebowitz, "What to Do When Employees Resist Change," *Supervision*, 1 August 1996.

Bambi, The Little Mermaid, Beauty and the Beast), animators at the Walt Disney Company naturally resisted the move to computer-generated (CG) animation. So Disney supported the difficult change by putting all of its animators through a six-month "CG Boot Camp," where they learned how to draw animated characters with computers.[43]

Finally, resistance to change can be managed through **coercion,** or the use of formal power and authority to force others to change. Because of the intense negative reactions it can create (e.g., fear, stress, resentment, sabotage of company products), coercion

Coercion using formal power and authority to force others to change should be used only when a crisis exists or when all other attempts to reduce resistance to change have failed.

4.2 What *Not* to Do When Leading Change

So far, you've learned how to execute a basic change process (unfreezing, change, refreezing) and how to manage resistance to change. Harvard Business School professor John Kotter argues that knowing what *not* to do is just as important as knowing what to do when it comes to achieving successful organizational change.[44]

Managers commonly make certain errors when they lead change. The first two errors occur during the unfreezing phase, when managers try to get the people affected by change to believe that change is really needed. The first and potentially most serious error is *not establishing a great enough sense of urgency*. Indeed, Kotter estimates that more than half of all change efforts fail because the people affected are not convinced that change is necessary. People will feel a greater sense of urgency if a leader in the company makes a public, candid assessment of the company's problems and weaknesses.

The second mistake that occurs in the unfreezing process is *not creating a powerful enough coalition*. Change often starts with one or two people. But change has to be supported by a critical and growing group of people to build enough momentum to change an entire department, division, or company. Besides top management, Kotter recommends that key employees, managers, board members, customers, and even union leaders be members of a *core change coalition* that guides and supports organizational change. Procter & Gamble Canada's CEO Tim Penner states that "our contribution to Canada… goes beyond our brands. From our long-term partnership with United Way, to our Junior Achievement volunteers in classrooms all over Canada, we continue to find ways to improve the quality of life in our communities… We encourage personal growth since our future success depends so much on developing the leaders of tomorrow." Clearly, P&G Canada is committing to explicit organizational change.

The next four errors that managers make occur during the change phase, when a change intervention is used to try to get workers and managers to change their behaviour and work practices. *Lacking a vision* for change is a significant error at this point. As you learned in Chapter 5, a *vision* is a statement of a company's purpose or reason for existing. A vision for change makes clear where a company or

Errors Managers Make When Leading Change

UNFREEZING

1. Not establishing a great enough sense of urgency.
2. Not creating a powerful enough guiding coalition.

CHANGE

3. Lacking a vision.
4. Undercommunicating the vision by a factor of ten.
5. Not removing obstacles to the new vision.
6. Not systematically planning for and creating short-term wins.

REFREEZING

7. Declaring victory too soon.
8. Not anchoring changes in the corporation's culture.

Source: J. P. Kotter, "Leading Change: Why Transformation Efforts Fail," *Harvard Business Review* 73, no. 2 (March–April 1995): 59.

department is headed and why the change is occurring. Change efforts that lack vision tend to be confused, chaotic, and contradictory. By contrast, change efforts guided by visions are clear and easy to understand and can be effectively explained in five minutes or less.

Undercommunicating the vision by a factor of ten is another mistake in the change phase. According to Kotter, companies mistakenly hold just one meeting to announce the vision. Or, if the new vision receives heavy emphasis in executive speeches or company newsletters, senior management then undercuts the vision by behaving in ways contrary to it. Successful communication of the vision requires that top managers link everything the company does to the new vision and that they "walk the talk" by behaving in ways consistent with the vision.

Furthermore, even companies that begin change with a clear vision sometimes make the mistake of *not removing obstacles to the new vision*. They leave formidable barriers to change in place by failing to redesign jobs, pay plans, and technology to support the new way of doing things.

CHANGE EFFORTS THAT LACK VISION TEND TO BE CONFUSED, CHAOTIC, AND CONTRADICTORY.

Another error in the change phase is *not systematically planning for and creating short-term wins.* Most people don't have the discipline and patience to wait two years to see if the new change effort works. Change is threatening and uncomfortable, so people need to see an immediate payoff if they are to continue to support it. Kotter recommends that managers create short-term wins by actively picking people and projects that are likely to work extremely well early in the change process.

The last two errors that managers make occur during the refreezing phase, when attempts are made to support and reinforce changes so that they stick. *Declaring victory too soon* is a tempting mistake in the refreezing phase. Managers typically declare victory right after the first large-scale success in the change process. Declaring success too early has the same effect as draining the gasoline out of a car: it stops change efforts dead in their tracks. With success declared, supporters of the change process stop pushing to make change happen. After all, why push when success has been achieved? Rather than declaring victory, managers should use the momentum from short-term wins to push for even bigger or faster changes. This maintains urgency

and prevents change supporters from slacking off before the changes are frozen into the company's culture.

The last mistake that managers make is *not anchoring changes in the corporation's culture.* An *organization's culture* is the set of key values, beliefs, and attitudes shared by organizational members that determines the "accepted way of doing things" in a company. As you learned in Chapter 3, changing cultures is extremely difficult and slow. According to Kotter, two things help anchor changes in a corporation's culture. The first is directly showing people that the changes have actually improved performance. The second is to make sure that the people who get promoted fit the new culture. If they don't, it's a clear sign that the changes were only temporary.

4.3 Change Tools and Techniques

Imagine your boss came to you and said, "All right, genius, you wanted it. You're in charge of turning around the division." How would you start? Where would you begin? How would you encourage change-resistant managers to change? What would you do to include others in the change process? How would you get the change process off to a quick start? Finally, what approach would you use to promote long-term effectiveness and performance? Results-driven change, the General Electric work-out, and organizational development are three change tools and techniques that can be used to address these issues.

One of the reasons that organizational change efforts fail is that they are activity-oriented rather than

Beyond Chicken Noodle

Your grandmother's old standby may cure your cold and heal your soul, but it isn't good enough to revive Campbell Soup Co.'s downturn or achieve its goal of expanding into global markets. Campbell's must make sure the famous red label remains the leader in soup. But that will mean change. Chicken soup may be food for the soul in Canada...

... but not so much for the Chinese. The company must learn the ins and outs of soup in different cultures and establish strategies for breaking into those markets. Some tips for transformation: All things are possible. See the situation straight. Have high standards and follow through. Take the time to get it right.

Source: J. Jargon, "Campbell's Chief Looks for Splash of Innovation," *The Wall Street Journal,* 30 May 2008, B8.

Exhibit 7.4

How to Create a Results-Driven Change Program

1. Set measurable, short-term goals to improve performance.
2. Make sure your action steps are likely to improve measured performance.
3. Stress the importance of immediate improvements.
4. Solicit help from consultants and staffers to achieve quick improvements in performance.
5. Test action steps to see if they actually yield improvements. If they don't, discard them and establish new ones.
6. Use resources you have or that can be easily required. It doesn't take much.

Source: R. H. Schaffer & H. A. Thomson, J.D, "Successful Change Programs Begin with Results," *Harvard Business Review on Change* (Boston: Harvard Business School Press, 1998), 189–213.

results-oriented. In other words, they focus primarily on changing company procedures, management philosophy, or employee behaviour. Typically, there is much buildup and preparation as consultants are brought in, presentations are made, books are read, and employees and managers are trained. There's a tremendous emphasis on "doing things the new way." But, with all the focus on "doing," almost no attention is paid to results, to seeing if all this activity has actually made a difference.

By contrast, **results-driven change** supplants the emphasis on activity with a laser-like focus on quickly measuring and improving results.[45] For example, top managers at Hyundai knew that if they were to compete successfully against the likes of Honda and Toyota, they would have to substantially improve the quality of their cars. So top managers guided the company's results-driven change process by increasing the number of quality teams from 100 to 865. Then, all employees were required to attend seminars on quality improvement and use the results of industry quality studies, such as those published annually by J.D. Power and Associates, as their benchmark. Before the change, a new Hyundai averaged 23.4 initial quality problems; after the results-driven change efforts, that number dropped to 9.6.[46]

Another advantage of results-driven change is that managers introduce changes in procedures, philosophy, or behaviour only if they are likely to improve measured performance. In other

words, changes are tested to see whether they actually make a difference. Consistent with this approach, Hyundai invested $30 million in a test centre where cars were subjected to a sequence of extremely harsh conditions to allow engineers to pinpoint defects and fix problems.[47]

A third advantage of results-driven change is that quick, visible improvements motivate employees to continue to make additional changes to improve measured performance. Exhibit 7.4 describes the basic steps of results-driven change.

The **General Electric workout** is a special kind of results-driven change. The "workout" involves a three-day meeting that brings together managers and employees from different levels and parts of an organization to quickly generate and act on solutions to specific business problems.[48] On the first morning, the boss discusses the agenda and targets specific business problems that the group will solve. The boss then leaves, and an outside facilitator breaks the group (typically 30 to 40 people) into five or six teams and helps them spend the next day and a half discussing and debating solutions. On day three, in what GE calls a "town meeting," the teams present specific solutions to their boss, who has been gone since day one. As each team's spokesperson makes specific suggestions, the boss has only three options: agree on the spot, say no, or ask for more information so that a decision can be made by a specific, agreed-on date.[49]

Organizational development is a philosophy and collection of planned change interventions designed to improve an organization's long-term health and performance. Organizational development takes a long-range approach to change; assumes that top management support is necessary for change to succeed; creates change by educating workers and managers to change ideas, beliefs, and behaviours so that problems can be solved in new ways; and emphasizes employee

Results-driven change
change created quickly by focusing on the measurement and improvement of results

General Electric workout a three-day meeting in which managers and employees from different levels and parts of an organization quickly generate and act on solutions to specific business problems

Organizational development a philosophy and collection of planned change interventions designed to improve an organization's long-term health and performance

Exhibit 7.5

General Steps for Organizational Development Interventions

1. **Entry**	A problem is discovered and the need for change becomes apparent. A search begins for someone to deal with the problem and facilitate change.
2. **Startup**	A change agent enters the picture and works to clarify the problem and gain commitment to a change effort.
3. **Assessment & feedback**	The change agent gathers information about the problem and provides feedback about it to decision makers and those affected by it.
4. **Action planning**	The change agent works with decision makers to develop an action plan.
5. **Intervention**	The action plan, or organizational development intervention, is carried out.
6. **Evaluation**	The change agent helps decision makers assess the effectiveness of the intervention.
7. **Adoption**	Organizational members accept ownership and responsibility for the change, which is then carried out through the entire organization.
8. **Separation**	The change agent leaves the organization after first ensuring that the change intervention will continue to work.

Source: W. J. Rothwell, R. Sullivan, and G. M. McLean, *Practicing Organizational Development: A Guide for Consultants* (San Diego: Pfeiffer & Co., 1995).

participation in diagnosing, solving, and evaluating problems.[50] As shown in Exhibit 7.5, organizational development interventions begin with the recognition of a problem. Then, the company designates a **change agent** to be formally in charge of guiding the change effort. This person can be someone from the company or a professional consultant. The change agent clarifies the problem, gathers information, works with decision makers to create and implement an action plan, helps to evaluate the plan's effectiveness, implements the plan throughout the company, and then leaves (if from outside the company) after making sure the change intervention will continue to work.

Organizational development interventions are aimed at changing large systems, small groups, or people.[51] More specifically, the purpose of *large system interventions* is to change the character and performance of an organization, business unit, or department. *Small group intervention* focuses on assessing how a group functions and helping it work more effectively to accomplish its goals. *Person-focused intervention* is intended to increase interpersonal effectiveness by helping people become aware of their attitudes and behaviours and acquire new skills and knowledge. Exhibit 7.6 describes the most frequently used organizational development interventions for large systems, small groups, and people.

Change agent the person formally in charge of guiding a change effort

Exhibit 7.6

Different Kinds of Organizational Development Interventions

LARGE SYSTEM INTERVENTIONS	
Sociotechnical systems	An intervention designed to improve how well employees use and adjust to the work technology used in an organization.
Survey feedback	An intervention that uses surveys to collect information from the members, reports the results of that survey to the members, and then uses those results to develop action plans for improvement.
SMALL GROUP INTERVENTIONS	
Team building	An intervention designed to increase the cohesion and cooperation of work group members.
Unit goal setting	An intervention designed to help a work group establish short- and long-term goals.
PERSON-FOCUSED INTERVENTIONS	
Counselling/coaching	An intervention designed so that a formal helper or coach listens to managers or employees and advises them on how to deal with work or interpersonal problems.
Training	An intervention designed to provide individuals with the knowledge, skills, or attitudes they need to become more effective at their jobs.

Source: W. J. Rothwell, R. Sullivan, and G. M. McLean, *Practicing Organizational Development: A Guide for Consultants* (San Diego: Pfeiffer & Co., 1995).

By the Numbers

$20 price for a tube of PlantLove lipstick

5 aspects of managing change with the experiential OR compression approach; stages of organizational decline

90% of people who will not change even if it's a matter of life or death

1859 year sewers were first installed in London

5 personality dimensions

10 number of minutes you get to pitch an idea in Adobe's Idea Champion Showcase

Visit **icanmgmt.com** to find the resources you need today!

Located at the back of the textbook are rip-out Chapter Review cards. Make sure you also go online to check out other tools that MGMT offers to help you successfully pass your course.

- Interactive Quizzes
- Key Terms Flashcards
- Audio Chapter Summaries
- PowerPoint Slides

- Interactive Games
- Crossword Puzzles
- "Reel to Reel" and "Biz Flix" videos
- Cases and Exercises

GLOBAL MANAGEMENT

What Is Global Business?

Global business is the buying and selling of goods and services by people from different countries. The Timex watch on my wrist as I write this chapter was purchased at a Wal-Mart in Manitcha. But since it was made in the Philippines, I participated in global business when I wrote Wal-Mart a cheque. Wal-Mart, for its part, had already paid Timex, which had paid the company that employs the Filipino managers and workers who made my watch.

Global business presents its own set of challenges for managers. How can you be sure that the way you run your business in one country is the right way to run that business in another? This chapter discusses how organizations answer that question. We will start by examining global business in two ways: first, by exploring its impact on Canadian businesses and then reviewing the basic rules and agreements that govern global trade. Next, we will examine how and when companies go global by examining the tradeoff between consistency and adaptation and discussing how to organize a global company. Finally, we will look at how companies decide where to expand globally, including finding the best business climate, adapting to cultural differences, and better preparing employees for international assignments.

Global business the buying and selling of goods and services by people from different countries

Learning Outcomes

1 discuss the impact of global business and the trade rules and agreements that govern it.

2 explain why companies choose to standardize or adapt their business procedures.

3 explain the different ways that companies can organize to do business globally.

4 explain how to find a favourable business climate.

5 discuss the importance of identifying and adapting to cultural differences.

6 explain how to successfully prepare workers for international assignments.

© Susan Van Etten

Of course, there is more to global business than buying imported products at Wal-Mart. After reading the next section, you should be able to

1   discuss the impact of global business and the trade rules and agreements that govern it.

1 Global Business, Trade Rules, and Trade Agreements

If you want a simple demonstration of the impact of global business, look at the tag on your shirt, the inside of your shoes, and the inside of your cell phone (take your battery out). Chances are, all of these items were made in different places around the world. As I write this, my shirt, shoes, and cell phone were made in Thailand, China, and Korea. Where were yours made?

*Let's learn more about **1.1 the impact of global business, 1.2 how tariff and nontariff trade barriers have historically restricted global business, 1.3 how global and regional trade agreements today are reducing those trade barriers worldwide**, and **1.4 how consumers are responding to those changes in trade rules and agreements**.*

1.1 The Impact of Global Business

Multinational corporations are corporations that own businesses in two or more

Multinational corporation a corporation that owns businesses in two or more countries

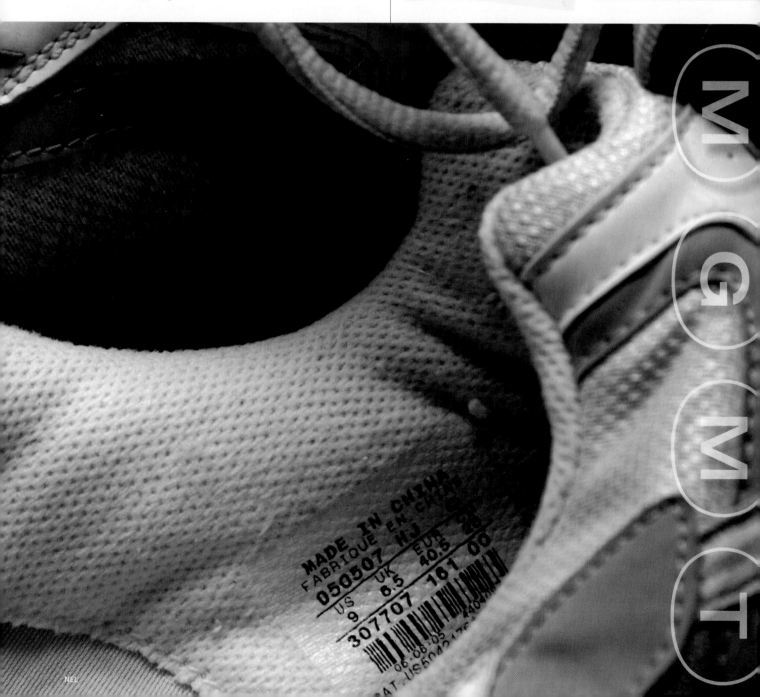

Foreign Direct Investment in Canada, 1998–2007 Cumulative at Year End

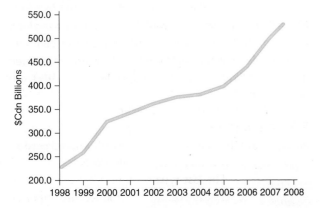

Sources: Statistics Canada: International Investment Position, May 2008 (http://www.investontario.com/siteselector/bcin_500.asp) Accessed 19 May 2010); Government of Canada, 9 March 2010. Canada Poised to Become "Tariff-Free Zone" for Manufacturers Thanks to Budget 2010. http://news.gc.ca/web/article=eng.co?m=index&nid=517440. Accessed 19 May 2010.

Direct foreign investment a method of investment in which a company builds a new business or buys an existing business in a foreign country

Trade barriers government-imposed regulations that increase the cost and restrict the number of imported goods

Protectionism a government's use of trade barriers to shield domestic companies and their workers from foreign competition

Tariff a direct tax on imported goods

Nontariff barriers nontax methods of increasing the cost or reducing the volume of imported goods

countries. In 1970, more than half of the world's 7,000 multinational corporations were headquartered in just two countries: the United States and the United Kingdom. Today, there are 77,175 multinational corporations, nearly 11.25 times as many as in 1970, and only 2,418, or 3.1 percent, are based in the United States.[1] Today, 53,072 multinationals, or 68.8 percent, are based in other countries (e.g., Germany, Italy, Canada, and Japan), while 20,238, or 26.2 percent, are based in developing countries (e.g., Colombia, South Africa, and Tunisia). So, today, multinational companies can be found by the thousands all over the world!

Another way to appreciate the impact of global business is by considering direct foreign investment. **Direct foreign investment** occurs when a company builds a new business or buys an existing business in a foreign country. U.S. steelmaker Nucor made a direct foreign investment when it purchased Harris Steel of Canada Ltd.[2] Of course, companies from many other countries also own businesses in Canada. Companies from the United Kingdom, Japan, Germany, the Netherlands,

the U.S., France, Switzerland, and Luxembourg have the largest direct foreign investment in Canada. Overall, foreign companies invest more than $500 billion a year to do business in Canada.

But direct foreign investment in Canada is only half the picture. Canada companies also have made large direct foreign investments in countries throughout the world. For example, Molson, the brewer of Molson X, paid $700 million to acquire Brewery Group, the fourth largest beer company in Mexico.[3] Canadian companies have made their largest direct foreign investments in the United Kingdom, the U.S., the Netherlands, and Australia. Note that there are many restrictions on foreign ownership in Canada. Broadcasting, aviation, liquor sales, mining, oil and gas, and pharmacies are only some of the industries where Canada restricts foreign ownership.[3]

So, whether foreign companies invest in the Canada or Canadian companies invest abroad, direct foreign investment is an increasingly important and common method of conducting global business.

1.2 Trade Barriers

Although today's consumers usually don't care where the products they buy come from (more on this in Section 1.4), national governments have traditionally preferred that consumers buy domestically made products in the hope that such purchases would increase the number of domestic businesses and workers. Indeed, governments have done much more than hope that you will buy from domestic companies. Historically, governments have actively used **trade barriers** to make it much more expensive or difficult (or sometimes impossible) for consumers to buy or consume imported goods. For example, the European Union places a 34 percent tax on frozen strawberries imported from China.[4] And the Canadian government imposes a tariff of 5 cents a litre on imported ethanol, which is blended with gasoline for use in automobiles.[5] By establishing these restrictions and taxes, the governments of the European Union, China, and the United States are engaging in **protectionism,** which is the use of trade barriers to protect local companies and their workers from foreign competition.

Governments have used two general kinds of trade barriers: tariff and nontariff barriers. A **tariff** is a direct tax on imported goods. Like the Canadian government's 5-cents-per-litre tax on imported ethanol, tariffs increase the cost of imported goods relative to that of domestic goods. **Nontariff barriers** are nontax methods of increasing the cost or reducing the volume of imported goods. There are five types of nontariff barriers: quotas, voluntary

Who Pays Tariffs?

Tariffs on foreign imports are supposed to preserve Canadian jobs, but 74 percent of shoes worn by Canadians are made outside Canada, suggesting that there aren't many Canadian jobs within the shoe industry to save. Still, Canada imposes a tax on imported shoes that can skyrocket to 32 percent, and the tariff creates $2 billion of revenue, which is more than auto tariffs. Who pays? Since low-end footwear bears the brunt of the tariff, it's mostly lower-income individuals who shop at retail outlets such as Wal-Mart Canada, where $5 of a $15 pair of tennis shoes may be duty.

Source: "Shot in the Foot," *The Wall Street Journal*, 6 September 2008, A10.

2/3, product price   *1/3, tariff*

© iStockphoto.com/Don Nichols

export restraints, government import standards, government subsidies, and customs valuation/classification. Because there are so many different kinds of nontariff barriers, they can be an even more potent method of shielding domestic industries from foreign competition.

Quotas are specific limits on the number or volume of imported products. For example, because of strict quotas, yearly imports of raw sugarcane into Canada are limited.[6] Since this is well below the demand for sugar in the Canada, domestic Canadian sugar prices are twice as high as sugar prices in the rest of the world.[7] Like quotas, **voluntary export restraints** limit the amount of a product that can be imported annually. The difference is that the exporting country rather than the importing country imposes restraints. Usually, however, the "voluntary" offer to limit exports occurs because the importing country has implicitly threatened to impose quotas. According to the World Trade Organization (see the discussion in Section 1.3), however, voluntary export restraints are illegal and should not be used to restrict imports.[8]

In theory, **government import standards** are established to protect the health and safety of citizens. In reality, such standards are often used to restrict or ban imported goods. For example, the U.S. banned the importation of nearly all Canadian beef. Ostensibly, the ban was to prevent transmission of mad cow disease (BSE), but the U.S. government was actually using this government import standard to protect the economic health of its beef farmers. Only after the World Trade Organization ruled that there was no scientific basis for

the ban did the U.S. allow Canadian beef to be imported without restrictions.[9]

Many nations also use **subsidies,** such as long-term, low-interest loans, cash grants, and tax deferments, to develop and protect companies in special industries. Not surprisingly, businesses complain about unfair trade practices when foreign companies receive government subsidies. For example, Embraer, the Brazilian jet airplane manufacturer, complained about subsidies provided to Canada's Bombardier jet manufacturer. This issue has been an ongoing dispute with many rulings made by the WTO. Meanwhile, the Canadian taxpayer picks up the subsidy costs.[10]

The last type of nontariff barrier is **customs classification.** As products are imported into a country, they are examined by customs agents, who must decide into which of nearly 9,000 categories they should classify a product (see the Official Harmonized Tariff Schedule of Canada at **http://www.cbsa-asfa .ca** for more information). Classification is important because the category assigned by customs agents can greatly affect the size of the tariff and whether the item is subject to import quotas. For example, the Canadian Border Services Agency has several customs classifications for imported shoes. Tariffs on imported leather or "nonrubber" shoes are about 10 percent, whereas tariffs on imported rubber shoes, such as athletic footwear or waterproof shoes, range from 20 to 84 percent.[11] The difference is large enough that some importers try to make their rubber shoes look like leather in hopes of receiving the nonrubber customs classification and lower tariff.

1.3 Trade Agreements

Thanks to the trade barriers described above, buying imported goods has often been much more expensive and difficult than buying domestic goods. During the 1990s, however, the regulations governing global trade were transformed. The most

Quota a limit on the number or volume of imported products

Voluntary export restraints voluntarily imposed limits on the number or volume of products exported to a particular country

Government import standard a standard ostensibly established to protect the health and safety of citizens but, in reality, often used to restrict imports

Subsidies government loans, grants, and tax deferments given to domestic companies to protect them from foreign competition

Customs classification a classification assigned to imported products by government officials that affects the size of the tariff and imposition of import quotas

significant change was that 124 countries agreed to adopt the **General Agreement on Tariffs and Trade (GATT)**. Although GATT itself was replaced by the **World Trade Organization (WTO)** in 1995, the changes that it made continue to encourage international trade. The WTO, headquartered in Geneva, Switzerland, administers trade agreements, provides a forum for trade negotiations, handles trade disputes, monitors national trade policies, and offers technical assistance and training for developing countries for its 150 member countries.

Through tremendous decreases in tariff and nontariff barriers, GATT made it much easier and cheaper for consumers in all countries to buy foreign products. First, tariffs were cut 40 percent on average worldwide by 2005. Second, tariffs were eliminated in 10 specific industries: beer, alcohol, construction equipment, farm machinery, furniture, medical equipment, paper, pharmaceuticals, steel, and toys. Third, stricter limits were put on government subsidies. Fourth, GATT established protections for intellectual property, such as trademarks, patents, and copyrights. Protection of intellectual property has become an increasingly important issue in global trade because of widespread product piracy. For example, 90 percent of the computer software and 95 percent of the video games in China are illegal pirated copies.[12] Finally, trade disputes between countries now are fully settled by arbitration panels from the WTO. In the past, countries could use their veto power to cancel a panel's decision, but now WTO rulings are complete and final.

The second major development that has reduced trade barriers has been the creation of **regional trading zones,** in which tariff and nontariff barriers are reduced or eliminated by treaties or agreements among countries within the trading zone. The largest and most important trading zones are in Europe

World Trade Organization

General Agreement on Tariffs and Trade (GATT) a worldwide trade agreement that reduced and eliminated tariffs, limited government subsidies, and established protections for intellectual property

World Trade Organization (WTO) as the successor to GATT, the only international organization dealing with the global rules of trade between nations. Its main function is to ensure that trade flows as smoothly, predictably, and freely as possible.

Regional trading zones areas in which tariff and nontariff barriers on trade between countries are reduced or eliminated

Maastricht Treaty of Europe a regional trade agreement between most European countries

(the Maastricht Treaty), North America (the North American Free Trade Agreement, or NAFTA), Central America (Central America Free Trade Agreement, or CAFTA-DR), South America (Union of South American Nations, or USAN), and Asia (the Association of Southeast Asian Nations, or ASEAN, and Asia-Pacific Economic Cooperation, or APEC). The map in Exhibit 8.1 shows the extent to which free trade agreements govern global trade.

In 1992, Belgium, Denmark, France, Germany, Greece, Ireland, Italy, Luxembourg, the Netherlands, Portugal, Spain, and the United Kingdom implemented the **Maastricht Treaty of Europe.** The purpose of this treaty was to transform their 12 different economies and 12 currencies into one common economic market, called the European Union (EU), with one common currency. Austria, Finland, and Sweden joined the EU in 1995, followed by Cyprus, the Czech Republic, Estonia, Hungary, Latvia, Lithuania, Malta, Poland, Slovakia, and Slovenia in 2004, and Bulgaria and Romania in 2007, bringing the total membership to 27 countries.[13] Croatia, Macedonia, and Turkey have applied and are still being considered for membership.[14] On 1 January 2002, a single common currency, the euro, went into circulation in 12 of the EU's members (Austria, Belgium, Finland, France, Germany, Greece, Ireland, Italy, Luxembourg, the Netherlands, Portugal, and Spain).

Prior to the treaty, trucks carrying products were stopped and inspected by customs agents at each border. Furthermore, since the required paperwork, tariffs, and government product specifications could be radically

Exhibit 8.1

Global Map of Regional Trade Agreements

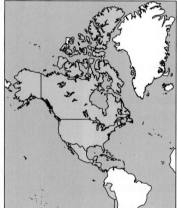

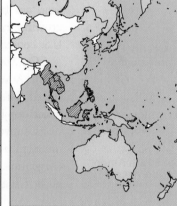

Maastricht Treaty of Europe Austria, Belgium, Bulgaria, Cyprus, the Czech Republic, Denmark, Estonia, Finland, France, Germany, Greece, Hungary, Ireland, Italy, Latvia, Lithuania, Luxembourg, Malta, the Netherlands, Poland, Portugal, Romania, Slovakia, Slovenia, Spain, Sweden, and the United Kingdom.

ASEAN Brunei Darussalam, Cambodia, Indonesia, Lao PDR, Malaysia, Myanmar, the Philippines, Singapore, Thailand, and Vietnam.

APEC Australia, Canada, Chile, the People's Republic of China, Hong Kong (China), Japan, Mexico, New Zealand, Papua New Guinea, Peru, Russia, South Korea, Taiwan, the United States, and all members of ASEAN except Cambodia, Lao PDR, and Myanmar.

NAFTA (North American Free Trade Agreement)
United States, Canada, and Mexico.

SACN (South American Community of Nations) (Proposed)
South America.

CAFTA-DR (Central America-Dominican Republic Free Trade Agreement)
Costa Rica, the Dominican Republic, El Salvador, Guatemala, Honduras, Nicaragua, and the United States.

USAN
Argentina, Brazil, Paraguay, Uruguay, Venezuela, Bolivia, Colombia, Ecuador, Peru, Guyana, Suriname, Chile

different in each country, companies often had to file 12 different sets of paperwork, pay 12 different tariffs, produce 12 different versions of their basic product to meet various government specifications, and exchange money in 12 different currencies. Likewise, open business travel was complicated by inspections at each border crossing. If you lived in Germany but worked in Luxembourg, your car was stopped and your passport was inspected twice every day as you travelled to and from work. Also, every business transaction required a currency exchange, for example, from German deutsche marks to Italian lira, or from French francs to Dutch guilders. Imagine all of this happening to millions of trucks, cars, and businesspeople, and you can begin to appreciate the difficulty and cost of conducting business across Europe before the Maastricht Treaty.

NAFTA, the **North American Free Trade Agreement** between the United States, Canada, and Mexico, went into effect on January 1, 1994. More than any other regional trade agreement, NAFTA has liberalized trade between countries so that businesses can plan for one market (North America) rather than for three separate markets (the United States, Canada, Mexico). One of NAFTA's most important achievements was to eliminate most product tariffs *and* prevent Canada, the United States, and Mexico from increasing existing tariffs or introducing new ones. Overall, both Mexican and Canadian exports to the United States have doubled

North American Free Trade Agreement (NAFTA) a regional trade agreement between the United States, Canada, and Mexico

since NAFTA went into effect. U.S. exports to Mexico and Canada have doubled, too, growing twice as fast as U.S. exports to any other part of the world.[15] In fact, Mexico and Canada now account for 36 percent of all U.S. exports.[16]

CAFTA-DR, the new **Central America Free Trade Agreement** between the United States, the Dominican Republic, and the Central American countries of Costa Rica, El Salvador, Guatemala, Honduras, and Nicaragua, went into effect in August 2005. With a combined population of 347.6 million, the CAFTA-DR countries together are the tenth largest U.S. export market in the world and the second-largest U.S. export market in Latin America after Mexico. U.S. companies export more than $19 billion in goods each year to the CAFTA-DR countries. Furthermore, U.S. exports to CAFTA-DR countries, which are increasing at 16 percent per year, are by far the fastest growing export market for U.S. companies.[17]

On May 23, 2008, 12 South American countries signed the **Union of South American Nations (USAN)** Constitutive Treaty, which united the former Mercosur (Argentina, Brazil, Paraguay, Uruguay, Venezuela) and Andean Community (Bolivia, Colombia, Ecuador, Peru) alliances along with Guyana, Suriname, and Chile. USAN aims to create a unified South America by permitting free movement between nations, creating a common infrastructure that includes an inter-oceanic highway, and establishing the region as a single market by eliminating tariffs by 2019. USAN is one of the largest trading zones in the world, encompassing 361 million people in South America with a combined gross domestic product of nearly $1 trillion.[18]

ASEAN, the **Association of Southeast Asian Nations,** and **APEC,** the **Asia-Pacific**

Central America Free Trade Agreement (CAFTA) a regional trade agreement between Costa Rica, the Dominican Republic, El Salvador, Guatemala, Honduras, Nicaragua, and the United States

Union of South American Nations (USAN) a regional trade agreement between Argentina, Brazil, Paraguay, Uruguay, Venezuela, Bolivia, Colombia, Ecuador, Peru, Guyana, Suriname, and Chile

Association of Southeast Asian Nations (ASEAN) a regional trade agreement between Brunei Darussalam, Cambodia, Indonesia, Lao PDR, Malaysia, Myanmar, the Philippines, Singapore, Thailand, and Vietnam

Asia-Pacific Economic Cooperation (APEC) a regional trade agreement between Australia, Canada, Chile, the People's Republic of China, Hong Kong, Japan, Mexico, New Zealand, Papua New Guinea, Peru, Russia, South Korea, Taiwan, the United States, and all members of ASEAN, except Cambodia, Lao PDR, and Myanmar

The Ambassador Bridge in Windsor is the busiest border crossing between Canada and the United States, carrying 25 percent of all trade between the two countries, or roughly $100 billion in annual trade going in both directions.

Source: P. Fessler, "Proposal for New Border Bridge Draws Critics," npr.org , available online at http://www.npr.org/templates/story/story.php?storyId=10298816 [accessed 6 August 2008].

© Rebecca Cook/Reuters/Landov

Economic Cooperation, are the two largest and most important regional trading groups in Asia. ASEAN is a trade agreement between Brunei Darussalam, Cambodia, Indonesia, Lao PDR, Malaysia, Myanmar, the Philippines, Singapore, Thailand, and Vietnam, which form a market of more than 558 million people. Canadian trade with ASEAN countries exceeds $78 billion a year. In fact, Canada is ASEAN's fifth largest trading partner (Japan is its largest), and ASEAN's member nations constitute the eighth largest trading partner of Canada. An ASEAN free trade area will begin in 2015 for the six original countries (Brunei Darussalam, Indonesia, Malaysia, the Philippines, Singapore, Thailand) and in 2018 for the newer member countries (Cambodia, Lao PDR, Myanmar, and Vietnam).[19]

APEC is a broader agreement that includes Australia, Canada, Chile, the People's Republic of China, Hong Kong (China), Japan, Mexico, New Zealand, Papua New Guinea, Peru, Russia, South Korea, Taiwan, the United States, and all the members of ASEAN except Cambodia, Lao PDR, and Myanmar. APEC's 21 member countries contain 2.6 billion people, account for 47 percent of all global trade, and have a combined gross domestic product of over $19 trillion. APEC countries began reducing trade barriers in 2000, though all the reductions will not be completely phased in until 2020.[20]

What $1 gets you in Canada

What $1 gets you in Japan *What $1 gets you in Switzerland*

1.4 Consumers, Trade Barriers, and Trade Agreements

The average worker earns nearly $54,930 a year in Switzerland, $59,590 in Norway, $38,980 in Japan, and $42,640 in Canada. Yet, after adjusting these incomes for how much they can buy, the Swiss income is equivalent to just $37,080, the Norwegian income to $40,420, and the Japanese income to $31,410![21] This is the same as saying that $1 of income can buy you only 68 cents' worth of goods in Switzerland and Norway, and 81 cents' worth in Japan. In other words, Canadians can buy much more with their incomes than those in other countries can.

One reason that Canadians get more for their money is that the Canadian marketplace has been one of the easiest for foreign companies to enter. Although some Canadian industries, such as farming, have been heavily protected from foreign competition by trade barriers, for the most part, Canadian consumers (and businesses) have had plentiful choices among Canadian-made and foreign-made products. More important, the high level of competition between foreign and domestic companies that creates these choices helps keep prices low in Canada. Furthermore, it is precisely the lack of choice and the low level of competition that keep prices higher in countries that have not been as open to foreign companies and products. For example, Japanese trade barriers are estimated to cost Japanese consumers more than $100 billion a year.[22]

So why do trade barriers and free trade agreements matter to consumers? They're important because free trade agreements increase choices, competition, and purchasing power and thus decrease what people pay for food, clothing, necessities, and luxuries. Accordingly, today's consumers rarely care where their products and services come from. Peter Germano, a jeweller who sells diamonds, says people don't care where the diamonds are from; they "just want to know which is cheaper."

And why do trade barriers and free trade agreements matter to managers? The reason, as you're about to read, is that while free trade agreements create new business opportunities, they also intensify competition, and addressing that competition is a manager's job.

How to Go Global?

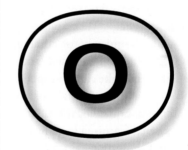

Once a company has decided that it *will* go global, it must decide *how* to go global. For example, if you decide to sell in Singapore, should you try to find a local business partner who speaks the language, knows the laws, and understands the customs and norms of Singapore's culture, or should you simply export your products from your home country? What do you do if you are also entering eastern Europe, perhaps starting in Hungary? Should you use the same approach in Hungary that you used in Singapore?

Although there is no magical formula for answering these questions, after reading the next two sections, you should be able to

2 explain why companies choose to standardize or adapt their business procedures.

3 explain the different ways that companies can organize to do business globally.

2 Consistency or Adaptation?

In this section, we return to a key issue: How can you be sure that the way you run your business in one country is the right way to run that business in another? In other words, how can you strike the right balance between global consistency and local adaptation?

Global consistency means that when a multinational company has offices, manufacturing plants, and distribution facilities in different countries, it will use the same rules, guidelines, policies, and procedures to run those offices, plants, and facilities. Managers at company headquarters value global consistency because it simplifies decisions. By contrast, a company with a **local adaptation** policy modifies its standard operating procedures to adapt to differences in foreign customers, governments, and regulatory agencies. Local adaptation is typically more important to the local managers who are charged with making the international business successful in their countries.

If companies lean too much toward global consistency, they run the risk of using management procedures poorly suited to particular countries' markets, cultures, and employees (i.e., a lack of local adaptation). MTV made this mistake when going global. According to Divya Gupta, president of Media Edge, which helps companies buy advertising in India, "MTV, when it first entered the country, made the mistake of coming in as MTV. No changes." MTV quickly learned from this mistake and stopped showing Western videos in international locations and started featuring local music and shows like *Mochilão* in Brazil, a travel show hosted by a popular model who backpacks to famous sites.[23]

If companies focus too much on local adaptation, however, they run the risk of losing the cost efficiencies and productivity that result from using standardized rules and procedures throughout the world. A decade into its development, MTV International was profitable, but not by much. While it had access to huge markets—in fact,

80 percent of MTV viewers are outside North America—access to those markets was slow to translate into large profits. Why? Because of the enormous cost of building new studios, acquiring new talent, and developing local content for so many different international markets.

3 Forms of Global Business

Historically, companies have generally followed the *phase model of globalization,* in which a company makes the transition from a domestic company to a global company in the following sequential phases: *3.1 exporting, 3.2 cooperative contracts, 3.3 strategic alliances,* and *3.4 wholly owned affiliates.* At each step, the company grows much larger, uses those resources to enter more global markets, is less dependent on home country sales, and is more committed in its orientation to global business. Some companies, however, do not follow the phase model of globalization.[24] Some skip phases on their way to becoming more global and less domestic. Others don't follow the phase model at all. These are known as *3.5 global new ventures.* This section reviews these forms of global business.[25]

3.1 Exporting

When companies produce products in their home countries and sell those products to customers in foreign countries, they are **exporting.** Located about 90 minutes from Shanghai, the city of Honghe is one of China's largest sweater producers. Half of its 100,000 citizens work in over 100 factories that produce about 200 million sweaters for export each year. The sweater export business generates $650 million/year in revenue.[26]

Exporting as a form of global business offers many advantages. It makes the company less dependent on sales in its home market and provides a greater degree of control over research, design, and production decisions. Though advantageous in a number of ways, exporting also has its disadvantages. The primary disadvantage is that many exported goods are subject to tariff and nontariff barriers that can substantially increase their final cost to consumers. A second disadvantage is that transportation costs can significantly increase the price of an exported product. Yet a third disadvantage: companies that export depend on foreign importers for product distribution. If, for example, the foreign importer makes a mistake on the paperwork that accompanies a shipment of imported goods, those goods can be returned to the foreign manufacturer at the manufacturer's expense.

Global consistency when a multinational company has offices, manufacturing plants, and distribution facilities in different countries and runs them all using the same rules, guidelines, policies, and procedures

Local adaptation when a multinational company modifies its rules, guidelines, policies, and procedures to adapt to differences in foreign customers, governments, and regulatory agencies

Exporting selling domestically produced products to customers in foreign countries

Bubbly Imports

Although you can build a plant to manufacture cars, textiles, or toys virtually anywhere in the world, some products must be imported because they can only be produced in one place. Chardonnay grapes, commonly used to make sparkling wine, can be grown anywhere you can plant a vineyard, but Champagne comes solely from one small region in France. Any wine has a unique characteristic called *terroir*, which comes from a combination of the grape variety and the soil and climate in which it is grown. The unique climate and chalky soil of the Champagne region makes Champagne unique. It cannot be replicated anywhere else in the world. The name Champagne, like Burgundy, is legally protected in France, where it can be used only on wines from that region. Other sparkling wines from California, Spain (Cava), and the Italian Piedmont (Asti) each have their own unique *terroir*. Drink and enjoy, but don't call it Champagne. Canada supports this approach to naming, mainly because it is hard to fight this logic, but also because Canada wants to claim the rights to Canadian Maple Syrup, and Rye Whiskey (among others).

Source: Office of Champagne, USA, available online at http://www.champagne.us [accessed 6 August 2008].

Canada used to be one of the most expensive places in the world to produce cars. But the fluctuating dollar and new contracts with workers are making production cheaper, prompting companies to rethink their strategies. Canadian automakers such as Chrysler are exporting Canadian-made cars to Europe, China, and Brazil. Chrysler is even moving some of its European production into the Canada. Moreover, foreign companies like BMW AG are ramping up their foreign direct investment in Canada, manufacturing their cars here for export to Europe.[27]

3.2 Cooperative Contracts

When an organization wants to expand its business globally without making a large financial commitment to do so, it may sign a **cooperative contract** with a foreign business owner who pays the company a fee for the right to conduct that business in his or her country. There are two kinds of cooperative contracts: licensing and franchising.

Under a **licensing** agreement, a domestic company, the *licensor*, receives royalty payments for allowing another company, the *licensee*, to produce its product, sell its service, or use its brand name in a particular foreign market. For example, brands like Coors Light, which consumers associate with an American company, are brewed in Canada by Molson under licence from the Coors Brewing Company in the United States. Licensing is favourable in this instance because of the complex distribution system in the various provinces of Canada.

One of the most important advantages of licensing is that it allows companies to earn additional profits

without investing more money. As foreign sales increase, the royalties paid to the licensor by the foreign licensee increase. Moreover, the licensee, not the licensor, invests in production equipment and facilities to produce the licensed product. Licensing also helps companies avoid tariff and nontariff barriers. Since the licensee manufactures the product within the foreign country, tariff and nontariff barriers don't apply.

The biggest disadvantage associated with licensing is that the licensor gives up control over the quality of the product or service sold by the foreign licensee. Unless the licensing agreement contains specific restrictions, the licensee controls the entire business from production to marketing to final sales. Many licensors include inspection clauses in their licence contracts, but closely monitoring product or service quality from thousands of miles away can be difficult. An additional disadvantage is that licensees can eventually become competitors, especially when a licensing agreement includes access to important technology or proprietary business knowledge.

A **franchise** is a collection of networked firms in

Cooperative contract an agreement in which a foreign business owner pays a company a fee for the right to conduct that business in his or her country

Licensing an agreement in which a domestic company, the licensor, receives royalty payments for allowing another company, the licensee, to produce the licensor's product, sell its service, or use its brand name in a specified foreign market

Franchise a collection of networked firms in which the manufacturer or marketer of a product or service, the franchisor, licenses the entire business to another person or organization, the franchisee

© iStockphoto.com/Andrew Dernie

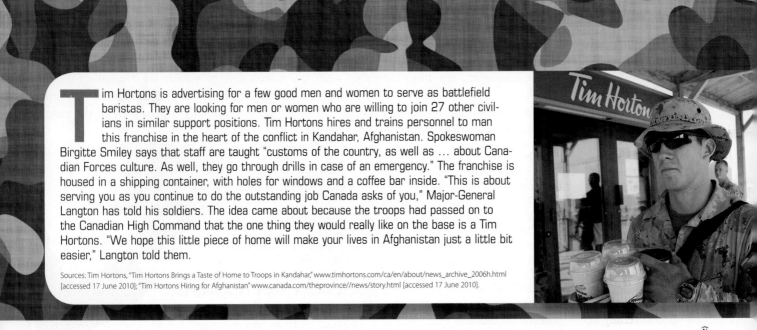

Tim Hortons is advertising for a few good men and women to serve as battlefield baristas. They are looking for men or women who are willing to join 27 other civilians in similar support positions. Tim Hortons hires and trains personnel to man this franchise in the heart of the conflict in Kandahar, Afghanistan. Spokeswoman Birgitte Smiley says that staff are taught "customs of the country, as well as ... about Canadian Forces culture. As well, they go through drills in case of an emergency." The franchise is housed in a shipping container, with holes for windows and a coffee bar inside. "This is about serving you as you continue to do the outstanding job Canada asks of you," Major-General Langton has told his soldiers. The idea came about because the troops had passed on to the Canadian High Command that the one thing they would really like on the base is a Tim Hortons. "We hope this little piece of home will make your lives in Afghanistan just a little bit easier," Langton told them.

Sources: Tim Hortons, "Tim Hortons Brings a Taste of Home to Troops in Kandahar," www.timhortons.com/ca/en/about/news_archive_2006h.html [accessed 17 June 2010]; "Tim Hortons Hiring for Afghanistan" www.canada.com/theprovince//news/story.html [accessed 17 June 2010].

which the manufacturer or marketer of a product or service, the *franchisor*, licenses the entire business to another person or organization, the *franchisee*. For the price of an initial franchise fee plus royalties, franchisors provide franchisees with training, assistance with marketing and advertising, and an exclusive right to conduct business in a particular location. More than 400 companies franchise their businesses to foreign franchise partners. Overall, franchising is a fast way to enter foreign markets. Over the last 20 years, franchisors have more than doubled their global franchises for a total of more than 100,000 global franchise units. We have to remember that the KFC or McDonald's restaurant in Indonesia, or Vietnam, is owned by a local business person, much the same as it is here at home in Canada.

Franchising has many advantages. However, franchisors face a loss of control when they sell businesses to franchisees who are thousands of miles away. And, while there are exceptions, franchising success may be somewhat culture-bound. In other words, because most global franchisors begin by franchising their businesses in similar countries or regions (Canada is by far the first choice for American companies taking their first step into global franchising), and because 65 percent of franchisors make absolutely no change in their business for overseas franchisees, that success may not generalize to cultures with different lifestyles, values, preferences, and technological infrastructures.

Strategic alliance an agreement in which companies combine key resources, costs, risk, technology, and people

Joint venture a strategic alliance in which two existing companies collaborate to form a third, independent company

3.3 Strategic Alliances

Companies forming **strategic alliances** combine key resources, costs, risks, technology, and people. The most common strategic alliance is a **joint venture**, which occurs when two existing companies collaborate to form a third company. The two founding companies remain intact and unchanged except that together they now own the newly created joint venture. One of the oldest and most successful global joint ventures is Fuji-Xerox, a joint venture between Fuji Film of Japan and U.S.-based Xerox Corporation, which makes copiers and automated office systems. More than 45 years after its creation, Fuji-Xerox employs over 42,000 people and has close to $9.1 billion in revenues.[28]

One of the advantages of global joint ventures is that, like licensing and franchising, they help companies avoid tariff and nontariff barriers to entry. Another advantage is that companies participating in a joint venture bear only part of the costs and the risks of that business. Many companies find this attractive because it is expensive to enter foreign markets and develop new products. For example, Arrow Energy, Ltd. is an oil and natural gas exploration and production company based in Calgary. They're partnering with Royal Dutch Shell PLC in a global joint venture that will mine natural gas from coal seams in Australia and export it for the global market. Global joint ventures can be especially advantageous to smaller local partners that link up with larger, more experienced foreign firms that can bring advanced management, resources, and business skills to the joint venture.[29]

Global joint ventures are not without problems, though. Because companies share costs and risks with their joint venture partners, they must also share profits. Managing global joint ventures can also be difficult because they represent a merging of four cultures: the country and organizational cultures of the first partner and the country and organizational cultures of the second partner. Often, to be fair to all involved, each partner in the global joint venture will have equal ownership and power. But this can result in power struggles and a lack of leadership. Because of these problems, companies forming global joint ventures should carefully develop detailed contracts that specify the obligations of each party. Such care is important because some estimate the rate of failure for global joint ventures as high as 70 percent.[30]

3.4 Wholly Owned Affiliates (Build or Buy)

Approximately one-third of multinational companies enter foreign markets through wholly owned affiliates. Unlike licensing arrangements, franchises, or joint ventures, **wholly owned affiliates** are 100 percent owned by the parent company. For example, Honda Motors of Canada in Cookstown, Ontario, is 100 percent owned by Honda Motors of Japan.

The primary advantage of wholly owned businesses is that the parent company receives all of the profits and has complete control over the foreign facilities. The biggest disadvantage is the expense of building new operations or buying existing businesses.

While the payoff can be enormous if wholly owned affiliates succeed, the losses can be immense if they fail because the parent company assumes all of the risk.

3.5 Global New Ventures

Companies used to evolve slowly from small operations selling in their home markets to large businesses selling to foreign markets. Furthermore, as companies went global, they usually followed the phase model of globalization. Recently, however, three trends have combined to allow companies to skip the phase model when going global. First, quick, reliable air travel can transport people nearly anywhere in the world within one day. Second, low-cost communication technologies, such as international e-mail, teleconferencing, phone conferencing, and the Internet, make it easier to communicate with global customers, suppliers, managers, and employees. Third, there is now a critical mass of businesspeople with extensive personal experience in all aspects of global business.[31] This combination of developments has made it possible to start companies that are global from inception. With sales, employees, and financing in different countries, **global new ventures** are companies that are founded with an active global strategy.[32]

Although there are several different kinds of global new ventures, all share two common factors. First, the company founders successfully develop and communicate the company's global vision from inception. Second, rather than going global one country at a time, new global ventures bring a product or service to market in several foreign markets at the same time. VistaPrint, a large printer in Canada, is actually headquartered in Lexington, Massachusetts. VistaPrint receives 15,000 orders a day from customers in 120 different countries, who design their business cards, brochures, and invitations online using 17 different VistaPrint Web sites, each representing a different language or location. Printing happens at two automated production facilities, one in the Netherlands and the other in Canada. Once printed, the products are cut and sized by robots and then packaged and delivered just three days after ordering. Regarding VistaPrint's commitment to worldwide customers, founder Robert Keane says, "It's often hard for startups

Wholly owned affiliates foreign offices, facilities, and manufacturing plants that are 100 percent owned by the parent company

Global new ventures new companies that are founded with an active global strategy and have sales, employees, and financing in different countries

© Kazuhiro Nogi/AFP/Getty Images

to find their way out of their home nation. But you have to—it's not that type of world anymore."[33]

Where to Go Global?

Deciding *where* to go global is just as important as deciding *how* your company will go global.

After reading the next three sections, you should be able to

4 explain how to find a favourable business climate.

5 discuss the importance of identifying and adapting to cultural differences.

6 explain how to successfully prepare workers for international assignments.

4 Finding the Best Business Climate

When deciding where to go global, companies try to find countries or regions with promising business climates.

*An attractive global business climate **4.1 positions the company for easy access to growing markets, 4.2 is an effective but cost-efficient place to build an office or manufacturing facility, and 4.3 minimizes the political risk to the company.***

4.1 Growing Markets

The most important factor in an attractive business climate is access to a growing market. Two factors help companies determine the growth potential of foreign markets: purchasing power and foreign competitors. **Purchasing power** is measured by comparing the relative cost of a standard set of goods and services in different countries. In Tokyo, a Coke costs $1.09.[34] Because a Coke costs only about $1.00 in Canada, the average Canadian would have slightly more purchasing power than the average Japanese. Purchasing power is strong in countries like Mexico, India, and China, which have low average levels of income. This is because basic living expenses, such as food, shelter, and transportation, are very inexpensive in those countries, so consumers still have money to spend after paying for necessities. Because basic living expenses are so low in China, Mexico, and India, purchasing power is strong, and millions of Chinese, Mexican, and Indian consumers increasingly have extra money to spend on what they want in addition to what they need.[35]

Consequently, countries with high and growing levels of purchasing power are good choices for companies looking for attractive global markets. As Exhibit 8.2 shows, Coke has found that the per capita consumption of Coca-Cola, or the number of Cokes a person drinks per year, rises directly with purchasing power. The more purchasing power people have, the more likely they are to purchase soft drinks.

The Big Mac Index

Every year since 1986, *The Economist* has published the Big Mac Index. The index compares the price for a Big Mac in dozens of countries around the world and uses its results to determine a country's purchasing power and value its exchange rate against the dollar (undervalued, overvalued, or right on the mark). Why the Big Mac? Well, like a Coke, the Big Mac is one of the few truly global consumer products. A McDonald's Big Mac sandwich costs an average of $3.65 in Canada, $3.90 in the United Kingdom, and $5.05 in Switzerland. Not all products are more expensive in other countries. In some, they are cheaper; for example, a Big Mac costs $1.41 in China and $2.66 in Mexico.

Source: "The Big Mac Index," *The Economist*, available online at http://www.economist.com/markets/indicators/displaystory.cfm?story_id=8649005.

Purchasing power a comparison of the relative cost of a standard set of goods and services in different countries

Exhibit 8.2

How Consumption of Coca-Cola Varies with Purchasing Power around the World

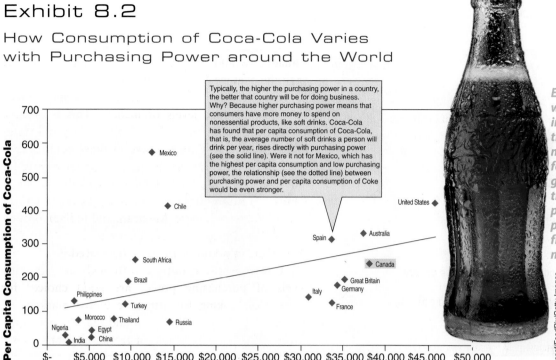

Typically, the higher the purchasing power in a country, the better that country will be for doing business. Why? Because higher purchasing power means that consumers have more money to spend on nonessential products, like soft drinks. Coca-Cola has found that per capita consumption of Coca-Cola, that is, the average number of soft drinks a person will drink per year, rises directly with purchasing power (see the solid line). Were it not for Mexico, which has the highest per capita consumption and low purchasing power, the relationship (see the dotted line) between purchasing power and per capita consumption of Coke would be even stronger.

Even Coca-Cola, which is available in over 200 countries, still has tremendous potential for further global growth. Currently, the Coca-Cola Company gets about 80 percent of its sales from its 16 largest markets.

© Judd Pilossof/FoodPix/Getty Images

Sources: "Rank Order—GDP—Per Capita," *The World Factbook* [online], available at http://www.cia.gov/cia/publications/factbook/rankorder/2004rank.html (accessed 7 September 2008), "2005 Annual Per Capita Consumption of All Company Beverage Products," *The Coca-Cola Company 2005 Annual Review* [online], available at http://www.thecoca-colacompany.com/ourcompany/ar/pdf/perCapitaConsumption2007.pdf, (accessed 6 August 2008).

The second part of assessing the growth potential of global markets involves analyzing the degree of global competition, which is determined by the number and quality of companies that already compete in a foreign market. Intel has been in China for twenty years not only because of the size of the potential market but also because there was almost no competition. Now that China is the third-largest computer chip market in the world, Intel faces competition from AMD, Intel's primary competitor, which entered China four years ago, and Shanghai Semiconductor Manufacturing International, a five-year-old Chinese company that manufactures low-end chips.[36]

4.2 Choosing an Office/Manufacturing Location

Companies do not have to establish an office or manufacturing location in each country they enter. They can license, franchise, or export to foreign markets, or they can serve a larger region from one country. But there are many reasons why a company might choose to establish a location in a foreign country. Some foreign offices are established through global mergers and acquisitions, such as the acquisition of IBM's Think Pad brand by Beijing-based computer maker Lenovo. In fact, while Lenovo maintains offices in both places,

top executives hold their monthly meetings at a different location each time—a strategy Bill Amelio, CEO of Lenovo, calls "worldsourcing." Other companies seek a tax haven (although this is more difficult for Canadian companies due to legal concerns), want to reflect their customer base, or strive to create a global brand. Although a company must be legally incorporated in one place, some companies have anywhere from 9 to 23 global hubs and don't regard any one as more central than another.[37]

Thus, the criteria for choosing an office/manufacturing location are different from the criteria for entering a foreign market. Rather than focusing on costs alone, companies should consider both qualitative and quantitative factors. Two key qualitative factors are workforce quality and company strategy. Workforce quality is important because it is often difficult to find workers with the specific skills, abilities, and experience that a company needs to run its business. Workforce quality is one reason that many companies doing business in Europe locate their customer call centres in the Netherlands. Workers in the Netherlands are the most linguistically gifted in Europe, with 73 percent speaking two languages, 44 percent speaking three languages, and 12 percent speaking more than three.[38]

Exhibit 8.3

World's Best Cities for Business

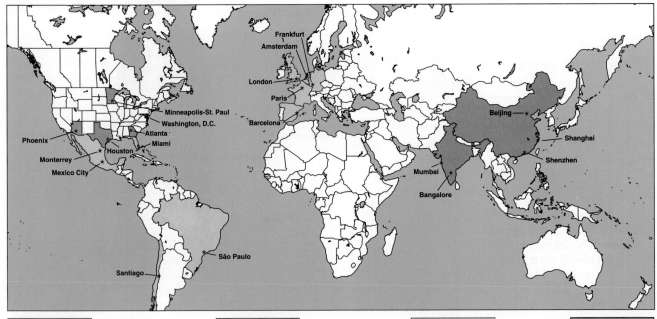

North America	Latin America	Europe	Asia-Pacific
1. Washington, D.C.	1. Santiago	1. London	1. Shanghai
2. Atlanta, GA	2. Miami	2. Paris	2. Beijing
3. Phoenix, AZ	3. São Paulo	3. Frankfurt	3. Shenzhen
4. Houston, TX	4. Monterrey (Mexico)	4. Barcelona	4. Bangalore
5. Minneapolis-St. Paul, MN	5. Mexico City	5. Amsterdam	5. Mumbai

Sources: "European Cities Monitor 2007," *Cushman & Wakefield* available online at http://www.berlin-partner.de/fileadmin/chefredaktion/documents/pdf_Presse/European_Investment_Monitor_2007.pdf, [accessed 18 September 2008]. K. Badenhausen, "Best Places for Business and Careers," *Forbes.com*, available online at http://www.forbes.com/lists/2005/05/05bestplaces.html [accessed 18 May 2010]. "Shanghai, Beijing, Shenzhen Top 3 in Best City Survey," *Fortune China*, available online at http://www.fortunechina.com/pdf/Best%20Cities%20Press%20Release%20(English)%202004.12.01.pdf [accessed 13 February 2007] R. Sridharan, "Best Cities, Really?" *Business Today*, 13 August 2006, 62. "Miami Is the Best City for Doing Business in Latin America, According to AmericaEconomia Magazine," *PR Newswire*, 24 April 2003.

A company's strategy is also important when choosing a location. For example, a company pursuing a low-cost strategy may need plentiful raw materials, low-cost transportation, and low-cost labour. A company pursuing a differentiation strategy (typically a higher priced, better product or service) may need access to high-quality materials and a highly skilled and educated workforce.

Quantitative factors such as the kind of facility being built, tariff and nontariff barriers, exchange rates, and transportation and labour costs should also be considered when choosing an office/manufacturing location. Each year, Cushman & Wakefield publishes its "European Cities Monitor" to help companies compare the pluses and minuses of the business climate in various cities, and similar information is available for other parts of the world. Exhibit 8.3 offers a quick overview of the best cities for business based on a variety of criteria. This information is a good starting point if your company is trying to decide where to put an international office or manufacturing plant.

4.3 Minimizing Political Risk

When managers think about political risk in global business, they envision burning factories and riots in the streets. Although political events such as these receive dramatic and extended coverage from the media, the political risks that most companies face usually are not covered as breaking stories on CTV and CBC. Nonetheless, the negative consequences of ordinary political risk can be just as devastating to companies that fail to identify and minimize that risk.[39]

When conducting global business, companies should attempt to identify two types of political risk: political uncertainty and policy uncertainty.[40] **Political uncertainty** is associated with the risk of major changes in political regimes that can result from war, revolution, death of political leaders, social unrest, or other influential events.

Political uncertainty
the risk of major changes in political regimes that can result from war, revolution, death of political leaders, social unrest, or other influential events

Emerging Markets: India

In many ways, India appears to be a global business nightmare. People speak dozens of different languages throughout the country. Getting around is a challenge due to a terrible infrastructure. Foreign companies must deal with tight regulations on foreign investment, slow bureaucratic culture, and the politics of family-owned big business. UPS delivery people, for example, must often ask for directions because there are no street numbers. Day-to-day traffic is worse than that on the busiest Canadian freeway: it can be hard to tell a parked car from a moving one. To top it all off, packages must be shrink-wrapped during monsoon season. That said, India—with 1.1 billion people, 9 percent annual economic growth, a growing middle class demanding imported goods, and cities full of entrepreneurs on the cutting edge of global business—is one of the hottest markets in the world. For example, India has eight million new cell phone subscribers per month. Like many of his fellow Indian expats, Arun Sarin, CEO of Vodafone Group PLC, left India in the 1970s because of limited business opportunities, but is now going home. India is a place companies cannot afford to ignore.

Sources: B. Stanley, "UPS Battles Traffic Jams To Gain Ground in India," *The Wall Street Journal*, 25 January 2008, A1; C. Bryan-Low, "To Revive Vodafone, CEO Bets on India," *The Wall Street Journal*, 22 February 2008, A1.

© Walter Bibikow/The Image Bank/Getty Images

Policy uncertainty refers to the risk associated with changes in laws and government policies that directly affect the way foreign companies conduct business.

Policy uncertainty is the most common—and perhaps most frustrating—form of political risk in global business. For example, the Kremlin has cleaned up Russia's once-inefficient auto industry, making it attractive to Western investors. Growth-starved auto companies like Renault have taken the bait. In fact, $80 million of private capital entered Russia in 2007. But such investment is a risk because 40 percent of the industry is owned by the Kremlin, making foreign investors subject to government policy. An example of what can happen as policy winds change: in February 2007, the Kremlin raided BP PLC and TNK-BP, its joint venture, and accused the foreign investor of industrial espionage.[41]

Several strategies can be used to minimize or adapt to the political risk inherent in global business. An *avoidance strategy* is used when the political risks associated with a foreign country or region are viewed as too great. If firms are already invested in high-risk areas, they may divest or sell their businesses. If they have not yet invested, they will likely postpone their investment until the risk shrinks. Exhibit 8.4 on the next page shows the long-term political risk for various countries in the Middle East (higher scores indicate less political risk). The following factors, which were used to compile these ratings, indicate greater political risk: government instability, poor socioeconomic conditions, internal or external conflict, military involvement in politics, religious and ethnic tensions, high foreign debt as a percentage of gross domestic product, exchange rate instability, and high inflation.[42] An avoidance strategy would likely be used for the riskiest countries shown in Exhibit 8.4, such as Iran and Lebanon, but would probably not be needed for the least risky countries, such as Israel, Jordan, or Oman. Risk conditions and factors change, so be sure to make risk decisions with the latest available information from resources such as the PRS Group (http://www.prsgroup.com), which supplies information about political risk to 80 percent of the *Fortune* 500 companies.

Control is an active strategy to prevent or reduce political risks. Firms using a control strategy lobby foreign governments or international trade agencies to change laws, regulations, or trade barriers that hurt their business in that country. Emerson Electric Co. had virtually no

Policy uncertainty the risk associated with changes in laws and government policies that directly affect the way foreign companies conduct business

Exhibit 8.4

Overview of Political Risk in the Middle East

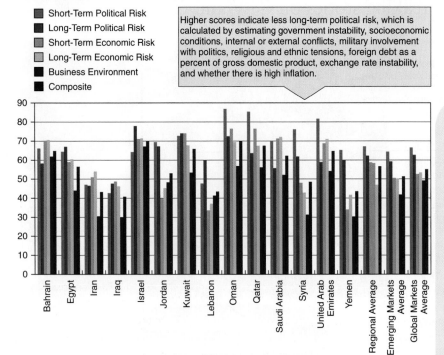

- ■ Short-Term Political Risk
- ■ Long-Term Political Risk
- ■ Short-Term Economic Risk
- ■ Long-Term Economic Risk
- ■ Business Environment
- ■ Composite

Higher scores indicate less long-term political risk, which is calculated by estimating government instability, socioeconomic conditions, internal or external conflicts, military involvement with politics, religious and ethnic tensions, foreign debt as a percent of gross domestic product, exchange rate instability, and whether there is high inflation.

Countries (x-axis): Bahrain, Egypt, Iran, Iraq, Israel, Jordan, Kuwait, Lebanon, Oman, Qatar, Saudi Arabia, Syria, United Arab Emirates, Yemen, Regional Average, Emerging Markets Average, Global Markets Average

Source: Middle East Overview Chart, Business Monitor International Country Risk Ratings, Business Monitor Online. © 2010 Business Monitor International.

business for its InSinkErator garbage disposals in Europe during the 1990s. The company lobbied European governments to convince them of the environmentally-friendly impact of a waste disposer over other methods of getting rid of food waste. Composting involves a lot of garbage trucks, and landfills emit poisonous methane. Garbage disposals are the cheapest method for disposing of food waste, they enable water-treatment plants to turn methane that comes through the sewer system into power, and they reduce the carbon footprint by reducing the amount of waste transported by trucks. Now Emerson sells over 100,000 disposals each year in Europe.[43]

Another method for dealing with political risk is *cooperation*, which involves using joint ventures and collaborative contracts such as franchising and licensing. Although cooperation does not eliminate the political risk of doing business in a country, it can limit the risk associated with foreign ownership of a business. For example, a German company forming a joint venture with a Chinese company to do business in China may structure the joint venture contract so that the Chinese company owns 51 percent or more of the joint venture.

National culture the set of shared values and beliefs that affects the perceptions, decisions, and behaviour of the people from a particular country

Where in the World...?

MoneySense, a Canadian financial website, publishes an interactive map with information on doing business around the world. The top 18 countries are rated for value and momentum. Slower grow countries usually have modest investment levels or requirements, which can make for terrific value. In May 2010, Apple passed Microsoft and all other companies in terms of market capitalization, but will the company double in value from its 2010 value of $245 billion? That kind of money can buy a lot of businesses in many of the 18 countries listed on the interactive map. Additionally, the "momentum" of the various countries is a measure of how fast they are growing. Certainly, India and China are growing faster than many other countries, but as indicated during the economic and worldwide banking crisis of 2009, some of these countries can have their momentum severely dented.

Sources: Rothery, N., Dec 2009. "Where in the World to Invest," http://www.moneysense.ca/2009/12/18/where-in-the-world-should-you-invest-2/ [accessed 16 June 2010]; Guglielmo, C. & Bass, D., 2010. "Apple Overtakes MicroSoft," http//:www.businessweek.com/news/2010-05-26/apple-overtakes-microsoft-in-market-capitalization-update3-html [accessed 16 June 2010].

Doing so qualifies the joint venture as a Chinese company and exempts it from Chinese laws that apply to foreign-owned businesses. However, as we saw with the BP-TNK joint venture in Russia, cooperation cannot always protect against *policy risk* if a foreign government changes its laws and policies to directly affect the way foreign companies conduct business.

5 Becoming Aware of Cultural Differences

National culture is the set of shared values and beliefs that affects the perceptions, decisions, and behaviour of the people from a particular country. The first step

Exhibit 8.5

Hofstede's Five Cultural Dimensions

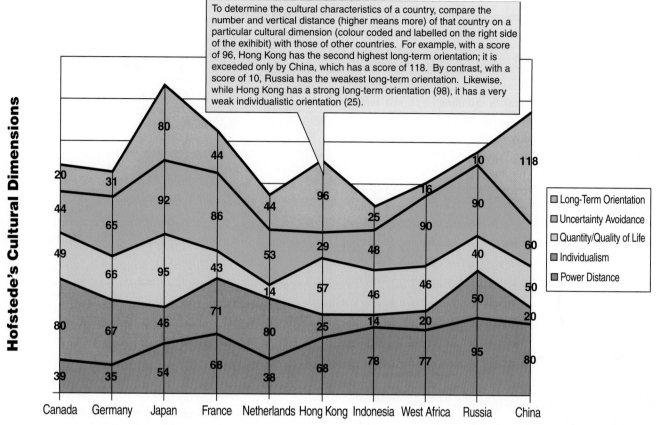

To determine the cultural characteristics of a country, compare the number and vertical distance (higher means more) of that country on a particular cultural dimension (colour coded and labelled on the right side of the exihibit) with those of other countries. For example, with a score of 96, Hong Kong has the second highest long-term orientation; it is exceeded only by China, which has a score of 118. By contrast, with a score of 10, Russia has the weakest long-term orientation. Likewise, while Hong Kong has a strong long-term orientation (98), it has a very weak individualistic orientation (25).

Hofstede's Cultural Dimensions

Legend:
- ☐ Long-Term Orientation
- ☐ Uncertainty Avoidance
- ☐ Quantity/Quality of Life
- ■ Individualism
- ■ Power Distance

Countries (x-axis): Canada, Germany, Japan, France, Netherlands, Hong Kong, Indonesia, West Africa, Russia, China

Source: G. H. Hofstede, "Cultural Constraints in Management Theories," *Academy of Management Executive* 7, no. 1 (1993): 81–94.

in dealing with culture is to recognize that there are meaningful differences. Professor Geert Hofstede spent 20 years studying cultural differences in 53 different countries. His research shows that there are five consistent cultural dimensions across countries: power distance, individualism, masculinity, uncertainty avoidance, and short-term versus long-term orientation.[44]

Power distance is the extent to which people in a country tolerate unequal distribution of power in society and organizations. In countries where power distance is weak, such as Denmark and Sweden, employees don't like their organization or their boss to have power over them or tell them what to do. They want to have a say in decisions that affect them. As Exhibit 8.5 shows, Russia and China, with scores of 95 and 80, respectively, are much stronger in power distance than Germany (35), the Netherlands (38), and Canada (39). Canada's power distance is relatively low, at 39, compared to the world average of 55. This may indicate a feeling of greater equality between societal levels, which include government, work organizations, and families. This orientation may reinforce cooperative interaction across power levels and may create a more stable cultural environment.

The tension between the province of Quebec and other Canadian provinces should be noted. Quebecers tend to be more private and reserved.

Individualism is the degree to which societies believe that individuals should be self-sufficient. In individualistic societies, employees put loyalty to themselves first and loyalty to their company and work group second. In Exhibit 8.5, the Netherlands (80), Canada (80), France (71), and Germany (67) are the strongest in individualism, while Indonesia (14), West Africa (20), and China (20) are the weakest. The majority of Canadians have "individualism" as their highest ranking dimension (80). Success tends to be measured by personal achievement; this is indicative of a society with a more individualistic attitude in which people have looser bonds with others. People are viewed as more self-reliant, and as focusing on themselves and their close family members. Canadians may be self-confident and open to discussions on general topics, but they place their personal privacy off limits to all but the closest of friends.

Quantity/quality of life (formerly known as *masculinity*) and *femininity* captures the difference between highly assertive and highly nurturing cultures. Quality-of-life cultures emphasize assertiveness, competition, material success, and achievement, whereas quality-of-life cultures emphasize the importance of relationships, modesty, caring for the weak, and quality of life. In Exhibit 8.5, Japan (95), Germany (66), and Canada (49) have the most masculine orientations, while the Netherlands (14) has the most feminine orientation. The terms "feminine" and "masculine" are not really appropriate today, but you will see them in many readings. They were originally used by Hofstede. The more common terms today are "quality of life" for feminine and "quantity of life" for masculine.

The cultural difference of *uncertainty avoidance* is the degree to which people in a country are uncomfortable with unstructured, ambiguous, unpredictable situations. In countries with strong uncertainty avoidance like Greece and Portugal, people tend to be aggressive and emotional and seek security (rather than uncertainty). In Exhibit 8.5, Japan (92), France (86), West Africa (90), and Russia (90) are strongest in uncertainty avoidance, while Hong Kong (29) is the weakest.

Short-term/long-term orientation addresses whether cultures are oriented to the present and seek immediate gratification or to the future and defer gratification. Not surprisingly, countries with short-term orientations are consumer driven, whereas countries with long-term orientations are savings driven. In Exhibit 8.5, China (118) and Hong Kong (96) have very strong long-term orientations, while Russia (10), West Africa (16), Indonesia (25), Canada (23), and Germany (31) have very strong short-term orientations. Canadians' lowest ranking dimension—"long-term orientation," at 23—compares to an average of 45 among the 23 countries surveyed. This low ranking may be indicative of Canadians' belief in meeting their obligations and tends to reflect an appreciation for cultural traditions, which may explain our acceptance of multiculturalism. To generate a graphical comparison of two different countries' cultures, go to **http://www.geert-hofstede .com/hofstede_dimensions.php**. Select a "home culture." Then select a "host culture." A graph comparing the countries on each of Hofstede's five cultural differences will automatically be generated.

Cultural differences affect perceptions, understanding, and behaviour. Recognizing cultural differences is critical to succeeding in global business. Nevertheless, as Hofstede pointed out, descriptions of cultural differences are based on averages—the average level of uncertainty avoidance in Portugal,

MGMT FACT

BILINGUALISM—A GROWING TREND

There are over 5 million people in Canada who speak more than one language. At least 35 percent of Canadians speak more than one language. Moreover, fewer than 2 percent of Canadians cannot speak at least one of the two official languages. Around 5.5 million people in Canada are able to speak both official languages. Bilingual, in Canada, generally refers to being able to speak both French and English; only 17 percent of Canadians, by this definition, are bilingual. More than half of Vancouverites and Torontonians were born outside Canada. This has led to a greater use of English as a second language, and also to a great deal of linguistic and cultural diversity. In Europe even more value is placed on the ability to speak multiple languages; more Europeans are multilingual, speaking three or more languages, than are bilingual. Being able to communicate in multiple languages is an important asset in any business and can help give a company the edge it needs to succeed in a competitive market.

Sources: City of Toronto, "Facts," http://www.toronto.ca/toronto_facts/diversity.htm; D. Todd, "Vancouver Teens Most Inter-Racial: Poll," *Vancouver Sun*, August 14, 2009.

the average level of power distance in Argentina, and so forth. Accordingly, says Hofstede, "If you are going to spend time with a Japanese colleague, you shouldn't assume that overall cultural statements about Japanese society automatically apply to this person."[45] Similarly, cultural beliefs may differ significantly from one part of a country to another.[46]

After becoming aware of cultural differences, the second step is deciding how to adapt your company to those differences. Unfortunately, studies investigating the effects of cultural differences on management practice point more to difficulties than to easy solutions. One problem is that different cultures will probably perceive management policies and practices differently. For example, blue-collar workers in France and Argentina, all of whom performed the same factory jobs for the same multinational company, perceived its company-wide safety policy differently.[47] French workers perceived that safety wasn't very important to the company, but Argentine workers thought that it was. The fact that something as simple as a safety policy can be perceived differently across cultures shows just how difficult it can be to standardize management practices across different countries and cultures.

6 Preparing for an International Assignment

An **expatriate** is someone who lives and works outside his or her native country. The difficulty of adjusting to linguistic, cultural, and social differences is the primary reason for expatriate failure in overseas assignments. The United States is the biggest destination for Canadians, with upwards of 1.5 million expatriates living there. The United Kingdom is the next largest destination, with almost 750,000 expats, followed by China, with 250,000. Some research has shown that large numbers of expatriates return home before they have successfully completed their assignments.[48] Of those who do complete their international assignments, about one-third are judged by their companies to be no better than marginally effective.[49]

Since the average cost of sending an employee on a three-year international assignment is $1 million, failure in those assignments can be extraordinarily expensive.[50]

The chances for a successful international assignment can be increased through **6.1 language and cross-cultural training** and **6.2 consideration of spouse, family, and dual-career issues.**

6.1 Language and Cross-Cultural Training

Pre-departure language and cross-cultural training can reduce the uncertainty that expatriates feel, the misunderstandings that take place between expatriates and natives, and the inappropriate ways that expatriates unknowingly behave when they travel to a foreign country. Indeed, simple things like using a phone, locating a public toilet, asking for directions, finding out how much things cost, exchanging greetings, or understanding what people want can become tremendously complex when expatriates don't know a foreign language or a country's customs and cultures.

Expatriates who receive pre-departure language and cross-cultural training make faster adjustments to foreign cultures and perform better on their international assignments.[51] Unfortunately, only one-third of the managers who go on international assignments are offered any kind of pre-departure training, and only half of those actually participate in the training![52] This is somewhat surprising given the failure rates for expatriates and the high cost of those failures. Furthermore, with the exception of some language courses, pre-departure training is not particularly expensive or difficult to provide. Three methods can be used to prepare workers for international assignments: documentary training, cultural simulations, and field experiences.

Documentary training focuses on identifying specific critical differences between cultures. For example, when 60 workers at Axcelis Technologies, were preparing to do business in India, they learned that while North Americans make eye contact and shake hands firmly when greeting others, Indians, as a sign of respect, do just the opposite, avoiding eye contact and shaking hands limply.[53]

After learning specific critical differences through documentary training, trainees can then participate in *cultural simulations,* in which they practise adapting to cultural differences. After the workers at Axcelis Technologies learned about key differences between their culture and India, they practised adapting to those differences by role playing. Some Axcelis workers would take the roles of Indian workers, while other Axcelis workers would play themselves and try to behave in a way consistent with Indian culture. As they role played, Indian music played loudly in the background, and they were coached on what to do or not do. Axcelis human resources director Randy Longo says, "At first, I was skeptical and wondered what I'd get out of the class. But it was enlightening for me."

Finally, *field simulation* training places trainees in an ethnic neighbourhood for three to four hours to talk to residents about cultural differences. For example, an electronics manufacturer prepared workers for assignments in South Korea by having trainees explore a nearby South Korean neighbourhood and talk to shopkeepers and people on the street about South Korean politics, family orientation, and day-to-day living practices.

6.2 Spouse, Family, and Dual-Career Issues

Not all international assignments are difficult for expatriates and their families, but the evidence clearly shows that how well an expatriate's spouse and family adjust to the foreign culture is the most important factor in determining the success or failure of an international assignment.[54] Barry Kozloff of Selection Research International says, "The cost of sending a family on a foreign assignment is around $1 million and their failure to adjust is an enormous loss."[55] Unfortunately, despite its importance, there has been little systematic research on what does and does not help expatriates' families successfully adapt. A number of companies, however, have

Expatriate someone who lives and works outside his or her native country

found that adaptability screening and intercultural training for families can lead to more successful overseas adjustment.

Adaptability screening is used to assess how well managers and their families are likely to adjust to foreign cultures. For example, Prudential Relocation Management's international division has developed an "Overseas Assignment Inventory" to assess the open-mindedness of

a spouse and family, respect for others' beliefs, sense of humour, and marital communication.

Only 40 percent of expatriates' families receive language and cross-cultural training, yet such training is just as important for the families of expatriates as for the expatriates themselves.[56] In fact, it may be more important because, unlike expatriates, whose professional jobs often shield them from the full force of a country's culture, spouses and children are fully immersed in foreign neighbourhoods and schools. Households must be run, shopping must be done, and bills must be paid. Unfortunately, expatriate spouse Laurel Larsen, despite two hours of Chinese lessons a week, hasn't learned enough of the language to communicate with the family's baby-sitter. She has to phone her husband, who became fluent in Chinese in his teens, to translate. Likewise, expatriates' children must deal with different cultural beliefs and practices, too. While the Larsens' three daughters love the private, international school that they attend, they still have had difficulty adapting to the incredible differences they perceive in inner China.[57]

ONLY **ONE-THIRD** OF THE **MANAGERS** WHO GO ON INTERNATIONAL ASSIGNMENTS ARE OFFERED ANY KIND OF **PRE-DEPARTURE TRAINING.**

Visit **icanmgmt.com** to find the resources you need today!

Located at the back of the textbook are rip-out Chapter Review cards. Make sure you also go online to check out other tools that MGMT offers to help you successfully pass your course.

- Interactive Quizzes
- Key Terms Flashcards
- Audio Chapter Summaries
- PowerPoint Slides

- Interactive Games
- Crossword Puzzles
- "Reel to Reel" and "Biz Flix" videos
- Cases and Exercises

86% of Canadian students surveyed found the interactive online quizzes valuable.

LEARNING YOUR WAY

We know that no two students are alike. **MGMT** was developed to help you learn **Principles of Management** in a way that works for you.

Not only is the format fresh and contemporary, it's also concise and focused. And **icanmgmt.com** is loaded with a variety of supplements, like audio chapter summaries, printable flashcards, and more!

At icanmgmt.com, you will find interactive flashcards, crossword puzzles, videos, interactive quizzing, and more to test your knowledge of key concepts. It includes plenty of resources to help you study, no matter what learning style you like best!

"I enjoy the cards in the back of the book and the fact that it partners with the website."

—Cassandra Jewell, Sir Sandford Fleming College

Visit **icanmgmt.com** to find the resources you need today!

Part 3 - Organizing

DESIGNING ADAPTIVE ORGANIZATIONS

Structure and Process

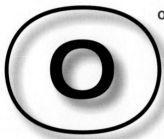

Organizational structure is the vertical and horizontal configuration of departments, authority, and jobs within a company. Organizational structure is concerned with vertical questions such as "Who reports to whom?" as well as horizontal questions such as "Who does what?" and "Where is the work done?" For example, Sony Corporation is a global company with operations all over the world as well as a number of divisions to handle different sectors of the company's business, each headed by its own president or CEO. Sony's North American headquarters is in New York City, but its many affiliated companies and operations span the continent. PlayStation products are developed and managed in Foster City, California, by Sony Computer Entertainment. Sony cameras and camcorders, TV and home theatre equipment, computers, MP3 players, headphones, and mobile phones are handled in San Diego by Sony Electronics. The Spider-Man films and the long-running *Jeopardy!* game show are brought to you by Sony Pictures Entertainment, headquartered in Culver City, California; while the music of Beyoncé and Avril Lavigne comes courtesy of Sony Music Entertainment.[1] Companies like Sony use organizational structure to set up departments and relationships among employees in order to make business happen. You can see Sony's organizational structure in Exhibit 9.1.

Organizational structure the vertical and horizontal configuration of departments, authority, and jobs within a company

Learning Outcomes

1 describe the departmentalization approach to organizational structure.

2 explain organizational authority.

3 discuss the different methods for job design.

4 explain the methods that companies are using to redesign internal organizational processes (i.e., intraorganizational processes).

5 describe the methods that companies are using to redesign external organizational processes (i.e., interorganizational processes).

© iStockphoto.com

166 *Part 3: Organizing*

NEL

Exhibit 9.1

Sony Corporation's Organizational Chart

	Consumer, Professional & Devices Group					Networked Products & Services Group						
Sony DADC	Professional Solutions Group	Semiconductor Business Group	Devices Solutions Business Group	Personal Imaging & Sound Business Group	Home Entertainment Business Group	Sony Network Entertainment	VAIO & Mobile Business Group	Sony Computer Entertainment	Sony Ericsson Mobile Communications	Sony Music Entertainment	Sony Pictures Entertainment	Sony Financial Holdings Group

Common Platforms

Headquarters

- Global Sales & Marketing Platform
- Manufacturing, Logistics, Procurement and CS Platform
- R&D, Common Software Platform

The organizational chart displays Sony's horizontal and vertical dimensions.

Source: "Sony Corp. Info: Organizational Data," http://www.sony.net/SonyInfo/CorporateInfo/Data/organization.html. [accessed June 7, 2010]

Exhibit 9.2

Process View of Microsoft's Organization

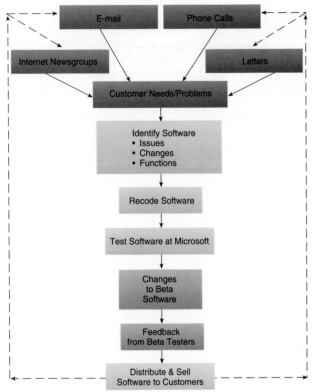

An **organizational process** is the collection of activities that transform inputs into outputs that customers value.[2] Organizational process asks: How do things get done? For example, Microsoft uses basic internal and external processes to write computer software, shown in Exhibit 9.2. The process starts when Microsoft gets external feedback from customers through Internet newsgroups, e-mail, phone calls, or letters. This information helps Microsoft understand customers' needs and problems and identify important software issues and needed changes and functions. Microsoft then rewrites the software, testing it internally at the company and then externally through its beta-testing process, where customers who volunteer or are selected by Microsoft give the company extensive feedback, which is then used to make improvements. After final corrections are made to the software, the company distributes and sells it to customers. They start the process again by giving Microsoft more feedback.

Organizational process the collection of activities that transform inputs into outputs that customers value

Organizational process is just as important as organizational structure, and you'll learn about both in this chapter.

Designing Organizational Structures

Procter & Gamble (P&G), the largest consumer packaged goods company in the world, owns some of the world's best-known brands, including Tide, Crest, Charmin, Pringles, and Pampers. P&G's product lines include 22 billion-dollar brands (which generate more than $1 billion in annual sales) and 20 half-billion-dollar brands (which generate more than $500 million in annual sales). Over the past decade, P&G has restructured its operations, segmenting its brands into three global business units (GBUs): Beauty and Grooming, Health and Well Being, and Household Care. Each GBU is responsible for all innovation, profitability, and shareholder returns for its own businesses and focuses solely on the brands and consumers in its own category as well as on competitors around the world. The organizational structure is also organized around geographic units (market development organizations) and global business services, which focus on delivering internal services. P&G's new design was meant to be global and local at the same time—something the company believes will be key to its future success.[3]

Why would a large company like P&G completely restructure its organizational design? What can be gained from such a change?

After reading the next three sections, you'll have a better understanding of the importance of organizational structure because you should be able to

1 describe the departmentalization approach to organizational structure.

2 explain organizational authority.

3 discuss the different methods for job design.

studiomode/GetStock.com

1 Departmentalization

Traditionally, organizational structures have been based on some form of departmentalization. **Departmentalization** is a method of subdividing work and workers into separate organizational units that take responsibility for completing particular tasks.[4]

Traditionally, organizational structures have been created by departmentalizing work according to five methods: **1.1 functional, 1.2 product, 1.3 customer, 1.4 geographic,** *and* **1.5 matrix.**

1.1 Functional Departmentalization

The most common organizational structure is functional departmentalization. Companies tend to use this structure when they are small or just starting out. **Functional departmentalization** organizes work and workers into separate units responsible for particular business functions or areas of expertise. A common functional structure might have individuals organized into accounting, sales, marketing, production, and human resources departments.

Not all functionally departmentalized companies have the same functions. The insurance company and the advertising agency shown in Exhibit 9.3 both have sales, accounting, human resources, and information systems departments, as indicated by the orange boxes. The purple and green boxes indicate the functions that are different. As would be expected, the insurance company has separate departments for life, auto, home, and health insurance. The advertising agency has departments for artwork, creative work, print advertising, and radio advertising. So the functional departments in a company that uses functional structure depend in part on the business or industry the company is in.

Functional departmentalization has some advantages. First, it allows work to be done by highly qualified specialists. While the accountants in the accounting department take responsibility for producing accurate revenue and expense figures, the engineers in research and development can focus their efforts on designing a product that is reliable and simple to manufacture. Second, it lowers costs by reducing duplication. When the engineers in research and development come up with that fantastic new product, they don't have to worry about creating an aggressive advertising campaign to sell it. That task belongs to the advertising experts and sales representatives in marketing. Third, with everyone in the same department having similar work experience or training, communication and coordination are less problematic for departmental managers.

Exhibit 9.3
Functional Departmentalization

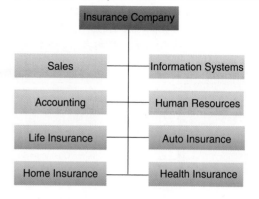

At the same time, functional departmentalization has a number of disadvantages. To start, cross-department coordination can be difficult. Managers and employees are often more interested in doing what's right for their function than in doing what's right for the entire organization. As companies grow, functional departmentalization may also lead to slower decision making and produce managers and workers with narrow experience and expertise.

1.2 Product Departmentalization

Product departmentalization organizes work and workers into separate units responsible for producing particular products or services. Exhibit 9.4 on the next page shows the product departmentalization structure used by United Technologies (UTC), which is organized along six different

Departmentalization subdividing work and workers into separate organizational units responsible for completing particular tasks

Functional departmentalization organizing work and workers into separate units responsible for particular business functions or areas of expertise

Product departmentalization organizing work and workers into separate units responsible for producing particular products or services

Exhibit 9.4

Product Departmentalization: United Technologies

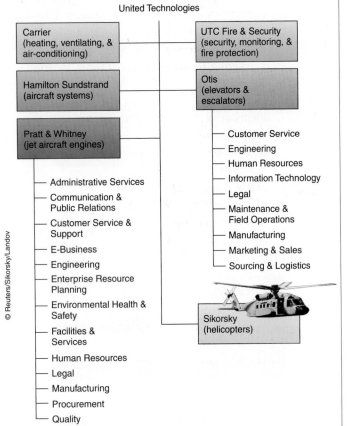

United Technologies

- Carrier (heating, ventilating, & air-conditioning)
- Hamilton Sundstrand (aircraft systems)
- Pratt & Whitney (jet aircraft engines)
  - Administrative Services
  - Communication & Public Relations
  - Customer Service & Support
  - E-Business
  - Engineering
  - Enterprise Resource Planning
  - Environmental Health & Safety
  - Facilities & Services
  - Human Resources
  - Legal
  - Manufacturing
  - Procurement
  - Quality

- UTC Fire & Security (security, monitoring, & fire protection)
- Otis (elevators & escalators)
  - Customer Service
  - Engineering
  - Human Resources
  - Information Technology
  - Legal
  - Maintenance & Field Operations
  - Manufacturing
  - Marketing & Sales
  - Sourcing & Logistics
- Sikorsky (helicopters)

© Reuters/Sikorsky/Landov

Source: United Technologies Corporation, *2009 Annual Report*, United Technologies, available online at http://www.utc.com/About+UTC/Company+Reports/2009+Annual+Report+English [accessed June 7, 2010].

product lines: Carrier, Hamilton Sundstrand, Otis, Pratt & Whitney, Sikorsky, and UTC Fire & Security.[5]

One of the advantages of product departmentalization is that, like functional departmentalization, it allows managers and workers to specialize in one area of expertise. Unlike the narrow expertise and experiences in functional departmentalization, however, managers and workers develop a broader set of experiences and expertise related to an entire product line. Likewise, product departmentalization makes it easier for top managers to assess work-unit performance. For example, because of the clear separation of its six different product divisions, United Technologies' top managers can easily compare the performance of its Carrier (heating, ventilating, air conditioning) and Otis (elevators and escalators) divisions. The divisions had similar

Customer departmentalization organizing work and workers into separate units responsible for particular kinds of customers

revenues—$11.4 billion for Carrier and $11.8 billion for Otis. However, when you examine profitability, Carrier's profits were $740 million compared to $2.4 billion for Otis.[6] Finally, decision making should be faster because managers and workers are responsible for the entire product line rather than for separate functional departments; in other words, there are fewer conflicts compared to functional departmentalization.

The primary disadvantage of product departmentalization is duplication. For example, you can see in Exhibit 9.4 that UTC's Otis elevators and Pratt & Whitney divisions both have customer service, engineering, human resources, legal, manufacturing, and procurement (similar to sourcing and logistics) departments. If United Technologies were instead organized by function, by contrast, one lawyer could handle matters related to both elevators and aircraft engines rather than working only on one or the other. Duplication like this often results in higher costs.

A second disadvantage is the challenge of coordinating across the different product departments. United Technologies would probably have difficulty standardizing its policies and procedures in product departments as different as the Carrier (heating, ventilating, and air-conditioning) and Sikorsky (military and commercial helicopters) divisions.

1.3 Customer Departmentalization

Customer departmentalization organizes work and workers into separate units responsible for particular kinds of customers. For example, as Exhibit 9.5 shows, the telecommunications company Sprint Nextel is organized into departments that cater to businesses, consumers, 4G mobile broadband operations, and product development.

The primary advantage of customer departmentalization is that it focuses the organization on customer needs rather than on products or business functions. Furthermore, creating separate departments to serve specific kinds of customers allows companies to specialize and adapt their products and services to customer needs and problems.

The primary disadvantage of customer departmentalization is that, like product departmentalization, it leads to duplication of resources. It can also be difficult to achieve coordination across different customer departments. Finally, the emphasis on meeting customers' needs may lead workers to make decisions that please customers but hurt the business.

Exhibit 9.5

Customer Departmentalization: Sprint Corporation

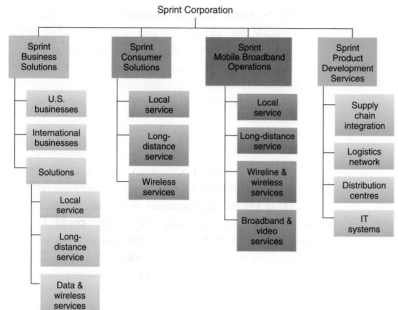

Source: "Overview," Sprint, available online at http://www.sprint.com/sprint/fastfacts/overview/index.html [accessed 1 May 2005].

1.4 Geographic Departmentalization

Geographic departmentalization organizes work and workers into separate units responsible for doing business in particular geographic areas. For example, Exhibit 9.6 shows the geographic departmentalization used by Coca-Cola Enterprises (CCE), the largest bottler and distributor of Coca-Cola products in the world. As shown in Exhibit 9.6, CCE has two regional groups: North America and Europe. As the table in the exhibit shows, each of these regions would be a sizable company by itself.

The primary advantage of geographic departmentalization is that it helps companies respond to the demands of different markets. This can be especially important when the company sells in different countries, as cultural preferences can vary widely. For example, CCE's geographic divisions sell products suited to taste preferences in different countries. CCE bottles and distributes the following products in Europe but not in Canada: Aquarius, BonAqua, Burn, Coca-Cola Light (which is somewhat different from Diet Coke), Diet Cherry Coke, Enviga, Nalu, Kinley, Lift, and Oasis.[7] Another advantage is that geographic departmentalization can reduce costs by locating unique organizational resources closer to customers. For instance, it is much cheaper for CCE

to build bottling plants in Belgium than to bottle Coke in England and then transport it across the English Channel to Belgium.

The primary disadvantage of geographic departmentalization is that it can lead to duplication of resources. For example, while it may be necessary to adapt products and marketing to different geographic locations, it's doubtful that CCE needs significantly different inventory tracking systems from location to location. Also, even more than with the other forms of departmentalization, it can be difficult to coordinate departments that are literally thousands of miles from one another and whose managers have very limited contact with one another.

> **Geographic departmentalization** organizing work and workers into separate units responsible for doing business in particular geographic areas

Exhibit 9.6

Geographic Departmentalization: Coca-Cola Enterprises

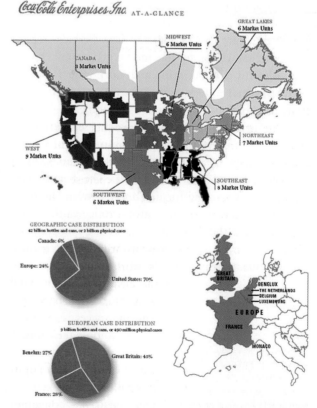

Source: "Territories of Operation, 2007 Annual Report," Coca-Cola Enterprises, available online at http://www.cokecce.com/brochures/cce_2007/index.html#territories [accessed 7 September 2008].

1.5 Matrix Departmentalization

Matrix departmentalization is a hybrid structure in which two or more forms of departmentalization are used together. The most common matrix combines the product and functional forms of departmentalization, but other forms may also be used. Exhibit 9.7 illustrates the matrix structure used by Procter & Gamble, which has more than 135,000 employees in 80 different countries. Across the top of Exhibit 9.7 are P&G's market development units (MDUs) which correspond to the five major geographic regions in which the company operates. These units are responsible for knowing the consumers and retailers in each geographic market. The global business units (GBUs) represent the company's three key brand areas; the reportable subsegments (included in the illustration are the billion-dollar brands associated with each) focus on specific brands, consumers, and competitors. Each GBU is responsible for the profitability, shareholder returns, and the innovation pipeline for its business. At the base of this organizational structure are Global Business Services (shared services that relate to the major geographic regions the company competes in) and Corporate Functions, which include functional departments that service and support the organization as a whole. To illustrate how the matrix organization works separately and together, let's use the example of a rollout of Pantene Shampoo, one of P&G's billion-dollar brands, in the United States and Latin America. The Beauty GBU would be responsible for determining what the brand stands for (e.g., Pantene gives you healthy, shiny hair) and for the associated marketing campaigns to communicate those benefits, as well as for product manufacturing using the global formula and package specifications. Each MDU focuses on ensuring that Pantene succeeds in its own region and makes modifications where necessary— for example, developing a smaller-size package for cost-sensitive consumers (in Latin America and the United States), or developing a large-size package suitable for warehouse stores such as Costco. The Global Business Centre in Costa Rica, serving both the United States and Latin America, provides support for accounting, employee payroll, order management, and logistics and systems operations. To summarize, P&G's organizational structure is designed to allow the company to "think globally" and "act locally."[8]

Several things distinguish matrix departmentalization from the other traditional forms of departmentalization.[9] First, most employees report to two bosses, one from each core part of the matrix. For example, in Exhibit 9.7, the manager responsible for Charmin in France would report both to the president for Global Baby & Family Care and to the president for Western Europe. Second, by virtue of their hybrid design, matrix structures lead to much more cross-functional interaction than other forms of departmentalization. In fact, while matrix workers are typically members of only one functional department (based on their work experience and expertise), they are also commonly members of several ongoing project, product, or customer groups. Third, because of the high level of cross-functional

> **Matrix departmentalization** a hybrid organizational structure in which two or more forms of departmentalization, most often product and functional, are used together

Exhibit 9.7

Matrix Departmentalization: Procter & Gamble

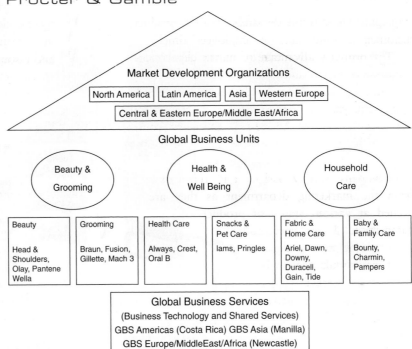

Source: "P&G Global Structure & Operations: Strength in Structure," available at http://www.pg.com/en_US/company/global_structure_operations/corporate_structure.shtml. [accessed 5 June 2010]. Used with permission by The Procter & Gamble Company.

interaction, matrix departmentalization requires significant coordination between managers in the different parts of the matrix. In particular, managers have the complex job of tracking and managing the multiple demands (project, product, customer, or functional) on employees' time.

The primary advantage of matrix departmentalization is that it allows companies to efficiently manage large, complex tasks like researching, developing, and marketing pharmaceuticals or carrying out complex global businesses. Efficiency comes from avoiding duplication. For example, rather than having an entire marketing function for each project, the company simply assigns and reassigns workers from the marketing department as they are needed at various stages of product completion. More specifically, an employee from a department may simultaneously be part of five different ongoing projects, but may be actively completing work on only a few projects at a time.

Another advantage is the pool of resources available to carry out large, complex tasks. Because of the ability to quickly pull in expert help from all the functional areas of the company, matrix project managers have a much more diverse set of expertise and experience at their disposal than do managers in the other forms of departmentalization.

The primary disadvantage of matrix departmentalization is the high level of coordination required to manage the complexity involved with running large, ongoing projects at various levels of completion. Matrix structures are notorious for confusion and conflict between project bosses in different parts of the matrix. At P&G, such confusion or conflict might occur between managers in the Global Fabric and Home Care Division and the president of operations in greater China. Disagreements or misunderstandings about schedules, budgets, available resources, and the availability of employees with particular functional

expertise are common. Another disadvantage is that matrix structures require much more management skill than the other forms of departmentalization.

Because of these problems, many matrix structures evolve from a **simple matrix,** in which managers in different parts of the matrix negotiate conflicts and resources directly, to a **complex matrix,** in which specialized matrix managers and departments are added to the organizational structure. In a complex matrix, managers from different parts of the matrix might report to the same matrix manager, who helps them sort out conflicts and problems.

2 Organizational Authority

The second part of traditional organizational structures is authority. **Authority** is the right to give commands, take action, and make decisions to achieve organizational objectives.[10]

*Traditionally, organizational authority has been characterized by the following dimensions: **2.1 chain of command, 2.2 line versus staff authority, 2.3 delegation of authority,** and **2.4 degree of centralization.***

2.1 Chain of Command

Turn back a few pages to Sony's organizational chart in Exhibit 9.1. If you place your finger on any position in the chart—say, the Home Entertainment Business Group (under Consumer, Professional and Devices Group)—you can trace a line upward to the company's CEO. This line, which vertically connects every job in the company to higher levels of management, represents the chain of command. The **chain of command** is the vertical line of authority that clarifies who reports to whom throughout the organization. People higher in the chain of command have the right, *if they so choose,* to give

> Matrix structures are notorious for confusion and conflict between project bosses in different parts of the matrix.

Simple matrix a form of matrix departmentalization in which managers in different parts of the matrix negotiate conflicts and resources

Complex matrix a form of matrix departmentalization in which managers in different parts of the matrix report to matrix managers, who help them sort out conflicts and problems

Authority the right to give commands, take action, and make decisions to achieve organizational objectives

Chain of command the vertical line of authority that clarifies who reports to whom throughout the organization

commands, take action, and make decisions concerning activities occurring anywhere below them in the chain. In the following discussion about delegation and decentralization, you will learn that managers don't always choose to exercise their authority directly.[11]

One of the key assumptions underlying the chain of command is **unity of command,** which means that workers should report to just one boss.[12] In practical terms, this means that only one person can be in charge at a time. Matrix organizations, in which employees have two bosses, automatically violate this principle. This is one of the primary reasons that matrix organizations are difficult to manage. Unity of command serves an important purpose: to prevent the confusion that might arise when an employee receives conflicting commands from two different bosses.

2.2 Line versus Staff Authority

A second dimension of authority is the distinction between line and staff authority. **Line authority** is the right to command immediate subordinates in the chain of command. For example, Sony CEO Howard Stringer has line authority over the head of Sony Entertainment Business Group, which contains Sony Pictures. Stringer can issue orders to that division president and expect them to be carried out. In turn, the head of Sony Entertainment Business Group can issue orders to his subordinates and expect them to be carried out.

Staff authority is the right to *advise* but not command others who are not subordinates in the chain of command. For example, a manager in human resources at Sony might advise the manager in charge of Sony's TV Business Group on a hiring decision but cannot order him or her to hire a certain applicant.

The terms *line* and *staff* are also used to describe different functions within the organization. A **line function** is an activity that contributes directly to creating or selling the company's products. So, for example, activities that take place within the manufacturing and marketing departments would be considered line functions. A **staff function,** such as accounting, human resources, or legal services, does not contribute directly to creating or selling the company's products but instead supports line activities. For example, marketing managers might consult with the legal staff to make sure the wording of a particular advertisement is legal.

2.3 Delegation of Authority

Managers can exercise their authority directly by completing the tasks themselves, or they can choose to pass on some of their authority to subordinates. **Delegation of authority** is the assignment of direct authority and responsibility to a subordinate to complete tasks for which the manager is normally responsible.

When a manager delegates work, three transfers occur, as illustrated in Exhibit 9.8. First, the manager transfers full responsibility for the assignment to the subordinate. According to Murray Martin, the Canadian CEO of Pitney Bowes Worldwide, the higher up you rise in an organization, the more you must be willing to delegate. "I think that if you are looking at companies that have long-term, continuous success, it is with CEOs that have been able to disperse power, rather than centralize power."[13] The challenge of delegation does not apply just to large organizations; small businesses and start-up ventures can also find delegation useful to support growth. For many entrepreneurs, letting go of day-to-day operations and decision making is not easy; even so, it is often critical to do so if the business is past the start-up phase and transitioning to growth. That

Exhibit 9.8

Delegation: Responsibility, Authority, and Accountability

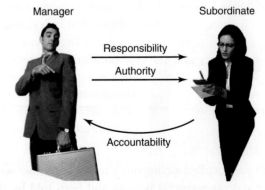

Manager   Subordinate

Responsibility

Authority

Accountability

Source: C. D. Pringle, D. F. Jennings, and J. G. Longenecker, *Managing Organizations: Functions and Behaviours* © 1990 Pearson Education, Inc. Adapted by permission of the author.

Unity of command
a management principle that workers should report to just one boss

Line authority the right to command immediate subordinates in the chain of command

Staff authority the right to advise, but not command, others who are not subordinates in the chain of command

Line function an activity that contributes directly to creating or selling the company's products

Staff function an activity that does not contribute directly to creating or selling the company's products, but instead supports line activities

Delegation of authority the assignment of direct authority and responsibility to a subordinate to complete tasks for which the manager is normally responsible is when owners need to be able to focus on developing and executing strategies for growth instead of devoting all their time to daily operations or to activities that could be carried out by others. This means that having the right people in place is vital to effective delegating. Alex Krohn, owner of Gossamer Threads Inc., a software and Web-hosting company based in Vancouver, believes that recruitment and building a solid team are needed for effective delegation to occur. That in turn means finding "the right people and make sure you can trust them to deliver the same quality of service you were providing."[14] To summarize, many managers find it difficult to delegate, but "the job of the leader is to conduct the orchestra, not play all the instruments."[15]

One reason it is difficult for some managers to delegate is that they often fear the task won't be done as well as if they did it themselves. However, one CEO says, "If you can delegate a task to somebody who can do it 75 percent to 80 percent as well as you can today, you delegate it immediately." Why? Many tasks don't need to be done perfectly; they just need to be *done*. And delegating tasks that someone else can do frees managers to assume other important responsibilities.

Delegating authority can generate a related problem: micromanaging. Sometimes managers delegate only to later interfere with how the employee is performing the task. "Why are you doing it that way? That's not the way I do it." But delegating full responsibility means that the employee—not the manager—is now completely responsible for task completion. Good managers need to trust their subordinates to do the job.

The second transfer that occurs with delegation is that the manager gives the subordinate full authority over the budget, resources, and personnel needed to do the job. To do the job effectively, subordinates must have the same tools and information at their disposal that managers had when they were responsible for the same task. In other words, for delegation to work, delegated authority must be commensurate with delegated responsibility.

The third transfer that occurs with delegation is the transfer of accountability. The subordinate now has the authority and responsibility to do the job and in return is accountable for getting the job done. In other words, managers delegate their authority and responsibility to subordinates in exchange for results.

2.4 Degree of Centralization

If you've ever called a company's toll-free number with a complaint or a special request and been told by the customer service representative, "I'll have to ask my manager," or "I'm not authorized to do that," you know that centralization of authority exists in that company. **Centralization of authority** is the location of most authority at the upper levels of the organization. In a centralized organization, managers make most decisions, even the relatively small ones. That's why the customer service representative you called couldn't make a decision without first asking the manager.

If you are lucky, however, you may have talked to a customer service representative at another company who said, "I can take care of that for you right now." In other words, the person was able to handle your problem without any input from or consultation with company management. **Decentralization** is the location of a significant amount of authority in the lower levels of the organization. An organization is decentralized if it has a high degree of delegation at all levels. In a decentralized organization, workers closest to problems are authorized to make the decisions necessary to solve the problems on their own.

© Fuse/Jupiterimages

Centralization of authority the location of most authority at the upper levels of the organization

Decentralization the location of a significant amount of authority in the lower levels of the organization

Decentralization has a number of advantages. It develops employee capabilities throughout the company and leads to faster decision making and more satisfied customers and employees. Bayshore Home Health is the largest provider of home and community health care services in Canada, with 50 locations across the country. The company has adopted a decentralized approach by encouraging employees to make decisions locally; management believes that "decision making is best when it is made as close to the client as possible."[16]

Another company in the health care industry, Trillium Health Centre (THC) in Ontario, has found much success with a decentralized organizational structure. THC is a merger of two hospitals, both of which had been operating under a traditional hierarchical structure, which is common in health care organizations. With the decentralized structure, each of the centre's 10 divisions has the ability to set

on equity (22.8 percent versus 16.6 percent), and return on sales (10.3 percent versus 6.3 percent). Surprisingly, the same study found that few large companies actually are decentralized. Specifically, only 31 percent of employees in these 1,000 companies were responsible for recommending improvements to management. Overall, just 10 percent of employees received the training and information needed to support a truly decentralized approach to management.[18]

With results like these, the key question is no longer *whether* companies should decentralize, but *where* they should decentralize. One rule of thumb is to stay centralized where standardization is important and to decentralize where standardization is unimportant. **Standardization** is solving problems by consistently applying the same rules, procedures, and processes. Kwik Kopy Printing Canada, a franchise business with 70 locations across Canada, uses a standardized process when recruiting and selecting potential franchisees. The company believes that selecting the right franchisees is a critical decision that affects brand awareness, the success of locations, and the company's overall financial performance. When a poor selection is made, it causes a ripple effect throughout the company; that is why management has a standardized system for dealing with this vital task. The selection process includes a series of personal interviews to assess the franchisee's skills, as well as profile testing to uncover the franchisee's strengths and weaknesses. Meetings with head office personnel and existing franchises are also part of the selection process. In addition, potential

> The key question is no longer **whether** companies should decentralize, but **where** they should decentralize.

its own vision, goals, and objectives and is supported by partnership councils led and chaired by staff and supported by management. The decision to employ a distributed leadership environment has been well received and has enhanced employee engagement on a collective level.[17] A study of 1,000 large companies found that those with a high degree of decentralization outperformed those with a low degree of decentralization in terms of return on assets (6.9 percent versus 4.7 percent), return on investment (14.6 percent versus 9.0 percent), return

Standardization
solving problems by consistently applying the same rules, procedures, and processes

franchisees must provide financial documentation to show they have sufficient equity to purchase the business. Kwik Kopy's president, Brett Harding, admits that to some the selection process may seem very long and structured. But, as he puts it, "No one gets married after the first date. Good franchising is about relationships."[19]

3 Job Design

1. "Welcome to McDonald's. May I have your order please?"
2. Listen to the order. Repeat it for accuracy. State the total cost. "Please drive to the second window."
3. Take the money. Make change.

4. Give customers drinks, straws, and napkins.

5. Give customers food.

6. "Thank you for coming to McDonald's."

Could you stand to do the same simple tasks an average of 50 times per hour, 400 times per day, 2,000 times per week, 8,000 times per month? Few can. Fast-food workers rarely stay on the job more than six months. Indeed, McDonald's and other fast-food restaurants have well over 100 percent employee turnover each year.[20]

The shape of a job is closely related to how happy and fulfilled an employee feels doing it. In this next section, you will learn about **job design**—the number, kind, and variety of tasks that individual workers perform in doing their jobs.

You will learn **3.1 why companies continue to use specialized jobs like the McDonald's drive-through job** *and* **3.2 how job rotation, job enlargement, job enrichment,** *and* **3.3 the job characteristics model are being used to overcome the problems associated with job specialization.**

3.1 Job Specialization

Job specialization occurs when a job is composed of a small part of a larger task or process. Specialized jobs are characterized by simple, easy-to-learn steps, low variety, and high repetition, like the McDonald's drive-through window job just described. One of the clear disadvantages of specialized jobs is that, being so easy to learn, they quickly become boring. This, in turn, can lead to low job satisfaction and high absenteeism and employee turnover, all of which are very costly to organizations.

Why, then, do companies continue to create and use specialized jobs? The primary reason is that specialized jobs are very economical. As we learned from Taylor and the Gilbreths in Chapter 2, economy is a key reason why the pioneers of scientific management sought to standardize tasks. Once a job has been specialized, it takes little time to learn and master. Consequently, when experienced workers quit or are absent, the company can replace them with new employees and lose little productivity. For example, next time you're at McDonald's, notice the pictures of the food on the cash registers. These pictures make it easy for McDonald's trainees to

quickly learn to take orders. Likewise, to simplify and speed operations, the drink dispensers behind the counter are set to automatically fill drink cups. Put a medium cup below the dispenser. Punch the medium drink button. The soft drink machine then fills the cup to within a half-inch of the top while that same worker goes to get your fries. At McDonald's, every task has been simplified in this way. Because the work is designed to be simple, wages can remain low since it isn't necessary to pay high salaries to attract highly experienced, educated, or trained workers.

3.2 Job Rotation, Enlargement, and Enrichment

Because of the efficiency of specialized jobs, companies are often reluctant to eliminate them. Consequently, job redesign efforts have focused on modifying jobs to keep the benefits of specialized jobs while reducing their obvious costs and disadvantages. Three methods—job rotation, job enlargement, and job enrichment—have been used to try to improve specialized jobs.[21]

Job rotation attempts to overcome the disadvantages of job specialization by

Job design the number, kind, and variety of tasks that individual workers perform in doing their jobs

Job specialization a job composed of a small part of a larger task or process

Job rotation periodically moving workers from one specialized job to another to give them more variety and the opportunity to use different skills

©Photodisc/Jupiterimages

periodically moving workers from one specialized job to another to give them more variety and the opportunity to use different skills. For example, an office receptionist who does nothing but answer phones could be systematically rotated to a different job, such as typing, filing, or data entry, every day or two. Likewise, a "mirror attacher" in an automobile plant might attach mirrors in the first half of the day's work shift and then install bumpers during the second half. Because employees simply switch from one specialized job to another, job rotation allows companies to retain the economic benefits of specialized work. At the same time, the greater variety of tasks makes the work less boring and more satisfying for workers.

Another way to counter the disadvantages of specialization is to enlarge the job. **Job enlargement** increases the number of different tasks that a worker performs within one particular job. So, instead of being assigned just one task, workers with enlarged jobs are given several tasks to perform. For example, an enlarged "mirror attacher" job might include attaching the mirror, checking to see that the mirror's power adjustment controls work, and then cleaning the mirror's surface. Though job enlargement increases variety, many workers report feeling more stress when their jobs are enlarged. Consequently, many workers view enlarged jobs as simply more work, especially if they are not given additional time to complete the additional tasks. In comparison, **job enrichment** attempts to overcome the deficiencies in specialized work by increasing the number of tasks and by giving workers the authority and control to make meaningful decisions about their work.[22]

3.3 Job Characteristics Model

In contrast to job rotation, job enlargement, and job enrichment, which focus on providing variety in job tasks, the **job characteristics model (JCM)** is an approach to job redesign that seeks to formulate jobs in ways that motivate workers and lead to positive work outcomes.[23] As shown in the far right column of Exhibit 9.9, the primary goal of the model is to create jobs that result in positive personal and work outcomes such as internal work motivation, satisfaction with one's job, and work effectiveness. Of these, the central concern of the JCM is internal motivation. **Internal motivation** is motivation that comes from the job itself rather than from outside rewards, such as a raise or praise from the boss. If workers feel that performing the job well is itself rewarding, then the job has internal motivation. Statements such as "I get a nice sense of accomplishment" or "I feel good about myself and what I'm producing" are examples of internal motivation.

Moving to the left in Exhibit 9.9, you can see that the JCM specifies three critical psychological states that must occur for work to be internally motivating. First, workers must *experience the work as meaningful;*

Job enlargement
increasing the number of different tasks that a worker performs within one particular job

Job enrichment
increasing the number of tasks in a particular job and giving workers the authority and control to make meaningful decisions about their work

Job characteristics model (JCM) an approach to job redesign that seeks to formulate jobs in ways that motivate workers and lead to positive work outcomes

Internal motivation
motivation that comes from the job itself rather than from outside rewards

---

Exhibit 9.9

Job Characteristics Model

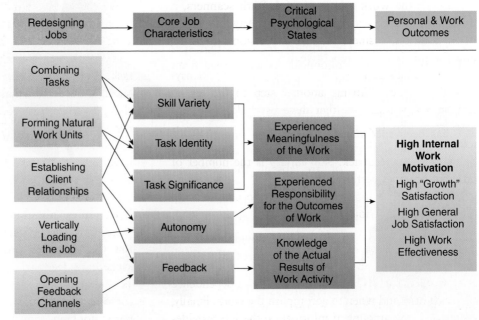

Source: J. RICHARD HACKMAN & GREG R. OLDHAM, WORK REDESIGN, 1st, ©1980. Printed and Electronically reproduced by permission of Pearson Education, Inc., Upper Saddle River, New Jersey.

Voznikevich Konstantin/Shutterstock

that is, they must view their job as being important. Second, they must *experience responsibility for work outcomes*—they must feel personally responsible for the work being done well. Third, workers must have *knowledge of results;* that is, they must know how well they are performing their jobs. All three critical psychological states must occur for work to be internally motivating.

For example, grocery store cashiers usually have knowledge of results. When you're slow, your checkout line grows long. If you make a mistake, customers point it out: "No, I think that's on sale for $2.99, not $3.99." Likewise, cashiers experience responsibility for work outcomes. At the end of the day, the register is totalled and the money is counted. Ideally, the money matches the total sales in the register. If the money in the till is less than what's recorded in the register, most stores make the cashier pay the difference. Consequently, most

To illustrate how the core job characteristics work together, let's use them to more thoroughly assess why the McDonald's drive-through window job is not particularly satisfying or motivating. To start, skill variety is low. Except for the size of an order or special requests ("no onions"), the process is the same for each customer. At best, task identity is moderate. Although you

WHY ISN'T THE DRIVE-THROUGH JOB PARTICULARLY SATISFYING OR MOTIVATING?

cashiers are very careful to avoid being caught short at the end of the day. Nonetheless, despite knowing the results and experiencing responsibility for work outcomes, most grocery store cashiers (at least where I shop) aren't internally motivated because they don't experience the work as meaningful. With scanners, it takes little skill to learn or do the job. Anyone can do it. In addition, cashiers have few decisions to make, and the job is highly repetitive.

What kinds of jobs produce the three critical psychological states? Moving another step to the left in Exhibit 9.9, you can see that these psychological states arise from jobs that are strong on five core job characteristics: skill variety, task identity, task significance, autonomy, and feedback. **Skill variety** is the number of different activities performed in a job. **Task identity** is the degree to which a job, from beginning to end, requires completion of a whole and identifiable piece of work. **Task significance** is the degree to which a job is perceived to have a substantial impact on others inside or outside the organization. **Autonomy** is the degree to which a job gives workers the discretion, freedom, and independence to decide how and when to accomplish the work. Finally, **feedback** is the amount of information the job provides to workers about their work performance.

take the order, handle the money, and deliver the food, others are responsible for a larger part of the process—preparing the food. Task identity will be even lower if the McDonald's has two drive-through windows because each drive-through window worker will have an even more specialized task. The first is limited to taking the order and making change, while the second just delivers the food. Task significance, the impact you have on others, is probably low. Autonomy is also very low: McDonald's has strict rules about dress, cleanliness, and procedures. But the job does provide immediate feedback, such as positive and negative customer comments, car horns honking, the amount of time it takes to process

Skill variety the number of different activities performed in a job

Task identity the degree to which a job, from beginning to end, requires the completion of a whole and identifiable piece of work

Task significance the degree to which a job is perceived to have a substantial impact on others inside or outside the organization

Autonomy the degree to which a job gives workers the discretion, freedom, and independence to decide how and when to accomplish the job

Feedback the amount of information the job provides to workers about their work performance

orders, and the number of cars in the drive-through. With the exception of feedback, the low levels of the core job characteristics show why the drive-through window job is not internally motivating for many workers.

What can managers do when jobs aren't internally motivating? The far left column of Exhibit 9.9 lists five job redesign techniques that managers can use to strengthen a job's core characteristics. *Combining tasks* increases skill variety and task identity by joining separate, specialized tasks into larger work modules. For example, some trucking firms are now requiring truck drivers to load their rigs as well as drive them. The hope is that involving drivers in loading will ensure that trucks are properly loaded, thus reducing damage claims.

Work can be formed into *natural work units* by arranging tasks according to logical or meaningful groups. Although many trucking companies randomly assign drivers to trucks, some have begun assigning drivers to particular geographic locations (e.g., Western Canada or Quebec) or to truckloads that require special driving skill (e.g., oversized loads, chemicals, etc.). Forming natural work units increases task identity and task significance.

Establishing client relationships increases skill variety, autonomy, and feedback by giving employees direct contact with clients and customers. In some companies, truck drivers are expected to establish business relationships with their regular customers. When something goes wrong with a shipment, customers are told to call drivers directly.

Vertical loading means pushing some managerial authority down to workers. For truck drivers, this means that they have the same authority as managers to resolve customer problems. In some companies, if a late shipment causes problems for a customer, the driver has the authority to fully refund the cost of that shipment (without first obtaining management's approval).

The last job redesign technique offered by the model, *opening feedback channels,* means finding additional ways to give employees direct, frequent feedback about their job performance.

Designing Organizational Processes

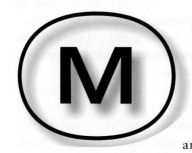

More than 40 years ago, Tom Burns and G.M. Stalker described how two kinds of organizational designs, mechanistic and organic, are appropriate for different kinds of organizational environments.[24] **Mechanistic organizations** are characterized by specialized jobs and responsibilities; precisely defined, unchanging roles; and a rigid chain of command based on centralized authority and vertical communication. This type of organization works best in stable, unchanging business environments. By contrast, **organic organizations** are characterized by broadly defined jobs and responsibility; loosely defined, frequently changing roles; and decentralized authority and horizontal communication based on task knowledge. This type of organization works best in dynamic, changing business environments.

The organizational design techniques described in the first half of this chapter—departmentalization, authority, and job design—are better suited for mechanistic organizations and the stable business environments that were more prevalent before 1980. In contrast, the organizational design techniques discussed next, in the second part of the chapter, are more appropriate for organic organizations and the increasingly dynamic environments in which today's businesses compete.

The key difference between these approaches is that mechanistic organizational designs focus on organizational structure while organic organizational designs are concerned with organizational process, or the collection of activities that transform inputs into outputs valued by customers.

After reading the next two sections, you should be able to

4   explain the methods that companies are using to redesign internal organizational processes (i.e., intraorganizational processes).

5   describe the methods that companies are using to redesign external organizational processes (i.e., interorganizational processes).

4 Intraorganizational Processes

An **intraorganizational process** is the collection of activities that take place within an organization to transform inputs into outputs that customers value.

*Let's take a look at how companies are using **4.1 re-engineering** and **4.2 empowerment** to redesign intraorganizational processes like these.*

4.1 Re-engineering

In their best-selling book *Re-engineering the Corporation*, Michael Hammer and James Champy define **re-engineering** as "the *fundamental* rethinking and *radical* redesign of business *processes* to achieve *dramatic* improvements in critical, contemporary measures of performance, such as cost, quality, service and speed."[25] Hammer and Champy further explained the four key words shown in italics in this definition. The first key word is *fundamental.* When re-engineering organizational designs, managers must ask themselves, "Why do we do what we do?" and "Why do we do it the way we do?" The usual answer is, "Because that's the way we've always done it." Fundamental rethinking involves getting behind "that's the way we've always done it" and

pursuing answers to these questions down to the foundations so that processes are actually achieving business goals. The second key word is *radical.* Re-engineering is about significant change, about starting over by throwing out the old ways of getting work done. The third key word is *processes.* Hammer and Champy noted that "most business people are not process oriented; they are focused on tasks, on jobs, on people, on structures, but not on processes." The fourth key word is *dramatic.* Re-engineering is about achieving quantum improvements in company performance.

An example from IBM Credit's operation illustrates how work can be reengineered.[26] IBM Credit lends businesses money to buy IBM computers. Previously, the loan process began when an IBM salesperson called the home office to obtain credit approval for a customer's purchase. The

> **Intraorganizational process** the collection of activities that take place within an organization to transform inputs into outputs that customers value
>
> **Re-engineering** fundamental rethinking and radical redesign of business processes to achieve dramatic improvements in critical measures of performance, such as cost, quality, service, and speed

In Plain English . . .

The definition of intraorganizational process tells you exactly what it is, but here's a quick example to help you get to "Oh, that's it."

The steps involved in an automobile insurance claim are a good example of an intraorganizational process:

1. Document the loss (i.e., the accident).
2. Assign an appraiser to determine the dollar amount of damage.
3. Make an appointment to inspect the vehicle.
4. Inspect the vehicle.
5. Write an appraisal and get the repair shop to agree to the damage estimate.
6. Pay for the repair work.
7. Return the repaired car to the customer.

© Bogdanov Olga/Itar-Tass/Landov

first department involved in the process took the credit information over the phone from the salesperson and recorded it on the credit form. The credit form was sent to the credit checking department, then to the pricing department (where the interest rate was determined), and on through a total of five departments. In all, it took the five departments six days to approve or deny the customer's loan. Of course, this delay cost IBM business. Some customers got their loans elsewhere. Others, frustrated by the wait, simply cancelled their orders.

Finally, two IBM managers decided to walk a loan straight through each of the departments involved in the process. At each step, they asked the workers to stop what they were doing and immediately process their loan application. They were shocked by what they found. From start to finish, the entire process took just 90 minutes! The six-day turnaround time was almost entirely due to delays in handing off the work from one department to another. The solution: IBM redesigned the process so that one person, not five people in five separate departments, now handles the entire loan approval process without any handoffs. Approval time dropped from six days to four hours and allowed IBM Credit to increase the number of loans it handled by a factor of 100!

Re-engineering changes an organization's orientation from vertical to horizontal. Instead of taking orders from upper management, lower- and middle-level managers and workers take orders from a customer who is at the beginning and end of each process. Instead of running independent functional departments, managers and workers in different departments take ownership of cross-functional processes. Instead of simplifying work so that it becomes increasingly specialized, re-engineering complicates work by giving workers increased autonomy and responsibility for complete processes.

In essence, re-engineering changes work by

changing **task interdependence,** the extent to which collective action is required to complete an entire piece of work. As shown in Exhibit 9.10, there are three kinds of task interdependence.[27] In **pooled interdependence,** each job or department independently contributes to the whole. In **sequential interdependence,** work must be performed in succession, as one group's or job's outputs become the inputs for the next group or job. Finally, in **reciprocal interdependence,** different jobs or groups work together in a back-and-forth manner to complete the process. By reducing the handoffs between different jobs or groups, re-engineering decreases sequential interdependence. Likewise, re-engineering decreases pooled interdependence by redesigning work so that formerly independent jobs or departments now work together to complete processes. Finally, re-engineering increases reciprocal interdependence by making groups or individuals responsible for larger, more complete processes in which several steps may be accomplished at the same time.

As an organizational design tool, re-engineering promises big rewards, but it has also come under severe criticism. The most serious complaint is that because it allows a few workers to do the work formerly done by many, re-engineering is simply a corporate code word for cost cutting and worker layoffs.[28] Likewise, for that reason, detractors claim that re-engineering hurts morale and performance. Today, even re-engineering gurus Hammer and Champy admit that roughly 70 percent of all re-engineering projects fail because of the effects on people in the workplace. Says Hammer, "I wasn't smart enough about that

Exhibit 9.10

Re-engineering and Task Interdependence

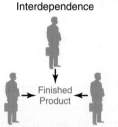

Pooled Interdependence

Finished Product

Sequential Interdependence

Finished Product

Reciprocal Interdependence

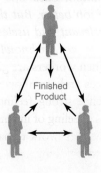

Finished Product

Nap? Or Free Lunch?

Forklift operators at Production Control Units (PCU) in Dayton, Ohio, used to compete to see who could take the longest on-the-job nap. Now they vie for who can come up with the best idea to improve their workplace and the company. Unproductive time lost the company over $4 million each year until PCU replaced their employee suggestion box with a Workplace Improvements Suggested by Employees (WISE) program. Individuals and groups who submit the best ideas see their ideas implemented and are rewarded with a prime parking spot or lunch on the company. The company saves money, and the employees are empowered to make a difference in their environment.

Source: R. Marshall, J. Talbott, and D. Bukovinsky, "Employee Empowerment Works at Small Companies, Too," *Strategic Finance* (September 2006): 34-38.

[the people issues]. I was reflecting my engineering background and was insufficiently appreciative of the human dimension. I've [now] learned that's critical."[29]

4.2 Empowerment

Another way of redesigning intraorganizational processes is through empowerment. **Empowering workers** means permanently passing decision-making authority and responsibility from managers to workers. For workers to be fully empowered, companies must give them the information and resources they need to make and carry out good decisions and then reward them for taking individual initiative.[30] Unfortunately, this doesn't happen often enough. As Michael Schrage, author and MIT researcher, wrote:

A warehouse employee can see on the intranet that a shipment is late but has no authority to accelerate its delivery. A project manager knows—and can mathematically demonstrate—that a seemingly minor spec change will bust both her budget and her schedule. The spec must be changed anyway. An airline reservations agent tells the Executive Platinum Premier frequent flier that first class appears wide open for an upgrade. However, the airline's yield management software won't permit any upgrades until just four hours before the flight, frequent fliers (and reservations) be damned. In all these cases, the employee has access to valuable information. Each one possesses the "knowledge" to do the job better. But the knowledge and information are irrelevant and useless. Knowledge isn't power; the ability to act on knowledge is power.[31]

When workers are given the proper information and resources and are allowed to make good decisions, they experience strong feelings of empowerment. **Empowerment** is a feeling of intrinsic motivation in which workers perceive their work to have meaning and perceive themselves to be competent, having an impact, and capable of self-determination.[32] Work has meaning when it is consistent with personal standards and beliefs. Workers feel competent when they believe they can perform an activity with skill. The belief that they are having an impact comes from a feeling that they can affect work outcomes. A feeling of self-determination arises from workers' belief that they have the autonomy to choose how best to do their work.

Empowerment can lead to changes in organizational processes because meaning, competence, impact, and self-determination produce empowered employees who take active, rather than passive, roles in their work.

5 Interorganizational Processes

An **interorganizational process** is a collection of activities that occur *among companies* to transform inputs into outputs that customers value. In other words, many companies work together to create a product or service that keeps customers happy. For example, when you purchase a pair of jeans from a retail clothing chain like American Eagle, you're not just buying from American Eagle—you're also buying from a network of suppliers in other countries and from that company's sourcing team, which generates the correct fabrics and the entire line of clothing

---

Empowering workers permanently passing decision-making authority and responsibility from managers to workers by giving them the information and resources they need to make and carry out good decisions

Empowerment feelings of intrinsic motivation, in which workers perceive their work to have impact and meaning and perceive themselves to be competent and capable of self-determination

Interorganizational process a collection of activities that take place among companies to transform inputs into outputs that customers value

The Virtual Office

Is the virtual workplace the way of the future? Over the past decade, the number of people who participate in virtual work has increased dramatically. Indeed, it is estimated that at least 10 percent of today's workforce telecommutes from home—three times the level of 2000. The reasons for this trend? Internet technology has made it possible for many employees to perform virtual work; employees are embracing the flexibility and autonomy that telecommuting provides; and organizations are realizing higher productivity and savings in labour and real estate costs. IBM, for example, saves $100 million a year by allowing 42 percent of its employees to work remotely. There are challenges, however, including these: employees must be helped to find the right work–life balance (working on holidays or weekends); workplace isolation must be overcome (wanting advice or simply missing social interaction); the lack of face-to-face communication must be compensated for (the volume of communication may be high but not necessarily efficient); and so must the lack of visibility (feeling that efforts are not being noticed or that it is more difficult to be promoted).

Source: J. Mulki, F. Bardhi, F. Lassk, and J. Nanavaty-Dahl, "Set Up Remote Workers to Thrive," *MIT Sloan Management Review*, October 1, 2009, http://sloanreview.mit.edu/the-magazine/articles/2009/fall/51116/set-up-remote-workers-to-thrive.

---

carried in American Eagle stores. That team then manufactures the first product prototypes and sends them to the company's design team for final inspection and possibly last-minute changes.

*In this section, you'll explore interorganizational processes by learning about **5.1 modular organizations** and **5.2 virtual organizations**.*[33]

5.1 Modular Organizations

Except for the core business activities that they can perform better, faster, and cheaper than others, **modular organizations** outsource all remaining business activities to outside companies, suppliers, specialists, or consultants. The term *modular* is used because the business activities purchased from outside companies can be added and dropped as needed, much like adding pieces to a three-dimensional puzzle. Exhibit 9.11 depicts a modular organization in which the company has chosen to keep training, human resources, sales, product design, manufacturing, customer service, research and development, and information technology as core business activities, but has

Modular organization
an organization that outsources noncore business activities to outside companies, suppliers, specialists, or consultants

outsourced the noncore activities of product distribution, Web page design, advertising, payroll, accounting, and packaging.

Exhibit 9.11

Modular Organization

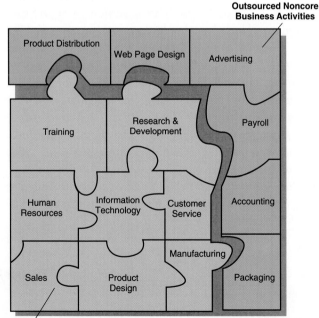

Modular organizations have several advantages. First, because modular organizations pay for outsourced labour, expertise, or manufacturing capabilities only when needed, they can cost significantly less to run than traditional organizations. For example, when Apple came up with its iPod digital music player, it outsourced the audio chip design and manufacture to SigmaTel in Austin, Texas, and final assembly to Asutek Computers in Taiwan. Doing so not only reduced costs and sped up production (beating Sony's Network Walkman to market), but also allowed Apple to do what it does best—design innovative products with easy-to-use software.[34] To obtain these advantages, however, modular organizations need reliable partners—vendors and suppliers that they can work closely with and trust.

Modular organizations have disadvantages, too. The primary disadvantage is the loss of control that occurs when key business activities are outsourced to other companies. Also, companies may reduce their competitive advantage in two ways if they mistakenly outsource a core business activity. First, as a result of competitive and technological change, the noncore business activities a company has outsourced may suddenly become the basis for competitive advantage. Second, related to that point, suppliers to whom work is outsourced can sometimes become competitors.

5.2 Virtual Organizations

In contrast to modular organizations, in which the interorganizational process revolves around a central company, a **virtual organization** is part of a network in which many companies share skills, costs, capabilities, markets, and customers with one another. Exhibit 9.12 shows a virtual organization in which, for "today," the parts of a virtual company consist of product design, purchasing, manufacturing, advertising, and information technology. Unlike modular organizations, in which the outside organizations are tightly linked to one central company, virtual organizations work with some companies in the network alliance but not with all. So, whereas a puzzle with various pieces is a fitting metaphor for a modular organization, a potluck dinner is an appropriate metaphor for a virtual organization. All participants bring their finest food dish but eat only what they want.

Another difference is that the working relationships between modular organizations and outside companies tend to be more stable and longer lasting than the shorter, often temporary relationships found among the virtual companies in a network alliance. The composition of a virtual organization is always changing. The combination of network partners that a virtual corporation has at any one time depends on the expertise needed to solve a particular problem or provide a

Exhibit 9.12

Virtual Organizations

Today, I'll have...

Purchasing

Product Design

Information Technology

Manufacturing

Advertising

© Mike Powell/Lifesize/Jupiterimages

Virtual organization
an organization that is part of a network in which many companies share skills, costs, capabilities, markets, and customers to collectively solve customer problems or provide specific products or services

specific product or service. This is why the business-person in the network organization shown in the photo is saying, "Today, I'll have . . . ." Tomorrow, the business could want something completely different. In this sense, the term *virtual organization* means the organization that exists "at the moment." Virtual organizations have a number of advantages. They let companies share costs. And, because members can quickly combine their efforts to meet customers' needs, they are fast and flexible.

As with modular organizations, a disadvantage of virtual organizations is that once work has been outsourced, it can be difficult to control the quality of work done by network partners. The greatest disadvantage, however, is that tremendous managerial skills are required to make a network of independent organizations work well together, especially since their relationships tend to be short and based on a single task or project. Virtual organizations are using two methods to solve this problem. The first is to use a *broker*. In traditional, hierarchical organizations, managers plan, organize, and control. But with the horizontal, interorganizational processes that characterize virtual organizations, the job of a broker is to create and assemble the knowledge, skills, and resources from different companies for outside parties, such as customers.[35] The second way to make networks of virtual organizations more manageable is to use a *virtual organization agreement* that, somewhat like a contract, specifies the schedules, responsibilities, costs, payouts, and liabilities for participating organizations.

Visit **icanmgmt.com** to find the resources you need today!

Located at the back of the textbook are rip-out Chapter Review cards. Make sure you also go online to check out other tools that MGMT offers to help you successfully pass your course.

- Interactive Quizzes
- Key Terms Flashcards
- Audio Chapter Summaries
- PowerPoint Slides

- Interactive Games
- Crossword Puzzles
- "Reel to Reel" and "Biz Flix" videos
- Cases and Exercises

86% of Canadian students surveyed prefer the 4LTR Press text and website combination to a traditional text.

LOG IN!

MGMT was designed for students just like you—busy people who want choices, flexibility, and multiple learning options.

MGMT delivers concise, electronic resources such as discipline-specific activities, flashcards, test yourself questions, crossword puzzles and more!

At **icanmgmt.com**, you'll find electronic resources such as **printable interactive flashcards, downloadable study aids, games, quizzes, and videos** to test your knowledge of key concepts. These resources will help supplement your understanding of core **Principles of Management** concepts in a format that fits your busy lifestyle.

"I really like how you use students' opinions on how to study and made a website that encompasses everything we find useful. Seeing this website makes me excited to study!"

—Abby Boston, Fanshawe College

Visit **icanmgmt.com** to find the resources you need today!

MANAGING TEAMS

Why Use Work Teams?

A growing number of organizations, two-thirds of executives in Canada, believe that they are significantly improving their effectiveness by establishing work teams.[1] But this has only been the case for the last 25 years. Procter & Gamble and Cummins Engine began using teams in 1962 and 1973, respectively. But many international companies, like Boeing, Caterpillar, Ford Motor Company, and General Electric, did not set up their first teams until the 1980s.[2] In other words, teams are a relatively new phenomenon, and there's still much for organizations to learn about managing them.

Work teams consist of a small number of people with complementary skills who hold themselves mutually accountable for pursuing a common purpose, achieving performance goals, and improving interdependent work processes.[3] Although work teams are not the answer for every situation or organization, if the right teams are used properly and in the right settings, teams can dramatically improve company performance and instill a sense of vitality in the workplace that is otherwise difficult to achieve.

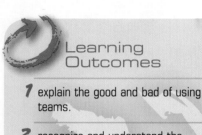

Learning Outcomes

1 explain the good and bad of using teams.

2 recognize and understand the different kinds of teams.

3 understand the general characteristics of work teams.

4 explain how to enhance work team effectiveness.

Work team a small number of people with complementary skills who hold themselves mutually accountable for pursuing a common purpose, achieving performance goals, and improving interdependent work processes

After reading the next two sections, you should be able to

1 explain the good and bad of using teams.

2 recognize and understand the different kinds of teams.

© iStockphoto.com

1 The Good and Bad of Using Teams

*Let's begin our discussion of teams by learning about **1.1 the advantages of teams, 1.2 the disadvantages of teams,** and **1.3 when to use and not use teams.***

1.1 The Advantages of Teams

Companies are making greater use of teams because they have been shown to improve customer satisfaction, product and service quality, employee job satisfaction, and decision making.[4] Teams help businesses increase *customer satisfaction* in several ways. For example, work teams can be trained to meet the needs of specific customers. Hewitt Associates, a consulting firm with offices in Calgary, Montreal, Toronto, and Vancouver, manages benefits administration for hundreds of multinational client firms. To ensure customer satisfaction, Hewitt re-engineered its customer service centre and created specific teams to handle benefits-related questions posed by employees of specific client organizations.[5] Businesses also create problem-solving teams and employee involvement teams to study ways to improve overall customer satisfaction and make recommendations for improvements. Teams like these typically meet on a weekly or monthly basis.

Teams also help firms improve *product and service quality* in several ways.[6] In contrast to traditional organizational structures where management is responsible

for organizational outcomes and performance, teams take direct responsibility for the quality of the products and services they produce. At Whole Foods, a supermarket chain with stores in Vancouver and Toronto that sells groceries and health foods, the 10 teams that manage each store are responsible for store quality and performance; they are also directly accountable because the size of their team bonus depends on the store's performance. Productive teams get an extra $1.50 to $2.00 per hour in every other paycheque.[7]

Another reason for using teams is that teamwork often leads to increased *job satisfaction*.[8] One reason that teamwork can be more satisfying than traditional work is that it gives workers a chance to improve their skills. This is often accomplished through **cross-training,** in which team members are taught how to do all or most of the jobs performed by the other team members. The advantage for the organization is that cross-training allows a team to function normally when one member is absent, quits, or is transferred. The advantage for workers is that cross-training broadens their skills and increases their capabilities while also making their work more varied and interesting. A second reason that teamwork is satisfying is that work teams often receive proprietary business information that is available only to managers at most companies. For example, Whole Foods has an "open books, open door, open people" philosophy.[9] Team members are given full access to their store's financial information and everyone's salaries, including those of the store manager and the CEO.[10] Team members also gain job satisfaction from unique leadership responsibilities that are not typically available in traditional organizations. For example, rotating leadership among team members can lead to more participation and cooperation in team decision making and improved team performance.[11]

Finally, teams share many of the advantages of group decision making discussed in Chapter 5. For instance, because team members possess different knowledge, skills, abilities, and experiences, a team is able to view problems from multiple perspectives. This diversity of viewpoints increases the odds that team decisions will solve the underlying causes of problems and not just address the symptoms. The increased knowledge and information available to teams also make it easier for

them to generate more alternative solutions, a critical part of improving the quality of decisions. Because team members are involved in decision-making processes, they are also likely to be more committed to making those decisions work. In short, teams can do a much better job than individuals in two important steps of the decision-making process: defining the problem and generating alternative solutions.

1.2 The Disadvantages of Teams

Although teams can significantly improve customer satisfaction, product and service quality, speed and efficiency in product development, employee job satisfaction, and decision making, using teams does not guarantee these positive outcomes. In fact, if you've ever participated in team projects in your classes, you're probably already aware of some of the problems inherent in work teams. Despite all of their promise, teams and teamwork are also prone to these significant disadvantages: initially high turnover, social loafing, and the problems associated with group decision making.

The first disadvantage of work teams is *initially high turnover*. Teams aren't for everyone, and some workers balk at the responsibility, effort, and learning required in team settings.

Social loafing is another disadvantage of work teams. **Social loafing** occurs when workers withhold their efforts and fail to perform their share of the work.[12] A 19th-century French engineer named Maximilian Ringlemann first documented social loafing when he found that one person pulling on a rope alone exerted an

© Image Source/Jupiterimages

Cross-training training team members to do all or most of the jobs performed by the other team members

Social loafing behaviour in which team members withhold their efforts and fail to perform their share of the work

average of 63 kilograms of force on the rope. In groups of three, the average force dropped to 53 kilograms per person. In groups of eight, the average dropped to just 31 kilograms per person. Ringlemann concluded that the larger the team, the smaller the individual effort. In fact, social loafing is more likely to occur in larger groups, where identifying and monitoring the efforts of individual team members can be difficult.[13] In other words, social loafers count on being able to blend into the background where their lack of effort isn't easily spotted. From team-based class projects, most students already know about social loafers or "slackers," who contribute poor, little, or no work whatsoever. Not surprisingly, a study of 250 student teams found that the most talented students are typically the least satisfied with teamwork because of having to carry slackers and do a disproportionate share of their team's work. Perceptions of fairness are negatively related to the extent of social loafing within teams.[14]

Finally, teams share many of the *disadvantages of group decision making* discussed in Chapter 5, such as groupthink. In *groupthink,* members of highly cohesive groups feel intense pressure not to disagree with one another so that the group can approve a proposed solution. Because groupthink restricts discussion and leads to consideration of a limited number of alternative solutions, it usually results in poor decisions. Also, team decision making takes considerable time, and team meetings can often be unproductive and inefficient. Another possible pitfall is *minority domination,* where just one or two people dominate team dis-

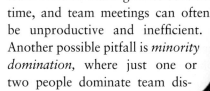

cussions, restricting consideration of different problem definitions and alternative solutions. Finally, team members may not feel accountable for the decisions and actions taken by the team.

1.3 When to Use Teams

As the two previous subsections made clear, teams have significant advantages *and* disadvantages. Therefore, the question is not *whether* to use teams, but *when* and *where* to use teams for maximum benefit and minimum cost. As Doug Johnson, associate director at the Center for the Study of Work Teams, puts it, "Teams are a means to an end, not an end in themselves."[15] Exhibit 10.1 on the next page provides some additional guidelines on when to use or not use teams.[16]

First, teams should be used when there is a clear, engaging reason or purpose for using them. Too many companies use teams because they're popular or because the companies assume that teams can fix all problems. Teams are much more likely to succeed if they know why they exist and what they are supposed to accomplish and more likely to fail if they don't.

Factors That Encourage People to Withhold Effort in Teams

1. **The presence of someone with expertise**. Team members will withhold effort when another team member is highly qualified to make a decision or comment on an issue.

2. **The presentation of a compelling argument**. Team members will withhold effort if the arguments for a course of action are very persuasive or similar to their own thinking.

3. **Lacking confidence in one's ability to contribute**. Team members will withhold effort if they are unsure about their ability to contribute to discussions, activities, or decisions. This is especially so for high-profile decisions.

4. **An unimportant or meaningless decision**. Team members will withhold effort by mentally withdrawing or adopting a "who cares" attitude if decisions don't affect them or their units, or if they don't see a connection between their efforts and their team's successes or failures.

5. **A dysfunctional decision-making climate**. Team members will withhold effort if other team members are frustrated or indifferent or if a team is floundering or disorganized.

Source: P. W. Mulvey, J. F. Veiga, and P. M. Elsass, "When Teammates Raise a White Flag," *Academy of Management Executive* 10, no. 1 (1996): 40–49

Exhibit 10.1

When to Use and When Not to Use Teams

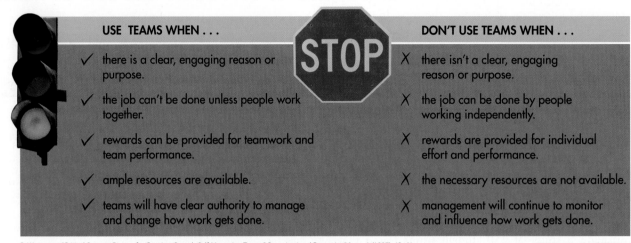

USE TEAMS WHEN . . .	DON'T USE TEAMS WHEN . . .
✓ there is a clear, engaging reason or purpose.	✗ there isn't a clear, engaging reason or purpose.
✓ the job can't be done unless people work together.	✗ the job can be done by people working independently.
✓ rewards can be provided for teamwork and team performance.	✗ rewards are provided for individual effort and performance.
✓ ample resources are available.	✗ the necessary resources are not available.
✓ teams will have clear authority to manage and change how work gets done.	✗ management will continue to monitor and influence how work gets done.

Source: R. Wageman, "Critical Success Factors for Creating Superb Self-Managing Teams," *Organizational Dynamics* 26, no. 1 (1997): 49–61.

© Hill Street Studios/Brand X Pictures/Jupiterimages / DDCoral/Shutterstock

Second, teams should be used when the job can't be done unless people work together. This typically means that teams are needed when tasks are complex, require multiple perspectives, or require repeated interaction with others to complete. If tasks are simple and don't require multiple perspectives or repeated interaction with others, however, teams should not be used.[17] For instance, production levels dropped by 23 percent when Levi Strauss (see http://www.levi.ca for store locations in Canada) introduced teams in its factories. Levi Strauss's mistake was assuming that teams were appropriate for garment work, where workers perform single, specialized tasks, like sewing zippers or belt loops. Because this kind of work does not require interaction with others, Levi Strauss unwittingly pitted the faster workers against the slower workers on each team. Arguments, infighting, insults, and threats were common between faster workers and the slower workers who held back team performance. One seamstress even had to physically restrain an angry coworker who was about to throw a chair at a faster worker who was constantly nagging her about her slow pace.[18]

Third, teams should be used when rewards can be provided for teamwork and team performance. Rewards that depend on team performance rather than individual performance are the key to rewarding team behaviours and efforts. You'll read more about team rewards later in the chapter, but for now it's enough to know that if the type of reward (individual versus team) is not matched to the type of performance (individual versus team), teams won't work.

Traditional work group a group composed of two or more people who work together to achieve a shared goal

2 Kinds of Teams

Let's continue our discussion of teams by learning about the different kinds of teams that companies use to make themselves more competitive. We look first at *2.1 how teams differ in terms of autonomy, which is the key dimension that makes one team different from another,* and then at *2.2 some special kinds of teams.*

2.1 Autonomy, the Key Dimension

Teams can be classified in a number of ways, such as permanent or temporary, functional or cross-functional. However, studies indicate that the amount of autonomy possessed by a team is the key difference among teams.[19] *Autonomy* is the degree to which workers have the discretion, freedom, and independence to decide how and when to accomplish their jobs.

Exhibit 10.2 shows how five kinds of teams differ in terms of autonomy. Moving left to right across the autonomy continuum at the top of the exhibit, traditional work groups and employee involvement groups have the least autonomy, semi-autonomous work groups have more autonomy, and, finally, self-managing teams and self-designing teams have the most autonomy. Moving from bottom to top along the left side of the exhibit, note that the number of responsibilities given to each kind of team increases directly with its autonomy. Let's review each of these kinds of teams and their autonomy and responsibilities in more detail.

The smallest amount of autonomy is found in **traditional work groups,** where two or more people work together to achieve a shared goal. In these groups, workers are responsible for doing the work or executing the task, but they do not have direct responsibility or

Exhibit 10.2
Team Autonomy Continuum

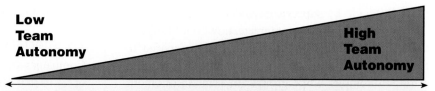

RESPONSIBILITIES	TRADITIONAL WORK GROUPS	EMPLOYEE INVOLVEMENT GROUPS	SEMI-AUTONOMOUS WORK GROUPS	SELF-MANAGING TEAMS	SELF-DESIGNING TEAMS
Control Design of					
Team					✓
Tasks					✓
Membership					✓
Production/Service Tasks					
Make Decisions				✓	✓
Solve Problems				✓	✓
Major Production/Service Tasks					
Make Decisions			✓	✓	✓
Solve Problems			✓	✓	✓
Information			✓	✓	✓
Give Advice/Make Suggestions		✓	✓	✓	✓
Execute Task	✓	✓	✓	✓	✓

Sources: R. D. Banker, J. M. Field, R. G. Schroeder, & K. K. Sinha, "Impact of Work Teams on Manufacturing Performance: A Longitudinal Field Study," *Academy of Management Journal* 39 (1996): 867–890: J. R. Hackman, "The Psychology of Self-Management in Organizations," in *Psychology and Work: Productivity, Change, and Employment*, ed. M. S. Pallak and T. Perlof (Wahsington, DC: American Psychological Association), 85–136.

control over their work. Workers report to managers who are responsible for their performance and who have the authority to hire and fire them, make job assignments, and control resources.

Employee involvement teams, which have somewhat more autonomy, meet on company time on a weekly or monthly basis to provide advice or make suggestions to management concerning specific issues such as plant safety, customer relations, or product quality.[20] Though they offer advice and suggestions, they do not have the authority to make decisions. Membership on these teams is often voluntary, but members may be selected because of their expertise. The idea behind employee involvement teams is that the people closest to the problem or situation are best able to recommend solutions.

Semi-autonomous work groups not only provide advice and suggestions to management but also have the authority to make decisions and solve problems related to the major tasks required to produce a product or service. Semi-autonomous groups regularly receive information about budgets, work quality and performance, and competitors' products. Furthermore, members of semi-autonomous work groups are typically

Employee involvement team team that provides advice or makes suggestions to management concerning specific issues

Semi-autonomous work group a group that has the authority to make decisions and solve problems related to the major tasks of producing a product or service

cross-trained in a number of different skills and tasks. In short, semi-autonomous work groups give employees the authority to make decisions that are typically made by supervisors and managers.

That authority is not complete, however. Managers still play a role, though much reduced compared to traditional work groups, in supporting the work of semi-autonomous work groups. In semi-autonomous work groups, managers ask good questions, provide resources, and facilitate performance of group goals.

Self-managing teams differ from semi-autonomous work groups in that team members manage and control *all* of the major tasks *directly related* to production of a product or service without first getting approval from management. This includes managing and controlling the acquisition of materials, making a product or providing a service, and ensuring timely delivery.

Self-designing teams have all the characteristics of self-managing teams, but they can also control and change the design of the teams themselves, the tasks they do and how and when they do them, and the membership of the teams.

2.2 Special Kinds of Teams

Companies are also increasingly using several other kinds of teams that can't easily be categorized in terms of autonomy: cross-functional teams, virtual teams, and project teams. Depending on how these teams are designed, they can be either low- or high-autonomy teams.

Cross-functional teams are intentionally composed of employees from different functional areas of the organization.[21] Because their members have different functional backgrounds, education, and experience, cross-functional teams usually attack problems from multiple perspectives and generate more ideas and alternative solutions, all of which are especially important when trying to innovate or do creative problem solving.[22] Cross-functional teams can be used almost anywhere in an organization and are often used in conjunction with matrix and product organizational structures (see Chapter 9). They can also be used with either part-time or temporary team assignments or with full-time, long-term teams.

Cessna, which manufactures airplanes using engines from Pratt & Whitney Canada, created cross-functional

Self-managing team
a team that manages and controls all of the major tasks of producing a product or service

Self-designing team
a team that has the characteristics of self-managing teams but also controls team design, work tasks, and team membership

Cross-functional team
a team composed of employees from different functional areas of the organization

---

Self-directed teams can have a high failure rate. In a study carried out at a western Canadian university, on a team project that was worth 40 percent of the final grade, each student was required to contribute to the final self-directed team project. Each team was to design and re-engineer a workplace process. The study found that despite explicit statements that they must contribute, several roles were not performed adequately, conflict was allowed to escalate to disruptive levels, and team efficacy was found to be extremely low.

On the other hand, research has shown that for Canadian companies such as Dofasco, Steel Case Equipment, Northern Telecom, LOF Glass, and Laurel Steel, results have been positive. The studies showed increased flexibility, productivity gains, improved quality, increased commitment, and improved customer service. The key, says, Michael Piczak, is the training and support of management for the implementation of the new Self-Directed Work Team process.

Pixland/Jupiterimages

Sources: G.H. Coetzer and R.T. Trimble, "An Empirical Examination of the Relationship Between Adult Attention Deficit, Cooperative Conflict Management, and Efficacy for Working in Teams," *American Journal of Business* 25, no. 1 (2010): 23–33; M.W. Piczak, "Self-Directed Work Teams: An Implementation Guide," http://www.spin.mohawkcollege.ca/courses/pizcakm/oh&s&sdwts.ppt.

teams for purchasing parts. With workers from purchasing, manufacturing engineering, quality engineering, product design engineering, reliability engineering, product support, and finance, each team addressed make-versus-buy decisions (make it themselves or buy from others), sourcing (who to buy from), internal plant and quality improvements, and the external training of suppliers to reduce costs and increase quality.[23]

Virtual teams are groups of geographically and/or organizationally dispersed coworkers who use a combination of telecommunications and information technologies to accomplish an organizational task.[24] Members of virtual teams rarely meet face-to-face; instead, they use e-mail, videoconferencing, and group communication software. For example, MySQL, an open source database software developer, has 320 workers in 25 countries, strewn from Montreal to the Ukraine. They communicate with one another using a company chat room (or Skype when live voice conversations are necessary) and are accountable for completing tasks on a program called Worklog. Oleksandr Byelkin lives in Lugansk, Ukraine; not only does he have poor phone service, but he also doesn't speak English very well. Even MySQL's holiday party was online.[25] Virtual teams can be employee involvement teams, self-managing teams, or nearly any kind of team discussed in this chapter. Virtual teams are often (but not necessarily) temporary teams that are set up to accomplish a specific task.[26] Ike Hall, an adjunct professor at Athabasca University's online MBA program (the largest MBA program in Canada), indicates that team projects and interactions carried out in a virtual environment can produce excellent results. There are certain skills that can be learned, and experience working in this manner can be very useful, given that Canadian businesses require executives who utilize more virtual teams.

The principal advantage of virtual teams is their flexibility. Employees can work with one another regardless of physical location, time zone, or organizational affiliation.[27] Because the team members don't meet in a physical location, virtual teams also find it much easier to include other key stakeholders such as suppliers and customers. Plus, virtual teams have certain efficiency advantages over traditional team structures. Because the teammates do not meet face-to-face, a virtual team typically requires a smaller time commitment than a traditional team does.[28] A drawback of virtual teams is that the team members must learn to express themselves in new contexts.[29] The give-and-take that naturally occurs in face-to-face meetings is more difficult to

achieve through video conferencing or other methods of virtual teaming. Indeed, several studies have shown that physical proximity enhances information processing in teams.[30] Therefore, some companies bring virtual team members together in offices or special trips on a regular basis to try to minimize these problems.

Project teams are created to complete specific, one-time projects or tasks within a limited time.[31]

Virtual team a team composed of geographically and/or organizationally dispersed coworkers who use telecommunication and information technologies to accomplish an organizational task

Project team a team created to complete specific, one-time projects or tasks within a limited time

Project teams are often used to develop new products, significantly improve existing products, roll out new information systems, or build new factories or offices. The project team is typically led by a project manager who has the overall responsibility for planning, staffing, and managing the team, which usually includes employees from different functional areas. Effective project teams demand both individual and collective responsibility.[32]

One advantage of project teams is that drawing employees from different functional areas can reduce or eliminate communication barriers. In turn, as long as team members feel free to express their ideas, thoughts, and concerns, free-flowing communication encourages cooperation among separate departments and typically speeds up the design process.[33] Another advantage of project teams is their flexibility. When projects are finished, project team members either move on to the next project or return to their functional units. For example, publication of this book required designers, editors, page compositors, and Web designers, among others. When the task was finished, these people applied their skills to other textbook projects. Because of this flexibility, project teams are often used with the matrix organizational designs discussed in Chapter 9.

Managing Work Teams

"Why did I ever let you talk me into teams? They're nothing but trouble."[34] Lots of managers have this reaction after making the move to teams. Many don't realize that this reaction is normal, both for them and for workers. In fact, such a reaction is characteristic

Norms informally agreed-on standards that regulate team behaviour

NASA Goddard Space Flight Center

of the *storming* stage of team development (discussed in Section 3.5). Managers who are familiar with these stages and with the other important characteristics of teams will be better prepared to manage the predictable changes that occur when companies make the switch to team-based structures.

After reading the next two sections, you should be able to

3   understand the general characteristics of work teams.

4   explain how to enhance work team effectiveness.

3 Work Team Characteristics

Understanding the characteristics of work teams is essential for making teams an effective part of an organization. Therefore, in this section you'll learn about **3.1 team norms, 3.2 team cohesiveness, 3.3 team size, 3.4 team conflict,** and **3.5 the stages of team development.**

3.1 Team Norms

Over time, teams develop **norms,** informally agreed-upon standards that regulate team behaviour.[35] Norms are valuable because they let team members know what is expected of them. At Nucor Steel (which purchased Harris Steel of Canada for $1.07 billion in 2007), work groups expect their members to get to work on time. To reinforce this norm, anyone who is late to work will not receive the team bonus for that day (assuming the team is productive). A worker who is more than 30 minutes late will not receive the team bonus for the entire week. Losing a bonus matters at Nucor because work group bonuses can easily double the size of a worker's take-home pay.[36]

Studies indicate that norms are one of the most powerful influences on work behaviour because they regulate the everyday actions that allow teams to function effectively. Effective work teams develop norms about the quality and timeliness of job performance, absenteeism, safety, and expression of ideas. Team norms are often associated with positive outcomes, such as stronger organizational commitment, more trust in management, and stronger job and organizational satisfaction.[37]

Norms can also influence team behaviour in negative ways. For example, most people would agree that damaging organizational property; saying or doing something to hurt someone at work; intentionally doing one's work badly, incorrectly, or slowly; griping about coworkers; deliberately breaking rules; or doing something to harm the company are negative behaviours. A study of workers from 34 teams in 20 different organizations found that teams with negative norms strongly influenced their team members to engage in these negative behaviours. In fact, the longer individuals were members of a team with negative norms and the more frequently they interacted with their teammates, the more likely they were to perform negative behaviours. Since team norms typically develop early in the life of a team, these results indicate how important it is for teams to establish positive norms from the outset.[38]

3.2 Team Cohesiveness

Cohesiveness is another important characteristic of work teams. **Cohesiveness** is the extent to which team members are attracted to a team and motivated to remain in it.[39] The level of cohesiveness in a group is important for several reasons. To start, cohesive groups have a better chance of

retaining their members. As a result, cohesive groups typically experience lower turnover.[40] In addition, team cohesiveness promotes cooperative behaviour, generosity, and a willingness on the part of team members to assist one another.[41] When team cohesiveness is high, team members are more motivated to contribute to the team because they want to gain the approval of other team members. For these reasons and others, studies have clearly established that cohesive teams consistently perform better.[42] Furthermore, cohesive teams quickly achieve high levels of performance. By contrast, teams low in cohesion take much longer to reach the same levels of performance.[43]

What can be done to promote team cohesiveness? First, make sure that all team members are present at team meetings and activities. Team cohesiveness suffers when members are allowed to withdraw from the team and miss team meetings and events.[44] Second, create additional opportunities for teammates to work together by rearranging work schedules and creating common workspaces. When task interdependence is high and team members have lots of chances to work together, team cohesiveness

Teams work best when you get to know each other outside of work.

© Rubberball/Jupiterimages

Cohesiveness the extent to which team members are attracted to a team and motivated to remain in it

tends to increase.[45] Third, engaging in nonwork activities as a team can help build cohesion. At a company where teams put in extraordinarily long hours coding computer software, the software teams maintained cohesion by doing "fun stuff" together. Team leader Tammy Urban says, "We went on team outings at least once a week. We'd play darts, shoot pool. Teams work best when you get to know each other outside of work—what people's interests are, who they are. Personal connections go a long way when you're developing complex applications in our kind of time frames."[46] Finally, companies build team cohesiveness by making employees feel that they are part of a special organization. For example, all the new hires at Disney World are required to take a course titled "Traditions One," where they learn the traditions and history of the Walt Disney Company (including the names of the seven dwarfs!). The purpose of Traditions One is to instill a sense of team pride in working for Disney.

3.3 Team Size

The relationship between team size and performance appears to be curvilinear. Very small or very large teams may not perform as well as moderately sized teams. For most teams, the right size is somewhere between six and nine members.[47] This size is conducive to high team cohesion, which has a positive effect on team performance, as discussed above. A team of this size is small enough for the team members to get to know one another and for each member to have an opportunity to contribute in a meaningful way to the success of the team. At the same time, the team is also large enough to take advantage of team members' diverse skills, knowledge, and perspectives. It is also easier to instill a sense of responsibility and mutual accountability in teams of this size.[48]

By contrast, when teams get too large, team members find it difficult to get to know one another, and the team may splinter into smaller subgroups. When this occurs, subgroups sometimes argue and disagree, weakening overall team cohesion. As teams grow, there is also a greater chance of *minority domination,* where just a few team members dominate team discussions. Even if minority domination doesn't occur, larger groups may not have time for all team members to share their input. And when team members feel that their contributions are unimportant or not needed, the result is less involvement, effort, and accountability to the team.[49] Large teams also face logistical problems such as finding an appropriate time or place to meet. Finally, the incidence of social loafing, discussed earlier in the chapter, is much higher in large teams.

Team performance can also suffer when a team is too small. Teams with just a few people may lack the diversity of skills and knowledge found in larger teams. Also, teams that are too small are unlikely to gain the advantages of team decision making (i.e., multiple perspectives, generating more ideas and alternative solutions, and stronger commitment) found in larger teams.

What signs indicate that a team's size needs to be changed? If decisions are taking too long, if the team has difficulty making decisions or taking action, if a few members dominate the team, or if the commitment or efforts of team members are weak, chances are the team is too big. In contrast, if a team is having difficulty coming up with ideas or generating solutions, or if the team does not have the expertise to address a specific problem, chances are the team is too small.

3.4 Team Conflict

Conflict and disagreement are inevitable in most teams. But this shouldn't surprise anyone. From time to time, people who work together are going to disagree about what and how things get done. What causes conflict in teams? Although almost anything can lead to conflict—casual remarks that unintentionally offend a team member, or fighting over scarce resources—the primary cause of team conflict is disagreement over team goals and priorities.[50] Other common causes of team conflict include disagreements over task-related issues, interpersonal incompatibilities, and simple fatigue.

Though most people view conflict negatively, the key to dealing with team conflict is not avoiding it, but

How to Have a Good Fight

- Work with more information to make discussion productive rather than contentious.
- Generate several alternative solutions. Two solutions will generate debate. More than two will generate productive discussion.
- Establish common goals.
- Use your sense of humour.
- Create and maintain a balance of power.
- Do not force consensus.

Source: K. M. Eisenhard, J. L. Kahwajy, and L. J. Bourgeois III, "How Management Teams Can Have a Good Fight", *Harvard Business Review* 75, no. 4 (July–August 1997): 77–85.

© iStockphoto.com/Walik

rather making sure that the team experiences the right kind of conflict. In Chapter 5, you learned about *c-type conflict*, or *cognitive conflict*, which focuses on problem-related differences of opinion, and *a-type conflict*, or *affective conflict*, which refers to the emotional reactions that can occur when disagreements become personal rather than professional.[51] Cognitive conflict is strongly associated with improvements in team performance, whereas affective conflict is strongly associated with decreases in team performance.[52] Why does this happen? With cognitive conflict, team members disagree because their different experiences and expertise lead them to different views of the problem and solutions. Indeed, managers who participated on teams that emphasized cognitive conflict described their teammates as "smart," "team players," and "best in the business." They described their teams as "open," "fun," and "productive." One manager summed up the positive attitude that team members had about cognitive conflict by saying, "We scream a lot, then laugh, and then resolve the issue."[53] Thus, cognitive conflict is also characterized by a willingness to examine, compare, and reconcile differences to produce the best possible solution.

By contrast, affective conflict often results in hostility, anger, resentment, distrust, cynicism, and apathy. Managers who participated on teams that emphasized affective conflict described their teammates as "manipulative," "secretive," "burned out," and "political."[54] Not surprisingly, affective conflict can make people uncomfortable and cause them to withdraw and decrease their commitment to a team.[55] Affective conflict also lowers the satisfaction of team members, may lead to personal hostility between coworkers, and can decrease team cohesiveness.[56] Although cognitive conflict is a benefit, affective conflict undermines team performance by preventing teams from engaging in the kinds of activities that are critical to team effectiveness.

So, what can managers do to manage team conflict? First, they need to realize that emphasizing cognitive conflict alone won't be enough. Studies show that cognitive and affective conflicts often occur together in a given team activity! Sincere attempts to reach agreement on a difficult issue can quickly deteriorate from cognitive to affective conflict if the discussion turns personal and tempers and emotions flare. While cognitive conflict is clearly the better approach to take, efforts to engage in cognitive conflict should be managed well and checked before they deteriorate and the team becomes unproductive.

Can teams disagree and still get along? Fortunately, they can. In an attempt to study this issue, researchers examined team conflict in twelve high-tech companies. In four of the companies, work teams used cognitive conflict to address problems but did so in a way that minimized the occurrence of affective conflict.

There are several ways teams can have a good fight.[57] First, work with more, rather than less, information. If data are plentiful, objective, and up-to-date, teams will focus on issues, not personalities. Second, develop multiple alternatives to enrich debate. Focusing on multiple solutions diffuses conflict by getting the team to keep searching for a better solution. Positions and opinions are naturally more flexible with five alternatives than with just two. Third, establish common goals. Remember, most team conflict arises from disagreements over team goals and priorities. Therefore, common goals encourage collaboration and minimize conflict over a team's purpose. Fourth, inject humour into the workplace. Humour relieves tension, builds cohesion, and just makes being in teams fun. Fifth, maintain a balance of power by involving as many people as possible in the decision process. And sixth, resolve issues without forcing a consensus. Consensus means that everyone must agree before decisions are finalized. Effectively, requiring consensus gives everyone on the team veto power. Nothing gets done until everyone agrees, which, of course, is nearly impossible. As a result, insisting on consensus usually promotes affective rather than cognitive conflict. If team members can't agree after constructively discussing their options, it's better to have the team leader make the final choice. Most team members can accept the team leader's choice if they've been thoroughly involved in the decision process.

3.5 Stages of Team Development

As teams develop and grow, they pass through four stages of development. As shown in Exhibit 10.3, those stages are forming, storming, norming, and performing.[58] Although not every team passes through each of these stages, teams that do tend to be better performers.[59] This holds true even for teams composed of seasoned executives. After a period of time, however, if a team is not managed well, its performance may start to deteriorate as the team begins a process of decline and progresses through the stages of de-norming, de-storming, and de-forming.[60]

Forming is the initial stage of team development. This is the getting-acquainted stage, during which team members first meet one another, form initial impressions, and try to get a sense of what it will be like to be part of the team. Some of the first team norms will be established during this stage, as team members begin to find out what behaviours will and won't be accepted by the team. During this stage, team leaders should allow time for team members to get to know one another, set early ground rules, and begin to set up a preliminary team structure.

Conflicts and disagreements often characterize the second stage of team development, **storming.** As team members begin working together, different personalities and work styles may clash. Team members become more assertive at this stage and more willing to state opinions. This is also the stage when team members jockey for position and try to establish a favourable role for themselves on the team. In addition, team members are likely to disagree about what the group should do and how it should do it. Team performance is still relatively low, given that team cohesion is weak and team members are still reluctant to support one another. Since teams that get stuck in the storming stage are almost always ineffective, it is important for team leaders to focus the team on team goals and on improving team performance. Team members need to be particularly patient and tolerant with one another in this stage.

During **norming,** the third stage of team development, team members begin to settle into their roles as team members. Positive team norms will have developed by this stage, and teammates should know what to expect from one another. Petty differences should have been resolved, friendships will have developed, and group cohesion will be relatively strong. At this point, team members will have accepted team goals, be operating as a unit, and, as indicated by the increase in performance, be working

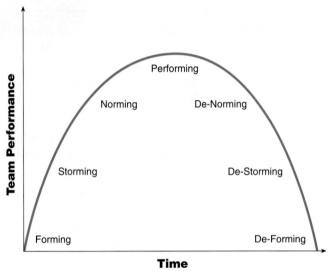

Exhibit 10.3

Stages of Team Development

Sources: J. F. McGrew, J. G. Bilotta, and J. M. Deeney, "Software Team Formation and Decay: Extending the Standard Model for Small Groups," *Small Group Research* 30, no. 2 (1999) : 209–234; B.W. Tuckman, "Development Sequence in Small Groups," *Psychological Bulletin* 63, no. 6 (1965): 384–399

Forming the first stage of team development, in which team members meet one another, form initial impressions, and begin to establish team norms

Storming the second stage of development, characterized by conflict and disagreement, in which team members disagree over what the team should do and how it should do it

Norming the third stage of team development, in which team members begin to settle into their roles, group cohesion grows, and positive team norms develop

together effectively. This stage can be very short and is often characterized by someone on the team saying, "I think things are finally coming together." Note, however, that teams may also cycle back and forth between storming and norming several times before finally settling into norming.

In the last stage of team development, **performing,** performance improves because the team has finally matured into an effective, fully functioning team. At this point, members should be fully committed to the team and think of themselves as members of a team and not just employees. Team members often become intensely loyal to one another at this stage and feel mutual accountability for team successes and failures. Trivial disagreements, which can take time and energy away from the work of the team, should be rare. At this stage, teams get a lot of work done, and it is fun to be a team member. But the team should not become complacent. Without effective management, its performance may begin to decline as it passes through the stages of de-norming, de-storming, and de-forming (these three stages are also known as adjourning.[61]

Mario Poirier/The Maple Leaf magazine, 23 September 2009, Vol. 12, No. 31, cover.

4 Enhancing Work Team Effectiveness

Making teams work is a challenging and difficult process. Nonetheless, companies can increase the likelihood that teams will succeed by carefully managing *4.1 the setting of team goals and priorities* and *4.2 how work team members are selected, 4.3 trained,* and *4.4 compensated.*[62]

4.1 Setting Team Goals and Priorities

In Chapter 5, you learned that having specific, measurable, attainable, realistic, and timely (i.e., S.M.A.R.T.) goals is one of the most effective means for improving individual job performance. Fortunately, team goals also improve team performance, especially when they are *specific* and *challenging*. In fact, team goals lead to much higher team performance 93 percent of the time.[63] For

> **Performing** the fourth and final stage of team development, in which performance improves because the team has matured into an effective, fully functioning team

Canada's RMC Team Work is Tops

A nine-member team from Canada's Royal Military College has beaten Sandhurst (Britain's Royal Military College) and West Point (U.S. Military Academy) three years in a row. The competition includes equipment inspection, tactical boat manoeuvring, marksmanship, first aid, river crossing, wall obstacles, radio communications, and other tasks that challenge the teams to their physical and mental limits. The team trained six days a week, on top of already demanding engineering academic courses and other military duties. It competed against 38 other teams from the United States, the United Kingdom, and—for the first time—a team from the National Military Academy of Afghanistan. "I am particularly impressed with the dedication of the cadets on the team," states Captain Kevin Wright, coach of the team. "They make tremendous sacrifices for the team." Without clear teamwork, no one person can finish the course. The team is only as strong as its weakest link and only as fast as its slowest member. Teamwork is emphasized at the Royal Military College of Canada; it is ingrained in the cadets to utilize these teamwork skills in their lifelong careers in the military or in civilian life.

Stefko, S. (2007). RMC Wins at Sandhurst competition - Again! *The Maple Leaf*, 10, no. 14 2007, Accessed 3 June 2010 from www.forces.gc.ca/site/commun/m.-fe/article-ang.asp?id=3062.

mgmt trend

example, Nucor Steel, with its Canadian affiliates, sets specific, challenging hourly goals for each of its production teams, which consist of first-line supervisors and production and maintenance workers. The average in the steel industry is tons of steel per hour. Nucor production teams have a goal of eight tons per hour, but get a 5 percent bonus for every ton over eight tons that they produce each hour. With no limit on the bonuses they can receive, Nucor's production teams produce an average of 35 to 40 tons of steel per hour![64]

Why is setting *specific* team goals so critical to team success? One reason is that increasing a team's performance is inherently more complex than just increasing one individual's job performance. For instance, consider that any team is likely to involve at least four different kinds of goals: each member's goal for the team, each member's goal for himself or herself on the team, the team's goal for each member, and the team's goal for itself.[65] In other words, without a specific, challenging goal for the team itself (the last of the four goals listed), team members may head off in all directions at once pursuing these other goals. Consequently, setting a specific, challenging goal *for the team* clarifies team priorities by providing a clear focus and purpose.

Challenging team goals affect how hard team members work. In particular, they greatly reduce the incidence of social loafing. When faced with reasonably difficult goals, team members necessarily expect everyone to contribute. Consequently, they are much more likely to notice and complain if a teammate isn't doing his or her share. In fact, when teammates know one another well, when team goals are specific, when team communication is good, and when teams are rewarded for team performance (discussed below), there is only a 1 in 16 chance that teammates will be social loafers.[66]

What can companies and teams do to ensure that team goals lead to superior team performance? One increasingly popular approach is to give teams stretch goals. *Stretch goals* are extremely ambitious goals that workers don't know how to reach.[67] The purpose of stretch goals is to achieve extraordinary improvements in performance by forcing managers and workers to throw away old, comfortable solutions and adopt radical, never-before-used solutions.[68]

Four things must occur for stretch goals to effectively motivate teams.[69] First,

Structural accommodation the ability to change organizational structures, policies, and practices in order to meet stretch goals

Bureaucratic immunity the ability to make changes without first getting approval from managers or other parts of an organization

TEAMS:

Ferraris of Work Design

teams must have a high degree of autonomy or control over how they achieve their goals. Second, teams must be empowered with control over resources such as budgets, workspaces, computers, or whatever else they need to do their jobs. Nick Mutton, EVP of Four Seasons Hotels and Resorts, indicates that tools are required to meet tough goals. These tools include rewarding staff for appropriate behaviours and making employees feel as respected and cared for as the guests."[70]

Third, teams need structural accommodation. **Structural accommodation** means giving teams the ability to change organizational structures, policies, and practices if doing so helps them meet their stretch goals. Finally, teams need bureaucratic immunity. **Bureaucratic immunity** means that teams no longer have to go through the frustratingly slow process of multilevel reviews and sign-offs to get management approval before making changes. Once granted bureaucratic immunity, teams are immune from the influence of various organizational groups and are accountable only to top management. Therefore, teams can act quickly and even experiment with little fear of failure.

4.2 Selecting People for Teamwork

Professor Edward Lawler says, "People are very naive about how easy it is to create a team. Teams are the Ferraris of work design. They're high performance but high maintenance and expensive."[71] It's almost impossible to have an effective work team without carefully selecting people who are suited for teamwork or for working on a particular team. A focus on teamwork (individualism-collectivism), team level, and team diversity can help companies choose the right team members.[72]

Are you more comfortable working alone or with others? If you strongly prefer to work alone, you may not be well suited for teamwork. Indeed, studies show that job satisfaction is higher in teams when team members prefer working with others.[73] An indirect way to measure someone's *preference for teamwork* is to assess the person's degree of individualism or collectivism. **Individualism-collectivism** is the degree to which a person believes that people should be self-sufficient and that loyalty to oneself is more important than loyalty to

one's team or company.[74] *Individualists*, who put their own welfare and interests first, generally prefer independent tasks in which they work alone. In contrast, *collectivists*, who put group or team interests ahead of self-interests, generally prefer interdependent tasks in which they work with others. Collectivists would also rather cooperate than compete and are fearful of disappointing team members or of being ostracized from teams. Given these differences, it makes sense to select team members who are collectivists rather than individualists. Indeed, many companies use individualism-collectivism as an initial screening device for team members. If team diversity is desired, however, individualists may also be appropriate, as discussed below. To determine your preference for teamwork, take the Team Player Inventory shown in Exhibit 10.4.

> **Individualism-collectivism** the degree to which a person believes that people should be self-sufficient and that loyalty to one's self is more important than loyalty to team or company

Exhibit 10.4

The Team Player Inventory

	STRONGLY DISAGREE				STRONGLY AGREE
1. I enjoy working on team/group projects.	1	2	3	4	5
2. Team/group project work easily allows others to not pull their weight.	1	2	3	4	5
3. Work that is done as a team/group is better than work done individually.	1	2	3	4	5
4. I do my best work alone rather than in a team/group.	1	2	3	4	5
5. Team/group work is overrated in terms of the actual results produced.	1	2	3	4	5
6. Working in a team/group gets me to think more creatively.	1	2	3	4	5
7. Teams/groups are used too often when individual work would be more effective.	1	2	3	4	5
8. My own work is enhanced when I am in a team/group situation.	1	2	3	4	5
9. My experiences working in team/group situations have been primarily negative.	1	2	3	4	5
10. More solutions/ideas are generated when working in a team/group situation than when working alone.	1	2	3	4	5

Reverse score items 2, 4, 5, 7, and 9. Then add the scores for items 1 to 10. Higher scores indicate a preference for teamwork, whereas lower total scores indicate a preference for individual work.

Team level is the average level of ability, experience, personality, or any other factor on a team. For example, a high level of team experience means that a team has particularly experienced team members. This does not mean that every member of the team has considerable experience, but that enough team members do to significantly raise the average level of experience on the team. Team level is used to guide selection of teammates when teams need a particular set of skills or capabilities to do their jobs well. For example, employees at Bombardier's Montreal plant are graduates of certified engineering schools in Quebec, or other provinces, and designers are registered professional engineers in the province.[75]

Whereas team level represents the average level or capability on a team, **team diversity** represents the variances or differences in ability, experience, personality, or any other factor on a team.[76] From a practical perspective, why is team diversity important? Professor John Hollenbeck explains, "Imagine if you put all the extroverts together. Everyone is talking, but nobody is listening. [By contrast,] with a team of [nothing but] introverts, you can hear the clock ticking on the wall."[77] Not only do strong teams have talented members (i.e., team level), but those talented members are also different in terms of ability, experience, or personality. For example, teams with strong team diversity on job experience have a mix of team members ranging from seasoned veterans to people with three or four years of experience to rookies with little or no experience. Team diversity is used to guide the selection of team members when teams must complete a wide range of different tasks or when tasks are particularly complex.

Once the right team has been put together in terms of individualism-collectivism, team level, and team diversity, it's important to keep the team together as long as practically possible. Interesting research by the National Transportation Safety Board shows that 73 percent of the serious mistakes made by jet cockpit crews are made the very first day that a crew flies together as a team and, of that 73 percent, 44 percent occur on their very first flight together that day (pilot teams fly two to three flights per day). Moreover, research has shown that fatigued pilot crews who have worked together before make significantly fewer errors than rested crews who have never worked together.[78] Their experience working together helps them overcome their fatigue and outperform new teams that have not worked together before. So, once you've created effective teams, keep them together as long as possible.

Team level the average level of ability, experience, personality, or any other factor on a team

Team diversity the variances or differences in ability, experience, personality, or any other factor on a team

Top 10 Problems Reported by Team Leaders

1. Confusion about their new roles and about what they should be doing differently.
2. Feeling they've lost control.
3. Not knowing what it means to coach or empower.
4. Having personal doubts about whether the team concept will really work.
5. Uncertainty about how to deal with employees' doubts about the team concept.
6. Confusion about when a team is ready for more responsibility.
7. Confusion about how to share responsibility and accountability with the team.
8. Concern about promotional opportunities, especially about whether the "team leader" title carries any prestige.
9. Uncertainty about the strategic aspects of the leader's role as the team matures.
10. Not knowing where to turn for help with team problems, as few, if any, of their organization's leaders have led teams.

Source: B. Filipczak, M. Hequet, C. Lee, M. Picard, and D. Stamps, "More Trouble with Teams." Training, October 1996: 21.

4.3 Team Training

After selecting the right people for teamwork, you need to train them. To be successful, teams need significant training, particularly in interpersonal skills, decision-making and problem-solving skills, conflict resolution skills, and technical training. Organizations that create work teams *often underestimate the amount of training* required to make teams effective. This mistake occurs frequently in successful organizations where managers assume that if employees can work effectively on their own, they can work effectively in teams. In reality, companies that successfully use teams provide thousands of hours of training to make sure that teams work. Stacy Myers, a consultant who helps companies implement teams, says, "When we help companies move to teams, we also require that employees take basic quality and business knowledge classes as well. Teams must know how their work affects the company, and how their success will be measured."[79]

Most commonly, members of work teams receive training in interpersonal skills. **Interpersonal skills** such as listening, communicating, questioning, and providing feedback enable people to have effective working relationships with others. Because of teams' autonomy and responsibility, many companies also give team members training in *decision-making and problem-solving skills* to help them do a better job of cutting costs and improving quality and customer service. Many organizations also teach teams *conflict resolution skills*. Delta Faucet Canada produces plumbing and mechanical devices. "Teams at Delta Faucet have specific protocols for addressing conflict. For example, if an employee's behaviour is creating a problem within a team, the team is expected to work it out without involving the team leader. Two team members will meet with the 'problem' team member and work toward a resolution. If this is unsuccessful, the whole team meets and confronts the issue. If necessary, the team leader can be brought in to make a decision, but . . . it is a rare occurrence for a team to reach that stage."[80] Firms must also provide team members with the *technical training* they need to do their jobs, particularly if they are being cross-trained to perform all of the different jobs on the team. Cross-training is less appropriate for teams of highly skilled workers. For instance, it is unlikely that a group of engineers, computer programmers, and systems analysts would be cross-trained for each other's jobs.

Team leaders need training, too, as they often feel unprepared for their new duties. New team leaders face myriad problems ranging from confusion about their new roles as team leaders (compared to their old jobs as managers or employees) to not knowing where to go for help when their teams have problems. The solution is extensive training.

4.4 Team Compensation and Recognition

Compensating teams correctly is very difficult. For instance, one survey found that only 37 percent of companies were satisfied with their team compensation plans and even fewer, just 10 percent, reported being "very positive."[81]

> **Interpersonal skills**
> skills, such as listening, communicating, questioning, and providing feedback, that enable people to have effective working relationships with others

The more each **team member** knows and can do, the better the **whole team** performs.

© Brand X Pictures/Jupiterimages

One of the problems, according to Monty Mohrman of the Center for Effective Organizations, is that "there is a very strong set of beliefs in most organizations that people should be paid for how well they do. So when people first get put into team-based organizations, they really balk at being paid for how well the team does. It sounds illogical to them. It sounds like their individuality and their sense of self-worth are being threatened."[82] Consequently, companies need to carefully choose a team compensation plan and then fully explain how teams will be rewarded. One basic requirement for team compensation to work is that the type of reward (individual versus team) must match the type of performance (individual versus team).

Employees can be compensated for team participation and accomplishments in three ways: skill-based pay, gainsharing, and nonfinancial rewards. **Skill-based pay** programs pay employees for learning additional skills or knowledge.[83]

These programs encourage employees to acquire the additional skills they will need to perform multiple jobs within a team and to share knowledge with others within their work groups.[84]

In **gainsharing** programs, companies share the financial value of performance gains such as productivity increases, cost savings, or quality improvements with their workers.[85] *Nonfinancial rewards* are another way to reward teams for their performance. These rewards, which can range from vacation trips to T-shirts, plaques, and coffee mugs, are especially effective when coupled with management recognition, such as awards, certificates, and praise.[86] Nonfinancial awards tend to be most effective when teams or team-based interventions, such as total quality management (see Chapter 18), are first introduced.[87]

Which team compensation plan should your company use? In general, skill-based pay is most effective for self-managing and self-directing teams performing complex tasks. In these situations, the more each team member knows and can do, the better the whole team performs. By contrast, gainsharing works best in relatively stable environments where employees can focus on improving productivity, cost savings, or quality.

Skill-based pay compensation system that pays employees for learning additional skills or knowledge

Gainsharing a compensation system in which companies share the financial value of performance gains, such as productivity, cost savings, or quality, with their workers

Visit **icanmgmt.com** to find the resources you need today!

Located at the back of the textbook are rip-out Chapter Review cards. Make sure you also go online to check out other tools that MGMT offers to help you successfully pass your course.

- Interactive Quizzes
- Key Terms Flashcards
- Audio Chapter Summaries
- PowerPoint Slides

- Interactive Games
- Crossword Puzzles
- "Reel to Reel" and "Biz Flix" videos
- Cases and Exercises

86% of Canadian students surveyed find PowerPoint notes a valuable way to help them study.

GET ONLINE

The easy-to-navigate website for **MGMT** offers guidance on key topics in **Principles of Management** in a variety of engaging formats. You have the opportunity to refine and check your understanding via interactive quizzes and flashcards. Videos and audio summaries provide inspiration for your own further exploration. And, in order to make **MGMT** an even better learning tool, we invite you to speak up about your experience with **MGMT** by completing a survey form and sending us your comments.

Get online and discover the following resources:
- Printable and Interactive PowerPoints
- Flashcards
- Interactive Quizzing
- Crossword Puzzles

"I think this book is awesome for students of all ages. It is a much simpler way to study."

—Yasmine Al-Hashimi, Fanshawe College

Visit **icanmgmt.com** to find the resources you need today!

MANAGING HUMAN RESOURCE SYSTEMS

Human resource management (HRM), or the process of finding, developing, and keeping the right people to form a qualified workforce, is one of the most difficult and important of all management tasks. This chapter is organized around the three parts of the human resource management process shown in Exhibit 11.1: attracting, developing, and keeping a qualified workforce.

Human resource management (HRM)
the process of finding, developing, and keeping the right people to form a qualified workforce

Exhibit 11.1

The Human Resource Management Process

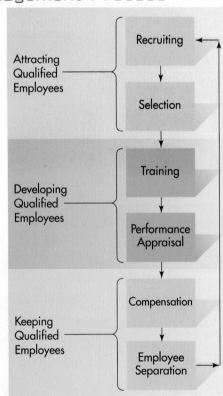

Attracting Qualified Employees
- Recruiting
- Selection

Developing Qualified Employees
- Training
- Performance Appraisal

Keeping Qualified Employees
- Compensation
- Employee Separation

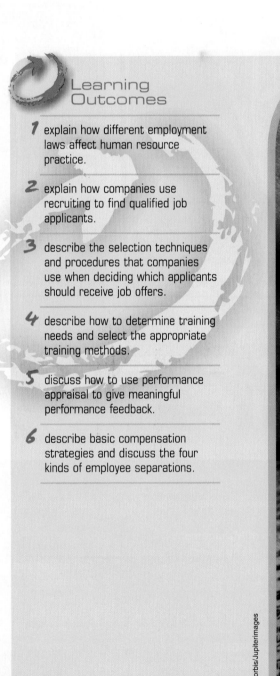

Learning Outcomes

1 explain how different employment laws affect human resource practice.

2 explain how companies use recruiting to find qualified job applicants.

3 describe the selection techniques and procedures that companies use when deciding which applicants should receive job offers.

4 describe how to determine training needs and select the appropriate training methods.

5 discuss how to use performance appraisal to give meaningful performance feedback.

6 describe basic compensation strategies and discuss the four kinds of employee separations.

© Corbis/Jupiterimages

This chapter will walk you through the steps of the HRM process. We explore how companies use recruiting and selection techniques to attract and hire qualified employees to fulfill those needs. Then we discuss how training and performance appraisal can develop the knowledge, skills, and abilities of the workforce. The chapter concludes with a review of compensation and employee separation, that is, how companies can keep their best workers through effective compensation practices and how they can manage the separation process when employees leave the organization.

The Legal Context

B

Before we explore how human resource systems work, you need to better understand the complex legal environment in which they exist. So we'll begin the chapter by reviewing the federal and provincial laws that govern human resource management decisions.

After reading the next section, you should be able to

1 explain how different employment laws affect human resource practice.

1 Employment Legislation

Canada's employment laws rest primarily with the provinces and territories. The federal government has laws that quite often mirror those of the provinces, but human rights, employment standards, labour relations, health and safety, employment equity, and other employment-related legislation belongs to the ten provinces and three territories. Canada's legal system is based on both British and French colonial law. The Constitution Act of 1867 (formerly known as the British North America Act) laid the foundation for our systems today. The Canadian Labour code, Part I, sets out industrial relations (bargaining rights, strikes, union certifications); Part II sets out occupational health and safety guidelines; Part III sets out standards for hours, wages, vacations, and holidays.[1]

To streamline the legal system somewhat, the governments in each jurisdiction have created special bodies, such as the B.C. Human Rights Tribunal, to enforce compliance and to assist in the interpretation of these complex laws. "Regulations" are also drafted, and they become part of the "act" or law in Canada. Regulations also help us interpret the law.

Most provinces have an employment (labour) standards act. Together these acts, which set out items that are defined in the Canadian Labour Code, may be specific to their particular province (e.g., St-Jean-Baptiste Day is a paid holiday in Quebec, whereas Remembrance Day is a paid holiday in Newfoundland and Labrador). Pay equity (equal pay for equal work) is another area found under employment standards acts. An employer cannot pay women differently who are performing the same work as men. The difficulty arises when we try to compare work of equal value. Should a nurse (a female-dominated job) be paid the same as a firefighter (a male-dominated job)?

The Canadian Charter of Rights and Freedoms was enacted under Pierre Trudeau's government in 1982. It is part of Canada's constitution, and it covers several fundamental freedoms that affect the workplace. Section 15a of the Charter prohibits discrimination along most of the lines we are familiar with (race, creed, colour, religion, gender, etc.); whereas Section 15b of the Charter allows certain hiring practices for "amelioration" of past injustices.[2] There are some additional areas where there are **bona fide occupational qualifications (BFOQs)**. For example, if Victoria's Secret hires models for its lingerie, it probably won't be taken to task for hiring women, as this would be seen as a BFOQ. In Burnaby and Richmond, B.C., there have been ongoing investigations and hearings dealing with gender discrimination against female firefighters for more than a dozen years (note we don't use the term fireman anymore).[3] The B.C. Supreme Court determined that a running-time standard (aerobic standard) for firefighters was not a BFOQ because it was not related to an individual's performance on the job; the same court ruled that there had been systematic discrimination on a prohibited ground.[4]

The provincial Human Rights Commissions in each province and territory have been established under the Canadian Human Rights Act. They are responsible for enforcing the Canadian Human Rights Act. The Canadian Human Rights Commission provides guidelines and support to the various provincial agencies.[5] The various Human Rights Commissions investigate and hold hearings on issues relating to complaints under the various labour acts. Let's explore employment legislation by reviewing **1.1 the major federal employment laws that affect human resource practice, 1.2 the concept of employment discrimination,** and **1.3 the laws regarding sexual harassment in the workplace.**

1.1 Federal Employment Laws

Exhibit 11.2 lists the major federal employment laws and their websites, where you can find more detailed information. The general effect of these laws, which are still evolving through court decisions, is that employers may not discriminate in employment decisions on the basis of sex, age, religion, colour, national origin, race, or disability. The intent is to make these factors irrelevant in employment decisions. Stated another way, employment decisions should be based on factors that are "job related," "reasonably necessary," or a "business necessity" for successful job performance. The only time that sex, age, religion, and the like can be used to make employment decisions is when they are considered a bona fide occupational qualification.

It is important to understand that these laws apply to the entire HRM process and not just to

Bona fide occupational qualification (BFOQ) an exception in employment law that permits sex, age, religion, and the like to be used when making employment decisions, but only if they are "reasonably necessary to the normal operation of that particular business."

Exhibit 11.2

Summary of Major Federal Employment Laws

Constitution Act (BNA) of 1867	http://laws.justice.gc.ca/en/const/index.html	Sets out basic federal and provincial responsibilities
Canadian Charter of Rights and Freedoms	http://laws.justice.gc.ca/en/charter	Sets out the 15 basic areas of freedoms in Canada
Canadian Human Rights Act	http://laws.justice.gc.ca/en/H-6/index.html	Act prohibiting discrimination on a number of grounds
Canadian Labour Code	http://laws.justice.gc.ca/enhttp://laws.justice.gc.ca/eng	Lays out responsibilities of each province and provides national guidelines
Employment Equity and Pay Equity Legislation	http://laws.justice.gc.ca/en/E-5.401/index.html	Requires equal pay for equal work
Workers Compensation Act (Manitoba)	http://web2.gov.mb.ca/laws/statutes/ccsm/w200e.php	Provincial act that lays out safety standards

Kateryna Dyellalova/Shutterstock

selection decisions (i.e., hiring and promotion). Thus, these laws also cover all training and development activities, performance appraisals, terminations, and compensation decisions. Employers who use sex, age, race, or religion to make employment-related decisions when those factors are unrelated to an applicant's or employee's ability to perform a job may face charges of discrimination from employee lawsuits or human rights tribunals. Each province has an act dealing with workplace safety. Requirements such as safety equipment, accident investigation, workplace hazardous materials information sheets (WHMIS), and safe work procedures are detailed in the various provincial acts. The various Workers' Compensation Acts (called WorkSafe BC in British Columbia) are administered by boards appointed by the provincial and territorial governments. The various boards set safety and health standards for employers and employees and conduct inspections to determine whether those standards are being met. Employers who do not meet standards may be fined.[6]

1.2 Employment Discrimination

Discrimination generally falls under one of the general headings contained in the Charter of Rights and Freedoms. Unfair discrimination typically leads to investigations by one of the provincial or territorial Human Rights Commissions. Discrimination may be intentional or unintentional. Generally, discrimination based on race, religion, ethnic origin, and so forth is easy to see. Unintentional discrimination is harder to see. Minimum height and weight requirements, which used to be common for police forces, can screen out females or Canadians of Asian origin, who tend to be shorter. Also, some job evaluation systems may include culturally (non-job-related) biased questions; and some job situations may discriminate against some cultures.

1.3 Sexual Harassment

Sexual harassment is prohibited by several laws, both federal and provincial. Sexual harassment does not have to be sexual in nature, although that sounds odd to most of us. It can also mean that someone is bothering you simply because you are a man or a woman. Making stereotypes about one gender or the other can be a form of sexual harassment.[7]

In some provinces the Human Rights Commission handles these cases; in other provinces, the Human Rights Tribunal does so. Most of these cases involve infractions of the Labour Code and are dealt with under the Human Rights Act. But in other cases, individuals—and employers—deal with these issues through the civil courts. *Alpaerts v Obront* was one case that found limited success in challenging the exclusive remedial jurisdiction of the Labour Code. The plaintiff alleged sexual harassment in her workplace to the point of constructive dismissal (i.e., intolerable circumstances). She sued for wrongful dismissal, alleging in part human rights violations by the employer. The case was allowed to proceed, partly on the basis that the plaintiff had a cause of action separate from the code violation. The court was concerned that if a code complaint had been brought at the same time, the result could have been different and a stay might have been merited.[8] None of the provinces—or, for that matter, the Canadian Human Rights Commission—will investigate without the formal filing of a complaint.

Sexual harassment occurs when employment outcomes, such as hiring, promotion, or simply keeping one's job, depend on whether an individual submits to being sexually harassed. For example, in a quid pro quo sexual harassment lawsuit against Costco, a female employee alleged that her boss groped her and bumped into her from behind to simulate sex. "He would tell her: 'You work with me and I'll work with you,' motioning to his private area."[9] The supervisor also allegedly told her that he would fire her if she reported his activities to upper management. In quid pro quo cases, requests for sexual acts are linked to economic outcomes (i.e., keeping a job). A **hostile work environment** occurs when unwelcome and demeaning sexually related behaviour creates an intimidating, hostile, and offensive work environment. There may be no economic injury—that is, requests for sexual acts aren't tied to economic outcomes. However, they can lead to psychological injury from a stressful work environment.

What should companies do to make sure that sexual harassment laws are followed and not violated?[10]

© Peter Finnie/iStockphoto.com

First, respond immediately when sexual harassment is reported. A quick response encourages victims of sexual harassment to report problems to management rather than to lawyers or a human rights tribunal. Furthermore, a quick and fair investigation may serve as a deterrent to future harassment. Next, take the time to write a clear, understandable sexual harassment policy that is strongly worded, gives specific examples of what constitutes sexual harassment, spells outs sanctions and punishments, and is widely publicized within the company. This lets potential harassers and victims know what will not be tolerated and how the firm will deal with harassment should it occur.

Next, establish clear reporting procedures that indicate how, where, and to whom incidents of sexual harassment can be reported. The best procedures ensure that a complaint will receive a quick response, that impartial parties will handle the complaint, and that the privacy of the accused and accuser will be protected. Students, who quite often have to deal with sexual harassment, can get help. The students at Simon Fraser University can go to a nonthreatening Human Rights Office representative to get help and guidance. Students at UBC can also receive help from the Equity Office in dealing with unwanted advances. Also, BCIT has a Harassment and Discrimination Advisory Office to help students and staff deal with these kinds of issues.[11]

Sexual harassment a form of discrimination in which unwelcome sexual advances, requests for sexual favours, or other verbal or physical conduct of a sexual nature occur while performing one's job; another form of sexual harassment is when employment outcomes, such as hiring, promotion, or simply keeping one's job, depend on whether an individual submits to sexual harassment

Hostile work environment a form of sexual harassment which unwelcome and demeaning sexually related behaviour creates an intimidating and offensive work environment

Finally, managers should also be aware that most provinces and many municipalities have their own employment-related laws and enforcement agencies. So compliance with federal law is often not enough. In fact, organizations can be in full compliance with federal law and at the same time be in violation of provincial or municipal sexual harassment laws.

Finding Qualified Workers

 Wade Miller, one of the founders of Manitoba's Pinnacle Staffing Solutions, says, "We thought we could do better and treat people differently." Recalls Mr. Miller, who left the Blue Bombers in April 2006 after an 11-year career: "Demographics are changing. As time goes by, there will be a need for businesses to find top talent. It's a good market segment to be in." Mr. Miller says that the philosophy at Pinnacle can be summed up by the phrase: "Great people create great organizations."[12]

After reading the next two sections, you should be able to

2 explain how companies use recruiting to find qualified job applicants.

3 describe the selection techniques and procedures that companies use when deciding which applicants should receive job offers.

2 Recruiting

Recruiting is the process of developing a pool of qualified job applicants. Let's examine **2.1 what job analysis is and how it is used in recruiting** and **2.2 how companies use internal recruiting** and **2.3 external recruiting to find qualified job applicants.**

2.1 Job Analysis and Recruiting

Job analysis is a "purposeful, systematic process for collecting information on the important work-related

aspects of a job."[13] Typically, a job analysis collects four kinds of information:

- work activities, such as what workers do and how, when, and why they do it;
- the tools and equipment used to do the job;
- the context in which the job is performed, such as the actual working conditions or schedule;
- the personnel requirements for performing the job, meaning the knowledge, skills, and abilities needed to do a job well.[14]

Job analysis information can be collected by having job incumbents and/or supervisors complete questionnaires about their jobs, by direct observation, by interviews, or by filming employees as they perform their jobs.

Job descriptions and job specifications are two of the most important results of a job analysis. A **job description** is a written description of the basic tasks, duties, and responsibilities required of an employee holding a particular job. **Job specifications,** which are often included as a separate section of a job description, are a summary of the qualifications needed to successfully perform the job. Exhibit 11.3 shows a job recruitment notice for a firefighter in the city of Calgary, Alberta.

Because a job analysis specifies what a job entails as well as the knowledge, skills, and abilities that are needed to do the job well, companies must complete a job analysis *before* beginning to recruit job applicants. Job analysis, job descriptions, and job specifications are the foundation on which all critical human resource activities are built. They are used during recruiting and selection to match applicant qualifications with the requirements of the job. It is therefore critically important that job descriptions be accurate. Unfortunately, they aren't always so. Apartment Investment & Management Co. (Aimco) discovered that its high turnover rate was due in part to poorly written job descriptions. The descriptions were more focused on education and

Recruiting the process of developing a pool of qualified job applicants

Job analysis a purposeful, systematic process for collecting information on the important work-related aspects of a job

Job description a written description of the basic tasks, duties, and responsibilities required of an employee holding a particular job

Job specifications a written summary of the qualifications needed to successfully perform a particular job

Exhibit 11.3

Job Recruitment Notice for a Firefighter for the City of Calgary, Alberta

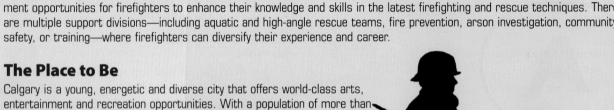

Looking for a challenging and exciting career? Firefighting may be for you ... We're looking for physically fit men and women—motivated individuals known for integrity, professionalism, and drive. Join our team of more than 1,200 firefighters dedicated to fire education, prevention, and safety.

Professionalism

A professional firefighting career offers excellent benefits, opportunities and job security. We can offer you the opportunity to be part of a highly-skilled team whose members are admired and valued by the community they serve and protect. Recruits are trained in-house to the highest international standards. We provide numerous professional development opportunities for firefighters to enhance their knowledge and skills in the latest firefighting and rescue techniques. There are multiple support divisions—including aquatic and high-angle rescue teams, fire prevention, arson investigation, community safety, or training—where firefighters can diversify their experience and career.

The Place to Be

Calgary is a young, energetic and diverse city that offers world-class arts, entertainment and recreation opportunities. With a population of more than a million people, it is one of the fastest-growing cities in North America. Calgary provides an unsurpassed quality of life for families. Its close proximity to the Rocky Mountains guarantees year-round adventure.

Pride. Professionalism. Teamwork. Respect. These are our core values. If you share them, review the links on this website and consider joining our team.

Resource: City of Calgary, "Firefighter Recruitment" (2010). http://content.calgary.ca/CCA/City+Hall/Business+Units/Calgary+Fire+Department/Firefighter+Recruitment/Firefighter+Recruitment.htm [accessed 19 June 2010]. Courtesy of the City of Calgary, 2010.

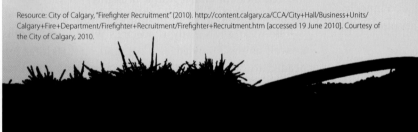

experience than actually explaining what an employee would do on the job and what the company culture is like. When they did explain the job, the descriptions were abstract and laden with jargon, making them unclear. Consequently, many new hires found themselves in an incompatible culture or in jobs they did not like or could not do.[15]

Job descriptions are also used throughout the staffing process to ensure that selection devices and the decisions based on these devices are job-related. For example, the questions asked in an interview should be based on the most important work activities identified by a job analysis. Likewise, during performance appraisals, employees should be evaluated in areas that a job analysis has identified as the most important in a job.

Job analyses, job descriptions, and job specifications also help companies meet the legal requirement that their human resource decisions be job-related. To be judged *job-related*, recruitment, selection, training, performance appraisals, and employee separations must be valid and be directly related to the important aspects of the job as identified by a careful job analysis. Job requirements, if they have the potential to discriminate against members of protected groups, must then meet the standards set in the *Meiorin* decision (*BC Public Service Relations Commission vs. BCBSEU*).[16] In *Meiorin* the Supreme Court of Canada found that the new job requirements were not based on job-related information and that the job analysis in that case was seriously flawed. Canadian Human Rights Commissions and courts recognize the U.S. *Uniform Guidelines for Employee Selection Procedures*. Additionally, the Canadian Society of Industrial Organizational Psychology has adapted the principles in the "Guidelines" for developing equitable selection systems in Canada.[17] In practice, if not in law, the starting point for defensible selection is an appropriate job analysis system.

2.2 Internal Recruiting

Internal recruiting is the process of developing a pool of qualified job applicants from people who already work in the company. Internal recruiting, sometimes called "promotion from within," improves employee commitment, morale, and motivation. Recruiting current employees also reduces recruitment startup time and costs, and because employees are already familiar with the company's culture and procedures, they are more likely to succeed in new jobs. Job posting and career paths are two methods of internal recruiting.

Job posting is a procedure for advertising job openings within the company to existing employees. A job description and requirements are typically posted on a bulletin board, in a company newsletter, or in an internal computerized job bank that is accessible only to employees.

A *career path* is a planned sequence of jobs through which employees may advance within an organization. For example, a person who starts as a sales representative may move up to sales manager and then to district or regional sales manager. Career paths help employees focus on long-term goals and development while also helping companies increase employee retention.

2.3 External Recruiting

External recuiting is the process of developing a pool of qualified job applicants from outside the company. External recruitment methods include advertising (newspapers, magazines, direct mail, radio, or television), employee referrals (asking current employees to recommend possible job applicants), walk-ins (people who apply on their own), outside organizations (universities, technical/trade schools, professional societies), employment services (state or private employment agencies, temporary help agencies, and professional search firms), special events (career conferences or job fairs), and Internet job sites. Which external recruiting method should you use? Studies show that employee referrals, walk-ins, newspaper advertisements, and state employment agencies tend to be used most frequently for office/clerical and production/service employees. By contrast, newspaper advertisements and college/university recruiting are used most frequently for professional/technical employees. When recruiting managers, organizations tend to rely most heavily on newspaper advertisements, employee referrals, and search firms.[18]

Companies are now hiring nontraditional people in non-traditional ways. One of these nontraditional ways is the Langley-based website 55pluspros.ca, which has been launched to help match older workers with employers seeking experienced and qualified professionals. "There are two reasons for this," Website founder Sherry Baker said in an interview. "There are more and more people retiring who realize that if they want to maintain their lifestyle, they'll have to make more money than what they get with their pension." Also, many are retiring in their mid-50s, when they're still healthy and energetic. They realize that they want to do something else more meaningful with their lives. "Most of them want to work part time, but they want to utilize their skills and training in a meaningful way" says Baker.[19] Baidu, a Beijing-based search engine company, seeks out the best web engineers by hosting an annual programming competition as a recruiting strategy.[20] Recently, the biggest change in external recruiting has been the increased use of the Internet. Some companies now recruit applicants through Internet job sites such as Monster.ca, Vancouverjobshop.ca, and BCJobs.ca. Companies can post job openings for 30 days on one of these sites for about half the cost of running an advertisement just once in a Sunday newspaper. Plus, Internet job listings generate nine times as many résumés as one ad in the Sunday newspaper.[21] And because these sites attract so many applicants and offer so many services, companies save by finding qualified applicants without having to use more expensive recruitment and search firms, which typically charge one-third or more of a new hire's salary.[22]

3 Selection

Once the recruitment process has produced a pool of qualified applicants, the selection process is used to determine which applicants have the best chance of performing well on the job. More specifically, **selection** is

Internal recruiting
the process of developing a pool of qualified job applicants from people who already work in the company

External recruiting
the process of developing a pool of qualified job applicants from outside the company

Selection the process of gathering information about job applicants to decide who should be offered a job

Preventing Brain Drain

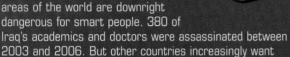

Recruiting and retaining the most skilled and knowledgeable workers is in every company's best interest. In a global economy that increasingly hinges on information rather than natural resources, it's also in every country's best interest. Some areas of the world are downright dangerous for smart people. 380 of Iraq's academics and doctors were assassinated between 2003 and 2006. But other countries increasingly want to attract the best talent. Saudia Arabia's king, for example, spent $12.5 billion on a new research university to cultivate talent at home. Countries can also attract talent globally by easing "tariffs" on incoming workers and making it easier for them to get work permits. Geoff Colvin, senior editor at *Fortune* magazine, says, "This international fight for talent will get much more serious. With luck it will lead to something new: a free market in brainpower."

Sources: G. Colvin, "The Battle for Brainpower," *Fortune* (10 December 2007) 34–35; C. Caulcutt, "Iraq's Deadly Brain Drain," France 24 (11 May 2008) available online at http://www.france24.com/en/20080510-iraqs-deadly-brain-drain-iraq (accessed 14 August 2008).

Validation the process of determining how well a selection test or procedure predicts future job performance. The better or more accurate the prediction of future job performance, the more valid a test is said to be.

Employment references sources such as previous employers or coworkers who can provide job-related information about job candidates

Background checks procedures used to verify the truthfulness and accuracy of information that applicants provide about themselves and to uncover negative, job-related background information not provided by applicants

the process of gathering information about job applicants to decide who should be offered a job. **Validation** is the process of determining how well a selection test or procedure predicts future job performance. The better or more accurate the prediction of future job performance, the more valid a test is said to be.

*Let's examine common selection procedures, such as **3.1 application forms and résumés, 3.2 references and background checks, 3.3 selection tests,** and **3.4 interviews.***

3.1 Application Forms and Résumés

The first selection devices that most job applicants encounter when they seek a job are application forms and résumés. Both contain similar information about an applicant, such as name, address, job and educational history, and so forth. Though an organization's application form often asks for information already provided by the applicant's résumé, most organizations prefer to collect this information in their own format for entry into a human resource information system.

Employment laws apply to application forms just as they do to all selection devices. Application forms may ask applicants for only valid, job-related information. Nonetheless, application forms commonly ask applicants for non-job-related information such as marital status, maiden name, age, or date of high school graduation. See various websites, such as the Alberta Human Rights Commission website (http://www.albertahumanrights.ab.ca) for assistance on pre-employment questions.[23] There's quite a bit of information that companies may not request in application forms, during job interviews, or in any other part of the selection process. Courts will assume that you consider all of the information you request of applicants, even if you don't. Be sure to ask only those questions that directly relate to the candidate's ability and motivation to perform the job.

Résumés also pose problems for companies but in a different way. Studies show that as many as one-third of job applicants intentionally falsify some information on their résumés and that 80 percent of the information on résumés may be misleading. Therefore, managers should verify the information collected via résumés and application forms by comparing it with additional information collected during interviews and other stages of the selection process, such as references and background checks, which are discussed next.

3.2 References and Background Checks

Nearly all companies ask an applicant to provide **employment references,** such as previous employers or coworkers, that they can contact to learn more about the candidate. **Background checks** are used to verify the truthfulness and accuracy of information that applicants provide about themselves and to uncover negative, job-related background information not provided by applicants. Background checks are conducted by contacting "educational institutions, prior employers, court

© Photos.com

GOOD TIP!

Don't Ask! (Topics to Avoid in an Interview)

1. *Gender, marital status, or family status.* Do not: ask the applicant to specify *Mr., Mrs., Miss,* or *Ms.* on an application form.

2. *Source of income.* Any inquiry concerning source of income must be job-related. You can request information about former employment. Avoid inquiries about other sources of income that may have a stigma attached to them, such as social assistance, disability pension, or child maintenance, unless you have a job-related reason for asking.

3. *Previous names.* Asking an applicant to provide previous names can cause the applicant to indirectly disclose marital status, gender, place of origin, or ancestry. "Any inquiry that requires an applicant to disclose this information would be contrary to the *Alberta Human Rights Act*, unless there is a business reason for doing so that is acceptable under the *Act*.

4. *Next of kin.* Asking for names of relatives or next of kin before hiring is not recommended. Such information can reveal the gender, marital status, place of origin, or ancestry of the applicant.

5. *Dependants and child care.* Avoid inquiries about an applicant's spouse, number of children or dependants, childcare arrangements, or plans to have children. The answers to these questions are usually not related to the job and can reveal gender and marital or family status. Inquiries that focus on willingness to work the required schedule, to work rotating shifts, or to relocate are clearly business-related and are acceptable.

6. *Age and date of birth.* It is not advisable to ask for applicant's date of birth or age, unless the applicant is under 18. In employment situations where there is a legal minimum age requirement, you can verify that the applicant meets the legal age requirement.

7. *Previous address.* It is not acceptable to request a previous address, unless it is for a business-related purpose that is acceptable under the act.

8. *Citizenship.* Citizenship is not specifically dealt with in the act. However, asking the applicant to reveal citizenship could require a non-Canadian applicant to disclose place of origin, which is protected under the act. Ask questions to solicit information that is related to the specific requirements of the job to be performed. Appropriate questions could include: Are you legally entitled to work in Canada? Are you a Canadian citizen or landed immigrant? Yes ___ No___ (Do not distinguish between the two.)

9. *Physical or mental disability.* It is not acceptable to ask questions that are not related to the specific job to be performed. With this in mind, it is contrary to the act to ask applicants to provide information about the general state of their physical or mental health, their appearance, or their height or weight.

10. *Sexual orientation.* Avoid inquiries about an applicant's sexual orientation. It is unacceptable to express a preference for an applicant to be heterosexual, homosexual, or bisexual unless you have a business-related reason for expressing a preference, and the reason is acceptable under the *Act*."

11. *Workers' Compensation.* Asking if the applicant has received or is receiving Workers' Compensation indirectly requires an applicant to provide information about a physical injury or disability. This can be contrary to the *Act*.

12. *Language ability.* It is appropriate to ask applicants if they have some proficiency in the languages that are specifically required for the job. The job description and employment advertisement should specify which languages are required. The level of language ability required should match the job requirements.

13. *Educational institutions.* You can request the names and addresses of academic, vocational, technical, and professional institutions attended and the nature and level of education received. Requiring information that reflects either the religious or racial affiliation of schools or other institutions attended is not advisable as it could reveal religious beliefs or race.

14. *Religious beliefs.* Avoid requesting information about applicants' religious beliefs, including which religious holidays and customs they observe, which church they attend, or whether their clothing is prescribed by their religion. It is permissible for an employer to specify the hours of work in a job advertisement. A job advertisement may indicate that the position will require shift, evening, or weekend work, or that it is functional 365 days per year. Courts and tribunals have said that the employer must make all efforts up to the point of undue hardship to accommodate the religious beliefs of an employee. In turn, the employee is expected to cooperate fully with the employer's efforts. Undue hardship may occur if accommodation would create the following conditions for an employer: an intolerable financial cost, serious disruption to a business or workplace, or other serious issues that cannot be overcome.

Source: Adapted from http://www.albertahumanrights.ab.ca/publications/bulletins_sheets_booklets/sheets/hr_and_employment/pre_employment_inquiries.asp with the permission of the Alberta Human Rights Commission. Note that each province will vary slightly.

© iStockphoto.com

records, police and governmental agencies, and other informational sources either by telephone, mail, remote computer access, or through in-person investigations."[24]

Unfortunately, previous employers are increasingly reluctant to provide references or background check information. While it is unlikely that Canadian employers will be sued for honestly providing unfavourable references, employers are quite vulnerable to being sued in cases where they knowingly hold back unfavourable information, especially if an employee is hired and subsequently causes harm to the new employer or its clients.[25] Many provide only dates of employment, positions held, and date of separation.

A former employer should not impede a former employee's job search. The Supreme Court of Canada ruled that employers have an obligation to act in good faith when an employee is terminated. In the case of *Jack Wallace v. The United Grain Growers*, the plaintiff was awarded 24 months' salary when it was found that the United Grain Growers neglected to provide a reference letter for him to secure a new job.[26]

With previous employers generally unwilling to give full, candid references and with negligent hiring lawsuits awaiting companies that don't get such references and background information, what can companies do? They can conduct criminal record checks, especially if the job for which the person is applying involves money, drugs, control over valuable goods, or access to the elderly, children with disabilities, or people's homes.[27] According to the Society for Human Resource Management, 96 percent of companies conduct background checks and 80 percent of companies go further and conduct criminal record checks.[28]

Next, ask applicants to sign a waiver that permits you to check references, run a background check, or contact anyone else with knowledge of their work performance or history. Likewise, ask applicants if there is anything they would like the company to know or if they expect you to hear anything unusual when contacting references.[29] This in itself is often enough to get applicants to share information that they typically withhold. When you've finished checking, keep the findings confidential to minimize the chances of a defamation charge.

Finally, many companies perform criminal background checks, and many more are starting to perform social media background checks. Certainly you should be careful about what you have on Facebook and or other sites such as MySpace. Anything that might embarrass you, or a potential employer, should seriously be considered for deletion.[30]

3.3 Selection Tests

Selection tests give organizational decision makers a chance to know who will likely do well in a job and who won't. The basic idea behind selection testing is to have applicants take a test that measures something directly or indirectly related to doing well on the job. The selection tests discussed here are specific ability tests, cognitive ability tests, biographical data, personality tests, work sample tests, and assessment centres.

Specific ability tests measure the extent to which an applicant possesses the particular kind of ability needed to do a job well. Specific ability tests are also called **aptitude tests** because they measure aptitude for doing a particular task well. For example, if you decide to go on for an MBA after you are through your undergraduate degree (and after you work for a few years), you will most likely be required to take the GMAT (Graduate Management Admissions Test). If you apply to law school in Canada, you will likely need to write the LSAT (Law School Admissions Test). These tests are examples of predictors of how well students will do in those graduate schools. Specific ability tests also exist for mechanical, clerical, sales, and physical work. For example, clerical workers have to be good at accurately reading and scanning numbers as they type or enter data. Exhibit 11.4 shows items similar to those found on the Minnesota Clerical Test, in which applicants have only a short time to determine whether the two columns of numbers and letters are identical. Applicants who are good at this are likely to do well as clerical or data entry workers.

Cognitive ability tests measure the extent to which applicants have abilities in perceptual speed, verbal comprehension, numerical aptitude, general reasoning, and spatial aptitude. In other words, these tests indicate how quickly and how well people understand words, numbers, logic, and spatial dimensions. Whereas specific ability tests predict job performance in only particular types of jobs, cognitive ability tests accurately predict job performance in almost all kinds of jobs.[31] Why is this so? The reason is that people with strong cognitive or mental abilities are usually good at learning new things, processing complex information, solving problems, and making decisions, and these

Specific ability tests (aptitude tests) tests that measure the extent to which an applicant possesses the particular kind of ability needed to do a job well

Cognitive ability tests tests that measure the extent to which applicants have abilities in perceptual speed, verbal comprehension, numerical aptitude, general reasoning, and spatial aptitude

Exhibit 11.4

Clerical Test Items Similar to Those Found on the Minnesota Clerical Test

NUMBERS/LETTERS		SAME	
		Yes	No
1. 3468251	3467251	O	O
2. 4681371	4681371	Yes O	No O
3. 7218510	7218520	Yes O	No O
4. ZXYAZAB	ZXYAZAB	Yes O	No O
5. ALZYXMN	ALZYXNM	Yes O	No O
6. PRQZYMN	PRQZYMN	Yes O	No O

Source: N. W. Schmitt and R. J. Klimoski, *Research Methods in Human Resource Management* (Mason, OH, South-Western, 1991). Used with permission from the authors.

abilities are important in almost all jobs.[32] In fact, cognitive ability tests are almost always the best predictors of job performance. Consequently, if you were allowed to use just one selection test, a cognitive ability test would be the one to use.[33] (In practice, though, companies use a battery of different tests because doing so leads to much more accurate selection decisions.)

Biographical data, or **biodata,** are extensive surveys that ask applicants questions about their personal backgrounds and life experiences. The basic idea behind biodata is that past behaviour (personal background and life experience) is the best predictor of future behaviour. Most biodata questionnaires have over 100 items that gather information about habits and attitudes, health, interpersonal relations, money, what it was like growing up in your family (parents, siblings, childhood years, teen years), personal habits, current home (spouse, children), hobbies, education and training, values, preferences, and work.[34] In general, biodata are very good predictors of future job performance, especially in entry-level jobs.

You may have noticed that some of the information requested in biodata surveys is related to those topics employers should avoid in applications, interviews, or other parts of the selection process. This information can be requested in biodata questionnaires provided that the company can demonstrate that the information is job-related (i.e., valid) and does not result in adverse impact against protected groups of job applicants. Biodata surveys should be validated and tested for adverse impact before they are used to make selection decisions.[35]

Work sample tests, also called *performance tests,* require applicants to perform tasks that are actually done on the job. So, unlike specific ability, cognitive ability, biographical data, and personality tests, which are indirect predictors of job performance, work sample tests directly measure job applicants' capability to do the job. For example, a computer-based work sample test has applicants assume the role of a real estate agent who must decide how to interact with virtual clients in a gamelike scenario. And, as in real life, the clients can be frustrating, confusing, demanding, or indecisive. In one situation, the wife loves the house but the husband hates it. The applicants, just like actual real estate agents, must demonstrate what they would do in these realistic situations.[36] This work sample simulation gives real estate companies direct evidence of whether applicants can do the job if they are hired. Work sample tests are generally very good at predicting future job performance; however, they can be expensive to administer and can be used for only one kind of job. For example, an auto dealership could not use a work sample test for mechanics as a selection test for sales representatives.

Assessment centres use a series of job-specific simulations that are graded by multiple trained observers to determine applicants' ability to perform managerial work. Unlike the previously described selection tests that are commonly used for specific jobs or entry-level jobs, assessment centres are most often used to select applicants who have high potential to be good managers. Assessment centres often last two to five days and require participants to complete a number of tests and exercises that simulate managerial work.

Biographical data (biodata) extensive surveys that ask applicants questions about their personal backgrounds and life experiences

Work sample tests tests that require applicants to perform tasks that are actually done on the job

Assessment centres a series of managerial simulations, graded by trained observers, that are used to determine applicants' capability for managerial work

© Radius Images/Jupiterimages

Exhibit 11.5

In-Basket Item for an Assessment Centre for Police Supervisors

The Justice Institute of British Columbia provides a Supervisory or Manager Centre "In-Basket" exercise that stimulates an e-mail inbox in a role play exercise. Police agencies submit current operational information, which is then used to custom-design the electronic e-mail exercise. Candidates log on, and assess and take action on documentation pertinent to their organization. All meetings and commitments can be entered into the electronic calendar contained in the program. Candidates are expected to answer all e-mail, "cc" the appropriate recipients, and send new e-mails in response to the problems posed. The In-Basket exercise can be accessed by a computer from anywhere in the world. Marking is a little easier (because there is less poor handwriting!), and both the administering organization and the candidate can monitor while the exercise is in progress.

Source: JIBC Police Academy, 2010. Welcome to te Assessment Centre electronic in-basket. Http://www.jibc.ca/police/programs/assessment_centre/assessment_centre_inbasket.htm. Accessed 26 June 2010.

Some of the more common assessment centre exercises are in-basket exercises, role plays, small-group presentations, and leaderless group discussions. An *in-basket exercise* is a paper-and-pencil test in which an applicant is given a manager's in-basket containing memos, phone messages, organizational policies, and other communications normally received by and available to managers. Applicants have a limited time to read through the in-basket, prioritize the items, and decide how to deal with each item. Experienced managers then score the applicants' decisions and recommendations. Exhibit 11.5 describes an in-basket exercise used by an assessment centre in B.C.

In a *leaderless group discussion,* another common assessment centre exercise, a group of six applicants is given approximately two hours to solve a problem, but no one is put in charge (hence the name "leaderless" group discussion). Trained observers watch and score each participant on the extent to which he or she facilitates discussion, listens, leads, persuades, and works well with others.

Are tests perfect predictors of job performance? No, they aren't. Some people who do well on selection tests will do poorly in their jobs. Likewise, some people who do poorly on selection tests (and therefore weren't hired) would have been very good performers. Nonetheless, valid tests will minimize these selection errors (hiring people who should not have been hired and not hiring people who should have been hired) while maximizing correct selection decisions (hiring people who should have been hired and not hiring people who should not have been hired). In short, tests increase the chances that you'll hire the right person for the job, that is, someone who turns out to be a good performer. So, although tests aren't perfect, almost nothing predicts future job performance as well as the selection tests discussed here.

3.4 Interviews

In **interviews,** company representatives ask job applicants job-related questions to determine whether they are qualified for the job. Interviews are probably the most frequently used and relied upon selection device. There are several basic kinds of interviews: unstructured, structured, and semistructured.

In **unstructured interviews,** interviewers are free to ask applicants anything they want, and studies show that they do. Because interviewers often disagree about which questions should be asked during interviews,

Interviews a selection tool in which company representatives ask job applicants job-related questions to determine whether they are qualified for the job

Unstructured interviews interviews in which interviewers are free to ask the applicants anything they want

© AP Images

Finding the Perfect Mate

While it may not be healthy to be married to your job, the process of finding one can often feel like dating. Sometimes it even looks like dating. An increasing number of retiring baby boomers and a shortage of skilled workers means that positions need to be filled more quickly, and some companies are turning to speed dating as a new interview strategy. Up to 200 candidates can appear for a daylong interviewing event, where they will spend five minutes each with various recruiters. Ill-fitting candidates can be eliminated early in the process, recruiters can easily remember candidates without searching through notes, and decisions are made more quickly.

Source: S. E. Needleman, "Speed Interviewing Grows as Skills Shortage Looms," *The Wall Street Journal* (6 November 2007), B15.

different interviewers tend to ask applicants very different questions.[37] Furthermore, individual interviewers even seem to have a tough time asking the same questions from one interview to the next. This high level of inconsistency lowers the validity of unstructured interviews as a selection device because comparing applicant responses can be difficult. As a result, unstructured interviews are about half as accurate as structured interviews at predicting which job applicants should be hired.

By contrast, with **structured interviews,** standardized interview questions are prepared ahead of time so that all applicants are asked the same job-related questions.[38] Structuring interviews also ensures that interviewers ask only for important, job-related information. Not only are the accuracy, usefulness, and validity of the interview improved, but the chances that interviewers will ask questions about topics that violate employment laws (the "Don't Ask!" box on page 217 has a list of these topics) are reduced.

The primary advantage of structured interviews is that comparing applicants is much easier because they are all asked the same questions. Structured interviews typically contain four types of questions: situational, behavioural, background, and job-knowledge. Situational questions ask applicants how they would respond in a hypothetical situation (e.g., "What would you do if…"). These questions are more appropriate for hiring new graduates, as they are unlikely to have encountered real work situations because of their limited experience. Behavioural questions ask applicants what they did in previous jobs that is similar to what is required for the job for which they are applying (e.g., "In your previous jobs, tell me about…"). These questions are more appropriate for hiring experienced

> **Structured interviews** interviews in which all applicants are asked the same set of standardized questions, usually including situational, behavioural, background, and job-knowledge questions

Exhibit 11.6

Guidelines for Conducting Effective Structured Interviews

Interview Stage	What to Do
 **Planning the Interview**	• Identify and define the knowledge, skills, abilities, and other (KSAO) characteristics needed for successful job performance. • For each essential KSAO, develop key behavioural questions that will elicit examples of past accomplishments, activities, and performance. • For each KSAO, develop a list of things to look for in the applicant's responses to key questions.
 **Conducting the Interview**	• Create a relaxed, nonstressful interview atmosphere. • Review the applicant's application form, résumé, and other information. • Allocate enough time to complete the interview without interruption. • Put the applicant at ease; don't jump right into heavy questioning. • Tell the applicant what to expect. Explain the interview process. • Obtain job-related information from the applicant by asking those questions prepared for each KSAO. • Describe the job and the organization to the applicant. Applicants need adequate information to make a selection decision about the organization.
 **After the Interview**	• Immediately after the interview, review your notes and make sure they are complete. • Evaluate the applicant on each essential KSAO. • Determine each applicant's probability of success and make a hiring decision.

Source: B.M. Farrell, "The Art and Science of Employment Interviews," *Personnel Journal* 65 (1986): 91–94; Catano et al. *Recruitment and Selection in Canada.* Toronto: Nelson Education, [2009], © 2010. p. 431.

individuals. Background questions ask applicants about their work experience, education, and other qualifications (e.g., "Tell me about the training you received at…"). Finally, job-knowledge questions ask applicants to demonstrate their job knowledge (e.g., for nurses, "Give me an example of a time when one of your patients had a severe reaction to a medication. How did you handle it?").[39]

Semistructured interviews are in between structured and unstructured interviews. A major part of the semistructured interview (perhaps as much as 80 percent) is based on structured questions, but some time is set aside for unstructured interviewing to allow the interviewer to probe into ambiguous or missing information uncovered during the structured portion of the interview.

How well do interviews predict future job performance? Contrary to what you've probably heard, recent evidence indicates that even unstructured interviews do a fairly good job.[40] When conducted properly, however, structured interviews can lead to much more accurate hiring decisions than unstructured interviews. In some cases, the validity of structured interviews can rival that of cognitive ability tests. But even more important, because interviews are especially good at assessing applicants' interpersonal skills, they work particularly well with cognitive ability tests. The combination (i.e., smart people who work well in conjunction with others) leads to even better selection decisions than using either alone.[41] Exhibit 11.6 provides a set of guidelines for conducting effective structured employment interviews.

Developing Qualified Workers

According to the Canadian Society for Training and Development, a typical investment in employee training increases productivity by an average of 17 percent, reduces employee turnover, and makes companies more profitable.[42] Giving employees the knowledge and skills they need to improve their performance is just the first step in developing employees, however. The second step, and not enough companies do this, is giving

Training developing the skills, experience, and knowledge employees need to perform their jobs or improve their performance

Needs assessment the process of identifying and prioritizing the learning needs of employees

employees formal feedback about their actual job performance.

After reading the next two sections, you should be able to

4 describe how to determine training needs and select the appropriate training methods.

5 discuss how to use performance appraisal to give meaningful performance feedback.

4 Training

Training means providing opportunities for employees to develop the job-specific skills, experience, and knowledge they need to do their jobs or improve their performance. Canadian companies spend more than 5 billion a year on training. To make sure those training dollars are well spent, companies need to **4.1 determine specific training needs, 4.2 select appropriate training methods,** and **4.3 evaluate training.**

4.1 Determining Training Needs

Needs assessment is the process of identifying and prioritizing the learning needs of employees. Needs assessments can be conducted by identifying performance deficiencies, listening to customer complaints, surveying employees and managers, or formally testing employees' skills and knowledge.

Note that training should never be conducted without first performing a needs assessment. Sometimes training isn't needed at all or isn't needed for all employees. Unfortunately, however, many organizations simply require all employees to attend training whether they need to or not. As a result, employees who aren't interested or don't need the training may react negatively during or after training. Likewise, employees who should be sent for training but aren't may also react negatively. Consequently, a needs assessment is an important tool for deciding who should or should not attend training. In fact, employment law restricts employers from discriminating on the basis of age, sex, race, colour, religion, national origin, or disability when selecting training participants. Just like hiring decisions, the selection of training participants should be based on job-related information.

4.2 Training Methods

Assume that you're a training director for a major oil company and that you're in charge of making sure all employees know to respond effectively in case of an oil spill off the Newfoundland and Labrador coast. Keep in mind the lessons learned from the BP oil spill in the Mexican Gulf during the early summer of 2010.[43] Exhibit 11.7 lists a number of training methods you could use: films and videos, lectures, planned readings, case studies, coaching and mentoring, group discussions, on-the-job training, role-playing, simulations and games, vestibule training, and computer-based learning. Which method would be best?

To choose the best method, you should consider a number of factors such as the number of people to be trained, the cost of training, and the objectives of the training. For instance, if the training objective is to impart information or knowledge to trainees, then you should use films and videos, lectures, and planned readings.

Exhibit 11.7

Training Objectives and Methods

TRAINING OBJECTIVE	TRAINING METHODS
Impart Information and Knowledge	• *Films and videos*. Films and videos share information, illustrate problems and solutions, and effectively hold trainees' attention.
	• *Lectures*. Trainees listen to instructors' oral presentations.
	• *Planned readings*. Trainees read about concepts or ideas before attending training.
Develop Analytical and Problem-Solving Skills	• *Case studies*. Cases are analyzed and discussed in small groups. The cases present a specific problem or decision, and trainees develop methods for solving the problem or making the decision.
	• *Coaching and mentoring*. Coaching and mentoring of trainees by managers involves informal advice, suggestions, and guidance. This method is helpful for reinforcing other kinds of training and for trainees who benefit from support and personal encouragement.
	• *Group discussions*. Small groups of trainees actively discuss specific topics. The instructor may perform the role of discussion leader.
Practise, Learn, or Change Job Behaviours	• *On-the-job training (OJT)*. New employees are assigned to experienced employees. The trainee learns by watching the experienced employee perform the job and eventually by working alongside the experienced employee. Gradually, the trainee is left on his or her own to perform the job.
	• *Role-playing*. Trainees assume job-related roles and practise new behaviours by acting out what they would do in job-related situations.
	• *Simulations and games*. Experiential exercises place trainees in realistic job-related situations and give them the opportunity to experience a job-related condition in a relatively low-cost setting. The trainee benefits from hands-on experience before actually performing the job, where mistakes may be more costly.
	• *Vestibule training*. Procedures and equipment similar to those used in the actual job are set up in a special area called a "vestibule." The trainee is then taught how to perform the job at his or her own pace without disrupting the actual flow of work, making costly mistakes, or exposing the trainee and others to dangerous conditions.
Impart Information and Knowledge; Develop Analytical and Problem-Solving Skills; and Practise, Learn, or Change Job Behaviours	• *Computer-based learning*. Interactive videos, software, CD-ROMs, personal computers, teleconferencing, and the Internet may be combined to present multimedia-based training.

Source: A. Fowler, "How to Decide on Training Methods," *People Management* 25, no. 1 (1995): 36.

In our example, trainees might read a manual or attend a lecture about how to seal a shoreline to keep it from being affected by the spill.

If developing analytical and problem-solving skills is the objective, then use case studies, coaching and mentoring, and group discussions. In our example, trainees might view a video documenting how a team handled exposure to hazardous substances, talk with first responders, and discuss what they would do in a similar situation.

If practising, learning, or changing job behaviours is the objective, then use on-the-job training, role playing, simulations and games, and vestibule training. In our example, trainees might participate in a mock shoreline cleanup to learn what do in the event oil comes to shore. This simulation could take place on an actual shoreline or on a video-game-like virtual shoreline.

If training is supposed to meet more than one of these objectives, then your best choice may be to combine one of the previous methods with computer-based training.

These days, many companies are adopting Internet training, or "e-learning." E-learning can offer several advantages. Because employees don't need to leave their jobs, travel costs are greatly reduced. Also, because employees can take training modules when it is convenient (in other words, they don't have to fall behind at their jobs to attend week-long training courses), workplace productivity should increase and employee stress should decrease. Finally, if the company's technology infrastructure can support it, e-learning can be much faster than traditional training methods.

There are, however, several disadvantages to e-learning. First, despite its increasing popularity, it's not always the appropriate training method. E-learning can be a good way to impart information, but it isn't always as effective for changing job behaviours or developing problem-solving and analytical skills. Second, e-learning requires a significant investment in computers and high-speed Internet and network connections for all employees. Finally, though e-learning can be faster, many employees find it so boring and unengaging that they may choose to do their jobs rather than complete e-learning courses when sitting alone at their desks. E-learning may become more interesting, however, as more companies incorporate gamelike features such as avatars and competition into their e-learning courses.

Dow Chemical Canada now has the ability to provide electronic learning or training to all its employees in through its Learn@dow .now Web-based training

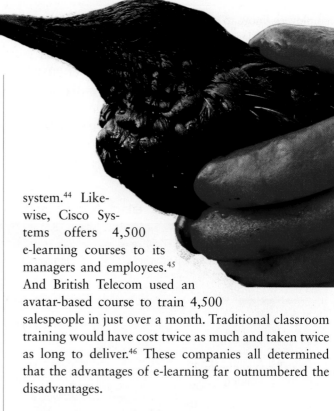

© Natalie Fobes/Stone/Getty Images

system.[44] Likewise, Cisco Systems offers 4,500 e-learning courses to its managers and employees.[45] And British Telecom used an avatar-based course to train 4,500 salespeople in just over a month. Traditional classroom training would have cost twice as much and taken twice as long to deliver.[46] These companies all determined that the advantages of e-learning far outnumbered the disadvantages.

4.3 Evaluating Training

After selecting a training method and conducting the training, the last step is to evaluate the training. Training can be evaluated in four ways: on *reactions* (how satisfied trainees were with the program), on *learning* (how much employees improved their knowledge or skills), on *behaviour* (how much employees actually changed their on-the-job behaviour because of training), or on *results* (how much training improved job performance, such as increased sales or quality, or decreased costs).[47] In general, if done well, training provides meaningful benefits for most companies. For example, a study by the Canadian Society for Training and Development shows that a training budget as small as $680 per employee can increase a company's total return on investment by 6 percent.[48]

5 Performance Appraisal

Performance appraisal is the process of assessing how well employees are doing their jobs. Most employees and managers intensely dislike the performance appraisal process. One manager says "I hate annual performance reviews. I hated them when I used to get them, and I hate them now that I give them. If I had to choose between performance reviews and paper cuts, I'd take paper cuts every time. I'd even take razor burns and the sound of fingernails on a blackboard."[49] Unfortunately, attitudes like

Performance appraisal the process of assessing how well employees are doing their jobs

Common Rating Errors

Central tendency error occurs when assessors rate all workers as average or in the middle of the scale.

Halo error occurs when assessors rate a particular worker as performing at the same level (good, bad, or average) in all parts of his or her job.

Leniency error occurs when assessors rate all workers as performing particularly well.

this are all too common. In fact, 70 percent of employees are dissatisfied with the performance appraisal process in their companies. Likewise, according to the Society for Human Resource Management, 90 percent of human resource managers are dissatisfied with the performance appraisal systems used by their companies.[50]

Let's explore how companies can avoid some of these problems with performance appraisals by 5.1 accurately measuring job performance and 5.2 effectively sharing performance feedback with employees.

5.1 Accurately Measuring Job Performance

Workers often have strong doubts about the accuracy of their performance appraisals—and they may be right. For example, it's widely known that assessors are prone to errors when rating worker performance. One of the reasons that managers make these errors is that they often don't spend enough time gathering or reviewing performance data. What can be done to minimize rating errors and improve the accuracy with which job performance is measured? In general, two approaches have been used: improving performance appraisal measures themselves, and training performance raters to be more accurate.

One of the ways companies try to improve performance appraisal measures is to use as many objective performance measures as possible. **Objective performance measures** are measures of performance that are easily and directly counted or quantified.

Common objective performance measures include output, scrap, waste, sales, customer complaints, and rejection rates.

But when objective performance measures aren't available, and frequently they aren't, subjective performance measures have to be used instead. Subjective performance measures require that someone judge or assess a worker's performance. The most common kind of subjective performance measure is the Graphic Rating Scale (GRS) shown in Exhibit 11.8 on page 226. Graphic rating scales are most widely used because they are easy to construct, but they are very susceptible to rating errors.

A popular alternative to graphic rating scales is the **Behaviour Observation Scale (BOS).** BOS requires raters to rate the frequency with which workers perform specific behaviours representative of the job dimensions that are critical to successful job performance. Exhibit 11.8 shows a BOS for two important job dimensions for a retail salesperson: customer service and money handling. Notice that each dimension lists several specific behaviours characteristic of a worker who excels in that dimension of job performance. (Normally, the scale would list seven to twelve items per dimension, not three as in the exhibit.) Notice also that the behaviours are good behaviours, meaning they indicate good performance, and the rater is asked to judge how frequently an employee engaged in those good behaviours. The logic behind the BOS is that better performers engage in good behaviours more often.

Not only do BOSs work well for rating critical dimensions of performance, but studies also show that managers strongly prefer BOSs for giving performance feedback; accurately differentiating between poor, average, and good workers; identifying training needs; and accurately measuring performance. And in response to the statement, "If I were defending a company, this rating format would be an asset to my case," attorneys strongly preferred BOSs over other kinds of subjective performance appraisal scales.[51]

The second approach to improving the measurement

Objective performance measures measures of job performance that are easily and directly counted or quantified

Behavioural observation scales (BOSs) rating scales that indicate the frequency with which workers perform specific behaviours that are representative of the job dimensions critical to successful job performance

© Image Source Pink/Jupiterimages

Exhibit 11.8

Subjective Performance Appraisal Scales

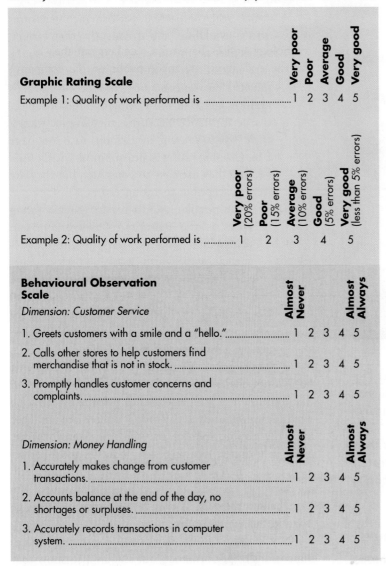

Graphic Rating Scale

	Very poor	Poor	Average	Good	Very good
Example 1: Quality of work performed is	1	2	3	4	5

	Very poor (20% errors)	Poor (15% errors)	Average (10% errors)	Good (5% errors)	Very good (less than 5% errors)
Example 2: Quality of work performed is	1	2	3	4	5

Behavioural Observation Scale

Dimension: Customer Service

	Almost Never				Almost Always
1. Greets customers with a smile and a "hello."	1	2	3	4	5
2. Calls other stores to help customers find merchandise that is not in stock.	1	2	3	4	5
3. Promptly handles customer concerns and complaints.	1	2	3	4	5

Dimension: Money Handling

	Almost Never				Almost Always
1. Accurately makes change from customer transactions.	1	2	3	4	5
2. Accounts balance at the end of the day, no shortages or surpluses.	1	2	3	4	5
3. Accurately records transactions in computer system.	1	2	3	4	5

of workers' job performance is **rater training**. The most effective is frame-of-reference training in which a group of trainees learns how to do performance appraisals by watching a videotape of an employee at work. Next, they evaluate the performance of the person in the videotape. A trainer (i.e., subject matter expert) then shares his or her evaluations, and trainees' evaluations are compared with the expert's. The expert then explains rationales behind his or her

evaluations. This process is repeated until the difference in evaluations given by trainees and evaluations by the expert are minimized. The underlying logic behind the frame-of-reference training is that by adopting the frame of reference used by an expert, trainees will be able to accurately observe, judge, and use the scale to evaluate performance of others.[52]

5.2 Sharing Performance Feedback

After gathering accurate performance data, the next step is to share performance feedback with employees. Unfortunately, even when performance appraisal ratings are accurate, the appraisal process often breaks down at the feedback stage. Employees become defensive and dislike hearing any negative assessments of their work, no matter how small. Managers become defensive, too, and dislike giving appraisal feedback as much as employees dislike receiving it.

What can be done to overcome the inherent difficulties in performance appraisal feedback sessions? Since performance appraisal ratings have traditionally been the judgments of just one person, the boss, one possibility is to use **360-degree feedback.** In this approach, feedback comes from four sources: the boss, subordinates, peers and coworkers, and the employees themselves. The data, which are obtained anonymously (except for the boss's), are compiled into a feedback report comparing the employee's self-ratings with those of the boss, subordinates, and peers and coworkers. Usually, a consultant or human resource specialist discusses the results with the employee. The advantage of 360-degree programs is that negative feedback ("You don't listen") is often more credible when it comes from several people.

Herbert Meyer, who has been studying performance appraisal feedback for more than 30 years, recommends a list of topics for discussion in performance appraisal feedback sessions listed in Exhibit 11.9.[53]

How these topics are discussed in a review session is important for its success. Managers can do three different things to make performance reviews as comfortable and productive as possible. First, managers should separate developmental feedback, which is designed to improve future performance, from administrative feedback, which is used as a reward for past performance, such as for raises. When managers give developmental feedback, they're acting as coaches, but when they give administrative feedback, they're acting as judges.

Exhibit 11.9

What to Discuss in a Performance Appraisal Feedback Session

- ✔ Overall progress—an analysis of accomplishments and shortcomings.
- ✔ Problems encountered in meeting job requirements.
- ✔ Opportunities to improve performance.
- ✔ Long-range plans and opportunities— for the job and for the individual's career.
- ✔ General discussion of possible plans and goals for the coming year.

Source: H. H. Meyer, "A Solution to the Performance Appraisal Feedback Enigma," *Academy of Management Executive* 5, no. 1 (1991): 68–76.

These roles, coaches and judges, are clearly incompatible. As coaches, managers are encouraging, pointing out opportunities for growth and improvement, and employees are typically open and receptive to feedback. But as judges, managers are evaluative, and employees are typically defensive and closed to feedback.

Second, Meyer suggests that performance appraisal feedback sessions be based on self-appraisals, in which employees carefully assess their own strengths, weaknesses, successes, and failures in writing. Because employees play an active role in the review of their performance, managers can be coaches rather than judges. Also, because the focus is on future goals and development, both employees and managers are likely to be more satisfied with the process and more committed to future plans and changes. And, because the focus is on development and not administrative assessment, studies show that self-appraisals lead to more candid self-assessments than traditional supervisory reviews.[54] See Exhibit 11.9 for a list of topics that Meyer recommends for discussion in performance appraisal feedback sessions.

Finally, what people do with the performance feedback they receive really matters. A study of 1,361 senior managers found that managers who reviewed their 360-degree feedback with an executive coach (hired by the company) were more likely to set specific goals for improvement, ask their bosses for ways to improve, and subsequently improve their performance.[55]

Managers need to receive feedback as well as give it. Not only does HCL Technologies, an outsourcer of technology services, have team members rate their bosses, but the evaluations are made public on the company's intranet to hold top managers accountable. This was the *boss's* idea.[56] A five-year study of 252 managers found that their performance improved dramatically if they met with their subordinates to discuss their 360-degree feedback ("You don't listen") and how they were going to address it ("I'll restate what others have said before stating my opinion"). Performance was dramatically lower for managers who never discussed their 360-degree feedback with subordinates and for managers who did not routinely do so (some managers did not review their 360-degree feedback with subordinates each year of the study). Why is discussing 360-degree feedback with subordinates so effective? These discussions help managers better understand their weaknesses, force them to develop a plan to improve, and demonstrate to the subordinates the managers' public commitment to improving.[57] In short, it helps to have people discuss their performance feedback with others, but it particularly helps to have them discuss their feedback with the people who provided it.

Keeping Qualified Workers

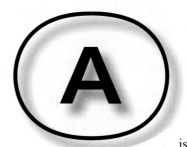

After Motorola's mobile devices division lost $1.2 billion in 2007, the company decided to split in half. In such times of transition and uncertainty, it is easy for a company to lose valuable employees as job security decreases and people seek opportunities elsewhere. In an effort to retain its human resources, Motorola established an incentive program that offered bonuses to employees in key roles who remained on the job and to their supervisors for keeping them there.[58]

After reading the next section, you should be able to

6 describe basic compensation strategies and discuss the four kinds of employee separations.

6 Compensation and Employee Separation

Compensation includes both the financial and the nonfinancial rewards that organizations give employees in exchange for their work. **Employee separation** is a broad term covering the loss of an employee for any reason. *Involuntary separation* occurs when employers decide to terminate or lay off employees. *Voluntary separation* occurs when employees decide to quit or retire. Because employee separations affect recruiting, selection, training, and compensation, organizations should forecast the number of employees they expect to lose through terminations, layoffs, turnover, or retirements when doing human resource planning.

Let's learn more about compensation and employee separation by examining the 6.1 compensation decisions that managers must make as well as 6.2 terminations, 6.3 downsizing, 6.4 retirements, and 6.5 turnover.

6.1 Compensation Decisions

There are three basic kinds of compensation decisions: pay level, pay variability, and pay structure.[59]

Pay-level decisions are decisions about whether to pay workers at a level that is below, above, or at current market wages. Companies use job evaluation to set their pay structures. **Job evaluation** determines the worth of each job by determining the market value of the knowledge, skills, and requirements needed to perform it. After conducting a job evaluation, most companies try to pay the going rate, meaning the current market wage. There are always companies, however, whose financial situation causes them to pay considerably less than current market wages. The child care industry, for example, has chronic difficulties filling jobs because it pays well below market wages. While the director of a child care centre in Canada would make between $31,579 and $48,731, a child care worker would make $10 to $15 per hour ($19,000–$29,000) according to PayScale.com. The pay for child care workers has gone up very little in the past 10 years.[60]

Some companies choose to pay above-average wages to attract and keep employees. *Above-market wages* can attract a larger, more qualified pool of job applicants, increase the rate of job acceptance, decrease the time it takes to fill positions, and increase the time that employees stay.[61]

Pay-variability decisions concern the extent to which employees' pay varies with individual and organizational performance. Linking pay to performance is intended to increase employee motivation, effort, and job performance. Piecework, sales commissions, profit sharing, employee stock ownership plans, and stock options are common pay-variability options. For instance, under **piecework** pay plans, employees are paid a set rate for each item produced up to some standard (e.g., 35 cents per item produced for output up to 100 units per day). Once productivity exceeds the standard, employees are paid a set amount for each unit of output over the standard (e.g., 45 cents for each unit above 100 units). Under a sales **commission** plan, salespeople are paid a percentage of the purchase price of items they sell. The more they sell, the more they earn.

Because pay plans such as piecework and commissions are based on individual performance, they can reduce the incentive that people have to work together. Therefore, companies also use group incentives (discussed in Chapter 10) and organizational incentives such as profit sharing, employee stock ownership plans, and stock options to encourage teamwork and cooperation.

With **profit sharing** employees receive a portion of the organization's profits over and above their regular compensation. The more profitable the company, the more profit is shared. Employees at Proform Concrete Services Inc. of Red Deer, Alberta, share profits with the company. Proform awards 15 percent of the company's

Perry Mastrovito/Creatas/Jupiterimages

Compensation the financial and nonfinancial rewards that organizations give employees in exchange for their work

Employee separation the voluntary or involuntary loss of an employee

Job evaluation a process that determines the worth of each job in a company by evaluating the market value of the knowledge, skills, and requirements needed to perform it

Piecework a compensation system in which employees are paid a set rate for each item they produce

Commission a compensation system in which employees earn a percentage of each sale they make

Profit sharing a compensation system in which a company pays a percentage of its profits to employees in addition to their regular compensation

How Do Options Work?

Options work like this. Let's say that you are awarded the right (or option) to buy 100 shares of stock from the company for $5 a share. If the company's stock price rises to $15 a share, you can exercise your options and make $1,000. When you exercise your options, you pay the company $500 (100 shares at $5 a share), but because the stock is selling for $15 in the stock market, you can sell your 100 shares for $1,500 and make $1,000. Of course, as the company's profits and share values increase, stock options become even more valuable to employees. Stock options have no value, however, if the company's stock falls below the option "grant price," the price at which the options have been issued to you. For instance, the options you have on 100 shares of stock with a grant price of $5 aren't going to do you a lot of good if the company's stock is worth $2.50. Why exercise your stock options and pay $5 a share for stock that sells for $2.50 a share in the stock market? (Stock options are said to be "underwater" when the grant price is lower than the market price.)

The Canadian Press (J.P. Moczulski)

© Mark Von Holden/FilmMagic/Getty Images

profits to its employees. The program is designed specifically to reward employees' loyalty and commitment.[62]

Employee stock ownership plans (ESOPs) compensate employees by awarding them shares of the company stock in addition to their regular compensation. By contrast, **stock options** give employees the right to purchase shares of stock at a set price. Proponents of stock options argue that this gives employees and managers a strong incentive to work hard to make the company successful. If they do, the company's profits and stock price increase, and their stock options increase in value. If they don't, profits stagnate or turn into losses, and their stock options decrease in value or become worthless.

The incentive has to be more than just a piece of paper, however. A study carried out by the Toronto Stock Exchange found that ESOP companies' five-year profit growth was 123 per cent higher, their net profit margin was 95 per cent higher, and productivity measured by revenue per employee was 24 per cent higher than for non-ESOP companies, among other benefits.[63]

Pay-structure decisions are concerned with internal pay distributions, meaning the extent to which people in the company receive very different levels of pay.[64] With *hierarchical pay structures*, there are big differences from one pay level to another. The highest pay levels are for people near the top of the pay distribution. The basic idea behind hierarchical pay structures is that large differences in pay between jobs or organizational levels should motivate people to work harder to obtain those higher-paying jobs. Many publicly owned companies have hierarchical pay structures by virtue of the huge amounts they pay their top managers and CEOs. For example, the average CEO now makes 364 times as much as the average worker, down from 525 times the pay of average workers just eight years ago. But with CEO pay packages averaging $18.8 million per year and average workers earning just $36,140, the difference is still incredible and can have a significant detrimental impact on employee morale.[65]

By contrast, *compressed pay structures* typically have fewer pay levels and smaller differences in pay between levels. Pay is less dispersed and more similar across jobs in the company. The basic idea behind compressed pay

> **Employee stock ownership plan (ESOP)** a compensation system that awards employees shares of company stock in addition to their regular compensation
>
> **Stock options** a compensation system that gives employees the right to purchase shares of stock at a set price, even if the value of the stock increases above that price

structures is that similar pay levels should lead to higher levels of cooperation, feelings of fairness and a common purpose, and better group and team performance.

So should companies choose hierarchical or compressed pay structures? The evidence isn't straightforward, but studies seem to indicate that there are significant problems with the hierarchical approach. The most damaging finding is that there appears to be little link between organizational performance and the pay of top managers.[66] Furthermore, studies of professional athletes indicate that hierarchical pay structures (e.g., paying superstars 40 to 50 times more than the lowest-paid athlete on the team) hurt the performance of teams and individual players.[67] Likewise, managers are twice as likely to quit their jobs when their companies have very strong hierarchical pay structures (i.e., when they're paid dramatically less than the people above them).[68] For now, it seems that hierarchical pay structures work best for independent work, where it's easy to determine the contributions of individual performers and little coordination with others is needed to get the job done. In other words, hierarchical pay structures work best when clear links can be drawn between individual performance and individual rewards. By contrast, compressed pay structures, in which everyone receives similar pay, seem to work best for interdependent work, which requires employees to work together. Some companies are pursuing a middle ground: combining hierarchical and compressed pay structures by giving ordinary workers the chance to earn more through ESOPs, stock options, and profit sharing.

6.2 Terminating Employees

Hopefully, the words "You're fired!" have never been directed at you. Lots of people hear them, however. During the worldwide economic and banking crisis of 2009, more than 473,200 Canadian workers were fired from their jobs in the first half of the year. Getting fired is a terrible thing, but many managers make it even worse by bungling the firing process, needlessly provoking the person who was fired and unintentionally inviting lawsuits. Though firing is never pleasant (and managers hate firings nearly as much as employees do), managers can do several things to minimize the problems inherent in firing employees.

First, in most situations, firing should not be the first option. Instead, employees should be given a chance to change their behaviour. When problems arise, employees should have ample warning and must be specifically informed as to the nature and seriousness of the trouble they're in. After being notified, they should be given sufficient time to change. If the problems continue, the employees should again be counselled about their job performance, what could be done to improve it, and the possible consequences if things don't change (e.g., written reprimand, suspension without pay, or firing). Sometimes this is enough to solve the problem. If the problem isn't corrected after several rounds of warnings and discussions, however, the employee may be terminated.[69]

Second, employees should be fired only for a good reason. Employers used to hire and fire employees under the legal principle of employment at will, which allowed them to fire employees for a good reason, a bad reason, or no reason at all. (Employees could also quit for a good reason, a bad reason, or no reason whenever they desired.) As employees began contesting their firings in court, however, the principle of wrongful discharge emerged. **Wrongful discharge** is a legal doctrine that requires employers to have a job-related reason to terminate employees. In other words, like other major human resource decisions, termination decisions should be made on the basis of job-related factors, such as violating company rules or consistently poor performance.

6.3 Downsizing

Downsizing is the planned elimination of jobs in a company. Whether it's because of cost cutting, declining market share, previous overaggressive hiring and growth, or outsourcing, companies typically eliminate jobs every year. A study completed by a University of Saskatchewan commerce professor indicates that the decision to downsize is not always made for economic reasons and that downsizing cannot be depended on to yield economic benefits. Professor Marc Mentzer analyzed data from 250 of Canada's largest companies. Downsizing is not always done for economic reasons or because the company needs to become more efficient for financial reasons. The study shows that contrary to common beliefs, the decision to downsize is unrelated to past performance. Profitable companies are no more likely to downsize than less profitable ones. Also, the study results show that downsized companies are no more likely to be profitable than companies that do not downsize.[70] Two-thirds of companies that downsize will downsize a second time within a year.

Another 15-year study of downsizing found that downsizing 10 percent of a company's workforce

Wrongful discharge a legal doctrine that requires employers to have a job-related reason to terminate employees

Downsizing the planned elimination of jobs in a company

produced only a 1.5 percent decrease in costs; that firms that downsized increased their stock price by only 4.7 percent over three years, compared with 34.3 percent for firms that didn't; and that profitability and productivity were generally not improved by downsizing.[71] Downsizing can also result in the loss of skilled workers who would be expensive to replace when the company grows again.[72] These results make it clear that the best strategy is to conduct effective human resource planning and avoid downsizing altogether. Indeed, downsizing should always be a last resort.

If companies do find themselves in financial or strategic situations where downsizing is required for survival, however, they should train managers in how to break the news to downsized employees, have senior managers explain in detail why downsizing is necessary, and time the announcement so that employees hear it from the company and not from other sources such as TV or newspaper reports.[73] Finally, companies should do everything they can to help downsized employees find other jobs. One of the best ways to do this is to use **outplacement services** that provide employment-counselling services for employees faced with downsizing. Outplacement services often include advice and training in preparing résumés, getting ready for job interviews, and even identifying job opportunities in other companies.

6.4 Retirement

Early retirement incentive programs (ERIPs) offer financial benefits to employees to encourage them to retire early. Companies use ERIPs to reduce the number of employees in the organization, to lower costs by eliminating positions after employees retire, to lower costs by replacing high-paid retirees with lower-paid, less-experienced employees, or to create openings and job opportunities for people inside the company.

Although ERIPs can save companies money, they can pose a big problem for managers if they fail to accurately predict which employees—the good performers or the poor performers—and how many will retire early. Consultant Ron Nicol says, "The thing that doesn't work is just asking for volunteers. You get the wrong volunteers. Some of your best people will feel they can get a job anywhere. Or you have people who are close to retirement and are a real asset to the company."[74] A "bigger than expected" response to the University of Waterloo's cost-cutting, early retirement package resulted in the loss of 340 faculty and staff members, about one-eighth of its employees, almost all of whom were senior faculty or senior administrators. This unexpected response to the ERIP offer represented a change that would normally occur over 10 years.[75]

Because of the problems associated with ERIPs, many companies are now offering **phased retirement**, in which employees transition to retirement by working reduced hours over a period of time before completely retiring. The advantage for employees is that they have more free time but continue to earn salaries and benefits without changing companies or careers. The advantage for companies is that it allows them to reduce salaries as well as hiring and training costs and retain experienced, valuable workers.[76]

6.5 Employee Turnover

Employee turnover is the loss of employees who voluntarily choose to leave the

Outplacement services employment-counselling services offered to employees who are losing their jobs because of downsizing

Early retirement incentive programs (ERIPs) programs that offer financial benefits to employees to encourage them to retire early

Phased retirement employees transition to retirement by working reduced hours over a period of time before completely retiring

Employee turnover loss of employees who voluntarily choose to leave the company

company. In general, most companies try to keep the rate of employee turnover low to reduce recruiting, hiring, training, and replacement costs. Not all kinds of employee turnover are bad for organizations, however. In fact, some turnover can actually be good. For instance, **functional turnover** is the loss of poor-performing employees who choose to leave the organization.[77] Functional turnover gives the organization a chance to replace poor performers with better workers. In fact, one study found that simply replacing poor-performing leavers with average workers would increase the revenues produced by retail salespeople in an upscale department store by $112,000 per person per year.[78] By contrast, **dysfunctional turnover,** the loss of high performers who choose to leave, is a costly loss to the organization.

Employee turnover should be carefully analyzed to determine whether good or poor performers are choosing to leave the organization. If the company is losing too many high performers, managers should determine the reasons and find ways to reduce the loss of valuable employees. The company may have to raise salary levels, offer enhanced benefits, or improve working conditions to retain skilled workers. One of the best ways to influence functional and dysfunctional turnover is to link pay directly to performance. A study of four sales forces found that when pay was strongly linked to performance via sales commissions and bonuses, poor performers were much more likely to leave (i.e., functional turnover). By contrast, poor performers were much more likely to stay when paid large, guaranteed monthly salaries and small sales commissions and bonuses.[79]

Functional turnover
loss of poor-performing employees who voluntarily choose to leave a company

Dysfunctional turnover loss of high-performing employees who voluntarily choose to leave a company

By the Numbers

1,200	number of firefighters who work for the city of Calgary, Alberta.
24	number of months of salary Jack Wallace received from his former employer when they failed to supply him with a reference letter.
123%	percent higher growth of ESOP companies in a TSE study compared to non-ESOP companies in a five-year period.
$31,579	amount a director of a child care centre in Canada might make per year.
15%	amount of profit Proform Concrete Services Inc. of Red Deer Alberta pays to employees.
473,200	number of Canadians who were fired in the first half of 2009.

Visit **icanmgmt.com** to find the resources you need today!

Located at the back of the textbook are rip-out Chapter Review cards. Make sure you also go online to check out other tools that MGMT offers to help you successfully pass your course.

- Interactive Quizzes
- Key Terms Flashcards
- Audio Chapter Summaries
- PowerPoint Slides

- Interactive Games
- Crossword Puzzles
- "Reel to Reel" and "Biz Flix" videos
- Cases and Exercises

TEST COMING UP? NOW WHAT?

With **MGMT** you have a multitude of study aids at your fingertips. After reading the chapters, check out these ideas for further help:

Chapter Review cards include learning outcomes, definitions, and visual summaries for each chapter.

Printable flashcards give you three additional ways to check your comprehension of key **Principles of Management** concepts.

Other great ways to help you study include **interactive games, audio summaries, quizzes,** and **flashcards.**

"I like the flashcards, the videos, and the quizzes. Great format! I love the cards in the back of the book!"

—Asha Thtodort, Algonquin College

Visit **icanmgmt.com** to find the resources you need today!

MANAGING INDIVIDUALS AND A DIVERSE WORKFORCE

As the composition of the Canadian population continues to change, so does workplace diversity. According to the 2006 census, around 20 percent of Canada's total population (about 6.2 million people) is foreign-born—the highest proportion since 1931. And that population's growth rate is four times faster than in the 2001 census. Canada is now second only to Australia in terms of multiculturalism (22 percent of Australia's population is foreign-born), and ranks higher than the United States (13 percent). Where are these newcomers to Canada coming from? The data tell us that 58 percent who arrived between 2001 and 2006 came from Asia and the Middle East and that almost all were in the 25 to 54 age group, injecting youth into Canada's society, including its labour market.[1] International immigration continues to fuel increases in Canada's population, especially in the Western provinces, signalling to managers that the face of Canada's workforce has been changing over the past decade. Exhibit 12-1 shows the projected changes to Canada's population over the next decade.

Other significant changes should also be mentioned, including the dramatic growth in the number of women in the paid workforce—a prominent social trend in Canada over the past half-century. In 2006, women accounted for 47 percent of the employed workforce in Canada, up from 37 percent in 1976. Also, the employment rate of women with children has experienced a sharp increase: 73 percent of all women with children under 16 and living at home are now part of the employed workforce, compared to only 39 percent in 1976.[2]

Other demographic changes continue to draw attention, including the aging of the baby boomers. The proportion of Canadians over 65 continues to increase and is expected to represent between 23 and 25 percent of the Canadian population by 2036 (compared to 14 percent in 2009). This aging of the population will affect the future composition of the Canadian workforce. In 2009, 69 percent of the Canadian population was

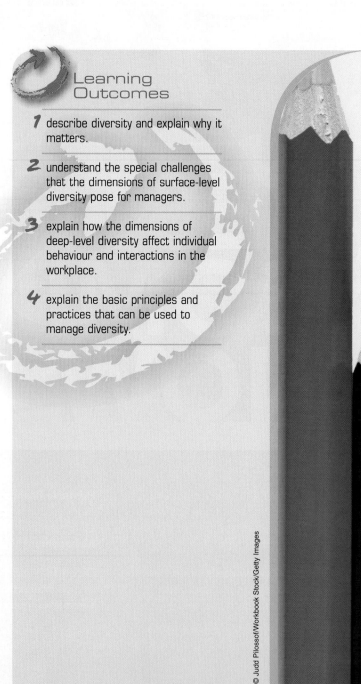

Learning Outcomes

1 describe diversity and explain why it matters.

2 understand the special challenges that the dimensions of surface-level diversity pose for managers.

3 explain how the dimensions of deep-level diversity affect individual behaviour and interactions in the workplace.

4 explain the basic principles and practices that can be used to manage diversity.

© Judd Pilossof/Workbook Stock/Getty Images

considered to be working-age; by 2026 this is expected to decline to 60 percent.[3]

Diversity and Why It Matters

D Diversity means variety. Therefore, **diversity** exists in an organization when there are a variety of demographic, cultural, and personal differences among the people who work there and the customers who do business there. For example, at Xerox Research Institute of Canada (XRIC) in Mississauga, there are 100 to 150 employees from 30 different countries. "It's like a United Nations here," say Yiliang Wu, a PhD who came to Canada from his native China in 1999 and is now a team leader at XRIC. "It is a wonderful place to work. The diversity is exciting and embracing. What counts here is the contribution you make, not where you came from."[4]

Diversity a variety of demographic, cultural, and personal differences among an organization's employees and customers

Exhibit 12.1

Visible Minority Groups in Canada, 2001 and 2017

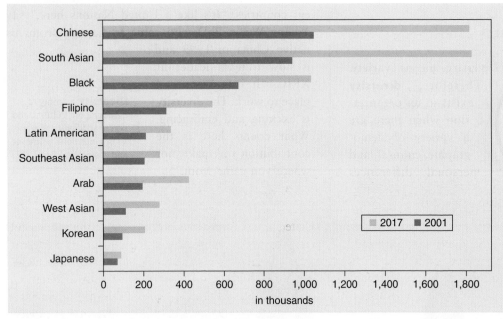

in thousands

Source: Statistics Canada, "Visible Minority Groups in Canada, 2001 and 2017," Canadian Demographics at a Glance 91-003-XWE 2007001 Released January 25, 2008. Available at http://www.statcan.gc.ca/pub/91-003-x/2007001/figures/4129878-eng.htm

After reading the next section, you should be able to

1   describe diversity and explain why it matters.

1 Diversity: Differences That Matter

You'll begin your exploration of diversity by learning **1.1 that diversity is not employment equity** and **1.2 how to build a business case for diversity.**

1.1 Diversity Is Not Employment Equity

A common misconception is that workplace diversity and employment equity are the same. However, these concepts differ in several critical ways, including their purpose, how they are practised, and the reactions they produce. In Canada, the term **employment equity** was introduced in 1984 to describe a planning process for achieving equality in all aspects of employment for four designated groups

in Canada: women, Aboriginal peoples, persons with disabilities, and members of visible minorities.[5] In contrast, diversity exists in organizations where a variety of demographic, cultural, and personal differences exist among the people who work there and the customers who do business there. So one key difference is that employment equity focuses more narrowly on demographics (gender, race, physical abilities), whereas diversity more broadly includes demographic as well as cultural and personal differences. A second difference is that employment equity is a process for actively creating diversity; however, diversity can exist even if organizations don't take purposeful steps to create it. For example, a McDonald's restaurant located near the University of British Columbia is more likely to have a more diverse group of employees than the McDonald's in Cochrane, Alberta.

A third important difference is that in Canada,

Employment Equity
an ongoing planning process used by an employer to eliminate barriers in an organization's employment procedures and to ensure appropriate representation of specific members of the workforce.

© Rachel Epstein/PhotoEdit Inc.

> A common misconception is that workplace **diversity** and employment **equity** are the same.

certain employers are subject to the Employment Equity Act, passed in 1986, which contains two federal Employment Equity programs: the Legislated Employment Equity Program (LEEP), which applies to federally regulated employers and all federal departments; and the Federal Contractors Program (FCP), for employers who have secured a federal goods and services contract of $200,000 or more and who have more than 100 employees. Under LEEP, by June 1 of every year, employers must submit employment equity reports that detail the representation of the designated groups within their workforce. Similarly, under the FCP, contractors must certify in writing their commitment to employment equity in order to bid on large government contracts.[6] By contrast, there is no federal or provincial legislation to oversee diversity; organizations that pursue diversity goals do so voluntarily.

Fourth, employment equity programs and diversity programs have different purposes. The purpose of employment equity is to "achieve equality in the workplace so that no person shall be denied employment opportunities or benefits for reasons unrelated to ability and in the fulfillment of goals, to correct the conditions of disadvantage in employment experienced by women, Aboriginal peoples, persons with disabilities, and visible minority people by

giving effect to the principle that employment equity means more than treating persons in the same way but also requires special measures and the accommodation of differences."[7] In contrast, the general purpose of diversity programs is to create a positive work environment where no one is advantaged or disadvantaged, where "we" is everyone, where everyone can do his or her best work, where differences are respected and not ignored, and where everyone feels comfortable.

A distinction should be made between Employment Equity in Canada and Affirmative Action in the United States. **Affirmative action** refers to the purposeful steps taken by an organization to create employment opportunities for women and minorities; it includes programs that compensate for past discrimination, which was widespread in the 1960s before affirmative action legislation was passed. Affirmative Action is required by law for private employers with 50 or more employees, and organizations that fail to uphold these laws may be required to: hire, promote, or give back pay to those not hired or promoted; reinstate those who were wrongly terminated; pay attorneys' fees and court costs for those who bring charges against them; and/or take other actions that make individuals whole by returning them to the condition or place they would have been had it not been for discrimination.[8] Thus, affirmative action is basically a punitive approach aimed at organizations that do achieve specific gender and race ratios in their workforces.[9]

Despite the overall success of affirmative action and employment equity in making workplaces much fairer than they used to be, the practice has drawn criticism from many people, especially when it comes to admissions quotas and hiring practices in institutions of higher education; government hiring practices; and the awarding of government contracts. Those who oppose these programs argue that giving preferential treatment to some groups at the expense of others is not fair; in particular, some Americans consider it unconstitutional.

1.2 Diversity Makes Good Business Sense

Those who support the idea of diversity in organizations often ignore its business aspects altogether, claiming

Affirmative action
purposeful steps taken by an organization to create employment opportunities for minorities and women

Generational Assets

A mix of older and younger workers may be critical to a company's success in our fast-paced, interconnected global marketplace. Gen-Xers and particularly millennials are flexible; learn new technologies and skills easily; are comfortable with crossing boundaries of space, time, and class; and tend to value collaboration. Baby boomers, while they can be slower to adapt to change, have experience and knowledge that are critical to a company's stability. The challenge? How to overcome generational differences in values, work methods, and communication styles within work groups. Capitalizing on the different strong points of each group and training employees on these differences are essential for success.

Sources: W. Boddie, J. Contardo, and R. Childs, "The Future Workforce: Here They Come," *The Public Manager* 36 (winter 2007) 25–28; E. White, "Age Is as Age Does; Making the Generation Gap Work for You," *The Wall Street Journal*, available online at http://online.wsj.com/article/SB121478926535514813.html [accessed 21 August 2008].

instead that diversity is simply the right thing to do. Yet diversity actually makes good business sense in several ways: cost savings, attracting and retaining talent, and driving business growth.[10] An increase of senior executive positions like "chief diversity officer" (CDO) suggests that more organizations are taking the business end of diversity seriously.[11]

Diversity experts have identified three strategic benefits of effectively managing workplace diversity.[12]

1. *Greater creativity and improved problem solving.* A diverse workforce that has variances in demographic variables such as age, gender, and ethnicity/ culture will also have different perspectives, skills, and talents, which aids in the performance of creative tasks and problem solving. In addition, employees who feel that diversity is supported in their organization tend to feel more valued and, as a result, tend to be more innovative. According to Marilyn Nagel, director of diversity at Cisco Systems Inc., "the link between innovation and diversity is clear. Companies that are more diverse regularly outperform companies that are not because they have stronger teamwork and a greater understanding of customers, partners, and suppliers."[13]

2. *Better insight into the needs of a diverse customer/client base.* As the market for goods and services continues to become more diverse, a diverse workforce with expanded cultural understanding becomes a competitive advantage to businesses that are intent on competing in the new global economy. Avon Company, realizing the importance of diversity, placed African-American and Hispanic managers in charge of

marketing to inner-city markets. This turned around what had been an unprofitable market segment.[14] Many successful companies have come to realize it is good business for a company's workforce to reflect its customer base.

3. *Enhanced ability to attract the best talent in a diverse labour market.* Optimizing human resources has become a competitive advantage for some organizations, and for some, that means competing to hire and retain the best talent from an increasingly diverse labour market. The assumption that talented individuals are attracted to organizations that value their abilities and that respond to their unique needs is one shared by many companies today, making diversity an important part of recruitment efforts today as diversity-friendly companies tend to attract better and more diverse job applicants.

The case for promoting workforce diversity is supported by various research, including a 2007 national survey of Canadians indicating that 77 percent of Canadian workers believe that diversity in culture and background contributes to innovation and creates a stronger business environment. Hadi Mahabadi, VP of the Xerox Research Centre of Canada, explains: "In the global economy of the 21st century, innovation will only thrive with the shared ideas of individuals with different backgrounds, areas of expertise and life experiences."[15]

A 2005 report presented by RBC Financial group makes an economic case for promoting diversity in Canada, taking into consideration demographic changes expected in the future, and presents three key reasons for addressing diversity. First, the report quantifies the untapped potential of today's workforce by calculating how much higher total incomes would be in Canada if the labour market experiences of immigrants were identical to those of workers born in Canada, and if women had the same labour market experiences as men. The result would be an extra $174 billion (or 21 percent increase) in personal income. Second, as baby boomers age and leave the workforce over the next two decades, immigration will continue to play an important role in the increase of the labour force in Canada. Even though immigration presently accounts for most of the net increase in the labour force, in the next 20 years, additional workers will be required beyond current immigration targets, and the focus should be on attracting highly skilled individuals to meet the needs of the Canadian workplace. Last, the study highlights the economic benefits associated with more diverse populations and suggests that the more developed an economy, the better equipped it is to benefit from a diverse population, with gains to productivity. To summarize, the more successful a company becomes in adopting a diversity approach, the better a position it will be in to deal with labour shortages and to capitalize on the skills and abilities of its employees.[16]

Overall, for many businesses today, the ability to manage and harness the benefits of today's diverse workforce is critical to remaining competitive in the changing global marketplace.

Diversity and Individual Differences

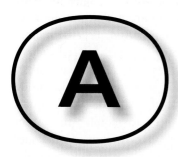

A survey that asked managers, "What is meant by diversity to decision-makers in your organization?" found that they most frequently mentioned race, culture, gender, national origin, age, religion, and regional origin.[17] When managers describe workers this way, they are focusing on surface-level diversity. **Surface-level diversity** consists of differences that are immediately observable, typically unchangeable, and easy to measure.[18] In other words, independent observers can usually agree on dimensions of surface-level diversity, such as another person's age, gender, race/ethnicity, or physical capabilities.

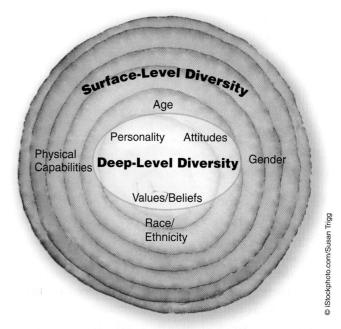

© iStockphoto.com/Susan Trigg

Most people start by using surface-level diversity to categorize or stereotype other people. But those initial categorizations typically give way to deeper impressions formed from knowledge of others' behaviour and psychological characteristics such as personality and attitudes.[19] When you think of others this way, you are focusing on deep-level diversity. **Deep-level diversity** consists of differences that are communicated through verbal and nonverbal behaviours and are learned only through extended interaction with others.[20] Examples of deep-level diversity include personality differences, attitudes, beliefs, and values. In other words, as people in diverse workplaces get to know one another, the initial focus on surface-level differences such as age, race/ethnicity, gender, and physical capabilities is replaced by deeper, more complex knowledge of coworkers.

If managed properly, the shift from surface- to deep-level diversity can accomplish two things.[21] First, coming to know and understand one another better can result in reduced prejudice and conflict. Second, it can lead to stronger social integration. **Social integration** is the degree to which group members are psychologically attracted to working with

Surface-level diversity differences such as age, gender, race/ethnicity, and physical disabilities that are observable, typically unchangeable, and easy to measure

Deep-level diversity differences such as personality and attitudes that are communicated through verbal and nonverbal behaviours and are learned only through extended interaction with others

Social integration the degree to which group members are psychologically attracted to working with one another to accomplish a common objective

one another to accomplish a common objective, or, as one manager put it, "working together to get the job done."

After reading the next two sections, you should be able to

2 understand the special challenges that the dimensions of surface-level diversity pose for managers.

3 explain how the dimensions of deep-level diversity affect individual behaviour and interactions in the workplace.

2 Surface-Level Diversity

Because age, gender, race/ethnicity, and physical disabilities are usually immediately observable, many managers and workers use these dimensions of surface-level diversity to form initial impressions and categorizations of coworkers, bosses, customers, or job applicants. Intentionally or not, sometimes those initial categorizations and impressions lead to decisions or behaviours that discriminate. Consequently, these dimensions of surface-level diversity pose special challenges for managers who are trying to create positive work environments where everyone feels comfortable and no one is advantaged or disadvantaged.

*Let's learn more about those challenges and the ways that **2.1 age, 2.2 gender, 2.3 race/ethnicity,** and **2.4 mental or physical disabilities can affect decisions and behaviours in organizations.***

2.1 Age

Age discrimination is treating people differently (e.g., in hiring and firing, promotion, and compensation decisions) because of their age. According to the Society for Human Resource Management, 53 percent of 428 surveyed managers believed that older workers "didn't keep up with technology," and 28 percent said that older workers were "less flexible." When 55-year-old Norman Abbott began his job search after being downsized, he was rejected for jobs he was well qualified for. "Age discrimination was alive and well, that was obvious," he says. He decided to take matters into his own hands, founding OE Quality Friction Inc., to manufacture brake pads.

So, what's reality and what's myth? Do older employees actually cost more? In some ways, they do. The older people are

Age discrimination treating people differently (e.g., in hiring and firing, promotion, and compensation decisions) because of their age

and the longer they stay with a company, the more the company pays for salaries, pension plans, and vacation time. But older workers cost companies less, too, because they tend to show better judgment, care more about the quality of their work, and have a greater sense of loyalty to their employer. They are also less likely to quit, show up late, or be absent, the cost of which can be substantial. In fact, the myth of older workers being sick more often is not the case: studies show that younger workers, especially those with young children, take more sick days.[22] A survey by Chicago outplacement firm Challenger, Gray & Christmas found that only 3 percent of employees age 50 and over changed jobs in any given year, compared to 10 percent of the entire workforce and 12 percent of workers ages 25 to 34. The study also found that while older workers make up about 14 percent of the workforce, they suffer only 10 percent of all workplace injuries and use fewer health-care benefits than younger workers with school-age children.[23] As for the widespread belief that job performance declines with age, the scientific evidence clearly refutes this stereotype. Performance does not decline with age regardless of the type of job.[24]

What can companies do to reduce age discrimination?[25] To start, managers need to recognize that age discrimination is much more pervasive than they probably think. Whereas "old" used to mean mid-50s, in today's workplace, "old" is closer to 40. When 773 CEOs were asked, "At what age does a worker's productivity peak?" the average age they gave was 43. Thus, age discrimination may be affecting more workers because perceptions about age have changed. In addition, age discrimination is more likely to occur with the aging of baby boomers simply because there are millions more older workers than there used to be. And, because studies show that interviewers rate younger job candidates as more qualified (even when they aren't), companies need to train managers and recruiters to make hiring and promotion decisions on the basis of qualifications, not age. Companies also need to monitor the extent to which older workers receive training. Companies are also monitoring and in many cases increasing the amount of training older workers receive. According to Statistics Canada, between 2002 and 2008 the proportion of employer-sponsored job-related training activities increased more among Canadians 35 to 64, compared to those 25 to 34.[26] Finally, companies need to ensure that younger and older workers interact with one another. One study found that younger workers generally hold positive views of older workers and that the

Exhibit 12.2

Average Earnings by Gender

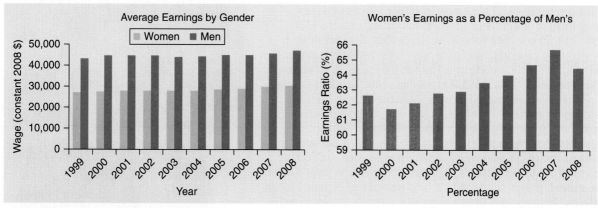

Source: Statistics Canada, Average earnings by sex and work pattern (All earners). Available at http://www40.statcan.gc.ca/l01/cst01/labor01a-eng.htm?sdi=average%20earnings%20sex%20work%20pattern [accessed 17 June 2010].

more time they spent working with older coworkers, the more positive their attitudes became.[27]

2.2 Gender

Gender discrimination occurs when people are treated differently because of their gender. Gender discrimination and racial/ethnic discrimination (discussed in the next section) are often associated with the so-called **glass ceiling,** the invisible barrier that prevents women and minorities from advancing to the top jobs in organizations.

To what extent do women face gender discrimination in the workplace? In some ways, there is much less gender discrimination than there used to be. According to data compiled by the Catalyst organization on women in management in Canada, in 2008, 39 percent of women held management positions (up from 35.4 percent in 2001), and 34.1 percent held senior management positions (up from 24.7 percent in 2001).[28] Since 1989, the number of women running businesses in Canada has risen 60 percent faster than those run by men, with an average annual growth rate of 3.3 percent.[29]

In fact, just over one-third of small and medium-sized enterprises in Canada are owned by women.[30] In addition, according to a 2009 Statistics Canada Labour Force Survey, there are more women than men in Canada's workforce (7.1 million women compared to 6.9 million men), but this is partly attributed to layoffs and cutbacks in male-dominated industries and the movement into self-employment, and the fact that labour rates are cheaper for women.[31]

Although progress has been made, gender discrimination is still found in Canada, as evidenced by the wage gap that still exists between women and men.

Women earn, on average, 80 cents for every dollar earned by a man, and in general, self-employed women do not earn as much as self-employed men. As of 2004, one-third of all women-run enterprises generated less than $50,000 in annual revenue (compared to 16.4 percent for men).[32] At higher levels in organizations, the glass ceiling appears to still be present for women. In 2007, only 5.8 percent of the top five senior positions at Canada's 100 largest companies were filled by women (down from 6.9 percent in 2006), and only 12 percent of corporate directorships in Canada are held by women.[33]

Is gender discrimination the sole reason for the slow rate at which women have been promoted to middle and upper levels of management and corporate boards? Some studies indicate that it's not.[34] In some instances, the slow progress appears to be due to career and job choices. Whereas men's career and job choices are often driven by the search for higher pay and advancement, women are more likely to choose jobs or careers that also give them a greater sense of accomplishment, more control over their work schedules, and easier movement in and out of the workplace.[35] Furthermore, women are historically much more likely than men to prioritize family over work at some time in their careers.

Beyond these reasons, however, it's likely that gender discrimination does play a role in women's slow progress into the higher levels of management. And even if you don't think so, many of the women you work with probably do.

Gender discrimination treating people differently because of their gender

Glass ceiling the invisible barrier that prevents women and minorities from advancing to the top jobs in organizations

The Judy Project

Judy Elder was a Toronto-based business leader who achieved great success at a relatively young age, reaching the top ranks of several large Canadian companies, including Microsoft Canada, IBM Canada, and Ogilvy One. She was known to be extremely passionate about the role women played in business, believing that there was plenty of room at the top for other women. After she passed away in 2002 at the age of 48, "The Judy Project— An Enlightened Leadership Forum for Executive Women," was established in her memory, in partnership with the Joseph L. Rotman School of Management at the University of Toronto. The annual week-long forum for a select group of senior executive women is a powerful and unique leadership-building experience led by CEOs and top academic thought leaders. "In a competitive environment," Colleen Moorehead, project co-founder and past president of E*Trade Canada, believes, "organizations thrive and grow on diversity of thinking and ideas. Selecting from 100% of available talent will always drive better results. Companies with diversity at the top, outperform their not so diverse peers where it counts, shareholder value. Corporate Canada can't afford to write-off 50% of its talent pool." The Judy Project's focus is to equip women to better navigate to the upper reaches of corporations while addressing the realities of the challenges that they face in seeking to be leaders of large organizations.

Courtesy of David Powell/Marketing Magazine.

Sources: M. Johne, "Dynamic soul inspires program," *The Globe and Mail*, 14 June 2001; L. Bogomolny, "Melting the Glass Ceiling," *Canadian Business Online*, 24 April 2006.

The Golf Divide

For decades, golf has been known as the great executive pastime—the white, male executive pastime. Today, however, many executive positions are held by women, who are less likely to be avid golfers, and techies and Silicon Valley executives, who prefer mountain biking, so corporate outings are becoming as diverse as their employees (soccer, cycling, etc.). Still, golf reigns as the activity of choice in many industries and is considered an ideal place to build and sustain business relationships. To get all types of businesspeople prepared to play, the PGA of America has a program called "Golf: For Business and for Life" that sponsors courses at colleges and universities, and the nonprofit Executive Women's Golf Association teaches the game to businesswomen, a growing number of whom are middle managers with executive aspirations.

Source: J. P. Newport and R. Adams, "Business Gold Changes Course," *The Wall Street Journal*, 26–27 May 2007, P1.

Indeed, one study found that more than 90 percent of executive women believed that the glass ceiling had hurt their careers.[36] In another study, 80 percent of women said they left their last organization because the glass ceiling had limited their chances for advancement.[37] A third study indicated that the glass ceiling is prompting more and more women to leave companies to start their own businesses.[38]

So, what can companies do to make sure that women have the same opportunities for development and advancement as men? One strategy is mentoring, or pairing promising female executives with senior executives from whom they can seek advice and support. A vice president at a utility company says "I think it's the single most critical piece to women advancing career-wise. In my experience you need somebody to help guide you and . . . go to bat for you."[39] In fact, 91 percent of female executives have a mentor at some point and feel their mentor was critical to their advancement.

Another strategy is to make sure that male-dominated social activities don't unintentionally exclude women. Nearly half (47 percent) of women in the work force believe that "exclusion from informal networks" makes it more difficult to advance their careers. By contrast, just 18 percent of CEOs thought this was a problem.[40] One final strategy is to designate a "go-to

> The evidence strongly indicates that there is **strong** and **persistent** racial and ethnic discrimination in the hiring processes of many organizations.

person" other than their supervisor that women can talk to if they believe that they are being held back or discriminated against because of their gender. Make sure this person has the knowledge and authority to conduct a fair, confidential internal investigation.[41]

2.3 Race/Ethnicity

Racial and ethnic discrimination occurs when people are treated differently because of their race or ethnicity. To what extent is racial and ethnic discrimination a factor in the workplace? And how is it addressed in the Canadian workplace? In Canada, the Canadian Human Rights Commission (CHRC) administers the Canadian Human Rights Act (CHRA) and is responsible for the compliance of employers under the Employment Equity Act. The CHRC reports that although the share of jobs held by visible minorities increased from 9.7 percent in 1997 to 14.9 percent in 2006, only 5.1 percent of visible minorities were represented in senior management positions. By sector, some gains have been made by visible minorities, most notably in the banking sector, where they held 23.5 percent of all jobs and 8.7 percent of all senior management positions.[42] As noted previously, the role of visible minorities in Canada's workplace continues to expand in the face of an aging Canadian workforce and a lower birth rate. By 2017, visible minorities are expected to represent about 20 percent of Canada's available workforce, and in some major cities the proportion will be closer to 50 percent. However, a national survey on career satisfaction and advancement of visible minorities in corporate Canada reported that visible minorities were more likely to perceive workplace barriers and lower levels of career satisfaction compared to white/Caucasian employees. Workplace barriers included the following: a perceived lack of fairness in terms of career advancement; inequality in performance standards; and fewer high-profile assignments. Given that career satisfaction is linked to productivity, the results are especially important for Canadian businesses—another reason to embrace diversity in the workplace.[43]

What accounts for the disparities between the percentages of minority groups in the general population and their smaller representation in management positions? Some studies have found that the disparities are due to pre-existing differences in training, education, and skills; when workers have similar skills, training, and education, they are much more likely to have similar jobs and salaries.[44]

Other studies, however, provide increasingly strong direct evidence of racial or ethnic discrimination in the workplace. For example, one study directly tested hiring discrimination by sending pairs of black and white males and pairs of Hispanic and non-Hispanic males to apply for the same jobs. Each pair had résumés with identical qualifications, and all were trained to present themselves in similar ways to minimize differences during interviews. The researchers found that the white males got three times as many job offers as the black males, and that the non-Hispanic males got three times as many offers as the Hispanic males.[45]

Another study, which used similar methods to test hiring procedures at 149 different companies, found that whites received 10 percent more interviews than blacks. Half of the whites interviewed received job offers, but only 11 percent of the blacks. And when job offers were made, blacks were much more likely to be offered lower-level positions, while whites were more likely to be offered jobs at higher levels than the jobs they had applied for.[46]

Critics of these studies point out that it's nearly impossible to train different applicants to give identical responses in job interviews and that differences in interviewing skills may have somehow accounted for the results. However, British researchers found similar kinds of discrimination just by sending letters of inquiry to prospective employers. As in the other studies, the letters were identical except for the applicant's race. Employers frequently responded to letters from Afro-Caribbean, Indian, or Pakistani "applicants" by indicating that the positions had been filled. By contrast, they often responded to white, Anglo-Saxon "applicants" by inviting them to face-to-face interviews. Similar results were found with Vietnamese and Greek "applicants" in Australia.[47] In short, the evidence indicates that there is strong and persistent racial and ethnic discrimination in the hiring processes of many organizations.

What can companies do to make sure that people of all racial and ethnic

Racial and ethnic discrimination treating people differently because of their race or ethnicity

backgrounds have the same opportunities?[48] Start by looking at the numbers. Compare the hiring rates of whites to the hiring rates for racial and ethnic applicants. Do the same thing for promotions within the company. See if nonwhite workers quit the company at higher rates than white workers. Also, survey employees to compare white and nonwhite employees' satisfaction with jobs, bosses, and the company, as well as their perceptions concerning equal treatment. Next, if the numbers indicate racial or ethnic disparities, consider employing a private firm to test your hiring system by having applicants of different races with identical qualifications apply for jobs in your company.[49]

Another step companies can take is to eliminate unclear selection and promotion criteria. Vague criteria allow decision makers to focus on non-job-related characteristics that may unintentionally lead to employment discrimination. Instead, selection and promotion criteria should spell out the specific knowledge, skills, abilities, education, and experience needed to perform a job well.

Finally, creating a culture that is visionary in its approach to diversity is key. It's not surprising that when it came time for PepsiCo to choose a new CEO, the board picked Indian-born Indra Nooyi. PepsiCo has a long history of diversity, stretching back to the end of World War II, when President Walter Mack hired Edward Boyd away from the National Urban League to head a team charged with launching a marketing program for African American consumers. In every area of the country where Boyd's team ran a marketing blitz, Pepsi sales increased, and soon Pepsi-Cola overtook market leader Coca-Cola in cities like Cleveland and Chicago. One of the most successful campaigns was a series of print advertisements titled "Leaders in Their Fields," which profiled the accomplishments

Disability an activity limitation or participation restriction associated with a physical or mental condition or health problem.

Disability discrimination treating people differently because of their disabilities

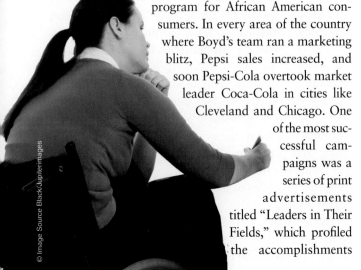

© Image Source Black/Jupiterimages

TECHNOLOGY = ABILITY

Individuals with disabilities face unique challenges in the workforce. Richard Saab became paralyzed from an aneurysm and was forced to forego his job as a cook because he could no longer stand. Following his recovery, he wanted to cook again. The Florida Department of Vocational Rehabilitation was able to assist him by acquiring a standing wheelchair, which enabled him to assume a position as a line chef again. Development of new assistive technologies not only helps people avoid workplace injury (for example, from poor ergonomic design at computer workstations) but also helps people with disabilities achieve their personal goals and contribute to the success of organizations.

Source: "Standing Wheelchair for a Chef," available online at http://www.workrerc.org [accessed 26 June 2008].

of professional and successful African Americans. Pepsi's print campaign was the first to shun the stereotypical images of African Americans used in print and other advertisements. As you can see from PepsiCo's history, it takes a long time and a lot of effort to create a culture of diversity. But good hiring practices contribute to such an organizational culture and make it easier to achieve what PepsiCo has.[50]

2.4 Mental or Physical Disabilities

One in every seven Canadians—that is more than 4.4 million people—is living with a disability.[51] A **disability** is defined as an activity limitation or participation restriction associated with a physical or mental condition or health problem.[52] In Canada, the most common types of disability involve pain, mobility, and agility—factors generally related to an aging population.[53] **Disability discrimination** occurs when people are treated differently because of their disabilities. To what extent is disability discrimination a factor in the workplace? In *The Business Case for Accessibility*, Bill Wilkerson summarizes the human resources potential of persons with disabilities in this way: "For far too many years, people with disabilities have been ignored in the marketplace. Yet this significant segment of the population is made up of many dedicated and talented people with much-needed abilities that have so far been under-utilized in the work environment."[54] Canadian statistics report that although 75.1 percent of working-age Canadians (those 14 to 64 years of age) were employed in 2006, only 53.5 percent of working-age

Sander Crombeen/Shutterstock

Work Force Health on the Decline

According to the Council for Disability Awareness, the general health of the American work force is declining because of age and questionable lifestyle choices (poor diet, lack of exercise, etc.). Rising obesity rates are causing back pain, hip and knee injury (often leading to joint replacement), and diabetes. Claims for depression and other nervous disorders, chronic bronchitis, and asthma are also increasing. Many companies are finding ways to accommodate workers. American Express has made its cafeteria wheelchair accessible and rearranged work schedules to coincide with the paratransit system. Sylvania has created flexible shifts for disabled employees, and General Motors enlists the help of an ergonomic specialist to help assign disabled workers to jobs that won't aggravate their ailments.

Source: M. P. McQueen, "Workplace Disabilities Are on the Rise," *The Wall Street Journal*, 1 May 2007, D1.

Canadians with disabilities were.[55] In terms of income levels, individuals with disabilities earn less than people without disabilities, and women with disabilities earn far less than men with disabilities. Anna MacQuarrie, director of policy and programs for the Canadian Association for Community Living, says that "about 750,000 Canadians live with intellectual disabilities and they are predominantly among the poorest of the poor in Canada."[56]

What accounts for the disparities between the employment and income levels of able people and people with disabilities? One factor is that as a group, individuals with disabilities often have lower levels of education than those without, and corresponding lower levels of employment. But education alone does not explain the employment and income gaps that exist. "Even with education, people with disabilities do not achieve the same general labour market outcomes as those without. Other serious barriers include negative attitudes, inaccessible infrastructure, and the lack of various supports."[57] Studies show that as long as companies make reasonable accommodations for disabilities (e.g., changing procedures or equipment), people with disabilities perform their jobs just as well as able people. They also have better safety records and are no more likely to be absent or quit their jobs.[58]

What can companies do to make sure that people with disabilities have the same opportunities as everyone else? A good place to start is to commit to providing reasonable workplace accommodations to current and prospective employees with disabilities. Workplace modifications can be resource specific (e.g., job redesign, modified work schedules, computer aids) or physical/structural (e.g., handrails, modified workstations, accessible washrooms).[59] Accommodations for disabilities needn't be expensive. According to the Job Accommodation Network, 71 percent of accommodations cost employers $500 or less, and 20 percent of accommodations don't cost anything at all.[60]

Finally, companies should actively recruit qualified workers with disabilities. In order to do so, Canadian employers need to overcome some misconceptions related to persons with disabilities. For example:

Myth: Persons with disabilities can't keep up with other workers.

Reality: 90 percent of persons with disabilities rated average or better on job performance than their non-disabled colleagues.

Myth: A person with a disability will miss a lot of work.

Reality: 86 percent of people with disabilities rated average or better on attendance than their non-disabled colleagues.

Myth: A person with a disability will have more accidents on the job.

Reality: 98 percent of people with a disability rate average or better in work safety compared to their non-disabled colleagues.

Myth: Persons with disabilities don't really want to work.

Reality: Staff retention is 72 percent higher among persons with disabilities.

If an employer can move beyond these myths, hiring individuals with disabilities can make economic sense based on a simple equation: employers need skilled workers; persons with disabilities are a largely untapped human resource available to meet today's growing labour and skill shortages; and persons with disabilities are a large, growing consumer market.[61]

3 Deep-Level Diversity

As you learned in Section 2, people often use the dimensions of surface-level diversity to form initial impressions about others. Over time, however, initial impressions based on age, gender, race/ethnicity, and mental or physical disabilities give way to deeper impressions based on behaviour and psychological characteristics. When we think of others this way, we are focusing on deep-level diversity, or the differences that can be learned only through extended interaction with others—for examples, differences in personality, attitudes, beliefs, and values. In short, recognizing deep-level diversity requires getting to know and understand one another better. And that matters because it can result in less prejudice, discrimination, and conflict in the workplace. These changes can then lead to better *social integration*, the degree to which organizational or group members are psychologically attracted to working with one another to accomplish a common objective.

Stop for a second and think about current or previous manager. What words would you use to describe him or her? Is your boss introverted or extraverted? Agreeable or disagreeable? Organized or disorganized? When you describe your manager or others in this way, you are describing dispositions and personality.

A **disposition** is the tendency to respond to situations and events in a predetermined

manner. **Personality** is the relatively stable set of behaviours, attitudes, and emotions displayed over time that makes people different from each other.[62] In other words, it is the person's core personality. In the last decade personality research conducted in different cultures, different settings, and different languages has shown that five basic dimensions of personality account for most of the differences in people's behaviours, attitudes, and emotions. The *Big Five Personality Dimensions* are extraversion, emotional stability, agreeableness, conscientiousness, and openness to experience.[63]

> Introverts and extraverts should be correctly matched to their jobs.

Extraversion is the degree to which someone is active, assertive, gregarious, sociable, talkative, and energized by others. In contrast to extraverts, introverts are less active, prefer to be alone, and are shy, quiet, and reserved. For the best results in the workplace, introverts and extraverts should be correctly matched to their jobs.

Emotional stability is the degree to which someone is not angry, depressed, anxious, emotional, insecure, or excitable. People who are emotionally stable respond well to stress. In other words, they can maintain a calm, problem-solving attitude in even the toughest situations (e.g., conflict, hostility, dangerous conditions, or extreme time pressures). By contrast, emotionally unstable people find it difficult to handle the most basic demands of their jobs under only moderately stressful situations and become distraught, tearful, self-doubting, and anxious. Emotional stability is particularly important for high-stress jobs such as police work, firefighting, emergency medical treatment, and piloting planes.

Agreeableness is the degree to which someone is cooperative, polite, flexible, forgiving, good-natured, tolerant, and trusting. Basically, agreeable people are easy to work with and be around, whereas disagreeable people are distrusting and difficult to work with and be around.

Conscientiousness is the degree to which someone is organized, hardworking, responsible, persevering, thorough, and achievement oriented. Ninety-two studies across five occupational groups (professionals, police, managers, sales, and skilled/semiskilled jobs) with a combined total of 12,893 study participants indicated that, on average, conscientious people are inherently more motivated and are better at their jobs.[64]

Openness to experience is the degree to which someone is curious, broad-minded, and open to new

---

Disposition the tendency to respond to situations and events in a predetermined manner

Personality the relatively stable set of behaviours, attitudes, and emotions displayed over time that makes people different from one another

Extraversion the degree to which someone is active, assertive, gregarious, sociable, talkative, and energized by others

Emotional stability the degree to which someone is not angry, depressed, anxious, emotional, insecure, and excitable

Agreeableness the degree to which someone is cooperative, polite, flexible, forgiving, good-natured, tolerant, and trusting

Conscientiousness the degree to which someone is organized, hardworking, responsible, persevering, thorough, and achievement oriented

Openness to experience the degree to which someone is curious, broadminded, and open to new ideas, things, and experiences; is spontaneous; and has a high tolerance for ambiguity

ideas, things, and experiences; is spontaneous; and has a high tolerance for ambiguity. People in marketing, advertising, research, or other creative jobs need to be curious, open to new ideas, and spontaneous.

Which of the Big Five Personality Dimensions has the largest impact on behaviour in organizations? The cumulative results indicate that conscientiousness is related to job performance across five different occupational groups (professionals, police, managers, sales, and skilled or semiskilled jobs).[65] In short, people "who are dependable, persistent, goal directed, and organized tend to be higher performers on virtually any job; viewed negatively, those who are careless, irresponsible, low-achievement striving, and impulsive tend to be lower performers on virtually any job."[66] The results also indicate that extraversion is related to performance in jobs, such as sales and management, that involve significant interaction with others. In people-intensive jobs like these, it helps to be sociable, assertive, and talkative and to have energy and be able to energize others. Finally, people who are extraverted and open to experience seem to do much better in training. Being curious and open to new experiences as well as sociable, assertive, talkative, and full of energy helps people perform better in learning situations.[67]

How Can Diversity Be Managed?

How much should companies change their standard business practices to accommodate the diversity of their workers? What do you do when a talented top executive has a drinking problem that only seems to affect his behaviour at company social events or when entertaining clients, where he has made inappropriate advances toward female employees? What do you do when, despite aggressive company policies against racial discrimination, employees continue to tell racial jokes and publicly post cartoons displaying racial humour? And, since many people confuse diversity with employment equity, what do you do to make sure that your company's diversity practices and policies are viewed as benefiting all workers and not just some workers?

White Males Lead Diversity?

At PricewaterhouseCoopers (PwC), the chief diversity officer, Chris Simmons, who is black, asked Keith Ruth to help lead the company's diversity effort. Ruth was surprised to be asked—because he is white. An emerging trend in managing diversity is to put white males in charge. The rationale is that unless white males are heavily involved and even champion diversity efforts, those efforts will not ever become part of the mainstream. PwC, Coca-Cola, and Georgia Power all have white men running diversity programs. For PwC's Simmons, it's an important step away from thinking that only women and minorities should be leading the diversity movement.

Source: E. White, "Diveristy Programs Look to Involve White Males as Leaders," *The Wall Street Journal*, 7 May 2007, B4.

No doubt about it, questions like these make managing diversity one of the toughest challenges that managers face.[68] Nonetheless, there are steps companies can take to begin to address these issues.

After reading the next section, you should be able to

4 explain the basic principles and practices that can be used to manage diversity.

4 Managing Diversity

As discussed earlier, diversity programs try to create a positive work environment where no one is advantaged or disadvantaged, where "we" is everyone, where everyone can do his or her best work, where differences are respected and not ignored, and where everyone feels comfortable. *Let's begin to address those goals by learning about 4.1 different diversity paradigms, 4.2 diversity principles, and 4.3 diversity training and practices.*

4.1 Diversity Paradigms

There are several different methods or paradigms for managing diversity: the discrimination and fairness paradigm, the access and legitimacy paradigm, and the learning and effectiveness paradigm.[69] The *discrimination and fairness paradigm,* which is the most common method of approaching diversity, focuses on equal opportunity, fair treatment, recruitment of minorities, and strict compliance with the equal employment opportunity laws. Under this approach, success is usually measured by how well companies achieve recruitment, promotion, and retention goals for women, people of different racial/ethnic backgrounds, or other underrepresented groups. For example, one manager says "If you don't measure something, it doesn't count. You measure your market share. You measure your profitability. The same should be true for diversity. There has to be some way of measuring whether you did, in fact, cast your net widely, and whether the company is better off today in terms of the experience of people of colour than it was a few years ago. I measure my market share and my profitability. Why not this?"[70] The primary benefit of the discrimination and fairness paradigm is that it generally brings about fairer treatment of employees and increases demographic diversity. The primary limitation is that the focus of diversity remains on the surface-level dimensions of gender, race, and ethnicity.

The *access and legitimacy paradigm* focuses on the acceptance and celebration of differences to ensure that the diversity within the company matches the diversity found among primary stakeholders such as customers, suppliers, and local communities. This is similar to the *business growth* advantage of diversity discussed earlier in the chapter. The basic idea behind this approach is attracting a broader customer base by creating a more diverse workforce. "We are living in an increasingly multicultural country, and new ethnic groups are quickly gaining consumer power. Our company needs a demographically more diverse work force to help us gain access to these differentiated segments."[71] Consistent with this goal, Ed Adams, vice president of human resources for Enterprise Rent-a-Car, says "We want people who speak the same language, literally and figuratively, as our customers. We don't set quotas. We say [to our managers], 'Reflect your local market.'"[72] The primary benefit of this approach is that it establishes a clear business reason for diversity. Like the discrimination and fairness paradigm, however, it focuses only on the surface-level diversity dimensions of gender, race, and ethnicity. Furthermore, employees who are assigned

responsibility for customers and stakeholders on the basis of their gender, race, or ethnicity may eventually feel frustrated and exploited.

Whereas the discrimination and fairness paradigm focuses on assimilation (having a demographically

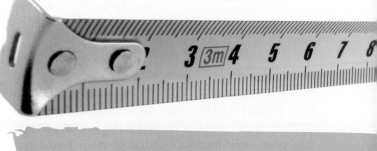

© Robert Bremec/iStockphoto.com

IF YOU DON'T MEASURE SOMETHING, . . .

GOOD TIP!

How to Create a Learning and Effectiveness Diversity Paradigm

1. Understand that a diverse work force will embody different perspectives and approaches to work. Value variety of opinion and insight.

2. Recognize both the learning opportunities and the challenges that the expression of different perspectives presents for your organization.

3. Set high standards of performance for everyone.

4. Create an organizational culture that stimulates personal development.

5. Encourage openness and a high tolerance for debate. Support constructive conflict on work-related matters.

6. Create an organizational culture in which workers feel valued.

7. Establish a clear mission and make sure it is widely understood. This keeps discussions about work differences from degenerating into debates about the validity of individual perspectives.

8. Create a relatively egalitarian, nonbureaucratic structure.

Source: D. A. Thomas and R. J. Ely, "Making Differences Matter: A New Paradigm for Managing Diversity," *Harvard Business Review* 74 (September–October 1996); 79–90.

---

representative workforce), and the access and legitimacy paradigm focuses on differentiation (having demographic differences inside the company match those of key customers and stakeholders), the *learning and effectiveness paradigm* focuses on integrating deep-level diversity differences, such as personality, attitudes, beliefs, and values, into the actual work of the organization. Aetna's 28,000 employees are diverse not only in terms of gender, ethnicity and race, but also by age group, sexual orientation, work styles and levels, perspective, education, skills, and other characteristics. Raymond Arroyo, head of diversity at Aetna, says, "Diversity at Aetna means treating individuals individually, leveraging everyone's best, and maximizing the powerful potential of our workforce." He adds, "Part of a top diversity executive's role in any organization is to integrate diversity into every aspect of a business, including the workforce, customers, suppliers, products, services and even into the community a business serves."[73]

The learning and effectiveness paradigm is consistent with achieving organizational plurality. **Organizational plurality** is a work environment where (1) all members are empowered to contribute in a way that maximizes the benefits to the organization, customers, and themselves, and (2) the individuality of each member is respected by not segmenting or polarizing people on the basis of their membership in a particular group.[74]

The learning and effectiveness diversity paradigm offers four benefits.[75] First, it values common ground. Dave Thomas of the Harvard Business School explains:

Holger Hill/fStop/Jupiterimages

"Like the fairness paradigm, it promotes equal opportunity for all individuals. And like the access paradigm, it acknowledges cultural differences among people and recognizes the value in those differences. Yet this new model for managing diversity lets the organization internalize differences among employees so that it learns and grows because of them. Indeed, with the model fully in place, members of the organization can say, 'We are all on the same team, with our differences—not despite them.'"[76]

Second, this paradigm makes a distinction between individual and group differences. When diversity focuses only on differences between groups, such as females versus males, large differences within groups are ignored.[77] For example, think of the women you know at work. Now, think for a second about what they have in common. After that, think about how they're different. If your situation is typical, the list of differences should be just as long as the list of commonalities if not longer. In short, managers can achieve a greater understanding of diversity and their employees by treating them as individuals and by realizing that not all employees want the same things at work.[78]

Third, because the focus is on individual differences, the learning and effectiveness paradigm is less likely to encounter the conflict,

> **Organizational plurality** a work environment where (1) all members are empowered to contribute in a way that maximizes the benefits to the organization, customers, and themselves, and (2) the individuality of each member is respected by not segmenting or polarizing people on the basis of their membership in a particular group

IT DOESN'T COUNT.

backlash, and divisiveness sometimes associated with diversity programs that focus only on group differences. Ray Haines, a consultant who has helped companies deal with the aftermath of diversity programs that became divisive, says, "There's a large amount of backlash related to diversity training. It stirs up a lot of hostility, anguish, and resentment but doesn't give people tools to deal with [the backlash]. You have people come in and talk about their specific ax to grind."[79] Not all diversity programs are divisive or lead to conflict. But, by focusing on individual rather than group differences, the learning and effectiveness paradigm helps to minimize these potential problems.

Finally, unlike the other diversity paradigms that simply focus on the value of being different (primarily in terms of surface-level diversity), the learning and effectiveness paradigm focuses on bringing different talents and perspectives *together* (i.e., deep-level diversity) to make the best organizational decisions and to produce innovative, competitive products and services.

4.2 Diversity Principles

Diversity paradigms are general approaches or strategies for managing diversity. Whatever diversity paradigm a manager chooses, diversity principles will help managers do a better job of *managing company diversity programs*.[80]

In a study of the Top 1000 Canadian companies and employers filing employment equity reports, researchers at the Richard Ivey School of Business identified nine action areas for managing diversity.[81]

Linking diversity to strategic business goals. At Alberta-based Syncrude Canada, understanding of the strategic value of diversity is expressed by the following equation: high job satisfaction = motivation = going above and beyond in times of change and growth = breakthrough business performance. In general, larger organizations are more likely to include diversity in their mission statement, to have a diversity council (that includes executives), to link diversity to business strategy, and to have a clear understanding of how diversity links to economic performance.

Including diversity in human resource planning. Organizations that understand how diversity can contribute to success will make strides to incorporate diversity in human resource planning. For example, Xerox Corporation traced the career path—specifically, the key jobs held by top executives in the company—and then set goals for placing women and visible minorities in those jobs in order to ensure diversity in future top executive candidates.

Recruiting a diverse workforce. Organizations can ensure that recruiting materials (ads, brochures, website), the recruiting process, and the pools used to identify potential hires are conducive to a diverse set of applicants. Innoversity, a Canadian nonprofit organization that works to create opportunities for visible minorities, created a showcase for artists and journalists from diverse ethnic groups to pitch their ideas to producers and broadcasters from across Canada. To reach growing hiring needs, Suncor Energy now recruits across the world, including in countries such as Venezuela and South Africa.[82]

Selecting a diverse workforce. To facilitate diversity in the selection process, organizations should utilize a structured interview process, use a diverse team to interview candidates, and identify ways that candidates can demonstrate job qualifications beyond traditional experiences. The University of British Columbia provides training to recruitment managers on employment equity in the interview process, and Corus Entertainment Inc. forwards job openings to organizations representing the disabled, such as the Canadian National Institute for the Blind.[83]

Training and developing a diverse staff. Research shows that women and visible minorities are more likely to be chosen for management positions in organizations that provide more training and development opportunities. This highlights critical elements needed for career advancement among a diverse workforce. TD Bank, for example, offers a training curriculum to help foreign-educated professionals integrate into the workforce, and also offers a mentoring and internship program.[84]

Maksym Bondarchuk/Shutterstock

Monitoring the effectiveness of staffing for diversity. Organizations that fall under Canada's Employment Equity Act are required to submit statistics annually to the federal government. However, other firms may also collect data to assess the level of workforce diversity by tracking the diversity of applicants, new hires, promotions, and turnover rates.

Providing work-life flexibility and *Creating an inclusive working environment.* Organizations offering flexible organizational structures and benefits to employees create a more inclusive workplace environment for employees with a variety of family situations. An inclusive work environment has been linked to increased productivity and profitability. Flexibility benefits might include these: flexible work scheduling, work-at-home options, job sharing, reduced work hours, a compressed work week, part-time employment, and an on-site or company-supported dependent care centre.

Senior executive support for diversity. Support from senior management can be critical for creating and promoting workplace diversity. Home Depot Canada created a Diversity and Inclusion Committee in 2007, led by the VP of Human Resources, to measure recruitment activities in relation to diverse groups and to increase the number of disabled employees. Calgary-based Agrium Inc., a leading retail supplier of agricultural products, seeks to establish a long-term, formal diversity and inclusiveness strategy for the company with a program led by the CEO and supported by the in-house Diversity Council.[85]

4.3 Diversity Training and Practices

Organizations use diversity training and several common diversity practices to manage diversity. There are two basic types of diversity training programs. **Awareness training** is designed to raise employees' awareness of diversity issues, such as the five dimensions discussed in this chapter, and to get employees to challenge underlying assumptions or stereotypes they may have about others. L'Oréal Canada has developed a training program where baby boomers and Generation X and Y employees meet to discuss their different expectations in the workplace. They also work in mixed-generation

Comstock/Jupiterimages

teams to learn about and appreciate one another's strengths and aptitudes.[86] At Shell Canada, senior management teams participate in gender-in-the-workplace training sessions to increase awareness of how gender differences affect communication and leadership styles. Also, all Shell employees are required to complete diversity-awareness training, which covers topics such as cross-cultural communication, discrimination, and the business case for inclusiveness.[87]

By contrast, **skills-based diversity training** teaches employees the practical skills they need for managing a

Awareness training training that is designed to raise employees' awareness of diversity issues and to challenge the underlying assumptions or stereotypes they may have about others

Skills-based diversity training training that teaches employees the practical skills they need for managing a diverse workforce, such as flexibility and adaptability, negotiation, problem solving, and conflict resolution

Mixed Messages

Managers need to think twice before communicating to today's diverse workforce, to ensure they consider the cultural context of the listener, as variations exist in language, tone, phonetics, and verbal and nonverbal cues across cultures. For example, in Canada, shaking your head horizontally means "no," but in India a similar gesture signifies understanding or "yes." A "thumbs-up" in Canada can mean *good job* or *good luck*, but in Australia, Thailand, and Iraq it is perceived as an obscene gesture. Canadians are also known to be very even-toned in their speech, a sign of respect and professionalism; however, other cultures communicate in a much more animated and boisterous tone, which may be perceived by Canadians as anger or agitation. With workforce diversity nearing record levels in Canada, managers must take note of cultural differences in order to reduce communication gaps and misunderstandings.

Sources: S. Tatla, "Thumbs Up Not Always a Sign of Approval," *Financial Post*, April 28, 2010, http://www.financialpost.com/Thumbs+always+sign+approval/2961001/story.html; B. Koerner, "What Does a Thumbs Up Mean in Iraq?" Slate.com, March 28, 2003, http://slate.msn.com/id/2080812.

diverse workforce such as flexibility and adaptability, negotiation, problem solving, and conflict resolution.[88] Retail chain Canada Safeway Limited provides employees with hands-on training materials and a resource library on the company's diversity website, which is available on the company intranet. Similarly, KPMG Canada has introduced an online diversity training program, mandatory for all employees, that includes customized module for employees, managers, and executive-level staff.[89]

Companies also use diversity audits, diversity pairing, and minority experiences for top executives to better manage diversity. **Diversity audits** are formal assessments that measure employee and management attitudes, investigate the extent to which people are advantaged or disadvantaged with respect to hiring and promotions, and review companies' diversity-related policies and procedures. Saskatchewan's electricity provider, SaskPower, measures the progress of its diversity-related recruitment goals through regular reporting to senior management. Similarly, the Royal Bank of Canada ensures that the company maintains a leadership role in diversity by preparing an annual diversity progress report in addition to its annual employment equity report.[90]

Diversity audits formal assessments that measure employee and management attitudes, investigate the extent to which people are advantaged or disadvantaged with respect to hiring and promotions, and review companies' diversity-related policies and procedures

Diversity pairing a mentoring program in which people of different cultural backgrounds, sexes, or races/ethnicities are paired together to get to know one another and change stereotypical beliefs and attitudes

Earlier in the chapter you learned that *mentoring,* pairing a junior employee with a senior employee, is a common strategy for creating learning and promotional opportunities for women. Diversity pairing is a special kind of mentoring. In **diversity pairing,** people of different cultural backgrounds, sexes, or races/ethnicities are paired for mentoring. The hope is that stereotypical beliefs and attitudes will change as people get to know one another as individuals.[91] HSBC Bank Canada established an Aboriginal mentorship program that paired senior-level executives with Aboriginal employees. Ernst & Young Canada has developed a number of unique "reverse mentoring" programs, including one where junior-level LGBT (lesbian, gay, bisexual, transgendered) employees mentor senior executives on issues relating to generational differences and sexual orientation. As well, its Coaching Our Leaders program pairs partners with mentors who are visible minorities or women to facilitate greater understanding on issues related to religion, culture, or gender.[92]

In summary, population trends and related growth in immigration levels in Canada suggest that managers must be aware of, and prepared to manage, the cultural diversity of the Canadian workforce. "Hence, opportunities exist for senior managers who wish to move their firms ahead in the competition for the next generation of talent. By developing a diverse internal pipeline to build the diverse top management teams of the future, senior executives can move their companies to the forefront of the Canadian business community in the area of diversity and inclusiveness."[93]

By the Numbers

30% visible minorities employed at Ernst & Young LLP.

42% jobs held by women in Canada in 1976.

1977 year that the Canadian Human Rights Act was passed.

7 diversity principles.

5 personality dimensions.

60 average age of baby boomers in 2010.

Visit **icanmgmt.com** to find the resources you need today!

Located at the back of the textbook are rip-out Chapter Review cards. Make sure you also go online to check out other tools that MGMT offers to help you successfully pass your course.

- Interactive Quizzes
- Key Terms Flashcards
- Audio Chapter Summaries
- PowerPoint Slides

- Interactive Games
- Crossword Puzzles
- "Reel to Reel" and "Biz Flix" videos
- Cases and Exercises

MOTIVATION

What Is Motivation?

What makes people happiest and most productive at work? Is it money, benefits, opportunities for growth, interesting work, or something else altogether? And if people desire different things, how can a company keep everyone motivated? It takes insight and hard work to motivate workers to join the company, perform well, and then stay with the company. Professor Marylene Gagne, of the John Molson School of Business in Montreal, indicates the importance of both intrinsic and extrinsic motivation to managers.[1]

So what is motivation? **Motivation** is the set of forces that initiates, directs, and makes people persist in their efforts to accomplish a goal.[2] *Initiation of effort* is concerned with the choices that people make about how much effort to put forth in their jobs. ("Do I really knock myself out for these performance appraisals or just do a decent job?") *Direction of effort* is concerned with the choices that people make in deciding where to put forth effort in their jobs. ("I should be spending time with my high-dollar accounts instead of learning this new computer system!") *Persistence of effort* is concerned with the choices that people make about how long they will put forth effort in their jobs before reducing or eliminating those efforts. ("I'm only halfway through the project, and I'm exhausted. Do I plough through to the end, or just call it quits?") Initiation, direction, and persistence are at the heart of motivation.

Motivation the set of forces that initiates, directs, and makes people persist in their efforts to accomplish a goal

 Learning Outcomes

1 explain the basics of motivation.

2 use equity theory to explain how employees' perceptions of fairness affect motivation.

3 use expectancy theory to describe how workers' expectations about rewards, effort, and the link between rewards and performance influence motivation.

4 explain how reinforcement theory works and how it can be used to motivate.

5 describe the components of goal-setting theory and how managers can use them to motivate workers.

6 discuss how the entire motivation model can be used to motivate workers.

© iStockphoto.com/Greg Epperson

After reading the next section, you should be able to

1 explain the basics of motivation.

1 Basics of Motivation

Take your right hand and point the palm toward your face. Keep your thumb and pinky finger straight and bend the three middle fingers so the tips are touching your palm. Now rotate your wrist back and forth. If you were in the Regent Square Tavern that hand signal would tell waitress Marjorie Landale that you wanted a Yuengling beer. Marjorie, who isn't deaf, would not have understood that sign a few years ago. But with a state school for the deaf nearby, the tavern always has its share of deaf customers, so she decided on her own to take classes to learn how to sign. At first, deaf customers would signal for a pen and paper to write out their orders. But after Marjorie signalled that she was learning to sign, "their eyes [would] light up, and they [would] finger-spell their order." Word quickly spread as the students started bringing in their friends, classmates, teachers, and hearing friends as well. Says Marjorie, "The deaf customers·are patient with my amateur signing. They appreciate the effort."[3]

What would motivate an employee like Marjorie to voluntarily learn a new language like American Sign

Language? (Sign language is every bit as much of a language as French or Spanish.) She wasn't paid to take classes in her free time. She chose to do it on her own. And while she undoubtedly makes more tip money with a full bar than with an empty one, it's highly unlikely that she began her classes with the objective of making more money. Just what is it that motivates employees like Marjorie Landale?

*Let's learn more about motivation by building a basic model of motivation out of **1.1 effort and performance, 1.2 need satisfaction,** and **1.3 extrinsic and intrinsic rewards.** Then we'll discuss **1.4 how to motivate people with this basic model of motivation.***

1.1 Effort and Performance

When most people think of work motivation, they think that working hard (effort) should lead to a good job (performance). Exhibit 13.1 shows a basic model of work motivation and performance, displaying this process. The first thing to notice about Exhibit 13.1 is that this is a basic model of work motivation *and* performance. In practice, it's almost impossible to talk about one without mentioning the other. Not surprisingly, managers often assume motivation to be the only determinant of performance when they say things such as "Your performance was really terrible last quarter. What's the matter? Aren't you as motivated as you used to be?" In fact, motivation is just one of three primary determinants of job performance. In industrial psychology, job performance is frequently represented by this equation:

$$\text{Job Performance} =$$
$$\text{Motivation} \times \text{Ability} \times \text{Situational Constraints}$$

In this formula, *job performance* is how well someone performs the requirements of the job. *Motivation,* as defined above, is effort, the degree to which someone works hard to do the job well. *Ability* is the degree to which workers possess the knowledge, skills, and talent needed to do a job well. And *situational constraints* are factors beyond the control of individual employees such as tools, policies, and resources that have an effect on job performance.

Since job performance is a multiplicative function of motivation times ability

Needs the physical or psychological requirements that must be met to ensure survival and well-being

times situational constraints, job performance will suffer if any one of these components is weak. Does this mean that motivation doesn't matter? No, not at all. It just means that all the motivation in the world won't translate into high performance when you have little ability and high situational constraints. So, while we will spend this chapter developing a model of work motivation, it is important to remember that ability and situational constraints affect job performance as well.

1.2 Need Satisfaction

In Exhibit 13.1, we started with a very basic model of motivation in which effort leads to job performance. But managers want to know, "What leads to effort?" Determining employee needs is the first step to answering that question.

Needs are the physical or psychological requirements that must be met to ensure survival and well-being.[4] As shown on the left side of Exhibit 13.2, a person's unmet need creates an uncomfortable, internal state of tension that must be resolved. For example, if you normally skip breakfast but then have to work through lunch, chances are you'll be so hungry by late afternoon that the only thing you'll be motivated to do is find something to eat. So, according to needs theories, people are motivated by unmet needs. But a need no longer motivates once it is met. When this occurs, people become satisfied, as shown on the right side of Exhibit 13.2.

Note: Throughout the chapter, as we build on this basic model, the parts of the model that we've already discussed will appear shaded in colour. Since we've already discussed the effort $\longrightarrow$ performance part of the model, those components are shown with a coloured background. When we add new parts to the model, they will have a white background. Since we're adding need satisfaction to the model at this step, the need-satisfaction components of unsatisfied need, tension, energized to

Exhibit 13.1

A Basic Model of Work Motivation and Performance

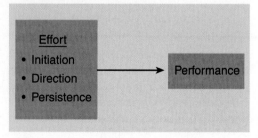

Exhibit 13.2

Adding Need Satisfaction to the Model

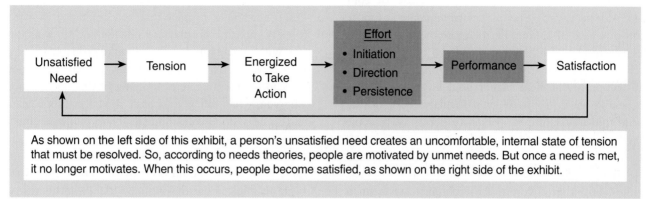

| Unsatisfied Need | → | Tension | → | Energized to Take Action | → | **Effort**
• Initiation
• Direction
• Persistence | → | Performance | → | Satisfaction |

As shown on the left side of this exhibit, a person's unsatisfied need creates an uncomfortable, internal state of tension that must be resolved. So, according to needs theories, people are motivated by unmet needs. But once a need is met, it no longer motivates. When this occurs, people become satisfied, as shown on the right side of the exhibit.

take action, and satisfaction are shown with a white background. This shading convention should make it easier to understand the work motivation model as we add to it in each section of the chapter.

Since people are motivated by unmet needs, managers must learn what those unmet needs are and address them. This is not always a straightforward task, however, because different needs theories suggest different needs categories. Consider three well-known needs theories. Maslow's Hierarchy of Needs suggests that people are motivated by *physiological* (food and water), *safety* (physical and economic), *belongingness* (friendship, love, social interaction), *esteem* (achievement and recognition),

and *self-actualization* (realizing your full potential) needs.[5] Alderfer's ERG Theory collapses Maslow's five needs into three: *existence* (safety and physiological needs), *relatedness* (belongingness), and *growth* (esteem and self-actualization).[6] McClelland's Learned Needs Theory suggests that people are motivated by the need for *affiliation* (to be liked and accepted), the need for *achievement* (to accomplish challenging goals), or the need for *power* (to influence others).[7]

Things become even more complicated when we consider the different predictions made by these theories. According to Maslow, needs are arranged in a hierarchy from low (physiological) to high (self-actualization), and

> ❝ Since people are motivated by **unmet needs**, managers must learn what those unmet needs are and **address them**. ❞

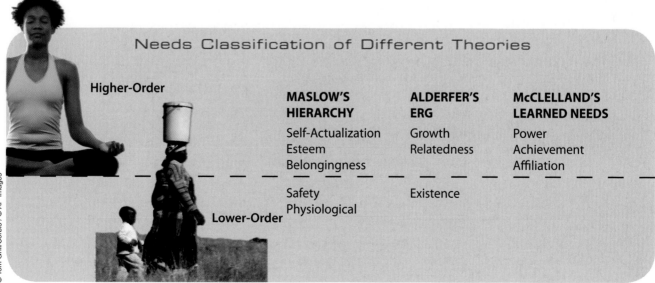

Needs Classification of Different Theories

Higher-Order

MASLOW'S HIERARCHY	ALDERFER'S ERG	McCLELLAND'S LEARNED NEEDS
Self-Actualization Esteem Belongingness	Growth Relatedness	Power Achievement Affiliation
Safety Physiological	Existence	

Lower-Order

people are motivated by their lowest unsatisfied need. As each need is met, they work their way up the hierarchy from physiological to self-actualization needs. By contrast, Alderfer says that people can be motivated by more than one need at a time. Furthermore, he suggests that people are just as likely to move down the needs hierarchy as up, particularly when they are unable to achieve satisfaction at the next higher need level. McClelland argues that the degree to which particular needs motivate varies tremendously from person to person, with some people being motivated primarily by achievement and others by power or affiliation. Moreover, McClelland says that needs are learned, not innate. For instance, studies show that children whose parents own a small business or hold a managerial position are much more likely to have a high need for achievement.[8]

So, with three different sets of needs and three very different ideas about how needs motivate, how do we provide a practical answer to managers who just want to know "What leads to effort?" Fortunately, the research simplifies things a bit. To start, studies indicate that there are two basic kinds of needs categories.[9] As you would expect, *lower-order needs* are concerned with safety and with physiological and existence requirements, whereas *higher-order needs* are concerned with relationships (belongingness, relatedness, and affiliation); challenges and accomplishments (esteem, self-actualization, growth, and

Extrinsic reward
a reward that is tangible, visible to others, and given to employees contingent on the performance of specific tasks or behaviours

achievement); and influence (power). Studies generally show that higher-order needs will not motivate people as long as lower-order needs remain unsatisfied.[10]

For example, imagine that you graduated from college six months ago and are still looking for your first job. With money running short (you're probably living on your credit cards) and the possibility of having to move back in with your parents looming (if this doesn't motivate you, what will?), your basic needs for food, shelter, and security drive your thoughts, behaviour, and choices at this point. But once you land that job, find a great place (of your own!) to live, and put some money in the bank, these basic needs should decrease in importance as you begin to think about making new friends and taking on challenging work assignments. In fact, once lower-order needs are satisfied, it's difficult for managers to predict which higher-order needs will motivate behaviour.[11] Some people will be motivated by affiliation, while others will be motivated by growth or esteem. Also, the relative importance of the various needs may change over time but not necessarily in any predictable pattern.

1.3 Extrinsic and Intrinsic Rewards

So, what leads to effort? In part, needs do. But rewards are important, too, and no discussion of motivation would be complete without considering them. Let's add two kinds of rewards, extrinsic and intrinsic, to the model in Exhibit 13.3.[12]

Extrinsic rewards are tangible and visible to others and are given to employees contingent on the performance of specific tasks or behaviours.[13] External agents (managers, for example) determine and control

Exhibit 13.3
Adding Rewards to the Model

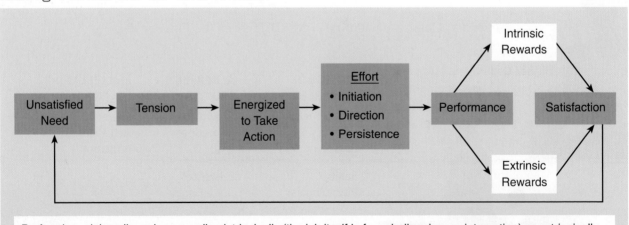

Performing a job well can be rewarding intrinsically (the job itself is fun, challenging, or interesting) or extrinsically (as you receive better pay or promotions, etc.). Intrinsic and extrinsic rewards lead to satisfaction of various needs.

Win-Win Motivation

Shari Adler took six months off from her job at Pfizer and spent it in Tanzania. But she wasn't on safari. She was working for the Tanzanian Ministry of Health. Adler reaped the benefits of Pfizer's paid volunteerism program, a strategy increasingly adopted by companies for a host of reasons. Younger workers want to see companies do more than write a cheque to help society. Moreover, meaningful volunteer opportunities help attract and retain workers who are motivated to use their job skills to help others in need. Paid volunteerism benefits companies too, since employees return with broader perspectives, more independence and confidence, and new skills that can enhance their motivation and on-the-job performance.

Source: S. E. Needleman, "The Latest Office Perk: Getting Paid to Volunteer," *The Wall Street Journal*, 29 April 2008, D1.

© Charles O. Cecil/Alamy

the distribution, frequency, and amount of extrinsic rewards such as pay, company stock, benefits, and promotions. For example, IKEA, the Sweden-based home furniture retailer, awarded its employees $80 million in bonuses to celebrate the company's 54 years of success. IKEA promoted the "Big Thank You" sale as a way to encourage customers to make purchases on its 54th anniversary, and all of the profits earned that day were distributed to its employees.[14]

Why do companies need extrinsic rewards? To get people to do things they wouldn't otherwise do. Companies use extrinsic rewards to motivate people to perform four basic behaviours: join the organization, regularly attend their jobs, perform their jobs well, and stay with the organization.[15] Think about it. Would you show up to work every day to do the best possible job that you could just out of the goodness of your heart? Very few people would. KPMG Canada, the accounting firm, now offers its employees paid sabbaticals, complete with benefits and a guaranteed job when they return. Deloitte & Touche LLP pressed ahead with its own new sabbatical program, even as Canada's recession deepened in 2009. It offered staff from across Canada a chance to work in Mozambique, Egypt, Ghana, and Latin America, where they will work with nonprofits on projects. The longer an employee perseveres, the greater the rewards.[16]

By contrast, **intrinsic rewards** are the natural rewards associated with performing a task or activity for its own sake. For example, aside from the external rewards

management offers for doing something well, employees often find the activities or tasks they perform interesting and enjoyable. Examples of intrinsic rewards include a sense of accomplishment or achievement, a feeling of responsibility, the chance to learn something new or interact with others, or simply the fun that comes from performing an interesting, challenging, and engaging task.

Which types of rewards are most important to workers in general? A number of surveys suggest that both extrinsic and intrinsic rewards are important. One survey found that the most important rewards were good benefits and health insurance, job security, a week or more of vacation (all extrinsic rewards), interesting work, the opportunity to learn new skills, and independent work situations (all intrinsic rewards). And employee preferences for intrinsic and extrinsic rewards appear to be relatively stable. Studies conducted over the last three decades have consistently found that employees are twice as likely to indicate that important and meaningful work matters more to them than what they are paid.[17]

1.4 Motivating with the Basics

So, given the basic model of work motivation based on needs and rewards in Exhibit 13.3, what practical steps can managers take to motivate employees to increase their effort?

Intrinsic reward a natural reward associated with performing a task or activity for its own sake

Well, *start by asking people what their needs are.* If managers don't know what workers' needs are, they won't be able to provide them the opportunities and rewards that can satisfy those needs. Tommy Lee Hayes-Brown, who is in charge of recognition programs at MetLife, which owns MetLife Canada, illustrates why it's important to be aware of employees' needs: "Let's say you decide to reward an employee's great performance with a ham. If he doesn't eat ham, it's not going to be all that meaningful."[18]

Next, *satisfy lower-order needs first.* Since higher-order needs will not motivate people as long as lower-order needs remain unsatisfied, companies should satisfy lower-order needs first. In practice, this means providing the equipment, training, and knowledge to create a safe workplace free of physical risks, paying employees well enough to provide financial security, and offering a benefits package that will protect employees and their families through good medical coverage and health and disability insurance.

Third, managers should *expect people's needs to change.* As some needs are satisfied or situations change, what motivated people before may not motivate them now. Likewise, what motivates people to accept a job (pay and benefits) may not necessarily motivate them once they have the job (the job itself, opportunities for advancement). Managers should also expect needs to change as people mature.[19] For older employees, benefits are as important as pay, which is always ranked as more important by younger employees. Older employees also rank job security as more important than personal and family time, which is more important to younger employees.[20]

Finally, *as needs change and lower-order needs are satisfied, create opportunities for employees to satisfy higher-order needs.* Recall that intrinsic rewards such as accomplishment, achievement, learning something new, and interacting with others are the natural rewards associated with performing a task or activity for its own sake.

Equity theory a theory that states that people will be motivated when they perceive that they are being treated fairly

And, with the exception of influence (power), intrinsic rewards correspond very closely to higher-order needs that are concerned with relationships (belongingness, relatedness, and affiliation) and challenges and accomplishments (esteem, self-actualization, growth, and achievement). Therefore, one way for managers to meet employees' higher-order needs is to create opportunities for employees to experience intrinsic rewards by providing challenging work, encouraging employees to take greater responsibility for their work, and giving employees the freedom to pursue tasks and projects they find naturally interesting.

How Perceptions and Expectations Affect Motivation

So we've now seen that people are motivated to achieve intrinsic and extrinsic rewards. When employees believe that rewards are not fairly awarded, or if they don't believe they can achieve the performance goals the company has set for them, they won't be very motivated.

After reading the next two sections, you should be able to

2 use equity theory to explain how employees' perceptions of fairness affect motivation.

3 use expectancy theory to describe how workers' expectations about rewards, effort, and the link between rewards and performance influence motivation.

2 Equity Theory

Fairness, or what people perceive to be fair, is a critical issue in organizations. **Equity theory** says that people will be motivated at work when they *perceive* that they are being treated fairly. In particular, equity theory stresses the importance of perceptions. So, regardless of the actual level of rewards people receive, they must also perceive that they are being treated fairly relative to others. For example, you learned in Chapter 11 that the average CEO now makes 364 times more than the average worker.[21] Many people believe that CEO pay is obscenely high and unfair. In 2008, the 60 CEOs of Canada's largest companies were paid more than $647 million, an average of almost $11 million each. It would take approximately 16,200 Canadians with an average income of $40,000 each to make as much as these CEOs did. Gwyn Morgan, Chairman of SNC-Lavalin Group Inc., the Montreal-based engineering company, takes the word "group" (in the company name) to heart. "When it comes to executive compensation, the board makes a point of regularly fine-tuning its pay policy according to what it believes are fair-minded, down-to-earth principles," he says. "The next thing we're going to do is examine longer periods of holding back incentive shares and putting more emphasis on long-term performance, even more than there has been" in order to ensure that people in the company feel that everyone is being recognized equitably.[22] Others believe that CEO pay is fair because if it were easier to find good CEOs, then CEOs would be paid much less. Equity theory doesn't focus on objective equity (i.e., that CEOs make 364 times more than blue-collar workers). Instead, it says that equity, like beauty, is in the eye of the beholder.

Let's learn more about equity theory by examining **2.1 the components of equity theory, 2.2 how people react to perceived inequities,** *and* **2.3 how to motivate people using equity theory.**

2.1 Components of Equity Theory

The basic components of equity theory are inputs, outcomes, and referents. **Inputs** are the contributions employees make to the organization. Inputs include education and training, intelligence, experience, effort, number of hours worked, and ability. **Outcomes** are what employees receive in exchange for their contributions to the organization. Outcomes include pay, fringe benefits, status symbols, and job titles and assignments. And, since perceptions of equity depend on comparisons, **referents** are others with whom people compare themselves to determine if they have been treated fairly. The referent can be a single person (comparing yourself with a coworker), or a generalized other (comparing yourself with "students in general," for example), or could be with yourself over time ("I was better off last year than I am this year"). Usually, people choose to compare themselves

Change in China

In Chapter 5, you learned about Geert Hofstede's studies of cultural differences. Hofstede studied China in the 1980s, when he found Chinese workers to be motivated by money (high masculinity), collectivist, and ill-inclined to offer suggestions to a supervisor (high power distance). Not so for the Chinese worker of today, who is individualist, values leisure time alongside salary, has plenty of ideas about how the company can improve, and shares them in culturally sensitive ways. This is important information for Western companies seeking to hire and motivate workers in China, as they might respond better to a recognition dinner than a bonus or a plaque.

Source: K. King-Metters and R. Metters, "Misunderstanding the Chinese Worker," *The Wall Street Journal*, 7 July 2008, R11.

© iStockphoto.com

to referents who hold the same or similar jobs or who are otherwise similar in gender, race, age, tenure, or other characteristics.[23]

According to equity theory, employees compare their outcomes (the rewards they receive from the organization) to their inputs (their contributions to the organization). This comparison of outcomes to inputs is called the **outcome/input (O/I) ratio.**

$$\frac{\text{OUTCOMES}_{\text{SELF}}}{\text{INPUTS}_{\text{SELF}}} = \frac{\text{OUTCOMES}_{\text{REFERENT}}}{\text{INPUTS}_{\text{REFERENT}}}$$

After an internal comparison in which they compare their outcomes to their inputs, employees then make an external comparison in which they compare their O/I ratio with the O/I ratio of a referent.[24] When people perceive that their O/I ratio is equal to the referent's O/I ratio, they conclude that they are being treated fairly. But, when people perceive that their O/I ratio is different from their referent's O/I ratio, they conclude that they have been treated inequitably or unfairly.

Inequity can take two forms, underreward and overreward. **Underreward** occurs when your O/I ratio is worse than your referent's

Inputs in equity theory, the contributions employees make to the organization

Outcomes in equity theory, the rewards employees receive for their contributions to the organization

Referents in equity theory, others with whom people compare themselves to determine if they have been treated fairly

Outcome/input (O/I) ratio in equity theory, an employee's perception of how the rewards received from an organization compare with the employee's contributions to that organization

Underreward a form of inequity in which you are getting fewer outcomes relative to inputs than your referent is getting

Exhibit 13.4

Adding Equity Theory to the Model

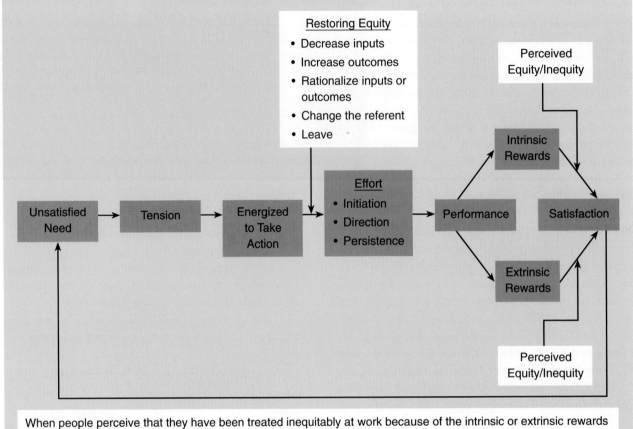

Restoring Equity
- Decrease inputs
- Increase outcomes
- Rationalize inputs or outcomes
- Change the referent
- Leave

Unsatisfied Need → Tension → Energized to Take Action → **Effort** • Initiation • Direction • Persistence → Performance → Intrinsic Rewards → Satisfaction

Performance → Extrinsic Rewards → Satisfaction

Perceived Equity/Inequity

Perceived Equity/Inequity

When people perceive that they have been treated inequitably at work because of the intrinsic or extrinsic rewards they receive relative to their efforts, they are dissatisfied (or frustrated or angry), their needs aren't met, and those reactions lead to tension and a strong need to take action to restore equity in some way (as explained in the "Restoring Equity" box).

O/I ratio. In other words, you are getting fewer outcomes relative to your inputs than your referent is getting. When people perceive that they have been underrewarded, they tend to experience anger or frustration.

By contrast, **overreward** occurs when your O/I ratio is better than your referent's O/I ratio. In this case, you are getting more outcomes relative to your inputs than your referent is. In theory, when people perceive that they have been overrewarded, they experience guilt. But, not surprisingly, people have a very high tolerance for overreward. It takes a tremendous amount of overpayment before people decide that their pay or benefits are more than they deserve.

Overreward a form of inequity in which you are getting more outcomes relative to inputs than your referent

2.2 How People React to Perceived Inequity

So what happens when people perceive that they have been treated inequitably at work? Exhibit 13.4 shows that perceived inequity affects satisfaction. In the case of underreward, this usually translates into frustration or anger; with overreward, the reaction is guilt. These reactions lead to tension and a strong need to take action to restore equity in some way. At first, a slight inequity may not be strong enough to motivate an employee to take immediate action. If the inequity continues or there are multiple inequities, however, tension may build over time until a point of intolerance is reached, and the person is energized to take action.[25]

When people perceive that they have been treated unfairly, they may try to restore equity by reducing inputs, increasing outcomes, rationalizing inputs or outcomes, changing the referent, or simply leaving. We will discuss these possible responses in terms of the inequity associated with underreward, which is much more common than the inequity associated with overreward.

People who perceive that they have been under-rewarded may try to restore equity by *decreasing or withholding their inputs (i.e., effort)*. When General Motors Canada asked for billions in Canadian aid from the federal and Ontario governments, it also planned to slash executive salaries by 10 percent and to cut benefits to hourly employees. Both the union and management felt that they had not earned their (by some estimates) large salaries. Chrysler Canada requested aid from the federal and provincial governments. Ford Canada did not, but it was cutting salaries and closing plants. GM has indicated that it will close down its Saturn plants, as well as eliminate the Pontiac division; Chrysler plans to close its Mercury division. The outcomes from these decisions are not considered inequitable by the workers.[26]

Increasing outcomes is another way people try to restore equity. This might include asking for a raise or pointing out the inequity to the boss and hoping that he or she takes care of it. Sometimes, however, employees may go to external organizations such as labour unions, federal agencies, or the courts for help in increasing outcomes to restore equity.

Another method of restoring equity is to *rationalize or distort inputs or outcomes*. Instead of decreasing inputs or increasing outcomes, employees restore equity by making mental or emotional adjustments to their O/I ratios or the O/I ratios of their referents. For example, suppose that a company downsizes 10 percent of its workforce. It's likely that the survivors, the people who still have jobs, will be angry or frustrated with company management because of the layoffs. If alternative jobs are difficult to find, however, these survivors may rationalize or distort their O/I ratios and conclude, "Well, things could be worse. At least I still have my job." Rationalizing or

distorting outcomes may be used when other ways to restore equity aren't available.

Changing the referent is another way of restoring equity. In this case, people compare themselves to someone other than the referent they had been using for previous O/I ratio comparisons. Since people usually choose to compare themselves to others who hold the same or similar jobs or who are otherwise similar (i.e., friends, family members, neighbours who work at other companies), they may change referents to restore equity when their personal situations change, such as a decrease in job status or pay.[27] Finally, when none of these methods are possible or restore equity, *employees may leave* by quitting their jobs, transferring, or increasing absenteeism.[28]

2.3 Motivating with Equity Theory

What practical steps can managers take to use equity theory to motivate employees? They can *start by looking for and correcting major inequities*. Among other things, equity theory makes us aware that an employee's sense of fairness is based on subjective perceptions. What one employee considers grossly unfair may not affect another employee's perceptions of equity at all. Although these different perceptions make it difficult for managers to create conditions that satisfy all employees, it's critical that they do their best to take care of major inequities that can energize employees to take disruptive, costly, or harmful actions such as decreasing inputs or leaving. So, whenever possible, managers should look for and correct major inequities.

Second, managers can *reduce employees' inputs*. Increasing outcomes is often the first and only strategy that companies use to restore equity, yet reducing employee inputs is just as viable a strategy. In fact, with dual-career couples working 50-hour weeks, more and more employees are looking for ways to reduce stress and restore a balance between work and family. Consequently, it may make sense to ask employees to do less, not more; to have them identify and eliminate the 20 percent of their jobs that doesn't increase productivity or add value for customers; and to eliminate company-imposed requirements that really aren't critical to the performance of managers, employees, or the company (e.g., unnecessary meetings and reports).

Finally, managers should *make sure decision-making processes are fair*. Equity theory focuses on **distributive justice**, the

> **Distributive justice** the perceived degree to which outcomes and rewards are fairly distributed or allocated

izmostock/GetStock.com

degree to which outcomes and rewards are fairly distributed or allocated. However, **procedural justice,** the fairness of the procedures used to make reward allocation decisions, is just as important.[29] Procedural justice matters because even when employees are unhappy with their outcomes (i.e., low pay), they're much less likely to be unhappy with company management if they believe that the procedures used to allocate outcomes were fair. For example, employees who are laid off tend to be hostile toward their employer when they perceive that the procedures leading to the layoffs were unfair. By contrast, employees who perceive layoff procedures to be fair tend to continue to support and trust their employers.[30] Also, if employees perceive that their outcomes are unfair (i.e., distributive injustice), but that the decisions and procedures leading to those outcomes were fair (i.e., procedural justice), they are much more likely to seek constructive ways of restoring equity such as discussing these matters with their manager. In contrast, if employees perceive both distributive and procedural injustice, they may resort to more destructive tactics such as withholding effort, absenteeism, tardiness, or even sabotage and theft.[31]

3 Expectancy Theory

Procedural justice the perceived fairness of the process used to make reward allocation decisions

Expectancy theory a theory that states that people will be motivated to the extent to which they believe that their efforts will lead to good performance, that good performance will be rewarded, and that they will be offered attractive rewards

Valence the attractiveness or desirability of a reward or outcome

Expectancy the perceived relationship between effort and performance

Instrumentality the perceived relationship between performance and rewards

One of the hardest things about motivating people is that rewards that are attractive to some employees are unattractive to others. **Expectancy theory** says that people will be motivated to the extent to which they believe that their efforts will lead to good performance, that good performance will be rewarded, and that they will be offered attractive rewards.[32]

*Let's learn more about expectancy theory by examining **3.1 the components of expectancy theory** and **3.2 how to use expectancy theory as a motivational tool.***

3.1 Components of Expectancy Theory

Expectancy theory holds that people make conscious choices about their motivation. The three factors that affect those choices are valence, expectancy, and instrumentality.

Valence is simply the attractiveness or desirability of various rewards or outcomes. Expectancy theory recognizes that the same reward or outcome—say, a promotion—will be highly attractive to some people, will be highly disliked by others, and will not make much difference one way or the other to still others. Accordingly, when people are deciding how much effort to put forth, expectancy theory says that they will consider the valence of all possible rewards and outcomes that they can receive from their jobs. The greater the sum of those valences, each of which can be positive, negative, or neutral, the more effort people will choose to put forth on the job.

Expectancy is the perceived relationship between effort and performance. When expectancies are strong, employees believe that their hard work and efforts will result in good performance, so they work harder. By contrast, when expectancies are weak, employees figure that no matter what they do or how hard they work, they won't be able to perform their jobs successfully, so they don't work as hard.

Instrumentality is the perceived relationship between performance and rewards. When instrumentality is strong, employees believe that improved performance will lead to better and more rewards, so they choose to work harder. When instrumentality is weak, employees don't believe that better performance will result in more or better rewards, so they choose not to work as hard.

Expectancy theory holds that for people to be highly motivated, all three variables—valence, expectancy, and instrumentality—must be high. Thus, expectancy theory can be represented by the following simple equation:

$$\text{Motivation} = \text{Valence} \times \text{Expectancy} \times \text{Instrumentality}$$

If any one of these variables (valence, expectancy, or instrumentality) declines, overall motivation will decline, too.

Exhibit 13.5 incorporates the expectancy theory variables into our motivation model. Valence and instrumentality combine to affect employees' willingness to put forth effort (i.e., the degree to which they are energized to take action), while expectancy

Exhibit 13.5

Adding Expectancy Theory to the Model

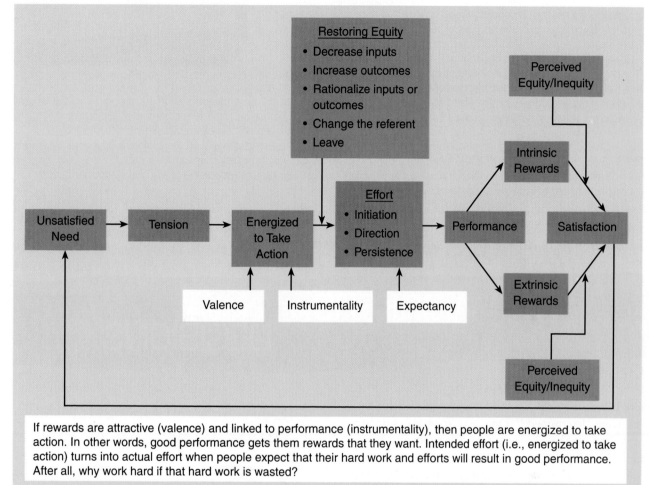

If rewards are attractive (valence) and linked to performance (instrumentality), then people are energized to take action. In other words, good performance gets them rewards that they want. Intended effort (i.e., energized to take action) turns into actual effort when people expect that their hard work and efforts will result in good performance. After all, why work hard if that hard work is wasted?

transforms intended effort ("I'm really going to work hard in this job") into actual effort. If you're offered rewards that you desire and you believe that you will in fact receive these rewards for good performance, you're highly likely to be energized to take action. However, you're not likely to actually exert effort unless you also believe that you can do the job (i.e., that your efforts will lead to successful performance).

3.2 Motivating with Expectancy Theory

What practical steps can managers take to use expectancy theory to motivate employees? First, they can *systematically gather information to find out what employees want from their jobs*. In addition to individual managers directly asking employees what they want from their jobs (see Subsection 1.4 "Motivating with the Basics"), companies need to survey their employees regularly to determine their wants, needs, and dissatisfactions. Since people consider the valence of all the possible

rewards and outcomes that they can receive from their jobs, regular identification of wants, needs, and dissatisfactions gives companies the chance to turn negatively valent rewards and outcomes into positively valent rewards and outcomes, thus raising overall motivation and effort. Therefore, employers should routinely survey employees to identify not only the range of rewards that are valued by most employees but also to understand the preferences of specific employees.

Second, managers can *take specific steps to link rewards to individual performance in a way that is clear and understandable to employees*. Unfortunately, most employees are extremely dissatisfied with the link between pay and performance in their organizations. In one study, based on a representative sample, 80 percent of the employees surveyed wanted to be paid according to a different kind of pay system! Moreover, only 32 percent of employees were satisfied with how their annual pay raises were determined, and only 22 percent

Time to Get Serious About Rewarding Employees

A top performer in an organization was rewarded with a one-week Caribbean cruise—with company executives. This was not a reward: the prospect of going on a cruise, especially with senior management, was her idea of hell. "I don't like schmoozing, I don't like feeling trapped, why couldn't they just give me the money?" she asked. Rewards come in many extrinsic forms—bonuses, trips to conferences, praise, dinner events, plaques—and many intrinsic forms—the pleasure of completing something that met personal needs, or executing a job to the highest standard. Money can be effective, but the dollar amount must fit the circumstances and be appropriate for the amount of effort. Two team members received financial rewards for exceptional work. One did the work in a week and received $25. The other, who worked on a major project for a year, received $1,500. They were equally "blown away" by their bonuses.

One young professional's high performance earned him a clock radio—emblazoned with the company's logo. That irked him. "I am happy to work for them. But I resent them thinking they can come into my bedroom and wake me up."

The best reward: the satisfaction that you derive when you feel—and can tell yourself—that you've made an important contribution. You have made a difference.

Source: Moses, B. (2010). Report on Business, 28 April 2010, *The Globe and Mail*. Accessed 19 May 2010 at http://www.theglobeandmail.com/report-on-business/managing/barbara-moses/time-to-get-serious-about-rewarding-employees/article1549639/

> IF MANAGERS WANT WORKERS TO HAVE STRONG EXPECTANCIES, THEY SHOULD EMPOWER THEM TO MAKE DECISIONS.

were happy with the way the starting salaries for their jobs were determined.[33] One way to make sure that employees see the connection between pay and performance (see Chapter 11 for a discussion of compensation strategies) is for managers to publicize the way in which pay decisions are made. This is especially important given that only 41 percent of employees know how their pay increases are determined.[34]

Finally, managers should *empower employees to make decisions if management really wants them to believe that their hard work and effort will lead to good performance.* If valent rewards are linked to good performance, people should be energized to take action. However, this works only if they also believe that their efforts will lead to good performance. One of the ways that managers destroy the expectancy that hard work and effort will lead to good performance is by restricting what employees can do or by ignoring employees' ideas. In Chapter 9, you learned that *empowerment* is a feeling of intrinsic motivation, in which workers perceive their work to have meaning and perceive themselves to be competent, to have an impact, and to be capable of self-determination.[35] So, if managers want workers to have strong expectancies, they should empower them to make decisions. Doing so will motivate employees to take active rather than passive roles in their work.

How Rewards and Goals Affect Motivation

When used properly, rewards motivate and energize employees. But when used incorrectly, they can demotivate, baffle, and even anger them. Goals are also supposed to motivate employees. But leaders who focus blindly on meeting goals at all costs often find that they destroy motivation.

 After reading the next three sections, you should be able to

4   explain how reinforcement theory works and how it can be used to motivate.

5   describe the components of goal-setting theory and how managers can use them to motivate workers.

6   discuss how the entire motivation model can be used to motivate workers.

4 Reinforcement Theory

Reinforcement theory says that behaviour is a function of its consequences, that behaviours followed by positive consequences (i.e., reinforced) will occur more frequently, and that behaviours followed by negative consequences, or not followed by positive consequences, will occur less frequently.[36] More specifically, **reinforcement** is the process of changing behaviour by changing the consequences that follow behaviour.[37]

Reinforcement has two parts: reinforcement contingencies and schedules of reinforcement. **Reinforcement contingencies** are the cause-and-effect relationships between the performance of specific behaviours and specific consequences. For example, if you get docked an hour's pay for being late to work, then a reinforcement contingency exists between a behaviour (being late to work) and a consequence (losing an hour's pay). A **schedule of reinforcement** is the set of rules regarding reinforcement contingencies such as which behaviours will be reinforced, which consequences will follow those behaviours, and the schedule by which those consequences will be delivered.[38]

Exhibit 13.6 (p. 268) incorporates reinforcement contingencies and reinforcement schedules into our motivation model. First, notice that extrinsic rewards and the schedules of reinforcement used to deliver them are the primary method for creating reinforcement contingencies in organizations. In turn, those reinforcement contingencies directly affect valences (the attractiveness of rewards), instrumentality (the perceived link between rewards and performance), and effort (how hard employees will work).

Let's learn more about reinforcement theory by examining 4.1 the components of reinforcement theory, 4.2 the different schedules for delivering reinforcement, and 4.3 how to motivate with reinforcement theory.

4.1 Components of Reinforcement Theory

As just described, *reinforcement contingencies* are the cause-and-effect relationships between the performance of specific behaviours and specific consequences. There are four kinds of reinforcement contingencies: positive reinforcement, negative reinforcement, punishment, and extinction.

Positive reinforcement strengthens behaviour (i.e., increases its frequency) by following behaviours with desirable consequences. By contrast, **negative reinforcement** strengthens behaviour by withholding an unpleasant consequence when employees perform a specific behaviour. Negative reinforcement is also called

avoidance learning because workers perform a behaviour to *avoid* a negative consequence. For example, at the Florist Network, company management instituted a policy of requiring good attendance for employees to receive their annual bonuses. Employee attendance improved significantly when excessive absenteeism threatened to result in the loss of $1,500 or more.[39] At Canada's SNC-Lavalin, employees who do not take any sick time receive a bonus of $1,500 just before Christmas. For every day that an employee is absent, $300 is deducted from that bonus.

By contrast, **punishment** weakens behaviour (i.e., decreases its frequency) by following behaviours with undesirable consequences. For example, the standard disciplinary or punishment process in most companies is an oral warning ("Don't ever do that again"), followed by a written warning ("This letter is to discuss the serious problem you're having with ... "), followed by three days off without pay ("While you're at home not being paid, we want you to think hard about ... "), followed by being fired ("That was your last chance"). Though punishment can weaken behaviour, managers have to be careful to avoid the backlash that sometimes occurs when employees are punished at work. For example, Frito-Lay began getting complaints from customers that they were finding potato chips with obscene messages written on them.

Reinforcement theory a theory that states that behaviour is a function of its consequences, that behaviours followed by positive consequences will occur more frequently, and that behaviours followed by negative consequences, or not followed by positive consequences, will occur less frequently

Reinforcement the process of changing behaviour by changing the consequences that follow behaviour

Reinforcement contingencies cause-and-effect relationships between the performance of specific behaviours and specific consequences

Schedule of reinforcement rules that specify which behaviours will be reinforced, which consequences will follow those behaviours, and the schedule by which those consequences will be delivered

Positive reinforcement reinforcement that strengthens behaviour by following behaviours with desirable consequences

Negative reinforcement reinforcement that strengthens behaviour by withholding an unpleasant consequence when employees perform a specific behaviour

Punishment reinforcement that weakens behaviour by following behaviours with undesirable consequences

Exhibit 13.6

Adding Reinforcement Theory to the Model

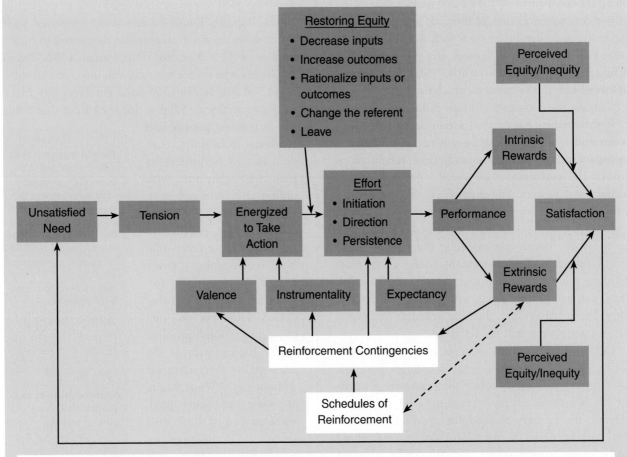

Extrinsic rewards and the schedules of reinforcement used to deliver them are the primary method for creating reinforcement contingencies in organizations. In turn, those reinforcement contingencies directly affect valences (the attractiveness of rewards), instrumentality (the perceived link between rewards and performance), and effort (how hard employees will work).

Frito-Lay eventually traced the problem to a potato chip plant where supervisors had fired 58 out of the 210 workers for disciplinary reasons over a nine-month period. The remaining employees were so angry over what they saw as unfair treatment from management that they began writing the phrases on potato chips with felt-tipped pens.[40]

Extinction is a reinforcement strategy in which a positive consequence is no longer allowed to follow a previously reinforced behaviour. By removing the positive consequence, extinction weakens the behaviour, making it less likely to occur. Based on the idea of positive reinforcement, most companies give company leaders and managers substantial financial rewards when the company performs well. Based on the idea of extinction, you would then expect that leaders and managers would not be rewarded (i.e., removing the positive consequence) when companies perform poorly. If companies really want pay to reinforce the right kinds of behaviours, then rewards have to be removed when company management doesn't produce successful performance.

4.2 Schedules for Delivering Reinforcement

As mentioned earlier, a *schedule of reinforcement* is the set of rules regarding reinforcement contingencies such

Extinction reinforcement in which a positive consequence is no longer allowed to follow a previously reinforced behaviour, thus weakening the behaviour

Exhibit 13.7

Intermittent Reinforcement Schedules

INTERMITTENT REINFORCEMENT SCHEDULES		
	FIXED	**VARIABLE**
INTERVAL (TIME)	Consequences follow behaviour after a fixed time has elapsed.	Consequences follow behaviour after different times, some shorter and some longer, that vary around a specific average time.
RATIO (BEHAVIOUR)	Consequences follow a specific number of behaviours.	Consequences follow a different number of behaviours, sometimes more and sometimes less, that vary around a specified average number of behaviours.

as which behaviours will be reinforced, which consequences will follow those behaviours, and the schedule by which those consequences will be delivered. There are two categories of reinforcement schedules: continuous and intermittent.

With **continuous reinforcement schedules,** a consequence follows every instance of a behaviour. For example, employees working on a piece-rate pay system earn money (consequence) for every part they manufacture (behaviour). The more they produce, the more they earn. By contrast, with **intermittent reinforcement schedules,** consequences are delivered after a specified or average time has elapsed or after a specified or average number of behaviours has occurred. As Exhibit 13.7 shows, there are four types of intermittent reinforcement schedules. Two of these are based on time and are called *interval reinforcement schedules,* while the other two, known as *ratio schedules,* are based on behaviours.

With **fixed interval reinforcement schedules,** consequences follow a behaviour only after a fixed time has elapsed. For example, most people receive their paycheques on a fixed interval schedule (e.g., once or twice per month). As long as they work (behaviour) during a specified pay period (interval), they get a paycheque (consequence). With **variable interval reinforcement schedules,** consequences follow a behaviour after different times, some shorter and some longer, that vary around a specified average time. On a 90-day variable interval reinforcement schedule, you might receive a bonus after 80 days or perhaps after 100 days, but the average interval between performing your job well (behaviour) and receiving your bonus (consequence) would be 90 days.

With **fixed ratio reinforcement schedules,** consequences are delivered following a specific number of behaviours. For example, a car salesperson might receive a $1,000 bonus after every 10 sales. Therefore,

a salesperson with only 9 sales would not receive the bonus until he or she finally sold a 10th car.

With **variable ratio reinforcement schedules,** consequences are delivered following a different number of behaviours, sometimes more and sometimes less, that vary around a specified average number of behaviours. With a 10-car variable ratio reinforcement schedule, a salesperson might receive the bonus after 7 car sales, or after 12, 11, or 9 sales, but the average number of cars sold before receiving the bonus would be 10 cars.

Which reinforcement schedules work best? In the past, the standard advice was to use continuous reinforcement when employees were learning new behaviours because reinforcement after each success leads to faster learning. Likewise, the standard advice was to use intermittent reinforcement schedules to maintain behaviour after it is learned because intermittent rewards are supposed to make behaviour much less subject to extinction.[41]

Continuous reinforcement schedule
a schedule that requires a consequence to be administered following every instance of a behaviour

Intermittent reinforcement schedule
a schedule in which consequences are delivered after a specified or average time has elapsed or after a specified or average number of behaviours has occurred

Fixed interval reinforcement schedule
an intermittent schedule in which consequences follow a behaviour only after a fixed time has elapsed

Variable interval reinforcement schedule
an intermittent schedule in which the time between a behaviour and the following consequences varies around a specified average

Fixed ratio reinforcement schedule an intermittent schedule in which consequences are delivered following a specific number of behaviours

Variable ratio reinforcement schedule
an intermittent schedule in which consequences are delivered following a different number of behaviours, sometimes more and sometimes less, that vary around a specified average number of behaviours

Research shows, however, that except for interval-based systems, which usually produce weak results, the effectiveness of continuous reinforcement, fixed ratio, and variable ratio schedules differs very little.[42] In organizational settings, all three produce consistently large increases over non-contingent reward schedules. So managers should choose whichever of these three is easiest to use in their companies.

4.3 Motivating with Reinforcement Theory

What practical steps can managers take to use reinforcement theory to motivate employees? University business professor Fred Luthans, who has been studying the effects of reinforcement theory in organizations for more than a quarter of a century, says that there are five steps to motivating workers with reinforcement theory: *identify, measure, analyze, intervene,* and *evaluate* critical performance-related behaviours.[43]

Identify means identifying critical, observable, performance-related behaviours. These are the behaviours that are most important to successful job performance. In addition, they must also be easily observed so that they can be accurately measured. *Measure* means measuring the baseline frequencies of these behaviours. In other words, find out how often workers perform them. *Analyze* means analyzing the causes and consequences of these behaviours. Analyzing the causes helps managers create the conditions that produce these critical behaviours, and analyzing the consequences helps them determine if these behaviours produce the results that they want. *Intervene* means changing the organization by using positive and negative reinforcement to increase the frequency

Photos.com / © iStockphoto.com/Andrea Tani/

Trashing the Workweek

Giving employees freedom to go to a baseball game on Wednesday afternoon might seem like a risky way to motivate them. But the Results-Only Work Environment (ROWE) approach, pioneered at Best Buy by Cali Ressler and Jodi Thompson, taps into employees' need for independence in order to get them to perform at their best. Lauren Larose from Victoria, BC, wrote to Ressler and Thompson stating that her first business co-op work term, with a government ministry, sucked. It was a great work environment, she said, but when her supervisor was out of the office she had nothing to do. The ROWE specialists responded that Lauren should try other communication (Twitter or texting) besides face-to-face taskings. They also suggested that Lauren mention to her supervisor that there are other projects that she would be interested in working on. "Self-motivation is something that all supervisors look for, and it sounds like you have it!" ROWE has boosted morale and productivity in many companies.

Source: S. Westcott, "Beyond Flextime: Trashing the Workweek", *Inc*, August 2008, 30–31; Globe Life, 30 March 2009. "Think Work Sucks?" Accessed 19 May 2010 at http://www.theglobeandmail.com/life/article690637.ece.

of these critical behaviours. *Evaluate* means evaluating the extent to which the intervention actually changed workers' behaviour. This is done by comparing behaviour after the intervention to the original baseline of behaviour before the intervention.

In addition to these five steps, managers should remember three other key things when motivating with reinforcement theory. *Don't reinforce the wrong behaviours.* Although reinforcement theory sounds simple, it's actually very difficult to put into practice. One of the most common mistakes is accidentally reinforcing the wrong behaviours. Sometimes managers reinforce behaviours that they don't want!

Managers should also *correctly administer punishment at the appropriate time.* Many managers believe that punishment can change workers' behaviour and help them improve their job performance. Furthermore, managers believe that fairly punishing workers also lets other workers know what is or isn't acceptable.[44] A danger of using punishment is that it can produce a backlash against managers and companies. But, if administered properly, punishment

ONE OF THE SIMPLEST, MOST EFFECTIVE WAYS TO MOTIVATE WORKERS…

can weaken the frequency of undesirable behaviours without creating a backlash.[45] To be effective, the punishment must be strong enough to stop the undesired behaviour and must be administered objectively (same rules applied to everyone), impersonally (without emotion or anger), consistently and contingently (each time improper behaviour occurs), and quickly (as soon as possible following the undesirable behaviour). In addition, managers should clearly explain what the appropriate behaviour is and why the employee is being punished. Employees typically respond well when punishment is administered this way.[46]

Finally, managers should *choose the simplest and most effective schedule of reinforcement*. When choosing a schedule of reinforcement, managers need to balance effectiveness against simplicity. In fact, the more complex the schedule of reinforcement, the more likely it is to be misunderstood and resisted by managers and employees. Since continuous reinforcement, fixed ratio, and variable ratio schedules are about equally effective, continuous reinforcement schedules may be the best choice in many instances by virtue of their simplicity.

5 Goal-Setting Theory

The basic model of motivation with which we began this chapter showed that individuals feel tension after becoming aware of an unfulfilled need. Once they experience tension, they search for and select courses of action that they believe will eliminate this tension. In other words, they direct their behaviour toward something. This something is a goal. A **goal** is a target, objective, or result that someone tries to accomplish. **Goal-setting theory** says that people will be motivated to the extent they accept specific, challenging goals and receive feedback that indicates their progress toward goal achievement.

*Let's learn more about goal setting by examining **5.1 the components of goal-setting theory** and **5.2 how to motivate with goal-setting theory.***

5.1 Components of Goal-Setting Theory

The basic components of goal-setting theory are goal specificity, goal difficulty, goal acceptance, and performance feedback.[47] **Goal specificity** is the extent to which goals are detailed, exact, and unambiguous. Specific goals, such as "I'm going to have a 3.0 average this semester," are more motivating than general goals, such as "I'm going to get better grades this semester."

Goal difficulty is the extent to which a goal is hard or challenging to accomplish. Difficult goals, such as "I'm going to have a 3.5 average and make the Dean's List this semester," are more motivating than easy goals, such as "I'm going to have a 2.0 average this semester."

Goal acceptance, which is similar to the idea of goal commitment discussed in Chapter 5, is the extent to which people consciously understand and agree to goals. Accepted goals, such as "I really want to get a 3.5 average this semester to show my parents how much I've improved," are more motivating than unaccepted goals, such as "My parents really want me to get a 3.5 average this semester, but there's so much more I'd rather do on campus than study!"

Performance feedback is information about the quality or quantity of past performance and indicates whether progress is being made toward the accomplishment of a goal. Performance feedback, such as "My prof said I need a 92 on the final to get an 'A' in that class," is more motivating than no feedback, "I have no idea what my grade is in that class."

Goal a target, objective, or result that someone tries to accomplish

Goal-setting theory a theory that states that people will be motivated to the extent to which they accept specific, challenging goals and receive feedback that indicates their progress toward goal achievement

Goal specificity the extent to which goals are detailed, exact, and unambiguous

Goal difficulty the extent to which a goal is hard or challenging to accomplish

Goal acceptance the extent to which people consciously understand and agree to goals

Performance feedback information about the quality or quantity of past performance that indicates whether progress is being made toward the accomplishment of a goal

...IS TO ASSIGN THEM SPECIFIC, CHALLENGING GOALS.

In short, goal-setting theory says that people will be motivated to the extent to which they accept specific, challenging goals and receive feedback that indicates their progress toward goal achievement.

How does goal setting work? To start, challenging goals focus employees' attention (i.e., direction of effort) on the critical aspects of their jobs and away from unimportant areas. Goals also energize behaviour. When faced with unaccomplished goals, employees typically develop plans and strategies to reach those goals. Goals also create tension between the goal, which is the desired future state of affairs, and where the employee or company is now, meaning the current state of affairs. This tension can be satisfied only by achieving or abandoning the goal. Finally, goals influence persistence. Since goals only go away when they are accomplished, employees are more likely to persist in their efforts in the presence of goals. Exhibit 13.8 incorporates goals into the motivation model by showing how they directly affect tension, effort, and the extent to which employees are energized to take action.

5.2 Motivating with Goal-Setting Theory

What practical steps can managers take to use goal-setting theory to motivate employees? One of the simplest, most effective ways to motivate workers is to *assign them specific, challenging goals.*

Second, managers should *make sure workers truly accept organizational goals.* Specific, challenging goals won't motivate workers unless they really accept, understand, and agree to the organization's goals. For this to occur, people must see the goals as fair and reasonable. Plus, they must trust management and believe that managers are using goals to clarify what is expected from them rather than to exploit or threaten them ("If you don't achieve these goals…"). Participative goal setting, in which managers and employees generate goals together, can help increase

Exhibit 13.8

Adding Goal-Setting Theory to the Model

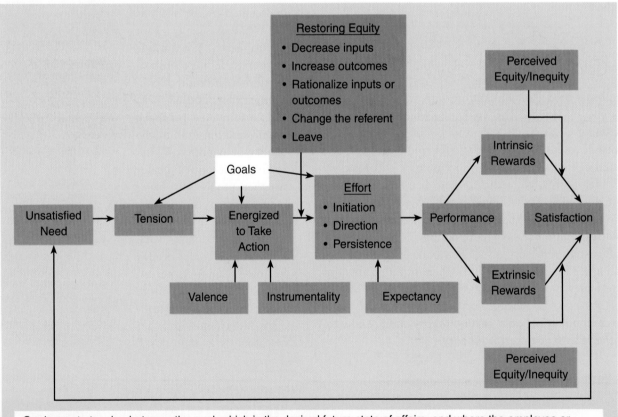

Goals create tension between the goal, which is the desired future state of affairs, and where the employee or company is now, meaning the current state of affairs. This tension can be satisfied only by achieving or abandoning the goal. Goals also energize behaviour. When faced with unaccomplished goals, employees typically develop plans and strategies to reach those goals. Finally, goals influence persistence.

trust and understanding and thus acceptance of goals. Furthermore, providing workers with training can help increase goal acceptance, particularly when workers don't believe they are capable of reaching the organization's goals.[48]

Finally, managers should *provide frequent, specific, performance-related feedback*. Once employees have accepted specific, challenging goals, they should receive frequent performance-related feedback so that they can track their progress toward goal completion. Feedback leads to stronger motivation and effort in three ways.[49] Receiving specific feedback that indicates how well they're performing can encourage employees who don't have specific, challenging goals to set goals to improve their performance. Once people meet goals, performance feedback often encourages them to set higher, more difficult goals. And, feedback lets people know whether they need to increase their efforts or change strategies in order to accomplish their goals. So, to motivate employees with goal-setting theory, make sure they receive frequent performance-related feedback so that they can track their progress toward goal completion.

6 Motivating with the Integrated Model

We began this chapter by defining motivation as the set of forces that initiates, directs, and makes people persist in their efforts to accomplish a goal. We also asked the basic question that managers ask when they try to figure out how to motivate their workers: "What leads to effort?" Though the answer to that question is likely to be somewhat different for each employee, the diagram on your Review Card for this chapter helps you begin to answer it by consolidating the practical advice from the theories reviewed in this chapter in one convenient location. So, if you're having difficulty figuring out why people aren't motivated where you work, check your Review Card for a useful, theory-based starting point.

Visit **icanmgmt.com** to find the resources you need today!

Located at the back of the textbook are rip-out Chapter Review cards. Make sure you also go online to check out other tools that MGMT offers to help you successfully pass your course.

- Interactive Quizzes
- Key Terms Flashcards
- Audio Chapter Summaries
- PowerPoint Slides

- Interactive Games
- Crossword Puzzles
- "Reel to Reel" and "Biz Flix" videos
- Cases and Exercises

LEADERSHIP

What Is Leadership?

1 If you've ever been in charge, or even just thought about it, chances are you've considered questions like: Do I have what it takes to lead? What are the most important things leaders do? How can I transform a poorly performing department, division, or company? Do I need to adjust my leadership depending on the situation and the employee? Why doesn't my leadership inspire people? If you feel overwhelmed at the prospect of being a leader, you're not alone—millions of leaders in organizations across the world struggle with fundamental leadership issues on a daily basis.

How does an ensemble of 100 or more musicians, all playing different parts at different times on different instruments, manage to produce something as beautiful as Beethoven's Fifth Symphony? (Or, if Gustav Mahler's "Symphony of a Thousand," is on the program, a lot more people might be involved!) The conductor, like a CEO, is responsible for managing all of this complexity and ensuring great output. But his or her job is about much more than just keeping the beat with a baton. According to Ramona Wis, author of *The Conductor as Leader: Principles of Leadership Applied to Life on the Podium*, conductors must also build connections between people, inspire them with vision, command their trust, and persuade them to participate in the ensemble at their very best.

Whether the end result is a stirring musical performance, innovation of new products, or increased profits, **leadership** is the process of influencing others to achieve group or organizational goals. The knowledge and

Leadership the process of influencing others to achieve group or organizational goals

Learning Outcomes

1 explain what leadership is.

2 describe who leaders are and what effective leaders do.

3 explain Fiedler's contingency theory.

4 describe how path-goal theory works.

5 explain the normative decision theory.

6 explain how visionary leadership (i.e., charismatic and transformational leadership) helps leaders achieve strategic leadership.

Bernd Vogel/Fancy/Jupiterimages

skills you'll learn in this chapter won't make the task of leadership less daunting, but they will help you navigate it.

After reading the next two sections, you should be able to

1 explain what leadership is.

2 describe who leaders are and what effective leaders do.

1 Leaders versus Managers

The Canadian academic and researcher Henri Mintzberg, from Montreal's McGill University, spent a lifetime trying to decide what it is that a manager does. His seminal work *Management: Folk Lore and Fiction*

helped define the difference between management and leadership. Managers make an unending series of decisions about doing things right. Leaders make decisions about doing the right thing.[1] In other words, leaders begin with the question, "What should we be doing?" while managers start with "How can we do what we're already doing better?" Leaders focus on vision, mission, goals, and objectives, while managers focus on productivity and efficiency. Managers see themselves as preservers of the status quo, while leaders see themselves as promoters of change and challengers of the status quo. Leaders, consequently, encourage creativity and risk taking. At Maddock Douglas, a firm that helps companies develop new products, President Louis Viton leads by encouraging creativity and risk-taking with

UNDERLED AND OVERMANAGED.

an annual "Fail Forward" award for ambitious ideas that end in disaster—even if they end up costing the company huge amounts of money. Viton says the latest "Fail Forward" winner produced a new product design that was a total embarrassment. . . . But she was trying to do something new and different and better. She went for it, and she won an award for it."[2]

Another difference is that managers have a relatively short-term perspective, while leaders take a long-term view. Managers are also more concerned with *means,* how to get things done, while leaders are more concerned with *ends,* what gets done. Managers are concerned with control and limiting the choices of others, while leaders are more concerned with expanding people's choices and options.[3] Finally, managers solve problems so that others can do their work, while leaders inspire and motivate others to find their own solutions.

Though leaders are different from managers, organizations need them both. Managers are critical to getting out the day-to-day work, and leaders are critical to inspiring employees and setting the organization's long-term direction. The key issue for any organization is the extent to which it is properly led and properly managed. As Mintzberg said in summing up the difference between leaders and managers, organizations are underled and overmanaged. They do not pay enough attention to doing the right thing, while they pay too much attention to doing things right.[4]

2 Who Leaders Are and What Leaders Do

"I don't know if it is a marriage made in heaven. But it is a match made in Canada," said Suncor's president. CEO Rick George was not shy about appealing to Canadian nationalism. Suncor Energy Inc. and Petro-Canada's proposed merger would create the country's largest energy company. "This will truly be a flagship Canadian corporation," he said at a Calgary news conference. His counterpart, CEO Ron Brenndenan of Petro-Canada, is not as extrovertive, but they will be running Canada's largest energy company.[5] Which one, George or Brenndenan, is likely to be more successful as a CEO? According to a survey of 1,542 senior managers, it's the extrovert. Forty-seven percent of those 1,542 senior managers felt that extroverts make better CEOs, while 65 percent said that being an introvert hurts a CEO's chances of success.[6] Clearly, senior managers believe that extroverted CEOs are better leaders. But are they? Not necessarily. In fact, a relatively high percentage of CEOs, 40 percent, are introverts. Canada's media giant Rogers is led by a shy man. "Though friends know him as gregarious, Mr. Rogers has often been considered the shy son of Ted." He continues to quietly head up the cable division at Rogers and serve as chairman of the trust that controls the family's voting shares while new CEO Nadir Mohamed takes the reins of the company.[7]

*So, what makes a good leader? Does leadership success depend on who leaders are, such as introverts or extroverts, or on what leaders do and how they behave? Let's learn more about who leaders are by investigating **2.1 leadership traits** and **2.2 leadership behaviours**.*

2.1 Leadership Traits

Trait theory is one way to describe who leaders are. **Trait theory** says that effective leaders possess a similar set of traits or characteristics. **Traits** are relatively stable characteristics, such as abilities, psychological motives, or consistent patterns of behaviour. For example, according to trait theory, leaders are taller and more confident and have greater physical stamina (i.e., higher energy levels) than nonleaders. Indeed, while just 14.5 percent of men are six feet tall, *58 percent* of *Fortune* 500 CEOs are six feet or taller.[8] Trait theory is also known as the "great person" theory because early versions of the theory stated

Trait theory a leadership theory that holds that effective leaders possess a similar set of traits or characteristics

Traits relatively stable characteristics, such as abilities, psychological motives, or consistent patterns of behaviour

that leaders are born, not made. In other words, you either have the right stuff to be a leader or you don't. And if you don't, there is no way to get it.

For some time, it was thought that trait theory was wrong and that there are no consistent trait differences between leaders and nonleaders or between effective and ineffective leaders. However, more recent evidence shows that "successful leaders are not like other people," that successful leaders are indeed different from the rest of us.[9] More specifically, leaders are different from nonleaders in the following traits: drive, the desire to lead, honesty/integrity, self-confidence, emotional stability, cognitive ability, and knowledge of the business.[10]

Drive refers to a high level of effort and is characterized by achievement, motivation, initiative, energy, and tenacity. In terms of achievement and ambition, leaders always try to make improvements or achieve success in what they're doing. Because of their initiative, they have a strong desire to promote change or solve problems. Leaders typically have more energy—they have to, given the long hours they put in and followers' expectations that they be positive and upbeat. Leaders are also more tenacious than nonleaders and are better at overcoming obstacles and problems that would deter most of us.

Successful leaders also have a stronger *desire to lead*. They want to be in charge and think about ways to influence or convince others about what should or shouldn't be done. *Honesty/integrity* is also important to leaders. *Honesty,* being truthful with others, is a cornerstone of leadership. Leaders won't be trusted if they are dishonest. When they are honest, subordinates are willing to overlook other flaws. *Integrity* is the extent to which leaders do what they say they will do. Leaders may be honest and have good intentions, but they also won't be trusted if they don't consistently deliver on what they promise.

Self-confidence, believing in one's abilities, also distinguishes leaders from nonleaders. Self-confident leaders are more decisive and assertive and are more likely to gain others' confidence. Moreover, self-confident leaders will admit mistakes because they view them as learning opportunities rather than as refutation of their leadership capabilities. This also means that leaders have *emotional stability.* Even when things go wrong, they remain even-tempered and consistent in their outlook and in the way they treat others. Leaders who can't control their emotions, who anger quickly or attack and blame others for mistakes, are unlikely to be trusted.

Leaders are also smart. Leaders typically have strong *cognitive abilities.* This doesn't mean that leaders are necessarily geniuses—far from it. But it does mean that leaders have the capacity to analyze large amounts of seemingly unrelated, complex information and see patterns, opportunities, or threats where others might not see them. Finally, leaders also know their stuff, which means they have superior technical knowledge about the businesses they run. Leaders who have a good *knowledge of the business* understand the key technological decisions and concerns facing their companies. More often than

Don't Judge a Leader by Her Chanel

How much do physical traits affect our perception of a person's ability to lead? One study showed that female candidates tend to fare worse in elections than their male opponents because of their gender ... and worse yet if they are perceived as unattractive. Although it is just as easy to judge a leader by the clothes he or she is wearing as it is to judge a book by its cover, it is best to focus on whether a person has strong personal—rather than physical—traits, such as persistence, attention to detail, efficiency, analytical skills, and high standards. One clear trend in the past 10 years is that more women are setting up their own businesses. Since 1981, the number of women who own their own firms has risen by 234 per cent, reaching 683,000 in 2006, according to Statistics Canada. The Canadian Imperial Bank of Commerce estimated the number of women business owners currently as more than 800,000.

Sources: J. N. Schubert and M. A. Curran, "Stereotyping Effects in Candidate Evaluation: The Interaction of Gender and Attractiveness Bias", available online at http://www3.niu.edu/~ti0jns1/mpsa2001_paper.htm [accessed 27 August 2008]; G. Anders, "Tough CEOs Often Most Successful, a Study Finds," *The Wall Street Journal*, 19 November 2007, B3; http://www.cbc.ca/money/story/2008/10/20/women-profit.html#ixzz0sCQZVPQc [accessed 18 June 2010].

Followers as Leaders

As more organizations become flatter, or adopt less hierarchical organizational structures, it is becoming increasingly clear that leaders and followers are dependent on one another. One thing good leaders need is good followers. Barbara Kellerman of Harvard University outlines five different types of followers and urges leaders to understand what kind of followers they have. Isolates and bystanders are not invested. They just do their jobs and tend to impede change. They can be useful for leaders who want to maintain the status quo but are otherwise dead weight. Good followers, by contrast, support a leader they've invested in. Consequently, they are good assets. Participants are self-motivated and driven to make a difference, activists are eager and will go the extra mile, while diehards will support their leader even if it means going down with the ship. But leaders beware: These types of followers can be a liability if you have not inspired their loyalty. So followers are leaders, too. As Kellerman notes, "While they may lack authority, at least in comparison with their superiors, followers do not lack power and influence."

Source: B. Kellerman, "What Every Leader Needs to Know About Followers," *Harvard Business Review* (December 2007): 84–91.

not, studies indicate that effective leaders have long, extensive experience in their industries. Canada's top female entrepreneur posted revenue approaching $2 billion in fiscal 2008, according to Canada's *Profit Magazine*. *Profit*, which has been tracking women in business since 1999, said that Rebecca MacDonald, who heads up the Energy Savings Income Fund, is the country's top female entrepreneur. Her company offers consumers fixed-rate energy contracts, and you must understand this complex business to be successful.[11]

2.2 Leadership Behaviours

Thus far, you've read about who leaders *are*. It's hard to imagine a truly successful leader who lacks all of these qualities. But traits alone are not enough to make a successful leader. Leaders who have all these traits (or many of them) must then take actions that encourage people to achieve group or organizational goals.[12] So we will now examine what leaders *do*, meaning the behaviours they perform or the actions they take to influence others to achieve group or organizational goals. When she interviewed the CEO of Procter & Gamble on the subject of leadership, Associated Press reporter Elise Amendola asked, "Are leaders born or made?" Debunking the "great person" theory, A.G. Lafley answered, "Clearly made. You choose to lead. You choose to want to make a difference, to make the world better in some meaningful way. Until that

choice is made, you don't have a leader. You have a lump of clay."[13]

Researchers at the University of Michigan, Ohio State University, and the University of Texas examined the specific behaviours that leaders use to improve the satisfaction and performance of their subordinates. Hundreds of studies were conducted and hundreds of leader behaviours were examined. At all three universities, two basic leader behaviours emerged as central to successful leadership: initiating structure (called *job-centred leadership* at the University of Michigan, and *concern for production* at the University of Texas) and considerate leader behaviour (called *employee-centred leadership* at the University of Michigan and *concern for people* at the University of Texas).[14] These two leader behaviours form the basis for

Leaders are shaped by the choices they make.

many of the leadership theories discussed in this chapter.

Initiating structure is the degree to which a leader structures the roles of followers by setting goals, giving directions, setting deadlines, and assigning tasks. A leader's ability to initiate structure primarily affects subordinates' job performance. In a recent work stoppage with the railways, CAW reached a tentative contract with VIA Rail, averting a strike. This is tough leadership, dealing with the paycheques of the workforce. CAW represents 2,200 customer service, train service, and maintenance workers across Canada. CAW representative Bob Chernecki says: "We feel just great about the settlement." CAW reached a tentative three-year deal "after a difficult and challenging round of negotiations."[15]

Consideration is the extent to which a leader is friendly, approachable, and supportive and shows concern for employees. Consideration primarily affects subordinates' job satisfaction. Specific leader consideration behaviours include listening to employees' problems and concerns, consulting with employees before making decisions, and treating employees as equals. Twenty-five years ago Wal-Mart's CEO, Lee Scott, received a lesson in the importance of consideration from founder Sam Walton. Scott, who was then in charge of a transportation unit, was known for his tough management style and for sending blistering memos. When "Mr. Sam" called him into his office, Scott found nine of his truck drivers there waiting for him. The drivers, who were taking advantage of Wal-Mart's open-door policy, had complained to Walton about the way Scott treated them and asked that he be fired. According to Scott, "They just wanted to do their work and be appreciated for it. So Mr. Walton asked me, with them there, if I could do it differently."[16] After agreeing that he could, Scott said that Walton "had me stand at the door as they were leaving and thank each one for having the courage to use the open door, which is one of the very basic principles of Wal-Mart."[17] That office is now Scott's, and Wal-Mart has the same open door through which any Wal-Mart employee can walk to talk with the CEO.

Although researchers at all three universities generally agreed that initiating structure and consideration were basic leader behaviours, their interpretation differed on how these two behaviours are related to each other and which are necessary for effective leadership. The University of Michigan studies indicated that initiating structure and consideration were mutually exclusive behaviours on opposite ends of the same continuum. In other words, leaders who wanted to be more considerate would have to do less initiating of

Exhibit 14.1

Blake/Mouton Leadership Grid

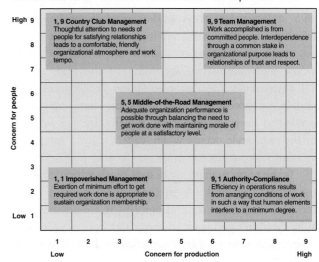

Source: R.R. Blake & A.A. McCanse, "The Leadership Grid®," *Leadership Dilemmas —Grid Solutions* (Houston: Gulf Publishing Company), 21. Copyright © 1991, by Scientific Methods, Inc. Reproduced by permission of Grid International, Inc.

structure (and vice versa). The University of Michigan studies also indicated that only considerate leader behaviours (i.e., employee-centred behaviours) were associated with successful leadership. By contrast, researchers at Ohio State University and the University of Texas found that initiating structure and consideration were independent behaviours, meaning that leaders can be considerate and initiate structure at the same time. Additional evidence confirms this finding.[18] The same researchers also concluded that the most effective leaders excelled at both initiating structure and considerate leader behaviours.

This "high-high" approach can be seen in the upper right corner of the Blake/Mouton leadership grid, shown in Exhibit 14.1. Blake and Mouton used two leadership behaviours—concern for people (i.e., consideration) and concern for production (i.e., initiating structure)—to categorize five different leadership styles. Both behaviours are rated on a 9-point scale, with 1 representing "low" and 9 representing "high." Blake and Mouton suggest that a "high-high" or 9,9 leadership style is the best. They call this style *team management* because leaders who use it display a high concern for people (9) and a high concern for production (9).

> **Initiating structure** the degree to which a leader structures the roles of followers by setting goals, giving directions, setting deadlines, and assigning tasks
>
> **Consideration** the extent to which a leader is friendly, approachable, and supportive and shows concern for employees

NEL

Chapter 14: Leadership   *279*

By contrast, leaders use a 9,1 *authority-compliance* leadership style when they have a high concern for production and a low concern for people. A 1,9 *country club* style occurs when leaders care about having a friendly enjoyable work environment but don't really pay much attention to production or performance. The worst leadership style, according to the grid, is the 1,1 *impoverished* leader, who shows little concern for people or production and does the bare minimum needed to keep his or her job. Finally, the 5,5 *middle-of-the-road* style occurs when leaders show a moderate amount of concern for both people and production.

Is the team management style, with a high concern for production and a high concern for people, really the best leadership style? Logically, it would seem so. Why wouldn't you want to show high concern for both people and production? Nonetheless, nearly 50 years of research indicates that there isn't one best leadership style. The best leadership style depends on the situation. In other words, no one leadership behaviour by itself and no one combination of leadership behaviours works well across all situations and employees.

Situational Approaches to Leadership

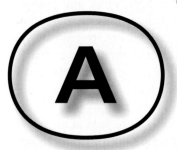

After leader traits and behaviours, the situational approach to leadership is the third major method used in the study of leadership. We'll review three major situational approaches to leadership—Fiedler's contingency theory, path-goal theory, and Vroom and Yetton's normative decision model. All assume that the effectiveness of any **leadership style,** the way a leader generally behaves toward followers, depends on the situation.[19]

According to situational leadership theories, there is no one best leadership style. But, one of these situational theories differs from the other three in one significant way. Fiedler's contingency theory assumes that leadership styles are consistent and

Leadership style the way a leader generally behaves toward followers

Contingency theory a leadership theory that states that in order to maximize work group performance, leaders must be matched to the situation that best fits their leadership style

difficult to change. Therefore, leaders must be placed in or "matched" to a situation that fits their leadership style. In contrast, the other situational theories assume that leaders are capable of adapting and adjusting their leadership styles to fit the demands of different situations.

After reading the next three sections, you should be able to

3 explain Fiedler's contingency theory.

4 describe how path-goal theory works.

5 explain the normative decision theory.

3 Putting Leaders in the Right Situation: Fiedler's Contingency Theory

Fiedler's **contingency theory** states that in order to maximize work group performance, leaders must be matched to the right leadership situation.[20] More specifically, the first basic assumption of Fiedler's theory is that leaders are effective when the work groups they lead perform well. So, instead of judging leaders' effectiveness by what the leaders do (i.e., initiating structure and consideration) or who they are (i.e., trait theory), Fiedler assesses leaders by the conduct and performance of the people they supervise. Second, Fiedler assumes that leaders are generally unable to change their leadership styles and that they will be more effective when their styles are matched to the proper situation. Third, Fiedler assumes that the favourableness of a situation for a leader depends on the degree to which the situation permits the leader to influence the behaviour of group members. Fiedler's third assumption is consistent with our definition of leadership as the process of influencing others to achieve group or organizational goals. In other words, in addition to

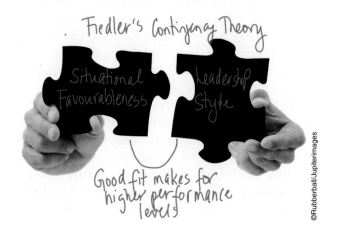

organization-wide communication also means finding ways to hear what people throughout the organization are feeling and thinking. This is important because most employees and managers are reluctant to share their thoughts and feelings with top managers. Surveys indicate that only 29 percent of first-level managers feel that their companies encourage employees to express their opinions openly. Another study of 22 companies found that 70 percent of the people surveyed were afraid to speak up about problems they knew existed at work.

Withholding information about organizational problems or issues is called **organizational silence.** Organizational silence occurs when employees believe that telling management about problems won't make a difference or that they'll be punished or hurt in some way for sharing such information.[45] Company hotlines, survey feedback, frequent informal meetings, surprise visits, and blogs are ways of overcoming organizational silence.

Company hotlines are phone numbers that anyone in the company can call anonymously to leave information for upper management. For example, Deloitte Touche Tohmatsu has a toll-free hotline for employees to call to report any kind of problem or issue within the company. Hotlines are particularly important because 44 percent of employees will not report misconduct. Why not? The reason is twofold: They don't believe anything will be done, and they "fear that the report will not be kept confidential."[46]

Survey feedback is information that is collected by survey from organization members and then compiled, disseminated, and used to develop action plans for improvement. Many organizations make use of survey feedback by surveying their managers and employees several times a year. At Four Seasons Hotels and Resorts, an employee opinion survey is conducted once a year to ensure that management keeps its finger on the pulse of what it considers one of its greatest assets, its corporate culture.[47] Similarly, FedEx utilizes an online survey, which is completely anonymous, to enable all employees to evaluate their managers and the overall environment at FedEx, including benefits, incentives, and working conditions. The results are compiled and then given back to each FedEx work group to decide where changes and improvements need to be made and to develop specific action plans to address those problems.

Frequent *informal meetings* between top managers and lower-level employees are one of the best ways for top managers to hear what others feel and think. Many people assume that top managers are at the centre of everything that goes on in organizations, but top managers commonly feel isolated from most of their lower-level managers and employees. Consequently, more and more top managers are scheduling frequent informal meetings with people throughout their companies.

Have you ever been around when a supervisor learns that upper management will be paying a visit? First there's panic, as everyone is told to drop what he or she is doing to polish, shine, and spruce up the workplace so that it looks perfect for the visit. Then, of course, top managers don't get a realistic look at what's going on in the company. Consequently, one of the ways to get an accurate picture is to pay *surprise visits* to various parts of the organization. These visits should not just be surprise inspections but should also be used as an opportunity to encourage meaningful upward communication from those who normally don't get a chance to communicate with upper management. Such surprise visits are now part of the culture at the Royal Mail, the United Kingdom's postal service. Chairman Allan Leighton frequently shows up unannounced at Royal Mail delivery offices. Leighton

Organizational silence when employees withhold information about organizational problems or issues

Company hotlines phone numbers that anyone in the company can call anonymously to leave information for upper management

Survey feedback information that is collected by surveys from organizational members and then compiled, disseminated, and used to develop action plans for improvement

says the initial reaction is always the same, "Oh s***, it's the chairman." However, Leighton isn't there to catch his employees doing something wrong. He's there to find out, right or wrong, what's really going on. Today, thanks in part to his communication with employees, the Royal Mail delivers 95 percent of first class mail in one day, better than any other postal service in the world, and now *earns*, not loses, a profit of 1.5 million pounds per day.

Blogs are another way to hear what people are thinking and saying both inside and outside the organization. A **blog** is a personal Web site that provides personal opinions or recommendations, news summaries, and reader comments. At Google, which owns the blog-hosting service Blogger, hundreds of employees are writing *internal blogs*. One

Blog a personal website that provides personal opinions or recommendations, news summaries, and reader comments

employee even wrote a blog for posting all the notes from the brainstorming sessions used to redesign the search page used by millions each day.[48] *External blogs*, written by people outside the company, can be a good way to find out what others are saying or thinking about your organization or its products or actions. Situations like this one make it increasingly important for companies to keep tabs on what others are saying about them. Some companies have created the new position of chief blogging officer to manage internal company blogs and to monitor what is said about the company and its products on external blogs.[49]

When a blog entry that was highly critical of the customer service at Home Depot drew more than 7,000 postings, new CEO Frank Blake posted a comment of his own indicating that he was establishing a "dedicated taskforce—working directly with me—that is ready and willing to address each and every issue raised on this [discussion] board."[50]

By the Numbers

75–95% estimated accuracy of information passing through organizational grapevines

$1 billion estimated value of the management coaching business

30 e-mails most people can read in 10–15 minutes

25% the amount that most people retain of what they hear

Visit **icanmgmt.com** to find the resources you need today!

Located at the back of the textbook are rip-out Chapter Review cards. Make sure you also go online to check out other tools that MGMT offers to help you successfully pass your course.

- Interactive Quizzes
- Key Terms Flashcards
- Audio Chapter Summaries
- PowerPoint Slides

- Interactive Games
- Crossword Puzzles
- "Reel to Reel" and "Biz Flix" videos
- Cases and Exercises

CONTROL

For all companies, past success is no guarantee of future success. Even successful companies fall short, face challenges, and have to make changes. **Control** is a regulatory process of establishing standards to achieve organizational goals, comparing actual performance to the standards, and taking corrective action when necessary to restore performance to those standards. Control is achieved when behaviour and work procedures conform to standards and company goals are accomplished.[1] Control is not just an after-the-fact process, however. Preventive measures are also a form of control.

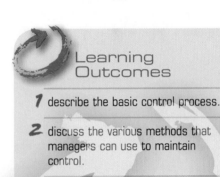

Learning Outcomes

1 describe the basic control process.

2 discuss the various methods that managers can use to maintain control.

3 describe the behaviours, processes, and outcomes that today's managers are choosing to control in their organizations.

Basics of Control

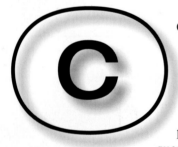

Control is important because there is so much at stake when a company fails to meet standards. Maple Leaf Foods Inc. is a meat processing company headquartered in Toronto. The company employs around 23,500 people at its operations across Canada and in the United States, the United Kingdom, and Asia, with sales of $5.2 billion in 2009. In August 2009, packaged meat products from Maple Leaf Foods were pinpointed as the source of a deadly, cross-Canada listeriosis outbreak that killed at least four people. Michael McCain, CEO of Maple Leaf, said that the company has a culture of food safety with standards "well beyond" what regulators require. "This week, our

Control a regulatory process of establishing standards to achieve organizational goals, comparing actual performance to the standards, and taking corrective action when necessary

© iStockphoto.com

best efforts failed," he said. "Tragically, our products have been linked to illness and loss of life." The internal control systems of Maple Leaf are augmented by external controls involving the Canadian Food Inspection Agency and provincial and local health authorities. Linda Smith, a spokesperson for Maple Leaf, said that 100 percent of recalled meats products were removed within days of the recall. "There is a very active effort to work with all of the food distribution customers," she said, "but it is not as direct because there are customers, and then those customers have customers," involving thousands of accounts. Although part of the system broke down, other parts worked very well. Certainly, some of the control standards failed at Maple Leaf; but other standards, for tracking through UPC/SSC codes and best-before dates,

were extremely useful control tools in containing this tragedy.[2]

 After reading the next section, you should be able to

1 describe the basic control process.

1 The Control Process

The basic control process 1.1 begins with the establishment of clear standards of performance; 1.2 involves a comparison of performance to those standards; 1.3 takes corrective action, if needed, to repair performance deficiencies; 1.4 is a dynamic, cybernetic process; and

1.5 consists of three basic methods: feedback control, concurrent control, and feedforward control. However, as much as managers would like, **1.6 control isn't always worthwhile or possible.**

1.1 Standards

The control process begins when managers set goals, such as satisfying 90 percent of customers or increasing sales by 5 percent. Companies then specify the performance standards that must be met to accomplish those goals. **Standards** are a basis of comparison for measuring the extent to which organizational performance is satisfactory or unsatisfactory. For example, many pizzerias use 30–40 minutes as the standard for delivery times. Since anything longer is viewed as unsatisfactory, they'll typically reduce the price if they can't deliver a hot pizza to you within that time period.

So how do managers set standards? How do they decide which levels of performance are satisfactory and which are unsatisfactory? The first criterion for a good standard is that it must enable goal achievement. If you're meeting the standard but still not achieving company goals, then the standard may have to be changed. There are many approaches to "standards." The Standards Council of Canada (SCC) is a federal Crown corporation that has a mandate to promote efficient and effective standardization in Canada. Located in Ottawa, the organization reports to Parliament through the Minister of Industry and oversees Canada's National Standards System. It is part of the International Organization

Maugli/Shutterstock

for Standards (ISO), which has 163 member countries. Because "International Organization for Standardization" would have different acronyms in different languages ("IOS" in English, "OIN" in French for Organisation Internationale de Normalisation), its founders decided to give it also a short, all-purpose name. They chose

Standards a basis of comparison for measuring the extent to which various kinds of organizational performance are satisfactory or unsatisfactory

Benchmarking the process of identifying outstanding practices, processes, and standards in other companies and adapting them to your company

"ISO," derived from the Greek isos, meaning "equal." Whatever the country, whatever the language, the short form of the organization's name is always ISO.[3]

Companies also determine standards by listening to customers' comments, complaints, and suggestions, or by observing competitors' products and services. Standards are also sometimes set by government authorities. Although the Canadian Food Inspection Agency typically establishes food standards, some companies are not satisfied by the government's slow response to food safety concerns. In order to monitor and enforce quality standards, they have turned to private regulators such as GlobalGap. The private regulator trend started in Europe in 1997 and has since caught on in Canada as companies like Wal-Mart and McDonald's have begun to buy only meat that has been certified by such regulators. GlobalGap has more than 100,000 producers representing 300 fruit products alone. BC Hothouse in Vancouver is a registered producer. Most meat packing plants in Alberta and Ontario are also producer-members of GlobalGap. With private regulators, companies can move more quickly to prompt growers to comply with the standards, improving food quality through the entire system.[4]

Standards can also be determined by benchmarking other companies. **Benchmarking** is the process of determining how well other companies (though not just competitors) perform business functions or tasks. In other words, benchmarking is the process of determining other companies' standards. When setting standards by benchmarking, the first step is to determine what to benchmark. Companies can benchmark anything from cycle time (how fast) to quality (how well) to price (how much). The next step is to identify the companies against which to benchmark your standards. The last step is to collect data to determine other companies' performance standards.

1.2 Comparison to Standards

The next step in the control process is to compare actual performance to performance standards. Although this sounds straightforward, the quality of the comparison largely depends on the measurement and information systems a company uses to keep track of performance. The better the system, the easier it is for companies to track their progress and identify problems that need to be fixed. One way for retailers to verify that performance standards are being met is to use secret shoppers, individuals who visit stores pretending to be customers but are really there to determine whether employees provide helpful customer service.

Secret shopper Cliff Fill recalls the fast-food restaurant where the workers discussed their dating plans as he stood in front of them ready to order. After ignoring him for 90 seconds (secret shoppers often carry timers with them), they turned to him and said, "We'll be done with our conversation in a minute and be with you."[5]

1.3 Corrective Action

The next step in the control process is to identify performance deviations, analyze those deviations, and then develop and implement programs to correct them.

Beta versions of software programs are a classic tool that developers use to monitor deviations from the standard and take corrective action *before* the product is released on the market. Microsoft has an internal program called Software Quality Metrics (SQM) that company software developers use when creating new software releases. SQM helps the developers determine how each change in the software code will affect the functionality of the program and uses a system of comparison charts to show how the changes will affect users of new software.[6]

1.4 Dynamic, Cybernetic Process

As shown in Exhibit 16.1, control is a continuous, dynamic, cybernetic process. Control begins by setting standards, measuring performance, and then comparing performance to the standards. If the performance deviates from the standards, then managers and employees analyze the deviations and develop and implement corrective programs that (hopefully) achieve the desired performance by meeting the standards. Managers must repeat the entire process again and again in an endless feedback loop (a continuous process). Thus, control is not a one-time achievement or result. It continues over time (i.e., it is dynamic) and requires daily, weekly, and monthly attention from managers to maintain performance levels at the standard. This constant attention is what makes control a cybernetic process. **Cybernetic** derives from the Greek word *kubernetes*, meaning "steersman," that is, one who steers or keeps on course.[7] The control process shown in Exhibit 16.1 is cybernetic because constant attention to the feedback loop is necessary to keep the company's activities on course.

1.5 Feedback, Concurrent, and Feedforward Control

The three basic control methods are feedback control, concurrent control, and feedforward control. **Feedback control** is a mechanism for gathering information about performance deficiencies after they occur. This information is then used to correct performance deficiencies or prevent future deficiencies. Study after study has clearly shown that feedback improves both individual and organizational performance. In most instances, any feedback is better than no feedback. If feedback has a downside, it's that it always occurs after the fact, after performance deficiencies have already occurred. Control can minimize the effects, but the damage is already done. The Canadian Aircraft Maintenance Engineer (AME) Licensing and Approved Training Organization (ATO) Systems are set by Transport Canada for

Exhibit 16.1

Cybernetic Control Process

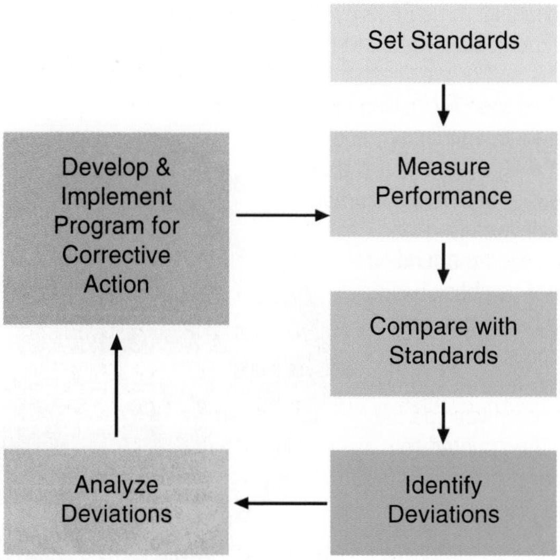

Source: Reprinted from H. Koontz & R. W. Bradspies, "Managing through Feedforward Control: A Future-Directed View," *Business Horizons* 15 (June 1972) 25–36, with permission from Elsevier.

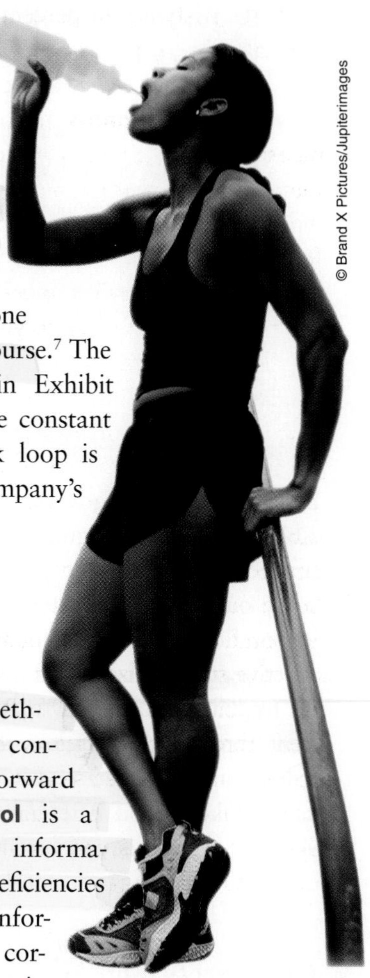

Cybernetic the process of steering or keeping on course

Feedback control a mechanism for gathering information about performance deficiencies after they occur

private firms. This government organization is responsible for controls, regulations, standards, policies, and procedures for aircraft in Canada. Private firms then carry out maintenance work under a feedback control system.[8]

Concurrent control addresses the problems inherent in feedback control by gathering information about performance deficiencies as they occur. Apple and Nike teamed up to create a real-time exercise feedback system called Nike + iPod. After a runner installs a sensor in her shoes, it transmits concurrent information to her iPod. The system measures time, distance, calories burned, and pace. Runners can actually track their efforts every moment of their run and make changes on the fly.[9] Concurrent control is an improvement over feedback because it attempts to eliminate or shorten the delay between performance and feedback about the performance.

Feedforward control is a mechanism for gathering information about performance deficiencies *before* they occur. In contrast to feedback and concurrent control, which provide feedback on the basis

Concurrent control a mechanism for gathering information about performance deficiencies as they occur, thereby eliminating or shortening the delay between performance and feedback

Feedforward control a mechanism for monitoring performance inputs rather than outputs to prevent or minimize performance deficiencies before they occur

Control loss the situation in which behaviour and work procedures do not conform to standards

of outcomes and results, feedforward control provides information about performance deficiencies by monitoring inputs, not outputs. Thus, feedforward control seeks to prevent or minimize performance deficiencies before they happen. Microsoft uses feedforward controls to try to prevent software problems before they occur. For example, when developing the latest version of its Windows Server software (for network and Internet computer servers), Microsoft taught 8,500 experienced programmers new methods for writing more reliable software code *before* asking them to develop new features for Windows Server software. Microsoft has also developed new software testing tools that let the programmers thoroughly test the code they've written (i.e., input) before passing the code on to others to be used in beta testing and then in final products.[10]

1.6 Control Isn't Always Worthwhile or Possible

Control is achieved when behaviour and work procedures conform to standards and goals are accomplished. By contrast, **control loss** occurs when behaviour and work procedures do not conform to standards.[11] Maintaining control is important because loss of control prevents organizations from achieving their goals. When

Automatic "Green"

Now you don't have to remember to turn down the thermostat when you leave the office in order to control energy costs. Software startup companies are creating "green software" programs that keep tabs on your energy use, turn off lights automatically, and figure out when it is cheapest to use energy for flexible tasks like cooling office space. The convenience doesn't come cheap: This author was responsible for a project that installed more than $7 million in automation heating, ventilating, and cooling (HVAC) systems at the University of British Columbia. Honeywell Canada provided the funding, on a pay-back basis, and everyone was a winner. The pay-back was guaranteed over a seven-year period and amounted to more than $1.2 million per year..

Source: J. Carlton, "To Cut Fuel Bills, Try High-Tech Help," *The Wall Street Journal*, 11 March 2008, B3.

© iStockphoto.com/Christine Balderas

control loss occurs, managers need to find out what, if anything, they could have done to prevent it. Usually, as discussed above, that means identifying deviations from standard performance, analyzing the causes of those deviations, and taking corrective action. Even so, implementing controls isn't always worthwhile or possible. Let's look at regulation costs and cybernetic feasibility to see why.

To determine whether control is worthwhile, managers need to carefully assess **regulation costs,** or costs associated with implementing or maintaining control. If a control process costs more than an an organization gains from its benefits, it may not be worthwhile. Thanks to technology, however, companies are finding it easier (i.e., more feasible) to control many more processes. For example, handwritten prescriptions can be difficult for pharmacists to read, but digital technology can be used to control the accuracy of prescriptions. Doctors can send prescriptions to the pharmacy electronically, and software can alert them to interactions with other drugs that might be harmful to a patient. Newfoundland and Labrador has started to link up 190 pharmacies in a provincial health department project. "A lot of drugs now do have serious interaction between them, and you obviously work with the pharmacy and doctors to try to avoid those," says St. John's pharmacist Chris Hollett. Remembers St. John's pharmacist Tom Healy: "We got a call from a drugstore in Conception Bay North that is also on the same centre of health information network, and he had a customer there who was trying to purchase a codeine product. But the prescription was also dispensed three days before, so we prevented a narcotic from being overdispensed."[12]

Another factor to consider is **cybernetic feasibility,** the extent to which it is possible to implement each of the three steps in the control process. If one or more steps cannot be implemented, then maintaining effective control may be difficult or impossible.

How and What to Control

The doors are locked on midnight-shift employees at 10 percent of Wal-Mart stores to keep out burglars and, some say, also to prevent employee theft. According to Mona Williams, Wal-Mart's vice president for communications, "Wal-Mart secures these stores just as any other business does that has employees working overnight. Doors are locked to protect associates and the store from intruders."[13] But many employees dislike the policy. When Michael Rodriguez injured his ankle at 3 A.M., he had to wait an hour for a store manager to show up to unlock the doors. Says Rodriguez, "Being locked in in an emergency like that, that's not right."[14] Wal-Mart's Mona Williams responds, "Fire doors are always accessible [and unlocked from the inside] for safety, and there will always be at least one manager in the store with a set of keys to unlock the doors."[15]

Does locking in midnight employees jeopardize or improve their safety? Is this policy a reasonable response to employee theft, which can often exceed a store's profits? If you were a Wal-Mart store manager, what would you do?

After reading the next two sections, you should be able to

2 discuss the various methods that managers can use to maintain control.

3 describe the behaviours, processes, and outcomes that today's managers are choosing to control in their organizations.

2 Control Methods

Managers can use five different methods to achieve control in their organizations: ***2.1 bureaucratic, 2.2 objective, 2.3 normative, 2.4 concertive,*** *and* ***2.5 self-control.***

2.1 Bureaucratic Control

When most people think of managerial control, what they have in mind is bureaucratic control. **Bureaucratic control** is top-down control, in which managers try to influence employee behaviour by rewarding or punishing employees for compliance or noncompliance with organizational policies, rules, and procedures. Most employees, however, would argue that bureaucratic managers emphasize punishment for

Regulation costs the costs associated with implementing or maintaining control

Cybernetic feasibility the extent to which it is possible to implement each step in the control process

Bureaucratic control the use of hierarchical authority to influence employee behaviour by rewarding or punishing employees for compliance or noncompliance with organizational policies, rules, and procedures

Spencer Grant/GetStock.com

noncompliance much more than rewards for compliance. For instance, when visiting the company's regional offices and managers, the president of a training company, who was known for his temper and for micromanaging others, would get some toilet paper from the restrooms and aggressively ask, "What's this?" When the managers answered, "Toilet paper," the president would scream that it was two-ply toilet paper that the company couldn't afford. When told of a cracked toilet seat in one of the women's restrooms, he said, "If you don't like sitting on that seat, you can stand up like I do!"[16]

As you learned in Chapter 2, bureaucratic management and control were created to prevent just this type of managerial behaviour. By encouraging managers to apply well-thought-out rules, policies, and procedures in an impartial, consistent manner to everyone in the organization, bureaucratic control is supposed to make companies more efficient, effective, and fair. Ironically, it frequently has just the opposite effect. Managers who use bureaucratic control often emphasize following the rules above all else.

Another characteristic of bureaucratically controlled companies is that due to their rule- and policy-driven decision making, they are highly resistant to change and slow to respond to customers and competitors. Recall from Chapter 2 that even Max Weber, the German philosopher who is largely credited with popularizing bureaucratic ideals in the late 19th century, referred to bureaucracy as the "iron cage." He said, "Once fully established, bureaucracy is among those social structures which are the hardest to destroy."[17]

2.2 Objective Control

In many companies, bureaucratic control has evolved into **objective control**, which is the use of observable measures of employee behaviour or output to assess performance and influence behaviour. Whereas bureaucratic control focuses on whether policies and rules are followed, objective control focuses on observing and measuring worker behaviour or output. There are two kinds of objective control: behaviour control and output control.

Behaviour control is regulating behaviours and actions that workers perform on the job. The basic assumption of behaviour control is that if you do the right things (i.e., the right behaviours) every day, then those things should lead to goal achievement. Behaviour control is still management-based, however, which means that managers are responsible for monitoring and rewarding or punishing workers for exhibiting desired or undesired behaviours. Companies that use global positioning satellite (GPS) technology to track where workers are and what they're doing are using behaviour control. GPS can also be used to modify the behaviour of other people. Two chronic Winnipeg car thieves were arrested after a series of break-ins and a police pursuit of a stolen vehicle. Youths with multiple car-theft convictions, who were deemed to be high-risk reoffenders, had been ordered to wear the ankle bracelets by the court. With the assistance of the Manitoba Probation Services electronic monitoring staff, people were able to use GPS to track the suspects. "Did they forget they were wearing the bracelets, or did they think that the satellites didn't work at night?" asks one observer.[18]

Instead of measuring what managers and workers do, **output control** measures the results of their efforts. Whereas behaviour control regulates, guides, and

Objective control the use of observable measures of worker behaviour or outputs to assess performance and influence behaviour

Behaviour control the regulation of the behaviours and actions that workers perform on the job

Output control the regulation of workers' results or outputs through rewards and incentives

measures how workers behave on the job, output control gives managers and workers the freedom to behave as they see fit as long as they accomplish pre-specified, measurable results. Output control is often coupled with rewards and incentives.

Three things must occur for output control and rewards to lead to improved business results. First, output control measures must be reliable, fair, and accurate. Second, employees and managers must believe that they can produce the desired results. If they don't, then the output controls won't affect their behaviour. Third, the rewards or incentives tied to outcome control measures must truly be dependent on achieving established standards of performance. This kind of output control can also be used for CEO salaries of not-for-profit organizations. Robert Bell, CEO of Toronto's sprawling University Health Network, has part of his salary tied to improving on a list of performance measures. As he runs through a spreadsheet, he indicates morbidity rates. "This is one of the best scores in Canada," he says proudly. "And we have the most complex patient load in Canada." Such accomplishments, he argues, are proof that pay-for-performance is a valuable output control measure. "My compensation is dramatically at risk," he says, "if we don't accomplish what the board thinks we should accomplish, I don't get as much salary."[19]

2.3 Normative Control

Rather than monitoring rules, behaviour, or output, another way to control what goes on in organizations is to use normative control to shape the beliefs and values of the people who work there. With **normative controls,** a company's widely shared values and beliefs guide workers' behaviour and decisions. For example, at Nordstrom, a Seattle-based department store chain, that ships to Canada, one value permeates the entire workforce from top to bottom: extraordinary customer service. On the first day of work at Nordstrom, trainees begin their transformation to the "Nordstrom way" by reading the employee handbook. Sounds boring, doesn't it? But Nordstrom's handbook is printed on *one side* of a 3-by-5-inch note card, shown in its entirety in Exhibit 16.2. That's it. No lengthy rules. No specifics about what behaviour is or is not appropriate. Just use your judgment.[20]

Normative controls are created in two ways. First, companies that use normative controls are very careful about whom they hire. While many companies screen potential applicants on the basis of their abilities, normatively controlled companies are just as likely to

Exhibit 16.2
Nordstrom's Employee Handbook

Welcome to Nordstrom's. We're glad to have you with our company. Our Number One goal is to provide outstanding customer service. Set both your personal and professional goals high. We have great confidence in your ability to achieve them.

Nordstrom Rules:

Rule #1: Use your good judgment in all situations.

There will be no additional rules. Please feel free to ask your department manager, store manager, or division general manager any question at any time.

Source: S. Williford, "Nordstrom Sets the Standard for Customer Service," *Memphis Business Journal,* 1 July 1996, 21.

screen potential applicants based on their attitudes and values. For example, before building stores in a new city, Nordstrom sends its human resource team into town to interview prospective applicants. In a few cities, the company cancelled its expansion plans when it could not find enough qualified applicants who embodied the service attitudes and values for which Nordstrom is known.[21]

Second, with normative controls, managers and employees learn what they should and should not do by observing experienced employees and by listening to the stories they tell about the company. At Nordstrom, many of these stories, which employees call "heroics," have been inspired by the company motto, "Respond to Unreasonable Customer Requests!"[22] "Nordies," as Nordstrom employees call themselves, like to tell the story about a customer who just had to have a pair of burgundy Donna Karan slacks that had gone on sale, but she could not find her size. The sales associate who was helping her contacted five nearby Nordstrom stores, but none had the customer's size. So rather than leave the customer dissatisfied with her shopping experience, the sales associate went to her manager for petty cash and then went across the street and paid full price for the slacks at a competitor's store. She then resold them to the customer at Nordstrom's lower sale price.[23] Obviously, Nordstrom would quickly go out of business if this were the norm. Nevertheless, this story makes clear the attitude that drives employee

Normative control
the regulation of workers' behaviour and decisions through widely shared organizational values and beliefs

performance at Nordstrom in ways that rules, behavioural guidelines, or output controls could not.

2.4 Concertive Control

Whereas normative controls are based on beliefs that are strongly held and widely shared throughout a company, **concertive controls** are based on beliefs that are shaped and negotiated by work groups.[24] Whereas normative controls are driven by strong organizational cultures, concertive controls usually arise when companies give autonomous work groups complete autonomy and responsibility for task completion. The most autonomous groups operate without managers and are completely responsible for controlling work group processes, outputs, and behaviour. Such groups do their own hiring, firing, worker discipline, work schedules, materials ordering, budget making and meeting, and decision making.

New York, David Hutchins is a frontline supervisor or "lead man" in the rolling mill, where steel from the furnace is spread thin enough to be cut into sheets. When the plant was under the previous ownership, if the guys doing the cutting got backed up, the guys doing the rolling—including Hutchins—would just take a break. He says, "We'd sit back, have a cup of coffee, and complain: 'Those guys stink.'" It took six months to convince the employees at the Auburn plant that the Nucor teamwork way was better than the old way. Now, Hutchins says, "At Nucor, we're not 'you guys' and 'us guys.' It's all of us guys. Wherever the bottleneck is, we go there, and everyone works on it."[25]

The second phase in the development of concertive control is the emergence and formalization of objective rules to guide and control behaviour. The beliefs and values developed in phase one usually develop into more objective rules as new members join teams.

 Concertive control is **not** established **overnight.**

Concertive control is not established overnight. Highly autonomous work groups evolve through two phases as they develop concertive control. In phase one, group members learn to work with one another, supervise one another's work, and develop the values and beliefs that will guide and control their behaviour. And because they develop these values and beliefs themselves, work group members feel strongly about following them.

In the steel industry, Nucor, which operates in Canada as the Harris Steel Canada Group (which it purchased in 2007), was long considered an upstart compared to the largest steel firms. Today, however, not only has Nucor managed to outlast many other mills, but the company has also bought out 13 other mills in the past five years. Nucor has a unique culture that gives real power to employees on the line and that fosters teamwork throughout the organization. This type of teamwork can be a difficult thing for a newly acquired group of employees to get used to. For example, at Nucor's first big acquisition in Auburn,

The clearer those rules, the easier it becomes for new members to figure out how and how not to behave.

Ironically, concertive control may lead to even more stress for workers to conform to expectations than bureaucratic control. Under bureaucratic control, most workers only have to worry about pleasing the boss. But with concertive control, their behaviour has to satisfy the rest of their team members. For example, one team member says, "I don't have to sit there and look for the boss to be around; and if the boss is not around, I can sit there and talk to my neighbour or do what I want. Now the whole team is around me and the whole team is observing what I'm doing."[26] Plus, with concertive control, team members have a second, much more stressful role to perform—that of making sure that their team members adhere to team values and rules.

2.5 Self-Control

Self-control, also known as **self-management,** is a control system in which managers and workers control their own behaviour.[27] Self-control does not result in anarchy, or a state in which everyone gets to do whatever he or she wants. In self-control or self-management, leaders and managers provide workers with clear boundaries within which they may guide and control their own goals and behaviours.[28] Leaders and managers also contribute to self-control by teaching others the skills

Concertive control
the regulation of workers' behaviour and decisions through work group values and beliefs

Self-control (self-management) a control system in which managers and workers control their own behaviour by setting their own goals, monitoring their own progress, and rewarding themselves for goal achievement

> If you control for just one thing, such as costs, then **other dimensions,** like marketing, customer service, and quality are likely to **suffer.**

they need to maximize and monitor their own work effectiveness. In turn, individuals who manage and lead themselves establish self-control by setting their own goals, monitoring their own progress, rewarding or punishing themselves for achieving or for not achieving their self-set goals, and constructing positive thought patterns that remind them of the importance of their goals and their ability to accomplish them.[29]

For example, let's assume you need to do a better job of praising and recognizing the good work that your staff does for you. You can use goal setting, self-observation, and self-reward to self-manage this behaviour. For self-observation, write "praise/recognition" on a 3-by-5-inch card. Put the card in your pocket. Put a check on the card each time you praise or recognize someone (wait until the person has left before you do this). Keep track for a week. This serves as your baseline or starting point. Simply keeping track will probably increase how often you do this. After a week, assess your baseline or starting point, and then set a specific goal. For instance, if your baseline was twice a day, you might set a specific goal to praise or recognize others' work five times a day. Continue monitoring your performance with your cards. Once you've achieved your goal every day for a week, give yourself a reward (perhaps a CD, a movie, lunch with a friend at a new restaurant) for achieving your goal.[30]

As you can see, the components of self-management, self-set goals, self-observation, and self-reward have their roots in the motivation theories you read about in Chapter 13. The key difference, though, is that the goals, feedback, and rewards originate from employees themselves and not from their managers or organizations.

3 What to Control?

In the first section of this chapter, we discussed the basics of the control process and that control isn't always worthwhile or possible. In the second section, we looked at the various ways in which control can be obtained. In this third and final section, we address an equally important issue, "What should managers control?" The way managers answer this question has critical implications for most businesses.

If you control for just one thing, such as costs, then other dimensions, like marketing, customer service, and quality, are likely to suffer. If you try to control for too many things, then managers and employees become confused about what's really important. In the end, successful companies find a balance that comes from doing three or four things right, like managing costs, providing value, and keeping customers and employees satisfied.

*After reading this section, you should be able to explain **3.1 the balanced scorecard approach to control and how companies can achieve balanced control of company performance by choosing to control 3.2 budgets, cash flows, and economic value added; 3.3 customer defections; 3.4 quality;** and **3.5 waste and pollution**.*

3.1 The Balanced Scorecard

Most companies measure performance using standard financial and accounting measures such as return on capital, return on assets, return on investments, cash flow, net income, and net margins. The **balanced scorecard** encourages managers to look beyond traditional financial measures to four different perspectives on company performance. How do customers see us (the customer perspective)? At what must we excel (the internal perspective)? Can we continue to improve and create value (the innovation and learning perspective)? How do we look to shareholders (the financial perspective)?[31]

The balanced scorecard has several advantages over traditional control processes that rely solely on financial measures. First, it forces managers at each level of the company to set specific goals and measure performance in each of the four areas. For example, Exhibit 16.3 (p. 326) shows that Nova Scotia Power Inc. uses different measures, at different levels in its organization, to determine whether it is meeting the standards it has set for itself. The four perspectives are financial, customer, internal, and

Balanced scorecard
measurement of organizational performance in four equally important areas: finances, customers, internal operations, and innovation and learning

Exhibit 16.3

Nova Scotia Power Inc.'s Balanced Score Card

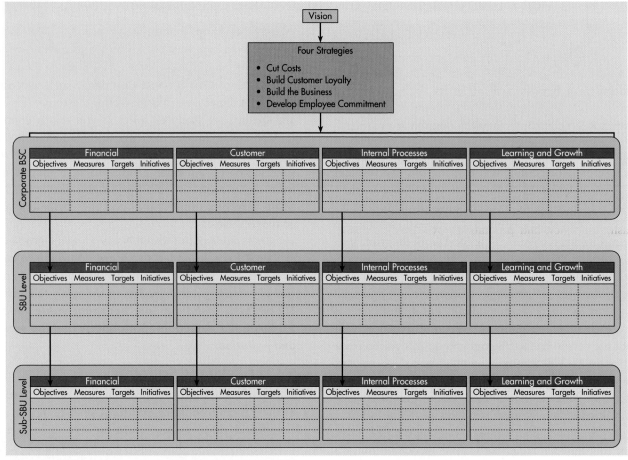

Source: Niven, P., 2006. Cascading the Balanced Scorecard : A Case Study on Nova Scotia Power, Inc., http://www.scribd.com/doc/3489336/Cascading-the-Balanced-Scorecard-A-Case-Study-on-Nova-Scotia-Power. Accessed 19 June 2010.

learning and growth. *Financial* perspectives are very common in businesses: they include ROI, profitability ratios, debt ratios, and so forth. The *customer* perspectives would include items such as getting 100 percent power 100 percent of the time—in other words, "What is the power outage rate, and how long do outages last?" *Internal* measures would include items such as preventive maintenance on-time performance, on-time, on-budget capital construction, and power frequency boundaries. *Learning and growth* perspectives deal with employee training, work-safe practices, innovations, and employee–management relations. Each of the corporation's strategic subunit (SBU), and subSBU (department) goals measures the four perspectives along the lines of the overall goals of Nova Scotia Power, which are to (1) cut costs,

Suboptimization performance improvement in one part of an organization at the expense of decreased performance in another part

(2) build customer loyalty, (3) build the business, and (4) develop employee commitment.

The second major advantage of the balanced scorecard approach to control is that it minimizes the chances of **suboptimization,** which occurs when performance improves in one area at the expense of decreased performance in others. Jon Meliones, chief medical director at a major children's hospital, says, "We could increase productivity…by assigning more patients to a nurse, but doing so would raise the likelihood of errors—an unacceptable trade-off."[32]

Let's examine some of the ways in which companies are controlling the four basic parts of the balanced scorecard: the financial perspective (budgets, cash flows, and economic value added), the customer perspective (customer defections), the internal perspective (total quality management), and the innovation and learning perspective (waste and pollution).

3.2 The Financial Perspective: Controlling Budgets, Cash Flows, and Economic Value Added

The traditional approach to controlling financial performance focuses on accounting tools such as cash flow analysis, balance sheets, income statements, financial ratios, and budgets. **Cash flow analysis** predicts how changes in a business will affect its ability to take in more cash than it pays out. **Balance sheets** provide a snapshot of a company's financial position at a particular time (but not the future). **Income statements,** also called profit and loss statements, show what has happened to an organization's income, expenses, and net profit (income less expenses) over a period of time. **Financial ratios** are typically used to track a business's liquidity (cash), efficiency, and profitability over time compared to other businesses in its industry. Finally, **budgets** are used to project costs and revenues, prioritize and control spending, and ensure that expenses don't exceed available funds and revenues. The Financial Review Card bound in the the back of this book contains tables that (a) show the basic steps or parts for cash flow analyses, balance sheets, and income statements; (b) list a few of the most common financial ratios and explain how they are calculated, what they mean, and when to use them; and (c) review the different kinds of budgets managers can use to track and control company finances.

By themselves, none of these tools—cash flow analyses, balance sheets, income statements, financial ratios, or budgets—tell the whole financial story of a business. They must be used together when assessing a company's financial performance. Since these tools are reviewed in detail in your accounting and finance classes, only a brief overview is provided here. Still, these are necessary tools for controlling organizational finances and expenses, and they should be part of your business toolbox.

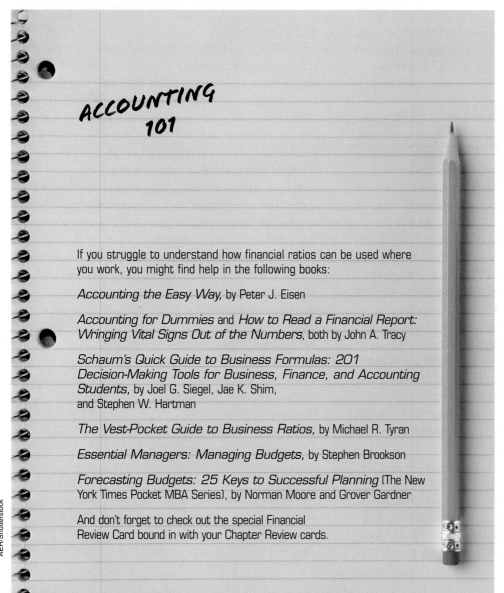

ACCOUNTING 101

If you struggle to understand how financial ratios can be used where you work, you might find help in the following books:

Accounting the Easy Way, by Peter J. Eisen

Accounting for Dummies and *How to Read a Financial Report: Wringing Vital Signs Out of the Numbers*, both by John A. Tracy

Schaum's Quick Guide to Business Formulas: 201 Decision-Making Tools for Business, Finance, and Accounting Students, by Joel G. Siegel, Jae K. Shim, and Stephen W. Hartman

The Vest-Pocket Guide to Business Ratios, by Michael R. Tyran

Essential Managers: Managing Budgets, by Stephen Brookson

Forecasting Budgets: 25 Keys to Successful Planning (The New York Times Pocket MBA Series), by Norman Moore and Grover Gardner

And don't forget to check out the special Financial Review Card bound in with your Chapter Review cards.

AER/Shutterstock

Cash flow analysis a type of analysis that predicts how changes in a business will affect its ability to take in more cash than it pays out

Balance sheets accounting statements that provide a snapshot of a company's financial position at a particular time

Income statements accounting statements, also called "profit and loss statements," that show what has happened to an organization's income, expenses, and net profit over a period of time

Financial ratios calculations typically used to track a business's liquidity (cash), efficiency, and profitability over time compared to other businesses in its industry

Budgets quantitative plans through which managers decide how to allocate available money to best accomplish company goals

Exhibit 16.4

Calculating Economic Value Added (EVA)

1. Calculate net operating profit after taxes (NOPAT).	$3,500,000
2. Identify how much capital the company has invested (i.e., spent).	$16,800,000
3. Determine the cost (i.e., rate) paid for capital (usually between 5 percent and 13 percent).	10%
4. Multiply capital used (Step 2) times cost of capital (Step 3).	(10% × $16,800,000) = $1,680,000
5. Subtract the total dollar cost of capital from net profit after taxes.	$3,500,000 NOPAT −$1,680,000 Total cost of capital $1,820,000 Economic value added

Though no one would dispute the importance of these four accounting tools, accounting research also indicates that the complexity and sheer amount of information contained in them can shut down the brain and glaze over the eyes of even the most experienced manager.[33] Sometimes there's simply too much information to make sense of. The balanced scorecard simplifies things by focusing on one simple question when it comes to finances: How do we look to shareholders? One way to answer that question is through something called economic value added.

Conceptually, **economic value added (EVA)** is not the same thing as profits. It is the amount by which profits exceed the cost of capital in a given year. It is based on the simple idea that capital is necessary to run a business and that capital comes at a cost. Although most people think of capital as cash, once it is invested (i.e., spent), capital is more likely to be found in a business in the form of computers, manufacturing plants, employees, raw materials, and so forth. And just like the interest that a homeowner pays on a mortgage or that a college student pays on a student loan, there is a cost to that capital.

The most common costs of capital are the interest paid on long-term bank loans used to buy all those resources, the interest paid to bondholders (who lend organizations their money), and the dividends (cash payments) and growth in stock value that accrue to shareholders. EVA is positive when company profits (revenues minus expenses minus taxes) exceed the cost of capital in a given year. In other words, if a business is to truly grow, its revenues must be large enough to cover both short-term costs (annual expenses and taxes) and long-term costs (the cost of borrowing capital from bondholders and shareholders). If you're a bit confused, the late Roberto Goizueta, the former CEO of Coca-Cola, explained it this way: "You borrow money at a certain rate and invest it at a higher rate and pocket the difference. It is simple. It is the essence of banking."[34]

Exhibit 16.4 shows how to calculate EVA. First, starting with a company's income statement, you calculate the net operating profit after taxes (NOPAT) by subtracting taxes owed from income from operations. (Remember, a quick review of an income statement is on the Financial Review Card bound at the back of your book). The NOPAT shown in Exhibit 16.4 is $3,500,000. Second, identify how much capital the company has invested (i.e., spent). Total liabilities (what the company owes) less accounts payable and less accrued expenses, neither of which you pay interest on, provides a rough approximation of this amount. In Exhibit 16.4, total capital invested is $16,800,000. Third, calculate the cost (i.e., rate) paid for capital by determining the interest paid to bondholders (who lend organizations their money), which is usually somewhere between 5 and 8 percent, and the return that stockholders want in terms of dividends and stock price appreciation, which is historically about 13 percent. Take a weighted average of the two to determine the overall cost of capital.

Economic value added (EVA) the amount by which company profits (revenues, minus expenses, minus taxes) exceed the cost of capital in a given year

In Exhibit 16.4, the cost of capital is 10 percent. Fourth, multiply the total capital ($16,800,000) from Step 2 by the cost of capital (10 percent) from Step 3. In Exhibit 16.4, this amount is $1,680,000. Fifth, subtract the total dollar cost of capital in Step 4 from the NOPAT in Step 1. In Exhibit 16.4, this value is $1,820,000, which means that our example company has created economic value or wealth this year. If our EVA number had been negative, meaning that the company didn't make enough profit to cover the cost of capital from bondholders and shareholders, then the company would have destroyed economic value or wealth by taking in more money than it returned.[35]

Why is EVA so important? First and most importantly, because it includes the cost of capital, it shows whether a business, division, department, profit centre, or product is really paying for itself. The key is to make sure that managers and employees can see how their choices and behaviour affect the company's EVA.

Second, because EVA can easily be determined for subsets of a company such as divisions, regional offices, manufacturing plants, and sometimes even departments, it makes managers and workers at all levels pay much closer attention to their segment of the business. When company offices were being refurbished at Genesco, a shoe company, a worker who had EVA training handed CEO Ben Harris $4,000 in cash. The worker explained that he now understood the effect his job had on the company's ability to survive and prosper. Since the company was struggling, he had sold the old doors that had been removed during remodelling so that the company could have the cash.[36] In other words, EVA motivates managers and workers to think like small-business owners

who must scramble to contain costs and generate enough business to meet their bills each month. And, unlike many kinds of financial controls, EVA doesn't specify what should or should not be done to improve performance. Thus, it encourages managers and workers to be creative in looking for ways to improve EVA performance.

Remember that EVA is the amount by which profits exceed the cost of capital in a given year. So the more that EVA exceeds the total dollar cost of capital, the better a company has used investors' money that year. Market value added (MVA) is simply the cumulative EVA created by a company over time.

Exhibit 16.5

Top 10 Canadian Companies by Market Value Added and Economic Value Added

	Market Value Added ($ Thousands)	Economic Value Added ($ Thousands)
Royal Bank of Canada	$ 25,770,000	$ 429,500
Bank of Nova Scotia	$ 19,534,200	$ 1,395,300
Toronto-Dominion Bank	$ 31,146,500	$ 889,900
Research in Motion	$ 42,163,520	$ 1,204,672
EnCana Corp.	$ 23,868,000	$ 918,000
Canadian National Railway	$ 71,411,200	$ 1,275,200
Teck Resources	$ 29,801,200	$ 1,146,200
Bank of Montreal	$ 9,334,000	$ 359,000
Great West Life Assurance	$ 9,922,000	$ 496,100
BCE Inc.	$ 6,720,000	$ 134,400

Sources: *Globe and Mail Report on Business,* "The Top 1000," 18 June 2010; H. Armitage, C. Ha, 2003, "The Pursuit of Value: EVA in Canada—An Uncertain Legacy," *Society of Management Accountants of Canada Magazine;* Stern Steward & Co., http://www.sternstewart.com [accessed 16 June 2010].

Thus, MVA indicates how much value or wealth a company has created or destroyed in total during its existence. The top ten Canadian companies by MVA and EVA are listed in Exhibit 16.5 (p. 329).

3.3 The Customer Perspective: Controlling Customer Defections

The second aspect of organizational performance that the balanced scorecard helps managers monitor is customers. It does so by forcing managers to address the question, "How do customers see us?" Unfortunately, most companies try to answer this question through customer satisfaction surveys, but these are often misleadingly positive. Most customers are reluctant to talk about their problems because they don't know who to complain to or think that complaining will not do any good. Indeed, a study by the Office of Consumer Affairs for South Australia found that 96 percent of unhappy customers never complain to anyone in the company.[37]

One reason that customer satisfaction surveys can be misleading is that sometimes even very satisfied customers will leave to do business with competitors. Rather than poring over customer satisfaction surveys from current customers, studies indicate that companies may do a better job of answering the question "How do customers see us?" by closely monitoring **customer defections**, that is, by identifying which customers are leaving the company and measuring the rate at which they are leaving. Unlike the results of customer satisfaction surveys, customer defections and retention do have a great effect on profits.

For example, very few managers realize that obtaining a new customer costs ten times as much as keeping a current one. In fact, the cost of replacing old customers with new ones is so great that most companies could double their profits by increasing the rate of customer retention by just 5 to 10 percent per year.[38] And, if a company can keep a customer for life, the benefits are even larger. According to Stew Leonard, owner of Stew Leonard's grocery store chain, "The lifetime value of a customer in a supermarket is about $246,000. Every time a customer comes through our front door I see, stamped on their forehead in big red numbers, '$246,000.' I'm never going to make that person unhappy with me. Or lose her to the competition."[39]

Beyond the clear benefits to the bottom line, the second reason to study customer defections is that customers who have left are much more likely than current customers to tell you what you were doing wrong. Finally, companies that understand why customers leave can not only take steps to fix ongoing problems, but can also identify which customers are likely to leave and make changes to prevent them from leaving.

3.4 The Internal Perspective: Controlling Quality

The third part of the balanced scorecard, the internal perspective, consists of the processes, decisions, and actions that managers and workers make within the organization. In contrast to the financial perspective of EVA and the outward-looking customer perspective, the internal perspective asks the question "At what must we excel?" Consequently, the internal perspective of the balanced scorecard usually leads managers to a focus on quality.

Quality is typically defined and measured in three ways: excellence, value, and conformance to expectations.[40] When the company defines its quality goal as *excellence,* managers must try to produce a product or service of unsurpassed performance and features. For example, Singapore Airlines is the best airline in the world by almost any standard. It has also

Customer defections
a performance assessment in which companies identify which customers are leaving and measure the rate at which they are leaving

mgmt trend

An Old Standby Is a Hot Trend

Vertical integration is making a comeback. In an effort to better control resources—namely, raw materials—some companies are buying suppliers who furnish critical components for important product lines. In 2006, Armour Holdings bought the textile manufacturer that supplied the super-strong fibres used in its armoured cars. Toyota took control of a key battery supplier for hybrid gasoline-electric engines. And Bridgestone Tire bought a rubber plantation in Indonesia. Watch the business press for articles on companies expanding vertically rather than horizontally.

Source: Timothy Aeppel, "A Hot Commodities Market Spurs Buying Spree by Manufacturers," *The Wall Street Journal,* 14 August 2006, A1, A7.

© iStockphoto.com/Steve Corrigan

© Xiaomei Chen/Newhouse News Service/Landov

received various "best airline" awards from the *Pacific Asia Travel Association, Travel+Leisure, Business Traveller, Conde Nast Traveller,* and *Fortune.*[41] Whereas many airlines try to cram passengers into every available inch on a plane, Singapore Airlines delivers creature comforts to encourage repeat business and customers willing to pay premium prices. On its newer planes, the first-class cabin is divided

to be less of a value. When a company emphasizes value as its quality goal, managers must simultaneously control excellence, price, durability, or other features of a product or service that customers strongly associate with value. Aldi, a German-based grocery store company with 7,500 stores worldwide, operates on the single principle of bringing maximum value to customers. Aldi stocks only 3 percent of the products that a typical grocery store carries, and most of its products are store brands. Customers bring their own bags and pick products off pallets rather than store shelves. Yet Aldi's store brands have consistently beaten the name brand rivals in taste and quality, and Aldi was voted the most trusted name in the grocery business in Germany, and its two founders (the Albrecht brothers) are the two richest men in Germany, thanks to this simple "value" approach to their business.[43]

When a company defines its quality goal as conformance to specifications, employees must base decisions and actions on whether services and

> ## The **internal perspective** asks the question "At what must we excel?"

into eight private mini-rooms, each with an unusually wide leather seat that folds down flat for sleeping, a 23-inch LCD TV that doubles as a computer monitor, and an adjustable table. These amenities and services are common for private jets but truly unique in the commercial airline industry.[42] Singapore Airlines was the first airline, in the 1970s, to introduce a choice of meals, complimentary drinks, and earphones in coach class. It was the first to introduce worldwide video, news, telephone, and fax services and the first to feature personal video monitors for movies, news, documentaries, and games. Singapore Airlines has had AC power for laptop computers for some time, and recently it became the first airline to introduce on-board high-speed Internet access.

Value is the customer perception that the product quality is excellent for the price offered. At a higher price, for example, customers may perceive the product

products measure up to the standard. In contrast to excellence and value-based definitions of quality that can be somewhat ambiguous, measuring whether products and services are "in spec" is relatively easy. Although conformance to specifications (i.e., precise tolerances for a part's weight or thickness) is usually associated with manufacturing, it can be used equally well to control quality in nonmanufacturing jobs. Exhibit 16.6 (p. 332) shows a checklist that a cook or restaurant owner would use to ensure quality when buying fresh fish.

The way in which a company defines quality affects the methods and measures that workers use to control quality. Accordingly, Exhibit 16.7 (p. 332) shows the advantages and disadvantages associated

Value customer perception that the product quality is excellent for the price offered

Exhibit 16.6

Conformance to Specifications Checklist for Buying Fresh Fish

QUALITY CHECKLIST FOR BUYING FRESH FISH		
FRESH WHOLE FISH	**ACCEPTABLE**	**NOT ACCEPTABLE**
Gills	✓ bright red, free of slime, clear mucus	✗ brown to greyish, thick, yellow mucus
Eyes	✓ clear, bright, bulging, black pupils	✗ dull, sunken, cloudy, grey pupils
Smell	✓ inoffensive, slight ocean smell	✗ ammonia, putrid smell
Skin	✓ opalescent sheen, scales adhere tightly to skin	✗ dull or faded colour, scales missing or easily removed
Flesh	✓ firm and elastic to touch, tight to the bone	✗ soft and flabby, separating from the bone
Belly cavity	✓ no viscera or blood visible, lining intact, no bone protruding	✗ incomplete evisceration, cuts or protruding bones, off-odour

© Paul Kay/Photolibrary/Getty Images

Sources: "A Closer Look: Buy It Fresh, Keep It Fresh," *Consumer Reports Online*, available online at http://www.seagrant.sunysb.edu/SeafoodTechnology/SeafoodMedia/CR02-2001/CR-SeafoodII020101.htm [accessed 20 June 2005]; "How to Purchase: Buying Fish," AboutSeaFood, available online at http://www.aboutseafood.com/faqs/purchase1.html [20 June 2005].

Exhibit 16.7

Advantages and Disadvantages of Different Measures of Quality

QUALITY MEASURE	ADVANTAGES	DISADVANTAGES
Excellence	Promotes clear organizational vision.	Provides little practical guidance for managers.
	Being/providing the "best" motivates and inspires managers and employees.	Excellence is ambiguous. What is it? Who defines it?
Value	Appeals to customers, who "know excellence when they see it."	Difficult to measure and control.
	Customers recognize differences in value.	Can be difficult to determine what factors influence whether a product/service is seen as having value.
	Easier to measure and compare whether products/services differ in value.	Controlling the balance between excellence and cost (i.e., affordable excellence) can be difficult.
Conformance to Specifications	If specifications can be written, conformance to specifications is usually measurable.	Many products/services cannot be easily evaluated in terms of conformance to specifications.
	Should lead to increased efficiency.	Promotes standardization, so may hurt performance when adapting to changes is more important.
	Promotes consistency in quality.	May be less appropriate for services, which are dependent on a high degree of human contact.

Source: C. A. Reeves and D. A. Bednar, "Defining Quality: Alternatives and Implications," *Academy of Management Review* 19 (1994): 419–445.

Exhibit 16.8

Four Levels of Waste Minimization

Waste Prevention & Reduction

Recycle & Reuse

Waste Treatment

Waste Disposal

© Imageshop/Jupiterimages

Source: Reprinted from D. R. May and B. L. Flannery, "Cutting Waste with Employee Involvement Teams," *Business Horizons* 38 (September–October 1995): 28–38, with permission from Elsevier.

with the excellence, value, and conformance to specification definitions of quality.

3.5 The Innovation and Learning Perspective: Controlling Waste and Pollution

The last part of the balanced scorecard, the innovation and learning perspective, addresses the question "Can we continue to improve and create value?" Thus, the innovation and learning perspective involves continuous improvement in ongoing products and services (discussed in Chapter 18); relearning and redesigning

the processes by which products and services are created (discussed in Chapter 7); and even things like waste and pollution minimization, an increasingly important area of innovation.

Exhibit 16.8 shows the four levels of waste minimization ranging from waste disposal, which produces the smallest minimization of waste, to waste prevention and reduction, which produces the greatest minimization.[44] The goals of the top level, *waste prevention and reduction,* are to prevent waste and pollution before they occur or to reduce them when they do occur. For example, United Parcel Service (UPS) (www .theupsstore.ca) uses a software program that helps drivers plan routes with only right turns to save driving time. The strategy also prevents environmental waste, since UPS saves three million gallons of fuel each year and reduces CO_2 emissions by 31,000 metric tons.[45] There are three strategies for waste prevention and reduction:

1. *Good housekeeping*—performing regularly scheduled preventive maintenance for offices, plants, and equipment and quickly fixing leaky valves and making sure machines are running properly so that they don't use more fuel than necessary are examples of good housekeeping.

2. *Material/product substitution*—replacing toxic or hazardous materials with less harmful materials. As part of its Pollution Prevention Pays program over the last 30 years, 3M eliminated 2.2 billion pounds of pollutants and saved $1 billion by using benign substitutes for toxic solvents in its manufacturing processes.[46]

3. *Process modification*—changing steps or procedures to eliminate or reduce waste. Terracycle is a manufacturer of plant food made from the castings (that is, the droppings) of red worms that have feasted on various types of organic waste. But rather than package the plant food in new bottles, Terracycle packages its product in used beverage containers and ships the bottles in recycled boxes to the retailers. The company's entire process operation is 100 percent geared toward reducing or eliminating waste.[47]

At the second level of waste minimization, *recycle and reuse,* wastes are reduced by reusing materials as

long as possible or by collecting materials for on- or off-site recycling. A growing trend in recycling is *design for disassembly,* where products are designed from the start for easy disassembly, recycling, and reuse once they are no longer usable. For example, the European Union (EU) is moving toward prohibiting companies from selling products unless most of the product and its packaging can be recycled.[48] Since companies, not consumers, will be held responsible for recycling the products they manufacture, they must design their products from the start with recycling in mind.[49] At reclamation centres throughout Europe, companies will have to be able to recover and recycle 80 percent of the parts that go into their original products.[50] Under the EU's end-of-life vehicle program, all cars built in Europe since June 2002 are already subject to the 80 percent requirement, which rose to 85 percent in 2006 and will be 95 percent by 2015 for autos. Moreover, effective in 2007, the EU requires auto manufacturers to pay to recycle all the cars they made between 1989 and 2002.[51]

Today, roughly 160 million cars in Europe are covered by these strict end-of-life regulations.[52]

At the third level of waste minimization, *waste treatment,* companies use biological, chemical, or other processes to turn potentially harmful waste into harmless compounds or useful by-products. For example, during "pickling," a process in the manufacture of steel sheets, the steel is bathed in an acid solution to clean impurities and oxides (which would rust) from its surface. Fortunately, Magnetics International found a safe, profitable way to treat the pickle juice, which it sprays into a 100-foot-high chamber at 1,200 degrees Fahrenheit to form pure iron oxide that can be transformed into a useful magnetic powder which is reused in electric motors, stereo speakers, and refrigerator gaskets.[53]

The fourth and lowest level of waste minimization is waste disposal. Wastes that cannot be prevented, reduced, recycled, reused, or treated should be safely disposed of in processing plants or in environmentally secure landfills that prevent leakage and contamination of soil and underground water supplies. For example, with the average computer lasting just three years, approximately 60 million computers come out of service each year. But with lead-containing cathode ray tubes in the monitors, toxic metals in the circuit

boards, paint-coated plastic, and metal coatings that can contaminate ground water, old computers can't just be thrown away.[54] Hewlett-Packard has started a unique computer disposal program that allows companies or individual computer users to recycle PCs and electronic equipment. Since 1987, HP has collected and recycled over 600 million pounds of used computer equipment. Between 1992 and 2005, they also collected over 91 million printer cartridges.

The materials found in these old components can be used to make new HP products as well as new airplane parts, shoe soles, wagons, and fence posts.[55] The service is available at **http://www.hp.com/hpinfo/ globalcitizenship/environment/recycle/index.html**. With three clicks and a credit card number (prices range from $13 to $34 per item), the old PC equipment will be picked up and properly disposed of. HP makes no profit from this service.

Visit **icanmgmt.com** to find the resources you need today!

Located at the back of the textbook are rip-out Chapter Review cards. Make sure you also go online to check out other tools that MGMT offers to help you successfully pass your course.

- Interactive Quizzes
- Key Terms Flashcards
- Audio Chapter Summaries
- PowerPoint Slides

- Interactive Games
- Crossword Puzzles
- "Reel to Reel" and "Biz Flix" videos
- Cases and Exercises

Part 5 - Controlling

MANAGING INFORMATION

A generation ago, computer hardware and software had little to do with managing business information. Rather than storing information on hard drives, managers stored it in filing cabinets. Instead of uploading daily sales and inventory levels by satellite to corporate headquarters, they mailed hardcopy summaries to headquarters at the end of each month. Instead of word processing, reports were typed on an electric typewriter. Instead of spreadsheets, calculations were made on adding machines. Managers communicated by sticky notes, not e-mail. Phone messages were written down by assistants and coworkers, not left on voice mail. Workers did not use desktop or laptop computers as a daily tool to get work done. Instead, they scheduled limited access time to run batch jobs on the mainframe computer (and prayed that the batch job computer code they wrote would work).

Today, a generation later, computer hardware and software are an integral part of managing business information. This is due mainly to something called **Moore's law.** Gordon Moore is one of the founders of Intel Corporation, which makes 75 percent of the integrated processors used in personal computers. In 1965, Moore predicted that computer-processing power would double and its cost would drop by 50 percent about every two years.[1] As Exhibit 17.1 (page 338) shows, Moore was right. Computer power, as measured by the number of transistors per computer chip, *has* more than doubled every few years. Consequently, the computer sitting in your lap or on your desk is not only smaller but also much cheaper and more powerful than the large mainframe computers used by *Fortune* 500 companies fifteen years ago. In fact, if car manufacturers had achieved the same power increases and cost decreases attained by computer manufacturers, a fully outfitted Lexus or Mercedes sedan would cost less than $1,000!

Moore's law the prediction that the cost of computing will drop by 50 percent every 18 months as computer-processing power doubles

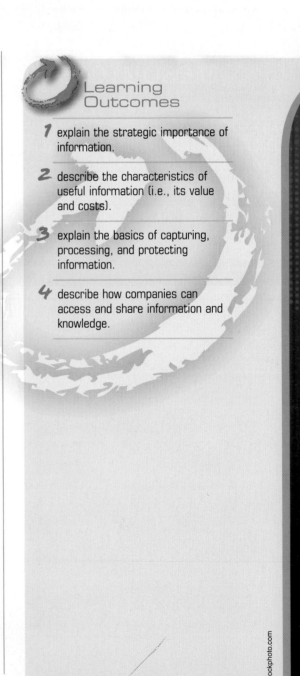

Learning Outcomes

1 explain the strategic importance of information.

2 describe the characteristics of useful information (i.e., its value and costs).

3 explain the basics of capturing, processing, and protecting information.

4 describe how companies can access and share information and knowledge.

© iStockphoto.com

Why Information Matters

Raw data are facts and figures. For example, 11, $452, 4, and 26,100 are some data that I used the day I wrote this section of the chapter. However, facts and figures aren't particularly useful unless they have meaning. For example, you probably can't guess what these four pieces of raw data represent, can you? And if you can't, these data are useless. That's why researchers make the distinction between raw data and information. Whereas raw data consist of facts and figures, **information** is useful data that can influence someone's choices and behaviour. One way to think about the difference between data and information is that information has context.

So what did those four pieces of data mean to me? Well, 11 stands for Channel 11, the local CBS affiliate on which I watched part of the men's PGA golf tournament. $452 is how much it would cost me to rent a minivan for a week if I go skiing over spring break. 4 is for the 4-gigabyte storage

Raw data facts and figures

Information useful data that can influence people's choices and behaviour

Exhibit 17.1

Moore's Law

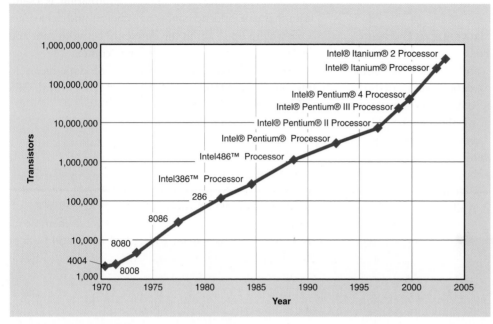

Source: "Moore's Law: Overviews," © Intel Corporation, available online at http://www.intel.com/technology/mooreslaw/index.htm [accessed 10 September 2008].

card that I want to add to my digital camera (prices are low, so I'll probably buy it). And 26,100 means that it's time to get the oil changed in my car.

After reading the next two sections, you should be able to

1 explain the strategic importance of information.

2 describe the characteristics of useful information (i.e., its value and costs).

1 Strategic Importance of Information

In today's hypercompetitive business environments, information is as important as capital (i.e., money) for business success, whether it's about furniture delivery, product inventory, pricing, or costs. It takes money to get businesses started, but businesses can't survive and grow without the right information. Information has strategic importance for organizations because

First-mover advantage
the strategic advantage that companies earn by being the first to use new information technology to substantially lower costs or to make a product or service different from that of competitors

it can be used to **1.1 obtain first-mover advantage** and **1.2 sustain a competitive advantage once it has been created.**

1.1 First-Mover Advantage

First-mover advantage is the strategic advantage that companies earn by being the first in an industry to use new information technology to substantially lower costs or to differentiate a product or service from that of competitors. By investing $90 billion over the last decade to replace copper coaxial lines with digital lines that feed high-speed cable modems and digital TV cable channels, cable companies convinced two out of every three high-speed Internet subscribers to choose cable over the DSL service provided by phone companies.[2] The phone companies are beginning to catch up. They now sign up more new high-speed Internet subscribers than cable providers. But does that mean that cable companies' first-mover advantage is slipping away? Well, not yet, as 57 percent of high-speed Internet subscribers still choose cable.[3] And with a growing subscriber base for residential phone service, the cable companies are now going after the phone companies' business customers, offering them high-speed Internet and business phone service.[4]

First-mover advantages like those established by high-speed Internet cable companies can be sizable. On average, first movers earn a 30 percent market share compared to 19 percent for the companies that follow.[5] Likewise, over 70 percent of market leaders started as first movers.[6]

1.2 Sustaining a Competitive Advantage

As described above, companies that use information technology to establish first-mover advantage usually have higher market shares and profits. According to the resource-based view of information technology shown in Exhibit 17.2, companies need to address three critical issues in order to sustain a competitive advantage through information technology. First, does

Exhibit 17.2

Using Information Technology to Sustain a Competitive Advantage

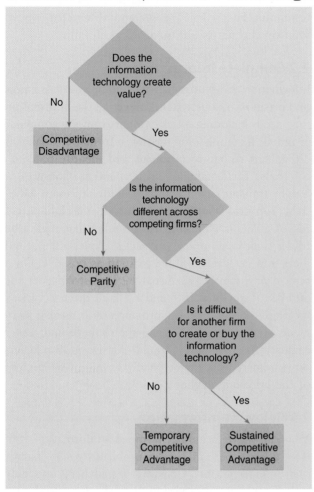

Does the information technology create value?
- No → **Competitive Disadvantage**
- Yes → **Is the information technology different across competing firms?**
  - No → **Competitive Parity**
  - Yes → **Is it difficult for another firm to create or buy the information technology?**
    - No → **Temporary Competitive Advantage**
    - Yes → **Sustained Competitive Advantage**

Source: Adapted from F. J. Mata, W. L. Fuerst, and J. B. Barney, "Information Technology and Sustained Competitive Advantage: A Resource-Based Analysis," *MIS Quarterly* 19, no. 4 (December 1995): 487–505. Reprinted by special permission by the Society for Information Management and the Management Information Systems Research Center at the University of Minnesota.

the information technology create value for the firm by lowering costs or providing a better product or service? If an information technology doesn't add value, then investing in it would put the firm at a competitive disadvantage to companies that choose information technologies that do add value.

Second, is the information technology the same or different across competing firms? If all the firms have access to the same information technology and use it in the same way, then no firm has an advantage over another (i.e., competitive parity).

Third, is it difficult for another company to create or buy the information technology used by the firm? If so, then the firm has established a sustainable competitive advantage over competitors through information

technology. If not, then the competitive advantage is just temporary, and competitors should eventually be able to duplicate the advantages the leading firm has gained from information technology. For more about sustainable competitive advantage and its sources, see Chapter 6 on organizational strategy.

In short, the key to sustaining a competitive advantage is not faster computers, more memory, and larger hard drives. The key is using information technology to continuously improve and support the core functions of a business. Thanks to innovative use of information technology and the largest private satellite network and database system in the world, Wal-Mart's costs are 10 percent lower than its competitors'.[7] Wal-Mart was one of the first retailers to use computers and bar codes to track sales and inventory data and then share those data with suppliers. Today, Wal-Mart's $4 billion supplier network, Retail Link, allows vendors like Ted Haedicke of Coca-Cola to "look at how much [and what kind of] Coke [has] sold . . . and at what prices at any store in the Wal-Mart system." He went on to say, "You can't do that with any other retailer today."[8]

Companies like Wal-Mart that achieve first-mover advantage with information technology and then sustain it with continued investment create a moving target that competitors have difficulty hitting.

2 Characteristics and Costs of Useful Information

Portsmouth, a scenic city of 190,000 on the southern coast of England, attracts 6.5 million visitors a year, primarily because of its historic role as the home of the British Royal Navy. To handle the crush of

visitors, Portsmouth relies on 320 buses, all equipped with computers and QDMA (quad-division multiple access) radio communication, which works reliably at speeds up to 250 miles per hour. Because the buses are networked, passengers waiting at bus stops can access a weatherproof computer terminal to find out when the next bus will arrive and what route that bus is taking. They can also check their e-mail, use trip planning software to determine which bus routes to take, or swipe a credit card to purchase tickets.[9]

As Portsmouth's bus system demonstrates, information is useful when it is **2.1 accurate, 2.2 complete, 2.3 relevant,** and **2.4 timely.** However, there can be significant **2.5 acquisition, 2.6 processing, 2.7 storage, 2.8 retrieval,** and **2.9 communication costs associated with useful information.**

2.1 Accurate Information

Information is useful when it is accurate. Portsmouth's QDMA computer system allows people to know exactly when their bus will arrive. Before relying on information to make decisions, you must know that the information is correct. But what if it isn't? For example, the restaurant business is notoriously difficult for two reasons. First, it's extremely competitive. Customers in any location typically have hundreds of restaurants from which to choose when dining out. Second, 60 percent of restaurants go out of business within three years. Why? Restaurant owners and managers typically have little accurate information about their businesses. Sure, they know whether they're losing money or not, but they don't know why. Restaurants often don't have accurate information regarding how much alcohol they sell, for example, wine versus beer versus hard liquor, nor do they have information regarding which food dishes, lobster versus swordfish, sell more or are more expensive to prepare. With Squirrel Systems Software, the Keg Restaurant, with locations in every major centre in Canada, can track this information and more. COO Jim Croteau sings the praises of this type of POS system. "Squirrel understands that technology needs to accommodate our unique requirements," he says. "Many of their staff come from the restaurant industry and share our sense of urgency. We're not in a one-size-fits-all industry." A similar software system allows one restaurant to track the costs of all its food products. It has found that sea bass sells 196 times in one month, whereas ahi tuna sells 89 times. Since the two fish cost the same, and both sell for $29, the restaurant has reduced costs and eliminated unsold food by cutting its ahi tuna orders in half.[10]

2.2 Complete Information

Information is useful when it is complete. Passengers on Portsmouth's bus system can get all the information they need (including a ticket) right from the computer terminal. Incomplete or missing information makes it difficult to recognize problems and identify potential solutions. For example, dispatchers at Con-way, a freight transportation company with offices in Montreal, Toronto, Winnipeg, Edmonton, and Halifax, are responsible for choosing truck routes that maximize trailer loads, minimize expenses (time, miles, and fuel), and get drivers home as soon as possible. On a typical day, Con-way's dispatchers must consider the number of trucks (2,100) and available drivers (varies), locations (200 across 25 provinces and states), shipments (typically 50,000), and the tonnage and trailer capacity for that day. Though Con-way's dispatchers do extremely well, they typically have only 85 percent of the information they need.[11]

2.3 Relevant Information

You can have accurate, complete information, but if it doesn't pertain to the problems you're facing, then it's irrelevant. Con-way dispatchers not only lacked complete information, they also lacked relevant information about their problems, such as last-minute changes in orders, weather, accidents, driver no-shows, and breakdowns. As a result, they ended up assigning longer, less efficient truck routes with less than full trucks that ultimately increased costs by $5 million per year. To address these issues, the company spent $3 million over five years to build a computerized truck route optimization system. This system tracks all customer shipment requests (which can be made as late as 5:15 P.M. each day for the next day's delivery) and communicates by satellite with each truck to monitor truck availability, loads, miles, fuel, weather, and accidents. Then, armed with all of this relevant

 Before relying on information to make decisions, you must **know** that the **information** is correct.

information, it cranks out optimal truck routes in just seven minutes. On an average day, this system allows Con-way to use 111 fewer trucks and 68 fewer drivers, drive 26,000 fewer miles, and increase the load in each truck by 370 revenue-generating pounds.[12]

2.4 Timely Information

Finally, information is useful when it is timely. News that your bus passed the stop ten minutes ago is not helpful in getting you where you want to go. To be timely, the information must be available when needed to define a problem or to begin to identify possible solutions. If you've ever thought, "I wish I had known that earlier," then you understand the importance of timely information and the opportunity cost of not having it.

2.5 Acquisition Costs

Acquisition cost is the cost of obtaining data that you don't have. For example, Acxiom, a billion-dollar company, with a major data centre in Toronto, gathers and processes data for direct-mail marketing companies. If you've received an unsolicited, preapproved credit card application recently (and who hasn't?), chances are Acxiom helped the credit card company gather information about you. Where does Acxiom get that information? Mainly from companies that sell consumer credit reports at a wholesale cost of $1 each. Acxiom also obtains information from retailers. Each time you use your credit card, checkout scanners gather information about your spending habits and product preferences. Many retailers sell this information to companies like Acxiom that use it for market research. So why pay for this information? The reason is that acquiring it can help credit card companies do a better job of identifying who will mail back a signed credit card application and who will simply shred it. The ability to target likely customers saves the companies money and effort in the end.[13]

2.6 Processing Costs

Companies often have massive amounts of data but not in the form or combination they need. Consequently, **processing cost** is the cost of turning raw data into usable information. eBay's data management system, which consists of only six data centres in the western U.S. (and a seventh in Vancouver), and is managed by less than a dozen administrators, is already pretty lean compared to other companies. By comparison, Hewlett Packard is moving to reduce its 85 data centres to six.[14] But eBay is shooting for automatic service-level management at scale, where data management would take place automatically as users do their part on the auction site. Paul Strong, who designs eBay's IT infrastructure, said, "Management is made easier by having fewer things to manage. By having patterns and fixing processes around them, you minimize variability, risk, and cost, and you maximize efficiency and to some degree agility."[15] Having fewer data centres means more efficient data processing and lower processing cost.

2.7 Storage Costs

Storage cost is the cost of physically or electronically archiving information for later use and retrieval. Google, Yahoo!, and Microsoft Live have incurred large storage costs to make it easy and fast for you to retrieve archived information. How costly can the storage for a simple Web search be? Well, consider that each time you conduct a Web search at Yahoo, 7,000 computers are activated to return the results of your search to you in less than 18/100 of a second.[16] And with the need for data storage doubling every 14 months, Yahoo!, Google, Microsoft, and other *Fortune* 500 companies are building server farms, large collections of networked computer servers in 750,000-square-foot buildings (seven times the size of a Costco), to keep up with demand.

2.8 Retrieval Costs

Retrieval cost is the cost of accessing already-stored and processed information. One of the most common misunderstandings about information is that it is easy and cheap to retrieve once the company has it. Not so. First, you have to find the information. Then, you've got to convince whoever

© iStockphoto.com/Ivan Kmit

Companies often have massive amounts of data, but not in the form or combination they need.

Acquisition cost the cost of obtaining data that you don't have

Processing cost the cost of turning raw data into usable information

Storage cost the cost of physically or electronically archiving information for later use and retrieval

Retrieval cost the cost of accessing already-stored and processed information

has it to share it with you. Then the information has to be processed into a form that is useful for you.

For example, more organizations are moving toward the paperless office. One challenge this move presents is how employees will retrieve various kinds of data that exist across a company, whether they come from an e-mail, a file record, a website, a word processing document, or an image. With this variety of information, how do you find what you need and find it quickly? One solution is Enterprise Content Management (ECM), a way of storing and providing access to unstructured information wherever it exists. Ulrich Kampffmeyer, former member of the board of directors of the Association for Information and Image Management, summed up the challenge well: "The most important job is to keep in-house information under control. The questions add up: where to put the thousands and thousands of e-mails, what to do with the electronically signed business correspondence, where to put taxation-relevant data, how to transfer information from the disorganized file system, how to consolidate information in a repository that everybody can use, how to get a single login for all the systems, how to create a uniform in-basket for all incoming information, how to make sure that no information is lost or ignored, etc. etc." Once this is accomplished, however, retrieval cost becomes quite low.[17]

2.9 Communication Costs

Communication cost is the cost of transmitting information from one place to another. For example, the most important information that an electric utility company collects each month is the information from the electric meter attached to the side of your house. Traditionally, electric companies employed meter readers to walk from house to house to gather information that would then be entered into company computers. Now, however, meter readers are losing their jobs to water, gas, and electric meters built with radio frequency (RF) transmitters (see Section 3.1 for more on this technology). The transmitters turn on when a meter reader drives by the house in a utility company van that has a laptop computer specially equipped to receive the RF signals. Such a van, travelling at legal speeds, can read 12,000 to 13,000 meters in an eight-hour day. By contrast, a meter reader on foot would record data from 500 meters per day.[18]

Communication cost
the cost of transmitting information from one place to another

Getting and Sharing Information

In 1907, Metropolitan Life Insurance, which now owns MetLife Canada, built a huge office building for its brand new, state-of-the-art information technology system. What was this great breakthrough in information management? Card files. That's right, the same card file systems that every library in Canada used before computers. Metropolitan Life's information technology consisted of 20,000 separate file drawers that sat in hundreds of file cabinets more than 15 feet tall. This filing system held 20 million insurance applications, 700,000 accounting books, and 500,000 death certificates. Metropolitan Life employed 61 workers who did nothing but sort, file, and climb ladders to pull files as needed.[19]

How we get and share information has clearly changed. Today, if storms, fire, or accidents damage policyholders' property, insurance companies write cheques on the spot to cover the losses. When policyholders buy a car, they call their insurance agent from the dealership to activate their insurance before driving off in their new car. And now, insurance companies are marketing their products and services to customers directly from the Internet.

Bloomberg/Getty Images

From card files to Internet files in just under a century, the rate of change in information technology is spectacular. After reading the next two sections, you should be able to

3 explain the basics of capturing, processing, and protecting information.

4 describe how companies can access and share information and knowledge.

3 Capturing, Processing, and Protecting Information

In this section, you will learn about the information technologies that companies use to 3.1 capture, 3.2 process, and 3.3 protect information.

3.1 Capturing Information

There are two basic methods of capturing information: manual and electronic. Manual capture of information is a slow, costly, labour-intensive process that entails recording and entering data by hand into a data storage device. Consequently, companies are relying more on electronic capture. They use electronic storage devices such as bar codes, radio frequency identification tags, and document scanners to capture and record data electronically.

Bar codes represent numerical data by varying the thickness and pattern of vertical bars. The primary advantage of bar codes is that the data they represent can be read and recorded in an instant with a handheld or pen-type scanner. Bar codes cut checkout times in half, reduce data entry errors by 75 percent, and save stores money because stockers don't have to go through the labour-intensive process of putting a price tag on each item in the store.[20]

Radio frequency identification (RFID) tags contain minuscule microchips and antennas that transmit information via radio waves.[21] Unlike bar codes, which require direct line-of-sight scanning, RFID tags are read by turning on an RFID reader that, like a radio, tunes into a specific frequency to determine the number *and* location of products, parts, or anything else to which the RFID tags are attached. Turn on an RFID reader, and every RFID tag within the reader's range (from several hundred to several thousand feet) is accounted for. Loblaw's has a new, 875,000-square-foot distribution centre in Ajax, just east of Toronto (that is about 13 football fields). Keeping track of 7,196 different products and 67,000 pallets is no small feat. Before

Loblaw's opened this large centre, a container of Yoplait yogurt travelled from an Ultima Foods plant to a Loblaw regional distribution warehouse and then on to a store. Along the way, the yogurt bided its time in trucks, on warehouse pallets, and, finally, found its way into a store and onto a shelf. By the time the yogurt made it to a dairy fridge, its month-long shelf life had ticked down to just 13 days, and no profits had been made in the first 17 days (though plenty of costs had by then been incurred). According to Rand Russell, the facility's general manager, a big innovation is called Vocollect. Order selecters driving "pallet jack" vehicles receive instructions from the central computer via wireless headsets. "Leaving the workers' hands free has increased their efficiency by 10 to 15 percent," estimates Russell. An even bigger technological wave is sweeping the world of warehousing: radio frequency identification. RFID is similar to an electronic bar code, but it can be read from a distance, which allows goods entering a building to be automatically logged into the central system. The technology tracks goods within a warehouse and automatically triggers orders when supplies run low. RFID can also be used to track expiry dates, or for "sourcing" in the event of food safety recalls.[22]

Electronic scanners, which convert printed text and pictures into digital images, have become an increasingly popular method of capturing data electronically because they are inexpensive and easy to use. The first requirement for a good scanner is a *document feeder* that automatically feeds document pages

Bar code a visual pattern that represents numerical data by varying the thickness and pattern of vertical bars

Radio frequency identification (RFID) tags tags containing minuscule microchips that transmit information via radio waves and can be used to track the number and location of the objects into which the tags have been inserted

Electronic scanners an electronic device that converts printed text and pictures into digital images

into the scanner or turns the pages (often with a puff of air) when scanning books or bound documents.[23] Text that has been digitized cannot be searched or edited like the regular text in your word processing software, however, so the second requirement for a good scanner is **optical character recognition** software to scan and convert original or digitized documents into ASCII (American Standard Code for Information Interchange) text or Adobe PDF documents. ASCII text can be searched, read, and edited with standard word processing, e-mail, desktop publishing, database management, and spreadsheet software, while PDF documents can be searched and edited with Adobe's Acrobat software.

3.2 Processing Information

Processing information means transforming raw data into meaningful information that can be applied to business decision making. Evaluating sales data to determine the best- and worst-selling products, examining repair records to determine product reliability, and monitoring the cost of long-distance phone calls are all examples of processing raw data into meaningful information. And with automated, electronic capture of data, increased processing power, and cheaper and more plentiful ways to store data, managers no longer worry about getting data. Instead, they scratch their heads about how to use the overwhelming amount of data that pours into their businesses every day. Furthermore, most managers know little about statistics and have neither the time nor the inclination to learn how to use them to analyze data.

One promising tool to help managers dig out from under the avalanche of data is data mining. **Data mining** is the process of discovering patterns and relationships in large amounts of data.[24] Data mining works by using complex algorithms such as neural networks, rule induction, and decision trees. If you don't know what those are, that's okay. With data mining, you don't have to. Most managers only need to know that data mining looks for patterns that are already in the data but are too complex for them to spot on their own.

Data mining typically splits a data set in half, finds patterns in one half, and then tests the validity of those patterns by trying to find them again in the second half of the data set. The data typically come from a **data warehouse** that stores huge amounts of data that have been prepared for data mining analysis by being cleaned of errors and redundancy. The data in a data warehouse can then be analyzed using two kinds of data mining. **Supervised data mining** usually begins with the user telling the data mining software to look and test for specific patterns and relationships in a data set. Typically, this is done through a series of "what if?" questions or statements. For instance, a grocery store manager might instruct the data mining software to determine if coupons placed in the Sunday paper increase or decrease sales. By contrast, with **unsupervised data mining,** the user simply tells the data mining software to uncover whatever patterns and relationships it can find in a data set. For example, State Farm Insurance (see statefarm.ca) used to have

pairs well with

...if you're a dad in a hurry after work.

PSL Images/GetStock.com / © Tim Boyle/Getty Images

Toronto Star/GetStock.com

three pricing categories for car insurance, depending on your driving record: preferred for the best drivers, standard for typical drivers, and nonstandard for the worst drivers. Now, however, it has moved to tiered pricing based on the 300 different kinds of driving records that its data mining software was able to discover. This allows State Farm to be much more precise in matching 300 different price levels to 300 different kinds of driving records.[25]

Unsupervised data mining is particularly good at identifying association or affinity patterns, sequence patterns, and predictive patterns. It can also identify what data mining technicians call data clusters.[26] **Association or affinity patterns** occur when two or more database elements tend to occur together in a significant way. Surprisingly, one company found that beer and diapers tended to be bought together between 5 and 7 P.M. The question, of course, was "why?" The answer, on further review, was fairly straightforward: fathers, who were told by their wives to buy some diapers on their way home, decided to pick up a six-pack for themselves, too.[27]

Sequence patterns occur when two or more database elements occur together in a significant pattern in which one of the elements precedes the other. Strat-Bridge provides data mining capability to professional sports teams so they can analyze their ticket sales in real time. Its StratTix software can help a team view up-to-the-minute seating charts to see which seats are selling and which are not. It provides teams with information about the people purchasing the tickets—for example, their geographic area and which source they used to purchase them (Ticketmaster, etc.). It also helps teams find the best time to market and promote games, and tells them what prices (at what times) will provide the best revenues. Stratbridge has deals with most teams in the National Hockey League, so when you go to the Rogers Arena in Vancouver to watch the Canucks, you know you are getting the best seat at the best price.[28]

Predictive patterns are just the opposite of association or affinity patterns. Whereas association or affinity patterns look for database elements that seem to go together, **predictive patterns** help identify database elements that are different. On the day after Thanksgiving, typically the busiest shopping day of the year, Wal-Mart's data

---

Association or affinity patterns when two or more database elements tend to occur together in a significant way

Sequence patterns when two or more database elements occur together in a significant pattern, but one of the elements precedes the other

Predictive patterns patterns that help identify database elements that are different

mining indicated that sales were unexpectedly slow for a boxed computer and printer combination that was offered at an extremely good price. Sales of this item were slow everywhere *except* one Wal-Mart store, where they greatly exceeded expectations. After noting the difference, headquarters called the store manager, who said that the products were displayed in an open box that made it clear to customers that the low price was for the computer *and* the printer. Sales took off at all stores after headquarters relayed this simple message: "Open the box."[29]

Data clusters are the last kind of pattern found by data mining. **Data clusters** occur when three or more database elements occur together (i.e., cluster) in a significant way. After analyzing several years' worth of repair and warranty claims, Ford Motor Company might find that, compared with cars built in its Mississauga plant, the cars it builds in Oakville (first element) are more likely to have problems with overtightened fan belts (second element) that break (third element) and result in overheated engines (fourth element), ruined radiators (fifth element), and payments for tow trucks (sixth element), which are paid for by Ford's three-year, 36,000 mile warranty.

Traditionally, data mining has been very expensive and very complex. Today, however, data mining services and analysis are much more affordable and within reach of most companies' budgets. And, if it follows the path of most technologies, it will become even easier and cheaper to use in the future.

3.3 Protecting Information

Protecting information is the process of ensuring that data are reliably and consistently retrievable in a usable format for authorized users but no one else. When customers purchase prescription medicine at CanadaDrugs.com, an online drugstore and health aid retailer, they want to be confident that their medical and credit card information is available only to them, the pharmacists at CanadaDrugs.com, and their doctors. See the extensive privacy policy (click "Privacy Policy" at **http://www .canadadrugs.com**) to make sure this is the case.

Companies like Canada Drugs.com find it necessary to protect information because of the numerous security threats to data and data security listed in

Data clusters when three or more database elements occur together (i.e., cluster) in a significant way

Protecting information the process of ensuring that data are reliably and consistently retrievable in a usable format for authorized users but no one else

You Are How You Type

A new form of biometrics involves identifying people by the way they type. After entering your ID and a code, BioPassword's artificial-intelligence software monitors your speed, how long you take before selecting the keys, and the rhythm you use to pound out your text. The more you use the software, the better it can identify *you* as the typist, making it nearly impossible for someone to hack into your computer. BioPassword is as accurate as finger and iris scans.

Source: J. Manez, "We Got the Beat," *Fast Company*, September 2006.

©Thinkstock/Jupiterimages

Exhibit 17.3. People inside and outside companies can steal or destroy company data in various ways, including denial-of-service Web server attacks that can bring down some of the busiest and best-run sites on the Internet; viruses and spyware/adware that spread quickly and can result in data loss and business disruption; keystroke monitoring, in which every mouse click and keystroke you make is monitored, stored, and sent to unauthorized users; password cracking software, which steals supposedly secure passwords; and phishing, where fake but real-looking e-mails and websites trick users into sharing personal information (usernames, passwords, account numbers) that leads to unauthorized account access. On average, 19 percent of computers are infected with viruses, 80 percent have spyware, and only one-third are running behind a protected firewall (discussed shortly). Studies show that the threats listed in Exhibit 17.3 are so widespread that automatic attacks will begin on an unprotected computer just 15 seconds after it connects to the Internet.[30]

As shown in the right-hand column of Exhibit 17.3, numerous steps can be taken to secure data and data networks. Some of the most important are authentication and authorization, firewalls, antivirus software for

Exhibit 17.3

Security Threats to Data and Data Networks

Security Problem	Source	Affects	Severity	The Threat	The Solution
Denial of service Web server attacks and corporate network attacks	Internet hackers	All servers	High	Loss of data, disruption of service, and theft of service.	Implement firewall, password control, server-side review, threat monitoring, and bug fixes; turn PCs off when not in use.
Password cracking software and unauthorized access to PCs	Local area network, Internet	All users, especially digital subscriber line and cable Internet users	High	Hackers take over PCs. Privacy can be invaded. Corporate users' systems are exposed to other machines on the network.	Close ports and firewalls, disable file and print sharing, and use strong passwords.
Viruses, worms, Trojan horses, and rootkits	E-mail, downloaded and distributed software	All users	Moderate to high	Monitor activities and cause data loss and file deletion. Compromise security by sometimes concealing their presence.	Use antivirus software and firewalls; control Internet access.
Spyware, adware, malicious scripts and applets	Rogue Web pages	All users	Moderate to high	Invade privacy, intercept passwords, and damage files or file system.	Disable browser script support; use security, blocking, and spyware/ adware software.
E-mail snooping	Hackers on your network and the Internet	All users	Moderate to high	People read your e-mail from intermediate servers or packets, or they physically access your machine.	Encrypt message, ensure strong password protection, and limit physical access to machines.
Keystroke monitoring	Trojan horses, people with direct access to PCs	All users	High	Records everything typed at the keyboard and intercepts keystrokes before password masking or encryption occurs.	Use antivirus software to catch Trojan horses, control Internet access to transmission, and implement system monitoring and physical access control.
Phishing	Hackers on your network and the Internet	All users, including customers	High	Fake, but real-looking, e-mails and Web sites that trick users into sharing personal information on what they wrongly thought was the company's website. This leads to unauthorized account	Educate and warn users and customers about the dangers. Encourage both not to click on potentially fake URLs, which might take them to phishing websites. Instead, have them type your company's URL into the Web browser.
Spam	E-mail	All users and corporations	Mild to high	Clogs and overloads e-mail servers and inboxes with junk mail. HTML-based spam may be used for profiling and identifying users.	Filter known spam sources and senders on e-mail servers; have users create further lists of approved and unapproved senders on their personal computers.
Cookies	websites you visit	Individual users	Mild to moderate	Trace Web usage and permit the creation of personalized Web pages that track behaviour and interest profiles.	Use cookie managers to control and edit cookies, and use ad blockers.

Sources: K. Bannan, "Look Out: Watching You, Watching Me," *PC Magazine,* July 2002, 99; A. Dragoon, "Fighting Phish, Fakes, and Frauds," *CIO,* 1 September 2004, 33; B. Glass, "Are You Being Watched?" *PC Magazine,* 23 April 2002, 54; K. Karagiannis, "DDoS: Are You Next?" *PC Magazine,* January 2003, 79; B. Machrone, "Protect & Defend," *PC Magazine,* 27 June 2000, 168–181.

PCs and e-mail servers, data encryption, and virtual private networks.[31] We will review those steps and then finish this section with a brief review of the dangers of wireless networks, which are exploding in popularity.

Two critical steps are required to make sure that data can be accessed by authorized users and no one else. One is **authentication,** that is, making sure users are who they claim to be.[32] The other is **authorization,** that is, granting authenticated users approved access to data, software, and systems.[33] When an ATM prompts you to enter your personal identification number (PIN), the bank is authenticating that you are you. Once you've been authenticated, you are authorized to access your funds and no one else's. Of course, as anyone who has lost a PIN or password or had one stolen knows, user authentication systems are not foolproof. In particular, users create security risks by not changing their default account passwords (such as birth dates) or by using weak passwords such as names ("Larry") or complete words ("football") that are quickly guessed by password cracker software.[34]

This is why many companies are now turning to **two-factor authentication,** which is based on what users know, such as a password, and what they have, such as a secure ID card. For example, to log onto their computer accounts, employees at one company must enter a password, such as a four-digit PIN, plus a secure number that changes every 60 seconds and is displayed on the tiny screen of the secure electronic ID (about the size of a pack of gum) they carry. For these same reasons, some companies are turning to biometrics for authentication. With **biometrics** such as fingerprint recognition or iris scanning, users are identified by unique, measurable body features.[35] Of course, since some fingerprint scanners can be fooled by fingerprint moulds, some companies take security measures even further by requiring users to simultaneously scan their fingerprint *and* insert a secure, smart card containing a digital file of their fingerprint. This is another form of two-factor authentication.

Unfortunately, stolen or cracked passwords are not the only way for hackers and electronic thieves to gain access to an organization's computer resources. Unless special safeguards are put in place, every time corporate users are online there's literally nothing between their personal computers and the Internet (home users with high-speed DSL or cable Internet access face the same risks). Hackers can access files, run programs, and control key parts of computers if precautions aren't taken. To reduce these risks, companies use **firewalls,** hardware or software devices that sit between the computers in an internal organizational network and outside networks such as the Internet. Firewalls filter and check incoming and outgoing data. They prevent company insiders from accessing unauthorized sites or from sending confidential company information to people outside the company. Firewalls also prevent outsiders from identifying and gaining access to company computers and data. If a firewall is working properly, the computers behind the company firewall literally cannot be seen or accessed by outsiders.

A **virus** is a program or piece of code that, without your knowledge, attaches itself to other programs on your computer and can trigger anything from a harmless flashing message to the reformatting of your hard drive to a systemwide network shutdown. You used to have to do or run something to get a virus, such as double-clicking an infected e-mail attachment. Today's viruses are much more threatening. In fact, with some viruses, just being connected to a network can infect your computer. *Antivirus software for personal computers* scans e-mail, downloaded files, and computer hard drives, disk drives, and memory to detect and stop computer viruses from doing damage. However, this software is effective only to the extent that users of individual computers have and use up-to-date versions. With new viruses appearing all the time, users should update their antivirus software weekly or, even better, configure their virus software to automatically check for, download, and install updates. By contrast, *corporate antivirus software* automatically scans e-mail attachments such as Microsoft Word documents, graphics, or text files as they come across the company e-mail server. It also monitors and scans all file downloads across company databases and

Authentication making sure potential users are who they claim to be

Authorization granting authenticated users approved access to data, software, and systems

Two-factor authentication authentication based on what users know, such as a password, and what they have in their possession, such as a secure ID card or key

Biometrics identifying users by unique, measurable body features, such as fingerprint recognition or iris scanning

Firewall a protective hardware or software device that sits between the computers in an internal organizational network and outside networks, such as the Internet

Virus a program or piece of code that, against your wishes, attaches itself to other programs on your computer and can trigger anything from a harmless flashing message to the reformatting of your hard drive to a systemwide network shutdown

network servers. So, while antivirus software for personal computers prevents individual computers from being infected, corporate antivirus software for e-mail servers, databases, and network servers adds another layer of protection by preventing infected files from multiplying and being sent to others.

Another way of protecting information is to encrypt sensitive data. **Data encryption** transforms data into complex, scrambled digital codes that can be unencrypted only by authorized users who possess unique decryption keys. There is nothing like having the freedom to take your information with you. We take for granted that we can hop on a plane with our laptops, visit a major client in a distant city, and wow them with our comprehensive full-colour presentation. But wait a minute—what if we relax in the supposed safety of a private airport lounge, look away for only a second, and our laptop disappears? Canada's privacy laws require that businesses protect personal information in their possession from unauthorized access or disclosure by taking appropriate security measures. Across Canada in 2008 there were 69,000 reported break-and-enters in businesses. Mercantile Mergers &

Acquisitions Corp. couldn't take that chance. As a brokerage firm that specializes in the merger business in Canada, it needed encryption software to protect sensitive client information. Mercantile evaluated five commercial encryption software packages and picked one that suited its purposes, was within its budget, and provided a cost-effective solution. If you want to learn more about encrypting your own files, download a free copy of Pretty Good Privacy from MIT (htpp://web.mit.edu/pgp).[36]

And, with people increasingly gaining unauthorized access to e-mail messages—e-mail snooping—it's also important to encrypt sensitive e-mail messages and file attachments. You can use a system called "public key encryption" to do so. First, give copies of your "public key" to anyone who sends you files or e-mail. Have the sender use the public key, which is actually a piece of software, to encrypt files before sending them to you. The only way to decrypt the files is with a companion "private key" that you keep to yourself.

Although firewalls can protect personal computers and network servers connected to the corporate network, people away from their offices (e.g., salespeople, business travellers, telecommuters who work at home) who interact with their company networks via the Internet face a security risk. Because Internet data are not encrypted, packet sniffer software (see Exhibit 17.3) easily allows hackers to read everything sent or received except files that have been encrypted before sending. Previously, the only practical solution was to have employees dial in to secure company phone lines for direct access to the company network. Of course, with international and long-distance phone calls, the costs quickly added up. Now, **virtual private networks (VPNs)** have solved this problem by using software to encrypt all Internet data at both ends of the transmission process. Instead of making long-distance calls, employees connect to the Internet. But, unlike typical Internet connections in which Internet data packets are unencrypted, the VPN encrypts the data sent by employees outside the company computer network, decrypts the data when they arrive within the company

The Value of a Disc

How valuable can two computer discs be? A package of 10 retails for $5.99, but two lost by British government workers could be as valuable as $2.5 billion. Why? Because they contained key personal data for about 25 million residents, and each record could be worth as much as $100 on the black market. You'd think one might insure such an item or at least encrypt the data. But they were sent through the office mail system with no protection other than easily-hacked passwords. Heads up! Although data is intangible, it's extremely valuable. So be careful how you handle it.

Source: B. Worthen, "Workers Losing Computer Data May Lack Awareness of Its Value," *The Wall Street Journal*, 27 November 2007, B3.

Alexander Kalina/Shutterstock

Data encryption the transformation of data into complex, scrambled digital codes that can be unencrypted only by authorized users who possess unique decryption keys

Virtual private network (VPN) software that securely encrypts data sent by employees outside the company network, decrypts the data when they arrive within the company computer network, and does the same when data are sent back to employees outside the network

network, and does the same when data are sent back to the computer outside the network.

Alternatively, many companies are now adopting Web-based **secure sockets layer (SSL) encryption** to provide secure off-site access to data and programs. If you've ever entered your credit card in a Web browser to make an online purchase, you've used SSL technology to encrypt and protect that information. SSL encryption is being used if a gold lock (Internet Explorer) or a gold key (Netscape) appears along the bottom of your Web browser. SSL encryption works the same way in the workplace. Managers and employees who aren't at the office simply connect to the Internet, open a Web browser, and then enter a user name and password to gain access to SSL-encrypted data and programs.

Finally, many companies now have wireless networks, which make it possible for anybody with a laptop and a wireless card to access the company network from anywhere in the office. Though wireless networks come equipped with security and encryption capabilities that, in theory, permit only authorized users to access the wireless network, those capabilities are easily bypassed with the right tools. Compounding the problem, many wireless networks are shipped with their security and encryption capabilities turned off for ease of installation.[37] Caution is important even when encryption is turned on because the WEP (Wired Equivalent Privacy) security protocol is easily compromised. If you work at home or are working on the go, extra care is critical because Wi-Fi networks in homes and public places like hotel lobbies are among the most targeted by hackers.[38] See the Wi-Fi Alliance Web site at **http://www.wi-fi.org** for the latest information on wireless security and encryption protocols that provide much stronger protection for your company's wireless network.

Secure sockets layer (SSL) encryption Internet browser–based encryption that provides secure off-site Web access to some data and programs

Executive information system (EIS) a data processing system that uses internal and external data sources to provide the information needed to monitor and analyze organizational performance

Intranets private company networks that allow employees to easily access, share, and publish information using Internet software

4 Accessing and Sharing Information and Knowledge

Today, information technologies allow companies to communicate data, share data, and provide data access to workers, managers, suppliers, and customers in ways that were unthinkable just a few years ago. *After reading this section, you should be able to explain how companies use information technology to improve **4.1 internal access and sharing of information, 4.2 external access and sharing of information,** and **4.3 the sharing of knowledge and expertise.***

4.1 Internal Access and Sharing

Executives, managers, and workers inside the company use three kinds of information technology to access and share information: executive information systems, intranets, and portals. An **executive information system (EIS)** uses internal and external sources of data to provide managers and executives the information they need to monitor and analyze organizational performance.[39] The goal of an EIS is to provide accurate, complete, relevant, and timely information to managers.

© Goodshoot/Jupiterimages

Managers at Lands' End Canada, the Web/mail-order company, use their EIS, which they call their "dashboard," to see how well the company is running. With just a few mouse clicks and basic commands such as *find, compare,* and *show,* the EIS displays costs, sales revenues, and other kinds of data in colour-coded charts and graphs. Managers can drill down to view and compare data by region, state/province, time period, and product. Lands' End's CIO Frank Giannantonio says, "Our dashboards include an early alert system that utilizes key performance metrics to target items selling faster than expected and gives our managers the ability to adjust product levels far earlier than they were able to do in the past."[40]

Intranets are private company networks that allow employees to easily access, share, and publish information using Internet software. Intranet websites are just like external websites, but the firewall separating the internal company network from the Internet permits only authorized internal access.[41] Companies

Intranets Are Evolving to Include:

- collaboration tools, like wikis, where team members can post all relevant information for a project they're working on together
- customizable e-mail accounts
- presence awareness (whether someone you are looking for on the network is in the office, in a meeting, working from home, etc.)
- instant messaging
- simultaneous access to files for virtual team members

typically use intranets to share information (e.g., about benefits) and to replace paper forms with online forms. Many company intranets are built on the Web model as it existed a decade ago. Companies like Motorola Canada, however, are building new systems based on the Web 2.0 model. The new intranet is collabourative like social media sites, allowing employees to network with one another beyond departmental boundaries and share their own information rather than just access company-published documents.

92% of the company's employees use Motorola's Intranet 2.0 and collectively contribute about 100,000 documents per day.[42]

Finally, **corporate portals** are a hybrid of executive information systems and intranets. While an EIS provides managers and executives with the information they need to monitor and analyze organizational performance, and intranets help companies distribute and publish information and forms within the company, corporate portals allow company managers and employees to access customized information *and* complete specialized transactions using a Web browser. Hillman Group Canada is the company that sells the nuts, bolts, fasteners, keys, and key cutting machines that you find in Home Depot, Lowes, Home Hardware, and nearly every other hardware store. Hillman's 1,800 employees produce products for 25,000 customers worldwide. Hillman's portal contains a real-time revenue report for every product with updated sales and production numbers on a continuous basis. Today, Hillman's portal contains 75 specialized reports that are accessed by 800 managers and employees.[43]

Corporate portal a hybrid of executive information systems and intranets that allows managers and employees to use a Web browser to gain access to customized company information and to complete specialized transactions

SURVEY SAYS

Reasons Why Companies Build Intranets (aka Employee Portals)

Companies are committed to intranets and are working hard to increase their usability. Here are the main reasons cited by survey respondents for why their companies are implementing (or considering) intranets:

94%	Let employees find information
50%	Enable collaboration and information sharing
44%	Automate business processes
40%	Reduce costs
25%	Provide secure, remote access to company data via the Web
17%	Provide online training

Source: Data from Forrester Research, as reported by A. Blackman, "Dated and Confused: Corporate Intranets Should Be Invaluable Employee Tools. Too Bad They Often Aren't," *The Wall Street Journal*, 14 May 2007, R5.

4.2 External Access and Sharing

Historically, companies have been unable or reluctant to let outside groups have access to corporate information. Now, however, a number of information technologies—electronic data interchange, extranets, Web services, and the Internet—are making it easier to share company data with external groups such as suppliers and customers. They're also reducing costs, increasing productivity by eliminating manual information processing (70 percent of the data output from one company, such as purchase orders, ends up as data input at another company, such as sales invoices or shipping orders), reducing data entry errors, improving customer service, and speeding communications.

With **electronic data interchange,** or **EDI,** two companies convert purchase and ordering information to a standardized format to enable direct electronic transmission of that information from one company's computer system to the other company's system. For example, when a Wal-Mart checkout clerk drags an Apple iPod across the checkout scanner, Wal-Mart's computerized inventory system automatically reorders another iPod through the direct EDI connection that its computer has with Apple's manufacturing and shipping computer. No one at Wal-Mart or Apple fills out paperwork. No one makes phone calls. There are no delays to wait to find out whether Apple has the iPod in stock. The transaction takes place instantly and automatically because the data from both companies were translated into a standardized, shareable, compatible format.

In EDI, the different purchasing and ordering applications in each company interact automatically without any human input. No one has to lift a finger to click a mouse, enter data, or hit the return key. An **extranet,** by contrast, allows companies to exchange information and conduct transactions by purposely providing outsiders with direct, Web browser–based access to authorized parts of a company's intranet or information system. Typically, user names and passwords are required to access an extranet.[44] For example, General Mills uses an extranet to provide Web-based access to its trucking database to 20 other companies that ship their products over similar distribution routes to make sure that its distribution trucks don't waste money by running half empty (or make late deliveries to customers because it waited to ship until the trucks were full). When other companies are ready to ship products, they log on to General Mills' trucking database, check the availability, and then enter the shipping load, place, and pickup time. By sharing shipping capacity on its trucks, General Mills can run its trucks fully loaded all the time. In several test areas, General Mills saved 7 percent on shipping costs (nearly $2 million) in the first year. Expanding the program company-wide is producing even larger cost savings.[45]

Finally, companies are reducing paperwork and manual information processing by using the Internet to electronically automate transactions with customers; this is similar to the way in which extranets are used to handle transactions with suppliers and distributors. For example, most airlines have automated the ticketing process by eliminating paper tickets altogether. Simply buy an e-ticket via the Internet, and then check yourself in online by printing your boarding pass from your personal computer or from a kiosk at the airport. Internet purchases, ticketless travel, and automated check-ins have together fully automated the purchase of airline tickets. Use of self-service kiosks is expanding, too. At the Canada Place Cruise Terminal in Vancouver, there are five car company kiosks to service the thousands of tourists that board Alaska cruise ships each year. For example, kiosks print rental agreements, permit upgrades to nicer cars, and allow customers to add additional drivers or buy extra insurance.[46]

In the long run, the goal is to link customer Internet sites with company intranets (or EDI) and extranets so that everyone—all the employees and managers within a company as well as the suppliers and distributors outside the company—who is involved in providing a service or making a product for a customer is automatically notified when a purchase is made. Companies that use EDI, extranets, and the Internet to share data with customers and suppliers achieve increases in productivity 2.7 times larger than those that don't.[47]

4.3 Sharing Knowledge and Expertise

At the beginning of the chapter, we distinguished between raw data, which consist of facts and figures, and information, which consists of useful data that influence someone's choices and behaviour. One more

Electronic data interchange (EDI) when two companies convert their purchase and ordering information to a standardized format to enable the direct electronic transmission of that information from one company's computer system to the other company's computer system

Extranets networks that allow companies to exchange information and conduct transactions with outsiders by providing them direct, Web-based access to authorized parts of a company's intranet or information system

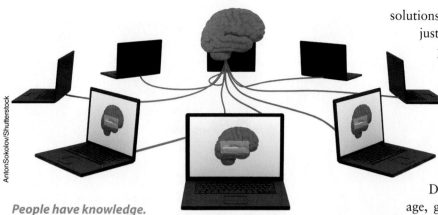

People have knowledge.
Computers contain data and information.

AntonSokolov/Shutterstock

solutions that might work. Though used by just 2 percent of physicians, medical DSS programs hold the promise of helping doctors make more accurate patient diagnoses. A British study of 88 cases misdiagnosed or initially misdiagnosed (to be correctly diagnosed much later) found that a medical DSS made the right diagnosis 69 percent of the time.[49] With a medical DSS, doctors enter patient data, such as age, gender, weight, and medical symptoms. The medical DSS then produces a list of diseases and conditions, ranked by probability, low or high, or by medical specialty, such as cardiology or oncology. For instance, when emergency room physician Dr. Harold Cross treated a 10-year-old boy who had been ill with nausea and dizziness for two weeks, he wasn't sure what was wrong because the boy had a healthy appetite, no abdominal pain, and just one brief headache. However, when the medical DSS that Dr. Cross used suggested a possible problem in the back of the boy's brain, he ordered an MRI scan that revealed a tumour which was successfully removed two days later.

important distinction needs to be made, namely, that data and information are not the same as knowledge. **Knowledge** is the understanding that one gains from information. Importantly, knowledge does not reside in information. Knowledge resides in people. That's why companies hire consultants and why family doctors refer patients to specialists. Unfortunately, it can be quite expensive to employ consultants, specialists, and experts. So companies have begun using two information technologies to capture and share the

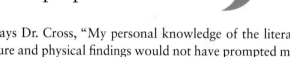

Knowledge does not reside in information.
Knowledge resides in people.

knowledge of consultants, specialists, and experts with other managers and workers: decision support systems and expert systems.

Whereas an executive information system speeds up and simplifies the acquisition of information, a **decision support system (DSS)** helps managers understand problems and potential solutions by acquiring and analyzing information with sophisticated models and tools.[48] Furthermore, whereas EIS programs are broad in scope and permit managers to retrieve all kinds of information about a company, DSS programs are usually narrow in scope and targeted toward helping managers solve specific kinds of problems. DSS programs have been developed to help managers pick the shortest and most efficient routes for delivery trucks, select the best combination of stocks for investors, and schedule the flow of inventory through complex manufacturing facilities.

It's important to understand that DSS programs don't replace managerial decision making; they *improve* it by furthering managers' and workers' understanding of the problems they face and the

Says Dr. Cross, "My personal knowledge of the literature and physical findings would not have prompted me to suspect a brain tumor."[50]

Expert systems are created by capturing the specialized knowledge and decision rules used by experts and experienced decision makers. They permit nonexpert employees to draw on this expert knowledge base to make decisions. Most expert systems work by using a collection of "if–then" rules to sort through information and recommend a course of action. For example, let's say that you're using your Bank of Montreal Master Card or your TD Visa card to help your spouse celebrate

Knowledge the understanding that one gains from information

Decision support system (DSS) an information system that helps managers understand specific kinds of problems and potential solutions and analyze the impact of different decision options using "what if" scenarios

Expert system an information system that contains the specialized knowledge and decision rules used by experts and experienced decision makers so that nonexperts can draw on this knowledge base to make decisions

a promotion. After dinner and a movie, the two of you stroll by a travel office with a Montreal poster in its window. Thirty minutes later, caught up in the moment, you find yourselves at the airport ticket counter trying to purchase last-minute tickets to Montreal. But there's just one problem. VISA didn't approve your purchase. In fact, the ticket counter agent is now on the phone with an VISA customer service agent.

So what put a temporary halt to your weekend escape to Montreal? An expert system that VISA calls "Authorizer's Assistant."[51] The first "if–then" rule that prevented your purchase was the rule "*if* a purchase is much larger than the cardholder's regular spending habits, *then* deny approval of the purchase." This if–then rule, just one of 3,000, is built into Royal Bank's VISA transaction-processing system, which handles thousands of purchase requests per second. Now that the VISA customer service agent is on the line, he or she is prompted by the Authorizer's Assistant to ask the ticket counter agent to examine your identification. You hand over your driver's licence and another credit card to prove you're you. Then the ticket agent asks for your address, phone number, Social Insurance number, and your mother's maiden name and relays the information to your bank. Finally, your ticket purchase is approved. Why? Because you met the last series of "if–then" rules. *If* the purchaser can provide proof of identity and *if* the purchaser can provide personal information that isn't common knowledge, *then* approve the purchase.

Visit **icanmgmt.com** to find the resources you need today!

Located at the back of the textbook are rip-out Chapter Review cards. Make sure you also go online to check out other tools that MGMT offers to help you successfully pass your course.

- Interactive Quizzes
- Key Terms Flashcards
- Audio Chapter Summaries
- PowerPoint Slides

- Interactive Games
- Crossword Puzzles
- "Reel to Reel" and "Biz Flix" videos
- Cases and Exercises

LOG IN!

MGMT was designed for students just like you—busy people who want choices, flexibility, and multiple learning options.

MGMT delivers concise, electronic resources such as discipline-specific activities, flashcards, test yourself questions, crossword puzzles and more!

At **icanmgmt.com**, you'll find electronic resources such as **printable interactive flashcards, downloadable study aids, games, quizzes, and videos** to test your knowledge of key concepts. These resources will help supplement your understanding of core **Principles of Management** concepts in a format that fits your busy lifestyle.

"I really like how you use students' opinions on how to study and made a website that encompasses everything we find useful. Seeing this website makes me excited to study!"

—Abby Boston, Fanshawe College

Visit **icanmgmt.com** to find the resources you need today!

MANAGING SERVICE AND MANUFACTURING OPERATIONS

Managing for Productivity and Quality

Furniture manufacturers, hospitals, restaurants, auto makers, airlines, and many other kinds of businesses struggle to find ways to produce quality products and services efficiently and then deliver them in a timely manner. Managing the daily production of goods and services, or operations management, is a key part of a manager's job. But an organization's success depends on the quality of its products and services as well as its productivity. Modelled after U.S.-based Southwest Airlines, Canada's WestJet Airlines has made a name for itself as the low-cost airline in Canada. It is now the second largest carrier in Canada. The company's success can be attributed to its commitment to cost control, high-growth revenue, and customer service. WestJet keeps its costs low by flying a single type of aircraft (the Boeing 737), by creating cost efficiencies in employee training, maintenance, and purchasing, and by keeping ground-handling charges low through subcontracting. Wherever possible, WestJet's strategy has been to focus on airports with competitive cost terms, and on niche routes where it is the only carrier to offer nonstop service and short-haul flights. This has allowed WestJet to eliminate costly in-flight amenities.[1] Want a meal on your flight? You can buy snacks à la carte or, better yet, pack your own meal. Need a pillow or blanket? You can purchase these for seven dollars. Want to visit the airport lounge? For $25 you can enter one of the open-access lounges that WestJet has partnered with

Learning Outcomes

1 discuss the kinds of productivity and their importance in managing operations.

2 explain the role that quality plays in managing operations.

3 explain the essentials of managing a service business.

4 describe the different kinds of manufacturing operations.

5 explain why and how companies should manage inventory levels.

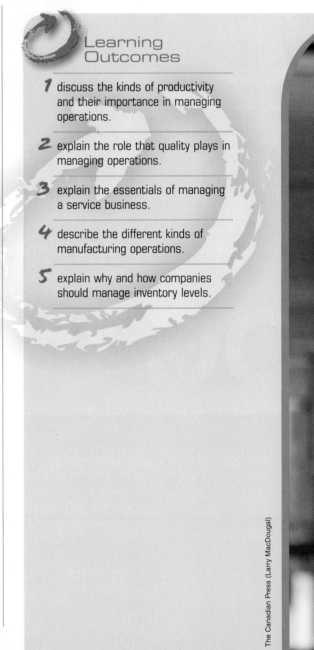

The Canadian Press (Larry MacDougal)

across the country.[2] As a result of its no-frills strategy, WestJet's costs are estimated to be 30 percent lower on domestic flights compared to rival Air Canada, allowing the airline to do more with less and to benefit from higher productivity.[3] In 2008, WestJet was in the top 10 among North American airlines for on-time performance, completion rate, and baggage ratio. It also reported one of the best pretax margins in the North American industry and an annual revenue growth of 19.9 percent.[4]

After reading the next two sections, you should be able to

1 discuss the kinds of productivity and their importance in managing operations.

2 explain the role that quality plays in managing operations.

1 Productivity

At their core, organizations are production systems. Companies combine inputs such as labour, raw materials, capital, and knowledge to produce outputs in the form of finished products or services. **Productivity** is a measure of performance that indicates how many

> **Productivity** a measure of performance that indicates how many inputs it takes to produce or create an output

inputs it takes to produce or create an output.

$$Productivity = \frac{Outputs}{Inputs}$$

The fewer inputs it takes to create an output (or the greater the output from one input), the higher the productivity. For example, a car's gas mileage is a common measure of productivity. A car that gets 60 kilometres (output) per litre (input) is more productive and fuel efficient than a car that gets 40 km per litre.

Let's examine **1.1 why productivity matters** and **1.2 the different kinds of productivity**.

1.1 Why Productivity Matters

Why does productivity matter? For companies, higher productivity—that is, doing more with less—results in lower costs for the company, lower prices, faster service, higher market share, and higher profits. For example, every second saved in the drive-through lane at fast-food restaurants increases sales by 1 percent. And with up to 75 percent of all fast-food restaurant sales coming from the drive-through window, it's no wonder that Wendy's (average drive-through time of 138.5 seconds), McDonald's (average time of 167.1 seconds), and Burger King (average time of 179.9 seconds) continue to look for ways to shorten the time it takes to process a drive-through order.[5] Productivity matters so much at the drive-through that McDonald's is experimenting with outsourcing. At roughly 50 McDonald's franchises around the U.S., drive-through orders are taken by someone at a California call centre. An operator can take orders from customers at restaurants in Honolulu one minute and from Gulfport, Mississippi, the next. During the 10 seconds it takes for a car to pull away from the microphone at the drive-through, a call centre operator can take the order of a different customer who has pulled up to the microphone at another restaurant, even if it's thousands of miles away. According to

Jon Anton, co-founder of Bronco Communications, which operates the call centre for McDonald's, the goal is "saving seconds to make millions" because more efficient service can lead to more sales and lower labour costs.[6]

The productivity of businesses within a country matters to that country because it results in a higher standard of living. A country's productivity measures the level of goods and services produced per worker per hour. This measure is important, because a positive relationship exists between productivity and standard of living.[7] Exhibit 18.1 illustrates this relationship. Companies that do more with less can raise employee wages without increasing prices or sacrificing normal profits. For households, that means additional income without loss of purchasing power. For businesses, higher productivity means profit growth; for governments, additional tax revenues can support health care, education, and/or social services.[8] Another benefit

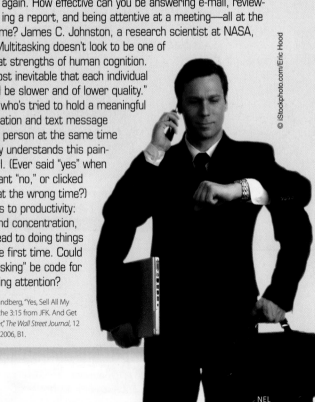

Multitasking to Higher Productivity?

Think multitasking—or doing multiple tasks *at the same time*—is the answer to increasing productivity? Think again. How effective can you be answering e-mail, reviewing a report, and being attentive at a meeting—all at the same time? James C. Johnston, a research scientist at NASA, says, "Multitasking doesn't look to be one of the great strengths of human cognition. It's almost inevitable that each individual task will be slower and of lower quality." Anyone who's tried to hold a meaningful conversation and text message another person at the same time probably understands this painfully well. (Ever said "yes" when you meant "no," or clicked "send" at the wrong time?) The keys to productivity: focus and concentration, which lead to doing things right the first time. Could "multitasking" be code for not paying attention?

Source: J. Sandberg, "Yes, Sell All My Stocks. No, the 3:15 from JFK. And Get Me Mr. Sister," *The Wall Street Journal*, 12 September 2006, B1.

> (Productivity matters because it results in a higher standard of living.)

© Comstock Images/Jupiterimages

© iStockphoto.com/Eric Hood

is that it makes products more affordable or better. It follows that those countries considered "richer" are the ones that can manufacture products and deliver services effectively.[9]

For the above reasons, the issue of productivity has garnered a fair amount of attention in Canada among economists and the business community at large. A 2009 Statistics Canada study indicates that over the past fifty years, business productivity has increased at a slightly lower rate than in the United States (4 percent per annum in Canada vs. 4.5 percent in the U.S.)[10] Before the mid-1980s, productivity growth in Canada was actually higher than in the U.S.; but since then, Canada's growth has slowed down and is now below that of the U.S. Experts point to business factors as the reason for Canada's lower productivity compared to the U.S. since 2000—specifically, to reduced investment in equipment, lower levels of innovation, a smaller high-tech industry, less worker training, and smaller production facilities.[11] The topic of productivity will continue to draw attention in Canada because "an improvement of even one percentage point in the annual growth rate of productivity, sustained for an extended period, can significantly improve the daily lives of Canadians. It can mean a more comfortable home, a more luxurious car, improved health services, more leisure or a cleaner environment. The upcoming decades will increasingly highlight this fact. Canada's aging society will increasingly depend on growth in productivity to maintain and improve its standard of living and quality of life."[12]

1.2 Kinds of Productivity

Two common measures of productivity are partial productivity and multifactor productivity. **Partial productivity** indicates how much of a particular kind of input it takes to produce an output.

$$\text{Partial productivity} = \frac{\text{Outputs}}{\text{Single kind of input}}$$

Labour is one kind of input that is frequently used when determining partial productivity. *Labour*

Exhibit 18.1

Standard of Living and Labour Productivity in Canada, 1961-2008 (Constant 2002 Dollars)

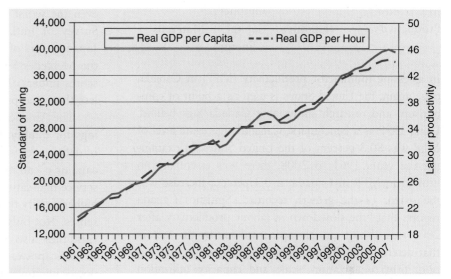

Source: "Standard of Living and Labour Productivity in Canada, 1961–2008 (constant 2002 dollars)," PRB 03-15E: Productivity: Its Increasing Influence over Canadians' Standard of Living and Quality of Life. Revised 5 November 2009. Daniel J. Shaw, Industry, Infrastructure and Resources Division, Parliamentary Information and Research Service, Library of Parliament. Reproduced with the permission of the Library of Parliament, 2010.

productivity typically indicates the cost or number of hours of labour it takes to produce an output. In other words, the lower the cost of the labour to produce a unit of output, or the less time it takes to produce a unit of output, the higher the labour productivity. For example, the automobile industry often measures labour productivity by determining the average number of hours of labour needed to completely assemble a car. The most productive auto manufacturers in the U.S. are Toyota and Chrysler. Both companies assemble a vehicle with 30.4 hours of labour. These two auto makers posted higher labour productivity than Honda (average 31.3 hours), General Motors (32.3 hours), and Ford (33.9 hours).[13] These results show that the Big 3 has made impressive strides in closing the productivity gap with Japanese auto makers building vehicles in North America.[14] Lower labour costs give auto makers an average cost advantage, which highlights the importance of productivity gains in this very competitive industry.

Partial productivity assesses how efficiently companies use only one input, such as labour, when creating outputs. Multifactor productivity is an overall measure of productivity that

> **Partial productivity**
> a measure of performance that indicates how much of a particular kind of input it takes to produce an output

assesses how efficiently companies use all the inputs it takes to make outputs. More specifically, **multifactor productivity** indicates how much labour, capital, materials, and energy it takes to produce an output.[15]

$$\frac{\text{Multifactor}}{\text{Productivity}} = \frac{\text{Outputs}}{\begin{array}{c}(\text{Labour} + \text{Capital} + \text{Materials} \\ + \text{Energy})\end{array}}$$

In assessing multifactor productivity (MFP) in Canada, once again, the United States is used as a point of comparison, and research shows that Canada lags behind. Using 1999 as a benchmark, Canada's aggregate level of MFP was 80.3 percent of the United States. In examining the years 1961 to 2008, there was essentially no growth in MFP in Canada; a 0.3 percent increase was the extent of the growth recorded. Statistics Canada reports that "the slowdown in labour productivity after 2000 was almost entirely accounted for by the factors that determine multifactor growth—technology, innovation, firm organization, scale and capacity utilization effect." Industries that contributed to declines in business sector MFP were mining, oil, and gas extraction and manufacturing; those associated with growth included finance, insurance, and real estate.[16]

Should managers use multiple or partial productivity measures? In general, they should use both. Multifactor productivity indicates a company's overall level of productivity relative to its competitors. In the end, that's what counts most. However, multifactor productivity measures don't indicate the specific contributions that labour, capital, materials, or energy make to overall productivity. To analyze the contributions of these individual components, managers need to use partial productivity measures. Doing so can help them determine what factors need to be adjusted or in what areas adjustment can make the most difference in overall productivity.

2 Quality

With the average new car costing more than $25,000, car buyers want to make sure that they're getting good quality for their money. Fortunately, as indicated by the number of problems per 100 cars (PP100), today's cars are of much higher quality than earlier models. In 1981, Japanese cars averaged 240 PP100. General Motors' cars averaged 670, Ford's averaged 740, and Chrysler's averaged 870 PP100! In other words, as measured by PP100, the quality of North American cars was two to three times worse than that of Japanese cars. In 2007, even the worst cars on the J.D. Power and Associates Survey of Initial Car quality beat the scores of the Japanese cars of decades ago. And high-quality cars like the Mercedes S-Class and Audi A8 even came in with scores under 100 (72 to be exact). That means there's less than one problem per car![17]

The American Society for Quality gives two meanings for **quality**. It can mean a product or service free of deficiencies, such as the number of problems per 100 cars, or it can mean the characteristics of a product or service that satisfy customer needs.[18] Today's cars are of higher quality than those produced 20 years ago in both senses. Not only do they have fewer problems per 100 cars, they also have a number of additional standard features (power brakes and steering, stereo/CD player, power windows and locks, air bags, cruise control, etc.).

In this part of the chapter, you will learn about **2.1 quality-related characteristics for products and services, 2.2 ISO 9000 and 14000, 2.3 the Baldrige National Quality Award,** *and* **2.4 total quality management.**

2.1 Quality-Related Characteristics for Products and Services

Quality products usually possess three characteristics: reliability, serviceability, and durability.[19] A breakdown occurs when a product quits working or doesn't do what it was designed to do. The longer it takes for a product to break down, or the longer the time between breakdowns, the more reliable the product. Consequently, many companies define product *reliability* in terms of the average time between breakdowns.

Serviceability refers to how easy or difficult it is to fix a product. The easier it is to maintain a working product or fix a broken product, the more serviceable that product is. The Reva NXR is the newest electric car to be built in India, the follow-up to the company's successful REVAi. The car is ideal for pollution-free city use. Several models, including the Intercity, can travel 160 kilometres on a single battery charge; they can also recharge 100 percent in 8 hours or, with the fast recharge option, in a mere 1.5 hours. The first charge in every car assembled comes from solar power. The vehicle has been designed to use around 80 percent fewer parts than a conventional vehicle. All in all, its operating costs are one-third those of a typical gasoline-powered car.[20] The Reva has high serviceability

Multifactor productivity an overall measure of performance that indicates how much labour, capital, materials, and energy it takes to produce an output

Quality a product or service free of deficiencies, or the characteristics of a product or service that satisfy customer needs

by virtue of a computerized diagnostic system that plugs into a portable electronic tool (PET) about the size of a personal digital assistant that assesses how well the car is running. Because the PET can be linked to a phone, customers can easily transmit their Reva's operational history to instantly find out if their car needs work and, if so, what kind.[21]

A product breakdown assumes that a product can be repaired. However, some products don't break down—they fail. *Product failure* means products can't be repaired, only replaced. *Durability* is defined as the mean time to failure. Thus, durability is a quality characteristic that applies to products that can't be repaired. Durability is crucial for products such as the defibrillation equipment used by emergency medical technicians, doctors, and nurses to restart patients' hearts. Imagine the lost lives (and lawsuits) that would occur if this equipment were prone to frequent failure!

While high-quality products are characterized by reliability, serviceability, and durability, services are different. There's no point in assessing the durability of a service because services don't last but are consumed the minute they're performed. For example, once a lawn service has mowed your lawn, the job is done until the mowers come back next week to do it again. Services also don't have serviceability. You can't maintain or fix a service. If a service wasn't performed correctly, all you can do is perform it again. Rather than serviceability and durability, the quality of service interactions often depends on how the service provider interacts with the customer. Was the service provider friendly, rude, or helpful? Five characteristics typically distinguish a quality service: reliability, tangibles, responsiveness, assurance, and empathy.[22]

Service reliability is the ability to consistently perform a service well. Studies clearly show that reliability matters more to customers than anything else when buying services. When you take your clothes to the dry cleaner, you don't want them returned with cracked buttons or wrinkles down the front. If your dry cleaner gives you back perfectly clean and pressed clothes every time, it's providing a reliable service.

Also, although services themselves are not tangible (you can't see or touch them), they are provided in tangible places. Thus, *tangibles* refer to the appearance of the offices, equipment, and personnel involved with the delivery of a service. One of the best examples of the effect of tangibles on the perception of quality is the restroom. When you eat at a fancy restaurant, you expect clean, if not upscale, restrooms. How different is your perception of a business, say a gas station, if it has clean restrooms rather than filthy ones?

Responsiveness is the promptness and willingness with which service providers give good service (your dry cleaner returning your laundry perfectly clean and pressed in a day or an hour). *Assurance* is the confidence that service providers are knowledgeable, courteous, and trustworthy. *Empathy* is the extent to which service providers give individual attention and care to customers' concerns and problems.

2.2 ISO 9000 and 14000

ISO, pronounced *eye-so,* comes from the Greek word *isos,* meaning "equal, similar, alike, or identical" and is also an acronym for the International Organization for Standardization, an international organization that helps set standards for 163 countries. The purpose of this agency is to develop and publish standards that facilitate the international exchange of goods and services.[23]

ISO 9000 is a series of five international standards, from ISO 9000 to ISO 9004, for achieving consistency in quality management and quality assurance in companies throughout the world. **ISO 14000** is a series of international standards for managing, monitoring, and minimizing an organization's harmful effects on

> **ISO 9000** a series of five international standards, from ISO 9000 to ISO 9004, for achieving consistency in quality management and quality assurance in companies throughout the world
>
> **ISO 14000** a series of international standards for managing, monitoring, and minimizing an organization's harmful effects on the environment

A high-tech electric Reva cruising the streets of Bangalore on World Environment Day.

© Dibyangshu Sarkar/AFP/Getty Images

the environment.[24] (For more on environmental quality and issues, see Section 3.5 of Chapter 16 on controlling waste and pollution.)

The ISO 9000 and 14000 standards publications are general and can be used for manufacturing any kind of product or delivering any kind of service. Importantly, the ISO 9000 standards don't describe how to make a better-quality car, computer, or widget. Instead, they describe how companies can extensively document (and thus standardize) the steps they take to create and improve the quality of their products. ISO 9000 certification is increasingly becoming a requirement for doing business with many companies.[25]

To become ISO certified, a process that can take months, a company must show that it is following its own procedures for improving production, updating design plans and specifications, keeping machinery in top condition, educating and training workers, and satisfactorily dealing with customer complaints.[26] Once a company has been certified as ISO 9000 compliant, an accredited third party will issue an ISO 9000 certificate that the company can use in its advertising and publications. Continued ISO 9000 certification is not guaranteed, however. Accredited third parties typically conduct periodic audits to make sure the company is still following quality procedures. If it is not, its certification is suspended or cancelled.

2.3 Baldrige National Quality Award

The Baldrige National Quality Award, which is administered by the U.S. government's National Institute for Standards and Technology, is given "to recognize U.S. companies for their achievements in quality and business performance and to raise awareness about the importance of quality and performance excellence as a competitive edge."[27] Each year, up to three awards may be given in these categories: manufacturing, service, small business, education, health care, and nonprofit.

The cost of applying for the Baldrige Award is $7,000 for manufacturing and service companies and $3,500 for small businesses.[28] Why does it cost so much just to apply? Because you get a great deal of information about your business in the process that will be useful even if you don't win. At a minimum, each company that applies receives an extensive report based on 300 hours of assessment from at least eight business and quality experts. Organizations receiving a site visit can benefit from up to 1,000 hours of in-depth review; however, additional fees do apply.

Businesses that apply for the Baldrige Award are judged on a 1,000-point scale based on the seven criteria in Exhibit 18.2.[29] Results is clearly the most important category, as it takes up 450 out of 1,000 points. In other words, in addition to the six other criteria, companies must show that they have achieved superior quality when it comes to products and services, customers, financial performance and market share, treatment of employees, organizational effectiveness, and leadership and social responsibility. This emphasis

Exhibit 18.2

Criteria for the Baldrige National Quality Award

2009–2010 CATEGORIES/ITEMS	POINT VALUES
1 LEADERSHIP	**120**
1.1 Senior Leadership	70
1.2 Governance and Social Responsibilities	50
2 STRATEGIC PLANNING	**85**
2.1 Strategy Development	40
2.2 Strategy Deployment	45
3 CUSTOMER	**85**
3.1 Customer Engagement	40
3.2 Voice of the Customer	45
4 MEASUREMENT, ANALYSIS, AND KNOWLEDGE MANAGEMENT	**90**
4.1 Measurement, Analysis, and Improvement of Organizational Performance	45
4.2 Management of Information, Information Technology, and Knowledge	45
5 WORKFORCE FOCUS	**85**
5.1 Workforce Engagement	45
5.2 Workforce Environment	40
6 PROCESS MANAGEMENT	**85**
6.1 Work Systems	35
6.2 Work Processes	50
7 RESULTS	**450**
7.1 Product Outcomes	100
7.2 Customer-Focused Outcomes	70
7.3 Financial and Market Outcomes	70
7.4 Workforce-Focused Outcomes	70
7.5 Process Effectiveness Outcomes	70
7.6 Leadership Outcomes	70
TOTAL POINTS 1,000	

Source: "Criteria for Performance Excellence," Baldrige National Quality Program 2009–2010, http://www.nist.gov/baldrige/publications/upload/2009_2010_Business_Nonprofit_Criteria.pdf.

on results is what differentiates the Baldrige Award from the ISO 9000 standards. The Baldrige Award indicates the extent to which companies have actually achieved world-class quality. The ISO 9000 standards simply indicate whether a company is following the management system it put in place to improve quality. In fact, ISO 9000 certification covers less than 10 percent of the requirements for the Baldrige Award.[30] Most companies that apply for the Baldrige Award do it to grow, prosper, and stay competitive.[31] Furthermore, the companies that have won the Baldrige Award have achieved superior financial returns. Since 1988, an investment in Baldrige Award winners would have outperformed the Standard & Poor's 500 stock index 80 percent of the time.[32]

2.4 Total Quality Management

Total quality management (TQM) is an integrated organization-wide strategy for improving product and service quality.[33] TQM is not a specific tool or technique but a philosophy or overall approach to management that is characterized by three principles: customer focus and satisfaction, continuous improvement, and teamwork.[34]

Although most economists, accountants, and financiers argue that companies exist to earn profits for shareholders, TQM suggests that customer focus and customer satisfaction should be a company's primary goals. **Customer focus** means that the entire organization, from top to bottom, should be focused on meeting customers' needs. The result of that customer focus should be **customer satisfaction,** which occurs when the company's products or services

meet or exceed customers' expectations. At companies where TQM is taken seriously, such as Enterprise Rent-a-Car, paycheques and promotions depend on keeping customers satisfied.[35] Enterprise measures customer satisfaction with a detailed survey called the Enterprise Service Quality index. Enterprise not only ranks each branch office by operating profits and customer satisfaction but also makes promotions to higher-paying jobs contingent on above-average customer satisfaction scores.

Continuous improvement is an ongoing commitment to increase product and service quality by constantly assessing and improving the processes and procedures used to create those products and services. How do companies know whether they're achieving continuous improvement? Besides higher customer satisfaction, continuous improvement is usually associated with reduced variation. **Variation** is a deviation in the form, condition, or appearance of a product from the quality standard for that product. The less a product varies from the quality standard, or the more consistently a company's products meet a quality standard, the higher the quality. At Freudenberg-NOK, a manufacturer of seals and gaskets for the automotive industry, continuous improvement means shooting for a goal of Six Sigma quality, meaning just 3.4 defective or nonstandard parts per million (PPM). Achieving this goal would eliminate almost all product variation. In a recent year, Freudenberg-NOK made over 200 million

© Comstock Images/Jupiterimages

Robotic Risk Management

Quality control is critical at a pharmacy. The wrong pill or the wrong dosage doesn't happen often, but when it does, it can be lethal to an unsuspecting patient and a costly mistake for the medical facility. Robots significantly reduce such errors. At $1 million each, they're an expensive fix. But Scott Beckman, VP of risk management and insurance for Advocate Health Care Network, says, "I'm going to find every savings I can to try to justify this expense. To me it's a no-brainer. It's a stellar piece of technology that can enhance patient safety and absolutely reduce errors, which means claims go down."

Source: R. Ceniceros, "Robots Reduce Errors in Dispensing Prescriptions," Business Insurance (28 April 2008): 30.

Total quality management (TQM) an integrated, principle-based, organization-wide strategy for improving product and service quality

Customer focus an organizational goal to concentrate on meeting customers' needs at all levels of the organization

Customer satisfaction an organizational goal to provide products or services that meet or exceed customers' expectations

Continuous improvement an organization's ongoing commitment to constantly assess and improve the processes and procedures used to create products and services

Variation a deviation in the form, condition, or appearance of a product from the quality standard for that product

seals and gaskets with a defect rate of 9 PPM, a rate that puts the company almost at its goal.[36] Furthermore, this represents a significant improvement from seven years ago when Freudenberg-NOK was averaging 650 defective PPM.[37]

The third principle of TQM is teamwork. **Teamwork** means collaboration between managers and nonmanagers, across business functions, and between the company and its customers and suppliers. In short, quality improves when everyone in the company is given the incentive to work together and the responsibility and authority to make improvements and solve problems. At Valassis, a printing company long famous for its use of teams, management turned to employees for additional suggestions when business fell during a recession. Teams offered so many ideas to cut costs and raise quality that the company was able to avoid layoffs.[38]

Customer focus and satisfaction, continuous improvement, and teamwork mutually reinforce one another to improve quality throughout a company. Customer-focused continuous improvement is necessary to increase customer satisfaction. At the same time, continuous improvement depends on teamwork from different functional and hierarchical parts of the company.

Managing Operations

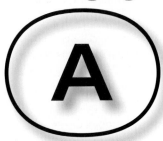

At the start of this chapter, you learned that operations management means managing the daily production of goods and services. Then you learned that to manage production, you must oversee the factors that affect productivity and quality. In this half of the chapter, you will learn about managing operations in service and manufacturing businesses.

Teamwork collaboration between managers and nonmanagers, across business functions, and between companies, customers, and suppliers

The chapter ends with a discussion of inventory management, a key factor in a company's profitability.

After reading the next three sections, you should be able to

3 explain the essentials of managing a service business.

4 describe the different kinds of manufacturing operations.

5 explain why and how companies should manage inventory levels.

3 Service Operations

Imagine that your digital camera suddenly stops working just as you are about to head out for spring break. You've got two choices. You can run to the closest Best Buy and buy a new camera, or you can try and have it fixed at Best Buy's repair department. Either way, you hope to end up with the same thing—a working camera. However, the first choice—getting a new digital camera—involves buying a physical product (a good); whereas the second—dealing with the repair department—involves buying a service.

Services differ from goods in several ways. First, goods are produced or made, but services are performed. In other words, services are almost always labour-intensive: someone typically has to perform the service for you. A repair shop could give you the parts needed to repair your digital camera, but you're still going to have a broken camera without the technician to perform the repairs. Second, goods are tangible, but services are intangible. You can touch and see that new camera, but you can't touch or see the service provided by the technician who fixed your camera. All you can "see" is that the camera works. Third, services are perishable and unstorable. If you don't use them when they're available, they're wasted. For example, if the

EuToch/Shutterstock

SUCCESS BEGINS WITH HOW WELL MANAGEMENT TREATS SERVICE EMPLOYEES.

repair department is backlogged on repair jobs, then you'll just have to wait until next week to get your camera repaired. You can't store an unused service and use it when you like. By contrast, you can purchase a good, such as motor oil, and store it until you're ready to use it.

Because services are different from goods, managing a service operation is different from managing a manufacturing or production operation. Let's look at 3.1 the service-profit chain and 3.2 service recovery and empowerment.

3.1 The Service-Profit Chain

One of the key assumptions in the service business is that success depends on how well employees—that is, service providers—deliver their services to customers. But success actually begins with how well management treats service employees, as the service-profit chain, depicted in Exhibit 18.3, demonstrates.[39]

The key concept behind the service-profit chain is *internal service quality,* meaning the quality of treatment that employees receive from a company's internal service providers such as management, payroll and benefits, human resources, and so forth. For example, Vancity, Canada's largest credit union, believes strongly that connecting directly with employees is vital for senior managers. It places a lot of emphasis on internal communications—specifically, on listening to employees. Vancity's culture centres around the concept that success starts with employees. Employees are not an afterthought; instead, they are a key group that the organization strives to impress every day. In fact, one performance measure that determines compensation for top executives at Vancity is results from employee surveys.[40]

As depicted in Exhibit 18.3, good internal service leads to employee satisfaction and service capability. *Employee satisfaction* occurs when companies treat employees in a way that meets or exceeds their expectations. In other words, the better employees are treated, the more satisfied they are, and the more likely they are to give high-value service that satisfies customers.

How employers treat employees is important because it affects service capability. *Service capability* is an employee's perception of his or her ability to serve customers well. When an organization serves its employees in ways that help them to do their jobs well, employees, in turn, are more likely to believe that they can and ought to provide high-value service to customers.

Finally, according to the service-profit chain shown in Exhibit 18.3, *high-value service* leads to *customer satisfaction* and *customer loyalty,* which, in turn, lead to *long-term profits and growth.* What's the link between customer satisfaction and loyalty, on the one hand, and profits, on the other? To start, the average business keeps only 70 to 90 percent of its existing customers each year. No big deal, you say? Just replace leaving customers with new customers. Well, there's one significant problem with that solution. It costs ten times as much to find a new customer as it does to keep an existing customer. Also, new customers typically buy only 20 percent as much as established customers. In fact, keeping existing customers is so cost-effective that most businesses could double their profits by simply keeping 5 percent more customers per year![41]

Exhibit 18.3

Service-Profit Chain

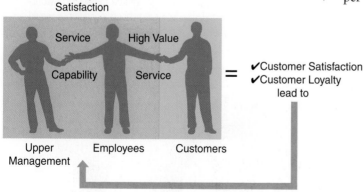

Internal Service Quality

Employee Satisfaction

Service Capability — High Value Service

= ✔Customer Satisfaction ✔Customer Loyalty lead to

Upper Management — Employees — Customers

Profit & Growth

Sources: R. Hallowell, L. A. Schlesinger, and J. Zornitsky, "Internal Service Quality, Customer and Job Satisfaction: Linkages and Implications for Management," *Human Resource Planning* 19 (1996): 20–31; J. L. Heskett, T. O. Jones, G. W. Loveman, W. E. Sasser, Jr., and L. A. Schlesinger, "Putting the Service-Profit Chain to Work," *Harvard Business Review* (March–April 1994): 164–174.

3.2 Service Recovery and Empowerment

When mistakes are made, when problems occur, and when customers become dissatisfied with the service they've received, service businesses must switch from the process of service delivery to the process of **service recovery,** or restoring customer satisfaction to strongly dissatisfied customers.[42] Service

Service recovery restoring customer satisfaction to strongly dissatisfied customers

recovery sometimes requires service employees not only to fix whatever mistake was made but also to perform heroic service acts that delight highly dissatisfied customers by far surpassing their expectations of fair treatment. For example, an executor of a family estate called a Vancouver branch of Vancity Credit Union requesting access to a deceased family member's safety deposit box. The executor lived on Vancouver Island, so an appointment was made to have the box removed. However, on the day of the appointment, the branch kept the executor waiting over 40 minutes only to discover that the safety deposit box was located at another branch. Needless to say, the executor was not happy about what he thought was a wasted trip. The manager, however, recognizing that the branch was entirely at fault, refunded the executor $100 to cover ferry costs and his wasted time as well as the $140 in administrative costs for removing the security box.[43]

Unfortunately, when mistakes occur, service employees often don't have the discretion to resolve customer complaints. Customers who want service employees to correct or make up for poor service are frequently told, "I'm not allowed to do that," "I'm just following company rules," or "I'm sorry, only managers are allowed to make changes of any kind." In other words, company rules prevent them from engaging in acts of service recovery meant to turn dissatisfied customers back into satisfied customers. The result is frustration for customers and service employees and lost customers for the company.

Now, however, many companies are empowering their service employees.[44] In Chapter 9, you learned that *empowering workers* means permanently passing decision-making authority and responsibility from managers to workers. With respect to service recovery, empowering workers means giving service employees the authority and responsibility to make decisions that immediately solve customer problems.[45] As part of Vancity's Service Recovery Program, employees are encouraged to "own" complaints and are empowered to take action and make decisions. Customer complaints and their resolution are tracked electronically. Each quarter, the Sales and Outstanding Service Committee review the feedback.[46] Empowering service workers does entail some costs, although they are usually less than the company's savings from retaining customers.

Make-to-order operation a manufacturing operation that does not start processing or assembling products until a customer order is received

4 Manufacturing Operations

Toyota makes cars, and Dell does computers. Shell produces gasoline, Bombardier makes aircraft, but Molson makes beer. The *manufacturing operations* of these companies all produce physical goods. But not all manufacturing operations, especially these, are the same. *Let's learn how various manufacturing operations differ in terms of* **4.1 the amount of processing that is done to produce and assemble a product** *and* **4.2 the flexibility to change the number, kind, and characteristics of products that are produced.**

4.1 Amount of Processing in Manufacturing Operations

Manufacturing operations can be classified according to the amount of processing or assembly that occurs after a customer order is received. The highest degree of processing occurs in **make-to-order operations**. A make-to-order operation does not start processing or assembling products until it receives a customer order. In fact, some make-to-order operations may not even order parts until a customer order is received. Not surprisingly, make-to-order operations produce or

What Qualifies as "Made in Canada?"

Some Canadian food manufacturers are becoming frustrated with the Canadian government's new "Product of Canada" and "Made in Canada" food labelling rules. For example, Ontario-based Chapman's Ice Cream has Canadian employees, uses milk from Canadian cows, and has its packaging made in Canada, yet the company doesn't qualify for the "Product of Canada" label because it uses some imported ingredients that are not available in Canada (cocoa beans, cane sugar, pineapple). Company president Penny Chapman says, "It's just plain stupid." According to her, although refined sugar and sweeteners are available in Canada, using those ingredients would price their ice cream out of the market.

Source: CBC News, "'Made in Canada' Rules Under Review," 22 May 2010.

Thomas M Perkins/Shutterstock

assemble highly specialized or customized products for customers.

For example, Dell has one of the most advanced make-to-order operations in the computer business. Because Dell has no finished goods inventory and no component parts inventory, its computers always have the latest, most advanced components, and Dell can pass on price cuts to customers. Plus, Dell can customize all of its orders, big and small. So whether you're ordering 5,000 personal computers for your company or just one personal computer for your home, Dell doesn't make the computers until you order them.

A moderate degree of processing occurs in **assemble-to-order operations.** A company using an assemble-to-order operation divides its manufacturing or assembly process into separate parts or modules. The company orders parts and assembles modules ahead of customer orders. Then, based on actual customer orders or on research forecasting what customers will want, those modules are combined to create semicustomized products. For example, when a customer orders a new car, General Motors may have already ordered the basic parts or modules it needs from suppliers. Based on sales forecasts, GM may already have ordered enough tires, air-conditioning compressors, brake systems, and seats from suppliers to accommodate nearly all customer orders on a particular day. Special orders from customers and car dealers are then used to determine the final assembly checklist for particular cars as they move down the assembly line.

The lowest degree of processing occurs in **make-to-stock operations** (also called build-to-stock). Because the products are standardized, meaning each product is exactly the same as the next, a company using a make-to-stock operation starts ordering parts and assembling finished products before receiving customer orders. Customers then purchase these standardized products—such as Rubbermaid storage containers, microwave ovens, and vacuum cleaners—at retail stores or directly from the manufacturer. Because parts are ordered and products are assembled before customers order the products, make-to-stock operations are highly dependent on the accuracy of sales forecasts. If sales forecasts are incorrect, make-to-stock operations may end up building too many or too few products, or they may make products with the wrong features or without the features that customers want. These disadvantages are leading many companies to move from make-to-stock to assemble-to-order systems.

4.2 Flexibility of Manufacturing Operations

A second way to categorize manufacturing operations is by **manufacturing flexibility,** meaning the degree to which manufacturing operations can easily and quickly change the number, kind, and characteristics of products they produce. Flexibility allows companies to respond quickly to changes in the marketplace (i.e., competitors and customers) and to reduce the lead time between ordering and final delivery of products. There is often a tradeoff between flexibility and cost, however, with the most flexible manufacturing operations frequently having higher costs per unit and the least flexible operations having lower costs per unit.[47] Some common manufacturing operations, arranged in order from the least flexible to the most flexible, are continuous-flow production, line-flow production, batch production, and job shops.

Most production processes generate finished products at a discrete rate. A product is completed, and then—perhaps a few seconds, minutes, or hours later—another is completed, and so on. By contrast, in **continuous-flow production,** products are produced continuously rather than at a discrete rate. Like a water hose that is never turned off and just keeps on flowing, production of the final product never stops. Liquid chemicals and petroleum products are examples of continuous-flow production. Because of their complexity, continuous-flow production processes are the most standardized and least flexible manufacturing operations.

Line-flow production processes are pre-established, occur in a serial or linear manner, and are dedicated to making one type of product. Line-flow production processes are inflexible because they are typically dedicated to manufacturing one kind of product. For example, nearly every city has a local bottling plant for soft drinks or beer. The processes or steps in bottling plants are serial, meaning they must occur in a particular order: sterilize; fill with soft drinks or beer; crown or cap bottles; check for underfilling and missing caps; apply label; inspect a final time; and then place bottles in cases, cases on pallets, and pallets on delivery trucks.[48]

Batch production involves the manufacture of large batches of different products in standard lot sizes. This production method is finding increasing use among restaurant chains. To ensure consistency in the taste and quality of their products, many restaurants have central kitchens, or commissaries, that produce batches of food such as mashed potatoes, stuffing, macaroni and cheese, rice, quiche filling, and chili, in volumes ranging from 10 to 200 litres. These batches are then delivered to restaurants, which serve the food to customers.

Finally, **job shops** are typically small manufacturing operations that handle special manufacturing processes or jobs. In contrast to batch production, which handles large batches of different products, job shops typically handle very small batches, some as small as one product or process per batch. Basically, each job in a job shop is different, and once a job is done, the job shop moves on to a completely different job or manufacturing process for, most likely, a different customer. For example, Leggett & Platt Machine Products in Carthage, Missouri, is a job shop that makes coil springs, innerspring units, welded metal grids, and various other parts for mattress manufacturers around the world. Since its inception, its 225 employees have made over 25,000 *different* parts; in other words, they have completed 25,000 different jobs for customers.[49]

5 Inventory

In 2006, when SUVs and pickup trucks accounting for nearly 80 percent of its sales, Chrysler was reluctant to stop making them—even when consumer demand dried up. Despite a lack of orders for SUVs and pickups, Chrysler kept building cars—cars that people didn't want—and ended up with nearly a four-month supply of inventory. In addition to what was already on dealer lots, the auto maker had 50,000 vehicles sitting on random storage lots around the midwestern United States.[50] In the automobile industry, excess inventory can cause a downward spiral. When automobile manufacturers continue to produce inventory just to keep factories running, production does not match "real" demand, and this leads to discounting by auto dealers and incentives offered by manufacturers. In some cases, brand image becomes tarnished.[51]

Inventory is the amount and number of raw materials, parts, and finished products a company has in its possession. Over the past few years, North American auto makers have experienced a wild ride, so to speak, facing the worst automotive sales results since the 1990s. Inventory management has become even more critical for auto makers. In the face of the automotive crisis, slowly over time, America's six biggest manufacturers—Nissan, Honda, GM, Ford, Chrysler, and Toyota—have all managed to maintain their inventories at adequate levels. Ford Motor Co. sales analyst George Pipas explains that "auto manufacturers have been pretty disciplined about gauging demand and keeping inventory under control. You can't just put the business on cruise control anymore."[52]

*In this section, you will learn about **5.1 the different types of inventory, 5.2 how to measure inventory levels, 5.3 the costs of maintaining an inventory,** and **5.4 the different systems for managing inventory.***

5.1 Types of Inventory

Exhibit 18.4 shows the four kinds of inventory a manufacturer stores: raw materials, component parts, work-in-process, and finished goods. The flow of inventory through a manufacturing plant begins when the purchasing department buys raw materials from

Line-flow production manufacturing processes that are pre-established, occur in a serial or linear manner, and are dedicated to making one type of product

Batch production a manufacturing operation that produces goods in large batches in standard lot sizes

Job shops manufacturing operations that handle custom orders or small batch jobs

Inventory the amount and number of raw materials, parts, and finished products that a company has in its possession

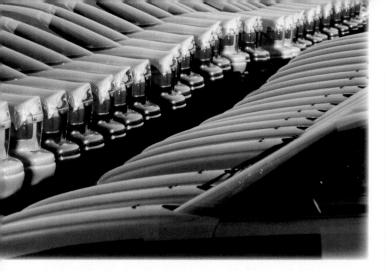

vendors. **Raw material inventories** are the basic inputs in the manufacturing process. For example, to begin making a car, automobile manufacturers purchase raw materials like steel, iron, aluminum, copper, rubber, and unprocessed plastic.

Exhibit 18.4

Types of Inventory

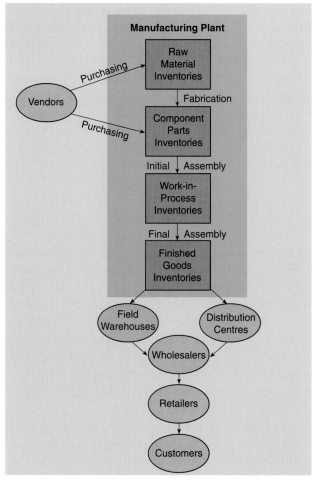

Source: From Markland / Vickery / Davis. *Operations Management*, 2E. © 1998 South-Western, a part of Cengage Learning, Inc. Reproduced by permission. www.cengage.com/permissions.

Next, raw materials are fabricated or processed into **component parts inventories,** meaning the basic parts used in manufacturing a product. For example, in an automobile plant, steel is fabricated or processed into a car's body panels, and steel and iron are melted and shaped into engine parts such as pistons or engine blocks. Some component parts are purchased from vendors rather than fabricated in-house.

The component parts are then assembled to make unfinished **work-in-process inventories,** which are also known as partially finished goods. This process is also called *initial assembly.* For example, steel body panels are welded to one another and to the frame of the car to make a "unibody," which comprises the unpainted interior frame and exterior structure of the car. Likewise, pistons, camshafts, and other engine parts are inserted into the engine block to create a working engine.

Next, all the work-in-process inventories are assembled to create **finished goods inventories,** which are the final outputs of the manufacturing process. This process is also called *final assembly.* For a car, the engine, wheels, brake system, suspension, interior, and electrical system are assembled into a car's painted unibody to make the working automobile, which is the factory's finished product. In the last step in the process, the finished goods are sent to field warehouses, distribution centres, or wholesalers, and then to retailers for final sale to customers.

5.2 Measuring Inventory

As you'll learn below, uncontrolled inventory can lead to huge costs for a manufacturing operation. Consequently, managers need good measures of inventory to prevent inventory costs from becoming too large. Three basic measures of inventory are average aggregate inventory, weeks of supply, and inventory turnover.

If you've ever worked in a retail store and had to take inventory, you probably weren't too excited about the process of counting every item in the store and storeroom. It's an extensive task that's a bit easier today because of bar codes that mark items and computers that can count and track them. Nonetheless, inventories still differ from day to day depending

Raw material inventories the basic inputs in a manufacturing process

Component parts inventories the basic parts used in manufacturing that are fabricated from raw materials

Work-in-process inventories partially finished goods consisting of assembled component parts

Finished goods inventories the final outputs of manufacturing operations

© Andersen Ross/Brand X Pictures/Jupiterimages

supply, meaning the number of weeks it would take for a company to run out of its current supply of inventory. In general, there is an acceptable number of weeks of inventory for a particular kind of business. Too few weeks of inventory on hand, and a company risks a **stockout**—running out of inventory. During a recent holiday season, the busiest shopping time of the year, retail and online stores ran out of Apple Computer's fast-selling iPods.[53] Apple issued a statement saying, "To try to meet the high demand, we're making and shipping iPods as fast as we can. So, if one store has run out, you may find iPods in another authorized iPod reseller."[54] Nevertheless, iPods were in such short supply that the iPod mini was selling for $380 on eBay, $130 over the suggested retail price. On the other hand, a business that has too many weeks of inventory on hand incurs high costs (discussed below). Excess inventory can be reduced only by cutting prices or temporarily stopping production.

Another common inventory measure, **inventory turnover,** is the number of times per year that a company sells or "turns over" its average inventory. For example, if a company keeps an average of 100 finished widgets in inventory each month, and it sold 1,000 widgets this year, then it turned its inventory 10 times this year.

In general, the higher the number of inventory turns, the better. In practice, a high turnover means that a company can continue its daily operations with just a small amount of inventory on hand. For example,

on when in the month or week they're taken. Because of such differences, companies often measure **average aggregate inventory,** which is the average overall inventory during a particular time period. Average

Uncontrolled inventory can lead to huge costs for a manufacturing operation.

aggregate inventory for a month can be determined by simply averaging the inventory counts at the end of each business day for that month. One way companies know whether they're carrying too much or too little inventory is to compare their average aggregate inventory to the industry average for aggregate inventory. For example, 72 days of inventory is the average for the automobile industry.

Inventory is also measured in terms of *weeks of*

Average aggregate inventory average overall inventory during a particular time period

Stockout the situation when a company runs out of finished product

Inventory turnover the number of times per year that a company sells or "turns over" its average inventory

let's take two companies, A and B, which have identical inventory levels (520,000 widget parts and raw materials) over the course of a year. If company A turns its inventories 26 times a year, it will completely replenish its inventory every two weeks and have an average inventory of 20,000 widget parts and raw materials. By contrast, if company B turns its inventories only two times a year, it will completely replenish its inventory every 26 weeks and have an average inventory of 260,000 widget parts and raw materials. So, by turning its inventory more often, company A has 92 percent less inventory on hand at any one time than company B.

The average number of inventory turns across all kinds of manufacturing plants is approximately 8 per year, although the average can be higher or lower for different industries.[55] For example, whereas the average auto company turns its entire inventory 13 times per year, some of the best auto companies more than double that rate, turning their inventory 27.8 times per year, or once every two weeks.[56] Turning inventory more frequently than the industry average can cut an auto company's costs by several hundred million dollars per year. Finally, it should be pointed out that even make-to-order companies like Dell turn their inventory. In theory, make-to-order companies have no inventory. In fact, they've got inventory, but you have to measure it in hours. For example, Dell turns its inventory 500 times a year in its factories, which means that on average it has 17 hours—that's hours and not days—of inventory on hand in its factories.[57]

©Stockbyte/Jupiterimages

Sharp Turns

How long do cars stay on dealers' lots? The new-vehicle "turn rate"—that is, the number of days a car sits on a dealer's lot before being sold—is a good indication of economic stability. The average retail turn rate for all vehicles is on average 63 days. In Canada, the automotive industry was happy to report that the turn rate reached a low of 51 days in October 2009 (12 days lower than in October 2008)—proof that the automobile industry was showing signs of economic recovery. Compact and midsize vehicle categories were in the top ten segments that had turn rates lower than the industry average. For example, the Ford Escape, Chevrolet Equinox, and Honda CR-V and Toyota RAV4, all part of the compact CUV (crossover utility vehicle) segment, had a turn rate below 50 days.

Sources: A. Wilson, "No More Push: How the Detroit 3 Finally Stopped Overproducing," *Automotive News*, 8 February 2010. "Turn Rate' Indicates Economic Recovery: J.D. Power," *Canadian Driver News*, 17 November 2009; H. Elliott, "Most Popular 2010 Cars," *Forbes*, 15 December 2009.

5.3 Costs of Maintaining an Inventory

Maintaining an inventory results in four kinds of costs: ordering, setup, holding, and stockout. **Ordering cost** is not the cost of the inventory itself but the costs associated with ordering the inventory. It includes the costs of completing paperwork, manually entering data into a computer, making phone calls, getting competing bids, correcting mistakes, and simply determining when and how much new inventory should be reordered. For example, ordering costs are relatively high in the restaurant business because 80 percent of food service orders (in which restaurants reorder food supplies) are processed manually. It's estimated that the food industry could save $6.6 billion if all restaurants converted to electronic data interchange (see Chapter 17).[58]

Setup cost is the cost of changing or adjusting a machine so that it can produce a different kind of inventory.[59] For example, 3M uses the same production machinery to make several kinds of industrial tape, but it must adjust the machines whenever it switches from one kind of tape to another. There are two kinds of setup costs: downtime and lost efficiency. *Downtime* occurs whenever a machine is not being used to process inventory. If it takes five hours to switch a machine from processing one kind of inventory to another, then five hours of downtime have occurred. Downtime is costly because companies earn an economic return only when machines are actively turning raw materials into parts or parts into finished products. The second setup cost is *lost efficiency*. Recalibrating a machine to its optimal settings after a switchover typically takes some time. It may take several days of fine-tuning before a machine finally produces the number of high-quality parts that it is supposed to. So, each time a machine has to be changed to handle a different kind of inventory, setup costs (downtime and lost efficiency) rise.

Holding cost, also known as *carrying* or *storage cost*, is the cost of keeping inventory until it is used or sold. Holding cost includes the cost of storage facilities, insurance to protect inventory from damage or theft, inventory taxes, the cost of obsolescence (holding inventory that is no longer useful to the company), and the opportunity cost of spending money on inventory that could have been spent elsewhere in the company. For example, it's estimated that U.S. airlines

Ordering cost the costs associated with ordering inventory, including the cost of data entry, phone calls, obtaining bids, correcting mistakes, and determining when and how much inventory to order

Setup cost the costs of downtime and lost efficiency that occur when a machine is changed or adjusted to produce a different kind of inventory

Holding cost the cost of keeping inventory until it is used or sold, including storage, insurance, taxes, obsolescence, and opportunity costs

have a total of $60 billion worth of airplane parts in stock for maintenance, repair, and overhauling their planes at any one time. The holding cost for managing, storing, and purchasing these parts is nearly $12.5 billion—or roughly one-fifth of the cost of the parts themselves.[60]

Stockout costs are the costs incurred when a company runs out of a product, as happened to Apple when it failed to have enough iPods during the holiday shopping season. There are two basic kinds of stockout costs. First, the company incurs the transaction costs of overtime work, shipping, and the like in trying to quickly replace out-of-stock inventories with new inventories. The second and perhaps more damaging cost is the loss of customers' goodwill when a company cannot deliver the products that it promised.

5.4 Managing Inventory

Inventory management has two basic goals. The first is to avoid running out of stock and thus angering and dissatisfying customers. Consequently, this goal seeks to increase inventory to a safe level that won't risk stockouts. The second goal is to have a minimum level of inventory. This goal is achieved by efficiently reducing inventory levels and costs as much as possible without impairing daily operations. The following inventory management techniques—economic order quantity (EOQ), just-in-time inventory (JIT), and materials requirement planning (MRP)—are different ways of balancing these competing goals.

Economic order quantity (EOQ) is a system of formulas that helps determine how much and how often inventory should be ordered. EOQ takes into account the overall demand (D) for a product while trying to minimize ordering costs (O) and holding costs (H). The formula for EOQ is

$$EOQ = \sqrt{\frac{2DO}{H}}$$

For example, if a factory uses 40,000 litres of paint a year (D), ordering costs (O)

are $75 per order, and holding costs (H) are $4 per litre, then the optimal quantity to order is 1,225 litres:

$$EOQ = \sqrt{\frac{2(40,000)(75)}{4}} = 1,225$$

And, with 40,000 litres of paint being used per year, the factory uses approximately 110 litres per day:

$$\frac{40,000 \; litres}{365 \; days} = 110$$

Consequently, the factory would order 1,225 new litres of paint approximately every 11 days:

$$\frac{1,225 \; litres}{110 \; litres \; per \; day} = 11.1 \; days$$

While EOQ formulas try to minimize holding and ordering costs, the just-in-time (JIT) approach to inventory management attempts to eliminate holding costs by reducing inventory levels to near zero. With a **just-in-time (JIT) inventory system,** component parts arrive from suppliers just as they are needed at each stage of production. By having parts arrive just in time, the manufacturer has little inventory on hand and thus avoids the costs associated with holding inventory.

To have just the right amount of inventory arrive at just the right time requires a tremendous amount of coordination between manufacturing operations and suppliers. One way to promote tight coordination under JIT is close proximity. Most parts suppliers for Toyota's JIT system at its Georgetown, Kentucky, plant are located within 200 miles of the plant. Furthermore, parts are picked up from suppliers and delivered to Toyota as often as 16 times a day.[61] A second way to promote close coordination under JIT is to have a shared information system that allows a manufacturer and its suppliers to know the quantity and kinds of parts inventory the other has in stock. Generally, factories and suppliers facilitate information sharing by using the same part numbers and names.

Manufacturing operations and their parts suppliers can also facilitate close coordination by using the Japanese system of kanban. **Kanban,** which is Japanese for "sign," is a simple ticket-based system that indicates when it is time to reorder inventory. Suppliers attach kanban cards to batches of parts. Then, when an assembly-line worker uses the first part out of a batch, the kanban card is removed. The cards are then collected, sorted, and quickly returned to the supplier, who begins resupplying the factory with parts that match the order information on the kanban cards. And, because prices and batch sizes are typically agreed to ahead of time, kanban tickets greatly reduce paperwork and ordering costs.[62]

A third method for managing inventory is **materials requirement planning (MRP)**. MRP is a production and inventory system that, from beginning to end, precisely determines the production schedule, production batch sizes, and inventories needed to complete final products. The three key parts of MRP systems are the master production schedule, the bill of materials, and inventory records. The *master production schedule* is a detailed schedule that indicates the quantity of each item to be produced, the planned delivery dates for those items, and the time by which each step of the production process must be completed in order to meet those delivery dates. Based on the quantity and kind of products set forth in the master production schedule, the *bill of materials* identifies all the necessary parts and inventory, the quantity or volume of inventory to be ordered, and the order in which the parts and inventory should be assembled. *Inventory records* indicate the kind, quantity, and location of inventory that is on hand or that has been ordered. When inventory records are combined with the bill of materials, the resulting report indicates what to buy, when to buy it, and what it will cost to order. Today, nearly all MRP systems are available in the form of powerful, flexible computer software.[63]

Which inventory management system should you use? EOQ formulas are intended for use with **independent demand systems**, in which the level of one kind of inventory does not depend on another. For example, because inventory levels for automobile tires are unrelated to the inventory levels of women's dresses, Sears could use EOQ formulas to calculate separate optimal order quantities for dresses and tires. By contrast, JIT and MRP are used with **dependent demand systems**, in which the level of inventory depends on the number of finished units to be produced. For example, if Yamaha makes 1,000 motorcycles a day, then it will need 1,000 seats, 1,000 gas tanks, and 2,000 wheels and tires each day. So, when optimal inventory levels depend on the number of products to be produced, use a JIT or MRP management system.

Materials requirement planning (MRP) a production and inventory system that determines the production schedule, production batch sizes, and inventory needed to complete final products

Independent demand system an inventory system in which the level of one kind of inventory does not depend on another

Dependent demand system an inventory system in which the level of inventory depends on the number of finished units to be produced

Visit **icanmgmt.com** to find the resources you need today!

Located at the back of the textbook are rip-out Chapter Review cards. Make sure you also go online to check out other tools that MGMT offers to help you successfully pass your course.

- Interactive Quizzes
- Key Terms Flashcards
- Audio Chapter Summaries
- PowerPoint Slides

- Interactive Games
- Crossword Puzzles
- "Reel to Reel" and "Biz Flix" videos
- Cases and Exercises

Endnotes

Chapter 1

1. K. Voigt, "Top Dogs," *The Wall Street Journal,* 15 March 2002, W1.
2. M. Herper and R. Langreth, "Dangerous Devices," *Forbes,* 27 November 2006, 94.
3. U.S. Commercial Service, "Market Report on Management Consulting Services," http://www.buyusa.gov/canada/en/marketintelligenceforusfirms.html; http://www.cmc-canada.ca/Media/PublicSectorDrivingVibrantCanadianConsultingMarket.cfm.
4. T. Peters, "The Leadership Alliance" (Pat Carrigan excerpt), *In Search of Excellence,* Video Arts distributor, 1985, videocassette.
5. Shouldice Hernia Center Newsletter 11, no. 1, http://www.shouldice.com/newsletter.htm.
6. K. Jaher, "Wal-Mart Seeks New Flexibility in Worker Shifts," *The Wall Street Journal,* 3 January 2007, A1.
7. D. A. Wren, A. G. Bedeian, and J. D. Breeze, "The Foundations of Henri Fayol's Administrative Theory," *Management Decision* 40 (2002): 906–918.
8. H. Fayol, *General and Industrial Management* (London: Pittman & Sons, 1949).
9. R. Stagner, "Corporate Decision Making," *Journal of Applied Psychology* 53 (1969): 1–13.
10. D. W. Bray, R. J. Campbell, and D. L. Grant, *Formative Years in Business: A Long-Term AT&T Study of Managerial Lives* (New York: Wiley, 1993).
11. "Retail Profile: Core Values, Planning, and Perspective Key to Success of Lululemon," *Canadian Retailer,* January–February 2010, 20.
12. A. Lashinsky, "Search and Enjoy," *Fortune,* 22 January 2007, 70.
13. "2010 Olympic & Paralympic Winter Games," http://www.tourismvancouver.com/visitors/vancouver/2010_olympics/2010_olympics; "The Vancouver 2010 Olympic Winter Games: By the Numbers," http://www.vancouver2010.com/olympic-news/n/news/the-vancouver-2010-olympic-winter-games-by-the-numbers_297556Ko.html; M. Cernetig, "A Glitch-Free Games?" *National Post,* 12 August 2009, http://www.financialpost.com/related/links/story.html?id=1883147; Canadian Tourism Commission, "2010 Media FAQ,"
http://mediacentre.canada.travel/media-faq; City of Vancouver Website. http://www.theglobeandmail.com/globe-investor/investment-ideas/features/experts-podium/olympian-like-effort-key-to-achieving-ones-financial-goals/article1468538, accessed May 3, 2010.
14. C. Cornell, "Running Room Goes South," *Profit Magazine,* April 2004, http://www.canadianbusiness.com/entrepreneur/exporting/article.jsp?content=20040408_161327_4380.
15. A. Warren, "The Small Stuff: It's the Little Things That Add Up—and Often Annoy," *The Wall Street Journal,* 10 May 2004, R9.
16. H. S. Jonas III, R. E. Fry, and S. Srivastva, "The Office of the CEO: Understanding the Executive Experience," *Academy of Management Executive* 4 (1990): 36–47.
17. R.B. Williams, "On-Boarding Increases Probability of Leaders' Success," *National Post,* May 2, http://network.nationalpost.com/NP/blogs/fpposted/archive/2010/05/02/on-boarding-increases-probability-of-leaders-success.aspx.
18. "Why Corporate Boardrooms Are in Turmoil," *The Wall Street Journal,* 16 September 2006, A7.
19. M. Porter, J. Lorsch, and N. Nohria, "Seven Surprises for New CEOS," *Harvard Business Review* (October 2004): 62.
20. M. Murray, "As Huge Firms Keep Growing, CEOs Struggle to Keep Pace," *The Wall Street Journal,* 8 February 2001, A1.
21. Q. Huy, "In Praise of Middle Managers," *Harvard Business Review* (September 2001): 72–79.
22. I. Barat, "Rebuilding After a Catastrophe: How Caterpillar is Responding to Tornado's Lesson," *The Wall Street Journal,* 19 May 2008, B1-2.
23. http://www.crm2day.com/content/t6_librarynews_1.php?news_id=118826.
24. T. Seideman, "Harnessing the Giant," *World Trade* 15 (2002): 28–29.
25. G. Will, "Waging War on Wal-Mart," *Newsweek,* 5 July 2004, 64.
26. J. Adamy, "A Menu of Options: Restaurants Have a Host of Ways to Motivate Employees to Provide Good Service," *The Wall Street Journal,* 30 October 2006, R1–R6.
27. S. Tully, "What Team Leaders Need to Know," *Fortune,* 20 February 1995, 93.
28. B. Francella, "In a Day's Work," *Convenience Store News,* 25 September 2001, 7.
29. L. Liu and A. McMurray, "Frontline Leaders: The Entry Point for Leadership Development in the Manufacturing Industry," *Journal of European Industrial Training* 28, no. 2–4 (2004): 339–352.
30. "What Makes Teams Work?" *Fast Company,* 1 November 2000, 109.
31. K. Hultman, "The 10 Commandments of Team Leadership," *Training & Development,* 1 February 1998, 12–13.
32. N. Steckler and N. Fondas, "Building Team Leader Effectiveness: A Diagnostic Tool," *Organizational Dynamics* (winter 1995): 20–34.
33. Tully, "What Team Leaders Need to Know."
34. H. Mintzberg, *The Nature of Managerial Work* (New York: Harper & Row, 1973).
35. P. Hales, "What Do Managers Do? A Critical Review of the Evidence," *Journal of Management Studies* 23, no. 1 (1986): 88–115.
36. http://www.canadastop100.com/index.html; http://www.eluta.ca/top-employer-mountain-equipment-co-op.
37. Francella, "In a Day's Work."
38. D. Deveau, "Blog Helps Boost Morale," *Canwest News Service,* November 5, 2009, http://www.working.com/regina/Blog+helps+boost+morale/2023946/story.html.
39. Y. I. Kane, "Toshiba's Plan for Life After HD DVD," *The Wall Street Journal,* 3 March 2008, B1-2.
40. J. Kohane. "Spirited Female CEOs Bottle Success," *Business Edge* 23, no. 5 (March 17, 2005), http://www.businessedge.ca/archives/article.cfm/spirited-female-ceos-bottle-success-8786.
41. M. Langley, "Changing Gears," *The Wall Street Journal,* 22 December 2006, A1.
42. J. Welch and G. Khermouch, "Can GM Save an Icon?" *Business Week,* 8 April 2002, 60.
43. A. Sharma, "Poor Reception: After Sprint and Nextel Merge, Customers and Executives Leave," *The Wall Street Journal,* 11 October 2006, A1; J. Gertzen, "Sprint Dodges Trouble with Deadline Reprieve," *Kansas City Star,* 19 June 2008.

44. L. A. Hill, *Becoming a Manager: Mastery of a New Identity* (Boston: Harvard Business School Press, 1992).

45. R. L. Katz, "Skills of an Effective Administrator," *Harvard Business Review* (September-October 1974): 90–102.

46. A. Bartlett and S. Ghoshal, "Changing the Role of Top Management: Beyond Systems to People," *Harvard Business Review* (May-June 1995): 132-142.

47. L. Schmidt and J. E. Hunter, "Development of a Causal Model of Process Determining Job Performance," *Current Directions in Psychological Science* 1 (1992): 89–92.

48. J. B. Miner, "Sentence Completion Measures in Personnel Research: The Development and Validation of the Miner Sentence Completion Scales," in *Personality Assessment in Organizations,* ed. H. J. Bernardin and D. A. Bownas (New York: Praeger, 1986), 147–146.

49. M. W. McCall, Jr., and M. M. Lombardo, "What Makes a Top Executive?" *Psychology Today,* February 1983, 26–31; E. van Velsor and J. Brittain, "Why Executives Derail: Perspectives across Time and Cultures," *Academy of Management Executive* (November 1995): 62–72.

50. McCall and Lombardo, "What Makes a Top Executive?"

51. K. Naj, "Corporate Therapy: The Latest Addition to Executive Suite Is Psychologist's Couch," *The Wall Street Journal,* 29 August 1994, A1.

52. P. Wallington, "Management2 Toxic!" *Financial Mail,* 28 July 2006, 48.

53. J. Sandberg, "Overcontrolling Bosses Aren't Just Annoying; They're Also Inefficient," *The Wall Street Journal,* 30 March 2005, B1.

54. J. Pfeffer, *The Human Equation: Building Profits by Putting People First* (Boston: Harvard Business School Press, 1996); J. Pfeffer, *Competitive Advantage through People: Unleashing the Power of the Work Force* (Boston: Harvard Business School Press, 1994).

55. D. Sankey, "You Need 'Skin' in the Game to Win," *Financial Post,* May 13, 2009, http://www.financialpost.com/story.html?id=1590365.

56. M. A. Huselid, "The Impact of Human Resource Management Practices on Turnover, Productivity, and Corporate Financial Performance," *Academy of Management Journal* 38 (1995): 635–672.

57. I. Fulmer, B. Gerhart, and K. Scott, "Are the 100 Best Better? An Empirical Investigation of the Relationship between Being a 'Great Place to Work' and Firm Performance," *Personnel Psychology* (Winter 2003): 965–993.

58. B. Schneider and D. E. Bowen, "Employee and Customer Perceptions of Service in Banks: Replication and Extension," *Journal of Applied Psychology* 70 (1985): 423–433; B. Schneider, J. J. Parkington, and V. M. Buxton, "Employee and Customer Perceptions of Service in Banks," *Administrative Science Quarterly* 25 (1980): 252–267.

Chapter 2

1. C. S. George, Jr., *The History of Management Thought* (Englewood Cliffs, NJ: Prentice Hall, 1972).

2. A. Erman, *Life in Ancient Egypt* (London: Macmillan & Co., 1984).

3. S. A. Epstein, *Wage Labor and Guilds in Medieval Europe,* (Chapel Hill: University of North Carolina Press, 1991).

4. R. Braun, *Industrialization and Everyday Life,* trans. S. Hanbury-Tenison (Cambridge: Cambridge University Press, 1990).

5. J. B. White, "The Line Starts Here: Mass-Production Techniques Changed the Way People Work and Live throughout the World," *The Wall Street Journal,* 11 January 1999, R25.

6. R. B. Reich, *The Next American Frontier* (New York: Times Books, 1983).

7. J. Mickelwait and A. Wooldridge, *The Company: A Short History of a Revolutionary Idea* (New York: Modern Library, 2003).

8. H. Kendall, "Unsystematized, Systematized, and Scientific Management," in *Scientific Management: A Collection of the More Significant Articles Describing the Taylor System of Management,* ed. C. Thompson (Easton, PA: Hive Publishing, 1972), 103–131.

9. United States Congress, House, Special Committee, *Hearings to Investigate the Taylor and Other Systems of Shop Management,* vol 3 (Washington D.C.: Government Printing Office, 1912).

10. A. Derickson, "Physiological Science and Scientific Management in the Progressive Era: Frederic S. Lee and the Committee on Industrial Fatigue," *Business History Review* 68 (1994): 483–514.

11. United States Congress, House, Special Committee, 1912.

12. F. W. Taylor, *The Principles of Scientific Management* (Elibron Classics, 1911) 26.

13. C. D. Wrege and R. M. Hodgetts, "Frederick W. Taylor's 1899 Pig Iron Observations," *Academy of Management Journal* 43 (2000): 1283-1291 J. R. Hough and M. A. White, "Using Stories to Create Change: The object lesson of Frederick Taylor's 'pig-tale,'" *Journal of Management* 27, no. 5 (2001) 585.

14. George, *The History of Management Thought.*

15. D. Ferguson, "Don't Call It 'Time and Motion Study,'" *IIE Solutions* 29, no. 5 (1997): 22–23.

16. P. Peterson, "Training and Development: The View of Henry L. Gantt (1861–1919)," *SAM Advanced Management Journal* (winter 1987): 20-23.

17. H. Gantt, "Industrial Efficiency," *National Civic Federation Report of the 11th Annual Meeting,* New York, 12 January 1991, 103.

18. M. Weber, *The Theory of Economic and Social Organization,* trans. by A. Henderson and T. Parsons (New York: The Free Press, 1947).

19. H. Verney, "Un grand ingénieur: Henri Fayol," *La fondateur de la doctrine administrative: Henri Fayol* (Paris: Dunod, 1925), as cited in Wren, "Henri Fayol As Strategist."

20. D. A. Wren, A. G. Bedeian, and J. D. Breeze, "The Foundations of Henri Fayol's Administrative Theory," *Management Decision* 40 (2002): 906–918.

21. Mary Parker Follett, *Mary Parker Follett—Prophet of Management: A Celebration of Writings from the 1920s,* ed. P. Graham (Boston: Harvard Business School Press, 1995).

22. D. Linden, "The Mother of Them All," *Forbes,* 16 January 1995, 75.

23. M. Losey, "HR Comes of Age," *HRMagazine* 43, no. 3 (1998): 40–53.

24. J. H. Smith, "The Enduring Legacy of Elton Mayo," *Human Relations* 51, no. 3 (1998): 221–249.

25. E. Mayo, *The Human Problems of an Industrial Civilization* (New York: Macmillan, 1933).

26. Ibid.

27. "Hawthorne Revisited: The Legend and the Legacy," *Organizational Dynamics* (winter 1975): 66–80.

28. E. Mayo, *The Social Problems of an Industrial Civilization* (Boston: Harvard Graduate School of Business Administration, 1945) 65–67.

29. C. I. Barnard, *The Functions of the Executive* (Cambridge, MA: Harvard University Press, 1938), 4.

30. J. Fuller and A. Mansour, "Operations Management and Operations Research: A Historical and Relational Perspective," *Management Decision* 41 (2003): 422–426.

31. D. Ashmos and G. Huber, "The Systems Paradigm in Organization Theory: Correcting the Record and Suggesting the Future," *Academy of Management Review* 12 (1987): 607–621; F. Kast & J. Rosenzweig, "General Systems Theory: Applications for Organizations and Management," *Academy of Management Journal* 15 (1972): 447–465; D. Katz and R. Kahn, *The Social Psychology of Organizations* (New York: Wiley, 1966).

32. R. Mockler, "The Systems Approach to Business Organization and Decision Making," *California Management Review* 11, no. 2 (1968): 53–58.

33. F. Luthans and T. Stewart, "A General Contingency Theory of Management," *Academy of Management Review* 2, no. 2 (1977): 181–195.

Chapter 3

1. Y. I. Kane, "Sony's Newest Display is a Culture Shift," *The Wall Street Journal*, 8 May 2008, B1.

2. R. Guth, "Videogame Giant Links with Sony, Snubbing Microsoft," *The Wall Street Journal*, 12 May 2003, A1; "Cost of Making Games Set to Soar," BBC News, 17 November 2005, http://news.bbc.co.uk/1/hi/technology/4442346.stm.

3. E. Romanelli and M. L. Tushman, "Organizational Transformation as Punctuated Equilibrium: An Empirical Test," *Academy of Management Journal* 37 (1994): 1141–1166.

4. C. Williams, A. Kondra, and C. Vibert, *Management*, 2nd Canadian Edition (Toronto: Nelson, 2008).

5. B. Jones, "The Changing Dairy Industry," Department of Agricultural & Applied Economics & Center for Dairy Profitability, http://www.aae.wisc.edu/jones/Presentations/Wisc&TotalDairyTrends.pdf; http://www.dairyinfo.gc.ca/index_e.php?s1=dff-fcil&s2=msp-lpl&s3=volume&page=hmp-hpl; http://www.dairyinfo.gc.ca/pdf/1920-2009.pdf.

6. N. Klym, "Digital Music Distribution," available online at http://cfp.mit.edu/groups/core-edge/docs/Digital-Music_Casestudy.pdf [accessed 25 July 2008]; "30 Products for 30 Years," *MacWorld*, June 2006, 15-16; T. Mennecke, "CD Sales, Shipments Down in 2005," *Slyck News*, 31 March 2006, http://www.slyck.com/news.php?story=1143; P. Burrows, "Microsoft Singing Its Own iTune," *BusinessWeek Online*, 11 July 2006, http://www.businessweek.com/technology/content/jul2006/tc20060706_956447.htm; http://www.nytimes.com/2010/02/26/arts/music/26arts-10BILLIONTHD_BRF.html; http://www.apple.com/hotnews/#section=itunes.

7. K. Yamagishi, "Japanese Makers Forge $1 Billion LCD Alliance," CNET News, August 31, 2004, http://news.cnet.com/Japanese-makers-forge-1-billion-LCD-alliance/2100-1041_3-5331665.html?tag=mncol; E. Ogg, "Flat-Panel TV Makers Sing the Discount Blues," CNET News, March 7, 2007, http://news.cnet.com/Flat-panel-TV-makers-sing-the-discount-blues/2100-1041_3-6165022.html.

8. "Consumer Products Brief—Kraft Foods Inc.: Price of Maxwell House Coffee to Rise 14% As Costs Increase," *The Wall Street Journal*, 15 December 2004, A16.

9. http://www2.conferenceboard.ca/weblinx/ibc/Default.htm.

10. Dr. S. Shaw, "Who Wants to Go Shopping?" *TechlifeMag.ca*, November 2007, http://www.nait.ca/techlife/32196.htm; http://www.vipedmonton.net/corporateconcierge

.htm; J. Bond, C. Thompson, E. Galinsky, and D. Prottas, 2002 *National Study of the Changing Workforce*, Families and Work Institute, http://www.familiesandwork.org/site/research/summary/nscw2002summ.pdf.

11. Industry Canada, "Privacy in the Digital Economy," http://www.ic.gc.ca/eic/site/ecic-ceac.nsf/eng/h_gv00045.html; Canadian Centre for Occupational Health and Safety, "Legislation, Bill C-45 Overview," http://www.ccohs.ca/oshanswers/legisl/billc45.html; http://www.cca-acc.com/news/government/billc45/summary.pdf; Province of Manitoba, "Employment Standards," February 18, 2010, http://www.gov.mb.ca/labour/standards/doc,unpaid-leave,factsheet.pdf; J. Koop and D. Kirby, "Canada: Increase in Climate Change Litigation in the U.S. Courts Could Spill Over into Canada," *Mondaq*, November 24, 2009, http://www.mondaq.com/canada/article.asp?articleid=89816; P. Webster, "The (Legal) Heat Is On: Why Companies Should Reveal Climate Impact," *Canadian Business Online*, March 26, 2007, http://www.canadianbusiness.com/after_hours/lifestyle_activities/article.jsp?content=20070326_85382_85382.

12. R. Johnston and S. Mehra, "Best-Practice Complaint Management," *Academy of Management Experience* 16 (November 2002): 145–154.

13. D. Smart and C. Martin, "Manufacturer Responsiveness to Consumer Correspondence: An Empirical Investigation of Consumer Perceptions," *Journal of Consumer Affairs* 26 (1992): 104.

14. http://www.priszm.com/index.php?id=1

15. S. A. Zahra and S. S. Chaples, "Blind Spots in Competitive Analysis," *Academy of Management Executive* 7 (1993): 7–28.

16. M. Frazier, "You Suck: Dyson, Hoover and Oreck Trade Accusations in Court, on TV as Brit Upstart Leaves Rivals in Dust," *Advertising Age*, 25 July 2005, 1.

17. CBC News, "Changing the Telephone Landscape," November 15, 2006, http://www.cbc.ca/news/background/voip; Statistics Canada, *The Daily*, "Residential Telephone Service Survey," April 23, 2008, http://www.statcan.gc.ca/daily-quotidien/080423/dq080423d-eng.htm; Industry Canada, "Telecommunications Service in Canada: An Industry Overview," http://www.ic.gc.ca/eic/site/smt-gst.nsf/vwapj/rt-sect3-1e.pdf/$FILE/rt-sect3-1e.pdf.

18. "One-on-One with Joe Parent, VP, Business Development and Marketing, Vonage Canada," *Canadian Business Online*, September 12, 2007, http://www.canadianbusiness.com/

innovation/article.jsp?content=20070912_114517_3396.

19. K. G. Provan, "Embeddedness, Interdependence, and Opportunism in Organizational Supplier-Buyer Networks," *Journal of Management* 19 (1993): 841–856.

20. C. Unninayar and N. P. Sindt, "Diamonds an Industry in Transition: Sometimes the Speed of Change Is Alarming," *Couture International Jeweler*, August–Sept 2003, 68–75; N. Gaouette, "Israel's Diamond Dealers Tremble: Diamond Colossus DeBeers Today Launches Fundamental Changes to $56 Billion Retail Market," *Christian Science Monitor*, 1 June 2001, http://www.csmonitor.com/2001/0601/p6s1.html.

21. N. Shirouzu, "Chain Reaction—Big Three's Outsourcing Plan: Make Parts Suppliers Do It," *The Wall Street Journal*, 10 June 2004, A1.

22. J. McCracken and P. Glader, "New Detroit Woe: Makers of Parts Won't Cut Prices: Some Can't Afford To," *The Wall Street Journal*, 2 March 2007 A1, A15.

23. D. Birch, "Staying on Good Terms," *Supply Management*, 12 April 2001, 36.

24. S. Parker and C. Axtell, "Seeing Another Viewpoint: Antecedents and Outcomes of Employee Perspective Taking," *Academy of Management Journal* 44 (2001): 1085–1100; B. K. Pilling, L. A. Crosby, and D. W. Jackson, "Relational Bonds in Industrial Exchange: An Experimental Test of the Transaction Cost Economic Framework," *Journal of Business Research* 30 (1994): 237–251.

25. "Carmakers Eye Economy with Unease," *USA Today*, 24 May 2004, B.06.

26. Health Canada, "Toy Safety," http://www.hc-sc.gc.ca/hl-vs/iyh-vsv/prod/toys-jouets-eng.php; Government of Canada, "Regulations Amending the Hazardous Products (Toys) Regulations," *Canada Gazette*, http://www.gazette.gc.ca/rp-pr/p1/2009/2009-06-20/html/reg5-eng.html; Canadian Toy Association, http://www.cdntoyassn.com/index.cfm.

27. B. Clarkson, "LCBO Campaign Tackles Elephant in the Room," *Toronto Sun*, December 10, 2009, http://www.torontosun.com/news/torontoandgta/2009/12/09/12098991.html; M. Kuburas, "LCBO Deflates Elephant in the Room," *Media in Canada*, December 2, 2009, http://www.mediaincanada.com/articles/mic/20091207/lcbo.html.

28. Canadian Press, "Environmental Group Seeks Forest Product Boycott," *Business Edge* 1, no. 11 (May 27, 2004), http://www.businessedge.ca/archives/article.cfm/environmental-group-seeks-forest-product-boycott-6108; M. DeSouza,

CanWest Global News Service, "Greenpeace Blasts Boreal Forest Destruction," September 25, 2008, http://www.theprovince.com/Green peace+blasts+boreal+forest+destruc tion/836502/story.html.

29. N. E. Boudette and J. A. White, "At GM, Curbing Inventories Calls for Juggling Act," *The Detroit Project,* http://www.detroitproject.com/ readmore/wsj_010803.htm.

30. C. Hymowitz, "Top Marketing Officers Find Getting Together Helps Them Do the Job," *The Wall Street Journal,* 11 January 2005, B1.

31. D. F. Jennings and J. R. Lumpkin, "Insights between Environmental Scanning Activities and Porter's Generic Strategies: An Empirical Analysis," *Journal of Management* 4 (1992): 791–803.

32. V. Vara, "Software Giants Seek Friends among Hackers," *The Wall Street Journal,* 3 August 2006, B1.

33. S. E. Jackson and J. E. Dutton, "Discerning Threats and Opportunities," *Administrative Science Quarterly* 33 (1988): 370–387.

34. B. Thomas, S. M. Clark, and D. A. Gioia, "Strategic Sensemaking and Organizational Performance: Linkages among Scanning, Interpretation, Action, and Outcomes," *Academy of Management Journal* 36 (1993): 239–270.

35. R. Daft, J. Sormunen, and D. Parks, "Chief Executive Scanning, Environmental Characteristics, and Company Performance: An Empirical Study," *Strategic Management Journal* 9 (1988): 123–139; V. Garg, B. Walters, and R. Priem, "Chief Executive Scanning Emphases, Environmental Dynamism, and Manufacturing Firm Performance," *Strategic Management Journal* 24 (2003): 725–744; D. Miller and P. H. Friesen, "Strategy-Making and Environment: The Third Link," *Strategic Management Journal* 4 (1983): 221–235.

36. Grant, "Comcast Plans Major Rollout."

37. D. Butcher, "Smartphones to Have 23 Percent Market Share by 2013: Study," *Mobile Marketer,* March 10, 2009, http://www.mobilemarketer. com/cms/news/research/2798.html; "Global Market for Smartphones and PDAs Worth $153.3 Billion in 2014," Electronics.ca Research Network Press Release, September 11, 2009, http://www.electronics.ca/presscenter/ articles/1190/1/Global-Market-For-Smartphones-And-PDAs-Worth-1533-Billion-In-2014-/Page1.html; J. Kinkaid, "Apple Has Sold 450,000 iPads, 50 million iPhones to Date," *TechCrunch,* April 8, 2010, http:// techcrunch.com/2010/04/08/apple-has-sold-450000-ipads-50-million-iphones-to-date.

38. A. Harrington, N. Hira, and C. Tkaczyk, "Hall of Fame: If Making the 100 Best List Is an Enormous Accomplishment, Consider How Tough It Is to Repeat the Feat Every Single Year," *Fortune,* 24 January 2005, 94; "SAS Makes the *Fortune* 'Hall of Fame,'" SAS Web Site, http://www.sas .com/news/feature/16jan05/fortune .html.

39. P. Elmer-DeWitt, "Mine, All Mine; Bill Gates Wants a Piece of Everybody's Action, but Can He Get It?" *Time,* 5 June 1995.

40. D. M. Boje, "The Storytelling Organization: A Study of Story Performance in an Office-Supply Firm," *Administrative Science Quarterly* 36 (1991): 106–126.

41. S. Walton and J. Huey, *Sam Walton: Made in America* (New York: Doubleday, 1992).

42. A. Davis, "Sky High: How WestJet Got There—and How You Can, Too," *Profit Magazine,* February 2004, http://www.canadianbusiness.com/ profit_magazine/article.jsp?con tent=20040213_171556_4580; P. Quinn, "WestJet Locks in Top Spot on Corporate Culture Honour Roll," *Financial Post,* January 30, 2008, http:// www.financialpost.com/working/story .html?id=241844.

43. D. R. Denison and A. K. Mishra, "Toward a Theory of Organizational Culture and Effectiveness," *Organization Science* 6 (1995): 204–223.

44. A. Davis, "Sky High: How WestJet Got There—and How You Can, Too," *Profit Magazine,* February 2004, http://www.canadianbusiness. com/profit_magazine/article.jsp?con tent=20040213_171556_4580; J. Kirby, "WestJet's Plan to Crush Air Canada," *Maclean's,* April 30, 2009, http://www2.macleans.ca/2009/04/30/ westjet%E2%80%99s-plan-to-crush-air-canada; P. Quinn, "WestJet Locks in Top Spot on Corporate Culture Honour Roll," *Financial Post,* January 30, 2008, http://www.financialpost .com/working/story.html?id=241844.

45. "Most Admired Corporates: #2—Four Seasons," *Financial Post,* December 3, 2008, http://www.financialpost.com/ working/story.html?id=1024072.

46. J. Sorenson, "The Strength of Corporate Culture and the Reliability of Firm Performance," *Administrative Science Quarterly* 47 (2002): 70–91.

47. A. Zuckerman, "Strong Corporate Cultures and Firm Performance: Are There Tradeoffs?" *Academy of Management Executive* (November 2002): 158.

48. *McDonald's Summary Annual Report* 2005, 2-4; D. Stires, "McDonald's Keeps Right on Cooking," *Fortune,* 17 May 2004, 102.

49. E. Schein, *Organizational Culture and Leadership,* 2d ed. (San Francisco: Jossey-Bass, 1992).

50. M. Parker, "M&A and Corporate Culture," *Canadian Business Online,* July 4, 2007, http://www .canadianbusiness.com/columnists/ marty_parker/article.jsp?con tent=20070619_150029_6476.

51. C. Leung, "Book Values," *Canadian Business Online,* October 10, 2005, http://www.canadianbusiness .com/companies/article.jsp?con tent=20051010_71494_71494.

52. "Employer Review: Yellow Pages Group Co.," *Eluta.ca.*

53. M. Parker, "Creating a Responsive and Adaptive Culture," *Canadian Business Online,* July 18, 2007, http://www.canadianbusiness.com/ columnists/marty_parker/article.jsp?con tent=20070710_125841_4696.

54. M. Parker, "M&A and Corporate Culture," *Canadian Business Online,* July 4, 2007, http://www .canadianbusiness.com/columnists/ marty_parker/article.jsp?con tent=20070619_150029_6476.

55. S. Islam, "Execs See Link to Bottom Line," *Financial Post,* November 19, 2008, http://www.financialpost.com/ story.html?id=1177050; A. Wahl, "Culture Shock: A Survey of Canadian Executives Reveals That Corporate Culture Is in Need of Improvement," http://www.waterstonehc.com/node/168.

56. C. Leung, "Culture Club: Effective Corporate Cultures," *Canadian Business Online,* October 9, 2006, http://www.canadianbusiness.com/ managing/employees/article.jsp?con tent=20061009_81277_81277.

Chapter 4

1. KPMG Forensic, "Integrity Survey 2005-2006," http://www.us.kpmg.com/ RutUS_prod/Documents/9/ForIntegrity Surv_WEB.pdf.

2. Deloitte LLP, "Social Networking and Reputational Risk in the Workplace: 2009 Ethics and Workplace Survey," http://www.deloitte.com/assets/ Dcom-UnitedStates/Local%20Assets/ Documents/us_2009_ethics_ workplace_survey_220509.pdf.

3. ASCLU and ChFC with Ethics Officer Association, "Technology and Ethics in the Workplace," 1998, http://www .bentley.edu/cbe/research/surveys/27 .cfm.

4. LRN, "LRN Ethics Study: Employee Engagement," 2007, http://www.ethics .org/files/u5/LRNEmployeeEngagement .pdf.

5. K. Tyler, "Do the Right Thing: Ethics Training Programs Help Employees Deal with Ethical Dilemmas," *HR Magazine* 50 (February 2005), available online at http://www.shrm.org/ hrmagazine/articles/0205/0205tyler.asp.

6. "2008 Report to the Nation on Occupational Fraud and Abuse," Association of Certified Fraud Examiners," available online at http://www.acfe.com/resources/publications.asp?copy=rttn [accessed 15 July 2008].

7. S. L. Robinson and R. J. Bennett, "A Typology of Deviant Workplace Behaviors: A Multidimensional Scaling Study," *Academy of Management Journal* 38 (1995): 555–572.

8. J. Norman, "Cultivating a Culture of Honesty," *The Orange County Register*, 23 October 2006.

9. S. Gaudin, "Computer Sabotage Case Back in Court," *Network World Fusion*, 19 April 2001, 12.

10. J. Bamfield, "The Global Retail Theft Barometer 2007" (Nottingham: Centre for Retail Research), http://www.globalretailtheftbarometer.com/ pdf/Global-Retail-Theft-Barometer-2007.pdf.

11. Retail Council of Canada, "The New Face of Retail Organized Crime," *Retail Organized Crime Report and Recommendations*, 2008, http://members.retailcouncil.org/advocacy/lp/issues/asr/2008_ROC_Report.pdf.

12. Retail Council of Canada, "Canadian Retail Security Survey," 2008, http://www.pwc.com/en_CA/ca/retail-consumer/publications/canadian-retail-security-survey-2007-en.pdf.

13. Retail Council of Canada, "The New Face of Retail Organized Crime."

14. CBC News, "Almost 1 in 5 Violent Incidents Occurs in Workplace: StatsCan," February 16, 2007; Statistics Canada, Canadian Centre for Justice Statistics Profile Series, *Criminal Victimization in the Workplace* by Sylvain Leseleuc (Ottawa: Statistics Canada, 2007).

15. W. Cragg and K. McKague, "Compendium of Ethics Codes and Instruments of Corporate Responsibility," Schulich School of Business York University, Toronto, 2003.

16. D. Palmer and A. Zakhem, "Bridging the Gap Between Theory and Practice: Using the 1991 Federal Sentencing Guidelines as a Paradigm for Ethics Training," *Journal of Business Ethics* 29, nos. 1–2 (2001): 77–84.

17. K. Tyler, "Do the Right Thing: Ethics Training Programs Help Employees Deal with Ethical Dilemmas," *HR Magazine* 50 (February 2005), http://www.shrm.org/hrmagazine/articles/0205/0205tyler.asp.

18. L. A. Hays, "A Matter of Time: Widow Sues IBM over Death Benefits," *The Wall Street Journal*, 6 July 1995.

19. S. Morris and R. McDonald, "The Role of Moral Intensity in Moral Judgments: An Empirical Investigation," *Journal of Business Ethics* 14 (1995): 715–726; B. Flannery and D. May, "Environmental Ethical Decision Making in the U.S. Metal-Finishing Industry," *Academy of Management Journal* 43 (2000): 642–662.

20. S. Sparks, "Federal Agents Seize Computers in 27 Cities as Part of Crackdown on Software Piracy," *The Wall Street Journal*, 12 December 2001, B4.

21. L. Kohlberg, "Stage and Sequence: The Cognitive-Developmental Approach to Socialization," in *Handbook of Socialization Theory and Research*, ed. D. A. Goslin (Chicago: Rand McNally, 1969); L. Trevino, "Moral Reasoning and Business Ethics: Implications for Research, Education, and Management," *Journal of Business Ethics* 11 (1992): 445–459.

22. L. Trevino and M. Brown, "Managing to be Ethical: Debunking Five Business Ethics Myths," *Academy of Management Executive* 18 (May 2004): 69–81.

23. L. T. Hosmer, "Trust: The Connecting Link between Organizational Theory and Philosophical Ethics," *Academy of Management Review* 20 (1995): 379–403.

24. M. R. Cunningham, D. T. Wong, and A. P. Barbee, "Self-Presentation Dynamics on Overt Integrity Tests: Experimental Studies of the Reid Report," *Journal of Applied Psychology* 79 (1994): 643–658; J. Wanek, P. Sackett and D. Ones, "Toward an Understanding of Integrity Test Similarities and Differences: An Item-Level Analysis of Seven Tests," *Personnel Psychology* 56 (winter 2003): 873–894.

25. H. J. Bernardin, "Validity of an Honesty Test in Predicting Theft among Convenience Store Employees," *Academy of Management Journal* 36 (1993): 1097–1108.

26. J. M. Collins and F. L. Schmidt, "Personality, Integrity, and White Collar Crime: A Construct Validity Study," *Personnel Psychology* (1993): 295–311.

27. W. C. Borman, M. A. Hanson, and J. W. Hedge, "Personnel Selection," *Annual Review of Psychology* 48 (1997): 299–337.

28. P. E. Murphy, "Corporate Ethics Statements: Current Status and Future Prospects," *Journal of Business Ethics* 14 (1995): 727–740.

29. Canadian Tire, "Our Code of Business Conduct," http://corp.canadiantire.ca/EN/AboutUs/Documents/code_of_business_conduct.pdf.

30. S. J. Harrington, "What Corporate America Is Teaching about Ethics," *Academy of Management Executive* 5 (1991): 21–30.

31. L. Bogomolny, "Good Housekeeping: How to Ensure Your Code of Ethics Is Effective," *Canadian Business Online*, March 1, 2004, http://www.canadianbusiness.com/article.jsp?content=20040301_58731_58731.

32. L. A. Berger, "Train All Employees to Solve Ethical Dilemmas," *Best's Review—Life-Health Insurance Edition* 95 (1995): 70–80.

33. "Leader's Guide: A Culture of Trust 2008," Lockheed Martin, http://www.lockheedmartin.com/data/assets/corporate/documents/ethics/2008_EAT_Leaders_Guide.pdf [accessed 17 July 2008].

34. L. Trevino, G. Weaver, D. Gibson, and B. Toffler, "Managing Ethics and Legal Compliance: What Works and What Hurts," *California Management Review* 41, no. 2 (1999): 131–151.

35. Boeing, "Ethics and Business Conduct Home," http://www.boeing.com/companyoffices/aboutus/ethics/hotline.html#howto.

36. Trevino, Weaver, Gibson, and Toffler, "Managing Ethics."

37. A. Countryman, "Leadership Key Ingredient in Ethics Recipe, Experts Say," *Chicago Tribune*, 1 December 2002, Business 1.

38. Bogomolny, "Good Housekeeping."

39. Ethics Research Center, "2009 National Business Ethics Survey," http://www.ethics.org/nbes/files/nbes-final.pdf.

40. G. Weaver and L. Trevino, "Integrated and Decoupled Corporate Social Performance: Management Commitments, External Pressures, and Corporate Ethics Practices," *Academy of Management Journal* 42 (1999): 539–552; G. Weaver, L. Trevino, and P. Cochran, "Corporate Ethics Programs as Control Systems: Influences of Executive Commitment and Environmental Factors," *Academy of Management Journal* 42 (1999): 41–57.

41. J. Salopek, "Do the Right Thing," *Training & Development* 55 (July 2001): 38–44.

42. Ethics Research Center, "2009 National Business Ethics Survey," http://www.ethics.org/nbes/files/nbes-final.pdf.

43. Ethics Research Center, "2007 National Business Ethics Survey," http://www.ethics.org/files/u5/The_2007_National_Business_Ethics_Survey.pdf.

44. M. P. Miceli and J. P. Near, "Whistleblowing: Reaping the Benefits," *Academy of Management Executive* 8 (1994): 65–72.

45. M. Master and E. Heresniak. "The Disconnect in Ethics Training," *Across the Board* 39 (September 2002): 51–52.

46. H. R. Bower, *Social Responsibilities of the Businessman* (New York: Harper & Row, 1953).

47. "Beyond the Green Corporation," *BusinessWeek*, 29 January 2007.

48. S. L. Wartick and P. L. Cochran, "The Evolution of the Corporate Social Performance Model," *Academy of Management Review* 10 (1985): 758–769.

49. J. Nocera, "The Paradox of Businesses as Do-Gooders," *The New York Times*, 3 February 2007, C1.

50. S. Waddock, C. Bodwell, and S. Graves. "Responsibility: The New Business Imperative," *Academy of Management Executive* 16 (2002): 132–148.

51. T. Donaldson and L. E. Preston, "The Stakeholder Theory of the Corporation: Concepts, Evidence, and Implications,"

Academy of Management Review 20 (1995): 65–91.

52. M. B. E. Clarkson, "A Stakeholder Framework for Analyzing and Evaluating Corporate Social Performance," Academy of Management Review 20 (1995): 92–117.

53. B. Agle, R. Mitchell, and J. Sonnenfeld, "Who Matters to CEOs? An Investigation of Stakeholder Attributes and Salience, Corporate Performance, and CEO Values," Academy of Management Journal 42 (1999): 507–525.

54. J. Wingrove, "Finger Lickin' Tofu: KFC Goes Vegan," Globe and Mail, June 4, 2008.

55. A. B. Carroll, "A Three-Dimensional Conceptual Model of Corporate Performance," Academy of Management Review 4 (1979): 497–505.

56. J. Lublin and M. Murrary, "CEOs Leave Faster Than Ever Before as Boards, Investors Lose Patience," The Wall Street Journal Interactive, 27 October 2000.

57. D. Woodruff, "Europe Shows More CEOs the Door," The Wall Street Journal, 1 July 2002.

58. L. Cameron, "Rumble at the Tim's Drive-Thru," Canadian Business, January 18, 2010, 13.

59. T. Howard, "Low-Carb Message Not Popular, but Sales Are Up," USA Today, 8 December 2003, 10B.

60. Scouts Canada, www.scouts.ca/dnn/Foundation/CorporateCampaign/Affinitycard/tabid/102/Default.aspx.

61. R. Spence, "What a Bargain: Do Successful Entrepreneurs Owe a Debt to the World?" Profit Magazine, December 2009.

62. K. Scannell, "Witness Says Police-Vest Maker Ignored Safety Concerns," The Wall Street Journal, 15 November 2004, C1.

63. L. Story, "Disney To Test Character Toys for Lead Paint," New York Times, September 10, 2007.

64. A. Holloway, "Sustain to Gain: Environmentally Friendly Companies," Canadian Business Online, January 30, 2006, http://www.canadianbusiness.com/markets/article.jsp?content=20060130_73968_73968.

65. Social Investment Organization, "Canadian Socially Responsible Investment Review 2008," http://www.socialinvestment.ca/documents/caReview2008.pdf.

66. P. Cunningham, "It Pays to Be Socially Responsible," Financial Post, February 12, 2007, http://www.financialpost.com/story.html?id=fbcde900-5cba-4f30-9775-ed4825f68424#ixzz0jFhem8r6.

67. H. Haines, "Noah Joins Ranks of Socially Responsible Funds," Dow Jones News Service, October 13, 1995.

68. J. Pereira, "Doing Good and Doing Well at Timberland," The Wall Street Journal, 9 September 2003, B1.

69. Cunningham, "It Pays to Be Socially Responsible."

70. R. Trudel and J. Cotte, "Does It Pay to Be Good?" MIT Sloan Management Review, January 8, 2009, http://sloanreview.mit.edu/the-magazine/articles/2009/winter/50213/does-it-pay-to-be-good.

Chapter 5

1. L. A. Hill, Becoming a Manager: Master a New Identity (Boston: Harvard Business School Press, 1992).

2. J. Jargon, "General Mills Sees Wealth via Health," The Wall Street Journal, 25 February 2008, A9.

3. E. A. Locke and G. P. Latham, A Theory of Goal Setting & Task Performance (Englewood Cliffs, NJ: Prentice Hall, 1990).

4. M. E. Tubbs, "Goal-Setting: A Meta-Analytic Examination of the Empirical Evidence," Journal of Applied Psychology 71 (1986): 474–483.

5. J. Bavelas and E. S. Lee, "Effect of Goal Level on Performance: A Trade-Off of Quantity and Quality," Canadian Journal of Psychology 32 (1978): 219–240.

6. C. Johnston, "Mike Weir Preparing for His Induction into Canadian Golf Hall of Fame," http://www.amherstdaily.com/Golf/2009-11-26/article-819646/Mike-Weir-preparing-for-his-induction-to-Canadian-Golf-Hall-of-Fame/1 J. Reed, "Mike Weir Hall of Famer," LondonOntarioGolf.com, December 1, 2009, http://www.londonontariogolf.com/inthenews/viewtopic.php?p=6155&sid=ad15d86b814d47513a8b992561a03ec2

7. Harvard Management Update, "Learn by 'Failing Forward,'" The Globe & Mail, 31 October 2000, B17.

8. C. C. Miller, "Strategic Planning and Firm Performance: A Synthesis of More Than Two Decades of Research," Academy of Management Performance 37 (1994): 1649–1665.

9. H. Mintzberg, "Rethinking Strategic Planning," Long Range Planning 27 (1994): 12–30; H. Mintzberg, "The Pitfalls of Strategic Planning," California Management Review 36 (1993): 32–47.

10. J. D. Stoll, "GM Sees Brighter Future," The Wall Street Journal, 18 January 2008, A3; D. Welch, "Live Green or Die," BusinessWeek, 26 May 2008, 36-41.

11. Mintzberg, "Pitfalls of Strategic Planning."

12. Locke and Latham, Theory of Goal Setting.

13. A. King, B. Oliver, B. Sloop, and K. Vaverek, Planning & Goal Setting for Improved Performance: Participant's Guide (Cincinnati, OH: Thomson Executive Press, 1995).

14. H. Klein and M. Wesson, "Goal and Commitment and the Goal-Setting Process: Conceptual Clarification and Empirical Synthesis," Journal of Applied Psychology 84 (1999): 885-886.

15. B. Scudamore, "Simplicity Breeds Success," Profit Magazine, October 2008, http://www.canadianbusiness.com/columnists/brian_scudamore/article.jsp?content=20081001_198719_198719&utm_source=business&utm_medium=rss

16. Scudamore, "Simplicity Breeds Success."

17. A. Pressman, "Ocean Spray's Creative Juices," BusinessWeek, 15 May 2006, 88–90.

18. A. Bandura and D. H. Schunk, "Cultivating Competence, Self-Efficacy, and Intrinsic Interest through Proximal Self-Motivation," Journal of Personality & Social Psychology 41 (1981): 586–598.

19. Locke and Latham, Theory of Goal Setting.

20. M. J. Neubert, "The Value of Feedback and Goal Setting over Goal Setting Alone and Potential Moderators of This Effect: A Meta-Analysis," Human Performance 11 (1998): 321–335.

21. E. H. Bowman and D. Hurry, "Strategy through the Option Lens: An Integrated View of Resource Investments and the Incremental-Choice Process," Academy of Management Review 18 (1993): 760–782.

22. M. Lawson, "In Praise of Slack: Time Is of the Essence," Academy of Management Executive 15 (2000): 125–135.

23. http://www.google.sh/intl/en/corporate

24. D. Forest and F. David, "It's Time to Redraft Your Mission Statement," Journal of Business Strategy, January–February 2003, 11–14, http://www.esf.edu/for/germain/David_8_12.pdf

25. http://www.starbucks.com/about-us/company-information/mission-statement

26. http://www.lululemon.com/about/culture; http://legion.ca/Home/mission_e.cfm

27.] S. Fife, "Break the Competitive Roadblock: Three Canadian Success Stories," Canadian Business Online, May 18, 2007, http://www.canadianbusiness.com/innovation/article.jsp?content=20070518_094759_4716; Leadership and Management Development Council of British Columbia, "Magnotta: Breaking New Ground with Innovative Marketing Strategies," December 2005, http://www.leadershipmanagement.bc.ca/pdf/MagnottaWinery_Eng[1].pdf; Magnotta.com http://www.magnotta.com/About.aspx

28. Industry Canada, Small Business Policy Branch, "Blue Falls Manufacturing: Turning Market Knowledge into a Competitive Edge," November 2006, http://leadershipmanagement.ca/pdf/BlueFallsManufacturing_Eng%5B1%5D.pdf

29. CBC News, "61% of Companies Monitor Workers' Web Surfing: Survey," April 19, 2007, http://www.cbc.ca/technology/story/2007/04/19/work-websurfing.html?ref=rss

30. M. Geist, "Computer and E-mail Workplace Surveillance in Canada: The Shift from Reasonable Expectation of Privacy to Reasonable Surveillance," *Canadian Bar Review* 82, no. 2 (August 2003), http://www.terremoto.ca/privacy/geist_report.pdf

31. R. Richmond, "It's 10 a.m. Do You Know Where Your Workers Are?" *The Wall Street Journal*, January 12, 2004, R1.

32. Adapted from quality procedure at G & G Manufacturing, Cincinnati, Ohio.

33. N. Humphrey, "References a Tricky Issue for Both Sides," *Nashville Business Journal* 11 (8 May 1995): 1A.

34. K. R. MacCrimmon, R. N. Taylor, and E. A. Locke, "Decision Making and Problem Solving," in *Handbook of Industrial & Organizational Psychology*, ed. M. D. Dunnette (Chicago: Rand McNally, 1976), 1397–1453.

35. Ibid.

36. A. Zimmerman, "Cricket Lee Takes on the Fashion Industry," *The Wall Street Journal*, 17 March 2008, R1.

37. *Consumers Reports Buying Guide: 2006*, 129–131.

38. P. Djang, "Selecting Personal Computers," *Journal of Research on Computing in Education* 25 (1993): 327.

39. "European Cities Monitor," Cushman & Wakefield Healy & Baker, 2007, available online at http://www.berlin-partner.de/fileadmin/chefredaktion/documents/pdf_Presse/European_Investment_Monitor_2007.pdf.

40. K. Blanchard, "The Critical Role of Teams," March 2006, http://www.kenblanchard.com/img/pub/pdf_critical_role_teams.pdf

41. I. L. Janis, *Groupthink* (Boston: Houghton Mifflin, 1983).

42. C. P. Neck and C. C. Manz, "From Groupthink to Teamthink: Toward the Creation of Constructive Thought Patterns in Self-Managing Work Teams," *Human Relations* 47 (1994): 929–952; J. Schwartz and M. L. Wald, "'Groupthink' Is 30 Years Old, and Still Going Strong," *The New York Times*, 9 March 2003, 5.

43. C. Ferraris and R. Carveth, "NASA and the Columbia Disaster: Decision-Making by Groupthink?," Proceedings of the 2003 Association for Business Communication Annual Convention, http://www.businesscommunication.org/conventions/Proceedings/2003/PDF/03ABC03.pdf.

44. C. Gallo, "How to Run a Meeting Like Google," *Business Week Online*, 8 September 2006, 15.

45. A. Mason, W. A. Hochwarter, and K. R. Thompson, "Conflict: An Important Dimension in Successful Management Teams," *Organizational Dynamics* 24 (1995): 20.

46. C. Olofson, "So Many Decisions, So Little Time: What's Your Problem?" *Fast Company*, 1 October 1999, 62.

47. Ibid.

48. R. Cosier and C. R. Schwenk, "Agreement and Thinking Alike: Ingredients for Poor Decisions," *Academy of Management Executive* 4 (1990): 69–74.

49. K. Jenn and E. Mannix, "The Dynamic Nature of Conflict: A Longitudinal Study of Intragroup Conflict and Group Performance," *Academy of Management Journal* 44, no. 2 (2001): 238–251; R. L. Priem, D. A. Harrison, and N. K. Muir, "Structured Conflict and Consensus Outcomes in Group Decision Making," *Journal of Management* 21 (1995): 691–710.

50. A. Van De Ven and A. L. Delbecq, "Nominal versus Interacting Group Processes for Committee Decision Making Effectiveness," *Academy of Management Journal* 14 (1971): 203–212.

51. A. R. Dennis and J. S. Valicich, "Group, Sub-Group, and Nominal Group Idea Generation: New Rules for a New Media?" *Journal of Management* 20 (1994): 723–736.

52. R. B. Gallupe and W. H. Cooper, "Brainstorming Electronically," *Sloan Management Review*, Fall 1993, 27–36.

53. Ibid.

54. G. Kay, "Effective Meetings through Electronic Brainstorming," *Management Quarterly* 35 (1995): 15.

Chapter 6

1. L. Kahney, "Inside Look at the Birth of the iPod," *Wired*, 21 July 2004, available online at http://www.wired.com/news/culture/0,64286-0.html, http://www.apple-history.com/?page=gallery&model=ipod; K. Hall, "Sony's iPod Assault Is No Threat to Apple," *BusinessWeek*, 13 March 2006, 53; N. Wingfield, "SanDisk Raises Music-Player Stakes," *The Wall Street Journal*, 21 August 2006, B4; "Growing Louder: Microsoft Plods after iPod Like a Giant — Powerful, Determined, Untiring," *Winston-Salem Journal*, 15 November 2006, D1-D2; A. Athavaley and R. A. Guth, "How the Zune Is Faring So Far with Consumers," *The Wall Street Journal*, 12 December 2006, D1, D7; P. Cruz, "US Top Selling Computer Hardware for January 2007," Bloomberg.com, available online at http://www.bloomberg.com/apps/news?pid=conewsstory&refer=conews&tkr=AAPL:US&sid=ap0bqJw2VpwI; J. Raphael, "Motorola's 2GHz Android Phone Means Business," PCWorld, June 11, 2010, http://www.pcworld.com/businesscenter/article/198636/motorolas_2ghz_android_phone_means_business.html;I. Fried, "Microsoft Claims Android Steps on Its Patents," CNET News, April 27, 2010, http://news.cnet.com/8301-13860_3-20003602-56.html; M. Ruhfass, "Bell Canada Now Offering RIM BlackBerry Pearl 3G 9100," Mobileburn.com, June 5, 2010, http://www.mobileburn.com/news.jsp?Id=9631.

2. J. Barney, "Firm Resources and Sustained Competitive Advantage," *Journal of Management* 17 (1991): 99–120; J. Barney, "Looking Inside for Competitive Advantage," *Academy of Management Executive* 9 (1995): 49–61.

3. J. Snell, "Apple's Home Run," *Macworld*, November 2006, 7.

4. J. D'Arcy and T. Davies, "The Walkman at 20," *Maclean's*, 30 August 1999, 10; K. Hall, "Sony's iPod Assault Is No Threat to Apple," *BusinessWeek*, 13 March 2006, 53.

5. Athavaley and Guth, "How the Zune Is Faring," D7.

6. S. H. Wildstrom, "ZUNE 2.0: PLAYING TOMORROW'S TUNE?," *Business Week*, 10 December 2007, 87.

7. J. Warren, "At New Web Store, Many Songs Sell for a Few Cents," *The Wall Street Journal*, 14 October 2006, P2.

8. R. Levine, "Napster's Ghost Rises," *Fortune*, 6 March 2006, 30; "30 Products for 30 Years," *MacWorld*, June 2006, 15-16.

9. S. Hart and C. Banbury, "How Strategy-Making Processes Can Make a Difference," *Strategic Management Journal* 15 (1994): 251–269.

10. R. A. Burgelman, "Fading Memories: A Process Theory of Strategic Business Exit in Dynamic Environments," *Administrative Science Quarterly* 39 (1994): 24–56; R. A. Burgelman and A. S. Grove, "Strategic Dissonance," *California Management Review* 38 (1996): 8–28.

11. R. Burgelman and A. Grove, "Strategic Dissonance," *California Management Review* (Winter 1996): 8–28.

12. E. Smith and M. Peers, "Cost Cutting Is an Uphill Fight at Warner Music," *The Wall Street Journal*, 24 May 2004, B1.

13. A. Fiegenbaum, S. Hart, and D. Schendel, "Strategic Reference Point Theory," *Strategic Management Journal* 17 (1996): 219–235.

14. "Most and Least Reliable Brands," *Consumer Reports*, available online at http://www.consumerreports.org/cro/money/resource-center/most-and-least-reliable-brands-5-07/cars/0507_brands_cars_1.htm.

15. S. Segan and E. Griffith, "The Best (and Worst) Tech Support in America," *PC Magazine*, 29 July 2008, available online at http://www.pcmag.com/article2/0,2817,2326603,00.asp.

16. D. J. Collis, "Research Note: How Valuable Are Organizational Capabilities?," *Strategic Management Journal* 15 (1994): 143–152.

17. CBC News, "Ottawa T & T Supermarket Opens to Huge Crowds,"

October 28, 2009, http://www.cbc.ca/canada/ottawa/story/2009/10/28/ottawa-091028.html.

18. A. Fiegenbaum and H. Thomas, "Strategic Groups as Reference Groups: Theory, Modeling and Empirical Examination of Industry and Competitive Strategy," *Strategic Management Journal* 16 (1995): 461–476.

19. R. K. Reger and A. S. Huff, "Strategic Groups: A Cognitive Perspective," *Strategic Management Journal* 14 (1993): 103–124.

20. CBC News, "RONA-Revy Home Centre Combo to Create Home Improvement Giant," May 14, 2001, http://www.cbc.ca/money/story/2001/05/14/ronaremy_tmc010514.html; RONA, http://www.rona.ca; CBC News, "Lowe's says Canadian Expansion "On Track"", September 21, 2006, http://www.cbc.ca/money/story/2006/09/21/lowes.html.

21. http://www.timbr.com

22. http://www.canac-marquis.com/Canac-Marquis-Grenier/client/fr/Accueil/Accueil.asp

23. "Auto Source Loses Money But Gains Experience," *Automotive Marketing*, May 1994, 20; Steven E. Bachand, "There's a Lot More to Canadian Tire," *Business Quarterly*, Spring 1995, 30–33, 36–39; Ian Brown, *Freewheeling: The Feuds, Broods, and Outrageous Fortunes of the Billes Family and Canada's Favourite Company* (Toronto: HarperCollins, 1989); "Trouble in Tireland," *Canadian Business*, November 1989, 95–109; "Canadian Tire's Journey South Is Uphill All the Way," *Business Week*, February 6, 1984, 88H.

24. *The Globe and Mail*, "Canadian Tire Lays Shopper Bob to Rest," November 9, 2009, http://www.theglobeandmail.com/globe-investor/canadian-tire-lays-shopper-bob-to-rest/article1357093; *The Globe and Mail*, "Canadian Tire Going Back to Basics," April 7, 2010, http://www.theglobeandmail.com/globe-investor/canadian-tire-going-back-to-basics/article1525372; *The Globe and Mail*, "A Chat with Canadian Tire's CEO," April 8, 2010, http://www.theglobeandmail.com/report-on-business/chat-with-canadian-tires-ceo/article1526416.

25. M. Lubatkin, "Value-Creating Mergers: Fact or Folklore?" *Academy of Management Executive* 2 (1988): 295–302; M. Lubatkin and S. Chatterjee, "Extending Modern Portfolio Theory into the Domain of Corporate Diversification: Does It Apply?" *Academy of Management Journal* 37 (1994): 109–136; M. H. Lubatkin and P. J. Lane, "Psst . . . The Merger Mavens Still Have It

Wrong!" *Academy of Management Executive* 10 (1996): 21–39.

26. "Who We Are," 3M, available online at http://solutions.3m.com/wps/portal/3M/en_US/our/company/information/about-us.

27. "About Samsung," Samsung, available online at http://www.samsung.com/us/aboutsamsung/index.html.

28. J. A. Pearce II, "Selecting among Alternative Grand Strategies," *California Management Review* (spring 1982): 23–31.

29. W. M. Bulkeley, "Staples Offers $3.6 Billion for Dutch Rival," *The Wall Street Journal*, 20 February 2008, A8.

30. "Subaru Archives Homepage," *Cars101.com*, available online at http://www.cars101.com/subaru_archives.html.

31. J. A. Pearce II, "Retrenchment Remains the Foundation of Business Turnaround," *Strategic Management Journal* 15 (1994): 407–417.

32. P. Eavis, "Sears Looks in Dire Shape," *The Wall Street Journal*, 30 May 2008, C14.

33. E. Taylor and C. Rauwald, "Daimler Scores Profit on Its Own," *The Wall Street Journal*, 15 February 2008, C7.

34. P. Wonacott, "Wal-Mart, Others Demand Lowest Prices, Managers Scramble to Slash Costs," *The Wall Street Journal*, 13 November 2003, A1.

35. M. Veverka, "Bigger and Better: Costco's Costly Expansion Is About to Pay Off—For Shoppers and Shareholders," *Barron's*, 12 May 2003, 28.

36. L. Tischler, "The Price Is Right," *Fast Company*, 1 November 2003, 83.

37. R. E. Miles and C. C. Snow, *Organizational Strategy, Structure, & Process* (New York: McGraw Hill, 1978); S. Zahra and J. A. Pearce, "Research Evidence on the Miles-Snow Typology," *Journal of Management* 16 (1990): 751–768; W. L. James and K. J. Hatten, "Further Evidence on the Validity of the Self Typing Paragraph Approach: Miles and Snow Strategic Archetypes in Banking," *Strategic Management Journal* 16 (1995): 161–168.

38. H. Greenberg, "Rivals Won't Let Tempur-Pedic Rest," *The Wall Street Journal*, 16-17 February 2008, B3.

39. M. Chen, "Competitor Analysis and Interfirm Rivalry: Toward a Theoretical Integration," *Academy of Management Review* 21 (1996): 100–134; J. C. Baum and H. J. Korn, "Competitive Dynamics of Interfirm Rivalry," *Academy of Management Journal* 39 (1996): 255–291.

40. Ibid.

41. S. Leung, "Wendy's Sees Green in Salad Offerings—More Sophistication, Ethnic Flavors Appeal to Women, Crucial to Building Market Share," *The Wall Street Journal*, 24 April 2003, B2.

42. M. Stopa, "Wendy's New-Fashioned Growth: Buy Hardee's," *Crain's Detroit Business*, 21 October 1996.

43. K. Crowe and H. Shachter, CBC News, "The Paradox of the Canadian Diet," January 20, 2004, http://www.cbc.ca/news/background/food/paradox.html.

44. Subway, available online at http://www.subway.com, 29 July 2008; N. Torres, "Full Speed Ahead," Entrepreneur.com, http://www.entrepreneur.com/magazine/entrepreneur/2007/january/172060.html.

45. G. Marcial, "How Wendy's Stayed Out of the Fire," *BusinessWeek*, 9 December 2002, 138.

46. D. Ketchen, Jr., C. Snow, and V. Street, "Improving Firm Performance by Matching Strategic Decision-Making Processes to Competitive Dynamics," *Academy of Management Executive* 18 (2004): 29–43.

47. S. Matthews, "Financial: Salads Help McD Post First U.S. Sales Gain in 14 Months," *Chicago Sun-Times*, 14 May 2003, 69.

Chapter 7

1. "Swedes to Use Body Heat to Warm Offices," ABC News, available online at http://abcnews.go.com/International/wireStory?id=410819 E. Yerger, "Company in Sweden Uses Body Heat to Warm Office Building," Unusual Things, available online at http://www.popfi.com/2008/01/14/company-to-use-body-heat-to-warm-office-building-2 D. Chazan, "Office block warmed by body heat," BBC News, available online at http://news.bbc.co.uk/2/hi/science/nature/7233123.stm.

2. T. M. Amabile, R. Conti, H. Coon, J. Lazenby, and M. Herron, "Assessing the Work Environment for Creativity," *Academy of Management Journal* 39 (1996): 1154–1184.

3. Ibid.

4. A. H. Van de Ven and M. S. Poole, "Explaining Development and Change in Organizations," *Academy of Management Review* 20 (1995): 510–540.

5. Amabile, et al., "Assessing the Work Environment for Creativity."

6. "Thinking About Tomorrow," *The Wall Street Journal*, 28 January 2008, R1.

7. P. Anderson and M. L. Tushman, "Managing through Cycles of Technological Change," *Research/Technology Management*, May–June 1991, 26–31.

8. R. N. Foster, *Innovation: The Attacker's Advantage* (New York: Summitt, 1986).

9. J. Burke, *The Day the Universe Changed* (Boston: Little, Brown, 1985).

10. "Industry Snapshot," *Time*, 5 December 2005, 110; W. Symonds, "Kodak: Is This the Darkest Hour?" *BusinessWeek Online*, 8 August 2006, 3.

11. M. L. Tushman, P. C. Anderson, and C. O'Reilly, "Technology Cycles, Innovation Streams, and Ambidextrous Organizations: Organization Renewal through Innovation Streams and Strategic Change," in *Managing Strategic Innovation and Change*, ed. M. L. Tushman and P. Anderson (New York: Oxford Press, 1997), 3–23.

12. "Blu Capabilities Still Up in the Air," Home Media Magazine, available online at http://www.nxtbook.com/ nxtbooks/questex/hom041308/#/2.

13. W. Abernathy and J. Utterback, "Patterns of Industrial Innovation," *Technology Review* 2 (1978): 40–47.

14. N. E. Boudette, E. Taylor, and L. Etter, "GM Expands Links to Ethanol," *The Wall Street Journal*, 14 January 2008, A6.

15. M. Schilling, "Technological Lockout: An Integrative Model of the Economic and Strategic Factors Driving Technology Success and Failure," *Academy of Management Review* 23 (1998): 267–284; M. Schilling, "Technology Success and Failure in Winner-Take-All Markets: The Impact of Learning Orientation, Timing, and Network Externalities," *Academy of Management Journal* 45 (2002): 387–398.

16. S. McBride and Y. I. Kane, "As Toshiba Surrenders: What's Next for DVDs?," *The Wall Street Journal*, 18 February 2008, available online at http://online.wsj.com/article/ SB120321618700574049.html?mod= MKTW; Y. I. Kane, "Toshiba Regroups After Losing DVD War," *The Wall Street Journal*, 20 February 2008, available online at http://online.wsj .com/article/SB120342115442976687 .html?mod=googlenews.

17. Amabile, et al., "Assessing the Work Environment for Creativity."

18. Ibid.

19. M. Csikszentmihalyi, *Flow: The Psychology of Optimal Experience* (New York: Harper & Row, 1990).

20. V. Vara, "Pleasing Google's Tech-Savvy Staff," *The Wall Street Journal*, 18 March 2008, B6.

21. S. Kirsner, "Adobe Idol," *Fast Company*, May 2007, 95.

22. K. Capell, "Thinking Simple at Philips," *Business Week*, 11 December 2006, 50.

23. K. M. Eisenhardt, "Accelerating Adaptive Processes: Product Innovation in the Global Computer Industry," *Administrative Science Quarterly* 40 (1995): 84–110.

24. Ibid.

25. E. Masamitsu, "This is My Job: Parachute Tester," *Popular Mechanics* 185 (June 2008): 174.

26. C. Salter, "Ford's Escape Route," *Fast Company*, 1 October 2004, 106.

27. L. Kraar, "25 Who Help the U.S. Win: Innovators Everywhere Are Generating Ideas to Make America a Stronger Competitor. They Range from a Boss Who Demands the Impossible to a Mathematician with a Mop," *Fortune*, 22 March 1991.

28. M. W. Lawless and P. C. Anderson, "Generational Technological Change: Effects of Innovation and Local Rivalry on Performance," *Academy of Management Journal* 39 (1996): 1185–1217.

29. G. Graff, "Plastics Firm Unlocks Value of Early Supplier Involvement," *Purchasing* 136 (14 June 2007) 5.

30. K. Kelly, "Older Harry Rates a PG-13: The Awkward, Lovelorn Hero of 'Goblet of Fire' May Lose Kids, Gain Broader Audience," *The Wall Street Journal*, 16 November 2005, B1.

31. B. Baumohl and W. Cole "The Perils of Having Way More than Enough," *Time*, 13 January 1997, 58; S. Forest, "Incredible Universe: Lost in Space," *BusinessWeek*, 4 March 1996, http:// www.businessweek.com/1996/10/ b346580.htm.

32. P. Strebel, "Choosing the Right Change Path," *California Management Review* (winter 1994): 29–51.

33. W. Weitzel and E. Jonsson, "Reversing the Downward Spiral: Lessons from W.T. Grant and Sears Roebuck," *Academy of Management Executive* 5 (1991): 7–22.

34. Ibid.

35. K. Lewin, *Field Theory in Social Science: Selected Theoretical Papers* (New York: Harper & Brothers, 1951).

36. A. Deutschman, "Making Change: Why Is It So Darn Hard to Change Our Ways?" *Fast Company*, May 2005, 52–62.

37. K. Lewin, *Field Theory in Social Science*.

38. A. B. Fisher, "Making Change Stick," *Fortune*, 17 April 1995, 121.

39. J. P. Kotter and L. A. Schlesinger, "Choosing Strategies for Change," *Harvard Business Review* (March– April 1979): 106–114; Harvard Business School Press, *Managing Change to Reduce Resistance* (Cambridge: Harvard Business School Press, 2005).

40. D. Sewell, "P&G Open to Outside Ideas, but No Kitty Swiffers," Report on Business, January 4, 2010, http:// www.theglobeandmail.com/report-on- business/pg-open-to-outside-ideas- but-no-kitt...

41. J. Neff, "P&G (Canada) Will Put 'up to' 20% of Budget in Digital in the Great North," http://customerlistening .typepad.com/customer_listening/2008/ 05/pg-canada-will.html.

42. PG.com, "Management Perspectives," http://www.pg.com/en_CA/company/ who_we_are/letter_penner.shtml.

43. B. Orwall, "Disney Decides It Must Draw Artists into Computer Age," *Wall Street Journal*, 23 October 2003, A1.

44. J. P. Kotter, "Leading Change: Why Transformation Efforts Fail," *Harvard Business Review* 73, no. 2 (March– April 1995): 59.

45. Harvard Business School Press, *The Results-Driven Manager: Getting People on Board* (Cambridge: Havard Business School Press, 2005).

46. M. Ihlwan, L. Armstrong, and M. Eidam, "Hyundai: Kissing Clunkers Goodbye," *Business Week*, 17 May 2004, 46.

47. Ibid.

48. R. N. Ashkenas and T. D. Jick, "From Dialogue to Action in GE WorkOut: Developmental Learning in a Change Process," in *Research in Organizational Change and Development*, vol. 6, ed. W. A. Pasmore and R. W. Woodman (Greenwich, CT: JAI Press, 1992), 267–287.

49. T. Stewart, "GE Keeps Those Ideas Coming," *Fortune*, 12 August 1991, 40.

50. W. J. Rothwell, R. Sullivan, and G. M. McLean, *Practicing Organizational Development: A Guide for Consultants* (San Diego, CA: Pfeiffer & Co., 1995).

51. Ibid.

Chapter 8

1. "World Investment Report, 2006," United Nations Conference on Trade & Development, http:// www.unctad.org/en/docs/ wir2006annexes_en.pdf

2. G. Samor, "Steelmaker Girds for Growth—Gerdau of Brazil Looks to Bulk Up Further in United States Market," *The Wall Street Journal*, 5 April 2005, B2.

3. FEMSA, "FEMSA Acquires Controlling Stake in Brazilian Brewer Kaiser," 16 Jan 2006, http://www.femsa.com/en/ press/news/news_20060310.htm.

4. J. Miller, "China's Low Fruit Prices Highlight EU's Vulnerabilities over Trade," *The Wall Street Journal*, 26 December 2006, A4.

5. GreenFacts Table 5: Applied Tariffs on Ethanol in Selected Countries, http:// www.greenfacts.org/en/biofuels/figtable- boxes/tarifs-ethanol.htm, Canada News Centre, "Canada Poised to Become 'Tariff-Free Zone' for Manufacturers Thanks to Budget 2010," March 9, 2010, http://news.gc.ca/web/article-eng .do?m=/index&nid=517449.

6. "Determination of Total Amounts and Quota Period for Tariff-Rate Quotas for Raw Cane Sugar and Certain Imported Sugars, Syrups, and Molasses," *Federal Register*, 15 April 2002, 18162.

7. J. Sparshott, "U.S. Sugar Growers Fear Losses from Free-Trade Push," *The Washington Times*, 24 March 2005, C07.

8. "Understanding the WTO," *World Trade Organization*, http://www.wto

.org/english/thewto_e/whatis_e/tif_e/
agrm9_e.htm [accessed 5 August 2008].

9. D. Poulin and K. Boame, "Mad Cow Disease and Beef Trade," November 12, 2009, http://www.statcan.gc.ca/pub/11-621-m/11-621-m2003005-eng.htm; S. Kosinski, "Canada Imports into the US," June 21, 2010, http://www1.foragebeef.ca/$foragebeef/frgebeef.nsf/all/news2892.

10. P. Lemieux, "Bombardier's Gain Is the Taxpayer's Loss—FP Comment," July 22, 2008, network.nationalpost.com/.../bombardier-s-gain-is-the-taxpayer-s-loss.aspx; "Americans Frown, Embraer Scraps with Bombardier and We Pick Up the Tab," August 14, 2008, http://www.canada.com/montrealgazette/news/business/story.html?id; CBC News, 2 April 2009. "A Transportation Giant Evolves," April 2, 2009, http://www.cbc.ca/canada/montreal/story/2009/04/02/f-bombardier-indepth-0402.html.

11. "Rocky Receives Customs Clarification on Imported Boots," *FN*, 31 March 2003.

12. H. Blodget, "How to Solve China's Piracy Problem: A Dozen Ideas. Maybe One Will Work," *Slate,* 12 April 2005, http://slate.msn.com/id/2116629/.

13. "The History of the European Union," *Europa—The European Union Online,* http://europa.eu.int/abc/history/index_en.htm; http://europa.eu/abc/european_countries/index_en.htm.

14. Ibid.

15. D. Luhnow, "Crossover Success: How NAFTA Helped Wal-Mart Reshape the Mexican Market" *The Wall Street Journal,* 31 August 2001, A1.

16. L.H. Teslik, "NAFTA's Economic Impact," Council on Foreign Relations, http://www.cfr.org/publication/15790/naftas_economic_impact.html#4.

17. "US Trade with the CAFTA-DR Countries," Office of the United States Trade Representative (July 2007), http://www.ustr.gov/assets/Trade_Agreements/Bilateral/CAFTA/Briefing_Book/asset_upload_file601_13191.pdf.

18. UNASUR, Union of South American Nations, http://www.comunidadandina.org/ingles/sudamerican.htm.

19. "Selected Basic ASEAN Indicators, 2005," *Association of Southeast Nations,* http://www.aseansec.org/stat/Table1.pdf; "Top Ten ASEAN Trade Partner Countries/Regions, 2005," *Association of Southeast Nations,* http://www.aseansec.org/Stat/Table20.pdf. "ASEAN Free Trade Area (AFTA)," *Association of Southeast Nations,* http://www.aseansec.org/12021.htm.

20. "Member Economies," Asia Pacific Economic Cooperation, http://www.apec.org/apec/member_economies/key_websites.html. "Frequently Asked Questions (FAQs)" *Asia-Pacific Economic Cooperation,* http://www.apec.org/apec/tools/faqs.html.

21. "The Big Mac Index," *The Economist,* http://www.economist.com/markets/indicators/displaystory.cfm?story_id=8649005.

22. "Freer Trade Cuts the Cost of Living," *World Trade Organization,* http://www.wto.org/english/thewto_e/whatis_e/10ben_e/10b04_e.htm.

23. MTV Brasil, http://mtv.terra.com.br/mochilao; MTV China, http://mtvchina.com; MTV India, http://www.mtvindia.com/sillypoint/sourav.php.

24. A. Sundaram and J. S. Black, "The Environment and Internal-Organization of Multinational Enterprises," *Academy of Management Review* 17 (1992): 729–757.

25. H. S. James, Jr., and M. Weidenbaum, *When Businesses Cross International Borders: Strategic Alliances & Their Alternatives* (Westport, CT: Praeger Publishers, 1993).

26. J. T. Areddy, "China's Export Machine Threatened by Rising Costs," *The Wall Street Journal,* 30 June 2008, A1.

27. J. D. Stoll, N. Shirouzu, and N. E. Boudette, "Detroit Sets Bold Goal: Exporting U.S. Cars," *The Wall Street Journal,* 8 April 2008, A1.

28. "Company Profile," Fuji Xerox, http://www.fujixerox.co.jp/eng/company/profile.html.

29. "Arrow, Shell Seal a Venture," *The Wall Street Journal,* 15 September 2008, http://online.wsj.com/article/SB122144583046434931.html.

30. "Joint Ventures," Encyclopedia of Business, 2nd ed., http://www.referenceforbusiness.com/encyclopedia/Int-Jun/Joint-Ventures.html#WHY_JOINT_VENTURES_FAIL.

31. M. W. Hordes, J. A. Clancy, and J. Baddaley, "A Primer for Global Start-Ups." *Academy of Management Executive* (May 1995): 7–11.

32. D. Pavlos, J. Johnson, J. Slow, and S. Young, "Micromultinationals: New Types of Firms for the Global Competitive Landscape," *European Management Journal* 21, no. 2 (April 2003): 164; B. M. Oviatt and P. P. McDougall, "Toward a Theory of International New Ventures," *Journal of International Business Studies,*(Spring 1994): 45; S. Zahra, "A Theory of International New Ventures: A Decade of Research," *Journal of International Business Studies* (January 2005): 20–28.

33. M. Copeland, "The Mighty Micro-Multinational," *Business 2.0,* 1 July 2006, 106.

34. *PriceCheckTokyo,* 10 February 2007, http://www.pricechecktokyo.com [accessed 6 August 2008].

35. D. Lynch, "Developing Nations Poised to Challenge USA as King of the Hill," *USA Today,* 8 February 2007, B.1; N. Srinivas, "Of Carats & Calories," *The Economic Times,* 29 December 2006.

36. F. Vogelstein, "How Intel Got Inside," *Fortune,* 4 October 2004, 127.

37. P. Dvorak, "Why Multiple Headquarters Multiply," *The Wall Street Journal,* 19 November 2007, B1; J. L. Yang, "Making Mergers Work," *Fortune,* 26 November 2007, 42.

38. "Customer Care in the Netherlands," The Netherlands Foreign Investment Agency, http://www.nfia.com/solutions.php?pageid=11 [accessed 13 February 2007] (content no longer available online).

39. J. Oetzel, R. Bettis, and M. Zenner, "How Risky Are They?" *Journal of World Business* 36, no. 2 (summer 2001): 128–145.

40. K. D. Miller, "A Framework for Integrated Risk Management in International Business," *Journal of International Business Studies* (2nd Quarter 1992): 311.

41. A. Osborn and D. Gauthier-Villars, "Twisty Road: Renault Deal in Russia Shows Kremlin Tactics," *The Wall Street Journal,* 21 March 2008, A1.

42. "Chapter 1: Political Outlook," *UAE Business Forecast Report* (2007 1st Quarter): 5–10.

43. I. Brat, "Going Global by Going Green," *The Wall Street Journal,* 26 February 2008, B1.

44. G. Hofstede, "The Cultural Relativity of the Quality of Life Concept," *Academy of Management Review* 9 (1984): 389–398; G. Hofstede, "The Cultural Relativity of Organizational Practices and Theories," *Journal of International Business Studies* (Fall 1983): 75–89; G. Hofstede, "The Interaction between National and Organizational Value Systems," *Journal of Management Studies* (July 1985) 347–357; M. Hoppe, "An Interview with Geert Hofstede," *Academy of Management Executive* (February 2004) 75–79; G.K. Stephens and C.R. Greer, "Doing Business in Mexico: Understanding Cultural Differences," *Organizational Dynamics*, Special Report, 1998.

45. R. Hodgetts, "A Conversation with Geert Hofstede," *Organizational Dynamics* (spring 1993): 53–61.

46. T. Lenartowicz and K. Roth, "Does Subculture within a Country Matter? A Cross-Cultural Study of Motivational Domains and Business Performance in Brazil," *Journal of International Business Studies* 32 (2001): 305–325.

47. M. Janssens, J. M. Brett, and F. J. Smith, "Confirmatory Cross-Cultural Research: Testing the Viability of a Corporation-Wide Safety Policy," *Academy of Management Journal* 38 (1995): 364–382.

48. J. S. Black, M. Mendenhall, and G. Oddou, "Toward a Comprehensive Model of International Adjustment: An Integration of Multiple Theoretical Perspectives," *Academy of Management*

Review 16 (1991): 291–317; R. L. Tung, "American Expatriates Abroad: From Neophytes to Cosmopolitans," *Columbia Journal of World Business,* 22 June 1998, 125; A. Harzing, "The Persistent Myth of High Expatriate Failure Rates," *International Journal of Human Resource Management* 6 (1995): 457–475; A. Harzing, "Are Our Referencing Errors Undermining Our Scholarship and Credibility? The Case of Expatriate Failure Rates," *Journal of Organizational Behavior* 23 (2002): 127–148; N. Forster, "The Persistent Myth of High Expatriate Failure Rates: A Reappraisal," *International Journal of Human Resource Management* 8 (1997): 414–433; A. McMullen, "Canada Tops Global Expats Survey of Best Countries," *National Post,* December 2, 2009, HYPERLINK "http://www.nationalpost.com/m/story.html?id=2292837&s=Today's%20Newspaper"http://www.nationalpost.com/m/story.html?id=2292837&s=Today's%20Newspaper.

49. J. Black, "The Right Way to Manage Expats," *Harvard Business Review* 77 (March–April 1999): 52; C. Joinson, "No Returns," *HR Magazine,* 1 November 2002, 70.

50. C. Joinson, "No Returns," *HR Magazine,* November 2002, 70.

51. J. S. Black and M. Mendenhall, "Cross-Cultural Training Effectiveness: A Review and Theoretical Framework for Future Research," *Academy of Management Review* 15 (1990): 113–136.

52. K. Essick, "Executive Education: Transferees Prep for Life, Work in Far-Flung Lands," *The Wall Street Journal,* 12 November 2004, A6.

53. P. W. Tam, "Culture Course— 'Awareness Training' Helps U.S. Workers Better Know Their Counterparts in India," *The Wall Street Journal,* 25 May 2004, B1.

54. W. Arthur, Jr., and W. Bennett, Jr., "The International Assignee: The Relative Importance of Factors Perceived to Contribute to Success," *Personnel Psychology* 48 (1995): 99–114; B. Cheng, "Home Truths about Foreign Postings; To Make an Overseas Assignment Work, Employers Need More Than an Eager Exec with a Suitcase. They Must Also Motivate the Staffer's Spouse," *BusinessWeek Online,* http://www.businessweek.com/careers/content/jul2002/ca20020715_9110.htm [accessed 16 July 2002].

55. M. Netz, "It's Not Judging—It's Assessing: The Truth about Candidate Assessments," *NRRE Magazine,* March 2004, http://rismedia.com/wp/2004-03-03/its-not-judging-its-assessing.

56. D. Eschbach, G. Parker, and P. Stoeberl, "American Repatriate Employees' Retrospective Assessments of the Effects of Cross-Cultural Training on Their Adaptation to International Assignments," *International Journal of Human Resource Management* 12 (2001): 270–287; "Culture Training: How to Prepare Your Expatriate Employees for Cross-Cultural Work Environments," *Managing Training & Development,* 1 February 2005.

57. J. Areddy, "Deep Inside China, American Family Struggles to Cope," *The Wall Street Journal,* 2 August 2005, A1.

Chapter 9

1. "Sony Corp. Info: Affiliated Companies," http://www.sony.net/SonyInfo/CorporateInfo/Data/organization.html.

2. M. Hammer and J. Champy, *Reengineering the Corporation: A Manifesto for Business Revolution* (New York: Harper & Row, 1993).

3. "P&G Media Kit 2009–2010," http://www.pg.com/en_US/downloads/media/2009_Media_Kit.pdf.

4. J. G. March and H. A. Simon, *Organizations* (New York: John Wiley & Sons, 1958).

5. "Company Overview," We are Always Moving: *United Technologies Corporation 2005 Annual Report,* available online at http://www.utc.com/annual_reports/2005/html [accessed 8 August 2008].

6. United Technologies Corporation, "2009 Annual Report," http://www.utc.com/About+UTC/Company+Reports/2009+Annual+Report+English.

7. Coca-Cola, "The Coca-Cola Company: Product Descriptions," http://www.virtualvender.coca-cola.com/ft/index.jsp.

8. P&G, "P&G Corporate Info Structure: Four Pillars," http://www.pg.com/jobs/corporate_structure/four_pillars.shtml.

9. L. R. Burns, "Adoption and Abandonment of Matrix Management Programs: Effects of Organizational Characteristics and Interorganizational Networks," *Academy of Management Journal* 36 (1993): 106–138.

10. H. Fayol, *General and Industrial Management,* trans. C. Storrs (London: Pitman Publishing, 1949).

11. M. Weber, *The Theory of Social and Economic Organization,* trans. and ed. A. M. Henderson & T. Parsons (New York: Free Press, 1947).

12. Fayol, *General and Industrial Management.*

13. K. Moore, "Murray Martin Talks to Karl Moore," *The Globe and Mail,* April 6, 2010, http://www.theglobeandmail.com/report-on-business/murray-martin-talks-to-karl-moore/article1525148.

14. A. Lopez-Pacheco, "Letting Go the Day-to-Day: It Starts with Building the Right Team," *Financial Post,* May 16, 2010, http://www.financialpost.com/Letting+starts+with+building+right+team/3038099/story.html.

15. M. Stern, "10 Worst Leadership Habits," *Canadian Business,* May 1, 2008, http://www.canadianbusiness.com/managing/career/article.jsp?content=20080312_198703_198703.

16. B. Cline, "Employees a Part of the Team," *Financial Post,* February 15, 2010, http://www.financialpost.com/Employees+part+team/2569169/story.html.

17. S. Bowness, "Healthy Leadership: Trillium Motivates from the Ground Up," *Canadian Business Online,* January 8, 2007, http://www.canadianbusiness.com/innovation/article.jsp?content=20070108_125019_6168.

18. E. E. Lawler, S. A. Mohrman, and G. E. Ledford, *Creating High Performance Organizations: Practices and Results of Employee Involvement and Quality Management in Fortune 1000 Companies* (San Francisco: Jossey-Bass, 1995).

19. B. Harding, "Globe and Mail Update," *Report on Business, The Globe and Mail,* May 23, 2005, http://www.theglobeandmail.com/report-on-business/article884122.ece.

20. S. Curry, "Retention Getters," *Incentive,* 1 April 2005.

21. R. W. Griffin, *Task Design* (Glenview, IL: Scott, Foresman, 1982).

22. F. Herzberg, *Work and the Nature of Man* (Cleveland, OH: World Press, 1966).

23. J. R. Hackman and G. R. Oldham, *Work Redesign* (Reading, MA: Addison-Wesley, 1980).

24. T. Burns and G. M. Stalker, *The Management of Innovation* (London: Tavistock, 1961).

25. Hammer and Champy, *Reengineering the Corporation.*

26. Ibid.

27. J. D. Thompson, *Organizations in Action* (New York: McGraw-Hill, 1967).

28. J. B. White, "'Next Big Thing': Re-Engineering Gurus Take Steps to Remodel Their Stalling Vehicles," *The Wall Street Journal Interactive Edition,* 26 November 1996.

29. Ibid.

30. G. M. Spreitzer, "Individual Empowerment in the Workplace: Dimensions, Measurement, and Validation," *Academy of Management Journal* 38 (1995): 1442–1465.

31. M. Schrage, "I Know What You Mean. And I Can't Do Anything about It," *Fortune,* 2 April 2001, 186.

32. K. W. Thomas and B. A. Velthouse, "Cognitive Elements of Empowerment," *Academy of Management Review* 15 (1990): 666–681.

33. G. G. Dess, A. M. A. Rasheed, K. J. McLaughlin, and R. L. Priem, "The New Corporate Architecture," *Academy of Management Executive* 9 (1995): 7–18.

34. G. McWilliams, "Apple Uses Software, Outsourcing to Gain Share As Sony Struggles to Grow," *The Wall Street Journal,* 10 March 2005, A1.

35. C. C. Snow, R. E. Miles, and H. J. Coleman, Jr., "Managing 21st Century Network Organizations," *Organizational Dynamics,* (winter 1992), 5–20.

Chapter 10

1. B. Dumaine, "The Trouble with Teams," *Fortune,* 5 September 1994, 86–92; M. Parker, "Rewarding Creativity, Effort, and Teamwork," Canadian Business Online, August 17, 2007, http://www.canadianbusiness.com/columnists/marty_parker/article.jsp?content=20070731_111735_5876.

2. J. Hoerr, "The Payoff from Teamwork—The Gains in Quality Are Substantial—So Why Isn't It Spreading Faster?" *BusinessWeek,* 10 July 1989, 56.

3. J. R. Katzenback and D. K. Smith, *The Wisdom of Teams* (Boston: Harvard Business School Press, 1993).

4. S. E. Gross, *Compensation for Teams* (New York: American Management Association, 1995); B. L. Kirkman and B. Rosen, "Beyond Self-Management: Antecedents and Consequences of Team Empowerment," *Academy of Management Journal* 42 (1999): 58–74; G. Stalk and T. M. Hout, *Competing against Time: How Time-Based Competition Is Reshaping Global Markets* (New York: Free Press, 1990); S. C. Wheelwright and K. B. Clark, *Revolutionizing New Product Development* (New York: Free Press, 1992).

5. J. Marquez, "Hewitt-BP Split May Signal End of 'Lift and Shift' Deals," *Workforce Management,* 29 December 2006, 3.

6. R. D. Banker, J. M. Field, R. G. Schroeder, and K. K. Sinha, "Impact of Work Teams on Manufacturing Performance: A Longitudinal Field Study," *Academy of Management Journal* 39 (1996): 867–890.

7. C. Fishman, "The Anarchist's Cookbook: John Mackey's Approach to Management Is Equal Parts Star Trek and 1970s Flashback," *Fast Company,* 1 July 2004, 70.

8. J. L. Cordery, W. S. Mueller, and L. M. Smith, "Attitudinal and Behavioral Effects of Autonomous Group Working: A Longitudinal Field Study," *Academy of Management Journal* 34 (1991): 464–476; T. D. Wall, N. J. Kemp, P. R. Jackson, and C. W. Clegg, "Outcomes of Autonomous Workgroups: A Long-Term Field Experiment," *Academy of Management Journal* 29 (1986): 280–304.

9. "Declaration of Interdependence," Whole Foods Market, available online at http://www.wholefoodsmarket.com/company/declaration.html [accessed 12 August 2008].

10. Ibid.

11. A. Erez, J. Lepine, and H. Elms, "Effects of Rotated Leadership and Peer Evaluation on the Functioning and Effectiveness of Self-Managed Teams: A Quasi-Experiment," *Personnel Psychology 55,* issue 4 (2002): 929.

12. R. Liden, S. Wayne, R. Jaworski, and N. Bennett, "Social Loafing: A Field Investigation," *Journal of Management* 30 (2004): 285–304.

13. J. George, "Extrinsic and Intrinsic Origins of Perceived Social Loafing in Organizations," *Academy of Management Journal* 35 (1992): 191–202.

14. T. T. Baldwin, M. D. Bedell, and J. L. Johnson, "The Social Fabric of a Team-Based M.B.A. Program: Network Effects on Student Satisfaction and Performance," *Academy of Management Journal* 40 (1997): 1369–1397.

15. C. Joinson, "Teams at Work," *HRMagazine,* 1 May 1999, 30.

16. R. Wageman, "Critical Success Factors for Creating Superb Self-Managing Teams," *Organizational Dynamics* 26, no. 1 (1997): 49–61.

17. D. A. Harrison, S. Mohammed, J. E. McGrath, A. T. Florey and S. W. Vanderstoep, "Time Matters in Team Performance: Effects of Member Familiarity, Entrainment, and Task Discontinuity on Speed and Quality," *Personnel Psychology* 56, no. 3 (August 2003): 633–669.

18. R. T. King, Jr., "Jeans Therapy: Levi's Factory Workers Are Assigned to Teams, and Morale Takes a Hit—Infighting Rises, Productivity Falls as Employees Miss the Piecework System," *The Wall Street Journal,* 20 May 1998, A1.

19. Kirkman and Rosen, "Beyond Self-Management."

20. S. Easton and G. Porter, "Selecting the Right Team Structure to Work in Your Organization," in *Handbook of Best Practices for Teams,* vol. 1, ed. G. M. Parker (Amherst, MA: Irwin, 1996).

21. R. J. Recardo, D. Wade, C. A. Mention, and J. Jolly, *Teams* (Houston: Gulf Publishing Co., 1996).

22. D. R. Denison, S. L. Hart, and J. A. Kahn, "From Chimneys to Cross-Functional Teams: Developing and Validating a Diagnostic Model," *Academy of Management Journal* 39, no. 4 (1996): 1005–1023.

23. J. Morgan, "Cessna Aims to Drive SCM to Its Very Core: Here Are 21 Steps and Tools It's Using to Make This Happen," *Purchasing,* 6 June 2002, 31.

24. A. M. Townsend, S. M. DeMarie, and A. R. Hendrickson, "Virtual Teams: Technology and the Workplace of the Future," *Academy of Management Executive* 13, no. 3 (1998): 17–29.

25. J. Hyatt, "MySQL: Workers in 25 countries with no HQ," *Fortune,* 1 June 2006, http://money.cnn.com/2006/05/31/magazines/fortune/mysql_greatteams_fortune/index.htm.

26. A. M. Townsend, S. M. DeMarie, and A. R. Hendrickson, "Are You Ready for Virtual Teams?" *HR Magazine* 41, no. 9 (1996): 122–126.

27. R. S. Wellins, W. C. Byham, and G. R. Dixon, *Inside Teams* (San Francisco: Jossey-Bass, 1994).

28. Townsend, DeMarie, and Hendrickson, "Virtual Teams."

29. W. F. Cascio, "Managing a Virtual Workplace," *Academy of Management Executive* 14 (2000): 81–90.

30. R. Katz, "The Effects of Group Longevity on Project Communication and Performance," *Administrative Science Quarterly* 27 (1982): 245–282.

31. D. Mankin, S. G. Cohen, and T. K. Bikson, *Teams and Technology: Fulfilling the Promise of the New Organization* (Boston: Harvard Business School Press, 1996).

32. A. P. Ammeter and J. M. Dukerich, "Leadership, Team Building, and Team Member Characteristics in High Performance Project Teams," *Engineering Management* 14, no. 4 (2002): 3–11.

33. K. Lovelace, D. Shapiro, and L. Weingart, "Maximizing Cross-Functional New Product Teams' Innovativeness and Constraint Adherence: A Conflict Communications Perspective," *Academy of Management Journal* 44 (2001): 779–793.

34. L. Holpp and H. P. Phillips, "When Is a Team Its Own Worst Enemy?" *Training,* 1 September 1995, 71.

35. S. Asche, "Opinions and Social Pressure," *Scientific American* 193 (1995): 31–35.

36. G. Smith, "How Nucor Steel Rewards Performance and Productivity," *Business Know How,* http://www.businessknowhow.com/manage/nucor.htm; "Nucor Agrees to Buy Harris Steeel of Canada for $1.07 Billion," New York Times, January 2, 2010, http://www.nytimes.com/2007/01/03/business/03steel.html.

37. S. G. Cohen, G. E. Ledford, and G. M. Spreitzer, "A Predictive Model of Self-Managing Work Team Effectiveness," *Human Relations* 49, no. 5 (1996): 643–676.

38. K. Bettenhausen and J. K. Murnighan, "The Emergence of Norms in Competitive Decision-Making Groups," *Administrative Science Quarterly* 30 (1985): 350–372.

39. M. E. Shaw, *Group Dynamics* (New York: McGraw Hill, 1981).

40. S. E. Jackson, "The Consequences of Diversity in Multidisciplinary Work Teams," in *Handbook of Work Group Psychology,* ed. M. A. West (Chichester, UK: Wiley, 1996).

41. A. M. Isen and R. A. Baron, "Positive Affect as a Factor in Organizational Behavior," in *Research in Organizational Behavior* 13, ed. L. L. Cummings and B. M. Staw (Greenwich, CT: JAI Press, 1991), 1–53.

42. C. R. Evans and K. L. Dion, "Group Cohesion and Performance: A Meta Analysis," *Small Group Research* 22, no. 2 (1991): 175–186.

43. R. Stankiewicsz, "The Effectiveness of Research Groups in Six Countries," in *Scientific Productivity*, ed. F. M. Andrews (Cambridge: Cambridge University Press, 1979), 191–221.

44. F. Rees, *Teamwork from Start to Finish* (San Francisco: Jossey-Bass, 1997).

45. S. M. Gully, D. S. Devine, and D. J. Whitney, "A Meta-Analysis of Cohesion and Performance: Effects of Level of Analysis and Task Interdependence," *Small Group Research* 26, no. 4 (1995): 497–520.

46. E. Matson, "Four Rules for Fast Teams," *Fast Company*, August 1996, 87.

47. F. Tschan and M. V. Cranach, "Group Task Structure, Processes and Outcomes," in *Handbook of Work Group Psychology*, ed. M. A. West (Chichester, UK: Wiley, 1996).

48. D. E. Yeatts and C. Hyten, *High Performance Self Managed Teams* (Thousand Oaks, CA: Sage Publications, 1998); H. M. Guttman and R. S. Hawkes, "New Rules for Strategic Development," *The Journal of Business Strategy* 25, no. 1 (2004): 34–39.

49. Yeatts and Hyten, *High Performance Self Managed Teams*; Guttman and Hawkes, "New Rules"; J. Colquitt, R. Noe, and C. Jackson, "Justice in Teams: Antecedents and Consequences of Procedural Justice Climate," *Personnel Psychology*, 1 April 2002, 83.

50. D. S. Kezsbom, "Re-Opening Pandora's Box: Sources of Project Team Conflict in the '90s," *Industrial Engineering* 24, no. 5 (1992): 54–59.

51. A. C. Amason, W. A. Hochwarter, and K. R. Thompson, "Conflict: An Important Dimension in Successful Management Teams," *Organizational Dynamics* 24 (1995): 20.

52. A. C. Amason, "Distinguishing the Effects of Functional and Dysfunctional Conflict on Strategic Decision Making: Resolving a Paradox for Top Management Teams," *Academy of Management Journal* 39, no. 1 (1996): 123–148.

53. K. M. Eisenhardt, J. L. Kahwajy, and L. J. Bourgeois III, "How Management Teams Can Have a Good Fight," *Harvard Business Review* 75, no. 4 (July–August 1997): 77–85.

54. Ibid.

55. C. Nemeth and P. Owens, "Making Work Groups More Effective: The Value of Minority Dissent," in *Handbook of Work Group Psychology*, ed. M. A. West (Chichester, UK: Wiley, 1996).

56. J. M. Levin and R. L. Moreland, "Progress in Small Group Research," *Annual Review of Psychology* 9 (1990): 72–78; S. E. Jackson, "Team Composition in Organizational Settings: Issues in Managing a Diverse Work Force," in *Group Processes and Productivity*, ed. S. Worchel, W. Wood, and J. Simpson (Beverly Hills, CA: Sage, 1992).

57. Eisenhardt, Kahwajy, and Bourgeois, "How Management Teams Can Have a Good Fight."

58. B. W. Tuckman, "Development Sequence in Small Groups," *Psychological Bulletin* 63, no. 6 (1965): 384–399.

59. Gross, *Compensation for Teams.*

60. J. F. McGrew, J. G. Bilotta, and J. M. Deeney, "Software Team Formation and Decay: Extending the Standard Model for Small Groups," *Small Group Research* 30, no. 2 (1999): 209–234.

61. Ibid.

62. J. R. Hackman, "The Psychology of Self-Management in Organizations," in *Psychology and Work: Productivity, Change, and Employment*, ed. M. S. Pallak and R. Perloff (Washington, DC: American Psychological Association, 1986), 85–136.

63. A. O'Leary-Kelly, J. J. Martocchio, and D. D. Frink, "A Review of the Influence of Group Goals on Group Performance," *Academy of Management Journal* 37, no. 5 (1994): 1285–1301.

64. Smith, "How Nucor Steel Rewards Performance and Productivity."

65. A. Zander, "The Origins and Consequences of Group Goals," in *Retrospections on Social Psychology*, ed. L. Festinger (New York: Oxford University Press, 1980), 205–235.

66. M. Erez and A. Somech, "Is Group Productivity Loss the Rule or the Exception? Effects of Culture and Group-Based Motivation," *Academy of Management Journal* 39, no. 6 (1996): 1513–1537.

67. S. Sherman, "Stretch Goals: The Dark Side of Asking for Miracles," *Fortune*, 13 November 1995, 231.

68. S. Kerr and S. Landauer, "Using Stretch Goals to Promote Organizational Effectiveness and Personal Growth: General Electric and Goldman Sachs," *Academy of Management Executive* (November 2004): 134–138.

69. K. R. Thompson, W. A. Hochwarter, and N. J. Mathys, "Stretch Targets: What Makes Them Effective?" *Academy of Management Executive* 11, no. 3 (1997): 48–60.

70. M. Parker, "Rewarding Creativity, Effort, and Teamwork," Canadian Business Online, August 17, 2007, URL won't open> http://www.canadianbusiness.com/colunmists/mary-parker/article.jsp?content=2007073...

71. Dumaine, "The Trouble with Teams."

72. G. A. Neuman, S. H. Wagner, and N. D. Christiansen, "The Relationship between Work-Team Personality Composition and the Job Performance of Teams," *Group & Organization Management* 24, no. 1 (1999): 28–45.

73. M. A. Campion, G. J. Medsker, and A. C. Higgs, "Relations between Work Group Characteristics and Effectiveness: Implications for Designing Effective Work Groups," *Personnel Psychology* 46, no. 4 (1993): 823–850.

74. B. L. Kirkman and D. L. Shapiro, "The Impact of Cultural Values on Employee Resistance to Teams: Toward a Model of Globalized Self-Managing Work Team Effectiveness," *Academy of Management Review* 22, no. 3 (1997): 730–757.

75. C. Fishman, "Engines of Democracy:" *Fast Company*, 1 October 1999, 174.

76. J. Bunderson and K. Sutcliffe, "Comparing Alternative Conceptualizations of Functional Diversity in Management Teams: Process and Performance Effects," *Academy of Management Journal* 45 (2002): 875–893.

77. J. Barbian, "Getting to Know You," *Training*, June 2001: 60–63.

78. J. Hackman, "New Rules for Team Building—The Times Are Changing—And So Are the Guidelines for Maximizing Team Performance," *Optimize*, 1 July 2002, 50.

79. Joinson, "Teams at Work."

80. K. Mollica, "Stay Above the Fray: Protect Your Time—and Your Sanity—by Coaching Employees to Deal with Interpersonal Conflicts on Their Own," *HR Magazine*, April 2005, 111.

81. S. Caudron, "Tie Individual Pay to Team Success," *Personnel Journal* 73, no. 10 (October 1994): 40.

82. Ibid.

83. Gross, *Compensation for Teams* 85.

84. G. Ledford, "Three Case Studies on Skill-Based Pay: An Overview," *Compensation & Benefits Review* 23, no. 2 (1991): 11–24.

85. J. R. Schuster and P. K. Zingheim, *The New Pay: Linking Employee and Organizational Performance* (New York: Lexington Books, 1992).

86. S. G. Cohen and D. E. Bailey, "What Makes Teams Work: Group Effectiveness Research from the Shop Floor to the Executive Suite," *Journal of Management* 23, no. 3 (1997): 239–290.

87. R. Allen and R. Kilmann, "Aligning Reward Practices in Support of Total Quality Management," *Business Horizons* 44 (May 2001): 77–85.

Chapter 11

1. Canada, Department of Justice, Canada Labour Code, June 4, 2010, http://laws.justice.gc.ca/en.
2. Government of Canada, Canadian Charter of Rights and Freedoms, 2010, http://laws.justice.gc.ca/en/charter.
3. "Female Firefighters All Off the Job," *Vancouver Province*, March 22, 2006, http://www.canada.com/theprovince/news/story.html?id=7817f631-f71c-4f55-8630-8589aebd718b; "Female Firefighters Walk Off Job in B.C. City, Alleging Harassment," CBC News, March 21, 2006, http://www.cbc.ca/canada/story/2006/03/21/firefighters-richmond060321.html#ixzz0sZm4R3eU; K. Bryce, "Nanaimo Fire Department Hires Its First Professional Female Firefighter," *Nanaimo Daily News*, May 27, 2010, http://www2.canada.com/nanaimodailynews/news/story.html?id=e43e59e9-2a9d-448f-8775-84d6d2c6734c.
4. Women's Legal Education and Action Fund, "Supreme Court Decides Fitness Test Discriminates Against B.C. Woman Firefighter," September 9, 1999, http://www.leaf.ca/media/releases/BCGSEU_Media_Release_September_9_1999.pdf.
5. Government of Canada, Canadian Human Rights Commission. http://www.chrc-ccdp.ca/links/default-en.asp.
6. Province of British Columbia, "WorkSafe BC: Regulation & Related Materials," 2010, http://www2.worksafebc.com/publications/OHSRegulation/Home.asp.
7. Canadian Bar Association, BC Branch, "Sexual Harassment," 2010, http://www.cba.org/bc/public_media/emplyment/271.aspx.
8. B. Etherington, ed., "Systematic Inequality and Workplace Culture: Challenging the Institutionalization of Sexual Harassment," *Canadian Labour and Employment Law Journal* 3 (1993), http://personnel.mcgill.ca/files/colleen.sheppard/Systemic_Inequality_Workplace.pdf; *Alpaerts v Obront* [1993] OJ #732 (QL) (OCJGD), http://www.isthatlegal.ca/index.php?name=jurisdiction2.small_claims_court_law_ontario.
9. B. Mims, "Suit Claims Costco Forced Woman to Quit After She Complained of Harassment," *Salt Lake Tribune*, 24 February 2005, C14.
10. Peirce, Smolinski, and Rosen, "Why Sexual Harassment Complaints Fall on Deaf Ears." H. Burnett-Nichols, "Sexual Harassment Best Practices: University Community as Partners," March 8, 2010, http://www.universityaffairs.ca/sexual-harassment-best-practices.aspx; "BCIT Harassment and Discrimination Policies," 2010, http://www.bcit.ca/harassment; "SFU Human Rights Policy," 2010, http://www.sfu.ca/humanrights/GuideforStudents.htm; UBC Equity Office, "UBC 2010," http://equity.ubc.ca/who/message-from-the-associate-vice-president-equity.
11. Province of Ontario, "The New Mandate of the Ontario Human Rights Commission," June 2010, http://www.ohrc.on.ca/en/commission/mission; http://www.isthatlegal.ca/index.php?name=jurisdiction2.small_claims_court_law_ontario; Simon Fraser University, "Protocol for Investigation: Human Rights Policy (GP18)," April 30, 2008, http://www.sfu.ca/humanrights/protocol/index.html; S. Katz, "Sexual Relations Between Students and Faculty: A Look at the Sexual Harassment Policies at Canadian Universities," January 10, 2010, http://www.universityaffairs.ca/sexual-relations-between-students-faculty.aspx.
12. M. Ryval, The Globe and Mail, March 31, 2009. http://www.theglobeandmail.com/report-on-business/article757128.ece.
13. R. D. Gatewood and H. S. Field, *Human Resource Selection* (Fort Worth, TX: Dryden Press, 1998).
14. Ibid.
15. E. White, "Job Ads Loosen Up, Get Real," *The Wall Street Journal*, 12 March 2007, B3.
16. *British Columbia (Public Service Employee Relations Commission) v. BCGSEU*, [1999] 3 S.C.R. 3 9 September 1999, http://csc.lexum.umontreal.ca/en/1999/1999scr3-3/1999scr3-3.html; V. Catano et al., *Recruitment and Selection in Canada* (Toronto: Nelson Education, 2009), 118; Ontario Human Rights Commission, "Sexual Harassment: What Can I Do?" 2010, http://www.ohrc.on.ca/en/issues/sexual_harassment.
17. J. Breaugh and M. Starke, "Research on Employee Recruitment: So Many Studies, So Many Remaining Questions," *Journal of Management* 26 (2000): 405–434.
18. "Website Offers Retirees a New Lease on Working Life," *The Vancouver Sun*, March 24, 2007, http://www.canada.com/vancouversun/news/archives/story.html?id=f1da0cd8-766d-4985-ac6a-aaccccde8a33.
19. J. T. Areddy, "China's Top Innovator Baidu Out-Googles Google," *The Wall Street Journal*, 25 July 2008, available online at http://online.wsj.com/article/SB121692051761181653.html [accessed 14 August 2008].
20. "Internet Recruitment Report," NAS Insights, available online at http://www.nasrecruitment.com/talenttips/NASinsights/InternetRecruitingReport06.pdf [accessed 14 August 2008].
21. K. Maher, "Corporations Cut Middlemen and Do Their Own Recruiting," *The Wall Street Journal*, 14 January 2003, B10.
22. Government of Alberta, Human Rights Commission, "A Recommended Guide for Pre-Employment Inquiries," 2010, http://www.albertahumanrights.ab.ca/publications/bulletins_sheets_booklets/sheets/hr_and_employment/pre_employment_inquiries.aspinquiries.
23. S. Adler, "Verifying a Job Candidate's Background: The State of Practice in a Vital Human Resources Activity," *Review of Business* 15, no. 2 (1993/1994): 3–8.
24. V. Catano et al., *Recruitment and Selection in Canada* (Toronto: Nelson Education, 2009), 326
25. *Wallace v. United Grain Growers Ltd.*, [1997] 3 S.C.R. 701. http://csc.lexum.umontreal.ca/en/1997/1997scr3-701/1997scr3-701.html.
26. M. Le, T. Nguyen, and B. Kleiner, "Legal Counsel: Don't Be Sued for Negligent Hiring," *Nonprofit World*, 1 May 2003, 14–15.
27. "Why It's Critical to Set a Policy on Background Checks for New Hires," *Managing Accounts Payable*, September 2004, 6; J. Schramm, "Future Focus: Background Checking," *HR Magazine*, January 2005.
28. C. Cohen, "Reference Checks," *CA Magazine*, November 2004, 41.
29. S. Marshall, "Spot Inflated Résumés with Simple Sleuthing," *Asian Wall Street Journal*, 7 April 2000, P3. M. Fitzgibbon, "Slaw, the Cooperative Canadian Weblog on All Things Legal," September 3, 2009, http://www.slaw.ca/2009/09/03/social-media-background-checks; BackCheck, "Criminal Record Check for Employment Screening," 2010, http://www.backcheck.ca; "NDP Candidate in B.C. Election Quits over Racy Photos in Facebook," CBC News, April 20, 2009, http://www.cbc.ca/canada/bcvotes2009/story/2009/04/20/bc-election-lam-facebook.html.
30. J. Hunter, "Cognitive Ability, Cognitive Aptitudes, Job Knowledge, and Job Performance," *Journal of Vocational Behavior* 29 (1986): 340–362.
31. F. L. Schmidt, "The Role of General Cognitive Ability and Job Performance: Why There Cannot Be a Debate," *Human Performance* 15 (2002): 187–210.
32. K. Murphy, "Can Conflicting Perspectives on the Role of g in Personnel Selection Be Resolved?" *Human Performance* 15 (2002): 173–186.
33. J. R. Glennon, L. E. Albright, and W. A. Owens, *A Catalog of Life History Items* (Greensboro, NC: The Richardson Foundation, 1966).
34. Gatewood and Field, *Human Resource Selection*.
35. I. Kotlyar and K. Ades, "HR Technology: Assessment Technology Can Help Match the Best Applicant to the Right Job," *HR Magazine*, 1 May 2002, 97.
36. M. S. Taylor and J. A. Sniezek, "The College Recruitment Interview: Topical

Content and Applicant Reactions," *Journal of Occupational Psychology* 57 (1984): 157–168.

37. R. Burnett, C. Fan, S. J. Motowidlo, and T. DeGroot, "Interview Notes and Validity," *Personnel Psychology* 51, no. X (1998): 375–396; M. A. Campion, D. K. Palmer, and J. E. Campion, "A Review of Structure in the Selection Interview," *Personnel Psychology* 50, no. 3 (1997): 655–702.

38. Campion et al., "A Review of Structure."

39. T. Judge, "The Employment Interview: A Review of Recent Research and Recommendations for Future Research," *Human Resource Management Review* 10, no. 4 (2000): 383–406.

40. J. Cortina, N. Goldstein, S. Payne, K. Davison, and S. Gilliland, "The Incremental Validity of Interview Scores Over and Above Cognitive Ability and Conscientiousness Scores," *Personnel Psychology* 53, no. 2 (2000): 325–351.

41. S. Livingston, T. W. Gerdel, M. Hill, B. Yerak, C. Melvin, and B. Lubinger, "Ohio's Strongest Companies All Agree That Training Is Vital to Their Success," *Cleveland Plain Dealer*, 21 May 1997, 30S; Rigzone, "Today's Trends: U.S., Canadian E&P Spending Estimates Rise," June 18, 2010, http://www.rigzone.com/news/article.asp?a_id=94873; Canadian Society for Training and Development, "Investing in People," 2010, http://www.cstd.ca/ResearchandResources/InvestinginPeople/tabid/81/Default.aspx.

42. The Oil Spill Training Company, http://oilspilltraining.com/home/index.asp; "BP Oil Spill Price Tag Hits $2 Billion," CBC News, June 21, 2010, http://www.cbc.ca/world/story/2010/06/21/bp-oil-well-cost.html.

43. S. Overby, "The World's Biggest Classroom," *CIO*, 1 February 2002, http://www.cio.com/article/30830/Dow_Chemical_The_World_s_Biggest_Classroom.

44. M. Totty, "Better Training through Gaming," *The Wall Street Journal*, 25 April 2005, R6.

45. J. Borzo, "Almost Human: Using Avatars for Corporate Training, Advocates Say, Can Combine the Best Parts of Face-to-Face Interaction and Computer-Based Learning," *The Wall Street Journal*, 24 May 2004, R4.

46. D. L. Kirkpatrick, "Four Steps to Measuring Training Effectiveness," *Personnel Administrator* 28 (1983): 19–25.

47. L. Bassi, J. Ludwig, D. McMurrer, and M. Van Buren, "Profiting from Learning: Do Firms' Investments in Education and Training Pay Off?" *American Society for Training and Development*, http://www.astd.org/NR/rdonlyres/91956A5E-6E57-44DD-AE5D-FCFFCDC11C3F/0/ASTD_Profiting_From_Learning.pdf; Canadian Society

for Training and Development, "Performance Improvement," 2010, http://www.cstd.ca/ResearchandResources/WebsitesArticles/tabid/297/Default.aspx.

48. J. Stack, "The Curse of the Annual Performance Review," *Inc.*, 1 March 1997, 39.

49. D. Murphy, "Are Performance Appraisals Worse Than a Waste of Time? Book Derides Unintended Consequences," *San Francisco Chronicle*, 9 September 2001, W1.

50. U. J. Wiersma and G. P. Latham, "The Practicality of Behavioral Observation Scales, Behavioral Expectation Scales, and Trait Scales," *Personnel Psychology* 39 (1986): 619–628; U. J. Wiersma, P. T. Van Den Berg, and G. P. Latham, "Dutch Reactions to Behavioral Observation, Behavioral Expectation, and Trait Scales," *Group & Organization Management* 20 (1995): 297–309.

51. D. J. Schleicher,, D. V. Day, B. T. Mayes, and R. E. Riggio, "A New Frame for Frame-of-Reference Training: Enhancing the Construct Validity of Assessment Centers," *Journal of Applied Psychology* (August 2002): 735–746.

52. H. H. Meyer, "A Solution to the Performance Appraisal Feedback Enigma," *Academy of Management Executive* 5, no. 1 (1991): 68–76; G. C. Thornton, "Psychometric Properties of Self-Appraisals of Job Performance," *Personnel Psychology* 33 (1980): 263–271.

53. D. A. Waldman, L. E. Atwater, and D. Antonioni, "Has 360 Feedback Gone Amok?" *Academy of Management Executive* 12, no. 2 (1998): 86–94.

54. J. Smither, M. London, R. Flautt, Y. Vargas, and I. Kucine, "Can Working with an Executive Coach Improve Multisource Feedback Ratings over Time? A Quasi-Experimental Field Study," *Personnel Psychology* (Spring 2003): 21–43.

55. J. McGregor, "The Employee is Always Right," *BusinessWeek*, 8 November 2007, available online at http://www.businessweek.com/globalbiz/content/nov2007/gb2007118_541063.htm [accessed 14 August 2008].

56. A. Walker and J. Smither, "A Five-Year Study of Upward Feedback: What Managers Do with Their Results Matters," *Personnel Psychology* (Summer 1999): 393–422.

57. W. Wong, "Motorola Introduces Worker Retention Incentives," Chicago Tribune (3 April 2008); M. Barnett and J. Cane, "Motorola Splits," Portfolio.com, 26 March 2008, available online at http://www.portfolio.com/news-markets/top-5/2008/03/26/Motorola-Splits [accessed 15 August 2008].

58. G. T. Milkovich and J. M. Newman, *Compensation*, 4th ed. (Homewood, IL: Irwin,1993).

59. Pay Scale Canada, "Hourly Rate Snapshot for Child Care / Day Care Worker," http://www.payscale.com/research/CA/Job=Child_Care_%2F_Day_Care_Worker/Hourly_Rate.

60. M. L. Williams and G. F. Dreher, "Compensation System Attributes and Applicant Pool Characteristics," *Academy of Management Journal* 35, no. 3 (1992): 571–595.

61. Proform Concrete Services Inc., "Profit Sharing Retirement Savings Program (PSRSP)," http://www.proformconcrete.com/profitsharing.htm.

62. C. Jensen, "Research and Legislation on ESOPs Could Have Positive Effects for Canada," Axiom News, January 19, 2009, http://www.axiomnews.ca/News-Archives/2009/January/January19.html.

63. M. Bloom, "The Performance Effects of Pay Dispersion on Individuals and Organizations," *Academy of Management Journal* 42, no. 1 (1999): 25–40.

64. "2007 Trends in CEO Pay," AFL-CIO, available online at http://www.aflcio.org/corporatewatch/paywatch/pay/index.cfm [accessed 15 August 2008]; C. Hymowitz, "Pay Gap Fuels Worker Woes," *The Wall Street Journal*, 28 April 2008, B8.

65. W. Grossman and R. E. Hoskisson, "CEO Pay at the Crossroads of Wall Street and Main: Toward the Strategic Design of Executive Compensation," *Academy of Management Executive* 12, no. 1 (1998): 43–57.

66. Bloom, "Performance Effects." National Unemployment Clock, 2010, http://www.keepjobsincanada.ca/learn-more/how-the-clock-works; "Canada Lost 129,000 Jobs in January: StatsCan," CBC News, February 6, 2009, http://www.cbc.ca/money/story/2009/02/06/januaryjobs.html#ixzz0sbRAATYf.

67. M. Bloom and J. Michel, "The Relationships among Organizational Context, Pay Dispersion, and Managerial Turnover," *Academy of Management Journal* 45 (2002): 33–42.

68. P. Michal-Johnson, *Saying Good-Bye: A Manager's Guide to Employee Dismissal* (Glenview, IL: Scott, Foresman & Co., 1985).

69. "Mass Layoffs in December 2007 and Annual Totals for 2007," Bureau of Labor Statistics News, 24 January 2008, available online at http://www.bls.gov/news.release/archives/mmls_01242008.pdf [accessed 15 August 2008].

70. M. Mentzer, "Downsizing Does Not Always Produce Results," Canadian Journal of Administrative Sciences 8, no. 12 (1996): 23–42, http://announcements.usask.ca/news/archive/1996/10/downsizing_stud.html.

71. J. R. Morris, W. F. Cascio, and C. E. Young, "Downsizing after All These Years: Questions and Answers about

Who Did It, How Many Did It, and Who Benefited from It," *Organizational Dynamics* 27, no. 3 (1999): 78–87.

72. K. Maher, "Hiring Freezes Cushion New Layoffs," *The Wall Street Journal*, 24 January 2008, A13.

73. K. E. Mishra, G. M. Spreitzer, and A. K. Mishra, "Preserving Employee Morale during Downsizing," *Sloan Management Review* 39, no. 2 (1998): 83–95.

74. J. Hilsenrath, "Adventures in Cost Cutting," *The Wall Street Journal*, 10 May 2004, R1.

75. University of Waterloo, "Early Retirement for 340," 2010, http://newsrelease.uwaterloo.ca/news.php?id=521.

76. M. Willett, "Early Retirement and Phased Retirement Programs for the Public Sector," *Benefits & Compensation Digest*, April 2005, 31.

77. D. R. Dalton, W. D. Todor, and D. M. Krackhardt, "Turnover Overstated: The Functional Taxonomy," *Academy of Management Review* 7 (1982): 117–123.

78. J. R. Hollenbeck and C. R. Williams, "Turnover Functionality versus Turnover Frequency: A Note on Work Attitudes and Organizational Effectiveness," *Journal of Applied Psychology* 71 (1986): 606–611.

79. C. R. Williams, "Reward Contingency, Unemployment, and Functional Turnover," *Human Resource Management Review* 9 (1999): 549–576.

Chapter 12

1. S. Proudfoot, "Immigrants Boost Population Growth: StatsCan," *CanWest News Service National Post*, March 26, 2009, http://www.vancouversun.com/Immigration+boosts+population+growth+StatsCan/1430563/story.html.

2. M. Almay, "Women in Canada: Work Chapter Updates," Statistics Canada, http://www.statcan.gc.ca/pub/89f0133x/89f0133x2006000-eng.htm.

3. Statistics Canada, "Population Count and Population Growth in Canada," http://www.statcan.gc.ca/pub/91-520-x/2010001/aftertoc-aprestdm1-eng.htm.

4. T. Belford, "Corporations Embrace Canada's Diverse Workforce," CanWest News Service, December 4, 2009, http://www.ottawacitizen.com/about-ottawa-citizen/Newcomers+strive+speak+office/2725088/Corporations+embrace+Canada+diverse+worceorce/2286018/story.html

5. Human Resources and Skills Development Canada, "What Is Employment Equity?" http://www.hrsdc.gc.ca/eng/lp/lo/lswe/we/information/what.shtml.

6. Ibid.

7. "*Employment Equity Act* Annual Report—2007," http://www.hrsdc.gc.ca/eng/labour/publications/equality/annual_reports/2007/page03.shtml.

8. Equal Employment Opportunity Commission, "Federal Laws Prohibiting Job Discrimination Questions and Answers," http://www.eeoc.gov/facts/qanda.html.

9. A.P. Carnevale and S.C. Stone, *The American Mosaic: An In-Depth Report on the Future of Diversity at Work* (New York: McGraw-Hill, 1995).

10. E. Orenstein, "The Business Case for Diversity," *Financial Executive*, May 2005, 22–25; G. Robinson and K. Dechant, "Building a Business Case for Diversity," *Academy of Management Executive* 11, no. 3 (1997): 21–31.

11. R. Rodriguez, "Diversity Finds its Place," *HR Magazine* 51, August 2008, available online at http://www.shrm.org/hrmagazine/articles/0806/0806rodriguez.asp.

12. A. Konrad, "Managing for Diversity and Inclusiveness: Results of the 2004–05 Ivey Strategic Diversity and Inclusiveness Survey," Richard Ivey School of Business, http://www.ivey.uwo.ca/faculty/Konrad_Report_07.pdf.

13. T. Worth, "The Business Case for Diversity: How Companies Keep Their Competitive Edge," *California Diversity*, November 2009, http://www.californiadiversitymagazine.org/the-business-case-for-diversity/#respond.

14. G. Robinson, K. Dechant. "Building a Business Case for Diversity," *Academy of Management Executive* 11, no. 3 (August 1997): 21-31, http://faculty.washington.edu/janegf/businesscasediversity.pdf.

15. Xerox News Room, "Canadians Name Diversity as Key Ingredient in Formula for Innovation Success," September 25, 2007, http://www.xerox.com/go/xrx/template/inv_rel_newsroom.jsp?subformat=print&Xcntry=CAN&Xlang=en_CA&ed_name=CAN_News_9_25_2007&format=article&view=newsrelease&app=Newsroom.

16. "The Diversity Advantage: A Case for Canada's 21st Century Economy," presented at the 10th International Metropolis Conference, Toronto, October 20, 2005, http://www.rbc.com/newsroom/pdf/20051020diversity.pdf.

17. M. R. Carrell and E. E. Mann, "Defining Workplace Diversity Programs and Practices in Organizations," *Labor Law Journal* 44 (1993): 743–764.

18. D. A. Harrison, K. H. Price, and M. P. Bell, "Beyond Relational Demography: Time and the Effects of Surface- and Deep-Level Diversity on Work Group Cohesion," *Academy of Management Journal* 41 (1998): 96–107.

19. D. Harrison, K. Price, J. Gavin, and A. Florey, "Time, Teams, and Task Performance: Changing Effects of Surface-and Deep-Level Diversity on Group Functioning," *Academy of Management Journal* 45 (2002): 1029–1045.

20. Harrison, Price, and Bell, "Beyond Relational Demography."

21. Ibid.

22. S. Baille-Ruder, "Hiring Older Workers," *Profit Magazine*, December 2004, http://www.canadianbusiness.com/entrepreneur/human_resources/article.jsp?content=20041203_140237_4856; D. Nebenzahl. "Employees over 55 Numbering in Millions, Yet Old Biases Stay Strong, Experts Say," *Vancouver Sun*, January 26, 2008, http://www.workplaceinstitute.org/node/20.

23. A. Fisher, "Wanted: Aging Baby-Boomers," *Fortune*, 30 September 1996, 204.

24. G. M. McEvoy and W. F. Cascio, "Cumulative Evidence of the Relationship between Employee Age and Job Performance," *Journal of Applied Psychology* 74 (1989): 11–17.

25. S. E. Sullivan and E. A. Duplaga, "Recruiting and Retaining Older Workers for the Millennium," *Business Horizons* 40 (12 November 1997): 65.

26. T. Knighton, F. Hujelah, J. Iacampo, and G. Werkneh, "Lifelong Learning Among Canadians Aged 18 to 64 Years: First Results from the 2008 Access and Support to Education and Training Survey," Statistics Canada Cat. no. 81-595-M, http://www.statcan.gc.ca/pub/81-595-m/81-595-m2009079-eng.htm

27. B. L. Hassell and P. L. Perrewe, "An Examination of Beliefs about Older Workers: Do Stereotypes Still Exist?" *Journal of Organizational Behavior* 16 (1995): 457–468.

28. "Women in Management in Canada, 1987–Present," *Catalyst*, http://www.catalyst.org/file/358/qt_women_mgmt_canada_1987-present.pdf; and http://www.catalyst.org/publication/400/women-in-management-in-canada-1987-present.

29. CIBC World Markets, "Women Entrepreneurs: Leading the Charge," 2005, http://www.cibc.com/ca/pdf/women-entrepreneurs-en.pdf.

30. E. Fisher and R. Reuber, "The State of Entrepreneurship in Canada," February 2010, http://www.ic.gc.ca/eic/site/sbrp-rppe.nsf/vwapj/SEC-EEC_eng.pdf/$file/SEC-EEC_eng.pdf.

31. Canadian Press, "Women Outnumber Men in Canadian Workforce," September 5, 2009, http://www.ctv.ca/servlet/ArticleNews/story/CTVNews/20090905/women_workforce_090905/20090905?hub=Canada.

32. CIBC World Markets, "Women Entrepreneurs: Leading the Charge," 2005, http://www.cibc.com/ca/pdf/women-entrepreneurs-en.pdf.

33. A. Pletsch, "Female Leaders: The Paternal Cycle," *Canadian Business Magazine*, June 16, 2008, http://www.canadianbusiness.com/

managing/career/article.jsp?con
tent=20080616_198711_198711;
L. Bogomolny, "Melting the Glass
Ceiling."

34. M. Bertrand and K. Hallock, "The
Gender Gap in Top Corporate Jobs,"
Industrial & Labor Relations Review
55 (2001): 3–21.

35. J. R. Hollenbeck, D. R. Ilgen, C.
Ostroff, and J. B. Vancouver, "Sex Differences in Occupational Choice, Pay,
and Worth: A Supply-Side Approach
to Understanding the Male-Female
Wage Gap," *Personnel Psychology* 40
(1987): 715–744.

36. Korn-Ferry International, 1993.

37. Department of Industry, Labor and
Human Relations, *Report of the
Governor's Task Force on the Glass
Ceiling Commission* (Madison, WI:
State of Wisconsin, 1993).

38. M. Fix, G. C. Galster, and R. J. Struyk,
"An Overview of Auditing for Discrimination," in *Clear and Convincing
Evidence: Measurement of Discrimination in America*, ed. M. Fix and R.
Struyk (Washington, DC: Urban Institute Press, 1993), 1–68.

39. B. R. Ragins, B. Townsend, and M.
Mattis, "Gender Gap in the Executive
Suite: CEOs and Female Executives
Report on Breaking the Glass Ceiling,"
Academy of Management Executive
12 (1998): 28–42.

40. N. Lockwood, "The Glass Ceiling:
Domestic and International Perspec-
tives," *HR Magazine*, 2004 Research
Quarterly, 2–10.

41. T. B. Foley, "Discrimination Lawsuits
Are a Small-Business Nightmare: A
Guide to Minimizing the Potential
Damage," *The Wall Street Journal*, 28
September 1998, 15.

42. Canadian Human Rights Commission
Annual Report, 2007, http://www.chrc-
ccdp.ca/publications/ar_2007_ra/page5-
en.asp.

43. Ryerson University Media Release,
"Catalyst and Ryerson University
Release New Study of More Than
17,000 Seasoned Professionals," June
28, 2007, http://www.ryerson.ca/news/
media/General_Public/20070629_
mrcatalyst.html.

44. D. A. Neal and W. R. Johnson,
"The Role of Premarket Factors
in Black-White Wage Differences,"
Journal of Political Economy 104, no.
5 (1996): 869–895.

45. Fix, Galster, and Struyk, "An Overview
of Auditing."

46. M. Bendick, Jr., C. W. Jackson, and
V. A. Reinoso, "Measuring Employment
Discrimination through Controlled
Experiments," in *African-Americans
and Post-Industrial Labor Markets*,
ed. J. B. Stewart (New Brunswick, NJ:
Transaction Publishers, 1997), 77–100.

47. P. B. Riach and J. Rich, "Measuring
Discrimination by Direct Experimental
Methods: Seeking Gunsmoke," *Journal

of PostKeynesian Economics* 14, no. 2
(winter 1991–1992): 143–150.

48. A. P. Brief, R. T. Buttram, R. M. Reizen-
stein, and S. D. Pugh, "Beyond Good
Intentions: The Next Steps toward
Racial Equality in the American Work-
place," *Academy of Management
Executive* 11 (1997): 59–72.

49. L. E. Wynter, "Business & Race:
Federal Agencies, Spurred on by
Nonprofit Groups, Are Increasingly
Embracing the Use of Undercover
Investigators to Identify Discrimination
in the Marketplace," *The Wall Street
Journal*, 1 July 1998, B1.

50. S. Capparell, *The Real Pepsi Challenge: The Inspirational Story of
Breaking the Color Barrier in American Business* (Reed Elsevier, 2007).

51. Canadian Press, "1 in 7 Canadians Live
with Disability: Statscan," December 3,
2007, http://www.thestar.com/article/
282097.

52. Statistics Canada, "Participation and
Activity Limitation Survey 2006:
Technical and Methodological Report,"
http://www.statcan.gc.ca/pub/89-628-x/
89-628-x2007001-eng.htm#1.

53. Canadian Press, "More Disabled
People in Canada: Report," December
28, 2009, http://www.cbc.ca/health/
story/2009/12/28/disabled-report-
canada.html?ref=rss.

54. B. Wilkerson, *The Business Case for
Accessibility* (Toronto: Queen's Printer
of Ontario, November 2001), http://
www.niagarafalls.ca/services/community_
health_and_wellness/disabilities_special_
needs/programs_services/pdf/business_
case_for_accessibility.pdf.

55. Human Resources and Skills Development Canada, "2009 Federal Disability
Report," http://www.hrsdc.gc.ca/eng/
disability_issues/reports/fdr/2009/
page01.shtml.

56. Canadian Press, "More Disabled People
in Canada."

57. Human Resources and Skills Development Canada, "2009 Federal Disability
Report."

58. R. Greenwood and V. A. Johnson,
"Employer Perspectives on Workers
with Disabilities," *Journal of
Rehabilitation* 53 (1987): 37–45.

59. Ibid.

60. "Low Cost Accommodation Solutions,"
Office of Disability Employment Policy,
available online at http://www.jan.wvu
.edu/media/LowCostSolutions.html
[accessed 21 August 2001].

61. Government of British Columbia,
"Workable Solutions: An Initiative of
the Minister's Council on Employment
for Persons with Disabilities," http://
www.mhr.gov.bc.ca/epwd/docs/Hand
book.pdf.

62. R. B. Cattell, "Personality Pinned
Down," *Psychology Today* 7 (1973):
40–46; C. S. Carver and M. F. Scheier,
Perspectives on Personality (Boston:
Allyn & Bacon, 1992).

63. J. M. Digman, "Personality Structure:
Emergence of the Five-Factor Model,"
Annual Review of Psychology 41
(1990): 417–440; M. R. Barrick and
M. K. Mount, "The Big Five Person-
ality Dimensions and Job Performance:
A Meta-Analysis," *Personnel Psy-
chology* 44 (1991): 1–26.

64. M. R. Barrick and M. K. Mount, "The
Big Five Personality Dimensions and Job
Performance," *Personnel Psychology*
44 (1991): 1–26. M. K. Mount and
M. R. Barrick, "The Big Five Personality
Dimensions: Implications for Research
and Practice in Human Resource
Management," *Research in Personnel
& Human Resources Management*
13 (1995): 153–200; M. K. Mount and
M. R. Barrick, "Five Reasons Why the
'Big Five' Article Has Been Frequently
Cited," *Personnel Psychology* 51
(1998): 849–857; D. S. Ones, M. K.
Mount, M. R. Barrick, and J. E. Hunter,
"Personality and Job Performance:
A Critique of the Tett, Jackson, and
Rothstein (1991) Meta-Analysis,"
Personnel Psychology 47 (1994):
147–156.

65. Barrick and Mount, "The Big Five
Personality Dimensions and Job
Performance." .

66. Mount and Barrick, "Five Reasons
Why the 'Big Five' Article Has Been
Frequently Cited." .

67. Mount and Barrick, "Five Reasons
Why the 'Big Five' Article Has Been
Frequently Cited."

68. Staff, "The Diverse Work Force," *Inc.*,
January 1993, 33.

69. D. A. Thomas and R. J. Ely, "Making
Differences Matter: A New Paradigm
for Managing Diversity," *Harvard
Business Review* 74 (September–
October 1996): 79–90.

70. D. A. Thomas and S. Wetlaufer, "A
Question of Color: A Debate on Race
in the U.S. Workplace," *Harvard Business Review* 75 (September–October
1997), 118–132.

71. Thomas and Ely, "Making Differences
Matter."

72. A. Fisher, "How You Can Do Better
on Diversity," *Fortune*, 15 November
2004, 60.

73. Aetna – 2005 Diversity Annual Report
(www.aetna.com) Obtained from
SHRM Research Department.

74. J. R. Norton and R. E. Fox, *The
Change Equation: Capitalizing on
Diversity for Effective Organizational
Change* (Washington, DC: American
Psychological Association, 1997).

75. Ibid.

76. Thomas and Ely, "Making Differences
Matter."

77. R. R. Thomas, Jr., *Beyond Race and
Gender: Unleashing the Power of
Your Total Workforce by Managing
Diversity* (New York: AMACOM,
1991).

78. Ibid.

79. S. Lubove, "Damned If You Do, Damned If You Don't: Preference Programs Are on the Defensive in the Public Sector, but Plaintiffs' Attorneys and Bureaucrats Keep Diversity Inc. Thriving in Corporate America," *Forbes*, 15 December 1997, 122.

80. L. S. Gottfredson, "Dilemmas in Developing Diversity Programs," in *Diversity in the Workplace*, ed. S. E. Jackson & Associates (New York: Guildford Press, 1992).

81. A. Konrad, C.Maurer, and Y. Yang, "Managing for Diversity and Inclusiveness: Results of the 2004–05 Ivey Strategic Diversity and Inclusiveness Survey," Richard Ivey School of Business, University of Western Ontario, http://www.ivey.uwo.ca/faculty/Konrad_Report_07.pdf.

82. Canada.com, "Forest Company Keys into Aboriginal Workforce," *Vancouver Sun*, April 5, 2008, http://www.canada.com/vancouversun/news/story.html?id=041ec56f-7401-4c40-bd09-e743548f69b2.

83. R. Caballero and R. Yerema, "Canada's Best Diversity Employers," March 23, 2010, http://www.eluta.ca/diversity-at-university-of-british-columbia and http://www.eluta.ca/diversity-at-corus-entertainment.

84. Canada.com, "Forest Company Keys into Aboriginal Workforce."

85. Caballero and Yerema, "Canada's Best Diversity Employers."

86. Caballero and Yerema, "Canada's Best Diversity Employers."

87. Ibid.

88. Carnevale and Stone, *The American Mosaic*.

89. Caballero and Yerema, "Canada's Best Diversity Employers."

90. Ibid.

91. J. R. Joplin and C. S. Daus, "Challenges of Leading a Diverse Workforce," *Academy of Management Executive* 11 (1997): 32–47.

92. Caballero and Yerema, "Canada's Best Diversity Employers."

93. Konrad, Maurer, and Yang, "Managing for Diversity and Inclusiveness."

Chapter 13

1. M. Gagne and E. Deci, "Self-Determination Theory and Work Motivation," *Journal of Organizational Behaviour* 26 (2005): 331–62.

2. J. P. Campbell and R. D. Pritchard, "Motivation Theory in Industrial and Organizational Psychology," in *Handbook of Industrial and Organizational Psychology*, ed. M. D. Dunnette (Chicago: Rand McNally, 1976).

3. P. Thomas, "Waitress Makes the Difference in Bringing Deaf to Pittsburgh," The *Wall Street Journal Interactive Edition*, 2 March 1999.

4. E. A. Locke, "The Nature and Causes of Job Satisfaction," in *Handbook of Industrial and Organizational*

Psychology, ed. M. D. Dunnette (Chicago: Rand McNally, 1976).

5. A. H. Maslow, "A Theory of Human Motivation," *Psychological Review* 50 (1943): 370–396.

6. C. P. Alderfer, *Existence, Relatedness, and Growth: Human Needs in Organizational Settings* (New York: Free Press, 1972).

7. D. C. McClelland, "Toward a Theory of Motive Acquisition," *American Psychologist* 20 (1965): 321–333; D. C. McClelland and D. H. Burnham, "Power Is the Great Motivator," *Harvard Business Review* 54, no. 2 (1976): 100–110.

8. J. H. Turner, "Entrepreneurial Environments and the Emergence of Achievement Motivation in Adolescent Males," *Sociometry* 33 (1970): 147–165.

9. L. W. Porter, E. E. Lawler III, and J. R. Hackman, *Behavior in Organizations* (New York: McGraw-Hill, 1975).

10. C. Ajila, "Maslow's Hierarchy of Needs Theory: Applicability to the Nigerian Industrial Setting," *IFE Psychology* (1997): 162–174.

11. M. A. Wahba and L. B. Birdwell, "Maslow Reconsidered: A Review of Research on the Need Hierarchy Theory," *Organizational Behavior & Human Performance* 15 (1976): 212–240; J. Rauschenberger, N. Schmitt, and J. E. Hunter, "A Test of the Need Hierarchy Concept by a Markov Model of Change in Need Strength," *Administrative Science Quarterly* 25 (1980): 654–670.

12. E. E. Lawler III and L. W. Porter, "The Effect of Performance on Job Satisfaction," *Industrial Relations* 7 (1967): 20–28.

13. Porter, Lawler, and Hackman, *Behavior in Organizations*.

14. "IKEA: Home is the most important place in the world," Ikea, 28 September 2008, available online at www.ikea.com.

15. Porter, Lawler, and Hackman, *Behavior in Organizations*.

16. J. S. Lublin, "Creative Compensation: A CEO Talks about His Company's Innovative Pay Ideas. Free Ice Cream, Anyone?," *The Wall Street Journal*, 10 April 2006, R6; Tavia Grant, "Worst of Times Might Be Best of Times to Take Off," *The Globe and Mail*, April 4, 2009, http://yoursabbatical.com/2009/04/04/wort-of-times-might-be-best-of-times-to-take-off

17. C. Caggiano, "What Do Workers Want?" *Inc.*, November 1992, 101–104; "National Study of the Changing Workforce," Families & Work Institute, available online at http://www.familiesandwork.org/summary/nscw.pdf [accessed 31 May 2005].

18. H. Dolezalek, "Good Job!: Recognition Training," *Training* (28 July 2008).

19. R. Kanfer and P. Ackerman, "Aging, Adult Development, and Work

Motivation," *Academy of Management Review* (2004): 440–458.

20. E. White, "The New Recruits: Older Workers," *The Wall Street Journal*, 14 January 2008, B3.

21. "2007 Trends in CEO Pay," AFL-CIO, available online at http://www.aflcio.org/corporatewatch/paywatch/pay/index.cfm [accessed 15 August 2008].

22. P. Froats, "CEO Compensation Increases," *Canadian Business Online*, July 15, 2008, http://blog.canadianbusiness.com/ceo-compensation-increases; B. Marotte, "SNC-Lavalin: Engineering a Fair-Minded Pay Policy," *The Globe and Mail, Report on Business*, November 24, 2009, http://www.theglobeandmail.com/report-on-business/board-games/snc-lavalin-engineerin...

23. C. T. Kulik and M. L. Ambrose, "Personal and Situational Determinants of Referent Choice," *Academy of Management Review* 17 (1992): 212–237.

24. J. S. Adams, "Toward an Understanding of Inequity," *Journal of Abnormal Social Psychology* 67 (1963): 422–436.

25. R. A. Cosier and D. R. Dalton, "Equity Theory and Time: A Reformulation," *Academy of Management Review* 8 (1983): 311–319; M. R. Carrell and J. E. Dittrich, "Equity Theory: The Recent Literature, Methodological Considerations, and New Directions," *Academy of Management Review* 3 (1978): 202–209.

26. "GM, Chrysler Ask for Billions in Canadian Aid," CBC News, February 21, 2009, http://www.cbc.ca/money/story/2009/02/20/carbailouts.html.

27. C. Chen, J. Choi, and S. Chi, "Making Justice Sense of Local-Expatriate Compensation Disparity: Mitigation by Local Referents, Ideological Explanations, and Interpersonal Sensitivity in China-Foreign Joint Ventures," *Academy of Management Journal* (2002): 807–817.

28. K. Aquino, R. W. Griffeth, D. G. Allen, and P. W. Hom, "Integrating Justice Constructs into the Turnover Process: A Test of a Referent Cognitions Model," *Academy of Management Journal* 40, no. 5 (1997): 1208–1227.

29. R. Folger and M. A. Konovsky, "Effects of Procedural and Distributive Justice on Reactions to Pay Raise Decisions," *Academy of Management Journal* 32 (1989): 115–130; M. A. Konovsky, "Understanding Procedural Justice and Its Impact on Business Organizations," *Journal of Management* 26 (2000): 489–512.

30. E. Barret-Howard and T. R. Tyler, "Procedural Justice as a Criterion in Allocation Decisions," *Journal of Personality & Social Psychology* 50 (1986): 296–305; Folger and Konovsky, "Effects of Procedural and Distributive Justice on Reactions to Pay Raise Decisions."

31. R. Folger and J. Greenberg, "Procedural Justice: An Interpretive Analysis of Personnel Systems," in *Research in Personnel and Human Resources Management*, Vol. 3, ed. K. Rowland and G. Ferris (Greenwich, CT: JAI Press, 1985); R. Folger, D. Rosenfield, J. Grove, and L. Corkran, "Effects of 'Voice' and Peer Opinions on Responses to Inequity," *Journal of Personality & Social Psychology* 37 (1979): 2253–2261; E. A. Lind & T. R. Tyler, *The Social Psychology of Procedural Justice* (New York: Plenum Press, 1988); Konovsky, "Understanding Procedural Justice and Its Impact on Business Organizations."

32. V. H. Vroom, *Work and Motivation* (New York: John Wiley & Sons, 1964); L. W. Porter and E. E. Lawler III, *Managerial Attitudes and Performance* (Homewood, IL: Dorsey Press & Richard D. Irwin, 1968).

33. P. V. LeBlanc and P. W. Mulvey, "How American Workers See the Rewards of Work," *Compensation & Benefits Review* 30 (February 1998): 24–28.

34. A. Fox, "Companies Can Benefit When They Disclose Pay Processes to Employees," *HR Magazine* 47 (July 2002): 25.

35. K. W. Thomas and B. A. Velthouse, "Cognitive Elements of Empowerment," *Academy of Management Review* 15 (1990): 666–681.

36. E. L. Thorndike, *Animal Intelligence* (New York: Macmillan, 1911).

37. B. F. Skinner, *Science and Human Behavior* (New York: Macmillan, 1954); B. F. Skinner, *Beyond Freedom and Dignity* (New York: Bantam Books, 1971); B. F. Skinner, *A Matter of Consequences* (New York: New York University Press, 1984).

38. A. M. Dickinson and A. D. Poling, "Schedules of Monetary Reinforcement in Organizational Behavior Management: Latham and Huber Revisited," *Journal of Organizational Behavior Management* 16, no. 1 (1992): 71–91.

39. R. Ho, "Attending to Attendance," *The Wall Street Journal Interactive*, 7 December 1998.

40. D. Grote, "Manager's Journal: Discipline without Punishment," *The Wall Street Journal*, 23 May 1994, A14.

41. J. B. Miner, *Theories of Organizational Behavior* (Hinsdale, IL: Dryden, 1980).

42. Dickinson and Poling, "Schedules of Monetary Reinforcement in Organizational Behavior Management."

43. F. Luthans and A. D. Stajkovic, "Reinforce for Performance: The Need to Go beyond Pay and Even Rewards," *Academy of Management Executive* 13, no. 2 (1999): 49–57.

44. K. D. Butterfield, L. K. Trevino, and G. A. Ball, "Punishment from the Manager's Perspective: A Grounded Investigation and Inductive Model," *Academy of Management Journal* 39 (1996): 1479–1512.

45. R. D. Arvey and J. M. Ivancevich, "Punishment in Organizations: A Review, Propositions, and Research Suggestions," *Academy of Management Review* 5 (1980): 123–132.

46. R. D. Arvey, G. A. Davis, and S. M. Nelson, "Use of Discipline in an Organization: A Field Study," *Journal of Applied Psychology* 69 (1984): 448–460; M. E. Schnake, "Vicarious Punishment in a Work Setting," *Journal of Applied Psychology* 71 (1986): 343–345.

47. E. A. Locke and G. P. Latham, *Goal Setting: A Motivational Technique That Works* (Englewood Cliffs, NJ: Prentice-Hall, 1984); E. A. Locke and G. P. Latham, *A Theory of Goal Setting and Task Performance* (Englewood Cliffs, NJ: Prentice-Hall, 1990).

48. G. P. Latham and E. A. Locke, "Goal Setting—A Motivational Technique That Works," *Organizational Dynamics* 8, no. 2 (1979): 68.

49. Ibid.

Chapter 14

1. W. Bennis, "Why Leaders Can't Lead," *Training & Development Journal* 43, no. 4 (1989); H. Mintzberg, "The Manager's Job: Folklore and Fact," in *Managing People and Organizations*, ed. John J. Garbarro (Cambridge: Harvard Business School Publications, 1992), http://www.uu.edu/personal/bnance/318/mintz.html; "The Man Who Invented Management: Why Peter Drucker's Ideas Still Matter," *Business Week*, November 2005, http://www.businessweek.com/magazine/content/05_48/b3961001.htm; H. Mintzberg, "Proven Models: 10 Managerial Roles," 2010, http://www.provenmodels.com/88/ten-managerial-roles/mintzberg,-henry.

2. L. Buchanan, "How the creative stay creative," *Inc.*, June 2008, 102–103.

3. A. Zaleznik, "Managers and Leaders: Are They Different?" *Harvard Business Review* 55 (1977): 76–78; A. Zaleznik, "The Leadership Gap," *The Washington Quarterly* 6 (1983): 32–39.

4. Bennis, "Why Leaders Can't Lead."

5. "Suncor, Petro-Canada Announce Merger," CBC News, March 23, 2009, http://www.cbc.ca/money/story/2009/03/23/suncor-petro-canada-merge.html#ixzz0sCN0BOJn.

6. D. Jones, "Not All Successful CEOs are Extroverts," *USA Today*, 7 June 2006, B.1.

7. G. Robertson, "How a Shy Guy and Matt Damon Are Helping Kids, One by One," *The Globe and Mail*, October 31, 2009, http://www.theglobeandmail.com/globe-investor/how-a-shy-guy-and-matt-damon-are-helping-kids-one-by-one/article1278592.

8. M. Gladwell, "Why Do We Love Tall Men?" *Gladwell.Com*, http://www.gladwell.com/blink/blink_excerpt2.html.

9. R. J. House and R. M Aditya, "The Social Scientific Study of Leadership: Quo Vadis?" *Journal of Management* 23 (1997): 409–473; T. Judge, R. Illies, J. Bono, and M. Gerhardt, "Personality and Leadership: A Qualitative and Quantitative Review," *Journal of Applied Psychology* (August 2002): 765–782; S. A. Kirkpatrick and E. A. Locke, "Leadership: Do Traits Matter?" *Academy of Management Executive* 5, no. 2 (1991): 48–60.

10. House and Aditya, "The Social Scientific Study of Leadership"; Kirkpatrick and Locke, "Leadership: Do Traits Matter?".

11. P. Demont, "Small Business Management: Profit Magazine's Top Woman Entrepreneur Passes $1.5B in Sales," CBC News, October 21, 2008, http://www.cbc.ca/money/story/2008/10/20/women-profit.html#ixzz0sCSVPpzK.

12. Kirkpatrick and Locke, "Leadership: Do Traits Matter?".

13. E. Amendola, "P&G CEO Wields High Expectations, but No Whip," *USA Today*, available online at http://www.usatoday.com/money/companies/management/2007-02-19-exec-pandg-usat_x.htm?loc=insterstitialskip [accessed 27 August 2008].

14. E. A. Fleishman, "The Description of Supervisory Behavior," *Journal of Applied Psychology* 37 (1953): 1–6; L. R. Katz, *New Patterns of Management* (New York: McGraw-Hill, 1961).

15. Canadian Press, "VIA Rail Strike Averted," June 27, 2010, http://www.cbc.ca/consumer/story/2010/06/27/via-strike-averted.html#ixzz0sCVFjl8o.

16. L. Grant, "Retail Giant Wal-Mart Faces Challenges on Many Fronts; Protests, Allegations Are Price of Success, CEO Says," *USA Today*, 11 November 2003, B.01.

17. Ibid.

18. P. Weissenberg and M. H. Kavanagh, "The Independence of Initiating Structure and Consideration: A Review of the Evidence," *Personnel Psychology* 25 (1972): 119–130.

19. R. J. House and T. R. Mitchell, "Path-Goal Theory of Leadership," *Journal of Contemporary Business* 3 (1974): 81–97; F. E. Fiedler, "A Contingency Model of Leadership Effectiveness," in *Advances in Experimental Social Psychology*, ed. L. Berkowitz (New York: Academic Press, 1964); V. H. Vroom and P. W. Yetton, *Leadership and Decision Making* (Pittsburgh: University of Pittsburgh Press, 1973); P. Hersey and K. H. Blanchard, *The*

Management of Organizational Behavior, 4th ed. (Englewood Cliffs, NJ: Prentice Hall, 1984); S. Kerr and J. M. Jermier, "Substitutes for Leadership: Their Meaning and Measurement," *Organizational Behavior & Human Performance* 22 (1978): 375–403.

20. F. E. Fiedler and M. M. Chemers, *Leadership and Effective Management* (Glenview, IL: Scott, Foresman, 1974); F. E. Fiedler and M. M. Chemers, *Improving Leadership Effectiveness: The Leader Match Concept*, 2d ed. (New York: John Wiley & Sons, 1984).

21. Fiedler and Chemers, *Improving Leadership Effectiveness.*

22. F. E. Fiedler, "The Effects of Leadership Training and Experience: A Contingency Model Interpretation," *Administrative Science Quarterly* 17, no. 4 (1972): 455; F. E. Fiedler, *A Theory of Leadership Effectiveness* (New York: McGraw-Hill, 1967).

23. L. S. Csoka and F. E. Fiedler, "The Effect of Military Leadership Training: A Test of the Contingency Model," *Organizational Behavior & Human Performance* 8 (1972): 395–407.

24. House and Mitchell, "Path-Goal Theory of Leadership."

25. Ibid.

26. B. M. Fisher and J. E. Edwards, "Consideration and Initiating Structure and Their Relationships with Leader Effectiveness: A Meta-Analysis," *Proceedings of the Academy of Management*, August 1988, 201–205.

27. M. Copeland, K. Crawford, J. Davis, S. Hamner, C. Hawn, R. Howe, P. Kaihla, M. Maier, O. Malik, D. McDonald, C. Null, E. Schonfeld, O. Thomas, and G. Zachary, "My Golden Rule," *Business 2.0,* 1 December 2005, 108.

28. E. White, "Art of Persuasion Becomes Key," *The Wall Street Journal,* 19 May 2008, B5.

29. J. C. Wofford and L. Z. Liska, "Path-Goal Theories of Leadership: A Meta-Analysis," *Journal of Management* 19 (1993): 857–876.

30. House and Aditya, "The Social Scientific Study of Leadership."

31. V. H. Vroom and A. G. Jago, *The New Leadership: Managing Participation in Organizations* (Englewood Cliffs, NJ: Prentice Hall, 1988).

32. C. Fishman, "How Teamwork Took Flight: This Team Built a Commercial Engine—and Self-Managing GE Plant—from Scratch," *Fast Company,* 1 October 1999, 188.

33. Ibid.

34. Ibid.

35. G. A. Yukl, *Leadership in Organizations,* 3d ed. (Englewood Cliffs, NJ: Prentice Hall, 1995).

36. B. M. Bass, *Bass & Stogdill's Handbook of Leadership: Theory, Research, and Managerial Applications* (New York: Free Press, 1990).

37. R. D. Ireland and M. A. Hitt, "Achieving and Maintaining Strategic Competitiveness in the 21st Century: The Role of Strategic Leadership," *Academy of Management Executive* 13, no. 1 (1999): 43–57.

38. P. Thoms and D. B. Greenberger, "Training Business Leaders to Create Positive Organizational Visions of the Future: Is It Successful?" *Academy of Management Journal* (Best Papers & Proceedings 1995): 212–216.

39. M. Weber, *The Theory of Social and Economic Organizations,* trans. R. A. Henderson and T. Parsons (New York: Free Press, 1947).

40. Eric Reguly, *The Globe and Mail Report on Business,* http://www.theglobeandmail.com/report-on-business/rob-magazine/ceo-of-the-year/article1375887.

41. D. A. Waldman and F. J. Yammarino, "CEO Charismatic Leadership: Levels-of-Management and Levels-of-Analysis Effects," *Academy of Management Review* 24, no. 2 (1999): 266–285.

42. K. B. Lowe, K. G. Kroeck, and N. Sivasubramaniam, "Effectiveness Correlates of Transformational and Transactional Leadership: A Meta-Analytic Review of the MLQ Literature," *Leadership Quarterly* 7 (1996): 385–425.

43. J. M. Howell and B. J. Avolio, "The Ethics of Charismatic Leadership: Submission or Liberation?" *Academy of Management Executive* 6, no. 2 (1992): 43–54.

44. A. Deutschman, "Is Your Boss a Psychopath?," *Fast Company,* July 2005, 44.

45. Howell & Avolio, "The Ethics of Charismatic Leadership."

46. Bass, "From Transactional to Transformational Leadership."

47. B. M. Bass, *A New Paradigm of Leadership: An Inquiry into Transformational Leadership* (Alexandra, VA: U.S. Army Research Institute for the Behavioral and Social Sciences, 1996).

48. Sylvia Fraser, "The Belinda Stronach Defence," *Toronto Life,* February 2006, http://www.torontolife.com/features/the-belinda-stronach-defense/?pageno=2; "Belinda Stronach Quits Politics for Magna," *Financial Post,* April 11, 2007, http://www.canada.com/nationalpost/news/story.html?id=3f2efd7c-0d10-477c-bf2c-4bb4ecda3abd&k=96098

49. Bass, "From Transactional to Transformational Leadership."

Chapter 15

1. E. E. Lawler III, L. W. Porter, and A. Tannenbaum, "Managers' Attitudes toward Interaction Episodes," *Journal of Applied Psychology* 52 (1968): 423–439; H. Mintzberg, *The Nature of Managerial Work* (New York: Harper & Row, 1973).

2. J. D. Maes, T. G. Weldy, and M. L. Icenogle, "A Managerial Perspective: Oral Communication Competency Is Most Important for Business Students in the Workplace," *Journal of Business Communication* 34 (1997): 67–80.

3. R. Lepsinger & A. D. Lucia, *The Art and Science of 360 Degree Feedback* (San Francisco: Pfeiffer, 1997).

4. E. E. Jones and K. E. Davis, "From Acts to Dispositions: The Attribution Process in Person Perception," in *Advances in Experimental and Social Psychology,* vol. 2, ed. L. Berkowitz (New York: Academic Press, 1965), 219–266; R. G. Lord and J. E. Smith, "Theoretical, Information-Processing, and Situational Factors Affecting Attribution Theory Models of Organizational Behavior," *Academy of Management Review* 8 (1983): 50–60.

5. J. Zadney and H. B. Gerard, "Attributed Intentions and Informational Selectivity," *Journal of Experimental Social Psychology* 10 (1974): 34–52.

6. J. Myers, "Noise Annoys in the Workplace," *The Globe and Mail Report on Business,* June 4, 2010, http://www.theglobeandmail.com/report-on-business/managing/weekend-workout/noise-annoys-in-the-workplace/article1592755.

7. A. Taylor, "GM Gets Its Act Together. Finally," *Fortune,* 5 April 2004.

8. H. H. Kelly, *Attribution in Social Interaction* (Morristown, NJ: General Learning Press, 1971).

9. J. M. Burger, "Motivational Biases in the Attribution of Responsibility for an Accident: A Meta-Analysis of the Defensive-Attribution Hypothesis," *Psychological Bulletin* 90 (1981): 496–512.

10. D. A. Hofmann and A. Stetzer, "The Role of Safety Climate and Communication in Accident Interpretation: Implications for Learning from Negative Events," *Academy of Management Journal* 41, no. 6 (1998): 644–657.

11. C. Perrow, *Normal Accidents: Living with High-Risk Technologies* (New York: Basic Books, 1984).

12. A. G. Miller and T. Lawson, "The Effect of an Informational Opinion on the Fundamental Attribution Error," *Journal of Personality & Social Psychology* 47 (1989): 873–896; J. M. Burger, "Changes in Attribution Errors over Time: The Ephemeral Fundamental Attribution Error," *Social Cognition* 9 (1991): 182–193.

13. F. Heider, *The Psychology of Interpersonal Relations* (New York: Wiley, 1958); D. T. Miller and M. Ross, "Self-Serving Biases in Attribution of Causality: Fact or Fiction?" *Psychological Bulletin* 82 (1975): 213–225.

14. J. R. Larson, Jr., "The Dynamic Interplay between Employees' Feedback-Seeking Strategies and

Supervisors' Delivery of Performance Feedback," *Academy of Management Review* 14, no. 3 (1989): 408–422.

15. C. Hymowitz, "Mind Your Language: To Do Business Today, Consider Delayering," *The Wall Street Journal*, 27 March 2006, B1.

16. G. L. Kreps, *Organizational Communication: Theory and Practice* (New York: Longman, 1990).

17. Ibid.

18. E. Beaton, "Frankly Speaking: Why It Pays to Tell Your Bosses What You Really Think of Them," *The Globe and Mail*, March 19, 2010, http://www.theglobeandmail.com/report-on-business/frankly-speaking/article1505364.

19. K. Voight, "Office Intelligence," *Asian Wall Street Journal*, 21 January 2005, P1.

20. L. Landro, "The Informed Patient: Hospitals Combat Errors at the 'Hand-Off,'" *The Wall Street Journal*, 28 June 2006, D1.

21. Kreps, *Organizational Communication: Theory and Practice*.

22. D. Therrien, "Rid Your Office of Backstabbers: How Good Managers Can Control Counterproductive Workplace Gossip," *Canadian Business Online*, November 22, 2004, http://www.canadianbusiness.com/managing/article.jsp?content=20041122_63827_63827.

23. W. Davis and J. R. O'Connor, "Serial Transmission of Information: A Study of the Grapevine," *Journal of Applied Communication Research* 5 (1977): 61–72.

24. W. C. Redding, *Communication within the Organization: An Interpretive View of Theory and Research* (New York: Industrial Communication Council, 1972).

25. D. T. Hall, K. L. Otazo, and G. P. Hollenbeck, "Behind Closed Doors: What Really Happens in Executive Coaching," *Organizational Dynamics* 27, no. 3 (1999): 39–53.

26. V. Galt, "Coaches Don't Always Demand More Pushups," *The Globe and Mail Report on Business*, May 5, 2007, http://www.theglobeandmail.com/report-on-business/article757302.ece.

27. A. Mehrabian, "Communication without Words," *Psychology Today* 3 (1968): 53; A. Mehrabian, *Silent Messages* (Belmont, CA: Wadsworth, 1971); R. Harrison, *Beyond Words: An Introduction to Nonverbal Communication* (Upper Saddle River, NJ: Prentice Hall, 1974); A. Mehrabian, *Non-Verbal Communication* (Chicago: Aldine, 1972).

28. C. A. Bartlett and S. Ghoshal, "Changing the Role of Top Management: Beyond Systems to People," *Harvard Business Review* (May-June 1995): 132–142.

29. T. Andrews, "E-Mail Empowers, Voice-Mail Enslaves," *PC Week*, 10 April 1995, E11.

30. A. Rawlins, "There's a Message in Every Email," *Fast Company* September 2007, http://www.fastcompany.com/magazine/118/theres-a-message-in-every-email.html?partner= rss-alert.

31. R. G. Nichols, "Do We Know How to Listen? Practical Helps in a Modern Age," in *Communication Concepts and Processes*, ed. J. DeVitor (Englewood Cliffs, NJ: Prentice Hall, 1971); P. V. Lewis, *Organizational Communication: The Essence of Effective Management* (Columbus, OH: Grid Publishing Company, 1975).

32. E. Atwater, *I Hear You*, revised ed. (New York: Walker, 1992).

33. R. Adler and N. Towne, *Looking Out/Looking In* (San Francisco: Rinehart Press, 1975).

34. T. Pittaway, "Dragons' Den: Fly Like a Dragon," *Profit Magazine*, October 2008, http://www.canadianbusiness.com/entrepreneur/managing/article.jsp?content=20081001_198708_198708; "Boston Pizza Quick Facts," http://www.bostonpizza.com/Libraries/General_Content_Files/Boston_Pizza_Quick_Facts.sflb.ashx.

35. C. Gallo, "Why Leadership Means Listening," *BusinessWeek Online* 31 January 2007, http://www.businessweek.com/smallbiz/content/jan2007/sb20070131_192848.htm.

36. B. D. Seyber, R. N. Bostrom, and J. H. Seibert, "Listening, Communication Abilities, and Success at Work," *Journal of Business Communication* 26 (1989): 293–303.

37. Atwater, *I Hear You*.

38. J. Sandberg, "Not Communicating with Your Boss? Count Your Blessings," *The Wall Street Journal*, 22 May 2007, B1.

39. P. Sellers, A. Diba, and E. Florian, "Get Over Yourself—Your Ego Is Out Of Control. You're Screwing Up Your Career," *Fortune*, 30 April 2001, 76.

40. H. H. Meyer, "A Solution to the Performance Appraisal Feedback Enigma," *Academy of Management Executive* 5, no. 1 (1991): 68–76.

41. C. Hymowitz, "Executives Who Build Truth-Telling Cultures Learn Fast What Works," *The Wall Street Journal*, 12 June 2006, B1.

42. C. Hymowitz, "Diebold's New Chief Shows How to Lead after a Sudden Rise," *The Wall Street Journal*, 8 May 2006, B1.

43. R. King, "No Rest for the Wiki," *Bloomberg Business Week*, April 26, 2010, http://www.businessweek.com/technology/content/mar2007/tc20070312_740461.htm.

44. A. Lashinsky, "Lights! Camera! Cue the CEO!" *Fortune*, 21 August 2006, 27.

45. E. Florian and W. Henderson, "Class of '01: Ellen Florian Spotlights Four

Retirees—Their Legacies, Their Plans, and What They've Learned That Can Help You Work Better," *Fortune*, 13 August 2001, 185.

46. K. Maher, "Global Companies Face Reality of Instituting Ethics Programs," *The Wall Street Journal*, 9 November 2004, B8.

47. M. Parker, "Corporate Culture: Emergence and Transformation," *Canadian Business Online*, January 18, 2007, http://www.canadianbusiness.com/columnists/marty_parker/article.jsp?content=20070606_125735_5612.

48. D. Kirkpatrick and D. Roth, "Why There's No Escaping the Blog," *Fortune (Europe)*, 24 January 2005, 64.

49. W. Ross, Jr., "What Every Human Resource Manager Should Know about Web Logs," *SAM Advanced Management Journal*, 1 July 2005, 4.

50. C. Martin and N. Bennett, "What to Do About Online Attacks: Step No. 1: Stop ignoring them," *The Wall Street Journal*, 10 March 2008, R6.

Chapter 16

1. R. Leifer and P. K. Mills, "An Information Processing Approach for Deciding upon Control Strategies and Reducing Control Loss in Emerging Organizations," *Journal of Management* 22 (1996): 113–137.

2. Canadian Food Inspection Agency, "HEALTH HAZARD ALERT: CERTAIN READY-TO-EAT DELI MEAT PRODUCTS PRODUCED AT ESTABLISHMENT 97B MAY CONTAIN LISTERIA MONO-CYTOGENES," August 19, 2009, http://www.inspection.gc.ca/english/corpaffr/recarapp/2008/20080819e.shtml; CTV News, "Complete List of Recalled Meats," September 6, 2008, http://www.ctv.ca/servlet/ArticleNews/story/CTVNews/20080821/maple_leaf_list_080821/20080821; CanWest News Service. "Deadly Listeriosis Outbreak Traced to Maple Leaf Meats," August 23, 2008, http://www.canada.com/cityguides/toronto/info/story.html?id=222b628d-8dc8-46af-b1dd-540; CBC News, "Meat Recall Could Cost Millions More," August 28, 2008, http://www.cbc.ca/canada/toronto/story/2008/08/25/maple-leaf-listeria.html#ixzz0sDiXnjOl864db14b8; "Deadly Outbreak Officially Tied to Maple Leaf Meats," *The Globe and Mail*, August 28, 2008, http://www.theglobeandmail.com/news/national/article705776.ece; N. Baer and L. Liepins, "Deadly Listeriosis Outbreak Traced to Maple Leaf Meats," *National Post*, August 24, 2008, http://www.nationalpost.com/news/Deadly+listeriosis+outbreak+traced+Maple+Leaf+meats/742696/story.html#ixzz0sDkVdfgl; CTV News, "Maple Leaf Foods Plant Linked to Listeria Outbreak,"

August 23, 2008, http://www.ctv.ca/
CTVNews/TopStories/20080823/
recall_listeria_080823.

3. http://www.scc.ca/en/about-scc.

4. J. W. Miller, "Private Food Standards
Gain Favor," *The Wall Street Journal*,
11 March 2008, B1; "GlobalGap
Passes Producer Landmark," May
27, 2010, http://www.fruitnet.com/
content.aspx?ttid=14&cid=6819;
CBC News, "BC Hot House Changes
Labeling on Mexican Produce," April
23, 2008, http://www.cbc.ca/canada/
british-columbia/story/2008/04/23/
bc-bchothouse-mexican-brand
.html#ixzz0sHTUArJ0.

5. B. Whitaker, "Yes, There Is a Job That
Pays You to Shop," *The New York
Times*, 13 March 2005, 8.

6. M. Foley, "Blame Vista Delay on
Quality?" *eWeek*, 3 April 2006, 33.

7. N. Wiener, *Cybernetics; Or Control
and Communication in the Animal and
the Machine* (New York: Wiley, 1948).

8. http://www.tc.gc.ca/eng/civilaviation/
standards/maintenance-aarpb-menu-
2534.htm.

9. J. Dalrymple and M. Honan, "Nike
to Add iPod Integration," *MacWorld*,
August 2006, 22-23.

10. R. Guth, "The To-Do List: Make Software More Reliable," *The Wall Street
Journal*, 17 November 2003, R4.

11. Leifer and Mills, "An Information Processing Approach for Deciding upon
Control Strategies and Reducing Control Loss in Emerging Organizations."

12. V. E. Knight, "Digital Prescriptions
Gain Favor," *The Wall Street Journal*,
17 June 2008, B2; "Newfoundland and
Labrador Pharmacy Network to Limit
Drug Errors, Abuse," http://news.sym-
patico.cbc.ca/local/nfld/nl_pharmacy_
network_to_limit_drug_errors_abuse/
ac0ee04c.

13. S. Greenhouse, "Workers Assail Night
Lock-Ins by Wal-Mart," *The New York
Times*, 18 January 2004, 1.

14. Ibid.

15. Ibid.

16. S. Shellenbarger, "Is the Awful Behavior
of Some Bad Bosses Rooted in Their
Past?" *The Wall Street Journal*, 17
May 2000, B1.

17. M. Weber, *The Protestant Ethic and
the Spirit of Capitalism* (New York:
Scribner's, 1958).

18. CBC News, "GPS Bracelets Lead to
Arrests of 2 Chronic Car Thieves,"
December 22, 2009, http://www.cbc
.ca/canada/manitoba/story/2009/12/22/
mb-police-chase-winnipeg
.html#ixzz0sHg4DPzz.

19. J. McFarland, "Hospitals Raise
Caution over Uniform Pay-for-
Performance Rules," *The Globe
and Mail*, April 29, 2010, http://
www.theglobeandmail.com/news/
national/hospitals-raise-caution-over-
uniform-pay-for-performance-rules/
article1529878.

20. A. DeFelice, "A Century of Customer
Love: Nordstrom Is the Gold Standard
for Customer Service Excellence,"
CRM Magazine, 1 June 2005, 42;
http://forums.redflagdeals.com/
nordstrom-now-ships-canada-812028;
http://shop.nordstrom.com/?origin=tab-
logo; http://shop.nordstrom.com/c/
6025407/...6pbo%3D6008488.

21. R. T. Pascale, "Nordstrom: Respond
to Unreasonable Customer Requests!,"
Planning Review 2 (May–June 1994):
17.

22. Ibid.

23. Ibid.

24. J. R. Barker, "Tightening the Iron Cage:
Concertive Control in Self-Managing
Teams," *Administrative Science Quar-
terly* 38 (1993): 408–437.

25. N. Byrnes, "The Art of Motivation,"
Business Week, 1 May 2006, 56–62;
D. Crofts and R. Delaney, "Nucor
Buys Canada's Harris Steel for $1.07
Billion," *Bloomberg News*, January 3,
2007, http://www.bloomberg.com/apps/
news?pid=newsarchive&sid=atc7t4wqg
N1Q&refer=us.

26. Barker, "Tightening the Iron Cage."

27. C. Manz and H. Sims, "Leading
Workers to Lead Themselves: The
External Leadership of Self-Managed
Work Teams," *Administrative Science
Quarterly* 32 (1987): 106–128.

28. J. Slocum and H. A. Sims, "Typology
for Integrating Technology, Organization and Job Design," *Human Relations* 33 (1980): 193–212.

29. C. C. Manz and H. P. Sims, Jr.,
"Self-Management as a Substitute for
Leadership: A Social Learning Per-
spective," *Academy of Management
Review* 5 (1980): 361–367.

30. C. Manz & C. Neck, *Mastering
Self-Leadership*, 3rd ed. (Upper Saddle
River, NJ: Pearson, Prentice Hall, 2004).

31. R. S. Kaplan & D. P. Norton, "Using
the Balanced Scorecard as a Strategic
Management System," *Harvard Busi-
ness Review* (January–February 1996):
75–85; R. S. Kaplan and D. P. Norton,
"The Balanced Scorecard: Measures
That Drive Performance," *Harvard
Business Review* (January–February
1992): 71–79. P. Niven, "Cascading the
Balanced Scorecard: A Case Study on
Nova Scotia Power, Inc.," http://www
.scribd.com/doc/3489336/Cascading-the-
Balanced-Scorecard-A-Case-Study-on-
Nova-Scotia-Power.

32. J. Meliones, "Saving Money, Saving
Lives," *Harvard Business Review*
(November–December 2000): 57–65.

33. M. H. Stocks and A. Harrell, "The
Impact of an Increase in Accounting
Information Level on the Judgment
Quality of Individuals and Groups,"
Accounting, Organizations & Society,
October–November 1995, 685–700.

34. B. Morris, "Roberto Goizueta and Jack
Welch: The Wealth Builders," *Fortune*,
11 December 1995, 80–94.

35. G. Colvin, "America's Best & Worst
Wealth Creators: The Real Champions
Aren't Always Who You Think. Here's
an Eye-Opening Look at Which Companies Produce and Destroy the Most
Money for Investors—Plus a New Tool
for Spotting Future Winners," *Fortune*,
18 December 2000, 207; "Introducing
the Wealth Added Framework (Relative Wealth Added (RWA) and Wealth
Added Index (WAI)," August 2009,
http://sternstewart.com/rankings/
SSGlobal1000/Introducing%20the%20
Wealth%20Added%20Framework.pdf.

36. E. Varon, "Implementation Is Not for
the Meek," *CIO*, 15 November 2002,
available online at http://www.cio.com/
article/31510/Strategic_Planning_
Implementation_Is_Not_for_the_Meek
[accessed 5 September 2008].

37. "Welcome Complaints," Office of
Consumer and Business Affairs, http://
www.ocba.sa.gov.au/businessadvice/
complaints/03_welcome.html.

38. C. B. Furlong, "12 Rules for Customer
Retention," *Bank Marketing* 5
(January 1993): 14.

39. M. Raphel, "Vanished Customers Are
Valuable Customers," *Art Business
News*, June 2002, 46.

40. C. A. Reeves and D. A. Bednar,
"Defining Quality: Alternatives and
Implications," *Academy of Manage-
ment Review* 19 (1994): 419–445.

41. "Our Achievements," Singapore
Airlines Web site, http://www
.singaporeair.com/saa/en_UK/content/
company_info/news/achievements.jsp.

42. S. Holmes, "Creature Comforts at
30,000 feet," *Business Week*, 18
December 2006, 138.

43. K. Nirmalya, " Strategies to Fight
Low-Cost Rivals," *Harvard Business
Review* 84, no. 12 (2006): 104–112;
World News, March 5, 2010, http://
article.wn.com/view/2010/03/05/
Aldi_groceries_for_moms.

44. D. R. May and B. L. Flannery, "Cut-
ting Waste with Employee Involvement
Teams," *Business Horizons*,
September–October 1995, 28–38.

45. J. Carlton, "To Cut Fuel Bills, Try
High-Tech Help," *The Wall Street
Journal*, 11 March 2008, B3.

46. M. Warner, "Plastic Potion No. 9," *Fast
Company*, September 2008, 88.

47. B. Burlingham, "The Coolest Little
Start-Up in America," *Inc.*, July 2006,
78–85.

48. M. Conlin and P. Raeburn, "Industrial
Evolution: Bill McDonough Has the
Wild Idea He Can Eliminate Waste.
Surprise! Business Is Listening,"
BusinessWeek, 8 April 2002, 70.

49. Ibid.

50. J. Sprovieri, "Environmental Management Affects Manufacturing Bottom
Line," *Assembly*, 1 July 2001, 24.

51. B. Byrne, "EU Says Makers Must
Destroy Their Own Brand End-of-Life
Cars," *Irish Times*, 23 April 2003, 52.

52. S. Power, "Take It Back: Where Do Cars Go When They Die? In Europe, They Have Little Choice," *The Wall Street Journal*, 17 April 2006, R6.

53. J. Szekely and G. Trapaga, "From Villain to Hero (Materials Industry's Waste Recovery Efforts)," *Technology Review*, 1 January 1995, 30.

54. "The End of the Road: Schools and Computer Recycling," Intel, http://www.intel.com/education/recycling_computers/recycling.htm.

55. B. Rose, "Where Old Computers Go: While Too Many Are Dumped Illegally, Sr. Center Salvages Thousands," *Press Democrat*, 18 June 2001, D1.

Chapter 17

1. R. Lenzner, "The Reluctant Entrepreneur," *Forbes*, 11 September 1995, 162–166.

2. M. Totty, "Who's Going to Win the Living-Room Wars? The Battle to Control Home Entertainment Is Heating Up," *The Wall Street Journal*, 25 April 2005, R1.

3. P. Grant & A. Schatz, "For Cable Giants, AT&T Deal Is One More Reason to Worry," *The Wall Street Journal*, 7 March 2006, A1.

4. P. Grant, "Cable Firms Woo Business in Fight for Telecom Turf," *Wall Street Journal*, 17 January 2007, A1.

5. R. D. Buzzell and B. T. Gale, *The PIMS Principles: Linking Strategy to Performance* (New York: Free Press, 1987); M. Lambkin, "Order of Entry and Performance in New Markets," *Strategic Management Journal* 9 (1988): 127–140.

6. G. L. Urban, T. Carter, S. Gaskin, and Z. Mucha, "Market Share Rewards to Pioneering Brands: An Empirical Analysis and Strategic Implications," *Management Science* 32 (1986): 645–659.

7. N. Buckley and S. Voyle, "Can Wal-Mart Conquer Markets outside the US?" *Financial Times*, 8 January 2003.

8. M. Garry and S. Mulholland, "Master of Its Supply Chain: To Keep Its Inventory Costs Low and Its Shelves Fully Stocked, Wal-Mart Has Always Invested Extensively—and First—in Technology for the Supply Chain," *Supermarket News*, 2 December 2002, 55.

9. S. Rupley, "A Moveable Mesh," *PC Magazine*, 21 September 2004, 94.

10. L. Tischler, "Tech for Toques," *Fast Company*, 1 May 2006, 68; Squirrel Systems, "Testimonials," 2010, htpp://www.squirrelsystems.com/about-squirrel-systems/TestimonialQuotes.htm.

11. R. Pastore, "Cruise Control," *CIO*, 1 February 2003, 60–66.

12. Ibid.

13. C. Quintanilla and L. Claman, "Acxiom Corporation—Chmn. & Pres. Interview," *CNBC/Dow Jones Business Video*, 21 November 2002.

14. P. Tam, "The Chief Information Officer's Job Isn't What It Used to Be; Just ask Hewlett-Packard's Randy Mott," *The Wall Street Journal*, 16 April 2007, R5.

15. J. N. Hoover, "How eBay Manages Its Data Centers," InformationWeek, 29 February 2008, available online at http://www.informationweek.com/news/internet/showArticle.jhtml?articleID=206901055 [accessed 10 September 2008].

16. S. Mehta, "Behold the Server Farm!" *Fortune*, 7 August 2006, 68.

17. M. Santosus, "Procter & Gamble's Enterprise Content Management (ECM) System," *CIO*, 15 May 2003, available online at http://www.cio.com/article/31920/Procter_Gamble_s_Enterprise_Content_Management_ECM_System [accessed 12 September 2008]; Ulrich Kampffmeyer, "Trends in Records, Document and Enterprise Content Management," Whitepaper. S.E.R. conference, Visegrád, September 28th, 2004.

18. T. Knauss, "Niagara Mohawk Meters to Send Readings by Radio; $100 Million Project Will Eventually Eliminate Need for Door-to-Door Readers," *The Post-Standard Syracuse*, 17 September 2002, A1.

19. S. Lubar, *Infoculture: The Smithsonian Book of Information Age Inventions* (Boston: Houghton, Mifflin, 1993).

20. Ibid.

21. B. Worthen, "Bar Codes on Steroids," *CIO*, 15 December 2002, 53.

22. J. Pachner, (2008) "This Little Yogurt Went to Market . . .," *Globe and Mail Report on Business*, October 31, 2008, htpp://www.theglobeandmail.com/report-on-business/rob-magazine/this-little-yogurt-went. . .

23. M. Stone, "Scanning for Business," *PC Magazine*, 10 May 2005, 117.

24. N. Rubenking, "Hidden Messages," *PC Magazine*, 22 May 2001, 86.

25. A. Carter and D. Beucke, "A Good Neighbor Gets Better," *BusinessWeek*, 20 June 2005, 16.

26. Rubenking, "Hidden Messages."

27. G. Saitz, "Naked Truth—Data Miners, Who Taught Retailers to Stock Beer Near Diapers, Find Hidden Sales Trends, a Science That's Becoming Big Business," *The Star-Ledger*, 1 August 2002, 041.

28. M. Overfelt, "A Better Way to Sell Tickets," *Fortune Small Business*, 1 December 2006, 76. M. Taormino, "Global Sports Buzz," January 17, 2010, http://www.globalsportsbuzz.com/2010/01.

29. B. Saporita, W. Boston, N. Gough, and R. Healy, "Can Wal-Mart Get Any Bigger? (Yes, a Lot Bigger . . . Here's How)," *Time*, 19 January 2003, 38.

30. B. Gottesman and K. Karagiannis, "A False Sense of Security," *PC Magazine*, 22 February 2005, 72.

31. F. J. Derfler, Jr., "Secure Your Network," *PC Magazine*, 27 June 2000, 183–200.

32. "Authentication," Webopedia.com, available online at http://www.webopedia.com/TERM/a/authentication.html [accessed 12 September 2008].

33. "Authorization," Webopedia.com, available online at http://www.webopedia.com/TERM/a/authorization.html [accessed 12 September 2008].

34. L. Seltzer, "Password Crackers," *PC Magazine*, 12 February 2002, 68.

35. B. Grimes, "Biometric Security," *PC Magazine*, 22 April 2003, 74.

36. W. Gross and M. Kisluk, "Security in Business: A Special Report" htpp://v1.theglobeandmail.com/partners/free/srsecurity/article_01.html; C. Payette, "Mercantile Mergers Locks and Loads with Drive Crypt," 2009, http://theglobeandmail.com/ervlet/story/RTGAM.20030131.gtcasesJan31?BNStroy/ein. . .; C. Atchison, (2008). "Security: Stop, Thief?" 2008, *Profit Magazine*, October 2008, http://www.canadianbusiness.com/entrepreneur/technology/article.jsp?content=20081001. . .

37. C. Metz, "Total Security," *PC Magazine*, 1 October 2003, 83.

38. J. DeAvila, "Wi-Fi Users, Beware: Hot Spots are Weak Spots," *The Wall Street Journal*, 16 January 2008, D1.

39. J. van den Hoven, "Executive Support Systems & Decision Making," *Journal of Systems Management* 47, no. 8 (March–April 1996): 48.

40. "Business Objects Customers Take Off with Performance Management; Management Dashboards Help Organizations Gain Insight and Optimize Performance," *Business Wire*, 4 April 2005.

41. "Intranet," Webopedia.com, available online at http://www.webopedia.com/TERM/i/intranet.html [accessed 26 August 2001].

42. S. Holz, "Bring Your Intranet Into the 21st Century," *Communication World*, January-February 2008, 14-18.

43. J. Ericson, "The Hillman Group Leverages Consolidated Reporting, Geographic Analysis to Support Its Hardware Manufacturing/Distribution Leadership," *Business Intelligence Review*, 1 March 2007, 12.

44. "Extranet," Webopedia.com, available online at http://www.webopedia.com/TERM/E/extranet.html [accessed 12 September 2008].

45. S. Hamm, D. Welch, W. Zellner, F. Keenan, and F. Engardio, "Down but Hardly Out: Downturn Be Damned, Companies Are Still Anxious to Expand Online," *BusinessWeek*, 26 March 2001, 126.

46. R. Ruggero, "Alaska Cruise Port Info for Vancouver, Canada," 2009, http://cruise-lines-routes.suite101.com/article.cfm/alaska_cruise_port_info_for_vancouver...

47. Hamm, Welch, Zellner, Keenan, and Engardio, "Down but Hardly Out."
48. K. C. Laudon and J. P. Laudon, *Management Information Systems: Organization and Technology* (Upper Saddle River, NJ: Prentice Hall, 1996).
49. J. Borzo, "Software for Symptoms," *The Wall Street Journal*, 23 May 2005, R10.
50. Ibid.
51. R. Hernandez, "American Express Authorizer's Assistant," *Business Rules Journal*, available online at http://www.bizrules.com/page/art_amexaa.htm [accessed 12 September 2008].

Chapter 18

1. 1999 Initial Public Offering Prospectus, http://www.westjet.com/pdf/investorMedia/financialReports/062899prospectus.pdf.
2. InFlight Experience," http://www.westjet.com/guest/en/experience/inflightExperience/buyOnBoard.shtml.
3. C. Sorensen, "WestJet's Big Plans to Conquer Air Canada and Then the World," *Maclean's*, May 27, 2010, http://www2.macleans.ca/2010/05/27/ready-for-takeoff/2.
4. WestJet 2008 Annual Report, http://www.westjet.com/pdf/investorMedia/financialReports/WestJet2008AR.pdf.
5. M. W. Nuckolls, "The Best in Drive-Thru '07: Building a Better Drive-Thru," QSR Magazine.com, http://www.qsrmagazine.com/reports/drive-thru_time_study.
6. M. Richtel, "The Long-Distance Journey of a Fast-Food Order," *The New York Times*, 11 April 2006, http://www.nytimes.com/2006/04/11/technology/11fast.html?ei=5090&en=fba08e17788e24c9&ex=1302408000&pagewanted=all.
7. "Solving (Almost) Canada's Productivity Puzzle," CBC News—Money, August 11, 2009, http://www.cbc.ca/money/story/2009/08/10/f-productivity-statistics-canada-study.html.
8. TD Economics Topic Paper, "Canada's Productivity Challenge," October 5, 2005, http://www.td.com/economics/topic/el1005_prod.pdf.
9. "Solving (Almost) Canada's Productivity Puzzle."
10. Statistics Canada, The Daily, "Study: Update on Long-Term Trends in Canada's Productivity Performance," August 4, 2009, http://www.statcan.gc.ca/daily-quotidien/090804/dq090804a-eng.htm.
11. "Solving (Almost) Canada's Productivity Puzzle."
12. D. Shaw, "Productivity: Its Increasing Influence over Canadians' Standard of Living and Quality of Life Industry," Library of Parliament, Infrastructure and Resources Division, November 5, 2009, p. 4, http://www2.parl.gc.ca/Content/LOP/ResearchPublications/prb0315-e.pdf.

13. B. Koenig, "Toyota and Chrysler Lead in Auto-Plant Efficiency," Bloomberg, June 5, 2008, http://www.bloomberg.com/apps/news?sid=aWdVR3oRciow&pid=newsarchive.
14. J. Neff, "Chrysler Ties Toyota for Most Productive Plants in North America," June 5, 2008, http://www.autoblog.com/2008/06/05/chrysler-ties-toyota-for-most-efficient-manufacturer-in-north-am.
15. "Multifactor Productivity," Bureau of Labor Satistics, http://stats.bls.gov/bls/productivity.htm.
16. J. Baldwin and W. Gu, "The Canadian Productivity Review: Productivity Performance in Canada, 1961 to 2008: An Update on Long-term Trends," August 2009, http://www.statcan.gc.ca/pub/15-206-x/15-206-x2009025-eng.pdf.
17. M. Rechtin "Porsche, Hyundai Score Big Gains in J.D. Power Quality Survey," *Auto Week*, 7 June 2006, http://www.autoweek.com/apps/pbcs.dll/article?AID=/20060608/FREE/60607007/1041&te.
18. "Basic Concepts," American Society for Quality http://www.asq.org/glossary/q.html.
19. R. E. Markland, S. K. Vickery, and R. A. Davis, "Managing Quality" (Chapter 7), *Operations Management: Concepts in Manufacturing and Services* (Cincinnati, OH: South-Western College Publishing, 1998).
20. http://www.revaglobal.com/HomeVideos.aspx?id=divHome.
21. G. Rao, "Computers to Be at the Heart of a Car," *Economic Times*, 12 February 2004.
22. L. L. Berry and A. Parasuraman, *Marketing Services* (New York: Free Press, 1991).
23. "FAQs—General,"International Organization for Standardization, http://www.iso.org/iso/en/faqs/faq-general.html.
24. "ISO 9000 and ISO 14000," International Organization for Standardization, http://www.iso.org/iso/iso_catalogue/management_standards/iso_9000_iso_14000.htm.
25. J. Briscoe, S. Fawcett, and R. Todd, "The Implementation and Impact of ISO 9000 among Small Manufacturing Enterprises," *Journal of Small Business Management* 43 (1 July 2005): 309.
26. R. Henkoff, "The Not New Seal of Quality (ISO 9000 Standard of Quality Management)," *Fortune*, 28 June 1993, 116.
27. "Frequently Asked Questions about the Malcolm Baldrige National Quality Award," National Institute of Standards & Technology, http://www.nist.gov/public_affairs/factsheet/baldfaqs.htm.
28. "Baldrige Award Application Forms," National Institute of Standards & Technology, http://www.baldrige.nist.gov/PDF_files/2008_Award_Application_Forms.pdf.

29. "Criteria for Performance Excellence," Baldrige National Quality Program 2008, http://www.quality.nist.gov/PDF_files/2008_Business_Criteria.pdf.
30. Ibid.
31. Ibid.
32. "NIST Stock Studies Show Quality Pays (Baldrige National Quality Award)," National Institute of Standards & Technology, http://www.quality.nist.gov/Stock_Studies.htm.
33. J. W. Dean, Jr., and J. Evans, *Total Quality: Management, Organization, and Strategy* (St. Paul, MN: West Publishing Co., 1994).
34. J. W. Dean, Jr., and D. E. Bowen, "Management Theory and Total Quality: Improving Research and Practice through Theory Development," *Academy of Management Review* 19 (1994): 392–418.
35. R. Allen and R. Kilmann, "Aligning Reward Practices in Support of Total Quality Management," *Business Horizons*, 1 May 2001, 77.
36. R. Carter, "Best Practices: Freudenberg-NOK/Cleveland, GA: Continuous Kaizens," *Industrial Maintenance & Plant Operations*, 1 June 2004, 10.
37. Ibid.
38. R. Levering, M. Moskowitz, L. Munoz, and P. Hjelt, "The 100 Best Companies to Work for," *Fortune*, 4 February 2002, 72.
39. R. Hallowell, L. A. Schlesinger, and J. Zornitsky, "Internal Service Quality, Customer and Job Satisfaction: Link-ages and Implications for Management," *Human Resource Planning* 19 (1996): 20–31; J. L. Heskett, T. O. Jones, G. W. Loveman, W. E. Sasser, Jr., and L. A. Schlesinger, "Putting the Service-Profit Chain to Work," *Harvard Business Review* (March-April 1994): 164–174.
40. A. Wahl, "Best Workplaces 2006: On the Money—Vancity," *Canadian Business Online*, April 10, 2006, http://www.canadianbusiness.com/managing/strategy/article.jsp?content=20060410_75926_75926.
41. R. Eder, "Customer-Easy Doesn't Come Easy," *Drug Store News*, 21 October 2002, 52.
42. L. L. Berry and A. Parasuraman, "Listening to the Customer—The Concept of a Service-Quality Information System," *Sloan Management Review* 38, no. 3 (spring 1997): 65; C. W. L. Hart, J. L. Heskett, and W. E. Sasser, Jr., "The Profitable Art of Service Recovery," *Harvard Business Review* (July-August 1990): 148–156.
43. Vancity Credit Union, "2002–2003 Accountability Report," https://www.vancity.com/lang/fr/AboutUs/OurBusiness/OurReports/AccountabilityReport/0203AccountabilityReport/CommitmentThree.

44. D. E. Bowen and E. E. Lawler III, "The Empowerment of Service Workers: What, Why, How, and When," *Sloan Management Review* 33 (Spring 1992): 31–39; D. E. Bowen and E. E. Lawler III, "Empowering Service Employees," *Sloan Management Review* 36 (Summer 1995): 73–84.

45. Bowen and Lawler III, "The Empowerment of Service Workers: What, Why, How, and When."

46. Vancity Credit Union, "2002–2003 Accountability Report."

47. G. V. Frazier and M. T. Spiggs, "Achieving Competitive Advantage through Group Technology," *Business Horizons* 39 (1996): 83–88.

48. "The Top 100 Beverage Companies: The List," *Beverage Industry*, July 2001, 30.

49. E. Gruber, "Cutting Time," *Modern Machine Shop*, March 2001, 102.

50. S. Silke Carty, "Chrysler Wrestles with High Levels of Inventory as Unsold Vehicles Sit on Lots," *USA Today*, 2 November 2006, http://www.usatoday.com/money/autos/2006-11-02-chrysler-high-inventory_x.htm?loc=interstitialskip; J. D. Stoll, "Chrysler Maintains Plan to Cut Production as Inventory Rises," *The Wall Street Journal*, 24 August 2006, http://www.wsj.com.

51. A. Wilson, "No More Push: How Detroit Stopped Overproducing," *Automotive News*, February 8, 2010, http://www.autonews.com/apps/pbcs.dll/article?AID=/20100208/RETAIL03/302089951.

52. N. Martinez, "Automakers Inventory Levels Kept at Bay Despite Extremely Dismal Sales," *Automotive News*, October 20, 2008, http://wot.motortrend.com/6301021/auto-news/automakers-inventory-levels-kept-at-bay-despite-extremely-dismal-sales/index.html.

53. N. Wingfield, "Out of Tune: iPod Shortage Rocks Apple," *The Wall Street Journal*, 16 December 2004, B1.

54. Ibid.

55. D. Drickhamer, "Reality Check," *Industry Week*, November 2001, 29.

56. D. Drickhamer, "Zeroing In on World-Class," *Industry Week*, November 2001, 36.

57. J. Zeiler, "The Need for Speed," *Operations & Fulfillment*, 1 April 2004, 38.

58. "About EFR," *Efficient Foodservice Response*, http://www.efr-central.com/aboutefr.html.

59. J. R. Henry, "Minimized Setup Will Make Your Packaging Line S.M.I.L.E.," *Packaging Technology & Engineering*, 1 February 1998, 24.

60. J. Donoghue, "The Future Is Now," *Air Transport World*, 1 April 2001, 78.

61. N. Shirouzu, "Why Toyota Wins Such High Marks on Quality Surveys," *The Wall Street Journal*, 15 March 2001, A1.

62. Ibid.

63. G. Gruman, "Supply on Demand; Manufacturers Need to Know What's Selling before They Can Produce and Deliver Their Wares in the Right Quantities," *Info World*, 18 April 2005.

Note: Entries in bold indicate key terms in the text.

LEARNING OUTCOMES

Review 1: Management Is . . .

> Good management is working through others to accomplish tasks that help fulfill organizational objectives as efficiently as possible.

Review 2: Management Functions

> Henri Fayol's classic management functions are known today as planning, organizing, leading, and controlling. Planning is determining organizational goals and a means for achieving them. Organizing is deciding where decisions will be made, who will do what jobs and tasks, and who will work for whom. Leading is inspiring and motivating workers to work hard to achieve organizational goals. Controlling is monitoring progress toward goal achievement and taking corrective action when needed. Studies show that performing the management functions well leads to better managerial performance.

Review 3: Kinds of Managers

> There are four different kinds of managers. Top managers are responsible for creating a context for change, developing attitudes of commitment and ownership, creating a positive organizational culture through words and actions, and monitoring their company's business environments. Middle managers are responsible for planning and allocating resources, coordinating and linking groups and departments, monitoring and managing the performance of subunits and managers, and implementing the changes or strategies generated by top managers. First-line managers are responsible for managing the performance of nonmanagerial employees, teaching direct reports how to do their jobs, and making detailed schedules and operating plans based on middle management's intermediate-range plans. Team leaders are responsible for facilitating team performance, fostering good relationships among team members, and managing external relationships.

Review 4: Managerial Roles

> Managers perform interpersonal, informational, and decisional roles in their jobs. In fulfilling the interpersonal role, managers act as figureheads by performing ceremonial duties, as leaders by motivating and encouraging workers, and as liaisons by dealing with people outside their units. In performing their informational role, managers act as monitors by scanning their environment for information, as disseminators by sharing information with others in the company, and as spokespeople by sharing information with people outside their departments or companies. In fulfilling decisional roles, managers act as entrepreneurs by adapting their units to incremental change, as disturbance handlers by responding to larger problems that demand immediate action, as resource allocators by deciding resource recipients and amounts, and as negotiators by bargaining with others about schedules, projects, goals, outcomes, and resources.

KEY TERMS

Management getting work done through others

Efficiency getting work done with a minimum of effort, expense, or waste

Effectiveness accomplishing tasks that help fulfill organizational objectives

Planning (management functions) determining organizational goals and a means for achieving them

Organizing deciding where decisions will be made, who will do what jobs and tasks, and who will work for whom

Leading inspiring and motivating workers to work hard to achieve organizational goals

Controlling monitoring progress toward goal achievement and taking corrective action when needed

Top managers executives responsible for the overall direction of the organization

Middle managers managers responsible for setting objectives consistent with top management's goals and for planning and implementing subunit strategies for achieving these objectives

First-line managers managers who train and supervise the performance of nonmanagerial employees who are directly responsible for producing the company's products or services

Team leaders managers responsible for facilitating team activities toward accomplishing a goal

Figurehead role the interpersonal role managers play when they perform ceremonial duties

Leader role the interpersonal role managers play when they motivate and encourage workers to accomplish organizational objectives

Liaison role the interpersonal role managers play when they deal with people outside their units

Monitor role the informational role managers play when they scan their environment for information

Disseminator role the informational role managers play when they share information with others in their departments or companies

Spokesperson role the informational role managers play when they share information with people outside their departments or companies

Entrepreneur role the decisional role managers play when they adapt themselves, their subordinates, and their units to change

Disturbance handler role the decisional role managers play when they respond to severe problems that demand immediate action

Resource allocator role the decisional role managers play when they decide who gets what resources

Negotiator role the decisional role managers play when they negotiate schedules, projects, goals, outcomes, resources, and employee raises

Technical skills the specialized procedures, techniques, and knowledge required to get the job done

Human skills the ability to work well with others

Conceptual skills the ability to see the organization as a whole, understand how the different parts affect each other, and recognize how the company fits into or is affected by its environment

Motivation to manage an assessment of how enthusiastic employees are about managing the work of others

How to Use the Card:

1. Look over the card to preview the new concepts you'll be introduced to in the chapter.

2. Read the chapter to fully understand the material.

3. Go to class (and pay attention).

4. Review the card one more time to make sure you've registered the key concepts.

5. Don't forget, this card is only one of many MGMT learning tools available to help you succeed in your management course.

Review 5: What Companies Look for in Managers

> Companies do not want one-dimensional managers. They want managers with a balance of skills. Managers need the knowledge and abilities to get the job done (technical skills), must be able to work effectively in groups and be good listeners and communicators (human skills), must be able to assess the relationships between the different parts of the company and the external environment and position their companies for success (conceptual skills), and should want to assume positions of leadership and power (motivation to manage). Technical skills are most important for lower-level managers, human skills are equally important at all levels of management, and conceptual skills and motivation to manage increase in importance as managers rise through the managerial ranks.

Review 6: Mistakes Managers Make

> Another way to understand what it takes to be a manager is to look at the top mistakes managers make. Five of the most important mistakes made by managers are being abrasive and intimidating; being cold, aloof, or arrogant; betraying trust; being overly ambitious; and failing to deal with specific performance problems of the business.

Review 7: The Transition to Management: The First Year

> Managers often begin their jobs by using more formal authority and less people management skill. However, most managers find that being a manager has little to do with "bossing" their subordinates. After six months on the job, the managers were surprised at the fast pace and heavy workload and that "helping" their subordinates was viewed as interference. After a year on the job, most of the managers had come to think of themselves not as doers but as managers who get things done through others. And, because they finally realized that people management was the most important part of their job, most of them had abandoned their authoritarian approach for one based on communication, listening, and positive reinforcement.

Review 8: Competitive Advantage through People

> Why does management matter? Well-managed companies are competitive because their workforces are smarter, better trained, more motivated, and more committed. Furthermore, companies that practise good management consistently have greater sales revenues, profits, and stock market performance than companies that don't. Finally, good management matters because good management leads to satisfied employees who, in turn, provide better service to customers. Because employees tend to treat customers the same way that their managers treat them, good management can improve customer satisfaction.

icanmgmt.com has great
review tools: flashcards, quizzes, games,
audio summaries, and self-assessments.

REVIEW card/

CHAPTER 2

LEARNING OUTCOMES

Review 1: The Origins of Management

> Management as a field of study is just 125 years old, but management ideas and practices have actually been used since 6000 B.C.E. From the ancient Sumerians to sixteenth-century Europe, there are historical antecedents for each of the functions of management discussed in this textbook: planning, organizing, leading, and controlling. However, there was no compelling need for managers until systematic changes in the nature of work and organizations occurred during the last two centuries. As work shifted from families to factories; from skilled labourers to specialized, unskilled labourers; from small, self-organized groups to large factories employing thousands under one roof; and from unique, small batches of production to large standardized mass production; managers were needed to impose order and structure, to motivate and direct large groups of workers, and to plan and make decisions that optimized overall company performance by effectively coordinating the different parts of organizational systems.

Review 2: Scientific Management

> Scientific management involved studying and testing different work methods to identify the best, most efficient ways to complete a job. According to Frederick W. Taylor, the father of scientific management, managers should follow four scientific management principles. First, study each element of work to determine the one best way to do it. Second, scientifically select, train, teach, and develop workers to reach their full potential. Third, cooperate with employees to ensure that the scientific principles are implemented. Fourth, divide the work and the responsibility equally between management and workers. Above all, Taylor felt these principles could be used to align managers and employees by determining a fair day's work, what an average worker could produce at a reasonable pace, and a fair day's pay (what management should pay workers for that effort). Taylor felt that incentives were one of the best ways to align management and employees.

Frank and Lillian Gilbreth are best known for their use of motion studies to simplify work. Whereas Taylor used time study to determine a fair day's work based on how long it took a "first-class man" to complete each part of his job, Frank Gilbreth used film cameras and micro chronometers to conduct motion studies to improve efficiency by eliminating unnecessary or repetitive motions. Henry Gantt is best known for the Gantt chart, which graphically indicates when a series of tasks must be completed to perform a job or project, but he also developed ideas regarding pay-for-performance plans (where workers were rewarded for producing more but were not punished if they didn't) and worker training (all workers should be trained and their managers should be rewarded for training them).

Review 3: Bureaucratic and Administrative Management

> Today, we associate bureaucracy with inefficiency and red tape. Yet, German sociologist Max Weber thought that bureaucracy—that is, running organizations on the basis of knowledge, fairness, and logical rules and procedures—would accomplish organizational goals much more efficiently than monarchies and patriarchies, where decisions were based on personal or family connections, personal gain, and arbitrary decision making. Bureaucracies are characterized by seven elements: qualification-based hiring; merit-based promotion; chain of command; division of labour; impartial application of rules and procedures; recording rules, procedures, and decisions in writing; and separating managers from owners. Nonetheless, bureaucracies are often inefficient and can be highly resistant to change.

The Frenchman Henri Fayol, whose ideas were shaped by his twenty-plus years of experience as a CEO, is best known for developing five management functions (planning, organizing,

KEY TERMS

Scientific management thoroughly studying and testing different work methods to identify the best, most efficient way to complete a job

Soldiering when workers deliberately slow their pace or restrict their work outputs

Motion study breaking each task or job into its separate motions and then eliminating those that are unnecessary or repetitive

Time study timing how long it takes good workers to complete each part of their jobs

Gantt chart a graphic chart that shows which tasks must be completed at which times in order to complete a project or task

Bureaucracy the exercise of control on the basis of knowledge, expertise, or experience

Integrative conflict resolution an approach to dealing with conflict in which both parties deal with the conflict by indicating their preferences and then working together to find an alternative that meets the needs of both

Organization a system of consciously coordinated activities or forces created by two or more people

System a set of interrelated elements or parts that function as a whole

Subsystems smaller systems that operate within the context of a larger system

Synergy when two or more subsystems working together can produce more than they can working apart

Closed systems systems that can sustain themselves without interacting with their environments

Open systems systems that can sustain themselves only by interacting with their environments, on which they depend for their survival

Contingency approach holds that there are no universal management theories and that the most effective management theory or idea depends on the kinds of problems or situations that managers are facing at a particular time and place

coordinating, commanding, and controlling) and fourteen principles of management (division of work, authority and responsibility, discipline, unity of command, unity of direction, subordination of individual interests to the general interest, remuneration, centralization, scalar chain, order, equity, stability of tenure of personnel, initiative, and *esprit de corps*). He is also known for his belief that management could and should be taught to others.

Review 4: Human Relations Management

> Unlike most people who view conflict as bad, Mary Parker Follett believed that it should be embraced rather than avoided. Of the three ways of dealing with conflict—domination, compromise, and integration— she argued that the latter was the best because it focuses on developing creative methods for meeting conflicting parties' needs.

Elton Mayo is best known for his role in the Hawthorne Studies at the Western Electric Company. In the first stage of the Hawthorne Studies, production went up because the increased attention paid to the workers in the study and their development into a cohesive work group led to significantly higher levels of job satisfaction and productivity. In the second stage, productivity dropped because the workers had already developed strong negative norms. The Hawthorne Studies demonstrated that workers' feelings and attitudes affected their work, that financial incentives weren't necessarily the most important motivator for workers, and that group norms and behaviour play a critical role in behaviour at work.

Chester Barnard emphasized the critical importance of willing cooperation in organizations and said that managers could gain workers' willing cooperation through three executive functions: securing essential services from individuals (through material, nonmaterial, and associational incentives), unifying the people in the organization with a clear purpose, and providing a system of communication. Barnard maintains that it is better to induce cooperation through incentives, clearly formulated organizational objectives, and effective communication throughout the organization than to impose it using managerial authority.

Review 5: Operations, Information, Systems, and Contingency Management

> Operations management uses a quantitative or mathematical approach to find ways to increase productivity, improve quality, and manage or reduce costly inventories. The manufacture of standardized, interchangeable parts, the graphical and computerized design of parts, and the accidental discovery of just-in-time management were some of the most important historical events in operations management.

Throughout history, organizations have pushed for and quickly adopted new information technologies that reduce the cost or increase the speed with which they can acquire, store, retrieve, or communicate information. Historically, some of the most important technologies that have revolutionized information management were the creation of paper and the printing press in the fourteenth and fifteenth centuries, the manual typewriter in 1850, cash registers in 1879, the telephone in the 1880s, time clocks in the 1890s, the personal computer in the 1980s, and the Internet in the 1990s.

A system is a set of interrelated elements or parts that function as a whole. Organizational systems obtain inputs from both general and specific environments. Managers and workers then use their management knowledge and manufacturing techniques to transform those inputs into outputs which, in turn, provide feedback to the organization. Organizational systems must also address the issues of synergy, open *versus* closed systems, and entropy.

Finally, the contingency approach to management clearly states that there are no universal management theories. The most effective management theory or idea depends on the kinds of problems or situations that managers or organizations are facing at a particular time. This means that management is much harder than it looks.

LEARNING OUTCOMES

Review 1: Changing Environments

> Environmental change, complexity, and resource scarcity are the basic components of external environments. Environmental change is the rate at which conditions or events affect change in a business. Environmental complexity is the number and intensity of external factors in an external environment. Resource scarcity is the scarcity or abundance of resources available in the external environment. As rates of environmental change increases, as the environment becomes more complex, and as resources become more scarce, managers become less confident that they can understand, predict, and effectively react to the trends affecting their businesses. According to punctuated equilibrium theory, companies experience periods of stability followed by short periods of dynamic, fundamental change, followed by a return to periods of stability.

Review 2: General Environment

> The general environment consists of events and trends that affect all organizations. Because the economy influences basic business decisions, managers often use economic statistics and business confidence indices to predict future economic activity. Changes in technology, which transforms inputs into outputs, can be a benefit or a threat to a business. Sociocultural trends such as changing demographic characteristics affect how companies run their businesses. Similarly, sociocultural changes in behaviour, attitudes, and beliefs affect the demand for a business's products and services. Court decisions and new federal and provincial laws have imposed much greater political/legal responsibility on companies. The best way to manage legal responsibilities is to educate managers and employees about laws and regulations as well as potential lawsuits that could affect a business.

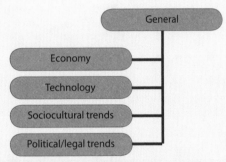

Review 3: Specific Environment

> The specific environment is made up of the five components shown here. Companies can monitor customers' needs by identifying customer problems after they occur or by anticipating problems before they occur. Because they tend to focus on well-known competitors, managers often underestimate their competition or do a poor job of identifying future competitors. Suppliers and buyers are very dependent on one another, and that dependence sometimes leads to opportunistic behaviour, in which one benefits at the expense of the other. Regulatory agencies affect businesses by creating rules and then enforcing them. Advocacy groups cannot regulate organizations' practices. Nevertheless, through public communications, media advocacy, and product boycotts, they try to convince companies to change their practices.

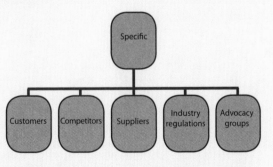

KEY TERMS

External environments all events outside a company that have the potential to influence or affect it

Environmental change the rate at which a company's general and specific environments change

Stable environment an environment in which the rate of change is slow

Dynamic environment an environment in which the rate of change is fast

Punctuated equilibrium theory a theory according to which companies go through long, simple periods of stability (equilibrium), followed by short periods of dynamic, fundamental change (revolution), and ending with a return to stability (new equilibrium)

Environmental complexity the number of external factors in the environment that affect organizations

Simple environment an environment with few environmental factors

Complex environment an environment with many environmental factors

Resource scarcity the abundance or shortage of critical organizational resources in an organization's external environment

Uncertainty extent to which managers can understand or predict which environmental changes and trends will affect their businesses

General environment the economic, technological, sociocultural, and political trends that indirectly affect all organizations

Specific environment the customers, competitors, suppliers, industry regulations, and advocacy groups that are unique to an industry and directly affect how a company does business

Business confidence indices indices that show managers' level of confidence about future business growth

Technology the knowledge, tools, and techniques used to transform input into output

Competitors companies in the same industry that sell similar products or services to customers

Competitive analysis a process for monitoring the competition that involves identifying competition, anticipating their moves, and determining their strengths and weaknesses

Suppliers companies that provide material, human, financial, and informational resources to other companies

Supplier dependence the degree to which a company relies on a supplier because of the importance of the supplier's product to the company and the difficulty of finding other sources for that product

Buyer dependence the degree to which a supplier relies on a buyer because of the importance of that buyer to the supplier and the difficulty of finding other buyers for its products

Opportunistic behaviour a transaction in which one party in the relationship benefits at the expense of the other

Relationship behaviour mutually beneficial, long-term exchanges between buyers and suppliers

Industry regulation regulations and rules that govern the business practices and procedures of specific industries, businesses, and professions

Advocacy groups groups of concerned citizens who band together to try to influence the business practices of specific industries, businesses, and professions

Public communications an advocacy group tactic that relies on voluntary participation by the news media and the advertising industry to get the advocacy group's message out

Media advocacy an advocacy group tactic that involves framing issues as public issues; exposing questionable, exploitative, or unethical practices; and forcing media coverage by buying media time or creating controversy that is likely to receive extensive news coverage

Product boycott an advocacy group tactic that involves protesting a company's actions by convincing consumers not to purchase its product or service

Environmental scanning searching the environment for important events or issues that might affect an organization

Cognitive maps graphic depictions of how managers believe environmental factors relate to possible organizational actions

Internal environment the events and trends inside an organization that affect management, employees, and organizational culture

Organizational culture the values, beliefs, and attitudes shared by members of the organization

Organizational stories stories told by members to make sense of events and changes in an organization and to emphasize culturally consistent assumptions, decisions, and actions

Organizational heroes people celebrated for their qualities and achievements within an organization

Company vision a business's purpose or reason for existing

Consistent organizational culture when a company actively defines and teaches organizational values, beliefs, and attitudes

Review 4: Making Sense of Changing Environments

> Managers use a three-step process to make sense of external environments: environmental scanning, interpreting information, and acting on it. Managers scan their environments based on their organizational strategies, their need for up-to-date information, and their need to reduce uncertainty. When managers identify environmental events as threats, they take steps to protect the company from harm. When managers identify environmental events as opportunities, they formulate alternatives for taking advantage of them to improve company performance. Using cognitive maps can help managers visually summarize the relationships between environmental factors and the actions they might take to deal with them.

Review 5: Organizational Cultures: Creation, Success, and Change

> Organizational culture is the set of key values, beliefs, and attitudes shared by members of an organization. Organizational cultures are often created by company founders and then sustained through telling organizational stories and celebrating organizational heroes. Adaptable cultures that promote employee involvement, make clear the organization's strategic purpose and direction, and actively define and teach organizational values and beliefs can help companies achieve higher sales growth, return on assets, profits, quality, and employee satisfaction. Organizational cultures exist on three levels: the surface level, where cultural artifacts and behaviours can be observed; just below the surface, where values and beliefs are expressed; and deep below the surface, where unconsciously held assumptions and beliefs exist. Managers can begin to change company cultures by focusing on the top two levels.

LEARNING OUTCOMES

Review 1: Workplace Deviance

> Ethics is the set of moral principles or values that define right and wrong. Workplace deviance is behaviour that violates important organizational norms about right and wrong and harms the organization or its workers. There are four different types of workplace deviance. Production deviance and property deviance harm the company, whereas political deviance and personal aggression harm individuals within the company.

Review 2: North American Ethics Guidelines and Legislation

> At the present time there is no national ethics legislation in Canada; however, an International Code of Ethics was released in 1997 to act as a guideline for Canadian businesses. Under the U.S. Sentencing Commission Guidelines, companies can be prosecuted and fined up to $300 million for employees' illegal actions.

Review 3: Influences on Ethical Decision Making

> Three factors influence ethical decisions: the ethical intensity of the decision, the moral development of the manager, and the ethical principles used to solve the problem. Ethical intensity is strong when decisions have large, certain, immediate consequences and when we are physically or psychologically close to those affected by the decision. There are three phases of moral maturity. At the preconventional level, decisions are made for selfish reasons. At the conventional level, decisions conform to societal expectations. At the postconventional level, internalized principles are used to make ethical decisions. Each of these phases has two steps within it. Managers can use a number of different principles when making ethical decisions: self-interest, personal virtue, religious injunctions, government requirements, utilitarian benefits, individual rights, and distributive justice.

Review 4: Practical Steps to Ethical Decision Making

> Employers can increase their chances of hiring ethical employees by testing all job applicants. Most large companies now have corporate codes of ethics. In addition to offering general rules, ethics codes must also provide specific, practical advice. Ethics training seeks to increase employees' awareness of ethical issues; make ethics a serious, credible factor in organizational decisions; and teach employees a practical model of ethical decision making. The most important factors in creating an ethical business climate are the personal examples set by company managers, the involvement of management in the company ethics program, a reporting system that encourages whistle-blowers to report potential ethics violations, and fair but consistent punishment of violators.

Review 5: To Whom Are Organizations Socially Responsible?

> Social responsibility is a business's obligation to benefit society. According to the shareholder model, a company's only social responsibility is to maximize shareholder wealth by maximizing company profits. According to the stakeholder model, companies must satisfy the needs and interests of multiple corporate stakeholders, not just shareholders. The needs of primary stakeholders, on which the organization relies for its existence, take precedence over those of secondary stakeholders.

Primary		Secondary
Governments	Suppliers	Media
Employees	Shareholders	Special Interest Groups
Customers	Local Communities	Trade Associations

KEY TERMS

Ethics the set of moral principles or values that defines right and wrong for a person or group

Ethical behaviour behaviour that conforms to a society's accepted principles of right and wrong

Workplace deviance unethical behaviour that violates organizational norms about right and wrong

Production deviance unethical behaviour that hurts the quality and quantity of work produced

Property deviance unethical behaviour aimed at the organization's property or products

Employee shrinkage employee theft of company merchandise

Political deviance using one's influence to harm others in the company

Personal aggression hostile or aggressive behaviour toward others

Ethical intensity the degree of concern people have about an ethical issue

Magnitude of consequences the total harm or benefit derived from an ethical decision

Social consensus agreement on whether behaviour is bad or good

Probability of effect the chance that something will happen and then harm others

Temporal immediacy the time between an act and the consequences the act produces

Proximity of effect the social, psychological, cultural, or physical distance between a decision maker and those affected by his or her decisions

Concentration of effect the total harm or benefit that an act produces on the average person

Preconventional level of moral development the first level of moral development in which people make decisions based on selfish reasons

Conventional level of moral development the second level of moral development in which people make decisions that conform to societal expectations

Postconventional level of moral development the third level of moral development in which people make decisions based on internalized principles

Principle of long-term self-interest an ethical principle that holds that you should never take any action that is not in your or your organization's long-term self-interest

Principle of personal virtue an ethical principle that holds that you should never do anything that is not honest, open, and truthful and that you would not be glad to see reported in the newspapers or on TV

Principle of religious injunctions an ethical principle that holds that you should never take any action that is not kind and that does not build a sense of community

Principle of government requirements an ethical principle that holds that you should never take any action that violates the law, for the law represents the minimal moral standard

Principle of utilitarian benefits an ethical principle that holds that you should never take any action that does not result in greater good for society

Principle of individual rights an ethical principle that holds that you should never take any action that infringes on others' agreed-upon rights

Principle of distributive justice an ethical principle that holds that you should never take any action that harms the least fortunate among us: the poor, the uneducated, the unemployed

Overt integrity test a written test that estimates job applicants' honesty by directly asking them what they think or feel about theft or about punishment of unethical behaviours

Personality-based integrity test a written test that indirectly estimates job applicants' honesty by measuring psychological traits, such as dependability and conscientiousness

Whistle-blowing reporting others' ethics violations to management or legal authorities

Social responsibility a business's obligation to pursue policies, make decisions, and take actions that benefit society

Shareholder model a view of social responsibility that holds that an organization's overriding goal should be to maximize profit for the benefit of shareholders

Stakeholder model a theory of corporate responsibility that holds that management's most important responsibility, long-term survival, is achieved by satisfying the interests of multiple corporate stakeholders

Stakeholders persons or groups with a "stake" or legitimate interest in a company's actions

Primary stakeholder any group on which an organization relies for its long-term survival

Secondary stakeholder any group that can influence or be influenced by a company and can affect public perceptions about its socially responsible behaviour

Economic responsibility the expectation that a company will make a profit by producing a valued product or service

Legal responsibility a company's social responsibility to obey society's laws and regulations

Ethical responsibility a company's social responsibility not to violate accepted principles of right and wrong when conducting its business

Discretionary responsibility the expectation that a company will voluntarily serve a social role beyond its economic, legal, and ethical responsibilities

Social responsiveness refers to a company's strategy for responding to stakeholders' economic, legal, ethical, or discretionary expectations concerning social responsibility

Reactive strategy a social responsiveness strategy in which a company does less than society expects

Defensive strategy a social responsiveness strategy in which a company admits responsibility for a problem but does the least required to meet societal expectations

Accommodative strategy a social responsiveness strategy in which a company accepts responsibility for a problem and does all that society expects to solve that problem

Proactive strategy a social responsiveness strategy in which a company anticipates responsibility for a problem before it occurs and does more than society expects to address the problem

Review 6: For What Are Organizations Socially Responsible?

> Companies can best benefit their stakeholders by fulfilling their economic, legal, ethical, and discretionary responsibilities. Being profitable, or meeting one's economic responsibility, is a business's most basic social responsibility. Legal responsibility consists of following a society's laws and regulations. Ethical responsibility means not violating accepted principles of right and wrong when doing business. Discretionary responsibilities are social responsibilities beyond basic economic, legal, and ethical responsibilities.

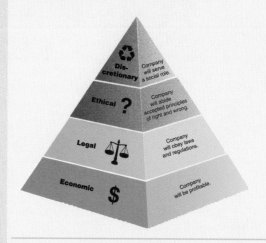

Review 7: Responses to Demands for Social Responsibility

> Social responsiveness is a company's response to stakeholders' demands for socially responsible behaviour. There are four social responsiveness strategies. When a company uses a reactive strategy, it denies responsibility for a problem. When it uses a defensive strategy, it takes responsibility for a problem but does the minimum required to solve it. When a company uses an accommodative strategy, it accepts responsibility for problems and does all that society expects to solve them. Finally, when a company uses a proactive strategy, it does much more than expected to solve social responsibility problems.

Review 8: Social Responsibility and Economic Performance

> Does it pay to be socially responsible? Sometimes it costs, and sometimes it pays. Overall, there is no clear relationship between social responsibility and economic performance. Consequently, managers should not expect an economic return from socially responsible corporate activities. If your company chooses to practise a proactive or accommodative social responsibility strategy, it should do so to better society and not to improve its financial performance.

LEARNING OUTCOMES

Review 1: Why Innovation Matters

> Technology cycles typically follow an S-curve pattern of innovation. Early in the cycle, technological progress is slow and improvements in technological performance are small. As a technology matures, however, performance improves quickly. Finally, as the limits of a technology are reached, only small improvements occur. At this point, significant improvements in performance must come from new technologies. The best way to protect a competitive advantage is to create a stream of innovative ideas and products. Innovation streams begin with technological discontinuities that create significant breakthroughs in performance or function. Technological discontinuities are followed by discontinuous change, in which customers purchase new technologies and companies compete to establish the new dominant design. Dominant designs emerge because of critical mass, because they solve a practical problem, or because of the negotiations of independent standards bodies. Because technological innovation both enhances and destroys competence, companies that bet on the wrong design often struggle, while companies that bet on the eventual dominant design usually prosper. When a dominant design emerges, companies focus on incremental change, lowering costs and making small but steady improvements in the dominant design. This focus continues until the next technological discontinuity occurs.

Review 2: Managing Innovation

> To successfully manage innovation streams, companies must manage the sources of innovation and learn to manage innovation during both discontinuous and incremental change. Since innovation begins with creativity, companies can manage the sources of innovation by supporting a work environment in which creative thoughts and ideas are welcomed, valued, and encouraged. Creative work environments provide challenging work; offer organizational, supervisory, and work group encouragement; allow significant freedom; and remove organizational impediments to creativity.

Discontinuous and incremental change require different strategies, as shown below. Companies that succeed in periods of discontinuous change typically follow an experiential approach to innovation. The experiential approach assumes that intuition, flexible options, and hands-on experience can reduce uncertainty and accelerate learning and understanding. A compression approach to innovation works best during periods of incremental change. This approach assumes that innovation can be planned using a series of steps and that compressing the time it takes to complete those steps can speed up innovation.

	Experiential Approach to Innovation: Managing Innovation During Discontinuous Change	Compression Approach to Innovation: Managing Innovation During Incremental Change
Environment	Highly uncertain discontinuous change—technological substitution and design competition	Certain incremental change—established technology (i.e., dominant design)
Goals	Speed Significant improvements in performance Establishment of new dominant design	Speed Lower costs Incremental improvements in performance of dominant design
Approach	Build something new, different, and substantially better	Compress time and steps needed to bring about small improvements
Steps	Design iterations Testing Milestones Multifunctional teams Powerful leaders	Planning Supplier involvement Shorten time of individual steps Overlapping steps Multifunctional teams

KEY TERMS

Organizational innovation the successful implementation of creative ideas in organizations

Creativity the production of novel and useful ideas

Organizational change a difference in the form, quality, or condition of an organization over time

Technology cycle a cycle that begins with the birth of a new technology and ends when that technology reaches its limits and is replaced by a newer, substantially better technology

S-curve pattern of innovation a pattern of technological innovation characterized by slow initial progress, then rapid progress, and then slow progress again as a technology matures and reaches its limits

Innovation streams patterns of innovation over time that can create sustainable competitive advantage

Technological discontinuity a scientific advance or a unique combination of existing technologies creates a significant breakthrough in performance or function

Discontinuous change the phase of a technology cycle characterized by technological substitution and design competition

Technological substitution the purchase of new technologies to replace older ones

Design competition competition between old and new technologies to establish a new technological standard or dominant design

Dominant design a new technological design or process that becomes the accepted market standard

Technological lockout when a new dominant design (i.e., a significantly better technology) prevents a company from competitively selling its products or makes it difficult to do so

Incremental change the phase of a technology cycle in which companies innovate by lowering costs and improving the functioning and performance of the dominant technological design

Creative work environments workplace cultures in which workers perceive that new ideas are welcomed, valued, and encouraged

Flow a psychological state of effortlessness, in which you become completely absorbed in what you're doing and time seems to pass quickly

Experiential approach to innovation an approach to innovation that assumes a highly uncertain environment and uses intuition, flexible options, and hands-on experience to reduce uncertainty and accelerate learning and understanding

Design iteration a cycle of repetition in which a company tests a prototype of a new product or service, improves on that design, and then builds and tests the improved prototype

Product prototype a full-scale, working model that is being tested for design, function, and reliability

Testing the systematic comparison of different product designs or design iterations

Milestones formal project review points used to assess progress and performance

Multifunctional teams work teams composed of people from different departments

Compression approach to innovation an approach to innovation that assumes that incremental innovation can be planned using a series of steps and that compressing those steps can speed innovation

Generational change change based on incremental improvements to a dominant technological design such that the improved technology is fully backward compatible with the older technology

Organizational decline a large decrease in organizational performance that occurs when companies don't anticipate, recognize, neutralize, or adapt to the internal or external pressures that threaten their survival

Change forces forces that produce differences in the form, quality, or condition of an organization over time

Resistance forces forces that support the existing state of conditions in organizations

Resistance to change opposition to change resulting from self-interest, misunderstanding and distrust, and a general intolerance for change

Unfreezing getting the people affected by change to believe that change is needed

Change intervention the process used to get workers and managers to change their behaviour and work practices

Review 3: Organizational Decline: The Risk of Not Changing

> The five-stage process of organizational decline begins when organizations don't recognize the need for change. In the blinded stage, managers fail to recognize the changes that threaten their organization's survival. In the inaction stage, management recognizes the need to change but doesn't act, hoping that the problems will correct themselves. In the faulty action stage, management focuses on cost cutting and efficiency rather than facing up to the fundamental changes needed to ensure survival. In the crisis stage, failure is likely unless fundamental reorganization occurs. Finally, in the dissolution stage, the company is dissolved through bankruptcy proceedings; by selling assets to pay creditors; or through the closing of stores, offices, and facilities. If companies recognize the need to change early enough, however, dissolution may be avoided.

Review 4: Managing Change

> The basic change process involves unfreezing, change, and refreezing. Resistance to change stems from self-interest, misunderstanding, and distrust as well as a general intolerance for change. It can be managed through education and communication, participation, negotiation, top management support, and coercion. Knowing what not to do is as important as knowing what to do to achieve successful change. Managers should avoid these errors when leading change: not establishing urgency, not creating a guiding coalition, lacking a vision, undercommunicating the vision, not removing obstacles to the vision, not creating short-term wins, declaring victory too soon, and not anchoring changes in the corporation's culture. Finally, managers can use a number of change techniques. Results-driven change and the GE workout reduce resistance to change by getting change efforts off to a fast start. Organizational development is a collection of planned change interventions (large system, small group, person-focused), guided by a change agent, that are designed to improve an organization's long-term health and performance.

Different Kinds of Organizational Development Interventions

LARGE SYSTEM INTERVENTIONS	
Sociotechnical systems	An intervention designed to improve how well employees use and adjust to the work technology used in an organization.
Survey feedback	An intervention that uses surveys to collect information from the members, reports the results of that survey to the members, and then uses those results to develop action plans for improvement.
SMALL GROUP INTERVENTIONS	
Team building	An intervention designed to increase the cohesion and cooperation of work group members.
Unit goal setting	An intervention designed to help a work group establish short- and long-term goals.
PERSON-FOCUSED INTERVENTIONS	
Counselling/coaching	An intervention designed so that a formal helper or coach listens to managers or employees and advises them on how to deal with work or interpersonal problems.
Training	An intervention designed to provide individuals with the knowledge, skills, or attitudes they need to become more effective at their jobs.

Source: W. J. Rothwell, R. Sullivan, & G. M. McLean, *Practicing Organizational Development: A Guide for Consultants* (San Diego: Pfeiffer & Co., 1995).

Refreezing supporting and reinforcing new changes so that they stick

Coercion using formal power and authority to force others to change

Results-driven change change created quickly by focusing on the measurement and improvement of results

General Electric workout a three-day meeting in which managers and employees from different levels and parts of an organization quickly generate and act on solutions to specific business problems

Organizational development a philosophy and collection of planned change interventions designed to improve an organization's long-term health and performance

Change agent the person formally in charge of guiding a change effort

REVIEW card/

LEARNING OUTCOMES

Review 1: Departmentalization

> There are five traditional departmental structures: functional, product, customer, geographic, and matrix. Functional departmentalization is based on the different business functions or types of expertise used to run a business. Product departmentalization is organized according to the different products or services a company sells. Customer departmentalization focuses its divisions on the different kinds of customers a company has. Geographic departmentalization is based on the different geographic areas or markets in which the company does business. Matrix departmentalization is a hybrid form that combines two or more forms of departmentalization, the most common being the product and functional forms. There is no single best departmental structure. Each structure has advantages and disadvantages.

Review 2: Organizational Authority

> Organizational authority is determined by the chain of command, line versus staff authority, delegation, and the degree of centralization in a company. The chain of command vertically connects every job in the company to higher levels of management and makes clear who reports to whom. Managers have line authority to command employees below them in the chain of command but have only staff, or advisory, authority over employees not below them in the chain of command. Managers delegate authority by transferring to subordinates the authority and responsibility needed to do a task; in exchange, subordinates become accountable for task completion. In centralized companies, most authority to make decisions lies with managers in the upper levels of the company. In decentralized companies, much of the authority is delegated to the workers closest to problems, who can then make the decisions necessary for solving the problems themselves.

Delegation: Responsibility, Authority, and Accountability

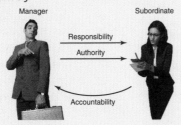

Source: C. D. Pringle, D. F. Jennings, and J. G. Longenecker, *Managing Organizations: Functions and Behaviours* © 1990. Adapted by permission of Pearson Education, Inc., Upper Saddle River, NJ.

Review 3: Job Design

> Companies use specialized jobs because they are economical and easy to learn and don't require highly paid workers. However, specialized jobs aren't motivating or particularly satisfying for employees. Companies have used job rotation, job enlargement, job enrichment, and the job characteristics model to make specialized jobs more interesting and motivating. The goal of the job characteristics model is to make jobs intrinsically motivating. For this to happen, jobs must be strong on five core job characteristics (skill variety, task identity, task significance, autonomy, and feedback), and workers must experience three critical psychological states (knowledge of results, responsibility for work outcomes, and meaningful work). If jobs aren't internally motivating, they can be redesigned by combining tasks, forming natural work units, establishing client relationships, vertical loading, and opening feedback channels.

KEY TERMS

Organizational structure the vertical and horizontal configuration of departments, authority, and jobs within a company

Organizational process the collection of activities that transform inputs into outputs that customers value

Departmentalization subdividing work and workers into separate organizational units responsible for completing particular tasks

Functional departmentalization organizing work and workers into separate units responsible for particular business functions or areas of expertise

Product departmentalization organizing work and workers into separate units responsible for producing particular products or services

Customer departmentalization organizing work and workers into separate units responsible for particular kinds of customers

Geographic departmentalization organizing work and workers into separate units responsible for doing business in particular geographic areas

Matrix departmentalization a hybrid organizational structure in which two or more forms of departmentalization, most often product and functional, are used together

Simple matrix a form of matrix departmentalization in which managers in different parts of the matrix negotiate conflicts and resources

Complex matrix a form of matrix departmentalization in which managers in different parts of the matrix report to matrix managers, who help them sort out conflicts and problems

Authority the right to give commands, take action, and make decisions to achieve organizational objectives

Chain of command the vertical line of authority that clarifies who reports to whom throughout the organization

Unity of command a management principle that workers should report to just one boss

Line authority the right to command immediate subordinates in the chain of command

Staff authority the right to advise, but not command, others who are not subordinates in the chain of command

Line function an activity that contributes directly to creating or selling the company's products

Staff function an activity that does not contribute directly to creating or selling the company's products, but instead supports line activities

Delegation of authority the assignment of direct authority and responsibility to a subordinate to complete tasks for which the manager is normally responsible

Centralization of authority the location of most authority at the upper levels of the organization

Decentralization the location of a significant amount of authority in the lower levels of the organization

Standardization solving problems by consistently applying the same rules, procedures, and processes

Job design the number, kind, and variety of tasks that individual workers perform in doing their jobs

Job specialization a job composed of a small part of a larger task or process

Job rotation periodically moving workers from one specialized job to another to give them more variety and the opportunity to use different skills

Job enlargement increasing the number of different tasks that a worker performs within one particular job

Job enrichment increasing the number of tasks in a particular job and giving workers the authority and control to make meaningful decisions about their work

Job characteristics model (JCM) an approach to job redesign that seeks to formulate jobs in ways that motivate workers and lead to positive work outcomes

Internal motivation motivation that comes from the job itself rather than from outside rewards

Skill variety the number of different activities performed in a job

Task identity the degree to which a job, from beginning to end, requires the completion of a whole and identifiable piece of work

Task significance the degree to which a job is perceived to have a substantial impact on others inside or outside the organization

Autonomy the degree to which a job gives workers the discretion, freedom, and independence to decide how and when to accomplish the job

Feedback the amount of information the job provides to workers about their work performance

Mechanistic organization an organization characterized by specialized jobs and responsibilities; precisely defined, unchanging roles; and a rigid chain of command based on centralized authority and vertical communication

Organic organization an organization characterized by broadly defined jobs and responsibility; loosely defined, frequently changing roles; and decentralized authority and horizontal communication based on task knowledge

Intraorganizational process the collection of activities that take place within an organization to transform inputs into outputs that customers value

Re-engineering fundamental rethinking and radical redesign of business processes to achieve dramatic improvements in critical measures of performance, such as cost, quality, service, and speed

Task interdependence the extent to which collective action is required to complete an entire piece of work

Pooled interdependence work completed by having each job or department independently contribute to the whole

Sequential interdependence work completed in succession, with one group's or job's outputs becoming the inputs for the next group or job

Reciprocal interdependence work completed by different jobs or groups working together in a back-and-forth manner

Empowering workers permanently passing decision-making authority and responsibility from managers to workers by giving them the information and resources they need to make and carry out good decisions

Empowerment feelings of intrinsic motivation, in which workers perceive their work to have impact and meaning and perceive themselves to be competent and capable of self-determination

Interorganizational process a collection of activities that take place among companies to transform inputs into outputs that customers value

Modular organization an organization that outsources noncore business activities to outside companies, suppliers, specialists, or consultants

Virtual organization an organization that is part of a network in which many companies share skills, costs, capabilities, markets, and customers to collectively solve customer problems or provide specific products or services

Review 4: Intraorganizational Processes

> Today, companies are using re-engineering and empowerment to change their intraorganizational processes. Re-engineering changes an organization's orientation from vertical to horizontal and its work processes by decreasing sequential and pooled interdependence and by increasing reciprocal interdependence. Re-engineering promises dramatic increases in productivity and customer satisfaction, but it has been criticized as simply an excuse to cut costs and lay off workers. Empowering workers means taking decision-making authority and responsibility from managers and giving it to workers. Empowered workers develop feelings of competence and self-determination and believe that their work has meaning and impact.

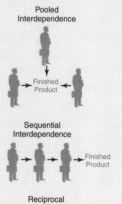

Review 5: Interorganizational Processes

> Organizations are using modular and virtual organizations to change interorganizational processes. Because modular organizations outsource all noncore activities to other businesses, they are less expensive to run than traditional companies. However, modular organizations require extremely close relationships with suppliers, may result in a loss of control, and could create new competitors if the wrong business activities are outsourced.

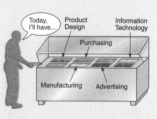

Virtual organizations participate in a network in which they share skills, costs, capabilities, markets, and customers. Virtual organizations can reduce costs, respond quickly, and, if they can successfully coordinate their efforts, produce outstanding products and service.

LEARNING OUTCOMES

Review 1: The Good and Bad of Using Teams

> In many industries, teams are growing in importance because they help organizations respond to specific problems and challenges. Teams have been shown to increase customer satisfaction (specific customer teams), product and service quality (direct responsibility), and employee job satisfaction (cross training, unique opportunities, and leadership responsibilities). Although teams can produce significant improvements in these areas, using teams does not guarantee these positive outcomes. Teams and teamwork have the disadvantages of initially high turnover and social loafing (especially in large groups). Teams also share many of the advantages (multiple perspectives, generation of more alternatives, and more commitment) and disadvantages (groupthink, time, poorly run meetings, domination by a few team members, and weak accountability) of group decision making. Teams should be used for a clear purpose, when the work requires that people work together, when rewards can be provided for both teamwork and team performance, when ample resources can be provided, and when teams can be given clear authority over their work.

ADVANTAGES AND DISADVANTAGES OF TEAMS

ADVANTAGES 👍	DISADVANTAGES 👎
☺ Customer satisfaction	☹ Initially high employee turnover
☺ Product and service quality	☹ Social loafing
☺ Speed and efficiency in product development	☹ Disadvantages of group decision making (groupthink, inefficient meetings, domination by a minority, lack of accountability)
☺ Employee job satisfaction	
☺ Better decision making and problem solving (multiple perspectives, more alternative solutions, increased commitment to decisions)	

Review 2: Kinds of Teams

> Companies use different kinds of teams to make themselves more competitive. Autonomy is the key dimension that makes teams different. Traditional work groups (which execute tasks) and employee involvement groups (which make suggestions) have the lowest levels of autonomy. Semi-autonomous work groups (which control major, direct tasks) have more autonomy, while self-managing teams (which control all direct tasks) and self-designing teams (which control membership and how tasks are done) have the highest levels of autonomy. Cross-functional, virtual, and project teams are common but are not easily categorized in terms of autonomy. Cross-functional teams combine employees from different functional areas to help teams attack problems from multiple perspectives and generate more ideas and solutions. Virtual teams use telecommunications and information technologies to bring coworkers together, regardless of physical location or time zone. Virtual teams reduce travel and work time, but communication may suffer since team members don't work face-to-face. Finally, project teams are used for specific, one-time projects or tasks that must be completed within a limited time. Project teams reduce communication barriers and promote flexibility; teams and team members are reassigned to their departments or new projects as old projects are completed.

KEY TERMS

Work team a small number of people with complementary skills who hold themselves mutually accountable for pursuing a common purpose, achieving performance goals, and improving interdependent work processes

Cross-training training team members to do all or most of the jobs performed by the other team members

Social loafing behaviour in which team members withhold their efforts and fail to perform their share of the work

Traditional work group a group composed of two or more people who work together to achieve a shared goal

Employee involvement team team that provides advice or makes suggestions to management concerning specific issues

Semi-autonomous work group a group that has the authority to make decisions and solve problems related to the major tasks of producing a product or service

Self-managing team a team that manages and controls all of the major tasks of producing a product or service

Self-designing team a team that has the characteristics of self-managing teams but also controls team design, work tasks, and team membership

Cross-functional team a team composed of employees from different functional areas of the organization

Virtual team a team composed of geographically and/or organizationally dispersed coworkers who use telecommunication and information technologies to accomplish an organizational task

Project team a team created to complete specific, one-time projects or tasks within a limited time

Norms informally agreed-on standards that regulate team behaviour

Cohesiveness the extent to which team members are attracted to a team and motivated to remain in it

Forming the first stage of team development, in which team members meet one another, form initial impressions, and begin to establish team norms

Storming the second stage of development, characterized by conflict and disagreement, in which team members disagree over what the team should do and how it should do it

Norming the third stage of team development, in which team members begin to settle into their roles, group cohesion grows, and positive team norms develop

Performing the fourth and final stage of team development, in which performance improves because the team has matured into an effective, fully functioning team

Structural accommodation the ability to change organizational structures, policies, and practices in order to meet stretch goals

Bureaucratic immunity the ability to make changes without first getting approval from managers or other parts of an organization

Individualism-collectivism the degree to which a person believes that people should be self-sufficient and that loyalty to one's self is more important than loyalty to team or company

Team level the average level of ability, experience, personality, or any other factor on a team

Team diversity the variances or differences in ability, experience, personality, or any other factor on a team

Interpersonal skills skills, such as listening, communicating, questioning, and providing feedback, that enable people to have effective working relationships with others

Skill-based pay compensation system that pays employees for learning additional skills or knowledge

Gainsharing a compensation system in which companies share the financial value of performance gains, such as productivity, cost savings, or quality, with their workers

Review 3: Work Team Characteristics

> The most important characteristics of work teams are team norms, cohesiveness, size, conflict, and development. Norms let team members know what is expected of them and can influence team behaviour in positive and negative ways. Positive team norms are associated with organizational commitment, trust, and job satisfaction. Team cohesiveness helps teams retain members, promotes cooperative behaviour, increases motivation, and facilitates team performance. Attending team meetings and activities, creating opportunities to work together, and engaging in non-work activities can increase cohesiveness. Team size has a curvilinear relationship with team performance: teams that are very small or very large do not perform as well as moderate-sized teams of six to nine members. Teams of this size are cohesive and small enough for team members to get to know each other and contribute in a meaningful way but are large enough to take advantage of team members' diverse skills, knowledge, and perspectives. Conflict and disagreement are inevitable in most teams. The key to dealing with team conflict is to maximize cognitive conflict, which focuses on issue-related differences, and minimize affective conflict, the emotional reactions that occur when disagreements become personal rather than professional. As teams develop and grow, they pass through four stages of development: forming, storming, norming, and performing. If a team is not managed well, its performance may decline after a period of time as the team regresses through the stages of de-norming, de-storming, and de-forming.

HOW TEAMS CAN HAVE A GOOD FIGHT

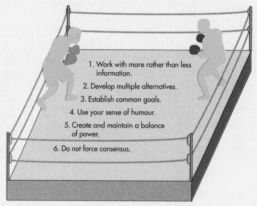

1. Work with more rather than less information.
2. Develop multiple alternatives.
3. Establish common goals.
4. Use your sense of humour.
5. Create and maintain a balance of power.
6. Do not force consensus.

Source: K. M. Eisenhardt, J. L. Kahwajy, and L. J. Bourgeois III, "How Management Teams Can Have a Good Fight," *Harvard Business Review* 75, no. 4 (July-August 1997): 77–85.

Review 4: Enhancing Work Team Effectiveness

> Companies can make teams more effective by setting team goals and managing how team members are selected, trained, and compensated. Team goals provide a clear focus and purpose, reduce the incidence of social loafing, and lead to higher team performance 93 percent of the time. Extremely difficult stretch goals can be used to motivate teams as long as teams have autonomy, control over resources, structural accommodation, and bureaucratic immunity. Not everyone is suited for teamwork. When selecting team members, companies should select people who have a preference for teamwork (individualism-collectivism) and should consider team level (average ability on a team) and team diversity (different abilities on a team). Organizations that successfully use teams provide thousands of hours of training to make sure that teams work. The most common types of team training are for interpersonal skills, decision-making and problem-solving skills, conflict resolution, technical training to help team members learn multiple jobs (i.e., cross training), and training for team leaders. Employees can be compensated for team participation and accomplishments in three ways: skill-based pay, gainsharing, and nonfinancial rewards.

LEARNING OUTCOMES

Review 1: Diversity: Differences That Matter

> Diversity exists in organizations when there are demographic, cultural, and personal differences among the people who work there and the customers who do business there. A common misconception is that workplace diversity and employment equity are the same. However, employment equity is more narrowly focused on demographics; while diversity is broader in focus (going beyond demographics); voluntary; and more positive in that it encourages companies to value all kinds of differences. Employment equity and diversity thus differ in purpose, practice, and the reactions they produce. Diversity also makes good business sense in terms of cost savings, attracting and retaining talent, and driving business growth (improving marketplace understanding and promoting higher-quality problem solving).

General Purpose of Diversity Programs

To create a positive work environment where

- no one is advantaged or disadvantaged.
- "we" is everyone.
- everyone can do his or her best work.
- differences are respected and not ignored.
- everyone feels comfortable.

Source: T. Roosevelt, "From Affirmative Action to Affirming Diversity," *Harvard Business Review* 68, no. 2 (1990): 107–117.

Review 2: Surface-Level Diversity

> Age, sex, race/ethnicity, and physical and mental disabilities are dimensions of surface-level diversity. Because those dimensions are (usually) easily observed, managers and workers tend to rely on them to form initial impressions and stereotypes. Sometimes this can lead to age, gender, racial/ethnic, or disability discrimination (i.e., treating people differently) in the workplace. In general, older workers, women, people of colour or different national origins, and people with disabilities are much less likely to be hired or promoted than white males. This disparity is often due to incorrect beliefs or stereotypes such as "job performance declines with age," "women aren't willing to travel on business," or "workers with disabilities aren't as competent as able workers." To reduce discrimination, companies can determine the hiring and promotion rates for different groups, train managers to make hiring and promotion decisions on the basis of specific criteria, and make sure that everyone has equal access to training, mentors, reasonable work accommodations, and assistive technology. Finally, companies need to designate a go-to person that employees can talk to if they believe they have suffered discrimination.

KEY TERMS

Diversity a variety of demographic, cultural, and personal differences among an organization's employees and customers

Employment Equity an ongoing planning process used by an employer to eliminate barriers in an organization's employment procedures and to ensure appropriate representation of specific members of the workforce.

Affirmative action purposeful steps taken by an organization to create employment opportunities for minorities and women

Surface-level diversity differences such as age, gender, race/ethnicity, and physical disabilities that are observable, typically unchangeable, and easy to measure

Deep-level diversity differences such as personality and attitudes that are communicated through verbal and non-verbal behaviours and are learned only through extended interaction with others

Social integration the degree to which group members are psychologically attracted to working with one another to accomplish a common objective

Age discrimination treating people differently (e.g., in hiring and firing, promotion, and compensation decisions) because of their age

Gender discrimination treating people differently because of their gender

Glass ceiling the invisible barrier that prevents women and minorities from advancing to the top jobs in organizations

Racial and ethnic discrimination treating people differently because of their race or ethnicity

Disability an activity limitation or participation restriction associated with a physical or mental condition or health problem.

Disability discrimination treating people differently because of their disabilities

Disposition the tendency to respond to situations and events in a predetermined manner

Personality the relatively stable set of behaviours, attitudes, and emotions displayed over time that makes people different from one another

Extraversion the degree to which someone is active, assertive, sociable, talkative, and energized by others

Emotional stability the degree to which someone is not angry, depressed, anxious, emotional, insecure, and excitable

Agreeableness the degree to which someone is cooperative, polite, flexible, forgiving, good-natured, tolerant, and trusting

Conscientiousness the degree to which someone is organized, hardworking, responsible, persevering, thorough, and achievement oriented

Openness to experience the degree to which someone is curious, broadminded, and open to new ideas, things, and experiences; is spontaneous; and has a high tolerance for ambiguity

Organizational plurality a work environment where (1) all members are empowered to contribute in a way that maximizes the benefits to the organization, customers, and themselves, and (2) the individuality of each member is respected by not segmenting or polarizing people on the basis of their membership in a particular group

Awareness training training that is designed to raise employees' awareness of diversity issues and to challenge the underlying assumptions or stereotypes they may have about others

Skills-based diversity training training that teaches employees the practical skills they need for managing a diverse workforce, such as flexibility and adaptability, negotiation, problem solving, and conflict resolution

Diversity audits formal assessments that measure employee and management attitudes, investigate the extent to which people are advantaged or disadvantaged with respect to hiring and promotions, and review companies' diversity-related policies and procedures

Diversity pairing a mentoring program in which people of different cultural backgrounds, genders, or races/ethnicities are paired together to get to know one another and change stereotypical beliefs and attitudes

Review 3: Deep-Level Diversity

> Deep-level diversity matters because it can reduce prejudice, discrimination, and conflict while increasing social integration. It consists of dispositional and personality differences that can be learned only through extended interaction with others. Research conducted in different cultures, settings, and languages indicates that there are five basic dimensions of personality: extraversion, emotional stability, agreeableness, conscientiousness, and openness to experience. Of these, conscientiousness is perhaps the most important because conscientious workers tend to be better performers on virtually any job. Extraversion is also related to performance in jobs that require significant interaction with others.

Review 4: Managing Diversity

> The three paradigms for managing diversity are the discrimination and fairness paradigm (equal opportunity, fair treatment, strict compliance with the law), the access and legitimacy paradigm (matching internal diversity to external diversity), and the learning and effectiveness paradigm (achieving organizational plurality by integrating deep-level diversity into the work of the organization). Unlike the other paradigms that focus on surface-level differences, the learning and effectiveness program values common ground, distinguishes between individual and group differences, minimizes conflict and divisiveness, and focuses on bringing different talents and perspectives together. What principles can companies use when managing diversity? Link diversity to strategic business goals. Include diversity in human resource planning. Recruit a diverse workforce. Select a diverse workforce. Train and develop a diverse staff. Monitor the effectiveness of staffing for diversity. Provide work–life flexibility. Create an inclusive working environment. Encourage senior executive support for diversity. The two types of diversity training are awareness training and skills-based diversity training. Companies also manage diversity through diversity audits and diversity pairing.

Paradigms for Managing Diversity

DIVERSITY PARADIGM	FOCUS	SUCCESS MEASURED BY	BENEFITS	LIMITATIONS
Discrimination & Fairness	Equal opportunity Fair treatment Recruitment of minorities Strict compliance with laws	Recruitment, promotion, and retention goals for underrepresented group	Fairer treatment Increased demographic diversity	Focus on surface-level diversity
Access & Legitimacy	Acceptance and celebration of differences	Diversity in company matches diversity of primary stakeholders	Establishes a clear business reason for diversity	Focus on surface-level diversity
Learning & Effectiveness	Integrating deep-level differences into organization	Valuing people on the basis of individual knowledge, skills, and abilities	Values common ground Distinction between individual and group differences Less conflict, backlash, and divisiveness Bringing different talents and perspectives together	Focus on deep-level diversity is more difficult to measure and quantify

LEARNING OUTCOMES

Review 1: Basics of Motivation

> Motivation is the set of forces that initiates, directs, and makes people persist in their efforts over time to accomplish a goal. Managers often confuse motivation and performance, but job performance is a multiplicative function of motivation times ability times situational constraints. Needs are the physical or psychological requirements that must be met to ensure survival and well-being. Different motivational theories (Maslow's Hierarchy of Needs, Alderfer's ERG Theory, and McClelland's Learned Needs Theory) specify a number of different needs. However, studies show that there are only two general kinds of needs, lower-order needs and higher-order needs. Both extrinsic and intrinsic rewards motivate people.

MOTIVATING TO INCREASE EFFORT

- **Start by asking people what their needs are.**
- **Satisfy lower-order needs first.**
- **Expect people's needs to change.**
- **As needs change and lower-order needs are satisfied, satisfy higher-order needs by looking for ways to allow employees to experience intrinsic rewards.**

Review 2: Equity Theory

> The basic components of equity theory are inputs, outcomes, and referents. After an internal comparison in which employees compare their outcomes to their inputs, they then make an external comparison in which they compare their O/I ratio with the O/I ratio of a referent, a person who works in a similar job or is otherwise similar. When their O/I ratio is equal to the referent's O/I ratio, employees perceive that they are being treated fairly. But, when their O/I ratio is different from their referent's O/I ratio, they perceive that they have been treated inequitably or unfairly. There are two kinds of inequity: underreward and overreward. Underreward, which occurs when a referent's O/I ratio is better than the employee's O/I ratio, leads to anger or frustration. Overreward, which occurs when a referent's O/I ratio is worse than the employee's O/I ratio, can lead to guilt but only when the level of overreward is extreme.

MOTIVATING WITH EQUITY THEORY

- **Look for and correct major inequities.**
- **Reduce employees' inputs.**
- **Make sure decision-making processes are fair.**

Review 3: Expectancy Theory

> Expectancy theory holds that three factors affect the conscious choices people make about their motivation: valence, expectancy, and instrumentality. Expectancy theory holds that all three factors must be high for people to be highly motivated. If any one of these factors declines, overall motivation will decline too.

MOTIVATING WITH EXPECTANCY THEORY

- **Systematically gather information to find out what employees want from their jobs.**
- **Take specific steps to link rewards to individual performance in a way that is clear and understandable to employees.**
- **Empower employees to make decisions if management really wants them to believe that their hard work and effort will lead to good performance.**

KEY TERMS

Motivation the set of forces that initiates, directs, and makes people persist in their efforts to accomplish a goal

Needs the physical or psychological requirements that must be met to ensure survival and well-being

Extrinsic reward a reward that is tangible, visible to others, and given to employees contingent on the performance of specific tasks or behaviours

Intrinsic reward a natural reward associated with performing a task or activity for its own sake

Equity theory a theory that states that people will be motivated when they perceive that they are being treated fairly

Inputs in equity theory, the contributions employees make to the organization

Outcomes in equity theory, the rewards employees receive for their contributions to the organization

Referents in equity theory, others with whom people compare themselves to determine if they have been treated fairly

Outcome/input (O/I) ratio in equity theory, an employee's perception of how the rewards received from an organization compare with the employee's contributions to that organization

Underreward a form of inequity in which you are getting fewer outcomes relative to inputs than your referent is getting

Overreward a form of inequity in which you are getting more outcomes relative to inputs than your referent

Distributive justice the perceived degree to which outcomes and rewards are fairly distributed or allocated

Procedural justice the perceived fairness of the process used to make reward allocation decisions

Expectancy theory a theory that states that people will be motivated to the extent to which they believe that their efforts will lead to good performance, that good performance will be rewarded, and that they will be offered attractive rewards

Valence the attractiveness or desirability of a reward or outcome

Expectancy the perceived relationship between effort and performance

Instrumentality the perceived relationship between performance and rewards

Reinforcement theory a theory that states that behaviour is a function of its consequences, that behaviours followed by positive consequences will occur more frequently, and that behaviours followed by negative consequences, or not followed by positive consequences, will occur less frequently

Reinforcement the process of changing behaviour by changing the consequences that follow behaviour

Reinforcement contingencies cause-and-effect relationships between the performance of specific behaviours and specific consequences

Schedule of reinforcement rules that specify which behaviours will be reinforced, which consequences will follow those behaviours, and the schedule by which those consequences will be delivered

Positive reinforcement reinforcement that strengthens behaviour by following behaviours with desirable consequences

Negative reinforcement reinforcement that strengthens behaviour by withholding an unpleasant consequence when employees perform a specific behaviour

Punishment reinforcement that weakens behaviour by following behaviours with undesirable consequences

Extinction reinforcement in which a positive consequence is no longer allowed to follow a previously reinforced behaviour, thus weakening the behaviour

Continuous reinforcement schedule a schedule that requires a consequence to be administered following every instance of a behaviour

Intermittent reinforcement schedule a schedule in which consequences are delivered after a specified or average time has elapsed or after a specified or average number of behaviours has occurred

Fixed interval reinforcement schedule an intermittent schedule in which consequences follow a behaviour only after a fixed time has elapsed

Variable interval reinforcement schedule an intermittent schedule in which the time between a behaviour and the following consequences varies around a specified average

Fixed ratio reinforcement schedule an intermittent schedule in which consequences are delivered following a specific number of behaviours

Review 4: Reinforcement Theory

> Reinforcement theory says that behaviour is a function of its consequences. Reinforcement has two parts: reinforcement contingencies and schedules of reinforcement. The four kinds of reinforcement contingencies are positive reinforcement and negative reinforcement, which strengthen behaviour, and punishment and extinction, which weaken behaviour. There are two kinds of reinforcement schedules, continuous and intermittent; intermittent schedules, in turn, can be divided into fixed and variable interval schedules and fixed and variable ratio schedules.

Review 5: Goal-Setting Theory

> A goal is a target, objective, or result that someone tries to accomplish. Goal-setting theory says that people will be motivated to the extent to which they accept specific, challenging goals and receive feedback that indicates their progress toward goal achievement. The basic components of goal-setting theory are goal specificity, goal difficulty, goal acceptance, and performance feedback. Goal specificity is the extent to which goals are detailed, exact, and unambiguous. Goal difficulty is the extent to which a goal is hard or challenging to accomplish. Goal acceptance is the extent to which people consciously understand and agree to goals. Performance feedback is information about the quality or quantity of past performance and indicates whether progress is being made toward the accomplishment of a goal.

Motivating with the Integrated Model

MOTIVATING WITH	MANAGERS SHOULD . . .
THE BASICS	• Ask people what their needs are. • Satisfy lower-order needs first. • Expect people's needs to change. • As needs change and lower-order needs are satisfied, satisfy higher-order needs by looking for ways to allow employees to experience intrinsic rewards.
EQUITY THEORY	• Look for and correct major inequities. • Reduce employees' inputs. • Make sure decision-making processes are fair.
EXPECTANCY THEORY	• Systematically gather information to find out what employees want from their jobs. • Take specific steps to link rewards to individual performance in a way that is clear and understandable to employees. • Empower employees to make decisions if management really wants them to believe that their hard work and efforts will lead to good performance.
REINFORCEMENT THEORY	• Identify, measure, analyze, intervene, and evaluate critical performance-related behaviours. • Don't reinforce the wrong behaviours. • Correctly administer punishment at the appropriate time. • Choose the simplest and most effective schedules of reinforcement.
GOAL-SETTING THEORY	• Assign specific, challenging goals. • Make sure workers truly accept organizational goals. • Provide frequent, specific, performance-related feedback.

Variable ratio reinforcement schedule an intermittent schedule in which consequences are delivered following a different number of behaviours, sometimes more and sometimes less, that vary around a specified average number of behaviours

Goal a target, objective, or result that someone tries to accomplish

Goal-setting theory a theory that states that people will be motivated to the extent to which they accept specific, challenging goals and receive feedback that indicates their progress toward goal achievement

Goal specificity the extent to which goals are detailed, exact, and unambiguous

Goal difficulty the extent to which a goal is hard or challenging to accomplish

Goal acceptance the extent to which people consciously understand and agree to goals

Performance feedback information about the quality or quantity of past performance that indicates whether progress is being made toward the accomplishment of a goal

LEARNING OUTCOMES

Review 1: Leaders Versus Managers

> Management is getting work done through others; leadership is the process of influencing others to achieve group or organizational goals. Leaders are different from managers. The primary difference is that leaders are concerned with doing the right thing, while managers are concerned with doing things right. Organizations need both managers and leaders. But, in general, companies are overmanaged and underled.

Managers
- Do things right
- Status quo
- Short term
- Means
- Builders
- Problem solving

Leaders
- Do the right things
- Change
- Long term
- Ends
- Architects
- Inspiring & motivating

Review 2: Who Leaders Are and What Leaders Do

> Trait theory says that effective leaders possess traits or characteristics that differentiate them from nonleaders. Those traits are drive, the desire to lead, honesty/integrity, self-confidence, emotional stability, cognitive ability, and knowledge of the business. These traits alone aren't enough for successful leadership; leaders who have many or all of them must also behave in ways that encourage people to achieve group or organizational goals. Two key leader behaviours are initiating structure, which improves subordinate performance, and consideration, which improves subordinate satisfaction. There is no ideal combination of these behaviours. The best leadership style depends on the situation.

Review 3: Putting Leaders in the Right Situation: Fiedler's Contingency Theory

> Fiedler's theory assumes that leaders are effective when their work groups perform well, that leaders are unable to change their leadership styles, that leadership styles must be matched to the proper situation, and that favourable situations permit leaders to influence group members. According to the Least Preferred Coworker (LPC) scale, there are two basic leadership styles. People who describe their LPC in a positive way have relationship-oriented leadership styles. By contrast, people who describe their LPC in a negative way have task-oriented leadership styles. Situational favourableness, which occurs when leaders can influence followers, is determined by leader-member relations, task structure, and position power. In general, relationship-oriented leaders with high LPC scores are better leaders under moderately favourable situations, while task-oriented leaders with low LPC scores are better leaders in highly favourable and unfavourable situations. Since Fiedler assumes that leaders are incapable of changing their leadership styles, the key is to accurately measure and match leaders to situations or to teach leaders how to change situational factors. Though matching or placing leaders in appropriate situations works well, re-engineering situations to fit leadership styles doesn't because of the complexity of the model, which makes it difficult for people to understand.

KEY TERMS

Leadership the process of influencing others to achieve group or organizational goals

Trait theory a leadership theory that holds that effective leaders possess a similar set of traits or characteristics

Traits relatively stable characteristics, such as abilities, psychological motives, or consistent patterns of behaviour

Initiating structure the degree to which a leader structures the roles of followers by setting goals, giving directions, setting deadlines, and assigning tasks

Consideration the extent to which a leader is friendly, approachable, and supportive and shows concern for employees

Leadership style the way a leader generally behaves toward followers

Contingency theory a leadership theory that states that in order to maximize work group performance, leaders must be matched to the situation that best fits their leadership style

Situational favourableness the degree to which a particular situation either permits or denies a leader the chance to influence the behaviour of group members

Leader-member relations the degree to which followers respect, trust, and like their leaders

Task structure the degree to which the requirements of a subordinate's tasks are clearly specified

Position power the degree to which leaders are able to hire, fire, reward, and punish workers

Path-goal theory a leadership theory that states that leaders can increase subordinate satisfaction and performance by clarifying and clearing the paths to goals and by increasing the number and kinds of rewards available for goal attainment

Directive leadership a leadership style in which the leader lets employees know precisely what is expected of them, gives them specific guidelines for performing tasks, schedules work, sets standards of performance, and makes sure that people follow standard rules and regulations

Supportive leadership a leadership style in which the leader is friendly and approachable, shows concern for employees and their welfare and treats them as equals, and creates a friendly climate

Participative leadership a leadership style in which the leader consults employees for their suggestions and input before making decisions

Achievement-oriented leadership a leadership style in which the leader sets challenging goals, has high expectations of employees, and displays confidence that employees will assume responsibility and put forth extraordinary effort

Normative decision theory a theory that suggests how leaders can determine an appropriate amount of employee participation when making decisions

Strategic leadership the ability to anticipate, envision, maintain flexibility, think strategically, and work with others to initiate changes that will create a positive future for an organization

Visionary leadership leadership that creates a positive image of the future that motivates organizational members and provides direction for future planning and goal setting

Charismatic leadership the behavioural tendencies and personal characteristics of leaders that create an exceptionally strong relationship between them and their followers

Ethical charismatics charismatic leaders who provide developmental opportunities for followers, are open to positive and negative feedback, recognize others' contributions, share information, and have moral standards that emphasize the larger interests of the group, organization, or society

Unethical charismatics charismatic leaders who control and manipulate followers, do what is best for themselves instead of their organizations, want to hear only positive feedback, share only information that is beneficial to themselves, and have moral standards that put their interests before everyone else's

Transformational leadership leadership that generates awareness and acceptance of a group's purpose and mission and gets employees to see beyond their own needs and self-interests for the good of the group

Transactional leadership leadership based on an exchange process, in which followers are rewarded for good performance and punished for poor performance

---

Review 4: Adapting Leader Behaviour: Path-Goal Theory

> Path-goal theory states that leaders can increase subordinate satisfaction and performance by clarifying and clearing the paths to goals and by increasing the number and kinds of rewards available for goal attainment. For this to work, however, leader behaviour must be a source of immediate or future satisfaction for followers and must complement and not duplicate the characteristics of followers' work environments. In contrast to Fiedler's contingency theory, path-goal theory assumes that leaders can and do change their leadership styles (directive, supportive, participative, and achievement oriented), depending on their subordinates (experience, perceived ability and internal or external locus of control) and the environment in which those subordinates work (task structure, formal authority system, and primary work group).

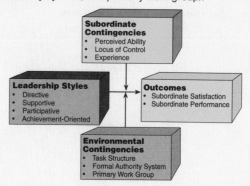

Review 5: Adapting Leader Behaviour: Normative Decision Theory

> The normative decision theory helps leaders decide how much employee participation should be used when making decisions. Using the right degree of employee participation improves the quality of decisions and the extent to which employees accept and are committed to decisions. The theory specifies five different decision styles or ways of making decisions: autocratic (AI or AII), consultative (CI or CII), and group (GII). The theory improves decision quality *via* the decision rules of quality, leader information, subordinate information, goal congruence, and problem structure. The theory improves employee commitment and acceptance *via* the decision rules of commitment probability, subordinate conflict, and commitment requirement. These decision rules help leaders improve decision quality and follower acceptance and commitment by eliminating decision styles that don't fit the decision or situation they're facing. Normative decision theory then operationalizes these decision rules in the form of yes/no questions, as shown in the decision tree displayed in Exhibit 14.8.

Review 6: Visionary Leadership

> Strategic leadership requires visionary, charismatic, and transformational leadership. Visionary leadership creates a positive image of the future that motivates organizational members and provides direction for future planning and goal setting. Charismatic leaders have strong, confident, dynamic personalities that attract followers, enable the leader to create strong bonds, and inspire followers to accomplish the leader's vision. Followers of ethical charismatic leaders work harder, are more committed and satisfied, are better performers, and are more likely to trust their leaders. Followers can be just as supportive and committed to unethical charismatics, but these leaders can pose a tremendous risk for companies. Unethical charismatics control and manipulate followers and do what is best for themselves instead of their organizations. Transformational leadership goes beyond charismatic leadership by generating awareness and acceptance of a group's purpose and mission and by getting employees to see beyond their own needs and self-interests for the good of the group. The four components of transformational leadership are charisma or idealized influence, inspirational motivation, intellectual stimulation, and individualized consideration.

LEARNING OUTCOMES

Review 1: Perception and Communication Problems

> Perception is the process by which people attend to, organize, interpret, and retain information from their environments. Perception is not a straightforward process. Because of perceptual filters such as selective perception and closure people exposed to the same information stimuli often end up with very different perceptions and understandings. Perception-based differences can also lead to differences in the attributions (internal or external) that managers and workers make when explaining workplace behaviour. In general, workers are more likely to explain behaviour from a defensive bias, in which they attribute problems to external causes (i.e., the situation). Managers, on the other hand, tend to commit the fundamental attribution error, attributing problems to internal causes (i.e., the worker associated with a mistake or error). Consequently, when things go wrong, it's common for managers to blame workers and for workers to blame the situation or context in which they do their jobs. Finally, this problem is compounded by a self-serving bias that leads people to attribute successes to internal causes and failures to external causes. So, when workers receive negative feedback from managers, they may become defensive and emotional and not hear what their managers have to say. In short, perceptions and attributions represent a significant challenge to effective communication and understanding in organizations.

BASIC PERCEPTION PROCESS

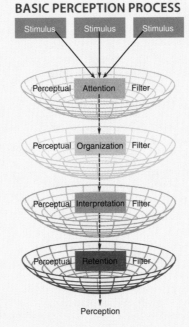

Review 2: Kinds of Communication

> Organizational communication depends on the communication process, formal and informal communication channels, one-on-one communication, and nonverbal communication. The major components of the communication process are the sender, the receiver, noise, and feedback. Senders often mistakenly assume that they can pipe their intended messages directly into receivers' heads with perfect clarity. Formal communication channels such as downward, upward, and horizontal communication carry organizationally approved messages and information. By contrast, the informal communication channel, called the "grapevine," arises out of curiosity and is carried out through gossip or cluster chains. There are two kinds of one-on-one communication. Coaching is used to improve on-the-job performance while counselling is used to communicate about non-job-related issues affecting job performance. Nonverbal communication, such as kinesics and paralanguage, accounts for as much as 93 percent of a message's content and understanding.

THE INTERPERSONAL COMMUNICATION PROCESS

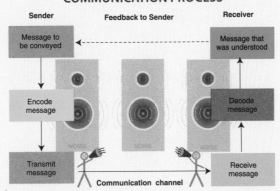

KEY TERMS

Communication the process of transmitting information from one person or place to another

Perception the process by which individuals attend to, organize, interpret, and retain information from their environments

Perceptual filters the personality-, psychology-, or experience-based differences that influence people to ignore or pay attention to particular stimuli

Selective perception the tendency to notice and accept objects and information consistent with our values, beliefs, and expectations while ignoring or screening out or not accepting inconsistent information

Closure the tendency to fill in gaps of missing information by assuming that what we don't know is consistent with what we already know

Attribution theory a theory that states that we all have a basic need to understand and explain the causes of other people's behaviour

Defensive bias the tendency for people to perceive themselves as personally and situationally similar to someone who is having difficulty or trouble

Fundamental attribution error the tendency to ignore external causes of behaviour and to attribute other people's actions to internal causes

Self-serving bias the tendency to overestimate our value by attributing successes to ourselves (internal causes) and attributing failures to others or the environment (external causes)

Encoding putting a message into a written, verbal, or symbolic form that can be recognized and understood by the receiver

Decoding the process by which the receiver translates the written, verbal, or symbolic form of a message into an understood message

Feedback to sender in the communication process, a return message to the sender that indicates the receiver's understanding of the message

Noise anything that interferes with the transmission of the intended message

Jargon vocabulary particular to a profession or group

Formal communication channel the system of official channels that carry organizationally approved messages and information

Downward communication communication that flows from higher to lower levels in an organization

Upward communication communication that flows from lower to higher levels in an organization

Horizontal communication communication that flows among managers and workers who are at the same organizational level

Informal communication channel ("grapevine") the transmission of messages from employee to employee outside of formal communication channels

Coaching communicating with someone for the direct purpose of improving the person's on-the-job performance or behaviour

Counselling communicating with someone about non-job-related issues that may be affecting or interfering with the person's performance

Nonverbal communication any communication that doesn't involve words

Hearing the act or process of perceiving sounds

Listening making a conscious effort to hear

Active listening assuming half the responsibility for successful communication by actively giving the speaker non-judgmental feedback that shows you've accurately heard what he or she said

Empathetic listening understanding the speaker's perspective and personal frame of reference and giving feedback that conveys that understanding to the speaker

Destructive feedback feedback that disapproves without any intention of being helpful and almost always causes a negative or defensive reaction in the recipient

Constructive feedback feedback intended to be helpful, corrective, and/or encouraging

Wikis websites that allow employees across an organization to edit and update documents in a quick and easy way, facilitating collaboration and interdepartment communication.

Online discussion forums the in-house equivalent of Internet newsgroups. By using Web- or software-based discussion tools that are available across the company, employees can easily ask questions and share knowledge with each other.

Video conferencing utilizes computer networks to transmit audio and video, allowing communication to take place at a distance.

Televised/videotaped speeches and meetings speeches and meetings originally made to a smaller audience that are either simultaneously broadcast to other locations in the company or videotaped for subsequent distribution and viewing

Organizational silence when employees withhold information about organizational problems or issues

Company hotlines phone numbers that anyone in the company can call anonymously to leave information for upper management

Survey feedback information that is collected by surveys from organizational members and then compiled, disseminated, and used to develop action plans for improvement

Blog a personal website that provides personal opinions or recommendations, news summaries, and reader comments

Review 3: Managing One-on-One Communication

❯ One-on-one communication can be managed by choosing the right communication medium, being a good listener, and giving effective feedback. Managers generally prefer oral communication because it provides the opportunity to ask questions and assess nonverbal communication. Oral communication is best suited to complex, ambiguous, or emotionally laden topics. Written communication is best suited for delivering straightforward messages and information. Listening is important for managerial success, but most people are terrible listeners. To improve your listening skills, choose to be an active listener (clarify responses, paraphrase, and summarize) and an empathetic listener (show your desire to understand, reflect feelings). Feedback can be constructive or destructive. To be constructive, feedback must be immediate, focused on specific behaviours, and problem-oriented.

Review 4: Managing Organization-Wide Communication

❯ Managers need methods for managing organization-wide communication and for making themselves accessible so that they can hear what employees throughout their organizations are feeling and thinking. Email, online discussion forums, wikis, televised/videotaped speeches and conferences, and videoconferences make it much easier for managers to improve message transmission and get the message out. By contrast, anonymous company hotlines, survey feedback, frequent informal meetings, and surprise visits help managers avoid organizational silence and improve reception by giving them the opportunity to hear what others in the organization feel and think. Monitoring internal and external blogs is another way to find out what people are saying and thinking about your organization.

REVIEW card/

CHAPTER 17

LEARNING OUTCOMES

Review 1: Strategic Importance of Information

> The first company to use new information technology to substantially lower costs or differentiate products or services often gains first-mover advantage, higher profits, and larger market share. Creating a first-mover advantage can be difficult, expensive, and risky, however. According to the resource-based view of information technology, sustainable competitive advantage occurs when information technology adds value, is different across firms, and is difficult to create or acquire.

Using Information Technology to Sustain a Competitive Advantage

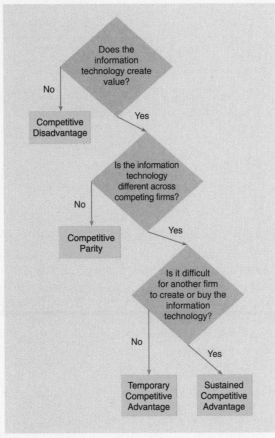

Source: Adapted from F. J. Mata, W. L. Fuerst, and J. B. Barney, "Information Technology and Sustained Competitive Advantage: A Resource-Based Analysis," *MIS Quarterly* 19, no. 4 (December 1995): 487–505. Reprinted by special permission by the Society for Information Management and the Management Information Systems Research Center at the University of Minnesota.

Review 2: Characteristics and Costs of Useful Information

> Raw data are facts and figures. Raw data do not become information until they are in a form that can affect decisions and behaviour. For information to be useful, it has to be reliable and valid (accurate), of sufficient quantity (complete), pertinent to the problems you're facing (relevant), and available when you need it (timely). Useful information does not come cheaply. The five costs of obtaining good information are the costs of acquiring, processing, storing, retrieving, and communicating information.

Review 3: Capturing, Processing, and Protecting Information

> Electronic data capture (bar codes, radio frequency identification [RFID] tags, scanners, and optical character recognition) is much faster, easier, and cheaper than manual data

KEY TERMS

Moore's law the prediction that the cost of computing will drop by 50 percent every 18 months as computer-processing power doubles

Raw data facts and figures

Information useful data that can influence people's choices and behaviour

First-mover advantage the strategic advantage that companies earn by being the first to use new information technology to substantially lower costs or to make a product or service different from that of competitors

Acquisition cost the cost of obtaining data that you don't have

Processing cost the cost of turning raw data into usable information

Storage cost the cost of physically or electronically archiving information for later use and retrieval

Retrieval cost the cost of accessing already-stored and processed information

Communication cost the cost of transmitting information from one place to another

Bar code a visual pattern that represents numerical data by varying the thickness and pattern of vertical bars

Radio frequency identification (RFID) tags tags containing minuscule microchips that transmit information via radio waves and can be used to track the number and location of the objects into which the tags have been inserted

Electronic scanners an electronic device that converts printed text and pictures into digital images

Optical character recognition the ability of software to convert digitized documents into ASCII (American Standard Code for Information Interchange) text or PDF documents that can be searched, read, and edited by word processing and other kinds of software

Processing information transforming raw data into meaningful information

Data mining the process of discovering patterns and relationships in large amounts of data

Data warehouse stores huge amounts of data that have been prepared for data mining analysis by being cleaned of errors and redundancy

Supervised data mining the process when the user tells the data mining software to look and test for specific patterns and relationships in a data set

Unsupervised data mining the process when the user simply tells the data mining software to uncover whatever patterns and relationships it can find in a data set

Association or affinity patterns when two or more database elements tend to occur together in a significant way

Sequence patterns when two or more database elements occur together in a significant pattern, but one of the elements precedes the other

Predictive patterns patterns that help identify database elements that are different

Data clusters when three or more database elements occur together (i.e., cluster) in a significant way

Protecting information the process of ensuring that data are reliably and consistently retrievable in a usable format for authorized users but no one else

Authentication making sure potential users are who they claim to be

Authorization granting authenticated users approved access to data, software, and systems

Two-factor authentication authentication based on what users know, such as a password, and what they have in their possession, such as a secure ID card or key

Biometrics identifying users by unique, measurable body features, such as fingerprint recognition or iris scanning

Firewall a protective hardware or software device that sits between the computers in an internal organizational network and outside networks, such as the Internet

Virus a program or piece of code that, against your wishes, attaches itself to other programs on your computer and can trigger anything from a harmless flashing message to the reformatting of your hard drive to a systemwide network shutdown

Data encryption the transformation of data into complex, scrambled digital codes that can be unencrypted only by authorized users who possess unique decryption keys

Virtual private network (VPN) software that securely encrypts data sent by employees outside the company network, decrypts the data when they arrive within the company computer network, and does the same when data are sent back to employees outside the network

capture. Processing information means transforming raw data into meaningful information that can be applied to business decision making. Data mining helps managers with this transformation by discovering unknown patterns and relationships in data. Supervised data mining looks for patterns specified by managers, while unsupervised data mining looks for four general kinds of data patterns: association/affinity patterns, sequence patterns, predictive patterns, and data clusters. Protecting information ensures that data are reliably and consistently retrievable in a usable format by authorized users but no one else. Authentication and authorization, firewalls, antivirus software for PCs and corporate e-mail and network servers, data encryption, virtual private networks (VPN), and Web-based secure sockets layer (SSL) encryption are some of the best ways to protect information. Be careful with wireless networks, which are easily compromised even when security and encryption protocols are in place.

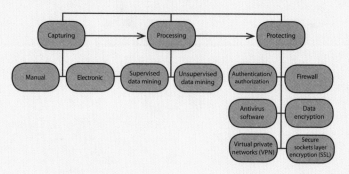

Review 4: Accessing and Sharing Information and Knowledge

> Executive information systems, intranets, and corporate portals facilitate internal sharing and access to company information and transactions. Electronic data interchange and the Internet allow external groups like suppliers and customers to easily access company information. Both decrease costs by reducing or eliminating data entry, data errors, and paperwork and by speeding up communication. Organizations use decision support systems and expert systems to capture and share specialized knowledge with nonexpert employees.

Secure sockets layer (SSL) encryption Internet browser–based encryption that provides secure off-site Web access to some data and programs

Executive information system (EIS) a data processing system that uses internal and external data sources to provide the information needed to monitor and analyze organizational performance

Intranets private company networks that allow employees to easily access, share, and publish information using Internet software

Corporate portal a hybrid of executive information systems and intranets that allows managers and employees to use a Web browser to gain access to customized company information and to complete specialized transactions

Electronic data interchange (EDI) when two companies convert their purchase and ordering information to a standardized format to enable the direct electronic transmission of that information

from one company's computer system to the other company's computer system

Extranets networks that allow companies to exchange information and conduct transactions with outsiders by providing them direct, Web-based access to authorized parts of a company's intranet or information system

Knowledge the understanding that one gains from information

Decision support system (DSS) an information system that helps managers understand specific kinds of problems and potential solutions and analyze the impact of different decision options using "what if" scenarios

Expert system an information system that contains the specialized knowledge and decision rules used by experts and experienced decision makers so that nonexperts can draw on this knowledge base to make decisions

LEARNING OUTCOMES

Review 1: Productivity

> Productivity is a measure of how many inputs it takes to produce or create an output. The greater the output from one input, or the fewer inputs it takes to create an output, the higher the productivity. Partial productivity measures how much of a single kind of input such as labour is needed to produce an output. Multifactor productivity is an overall measure of productivity that indicates how much labour, capital, materials, and energy are needed to produce an output.

$$\text{Partial productivity} = \frac{\text{Outputs}}{\text{Single kind of input}}$$

$$\text{Multifactor productivity} = \frac{\text{Outputs}}{(\text{Labour} + \text{Capital} + \text{Materials} + \text{Energy})}$$

Review 2: Quality

> Quality can mean a product or service free of deficiencies or the characteristics of a product or service that satisfy customer needs. Quality products usually possess three characteristics: reliability, serviceability, and durability. Quality service means reliability, tangibles, responsiveness, assurance, and empathy. ISO 9000 is a series of five international standards for achieving consistency in quality management and quality assurance, while ISO 14000 is a set of standards for minimizing an organization's harmful effects on the environment. The Baldrige National Quality Award recognizes U.S. companies for their achievements in quality and business performance. Each year, three Baldrige Awards may be given for manufacturing, service, small business, education, health care, and nonprofit. Total quality management (TQM) is an integrated organization-wide strategy for improving product and service quality. TQM is based on three mutually reinforcing principles: customer focus and satisfaction, continuous improvement, and teamwork.

Review 3: Service Operations

> Services are different from goods. Goods are produced, tangible, and storable. Services are performed, intangible, and perishable. Likewise, managing service operations is different from managing production operations. The service-profit chain indicates that success begins with internal service quality, meaning how well management treats service employees. Internal service quality leads to employee satisfaction and service capability, which, in turn, lead to high-value service to customers, customer satisfaction, customer loyalty, and long-term

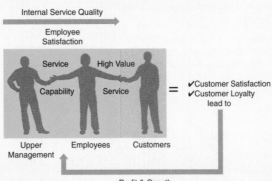

Service-Profit Chain

Sources: R. Hallowell, L. A. Schlesinger, and J. Zornitsky, "Internal Service Quality, Customer and Job Satisfaction: Linkages and Implications for Management," *Human Resource Planning* 19 (1996): 20–31; J. L. Heskett, T. O. Jones, G. W. Loveman, W. E. Sasser, Jr., and L. A. Schlesinger, "Putting the Service-Profit Chain to Work," *Harvard Business Review* (March–April 1994): 164–174.

profits and growth. Keeping existing customers is far more cost-effective than finding new ones. Consequently, to prevent disgruntled customers from leaving, some companies are empowering service employees to perform service recovery—restoring customer satisfaction to strongly

KEY TERMS

Productivity a measure of performance that indicates how many inputs it takes to produce or create an output

Partial productivity a measure of performance that indicates how much of a particular kind of input it takes to produce an output

Multifactor productivity an overall measure of performance that indicates how much labour, capital, materials, and energy it takes to produce an output

Quality a product or service free of deficiencies, or the characteristics of a product or service that satisfy customer needs

ISO 9000 a series of five international standards, from ISO 9000 to ISO 9004, for achieving consistency in quality management and quality assurance in companies throughout the world

ISO 14000 a series of international standards for managing, monitoring, and minimizing an organization's harmful effects on the environment

Total quality management (TQM) an integrated, principle-based, organization-wide strategy for improving product and service quality

Customer focus an organizational goal to concentrate on meeting customers' needs at all levels of the organization

Customer satisfaction an organizational goal to provide products or services that meet or exceed customers' expectations

Continuous improvement an organization's ongoing commitment to constantly assess and improve the processes and procedures used to create products and services

Variation a deviation in the form, condition, or appearance of a product from the quality standard for that product

Teamwork collaboration between managers and nonmanagers, across business functions, and between companies, customers, and suppliers

Service recovery restoring customer satisfaction to strongly dissatisfied customers

Make-to-order operation a manufacturing operation that does not start processing or assembling products until a customer order is received

Assemble-to-order operation a manufacturing operation that divides manufacturing processes into separate parts or modules that are combined to create semicustomized products

Make-to-stock operation a manufacturing operation that orders parts and assembles standardized products before receiving customer orders

Manufacturing flexibility the degree to which manufacturing operations can easily and quickly change the number, kind, and characteristics of products they produce

Continuous-flow production a manufacturing operation that produces goods at a continuous, rather than a discrete, rate

Line-flow production manufacturing processes that are pre-established, occur in a serial or linear manner, and are dedicated to making one type of product

Batch production a manufacturing operation that produces goods in large batches in standard lot sizes

Job shops manufacturing operations that handle custom orders or small batch jobs

Inventory the amount and number of raw materials, parts, and finished products that a company has in its possession

Raw material inventories the basic inputs in a manufacturing process

Component parts inventories the basic parts used in manufacturing that are fabricated from raw materials

Work-in-process inventories partially finished goods consisting of assembled component parts

Finished goods inventories the final outputs of manufacturing operations

Average aggregate inventory average overall inventory during a particular time period

Stockout the situation when a company runs out of finished product

Inventory turnover the number of times per year that a company sells or "turns over" its average inventory

Ordering cost the costs associated with ordering inventory, including the cost of data entry, phone calls, obtaining bids, correcting mistakes, and determining when and how much inventory to order

Setup cost the costs of downtime and lost efficiency that occur when a machine is changed or adjusted to produce a different kind of inventory

Holding cost the cost of keeping inventory until it is used or sold, including storage, insurance, taxes, obsolescence, and opportunity costs

Stockout costs the costs incurred when a company runs out of a product, including transaction costs to replace inventory and the loss of customers' goodwill

Economic order quantity (EOQ) a system of formulas that minimizes ordering and holding costs and helps determine how much and how often inventory should be ordered

Just-in-time (JIT) inventory system an inventory system in which component parts arrive from suppliers just as they are needed at each stage of production

Kanban a ticket-based JIT system that indicates when to reorder inventory

Materials requirement planning (MRP) a production and inventory system that determines the production schedule, production batch sizes, and inventory needed to complete final products

Independent demand system an inventory system in which the level of one kind of inventory does not depend on another

Dependent demand system an inventory system in which the level of inventory depends on the number of finished units to be produced

dissatisfied customers—by giving them the authority and responsibility to immediately solve customer problems. The hope is that empowered service recovery will prevent customer defections.

Review 4: Manufacturing Operations

> Manufacturing operations produce physical goods. Manufacturing operations can be classified according to the amount of processing or assembly that occurs after receiving an order from a customer.

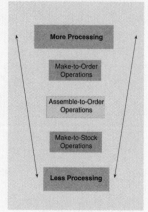

Manufacturing operations can also be classified in terms of flexibility, the degree to which the number, kind, and characteristics of products can easily and quickly be changed. Flexibility allows companies to respond quickly to competitors and customers and to reduce order lead times, but it can also lead to higher unit costs.

Review 5: Inventory

> There are four kinds of inventory: raw materials, component parts, work-in-process, and finished goods. Because companies incur ordering, setup, holding, and stockout costs when handling inventory, inventory costs can be enormous. To control those costs, companies measure and track inventory in three ways: average aggregate inventory, weeks of supply, and turnover. Companies meet the basic goals of inventory management (avoiding stockouts and reducing inventory without hurting daily operations) through economic order quantity (EOQ) formulas, just-in-time (JIT) inventory systems, and materials requirement planning (MRP).

$$EOQ = \sqrt{\frac{2DO}{4}}$$

Use EOQ formulas when inventory levels are independent, and use JIT and MRP when inventory levels are dependent on the number of products to be produced.

Notes